BRITISH WRITERS

BRITISH WRITERS

Edited under the auspices of the British Council

IAN SCOTT-KILVERT
General Editor

VOLUME V

ELIZABETH GASKELL

TO

FRANCIS THOMPSON

CHARLES SCRIBNER'S SONS / NEW YORK

Library of Congress Cataloging in Publication Data (Revised)

Main entry under title:

British writers.

Includes bibliographies and index.
CONTENTS: v. 1. William Langland to the English
Bible—v. 2. Thomas Middleton to George Farquhar
—[etc.]—v. 5. Elizabeth Gaskell to Francis Thompson.
1. English literature—History and criticism.
2. English literature—Bio-bibliography. 3. Authors,
English—Biography. I. Scott-Kilvert, Ian.
II. Great Britain. British Council.
PR85.B688   820'.9   78-23483   AACR2
ISBN 0-684-15798-5 (v. 1)   ISBN 0-684-16635-6 (v. 4)
ISBN 0-684-16407-8 (v. 2)   ISBN 0-684-16636-4 (v. 5)
ISBN 0-684-16408-6 (v. 3)

Editorial Staff

List of Subjects in Volume V

Introduction

British Writers is designed as a work of reference to complement *American Writers*, the eight-volume set of literary biographies of authors past and present, which was first published in 1974. In the same way as its American counterpart, which first appeared in the form of individual pamphlets published by the University of Minnesota Press, the British collection originates from a series of separate articles entitled *Writers and Their Work*. This series was initiated by the British Council in 1950 as a part of its worldwide program to support the teaching of English language and literature, an activity carried on both in the English-speaking world and in many countries in which English is not the mother tongue.

The articles are intended to appeal to a wide readership, including students in secondary and advanced education, teachers, librarians, scholars, editors, and critics, as well as the general public. Their purpose is to provide an introduction to the work of writers who have made a significant contribution to English literature, to stimulate the reader's enjoyment of the text, and to give students the means to pursue the subject further. The series begins in the fourteenth century and extends to the present day, and is printed in chronological order according to the date of the subject's birth. The articles are far from conforming to a fixed pattern, but speaking generally each begins with a short biographical section, the main body of the text being devoted to a survey of the subject's principal writings and an assessment of the work as a whole. Each article is equipped with a selected bibliography that records the subject's writings in chronological order, in the form both of collected editions and of separate works, including modern and paperback editions. The bibliography concludes with a list of biographical and critical publications, including both books and articles, to guide the reader who is interested in further research. In the case of authors such as Chaucer or Shakespeare, whose writings have inspired extensive criticism and commentary, the critical section is further subdivided and provides a useful record of the new fields of research that have developed over the past hundred years.

British Writers is not conceived as an encyclopedia of literature, nor is it a series of articles planned so comprehensively as to include every writer of historical importance. Its character is rather that of a critical anthology possessing both the virtues and the limitations of such a grouping. It offers neither the schematized form of the encyclopedia nor the completeness of design of the literary history. On the other hand it is limited neither by the impersonality of the one nor the uniformity of the other. Since each contributor speaks with only one voice out of many, he is principally concerned with explaining his subject as fully as possible rather than with establishing an order of merit or making "placing" comparisons (since each contributor might well "place" differently). The prime task is one of presentation and exposition rather than of assigning critical praise or censure. The contributors to the first volume consist of distinguished literary scholars and critics—later volumes include contributions by poets, novelists, historians, and biographers. Each writes as an enthusiast for his subject, and each sets out to explain what are the qualities that make an author worth reading.

The fourth volume of *British Writers* dealt in the main with the romantic poets and critics and with the fiction and other prose of the Regency period. But because of the chronological dovetailing of the romantic era and its successor, the same volume also included authors such as Tennyson, the Brownings, Disraeli, Carlyle, and Macaulay, who, although sufficiently close to the romantics to have felt their influence strongly, are generally regarded as characteristically Victorian.

The present volume consists of essays on "Victorian literature" in the sense that scarcely any of the writers discussed had begun to publish before the beginning of Queen Victoria's reign, and almost all of them had ceased to do so by the time of her death. Volumes V and VI will likewise overlap, but for the opposite reason to the one mentioned above. This is that while a number of major authors, notably Hardy, James, Shaw, Kipling, and Conrad, had already established a reputation before the end of the nineteenth century, their literary achievements may be regarded as extending to a significant degree into the twentieth.

The 1830's and 1840's were a period of intense social unrest and intellectual ferment throughout Europe. In England these discontents were mainly the product of the Industrial Revolution, which had brought poverty, unemployment, overcrowding, and the exploitation of women and children. The Industrial Revolution had in fact been in progress in England for well over half a century, but it had not hitherto engaged the attention of writers and intellectuals in practical terms. Poets, novelists, philosophers, and reformers had of course been aware of poverty and suffering but had confined themselves to abstract questions of political rights and constitutional reforms. But it soon became clear that the eagerly awaited Reform Bill of 1832 had merely transferred political power from the land-owning to the manufacturing interest, whose economic policies had greatly contributed to the very conditions against which the working classes were protesting. The opening chapter of Carlyle's pamphlet *Chartism* (1839) is entitled "The Condition of England Question"; and throughout the turbulent 1830's and hungry 1840's this question haunted the imagination not merely of the compassionate and humane but rather of all classes of society. The problem was how to relieve the immediate and undoubted hardships without sacrificing the English tradition of gradual and constitutional change.

The fears aroused by this continuing crisis were felt in every sector of Victorian thought—in politics, economics, religion, philosophy, science, literature, and art. Sympathies were divided, and the various theories and systems that were devised to meet the challenge were as numerous as they were mutually antithetical. Nevertheless it is worth the effort to disentangle the principal strands of thought.

In political terms, the initiative was at that time held by the Utilitarians and the apostles of laissez-faire economics. Originally the Utilitarians, in pursuit of their ideal of the greatest happiness of the greatest number, had supported the extension of education and of the vote, the control of bread prices, and many other political and social reforms. But since Jeremy

Bentham had admitted into his program the economic doctrines of Adam Smith and had come to regard the factory system as the prime agent of civilization and economic advancement, Utilitarian doctrine seemed designed to create a working class that would be entirely submissive to the needs of production. It was this outlook, the social and educational creed of Mr. Gradgrind, which Dickens attacked so eloquently in *Hard Times*. Macaulay, as a prominent Whig member of Parliament and supporter of the Reform Bill, opposed the kind of state intervention that the Utilitarians favored and upheld the classical laissez-faire solution. He considered that the duty of government was to protect persons and property and leave the stage free for enlightened self-interest to create wealth. While he could not deny the hardships that the masses were suffering, he was ready to argue that the future was bright and that even the most deprived classes of the day were immeasurably better off than their ancestors. Moreover Macaulay belonged to a family of the Clapham Sect of Evangelicals, and even the more philanthropic members of the sect were committed to the doctrine of self-help and to the belief that poverty was ordained.

There was no lack of opposition to the Utilitarian view of life, but it was much divided. Carlyle, in his essay "Signs of the Times," had been one of the very first to recognize both the nature of his era as "the mechanical age" and its attendant dangers. "They cease to worship God or virtue, and substitute the ignoble alternative, profit. Our true Deity is mechanism." Yet he himself believed no less passionately in the necessity for personal salvation, insisted that idleness is a crime as well as a sin, and proclaimed the doctrine of work for the good of the spirit. Disraeli, in his novel *Sybil,* with its dramatic vision of an England split into two nations, rich and poor, was pursuing a specific political objective. His aim was an alliance between the populace and a reformed aristocracy to oppose the Whigs and their power base, the new business and manufacturing interest. Charles Kingsley's *Alton Locke* and Elizabeth Gaskell's *Mary Barton* were the work of authors who did not themselves belong to the oppressed classes but who wrote from a humanitarian standpoint and from a knowledge of the poverty and injustices which they were describing.

Matthew Arnold offers a different diagnosis of the problem, with his famous division of English society into Barbarians (the aristocracy), Philistines (the middle class), and Populace (the workers). The first he judged to have had their chance and missed it, the third to lack the power to act. It was the Philistines who could save the day and who could themselves be saved. So, for their own good, he castigated them for their materialism, puritanism, and the sheer ugliness of their lives; their preference for the Hebraic rather than for the Hellenic ideal.

Religion also played a significant part in the national debate, especially in the 1830's, when the Oxford Movement was at its height. The influence of the movement on religion has been compared by David Daiches to that of Wordsworth on poetry at the beginning of the century, "a romantic rebellion against the perfunctory unimaginative routine into which the Church of England had fallen." Its supporters feared, as Carlyle had done, the threat to spiritual values from the rising tide of materialism. They also feared the growth of liberal theology and the progressive secularizing of religious history and suspected that neither the Church of England nor the Dissenters could inspire the revival of faith which was needed to combat these tendencies. However, the movement was only one manifestation of a widely felt need to review the position of Anglican Protestantism vis-a-vis the rest of Christendom. Later, Protestantism itself, with its dependence on personal conviction and individual interpretation of the Bible, was to experience a crisis of faith arising from the Higher Criticism of the Scriptures and from scientific discoveries, especially in the fields of geology, biology, and zoology, which seek to explain the origins of man and the history of the universe. All the leading intellectual figures of the age, Carlyle, Ruskin, Newman, Arnold, Mill, George Eliot, to name only those closely associated with literature, experienced such crises of belief, as their memoirs and other writings bear witness.

The severity of these intellectual and spiritual ordeals may account for the undoubted fact that the major achievements of Victorian literature are found in prose. The romantic poets had elevated the writing of poetry, in T. S. Eliot's phrase, into a kind of raid upon the absolute and its result as a revelation. The Victorian poets could not emulate the power of their predecessors to explore new worlds of experience, nor, with rare exceptions, to match the direct impact of their writing. The dominant mood is now elegiac or pastoral. The poet withdraws in private grief, or doubt, or sensuous reverie from the busy world, "with its sick hurry, its divided aims." Such is the impression we frequently receive from Tennyson, Arnold, D. G. Rossetti, or Morris—witness *The Lotus Eaters* or *The Scholar Gipsy*. The exceptions are those poets whose poetry reflects not a mood but a spiritual or intellectual stress, directly confronted, such as Emily Brontë, Clough, or Hopkins.

The novelists were cast for an easier role: that of reporting or representing situations, not providing revelation. The novel was now becoming what the drama had been for the Elizabethans—the popular, all-embracing literary medium. It could absorb not only the most urgent social topics, but also, as the theater had done, history, crime, domestic relationships, melodrama, farce. It spoke not only to the literate public but even to the illiterate who attended Dickens' readings.

Of all practitioners of the novel, Dickens now appears to us the most complete embodiment of his time. True, he speaks only with unchallenged authority for the middle and lower-middle classes: elsewhere he improvises with the idiosyncratic power of a great artist; but one could not claim for him, as for Shakespeare or Tolstoy, that he is a master of dialogue for all mankind. But he remains the writer who succeeded better than any other contemporary in shaping his novels so as to express the exuberance and diversity of his genius. Barbara Hardy's essay begins with a study of the development of his style, from the sharp vision of his early journalism to the far more elaborate arts of narrative, scene-setting, and character portrayal which he gradually evolved. She discusses all the novels individually and finally considers the immensely diverse range of effects which Dickens attempts in the second half of his career, especially in exploring the inner life of his characters.

Thackeray also served his apprenticeship to fiction as a journalist, but like so many of his contemporaries he was acutely aware of social inequalities and views these from a very different standpoint to that of Dickens. His approach is more consistently satirical and his canvas deliberately narrower: in particular he focusses his attention on the English caste system as seen in London society and in the rural community. John Carey reviews his large and extremely variegated output in detail, but places *Vanity Fair* in a class by itself as one of the two or three outstanding English novels of the nineteenth century. Although subsequent books display other facets of Thackeray's gifts, he regrets that the later works were inclined to turn away from the disturbing insights that had inspired Thackeray's satirical masterpiece.

George Eliot, especially in her last two novels, *Middlemarch* and *Daniel Deronda*, was recognized by her contemporaries as having brought an intellectual weight and distinction to the English novel which it had previously lacked. She also possessed the gift, rarely displayed by her predecessors, of making daily business or professional life both interesting and capable of affording important insights into character. Henry James praised *Middlemarch* as the first English novel to display an organized, molded, balanced composition, gratifying the reader with a sense of design and construction; and Lettice Cooper endorses the general verdict that this represents the full flower of George Eliot's genius. She notes the shrewdness of her subject's comedy by contrast with the solemnity of her letters and sums up with the judgment that moral concern for her characters is of the very essence of George Eliot's fiction and that it is on the urgency of their moral choices that the tension of her plots depends.

Mrs. Gaskell's first novel, *Mary Barton*, appeared in 1848, three years after Disraeli's *Sybil, or The Two Nations*. The events on which it is based had taken place some nine years earlier, at a time of great industrial distress in Manchester; and her book presents a far more realistic and convincing picture of the life of the poor of that period than Disraeli's, notwithstanding the eloquence and intellectual range of the latter. This was the most politically engaged of all Mrs. Gaskell's books. Miriam Allott's essay demonstrates how Mrs. Gaskell's gifts developed as a mediator seeking to bring Christian compassion to bear upon the problems arising, on the one hand, from class antagonisms and, on the other, from the sufferings of women, as in *Ruth* and *Sylvia's Lovers*. But besides her contribution to the novel of social protest, Mrs. Gaskell also belongs to the tradition of Jane Austen as an observer of the foibles of rural society; and in naming her as the least stuffy of Victorians, Miriam Allott pays tribute to her gifts as a creator of social comedy in *Cranford* and still more in the unfinished *Wives and Daughters*.

The peculiar genius and circumstances of the Brontë sisters marks them off sharply from the other major English novelists of the period. They led exceptionally isolated lives, but they enjoyed an intense independence and sense of freedom—the freedom of spirit and a freedom especially associated with their love of the moors—and their gifts were reinforced by an extraordinary strength of inner conviction. The present study includes a large proportion of biographical material. Winifred Gérin is at pains to stress the close partnership of the four children in their early years and the importance of their juvenilia in shaping their creative powers as mature writers. Her account

of their youthful epics of Angria (Charlotte and Branwell) and of Gondal (Emily and Anne) makes it clear how they grew up with a vivid picture of a fantasy adult world which heightened their youthful imaginations and passions; while in later life these were hardly ever modified by firsthand acquaintance with the emotions of others. In the critical section of the essay the author notes the importance of the five novelettes written by Charlotte in her early twenties as preliminary sketches for her later books. She goes on to review all the sisters' novels and discusses the text of Emily's poems and the crucial importance of the Hatfield edition.

Trollope enjoys a secure reputation as the unpretentious but highly skilled craftsman of Victorian fiction. Henry James remarked that "his great, his inestimable merit was a complete appreciation of the usual," and he has left behind a fictional world so apparently solid that his popularity with the modern reader and viewer has never waned. Trollope does not explore moral problems with the penetration of George Eliot, but Hugh Sykes Davies pays especial tribute to his use of the moral imagination in the portrayal of his characters. Apart from the Barchester cycle and the political novels grouped around the Pallisers, he singles out *The Way We Live Now* and *The Claverings* as Trollope's two finest achievements.

Meredith's writings have not worn well in the twentieth century, and it is significant that he is not included in the *Select Bibliographical Guide* to the English novel. His gifts as a poet gave his novels an unusual richness in figurative language; but he lacked discrimination in using it, and so many readers might be inclined to agree with a contemporary reviewer who remarked that "his pages so teem with magnificent epigrams...and fantastic locutions that the mind would welcome dullness as a glad relief." Phyllis Bartlett finds the best of his writing in the early novel *The Ordeal of Richard Feverel*, in *Beauchamp's Career*, and above all in *The Egoist*, a powerfully conceived put-down of the Victorian aristocratic hero: it is certainly on this novel that Meredith's fame principally rests today.

In his late thirties, Matthew Arnold almost entirely abandoned the writing of poetry and thereafter devoted himself to the criticism of literature and society: posterity has on the whole approved his decision by regarding him as a distinguished poet but a major critic, the outstanding intermediate figure among poet-critics between Coleridge and T. S. Eliot. In the Victorian age his criticism is preeminent,

INTRODUCTION

together with Newman's, for its persuasive and moderate approach, by comparison with the more strident exhortations of most contemporary publicists. Kenneth Allott divides his attention equally between the poetry and the prose and notes the perpetual tug of war between the Celtic and the Teutonic elements in Arnold's makeup, a tension which is reflected alike in his poetry and his career.

Arthur Hugh Clough was never a popular writer in his own century, but his manifest integrity and clear vision of the intellectual and spiritual crises which beset the Victorian intellectual have steadily won him respect as a decidedly original minor poet. His determination to contribute a new realism to poetry, to write in colloquial terms of ordinary feelings and of the obvious rather than the rare facts in human experience commends him to modern taste. Isobel Armstrong explains how Arnold's poetic stance was precisely the opposite of Clough's, with the former striving to remove poetry as far as possible from the commonplace. She discusses Clough's technical originality, especially his use of the hexameter, and sees in him a poet who looks at once backward to the eighteenth and forward to the twentieth century.

Hopkins' position in the Victorian literary scene is unique: that of a strikingly original poet whose work was unknown except to a handful of friends and was not published until thirty years after his death. Hopkins, moreover, remained uninfluenced by contemporary poetic fashions, nor has he attracted disciples since his reputation became established. As befits the subject, Graham Storey provides the most detailed study in the present volume of poetic technique and of the use of language. He discusses the terms "in-stress" and "in-scape," which are crucial to the understanding of Hopkins' conception of poetry; and he examines the nature and the use of "sprung rhythm," which first appears in *The Wreck of the Deutschland.* He also discusses the relation of Hopkins' religious vocation to his poetry. In general he judges that few poets have communicated so strongly both excitement at natural beauty and its opposite, intimate knowledge of the terrors of despair. In assessing the remarkable stature which Hopkins' reputation has attained since his writings became known to the world, he concludes that his innovations were too extreme for him to have been accepted at a just valuation by his contemporaries, and hence that the delay in publication has worked in his favor.

Edward Lear and Lewis Carroll tend to be paired by literary historians as Victorian solitaries who possessed exceptional talents in writing for children

and extended the range both of English humor and of the language by pioneering the writing of nonsense verse and prose. Joanna Richardson explains how Lear's epilepsy, indifferent health, and unattractive appearance impelled him to lead the life of a traveling painter, although he yearned for domesticity. His verses—and especially his limericks—for all lightness of touch and spontaneity also disclose his awareness of his physical handicaps and of the harshness of society. The essay is particularly appreciative of the delightful quality of Lear's letters, as remarkable for their descriptions as for their wit.

Both Lear's and Carroll's writings have always been recognized as peculiarly English. In European literature there is scarcely any parallel to the nonsense tradition, but in England there are clear antecedents in the patter of Elizabethan clowns and fools, above all in Shakespeare. Lewis Carroll is a more inventive coiner of words than Lear, and in the *Alice* books his dialogue probes depths of meaning which have kept specialists in logic, linguistics, and semantics busy for the past century. Derek Hudson points out how *Alice in Wonderland,* although inspired by the famous Oxford river trip of 1862, was no sudden creation. It had been prepared for many years by means of sketches of childhood impressions and fantasies and practice in the parody of verse and prose. The essay also discusses Carroll's other poems, and his last, though less successful, tale, *Sylvie and Bruno.*

The qualities that the four poets known as the Pre-Raphaelites—Dante Gabriel Rossetti, Christina Rossetti, William Morris, and Algernon Charles Swinburne—can be shown to share are comparatively few, and the differences in their writings are more marked than the resemblances. The artists of the movement originally championed simplicity, freshness, and accuracy in the handling of detail in their subjects. Dante Gabriel Rossetti was the only painter among them who had studied Dante, and his attitude to the treatment of detail embodies a feeling for the symbolic and sacramental significance of objects such as is found in medieval art and religion. But his poetry, small though his output was, displays a surprising diversity, and the particularization of objects by no means dominates his writing. Oswald Doughty's essay describes the many facets and contrasting qualities of Rossetti's verse—the dramatic simplicity of *My Sister's Sleep,* the timeless mystery of *The Burden of Nineveh,* and the sinister regions of mythology where love meets death, as in *Astarte Syriaca.*

Christina Rossetti experienced the influence of both

the Pre-Raphaelite group and the Oxford Movement. Her poetry displays much of the technical skill and economy of form of her brother's and also shares something of its rich pictorial quality, but it stops short of the sensual and overlush effects in which Dante Gabriel sometimes indulges. Georgina Battiscombe gives a detailed account both of her secular and her devotional poetry, and compares her position with that of Emily Brontë, suggesting that Christina may be regarded as a Christian without being a mystic, and Emily as a mystic but not necessarily a Christian. Elsewhere she firmly rebuts the attempts of some biographers to extrapolate Christina's personal relationships from the evidence of her poems.

Poetry was only one of Morris' many creative activities, and his first book of poems is the only one that displays much kinship to the artistic aims of the Pre-Raphaelites. Thereafter his connections with Rossetti were personal rather than literary. Philip Henderson creates an attractive portrait of the generosity and idealism of Morris' temperament and describes the extraordinary versatility of his achievement as a narrative poet, prose writer, designer of wallpaper, furniture, textiles, and typography, and as an evangelist for socialism.

Historically the most interesting member of the Pre-Raphaelite group is Swinburne. His idealization of freedom in the sphere of politics and morals, his championship of oppressed nationalities, and his hostility to authoritarian religions hark back to the patrician individualism of Byron, Shelley, and Landor. His determination to violate the decorum of mid-Victorian literature, his interest in Baudelaire and Sade, and his writings on the doctrine of art for art's sake foreshadow the development of the Aesthetic, Symbolist, and Decadent movements in Britain. Ian Fletcher devotes a large part of his essay to the earliest and best of his compositions, *Atalanta in Calydon* and *Poems and Ballads* (1866); but in praising his virtuosity as a metrical innovator, he remarks on how his notorious tendency to subordinate sense to sound offsets the diversity of his experiments and quickly dulls the response. He also gives an appreciation of Swinburne's little-known prose fiction and singles out his book on Blake as his most lasting achievement in criticism.

Both Carlyle and Ruskin, the two great Victorian prophets of change, withdrew into a melancholy isolation in later life and composed their autobiographies. But if one compares the writings of each in their prime, it is Ruskin who must appear to a modern reader by far the more illuminating commentator, especially on developments in the late nineteenth century in the areas taken up in literature, art, politics, and sociology. Ruskin begins by condemning the Victorian industrial system because it made slaves of its workmen; and in this context he is close to the Pre-Raphaelite view that the creation of beauty is a duty owed to society. It is easy to see how this theory developed (though not through Ruskin) into the Aesthetic concept of art for art's sake, and hence the Aesthetic tenet that the creation of beauty is a duty owed to oneself. Ruskin exerts a further hold upon posterity through his essay *Unto This Last,* written as early as 1860, which was to become a seminal document in the evolution of the British Labour Party. Peter Quennell's essay skillfully steers the reader through the wide range and numerous inconsistencies of Ruskin's doctrines. He stresses a point that is sometimes overlooked, namely the excellence of Ruskin's descriptive prose and his originality among his contemporaries in treating criticism as a record of personal adventure not only among artistic masterpieces but among the beauties of the natural world. Ruskin continually developed his sensibilities both to art and to natural objects to a degree that Carlyle never attempted.

In the last three decades of Queen Victoria's reign, many of the historical factors that had originally shaped the character of the Victorian era changed or disappeared. The Condition of England Question had in some respects lost its urgency; in others, it had been transformed; the balance of power between the classes and especially between employers and employed had significantly shifted.

And in the spheres of literature, art, and ideas, the signs of change were still more apparent. Scientific discoveries had revolutionized the very concept of knowledge and accentuated the general impression that certainty on any question—intellectual, ethical, or artistic—was becoming increasingly unattainable, and hence that judgments must be relative. In spite of a vast growth in resources, man was not creating a more beautiful, but an uglier, world, so that writers and artists felt themselves more and more disillusioned with or alienated from their public. The conception of art defended by Ruskin and the Pre-Raphaelites had been that the technical content of a work of art must be seen as one with the ethical, and that artistic pleasure should be shared by the whole community—as in these writers' idealized visions of the Middle Ages. The Aesthetes, who succeeded them, were intensely conscious of being a minority and regarded aesthetic experience essentially as an individual matter. "The first step towards seeing the object as it really is," wrote Pater—thus upstaging Arnold—"is to know one's own impression of it as it really is.... What is this song or picture to me?"

Ian Fletcher provides a thorough exposition of Pater's criticism, discussing both its strengths and its weaknesses. He notes how, unlike his contemporaries but anticipating modern historiography, Pater stresses the continuity of the Renaissance with both the Middle Ages and modern times. Discussing *Marius the Epicurean*, he draws attention to the resemblances between late imperial Rome and Victorian England and sees in the novel a projection of Pater's inner life, a presentation through imaginary diaries and lectures of modes of belief that appealed to the author. What clearly distinguishes Pater's type of criticism from that of an Arnold or a Leavis is that it remains fixed on the work of art in itself and does not attempt to move beyond to its wider or deeper human relevance.

Pater guarded his hedonistic philosophy behind the lifestyle of a recluse. The significance of Oscar Wilde's career lies as much in its tragic public aspects as in his writings: he was willing to present his views on art and the artist upon the stage of real life. John Stokes's essay marshals with a welcome lucidity the frequently paradoxical sequence of Wilde's ideas, drawn from his lectures, essays, fiction, plays, and conversation. One of this essay's principal themes concerns Wilde's fulfillment of the artist's role in a repressive and Philistine society. The artist, Wilde contended, has exceptional needs and can fulfill himself only through his art. Yet to judge his fulfillment in terms of production alone would be to accept the values of the Philistine, and thus the artist finds his true fulfillment in style, in his very refusal to produce: he seeks to be somebody rather than to do something. This conception is akin to Baudelaire's idea of the dandy, which enables the artist to scorn the Philistine precepts of convention-bound morality, material production, and originality as the measure of social progress. In terms of Wilde's own career and the plot of such a book as *Dorian Gray*, it is easy to see how these ideas lead to the indulgence of fantasy, disguise, and the enactment of a double life.

The two novelists of the period discussed here present a striking contrast: Stevenson, the creator of historical and adventure stories; Gissing, the realist. G.B. Stern's account of Stevenson is as much biographical as critical. In her treatment of the novels, she pays particular attention to Stevenson's power in presenting the peculiar energy and fascination displayed by evil characters: Long John Silver, the Master of Ballantrae, and Mr. Hyde. She also stresses Stevenson's gifts of style and his awareness of the technical demands of novel writing which attracted the admiration of Henry James.

George Gissing, as befits a disciple of Dickens and one of his best critics, is a late contributor to the Condition of England Question. While he undoubtedly observed and experienced poverty at first hand for many years, his descriptions lack the Dickensian power to bring a scene instantly to life. And although he possessed a keen and compassionate social conscience, he could not conceal his temperamental lack of sympathy for the uneducated. Still, it is noteworthy that there has been a revival of interest during recent years in his novels, many of which are once more in print. A. C. Ward examines the nature of Gissing's realism, which differed from that of Zola, and notes how his writing regains its vitality whenever he deals with characters who speak his own language. The essay rates *New Grub Street* as the best of his novels, but reserves its highest praise for the book that has always attracted most readers, the semi-autobiographical *Private Papers of Henry Ryecroft*. Here at last the author hit upon a theme to use his descriptive powers on subjects that were closer to his heart.

The series was founded by Laurence Brander, then director of publications, at the British Council. The first editor was T. O. Beachcroft, himself a distinguished writer of short stories. His successors were the late Bonamy Dobrée, formerly Professor of English Literature at the University of Leeds; Geoffrey Bullough, Professor Emeritus of English Literature, King's College, London, and author of *The Narrative and Dramatic Sources of Shakespeare*; and since 1970 the present writer. To these founders and predecessors *British Writers* is deeply indebted for the design of the series, the planning of its scope, and the distinction of their editorship, and I personally for many years of friendship and advice, and invaluable experience generously shared.

—Ian Scott-Kilvert

Chronological Table

1770 Boston Massacre
Edmund Burke's *Thoughts on the Cause of the Present Discontents*
Oliver Goldsmith's *The Deserted Village*
Death of Thomas Chatterton
Ludwig van Beethoven born
William Wordsworth born

1771 Arkwright's first spinning mill founded
Deaths of Thomas Gray and Tobias Smollett
Walter Scott born

1772 Samuel Taylor Coleridge born

1773 Boston Tea Party
Goldsmith's *She Stoops to Conquer*
Johann Wolfgang von Goethe's *Götz von Berlichingen*

1774 The first Continental Congress meets in Philadelphia
Goethe's *Sorrows of Young Werther*
Death of Oliver Goldsmith
Robert Southey born

1775 Burke's speech on American taxation
American War of Independence begins with the battles of Lexington and Concord
Samuel Johnson's *Journey to the Western Islands of Scotland*
Richard Brinsley Sheridan's *The Rivals* and *The Duenna*
Beaumarchais's *Le Barbier de Seville*
James Watt and Matthew Boulton begin building steam engines in England
Jane Austen born
Charles Lamb born
Walter Savage Landor born
Matthew Lewis born

1776 American Declaration of Independence
Edward Gibbon's *Decline and Fall of the Roman Empire* (1776–1788)
Adam Smith's *Inquiry into the Nature & Causes of the Wealth of Nations*
Thomas Paine's *Common Sense*
Death of David Hume
John Constable born

1777 Maurice Morgann's *Essay on the Dramatic Character of Sir John Falstaff*

Sheridan's *The School for Scandal* first performed (published 1780)
General Burgoyne surrenders at Saratoga

1778 The American colonies allied with France
Britain and France at war
Captain James Cook discovers Hawaii
Death of William Pitt, first earl of Chatham
Deaths of Jean Jacques Rousseau and Voltaire
William Hazlitt born

1779 Johnson's *Prefaces to the Works of the English Poets* (1779–1781); reissued in 1781 as *The Lives of the Most Eminent English Poets*
Sheridan's *The Critic*
Samuel Crompton invents the spinning mule
Death of David Garrick

1780 The Gordon riots in London

1781 Charles Cornwallis surrenders at Yorktown
Immanuel Kant's *Critique of Pure Reason*
Friedrich von Schiller's *Die Räuber*

1782 William Cowper's "The Journey of John Gilpin" published in the *Public Advertiser*
Pierre de Laclos's *Les Liaisons dangereuses*
Rousseau's *Confessions* published posthumously

1783 American War of Independence ended by the Definitive Treaty of Peace, signed at Paris
William Blake's *Poetical Sketches*
George Crabbe's *The Village*
William Pitt the younger becomes prime minister
Henri Beyle (Stendhal) born

1784 Beaumarchais's *Le Mariage de Figaro* first performed (published 1785)
Death of Samuel Johnson

1785 Warren Hastings returns to England from India

James Boswell's *The Journal of a Tour of the Hebrides, with Samuel Johnson, LL.D.*

Cowper's *The Task*

Edmund Cartwright invents the power loom

Thomas De Quincey born

Thomas Love Peacock born

1786 William Beckford's *Vathek* published in English (originally written in French in 1782)

Robert Burns's *Poems Chiefly in the Scottish Dialect*

Wolfgang Amadeus Mozart's *The Marriage of Figaro*

Death of Frederick the Great

1787 The Committee for Abolition of the Slave Trade founded in England

The Constitutional Convention meets at Philadelphia; the Constitution is signed

1788 The trial of Hastings begins on charges of corruption of the government in India

The Estates-General of France summoned

U. S. Constitution is ratified

George Washington elected president of the United States

Giovanni Casanova's *Histoire de ma fuite* (first manuscript of his memoirs)

The *Daily Universal Register* becomes the *Times* (London)

George Gordon, Lord Byron born

1789 The Estates-General meets at Versailles

The National Assembly (Assemblée Nationale) convened

The fall of the Bastille marks the beginning of the French Revolution

The National Assembly draws up the Declaration of Rights of Man and of the Citizen

First U. S. Congress meets in New York

Blake's *Songs of Innocence*

Jeremy Bentham's *Introduction to the Principles of Morals and Legislation* introduces the theory of utilitarianism

Gilbert White's *Natural History of Selborne*

1790 Congress sets permanent capital city site on Potomac River

First U.S. Census

Burke's *Reflections on the Revolution in France*

Blake's *The Marriage of Heaven and Hell*

Edmund Malone's edition of Shakespeare

Death of Benjamin Franklin

1791 French royal family's flight from Paris and capture at Varennes; imprisonment in the Tuileries

Bill of Rights is ratified

Paine's *The Rights of Man* (1791–1792)

Boswell's *Life of Johnson*

Burns's *Tam o' Shanter*

The *Observer* founded

1792 The Prussians invade France and are repulsed at Valmy

September massacres

The National Convention declares royalty abolished in France

Washington reelected

New York Stock Exchange opens

Mary Wollstonecraft's *A Vindication of the Rights of Woman*

William Bligh's voyage to the South Seas in H.M.S. *Bounty*

Percy Bysshe Shelley born

1793 Trial and execution of Louis XVI and Marie Antoinette

France declares war against England

The Committee of Public Safety (Comité de Salut Public) established

Eli Whitney devises the cotton gin

William Godwin's *An Enquiry Concerning Political Justice*

Blake's *Visions of the Daughters of Albion* and *America*

Wordsworth's *An Evening Walk* and *Descriptive Sketches*

1794 Execution of Georges Danton and Maximilien de Robespierre

Paine's *The Age of Reason* (1794–1796)

Blake's *Songs of Experience*

Ann Radcliffe's *The Mysteries of Udolpho*

Death of Edward Gibbon

1795 The government of the Directory established (1795–1799)

Hastings acquitted

Landor's *Poems*

Death of James Boswell
John Keats born
Thomas Carlyle born

1796 Napoleon Bonaparte takes command in Italy
Matthew Lewis' *The Monk*
John Adams elected president
Death of Robert Burns

1797 The peace of Campo Formio: extinction of the Venetian Republic
X. Y. Z. Affair
Mutinies in the Royal Navy at Spithead and the Nore
Blake's *Vala, Or the Four Zoas* (first version)
Deaths of Edmund Burke, Mary Wollstonecraft, and Horace Walpole
Franz Schubert born

1798 Napoleon invades Egypt
Horatio Nelson wins the battle of the Nile
Wordsworth and Coleridge's *Lyrical Ballads*
Landor's *Gebir*
Thomas Malthus' *Essay on the Principle of Population*

1799 Napoleon becomes first consul
Pitt introduces first income tax in Great Britain
Sheridan's *Pizarro*
Honoré de Balzac born
Thomas Hood born
Alexander Pushkin born

1800 Thomas Jefferson defeats John Adams for the presidency
Alessandro Volta produces electricity from a cell
Library of Congress established
Death of William Cowper
Thomas Babington Macaulay born

1801 First census taken in England

1802 The Treaty of Amiens marks the end of the French Revolutionary War
The *Edinburgh Review* founded

1803 England's war with France renewed
The Louisiana Purchase
Robert Fulton propels a boat by steam power on the Seine
Hector Berlioz born

1804 Napoleon crowned emperor of the French
Jefferson reelected

Blake's *Milton* (1804–1808) and *Jerusalem*
The Code Napoléon promulgated in France
Beethoven's "Eroica" Symphony
Schiller's *Wilhelm Tell*
Benjamin Disraeli born
Nathaniel Hawthorne born

1805 Napoleon plans the invasion of England
Battle of Trafalgar
Battle of Austerlitz
Beethoven's *Fidelio* produced for the first time
Scott's *The Lay of the Last Minstrel*

1806 Scott's *Marmion*
Death of William Pitt
Death of Charles James Fox
Elizabeth Barrett born

1807 France invades Portugal
Aaron Burr tried for treason and acquitted
Byron's *Hours of Idleness*
Charles and Mary Lamb's *Tales from Shakespeare*
Thomas Moore's *Irish Melodies*
Wordsworth's *Ode on the Intimations of Immortality*

1808 National uprising in Spain against the French invasion
The Peninsular War begins
James Madison elected president
Covent Garden theater burned down
Goethe's *Faust*, part I
Beethoven's Fifth Symphony completed
Lamb's *Specimens of English Dramatic Poets*

1809 Drury Lane theater burned down and rebuilt
The *Quarterly Review* founded
Byron's *English Bards and Scotch Reviewers*
Byron sails for the Mediterranean
Francisco Goya's *Los Desastres de la Guerra* (1809-1814)
Edward FitzGerald born
Edgar Allan Poe born
Alfred Tennyson born

1810 Crabbe's *The Borough*
Scott's *The Lady of the Lake*
Fréderic Chopin born
Elizabeth Gaskell born
Robert Schumann born

CHRONOLOGICAL TABLE

1811 **The Regency of George IV (1811–1820)**
Luddite Riots begin
Coleridge's *Lectures on Shakespeare* (1811–1814)
Jane Austen's *Sense and Sensibility*
Shelley's *The Necessity of Atheism*
John Constable's *Dedham Vale*
Franz Liszt born
William Makepeace Thackeray born

1812 Napoleon invades Russia; captures and retreats from Moscow
U. S. declares war against England
Henry Bell's steamship *Comet* is launched on the Clyde river
Madison reelected
Byron's *Childe Harold*, cantos I–II
The Brothers Grimm's *Fairy Tales* (1812–1815)
Hegel's *Science of Logic*
Robert Browning born
Charles Dickens born
Edward Lear born

1813 Wellington wins the battle of Vitoria and enters France
Jane Austen's *Pride and Prejudice*
Byron's *The Giaour* and *The Bride of Abydos*
Shelley's *Queen Mab*
Southey's *Life of Nelson*
Giuseppe Verdi born
Richard Wagner born

1814 Napoleon abdicates and is exiled to Elba; Bourbon restoration with Louis XVIII
Treaty of Ghent ends the war between Britain and U. S.
Jane Austen's *Mansfield Park*
Byron's *The Corsair* and *Lara*
Scott's *Waverley*
Wordsworth's *The Excursion*

1815 Napoleon returns to France (the Hundred Days); is defeated at Waterloo and exiled to St. Helena
U.S.S. *Fulton*, the first steam warship, built
Scott's *Guy Mannering*
Schlegel's *Lectures on Dramatic Art and Literature* translated
Wordsworth's *The White Doe of Rylstone*
Anthony Trollope born

1816 Byron leaves England permanently

The Elgin Marbles exhibited in the British Museum
James Monroe elected president
Jane Austen's *Emma*
Byron's *Childe Harold*, canto III
Coleridge's *Christabel. Kubla Khan: A Vision. The Pains of Sleep*
Benjamin Constant's *Adolphe*
Goethe's *Italienische Reise*
Peacock's *Headlong Hall*
Scott's *The Antiquary*
Shelley's *Alastor*
Rossini's *Il Barbiere di Siviglia*
Death of Richard Brinsley Sheridan
Charlotte Brontë born

1817 *Blackwood's Edinburgh* magazine founded
Jane Austen's *Northanger Abbey* and *Persuasion*
Byron's *Manfred*
Coleridge's *Biographia Literaria*
Hazlitt's *The Characters of Shakespeare's Plays* and *The Round Table*
Keats's *Poems*
Peacock's *Melincourt*
David Ricardo's *Principles of Political Economy and Taxation*
Death of Jane Austen
Death of Mme. de Staël
Branwell Brontë born
Henry David Thoreau born

1818 Byron's *Childe Harold*, canto IV, and *Beppo*
Hazlitt's *Lectures on the English Poets*
Keats's *Endymion*
Peacock's *Nightmare Abbey*
Scott's *Rob Roy* and *The Heart of Midlothian*
Shelley's *The Revolt of Islam*
Mary Shelley's *Frankenstein*
Emily Brontë born
Karl Marx born
Ivan Sergeyevich Turgenev born

1819 The *Savannah* becomes the first steamship to cross the Atlantic (in 26 days)
Peterloo massacre in Manchester
Byron's *Don Juan* (1819–1824) and *Mazeppa*
Crabbe's *Tales of the Hall*
Géricault's *Raft of the Medusa*
Hazlitt's *Lectures on the English Comic Writers*

Arthur Schopenhauer's *Die Welt als Wille und Vorstellung (The World as Will and Idea)*

Scott's *The Bride of Lammermoor* and *A Legend of Montrose*

Shelley's *The Cenci,* "The Masque of Anarchy," and "Ode to the West Wind"

Wordsworth's *Peter Bell*

Queen Victoria born

Arthur Hugh Clough born

Marian Evans (George Eliot) born

Herman Melville born

John Ruskin born

Walt Whitman born

1820–1830 Reign of George IV

1820 Trial of Queen Caroline

Cato Street Conspiracy suppressed; Arthur Thistlewood hanged

Monroe reelected

Missouri Compromise

The *London* magazine founded

Keats's *Lamia, Isabella, The Eve of St. Agnes, and Other Poems*

Hazlitt's *Lectures Chiefly on the Dramatic Literature of the Age of Elizabeth*

Charles Maturin's *Melmoth the Wanderer*

Scott's *Ivanhoe* and *The Monastery*

Shelley's *Prometheus Unbound*

Anne Brontë born

1821 Greek War of Independence begins

Liberia founded as a colony for freed slaves

Byron's *Cain, Marino Faliero, The Two Foscari,* and *Sardanapalus*

Hazlitt's *Table Talk* (1821–1822)

Scott's *Kenilworth*

Shelley's *Adonais* and *Epipsychidion*

Death of John Keats

Death of Napoleon

Charles Baudelaire born

Feodor Dostoyevsky born

Gustave Flaubert born

1822 The Massacres of Chios (Greeks rebel against Turkish rule)

Byron's *The Vision of Judgment*

De Quincey's *Confessions of an English Opium-Eater*

Peacock's *Maid Marian*

Scott's *Peveril of the Peak*

Shelley's *Hellas*

Death of Percy Bysshe Shelley

Matthew Arnold born

1823 Monroe Doctrine proclaimed

Byron's *The Age of Bronze* and *The Island*

Lamb's *Essays of Elia*

Scott's *Quentin Durward*

1824 The National Gallery opened in London

John Quincy Adams elected president

The *Westminster Review* founded

Beethoven's Ninth Symphony first performed

James Hogg's *The Private Memoirs and Confessions of a Justified Sinner*

Landor's *Imaginary Conversations* (1824–1829)

Scott's *Redgauntlet*

Death of George Gordon, Lord Byron

1825 Inauguration of steam-powered passenger and freight service on the Stockton and Darlington railway

Bolivia and Brazil become independent

Alessandro Manzoni's *I Promessi Sposi* (1825–1826)

1826 André-Marie Ampère's *Mémoire sur la théorie mathématique des phénomènes électrodynamiques*

James Fenimore Cooper's *The Last of the Mohicans*

Disraeli's *Vivian Gray* (1826–1827)

Scott's *Woodstock*

1827 The battle of Navarino ensures the independence of Greece

Josef Ressel obtains patent for the screw propeller for steamships

Heinrich Heine's *Buch der Lieder*

Death of Ludwig van Beethoven

Death of William Blake

1828 Andrew Jackson elected president

Death of Franz Schubert

Henrik Ibsen born

George Meredith born

Dante Gabriel Rossetti born

Leo Tolstoy born

1829 The Catholic Emancipation Act

Robert Peel establishes the metropolitan police force

Greek independence recognized by Turkey

Balzac begins *La Comédie humaine* (1829–1848)

Peacock's *The Misfortunes of Elphin*
J. M. W. Turner's *Ulysses Deriding Polyphemus*

1830–1837 Reign of William IV

1830 Charlex X of France abdicates and is succeeded by Louis-Philippe
The Liverpool-Manchester railway opened
Tennyson's *Poems, Chiefly Lyrical*
Death of William Hazlitt
Camille Pissarro born
Christina Rossetti born

1831 Michael Faraday discovers electromagnetic induction
Charles Darwin's voyage on H. M. S. *Beagle* begins (1831–1836)
The Barbizon school of artists' first exhibition
Nat Turner slave revolt crushed in Virginia
Peacock's *Crotchet Castle*
Stendhal's *Le Rouge et le noir*
Edward Trelawny's *The Adventures of a Younger Son*

1832 The first Reform Bill
Samuel Morse invents the telegraph
Jackson reelected
Disraeli's *Contarini Fleming*
Goethe's *Faust*, part II
Tennyson's *Poems, Chiefly Lyrical*, including "The Lotus-Eaters" and "The Lady of Shalott"
Death of Johann Wolfgang von Goethe
Death of Sir Walter Scott
Charles Lutwidge Dodgson (Lewis Carroll) born
Édouard Manet born
Leslie Stephen born

1833 Robert Browning's *Pauline*
John Keble launches the Oxford Movement
The Factory Act
American Anti-Slavery Society founded
Lamb's *Last Essays of Elia*
Carlyle's *Sartor Resartus* (1833–1834)
Pushkin's *Eugene Onegin*
Mendelssohn's Italian Symphony first performed
Johannes Brahms born

1834 Abolition of slavery in the British Empire
Louis Braille's alphabet for the blind

The Factory Act
Balzac's *Le Père Goriot*
Nikolai Gogol's *Dead Souls*, part I (1834–1842)
Death of Samuel Taylor Coleridge
Death of Charles Lamb
William Morris born

1835 Hans Christian Andersen's *Fairy Tales* (1st series)
Robert Browning's *Paracelsus*
Alexis de Tocqueville's *De la Democratie en Amerique* (1835–1840)
Samuel Langhorne Clemens (Mark Twain) born

1836 Texas becomes independent from Mexico and U. S. recognizes Republic of Texas
Martin Van Buren elected president
Dickens' *Sketches by Boz* (1836–1837)
Landor's *Pericles and Aspasia*

1837–1901 Reign of Queen Victoria

1837 Isaac Pitman publishes his system of shorthand
Carlyle's *The French Revolution*
Dickens' *Oliver Twist* (1837–1838) and *Pickwick Papers*
Disraeli's *Venetia* and *Henrietta Temple*
Death of John Constable
Death of Alexander Pushkin
Algernon Charles Swinburne born

1838 Chartist movement in England
National Gallery in London opened
Elizabeth Barrett Browning's *The Seraphim and Other Poems*
Dickens' *Nicholas Nickleby* (1838–1839)
Georges Bizet born

1839 Louis Daguerre perfects process for producing an image on a silver-coated copper plate
Faraday's *Experimental Researches in Electricity* (1839–1855)
First Chartist riots
Opium War between Great Britain and China
Carlyle's *Chartism*
Chopin's twenty-four *Preludes*
Stendhal's *La Chartreuse de Parme*
Paul Cézanne born
Walter Horatio Pater born

1840 Canadian Act of Union
Queen Victoria marries Prince Albert
Charles Barry begins construction of

the Houses of Parliament (1840-1852)
William Henry Harrison elected president
Robert Browning's *Sordello*
Richard Henry Dana's *Two Years Before the Mast*
Thomas Hardy born
Claude Monet born
Auguste Rodin born
Peter Ilyich Tchaikovsky born

1841 New Zealand proclaimed a British colony
James Clark Ross discovers the Antarctic continent
Punch founded
New York Tribune founded
John Tyler succeeds to the presidency after the death of Harrison
Carlyle's *Heroes and Hero-Worship*
Dickens' *The Old Curiosity Shop*
Ralph Waldo Emerson's *Essays, First Series*
Henry Wadsworth Longfellow's *Ballads and Other Poems*
Edgar Allan Poe's "The Murders in the Rue Morgue"
Anton Dvořák born
Pierre Auguste Renoir born

1842 Chartist riots
Income tax revived in Great Britain
The Mines Act, forbidding work underground by women or by children under the age of ten
Charles Edward Mudie's Lending Library founded in London
Dickens visits America
Robert Browning's *Dramatic Lyrics*
Gogol's *Dead Souls*, part II (1842-1852)
Macaulay's *Lays of Ancient Rome*
Tennyson's *Poems*, including "Morte d'Arthur," "St. Simeon Stylites," and "Ulysses"
Wordsworth's *Poems*
Death of Stendhal

1843 Marc Isambard Brunel's Thames tunnel opened
The *Economist* founded
Carlyle's *Past and Present*
Dickens' *A Christmas Carol*
Kierkegaard's *Either/Or*
John Stuart Mill's *Logic*

Macaulay's *Critical and Historical Essays*
John Ruskin's *Modern Painters* (1843–1860)
Wagner's *The Flying Dutchman* performed in Dresden
Death of Robert Southey
Edvard Grieg born
Henry James born

1844 Rochdale Society of Equitable Pioneers, one of the first consumers' cooperatives, founded by twenty-eight Lancashire weavers
James K. Polk elected president
Elizabeth Barrett Browning's *Poems*, including "The Cry of the Children"
Dickens' *Martin Chuzzlewit*
Disraeli's *Coningsby*
Dumas's *The Three Musketeers*
Turner's *Rain, Steam and Speed*
Robert Bridges born
Friedrich Wilhelm Nietzsche born

1845 The great potato famine in Ireland begins (1845–1849)
Disraeli's *Sybil*
Dumas's *The Count of Monte Cristo*
Poe's *The Raven and Other Poems*
Wagner's *Tannhäuser* performed in Dresden
Death of Thomas Hood

1846 Repeal of the Corn Laws
Mexican War (1846–1848)
The *Daily News* founded (edited by Dickens the first three weeks)
Elias Howe's sewing machine patented
Standard-gauge railway introduced in Britain
Balzac's *La Cousine Bette*
The Brontës' pseudonymous *Poems by Currer, Ellis and Acton Bell*
Lear's *Book of Nonsense*
Melville's *Typee*

1847 The California gold rush begins
The Mormons, led by Brigham Young, found Salt Lake City
The Ten Hours Factory Act
James Simpson uses chloroform as an anesthetic
Anne Brontë's *Agnes Grey*
Charlotte Brontë's *Jane Eyre*
Emily Brontë's *Wuthering Heights*

CHRONOLOGICAL TABLE

Emerson's *Poems*
Tennyson's *The Princess*
Balzac's *Le Cousin Pons*

1848 The year of revolutions in France, Germany, Italy, Hungary, Poland
Marx and Engels issue *The Communist Manifesto*
The Chartist Petition
The Pre-Raphaelite Brotherhood founded
Zachary Taylor elected president
Anne Brontë's *The Tenant of Wildfell Hall*
Dickens' *Dombey and Son*
Dumas's *La Dame aux Camélias*
Elizabeth Gaskell's *Mary Barton*
Macaulay's *History of England* (1848–1861)
Mill's *Principles of Political Economy*
Thackeray's *Vanity Fair*
Death of Emily Brontë

1849 Bedford College for women founded
Arnold's *The Strayed Reveller*
Charlotte Brontë's *Shirley*
Ruskin's *The Seven Lamps of Architecture*
Death of Anne Brontë
Death of Fréderic Chopin
Death of Edgar Allan Poe
August Strindberg born

1850 The Public Libraries Act
First submarine telegraph cable laid between Dover and Calais
Millard Fillmore succeeds to the presidency after the death of Taylor
Elizabeth Barrett Browning's *Sonnets from the Portuguese*
Carlyle's *Latter-Day Pamphlets*
Dickens' *Household Words* (1850–1859) and *David Copperfield*
Nathaniel Hawthorne's *The Scarlet Letter*
Charles Kingsley's *Alton Locke*
The Pre-Raphaelites publish the *Germ*
Tennyson's *In Memoriam*
Thackeray's *The History of Pendennis*
Wordsworth's *The Prelude*
Death of Honoré de Balzac
Death of William Wordsworth
Guy de Maupassant born
Robert Louis Stevenson born

1851 The Great Exhibition opens at the Crystal Palace in Hyde Park
Louis Napoleon seizes power in France
Gold strike in Victoria incites Australian gold rush
Elizabeth Gaskell's *Cranford* (1851–1853)
Melville's *Moby Dick*
Hawthorne's *The House of the Seven Gables*
Meredith's *Poems*
Ruskin's *The Stones of Venice* (1851–1853)
Verdi's *Rigoletto* produced in Venice

1852 The Second Empire proclaimed with Napoleon III as emperor
The Niagara Falls Bridge constructed
David Livingstone begins to explore the Zambezi (1852–1856)
Franklin Pierce elected president
Arnold's *Empedocles on Etna*
Harriet Beecher Stowe's *Uncle Tom's Cabin*
Thackeray's *The History of Henry Esmond, Esq.*
George Moore born

1853 Crimean War (1853–1856)
Arnold's *Poems*, including "The Scholar Gypsy" and "Sohrab and Rustum"
Charlotte Brontë's *Villette*
Elizabeth Gaskell's *Ruth*
Hawthorne's *Tanglewood Tales for Girls and Boys*
Verdi's *Il Trovatore* and *La Traviata*
Vincent van Gogh born

1854 Frederick D. Maurice's Working Men's College founded in London with more than 130 pupils
Abraham Gesner manufactures kerosene
Battle of Balaklava
Dickens' *Hard Times*
Theodor Mommsen's *History of Rome* (1854–1856)
Tennyson's "The Charge of the Light Brigade"
Thoreau's *Walden*
Florence Nightingale in the Crimea (1854–1856)
Arthur Rimbaud born
Oscar Wilde born

1855 David Livingstone discovers the Victoria Falls
Robert Browning's *Men and Women*
Elizabeth Gaskell's *North and South*
Tennyson's *Maud*
Thackeray's *The Newcomes*
Trollope's *The Warden*
Whitman's *Leaves of Grass*
Death of Charlotte Brontë

1856 The Treaty of Paris ends the Crimean War
Henry Bessemer's steel process invented
James Buchanan elected president
Flaubert's *Madame Bovary* (1856; new edition in book form, 1857)
Death of Robert Schumann
Sigmund Freud born
George Bernard Shaw born

1857 The Indian Mutiny begins; crushed in 1858
The *Atlantic Monthly* founded
Dred Scott decision, involving legal status of slaves
The Matrimonial Causes Act
Baudelaire's *Les Fleurs du mal*
Charlotte Brontë's *The Professor*
Elizabeth Barrett Browning's *Aurora Leigh*
Dickens' *Little Dorritt*
Elizabeth Gaskell's *The Life of Charlotte Brontë*
Thomas Hughes's *Tom Brown's School Days*
Trollope's *Barchester Towers*
Joseph Conrad born
Edward Elgar born
George Gissing born

1858 Carlyle's *History of Frederick the Great* (1858–1865)
Arthur Hugh Clough's *Amours de Voyage* first published
George Eliot's *Scenes of Clerical Life*
Morris' *The Defence of Guinevere*
Trollope's *Dr. Thorne*
Giacomo Puccini born

1859 John Brown raids Harper's Ferry and is executed
Edwin Drake drills the first oil well in Pennsylvania
Charles Darwin's *The Origin of Species*
Dickens' *A Tale of Two Cities*
George Eliot's *Adam Bede*

FitzGerald's *The Rubaiyat of Omar Khayyám*
Meredith's *The Ordeal of Richard Feverel*
Mill's *On Liberty*
Samuel Smiles's *Self-Help*
Tennyson's *Idylls of the King*
Death of Thomas De Quincey
Death of Thomas Babington Macaulay
A. E. Housman born
Francis Thompson born

1860 Giuseppe Garibaldi's "Thousand" liberate Sicily and Naples
Abraham Lincoln elected president
The *Cornhill* magazine founded with Thackeray as editor
William Wilkie Collins' *The Woman in White*
George Eliot's *The Mill on the Floss*
Anton Chekhov born

1861 American Civil War begins
Victor Emmanuel II of Sardinia proclaimed king of Italy
Louis Pasteur presents the germ theory of disease
Arnold's *Lectures on Translating Homer*
Dickens' *Great Expectations*
George Eliot's *Silas Marner*
Meredith's *Evan Harrington*
Francis Turner Palgrave's *The Golden Treasury*
Trollope's *Framley Parsonage*
Peacock's *Gryll Grange*
Death of Prince Albert
Death of Elizabeth Barrett Browning
Death of Arthur Hugh Clough

1862 George Eliot's *Romola*
Victor Hugo's *Les Misérables*
Meredith's *Modern Love*
Christina Rossetti's *Goblin Market*
Ruskin's *Unto This Last*
Trollope's *Orley Farm*
Turgenev's *Fathers and Sons*
Death of Henry David Thoreau
Claude Debussy born

1863 Thomas Huxley's *Man's Place in Nature*
Lincoln's Gettysburg Address
Emancipation Proclamation
Ernest Renan's *La Vie de Jésus*
Berlioz's *Les Troyens* produced in Paris
Manet's *Le Déjeuner sur l'herbe*
Tolstoy's *War and Peace* (1863–1869)

Death of William Makepeace Thackeray

1864 The Geneva Red Cross Convention signed by twelve nations
Robert Browning's *Dramatis Personae*
John Henry Newman's *Apologia pro vita sua*
Tennyson's *Enoch Arden*
Trollope's *The Small House at Allington*
Death of Nathaniel Hawthorne
Death of Walter Savage Landor
Henri de Toulouse-Lautrec born

1865 Assassination of Lincoln; Andrew Johnson succeeds to the presidency
American Civil War ends
13th Amendment abolishes slavery in the United States
Massachusetts Institute of Technology opened
Arnold's *Essays in Criticism* (1st series)
Carroll's *Alice's Adventures in Wonderland*
Dickens' *Our Mutual Friend*
Meredith's *Rhoda Fleming*
A. C. Swinburne's *Atalanta in Calydon*
Wagner's *Tristan und Isolde* first produced in Munich
Death of Elizabeth Gaskell
Rudyard Kipling born
William Butler Yeats born

1866 Alfred Nobel invents dynamite
Austria at war with Prussia
First successful transatlantic telegraph cable laid
Dostoyevsky's *Crime and Punishment*
George Eliot's *Felix Holt, the Radical*
Elizabeth Gaskell's *Wives and Daughters*
Ibsen's *Brand*
Swinburne's *Poems and Ballads*
Death of Thomas Love Peacock
Herbert George (H. G.) Wells born

1867 The second Reform Bill
Arnold's *New Poems*
Bagehot's *The English Constitution*
Carlyle's *Shooting Niagara*
Marx's *Das Kapital* (vol. I)
Ibsen's *Peer Gynt*
Trollope's *The Last Chronicle of Barset*
Verdi's *Don Carlos* produced in Paris
Death of Charles Baudelaire

Arnold Bennett born
John Galsworthy born
Luigi Pirandello born

1868 Gladstone becomes prime minister (1868–1874)
Johnson impeached by House of Representatives; acquitted by Senate
Ulysses S. Grant elected president
Robert Browning's *The Ring and the Book* (1868–1869)
Collins' *The Moonstone*
Dostoyevsky's *The Idiot*
Wagner's *Die Meistersinger* produced in Munich
Norman Douglas born

1869 The Suez Canal opened
Girton College, Cambridge, founded
Arnold's *Culture and Anarchy*
Flaubert's *L'Education sentimentale* (dated 1870)
Mill's *The Subjection of Women*
Trollope's *Phineas Finn*
Wagner's *Rheingold* produced in Munich
Death of Hector Berlioz
André Gide born
Henri Matisse born

1870 The Franco-Prussian War begins
The Elementary Education Act establishes schools under the aegis of local boards
Heinrich Schliemann begins to excavate Troy
Dickens' *Edwin Drood*
Disraeli's *Lothair*
Morris' *The Earthly Paradise*
Dante Gabriel Rossetti's *Poems*
Death of Charles Dickens
Death of Alexandre Dumas (père)
Lenin born

1871 The Paris Commune
The Treaty of Frankfurt ends the Franco-Prussian war
Trade unions legalized
Newnham College, Cambridge, founded for women students
Carroll's *Through the Looking Glass*
Darwin's *The Descent of Man*
Meredith's *The Adventures of Harry Richmond*
Swinburne's *Songs Before Sunrise*
Verdi's *Aida* produced in Cairo

Marcel Proust born
Paul Valéry born

1872 Samuel Butler's *Erewhon*
George Eliot's *Middlemarch*
Grant reelected
Hardy's *Under the Greenwood Tree*
Turgenev's *A Month in the Country* first performed

1873 E. Remington and Sons begins manufacturing typewriters
Arnold's *Literature and Dogma*
Mill's *Autobiography*
Pater's *Studies in the History of the Renaissance*
Tolstoy's *Anna Karenina* (1873–1877)
Trollope's *The Eustace Diamonds*
Death of John Stuart Mill
Ford Madox Ford born

1874 Disraeli becomes prime minister
Hardy's *Far from the Madding Crowd*
James Thomson's *The City of Dreadful Night*
Gilbert Keith (G. K.) Chesterton born
Winston Churchill born
William Somerset Maugham born

1875 Britain buys Suez Canal shares
Trollope's *The Way We Live Now*
Bizet's *Carmen* produced in Paris
Death of Hans Christian Andersen
Death of Georges Bizet
Rainer Maria Rilke born

1876 Bell transmits first message on the telephone
F. H. Bradley's *Ethical Studies*
George Eliot's *Daniel Deronda*
Henry James's *Roderick Hudson*
Meredith's *Beauchamp's Career*
Morris' *Sigurd the Volsung*
Trollope's *The Prime Minister*
Twain's *The Adventures of Tom Sawyer*
Brahms's *First Symphony*
Wagner's *Götterdämmerung* and *Siegfried* produced in Bayreuth
George Macauley Trevelyan born

1877 Russia and Turkey at war
Edison invents the phonograph record
Rutherford B. Hayes elected president after Electoral Commission awards him disputed votes
Ibsen's *Pillars of Society*
Henry James's *The American*

Zola's *L'Assommoir*
Cézanne shows sixteen pictures at the third impressionist exhibition

1878 The Congress of Berlin ends the Russo-Turkish War
Electric street lighting introduced in London
A. A. Pope manufactures the first American bicycles
Hardy's *The Return of the Native*
Swinburne's *Poems and Ballads. Second Series*

1879 Somerville College and Lady Margaret Hall opened at Oxford for women
The London telephone exchange built
Gladstone's Midlothian campaign (1879–1880)
Browning's *Dramatic Idyls*
Ibsen's *A Doll's House*
Meredith's *The Egoist*
Albert Einstein born
Edward Morgan (E. M.) Forster born
Josef Stalin born

1880 Gladstone's second term as prime minister (1880–1885)
James A. Garfield elected president
Louis Pasteur discovers streptococcus
Browning's *Dramatic Idyls Second Series*
Disraeli's *Endymion*
Dostoyevsky's *The Brothers Karamazov*
Hardy's *The Trumpet-Major*
James Thomson's *The City of Dreadful Night*
Zola's *Nana*
Death of George Eliot
Death of Gustave Flaubert
Jacob Epstein born

1881 Garfield assassinated; Chester A. Arthur succeeds to the presidency
Ibsen's *Ghosts*
Henry James's *The Portrait of a Lady* and *Washington Square*
D. G. Rossetti's *Ballads and Sonnets*
Death of Thomas Carlyle
Death of Benjamin Disraeli
Béla Bartók born
Pablo Picasso born

1882 Triple Alliance formed between German empire, Austrian empire, and Italy

Leslie Stephen begins to edit the *Dictionary of National Biography*

Married Women's Property Act passed in Britain

Britain occupies Egypt and the Sudan

Ibsen's *An Enemy of the People*

Wagner's *Parsifal*

Deaths of Charles Darwin, Ralph Waldo Emerson, D. G. Rossetti, Anthony Trollope

James Joyce born

Franklin Delano Roosevelt born

Virginia Woolf born

1883 Uprising of the Mahdi: Britain evacuates the Sudan

Metropolitan Opera, New York, opens

Royal College of Music opens

T. H. Green's *Ethics*

Nietzsche's *Thus Spake Zarathustra* published sequentially, with entire work appearing in 1891

Stevenson's *Treasure Island*

Deaths of Edward Fitzgerald, Karl Marx, Ivan Turgenev, Richard Wagner

1884 The Mahdi captures Omdurman: General Gordon appointed to command the garrison of Khartoum

The *Oxford English Dictionary* begins publishing

The Fabian Society founded

Hiram Maxim's recoil-operated machine gun invented

Ibsen's *The Wild Duck*

Twain's *Adventures of Huckleberry Finn*

Sean O'Casey born

1885 The Mahdi captures Khartoum: General Gordon killed

Gottlieb Daimler invents an internal combustion engine

Pasteur perfects vaccine for rabies

Marx's *Das Kapital* (vol. II)

Meredith's *Diana of the Crossways*

Maupassant's *Bel-Ami*

Pater's *Marius the Epicurean*

Tolstoy's *The Power of Darkness*

Zola's *Germinal*

Death of Victor Hugo

D. H. Lawrence born

Ezra Pound born

1886 The Canadian Pacific Railway completed

Gold discovered in the Transvaal

The Statue of Liberty dedicated

Linotype first used in the New York *Herald-Tribune*

Ibsen's *Rosmersholm*

Henry James's *The Bostonians* and *The Princess Casamassima*

Nietzsche's *Beyond Good and Evil*

Rimbaud's *Illuminations*

Stevenson's *The Strange Case of Dr. Jekyll and Mr. Hyde*

Death of Franz Liszt

1887 Queen Victoria's Golden Jubilee

Hardy's *The Woodlanders*

Verdi's *Otello*

Zola's *La Terre*

1888 Henry James's *The Aspern Papers*

Kipling's *Plain Tales from the Hills*

Rimsky-Korsakov's *Scheherazade*

Strindberg's *Miss Julie*

Death of Matthew Arnold

Death of Edward Lear

T. S. Eliot born

Thomas Edward (T. E.) Lawrence born

Kathleen Beauchamp (Kathleen Mansfield) born

1889 George Eastman produces a celluloid roll film

Yeats's *The Wanderings of Oisin*

Death of Robert Browning

Death of Gerard Manley Hopkins

Charles Chaplin born

1890 Morris founds the Kelmscott Press

Ibsen's *Hedda Gabler*

William James's *The Principles of Psychology*

Henry James's *The Tragic Muse*

Morris' *News From Nowhere*

Tolstoy's *The Kreutzer Sonata*

Death of John Henry Newman

Death of Vincent Van Gogh

Charles De Gaulle born

1891 Gissing's *New Grub Street*

Hardy's *Tess of the d'Urbervilles*

Wilde's *The Picture of Dorian Gray*

Death of Herman Melville

Death of Arthur Rimbaud

1892 Conan Doyle's *The Adventures of Sherlock Holmes*

Shaw's *Widower's Houses*

Toulouse-Lautrec's *At the Moulin de la*

Galette
Zola's *La Débâcle*
Wilde's *Lady Windermere's Fan*
Death of Alfred, Lord Tennyson
Death of Walt Whitman

1893 Fridtjof Nansen leads three-year expedition that fails to reach the North Pole
The World's Columbian Exposition opens in Chicago
Tchaikovsky's "Pathetic" Symphony
Verdi's *Falstaff*
Wilde's *A Woman of No Importance* and *Salomé*
Death of Guy de Maupassant
Death of Peter Ilyich Tchaikovsky

1894 Trial and conviction of Alfred Dreyfus
Kipling's *The Jungle Book*
Moore's *Esther Waters*
Marx's *Das Kapital* (vol. III)
The Yellow Book begins to appear quarterly
Shaw's *Arms and the Man*
Deaths of Walter Pater, Robert Louis Stevenson, Christina Rossetti
Aldous Huxley born
John Boynton (J. B.) Priestley born

1895 Trial and imprisonment of Oscar Wilde
Roentgen discovers X rays
William Ramsey announces discovery of helium
Marconi sends first wireless telegraph signals
The National Trust founded
Conrad's *Almayer's Folly*
Hardy's *Jude the Obscure*
Wells's *The Time Machine*
Wilde's *The Importance of Being Earnest*
Yeats's *Poems*

1896 The Nobel Prizes established
First modern Olympic Games held in Athens
Failure of the Jameson Raid on the Transvaal
Chekhov's *The Seagull*
Housman's *A Shropshire Lad*
Ibsen's *John Gabriel Borkman*
Puccini's *La Bohème*
Death of William Morris
Death of Alfred Nobel

1897 Queen Victoria's Diamond Jubilee
The Klondike Gold Rush begins
Conrad's *The Nigger of the Narcissus*
Havelock Ellis' *Studies in the Psychology of Sex* begins publication
Henry James's *The Spoils of Poynton* and *What Maisie Knew*
Kipling's *Captains Courageous*
Rostand's *Cyrano de Bergerac*
Shaw's *Candida*
Wells's *The Invisible Man*
Death of Johannes Brahms

1898 Kitchener defeats the Mahdist forces at Omdurman: the Sudan re-occupied
Pierre and Marie Curie discover radium
Count von Zeppelin builds an airship
Construction of the Paris Métro system begins
Chekhov's *Uncle Vanya*
Hardy's *Wessex Poems*
Henry James's *The Turn of the Screw*
Shaw's *Caesar and Cleopatra*
Wells's *The War of the Worlds*
Wilde's *The Ballad of Reading Gaol*
Death of Lewis Carroll
Death of William Ewart Gladstone

1899 The Boer War begins
Elgar's *Enigma Variations*
Ernst Haeckel's *The Riddle of the Universe*
Kipling's *Stalky and Co.*
Tolstoy's *Resurrection*

1900 The Boxer rising in China
Max Planck presents his first paper on quantum theory
Arthur Evans begins to excavate at Cnossus
Conrad's *Lord Jim*
Elgar's *The Dream of Gerontius*
Freud's *The Interpretation of Dreams*
Shaw's *Three Plays for Puritans*
Deaths of Friedrich Nietzsche, John Ruskin, Oscar Wilde

1901 Death of Giuseppe Verdi

1903 Death of George Gissing
Death of Camille Pissarro

1904 Deaths of Leslie Stephen, Anton Chekhov, Anton Dvořák

1907 Death of Francis Thompson

1909 Death of Algernon Charles Swinburne
Death of George Meredith

List of Contributors

KENNETH ALLOTT. Andrew Cecil Bradley Professor of Modern English Literature, University of Liverpool (1964–1973). Publications include *Collected Poems* (1975); *Matthew Arnold*, Writers and Their Background series; and editions of *The Complete Poems of Matthew Arnold*, Longman's Annotated English Poets series; and *Robert Browning: Selected Poems*. **Matthew Arnold.**

MIRIAM ALLOTT. Andrew Cecil Bradley Professor of Modern English Literature, University of Liverpool (1974–1981); Professor of English, Birkbeck College, University of London (1979–   ). Publications include *The Complete Poems of John Keats*, Longman's Annotated English Poets series; *Matthew Arnold: Selected Poems and Prose*; *The Complete Poems of Matthew Arnold* (second edition), Longman's Annotated English Poets series; *Essays on Shelley*; and essays on the romantic poets and nineteenth- and twentieth-century fiction. **Elizabeth Gaskell.**

ISOBEL MAIR ARMSTRONG. Professor of English, University of Southampton (1979–   ). Publications include *Language as Living Form in Nineteenth Century Poetry*; *Robert Browning*, Writers and Their Background series; and editions of *Victorian Scrutinies; Reviews of Poetry 1830–1970; The Major Victorian Poets: Reconsiderations*; and (with Roger Mansfield) two anthologies of poetry, *Every Man Will Shout* and *A Sudden Line*. **Arthur Hugh Clough.**

PHYLLIS BARTLETT. Professor Emerita of English, Queens College, City University of New York (1967–1973). Publications include *Poems of Process*, a study of English and American poets; and editions of *The Poems of George Chapman* and *The Poems of George Meredith*. **George Meredith.**

GEORGINA BATTISCOMBE. Biographer. Publications include *Charlotte Mary Yonge; Mrs. Gladstone; John Keble* (James Tait Black Prize, 1963); *Queen Alexandra; Lord Shaftesbury; Reluctant Pioneer* (biography of Elizabeth Wordsworth); *Christina Rossetti; Two on Safari* (travel); and articles in the *Dictionary of National Biography* and *Theology*. **Christina Rossetti.**

PETER HERBERT BUTTER. Regius Professor of English Language and Literature, University of Glasgow (1965–   ). Publications include *Shelley's Idols of the Cave; Edwin Muir: Man and Poet*; and editions of Shelley's *Alastor, Prometheus Unbound and Other Poems; Selected Letters of Edwin Muir; and Selected Poems of William Blake*. **Francis Thompson.**

JOHN CAREY. Merton Professor of English Literature, University of Oxford (1976–   ). Publications include *The Violent Effigy: A Study of Dickens' Imagination; Thackeray: Prodigal Genius; John Donne: Life, Mind and Art*; and editions of *The Complete Poems of John Milton* (with Alastair Fowler); James Hogg's *Confessions of a Justified Sinner; and Andrew Marvell*, Penguin Critical Anthologies series. Translation of Milton's *Christian Doctrine*. **William Makepeace Thackeray.**

LETTICE ULPHA COOPER, OBE. Novelist and biographer. President, English Centre of PEN (1977–1979). Publications include *We Have Come to a Country; The New House; National Provincial; Fenny; Late in the Afternoon; Desirable Residence* (all fiction); *Robert Louis Stevenson* (biography). **George Eliot.**

OSWALD DOUGHTY. Formerly Professor of English Literature, University of Cape Town. Publications include *D. G. Rossetti: A Victorian Romantic*; and editions of *The Poems of D. G. Rossetti* and (with J. R. Wahl) *The Letters of D. G. Rossetti*. **Dante Gabriel Rossetti.**

IAN FLETCHER. Professor of English Literature, University of Reading (1978–   ). Publications include *Romantic Mythologies; The Decadent Movement of the 1890's*; and essays on William Butler Yeats and his circle. **Walter Horatio Pater; Algernon Charles Swinburne.**

WINIFRED GÉRIN, FRSL. Biographer and critic. Publications include *Anne Brontë; Branwell Brontë; Charlotte Brontë: The Evolution of Genius* (James Tait Black Prize, 1967; W. H. Heinemann Award, 1968; British Academy Rose Mary Crawshaw Prize, 1968); and *Emily Brontë*. Editions include *Five Novelettes of Charlotte Brontë*. **The Brontës.**

PHYLLIS GROSSKURTH. Professor of English, University of Toronto (1975–   ). Publications include *John Addington Symonds* (Governor-General's Award for Nonfiction, 1965); *Havelock Ellis*; and articles in the *Times Literary Supplement* and *New York Review of Books*. **Leslie Stephen.**

BARBARA HARDY. Professor of English, Birkbeck College, University of London. Publications include *The Novels of George Eliot: A Study in Form; The Appropriate Form; An Essay on the Novel; "Middlemarch": Critical Approaches to the Novel; Critical Essays on George Eliot; The Moral Art of Dickens; The Exposure of Luxury: Radical Themes in Thackeray; A Reading of Jane Austen; Tellers and Listeners: The Narrative Imagination; The Advantage of Lyric;* and *Particularities: Readings in George Eliot*. Editions of George Eliot's *Daniel Deronda*, Penguin English Library series; *The Trumpet Major*; and *A Laodicean*, New Wessex series. **Charles Dickens.**

PHILIP HENDERSON. Biographer and critic. Publications include *Christopher Marlowe; Swinburne: The Portrait of a Poet;* and *William Morris*. **William Morris.**

DEREK HUDSON, FRSL. Biographer and critic. Editorial staff, the *Times* (London) (1939–1949); Literary Editor, the *Spectator* (1949–1953); Editorial staff, Oxford University Press (1955–1975); Literary Adviser, Oxford University Press (1965–1975). Publications include the biographies *W. M. Praed; Thomas Barnes of "The Times"; Martin Tupper; Lewis Carroll; A. J. Munby (Munby Man of Two Worlds); Charles Keene; Arthur Rackham; Sir Joshua Reynolds;* and *Sir Gerald Kelly*. **Lewis Carroll.**

PETER QUENNELL, CBE. Biographer and editor. Editor, *Cornhill* magazine (1944–1951) and (with Alan Hodge) *History Today* (1958–1979). Publications include *Byron: The Years of Fame; Byron in Italy*; biographical studies of Shakespeare, Pope, Hogarth, and Samuel Johnson; *The Sign of the Fish; The Marble Foot;* and *The Wanton Chase* (all three autobiographies); and two collections of essays. **John Ruskin.**

JOANNA RICHARDSON, FRSL. Publications include *Fanny Brawne; Théophile Gautier: His Life and Times; Princesse Mathilde; Verlaine; Victor Hugo; Zola; Keats and His Circle*. Editions of *FitzGerald: Selected Works*, Reynard Library series. Translations of *Baudelaire; Verlaine*, Penguin Poets series; and Théophile Gautier's *Mademoiselle de Maupin*, Penguin Classics series. **Edward Lear.**

GLADYS BRONWEN STERN. Novelist, playwright, and biographer. Publications include *Children of No Man's Land; Tents of Israel; Mosaic, A deputy Was King; Shining and Free; The Matriarch* (all fiction); *Another Part of the Forest* and *All in Good Time* (both autobiographies); *No Son of Mine* (biography of Robert Louis Stevenson); and (with Frank Vosper) *The Martriarch* (drama). **Robert Louis Stevenson.**

JOHN STOKES. Lecturer in English, University of Warwick (1973–   ). Publications include *Resistible Theatres: Enterprise and Experiment in the Late Nineteenth Century; The Decadent Consciousness: A Hidden Arhive of Late Victorian Literature;* "Oscar Wilde" in *Anglo-Irish Literature: A Review of Research*; articles on Henry James, Eleanora Duse, and Sarah Bernhardt. **Oscar Wilde.**

GRAHAM STOREY. Reader in English, University of Cambridge (1981-   ). University Lecturer since 1965 and Fellow of Trinity Hall. Vice President, Gerard Manley Hopkins Society (1971). Publications include *A Preface to Hopkins*; article on Hopkins in *English Poets: Select Bibliographical Guides*. Editions include *Journals and Papers of Gerard Manley Hopkins* (edited by Humphry House; completed by Graham Storey); and *Selected Verse and Prose of Gerard Manley Hopkins*. Joint General Editor of the Pilgrim edition of *The Letters of Charles Dickens* since 1965. **Gerard Manley Hopkins.**

HUGH SYKES DAVIES. Lecturer in English Literature, University of Cambridge (1936–1967); Director of Studies in English, St. John's College, Cambridge (1936–1965). Publications include *The Poets and Their Critics* and articles on Lucretius, Layamon, Swift, Wordsworth, and Surrealism. Other publications are *Petron*, a sequence of prose peoms, and three novels. **Anthony Trollope.**

A. C. WARD. Critic. Publications include *All Illustrated History of English Literature* and *Companion to Twentieth Century Literature*. **George Gissing.**

ELIZABETH GASKELL

(1810-1865)

Miriam Allott

INTRODUCTION

ELIZABETH GASKELL's writings reflect her sanguine, uncomplicated temperament and her quick human sympathies. Like many of her contemporaries, she was conscious of the painful effects of Victorian social and religious upheaval, but she is almost alone among them in betraying so few signs of personal disequilibrium. Her private life—she married a hardworking Unitarian minister in Manchester and brought up four daughters—remained happy, and her writing always kept its natural ease and vivacity. Her sincerity and lack of pretension impressed everyone when she made her literary debut with *Mary Barton* in 1848, at the age of thirty-eight. Thomas Carlyle's wife, Jane, a fellow guest at dinner with Charles Dickens in 1849, described her afterward as "a natural unassuming woman whom they have been doing their best to spoil by making a lioness out of her." "They" did not succeed, for Frederick Greenwood, who met her shortly before her death in 1865—he was the young editor of the *Cornhill* magazine who supplied the notes for the unfinished final installment of her last novel, *Wives and Daughters*—wrote later: "In my recollections of her there is no 'brilliance' of any kind, but a large, firm, homely figure, furnished far beyond the common with a kindly wisdom." At the height of her fame, one of her friends tells us, "She was more proud of her cows and poultry, pigs and vegetables, than of her literary triumphs."

In the intervals of her busy housekeeping, Mrs. Gaskell managed to write six novels, several *nouvelles*, a biography, about thirty short stories, a number of sketches and articles, and a few poems. The poetry is dead, but many of the other works are still highly readable. Four are recognized as English classics: *Cranford* (1853), an engaging series of sketches depicting early Victorian life in the small Cheshire town of Knutsford; *Cousin Phillis* (1864), a pastoral idyll also set in the Knutsford countryside; *Wives and Daughters* (1866), a comedy of provincial life and manners that illustrates its author's sense of character and her shrewd amusement at social pretension; and *The Life of Charlotte Brontë* (1857), at once a memorial to a friend and one of the most moving biographies in English.

Mrs. Gaskell was not a thinker or, as we should say now, an "intellectual," but the humanitarian principles of her Unitarian upbringing quickened her compassion for the victims of social conflict so that she was often drawn to write about situations and incidents more explosively than she realized. In *Mary Barton* (1848) and *North and South* (1855) she tried to make her readers understand the suffering experienced on both sides in the industrial disputes of the 1830's and 1840's. In *Ruth* (1853) and *Sylvia's Lovers* (1863) her subject was the suffering undergone by those whose love affairs conflicted with social convention. These are ambitious novels, interesting in spite of all their imperfections; but they show that if her heart was in the right place, her intellectual equipment was amateurish. She had no real idea of the complexity of the economic issues—only a vague sense of how received ideas based on so-called economic laws, on the one hand, and ingrained prejudices based on traditional patterns of behavior, on the other, made industrial problems difficult to solve; and she was too securely protected by the customary moral half-truths of her own age and class to treat situations like Ruth's with the unsentimental honesty they required.

Her simple advocacy of Christian forgiveness, understanding, and love won her a grateful audience, but we cannot wonder that she several times found herself—to her dismayed surprise—the center of violent public controversy, or that we do not read her social novels today for any far-reaching analysis of the situations that drove her to write them. Her unthinking but generous warmth of feeling also got her into trouble over *The Life of Charlotte Brontë*. She had to face the consequences of attacking the cruelty and injustice of people who were still alive, and could readily be identified from her descriptions.

Henry James, who enjoyed Mrs. Gaskell's books, rightly felt that her genius was "obviously the offspring of her affections, her feelings, her associations," that it was "little of an intellectual matter" and, indeed, "little else than a peculiar play of her personal character." It is for exactly these qualities that her humane testimony is so valuable in helping us to understand the atmosphere of the age in which she lived. When she began writing in the 1840's, many people were deeply troubled about the fate of England. The Chartist uprisings of the 1830's and 1840's—which prompted two other novelists, Benjamin Disraeli and Charles Kingsley, to express their views polemically in such works as *Sybil* (1845) and *Alton Locke* (1850)—brought home to thousands of ordinary men and women the hard facts of beggary and starvation. Mrs. Gaskell in her social novels voices the good intentions and modest insight of the "aroused" decent citizen, while in the rest of her action she celebrates the quiet country life that she valued and that industrial civilization, spreading with the railroads, was already beginning to threaten with disintegration.

Her feeling for nature and the countryside is the source of her most immediately attractive work. Once she had come to share her husband's life in the Manchester soot, Mrs. Gaskell never returned to the country existence that she remembered with a radiance around it. Consequently, when she describes meadows in spring, an orchard in late summer, or a garden full of flowers, she writes with a special charm that is hardly self-regarding enough to be described as nostalgic. It was certainly her portrayal of country life and country people that appealed to George Eliot, who acknowledges a debt to *Cranford*, read "for the first time in 1857, when I was writing the *Scenes of Clerical Life*," and to "the earlier chapters of *Mary Barton*," reread "the next year, when I was writing *Adam Bede*."

George Eliot must also have appreciated the "Dutch fidelity" of Mrs. Gaskell's description of interiors—especially of the living rooms, studies, and kitchens that enliven with their detail her commentary on their owners' moral life. In the tranquil "house-place" of *Cousin Phillis*, "everything that ought to be black and polished" is so; "such things as were to be white and clean" are "spotless in their purity"; the quiet hours are measured by the double tick of the old clock; the cat sleeps on the crimson rug before the blazing fire; and the light flickers on the snowy flags, the mended stockings, the copy of Dante, and Phillis' knitting. With her eye for this kind of particularity, her commonsensical but not insensitive wisdom, her easy-flowing narrative style, and her genuine storyteller's gift, Mrs. Gaskell secures an important secondary place for herself in the history of the English novel. In *Wives and Daughters* all her talents are at last focused to produce what may be more than a minor achievement. At her best she combines the shrewd observation that delights us in Jane Austen with the social conscience of a more earnest age: her works help to prepare the way for the widened range and the stiffer texture of the great works of nineteenth-century fiction.

We sometimes forget that Elizabeth Cleghorn Gaskell was born not at Knutsford but in London at Cheyne Walk, Chelsea, on 29 September 1810. Her father, William Stevenson (descended from the poet James Thomson), was himself a gifted man; once a Unitarian minister (he resigned his ministry, like Mr. Hale in *North and South*), he combined farming, writing, and teaching before being appointed keeper of the records to the Treasury. His wife, Elizabeth Holland, who died thirteen months after her daughter was born, provided the Knutsford connection. Her father, Samuel Holland, a member of an old Lancashire family, farmed his own land at Sandlebridge, just two miles outside Knutsford in Cheshire—Woodley in *Cranford* and Heathbridge in *Cousin Phillis* are among Mrs. Gaskell's many fictional portraits of the real Sandlebridge—and her sister, Hannah Lumb, lived at Heathside in Knutsford itself. It was to this sister that Elizabeth Gaskell was sent as a baby. With her aunt she spent a happy childhood, absorbing the impressions that were to make "Cranford" famous as she rode with her uncle, Dr. Peter Holland, on his country rounds (like Molly and Dr. Gibson in *Wives and Daughters*), listened to the friends who came to tea with her "darling Aunt Lumb," or walked on Sundays to the Unitarian chapel on the hillside.

This Knutsford period ended in 1825, when Elizabeth was sent for two years to a school at Stratford-on-Avon ("I was brought up by the river Avon in

Warwickshire," says Signora Brunoni in *Cranford*); two years more were spent in London nursing her father until his death in 1829; and from then until her marriage in 1832 she lived with Anne Turner, the daughter of a Unitarian minister connected with her family, first in Newcastle on Tyne, then in Edinburgh (the setting for the "frame" story in *Round the Sofa*), and finally in Manchester, where Anne's sister was married to the Reverend John Gooch Robberds, minister of Cross Street Unitarian Chapel. Their fellow guest here was the minister's handsome assistant, William Gaskell, who was eventually to succeed him as senior minister and remain at Cross Street for the rest of a long, active life, surviving his wife by eighteen years and becoming widely known for his philanthropy and as a lecturer in English literature and history at Manchester College. He and Elizabeth married after a short courtship in 1832— her good looks at this time are preserved in W. J. Thompson's miniature and David Dunbar's bust (now in the Arts Library at Manchester University) —and after their honeymoon at Ffestiniog in Wales, they settled, on Elizabeth's twenty-second birthday, into the first of their Manchester homes.

In the interval of sixteen years before her first book appeared, Mrs. Gaskell bore six children—of whom four survived—worked among the Manchester poor, and made the first of many continental visits. It was one of the few on which her husband accompanied her, for as the years went on, he became increasingly engrossed in his work. But it was he who encouraged her to find solace in writing when their only boy died at nineteen months from scarlet fever in 1845—a loss that haunted her all her life. She had already collaborated with him on a poem "in the Crabbe manner" about the Manchester poor, and had herself written the prose sketch "Clopton Hall" (1840).

When *Mary Barton* came out in 1848, Mrs. Gaskell's reputation was established at once, and she appears henceforth on the Victorian scene as a minor celebrity. In 1850, Dickens asked her to write for his new periodical, *Household Words*. She complied with "Lizzie Leigh," and for the next thirteen years remained a regular contributor to Dickens' periodicals. Her short stories, briefly noticed later, have faults of melodrama and sentimentality, but many of them are still very readable. Certainly they succeeded in their chief purpose—to keep the pot boiling and provide a Victorian lady with pin money.

The year 1850 was also the year of Mrs. Gaskell's momentous meeting with Charlotte Brontë. Utterly different in their circumstances as they were—the one lonely, plain, and intense, the other successful, healthy, graceful, and beloved—the two women immediately became friends, and after Charlotte's death five years later, it was to Mrs. Gaskell that Patrick Brontë entrusted the first reliable account of his daughter's life and work.

The publication of *The Life of Charlotte Brontë* in 1857 roughly bisects a writing life that from 1848 to its close in 1865 had few ups and downs. As a popular and successful novelist in the 1850's, Mrs. Gaskell kept more or less open house in Manchester. She traveled abroad whenever she could, often staying with a friend, the Englishwoman Madame Mary Mohl, who kept a salon in Paris. In Rome in 1857 she added to her American friendships—Charles Eliot Norton and Harriet Beecher Stowe were already regular correspondents—the sculptor William Wetmore Story. At home in Manchester, at 42 Plymouth Grove, where she and her husband finally settled in 1850, she received among her frequent visitors John Ruskin, Dickens, and Carlyle, all of whom fell under the spell of her personality.

Something of Mrs. Gaskell's personal charm can be glimpsed in her unstuffy, gossipy letters to her daughters when she was separated from them. In one of them she gaily describes a typically busy week: the Carlyles coming to stay, other guests due, half her domestic staff ill, and the cook leaving to get married. It is not surprising that she was sometimes glad to escape for seclusion either to her favorite Silverdale, where in a "queer, pretty crampy house" by the sands of Morecambe Bay, with the fells in the background, she could write without interruption, or else to Lea Hurst, "so very lovely and still," home of Florence Nightingale's family, where in 1854 she found strength to wrestle with the installments of *North and South*.

It was only at the close of her life that Mrs. Gaskell realized an old dream of a country retreat of her own, and bought—and then it was partly as a surprise for William—a pleasant house standing on four acres of ground at Alton in Hampshire. She was not to enjoy it for long. After tea there on 12 November 1865, barely four months after its purchase, she suddenly collapsed and died while talking to members of her family. She left the final passages of *Wives and Daughters* unfinished. Her body was taken back to Manchester and then on for burial to the Unitarian chapel at Knutsford.

THE NOVELS

WE cannot properly speak of development in connection with Mrs. Gaskell's art, although she improves technically in her later books and is better at disguising her weaknesses of construction. *Sylvia's Lovers* (1863) moves firmly to its climax, flagging only once this is over; *Cousin Phillis* (1864) faultlessly maintains its minor emotional key; and *Wives and Daughters* (1866), a novel that is on an ambitious scale and unusually mature in its assessment of character, combines a wide range of materials into a firm and pleasing narrative. But Mrs. Gaskell's first two books, *Mary Barton* (1848) and *Cranford* (1853), show no less than these later ones the characteristic qualities of her talent. Had she lived longer, it is unlikely that her work would have altered greatly—such changes are more normal in the careers of the "poetic" writer or the "sage" (Henry James and George Eliot, for example). So it seems reasonable in discussing her novels to arrange them in accordance with their themes and subject matter instead of in chronological order.

Although *Mary Barton*, Mrs. Gaskell's first novel, is separated by nearly seven years from *North and South* (1855), the two books are closely connected—indeed, the second depends to a great extent on the first for its form. Both books deal with Manchester labor troubles, but there is a difference in emphasis. In *Mary Barton* the cotton workers, rather than their employers, are the central figures, and it is with them that we are chiefly invited to sympathize. In *North and South* Mrs. Gaskell, anxious to allay criticism by impartiality, shows a prejudiced "outsider," a young girl who is a southerner, gradually overcoming her hostility to the hardheaded northern master manufacturers: "North" and "South," as well as employers and employed, are to be reconciled, Mrs. Gaskell urges, by the exercise of mutual understanding and Christian charity.

These books are examples of a new kind of fiction first appearing in the troubled 1840's. Disraeli in *Coningsby* (1844) and *Sybil* (1845), Charles Kingsley in *Yeast* (1848) and *Alton Locke* (1850), and Dickens in *Bleak House* (1853) and *Hard Times* (1854) are all concerned with the distressing contrast between the lives of the rich and the poor, the "two nations," as Disraeli calls them in *Sybil*. Mrs. Gaskell shares the concern of these novelists with the "condition of England" question, but unlike them she tries hard to handle her subject with the compassionate detachment of the "pure" novelist. If she fails to turn her social novels into successful works of art, it is not because she has a "patented" point of view of her own to preach, but because she does not see far enough into the life that she is struggling to present.

Mary Barton

Mary Barton is set in Manchester during the lean years on either side of 1840. Bad harvests and falling wages had culminated in the acute distress of 1839, when the great Chartist petition signed by well over a million people was rejected by Parliament, with violent results throughout industrial England. Mrs. Gaskell makes this the turning point in the life of a cotton worker, John Barton, showing how it eventually pushes him down to ruin and crime. Indeed, she may not have realized just how strong an indictment of laissez-faire economics was her "thorough specimen of a Manchester man," with his slightly stunted body and his "wan colourless face" betraying the privations of his childhood, his strong features expressing "extreme earnestness," his unanswerable assertions—"It's the poor, and the poor only, as does things for the poor"—and his bitter questions about the employers—"Have they ever seen a child o' ther'n die for want of food?" What finally breaks him is his bewilderment at the discrepancy between the facts of his experience and the employers' professions of Christianity. When, driven to desperation, he at last carries out a trade union "assassination," it is still this failure to square belief and action that perplexes his dying consciousness.

"Round the character of John Barton all the others formed themselves," Mrs. Gaskell tells us, and she seeks to relate the private destinies of her supporting characters to the public events that destroy him. The decline of their fortunes is thoroughly convincing. At first there is the decent cheerfulness of the workers' rare outing on a May evening in Green Heys Fields outside the town—a pastoral opening in Mrs. Gaskell's favorite style. The home to which the Bartons return with their friends, the Wilsons, is clean and bright with its geraniums, its blue-and-white-check curtains, and the warm glow of its fire. Money is sufficient for "fresh eggs . . . nice ham . . . a pennyworth of milk." Mrs. Gaskell's description of the humble pleasures of the poor is partly an encouragement to Dickensian coziness; but it is also intended to heighten the contrast when Mrs. Barton is dead, John Barton is out of work, and Mary comes home from dressmaking to a room that is "dingy and comfortless." There is no money to buy fuel for the fire; and in place of the friendly Wilsons, there are only the "strange faces of pale men," men of the trade unions "ready for anything, made ready by want." Her description of a starving family in chapter 6 is a gallant attempt at a truthful unsentimentality.

But Mrs. Gaskell's great technical triumph in this book is her management of the chain of events leading from the murder of Harry Carson, the employer's son, to the trial of Jem Wilson at Liverpool assizes—an achievement that owes nothing to her "social purpose." Mary Barton—reminding us a little of Jeanie Deans in *The Heart of Mid-Lothian* (1818)—sets off to Liverpool to find Will, the one man who can prove Jem's alibi: she must save her lover without betraying her father, a situation full of strong dramatic possibilities. Her journey by train (a great undertaking to such a woman at the time), her alternations of hope and despair on learning that Will's ship is far out in the Mersey, her long chase after him in the fishermen's boat, Will's voice at last calling out reassurance from the tall merchantman, his part in the dramatic climax at the trial—all this is satisfactory storytelling, handled without a sign of the novice.

A quality of solidity is given to the whole narrative by the Lancashire dialect and the author's close observation of the stubborn, friendly Manchester folk. We may be inclined to smile at the happy endings contrived for many of the characters, and to doubt the reality of the reconciliation scene between the bereaved manufacturer and his son's murderer; but these reservations do not seriously interfere with a total effect of honesty within the limits of a rather conventional understanding.

North and South

Although many voices were raised in praise of *Mary Barton* (Carlyle and Dickens were among the enthusiasts), Mrs. Gaskell was worried by the strictures of those who felt, as one reviewer did, that she showed a "morbid sensibility to the condition of operatives." W. R. Greg condemned her "fatally false idea" that "the poor are to look to the rich and not to themselves for relief and rescue," and declared that the employers ought to have been given credit for various benevolent schemes that they had already tried to put into practice. These criticisms she took the more seriously because she could not really appraise them. They will explain why six years

later in *North and South*, her second attack on the theme of relations between capital and labor (*Cranford* and *Ruth* had appeared in the interval), she chose a narrative device that would reduce the chance of a similar misunderstanding—she was shocked at the idea of herself "setting class against class"—and at the same time vividly bring home to her readers the dangers of imperfect human sympathies. She tells her story mainly from the point of view of Margaret Hale, a young girl brought up in the modest gentility of a vicarage in the South, with little experience of the outside world beyond occasional visits to London.

Margaret Hale comes into contact with the North when her father resigns his living for conscientious reasons and travels to "Milton-Northern," where he hopes to find employment as a tutor through the influence of an old college friend. We see this new world through Margaret's eyes. Everything appears more "purposelike." The carts are made with more iron and less wood and leather; clothes are "more enduring, not so gay and pretty," while smock frocks have totally disappeared because they get entangled in machinery. The people, who hurry through the streets with a preoccupied air, live in "long, straight hopeless streets of regularly-built houses" that in autumn and winter are swathed in "white wreaths of unwholesome mist."

> "Oh, Margaret! are we to live here?" asked Mrs Hale in blank dismay.
> Margaret's heart echoed to the dreariness of the tone in which this question was put.[1]
>
> (ch. VIII)

Perhaps this is how Mrs. Gaskell herself felt when she settled in her first Manchester home.

At this point in the story, Mrs. Gaskell seems more interested in contriving the debate between capital and labor than in keeping a firm hold on her narrative. Chapters such as "What Is a Strike?" and "Masters and Men" are typical. Margaret listens sympathetically to the workingman Nicholas Higgins, and to his daughter Bessy, who is dying of consumption brought on by her hard life in the mills—the strikes that her father defends mean only misery and starvation to her. Then it is the turn of

---

[1]All quotations from the novels and from *The Life of Charlotte Brontë* are taken from C. K. Shorter, ed., *The Novels and Tales*, 11 vols. (London, 1906–1919).

Margaret's father's pupil, the rising manufacturer Mr. Thornton. "What in the world do manufacturers want with classics, or literature . . . ?" asks Margaret scornfully; but it is through Thornton, whom she first dislikes and then passionately loves, that she eventually comes to understand the viewpoint of the better employers.

North and South hardly exists as an imaginative achievement if it is to be judged by its debates on economics and its melodramatic plotting. One understands why Dickens was irritated by the long, drawn-out installments for *Household Words*. All the same, it is in many respects a more interesting kind of work than *Mary Barton*, if only because of Mrs. Gaskell's bold presentation of the hero and heroine, two individuals who forge for themselves a strong personal relationship in spite of wide differences in temperament, background, and ideals. *North and South* is not, as some critics have thought, a Victorian *Pride and Prejudice*. Instead of looking back to Elizabeth Bennet and Darcy, Margaret and Thornton look forward—as do George Eliot's Felix Holt and Esther Lyon—to the emotional entanglements of a later age, when the pattern of society adds new complications to the relationships between men and women. D. H. Lawrence's contentious lovers are their twentieth-century descendants.

At first sight the social theme in *Ruth* seems to link this novel more closely with *Mary Barton* and *North and South* than with *Sylvia's Lovers*, especially since the latter deserts a contemporary Lancashire setting for the Yorkshire coast toward the end of the eighteenth century. But the moral issues in *Sylvia's Lovers* are somewhat similar to those in *Ruth*, and both heroines endure lifelong suffering because of a youthful passion. Ruth, a penniless, seventeen-year-old seamstress, is seduced and abandoned by a "gentleman," and finds herself with a child to look after. The rest of her life is spent in bringing up her young son and in repentantly practicing self-sacrifice. Sylvia, after losing her lover to the press-gang, is coerced into marriage with his rival, who puts it about that the man he is supplanting has been drowned. When the "drowned" lover returns, Sylvia is torn by her passion for him, her hatred of her husband, and her love for the child of her marriage.[2]

The two novels are also linked by a common origi-

nating "germ." Mrs. Gaskell was familiar with the poetry of George Crabbe, whose "Ruth"—one of the stories contained in his *Tales of the Hall*—relates how a country girl is abandoned by her lover. The lover, moreover, is snatched away by the press-gang:

> . . . gangs came pressing till they swept the shore:
> Our youth was seized and quickly sent away . . .
> There were wives, maids, and mothers on the beach,
> And some sad story appertain'd to each.[3]
>
> (174–175; 179–180)

In these lines Mrs. Gaskell may have found a hint for her own vivid dramatization of the confusion and despair on the beaches in *Sylvia's Lovers* when the "Press" strikes. Not only is Sylvia's lover taken, but her father is arrested for retaliating against the gang, and hanged.

Ruth

There is always a vast difference between the original "germ" and the final form of any work. *Sylvia's Lovers* and *Ruth* travel in their separate directions far away from Crabbe's story. In *Ruth* the familiar theme of the seduced girl and her fatherless child is the basis of a plea for human sympathy, although the novelist's wish to describe human behavior honestly is still crippled by conventional notions about retribution. Mrs. Gaskell fights hardest against these notions when she takes up the cause of Ruth's illegitimate child. Ruth is taken in by the crippled Dissenting minister Thurstan Benson, and it is through him that Mrs. Gaskell puts her case. She sees to it that his arguments are strong enough to persuade even his conventionally minded sister, Faith, that the arrival of the baby will make Ruth "forget herself, and be thoughtful for another." "I think you, Thurstan, are the first person I ever heard rejoicing over the birth of an illegitimate child," says Faith in her first shocked surprise. "It appears to me, I must own, rather questionable morality." But she accepts his decision and Ruth's son, unlike the child in Crabbe's story,

> A creature doom'd to shame! in sorrow born;
> A thing that languished nor arrived at age
> When the man's thoughts with sin and pain engage . . .
>
> (417–419)

---

[2]The situation has some elements in common with Mrs. Gaskell's short story "The Manchester Marriage" (1858) and with Alfred Tennyson's *Enoch Arden* (1864).

[3]From A. C. Ward, ed., *George Crabbe. Poems*, vol. II (Cambridge, 1906).

is eventually cherished by both the Bensons as a means of hastening his mother's moral and emotional recovery. "About the child . . . *I have no doubt,*" Dean Arthur Stanley's mother wrote emphatically when the book appeared.

Few readers felt the same way about the book as a whole. The enlightened thought Mrs. Gaskell too timid; the unenlightened were horrified. For the former Ruth's long repentance, followed by her death while nursing her seducer in a typhus epidemic, was too much. "Why should she die?" asked Charlotte Brontë. Arthur Hugh Clough thought that "such overpowering humiliation" ought not to be demanded of a girl "not really guilty though misguided." W. R. Greg, the critic of *Mary Barton,* pointed out in his essay "The False Morality of Lady Novelists" (1859) that the "fallen woman" in contemporary literature is "punished without discrimination as the most sunk of sinners" and is usually represented "as acquiescing in the justice of the sentence." Mrs. Gaskell meant to correct these views, he thought, but her ideas "were not quite clear or positive enough" for her "to carry out boldly or develop fully the conception she had formed." Some readers regretted the Dissenting minister's decision to conceal the truth about Ruth and to pass her off as a widow when she came to live with him and his sister. They felt he should have told the truth from the beginning—he would have avoided deceit and forestalled the unhappy consequences of the truth coming out later. (When this happens, Ruth is ostracized by the hitherto friendly townsfolk, and her son is made miserable; only by sacrificing herself to the typhus victims does she win back respect.)

Other reactions were more conventional. "I must be an improper person without knowing it," Mrs. Gaskell wrote when she heard that two members of the congregation in her husband's chapel had burned the book and a third had forbidden his wife to read it. "Well, the Bible has been burnt," was Archdeacon Hare's impatient comment on this behavior.

*Ruth'*s modern readers may wonder what all the fuss was about, perhaps forgetting how much of a pioneer Mrs. Gaskell really was, especially in exposing the double moral standard for men and women (Ruth's lover eventually runs for office in a local election). They may feel, with some justification, that the author's infatuation with the emotional cliché makes her treatment of Ruth almost indistinguishable in its moral tone from, say, Dickens' treatment of Little Emily in *David Copperfield.* Her plotting is

certainly affected by this weakness: a series of far-fetched coincidences brings Ruth's secret to light, thrusts her lover back into her life, and finally transforms him into a sick man whom she nurses without his knowing it.

But many aspects of the book escape the blight. The crippled minister, his outspoken sister, and their loyal North Country maid Sally are all good, firm portrayals in Mrs. Gaskell's best manner. She is at home, too, in the description of the serenity of their spotless house. George Eliot liked the account of Ruth's bedroom, where the "white dimity bed, and the walls stained green had something of the colouring and purity . . . of a snowdrop," while the floor, stained rich dark brown, "suggested the idea of the garden-mould out of which the snowdrop grows." In the early scenes in Wales, where Ruth is living with her lover (the scene of Mrs. Gaskell's own honeymoon), the author succeeds in convincing us of her heroine's essential innocence, especially in suggesting a harmony between the experience of passion and the beauty of the physical world. There is still something a little too ladylike in Mrs. Gaskell's approach, a touch of false refinement betrayed in her phrasing, as the last quotations show; but in context she triumphs over this weakness by the naive freshness of the current of feeling:

Their breakfast hour was late . . . but Ruth was up betimes and out and away, brushing the dew drops from the short crisp grass; the lark sang high above her head, and she knew not if she moved or stood still, for the grandeur of this beautiful earth absorbed all idea of separate and individual existence. Even the rain was a pleasure to her . . . she watched the heather darken on the heathery mountainside, and then the pale golden gleam which succeeded. There was no change or alteration of nature that had not its own peculiar beauty. . . .

(ch. V)

This may not be a very exalted style of writing, but for the most part it is surprisingly serviceable.

Sylvia's Lovers

In this novel the attempt to evoke the past in a setting of countryside and sea, among the homely lives of Yorkshire farmers and shopkeepers, allows Mrs. Gaskell's imagination room to work more freely than in *Ruth.* Emancipated from the pressure of contemporary social problems, she enjoys establishing the flavor of her period—the 1790's, when Whitby shipowners made fortunes from the whaling trade, and press-gangs served the Admiralty by seizing men to fill unmanned ships. She takes pleasure in describing the Yorkshire coast near Whitby, noticing "the moorland heights swelling one behind the other" above the banks of the Dee, the nearer ones colored "russet brown with the tints of the fading bracken," and "the river itself . . . swelling and chafing with the incoming tide" until its waters rush over the feet of the watching crowd on the staithes. She enjoys, too, imitating the Yorkshire dialect, especially in the conversation of old Daniel, Sylvia's father:

"Women's well enough i' their way . . . but a man may have too much on 'em. Now there's me, leg-fast these four days, and a'll make free to say to yo', a'd rather a deal ha' been loading dung i't wettest weather; an' a reckon it's th' being wi' nought but women as tires me so; they talk so foolish it gets in't bones. . . ."

(ch. V)

Mrs. Gaskell seems free, too, in this novel to make her characters interestingly complex. Sylvia's husband, Philip, suffers through his own contradictory impulses; Charley Kinraid, her early lover, who is gay and appealing in youth, fades and becomes commonplace in middle age; the members of Sylvia's household—her stubborn father, her shrewd Yorkshire mother, the rugged countryman Kester—stand out as sharply differentiated human beings.

Sylvia herself is one of Mrs. Gaskell's most lifelike heroines. When we see her first, as a country girl walking barefoot to town "to choose her first cloak"—it must be scarlet instead of the useful gray recommended by her mother—she is lighthearted, "affectionate, wilful, naughty, tiresome, charming, anything in fact at present, that the chances of an hour called out." But maturity is pitilessly forced on her by the loss of her lover, her father's death, and her unhappiness in marriage. The inner strength that she has developed triumphs when she overcomes her passion for Kinraid. She sends him away, in obedience to her marriage vows, for the sake of the child. It is the child's cry that interrupts her first rapture at seeing her old lover again:

". . . it is his child—I'd forgotten that—forgotten all. I'll make my vow now, lest I lost mysel' again. I'll never forgive yon man, nor live with him as his wife again. All that's done and ended. He's spoilt my life—he's spoilt it for as long as iver I live on this earth; but neither yo' nor him shall spoil my soul. It goes hard wi' me, Charley, it does indeed. I'll give yo' one kiss—one little kiss—and then, so help me God . . . I'll niver see yo' again on this side heaven . . . I'm bound and tied, but I've sworn my oath to him as well as yo': there's things I will do, and there's things I won't. . . ."

(ch. XXXIII)

The book should have ended here, for the plot runs wild in the remaining twelve chapters. In these Sylvia's husband remorsefully joins the army, saves Kinraid's life on a battlefield where both are fighting, is disfigured by wounds, has a spell as a pensioner in an almshouse, returns to live unrecognized in a poor hut near his old home, and finally dies in Sylvia's arms, consoled by the knowledge that all is forgiven.

Unlikely as it may seem from this summary, Philip is well drawn. At first angular, priggish, and possessive, he is slowly dignified by his passion, by the guilt and suffering that he endures in his marriage, and by the despair that finally drives him away. His redemption is best forgotten.

Cousin Phillis and Wives and Daughters were published after Ruth and Sylvia's Lovers, in the last two years of Mrs. Gaskell's life. In them she strokes in English country life with that blend of pathos and shrewd humor that first delighted her readers ten years before, when her Cranford papers were appearing in Household Words. All three books are full of her early memories of Knutsford. So long as this remains her subject, no missionary zeal strains her language, distorts her narrative, or interferes with her sensitive representation of feeling—the exaggerated pathos of Ruth and the false heroics that spoil North and South are blessedly absent.

Cranford

An atmosphere of potpourri and lavender is associated with memories of Cranford; but on coming to the book again, one is struck in the first place by its tact of presentation and the happy discretion of its style. It is a small masterpiece achieved through emotional understatement, the manner exactly suiting the subject matter, since Cranford is a place of low tones and quiet economies. At the same time piquancy is given to the narrative by Mrs. Gaskell's calculated heightening of her entertaining incidents. She herself seems to have enjoyed Cranford best among her books. "It is the only one . . . I can read again," she wrote, adding, "It is true, too, for I have seen the cow that wore the grey-flannel jacket— and I know the cat that swallowed the lace that belonged to the lady, that sent for the doctor. . . ." Of course the point about "truth" is not to be taken at its face value. Mrs. Gaskell as a novelist very well knew that in these episodes her creative imagination had been at work transforming the facts of experience and adding to their humorous or pathetic effect.

Mrs. Gaskell's readers seem to have shared her preference, for *Cranford* has gone into more than 170 editions since 1853. "*Cranford* is known and loved from Maine to California," wrote Charles Eliot Norton from America in 1858. In England, too, there were thousands of admirers. In a letter to John Ruskin, Mrs. Gaskell explains that she had meant to write only the first paper ("so killed Captain Brown very much against my will"), but was encouraged to carry on in answer to the demand. Dickens, as editor of *Household Words*, was naturally delighted, objecting only to the amusing reference to himself that occurs in the celebrated duel between Miss Deborah Jenkins and Captain Brown over the relative merits of Samuel Johnson and the author of *The Pickwick Papers*, a work supposed to be "just out" when the story opens. "Aren't they famously good?" asks the Captain as the *Pickwick* installments appear. Miss Jenkins disagrees: ". . . I don't think they are by any means equal to Dr Johnson. Still perhaps the author is young. Let him persevere, and who knows what he may ever become if he will take the great Doctor for his model?"

Although *Cranford* is based on actual experience, the "truth" of which Mrs. Gaskell speaks is not simply documentary. The narrator, Mary Smith, is a fictional persona for Mrs. Gaskell's youthful self, while the "Amazons" are an imaginative re-creation of the relatives and friends surrounding her beloved "Aunt Lumb." Mrs. Gaskell is content to capture their essential qualities, especially in her half-fanciful, half-humorous anecdotes about the economies and eccentricities of the spinster sisters, Miss Deborah and Miss Matty Jenkins. One would need to quote at length to give a just idea of the flavor of these stories, for the writer gets her effect by an accumulation of delicately fine strokes. Still, some hint may be given in the following passages, where Mrs. Gaskell neatly summarizes *Cranford*'s most genteel social customs:

. . . there were rules and regulations for visiting and calls; and they were announced to any young people who might be staying in the town, with all the solemnity with which the old Manx laws were read once a year on the Tinwald Mount.

"Our friends have sent to inquire how you are after your

journey to-night, my dear" (fifteen miles, in a gentleman's carriage); "they will give you some rest to-morrow, but the next day, I have no doubt, they will call; so be at liberty after twelve—from twelve to three are our calling hours."

(ch. I)

Then, after they had called:

"It is the third day; I dare say your mamma has told you, my dear, never to let more than three days elapse between receiving a call and returning it; and also, that you are never to stay longer than a quarter of an hour."

"But am I to look at my watch? How am I to find out when a quarter of an hour has passed?"

"You must keep thinking about the time, my dear, and not allow yourself to forget it in conversation."

As everybody had this rule in their minds, whether they received or paid a call, of course no absorbing subject was ever spoken about. We kept ourselves to short sentences of small talk, and were punctual to our time.

(ch. I)

We are made to see that gentility and poverty are perfectly compatible:

The Cranfordians had that kindly *esprit de corps* which made them overlook all deficiencies in success when some among them tried to conceal their poverty. When Mrs Forrester, for instance, gave a party in her baby-house of a dwelling, and the little maiden disturbed the ladies on the sofa by a request that she might get the tea-tray out from underneath, every one took this novel proceeding as the most natural thing in the world; and talked on about household forms and ceremonies as if we all believed that our hostess had a regular servants' hall, second table, with housekeeper and steward, instead of the one little charity-school maiden, whose short ruddy arms could never have been strong enough to carry the tray upstairs, if she had not been assisted in private by her mistress, who now sat in state, pretending not to know what cakes were sent up, though she knew, and we knew, and she knew that we knew, and we knew that she knew that we knew, she had been busy all the morning making tea-bread and sponge cakes.

(ch. I)

By way of contrast, there is the drawing room of the Honorable Mrs. Jamieson, pillar of Cranford society, who keeps a manservant (the surly tyrant Mr. Mulliner) and a dog (Carlo), and whose slightest word on the *convenances* is law to the Cranford ladies.

The furniture was white and gold; not the later style, Louis Quatorze, I think they call it, all shells and twirls; no,

Mrs Jamieson's chairs and tables had not a curve or bend about them. The chair and table legs diminished as they neared the ground, and were straight and square in all their corners. The chairs were all a-row against the walls, with the exception of four or five which stood in a circle round the fire. They were railed with white bars across the back, and knobbed with gold; neither the railings nor the knobs invited to ease. There was a japanned table devoted to literature, on which lay a Bible, a Peerage, and a Prayer-Book. There was another square Pembroke table dedicated to the Fine Arts, on which were a kaleidoscope, conversation-cards, puzzle-cards (tied together to an interminable length with faded pink satin ribbon), and a box painted in fond imitation of the drawings which decorate tea-chests. Carlo lay on the worsted-worked rug, and ungraciously barked at us as we entered. Mrs Jamieson stood up, giving us each a torpid smile of welcome, and looking helplessly beyond us at Mr Mulliner, as if she hoped he would place us in chairs, for, if he did not, she never could. I suppose he thought we could find our way to the circle round the fire, which reminded me of Stonehenge, I don't know why.

(ch. VIII)

The Cranford ladies are tremulous when Mrs. Jamieson assembles them in this room to take tea and meet her sister-in-law, Lady Glenmire, widow of a baron and one who "might have sat down to tea with a coronet, instead of a cap, on her head." Conversation is at first rather strained:

We were thinking what we could talk about, that should be high enough to interest My Lady. There had been a rise in the price of sugar, which, as preserving-time was near, was a piece of intelligence to all our housekeeping hearts, and would have been the natural topic if Lady Glenmire had not been by. But we were not sure if the peerage ate preserves—much less knew how they were made. At last, Miss Pole, who had always a great deal of courage and *savoir faire*, spoke to Lady Glenmire, who on her part had seemed just as much puzzled to know how to break the silence as we were.

"Has your ladyship been to Court lately?" asked she; and then gave a little glance round at us, half timid and half triumphant, as much as to say, "See how judiciously I have chosen a subject befitting the rank of the stranger."

"I never was there in my life," said Lady Glenmire, with a broad Scotch accent, but in a very sweet voice. And then, as if she had been too abrupt, she added: "We very seldom went to London—only twice, in fact, during all my married life; and before I was married my father had far too large a family" (fifth daughter of Mr Campbell was in all our minds, I am sure) "to take us often from our home even to Edinburgh. Ye'll have been in Edinburgh, maybe?" said she, suddenly brightening up with the hope of a common

interest. We had none of us been there; but Miss Pole had an uncle who once had passed a night there, which was very pleasant. . . .

(ch. VIII)

Mrs. Gaskell cat-steps her way through the perils of sentiment by the merest hint that she is aware that decayed gentlewomen are in some way absurd. It is partly through their dialogue that she makes Miss Matty and Miss Deborah as familiar to us as Jane Austen's Miss Bates and George Eliot's Mrs. Poyser. "Two people we know going to be married," says Miss Matty when Lady Glenmire upsets everyone by engaging herself to Mr. Hoggins. "It's coming very near!" "It is very pleasant dining with a bachelor," she sighs while visiting her girlhood suitor who is now over seventy, "I only hope it is not improper; so many pleasant things are!"

Mary Smith's commentary also helps to establish the Cranford atmosphere, for she identifies herself lovingly with the town and its inhabitants, sharing in their decorous entertainments and practicing the "elegant economy" that "made us very peaceful and satisfied. . . . If we walked to or from a party it was because the night was *so* fine, or the air *so* refreshing, not because sedan chairs were expensive. . . ." By combining dialogue and author's commentary in this way, Mrs. Gaskell produces her memorable episodes: the cow losing its coat through falling into a lime pit and wearing a flannel jacket afterward for warmth; Miss Pole arriving on Miss Matty's doorstep with her "silver" in a little basket, determined to sit up all night during the robbery scare; the excitement fluttering the Cranford ladies on the arrival of the magician "Signor Brunoni," giving way to compassion when they find he is only poor, sick Samuel Brown; Miss Matty losing her tiny annuity after the failure of Drumbleton Bank and bravely setting up shop in her own front parlor.

The innocence of life in this "version of pastoral" is a large part of its enduring appeal. There are certain links with Charles Lamb and Winthrop Praed. It is easy to see why a young American complimented herself by thinking at the time that *Cranford* was the portrait of a New England town that she had once known. William Makepeace Thackeray's daughter, Lady Ritchie, herself an accomplished author, accounted for its popularity by saying, "We all have a Cranford somewhere in our lives." She meant that in some moods we should all like to have one.

Cousin Phillis

Cousin Phillis, a short idyll with Wordsworthian overtones, is more subtle in feeling than *Cranford;* indeed, it is one of Mrs. Gaskell's finest pieces of prose. She links her heroine with the figure in William Wordsworth's Lucy poems—the young cousin who tells Phillis' story thinks of her as "a maiden whom there were few to love and none to praise"—and her writing captures some of the appropriate freshness and ease. The steady cycle of the seasons provides a commentary on the troubled human emotions in the foreground, and the restraint of the narrative adds to its poignancy.

Mrs. Gaskell hints unobtrusively at the way modern industrial changes may disturb the quietest of country lives. She brings an amiable, worldly engineer, Holdsworth, to Phillis' home at Hope Farm along with the new railroad that he is helping to build. The values that he unwittingly threatens she presents through the various members of Phillis' family. Phillis' father, the Reverend Ebenezer Holman, is both farmer and minister, uniting simple religious faith with physical toughness and practical good sense. He works by day with his men in the fields, and then, "suddenly changing the tone of his deep bass voice to an odd suggestion of Chapels and preachers," he gives out the evening psalm.

There we five stood, bareheaded, excepting Phillis, in the tawny stubble-field, from which all the shocks of corn had not yet been carried—a dark wood on one side, where the wood-pigeons were cooing; blue distance seen through the ash-trees on the other. . . .

(pt. 1)

Phillis herself is first seen with "the westering sun full on her," gazing steadily at the newcomer with "large, quiet eyes," her plain, dark-blue cotton dress setting off her fairness. The fowls peck around her in the yard, the bright milk cans glitter as they sweeten in the sun, the court is full of flowers crowding up the walls and over the turf—"I fancy that my Sunday coat was scented for days afterwards," says her cousin Paul, "by the bushes of sweetbriar and the fraxinella that scented the air." Her closeness to the natural world is emphasized when Holdsworth is called away to Canada. She fails with the fading year, weeping in "the lonely leafless orchard." When Paul, foolishly but with the best intentions, encourages her to believe in Holdsworth's affection, she sings for happiness like birds in spring:

I never saw her so happy or so lovely . . . her sun-bonnet fallen back on her neck, her hands full of delicate wood-flowers . . . intent on sweet mockery of some bird. . . . She had done it often at my request the spring before, but this year she really gurgled, and whistled, and warbled, just as they did out of the very fulness and joy of her heart.

(pt. 4)

Sorrow and sickness overcome her after the report of Holdsworth's marriage, but her natural resilience pulls her through. "Now Phillis," says Betty, the strong-minded maid who reminds us of Sally in *Ruth*, "we ha' done a' we can for you, and the doctors has done a' they can for you, and more than you deserve, too, if you don't do something for yourself." It is pleasant to find a Victorian heroine agreeing, as Phillis does, that she had better try to get back to normal. Her story ends with her determined words, "I can and I will."

Wives and Daughters

Anyone who has not read this admirable novel should do so without delay. It is Mrs. Gaskell's masterpiece, needing neither allowance nor apology, and it is the only novel she wrote (*Cranford* is a series of sketches) with which a contemporary reader will feel at home. In some respects it is reminiscent of Anthony Trollope. It is written with the humorous social observation and apparent lack of effort that make his books so readable. It chronicles day-to-day life in early Victorian country society with a light irony that gives an extra dimension to the representation of character and adds a touch of satiric wit to the pleasantly absorbing story. Mrs. Gaskell gives the impression throughout that she is seeing her subject from inside. From the moment the scene opens in Molly Gibson's little bedroom at Hollingford (which is Knutsford again, of course) on the great day of Lady Cumnor's annual garden party up at the Towers, to the close of the book, when Molly, now grown up, has survived the trials of her father's remarriage and her half sister's waywardness, and has also won the heart of the squire's son, the narrative flows along with assurance, expansive but never out of control.

Mrs. Gaskell produces her "criticism of life" by contrasting the stateliness of existence at Cumnor Towers and the dignified orderliness of Hamley Hall with the pinching of the genteel bourgeois home, where Dr. Gibson's second wife insists on the "new-fangled notion of six o'clock dinner," depriving her husband of his favorite meal of bread and cheese for the sake of "some little dainty" that will "not scent the house." But it was probably in drawing Mrs. Gibson herself that Mrs. Gaskell took most pleasure. There is a touch of the devil in her skill here that is the more gratifying for being almost unexpected. With her prettiness and her disingenuous air of unselfishness, Mrs. Gibson is one of the best things in the book. The two girls are also well drawn—Mrs. Gibson's own attractive, willful daughter, Cynthia, who recalls the heroine in *Sylvia's Lovers* (and more distantly Charlotte Brontë's *Shirley*), and her stepdaughter, Molly, who is perhaps closer to the serious-minded heroines of Mrs. Gaskell's earlier tales.

There may be an element of autobiography in the account of Molly's relationship with her stepmother, for we know that Mrs. Gaskell was unhappy during her visits to her own father in London after his remarriage. But her imaginative insight in this book is more remarkable than the use she makes of personal experience. She was never as close to her father as Molly is to Dr. Gibson, but this does not in the least prevent her from sensitively distinguishing the different kinds of affection that a closely united father and daughter may have for each other. Molly's passionate idealization of her father, which increases her emotional disturbance on his remarriage, is contrasted with his own troubled feelings of responsibility and love. The discrepancy between his professional competence as a doctor and his lack of wisdom in managing his personal affairs is completely convincing. In reading about these people and tracing the crosscurrents of feeling underlying the general surface comedy, we recognize that in *Wives and Daughters* Mrs. Gaskell's art has taken on depth and perhaps come of age.

Some idea of the neat satire enlivening this portrait of provincial society will appear in these passages describing how Dr. Gibson becomes engaged to the pretty widow Mrs. Kirkpatrick. (Up to now his future wife has been acting as paid companion to Lady Cumnor at the Hall. Her daughter is away at school.)

"Is he going to offer?" thought she, with a sudden palpitation, and a conviction of her willingness to accept a man whom an hour before she had simply looked upon as one of the category of unmarried men to whom matrimony was possible.

He was only going to make one or two medical inquiries; she found that out very speedily, and considered the conversation as rather flat. . . .

(ch. X)

Unknown to her, Dr. Gibson has at this moment made up his mind to propose. He finds an excuse to linger.

"It's very stormy weather," said he.

"Yes, very. My daughter writes me word that for two days last week the packet could not sail from Boulogne."

"Miss Kirkpatrick is at Boulogne, is she?"

"Yes, poor girl. . . . A young daughter is a great charge, Mr Gibson, especially when there is only one parent to look after her."

"You are quite right," said he, recalled to the remembrance of Molly; . . .

"You are thinking of your own daughter. . . . Dear child! . . . How I should like to see her!"

"I hope you will. I should like you to see her. I should like you to love my poor little Molly,—to love her as your own—" He swallowed down something that rose in his throat, and was nearly choking him.

"Is he going to offer? *Is* he?" she wondered; and she began to tremble in the suspense before he next spoke.

"Could you love her as your daughter? Will you try? Will you give me the right of introducing you to her as her future mother; as my wife?"

There! he had done it—whether it was wise or foolish—he had done it; but he was aware that the question as to its wisdom came into his mind the instant that the words were said past recall.

She hid her face in her hands.

"Oh! Mr Gibson," she said; and then, a little to his surprise, and a great deal to her own, she burst into hysterical tears: it was such a wonderful relief to feel that she need not struggle any more for a livelihood.

(ch. X)

Less excision than usual is necessary to do justice to the effect Mrs. Gaskell wanted to achieve here, and generally her dialogue and the style of her commentary in this novel are lively and economical. But her comic scenes are always better than her serious ones. In describing the troubles at Hamley Hall—which include family quarrels, illness, and death—she often falls victim to her weakness for platitude, and only rarely rises above a usefully informative level of prose. Fortunately it is her humor that leaves the strongest impression on us; and the book closes, appropriately enough, on the image of Mrs. Gibson, self-centered as ever, gesticulating romantically at Roger Hamley and totally unaware that Molly behind her, and Roger outside the window, are eagerly trying to get a glimpse of each other by dodging from side to side of her "perpetually moving arms." Mrs. Gaskell's mood and style were at their gayest in this last episode, written just as she was about to break off her novel for the last time before her death.

THE LIFE OF CHARLOTTE BRONTË

No ONE who has read *The Life of Charlotte Brontë* can ever forget it. In the first place the material itself is extraordinary. Even in bare outline the story of the three Brontë sisters, Charlotte, Emily, and Anne, and their brother, Branwell, has the intensity of tragic experience. Mrs. Gaskell must have felt this when she first met Charlotte in 1850 and was overwhelmed by the quiet confidences of the "little lady in a black silk gown." She dashed down her impressions in a letter that shows dramatically her immediate response to the contrast between, on the one hand, the Brontës' loneliness, frustration, and fatal disease, and, on the other, the compensating vigor of their creative imagination.

Just after Charlotte's death in 1855 Mrs. Gaskell wrote to George Smith (he was Charlotte Brontë's publisher), asking for a copy of "Richmond's portrait of Miss Brontë." After explaining how much she "honoured and loved her," she went on, "If I live long enough, and no one is living whom such a publication would hurt, I will publish what I know of her, and make the world . . . honour the woman as much as they admired the writer." Two weeks later she received the letter from Charlotte's father asking her to write an account of his daughter's life and work. She set to work at once, and finished the book after two laborious years.

If the material is remarkable, so is Mrs. Gaskell's treatment of it. "It is perhaps as difficult to write a good life as to live one," wrote Lytton Strachey in the preface to his book *Eminent Victorians* (1918); he was thinking of the "two fat volumes, with which it is our custom to commemorate the dead. . . . They are as familiar as the cortège of the undertaker, and wear the same air of slow, funereal barbarism."

From this lugubriousness Mrs. Gaskell's biography is entirely free. She respects Charlotte Brontë as a human being and is deeply moved by her tale. She is not tongue-tied by respect, as Stanley is in his *Life and Correspondence of Thomas Arnold* (1844) or John Cross in his *George Eliot's Life* (1885–1886). She does not present us with a graven image or a pattern for imitation. She tells us how, when she visited Haworth in 1853, she walked every day with Charlotte on the moors—"Oh! those high, wild desolate moors, up above the whole world and the very realms of silence"—and how each evening they would sit together by the fire in the little parlor, where the four children had once walked around and around the table making up their poems and tales, and that Charlotte had now tried to make cheerful with pictures and fresh crimson curtains. They would speak of the past, and of Emily, "about whom she was never tired of talking, nor I of listening." Old Mr. Brontë would appear from time to time, still treating Charlotte like a child, "but when she had left the room, then all his pride in her genius and her fame came out"; and he would make Mrs. Gaskell repeat remarks from admiring reviews "over and over again as if he desired to impress them on his memory."

Some facts and opinions about the people in the story Mrs. Gaskell did try to suppress, either because of scruples about hurting their feelings or because they themselves took offense. In the third edition she toned down her account of the Brontë girls' schooldays because objections were raised by relatives of the principal of the school, the Reverend Carus Wilson. She also omitted certain remarks about the woman with whom Branwell fell in love because a libel action was threatened.[4] Her decision to omit references to Charlotte's passion for M. Heger, the Brussels teacher, was entirely her own—here she wished above all, one feels, to avoid inflicting unmerited distress on people who were still alive, especially Charlotte's husband, the Reverend Arthur Nicholls.

With these understandable exceptions, Mrs. Gaskell makes full use of personal papers and documents, relying most of all on Charlotte's letters. "Her language . . . is so powerful and living," she felt, "that it would be a shame not to express everything that can be in her own words." So it is through Charlotte that we learn of the journeys to Brussels in search of education, the abortive scheme to found a school at the parsonage, Branwell's moral disintegration and death, the first attempts at publication

[4]These and other details are incorporated in Margaret Lane's *The Brontë Story* (1953), which is a careful reworking of Mrs. Gaskell's original material.

by "Currer, Ellis and Acton Bell," Emily's illness and death, followed so soon by Anne's, and Charlotte's anguish alone in the silent parlor at Haworth.

Mrs. Gaskell tells us that she understood Charlotte's life "the better for seeing the place where it had been spent, the place where she had loved and suffered." It is just this understanding that she transmits to her readers. Indeed, by keeping her attention steadily on the facts and presenting them with all her novelist's imaginative skill and compassion, she tells us even more than she intended to about Charlotte and about Emily—that "remnant of the Titans," as she calls her. It is pleasant to reflect that all subsequent books about the Brontës still go back in the first place to the pioneer work of this kind, sensible, mid-Victorian lady, who felt so poignantly the fate of Charlotte and her family, and worked so hard to leave behind a fitting commemoration of her friend and fellow novelist.

CONCLUSION

It is easy to see why Dickens called Mrs. Gaskell his "Scheherazade." She hardly ever fails to keep the reader wondering what will happen next, even when he or she is drawn into the wildest melodrama—as so often happens in her short stories. A love of Gothic sensationalism, hinted at in the plots of her novels, lets itself go in the ghosts and murders and robbers, the blood and the revenge that crowd these tales. They vary greatly in merit, but at least two of them are notable, if only because they have impressed some famous people in a variety of ways. The first, *The Moorland Cottage* (1850), combines dramatic action and moral conflict in a pastoral setting. The second, "The Old Nurse's Story" (1852), tells of ghosts and presences haunting an old country house. When Matthew Arnold, according to his sister Jane, was "stretched at full length on a sofa reading a Christmas tale of Mrs. Gaskell, which moves him to tears, and the tears to complacent admiration of his own sensibility," it was *The Moorland Cottage* that so affected him. What is more, Mrs. Gaskell's handling of the brother-and-sister relationship between Edward and Maggie must have influenced George Eliot's later drawing of Tom and Maggie in *The Mill on the Floss* (1860).

When Charlotte Brontë received her copy of *The Moorland Cottage*, she admired it so much that she sent Mrs. Gaskell a copy of *Wuthering Heights* in

return. It is very probable that Lockwood's dream about the ghostly child in the storm, wailing to be let in, provided a "germ" for "The Old Nurse's Story," for here too there is the lost spirit of a child, "with the terrible wound in its shoulder," wailing outside in the snow and battering "soundlessly" on the glass. It is hard to believe that this story was unknown to Henry James, for his own terrifying story of possession, "The Turn of the Screw," has many elements in common with it. James's haunted children, Miles and Flora, like Mrs. Gaskell's Rosamund, are drawn out across the snow in the wake of a restless and predatory power, a power that James's governess repels with the same passionate intensity as Mrs. Gaskell's "old Nurse," Hester.

Mrs. Gaskell is working more or less within her range in these and some other stories—for example, "Mr. Harrison's Confessions," "The Manchester Marriage," and "Six Weeks at Heppenheim." But this is not always true of her other tales, nor indeed of her most important work. Perhaps we notice her weaknesses most in her social novels, where we often find her going beyond her intellectual grasp of situation or, what is worse, of feeling, and where we are sometimes made uncomfortably aware of the incongruity between her subject matter and her method of presenting it. Even in her idyllic passages, where she tries to make us feel for ourselves the essential simplicity and goodness of "natural" life (in contrast with the frustrating complexity of industrial city existence), there are touches of false refinement that spoil the phrasing.

Mrs. Gaskell's mental limitations are responsible for these faults, but she finds ways of making us forget them in her nonsocial works. In *Cranford* her delicate mixture of sentiment and humor promotes an unusual "awareness" of attitude and gives her writing the poise and expertise that we sometimes find in good "society verse"—Praed's "The Belle of the Ball-Room," perhaps, or "The Vicar." In *Wives and Daughters* her humor, with its touch of agreeable malice, makes a useful curb for her emotionalism, permitting her to stand at a sufficient distance to discriminate among the various levels of feeling in her characters. Its function as a brake is taken over in *The Life of Charlotte Brontë* by facts—if Mrs. Gaskell's intelligence did not tell her on this occasion that her material needed no emotional heightening, her moral integrity certainly did so.

Mrs. Gaskell is not a major novelist. Her way of

looking at life is restricted by the limitations of her intellect and imagination, and her narrative technique is not always free from cliché. Nevertheless, her art is an important minor achievement. Standing some way behind her great Victorian fellow novelists—Dickens, George Eliot, Thackeray, and Trollope all tower above her—she still impresses us by the genuineness of her sensibility, the warmth of her personal sympathy, and the liveliness with which she writes about the things that she believed to be important and wanted very much to set right. She is the least stuffy of Victorians, and we should be grateful to her for letting us see that even in her own day, good humor and conscientious scruple were not necessarily incompatible. She tried to "instruct and delight" in accordance with a critical precept that is no longer fashionable. It is a tribute to the real quality of her talent that her books should still appeal to us as much as they do.

SELECTED BIBLIOGRAPHY

I. BIBLIOGRAPHY. J. A. Green, *A Bibliographical Guide to the Gaskell Collection in the Moss Side Library* (Manchester, 1911); M. Sadleir, *Excursions in Victorian Bibliography* (London, 1922); G. de Witt Sanders, *Elizabeth Gaskell* (New Haven, Conn., 1929), includes C. S. Northrup's comprehensive checklist of Gaskell's writings (with her contributions to periodicals) as well as early reviews of her books and articles and books about her; M. L. Parrish, *Victorian Lady Novelists: George Eliot, Mrs. Gaskell, the Brontë Sisters* (New York, 1933), first eds. of Gaskell formerly in the library of M. L. Parrish at Dormy House, Pine Valley, N. J., and now in the Princeton University Library, described and annotated.

II. COLLECTED WORKS. *The Novels and Tales*, 7 vols. (London, 1872–1873), first collected ed., illus. by G. Du Maurier—some of the short stories are omitted; A. W. Ward, ed., *The Works*, 8 vols. (London, 1906), the Knutsford ed., contains excellent introductory essays and a substantial biography in vol. I, but does not include *The Life of Charlotte Brontë* or Gaskell's verse; C. K. Shorter, ed., *The Novels and Tales*, 11 vols. (London, 1906–1919), the World's Classics, contains many of Gaskell's occasional writings and includes the poems as well as *The Life of Charlotte Brontë*—Shorter's intros. are less informative than Ward's but his ed. is the most inclusive to date; J. Whitehill, ed., *Letters of Mrs. Gaskell and Charles Eliot Norton, 1855–1865* (Oxford, 1932); J. A. V. Chapple and A. Pollard, eds., *The Letters of Mrs. Gaskell* (Manchester, 1966).

III. SEPARATE WORKS. (The titles of the periodicals

Household Words and *All the Year Round* are abbreviated *HW* and *AYR*, respectively.) C. M. Mills, *Life in Manchester* (Manchester, 1848), contains "Libbie Marsh's Three Eras," "The Sexton's Hero," and "Christmas Storms and Sunshine," three early tales originally published in *Howitt's Journal* (June 1847–January 1848)—Gaskell did not use this pseudonym again; *Mary Barton*, 2 vols. (London, 1848), novel, in T. Seccombe, ed. (London, 1912), the Everyman's Library; *The Moorland Cottage* (London, 1850), novella, with illus. by B. Foster; *Cranford* (London, 1853), novel, originally published in *HW* (September 1851–May 1853); *Ruth*, 3 vols. (London, 1853), novel; *North and South*, 2 vols. (London, 1855), novel, originally published in *HW* (September 1854–January 1855), in E. A. Chadwick, ed. (London, 1914), the Everyman's Library; *Lizzie Leigh and Other Tales* (London, 1855), short stories including "The Well of Pen-Morfa" (*HW*, 1850), "The Heart of John Middleton" (*HW*, 1850), "Mr. Harrison's Confessions" (*Ladies' Companion*, 1851), and "The Old Nurse's Story" (*HW*, Christmas 1852).

The Life of Charlotte Brontë, 2 vols. (London, 1857), biography, in M. Sinclair, ed. (London, 1908), the Everyman's Library; *My Lady Ludlow* (New York, 1859), novel; *Round the Sofa*, 2 vols. (London, 1859), short stories, links "My Lady Ludlow" (*HW*, 1858), "The Doom of the Griffiths" (*Harper's New Monthly* magazine, 1858), and four other tales by means of a "frame" story set in Edinburgh; *Right at Last and Other Tales* (London, 1860), short stories, includes "The Manchester Marriage" (*HW*, Christmas 1858) and "Lois the Witch" (*AYR*, 1859); *Lois the Witch and Other Tales* (Leipzig, 1861), short stories, repr. four earlier tales and adds "The Grey Woman" (*AYR*, 1861); *A Dark Night's Work* (London, 1863), novella, originally published in *AYR* (January–February 1863); *Sylvia's Lovers*, 3 vols. (London, 1863), novel, in T. Seccombe, ed. (London, 1911), the Everyman's Library; *Cousin Phillis* (New York, 1864), novella, originally published in *Cornhill* magazine (November 1863–February 1864); *Cousin Phillis and Other Tales* (London, 1865), short stories, in T. Seccombe, ed. (London, 1912), the Everyman's Library; *The Grey Woman and Other Tales* (London, 1865), short stories, repr. some earlier tales and adds "Curious if True" (*Cornhill* magazine, 1861) and "Six Weeks at Heppenheim" (*Cornhill* magazine, 1862); *Wives and Daughters*, 2 vols. (London, 1866), novel, originally published in *Cornhill* magazine (August 1864–January 1866); *"My Diary": The Early Years of My Daughter Marianne* (London, 1923), written March 1835–October 1838—only fifty copies privately printed.

IV. BIOGRAPHICAL AND CRITICAL STUDIES. W. R. Greg, *Mistaken Aims and Attainable Ideals of the Artizan Class* (London, 1876), repr. an 1849 review of *Mary Barton* from *Edinburgh Review*; J. Forster, *The Life of Charles Dickens*, 3 vols. (London, 1872–1874); G. Hogarth and M. E. Dickens, eds., *Letters of Charles Dickens*, 3 vols. (London, 1880–1882), many useful references to Gaskell; E. Montégut, *Écrivains modernes de l'Angleterre*, 2nd ser. (Paris, 1889), contains discussions of *Mary Barton, Ruth,* and *North and South*, repr. from *Revue des deux mondes;* C. K. Shorter, *Charlotte Brontë and Her Circle* (London, 1896), provides information on Gaskell's friendship with Charlotte Brontë; M. Oliphant et al., *Women Novelists of Queen Victoria's Reign* (London, 1897), contains a chapter on Gaskell by E. Lyall (A. E. Bayly); G. A. Payne, *Mrs. Gaskell and Knutsford* (Manchester, 1900; 2nd ed., 1906); L. Cazamian, *Le Roman social en Angleterre, 1830–1850* (Paris, 1904); M. J. Shaen, *Memorials of Two Sisters: Susannah and Catherine Winkworth* (London, 1908), contains interesting personal reminiscences of Gaskell by two of her closest friends; E. Chadwick, *Mrs. Gaskell: Haunts, Homes and Stories* (London, 1910; rev. ed., 1913); J. J. van Dullemen, *Mrs. Gaskell: Novelist and Biographer* (Amsterdam, 1924); G. A. Payne, *Mrs. Gaskell: A Brief Biography* (Manchester, 1929); G. de Witt Sanders, *Elizabeth Gaskell* (New Haven, Conn., 1929); A. S. Whitfield, *Mrs. Gaskell: Her Life and Work* (London, 1929); E. Haldane, *Mrs. Gaskell and Her Friends* (London, 1930), makes good use of Gaskell's letters, especially the Gaskell correspondence in the Brotherton Library, Leeds.

D. Cecil, *Early Victorian Novelists* (London, 1934), contains an essay on Gaskell; A. B. Hopkins, "Mrs. Gaskell in France, 1849–1900," in *Publications of the Modern Language Association* 53 (1938), 545–574; Y. Ffrench, *Mrs. Gaskell* (London, 1949), a short general intro., in the English Novelists series; A. B. Hopkins, *Elizabeth Gaskell, Her Life and Work* (London, 1952), still the best biography but should be read in conjunction with the 1966 ed. of her letters, contains a full bibliography; H. P. Collins, "The Naked Sensibility," in *Essays in Criticism* 3 (1953), 60–72; M. Lane, *The Brontë Story: A Reconsideration of Mrs. Gaskell's Life of Charlotte Brontë* (London, 1953); M. L. Astaldi, *La signora Gaskell* (Rome, 1954); the Gaskell Committee, comp., *Knutsford and Mrs. Gaskell* (Derby–Cheltenham, 1960); A. Pollard, *Mrs. Gaskell: Novelist and Biographer* (Manchester, 1965), a deliberately uncomplicated account of "a major minor novelist"; E. Wright, *Mrs. Gaskell: A Basis for Reassessment* (London, 1965), claims that Gaskell is less an intuitive storyteller than a serious, self-conscious artist; J. McVeagh, *Elizabeth Gaskell* (London, 1969); J. G. Sharps, *Mrs. Gaskell's Observation and Invention: A Study of Her Non-Biographic Works* (London, 1970), the most detailed and methodically documented survey of her work; P. Beer, *Reader, I Married Him, A Study of the Women Characters of Jane Austen, Charlotte Brontë, Elizabeth Gaskell and George Eliot* (London–New York, 1974); W. A. Craik, *Elizabeth Gaskell and the English Provincial Novel* (London, 1975), a study of her novels in relation to major provincial novelists of the nineteenth century, notably the Brontës, Anthony Trollope, George Eliot, and Thomas Hardy (they all write of a world that is—in no dismissive sense—provincial).

WILLIAM MAKEPEACE THACKERAY
(1811-1863)

John Carey

INTRODUCTION

Vanity Fair is arguably the greatest English novel of the nineteenth century, and the only one that, in epic sweep, can challenge comparison with the masterpieces of Stendhal and Leo Tolstoy. That alone would make William Makepeace Thackeray worth studying. But he had, also, an extremely likable personality—wry, warm, disillusioned, self-deprecating—that colors almost everything he wrote. As with a handful of other great writers—Samuel Johnson, Robert Louis Stevenson, G. K. Chesterton, George Orwell among them—it is eventually not just the writer but the man that you value.

Like Honoré de Balzac, from whom he learned, and whose *Cousine Bette* influenced *Vanity Fair*, Thackeray was imaginatively excited by the externals of life—what people wore, ate, earned, spent; their jobs, marriages, postal addresses, and social connections. These data teem in his fiction: he can evoke whole careers and genealogies in a few sentences. Behind his main characters we glimpse swarms of remoter figures, not nightmarish or fantastic, as in Charles Dickens, but busily pursuing realistic vocations. For the first time in English literature, Thackeray gives us a sense of living in a crowded and diverse world.

His ideas, too, are more modern than those of any previous novelist. Thomas Carlyle said that he had no convictions, and that is true—but only because Thackeray realized that convictions come easiest to those who are dull, self-satisfied, and unseeing. He questioned, at some time or other, the value of almost everything his Victorian contemporaries held dear—including literature and art. The notion that painters or writers were more loftily engaged than ordinary people and consequently should not have to earn their living, provide for their children, or treat their fellow men with decent consideration, attracted his untiring scorn. A literary man, he declared, was no better or worse than a man writing in a ledger. He loved poking fun at the cult of romantic genius (of which Byron was for him the most deplorable example). He disparaged classical culture and the educational system based on it. He found William Shakespeare's tragedies boring and exaggerated, and he insisted that nothing was so overrated as the fine arts.

Like our age, he found doubt in religion easier than certainty. The God his countrymen worshiped caused him grave misgivings, and he pointed out that the Old Testament was largely a chronicle of crimes and slaughters sanctioned by the Almighty. In ethics, too, he tended to skepticism. Moral choice, he suggested, was illusory, and moral judgment consequently misguided. When one considered the unequal fortunes of men and how completely genetic factors and environment mastered their actions, the concepts of vice and virtue, as generally understood, became irrelevant, as did punishment. The loyalty of Englishmen to their country and their readiness to fight for it were other nineteenth-century ideals he eyed quizzically. Patriotism, he said, was the faith of dullards. His poem "The Chronicle of the Drum" calls war "The noble art of murdering" and ridicules poets and historians who glorify it. He distrusted all political dogma, decrying the "humbug" of both right and left. Since selfishness was the universal human motive, any change in the distribution of wealth was likely, he argued, to end in a system as unjust as the one it had replaced.

His unflattering opinions of life displeased the Victorians. John Ruskin complained that he "settled like a meat fly on whatever one had got for dinner and made one sick of it." We are likelier to regret that he did not remain faithful to his disturbing insights. As time went on, he suppressed his satirical side for the sake of popularity. Even before that happened, his basic lack of conviction made him irresolute. The skeptical views, summarized above, alternate in his writing with postures that are rigid, pompous, and conservative. Instead of confronting this dilemma, he tended increasingly to shuffle off into jocular cynicism and conformity. His flippant side shows up in his light verse, which is often both comic and winningly irresponsible. Significantly, his poem "A Failure" defines life as "a laugh disguising a defeat." These shortcomings and inconsistencies, however, only make him a more authentic and recognizable human being. He had no pretensions to systematic thought; indeed, he mistrusted it, for he believed that every human viewpoint was isolated, limited, and personal. "A distinct universe," he said, "walks about under your hat and under mine." Ultimately all his writing is a study of the factors—pride, greed, selfishness, class—that divide people from one another. But he does not hold out any hope that things could be very different. He was too realistic to be an optimist.

LIFE

THACKERAY'S life encompassed unusually violent ups and downs of fortune, and these developed his awareness of the sharp divisions between different social groups. He began opulently. His father, Richmond Makepeace Thackeray, was highly placed in the East India Company, with a palatial residence near the Esplanade in Calcutta, where William Makepeace Thackeray, his only legitimate child, was born on 18 July 1811. William retained only vague memories of India—ballrooms, fireworks, elephant rides—for his father soon died, and at the age of five he was sent back to school in England. Meanwhile, his mother stayed in India, taking as her second husband an officer in the Bengal Engineers, Henry Carmichael-Smyth. She had known and loved him as a girl, but her family had prevented the match on financial grounds and married her off to Thackeray's wealthy father. Nearly four years passed before she and her new husband rejoined young William in England.

This period of separation marked Thackeray deeply. School was horrible. He never forgot the misery, the canings, the fat yellow soap floating in ice and water each morning. Every night he prayed that he might dream of his mother. His later fictional portraits of her—Helen Pendennis, Rachel Esmond —show the sacred place she occupied in his imagination. The story of her family's mercenary treatment of her gave him a phobia about money-marriages that is apparent in the novels.

In 1822, he went to Charterhouse, his stepfather's old school. He found it brutal, snobbish, and depraved, and he made little progress as a student. Being nearsighted, he was no good at games, and his nose was broken in a fight, which disfigured him for life. His hostility to public schools and classical education was bred at Charterhouse. However, his memories of it grew rosier with the years, and it features much in his books—most celebratedly as Grey Friars in *The Newcomes*. It was at school that he began making comic sketches to amuse his classmates. Drawing and, to a lesser degree, painting remained lifelong passions: he often felt he should have been an artist, not a writer.

Leaving Charterhouse, Thackeray entered Trinity College, Cambridge, in 1829, where he was again a failure academically. As the heir to his father's fortune, he could afford to cut an aristocratic figure. He mixed with gilded youths and cultivated his taste in wines, fine foods, jewelry, and cigars. At the time, rich Anglo-Indians were envied and somewhat shunned in good English circles, and this quickened Thackeray's desire to hobnob with young men of rank. He scorned the humbler, hard-working undergraduates, telling his mother that they "smelt of the shop."

He spent his first long vacation in Paris—a turning point in his life, for he fell in love with the city and the glittering realms of opera and ballet that he found there. Marie Taglioni, the great ballerina, enchanted him: she always remained one of his ideals. At Frascati's he discovered the excitement of *rouge et noir*, and he returned from Paris a compulsive gambler. Over the next four years his gaming debts mounted dizzily. He fell victim to a group of professional cardsharpers who descended on Cambridge and tricked him out of a large part of his patrimony. Sharks, gulls, and foolish young wastrels were to become, when he turned to writing, constant inhabitants of his fictional world.

After five terms he abandoned Cambridge and began a life of leisured idleness. He sailed up the Rhine and spent six months in Weimar, captivated by the cultured, old-world society with its sedan chairs and court entertainments. It seemed a fragment of the eighteenth century, miraculously preserved, and his memories of it helped to kindle his affection for that historical period. Back in London, he started legal studies at the Middle Temple, but soon gave them up, preferring the comforts of luxurious gaming houses and brothels. He studied art, rather negligently, in Paris, and he bought up an ailing London paper, the *National Standard*, which he ran for a few months until it collapsed, learning the rudiments of journalism from William Maginn, one of the "low literary men" whom Thackeray always felt distaste for, even when his livelihood depended on them.

At the end of 1833, disaster struck. The Indian banks in which his stepfather had invested Thackeray's fortune failed, and he was suddenly poor. To make matters worse, he fell in love with a penniless girl, Isabella Shawe, daughter of an Irish military widow living in Paris. Her mother's mercenary opposition to their union (fictionalized, much later, in *Philip*) was bound, given Thackeray's views on money and marriage, to drive him into wedlock. But much as he loved Isabella, he soon realized how unwise their marriage had been. She was a sweet, limp little thing (Amelia in *Vanity Fair* is partly modeled on her) and could offer Thackeray no intellectual companionship. For her mother, he developed a profound loathing: she permanently poisoned his view of mothers-in-law and the Irish. Despite these drawbacks, his early wedded life with Isabella was blissful, and he celebrated it in the "Ballad of Bouillabaisse," where his memory of his young bride is characteristically mingled with wining and dining and the Parisian elegancies he so loved.

To earn his living in these anxious years Thackeray turned to journalism. His stepfather secured him the job of Paris correspondent on a radical London paper, the *Constitutional*, in which capacity he was expected to express abhorrence of Louis Philippe and to champion liberty against French despotism. In 1837, the paper ceased publication, and Thackeray became a free-lance writer. He wrote under tremendous pressure, but enjoyed the challenge. "I love to have the press thumping, clattering, and banging in my rear," he declared; "it creates the necessity which always makes me work best." Certainly the sketches, reviews, and articles that he dashed off during the next ten years contain much of his most brilliant and vivacious writing, though they are virtually unknown today. He wrote for various periodicals, most notably the conservative *Fraser's* and, from 1844 onward, the left-wing *Punch*. He adopted the facetious nom de plume Michael Angelo Titmarsh, partly as a protest against undue solemnity and partly to keep an amused, gentlemanly distance from the business of authorship.

As a relief from the strain of hack work he turned increasingly to clubland, bachelor society, and the joys of haute cuisine, leaving his wife to cope with the trials of motherhood alone. Their eldest child, Anne, had been born in 1837; a second daughter, Jane, was born in 1838, but died within a year. Shortly after Isabella had given birth to their third child, Harriet, in 1840, Thackeray left for a continental pleasure trip. In retrospect he blamed himself severely for this neglect. Isabella suffered acute depression following Harriet's birth, and attempted suicide by throwing herself into the sea when Thackeray was taking her to visit her mother in Ireland. He accompanied her to the continent, seeking a cure for her mental breakdown, but none was found. She remained hopelessly insane for the rest of her long life, and in 1845 was placed in a home at Camberwell. Thackeray's self-reproach is reflected in his account of George's desertion of Amelia in *Vanity Fair*, but the tragedy had more far-reaching effects on him than this. He felt prematurely aged and became a prey to nostalgia. Also, he depended more and more on wine and gastronomic excesses to keep himself going. His girth increased accordingly—he was, as he put it, a "Big Blubber man"—and this, together with his exceptional height and piping treble voice, gave him, in his maturity, rather a distinctive social presence.

Meanwhile, he went on struggling to earn a living by his pen. He begged advances from his publishers, and was reduced to humiliating expedients—depositing, on one occasion, his household silverware with them as security. The knowledge of genteel poverty displayed in the closing chapters of *The Newcomes* was firsthand. But his reputation grew steadily. By 1845 he was earning £1,200 a year, and was able to rent a house in Kensington, so that his daughters, who had been boarded with his mother in Paris, could come and live with him. In February 1845 he began the first draft of *Vanity Fair*.

Published in monthly parts from January 1847 to July 1848, this novel made him a celebrity. Its success, however, did not have a wholly beneficial effect on his writing. He found himself courted by the great and a frequent guest in their grand houses. Society hostesses competed for him. "I reel from dinner party to dinner party. I wallow in turtle and swim in Shampang," he wrote jocularly to a friend. He felt that he had won his way back to the patrician status he had enjoyed before he lost his fortune, and he came to feel ashamed of the "misanthropical" and satirical strains in his work. He parted company with *Punch*, describing its leading light, Douglas Jerrold, as a "savage little Robespierre," and he decided to strike a "kinder" and more solemn note in his books. To be "comic and grinning" was now, he decided, "below my rank in the world."

The loss of sparkle in his writing after *Vanity Fair* can be traced to this deliberate change of policy and also to a sudden decline in his health. He had suffered for some time from digestive disorders and from the painful aftermath of a venereal infection—a relic of his prodigal youth. Then, in September 1849, he was stricken with a near-fatal illness, diagnosed as "bilious fever" but probably typhoid, from which he made a slow recovery. Another source of upset was his frustratingly unphysical love affair, extending over several years, with Jane Brookfield, the wife of his clergyman friend Henry Brookfield. Eventually Thackeray realized that Jane had merely played with his affections and never intended to be unfaithful to her husband. The knowledge hurt him: "the thought I have been made a fool of is the bitterest of all," he wrote. He felt resentful toward Henry Brookfield too, believing he had treated Jane tyrannically. The coarsely inconsiderate husband Lord Castlewood, in *Henry Esmond*, is a stab at Brookfield.

The softening of Thackeray's mind after *Vanity Fair* and his obsequious relations with high society are sadly apparent in his sentimental lectures *The English Humourists*, written during 1851. He gave them before a genteel audience in Willis's Rooms, St. James's, a fashionable venue, and the third lecture (as Charlotte Brontë sardonically records) was postponed for a week because it clashed with Ascot. As his social views became more complacent and his prosperity increased, he found writing less and less attractive. It became a joyless grind, and he groaned over the dullness of it, complaining that he had no new ideas. Money seemed the only worthwhile goal. Seized with the urge to amass a fortune that he could leave to his daughters, he toured the English cities with his lectures and, in 1852, took them to America, netting handsome profits.

The disasters of the Crimean War in 1854–1855 put a stop, temporarily, to Thackeray's flirtation with England's governing class. Indignant at the appalling mismanagement, he joined the Administrative Reform Association, demanding that the educated middle classes should take over the running of the country, and with this in mind he stood for Parliament at the Oxford election in 1857, but he was defeated. To express his new impatience with monarchy and aristocracy he wrote his series of lectures *The Four Georges*, with which he made his second American tour in 1855. The lectures antagonized

some highly placed friends, but Thackeray's brief return to the radical attitudes of his *Punch* period did not signal any real inclination toward democracy. It always alarmed him to think of the masses having power. Significantly, he was much less taken with America on his second trip than on his first: "the rabble supremacy turns my gorge," he remarked.

The great success of his final years was his editorship of the *Cornhill* magazine, launched in 1859, which allowed him to present his ideal of the middle-class gentleman to a large audience. He carefully censored the paper's political views, cutting short the serialization of Ruskin's *Unto This Last*, which had offended readers by its attacks on orthodox political economy. Sales of the *Cornhill* soared, as did the editor's salary, and Thackeray was able to build himself a splendid house, in his beloved Queen Anne style, at Palace Green, Kensington.

These last years also saw a rift between Thackeray and his great rival Dickens. At bottom he had always disliked Dickens and envied his unmatchable popularity. He objected to Dickens' sentimentalization of low and criminal types (Nancy, in *Oliver Twist*, for instance), his dandified dress, and his rabble-rousing politics. Dickens was not, in his eyes, a gentleman—though he acknowledged his genius. When a young friend of Dickens, Edmund Yates, wrote a sarcastic article referring to Thackeray's leftward swing in *The Four Georges*, a furious row ensued, which ended with Thackeray severing relations with Dickens and getting Yates expelled from the Garrick Club.

The two novelists did not speak again until late in 1863 when, seeing Dickens in the Athenaeum, Thackeray ran to him and shook his hand. A few days later, coming home late from dinner on Christmas Eve, Thackeray suffered an apoplectic stroke and died instantly. By his own request he was buried in Kensal Green next to his infant daughter Jane, who had always held a special place in his heart. His mother, whose influence on him had been so great, lived for one more year, and was laid to rest on Christmas Eve 1864, beside her son.

EARLY WORKS, 1837–1843

WHAT spoils Thackeray's earliest works is that he is so keen to sound superior to what he is writing about that you wonder why he is writing about it at all. He chooses lower-class subjects and treats them in a way that amounts to a protracted sneer. This is understandable, given his recent fall from fortune, but it is still regrettable. "The Professor" (1837), his first published story, is a facetious, disparaging account of a romance between two h-dropping cockneys; *The Yellowplush Correspondence* (1837–1838) is the memoir of a mercenary, snobbish footman, couched in uneducated spelling; "Barber Cox" (1840) is the tale of a barber and his wife who come into a fortune and make fools of themselves by trying to live like gentlefolk; "The Fatal Boots" (1839) is the autobiography of an unbelievably base, cowardly, and bullying youth, intent on marrying for money. Fortunately, even these works have stretches where, despite himself, Thackeray has allowed his imagination to become engaged. The details of the oyster shop in "The Professor," with the gas lamps gleaming on the ruby lobsters; the portrait in "Yellowplush" of the smooth, revered old hypocrite, the Earl of Crabs; and in "Barber Cox" the chaos of dirt and glitter backstage at the ballet: all open up subjects that Thackeray was to pursue later. The most remarkable early piece in this respect is "Captain Rook and Mr. Pigeon" (1840), a tale of a dandy card-sharper and his victim, which is based on Thackeray's own dearly bought experience and bristles with incidents and items of food, clothing, and jewelry that were to become fixtures in his fictional workshop.

Two early works that shift the focus to the middle classes and adopt a more sympathetic attitude are *The Bedford-Row Conspiracy* (1840) and *Samuel Titmarsh and the Great Hoggarty Diamond* (1841). The first, an adaptation of a *nouvelle* by Charles de Bernard, follows the fortunes of John Perkins, a good-natured but simple young barrister, and his sweetheart, Lucy. Thackeray directs his satire against the establishment figures who confront these two—notably William Scully, a double-dealing Whig MP, and General Gorgon, a haughty Tory militia officer whose wife, Lady Gorgon, resembles a "healthy, broad-flanked, Roman-nosed white dray-horse." Giving yourself airs and living above your station are anathema in all these works, and the Gorgons exhibit them on a grand scale.

Sam Titmarsh in *The Great Hoggarty Diamond* belongs to the clerkly, commercial-traveler class and is presented as a likable chap who improbably falls in with some aristocrats while shopping. They take to him because he is cocky, yet respectful, and disdains affectation. Eventually Sam goes bankrupt through speculation, and his infant son dies, whereupon Lord and Lady Tiptoff generously employ him as their steward while his wife, Mary (an angelic girl who,

though poor, is voted a true lady by everyone), is taken on by the Tiptoffs as a wet nurse. This rather absurd tale, with its stress on humility and charity, is in some respects (such as the child's death) autobiographical, and for Thackeray to cast himself as Titmarsh suggests his worries about class. While scorning those who aped their betters, he was unsure where, in the social scale, he himself fitted. He realized that he had made a fool of himself by acting the grandee at Cambridge, so he adopted, defensively, a jauntily unpretentious persona.

The most successful of these social fictions is *A Shabby Genteel Story* (1840), which brings two parts of Thackeray's past life into fruitful conflict. The heroine, Caroline Gann, is an idealized portrait of Isabella. Set against her is her villainous seducer, Brand Firmin (alias George Brandon), based on Harry Matthew, a young roué who had been Thackeray's idol at Cambridge. Caroline, though pure-souled, comes, like Isabella, from a grubby background and has coarse relatives. Her stepmother (modeled on Mrs. Shawe) is a military widow of the deepest vulgarity, perpetually boasting of her noble lineage, and her father, James Gann, is a bankrupt oil merchant, eking out a flyblown existence in his wife's Margate boardinghouse. Thackeray's portrayal of the dirt and meanness in the Gann family shows his recoil from the kind of people his marriage had dragged him down among, and his depiction of Firmin shows his disenchantment with his Cambridge values. A snobbish idler and glutton, contemptuous of the *canaille*, Firmin is presented by Thackeray as a typical product of the "accursed system" of public school and university education that teaches, we are told, selfishness, irreligion, and scorn for natural affections. Yet Firmin is also, Thackeray assures us, "innately a gentleman," and his polished mockery of the Ganns is close to Thackeray's own style. This tension, suggesting Thackeray's divided feelings about his affluent past, lends complexity to the tale. The minor figures are profusely imagined—Andrew Fitch, for instance, the rhapsodic cockney painter, or the decayed James Gann, with his telescope for examining the bathing machines from the esplanade. For the first time in Thackeray's work, this story makes us aware of the varied, receding depths of other lives, beyond the doings of the main characters.

Though Thackeray was still, at this stage, unsure of his own stance as a writer, he was quite clear where others had gone wrong, and he developed a talent for burlesque. Exaggeration and unreality are what he derides in the authors he picks on, and his burlesques build up their own fantastic momentum accordingly. *The Tremendous Adventures of Major Gahagan* (1838–1839) ridicules military adventure novels, particularly those with an Indian setting, through the person of Major Goliah O'Grady Gahagan, commander of the Ahmednuggar Irregular Horse, who kills four tigers with his bare hands, enters the enemy camp disguised with bootblacking, and performs other valorous feats—for all of which we have only the major's decidedly questionable word. Throughout, Thackeray makes great play with the routine articles of local color and the scattering of Hindustani words by which novelists strive to convey the mysterious East.

Much less funny is *Catherine* (1839–1840), the story of the "idlest, dirtiest and most passionate little minx" of a servant girl, who is ruined, betrayed, and finally burned at the stake for murdering her husband. Thackeray based it on an actual case, and meant it as an attack on the "Newgate School" of novelists (a category in which he included Dickens), which glamorized the lives of criminals. He admitted, though, a "sneaking kindness" for his heroine, and the book outgrows its satirical purpose. Set in the early eighteenth century, it is the earliest of Thackeray's stories to show his fascination with the luxuriously artificial life of Europe in that period, epitomized in Catherine's seducer, the shady nobleman von Galgenstein, with his ruffles and rings, and the "chestnut-coloured, orange-scented pyramid of horsehair" that forms his wig.

Thackeray's series of *Punch's Prize Novelists* (1847) added to the tally of his burlesques. It includes brilliant take-offs of Bulwer-Lytton's *Eugene Aram* and Benjamin Disraeli's *Coningsby*, and a piece called "Crinoline" by Jeames Plush Esq. (the footman from *Yellowplush*), which exposes, through Jeames's enthusiasm, the vulgarity and ignorance upon which novels of high society depend for their appeal:

Add I the penn of the hawther of a Codlingsby himself, I coodnt dixcribe the gawjusness of their aboad. They add twenty-four footmen in livery, besides a boy in codroys for the knives & shoes. They had nine meals aday—Shampayne and pineapples were served to each of the young ladies in bed before they got up.[1]

(vol. VIII, pp. 91–92)

[1]All quotations of prose and verse are from *The Works*, 26 vols. (London, 1910–1911).

As this suggests, Thackeray was always just as interested in the motives and social conditions that produce and popularize literature and art as he was in literature and art themselves. The topic satisfied his instinct to dissect society. It is treated in sketches like "The Fashionable Authoress" and "The Artists" (both 1841), where he harps on the insincerity of newspaper editors and reviewers (a favorite grumble) and describes in his zestful, knowing, impressionistic way the lives of the painting fraternity and the London districts they frequent. Also in this line, though more factual, is "Half-a-Crown's Worth of Cheap Knowledge" (1839)—a survey based on a reading of several penny and twopenny newspapers produced for the working class. The liveliness of the original idea is, unfortunately, counteracted by Thackeray's scornful response both to the radical political papers in his sample and to the "inconceivably dirty" journals like the *Town*, which circulated information about gin shops, barmaids, pawnbrokers, and tripe vendors. Still, as Thackeray was writing for *Fraser's*, a more liberal stance could scarcely be expected.

This brings us to Thackeray's role as social observer, which accounts for his most enjoyable writing in these years. In *The Paris Sketch Book* (1840) he presents France as a ridiculous but lovely playground and the French as absurd political animals whose nature it is to knock down omnibuses and build barricades. On the other hand, they are far more cultured and artistic, Thackeray emphasizes, than the English. A theme uniting the book is the healthiness of the commonplace, by comparison with high or romantic art. Thackeray scoffs at Racine, Victor Hugo, George Sand, and the German mystics and transcendentalists, and ridicules the ostentation of Versailles with its "thousands of yards of the worst pictures the eye has ever looked on." The circus or the spectacles at Franconi's, where the battles of the Empire were replayed for a popular audience, seem to him by contrast "good and right-hearted."

Apart from the *Sketch Book* there are three other outstanding pieces of similar date that exploit Thackeray's quick eye for foreign culture. *The Second Funeral of Napoleon* (1841), which he thought, with some reason, his best thing so far, gives a marvelously deflating account of the ceremonial surrounding the collection of Napoleon's body from St. Helena and its conveyance to Les Invalides; "Shrove Tuesday in Paris" (1841) describes a masked ball where Thackeray met a young woman called Madame Pauline, ex-governess to an English family, who, some have conjectured, became his mistress and contributed to his portrait of Becky Sharp; and "Memorials of Gormandising" (1841) takes us on a lyrical tour of the Café Foy, the Trois Frères, the Rocher de Cancale, and other temples of Parisian haute cuisine. Any of these pieces would be a good place for someone ignorant of Thackeray to start reading him, and so would "Going to See a Man Hanged" (1840), where the subject is, for a change, English—the public execution of the murderer Courvoisier in July 1840. In its vividness and mastery of atmosphere this challenges comparison with George Orwell's "A Hanging."

Finally, art criticism was a branch of his trade that Thackeray relished, for it went some way to answering his wish to be a painter himself. He wrote about pictures and exhibitions for several magazines, employing a chatty, discursive, irreverent manner that still retains, when we read it, some of the fun and sparkle of the day it was written. He adopted this tone quite deliberately, to express his distrust of sublimity and aggrandizement and his opinion that art should be rooted in everyday life. To the same end his picture reviews give glimpses of the author strolling out of the National Gallery for a cigar, or bolting gin and ham sandwiches while he writes up his copy, and they use commonplace language (alluding to Hill's "spinach pastures" or to Stone's painting of a dog "with no more bones than an apple dumpling") to keep the knockabout, forthright figure of Michael Angelo Titmarsh in the front of the reader's mind.

MATURING YEARS, 1843–1848

As he grew more confident, Thackeray's involvement in what he was writing about became richer and deeper. In these years, too, his association with *Punch* sharpened his sense of society's shams and injustices, while the breakdown of his marriage made him more reflective about the effects of time on people and about the loves and choices that shape our lives.

In the series of short stories called *Men's Wives* (1843), which show his increased misgivings about marriage and women, we can feel a new sympathy in the characterization that clearly foreshadows a full-scale novel. "Mr. and Mrs. Frank Berry" is set in Versailles, where the narrator comes across a former school friend, now married and living in a house in the Avenue de Paris, a crumbling old pleasure dome with a grotto, a fountain, plaster-of-Paris nymphs, damp Cupids, and cracked gilt cornices. The presiding genius of this ruin, reflecting its genteel decay, is the friend's wife, Mrs. Berry, a skinny killjoy with no lips—her mouth a mere "feeble pucker" in her face. Berry is dominated by this specter, and the point of the story is the contrast between his feeble manhood and the bonny lad the narrator remembers at Slaughter House School (Charterhouse), who once vanquished Biggs, the school champion, in an epic scrap, when raspberry tarts and ginger beer changed hands prodigiously in wagers. (This fight represents an early version of that between Dobbin and Cuff in *Vanity Fair*.)

"The Ravenswing," a novelette, also anticipates Thackeray's masterpiece in numerous details, and its heroine, Morgiana, combines characteristics of both Becky and Amelia. But the imaginative heart of the piece lies in the aura of theatrical reminiscence that Thackeray weaves around the characters. Morgiana goes on the stage, and is rapturously received in *The Brigand's Bride*, an opera by Sir George Thrum (a figure based partly on Sir George Smart, one of the leading musical impresarios of the day), and Morgiana's mother, behind the bar of the Bootjack Hotel, is surrounded by mementos of early nineteenth-century dancers, evoking the wonderland of tutus and bouquets that Thackeray so loved. At the end we enter another of Thackeray's dream realms—the German Rhineland. The narrator spots Morgiana, her little boy, and her faithful old suitor, to whom she is now married, at a café in Koblenz, where the stepfather is cramming the boy with cherries and cakes—a scene replayed by Amelia, little George, and Dobbin in the "Am Rhein" chapter of *Vanity Fair*.

In violent contrast is "Dennis Haggarty's Wife," a savage piece, expressing Thackeray's hatred of his mother-in-law and exasperation at his wife's decline. Haggarty marries the daughter of a pretentious, lodging-house-haunting Irish widow, glistening with cheap baubles, and the narrator later finds him and his wife occupying a wretched cottage near Dublin. The place stinks of onions and peat smoke, and Mrs. Haggarty, now blind and ravaged by smallpox, puts on for the visitor a ghastly show of simpering affectation, waving a lace handkerchief before her scarred features, and screeching the girlish ballads with which she used to captivate Haggarty. Eventually mother and daughter take all Haggarty's money and decamp, leaving him broken with grief. Thackeray's failed marriage and lost fortune take on here, it seems, the fictional guise of cause and effect.

The hazards of wedlock occupy Thackeray in several other pieces. "Bob Robinson's First Love" (1845) is about a lad who plans to elope with his tutor's daughter until his uncle, an apoplectic, dandified little military man, dashes to the rescue in his yellow post chaise and cuts short the romance. (Major Pendennis' mission to save his nephew is clearly anticipated.) "Bluebeard's Ghost" (1843), which is about a young widow's unmerited devotion to her dead partner, looks forward to Amelia's mourning for George, and her slighted wooer, Captain Whiskerfield, with his virtues and his squint, foreshadows Dobbin. Thackeray's love for Jane Brookfield and his jealousy of her loyalty to her spouse find an outlet in this tale too, as they do in the twin stories "The Partie Fine" (1844) and "Arabella," which concern an undeserving husband and his sweet, faithful wife, who is left at home to do the sewing while he is out on a spree. "The Partie Fine," with its gas lamps, actresses, and elegant nightlife, is in effect a more sardonic and observant version of "Memorials of Gormandising."

Thackeray's interest in rogues' lives and in the eighteenth century (as exhibited in *Catherine*), his personal worries about the harmful effects of doting mothers and gentlemanly education, his fascination with gambling, and his phobia about lying Irishmen all come together in *Barry Lyndon* (1844), his most successful piece of fiction of these years. Lyndon starts out as a spoiled, naive youth, but his experiences turn him into an unscrupulous adventurer. He flees from home, thinking he has killed a man in a duel, is rooked by cardsharpers (that unavoidable Thackerayan fate), enlists, fights at Minden, finds himself press-ganged into Frederick the Great's army, becomes a professional gambler, travels round Europe running a faro bank with his uncle, returns to Ireland where he terrorizes Honoria, countess of Lyndon, into marrying him, squanders her estate, and dies in the Fleet prison of delirium tremens.

Lyndon tells his own story, and the reader has to guess at the truth through a fog of lies and boasts. But Thackeray's attitude to his antihero is enrichingly divided. He allows Lyndon real courage and spirit, and Lyndon's social criticisms (his scorn, for instance, for young diplomats: "little pink-faced boys from school with no other claim than mamma's title") reflect Thackeray's. His accounts of eighteenth-century life show Thackeray's imagina-

tion deeply stirred—the young bloods shaking their Mechlin ruffles over the green tables at faro; the brutalized soldiery, flogged into battle, their hair plastered with flour and candle grease; the dandies with rouged cheeks and apricot velvet coats and white fishskin sword-scabbards; the ladies with hoopskirts eighteen feet in circumference. Through these glamorous externals Thackeray felt that he had reentered a world that was more dashing and depraved, more cruel and courtly, than the Victorian era.

Social pretension, that bugbear of the young Thackeray, is a root evil in *Barry Lyndon*. Barry's mother dresses him like a little lord, keeps a footman, and otherwise encourages the boy's fatal ambitions. Two near-contemporary stories, *Mrs. Perkins's Ball* (1847) and *A Little Dinner at Timmins's* (1848) (which Orwell called "one of the best comic short stories ever written"), similarly attack the middle classes for getting above their station. Perkins and Timmins, both distantly related to noble persons, both allow this to seduce them into throwing grand entertainments in their ridiculously cramped suburban villas, with catastrophic results. But Thackeray's main assault on swanks and toadies comes in the *Book of Snobs* (1848 and 1852) (first published in *Punch* in 1846–1847 as *The Snobs of England*)—a scintillating indictment of English society, shot through with the *Vanity Fair* spirit. University snobs and military snobs, clerical snobs and city snobs, sporting snobs and holidaying snobs—the categories proliferate, showing us a nation of emulous dupes and fools, rotten with pride and peerage-worship. Thackeray, for all his flippancy, has his finger on the great acquisitive pulse of mid-nineteenth-century England. It is a documentary that keeps sliding sympathetically into fiction, as Thackeray fleshes out his victims with lives, loves, and personal identities. But there is no mistaking the work's radical animus. Thackeray's remedy for the ills he portrays is social equality: "the table of ranks and degrees is a lie, and should be flung into the fire." A tradesman is as good as you, and you are as good as a lord: let us be done with cringing and crawling and court circulars. That is Thackeray's message in the mid-1840's, and we can well understand why, ten years later, he had come to hate the *Book of Snobs* and said he could not bear to read a word of it.

Thackeray's social reporting for *Punch* in this period exposes some of the destitution and starvation upon which the affluent society of the *Book of*

Snobs was built. His articles show his awareness of a side of life that readers of his novels would suppose he was completely blind to. "The Curate's Walk" (November–December 1847) recounts a visit, in the company of clergyman Brookfield, to some artisan dwellings—a bookbinder's, a shoemaker's—in Great Guelph Street. In one, only the children are at home, with some pieces of dry bread and a jug of water to sustain them during the day; in another, the visitors find an emaciated woman and her shriveled baby. Thackeray's tone is uneasy, striving to retain balance, and making one or two unhappy attempts at jocularity. Dickens, less guarded in his response to such scenes, wrote to say that he had "cried most bitterly" over the article. In "Waiting at the Station" (March 1850), a companion piece, Thackeray interviews a group of poor women emigrants, off to seek a better life in Australia, and expresses his shame at the "bitter cold and hunger, constant want and unavailing labour" that have driven them out of their own country. By contrast, "A Dinner in the City" (December 1847) describes the gargantuan consumption of foodstuffs at one of the great livery companies' entertainments—the guests working their jaws in a dizzy mist of gluttony, while rich fluids stream down their chins. News of the popular revolutions of 1848 on the continent alarmed this prosperous section of the community, and Thackeray gives us a glimpse of their fright in "A Club in an Uproar" (March 1848), set in one of those bow-windowed conservative havens so favored in his later writing. He watches the members snatching the newly arrived newspapers in panic, and he notices, while listening to their talk, how bloodthirsty and oppressive fear makes them.

Thackeray was honest enough to acknowledge, though, that his own tastes and instincts, as well as his background, united him with such people, rather than with society's victims. To express his impatience with his own snobbishness while simultaneously indulging it, he invented the persona of the Fat Contributor, whose travels in England and abroad amused *Punch* readers in 1844 and 1845. The Fat Contributor's prejudices are often identical with Thackeray's, but his pomposity and egotism are also unsparingly delineated.

The same uncomfortable sense that he is alienated from the lower orders, and that they arouse his sympathy and his distaste in almost equal quantities, can be felt throughout *The Irish Sketch Book* (1843). In his tour of Ireland, Thackeray found an unprecedented display of beggary, dirt, inefficiency, idleness, superstition, idolatry, and blackguardism—which, as he well realizes, is only another way of saying that he found starvation, unemployment, and their natural consequences. His confused reactions—now furious, now compassionate—are recorded with scrupulous frankness. He is "perpetually made ashamed of being happy," yet the beggars howling for his money exasperate him, and he suggests, only half humorously, that policemen should be stationed near the beauty spots to drive such "vermin" away or fling them into the sea. Meanwhile, the Irish landscape—the huge red moon over "white purple flats" at the mouth of the Shannon; the lean, solitary crags at the Giant's Causeway—keep exciting his painter's eye, though he is far from bowled over by the tourist attractions, retaining a chaffing, cockney matter-of-factness in the face of sublimity.

This also pervades his finest travel book, *Notes of a Journey from Cornhill to Grand Cairo* (1846)—the record of a Mediterranean voyage sponsored by the Peninsular and Oriental Steam Navigation Company. Offhand, haphazard, full of sun and surprises, it radiates life the more strongly because it gives its attention to undignified things—greasy food, bedbugs, primitive modes of transport—at the expense of the great buildings and works of art en route, which Thackeray tends to find tedious. Yet even when bored, he makes you feel what it was like to be there, through the brilliant scatter of impressions he records—the tawdry chapels, with their striped calico, gilt paper, and snuffling priests, in the Holy Land; the women in Smyrna, shuffling about in "black nosebags" and yellow slippers; the melon boats heaped with golden fruit on the Bosphorus. Enlivening, too, are Thackeray's robust social views—his reflections on the offensiveness of the English abroad; or his resistance to the "magic" of the Orient, which he sees as a compound of despotism, sensuality, and female enslavement. For the newcomer to Thackeray, this book is an ideal starting point: it sparkles with his vivacity, irreverence, and swift coloring.

VANITY FAIR

WHEN Thackeray talks about *Vanity Fair* (1848) in his letters, we notice an intriguing inconsistency. On the one hand, he maintains that it is a darkly moral tale, that all its characters (except William Dobbin) are meant to be "odious"—greedy, mean, and godless—and that their story should leave us "dissatisfied and unhappy," as "we ought to be with our own and all other stories." Yet writing to Jane Brookfield from Brussels, he expresses delight at revisiting the scenes these characters have frequented: "How curious it is! I believe perfectly in all those people, and feel quite an interest in the Inn in which they lived." This vacillation between imaginative involvement and satirical detachment can be readily detected in the story itself. It is one of the things that keeps a reader's interest in it fresh, and it gives Thackeray scope for the irony and the tenderness that were both natural to him.

He does not make us feel simple approval or disapproval of any of his main figures—least of all Becky Sharp, who is the most interesting character he ever created (and the most objectionable to the Victorian reading public, whose prejudice deterred him from trying anything so intelligent again). Clever, brave, underprivileged, selfish, heartless, and amoral, Becky has the unpredictable quality of a living mind. She could surprise even her creator. When Rawdon Crawley, Becky's husband, rushes in and knocks Lord Steyne down in the great discovery scene (chapter 53), Becky, though aghast, feels a thrill of admiration at seeing her husband "strong, brave, and victorious"—and this reaction, so revealing of Becky's inner needs, came to Thackeray out of the blue, causing him to slap the table and cry out, "*That* is a touch of genius!" Becky, too, expresses Thackeray's resentment against English society, especially the ruling class, as she hoodwinks the purse-proud Crawleys or triumphs over the insolent, aristocratic Bareacres (chapter 32). Her one unforgivable defect is her lack of motherly love (much worse in Thackeray's eyes—and ours—than her adultery with Lord Steyne or her murder of Jos Sedley, supposing she is guilty of these).

On the contrary, motherly love is practically Amelia Sedley's only virtue. Apart from that, she is an empty little thing, and her self-indulgent devotion to George Osborne's memory is positively annoying. But as she clings to her little son, or, having relinquished him to the Osbornes, toils half across London to see the light in his bedroom window, she shows a capacity for love that makes Becky, by comparison, seem scarcely alive at all. That Thackeray, the deserted child, who used to pray that he would dream of his mother, should make motherliness the pivot of his story suggests the depths from which its planning came.

Amelia's failings of character and intelligence, for which maternal love has to compensate, make her unworthy of Dobbin's devotion, and, when roused, he tells her this (chapter 66). Yet she has only to cry for help, and Dobbin comes running once more. Thackeray declared that such an attachment should lessen our regard for Dobbin. We should see, he told the critic Robert Bell, that Dobbin's love is "vanity," and Dobbin "a fool for his pains." No doubt Thackeray sometimes felt like that about himself, looking back on his love for Isabella; but, of course, we do not agree. We do not expect men to fall in love with "worthy" women, and, besides, we recognize that it is Dobbin's nobility that makes him value other people (George Osborne, as well as Amelia) more highly than he values himself. His character illustrates the close connection between modesty and magnanimity.

George, though not the paragon Dobbin takes him for, is not just contemptible either—or, rather, Thackeray makes us feel his youth and callowness so acutely that we blush for him at his worst moments rather than indulging in anything as simple as blame. When he boasts of the dinner he gave the Bareacres ("rather a nice thing"), or demands of Amelia at the opera ("Emmy, why didn't you have a bouquet?") in chapter 29, his vanity and his wish that his wife should do him credit expose themselves so naively that we feel almost protective in the face of such innocence. He is redeemingly capable of shame (see the end of chapter 29, describing his feelings on the eve of Waterloo), and he dies heroically.

About Rawdon Crawley our feelings are again divided. A stupid young heavy dragoon, with savage little eyes, he is also affectionate, fearless, and vulnerable. When we watch him, before Waterloo, toting up his assets, for Becky's benefit, in his big schoolboy handwriting, and going off to battle in a shabby uniform to preserve the better one for his widow; or when later he is shown playing with little Rawdon (chapter 37), cramming his nursery with toys and giving him rides on his chest while the child uses his great mustache as driving reins, we appreciate the essential healthiness of Rawdon's nature. But these winning scenes cannot disguise the fact that he is a fraud and a parasite, whose idleness and dishonesty ruin others. Raggles goes to prison, and his children are flung on the street, because Rawdon wishes to "live well on nothing a year" (chapter 37).

The impact of *Vanity Fair* comes partly from the lifelike complications of these main characters, but even more so from the swarm of minor ones. It is an affirmation of the fertility and fascination of human life, and in this respect its puritanical title (taken from John Bunyan's *Pilgrim's Progress*) is wildly inappropriate. Of course, some members of its huge cast do display the vanity of mankind's aspirations, but love and goodness are much in evidence too—witness Major and Mrs. O'Dowd (through whose shining qualities Thackeray atones for his former treatment of Irish military types); or poor Briggs, weeping over her momentos of the young writing master she loved at eighteen; or tough old Macmurdo, sticking by Rawdon in his distress and touched by his love for his boy; or the young stockbrokers who, when Sedley's effects go under the hammer, buy up his spoons and forks and send them to Mrs. Sedley—a gesture that reduces the old man to tears. Even the wholly worthless characters are not viewed morosely but with keen enjoyment. They are either spectacularly dissolute, like Lord Steyne, or comic, like Jos Sedley, or both, like old Sir Pitt Crawley.

Thackeray surveys this variegated crowd with an exuberant but penetrating gaze. He shows us how little his human beings understand their true motives and how much selfishness is involved even in their kindest acts. His most searing portrait is of old Osborne, a baffled, tigerish man whose one generous feeling, his love for his son, is inextricably enmeshed with self-regard—so that he is horribly torn, when George dies, between grief that he will see his son no more and rage that his desire to avenge himself on the disobedient boy should have been balked.

By combining a broad canvas with intricate personal studies like this, *Vanity Fair* is able to perform one of the main functions of the novel form—it helps its readers to cope with life. As temporary inhabitants of an unknowably complex world, we are all (if we think at all) threatened by feelings of insignificance and self-obliteration. The novelist's task is to save us from this abyss by enthroning us at the perceptual center of an alternative but recognizable world that, through his guidance, we can dominate and understand, and in which we may gain the knowledge and confidence to survive when we return to the world of actuality. The multiplication of minor figures in *Vanity Fair* serves the purpose of making the fictional world seem as profuse and disorganized as the world in which we live, and so it increases the illusion of control we get when we are able to fit it inside our heads.

The other purpose of Thackeray's crowd of extras is that they seem to authenticate by their presence the main action. Thackeray invents a history for the Gaunt family (chapter 47); for instance, he shows us Gaunt Square with its statue in Roman costume of the eighteenth-century Lord Gaunt, who fought at Minden; tells us of Lord George Gaunt, "the brilliant dandy diplomatist of the Congress of Vienna," now locked in a madhouse and playing with children's toys; and pretends that there is a present-day Lord Steyne who lives in Naples. And he concocts this whole fascinating rigmarole (taking up page after page and quite unconnected with the story) simply to supply the Lord Steyne who crosses Becky's path with credentials of actual existence. Equally typical of the method is the family called Scape—prosperous Anglo-Indians who encounter financial troubles and have to go and live in Boulogne—who occupied, we are told, Jos's Gillespie Street house before he moved in (chapter 60). Jos's move is a minor incident, but Thackeray invents a whole family of displaced persons to give it verisimilitude. The principle behind this prolific realism is not just that the more lies you tell the more you will be believed but also that the most circumstantial lies succeed best.

This brings us to Thackeray's treatment of the Battle of Waterloo. By selecting a major historical event as his topic, a novelist—provided he can carry it off—adds greatly to the stature of his book, since he creates for his readers the illusion that they are viewing, from a commanding eminence, a decisive moment in the world's destiny. In real life, wars and revolutions sweep over individuals, leaving them with only a vague sense of the impersonal forces that have engulfed them. This unregarding impetus of history is one of Thackeray's themes in *Vanity Fair*. When the eagles of Napoleon Bonaparte disembark at Cannes, they bring ruin to the little corner of Bloomsbury where Amelia and her family live (chapter 18). But the novelist, if he is sufficiently gifted and intrepid, can turn the tables on history, treating it as masterfully as it treats us and restoring to his readers a sense of superiority to historical events. The greatness of *Vanity Fair* accrues to a considerable degree from the magnitude of its subject; and not until *Denis Duval* (his last and unfinished novel) did Thackeray again choose a subject (the French Revolution) that might have sustained a comparable achievement.

But a big subject brings perils too, increasing the risk of falsity and bombast; and for Thackeray there was an additional problem of artistic integrity, for having no personal experience of battle he thought it would be bogus to write about it. To launch into scenes of shot and shell would be to usurp the glamor of militarism without its dangers, like the clownish Jos Sedley. Accordingly, he decided on a behind-the-scenes view of hostilities—a wartime version of the backstage life he always found so appealing (chapter 30). We see Peggy O'Dowd getting her husband's kit together; the distraught Emmy holding the blood-red sash to her bosom as George packs. We watch the troops march away; hear the thunder of the cannon; see the fugitives and the cartloads of wounded arriving back in Brussels. But of the battle itself we hear only later, in hints and anecdotes.

By this means Thackeray remains true to his central idea, which was to show the effects of war upon the noncombatants. He also gains greatly in suspense, achieving that muted, devastating end to chapter 32—the news of George's death—that is one of the supreme moments in English fiction. In this part of the book, too, we find Thackeray's most telling use of minor characters. Through them he creates the impression of the panic-stricken activity on the battle's edge. In fact, the subsidiary figures he introduces for this purpose are remarkably few: Isador, Jos's servant, fancying what a dash he will cut in his master's lace coat after the French victory; the fugitive Belgian hussar, sweetheart of the Osbornes' cook, who arrives in the kitchen spreading alarm; the Bareacres, fuming and trembling in their immobilized carriage. But through these few, vividly caught figures, and the clutter of circumstantial detail around them, Thackeray conveys, in chapter 32, the bustle of a whole threatened city.

The idea that *Vanity Fair* was not prefigured at all by Thackeray's earlier writings will not, as we have seen, stand much scrutiny. Its satire, and the broad range of its characterization, which make it virtually the portrait of a nation, connect it clearly with the *Book of Snobs*; its continental scenarios reflect enthusiasms Thackeray had long been voicing; and the choice of Becky as a central figure reminds us of the rogues' lives (*Catherine, Barry Lyndon*) that had intrigued him for some years. After *Vanity Fair*, he never again placed a character so dubious, tainted, and controversial in a leading role, and that is an indication of the great change that came over his fiction.

But though hindsight allows us to identify the growth points of *Vanity Fair* in the miscellaneous

productions that preceded it, its advent is still astonishing. We should never have guessed that Thackeray was on the point of writing a masterpiece so ripe, sustained, and serious, or so rich in characters who overcome their creator's criticisms and achieve a life of their own. Had Thackeray followed *Vanity Fair* with four or five books of equal quality, he would be England's greatest novelist. In the event, enjoyable though much of his later work is, he never reached such heights again.

PENDENNIS *AND* THE NEWCOMES

The History of Pendennis (1848–1850) and *The Newcomes* (1853–1855) are appropriately treated together. Characters from one recur in the other, so that they may be said to depict the same extended social circle. Thackeray grew fonder, as time went on, of linking his stories together in this way. Already in *Barry Lyndon* (chapter 5) he had reintroduced Galgenstein, the German recruiting officer, from *Catherine*, and in his later works his reversion to old names and faces becomes almost obsessive. This has struck some critics as a sentimental indulgence. But it is more intelligently seen as a bid to extend the authenticity of his fictional world by giving us a fuller understanding of the lives and ancestries of the figures who pass through his pages, so that our grasp of social complications and the interactions of class and personality may be deepened.

After *Vanity Fair*, the chief disappointment for readers of these two novels is Thackeray's apparent loss of satirical edge. As we have seen, his retreat from satire was quite deliberate, and his attempt to appeal instead to the hearts and tear ducts of his Victorian public, in such scenes as the deaths of Helen Pendennis and Colonel Newcome, is, for a modern audience, distinctly trying. But though he made his fictions softer, Thackeray had not, essentially, changed very much. He hid his satirical awareness rather than lost it, and the harsh comments he offers about his fictional characters in private correspondence can surprise readers who have taken the cordial tone of the novels at face value. We find him confessing, in letters, that he does not like "dearest Laura," and that Arthur Pendennis' admiration for her shows "he is a weak character and led by women." Such opinions should encourage us to look more suspiciously at the post-*Vanity Fair* novels, and consider ways of reading them that are less flattering to the participants than Thackeray's generally bland treatment might suggest.

Pendennis and *The Newcomes* (along with *The Virginians* and *Philip*) are all stories about a youth of generous instincts (Pen, Clive, Harry, Philip) who is corrupted by relatives and by snobbery, and develops into a cynic or a wastrel or both. Thackeray, looking back, felt that this was how he had developed in his younger days, and all the stories have a greater or lesser autobiographical ingredient.

Pen's corrupters are his mother and his uncle, Major Pendennis. Chapter 2 is important to our understanding of the story, for there we learn that Pen's father was an apothecary in Bath, who made money, bought a small estate and bogus family portraits, married Helen Thistlewood, "a very distant relative of the noble house of Bareacres" (the abominable Bareacres of *Vanity Fair*), and set up as a gentleman. Social pretension is, accordingly, instilled in Pen as a child (as it was in the young Barry Lyndon). The "vice" of his mother (the Bareacres' relative) is, we are told, pride in her family, and this "unfortunate superstition and idol-worship" caused "a great deal of the misfortune which befell" her son. "Vice" is hardly a word we should associate with the angelic mother-figure Helen Pendennis, as she is later developed; but this clear early statement alerts us to the satirical element in Thackeray's initial conception of the character, which his subsequent sanctification rather glossed over.

Major Pendennis is an even greater snob than Helen, and together they break off, in the first part of the story, Pen's "unsuitable" attachment to an actress, Miss Fotheringay. Thackeray does not simplify the social issues here by putting Helen and the major in the wrong. The match with Miss Fotheringay really would have been a mistake, because she is coarse and stupid, and her father is a drunk. Yet Pen's passion for her is genuine and has all the agony of first love. He never, in the rest of the novel, feels anything so deeply again. The barrier between the middle and the lower classes, Thackeray wants to show us, is sustained by pride and snobbery, yet it also reflects—and perpetuates—real social differences, so that if the middle class step across it they find themselves among people whose speech and habits repel them. It is this kind of uncomfortable truth, distasteful to our liberal instincts, that the later Thackeray is keen to bring out.

There is a barrier between the middle and the upper classes, too, and Pen tries to cross this next. Encouraged to think well of himself by his mother and uncle, he mixes with aristocrats at university, neglects his studies, runs up debts, and leaves in disgrace, unqualified for any employment (just as Thackeray had done). Thackeray condemns his "wicked extravagance and idleness," but he also presents Pen's profligacy as the overflow of a free and generous spirit, which scorns anything mean. As in the Fotheringay episode, Pen's natural impulses are shown to run counter to cautious, worldly class considerations, and they land him in a mess.

This pattern is repeated in the affair with Fanny Bolton, daughter of a lodgekeeper and Pen's second lower-class love. This time, however, conscious of the difference in their stations and hardened by his experience of the world, he feels ashamed of his passion, suppresses it, contracts a fever, and almost dies—being pulled through only by the devoted nursing of Fanny, who is dismissed ignominiously, like a presumptuous servant, when Helen Pendennis arrives on the scene.

This is the novel's emotional climax, and Thackeray discusses at some length (chapter 51) whether Pen was justified in stifling his fondness for a "penniless girl out of the kitchen." He is sarcastic about the "respectable" persons who will applaud Pen's circumspection, and he suggests that a blind, self-sacrificing love on Pen's part might have been nobler. But in the end Thackeray comes to no decision: "in fine, let this be a reserved point, to be settled by the individual moralist who chooses to debate it." This cannot help but strike us as shuffling and equivocal. For if Thackeray is not prepared to say that Pen ought to have flouted respectability, then by what right is he sarcastic at respectability's expense? He wishes, it seems, to remain comfortably ensconced in his middle-class values, but to have the pleasure of poking fun at them at the same time.

Our suspicion that Thackeray's protests against class barriers are insincere is deepened by the support for them that Pen's friend George Warrington expresses. A ludicrous concoction of bluff heartiness, Warrington is evidently intended by Thackeray as an absolutely dependable spokesman on social and moral issues, and he gives it firmly as his opinion (chapter 61) that a "high-souled man" doesn't associate with housemaids, laundresses, or the like—or, if he does, "bitterly rues it afterwards." What's more, Warrington has reason to know, for he reveals (chapter 57) that he married, at eighteen, a woman of "low degree," discovered too late that she was a "boor," and eventually had to settle all his money on her and her children, provided that they would "hide themselves away." This melodramatic flashback is the only attempt the novel makes to examine the actual results of marrying out of one's class, and its handling of the question necessarily appears evasive by consequence.

Evasive, too, is the story's winding-up. By a crude plot mechanism Pen is rescued at the last moment from the natural consequences of his worldliness. We see him growing more and more cynical, sucking up to aristocrats whom he secretly despises, and aspiring to a seat in Parliament. But Blanche Amory, the rich girl whom he plans to marry—though he does not love her—is opportunely revealed as the daughter of a returned convict, and Pen, in a final flurry of pseudoreligious uplift, weds instead his stepsister Laura, who appears as a sort of reincarnation of his mother ("arms as tender as Helen's once more enfolded him," in chapter 74).

The impression *Pendennis* leaves, then, is of halfhearted social criticism, coupled with a genial but condescending attitude to its characters (particularly those representing the world of journalism—Bacon, Bungay, Shandon) that contrasts with the sharper vision of *Vanity Fair*.

From a technical viewpoint, *The Newcomes* illustrates even better than *Pendennis* the extraordinarily roundabout manner of narration that Thackeray developed in his fiction—the wanderings to and fro in time, the side-turnings and interpolations, the letters from people we know nothing about, the passersby who somehow catch Thackeray's attention and are fascinatedly pursued far away from the main story. These tactics can exasperate readers unprepared to trust themselves to Thackeray's "discursive muse," but their purpose is to enhance realism by creating the impression of an actual world of bustle and gossip, flooding over and around the foreground characters, into which Thackeray is free to dip at any point.

In subject matter, *The Newcomes*, like *Pendennis*, is largely about the styles and conventions that separate people from one another. Its most touching scene (chapter 21) shows Colonel Newcome, bewildered by Clive's avant-garde artistic tastes and feeling estranged from his son, standing before the pictures in the National Gallery "desperately praying to comprehend them." Mostly, though, the separating factor the novel examines is not taste or age, as here,

but class. It resembles *Pendennis*, again, in warning its readers at the start that the class aspirations of its characters are bogus: they are "jackdaws" in "peacocks' feathers" (chapter 1). The name "Newcome" itself suggests their parvenu status. The father of Colonel Newcome and his two half brothers was, we learn, in trade as a cloth merchant.

When this humble origin is kept in mind, the half brothers Sir Brian and Hobson can readily be seen as social climbers, especially the former, who (like Pendennis' father) marries an aristocratic girl (the granddaughter, we are told, of old Lady Kew, who is sister to Lord Steyne of *Vanity Fair*). It is the pride of Sir Brian's family that generates catastrophe in the book. His son Barnes is an odious dandy, whose lofty ways infuriate the simple, honest colonel; and Barnes's sister, the lovely Ethel, is destined by her family to marry the young Lord Kew—another bitter pill for the colonel, for he wants her to marry his son Clive, seeing quite well that the two young people are mutually attracted. As the colonel has to stomach more and more indignities from his wealthy relations, hatred and thirst for revenge gradually take possession of him, and he engages recklessly in the Indian moneymaking schemes that bring him to ruin.

Thackeray does not succeed, though, in showing the poisoning of the colonel's heart convincingly. We are informed that "hate and suspicion had mastered him" (chapter 64), but in fact he remains, to our eyes, the rather poignant old duffer he has always been. The Thackeray of *Vanity Fair*, who showed poverty embittering old Sedley and his wife, would have been equal to the task, but the softer, new-style Thackeray cannot bring himself to do it.

More successfully handled is the corruption of Clive by his loving and munificent father. Clive's wealthy indolence and his toying with an artistic career are described so indulgently by Thackeray (who was remembering his own youth) that we are deceived into thinking he approves. And of course, in a way, he does. He warms nostalgically to Clive's hedonism, while recognizing that it is morally indefensible. Gradually we are brought to see that Clive is a spoiled, bored, aimless lad, a parasitic "capitalist" (as Thackeray calls him in chapter 50), with no function, no talent, and no inclination to earn his living. He has not even the energy to choose a wife for himself: his father does it for him, marrying him off (partly to spite Ethel) to the colorless

WILLIAM MAKEPEACE THACKERAY

Rosey Mackenzie. So this novel, unlike *Pendennis*, does not shirk the disastrous marriage toward which the logic of the plot leads the hero, and the subsequent domestic scenes (chapters 73–75, 78–80) are the most powerful Thackeray had written since *Vanity Fair*, with Clive and his father being hounded by Rosey's coarse, tyrannical mother (based, needless to say, on Thackeray's own mother-in-law).

These scenes alone would make *The Newcomes* superior to *Pendennis*. True, it is sometimes evasive, like that novel. We are never quite sure, for example, how culpable the colonel's pride in social rank is meant to appear. His lofty patronage of J. J., the artistic genius whose father is a butler, seems intended as amiable stuffiness, less blameworthy, somehow, than the pride of his half brothers. With certain, favored individuals Thackeray is prepared, it seems, to take an indulgent view of such snobbery. But this, though inconsistent, has the advantage of allowing him a richer sense of the mixture of good and bad within people. In this respect, Lord Kew is one of the triumphs of Thackeray's later art, for in Kew he shows us how a man can be noble-minded and generous, yet also dangerously wrong on every social issue. Kew defends money-marriage (chapter 30). He puts a stop to the affair between penniless Jack Belsize and Clara Pulleyn—though they love each other—and he supports Clara's family in marrying her to Barnes Newcome, whom she hates (chapter 29). When the marriage comes to grief (chapter 58), Kew's ineptitude appears plainly. He is also shown up by Ethel. For when he reprimands her for flirting at the ball (chapter 34), she confronts him with a letter giving details of his own dissolute youth, and having exposed his double standard of morality, she breaks off her engagement to him. In these transactions Kew is stupid, unjust, and hypocritical, but Thackeray's skill lies in presenting him at the same time as gallant and honorable. He is a true product of his class, reflecting its virtues and its faults, which are inextricably intertwined.

The complications surrounding Kew also bring into the novel its most exciting minor characters—the shady, scandalous, arty set headed by the Duchesse d'Ivry (chapters 31, 33–34, 36). Some of them, we are told, knew Becky in her Gaunt House days. They breathe the atmosphere of *Vanity Fair*, and contrast sparklingly with the unfortunately more preponderant characters (Pen, Laura, Warrington) who insert themselves into *The Newcomes* from *Pendennis*.

HENRY ESMOND *AND* THE VIRGINIANS

THACKERAY's fascination with the eighteenth century, which these two novels indulge, was a mixture of attraction and repulsion. Years back, in some of his early *Times* (London) reviews, he had remarked that there was no "meaner page in history" than that period. He envisaged it as a garish cavalcade, rife with corruption and intrigue. To the Victorians, eighteenth-century gentlefolk—duelists, murderers, rakes—must seem, he confessed in his *English Humourists* lectures (1853), as savage as ancient Britons. Yet this wildness added spice to his notion of the "grand Old World," where gentlemen were still gentlemen and the leveling effect of railways and parliamentary democracy had not yet been felt. In those days, he records half-wistfully in *Henry Esmond* (book I, chapter 12), men of breeding would spend a quarter of their time at cards, and another at drink, and could often write no more than their names. They rode roughshod over justice. Lord Mohun, Lord Castlewood's slayer, is released unpunished; and the same day, we are reminded, a woman is hanged at Tyburn for shoplifting (book II, chapter 2). Such enormities gave Thackeray a pleasurable frisson, allowing him to escape, in fancy, from the moral restrictions imposed by civilization.

One interest in *Henry Esmond* (1852), then, is that it introduces us to yet another Victorian fantasy world, as liberating for its inventor as Tennyson's Arthurian Britain or Browning's Italy. A further thing *Henry Esmond* can teach us, alas, is how transient literary judgments are. Though the book seems, as George Orwell put it, "barely readable" nowadays, it was for long considered a masterpiece. George Saintsbury pronounced Beatrix "the one complete woman in English prose fiction." Most moderns would presumably award that title to Molly Bloom. But even if we could not expect that of Saintsbury, it still seems astonishing that he should have imagined Beatrix a worthier claimant than Charlotte Brontë's or George Eliot's heroines—or, indeed, more deserving than Becky Sharp. Beatrix is, in fact, a purely masculine confection, got up to appease the male taste for willful, pettish young women. The book as a whole has all the falsity of costume drama, without the thrills—for Thackeray affects the reserve of a polished Augustan gentleman, and the various campaigns Esmond fights in are relayed to us in self-deprecating summaries that studiously exclude anything that might excite.

It is worth remembering, though, that Thackeray said, apropos of *Henry Esmond*, "it is the unwritten part of books that would be the most interesting." If, taking the hint, we look beneath the surface of this austere and courtly narrative, we come upon orgies of wish-fulfillment, as extravagant as anything we could find in pantomime or fairy tale. Esmond, the waif who is really a lord's son, belongs to the world of goosegirl princesses, and he is also Oedipus—a dashing Oedipus in wig and regimentals, who weds his mother and prospers.

To take these themes separately—first, the sexual one. When little orphaned Henry Esmond, twelve years old, first sets eyes on Rachel, she is a dazzling vision of motherhood, with two children of her own and a grand, haughty husband, Viscount Castlewood. Henry loves her as a son, and she is repeatedly identified as his surrogate "mother." But as time goes on the relative ages of son and mother are reversed, so that he becomes senior. Already by book I, chapter 9 he is acting as Rachel's "tutor"; he seems "older" than her by book II, chapter 6; and by book III, chapter 4 he feels like the "grandfather" of the whole family. So when he marries Rachel at the end (when, if we stop to work it out, we find that he is thirty-five and she forty-three), he seems a rather mature husband for her, and she looks younger than her own daughter. Clearly something perverse and subliminal is afoot here, such as is normally countenanced only in the confused, private world of dreams. Thackeray's ardent love for his mother, with its crisis of early separation and blissful reunion, has procured satisfaction for itself within the innocuous confines of a historical novel, leaving evident traces of the miraculous and the unnatural. Victorian reviewers were quick to scent something indecent about Henry's marriage. It "affects us somewhat like a marriage with his own mother," objected the *Athenaeum*.

Mrs. Carmichael-Smyth's suspicious vigilance in the matter of the governesses Thackeray hired for his daughters perpetuated an element of sexual jealousy in the mother-son relationship, which is reflected in Rachel's anger about Nancy (book I, chapter 8), as it had been in Helen Pendennis' treatment of Fanny Bolton. Meanwhile, young Thackeray's guilt over his resentment of Carmichael-Smyth (he thought his mother's second marriage "immodest" and was "disgusted" to hear his stepfather snoring in her room) finds fictional atonement in Henry's noble behavior toward Rachel's husband, Castlewood. Here, too, the resolution of difficulties has the perfection and self-glorification of a child's dream. Though the stepfather is unworthy, the child fights and is wounded on his behalf (book I, chapter 14); the "mother" unfairly blames the child for her husband's death (book II, chapter 1), but kneels and "worships" him when she discovers the truth (book III, chapter 2).

In the region of social, as of sexual, relations the story offers gratifications normally available only in dream or daydream. For Henry discovers (book I, chapter 14) that he is the real Lord Castlewood—the legitimate son of the third viscount. Out of consideration for Rachel and her children, though, who would be disinherited if he claimed the title, he conceals his identity, experiencing a "glow of righteous happiness" as he does so. When his secret comes out, the aristocrats who have slighted him do him homage. Rachel's daughter, the haughty Beatrix, previously scornful of humble Colonel Esmond's advances, repents her mistake; her betrothed, the great Duke of Hamilton, unbends, deeming it an "honour" to know Esmond; and the foppish, dissolute son of James II, arriving on the scene, to make his unsuccessful bid for the English throne, appears, as Rachel's son Frank exclaims, far less like a king than Esmond (book III, chapter 9). *Henry Esmond* represents, then, the acme of middle-class wish-fulfillment, for it offers a hero who is nobler than the nobles, yet voluntarily remains a commoner. Esmond, at the end, emigrates to the New World, rejecting the institutions of monarchy and peerage altogether.

The Virginians (1857–1859) continues the story. Its twin heroes, Harry and George Warrington, are Henry Esmond's grandsons, born in America, and when they return to England they find themselves treated with mercenary calculation by the present inheritors of the Castlewood estates. Of all Thackeray's longer fictions, this is the least successful. The characters do not gain our sympathy, and their activities seem mostly trivial. Thackeray's eighteenth-century idyll has gone sour: the round of drinking, betting, and courtliness now strikes even its chronicler as tedious. The English historical figures, in their period dress, are pale ghosts of the troop who once reveled and fought in *Barry Lyndon*, and the American scenes are featureless voids. Thackeray is sick of writing novels, and admits it (book I, chapter 18). He dawdled over the plot, so that the American War of Independence (with George fighting for the English, and Harry for the Americans) has to be polished off in a couple of chapters at the end, instead of supplying a central feature.

The plan of the book rests on a number of contrasts. The raw young world of the Virginians comes up against the dissipated routines of the English aristocracy. Savage forests, Indians, and scalpings give way to powder, brocade, and wax candles. The twins themselves are markedly dissimilar. Harry, dashing and soldierly, is corrupted by English life, drinking and gambling his way to a debtors' prison before the end of the first half. George, more thoughtful, marries into the kindly Lambert family, who stand for middle-class virtue in opposition to the arrogant Castlewoods. Meanwhile, in the American scenes, George, Harry, and their mother, Rachel (widowed daughter of Henry Esmond), bring the pride and exclusiveness of the English class system into contention with a sturdy, rebellious land. Rachel, a Negro-whipping despot, retains an English upper-class contempt for books and brains, as against blood, and spurns Harry for eventually marrying Hetty Mountain, her housekeeper's daughter. Set against Rachel is her neighbor George Washington, whom young George absurdly challenges to a duel when he suspects that he is presumptuously aspiring to Rachel's hand.

These contrasts might have endued the novel with genuine conflict and variety—yet they are the qualities it conspicuously lacks. Thackeray cannot manage the switches of viewpoint such a plan would demand. His tone remains equable, lofty, and complacent. He applauds the lordly ways of his young gentlemen—as when Harry treats the lawyer Draper with open contempt (book I, chapters 46–48), or when George is deliberately offensive to Garrick, on the grounds that he is merely an actor (book II, chapter 31). Such displays of class distinction warm Thackeray's heart now. He no longer even pretends to deplore them, as he did in *Pendennis*. On the contrary, he disparages, by comparison, modern egalitarianism, declaring that he finds it objectionable to be hailed as a fellow author by "Tom Garbage" (book I, chapter 43). The defiant impudence of this social comment (which could be matched in the flaunted snobbishness of a twentieth-century reactionary like Evelyn Waugh) is ultimately an expression of wounded feeling, traceable in Thackeray's case to upset over the Garrick Club affair and to resentment at his own obligation to turn out novels—by now a hated chore. What he could seldom bring himself to investigate was the contradiction between his dislike of aristocratic pride (as exhibited in this novel by the Castlewoods) and his approval of middle-class pride (as exhibited by Harry, George, and himself).

But some things worthy of Thackeray can be salvaged from *The Virginians*. The book improves, the further we get from the main story. The incidental characters have more life than the central ones—hook-nosed Mrs. Quiggett, for example, laughing her strident laugh "like a venerable old cockatoo," till her ribs seem to jingle; or Museau, the French officer who helps George to escape, and who plays an asthmatic flute, while dreaming of his native Normandy and tripes à la mode de Caen.

Among the Castlewoods, Maria, the woman who inveigles Harry into a liaison, bears the closest relation to Thackeray's deeper fears and obsessions. Being considerably older than Harry, she is the menacing counterpart of the mother-bride celebrated in *Henry Esmond*. Thackeray transforms her into a siren—eyes cold as fishponds—dragging men to the depths and crunching their bones (book I, chapter 18). This horror (a recurrent one with Thackeray) is compounded by the offensive detailing of Maria's physique. Her teeth are allegedly false (whether they are or not becomes an important factor in the intrigue), and when she is taken sick in the coach (book I, chapter 20), she visibly decays, her eyelids growing wrinkled and her yellow cheeks betraying their metallic streaks of rouge. The contemplation of female decomposition leads Thackeray to one of his greatest pieces of associative writing (the penultimate paragraph of book I, chapter 26), where women and love merge with ashes, corpses, and ghouls, dead limbs stick out from sofa cushions, and death's-head moths flutter over winding sheets.

The mood of generalized reverie in this passage, turning from a single story to muse upon the countless other stories that might be told, became increasingly congenial to Thackeray. Its inherent expansiveness was one factor that gradually unfitted him for the novelist's task, because it made him impatient of any single novel's confines.

WILLIAM MAKEPEACE THACKERAY

Roundabout Papers (1860–1863), which Thackeray started to write when he undertook the editorship of the *Cornhill* magazine, provided the ideal medium for his wandering, later mood. They are full of nostalgia. He remembers his boyhood and the incidentals that are, for children as for writers, all-important: the jam tarts and brandyballs, the treasured marbles and pencil cases, the stagecoach rides. He muses upon his passion for pantomimes (which he never outgrew) and upon the vanished ballet dancers and opera singers—Marie Taglioni, Maria Caradori, Pauline Duvernay, and lovely Ronzi de Begnis—who shimmered through his youthful dreams. He remembers being behind the scenes at the opera in 1828 and seeing the great Henriette Sontag let her hair fall over her shoulders, ready for her murder scene with Domenico Donzelli in *Otello*; and further back, he remembers the day George IV was crowned, and how he sat reading in the summerhouse at his great-grandmama's, in a town that might have come out of a Jane Austen novel; and further back still, lies that aching memory of a small boy parting from his mother on the river steps at Calcutta, before he had seen England at all.

There are loving evocations of his travels in Europe and America: Paris; Weimar, where as a youth he met Goethe; the little city of Chur in the Grisons, with its vines and great moldering gates; New Orleans in springtime, when the orchards flush with peachblossom, and sweet herbs sprout to flavor the juleps. The Low Countries, the setting for much of his greatest novel, have a special hold over him. His painter's eye delights in their wide landscapes—the pea-green canals appear so full that a pailful of water would overset them. And in their galleries are the masterpieces of Peter Paul Rubens and Rembrandt, which he has stood before for hours.

These subjects jostle together with a host of other chance interests, so that we seem to watch Thackeray riffling aimlessly but wistfully through a lifetime's joys and sorrows. On social questions he takes, as we might expect, an amused, tolerant line. The essay "On Ribbons" starts out as if it were going to advocate the abolition of titles and decorations, but by the end Thackeray is content that the "Ornamental Classes" (as he calls the aristocracy) should retain their splendors. In "On a Chalk Mark on the Door" he again upholds social divisions, and does it

again with the wry humor of a man who recognizes that in an ideal world things would be different. It is natural, he says, that servants should hang together, tell lies on behalf of their fellows, and adopt a hypocritical air before their masters. Indeed, that is what is required of them, for if servants were to speak their minds, few employers would find it palatable. We must realize, he observes, that servants have their own dependents and loyalties in "the vast, silent, poverty-stricken world outside your comfortable kitchen fire, the world of darkness, and hunger, and miserable cold, and dank, flagged cellars, and huddled straw, and rags, in which pale children are swarming." Thackeray sees how guilty and fragile are the privileges of his own class: it is part of his realism.

The Four Georges (1860), another product of this Indian summer of Thackeray's genius, shares the musing tone of the *Roundabout Papers*. Though a historical work, describing the origins of the Hanoverian line and the manners of English society from the reign of George I to that of George IV, it has the imaginative breadth of fiction and the informality of personal monologue. Thackeray looks back over the revolutions that, almost within living memory, have changed his world—the American Revolution, the French Revolution, and the "silent revolution" of early nineteenth-century England, which has brought industrialization, created the urban mass with its political discontents, and inaugurated the conflict between capital and labor. Thackeray is not concerned to analyze the social implications of all this: his brain was not analytic. Instead, he spreads before us a patchwork of a departed age—the glamor and bustle, the cards and coaches, the flaring lights and gilding of the "vast, busy, brilliant" society. This is Thackeray's last visit to the eighteenth century (except for the unfinished *Denis Duval*), and his divided feelings about it are more acute than ever. He deplores its depravity, its flaunting vice, its brutality to the common people. He declares himself appalled by its excesses. Yet he also fancies that it was a "merrier" England, and we cannot miss the enchantment in his accounts of that "brilliant, jigging, smirking Vanity Fair." It seems, curiously, closer to him than the Victorian age. As he grew older, he lived increasingly in the past, and his own youth—affluent and carefree—seemed to merge with the eighteenth-century world. He had, after all, grown up under the last of the Georges. He had known a lady, he tells us, who had been patted on the head by George I and had knocked on Dr. Johnson's door. His celebration of that bygone era is, in the last resort, personal and possessive. That is why his denunciations of it are so tinged with love.

This quality of involvement, which makes him see and feel the pros and cons deeply, reminds us of *Vanity Fair*, and *The Four Georges* is in some ways his richest achievement since that novel. But the most fascinating (and the most undervalued) of his late works is *Lovel the Widower* (1860), which recasts in the form of a novel (or, rather, of a complex narrative monologue) an unsuccessful play Thackeray had written, *The Wolves and the Lamb*. Like the *Roundabout Papers* and *The Four Georges*, *Lovel the Widower* escapes from the restrictions of the novel form, which Thackeray had come to find oppressive. It does so partly by keeping its characters somewhat flat, so that they belong to fable or burlesque rather than novel, but chiefly by enfolding them within the bewilderingly prolific stream-of-consciousness of the narrator, Mr. Batchelor, who wanders backward and forward in time, and who surrounds Fred Lovel's story in a radiant mist of his own memories and regrets.

Batchelor has, of course, much in common with Thackeray—or, rather, with the composite, fantasized Thackeray who lives in and through his stories. He has had an unhappy love affair with Glorvina O'Dowd (the girl who angles for Dobbin in *Vanity Fair*); a friend of his youth was Warrington (from *Pendennis*); another was Honeyman (from *The Newcomes*). His career (misspent college days, extravagance, debts, early struggles for a living) is a representative one, combining elements from Thackeray's own with those of his various heroes. We seem to have penetrated to the substrata of Thackeray's imagination and to be stumbling on fragments and figures we have met before in other guises. For example, Batchelor's landlord, Captain Prior, a drunken ex-paymaster in the queen of Portugal's service who is now a clerk to a coal merchant, is a battered mutation of Howard Walker from "The Ravenswing" in *Men's Wives*.

The story combines two themes that have always attracted Thackeray—the scheming female with a bohemian past (Becky) and the love of a gentleman for a lower-class girl (Miss Fotheringay and Fanny Bolton). But these themes are given a new, socially emancipating turn. For this time the scheming female wins, and the gentleman marries her, defying snobbish objections. Elizabeth Prior, the heroine, has

been a dancer, twirling in spangles in the corps de ballet at the Prince's Theatre, and then traipsing home to cook mutton broth for her worthless old pa. She has lived by her wits, picking up French and Italian and becoming a governess in the family of the wealthy widower Lovel. Batchelor and Lovel's butler, Dick Bedford, both fall for her, but she keeps them on a string and succeeds in marrying her employer, to the horror of his mother-in-law, Lady Baker. Batchelor ends up feeling cowardly and class-bound, for he hesitated when he might have won Elizabeth; and he is conscious of his inferiority to Dick Bedford, who knocks down a relative of Lovel's for pestering her. Bedford was modeled on Thackeray's own butler, Samuel James, a widely read, self-educated man, whom Thackeray much admired and, according to his daughter, treated rather as a friend than as a servant.

The Adventures of Philip on His Way Through the World (1861–1862), the most closely autobiographical of his novels, handles the class question more warily. It is a continuation of *A Shabby Genteel Story*, narrated by Arthur Pendennis. Philip, the son of Dr. Firmin, is a typical Thackerayan young gent —a high-handed but noble-minded fellow who loses his fortune, has to drudge at journalism for a living, and yet feels he is a cut above the people he works for. His life in Paris, wooing of Charlotte, and hostilities with his mother-in-law are all richly atmospheric parts of the novel drawn from Thackeray's personal memories. A key figure in the fiction is Caroline Gann, the girl Dr. Firmin seduced in *A Shabby Genteel Story*, who is now a sick-nurse. We are told she had a baby by Dr. Firmin, and it died. She nurses Philip through a childhood illness and is seized with the delusion that he is really her child. Accordingly, she sacrifices her welfare for him and conceals the fact that Dr. Firmin went through a form of marriage with her, so as not to deprive Philip of his inheritance. Further, when the blackmailing Tufton Hunt, who wants Caroline to expose Dr. Firmin, gets hold of a document Firmin has forged, Caroline steals it from him and destroys it, thus preserving the good name of the Firmins.

Philip does not know of Caroline's sacrifice and treats her with kindly condescension, as a natural inferior. Moreover she acquiesces in this. When the Pendennises, who are Philip's friends, offer her a home, she refuses, insisting she is not fit company for them. "My parents did not give me the education you have had ma'am," she tells Mrs. Pendennis, and she addresses the Pen children as "Miss" and "Master" (book II, chapter 2). We are clearly meant to regard this as commendable and realistic on her part. Pen and his wife agree in private that Caroline, "good as she is," is not a "fitting companion" for Philip (book II, chapter 12), and it is her peculiar virtue, in Philip's eyes, that she "makes no pretence at equality" (book II, chapter 14). Caroline is thus an ideal lower-class person, from the middle-class viewpoint, for she is loyal yet subservient. She dies an appropriately selfless death, catching an infection from a patient she is nursing (book II, chapter 23).

The importance of all this is that it reveals as sham Thackeray's intermittent regrets about Philip's "hauteur and arrogance." For his hauteur and arrogance consist only in maintaining that lower-class people, such as his employer, the self-educated Mugford (book II, chapter 14), are not fit to be his friends—and this, as the Caroline episode demonstrates, is the novel's official view. Thackeray also depicts Philip as a sturdy egalitarian, on the grounds that he refuses to kowtow to Lord Ringwood. To Philip, we are assured, "all folk were alike, great and small" (book I, chapter 19). But, as Caroline and Mugford could testify, that is simply untrue. What it boils down to is that all folk are alike if the folk concerned are the middle and upper classes, but not if they are the middle and lower classes.

This snobbery, it might be retorted, is to be laid not to Thackeray's charge but to Pendennis' since he relates the story and is responsible for all the comments on Philip's behavior. And there are, indeed, indications that Thackeray sees, and means us to see, the social issues more fully than the smug Pendennis or the arrogant Philip do. Thus the woman Philip insults at Mugford's party (book II, chapter 15)—an ex-actress now married to a wealthy tailor named Woolsey—is, the keen reader of Thackeray realizes, none other than Morgiana from "The Ravenswing." This is perhaps the finest instance of Thackeray purposefully reusing a character from another story, for we know the worth of Morgiana and her husband, and can see Philip's rudeness from their angle. Thackeray does not mean us to miss, either, the superior magnanimity of the socially inferior characters, Caroline and Mugford (who forgives Philip and gives him his job back in book II, chapter 22). For all this, Thackeray compromises on the class issue. He is not prepared openly to disown Pendennis' "realistic" view of the gulf between the middle and lower classes. Further, the story's disparaging treatment of the dark-skinned Grenville Woolcomb

(a deliberately offensive surname), which is repellent to modern readers, clearly recalls Thackeray's observations about the inferiority of blacks to whites on his American trip.

Of *Denis Duval* (1864), Thackeray's last novel, there is less to say, for he died after completing only eight chapters. A tale of smugglers and spies, highwaymen and sea fights, it represents a bid on Thackeray's part to break away from the repeated remodelings of his own youth, which stretch from *Pendennis* to *Philip*. Beginning in mid-eighteenth-century Rye, where Duval grows up, it was to culminate on the streets of revolutionary France, and Duval, a poor boy who becomes an admiral, was to claim as his bride his childhood love, the aristocratic Agnes de Saverne. Despite this highly charged subject matter, the narrative is dilatory and "roundabout" in Thackeray's late manner, being presented as the reminiscences of Duval, written after retirement. "Why do I make zigzag journeys? 'Tis the privilege of old age to be garrulous," Duval explains in mitigation.

That explanation is distinctly complacent, as is the narrative method it excuses—a method designed not to come to grips with experience but to savor it from a serene distance. In other words, Thackeray's late manner had, in addition to its undoubted personal charms, deeply conservative political implications that were, for its original public, part of its appeal.

CONCLUSION

It is no exaggeration to say that without a knowledge of Thackeray it is impossible to understand Victorian England. True, there are large areas of the historical picture that he virtually ignores—the slums, the factories, the rural community, the great imperialist adventure. But the fact that he can ignore them is itself historically significant, and he presents more fully than any other writer the social mores of the middle and upper-middle classes, which were to dominate the age. Moreover, born as he was on a watershed between two historical periods, he allows us a unique awareness of what was involved in the transition from the Regency to the Victorian era, from the aftermath of romanticism and revolution to mid-century stability. His works illustrate this transition as well as describe it, which is why we notice a loss of vivacity and irony when we pass from the early miscellaneous writings to the large-scale novels that followed *Vanity Fair*.

But his writings are not, of course, just an illustration of social history. They are the record of a vast imaginative enterprise—an expanding universe of people and places, evoked in his swift, brilliant, seemingly careless manner. Within this expanse we can identify particular regions of space and time—Paris, the old German provinces, the eighteenth century, the demimonde of ballet dancers and opera singers—that had an appeal for him at once worldly and poetic, escapist and eagerly documentary.

He was continually aware of the inadequacy of language, and that is why we have the hundreds of sketches and drawings, which are an integral part of his vision and, especially in a work like *A Journey from Cornhill to Grand Cairo*, provide an essential complement to the written word. He was aware, too, of the artificiality of the whole fictional endeavor, and this, together with his pursuit of realism, led to his experiments in oblique and circuitous methods of narration and to the evolution of a highly personal voice that (as in *Lovel the Widower*) eventually threatened to swamp the novel altogether. It is, finally, in the four volumes of his *Letters and Private Papers*, which no lover of Thackeray should miss, that we find this voice at its most uninhibited. Unflaggingly enjoyable, they offer on page after page that mingling of enchantment and disenchantment, flippancy and seriousness, quick observation and caricature, for which the only adjective is—Thackerayan.

SELECTED BIBLIOGRAPHY

I. BIBLIOGRAPHY. "Lewis Melville" [Lewis Saul Benjamin], *William Makepeace Thackeray*, 2 vols. (London, 1910); H. S. Van Duzer, *A Thackeray Library* (New York, 1919); D. Flamm, ed., *Thackeray's Critics. An Annotated Bibliography of British and American Criticism, 1836–1901* (Chapel Hill, N. C., 1966), with intro. by D. Flamm; J. E. Olmsted, ed., *Thackeray and His Twentieth-Century Critics. An Annotated Bibliography, 1900–1975* (New York–London, 1977), with intro by Olmsted. *Note:* There is no full, definitive bibliography. Important Thackeray collections, which have been cataloged, are housed at Princeton University (Parrish Collection) and in the New York Public Library (Berg Collection).

II. COLLECTED WORKS. *Miscellanies: Prose and Verse*, 4 vols. (London, 1855–1857; repr. 1861, 1865), this selection was made by Thackeray himself; for other collections of miscellaneous essays and stories see the *Cambridge Bibliography of English Literature*, vol. III (1969), cols. 856–859; *Works*, 22 vols. (London, 1867–1869; 2 supp. vols., 1885–1886), the Library ed.; *Works*, 26 vols. (London, 1878–1886), with a memoir by Sir L. Stephen; *Works*, 13 vols. (London, 1898), the Biographical ed., with biographical intros. by Thackeray's daughter Anne Ritchie; *The Works*, 17 vols. (London, 1908), the Oxford ed., intros. by G. Saintsbury, with original and rev. readings, and additional material; *The Works*, 26 vols. (London, 1910–1911), the Centenary ed., with biographical intros. by Lady Ritchie, and a memoir by Sir L. Stephen; G. N. Ray, coll. and ed., *The Letters and Private Papers*, 4 vols. (Cambridge, Mass., 1945–1946); G. N. Ray, ed., *W. M. Thackeray* (Urbana, Ill., 1955), contributions to the *Morning Chronicle*.

III. SEPARATE WORKS. [Goliah Gahagan], "The Professor. A Tale," short story, first published in *Bentley's Miscellany* (July 1837); *The Yellowplush Correspondence* (Philadelphia, 1838), comic pieces, first published in *Fraser's* magazine (November 1837–August 1838), repr. in *Comic Tales and Sketches* (London, 1841) as *Papers by Mr. Yellowplush*; "Strictures on Pictures," art criticism, first published in *Fraser's* magazine (June 1838); *Some Passages in the Life of Major Gahagan*, burlesque short novel, first published in the *New Monthly* magazine (February 1838–February 1839), repr. as *The Tremendous Adventures of Major Gahagan* in *Miscellanies*, vol. I (London, 1855); "Half-a-Crown's Worth of Cheap Knowledge," survey, first published in *Fraser's* magazine (March 1839); "Stubb's Calendar: or, The Fatal Boots" (New York, 1850), comic story, first published in Cruikshank's *Comic Almanack* (London, 1839), repr. as "The Fatal Boots" in *Miscellanies*, vol. I (London, 1855); *Catherine, A Story*, by Ikey Solomons, Esq., Junior, short novel, first published in *Fraser's* magazine (May 1839–February 1840).

The Bedford-Row Conspiracy, short novel, first published in the *New Monthly* magazine (January–April 1840); [Mr. Titmarsh], *The Paris Sketch Book*, 2 vols. (London, 1840), prose sketches; [Michael Angelo Titmarsh], "A Pictorial Rhapsody," art criticism, first published in *Fraser's* magazine (June 1840); *An Essay on the Genius of George Cruikshank* (London, 1840), art criticism, first published in the *Westminster Review* (June 1840); "Going to See a Man Hanged," journalism, first published in *Fraser's* magazine (August 1840); *A Shabby Genteel Story* (New York, 1857), short novel, first published in *Fraser's* magazine (June–October 1840); "Barber Cox and the Cutting of His Comb," comic story, first published in G. Cruikshank's *Comic Almanack* (London, 1840), repr. as "Cox's Diary" in *Miscellanies*, vol. I (London, 1855); "Captain Rook and Mr. Pigeon," "The Fashionable Authoress," "The Artists," prose sketches, first published in K. Meadows, *Heads of the People* (London, 1840–1841).

"On Men and Pictures: A Propos of a Walk in the

Louvre," art criticism, first published in *Fraser's* magazine (July 1841); "Shrove Tuesday in Paris," journalism, first published in *Britannia* (June 1841); [Mr. M. A. Titmarsh], *The Second Funeral of Napoleon . . . and The Chronicle of the Drum* (London, 1841), reportage; [M. A. Titmarsh], "Memorials of Gormandising, In a Letter to Oliver Yorke, Esq.," culinary journalism, first published in *Fraser's* magazine (June 1841); *The Great Hoggarty Diamond* (New York, 1848), short novel, first published in *Fraser's* magazine (September–December 1841) as *The History of Samuel Titmarsh and the Great Hoggarty Diamond. Edited and Illustrated by Sam's Cousin, Michael Angelo;* "Miss Tickletoby's Lectures on English History," comic journalism, first published in *Punch* (July–October 1842); "The Fitz-Boodle Papers," comic journalism, first published in *Fraser's* magazine (June 1842–February 1843) as "Fitz-Boodle's Confessions," repr. in *Miscellanies*, vol. IV (London, 1857), as "The Fitz-Boodle Papers"; [George Fitz-Boodle], *Men's Wives*, short stories and a novelette, first published in *Fraser's* magazine (March–November 1843); [M. A. Titmarsh], *The Irish Sketch Book*, 2 vols. (London, 1843), travel; [M. A. Titmarsh], "Bluebeard's Ghost," short story, first published in *Fraser's* magazine (October 1843).

[Fitz-Boodle], *The Luck of Barry Lyndon, A Romance of the Last Century*, 2 vols. (New York, 1852), novel, first published in *Fraser's* magazine (January–December 1844), rev. as *The Memoirs of Barry Lyndon, Esq.* (New York, 1856), also in M. Anisman, ed. (New York, 1971); "The History of the Next French Revolution," satirical journalism, first published in *Punch* (February–April 1844); [Lancelot Wagstaff, Esq.], "The Partie Fine," short story, first published in the *New Monthly* magazine (May 1844); [Mr. Wagstaff], "Greenwich—Whitebait," journalism, first published in the *New Monthly* magazine (July 1844); [Titmarsh], "Little Travels and Roadside Sketches," travel, first published in *Fraser's* magazine (May 1844–January 1845); "The Fat Contributor Papers," journalism, first published in *Punch* (August 1844–October 1845) as "Wanderings of Our Fat Contributor"; [Lancelot Wagstaff, Esq.], "Bob Robinson's First Love," short story, first published in the *New Monthly* magazine (August 1845); [Michael Angelo Titmarsh], *A Legend of the Rhine*, comic journalism, first published in G. Cruikshank's *Table-Book* (June–December 1845).

[Michael Angelo Titmarsh, Esq.], *Jeames's Diary, or, Sudden Wealth* (New York, 1846), comic journalism, first published in *Punch* (August 1845–January 1846), repr. in *Miscellanies*, vol. II (London, 1855), as *The Diary of C. Jeames De La Pluche, Esq.; Notes of a Journey from Cornhill to Grand Cairo . . . by Mr. M. A. Titmarsh* (London, 1846), travel; *The Book of Snobs* (incomplete, London, 1848; complete, New York, 1852), satire, first published in *Punch* (February 1846–February 1847) as *The Snobs of England, By One of Themselves*, also in J. Sutherland, ed. (Santa Lucia, 1978); [M. A. Titmarsh], *Mrs. Perkins's Ball*

(London, 1847), short novel; *Punch's Prize Novelists*, burlesque, first published in *Punch* (April–October 1847); *Sketches and Travels in London* (London, 1856), journalism, first published in *Punch* (November 1847–March 1850) as *Travels in London; Vanity Fair. A Novel Without a Hero* (London, 1848), novel, first published in 20 monthly parts (January 1847–July 1848), also in G. Tillotson and K. Tillotson, eds. (London, 1963), and J. I. M. Stewart, ed. (Harmondsworth, 1972); *A Little Dinner at Timmins's*, short novel, first published in *Punch* (May–July 1848); [Mr. M. A. Titmarsh], *Our Street* (London, 1848), prose sketches; *The History of Pendennis. His Fortunes and Misfortunes, His Friends and His Greatest Enemy*, 2 vols. (London, 1849–1850), novel, first published in 24 monthly parts (November 1848–December 1850), also in D. Hawes, ed. (Harmondsworth, 1972); "Mr. Brown's Letters to a Young Man About Town," journalism, first published in *Punch* (March–August 1849); [Mr. M. A. Titmarsh], *Doctor Birch and His Young Friends* (London, 1849), prose sketches.

[Mr. M. A. Titmarsh], *Rebecca and Rowena, A Romance Upon Romance* (London, 1850), parody; [Mr. M. A. Titmarsh], *The Kickleburys on the Rhine* (London, 1850), short novel; *The History of Henry Esmond, Esq. A Colonel in the Service of Her Majesty Q. Anne. Written by Himself*, 3 vols. (London, 1852), novel; *The English Humourists of the Eighteenth Century* (London, 1853), lectures; [Arthur Pendennis, Esq., ed.], *The Newcomes. Memoirs of a Most Respectable Family*, 2 vols. (London, 1854–1855; rev. 1863), novel, first published in 24 monthly parts (October 1853–August 1855); *Ballads* (London, 1855), poems; [Mr. M. A. Titmarsh], *The Rose and the Ring . . . A Fire-side Pantomime for Great and Small Children* (London, 1855), children's story.

The Virginians. A Tale of the Last Century, 2 vols. (London, 1858–1859), novel, first published in 24 monthly parts (November 1857–September 1859); *Lovel the Widower* (London, 1861), novel, first published in the *Cornhill* magazine (January–June 1860); *The Four Georges: Sketches of Manners, Morals, Court and Town Life* (New York, 1860; London, 1861), lectures; *Roundabout Papers* (London, 1863), essays, first published in the *Cornhill* magazine (January 1860–November 1863), also in J. E. Wells, ed. (New York, 1925); *The Adventures of Philip on His Way Through the World*, 3 vols. (London, 1862), novel, first published in the *Cornhill* magazine (January 1861–August 1862); *Denis Duval* (New York, 1864; London, 1867), unfinished novel, first published in the *Cornhill* magazine (March–June 1864).

IV. BIOGRAPHICAL AND CRITICAL STUDIES. A. Trollope, *Thackeray* (London, 1879), in the English Men of Letters series, a portrait of Thackeray by a friend; G. Saintsbury, *A Consideration of Thackeray* (Oxford, 1931), a repr. of the intros. to the Oxford ed. of *The Works*; R. Las Vergnas, *Thackeray. L'Homme, le penseur, le romancier* (Paris, 1932); D. Cecil, *Early Victorian Novelists* (London, 1934);

J. W. Dodds, *Thackeray. A Critical Portrait* (New York, 1941); J. Y. T. Greig, *Thackeray: A Reconsideration* (Oxford, 1950), unsympathetic; G. N. Ray, *The Buried Life* (London, 1952), suggests real-life originals for many of Thackeray's characters; G. Tillotson, *Thackeray the Novelist* (London, 1954), a perceptive study, particularly good on Thackeray's style; K. Tillotson, *Novelists of the Eighteen-Forties* (Oxford, 1954); G. N. Ray, *Thackeray. The Uses of Adversity* (London–New York, 1955); G. N. Ray, *Thackeray. The Age of Wisdom* (London–New York, 1958), the standard biography, authorized by the Thackeray family; the 1955 vol. carries the story up to *Vanity Fair*; the 1958 vol. completes it; J. Loofbourow, *Thackeray and the Form of Fiction* (Princeton, N. J., 1964); G. Tillotson and D. Hawes, eds., *Thackeray: The Critical Heritage* (London, 1968), invaluable for tracing the growth of Thackeray's reputation; J. S. McMaster, *Thackeray. The Major Novels* (Manchester, 1971); B. Hardy, *The Exposure of Luxury. Radical Themes in Thackeray* (London, 1972), a brilliant study, if at times overly moralistic; J. A. Sutherland, *Thackeray at Work* (London, 1974), reconstructs Thackeray's working methods from a study of the MSS; J. Carey, *Thackeray: Prodigal Genius* (London, 1977), argues for the superior imaginative vitality of the younger Thackeray; E. F. Harden, *The Emergence of Thackeray's Serial Fiction* (London, 1979), the closest study of the MSS to date, somewhat indigestible; A. Monsarrat, *An Uneasy Victorian: Thackeray the Man 1811–1863* (London, 1980), sympathetic and lively, but adds little to G. N. Ray.

CHARLES DICKENS

(1812-1870)

Barbara Hardy

ONE of the greatest modern writers, James Joyce, claimed that Dickens has entered into the language more than any writer since Shakespeare.[1] This is not mere praise. Like Shakespeare, Dickens brims with originality but expresses and addresses human nature at large. Like Shakespeare, he is fully in possession of himself, creating an art that is powerfully personal and generously accessible. Like Shakespeare, he creates a flexible language for self-expression and imaginative creativity that commands admiration for its brilliance and virtuosity. Like Shakespeare, he creates a unique and independent-seeming world, allowing us to use that time-worn term "world" with precision.

Dickens has entered into the art and consciousness of modern writers such as Joyce, T. S. Eliot, Evelyn Waugh, George Orwell, and Angus Wilson, but has also been assimilated without too much damage into popular culture and media such as film, radio, and television. His myths are old and new, Victorian and modern. Pickwick, Mrs. Gamp, Quilp, and Oliver Twist are only a few of his many popular fictions, individual and typical, comic and terrible. Such characters can stand as models or reminders of his own genius, for, like their author, they combine peculiarity with ordinariness. Their ancestors are Falstaff, Lady Macbeth, Iago, and Hamlet; like them, they speak with the force and simplicity of moral abstractions but are imagined as individuals with appropriate voice and form. They carry history with them: it is hard to think of the wretched Victorian orphan or the workhouse without remembering Oliver and his porridge bowl, of the Victorian capitalist without remembering Dombey and his son, of sly or brutal crime without remembering Fagin and Bill Sikes, of prison without remembering the Dorrits, of the newly rich without remembering the Veneer-

ings, of cant and prudishness without Podsnap. Their very names are vivid metonymies. For many readers, Dickens is not only a great novelist but a history book. Victorian England is his "best of times" and "worst of times," though the sentence in which he used those words at the beginning of *A Tale of Two Cities* (1859) was not referring to his epoch or his society. His fictions are packed with social information and social passion.

Although he is a great entertainer and comic genius, we have come to know him as a famous example of the wounded artist, whose sicknesses were shed in great art, whose very grudges against family and society linked him through personal pains with larger public sufferings. Dickens was born in Landport, Portsea, on 7 February 1812, second son of John Dickens, a clerk in the Navy Pay Office, whose improvidence led to imprisonment in the Marshalsea for debt. Dickens was sent to work at the age of twelve in Warren's Blacking Warehouse. After his father's release he went back to school, then into an attorney's office. He spent much of his time exploring the busy and varied life of London and decided to become a journalist. He mastered a difficult system of shorthand and by March 1832, at the age of twenty, he was a general and parliamentary reporter. His father's fecklessness became the comic insouciance of Micawber; the prison became a fictional fact and a myth; the humiliation was a creative obsession; the journalism was his apprenticeship. In 1829 he met and soon fell in love with Maria Beadnell, but her parents found him socially inferior: her looks and temperament, their young love, and his subsequent encounter with her in middle age provided the bittersweet tones and trials of David Copperfield's love for Dora and the not-quite-blighted exuberance of Flora Finching in *Little Dorrit* (1855–1857). After Dickens joined the *Morning Chronicle* in 1833, his first sketch, "A Dinner at Poplar," was published, and others followed. He traveled the country report-

[1]"The Centenary of Charles Dickens," in *Journal of Modern Literature*, 5, no. 1 (February 1976).

ing meetings and by-elections, enjoyed a rapidly expanding social life, and in April 1836, two months after the publication of *Sketches by Boz*, married Catherine Hogarth. He next contracted to write a serial, which became *Pickwick Papers* (1836–1837), and, with the death of the artist Seymour, began his long association with Phiz. He had already agreed to edit *Bentley's Miscellany*, in which *Oliver Twist* appeared in 1837–1839.

Early in 1837 the first of his ten children was born, and in May Catherine's sister Mary, who had lived with them since their marriage, died. Dickens' intense grief was memorialized in the nearly fatal illness of Rose Maylie in *Oliver Twist*, and lasted until his death. In 1838 he visited the "cheap schools of Yorkshire," about which he wrote in *Nicholas Nickleby* (1838–1839), and about this time he met the philanthropist Angela Burdett Coutts and put his social concern and energy to work for her causes. (They established a Home for Fallen Women in 1847.) By the late 1830's he was a literary lion, but his radical intensity survived success and social prestige, and he continued to attack privilege, patronage, snobbery, injustice, and inhumanity.

Having expanded the original idea of *Master Humphrey's Clock* (1840–1841)—papers supposedly written in a weekly gathering and put in an old-fashioned clock kept in Master Humphrey's queer old house—into the full-length narrative of *The Old Curiosity Shop* (1840–1841) and at last got down to the writing of *Barnaby Rudge* (1841), Dickens continued to voice his detestation of the employment of children in the mines and condemned factory conditions, writing lampoons against the Tories who opposed humane legislation. In 1842 he visited America. Fêted and lionized to the point of exhaustion, he found much to praise and much to hate, and *American Notes* (1842) and *Martin Chuzzlewit* (1843–1844) were fed by his violently mixed responses. In 1844–1845 he went to Italy, where the bells of Genoa provided him with the title for *The Chimes* (1844), the "little book" that struck "a great blow for the poor." On his return he had a short period as editor of the *Daily News* and campaigned for improvements in the ragged schools (voluntary institutions providing free instruction for children of the poor) and for the abolition of public hangings.

Dombey and Son (1846–1848) was written partly in Paris and Lausanne, and after *David Copperfield* (1849–1850) Dickens started his own magazine, *Household Words*, whose tone and temper were his own—humanitarian and radical. Authorial and edi-

torial activities were somehow combined with amateur theatricals, frequently in aid of charity. In 1851 he moved to Tavistock House, which was large enough for his family (and for the Hogarths, his wife's family, when he was away), and began *Bleak House* (1852–1853) in the following year. At Christmas 1853 he read *A Christmas Carol* (1843) to an audience of 2,000; and the next year the falling sales of *Household Words* were boosted by the publication of *Hard Times* (1854). Dickens pleaded urgently in his magazine for improvements in sanitation following the cholera epidemic in 1854.

He pilloried Palmerston and the government for the appalling mismanagement of the Crimean War, the central attack on inefficiency being sustained in *Little Dorrit* (1855–1857). He bought the house that he had coveted since childhood, Gad's Hill Place, near Rochester, but by 1857 it was becoming clear that his marriage was at an end. He turned frantically to the idea of undertaking a series of readings from his books, but the crisis with Catherine had been reached. Urged by her mother, she left him, and rumors got abroad that Ellen Ternan, a young actress whom he had met during his production of Wilkie Collins' *The Frozen Deep*, was his mistress. This provoked Dickens to a public and personal assertion of their innocence, a famous and characteristic act of indiscretion.

In April 1859 he brought out a new magazine, *All the Year Round*, which opened with *A Tale of Two Cities*, but sales fell, and it needed *Great Expectations* (1860–1861) to restore them. Dickens' creative restlessness continued, but with more and more manic public readings his health deteriorated. After the mid-1860's Ellen Ternan stayed periodically at Gad's Hill. On 9 June 1865 Dickens was involved in a railway accident that is mentioned in the postscript to *Our Mutual Friend* (1864–1865), but he went on reading, even going to America in 1867–1868. Financially successful but physically battered, he refused to heed the warnings—partial paralysis, inability to read street signs on his left side, increasing lameness in the left foot—and undertook another series of readings in 1870. On 15 March he gave a last reading of *A Christmas Carol*. He died on 9 June 1870, leaving *Edwin Drood* unfinished, in a final coup de theatre.

Like all lives, Dickens' is full of loose ends and contradictions. He is the great novelist of childhood, whose demands and disappointments alienated his own children; the great sentimental celebrant of domestic life, whose separation from his wife incurred painful publicity; the defender of sexual morals, whose love for Ellen Ternan stimulated speculations of every kind. He was also a novelist who loved to devise plots that hinged on secrecy and disclosure and who succeeded in keeping secret his own private life. As an amateur of detection, he might have enjoyed or deplored the literary detective work that has failed to discover the nature of his relationship with Ellen Ternan. K. J. Fielding suggested (in his British Council pamphlet on Dickens, Writers and Their Work series, no. 37) that Dickens' critics have not used recent biographical revelations with precision and definiteness; and this is still true, with the exception of Angus Wilson. Dickens' later heroines, for instance, are too often crudely identified as images of Ellen, and though her name connects itself irresistibly with the names of Estella, Bella, and Helena Landless, their originality and spirit were not new in his novels. Edith Dombey and Louisa Gradgrind are also brilliantly lucid instances of their author's insight into women's sexuality, aggression, and pride, and of his capacity to bring out these qualities in ideological, as well as psychological, significance. Dickens' life was not at all like a Dickens novel, though his energy, his egocentricity, and his histrionic virtuosity mark both the life and the work.

Dickens' career has twin stamps of power. The end is plainly present in the beginning, and the end has progressed far beyond the beginning. Great artists find forms for their individuality, while always exhibiting that improvability so rare in human experience. Like many other novelists—Defoe, Richardson, Fielding, Thackeray, George Eliot, Zola, and Henry James—Dickens began as a journalist, then moved from fact to fiction. Like his own David Copperfield, he first wrote in bondage to other men's words. His work as a parliamentary reporter trained him in attention, speed, and precision. As he listened and wrote, he was educating his response to words, rhythms, eloquence, and personality. From reporting, he moved on to the freer forms of journalism, and *Sketches by Boz* provides us with a collection of essays that shows the evolution of the prose writer, the storyteller, the creator of character, and the analyst of environments and objects. Of course, Dickens never gave up journalism, and his career as a novelist developed together with editorial labors, journalistic essays, and speeches. But *Sketches by Boz* offers a lucid example of a novelist learning and developing his special novelistic powers. We could turn this statement on its head and praise *Sketches* as

great journalism, sharp in observation, animated in language, recording signs while interpreting their meanings. However, there is more to this book than impressive reporting.

Dickens is a dynamic presenter of the world of the city. At times it seems as if the actual environment of rapid social and economic change helped to develop his mastery of flux. In *Sketches* we see an energetic meeting of artist and subject. Whatever building, street, or institution Dickens describes, he more than describes. He is a vivid observer of the mobility of surfaces, and the many surfaces in *Sketches by Boz* are truthfully designed not to be static. Dickens knows that so-called solid objects do not present themselves in a still world, but as moving aspects of social mutability. He seizes and particularizes moments and movements. When he describes dirty London streets, for instance, in chapter 2 of the section entitled "The Streets—Night," we are told that "just enough damp" is "gently stealing down" to make the pavements greasy. The gas lamps are said to look more luminous because of "the heavy lazy mist, which hangs over every object." Description in *Sketches* is consistently cinematic, animated by Dickens' refusal to paint a static scene. Where there is an apparent exception, it proves the rule, since its stillness is emphatic. Here is a short description of a room that is waiting for a tenant, and thus is unnaturally void and placid:

It was a neat, dull little house, on the shady side of the way, with new, narrow floorcloth in the passage, and new, narrow stair-carpets up to the first floor. The paper was new, and the paint was new, and the furniture was new; and all three, paper, paint, and furniture, bespoke the limited means of the tenant. There was a little red and black carpet in the drawing room, with a border of flooring all the way round; a few stained chairs and a Pembroke table. A pink shell was displayed on each of the little sideboards, which, with the addition of a tea-tray and caddy, a few more shells on the mantelpiece, and three peacock's feathers tastefully arranged above them, completed the decorative furniture of the apartment.[2]

("Our Parish," ch. 7)

Dickens, like Henry James, knew that human beings can't be separated from their personal environments of clothes, accessories, furniture, rooms, and houses. The only cold, still things are those

[2]All quotations from the works are from *The New Oxford Illustrated Dickens*, 21 vols. (London, 1947–1958).

waiting to be peopled. There is a sense in which even this quiet scene refuses to stay quite still. Its quietness is a Dickensian quietness, alert and tense. This is an early essay, but its language is strikingly Dickensian in insistent repetition and mounting rhythm, which transforms fact into poetry. Dickens has an eye for the odd particular, like the pink shell and the peacock feathers, which not only provides selective vividness and focus but conveys a precise sense of social ways and means. The eye and voice of the mature Dickens are apparent from his very first exercises, despite occasional uneconomical phrasing. Here is the germ of the bravura set pieces of the late Dickens, the repetitions that stylize and signify the veneer of the Veneerings in *Our Mutual Friend*, though he is as yet relatively restrained, unpracticed in exaggeration and in the stylizations that mark the poetic prose of the later novels.

Although Dickens is not yet engaged with psychological subtlety, the "I" of his anonymous but animated reporter has some psychological dimension. The observer here is constantly recording and responding to social change. Scotland Yard, for instance, like most of the places and buildings, is described historically, in terms of what it was and what it has become during a specified period of time. The observer in *Sketches* is closely attentive to the erosions and accretions that unbuild and rebuild a great city, changing the scene from day to day, if we watch with conscientious concentration. This sense of historical motion is one of the remarkable achievements of *Sketches* and is recognizably a beginning of a form and a theme that continues throughout the novels, rising into prominence in *Dombey and Son* and later works. But it is given individuality and personality by being attached to personal memory. History is vivid here because it is observed through particular eyes, particular ears, and a particular memory. It is also presented through an intelligent inference of the future from the past, active and impassioned. Dickens makes his novelist-character David Copperfield observe that observation may be called a quality of creative power. David is provided with marvelously vivid things to observe and makes us observe them as signifiers of Dickens' power: the tall fowls, the greenness of the churchyard's grass, the wrinkled wax Peggotty kept for her thread, the workbox with a view of St. Paul's pink dome, and the rough red of Peggotty's skin blended with the smooth red velvet of the parlor footstool. All these things are described as objects originally observed, well enough in the past to be remembered. The novelist makes his novelist fully comprehend this process: "If it should appear from anything I may set down in this narrative that I was a child of close observation, or that as a man I have a strong memory of my childhood, I undoubtedly lay claim to both of these characteristics."

The descriptions in *Sketches* are individualized by Dickens' brilliant layering of visual experience: objects and places are not visualized baldly, as if seen for the first time, or for a once-and-only time. They are objects seen as remembered. This complication of simple visual record is not only animated but true to writing experience, which superimposes image on experience. Objects in fiction are inevitably remembered, and rely, too, on the reader's memory. Dickens' wandering Londoner also introduces a further layer of comparative experience. The author analyzes the activity of intelligence and imagination:

We never see any very large, staring, black Roman capitals, in a book, or shop-window, or placarded on a wall, without their immediately recalling to our mind an indistinct and confused recollection of the time when we were first initiated in the mysteries of the alphabet. We almost fancy we see the pen's point following the letter, to impress its form more strongly on our bewildered imagination; and wince involuntarily, as we remember the hard knuckles with which the reverend old lady who instilled into our mind the first principles of education for ninepence per week, or ten and sixpence per quarter, was wont to poke our juvenile head occasionally, by way of adjusting the confusion of ideas in which we were generally involved. The same kind of feeling pursues us in many other instances, but there is no place which recalls so strongly our recollections of childhood as Astley's. It was not a "Royal Amphitheatre" in those days, nor had Ducrow arisen to shed the light of classic taste and portable gas over the sawdust of the circus; but the whole character of the place was the same, the pieces were the same, the clown's jokes were the same, the riding-masters were equally grand, the comic performers equally witty, the tragedians equally hoarse, and the "highly-trained chargers" equally spirited. Astley's has altered for the better—we have changed for the worse. Our histrionic taste is gone, and with shame we confess, that we are far more delighted and amused with the audience, than with the pageantry we once so highly appreciated.

("Scenes," ch. 11)

This apparently straightforward introduction is far from simple: it joins the two experiences of childhood learning and childhood play, through a deceptively informal and rambling structure of recall, which masks analysis and abstraction in a characteristically Dickensian fashion. If we compare Dickens with George Eliot or Marcel Proust, he is relaxed, informal, unanalytic, but the implication of his juxtaposed particulars is essentially identical with the explicit concepts they articulate and generalize. It is easy to underrate Dickens' intelligence, because his habit is hardly ever that of analytic or generalized discourse. His vivid particulars are cunningly linked in contrasts and comparisons that reveal psychological intuition by the very way in which he inquires, answers, suggests, and informs. Not that conceptual language is absent: notice the careful use of phrases like "indistinct and confused recollection," "we almost fancy," and "bewildered imagination."

Sketches by Boz is also animated by Dickens' range of comedy. The theatrical influence, which many critics have noticed, is shown very clearly in the sketch of Astley's in chapter 11. Dickens describes comedy in a way that seems infected by the experience he reports. His actresses and clowns are larger than life, but the exaggeration and mannerism are surely inspired by their actual theatrical origins. A personal sense of the ridiculous is always available: the observer moves rapidly from precise theatrical report, amused and amusing, to travesty and fantasy: "By the way, talking of fathers, we should very much like to see some piece in which all the dramatis personae were orphans. Fathers are invariably great nuisances on the stage." "By the way" introduces a casual-seeming digression, which expands and generates drama as Dickens rapidly throws off two tiny, funny, scornful scenes of implausible family discovery, complete with stagey dialogue and gesture:

"It is now nineteen years, my dear child, since your blessed mother (here the old villain's voice falters) confided you to my charge. You were then an infant," &c., &c. Or else they have to discover, all of a sudden, that somebody whom they have been in constant communication with, during three long acts, without the slightest suspicion, is their own child: in which case they exclaim, "Ah! what do I see? This bracelet! That smile! These documents! Those eyes! Can I believe my senses?—It must be!—Yes—it is, it is my child!"—"My father!" exclaims the child; and they fall into each other's arms, and look over each other's shoulders, and the audience give three rounds of applause.

("Scenes," ch. 11)

Dickens' affective range includes pathos as well as fun. One of the most interesting seminal sketches, "The Pawnbroker's Shop," shows this pathos at its best, not existing as a crude rhetorical device to force strong response from the reader, but dramatized in a compressed vignette that arrives at sympathy through analysis. There is analysis as well as persuasion, forcing understanding as well as pity. At the end of this sketch Dickens uses a scenic division and contrast (a device he develops in the novels). In a split-scene sketch of the shop he describes two girls, one still virtuous and the other "whose attire, miserably poor but extremely gaudy . . . bespeaks her station." The virtuous girl, with her mother, is pawning a gold chain and a "forget-me-not" ring, and the prostitute catches sight of the trinkets and bursts into tears, in a variation of the theme of Holman Hunt's *The Awakening Conscience* (1851–1853). Dickens is carefully using a sentimental genre-piece in order to make a point about social corruption. The narrator infers that the first girl is no novice, because of the way she and her mother answer questions and bargain with the pawnbroker. They have some delicacy, standing back to "avoid the observation even of the shopman" but are not too humiliated, "for want has hardened the mother, and her example has hardened the girl, and the prospect of receiving money, coupled with a recollection of the misery they have both endured from the want of it," has made them what they are. The prostitute represents a further stage in what Dickens calls degradation, but we are told that there are still "chords in the human heart" that vibrate to past associations. In case we have still not got the point or may mistake this for a stark contrast between virtue and vice, Dickens dissolves the antithesis and presents a series:

There has been another spectator, in the person of a woman in the common shop; the lowest of the low; dirty, unbonneted, flaunting, and slovenly. Her curiosity was at first attracted by the little she could see of the group; then her attention. The half-intoxicated leer changed to an expression of something like interest, and a feeling similar to that we have described, appeared for a moment, and only a moment, to extend itself even to her bosom.

("Scenes," ch. 23)

Being Dickens, he ends by explicit comment, asking "how soon these women may change places" and seeing all three as representing different stages of deterioration. The act of reporting social conditions makes a discovery about social conditioning.

Sketches by Boz is a three-part collection, which grows in complexity and creativity, beginning with

"Our Parish," moving into "Scenes," where description and animated topography are joined, and continuing with "Characters." The art of the novelist is developing. Some of the pieces in "Characters" tilt the character sketch in the direction of narrative, as in "The Misplaced Attachment of Mr. John Dounce," and it seems inevitable that *Sketches* should conclude with the fiction of "Tales."

In some ways *Sketches* is, for all its discontinuity, morally and sociologically more unified and probing than *Pickwick Papers.* Begun as a series of sketches, *Pickwick Papers* came to achieve narrative unity and continuity, but in a form that often divides comedy from pathos. In the inset tales that are narrated or read, following the eighteenth-century tradition on which Dickens was reared, Pickwick and his friends are given a literary supplement to their tour of investigation. It is a dark, grim, tragic supplement, telling of madness, crime, death, poverty, and misery. Pickwick's responses are always tellingly obtuse. It is not until he is himself involved with the institutions of law and the prison that he begins to feel and understand. This may be a gradual discovery, made by the author in the process of developing continuity, but the effect is to departmentalize the grim and the comic materials, as in Victorian melodrama. Still, the underworld is present, and Pickwick's innocence is not to remain intact. There are also other compressed but conspicuous assertions of the underworld, in the black humor of Jingle's telegraphese and Sam Weller's anecdotes, which present deaths, murders, marital disaster, servants' wretchedness, fear, pain, drugs, horror, in the guise of joke— "There's nothin so refreshin as sleep, sir, as the servant-girl said afore she drank the egg-cupful of laudanum."

For the most part, the comedy of the novel lies apart from its pathos, and the various kinds of comedy—jokes, farce, comedy of humors, visual anecdote, social satire—seem to lie apart from each other. The episodic structure of the action, with its many narrative interruptions, shows Dickens' form at its most informal, and Dickens himself declared that he thought of it "as being a book by itself and quite unlike his other work."[3] *Pickwick Papers* makes no use of fantasy in its main action but up to a point it can be, and frequently has been, read as a fable. But what kind of fable? It proffers pastoral and domestic symbols of the good life, and its events and characters present moral concepts through simplification. Social and psychological complication are avoided. Like fable, it has a simply extractable point, and the story of Pickwick's journey from innocence to experience makes no attempt to show the difficulties and subtleties of leading the good life or passing ethical judgments. Insofar as it is a fable, it permits an evasiveness that is not present in the later novels. Moreover, to call it a fable is to pick on certain features and ignore others, and much of the description and narration is weak and tedious. It is much easier to see the structure and statement of *Pickwick Papers* at a considerable distance from the full text itself, and if we are to understand and judge its individual qualities as a work of art, and if we are to see its place in Dickens' work, we should keep close to its detail and try to say something about its variety. We must not lay stress on its resemblance to *Don Quixote,*[4] or its mythical rendering of the Fall,[5] or its revelations of the transcendent possibilities of human goodness,[6] without acknowledging the existence of materials that do not fit into mythical patterns.

Much of the power of *Pickwick Papers* resides in parts rather than in the whole, and in parts not very strongly attached to each other in feeling or moral argument. Criticism and irony are present in its comedy, but by no means in all the comic scenes or in all the comic characters. Dickens is often conventional in his comedy of humors and in farce, though he is strong in comic and macabre wit, joke, and anecdote. Where the comedy is neither satiric nor dark, it is frequently arch, jolly, or sentimental, as in the cozily convivial Dingley Dell scenes or the farcical episodes of Pickwick on the ice or in the wrong double-bedded room, where the illustrator's vivid compression shows up the flatness and feebleness of the prose narrative, or the scenes displaying the humors of Tupman and Snodgrass, where neither character nor action has the satiric bite or comic power of the theatrical source in Ben Jonson.

Even if we grant Dickens the excuse of an awkwardly imposed and improvised form, in which he gradually discovered a theme and a continuity,

[3]Phillip Collins, ed., *Dickens: Interviews and Recollections,* 2 vols. (London, 1981), vol. I, p. 163.

[4]Ernest Simmons, *Dostoevsky: The Making of a Novelist* (London, 1940), p. 210.
[5]W. H. Auden, *The Dyer's Hand and Other Essays* (London, 1963), "Dingley Dell and The Fleet," pp. 407–428.
[6]S. Marcus, *Dickens from Pickwick to Dombey* (London, 1965), "The Blest Dawn," pp. 13–53, particularly pp. 18 and 51–53.

Pickwick Papers is an erratic novel. The "amusing and pleasant" adventures are sealed off, for most of the action, from the episodes showing want and misery. The grotesque and zany comedy of the Wellers, the Fat Boy, the medical students, Jingle, and the lawyers allow Dickens' imagination of misery to appear, but in a fragmented and flippant form. The fragmentation has its significance, showing Dickens' divided vision of a society he deplored and individual possibilities he celebrated. Dingley Dell's final celebratory reconciliations, moreover, are triumphs of middle-class morality: Sam refuses to marry until it is convenient for his master, and Tony Weller tries to make over his money to Pickwick. The adventures of the Pickwick Club are neither Odyssean nor Quixotic. Dickens aspires toward social criticism, but seems to edit rather than assimilate the intransigent materials of social reality.

In writing *Oliver Twist* Dickens was influenced by "Newgate" novels dealing with criminals, such as Bulwer Lytton's *Eugene Aram* (1832) and Ainsworth's *Rookwood* (1834), but despite Dickens' own tendency toward melodrama, *Oliver Twist* breaks new ground in moral purpose and realism.

In *Oliver Twist* the incorruptible innocence is that of youth, not age. Dickens takes up that subject of character conditioned by environment imaged in "The Pawnbroker's Shop" and absent in *Pickwick*. Oliver is one of several angelic children—Nell, Barnaby, Paul, and Florence—who embody virtue. Their radiance and purity are heightened and threatened by the darkness and deformity that surround them. Dickens tells us that he wanted Oliver to represent the strength of virtue in the fallen world: he is neglected, imprisoned, and isolated. He wanders in an unknown country and an unknown city, picking up dangerous helpers and teachers. He is involved in cruelty, misery, and nightmare, and his child's point of view, both realistically and symbolically innocent, brings us close to the sensations of helplessness and panic. It is easy to speak of Dickens' virtuous characters as emblematic—which they are—but it is essential to notice his affective powers, which are highly developed in *Oliver Twist*. Its control and unity of theme and feeling distinguish it sharply from *Sketches*, which for all its excellence was a collection of magazine and newspaper pieces,[7]

blended by an original talent, and from *Pickwick Papers*, where power is generated slowly and remains fitful. I do not agree with those critics who locate the beginnings of a unified theme in *Martin Chuzzlewit*, which deals centrally with selfishness, or *Dombey and Son*, which deals with pride. It is true that Dickens spoke explicitly about giving these novels a ruling subject, and that in them he marshals scene, image, and character into illustrative action. But as D. H. Lawrence reminds readers who are inclined to trust overmuch in the artist, the proof lies in the tale, and *Oliver Twist* is as wholly bent on pursuing a subject as are the later novels, though more mutedly. That subject is the relationship of the individual to his environment, and it is one that Dickens considered, explicitly and implicitly, in all his subsequent novels. The focus on moral abstractions like selfishness and pride has overimpressed critics, from John Forster onward.

In the first chapter of *Oliver Twist* Dickens cunningly and movingly modulates from comedy to pathos and from pathos to satire. He takes us from the drunken old woman to the dying mother, exclaiming, "Let me see the child, and die," and the brusque, habituated, but not totally calloused doctor. Dickens is learning to break down the barriers between pathos and comedy, and in doing so achieves not only structural continuity but also a control of pathos. Such rapid switches help in all the later novels to hold together disparate effects, to provide variety and unity, and to give that double opportunity for comedy and pathos that Dickens admired in stage melodrama. I don't want to make the act of combination sound mechanically adroit, because at its best it brings about imaginative cohesion. There are more powerful instances, as in the horrifying juxtapositions of Chadband's gross appetite and grosser language with the delicacy of Jo, Dickens' text, object, and victim, in *Bleak House*; or of the neighborhood of Mrs. Sparsit to Louisa Bounderby's moral crisis in the storm, in *Hard Times*; or of the interwoven dark and light threads of feeling in Merdle's suicide, in *Little Dorrit*. But it is in *Oliver Twist* that we first feel that proximity of laughter and pity, or amusement and horror, so congenial to Dickens. There is more here than the thrilling emotional collocation or the earthing of satire and pathos. Dickens, like all great artists, analyzes as he creates, discovers as he entertains.

In the harsh humor of the opening workhouse scene of *Oliver Twist* Dickens has left far behind the Fat Boy's simple rhetorical intent in *Pickwick Papers*

---

[7]Beginning with "A Dinner at Poplar Walk," in *Monthly* magazine, n.s. 16 (December 1833), pp. 117–624, and ending with "Vauxhall Gardens by Day" (*Sketches by "Boz"*), *Morning Chronicle* 26, n.s. no. 4 (October 1836).

to "make our flesh creep." His imagination puts together facets of a particular place at a particular time, a bad place at a bad time, an English workhouse just after the Poor Law Act of 1834. Through the brilliant sleights-of-hand of his metonymies, the edifice is built and peopled. There are the representatives of officialdom, molded by their roles, face to face with the representatives of the poor, molded by their conditions. Dickens' method is to make character illustrative while preserving it from abstraction. The characters in *Oliver Twist*, like the women in "The Pawnbroker's Shop," exhibit the hardening and perverting social process, a draining away of humanity. In the first chapter, mother and child are presented in the timeless anonymity of birth and death, through a single imperative, "Let me see the child, and die." The sentence is not banal speech. It sums up the mother's instinctive desire to see the newborn baby, and takes a short stride from birth to death: the two experiences encompassed in one sentence give this character a little life, but enough. The old pauper is presented with the same economy. She gives her grim advice, "Think what it is to be a mother, there's a dear young lamb, do"—exactly what Oliver's mother is doing—and reminisces in beery vein on her experiences of birth, death, and workhouse misery. And the doctor, drawing the official line at not "being bothered" if the baby gives trouble, as he knows it's likely to do, is sufficiently deflected from his professional humor by a glint of particular response after he puts on "his gloves with great deliberation": "She was a good-looking girl, too; where did she come from?" The time and the place bring these people together; with apparently effortless art Dickens observes how time and place have made and unmade them.

Dickens' subject is conditioned human nature. At the center of the moral action is the virtuous and innocent child, created in a successful blend of myth and particularity. The innocence of the child comes to the Victorian and modern reader out of Christian tradition and social fact, with the simple vividness of a famine poster. Its fabulous simplicity is supported by psychological vividness. One of Dickens' few strengths as a psychological novelist is his rendering of childhood sensibility. The idealized nature of Oliver is conveyed or licensed—neither metaphor is quite right—in a medium of feeling. Oliver feels timidity, starving bravado, isolation, horror, fear, relief, shame, nightmare, and loving reciprocity. These passions are animated in a continuum, to

which the reader's response is fluent and varied. It is sometimes suggested—by Henry James, for instance—that Oliver's sustained gentlemanliness is unconvincing, and Dickens was himself uneasily aware that this might be so. But, as so often, he is straddling fable and realism. It was not his purpose to create a totally accurate portrait of a foundling, but to combine such a portrait with an image of original virtue.

Dickens shows Oliver's resistance and courage as the product of heredity, just as Shakespeare makes Perdita's royal nature transcend her rustic nurture, but there is more to Oliver's moral style than a romantic theory of heredity. Dickens' exploration of the conditioned character relies on the presence of a controlling fable or fantasy about the unconditioned and unconditional. From *Pickwick* onward there is a double vision: a vision of the power and terror of the real world and a vision of the power and glory of human love. The first vision is shown realistically, the second idealistically. After *Pickwick*, the ideal virtue is not presented so emblematically as to be set apart from the social environment in which it is placed. Oliver escapes the environment's dangers, as only angelic children may escape, but we feel the existence of a real threat. *Oliver Twist* is not only concerned with its hero, but with the perverted population that surrounds him. The members of the thieves' gang have different fates, marked on a descending scale. The brilliant child's play of Fagin's schooling is a paradigm of environment and conditioning. Rose Maylie and her protected middle-class world offer an escape to Nancy, much in the style of a paternalist employer or a welfare organization, but Nancy truthfully says that she was brought up in the streets and cannot get out of them. The tension between her environment and her struggling virtue kills her; the murder is no simple climax in a crime story or a moral tale, but tells a truth about a death struggle between nature and nurture, self and society.

The plot to corrupt Oliver is sometimes condemned for weakness and implausibility. It is true that explanation and exposition are huddled up at the end of the novel, but this novel is a social parable, and Monks's plot to corrupt his half brother is part of a total pattern that includes the workhouse, the baby farm, the thieves' den, the Brownlow home, and the criminality of Sikes. Dickens comes close to endangering Oliver's idealized virtue in the great temptation scene in chapter 18. The child is being carefully brainwashed, first cunningly cold-shouldered and isolated, then cunningly brought into the deadly warmth of the thieves' family circle. Here he shows all the susceptibility of the return from exile as clearly as, say, Rubashov, the hero of Arthur Koestler's *Darkness at Noon*. It is no good remembering the diabolical suggestiveness of Fagin's fork if we forget the familiar sausage on its prong. Dickens symbolizes his moral action, but also domesticates it:

Oliver was but too glad to make himself useful; too happy to have some faces, however bad, to look upon; too desirous to conciliate those about him when he could honestly do so; to throw any objection in the way of this proposal. So he at once expressed his readiness; and, kneeling on the floor, while the Dodger sat upon the table so that he could take his foot in his lap, he applied himself to a process which Mr. Dawkins designated as "japanning his trotter-cases."

(ch. 18)

Oliver's invulnerability remains, but Dickens brings it into intimate connection with the brute force and insidious persuasiveness of a society that makes criminals. His is not an isolated fable. At the other extreme of the moral action is Sikes, who also shows Dickens' interest in corruptibility, as well as his insight into moral extremity. The extreme of vice is shown as a derivation of complex human nature. Dickens describes Sikes as an utterly hardened character: "Whether every gentler human feeling is dead within such bosoms, or the proper chord to strike has rusted and is hard to find, I do not know."[8] And the extreme violence and resolution in outward action is fully expressive of the extremity of character.

If Dickens sees Sikes as dead or rusted in gentler human feelings, he most certainly does not show him only as the violently outraged and jealous murderer played on by events and by Fagin. The flight of Sikes is a behavioristic display of strong but mixed and unclassified passions. The author contrives expressive actions that symbolize, precipitate, and blend the passions. The result is twofold: not only is tension sustained and renewed after the murder, but the interest is given a human focus, and the character of Sikes expands in a form of psychological melodrama where the stage is both interior and exterior. The events themselves are exciting: the pursuit, the flight, the fire, the trap, the death. The inner register is also exciting and especially so for not being simple

[8]From "The Author's Preface to the Third Edition" (1841).

or predictable. Dickens is not showing us a brute nor indeed is he evoking easy compassion for a hunted man, but he is keeping Sikes (and us) in touch with certain common features of human feeling: loneliness, alienation, need for human contact and activity, repression, energy, and fear. Being Dickens, he uses a whole range of effects, from the ironic grim comedy of the cheapjack who finds the bloodstain on Sikes's hat to the symbolic fire fighting at the end. In the fire we have the most successful external showing of something too subtle and complex to be analyzed or given a single name. Sikes seizes on the fire as an opportunity to use his energy and join it with that of other people. His is a pleasure, familiar in guilty or alienated states, in which participation in something detached from personal problems gives relief. Dickens also emphasizes the release of sheer physical energy, which keeps us in touch with the man's brutality and loss of gentle human feeling. In Coleridgean terms we are kept on the "highroad" of human passions and induced to feel a kind of sympathy, empathy rather than pity. The violent action is given an inner life of nerves and feelings.

For now, a vision came before him, as constant and more terrible than that from which he had escaped. Those widely staring eyes, so lustreless and so glassy, that he had better borne to see them than think upon them, appeared in the midst of the darkness; light in themselves, but giving light to nothing. There were but two, but they were everywhere. If he shut out the sight, there came the room with every well-known object—some, indeed, that he would have forgotten, if he had gone over its contents from memory—each in its accustomed place. The body was in *its* place, and its eyes were as he saw them when he stole away. He got up, and rushed into the field without. The figure was behind him. He re-entered the shed, and shrunk down once more. The eyes were there, before he had laid himself along.

(ch. 48)

So far this is brilliant criminal psychology: the involuntary imagery of strong passion realizes and substantiates the macabre presentation of the body with the carefully placed "its" and the telling selection of the eyes. This kind of inner drama is found over and over again in Dickens: it is there at the end of this novel in Fagin's analyzed perceptions in the court (also playing a variant on the image of eyes), in the analysis of Jonas Chuzzlewit's guilty terrors, in Scrooge's nightmare of death, and in many other instances. Robert Garis, one of the few critics to pay any attention to the feelings in fiction, suggests that Dickens is especially good at showing the passion of anger. To this we must add guilt and fear, or better, guilty fear. Dickens blends the extraordinary and the ordinary in his rendering of extreme states of sensation and passion. After the paragraph just quoted comes this:

And here he remained, in such terror as none but he can know, trembling in every limb, and the cold sweat starting from every pore, when suddenly there arose upon the night-wind the noise of distant shouting, and the roar of voices mingled in alarm and wonder. Any sound of men in that lonely place, even though it conveyed a real cause of alarm, was something to him. He regained his strength and energy at the prospect of personal danger; and, springing to his feet, rushed into the open air.

The broad sky seemed on fire. Rising into the air with showers of sparks, and rolling one above the other, were sheets of flame, lighting the atmosphere for miles round, and driving clouds of smoke in the direction where he stood. The shouts grew louder as new voices swelled the roar, and he could hear the cry of Fire! mingled with the ringing of an alarm-bell, the fall of heavy bodies, and the crackling of flames as they twined round some new obstacle, and shot aloft as though refreshed by food. The noise increased as he looked. There were people there—men and women—light, bustle. It was like new life to him. He darted onward—straight, headlong—dashing through brake and briar, and leaping gate and fence as madly as the dog, who careered with loud and sounding bark before him.

He came upon the spot. There were half-dressed figures tearing to and fro, some endeavouring to drag the frightened horses from the stables, others driving the cattle from the yard and out-houses, and others coming laden from the burning pile, amidst a shower of falling sparks, and the tumbling down of red-hot beams. The apertures, where doors and windows stood an hour ago, disclosed a mass of raging fire; walls rocked and crumbled into the burning well; the molten lead and iron poured down, white-hot, upon the ground. Women and children shrieked, and men encouraged each other with noisy shouts and cheers. The clanking of the engine-pumps, and the spirting and hissing of the water as it fell upon the blazing wood, added to the tremendous roar. He shouted, too, till he was hoarse; and, flying from memory and himself, plunged into the thickest of the throng.

Hither and thither he dived that night: now working at the pumps, and now hurrying through the smoke and flame, but never ceasing to engage himself wherever noise and men were thickest. Up and down the ladders, upon the roofs of buildings, over floors that quaked and trembled with his weight, under the lee of falling bricks and stones, in every part of that great fire was he; but he bore a charmed life, and had neither scratch nor bruise, nor weariness nor thought, till morning dawned again, and only smoke and blackened ruins remained.

(ch. 48)

Dickens tells us that Sikes is energized at the thought of personal danger, that it is like new life, that he is escaping from memory and himself, but he also leaves much to the action's eloquence. It tells us that Sikes could only escape from one torment into another, that he needed men and women, that a delirium of action worked, but did not last. It is a perfect instance of Dickens contriving an event that despite melodramatic violence and improbability makes itself accepted because it is such a good carrier of passion. That makes it sound too static: it is, rather, a generator of passion. We see an aspect of guilt and fear; we also see the needs, sensations, and perceptions that join Sikes with common humanity. I need not labor the additional work that Dickens gets out of his action: the fire fighting gives symbolic expression to violence, destructiveness, desperation, and ruin; Sikes needs the fire, he is also like the fire—burning, raging, rocking, and breaking.

Oliver Twist does not lack flaws; Dickens is always weak in his handling of the tender passions, and the portrayals of charity and love here are feebly articulated in comparison with the handling of fear and terror. The pastoral scenes are banal. The excursus on the illness of Rose Maylie is an all-too-vivid example of the flexibility of large, loose, baggy Victorian novels, which allowed Dickens a space to indulge a private grief for his sister-in-law's death. But it achieves affective subtlety and grasps a central subject.

In *Nicholas Nickleby* (1838–1839) there is a similar weakness and a similar strength, but Dickens is beginning to develop and expand his versatility in creating character. To isolate particular themes is misleading: the novel makes a devastatingly harsh and grotesque indictment of education, but this occupies a relatively small part of the action; it is concerned in many ways with theatricality and role playing, but to relate this theme to all characters and all events is to lose depth in surface. At the center of the novel, in both typicality and emotional complexity, stands Ralph Nickleby. Like Sikes, he is an example of Dickens' imaginative capacity for creating human monsters and monstrous humans. Ralph can be seen in some lights as fabulous, in others as realistic: he is both. Dickens, like Jane Austen, creates caricatures not simply, as terms of art, but complexly, as aspects of life. Dickens postulates a human nature that is warped, hardened, drained, chilled. The simplifications of character are not properly described in terms of literary choice or literary convention, though we have to acknowledge the Victorian concern with comic and eccentric character, and Dickens' own heady oscillations from laughter to violence. The simplifications of character are present in Dickens, however, as T. A. Jackson observed long ago, because he was reflecting the reifications of society. Like all great novelists of the nineteenth century, Dickens meditates consciously and unconsciously on the key question that Henry James put in the words of Madame Merle in *The Portrait of a Lady* (1881): "What shall we call our 'self'? Where does it begin? Where does it end? It overflows into everything that belongs to us—and then it flows back again" (ch. 19).

Ralph Nickleby's complexity is an example of Dickens' imaginative handling of character and his awareness of nature and social shaping. We may at first sight take Ralph's detestation of Nicholas for an instinctive loathing of goodness by evil, but the novel eventually lets us know that there is a much more plausible and simple human cause in Ralph's reawakened sexual jealousy. Part of the complexity of this characterization—standing out, as it does, in an action that has few complex characters—lies in the way in which Dickens slowly unfolds causality and, with it, nature. He begins with a brief and unrevealing summary of the Nickleby family history, disclosing little about the elder brother, but Ralph is slowly revealed as a monster who has been made monstrous by a social structure built on the values of avarice and greed. Throughout the novel Dickens lets slivers of light fall on Ralph: we are told at first that his heart has rusted and is "only a piece of cunning mechanism, and yielding not one throb of hope, or fear, or love, or care, for any living thing," but it turns out to be capable, after all, of one or two throbs.

Chapter 19 ends with a small incident, reminiscent of the pawned forget-me-not ring and *The Awakening Conscience*. Kate has just got into the coach after the dinner party at Ralph Nickleby's, and as the door closes, a comb falls out of her hair. Ralph picks it up and sees her face picked out in the lamplight, especially a "lock of hair that had escaped and curled loosely over her brow." Ralph is moved by "some

dormant train of recollection," reminded of his dead brother's face "with the very look it bore on some occasion of boyish grief." Dickens then rises into the crescendo and climax: "Ralph Nickleby, who was proof against all appeals of blood and kindred—who was steeled against every tale of sorrow and distress—staggered while he looked and went back into his house, as a man who had seen a spirit from some world beyond the grave." But as it happens, Dickens has already shown Ralph as a little moved, and the earlier instance is one of those tiny realistic touches that are worth ten of the more melodramatic scenes from the inner life. Slightly earlier, at the end of Ralph's dinner party, Kate is weeping, and Dickens makes the point that Ralph is vulnerable—not very, but slightly—because his ruling passion is for the moment not involved:

> Ralph would have walked into any poverty-stricken debtor's house, and pointed him out to a bailiff, though in attendance upon a young child's death-bed, without the smallest concern, because it would have been a matter quite in the ordinary course of business, and the man would have been an offender against his only code of morality. But, here was a young girl, who had done no wrong save that of coming into the world alive; who had patiently yielded to all his wishes; who had tried hard to please him—above all, who didn't owe him money—and he felt awkward and nervous.
>
> (ch. 19)

It is moments like these that create a sense of emotional wholeness and sequence in the flat characters. They also show the human surplus, the vital remnants of nature not wholly perverted. Notice how completely unsentimental this last observation is; it even allows us a flash of contempt for Ralph, the denatured man being invoked in order to explain the surplus touch of nature. It contrasts strongly with the incident of the lock of hair in the lamplight, which belongs less to the truthful observations of psychology than to the crude melodrama of the inner life.

Nicholas Nickleby is a larger and looser novel than *Oliver Twist*, and although the concern with the making of men by society is a dominant theme, there are many facets of the action that sparkle with an independent glitter. The long and episodic novel has more scope for weakness than *Oliver Twist*, but its dangerous areas are the same. The presentation of the romantic heroine, Kate Nickleby, is often fortunately obscured by the comedy or violence of context. The febrile comic play of the Mantalinis or the sinister predatoriness of the high-life seducers compensate for what is at best a shadowy stereotype of womanly beauty and virtue. The same excess and sentimentality pump up the benevolent figures of the Cheeryble brothers: Dickens' defense of their realism by reference to their reality is singularly beside the point. Nicholas himself, like David Copperfield, is in the direct line of descent from the heroes of the eighteenth-century adventure novels of Fielding and Smollett, which Dickens had read and admired. Dickens has David imagine himself as "a child's Tom Jones," and some of Dickens' other heroes can be similarly described. Pickwick and Oliver have mythic pretensions, Nicholas has none. He is the most neutral of a line that includes David Copperfield and Pip, who become more complicated in moral and psychological life. Nicholas is a Victorian version of the eighteenth-century rogue hero, with most of the rogue removed. His personal adventures are circumscribed, but Dickens exploits his neutrality. Nicholas' blandness as a character almost passes without notice because he is so often the observer or the object of stronger emotional action. He provides a context, for example, for the strong theatrical comedy of the Crummles family and troupe.

Dickens dedicated the novel to the great tragic actor W. C. Macready, and the assimilation of drama to narrative that began in *Sketches by Boz* becomes fully developed in a novelistic action of farce and melodrama and an exuberant criticism of theatricality in character. Nicholas provides a foil and an object for Ralph Nickleby's sharply observed moral jealousy: the emotional variety of one character throws into relief the nullity of the other, but also compensates for it. Nicholas is also a neutral point of view for presenting the most famous topical satire in the novel, the attack on the brutal Yorkshire schools that was one of the first examples of Dickens' socially effective propaganda. Comedy is often blended with pathos and grotesque horror in the characters of the Squeers family, and in some of the educational dialogue, but the Squeers' schoolroom is like an inferno, often unrelieved by humor and particularized by hideous physical detail, like Bolder's wart-covered hands and the boys' "foul appearance of dirt, disorder, and disease." Dickens actually uses the words "incipient Hell" after descriptions that show that his sense of horror works not only rhetorically but critically:

Pale and haggard faces, lank and bony figures, children with the countenances of old men, deformities with irons upon their limbs, boys of stunted growth, and others whose long meagre legs would hardly bear their stooping bodies, all crowded on the view together; there were the bleared eye, the hare-lip, the crooked foot, and every ugliness or distortion that told of unnatural aversion conceived by parents for their offspring, or of young lives which, from the earliest dawn of infancy, had been one horrible endurance of cruelty and neglect. There were little faces which should have been handsome, darkened with the scowl of sullen dogged suffering; there was childhood with the light of its eye quenched.

(ch. 8)

One of the isolated glories of *Nicholas Nickleby* reminds us of the richness of local story telling in *Pickwick Papers*. It is hard to relate Mrs. Nickleby's comic story telling to the novel's social concern, and imprecise to take it as evidence of the theatrical theme, since she has so much in common with other Dickensian narrators, like the Bagman and Mrs. Gamp. She is sufficiently stereotyped to arouse expectation, sufficiently inventive and versatile to cause surprise. Dickens, like George Eliot, if more roughly, divides characters into egoists and altruists, and Mrs. Nickleby is one of his great egocentric tellers. She constitutes a perpetual challenge to the notion of organic unity that still haunts Dickens criticism, and resembles Dickens' great villains, Fagin, Quilp, the Brasses, or Uriah Heep, in her rapturous vitality. But the vitality is not naive: Dickens is like all great storytellers in his interest in the act and art of story telling. Mrs. Nickleby's total unawareness of communication is expressive of her self-aggrandizing intent and her sheer dottiness, itself a mark of mindlessness in a novel that takes some interest in differentiating between minds. She is comically guilty of all the narrative sins, as she rambles, forgets, stumbles, misses the point, and loses a sense of her listeners, but nourishes our delight in the zany and the absurd. Her narrative is creative, disordered, but crammed with gorgeous particulars:

"I really am very subject to colds, indeed—very subject. I had a cold once," said Mrs. Nickleby, "I think it was in the year eighteen hundred and seventeen; let me see, four and five are nine, and—yes, eighteen hundred and seventeen, that I thought I should never get rid of. I was only cured at last by a remedy that I don't know whether you happened to hear of, Mr. Pluck. You have a gallon of water as hot as you can possibly bear it, with a pound of salt and six pen'orth of the finest bran, and sit with your head in it for twenty minutes every night just before going to bed; at least, I don't mean your head—your feet.

(ch. 27)

Although these anecdotes show Dickens' freedom of comic effect, they are tethered within a local context. This story, for instance, is ironically placed in a scene where the listeners are Sir Mulberry Hawk's aides, Pyke and Pluck, just as the story in the previous chapter, about the hackney coach, was told to Sir Mulberry and Lord Verisopht. Mrs. Nickleby is allowed to take off on her fine flights for our pleasure, but her narrative is brought into connection with plot. Her solipsism has dramatic consequences. Dickens is reworking the comic anecdote but with a new control.

In 1840 Dickens began to bring out *Master Humphrey's Clock*, a weekly miscellany of fictitious papers given a tenuous unity by the device of the old clock, at once a repository and a reminder of time. The scheme was abandoned, but out of it grew *The Old Curiosity Shop*, one of his most popular and uneven novels. As in *Pickwick Papers*, the unevenness is largely one of language: the grotesque and comic parts have individuality, the solemn and serious parts none. What Gerard Manley Hopkins calls "the rehearsal" of "self" is restricted to certain affective areas, and the restriction is especially marked in a novel where the tender emotions are so central to plot and action. Nell's adventures and feelings are very much more prolonged and active than those of Oliver, as she is dramatized in a long ordeal of living and dying. She is nearer adulthood than Oliver and is given a whole range of moral and psychological experience that raises expectations Dickens cannot satisfy. It is hard, if not impossible, to separate conception and language: there is a correlation of weak language with certain emotional and moral areas. In the famous deathbed scene, there is stock response, strong demand for pity, no particularity, and every stop pulled out—child, nature, hearth, beauty:

She was dead. Dear, gentle, patient, noble Nell was dead. Her little bird—a poor slight thing the pressure of a finger would have crushed—was stirring nimbly in its cage; and the strong heart of its child-mistress was mute and motionless for ever.

Where were the traces of her early cares, her sufferings, and fatigues? All gone. Sorrow was dead indeed in her, but peace and perfect happiness were born; imaged in her tranquil beauty and profound repose.

And still her former self lay there, unaltered in this change. Yes. The old fireside had smiled upon that same sweet face; it had passed like a dream through haunts of misery and care.

(ch. 71)

Since Dickens depends so much on the solemn and intense appeal to ideals of virtue, such banality of feeling is a gross defect. It is true that some aspects of religious, aesthetic, and domestic values are dated and counterproductive, but this is not the central issue. When Oscar Wilde said it took a heart of stone not to laugh at Little Nell, he was responding to Dickens' banal language and sentimental indulgence, two sides of the same coin of cant appeal. It does not do to defend such simplifications on the grounds that the characters have a mythical or fairy-tale appeal. In the real fairy tale or folk tale, there is simplicity, bareness, matter-of-factness, particularity, and reticence. The heroes and heroines of folk tale are unaccompanied by wholesale emotional and moral solicitation: the reader is not held to ransom for sympathy. Dickens is to move toward particularities of fact and feeling in *Dombey and Son* and *Bleak House*, but he has not yet arrived at them in *The Old Curiosity Shop*.

At the beginning the narrator notices the power of visual objects to impress the mind:

I am not sure I should have been so thoroughly possessed by this one subject, but for the heaps of fantastic things I had seen huddled together in the curiosity-dealer's warehouse. These, crowding on my mind, in connection with the child, and gathering round her, as it were, brought her condition palpably before me.

(ch. 1)

This rare technical and psychological comment reminds us of particularity. Where the novel fails, there is generalization, abstraction, banality, and nothing palpable. Where it succeeds, in the vigorous comic horrors of Quilp and the Brasses, Mrs. Jarvey's waxworks, the desolate and hideous industrial imagery, the compassionate comedy of the marchioness, Dickens is giving us the particulars of sense and emotion, not making large, flamboyant gestures and stock appeal. As Aldous Huxley says in his essay "Vulgarity in Literature" (1930), "Nell's virtues are marooned, as it were, in the midst of a boundless waste of unreality; isolated, they fade and die. Even her sufferings and death lack significance because of this isolation."

Out of *Master Humphrey's Clock* also came *Barnaby Rudge*, Dickens' first historical novel, ambitious in its research and its topicality, as he recreated the revolutionary and religious struggles of the Gordon Riots (1780) at the time of the industrial and religious unrest and Chartist and Protestant associations of the late 1830's and early 1840's. Plot mysteries are central but too obscurely dramatized to provide puzzle or tension. There is very little comedy, though Dickens gives a central place to a virulent attack on women, which dramatizes two extremes of women's "absurdity": the comely and rebellious shrew Mrs. Varden, rebuked and converted into a good wife, and the hysterical, man-eating, ugly spinster, her maid Miggs. Some pressure of personal feeling seems present in this aggressive satire, which is compounded by the approval lavished on the stock heroine in the high-life love story and on the arch Dolly Varden with her homely John in the low-life romance. Most powerful are the portraits of villainy. Dennis the hangman is animated by a colloquial style and black humor:

"I've heerd a eloquence on them boards—you know what boards I mean—and have heerd a degree of mouth given to them speeches, that they was as clear as a bell, and as good as a play. There's a pattern! And always, when a thing of this natur's to come off, what I stand up for, is, a proper frame of mind. Let's have a proper frame of mind, and we can go through with it, creditable—pleasant—sociable. Whatever you do (and I address myself, in particular, to you in the furthest), never snivel."

(ch. 65)

In striking contrast is the polished hypocrite, Sir John Chester, and here too the energetic particularity of character derives directly from language. Chester anticipates the devastating but amusing effrontery and hypocrisy of Skimpole in *Bleak House* and, like Dennis, is a character who is not treated humorously but created as a humorist. His son, Edward, is unparticularized in every way and speaks a banal language that registers neither feeling nor character: "I will endeavour earnestly and patiently, if ever man did, to open some prospect for myself, and free you from the burden you fear I should become if I married one whose worth and beauty are her chief endowments." His father is thoroughly imagined, particularized by gesture and accessory, as he moves in his seat, lays down the paper, and pares his nails with an elegant little knife, and by superciliousness of style and aggressions of irony and wit: "You have to thank me, Ned, for being of good family; for your mother, charming person as she was, and almost broken-hearted, and so forth, as she left me, when she was prematurely compelled to become immortal—had nothing to boast of in that respect" (ch. 15).

Where Dickens has a sense of character, he has a sense of style. As is commonly observed, the pattern of character and theme is unified. Barnaby's weak brain parallels that of Lord George Gordon, and the Willett father and son parallel the Chesters. The characters take their part, personally and illustratively, in the central action of the riots, which are shown with a considerable mastery of description and detail. This formal responsiveness, however, seems less important than the political interest it conveys. Dickens' sense of compassion is present, but shadowed by a fear of social disturbance. That disturbance is dramatized in highly effective crowd scenes and satirized incisively through caricature. The ineffective lord mayor of London and the civic chaos are done with painfully accurate comedy, and the survey of political motive and character—loyal, disloyal, cynical, idealistic, naive, brutal, manipulative—is brilliantly imaged, for instance, in Gashford, the treacherous secretary, the well-meaning Lord George Gordon, and the parodying figure of Barnaby. In Barnaby Rudge himself, the image of the virtuous child has been transformed into that of the susceptible and pathetic fool. Sentimental by Shakespearean standards, like his predecessor Smike in *Nicholas Nickleby*, Barnaby gives Dickens a double opportunity. In this poor fool, Dickens caricatures and indicts what he saw as the exciting mindlessness of revolution, and Barnaby's central position as eponymous hero draws attention to his rhetorical function. He also gives Dickens congenial psychological material for fantasy and wildness, important in a novel that almost entirely lacks any rendering of interior life. Barnaby's dreams and madness give a release and relief that are welcome in this novel where there is no free comedy.

The financial success of *American Notes* persuaded Dickens to send Martin Chuzzlewit to America. He was obviously intent on extending and intensifying his satire, which was based on social observation but stimulated by the abuse he had suffered in the American press. The results were immediate: an increase in the English sales of some 3,000, and more American abuse for the aggressive caricature and criticism. America provided him with a national emblem of self-aggrandizement.

Martin Chuzzlewit presents a coherently worked-out theme, the theme of self. The impersonations of the elder Chuzzlewit, the exiles of Martin, Mark Tapley, Tom Pinch, the attempted murder of Anthony Chuzzlewit, and the murder of Tigg Montague, the speculator and blackmailer, are all caused by selfishness or unselfishness. Selfishness is given its form of Nemesis, including Pecksniff's deceit and hubris, the punishment of Mercy in her marriage to Jonas, the ordeal of Martin in Eden, and the stern advice given to Mrs. Gamp. On the credit side there are the rewards of Tom, Ruth, John Westlock, Mark Tapley, and the young Martin. The theme expresses itself actively—apart from the content of character—in the demonstration of a change of heart and moral causality.

The important part of the action that runs right through the novel is the impersonation of old Chuzzlewit, and its consequences in the duping of Pecksniff and the exile of Martin. It provides some mystery, some irony, and some scenes that enact the humors. There is the hypocritical domestic show put on for Martin's benefit, several scenes of moral antithesis between young Martin and Tom Pinch, the splendid quarrel scene in which the predatory Chuzzlewit hypocrites fall out, the scene where old Chuzzlewit lies to Pecksniff while Pecksniff is lying to him. Such scenes are frequent at the beginning, then thin out and reappear in a conspicuous huddle toward the end when we have the revelation of Martin's trick, the exposure of Pecksniff, and the general apportionment of rewards and punishments. This one overarching piece of action does indeed overarch. It is important at the beginning and end but strays more or less out of sight for a large part of the novel, and when it does appear it is markedly unproductive of tension. There are indeed so few rising intonations of curiosity, doubt, and expectation at the beginning of the novel that it is not surprising that it was not a success as a serial; though no doubt all the other reasons that have been suggested for this relative failure—disappointment with *Barnaby Rudge*, reviewers' hostility to *American Notes*, the change to monthly publication, harshness of satire, lack of pathetic children and deaths—may also be important. But the striking difference between this novel and almost all Dickens' others is this absence of initial tension.

Incident and human emotional center are both present, for instance, in the death of Mrs. Dombey, the mystery of Esther's birth, Pip's encounter with Magwitch, the first river scene in *Our Mutual Friend*. Sometimes the incident alone is arresting, as in the workhouse scene in the first chapter of *Oliver Twist*. Sometimes the introductory scene is symbolic, as in *Bleak House* and *Little Dorrit*. But in all these novels we also move swiftly forward to a strong human identification. Leaving aside the tiresome exercise in sarcasm that is the prelude to *Martin Chuzzlewit*, there is no exciting incident in the early chapters. There are few strongly exciting situations anywhere in the novel, apart from Martin's trip to Eden and the criminal career of Jonas Chuzzlewit, and neither of these sources of tension is anticipated by any early trailers.

The human center is missing too: the most interesting and conspicuous character is Pecksniff, one of Dickens' most brilliant and hideous comic stereotypes. Martin is too neutral and uninteresting, and is scarcely ever seen from the inside until his crisis of conversion. The one character whose emotions are dramatized with any strength is Tom Pinch, and he is not only a grossly sentimental figure but is also given practically nothing to do. In these three characters, as they appear, there seems to be no potentiality for tense action or emotional identification; but the big wasted opportunity is in the conflict and impersonation of old Martin. This impersonation is neither prominent nor productive of mystery, plot influence, or dramatic irony. Boffin's assumed humor in *Our Mutual Friend* is motivated, influential, and provides a heightened moral symbol of the prevailing evil in the novel. Martin's impersonation is weakly motivated and has barely more than a concluding pantomimic resolution in action.

If the moral content does not terminate in action, what makes the incident of the early parts of the novel? There are brilliant comic scenes with lively satire, linguistic humor, and farce, but although these scenes usually have thematic relevance, they seldom move beyond a self-contained action that raises no questions and leaves no disturbing loose ends. There is some attempt at the moral conflict that in other novels produces its tension, in personal relationships that form a moral antithesis (Nicholas and Smike, Dombey and Florence, Hexam and Lizzie), but the moral antithesis in *Martin Chuzzlewit* is thin and formal. There is the moral opposition of old Martin and Pecksniff, and of young Martin with Tom Pinch and Mark Tapley. None of these morally significant pairs is shown in the tension of personal relations: there is no human antagonism, or love, or fear, or any of the conflicting emotions that mark the relations of Oliver and Fagin, or Pip and Magwitch, or Florence and Dombey, where the moral antithesis is complicated and mutated in human relations. The only parts of *Chuzzlewit* that show a personal as well as a moral conflict are either presented offstage in exposition, like the relationship between Martin and his grandfather, or are not explored for moral antithesis. Mary's relation to the sadistic Jonas, with its pleas and cries on behalf of outraged sacred womanhood, or the relation of Mary Graham to Pecksniff in his role of repulsive furtive lecher, are not moving as moral demonstrations.

These two structures of character bring out the mixture of styles and powers in this novel. Mercy is translated from her satiric and comic role into the area of romantic melodrama, where a different treatment is applied in response to a new affective demand. Dickens fails to create any continuity of character, simply grafting a new set of characteristics onto an old one, interestingly shifting the name from Merry to Mercy. In *David Copperfield* and Betsey Trotwood, he succeeds in integrating comic and serious functions, but in *Martin Chuzzlewit* he can only manage one register at a time. When the new Mercy is created, there is another disjunction because Dickens fails to handle the experiences of love and suffering but manages excellently with those of guilt and criminal fear. Mercy fails to create pity, but Jonas creates that blend of horrified expectation and surprise that Dickens so powerfully manipulated as early as *Oliver Twist*. Similarly Mary Graham's appeal as victim is null compared with Pecksniff's as grotesque seducer. There are, and remain, certain emotions that Dickens fails to imagine: the weak language used for Mary and Mercy contrasts with the bizarre and novel language used for Pecksniff and Jonas. Dickens is not alone among great writers in this unevenness of imagination. Ben Jonson's virtuous characters in *Volpone* are feebly articulated compared with those conceived as strong grotesques, and both Thackeray and George Eliot reveal spots of commonness in certain areas of pathos and admiration. The reasons for such inequalities are a matter of speculation: the artistic experience suggests that certain emotions are congenial and others not, but such congeniality is probably in part personal and in part social. Dickens and Thackeray, for instance, are what may be carefully called typically

Victorian in their occasional stereotyping of womanly virtue, but Thackeray is a more radical analyst of the duplicities and mutabilities of what we call love than is Dickens.

Martin Chuzzlewit, then, succeeds in harsh and exuberant satire, in the manipulation of an externally and internally exciting crime story, and in the creation of great comic characters, such as Pecksniff and Mrs. Gamp. Mrs. Gamp is Mrs. Nickleby's successor, a powerful and disturbing teller of tales, providing a series of marvelously comic anecdotes that do much more than entertain, being fully expressive of character and playing a surprising part in the plot. Both Mrs. Gamp and Mrs. Harris play a cunningly devised part in the revelation scene and its listener's response, but Mrs. Gamp's last story forms a fine example of Dickens' not altogether successful attempt to integrate effects:

"Which, Mr. Chuzzlewit," she said, "is well beknown to Mrs. Harris as has one sweet infant (though she *do* not wish it known) in her own family by her mother's side, kep in spirits in a bottle; and that sweet babe she see at Greenwich Fair, a-travelling in company with the pink-eyed lady, Prooshan dwarf, and livin' skelinton, which judge her feelins when the barrel organ played, and she was showed her own dear sister's child, the same not being expected from the outside picter, where it was painted quite contrairy in a livin' state, a many sizes larger, and performing beautiful upon the Arp, which never did that dear child know or do: since breathe it never did, to speak on, in this wale! And Mrs. Harris, Mr. Chuzzlewit, has knowed me many year, and can give you information that the lady which is widdered can't do better and may do worse, than let me wait upon her, which I hope to do. Permittin' the sweet faces as I see afore me."

(ch. 52)

There is a falling off, as old Martin addresses his didactic speech to "the astonished Mrs. Gamp," "hinting at the expediency of a little less liquor, and a little more regard for her patients, and perhaps a trifle of additional honesty." Mrs. Gamp is an impermeable and incorrigible character—unlike young Martin and Mark Tapley—and the final exchange shows the insulation of modes and styles and Dickens' awareness of a need to bring them closer together.

In *A Christmas Carol* Scrooge sees his own image in the most literal fashion, moving back in time and confronting himself at different stages in his process of deterioration. There is his old self, the child, loving and innocent opposite of the unloving old sophist. There is the transitional self, committed to loveless rationalism but still holding some few warm contacts with the past. There is his mirror image, the present self, who echoes his own words and sentiments but in a context newly charged with feeling. The doubles, like the ghosts, are all potent in different ways, and indeed the ghosts are not only aspects of Christmas but also aspects of Scrooge: his past, his present, and his suggestive anonymous future. The return to childhood restores him to the first springs of love in a way reminiscent of Wordsworth and George Eliot; the personal past is a tradition that can keep alive the feeling child, father of the rational man. It also gives a brief glimpse of the deprived and isolated child. Instead of a recognition of causality—though that is obliquely present—we have in Scrooge himself the equally effective stirring of love and pity. He sees his sister, rather as Silas Marner remembers his sister after he first sees Eppie, and the link is made with old affection and old sorrow. He "feels pity for his former self" and the pity brings with it the first movement of imaginative self-criticism. He identifies his old sorrow with sorrow outside himself: "There was a boy singing a Christmas Carol at my door last night. I should like to have given him something: that's all" (stave 2). This is of course the carol that gives the story its name, and also its theme: "God bless you, merry gentlemen, may nothing you dismay." Scrooge threatens the boy with his ruler, rejects the blessing, and Christmas brings him a strong but salutary dismay.

The Ghost of Christmas Past acts as devil's advocate, and his timing is admirable. Scrooge is identifying himself with his former self at Fezziwig's ball: "His heart and soul were in the scene, and with his former self. He corroborated everything, remembered everything, enjoyed everything, and underwent the strangest agitation" (stave 2). The Ghost pours cold water on the apprentices' gratitude: "A small matter . . . to make these silly folks so full of gratitude. . . . He has spent but a few pounds of your mortal money: three or four perhaps." So Scrooge is forced to defend the generous spirit, heated by the remark, and speaking unconsciously like his former, not his latter, self: "The happiness he gives, is quite as great as if it cost a fortune." Then he suddenly remembers his present self and, gently urged by his ghostly analyst, moves toward self-criticism. The process is continued by the Ghost, in stave 3, who

answers Scrooge's question about Tiny Tim: "If he be like to die, he had better do it, and decrease the surplus population." When Scrooge is overcome "with penitence and grief" at his own words, the Ghost comes in quickly with the grave rebuke: "Forbear that wicked cant until you have discovered What the surplus is, and Where it is." The Ghost employs the same mimicry when he shows the terrible children, Want and Ignorance. Scrooge's newborn horror, like his compassion, is answered by his own words: "Are there no prisons? . . . Are there no workhouses?" This technique of exact quotation comes decorously enough in the Christmas present, rubbing Scrooge's nose in his very recent refusal to give to the portly gentleman. The arguments for charity were also presented in personification ("Want is keenly felt, and Abundance rejoices") but they have to be acted out for the unimaginative man, forcing him to walk through the crowds and see them composed not of ciphers but of individuals. All the elements in this brief masque are appropriate. They show to the hardened man the need and love in his own past; they show to the old killjoy his dead capacity for joy. Having indicated causality and change, the show ends with a memento mori, cold, solitary, and repulsive, in the new perspective of feeling. Effective argument is implied in the dramatic reclamation by love and fear, and we are left with the urgent question, Is reclamation still possible? which makes the modulation from nightmare to fantasy. The fantasy has a realistic suggestion of hypnotic therapy.

One might suggest that the poise and control of fable and feeling in *A Christmas Carol* constitute a turning point in Dickens' development. The novels that follow are all great novels, with the exception of *A Tale of Two Cities*. They show a balance of the various Dickensian interests—in social satire, love story, psychological and moral fable, and plot mystery. Linguistic variety and brilliance are more sustained, and Dickens has learned to carry into the serious style the figurative brilliance that was once reserved for his comic effects. The tautness of *A Christmas Carol*, outstanding of all five of the Christmas books written between 1843 and 1848, may well have helped to break down the barriers that previously existed between his different stylistic registers of thinking and feeling. *Dombey and Son* also benefits from Dickens' total social commitment in the Christmas books and returns him wholeheartedly to criticism of the unjust and acquisitive society.

Dombey embodies pride, but it is sharply and diagnostically shown as a capitalistic pride, the paternal pride acting in the interest of transactional possessiveness and expansion. The novel also shows Dickens' most impressive use of his affective medium.

The symbolic use of that great Victorian symbol, the railway, shows Dickens' fusion of social and psychological drama. The railway is connected with the whole industrial scene of the novel, and we see it grow, make changes, employ real people. Dickens makes quite plain the gap between the railway's symbolic rendering of Dombey and its larger life. Dickens picks up, for instance, the violence of its noise, the iron way, and its speed. He also makes it quite plain that Dombey's sensations and feelings are selecting the symbolic points, that the train's journey, landscape, and effects are not wholly or simply as Dombey interprets them: "He found no pleasure or relief in the journey. Tortured by these thoughts he carried monotony with him, through the rushing landscape, and hurried headlong, not through a rich and varied country, but a wilderness of blighted plans and gnawing jealousies" (ch. 20). Dombey chooses the dark, but there exists the light; there is a wilderness without like the wilderness within, but there are also richness and variety. When Dombey moves into the industrial horrors, Dickens makes explicit what was formerly implicit:

There are dark pools of water, muddy lanes, and miserable habitations far below. There are jagged walls and falling houses close at hand, and through the battered roofs and broken windows, wretched rooms are seen, where want and fever hide themselves in many wretched shapes, while smoke and crowded gables, and distorted chimneys, and deformity of brick and water penning up deformity of mind and body, choke the murky distance. As Mr. Dombey looks out of his carriage window, it is never in his thoughts that the monster who has brought him there has let the light of day in on these things: not made or caused them.

(ch. 20)

The railway links Dombey with Carker. Carker is afraid of death, and throughout the description of his flight, Dickens incorporates the unknown object of the fear into the fear itself. Carker feels alienated chiefly because he has been mortified and hit where he felt most confident, in his sexual vanity. He also feels alienated because he is in a foreign country. And Dickens makes his very self-consciousness increase the feeling of dissociation in a perceptive

stroke: "The dread of being hunted in a strange remote place, where the laws might not protect him—the novelty of the feeling that it was strange and remote, originating in his being left alone so suddenly amid the ruins of his plans" (ch. 55). Like Sikes, the character opens out, largely by means of acutely rendered new feeling. The whole episode is also an inner melodrama of violent fear and desperate turmoil of feeling—the violence is right for Carker, as it was for Sikes, and once more keeps sensational action and passion on the highroad of human experience. This symbolism of feeling is more subtle than anything in *Oliver Twist*. Pre-echo replaces explicit anticipation, sensation is excitingly in advance of explication. We do not understand why Carker feels a rush, hears a bell, and is aware of a sweep of "something through the air" until he comes to be killed by the train, and symbol is discovered at the moment of climax. The imagery of the river and the wild waves is assertive in its recurrences, but Dickens is slowly learning the effectiveness of suggestion. As so often, his strengths and weaknesses are close neighbors. The exaggerated unconventional language of the serious loves in *Martin Chuzzlewit* was accompanied by the parody of amorous intensity and hyperbole in the exclamations and personifications in Moddle's style. One of the difficulties of judging Dickens' language of feeling lies in such intimate mingling of success and failure, so conspicuous in *Dombey and Son*.

The account of Paul's death, for instance, concludes with an intense appeal to stock response, through a generalized imagery, a series of exclamations, and the climactic invocation of childhood, the garden of Eden, and immortality. As so often, Dickens accumulates in the hope of intensifying, but diffuses and stereotypes:

The golden ripple on the wall came back again, and nothing else stirred in the room. The old, old fashion! The fashion that came in with our first garments, and will last unchanged until our race has run its course, and the wide firmament is rolled up like a scroll. The old, old fashion—Death!

Oh thank GOD, all who see it, for that older fashion yet, of Immortality! And look upon us, angels of young children, with regards not quite estranged, when the swift river bears us to the ocean!

(ch. 16)

Earlier in this chapter, Dickens is writing with a constant attention to emotional particulars, recording the experience of pain and death from the inside, solidifying and realizing the imagery of the wild waves through the drama of the dying child's imagination:

When the sunbeams struck into his room through the rustling blinds, and quivered on the opposite wall like golden water, he knew that evening was coming on, and that the sky was red and beautiful. As the reflection died away, and a gloom went creeping up the wall, he watched it deepen, deepen, deepen into night. Then he thought how the long streets were dotted with lamps, and how the peaceful stars were shining overhead. His fancy had a strange tendency to wander to the river, which he knew was flowing through the great city; and now he thought how black it was, and how deep it would look, reflecting the hosts of stars—and more than all, how steadily it rolled away to meet the sea.

As it grew later in the night, and footsteps in the street became so rare that he could hear them coming, count them as they passed, and lose them in the hollow distance, he would lie and watch the many-coloured ring about the candle, and wait patiently for day. His only trouble was, the swift and rapid river. He felt forced, sometimes, to try to stop it—to stem it with his childish hands—or choke its way with sand—and when he saw it coming on, resistless, he cried out! But a word from Florence, who was always at his side, restored him to himself; and leaning his poor head upon her breast, he told Floy of his dream, and smiled.

(ch. 16)

Dickens' handling of feeling moves between these opposites, of generalization and particularity. The incisive account in which the river is physically and socially actualized, then vividly used as an emotional symbol of dying, in the notation of panic and passivity, lapses into that concluding flourish at the end of the chapter.

A similarly teasing combination of effects marks the treatment of Edith Dombey, another of the novel's triumphs. Edith is one of Dickens' most subtle portraits of a woman, psychologically and socially imagined with zest, thoroughness, and precision. The novel's indictment of the patriarchal assumptions of Victorian capitalism depends largely on this piece of characterization, since Florence Dombey—the commercially invisible "daughter"—is conceived too simply and prettily in terms of the angelic child, scarcely endorsing, let alone dramatizing, the feminist implications so radically if erratically present in this novel. Dickens' rejection of capitalist inheritance of power represents a brilliant insight into the nature of sexual politics, but it is not sustained in

all the ramifications of character and action. Perhaps nowhere else—with the possible exception of the treatment of Louisa in *Hard Times*—does Dickens make such a rejection of patriarchy as he does through Edith's sense of the market and its values, her doomed and modern attempt to talk to her husband about the survival of relationship, and her highly economical sexual and social revenge on the exploitations of both husband and seducer.

The analysis and criticism, central in the very title of the novel, is supported by scenic particulars, as in the scene in Edith's boudoir (chapter 40), where the deliberate disarray of clothing and ornament image a cosmetic flouting of the conventions she has so lucidly recognized. But her language and behavior are conceived in a way that is often stagey and banal:

It was that of a lady, elegantly dressed and very handsome, whose dark proud eyes were fixed upon the ground, and in whom some passion or struggle was raging. For as she sat looking down, she held a corner of her under lip within her mouth, her bosom heaved, her nostril quivered, her head trembled, indignant tears were on her cheek, and her foot was set upon the moss as though she would have crushed it into nothing.

(ch. 27)

Dickens' strengths and weaknesses are sometimes juxtaposed, sometimes closely interwoven. This unevenness takes a promising form in *Dombey and Son*. In *Pickwick* and even in *Martin Chuzzlewit*, banality or feebleness were separated from originality and power, but in *Dombey and Son* weaknesses and strengths tend to be married. Dickens can use stagey dialogue or description to embody subtle insights into character and society: it is no longer possible to relate weakness of style to weakness of idea. Such mingling of effects may trouble the critic, but it is productive. The deathbed of Jo, in *Bleak House*, in many ways close to the rituals and images of feeling in the deathbed of Paul, shows the effective crossing of particularity with generalization.

Like *Dombey and Son*, *David Copperfield* belongs to the maturity of Dickens' art. There is less explicit social criticism in this novel than in the other writing; his eye was on his own domestic and spiritual adventures, not on social injustice. Being the man he was, seeing his own life necessarily involved some social criticism, but this emerges implicitly and often unconsciously. There are some exceptions. The book contains some hard nuggets of topical concern, usually extractable and conspicuous: the plea for prostitutes and their reclaim, the satire on the law, the criticism of model prisons, the interest in emigration. These mostly appear as tractlike forms within the continuum of the novel, not digressions but certainly statements in a different mode. We may feel that the treatment of Emily's seduction suffers from being part of a generalized case about fallen women, but we are likely to applaud the formalized little coda about prison reform, which allows the three villains to take a final bow and creates a new piece of satirical irony. These embedded tracts are few. More typical and more interesting is the revelation of Dickens' implicit social attitudes, often remaining well below the conscious level of criticism.

In Dickens' other study of psychological growth, *Great Expectations,* the psychological concerns are socially expressive: Pip's humiliations, ambitions, illusions, snobbishness, gentlemanliness, and fall and rise are all recognizable social symbols. The novel is at once a portrait of an individual character and a strong generalization. In *David Copperfield,* because Dickens is closer to his hero and in a position where he found it hard to be distanced and objective, the relation of psychology to social expression is markedly different. David often reveals—or rather betrays—Victorian limitations that the author does not see but that the modern reader certainly does. David's dissatisfaction with Dora's housekeeping, for instance, is very plainly characteristic of both his sex and age, an expectation and a need that it never occurs to him to question or criticize. Dickens takes very great pains to show David's painful attempts, after intolerant and demanding mistakes, to accept Dora as she is, and the tolerance and compromise are clearly meant to be seen as meritorious. In a sense they are, but modern readers will set aside the limited assumption that every man deserves a good housekeeper, and sympathize with the undated and moving residue—David's difficult decision to accept another human being for what she is, which is not what he wants or needs.

Dickens makes David's observation and sensibility act as a sensitive register for the novel's several actions. At times the response is unsurprising, but at others it is interestingly marked, as on the occasion when Dickens gives the last word to Uriah Heep after David has observed, rather priggishly and very inaccurately, that "greed and cunning" always "overreach themselves. It is as certain as death." Heep replies:

"Or as certain as they used to teach at school (the same school where I picked up so much umbleness), from nine o'clock to eleven, that labour was a curse; and from eleven o'clock to one, that it was a blessing and a cheerfulness, and a dignity, and I don't know what all, eh?" said he with a sneer. "You preach about as consistent as they did. Won't umbleness go down?"

(ch. 52)

Since the novel ends with umbleness going down splendidly, albeit in prison, this riposte seems to mark a rare division between Dickens and David. It certainly marks Dickens' imaginative recognition of the social significance of Heep and the socially determined nature of the ethics of industry. Dickens is not perhaps entirely behind the comment, for he does use his art to celebrate the certainty of vice's downfall, and he does elsewhere preach the blessedness and dignity of labor pretty loudly, but the passage marks a fruitful uncertainty, a movement of the critical imagination beyond those historical limitations that operated on it.

Critics such as Gwendolyn Needham and Edgar Johnson have praised *David Copperfield* for its powers of thematic unification and control of idea. It has also been praised for its coherent analysis of "the undisciplined heart," the phrase in which Annie Strong sums up her youthful, irrational, and amoral feeling, and which stirs David to self-recognition and diagnosis. Almost every character, problem, and episode can be seen as an illustration of this theme. What I want to question is that the idea and its ramifications are sources of strength. G. K. Chesterton, whose criticism combines effusiveness with much insight, said that Dickens' characters were often implausible but still possessed the power to shake us profoundly. I believe that it is not so much the explicit moral and psychological study of the heart and its discipline that gives *David Copperfield* its strength and its vitality, as certain intense local shafts that strike deep as insights and revelations.

Once David sees that his heart is undisciplined, the path ahead is fairly smooth and straight, and Dickens, here as elsewhere, illustrates the moral and psychological fallacy of identifying diagnosis with remedy. Once Martin Chuzzlewit, Scrooge, David, and Pip arrive at self-knowledge, they proceed to improvement and conversion. The actual concept of the disciplined heart seems crude and owes much to the impression made on us by another and easier kind of discipline, the discipline of action. We see David's grit and professional industry emerging from the ordeal set him by Betsey Trotwood, his fairy godmother; and by a kind of sideways shift, we may well ignore the absence of much dramatic evidence for the emotional discipline that Annie and David tell of, but do not show, in their change of heart. Annie's narrative is a summary of action and feeling, made in retrospect when she confesses to her husband. David's narrative is addressed to the reader. We are meant to feel and approve David's attempts to discipline his own demands for comfort, rational companionship, and a profound love, and to accept the deficiencies of Dora and of his marriage. Behind the pages of narrative lie Dickens' own hard and fatigued attempts to live with his own marriage, but the toughness and wryness of this experience of accepting uncomfortable life remain largely unrealized and unarticulated.

The psychological interest is erratic, appearing in spots rather than stretches, especially once we follow David into the adult world, but it is arrestingly present. David tells Dora that he has been trying to change her, has seen his error, and has decided not "to try any more." Dora's response is one of the many small details that make her character interesting:

"It's better for me to be stupid than uncomfortable, isn't it?" said Dora.

"Better to be naturally Dora than anything else in the world."

"In the world! Ah Doady, it's a large place!"

(ch. 48)

One moment like this is more delicate and moving than all the loudly whispered hints about her last talk with Agnes.

David Copperfield has a vitality that possesses comic and serious dimensions. The same is true of the comic characters. In this novel, the jokes do not explode to leave no trace. When Micawber speaks, the style is the man:

"Under the impression," said Mr. Micawber, "that your peregrinations in this metropolis have not as yet been extensive, and that you might have some difficulty in penetrating the arcana of the Modern Babylon in the direction of the City Road—in short," said Mr. Micawber, in another burst of confidence, "that you might lose yourself—I shall be happy to call this evening, and install you in the knowledge of the nearest way."

(ch. 11)

Micawber's celebrated "in short" does not merely show up the inflation and grandiose circumlocution of his grand flights, but cuts them short and modifies their grandiosity. The hollow men in Dickens, like Pecksniff and Chadband, irritate the reader into deflating and translating their flights; Micawber is given the ability to deflate himself, and the stylistic deflation that follows the "in short" signals the descent to practical matters. The reader who properly attends to the style is not too startled at Micawber's final triumphs. The comedy here, as in other characters, is subtly deceptive and subtly revealing. The reader has to learn, with David, to see beneath the comic simplifications, to learn, for instance, that Mrs. Micawber's elasticity is not ludicrous, but guarantees her much-vaunted but genuine constancy, or that Betsey Trotwood's comic spinsterishness is neither comic nor simple. Dickens is learning to use comedy not simply for farce and satire, but most originally to create surface effects and to trip us into feeling the depths beneath. His apparently end-stopped jokes and his apparently static caricatures are dynamic and complex.

This kind of comedy is appropriately used in a novel of memory, a novel that explores the past, reenacts it, and explores its meanings. The past sensations and feelings are presented as things remembered, and the effect of the double vision of David the past child and David the man in the present works in the same way as the comic duplicity. The rhythm of the novel depends largely on the relation between the time past and present, a relation that is made very emphatic in the several "retrospects" where, by a fine stroke of linguistic imagination, Dickens uses the present tense to express what is most visibly presented as the rapid passing of time in the past, a present tense that speaks with a sad and faintly mocking voice of what was vivid and now has faded, a perfect vehicle for the ironies of nostalgic remembering, reliving, questioning, and burying:

Next day, too, when we all go in a flock to see the house—our house—Dora's and mine—I am quite unable to regard myself as its master. I seem to be there, by permission of somebody else. I half expect the real master to come home presently, and say he is glad to see me. Such a beautiful little house as it is, with everything so bright and new; with the flowers on the carpets looking as if freshly gathered, and the green leaves on the paper as if they had just come out; with the spotless muslin curtains, and the blushing rose-coloured furniture, and Dora's garden hat with the blue ribbon—do I remember, now, how I loved her in such another hat when I first knew her!—already hanging on its little peg; the guitar-case quite at home on its heels in a corner; and everybody tumbling over Jip's Pagoda, which is much too big for the establishment.

(ch. 43)

Some of the most complex writing, which blends comedy and pathos, is in these passages, and it is in them that the powerfully articulated themes of mutability and memory are expressed. *David Copperfield* is a novel of "the silent gliding on . . . of existence," the memory of "the unseen, unfelt progress of . . . life," "of the river," and "the journey." The gliding is halted, the progress held up, the river stopped, and the journey interrupted, in four great punctuating chapters, placed arrestingly at the ends of installments, where the theme becomes explicit, the narrative summary conveniently made, and the sensations of memory movingly created out of that "historic present" that uses the language of time present to dramatize time past and delicately fuses and defines layers of experience. It is the unity of feeling emphasized by Schlegel and Coleridge to replace the rigidities of neoclassical concepts of form that seems most appropriately invoked to describe the structure, the subject, and the appeal of *David Copperfield*.

Bleak House was published in monthly parts, beginning in March 1852. It is one of the most thoroughly studied of Dickens' novels. Scholars have collated the fiction with the facts of history and concluded that this is a highly topical novel, in its Carlylean symbolism of fire and fog, and all its documentary materials. "Documentary" is a misleading word: Dickens was a novelist, not only a reporter. He took such contemporary events and problems as the Manning case (which was the source for the murder of Tulkinghorn), the charitable efforts of Mrs. Chisholm's Family Colonisation Society, the Oxford Movement (violently and irreverently parodied in Mrs. Pardiggle and her unfortunate sons), scandals about sanitation and cholera, and the criticisms of chancery, and reinvented them for his novel. By his own reassembly of these materials, he revealed his social diagnosis. John Carey has discussed Dickens' ambivalence and inconsistency in moral attitude, but *Bleak House* is lucid and consistent. Chancery and a great house and the brickmakers and the frightful slums of Tom All Alone's

are inextricably joined: rank, wealth, and ease are responsible for ignorance, poverty, and pain. And if the reason will not see and accept such connections, the body will—the disease that does not know its place acts as a violent physiological metaphor for the oneness of the body politic. The fog is commonly celebrated as the controlling image of the novel, but it is really only one instance and aspect of that bleakness—cold, wet, and filthy—announced in the title. The house of England does not shelter its citizens from cruel weathers. Cold, wet, fog, and dirt are sensed as presences throughout a novel that not only makes us laugh, cry, and wait, as Dickens advised Wilkie Collins a novel should, but also makes us feel and smell.

From the very beginning of the novel, with its verbless bird's-eye view of the Thames and London, our senses are agitated. The fog's chill and blur are felt and seen—and, indeed, the beginning of the novel would be thin and allegorical if this were not so, for most of the equations and interpretations of the setting drawn by the critics are explicitly announced by Dickens himself. Some readers have felt Dickens' explicitness an irritant: he leaves little to be inferred, but puts the case at the top of his voice, repeats it in capital letters, and then adds an extra gloss in a footnote. These novels were read to groups of illiterates as Thackeray's and George Eliot's never were, and much can be forgiven a writer whose sympathy and entertainment have reached so many people. We move through the novel, feeling fog, damp, filth, and slime, and then, when the sensations of revulsion are held up by Esther's orderly housekeeping or Chadband's gluttonous delight, we feel the impact of the interruption. Dickens animates his simple and schematic symbol, and involves us in a close and concrete relation with places, events, and characters. As with his Fat Boy in *Pickwick*, he wants to make our flesh creep by the contaminating exposures of *Bleak House*.

He moves us through disgust and pity, but also through comedy. Most of it is strongly satirical. Mrs. Jellyby, Mr. Turveydrop, the Pardiggles, Chadband, and Harold Skimpole are contemptuously ridiculed instances of heartless and complacent survivals among so many victims. The character of Mrs. Bayham Badger is the nearest we get to a comedy in which criticism is subdued by delight: "'Mrs. Badger has been married to three husbands—two of them highly distinguished men,' said Mr. Badger, summing up the facts; 'and, each time, upon the twenty-first of March at Eleven in the forenoon!'" (ch. 12). This has the old wild touch of superfluous detail; though Mrs. Badger is a type of solipsist seclusion and survival, and her best scene is carefully placed before the passage revealing the love of Ada and Richard, it has a gaiety that is rare in this dark novel. The grimness of satire is sustained in the rhetoric and language of the omniscient narrator who shares the story telling with Esther. The language used is often hortatory, even forensic. The reader is addressed and pressed, often in the manner of a prosecuting counsel, judge, or interrogator persuading, accusing, questioning, informing, summing up. The range of tone and feeling in this cross-examination is considerable. There is dry irony: "Mr. Vholes is a very respectable man. He is allowed by the greater attorneys who have made good fortunes, or are making them, to be a most respectable man"; and acid astringency: "The one great principle of the English law is, to make business for itself." The voice can shed both dryness and irony in passionate vituperation, as when the present tense gives up transitive verbs in despair on the occasion of Jo's death: "Dead, your Majesty. Dead, my lords and gentlemen. Dead, Right Reverends and Wrong Reverends of every order. Dead, men and women, born with Heavenly compassion in your hearts. And dying thus around us every day" (ch. 47).

The stark descriptions and direct address of this threnody are of course contrasted with the placid tones of Esther's narrative. One of Esther's many disadvantages as narrator/heroine is her total lack of irony or humor, a disadvantage she shares with other virtuous models in Dickens and George Eliot, but which is here peculiarly distinct and limiting, because she is a storyteller contrasted with the flexibility and force of the other narrator. Dickens is making an experiment in narrative structure (the best account of this can be found in W. J. Harvey's essay in *Dickens and the Twentieth Century*). We move from the limited vision and feeling of Esther to the larger, darker vision whose detachment is underlined by the present tense that bleakly records the way things are. The detachment has both passion and judgment, and is rather like the detachment one would expect of a recording angel. The division between the two narratives makes particularly plain that awkward separation between the optimistic record of the individual heart and the black record of the social historian.

Esther's story shows the energy of virtue and its final happy success; the social record shows the energy of destructive injustice. We are left with the constructiveness of the good housekeeper and the good doctor, rewarded with each other, cozily settled in their rustic version of "Bleak House," whose "doll's rooms" strike some readers as an impropriety after Tom All Alone's. Dickens does disturb the final harmony with the discords of Caddy's deaf-and-dumb child and Ada's mourning, but the strongest chords are those expressing peace, beauty restored, pain soothed, virtue recognized, energy activated, the wind never in the east. Dickens does not make his final passages ironical, and we drop down from the powerful indictment to this weak doll's-house reassurance. It is not only that Dickens tends to conventionalize his ending, but perhaps that his mind was divided. He found it possible to feel boundless hope in the human heart, little in societies and institutions. *Bleak House* suggests that as soon as generous impulse becomes institutionalized charity, it kills the love of individuals by individuals. So it is understandable, if depressing, to find that the conclusion of the novel seems so congratulatory. The reconciliation is too tiny, too unrepresentative, to emerge from this novel. The sense of its restriction is increased by Esther's own unreality: if there is indeed hope to be found in human hearts, let them be more complex and more eroded by experience than Miss Summerson's. Her symbolic name and fairy-tale associations with Dame Durden and the rest do not make her a character with genuine mythological weight, but sentimentalize good works by excessive solicitude, admiration, and complacency. Some of the responses that the author demands for the heroine are precluded by her role as ostentatiously modest narrator. We can only be glad that it was David and not Agnes who told the story of *David Copperfield*.

In the next few novels Dickens takes pains to avoid any suggestion of an easy solution. *Hard Times, Little Dorrit, A Tale of Two Cities*, and *Great Expectations* limit their concluding demands on the reader and do not expect us to settle down and see everything and everyone as now prospering after all that pain. The sense of reality begins in *Hard Times* with a toughening of moral humors in the two chief women characters. Sissy Jupe is a more subdued type of womanly virtue than Esther, and we are asked to concentrate not on Sissy but on Louisa, a psychologically realistic character who does not tax our credulity or our faith. Like Edith Dombey, to whom she is related, Louisa is a case of repressed passion and vision. She sees the highest, but pride, self-contempt, and doubt drive her into following the lowest. She perversely represses her capacity for virtue and tries to act out the utilitarian disregard for feeling that her education has held up as a model. She is also moved by her love for her brother and does not follow Edith's earlier course of punishing herself and her male aggressors, and is indeed moved by Harthouse (and he by her and by Sissy) as Edith never is by Carker. Harthouse is a less stagey and a more compressed version of Carker, a study in perverted ennui, who is a sketch for Eugene Wrayburn. Louisa is also exposed to experience not simply as a victim, like Esther Summerson, but as a susceptible and malleable human being who has a capacity for damnation.

Though the treatment of the working-class characters and industrial problems is sentimental and crass, the virtue of *Hard Times* lies in a new kind of truthfulness about social conditioning of character. We do not find, as in *Bleak House*, the anatomy of destructiveness followed by a small-scale model of construction. The humors of the self-made man *gloriosus* in Bounderby, and of the convertible utilitarian in Gradgrind, are incisive and spirited, very much in the manner of those Jonsonian humors whose very narrowness produces a pressure of vitality. The presentation of the circus with its symbols of pastime, joy, and goodhearted sleaziness is effective within the limits of the fable and, in spite of its embarrassing lisping innocence, responds adequately enough to the countersymbol of the fact-choked and fact-choking schoolroom. The novel lacks a proper adult paradigm for the imaginative and sensual life denied by Gradgrind, but so much of the focus is on the child's education that this passes almost without notice. That it does not escape entirely without notice is perhaps a tribute to the delineation of passion, repression, and conflict in Louisa. Dickens cannot really be said to explore her inner life, but he manages very skillfully, as with Dombey, to imply it.

Louisa does not go right down to the bottom of Mrs. Sparsit's gloatingly imagined moral staircase, but her redemption is treated with some sternness, and there is no falsely triumphant climax. The anatomy of a heartless education and a heartless industrialism, linked by the criterion of efficiency, concludes with no more than a sad and sober appraisal:

Herself again a wife—a mother—lovingly watchful of her children, ever careful that they should have a childhood of the mind no less than a childhood of the body, as knowing it to be even a more beautiful thing, and a possession, any hoarded scrap of which, is a blessing and happiness to the wisest? Did Louisa see this? Such a thing was never to be.

(book 3, ch. 9)

The last words to the Dear Reader, which recall the end of *The Chimes*, though discussing the possibility of remedy, are free from optimistic flights: "It rests with you and me, whether, in our two fields of action, similar things shall be or not." Dickens looks forward to rebirth—in the lives of children still unborn and in deathbed repentance—but he denies Louisa a brave new life; the quiet and almost matter-of-fact language is true to the experience of the novel. His liking for cheers and congratulations at the end is subdued, as he suggests that Louisa's future will be undertaken "as part of no fantastic vow, or bond, or brotherhood or sisterhood . . . but simply as a duty to be done." It is particularly satisfying that Dickens avoids the pendulum-swing so grossly offensive in *Bleak House*; he does not offer the language and symbolism of strong feeling and vivid fancy in reaction to the world and values of hard fact. He matches heartless rationality with a rational warmth. The very last words of the novel are placed in a context of age and death: "We shall sit with lighter bosoms on the hearth, to see the ashes of our fires turn grey and cold." The image of dying fires is wholly sensitive to Coketown and remembers its ashes, in contrast to the way that Esther's little "Bleak House" depended on ignoring the larger bleakness.

Little Dorrit is a bigger and more complex venture than *Hard Times*, but the new sensibility and toughness remain and grow. Dorrit herself is no complex psychological study, but a very effective character who manages at once to be symbolic and yet also subject to time and place. She has a certain grotesqueness—stunted and sexless—that helps to stylize her as an image of virtue and to make her a more natural prison-child. She is Dickens' most successfully heroic character since Oliver Twist. And she is helped by sharing the interest of the novel with Arthur Clennam, victim of another kind of imprisonment, and a character with more inner life than we have found up to now. He too is responsively and convincingly stunted by environment, and extricates himself slowly and exhaustedly. The virtue and energy Dickens celebrates in this novel are hard-won and battered. Here too the ending is triumphant only in a muted way and has a rational sobriety and lack of crescendo. Arthur and Dorrit, like Louisa, move into a "modest" life. The last sentence of the novel, one of the most sensitive Dickens ever wrote, musters our sympathy but makes no attempt to wipe out our recollection of all that has happened. It is framed by the restlessness, dissatisfactions, and irresoluteness that have marked so much of the action: "They went quietly down into the roaring streets, inseparable and blessed; and as they passed along in sunshine and shade, the noisy and the eager, and the arrogant and the froward and the vain, fretted and chafed, and made their usual uproar" (book 2, ch. 34).

The whole novel is not written or imagined with such rational and complex control. There are flights of pity and ecstasy where Dickens is at his worst. When the Dorrit brothers die, for instance, Dickens has some excellent individual touches of act and feeling, in the account of the old man sending off his trinkets and clothing to be pawned, and in the image of death: "Quietly, quietly, all the lines of the plan of the great Castle melted." But he moves off into the banalities of prayer—an act he simply cannot fathom—and into a paradisal imagery that rings hollow: "The two brothers were before their Father; far beyond the twilight judgments of this world; high above its mists and obscurities." Some of the appeals on behalf of Dorrit's frailty and goodness also fall into banality. I emphasize such sentimental patches because I do not want to imply that the late Dickens is entirely in control of himself, his characters, and his readers. There is sentimentality, but it is not used to solve problems, reach conclusions, or venture a grandiose finality.

Little Dorrit is like *Bleak House* in its centripetal symbolism. The novelist draws our attention at almost every point to the insistent symbol of imprisonment. When we have mentioned the dark stench of the French prison, with dazzling light outside and its microcosmic image of class and power, the travelers in quarantine talking explicitly of prison, the Marshalsea, Dorrit's conceit of the grand European tour that is so like imprisonment, the blatant but striking comparison of the St. Bernard hostel to a prison, Mrs. Clennam's room, and repressive religion, we have made no observations that the novelist does not make repeatedly and clearly for us. The scene has widened: England is like a Bleak House, human life and civilization are like a prison. The sensuous life of

the symbolism is more thinly intellectual, more obviously worked out in simple equations, though it has a dimension of feeling, perhaps shown most vividly in the depression and restricted energies of Clennam, a prisoner almost incapable of stretching and moving into life. Dickens, like Henry James, makes the characters themselves do much of the symbol making, and this increases the explicitness but is at times less than plausible.

The most successful piece of institutional portraiture is not the prison, but Dickens' presentation of the civil service, then the citadel of ease and privilege, unassailed by competition, as the Circumlocution Office. Dickens creates a devastating analysis in a daring exposition—by now he could risk making speeches in the novels—and very funny satirical portraiture. The Tite Barnacle family is animated by satire that is heralded by Dickens' introductory exegis unfolding "the Whole Science of Government." After eleven paragraphs of sardonic commentary Dickens feels free to use ridicule:

He had a superior eye-glass dangling round his neck, but unfortunately had such flat orbits to his eyes, and such limp little eyelids, that it wouldn't stick in when he put it up, but kept tumbling out against his waistcoat buttons with a click that discomposed him very much.

(book 1, ch. 10)

The eyeglass and the limp little eyelids caricature the affectation and feebleness of this ruling class, but there is the extra comic detail so dear to Dickens in the flat orbits of the eyes. The language accurately imitates upper-class vagueness and polite exclamatoriness in its many "I says" and "Look heres" accompanied by the mannerism of the clicking eyeglass. Light comedy is not an end in itself; the lightness here suggests the silliness and frivolity of what is described. The levity is part of reproach and bitter criticism. It is also found in *Little Dorrit*'s less grim and harsh comedy. It would be hard to imagine Flora Finching and her aunt, for instance, in *Bleak House.*

In *Little Dorrit* and *Bleak House* the comic is often neighbor to the grim or pathetic. In *Bleak House* we pass innocently from chat about tainted chops to the grisly scene of spontaneous combustion. In these novels Dickens seems to be able to infect one feeling with another, so that we scarcely know whether to call the fun grisly or the horror the more macabre for the presence of laughter. Dickens' imagination was always attracted by mixtures of feeling, and the mixtures grow richer in the late novels. The suicide of

Merdle, the financier whose soiled name, taken from *merde*, gives him away, is preluded by some light comedy of manners in Fanny's drawing room. It must be remembered that Fanny is a recent graduate from prison:

> "I thought I'd give you a call, you know."
>
> "Charmed, I am sure," said Fanny.
>
> "So I am off," added Mr. Merdle, getting up. "Could you lend me a penknife?"
>
> It was an odd thing, Fanny smilingly observed, for her who could seldom prevail upon herself even to write a letter, to lend to a man of such vast business as Mr. Merdle. "Isn't it?" Mr. Merdle acquiesced; "but I want one; and I know you have got several little wedding keepsakes about, with scissors and tweezers and such things in them. You shall have it back tomorrow."
>
> "Edmund," said Mrs. Sparkler, "open (now, very carefully, I beg and beseech, for you are so very awkward) the mother of pearl box on my little table there, and give Mr. Merdle the mother of pearl penknife."
>
> "Thank you," said Mr. Merdle; "but if you have got one with a darker handle, I think I should prefer one with a darker handle."
>
> "Tortoise-shell?"
>
> "Thank you," said Mr. Merdle; "yes. I think I should prefer tortoise-shell."
>
> (book 2, ch. 24)

Undertaking not to get ink on the knife, he goes off to kill himself. Both *Bleak House* and *Little Dorrit* are novels of multiple action, organized not only by central symbols but by an operatic intricacy of plot, which is slowly and mysteriously wound and rapidly unwound. As early as *Oliver Twist* and *Barnaby Rudge* Dickens had used complicated intrigue, mystery, and unraveling, but in *Bleak House* and *Little Dorrit* such plots cover a huge range of characters, and the mystery and final revelation involve almost everyone of importance. Separate threads of action, character, and society are gathered up in plot as well as symbolism and theme. The last curtain can then be economically inclusive. The argument takes in the love story, the criminal adventure, and the satire on institutions. Dickens often creates a symbol that figures his structure as well as contributing to it. For example, the imagery of roads begins in the first chapter of *Little Dorrit*, and the prison-keeper sings, "Who passes by this road so late? Compagnon de la Majolaine," in a suitable overture for a novel concerned with many journeys. In the late novels journeys are not what they were in early Dickens, now forming only a part, not mapping the total trajectory. The shadows of the future, the approaching strangers, and the hysterically mounting echoes cast typically dark and ominous gloom in the dark novels. The episodic structure of journey-novels gives way to the symbol of the journey.

A Tale of Two Cities contains not only this imagery of an ominous future, in which the sound of revolution is gathering, but something of the prison mood and claustrophobia of *Dorrit*. It is chiefly interesting for feeling and atmosphere, and stands out, like *Barnaby Rudge* among the early novels, as a tale of action and adventure. It is also, as *Barnaby Rudge* is not, a rather feeble novel. It is bound together by symbolism and plot, it has some interesting psychological ideas, but no satiric or comic power and very little character interest. Its contemporaneity is plain in the fine opening oratory and in its Carlylean inspiration and source. It is stark in moral action, simple in feeling, quite a good novel to read in childhood, but one that does not wear well into adult life. Its most characteristic defect is in language. Like George Eliot's *Romola* (1861–1862), it suffers from the double artificiality of mimicking the language of another time and another country. Dickens usually relies heavily on the colors of language, but in this novel the characters' speech is stilted and characterless. Even where it is relieved by pseudotranslation from the French, of a mildly entertaining kind, the relief soon palls. There are some good passages, like Manette's traumatic reversions to prison life or the knitting of Madame Defarge (another emblem of tragic destiny), and there is the good idea, which degenerates into mere plot manipulations, of the physical likeness and moral unlikeness of Darnay and Carton. But the flatness and hollowness of character and reliance on external action are not typical of this period, or even of Dickens' work as a whole. It belongs with some of his feebly melodramatic stories such as *Hunted Down* (1859), which also lack density of language and character.

This lapse is followed by *Great Expectations*, one of Dickens' finest novels. It is remarkably dense and subtle in its dramatic psychology. It is a profound study of the theme of the bad mother and the unloved child, which Edmund Wilson has related to Dickens' own feelings of hostility and deprivation. Once more we have a solitary orphan, no longer the victim of impersonal institutions, but uncomfortably shuttling between the unloving and effective Mrs. Joe and the loving and ineffective Joe. The personal story is certainly not shut off from society, and it offers a complex analysis through character, plot, symbol, and fable. The grotesque characters of Miss Havisham and Magwitch are brought together in a conflict of class and wealth that accumulates its farce through many particulars.

The plot is one of Dickens' best, at once intricate and lucid, highly original yet commanding the immediate assent of fable. Pip moves innocently into the convict's orbit of gratitude, need, ambition, and power, when he first innocently and spontaneously blesses the broken "wittles" and hopes that Magwitch is enjoying the stolen food. The convict chokes at the first words of hospitality and love he has ever heard, and Pip's life begins to be ironically remade. At first, before he comes into money, he submits to a growing consciousness of class that destroys his spontaneous warmth and generosity. When he is contemptuously fed like a dog in Miss Havisham's yard, he begins his hard education in class antagonism and great expectations. This is the loss of innocence in a world where love requires the right manners, the right accent, the right clothes, and the right income. Dickens sets up this world and explores it with irony and regret. Magwitch is the fairy godfather who pays for Pip's education and thus lets him act out the fantasy of becoming a gentleman who will please Estella. It is a novel where separate fantasies struggle and defeat each other: Miss Havisham's mad dream of creating a heartless girl who will act out her need for sexual revenge locks with the convict's fantasy of making the gentleman he himself can never be. The plots of Magwitch and Miss Havisham, and their intentions and fantasies, cross. Magwitch has made a gentleman who cannot stand his table manners; Miss Havisham finds that the destruction of the heart means that Estella can make no exception for her. Pip's discovery of his real benefactor is one of the best recognition scenes in Dickens, because its shock also marks a moment of moral discovery. It leads to the conversion of Pip, to his forced intimacy with Magwitch, which, after all, becomes love.

Estella's education and perversion—a little like Louisa's—are shown from the outside, as is her eventual change of heart. Pip's is shown from the inside, in a confessional self-analysis in which he bares his secret life and its causality. It is easy to overrate this analysis, simply because it is on a larger scale and more detailed than anything else in Dickens. But it has its weakness: Pip is too clearly and completely aware of the social and emotional forces that have made him what he is. His process and motivation are available to him in a way that is not implausible, but is just not related to his individual limitations. It is a first-person novel that could really do with an omniscient author possessed of more wisdom than the hero. Pip is not endowed with anything like the sensitive register of consciousness that we find in, say, George Eliot's Maggie Tulliver or most of the central characters of Henry James. He is not shown, like them, in a fine psychic notation that imitates the workings of the brain that feels and the heart that thinks. We do not see him breaking down old categories and emerging into new ones, like Maggie or James's Strether. This is, of course, an invidious comparison, but I make it in order to stress that *Great Expectations* is a great psychological novel of Dickens' own kind. Here he explores the inner life more tenaciously than anywhere else, but it is not the kind of psychological novel that imitates the activity of the mind. It describes and symbolizes the moral life but does not analyze its processes.

Great Expectations, like *David Copperfield*, is a novel of memory, and as such blurs character and personality in a way both convenient and evasive. Pip's story is told through the medium of recollection, and Pip is not shown as an unpleasant and obtuse snob, but always seen through the memory and sensibility of his unsnobbish older self. This technique makes his development and change of heart rather remote and shadowy, though there are impressive moments of moral feeling, as when he suddenly sees himself in relation to Joe and Magwitch, as someone who has failed in love and loyalty. As so often in Dickens, the outline of development and upheaval is firm and plain, the detail omitted. We see the moral action in the simple action of a fable: Pip is moved by seeing his opposite in Magwitch, his double in Estella; Miss Havisham is moved by recognizing in Pip a victim of love like herself. We tend to overlook the absence of a direct dramatization of the unregenerate Pip, and he is really much the same all the way through, imaginative, sensitive, self-critical, telling us but not showing us that he was different once. The places where the unconverted Pip shows through tend, not surprisingly, to be in dialogue, like the passage where he tries to tell Biddy that it would be a good thing if Joe could attempt some self-improvement. The first-person narrative is something Dickens never used with the ease and consistency of Charlotte Brontë or Thackeray.

One of the successes of the novel, however, is its fusion of the individual story with the social indictment. Dickens shows in Pip the natural unconditioned life of the heart and the socially destructive process that weakens and distorts it, transforming instinct into calculation, human love into manipulation, generosity into greed, spontaneity into shame and ambition. Though he may be thought to soften the class issue by the pastoral image of Joe and his forge, which begs the whole question of economic determinism, he also produces some striking criticisms and ironies. Pip's ambitions as he climbs to the top are soiled by the tainted money typical of his society, but the process and some of the social and emotional changes involved will be relevant in a meritocracy. Joe and Biddy are not often patronized; they have dignity and toughness; they are not babies like Sleary, but inhabit the adult world. The end originally planned by Dickens would have kept Estella and Pip apart, though even this version reveals optimism in Pip's ability to break with his social conditioning and start again, with the far from slight advantage of a good bourgeois education. But both the old and the revised endings are modest and unassuming, like those of *Hard Times* and *Little Dorrit:* Pip and Estella are sad and scarred, and the last words of the book evoke darkness as well as light. Dickens simplifies the social issues, certainly, but the indictment of society remains.

Our Mutual Friend is also a conversion story with social significance. It too deals with class, wealth, and social mobility. Plot and moral action are tightly bound in a multiple action that takes us back to *Bleak House* and *Little Dorrit*. Like *Great Expectations* it concerns a moral ordeal and test, though in this novel the test is set by the characters. The plot makers within the novel are not frustrated, or perverse, or innocent, and they come out as rather flat, like Harmon Rokesmith, or as cozy caricatures, like the Boffins. Harmon stages the pseudoconversion of Boffin, the Golden Dustman whose heart of gold becomes—Midaslike—chilled and hardened. This impersonated corruption acts as a test and a warning to Bella Wilfer, a nice girl with mercenary leanings. The false conversion brings about the true one, and Bella rejects money and chooses love. In this novel Dickens separates the subjects of money and class, dealing with them in different actions, though there is

plenty of linking material in the chorus of Veneerings and Podsnaps. The story of Bella and the Boffins might have involved class but is simply a fable about love and money, whereas the story of Lizzie Hexam and her rival lovers deals expressly with problems of changing social strata. Bradley Headstone, the repressed, respectable, and passionate schoolmaster, is opposed to Eugene Wrayburn, the idle, debilitated, able, and perverse gentleman. Backed by Charley, Lizzie's clever and ambitious brother, these characters act out a splendid crime of passion, which is thickly detailed and documented as determined by social forces.

The several mysteries, some overt, some covert, are less unified than the action of *Bleak House:* there is the impersonation of Rokesmith by Harmon, the impersonation of a miser by Boffin, which goes back to *Martin Chuzzlewit*, the story of the crime, and rich supporting material, grotesque, comic, pathetic, and satiric. The best thing in the novel is the psychological study of crime, not exactly new in Dickens—who had long ago shown Sikes's solitude and guilt as he fights the fire and listens to the cheapjack selling stain remover, and a little later, Jonas Chuzzlewit and his telltale heart—but new in its careful sociological backing. In the analysis of Bradley he moves out of the so-called criminal classes to draw a new kind of meritocratic monster whose violence, repression, and jealousy are part of a deadly struggle for respectability and sexuality in a not very intelligent man of strong passions with a need for social conformity. Dickens' method seems deceptively simple, using sociopsychological analysis, on the one hand, and expressive stage gestures like the beating of a hand on a stone, on the other. But what is admirable and far from simple is the blend of thriller and social criticism with the control of contrary feelings, such as we find in the scene with the tortoise-shell penknife. During the scene in Bradley's schoolroom, for instance, Rogue Riderhood enters in the grimly ridiculous guise of a friendly visitor wanting to put the children through their paces. The well-drilled chorus of children chirping their facts speaks fully for the education that has shaped Bradley, and provides just the right surface of innocent routine that Riderhood can threateningly play with and then destroy, after a tensely mounting examination not unlike his namesake Red Ridinghood's interrogation of the wolf.

But the novel as a whole lacks the force of such individual scenes. Despite the story of crime and punishment, the character of Wrayburn, and the excellent comedy of Wegg and Venus, a pair of morality grotesques, there is much flat, undeveloped action and softness of character, with an unsatisfactory relation between the whole and its parts. Wrayburn marries Lizzie, perhaps to denote a new flexibility in attitudes to marriage between the classes, as Humphry House suggests, though with crucial stages in his conflict and decision blurred by grave illness and a symbolic rescue from death and the river. His marriage is finally approved by Twemlow, a choric character of some importance, a "real" gentlemen among the upstart rich, and an interesting new stereotype created by Dickens, the *gentleman* with a heart of gold. Although the novel is bristling with convincing social victims like Charley Hexam and Bradley, its converted or virtuous characters are much less credible. Dickens' densely documented analysis of Bradley only shows up the dreaminess of such figures as Bella and the Boffins, and even Eugene has to be helped over the tricky area of decision by symbolic action. The striking and impressive figures of the Podsnaps, the Lammles, and the Veneerings act out their own little drama and thus become much more than a comic chorus; they create a satiric action that is much closer to Thackeray's powerful caricature of a whole world, in *The Newcomes* (1854–1855), than anything else in Dickens. If *Bleak House* moves us through pity and disgust and *Little Dorrit* through ironic claustrophobia, *Our Mutual Friend* moves us through the sharpest and most strident criticism Dickens ever created. It is satire that appears on the margin of previous novels but takes over in this novel; it creates a world in which the benevolent softnesses of Mr. Wilfer the Cherub, and Bella's baby, and Wrayburn's marriage, and little Johnny's words in the Children's Hospital about "the boofer lady," shrivel up before our eyes. The best that we can find in this world is the likely alliance of the Lammles, taken in and making the best of things, or of Jenny Wren, with her sustaining fantasy of the father who is a bad child.

Dickens creates such a powerful anatomy of a corrupting society, ruled and moved by greed and ambition, that the wish-fulfilling fantasies of virtue and conversion are too fragile to support faith. That contemptuous insight out of which he drew Podsnap's humors and the rich (but not excremental) dustheaps where the scavenging Wegg prods with his wooden leg is realized in sensuous detail and appropriate language. Dickens can make virtue lisp like a baby or rhapsodize like a saint, but it seldom speaks with the unerring individual tones of Podsnap's loud, patronizing complacency, or the drunken ellipses of Doll's, or the soaring "tones of moral grandeur" of the Lammles' duet. Virtue often speaks in the neutral language that expresses neither personality nor class, as in Mrs. Boffin or Lizzie, where style glosses over the social difficulties of class and marriage. Boffin the miser is so much more sharply incised in manners and speech—"Scrunch or be scrunched"—than Boffin the good old man that it is not surprising that George Gissing (mistakenly) thought Dickens must have really intended to make the Golden Dustman a study in deterioration. Betty Higden is endowed with a certain life because she is given a language, and she is perhaps the most effective instance of virtuous energy in the book. The others are either nonentities or unappealing: Bella does not want to be the doll in the doll's house, but her marriage and maternity are nothing if not embarrassingly doll-like. Neither the action nor the psychology of individual goodness is strong enough to heal those sore spots shown and painfully touched in pity and violence and satire.

Dickens died after six monthly parts of *Edwin Drood* had come out. This last novel begins as a more concentrated and specialized mystery story than anything else he wrote, and it is likely that the central interest would have developed from the contrast between John Jasper's respectable public life and his secret drug-taking criminality, perhaps related to the practices of the Thugs, in which there was some contemporary interest. Edmund Wilson gives a good account of those many scholarly speculations that naturally sprang up to complete a detective story left unfinished. It is tempting but dangerous to suggest, as some have done, that Jasper is to be a study in dual personality, and I can see little in the suggestion that the detective, Datchery, is Helena Landless in disguise, but the novel's chief pleasure must lie in such speculations. It also has the interest of muted language and character. It is probably the one Dickens novel from which one could quote passages not immediately recognizable as Dickensian; and two of its characters, Mr. Grewgious and Mr. Crisparkle, are interestingly sober treatments of eccentrics who would in an earlier novel have been more exaggeratedly comic: Dickens develops them steadily and respectfully, in an almost Trollopian combination of the serious and slightly comic portrait. But it is only a marvelous fragment, the unfinished novel of an author who wrote hand to mouth, even if with a sense of design.

Robert Garis, in *The Dickens Theatre*, has discussed that frank and open theatricality with which Dickens presents and animates his work. Theatricality is a useful word to describe the vitality and flourish of his appearances as an author, and useful too in defining the limits of his art. We should insist on these limits not because Dickens has been overpraised, but in order to try to recognize his individuality. He is theatrical, for instance, in his use of external action. His stage is not often the lonely stage of soliloquy, but a stage crowded with the lively, stereotyped, stagey, concrete, simplified, physically exciting actions of actors. Dickens provides not only script and stage directions but movement and performances too. His novels are like plays in action. But in the novels from *Dombey and Son* onward, he seems to be pushing this theatrical and extrovert art beyond the limits of theatricality. The attempt to imply the inner life of characters can be traced back to Sikes and Ralph Nickleby but becomes fully developed in Dombey and Edith, who are shown stagily but subtly. It continues in the figure of Esther Summerson whom Dickens is trying to create from the inside, though often with the unhappy result of making a reserved and introspective character behave like a self-conscious puppet. *Bleak House* is a valiant failure in an attempt to show the inner life of a human being in one part of the novel, and an impersonal, fierce vision of social injustice in the other. In *Hard Times* he places his analysis of the inner life most courageously and effectively in a simple fable and shows it, as in *Dombey and Son*, not through the technique of enlarged soliloquy, where he is generally weak, but through implication and reticence, where he is strong.

The psychology becomes more complex and mobile in content as he goes on experimenting in form: in *Little Dorrit* we have the inner self of Clennam's vivid ordinariness, and Dickens moves from this success to others, in Pip and Wrayburn. He is exploring a kind of character really belonging to another kind of novel, very far from theatrical, that novel of inner action written by Charlotte Brontë, George Eliot, George Meredith, and Henry James, where the very form of the novel takes on the imprint of consciousness. Dickens' persistent experiments are marked by a limitation. He is apparently not trying to write whole novels of inner action, but inserting this inner analysis of complexity into *his* kind of novel, placing its subtlety under the spotlight that glares on the Dickens stage. Sometimes he can only bring it off for short stretches, as with the childhood of David; sometimes he manages the marvelous sleight-of-hand that makes us feel we have had full access to the conflicts of Dombey, Edith, and Louisa. Sometimes he creates the dense particularity of Pip, Clennam, Wrayburn. But it is a dense particularity revealed by his own weird spotlight. And it keeps strange company, which is not complex, or dense, or always very individualized. It is the story of an inner life, rather than the presentation of an inner life.

It points to three things: first, to that theatrical and extrovert nature of his genius. Next, it reveals his delight in difficulty, in the strenuousness spoken of by Henry James that shows itself so energetically in Dickens' attempt to push beyond the frontiers of his genius. Finally, it is no accident that in those novels where he succeeds in actualizing a central character, we feel least troubled by the duality and disparity of his analysis of the individual and the society. His developing interest in psychology seems at times to go against the grain of his genius, but in fact his sociological imagination needed the particulars of a sense of character and is badly betrayed and isolated when Dickens fails to anatomize the single heart. It is that powerful sociological imagination that triumphs most truthfully when Dickens succeeds in piercing through to the inner life. Dickens the man was often muddled, inconsistent, and neurotic in his responses to political problems and social experience, but at its best his art overcame or sublimated the weaknesses of the artist.

SELECTED BIBLIOGRAPHY

This bibliography has been compiled by Graham Handley of the Department of English at Birkbeck College, University of London. He would like to acknowledge the bibliographies of K. J. Fielding, T. Blount, and M. Slater in the British Council's Writers and Their Work studies of Dickens, as well as the generous help of A. Sanders, present editor of *The Dickensian*.

Items marked with an asterisk (*) are *essential reading;* those marked with a cross (+) are *strongly recommended.*

I. BIBLIOGRAPHY. Detailed bibliographical information is also found in the *New Cambridge Bibliography of English Literature*, vol. III, pp. 779–850; this entry, by P. Collins, was separately issued by the Dickens Fellowship in 1970. F. G. Kitton, *Dickensiana: A Bibliography of the Literature Relating to Dickens and His Writings* (London, 1886); F. G. Kitton, *The Novels of Charles Dickens: A Bibliography and a Sketch* (London, 1897); F. G. Kitton,

The Minor Writings of Charles Dickens: A Bibliography and a Sketch (London, 1900), *Hard Times* included; W. G. Wilkins, *First and Early American Editions of the Works of Dickens* (Cedar Rapids, Iowa, 1910); T. Hatton and A. H. Cleaver, *A Bibliography of the Periodical Works of Charles Dickens: Bibliographical, Analytical and Statistical* (London, 1933); W. Miller, *The Dickens Student and Collector: A List of Writings about Charles Dickens and His Works, 1836–1945* (London, 1946), supplements 1947 and 1953, includes contemporary reviews, dramatizations, and plagiarisms of Dickens; *G. H. Ford and L. Lane, Jr., eds., *The Dickens Critics* (Ithaca, N. Y., 1961), discussions and list of Dickens criticism 1840–1960; +L. Stevenson, ed., *Victorian Fiction: A Guide to Research* (Cambridge, Mass., 1964), contains "Charles Dickens" by A. B. Nisbet, a comprehensive coverage of criticism and scholarship; +G. H. Ford, ed., *Victorian Fiction: A Second Guide to Research* (New York, 1978), as the preceding, with P. Collins evaluating criticism from 1963 to 1975; J. Gold, *The Stature of Dickens: A Centenary Bibliography* (Toronto, 1971); *Victorian Bibliography*, published annually in June issue of *Victorian Studies*, Bloomington, Ind., cumulative vols. cover 1932–1964; +*The Year's Work in Dickens Studies*, published annually in *The Dickensian* (1968–   ); *The Dickens Checklist*, published quarterly in each issue of *The Dickens Studies Newsletter* (1970–   ), covers books, articles, reprints, dissertations; A. E. Dyson, ed., *The English Novel: Select Bibliographical Guides* (London, 1974), see "Dickens," by M. Slater, a survey of scholarship and criticism 1836–1971; R. C. Churchill, *Bibliography of Dickensian Criticism, 1836–1975* (New York and London, 1975).

II. Collected Editions. *Works*, 17 vols. (London, 1847–1868), first "cheap" ed., some new prefaces by Dickens; *Library Edition*, 22 vols. (London, 1858–1859), reiss. 1861–1874 in 30 vols.; *The Charles Dickens Edition*, 21 vols. (London, 1867–1874), descriptive headlines on right-hand pages; *Household Edition*, 22 vols. (London, 1871–1879), issued in monthly parts; *MacMillan Edition*, 21 vols. (London, 1892–1925), intros. by C. Dickens, Jr., includes *Letters*, ed. by G. Hogarth and M. Dickens; *Gadshill Edition*, 36 vols. (London, 1897–1908), intro. and notes by A. Lang, includes many uncollected articles; *National Edition*, 40 vols. (London, 1906–1908), ed. by B. W. Matz; *Nonesuch Edition*, 23 vols. (London, 1937–1938), includes 3-vol. *Letters*, ed. by W. Dexter, and 2-vol. *Collected Papers*; +*The New Oxford Illustrated Dickens*, 21 vols. (London, 1947–1958); *K. Tillotson and J. Kinsley, gen. eds., *Clarendon Edition*, 5 vols. (London, 1966–   ), definitive texts, includes textual variants, author's number plans, relevant bibliographical material, *Oliver Twist*, *Edwin Drood*, *Dombey and Son*, *Little Dorrit*, *David Copperfield* published so far.

III. Separate Works. *Sketches by Boz*, 2 vols. (London, 1838), essays; 2nd series, 1 vol. (1836); both series, 1 vol. (1839); *The Posthumous Papers of the Pickwick Club, edited by "Boz"* (London, 1837), novel, issued serially

(April 1836–November 1837); *Oliver Twist, or The Parish Boy's Progress*, 3 vols. (London, 1838), novel, issued serially in *Bentley's Miscellany* (February 1837–April 1839), also in *Clarendon ed. by K. Tillotson (1966), and +Penguin English Library ed. by P. Fairclough, intro. by A. Wilson (1966); *The Life and Adventures of Nicholas Nickleby* (London, 1839), novel, issued in 20 monthly parts (April 1838–October 1839), also in *Penguin English Library ed. by M. Slater (1978).

Master Humphrey's Clock, 3 vols. (London, 1840–1841), novels, sketches, short stories, issued in 88 weekly parts and in monthly parts (4 April 1840–27 November 1841); *The Old Curiosity Shop* (London, 1841), novel, issued serially in the *Clock* from 25 April 1840, also in +Penguin English Library ed. by A. Easson, with intro. by M. Andrews (1972); *Barnaby Rudge: A Tale of the Riots of 'Eighty* (London, 1841), novel, issued serially in the *Clock* from 13 February 1841, also in +Penguin English Library ed. by G. Spence (1973); *American Notes, for General Circulation*, 2 vols. (London, 1842), travel; *The Life and Adventures of Martin Chuzzlewit* (London, 1844), novel, issued in 20 monthly parts (January 1843–July 1844), also in +Penguin English Library ed. by P. N. Furbank (1968); *A Christmas Carol: In Prose* (London, 1843), first of the Christmas books; *The Chimes: A Goblin Story* (London, 1844), second of the Christmas books; *The Cricket on the Hearth: A Fairy Tale of Home* (London, 1845), third of the Christmas books.

The Battle of Life (London, 1846), fourth of the Christmas books; *Pictures from Italy* (London, 1846), travel, first published in the *Daily News* (21 January–2 March 1846), with some differences, as seven "Travelling Letters"; *Dealings with the Firm of Dombey and Son, Wholesale, Retail, and for Exportation* (London, 1848), novel, first issued in 20 monthly parts (October 1846–April 1848), also in *Clarendon ed. by A. Horsman (1974), and +Penguin English Library ed. by P. Fairclough, with intro. by R. Williams (1970); *The Haunted Man and the Ghost's Bargain* (London, 1848), fifth and last of the Christmas books, also in +Penguin English Library ed. by M. Slater, *Christmas Books*, vol. II (Harmondsworth, 1971).

The Personal History, Adventures, Experience, and Observation of David Copperfield: The Younger of Blunderstone Rookery (Which He Never Meant to Be Published on Any Account) (London, 1850), novel, issued in 20 monthly parts (May 1849–November 1850), also in *Clarendon ed. by N. Burgis (1981), Riverside ed. by G. H. Ford (Boston, 1958), and +Penguin English Library ed. by T. Blount (1966); *A Child's History of England*, 3 vols. (London, 1852–1854), history, first appeared in *Household Words* (25 January 1851–10 December 1853); *Bleak House* (London, 1853), novel, issued in 20 monthly parts (March 1852–September 1853), also in +Norton Critical ed. by G. H. Ford and S. Monod (New York, 1977), and Penguin English Library ed. by N. Page, with intro. by J. H. Miller (1971); *Hard Times: For These Times* (London, 1854), novel, first appeared in *Household Words* in weekly installments (1 April–12 August 1854), also in +Norton Critical ed. by G. Ford and S. Monod (New York, 1966), and +Penguin English Library ed. by D. Craig (1969).

Little Dorrit (London, 1857), novel, issued in 20 monthly parts (December 1855–June 1857), also in *Clarendon ed. by H. P. Sucksmith (1976), +Penguin English Library ed. by J. Holloway (1967), College Classics in English ed. by R. D. McMaster (1969); *The Lazy Tour of Two Idle Apprentices* (London, 1857), travel, in collaboration with W. Collins, first appeared in *Household Words* in weekly installments (3–31 October 1857); *Reprinted Pieces* (London, 1858), vol. VIII of the Library ed., includes 31 articles from *Household Words*; *A Tale of Two Cities* (London, 1859), novel, first published in *All the Year Round* in weekly installments (30 April–26 November 1859), also in +Penguin English Library ed. by G. Woodcock (1970); *Hunted Down* (London, 1859), short story, first appeared in the *New York Ledger* (20–27 August, and 3 September 1859) and in *All the Year Round* (4–11 August 1860).

Great Expectations, 3 vols. (London, 1861), novel, first published in *All the Year Round* in weekly installments (1 December 1860–3 August 1861), also in +Penguin English Library by A. Calder (1965); *The Uncommercial Traveller* (London, 1861), essays, from *All the Year Round*, included in the Gadshill ed. (1908); *Our Mutual Friend* (London, 1865), novel, issued in 20 monthly parts (May 1864–November 1865), also in +Penguin English Library ed. by S. Gill (1971); *George Silverman's Explanation* (London, 1868), short story, first appeared in the *Atlantic Monthly* (January–March 1868) and in *All the Year Round* (1, 15, 29 February 1868); *Holiday Romance* (London, 1868), children's story, first appeared in *Our Young Folks* (January–May 1868) and in *All the Year Round* (25 January–4 April 1868); *The Mystery of Edwin Drood* (London, 1870), unfinished novel, first issued in monthly parts (April–September 1870), designed for 12 parts, also in *Clarendon ed. by M. Cardwell (1972), and +Penguin English Library ed. by A. J. Cox, with intro. by A. Wilson (1974).

Note: MSS of most of the novels are in the Forster Collection at the Victoria and Albert Museum. The MS of *Great Expectations* is in the Wisbech Museum; that of *Our Mutual Friend* is in the Pierpont Morgan Library, New York City.

In addition to his journalism and magazine contributions in the early part of his career, Dickens realized his ambition to edit his own periodical with *Household Words* (March 1850–May 1859) and *All the Year Round* (April 1859 until his death in June 1870). The book in which are recorded authors and payments for articles in *Household Words* is at Princeton, ed. by A. Lohrli (Toronto, 1973). H. Stone edited *The Uncollected Writings of Charles Dickens in "Household Words" 1850–1859*, 2 vols. (London, 1969).

IV. LETTERS, SPEECHES, READINGS. W. Dexter, ed., *The Letters of Charles Dickens*, 3 vols. (London, 1938), part of the Nonesuch ed. listed in COLLECTED EDITIONS; E. Johnson, ed., *Letters from Charles Dickens to Angela Burdett Coutts, 1841–1862* (London, 1953), first published as *The Heart of Charles Dickens* (New York, 1952); *K. J. Fielding, ed., *The Speeches of Charles Dickens* (London, 1960), definitive text, supplementary material by P. Collins and D. A. Roos in *The Dickensian* (May 1977); *H. House, G. Storey, K. Tillotson et al., eds., *The Letters of Charles Dickens* (Oxford, 1965–), the Pilgrim ed., when completed will contain more than 13,000 letters, 5 vols. issued so far; *P. Collins, ed., *Charles Dickens: The Public Readings* (London, 1975), first complete ed. of texts of the public readings.

V. PERIODICALS DEVOTED TO DICKENS. +*The Dickensian* (London, 1905–), index to first 70 vols. by F. T. Dunn (1976); *Dickens Studies* (Boston, 1965–1969); *Dickens Studies Annual* (Carbondale, Ill., 1970–); +*The Dickens Studies Newsletter* (Louisville, Ky., 1970–).

VI. BIOGRAPHIES. *J. Forster, *The Life of Charles Dickens*, 3 vols. (London, 1872–1874), rev. ed., 2 vols. (1876), new one-vol. ed. by J. W. T. Ley (1928), new two-vol. ed. by A. J. Hoppé (1969), both later eds. with additional material; G. Dolby, *Charles Dickens as I Knew Him* (London, 1885), Dickens' reading tours; M. Dickens, *Charles Dickens, by His Eldest Daughter* (London, 1885), issued also as *My Father as I Recall Him* (1897); J. W. T. Ley, *The Dickens Circle* (London, 1918); H. F. Dickens, *Memories of My Father* (London, 1928); G. Storey, *Dickens and Daughter* (London, 1939), Kate Dickens' reminiscences; U. Pope-Hennessy, *Charles Dickens 1812–1870* (London, 1945); +E. Johnson, *Charles Dickens, His Tragedy and Triumph* (New York, 1952; repr. 1965; rev. ed. 1977); A. Nisbet, *Dickens and Ellen Ternan* (Berkeley, 1952; Cambridge, 1953); A. A. Adrian, *Georgina Hogarth and the Dickens Circle* (London, 1957); J. B. Priestley, *Charles Dickens: A Pictorial Biography* (London, 1961); M. Fido, *Charles Dickens: An Authentic Account of His Life and Times* (London, 1970); *A. Wilson, *The World of Charles Dickens* (London, 1970); N. MacKenzie and J. MacKenzie, *Dickens: A Life* (London, 1979).

VII. GENERAL CRITICISM. G. Gissing, *Charles Dickens* (London, 1898); +G. K. Chesterton, *Charles Dickens* (London, 1906); A. C. Swinburne, *Charles Dickens* (London, 1913); A. C. Quiller-Couch, *Dickens and Other Victorians* (Cambridge, 1925); +E. M. Forster, *Aspects of the Novel* (London, 1927); D. Cecil, *Early Victorian Novelists* (London, 1934); *G. Orwell, *Inside the Whale* (London, 1940), an important essay, repr. in Orwell's *Critical Essays* (London, 1954); *E. Wilson, *The Wound and the Bow* (Boston, 1941), the essay "Dickens: the Two Scrooges" helped revitalize Dickens criticism; +S. Monod, *Dickens Romancier* (Paris, 1953), repr. as *Dickens the Novelist* (Norman, Okla., 1968), first major focus on the MSS and proofs of the novels; +K. J. Fielding, *Charles Dickens: A Critical Introduction* (London, 1958; rev. ed. 1965); +J. H. Miller, *Charles Dickens: The World of His Novels*

(Cambridge, Mass., 1958); +J. Cross and G. Pearson, eds., *Dickens and the Twentieth Century* (London, 1962), essays on each work by leading critics; +R. Garis, *The Dickens Theatre: A Reassessment of the Novels* (London, 1965); H. M. Daleski, *Dickens and the Art of Analogy* (London, 1970); A. E. Dyson, *The Inimitable Dickens: A Reading of the Novels* (London, 1970); +B. Hardy, *The Moral Art of Dickens* (London, 1970); F. R. Leavis and Q. D. Leavis, *Dickens the Novelist* (London, 1970); +J. Lucas, *The Melancholy Man: A Study of Dickens' Novels* (London, 1970; rev. 1980); A. Nisbet, ed., Dickens centennial issue of *Nineteenth Century Fiction* (March 1970); +M. Slater, ed., *Dickens 1970* (London, 1970); H. P. Sucksmith, *The Narrative Art of Charles Dickens: The Rhetoric of Sympathy and Irony in His Novels* (London, 1970); S. Wall, ed., *Charles Dickens: A Critical Anthology* (Harmondsworth, 1970); J. Kincaid, *Dickens and the Rhetoric of Laughter* (London, 1971); A. Nisbet and B. Nevius, eds., *Dickens Centennial Essays* (London, 1971); +J. Carey, *The Violent Effigy: A Study of Dickens's Imagination* (London, 1973).

VIII. STUDIES OF SPECIAL ASPECTS OF DICKENS' WORK. W. M. C. Kent, *Dickens as a Reader* (London, 1872), repr. with intro. by P. Collins (1971); F. G. Kitton, *Dickens and His Illustrators* (London, 1899; repr. Amsterdam, 1972); +H. House, *The Dickens World* (London, 1941); *J. Butt and K. Tillotson, *Dickens at Work* (London, 1957), close analysis of Dickens' MSS, corrected proofs, number plans; J. Butt, ed., *A Review of English Literature: Dickens Number* (July 1961); *P. Collins, *Dickens and Crime* (London, 1962; new ed., 1964); *P. Collins, *Dickens and Education* (London, 1963); R. H. Dabney, *Love and Property in the Novels of Dickens* (London, 1967); G. L. Brook, *The Language of Dickens* (London, 1970); +M. Slater, ed., *Dickens and Fame 1870-1970* (London, 1970); A. Welsh, *The City of Dickens* (London, 1971); J. Gold, *Charles Dickens: Radical Moralist* (London, 1972); W. Oddie, *Dickens and Carlyle* (London, 1972); R. Barnard, *Imagery and Theme in the Novels of Charles Dickens* (London, 1974); A. Harbage, *A Kind of Power: The Shakespeare-Dickens Analogy* (London, 1975); B. Hardy, *Tellers and Listeners: The Narrative Imagination* (London, 1975); F. Kaplan, *Dickens and Mesmerism: The Hidden Springs of Action* (London, 1975); G. Steward, *Dickens and the Trials of the Imagination* (London, 1975); D. DeVries, *Dickens's Apprentice Years* (New York, 1976); +R. L. Patten, *Charles Dickens and His Publishers* (London, 1978); +M. Slater, ed., *Dickens on America and the Americans* (London, 1978); N. Pope, *Dickens and Charity* (London, 1978); F. S. Schwarzbach, *Dickens and the City* (London, 1979); H. Stone, *Dickens and the Invisible World* (London, 1979); +J. R. Cohen, *Dickens and His Original Illustrators* (London, 1980); Dennis Walder, *Dickens and Religion* (London, 1981); +P. Collins, ed., *Dickens: Interviews and Recollections*, 2 vols. (London, 1981).

IX. STUDIES OF INDIVIDUAL NOVELS. See particularly:

+P. Collins, ed., +*Dickens: The Critical Heritage* (London, 1971); +T. W. Hill, explanatory notes in *The Dickensian—Dombey and Son* (1942), *David Copperfield* (1943), *Bleak House* (1943-1944), *The Mystery of Edwin Drood* (1944), *A Tale of Two Cities* (1945), *Little Dorrit* (1945-1946), *Our Mutual Friend* (1947), *Hard Times* (1952), *Great Expectations* (1957-1960).

Sketches by Boz. J. H. Miller, *Charles Dickens and George Cruikshank* (London, 1971); G. Smith, *The Other Nation: The Poor in English Novels of the 1840's and 1850's* (London, 1980).

Pickwick Papers. R. L. Patten, ed., intro. and notes in Penguin English Library ed. (London, 1972).

Oliver Twist. The Dickensian (1974), *Oliver Twist* issue; *P. Collins, *Charles Dickens: The Public Readings* (London, 1975), contains description of Dickens' own fascination with the "Sikes and Nancy" text and his performance.

Nicholas Nickleby. M. Slater, "The Composition and Monthly Publication of Nicholas Nickleby," accompanies the Scolar Press facs. of the part issue (London, 1973); S. Marcus, *Dickens from Pickwick to Dombey* (London, 1965).

The Old Curiosity Shop. A. Easson, "From Manuscript to Print," *Dickens Studies Annual* (1970).

Barnaby Rudge. S. Marcus, see under *Nicholas Nickleby*; G. Thurley, *The Dickens Myth* (London, 1976).

Martin Chuzzlewit. S. Marcus, see under *Nicholas Nickleby*; J. Butt, *Pope, Dickens and Others* (London, 1969); C. Woodring, "Change in *Martin Chuzzlewit*," in *Nineteenth Century Literary Perspectives*, ed. C. de L. Ryals (London, 1974).

The Battle of Life. J. Butt, see under *Martin Chuzzlewit*; +M. Slater, intro. to Penguin English Library *Christmas Books*, vol. II (Harmondsworth, 1971); D. Thomas, *Dickens: Selected Short Fiction* (Harmondsworth, 1976).

Dombey and Son. K. Tillotson, *Novels of the Eighteen-Forties* (Oxford, 1954; repr. 1961); S. Marcus, see under *Nicholas Nickleby*; J. Lucas, "Dickens and *Dombey and Son*," in *Tradition and Tolerance in Nineteenth Century Fiction*, eds. J. Goode, D. Howard, and J. Lucas (London, 1966); L. Lerner, "An Essay on *Dombey and Son*," in *The Victorians*, ed. L. Lerner (London, 1978); P. Ingham, "Speech and Non-communication in *Dombey and Son*," *Review of English Studies* (May 1979).

David Copperfield. V. Woolf, "David Copperfield" (1925), in Dickens volume of Penguin Critical Anthologies, ed. S. Wall (London, 1970); P. Collins, *Charles Dickens: David Copperfield* (London, 1977).

Bleak House. M. D. Zabel, "Dickens: The Undivided Imagination," in *The Dickens Critics*, eds. G. Ford and L. Lane (London, 1961); H. P. Sucksmith, "Dickens at Work on *Bleak House*," *Renaissance and Modern Studies*, 9 (1965); +A. Y. Wilkinson, "*Bleak House*: From Faraday to Judgement Day," *Journal of English Literary History*, 34 (June 1967); J. Korg, ed., *Twentieth Century Interpretations of "Bleak House"* (Englewood Cliffs, N. J., 1968);

+A. E. Dyson, ed., *Dickens: Bleak House* (London, 1969); G. Smith, *Charles Dickens: Bleak House* (London, 1974); M. Ragussis, "The Ghostly Signs of *Bleak House*," *Nineteenth Century Fiction,* 34 (December 1979).

Hard Times. G. B. Shaw, "Introduction" (1912), repr. in *The Dickens Critics,* eds. G. Ford and L. Lane (London, 1961); P. E. Gray, ed., *Twentieth Century Interpretations of "Hard Times"* (Englewood Cliffs, N.J., 1969); A. Easson, *"Hard Times": Critical Commentary and Notes* (London, 1973).

Little Dorrit. L. Trilling, "*Little Dorrit*," *Kenyon Review,* 15 (Autumn 1953), repr. as intro. to New Oxford Illustrated ed. and in *The Dickens Critics,* eds. G. Ford and L. Lane (London, 1961); P. D. Herring, "Dickens' Monthly Number Plans for *Little Dorrit*," in *Modern Philology,* 64 (August 1966); J. C. Reid, *Charles Dickens: Little Dorrit* (London, 1967); +C. P. Snow, "Dickens and the Public Service," in *Dickens 1970,* ed. M. Slater (London, 1970); W. Myers, "The Radicalism of *Little Dorrit*," in *Literature and Politics in the Nineteenth Century,* ed. J. Lucas (London, 1971); P. J. M. Scott, *Reality and Comic Confidence in Charles Dickens* (London, 1979).

A Tale of Two Cities. M. D. Zabel, *Craft and Character in Modern Fiction* (New York, 1957); C. E. Beckwith, ed., *Twentieth Century Interpretations of "A Tale of Two Cities"* (New York, 1972); +A. Sanders, *The Victorian Historical Novel (1840–1880)* (London, 1979).

Great Expectations. +G. B. Shaw, "Introduction" and "Postscript" to *Great Expectations* (London, 1937), restores Dickens' alternative ending to the novel; D. Van Ghent, *The English Novel: Form and Function* (New York, 1953), includes "On *Great Expectations*," also in *Dickens:*

Modern Judgements, ed. A. E. Dyson (London, 1968); R. Lettis and W. E. Morris, eds., *Assessing Great Expectations: Materials for Analysis* (San Francisco, 1963); H. Stone, "The Genesis of a Novel: *Great Expectations*," in *Charles Dickens 1812–1870,* ed. E. W. F. Tomlin (London, 1969); +G. Martin, "A Study Guide to *Great Expectations*" and "*Great Expectations*," units 6 and 7 of the Open University Course, *The Nineteenth Century Novel and Its Legacy* (London, 1973); A. L. French, "Beating and Cringing: *Great Expectations*," *Essays in Criticism,* 24 (April 1974).

Our Mutual Friend. R. Morse, "*Our Mutual Friend*," *Partisan Review,* 16 (March 1949), repr. in *The Dickens Critics,* eds. G. Ford and L. Lane (London, 1961), and in *Dickens: Modern Judgments,* ed. A. E. Dyson (London, 1968); J. H. Miller, *The Form of Victorian Fiction* (Notre Dame, 1970; repr. 1979); +U. C. Knoepflmacher, *Laughter and Despair: Readings in Ten Novels of the Victorian Era* (Berkeley–Los Angeles, 1971), especially "*Our Mutual Friend:* Fantasy as Affirmation"; G. Stewart, *Dickens and the Trials of the Imagination* (Cambridge, Mass., 1974); R. Altick, "Education, Print and Paper in *Our Mutual Friend,*" in *Nineteenth Century Literary Perspectives: Essays in Honor of Lionel Stevenson,* ed. C. de L. Ryals (Durham, N.C., 1974); R. Mundhenk, "The Education of the Reader in *Our Mutual Friend,*" in *Nineteenth Century Fiction,* 34 (June 1979); A. Sanders, "'Come Back and Be Alive': Living and Dying in *Our Mutual Friend,*" *The Dickensian* (Autumn 1979).

Edwin Drood. G. H. Ford, "Dickens's Notebook and *Edwin Drood,*" in *Nineteenth Century Fiction,* 6 (December 1952).

EDWARD LEAR

(1812-1888)

Joanna Richardson

LIFE

EDWARD LEAR was born in Holloway, a picturesque village north of London, on 12 May 1812. He was the twentieth of the twenty-one children of Ann Skerrett and Jeremiah Lear. Mr. Lear was of Danish origin. "My own name," Edward would explain, "is really LØR, but my Danish Grandfather picked off the two dots and pulled out the diagonal line, and made the word Lear." His Danish grandfather had become a naturalized Englishman; Lear's father was conventional enough to be a stockbroker in the City of London. And nothing could have been more English than Edward's own first memory: it was the summer of 1815; he was just three years old, and he was wrapped in a blanket and taken out of bed to see the illuminations celebrating Waterloo.

He once declared that he could remember "every particle" of his life from the time he was four years old; his earliest recollections were probably quite happy. The house was large and comfortable, the family well-to-do; there were pleasant drives through the Highgate lanes and walks on Hampstead Heath. In the big painting room at Bowman's Lodge (the house has long since been destroyed), Edward pored over illustrated books of natural history and learned how to draw and paint from his sister Sarah.

Soon after his seventh birthday, he began to suffer from what he was to call the "terrible demon," the epilepsy which pursued him for the rest of his life. Its attacks were frequent (sometimes as many as eighteen in a month); and it had a deep effect on his character. "It is," he wrote, "a most merciful blessing that I have kept up as I have, and have not gone utterly to the bad mad sad." His infirmity made him embarrassed in the presence of strangers, reticent, and often deeply depressed. It also made him gentle and considerate; and it was to help him, as a man, to understand the problems and needs of childhood, and to be perfectly at ease with children. "He knew a great deal about children," wrote one who remembered him, J. St. Loe Strachey,

and they knew that he knew it, and he knew that they knew that he knew it, and so a complete and (as he might have said) abject harmony was established. The sympathy of which I speak is written large in all Mr. Lear's books; in every word of the letterpress and in every line, deep or narrow, straight or wavy, of his drawings. It was also shown in his personality. . . . I have a peculiarly vivid recollection of seeing Lear when he was stopping at my father's house, when I was about 8 or 9 years old. . . . I remember perfectly the towering, bearded, spectacled man, standing in the drawing-room at Sutton Court, and talking in a way which made one feel at once that he was "all right." . . .

Lear was not only beset in childhood by epilepsy; he was already liable to attacks of asthma and bronchitis. His sight was poor, and he was very conscious that his nose was large and that he was plain. These were personal causes for sadness; but, when he was thirteen, disaster struck the whole Lear family. Mr. Lear went bankrupt, the house at Highgate had to be sold, the servants and the carriages dispersed. Mr. Lear was imprisoned, and his wife moved the family into London, within reach of the jail. The two eldest sons emigrated to America, the third son went as a medical missionary to West Africa, and some of the daughters were sent out to earn their living as governesses and companions. Several of them died, unable to bear the hardships of their new life. Four years later, having paid off Jeremiah's debts, Mrs. Lear retired with him to Gravesend. She seems to have been more devoted to her husband than to her children. From the moment of the tragedy, she had entrusted Edward to his eldest sister, Ann. His education and upbringing lay entirely in her hands.

Ann was fortunate in having a small private income (her grandmother had left her £300 a year). She was high-principled, gentle, and extremely understanding. As Lear would write later, "she has always been as near to Heaven as it is possible to be."[1] But he was too frail to go to school, and Ann's teaching could only be a poor substitute for education. "Please believe," Lear once explained, "that the irritation of an artist's life produces much which works its possessor bitterness, when that individual's brain has been so little guided in youth as mine was."

He spent much time writing verse and studying books of natural history; he worked hard at drawing and painting. At the age of fifteen he began to earn his living as a draftsman. He made morbid disease drawings for doctors and hospitals, and he colored prints, screens, and fans. By the time he was eighteen he was taking pupils. Soon afterward, through a friend he was asked by the Zoological Society to draw the parrots in the London Zoo. The result was *Illustrations of the Family of Psittacidae, or Parrots:* a magnificent folio with 42 colored lithographs of birds. It appeared in 1832; and the delicacy and beauty of the drawings led Dr. J. E. Gray of the British Museum to ask Lear to illustrate his volume *Tortoises, Terrapins and Turtles* (which eventually appeared in 1872). The parrot book was to have a result of far more importance. The earl of Derby, an eager naturalist, had assembled a private menagerie at his country house, Knowsley Hall, near Liverpool. He wanted to publish a book about his collection, and needed a suitable artist to illustrate it. Lear was recommended. Lord Derby watched him at work in the Parrot House in the Zoological Gardens, and commissioned him at once to come to Knowsley. Lear spent most of the next four years in the enormous stately house in Lancashire, drawing the menagerie and finding friends and patrons he could hardly otherwise have met. The product of his four years' work appeared in 1846: a handsome volume called *Gleanings from the Menagerie and Aviary at Knowsley Hall.*

During those four years, Lear had also stumbled on his immortality. A "valued friend" had shown him a children's book called *Anecdotes and Adventures of Fifteen Gentlemen,* and he had pointed out a limerick:

There was an Old Man of Tobago,
Liv'd long on rice-gruel and sago;
But at last, to his bliss,
The physician said this—
"To a roast leg of mutton you may go."[2]

The limerick caught Lear's imagination; and, urged on by the grandchildren of Lord Derby, who showed their quite "uproarious delight," he struck off one limerick after another. The nonsense poet had found himself. The first *Book of Nonsense* appeared in 1846, the same year as the book on the Knowsley menagerie.

During his years at Knowsley, Lear had traveled to the Lakes and to Ireland. His growing interest in landscape, and his indifferent eyesight, led him to make an important decision. He would do no more exacting drawings of parrots and turtles. He would earn his living by landscape painting; he would improve his health by living in a southern climate. His decision to go abroad for an indefinite period must have hurt his sister Ann; and Lear felt a certain guilt at leaving her to an empty life. But in 1837 he set out for Italy, and there he stayed for the next three years. The first result, *Views in Rome and Its Environs,* a fine collection of lithographs, was published in 1841.

It was in Rome in 1845 that he met a handsome, ebullient, gifted Irishman, Chichester Fortescue, who was just down from Oxford and making the Grand Tour before he entered Parliament. "Lear a delightful companion," wrote Fortescue, "full of *nonsense,* puns, riddles, everything in the shape of fun. . . . I don't know where I have met anyone to whom I have taken so great a liking." The liking was mutual. Lear and Fortescue were drawn to each other at once, and their friendship continued until Lear's death.

Circumstances had made it hard for Lear to lead a normal life. As a friend observed, he needed marriage, "especially if it should give him children of his own instead of all the world's." Lear probably knew that he needed marriage; but his epilepsy and plainness seemed to him to put it out of the question. When Fortescue once complained of loneliness, Lear answered: "*You,* it appears to me, might put an end to all chance of such blacknesses, by asking any young Lady to marry you, which if *you* asked her

[1]All quotations from the letters are from Lady Strachey, ed., *Letters of Edward Lear* (London, 1907), and her edition of *Later Letters of Edward Lear* (London, 1911).

[2]All quotations from the poems are from H. Jackson, ed., *The Complete Nonsense of Edward Lear* (London, 1947).

she instantly *would*, whereas if *I* asked her she instantly *wouldn't*." For most of his life Lear refused to think of marriage; but he was affectionate by nature, and he longed for close relationships. Chichester Fortescue and, later, Franklin Lushington, the judge, were the two dearest friends in his life; and in these friendships he found considerable happiness. But his happiness could not be complete. He could not be everything to Fortescue, who enjoyed a late but perfect marriage to Countess Waldegrave. "Every marriage of people I care about," wrote Lear, in dejection, "rather seems to leave one on the bleak shore alone." As for Lushington, for whom he conceived an even deeper love, he did not merely get married: he was incapable of showing Lear affection. "I am older than Babylon in many ways," wrote Lear, in misery. "I wish sometimes I grew hard and old at heart, it would I fancy save a deal of bother."

But if his closest friendships gave him only partial pleasure, Lear did enjoy professional success. When his *Illustrated Excursions in Italy* appeared in 1846, he himself was in London; and Queen Victoria summoned him to Osborne, in the Isle of Wight, to give her a course of twelve drawing lessons. Prince Albert showed him the model of Osborne House, part of which was still under construction; and the queen herself made a deep impression on him. Nearly forty years later, he wrote warmly:

To my mind, [she] is one of the most remarkable women of this century or perhaps any other. . . . She is a true and fine woman in every respect. . . . I don't know if it is proper to call a sovereign a duck, but I cannot help thinking H. M. a dear and absolute duck, and I hope she may live yet thirty or forty more years, for every year she lives will be a blessing to her country. . . .

Queen Victoria's drawing master returned to Rome late in 1846; and the following spring, with John Proby, later earl of Carysfort, he toured Sicily (his drawings of it were to be published fifty years after his death). That summer with the same companion he toured Calabria and Naples; and his accounts of these tours appeared, with many lithographs, in 1852 as *Journals of a Landscape Painter in Southern Calabria*.

For the last ten years Lear had made Rome his headquarters; in 1848 the political situation grew disturbing, and he decided it was time to move. "I strongly long to go to Egypt for the next winter as ever is," he wrote Fortescue on 12 February:

I am crazy about Memphis & On & Isis and crocodiles and opthalmia & nubians, and simooms & sorcerers, & sphingidae. Seriously the contemplation of Egypt must fill the mind, the artistic mind I mean, with great food for the rumination of long years. . . .

He stayed briefly in Corfu, and then, on the invitation of Sir Stratford Canning, the British ambassador in Turkey, he went to Athens and to Constantinople; he traveled on to Albania, Malta, and Egypt. During 1848 and 1849 he covered the whole Greek peninsula from Salonika in the northeast to Sunium in Attica. For the next two years he made lithographs from his sketches and wrote up his diaries. The result was *Journals of a Landscape Painter in Albania etc.*, which appeared in 1851. It was well received, and rightly, for it was illustrated with style and written with infectious, original gusto; and those who knew Lear's infirmities must have respected him for his willingness to live rough and his constant eagerness for adventure.

From 1849 to 1853 Lear was living in England. During the winters he worked in London, and held exhibitions (his painting *Claude Lorrain's House on the Tiber* was hung at the Royal Academy in 1850); and in the summer he visited friends in the country. Among these friends were the Tennysons, in the Isle of Wight. But, left to himself, in an English winter, Lear was sometimes unable to work, and weighed down by his inescapable melancholy. Fortescue suggested marriage. "No, my dear Fortescue," answered Lear,

I don't mean to marry—never. . . . In my case I should paint less and less well, and the thought of annual infants would drive me wild. . . . I only wish I could dub and scrub myself into what I wish to be, and what I might be I fear if I took proper pains. But chi sa? How much will be allowed for *nature*, and early impressions, and iron early tuition? Looking back, I sometimes wonder I am even what I am. I often wonder how I have made so many certainly real friends as I have. . . .

(23 January 1853)

One of his real friends had recently come into his life: Holman Hunt, the Pre-Raphaelite painter. Hunt was fifteen years younger than Lear, but Lear looked up to him with the admiration of a pupil, and came to believe himself, as a landscape painter, to be a child of the Pre-Raphaelite school. It was during a stay with Holman Hunt that he conceived the idea of illustrating Tennyson's poems; the project was to occupy him, intermittently, for the rest of his life. "I don't want to be a sort of pictorial Boswell," Lear explained, "but to be able to reproduce certain lines of poetry in form and colour." None of Tennyson's contemporaries more nearly reproduced his verbal pictures than Lear did in *Poems by Alfred, Lord Tennyson* (1889).

In 1855, at last, Lear settled in Corfu; and though he made numerous journeys, Corfu remained his headquarters for the next three years. But his unequal friendship with Lushington (who was preoccupied with his work as a judge) was a constant source of anxiety; and, in his noisy lodgings, feeling little but dislike for the limited society of the island, he was more frustrated and miserable than ever:

Just figure to yourself [he told Fortescue] the condition of a place where you never have any breath or extent of intellectual society, & yet cannot have any peace or quiet. . . .

The constant walking and noise overhead prevents any application to any sort of work, & it is only from 6 to 8 in the morning that I can attend really to anything. . . . And then, if I can't sleep, my whole system seems to turn into pins, cayenne-pepper, & vinegar & I suffer hideously. You see I have no means of carrying off my irritation: others have horses, or boats, in short:—I have only walking, and that is beginning to be impossible alone. . . .

(6 June 1857)

From 1858 to 1860 Lear was living in Rome; from 1861 to 1864 he was in Corfu. In 1867, he settled for three years in Cannes. The long list of his wanderings emphasizes his persistent loneliness. But at last, in the winter of 1870, at the age of fifty-eight, when he had saved some £3,000, he began to look for a permanent home. He chose San Remo, bought some land, and arranged for a house to be built. He spent the summer of 1870 at a hotel in the mountains near Turin, writing up his Egyptian journals and preparing *Nonsense Songs, Stories, Botany and Alphabets* (which appeared in 1871). When he returned to San Remo that autumn, he found his house, the Villa Emily, rapidly nearing completion. Two "damsels" were soon making curtains, the carpets were laid, and Lear moved in with his servant Giorgio, and the bandy-legged gardener Giuseppe; before long the household received the distinguished addition of Foss, the cat. A new book, *More Nonsense, Pictures, Rhymes, Botany*, was published just before Christ-

mas 1871. It belied the feelings of its author. "I am very glad you all like the 'More Nonsense,'" Lear wrote to Fortescue. "It is queer (and you would say so if you saw me) that I am the man as is making some three or four thousand people laugh in England all at one time,—to say the least, for I hear 2,000 of the new Nonsense are sold."

Early in 1872, Lear's relative domestic peace was broken. His friend Lord Northbrook, who had just been appointed viceroy of India, offered to take him to India, give him a year's sightseeing, and pay for his journey back to San Remo. To an elderly man who had recently settled in a house of his own, the prospect must have seemed a little daunting; but in 1873, Lear embarked on his two-year tour of India and Ceylon (his viceregal travels were described in his *Indian Journal*, published as recently as 1953). In 1877 appeared *Laughable Lyrics*, the last book of nonsense to be published in his lifetime. In 1881, when a new "diametrical damnable blazing 5 Story Hotel" was built at the end of his garden and his peace and privacy were gone, he moved from the Villa Emily to the Villa Tennyson, San Remo. He continued his landscape painting, for, as he observed, "a man can but 'try,' and the mere act of 'trying' goes, I take it, a long way to stave off mental and fizzicle maladies." But his melancholy would not leave him. He failed to take his chance of happiness when at last it came: he failed to ask Augusta Bethell in marriage; and in his nonsense, as will be seen, lies the record of his love and of his failure.

He waited for death with equanimity:

I cannot say I find any terror in the contemplation of death [he told Fortescue in 1882]; I have lived to ascertain positively that much of the evil of my life has arisen from congenital circumstances over which I—as a child—could have had no control; a good deal too has been the result of various ins and outs of life vagaries, and what is called chance—which chance I don't believe in, for if I did I must give up all idea of a God at all. I know also that I owe an immensity to the assistance of friends; and neither do I put that down to chance. So, on the whole, I am tolerably placid. . . .

Two years later, he wrote sadly to the same correspondent: "The grasshopper has become a burden, and the quick-pace downhill transit to indifference and final apathy is more and more discernible as month follows month."

Edward Lear died on 29 January 1888. He was buried at San Remo.

THE ARTIST, TOPOGRAPHER, AND LETTER-WRITER

SUCH is the outline of Lear's life. "And thinking over all," he wrote, "I have long since come to the conclusion that we are *not wholly* responsible for our lives, *i.e.,* our acts, *in so far as* congenital circumstances, physical or psychical, over which we have no absolute control, prevent our being so." Lear's destiny had virtually been decided for him. He was convinced he could not marry; he had to live abroad; he was compelled to travel constantly, not only in search of subjects for his brush, but in search of temporary forgetfulness. "I am convinced of this more and more," he told Fortescue in 1859. "If you have a wife, or are in love with a woman, . . . then you may stay in any place and in any circumstances. . . . But if you are absolutely alone in the world, and likely to be so, then move about continually and never stand still."

Lear himself very rarely stood still. He traveled with astonishing energy, considering his ill health, to produce his pictures and travel books. And here, perhaps, it is time to consider the artist and the "Globular foolish Topographer."

Lear's immortality as a writer of nonsense has obscured his very real gifts as a serious draftsman and an artist. His *Illustrations of the Family of Psittacidae, or Parrots* had been of more than ornithological interest. Lear's delicate likeness of the salmon-crested cockatoo had been a picture in its own right; his red and yellow macaw, with the vain and stupid look in its little eye, had shone quite unforgettably from the page; and it had been hard to choose between the pair of glowing crimson-winged parakeets and the New Holland parakeets, subtle and almost Chinese in effect. Lear's watercolors of foreign lands were less intense in hue; but they showed a delicate color sense, a sophisticated simplicity. His painting of the Euboean landscape near Castella (reproduced in *Later Letters of Edward Lear*) suggests how exquisitely dreamy, how subtly Romantic he could be. The illustrations in his *Indian Journal* show that he used the medium with decision and fluency, and his meticulous notes: "Temples. Brown oker," or "River more intricate, and brighter," reveal how he insisted on accuracy.

But it is not true that in his landscapes, the pupil of Holman Hunt paid Pre-Raphaelite attention to minutiae. His details may be scrupulously accurate, but he limits them to essentials, and some of his impressionistic lithographs suggest the rich, strange world that we sometimes see in the paintings of Samuel Palmer. Lear is especially sensitive to the forms of trees: to "the endlessly varying groups of olive trees," the "wildly twisted olive-trunks" in the Ionian Islands. He loves the contrast between the cumulus olive and the spiral cypress. He is haunted too by the barren, jagged rocks, by cliffs and caves reflected in the sea, by the grim heights of Sappho's Leap, the majestic, ruined walls of ancient Samos. The lithographs in his *Journals of . . . Southern Calabria* catch the fairytale romance of the square, towering rock of Palizzi, and the double fortress rock of Rocella. The lithographs in the *Illustrated Excursions in Italy* show no Victorian insistence on trivia: they are drawn freely, in the grand manner, and it is clear that the hillside town of Citta di Penna, the clouded silhouette of Città d'Antino, struck deep at Lear's imagination:

> Illyrian woodlands, echoing falls
> Of water, sheets of summer glass,
> The long divine Peneïan pass,
> The vast Akrokeraunian walls,
>
> Tomohrit, Athos, all things fair,
> With such a pencil, such a pen,
> You shadow forth to distant men,
> I read and felt that I was there.

As Tennyson emphasized in his poem "To E. L., on his Travels in Greece," Lear did more than record the facts: he recalled an atmosphere. In his lithograph of Tempe, in his painting of the pale blue and violet mountains of Thermopylae, in his impressions of the crags of Suli, the huddled mountain buildings of Pentedatilo, we feel a haunting, melancholy, deeply romantic poetry. It is, at times, akin to that of "The Princess" and "Oenone"; and it confirms how perfectly Lear was suited to his task of illustrating Tennyson. But the poetry that Lear expressed in painting was not merely Tennysonian. It was poetry which was natural to himself.

If Lear deserves far more acclaim for his natural history illustrations, for his accomplishments as a landscape artist, he also deserves more recognition as a writer of travel books. He himself dismissed the Albanian journal as "memoranda of an artist's mere tour of search among the riches of far-away Landscape"; and the remark contains a certain truth. Lear's travel books are, first and foremost, the works of a draftsman and painter. "You have majestic cliff-girt shores," he writes of Albania; "castle-crowned heights, and gloomy fortresses; palaces glittering with gilding and paint; mountain-passes such as you encounter in the snowy regions of Switzerland; deep bays, and blue seas with bright, calm isles resting on the horizon." The Tennysonian vision was, nonetheless, the vision of Lear the artist. Lear's visual sense is always evident: he has an eye for color, form, and composition. In Corsica he finds it good "to sit below huge brown-armed trees, full-foliaged, shading a green slope of freshest turf and fern." In India he revels in "the rich colour of woods, ilex and pine, and the vast blue space of hollow mountain."

Lear's books of travel are certainly searches for the riches of landscape; but they are not merely that. They are amused, appreciative, gay. Lear revels in the "torrents of pigs" rushing down from the hills for their supper in Arezzano; he is amused by his primitive lodgings: "a large raftered room, of a bewildering aspect, . . . strewed with articles of female dress, intermixed rather oddly with fowls of all sizes, fluttering about in every direction, over and under two very misshapen beds." At Trasacco, he records, "we stood at the end of a fearfully hot slip of white pebbles, bordered by a fringe of meditative green frogs." At Città di Penna he was woken at daybreak "when a sound of Choc! choc! choc! pervaded the room, and forthwith numbers of little chanticleers rushed from all corners." And, touring the Ionian Islands, describing the Plain of Currant-Vines near Galáro, the familiar Lear breaks through at last: the Plain, he decides, "may be, in truth, called one unbroken continuance of future currant-dumplings and plum-puddings." Lear's nonsense is never very far away.

It is certainly never far from his letters; and his correspondence was massive. "Every human being," he wrote, "capable of writing ever since the invention of letters must have written to me, with a few exceptions perhaps, such as the prophet Ezekiel, Mary Queen of Scots, and the Venerable Bede." The number of his correspondents puzzled him. "Either all my friends must be fools or mad; or . . . there must be more good qualities about this child than he ever gives or has given himself credit for possessing." The fact was that he was immensely endearing. It *was* pleasant to know Mr. Lear and to receive a letter in his "meandering mash-potato manner"; and so the volume of correspondence was such that in 1864 Lear declared: "I abhor the sight of a pen, and if I

were an angel I would immediately moult all my quills for fear of their being used in calligraphy."

Lear's letters are inimitable, and he was an industrious writer. It is strange that there are only two published volumes of his correspondence. But since they cover forty years of his life (1847–1887), and since the letters are nearly all addressed to Chichester Fortescue—one of the few, wrote Lear, "who understand this queer child"—they bring us very close to the writer.

They reveal, more than anything else, Lear's constant loneliness. "I think," he wrote to Lady Waldegrave in 1870, "as I can't help being alone it is perhaps best to be altogether, jellyfish-fashion caring for nobody." The remark, made in desperation, did not ring true. For the letters, which show us Lear's loneliness, also make it plain that he was intensely affectionate. He had no time for a vapid, superficial social life; but he loved his family, he was devoted to children, and he was very fond of his friends. "I am coming to England fast as I can," he wrote to Fortescue, when Lushington proved an unresponsive companion.

Why are you coming say you? because I can't stay here any longer—without seeing friends & having some communion of heart & spirit—with one who should have been this to me, I have none. . . . And I can't bear it. And I want to see my sister. . . . And *you*. And my dear Daddy Holman Hunt, & other people. So I'm off.

(1 May 1857)

Lear was a deeply serious man; and the letters he wrote to Fortescue (then Lord Carlingford) on the death of his wife show the gentle understanding, the complete, affectionate sympathy he was capable of feeling.

However, he did not enjoy any one complete relationship; he was never supremely important to another human being. And this ultimate lack of love was the bane of Lear's life. Time and again, in his correspondence, he bursts out in depression. "I must leave off, I feel like 5 nutmeg-graters full of baked eggshells—so dry & cold & miserable." "For all I write cheerfully I am as savage and black as 90,000 bears." Sometimes he seeks refuge from his loneliness in his books and correspondence:

I am writing this from Certosa del Pesio, a Mountain Pension twenty-four hours above S. Remo, to which . . . I have come for a week or two to be out of the great heat by the sea-shore, to complete my child's nonsense-book for Xmas, and to write letters, and a fair copy of two Egyptian journals, 1854 and 1867, for future publication.

(6 July 1870)

Sometimes he attempts to forget his loneliness in his painting, working long hours in his studio, or tramping miles to record a landscape. "Did I tell you of my visit to Oudesh, vulgarly called Gozo?" he asks Lady Waldegrave in 1866. "I drew every bit of it, walking fifteen or twenty miles a day." And then, again, Lear attempts to be philosophic about his solitude. "As I grow older," he writes,

I as it were prohibit regrets of all sorts, for they only do harm to the present and thereby to the future. By degrees one is coming to look on the whole of life past as a dream, and one of no very great importance either if one is not in a position to affect the lives of others particularly.

It was a brave but futile attempt to pretend indifference.

But though Lear's gayest letters are still permeated with sadness, though they leave a haunting sense of melancholy, they are far from being a mere record of natural grievances. They have an unmistakable style; only Lear could have written them. They are intimate, fluent, vivid, discursive, and, as he would say, "spongetanious."

And here and there in his correspondence, when he is particularly moved, Lear finds himself, suddenly, writing poetry. Like many sensitive people, he tries to hide his feelings under a cloak of flippancy, but the feelings carry him away. In Damascus, on 27 May 1858, he sat down to write to Lady Waldegrave, and to tell her about his visit to Jerusalem. He was moved to write one of the finest of his letters:

There is enough in Jerusalem to set a man thinking for life, & I am deeply glad I have been there. O my nose! O my eyes! O my feet! How you all suffered in that vile place! for let me tell you, physically Jerusalem is the foulest and odiousest place on earth. A bitter doleful soul-ague comes over you in its streets. And your memories of its interior are but horrid dreams of squalor & filth, clamour & uneasiness, hatred & malice & all uncharitableness. But the outside is full of melancholy glory, exquisite beauty & a world of past history of all ages:—every point forcing you to think on a vastly dim receding past, or a time of Roman war & splendour, (for Aelia Capitolium was a fine city) or a smash of Moslem & Crusader years, with long long dull winter of deep decay through centuries of misrule. The Arab & his sheep are alone the wanderers on the pleasant

vallies & breezy hills round Zion: the file of slow camels all that brings to mind the commerce of Tyre and other bygone merchandize. . . .

Poetry lay deep in Lear: a sense of significance, of the natural music of writing. He had a strong sense of color too; and the landscape painter's letters are punctuated with bright little pictures: like the verbal watercolor of the way to Ramleh, "through one almighty green lovely cornfield," with "the long unbroken line of blue-lilac hills." "Nubia delighted me," he writes from Cairo. "Sad, stern, uncompromising landscape, dark ashy purple lines of hills, piles of granite rocks, fringes of palm and ever and anon astonishing ruins of oldest temples: above all wonderful Abou Simbel, which took my breath away." "Imagine 16 worlds of gardens rolled out flat," he writes to Lady Waldegrave, "with a river and a glittering city in the middle, & you have a sort of idea of what the Damascus pianura is like." And then, sitting in Trieste in November 1861, he tells Fortescue:

I shall employ my last hours on earth, —*i.e.* before I embark on the oshun, in writing to you. . . .

All the traffic of Trieste is like gold & silver set in lapis lazuli & emerald, & the air is as lovely as the wision & spectacles. . . .

For with this sense of poetry, this sense of form and color, went a sense of humor: sometimes gentle, sometimes wild, and at times disguising some profound affection or depression. After a visit to Farringford in 1859, when he had enjoyed the comfort of a normal domestic life and the motherly care of Mrs. Tennyson, Lear wrote to Fortescue:

I should think, computing moderately, that 15 angels, several hundreds of ordinary women, many philosophers, a heap of truly wise and kind mothers, 3 or 4 minor prophets, and a lot of doctors and school-mistresses, might all be boiled down, and yet their combined essence fall short of what Emily Tennyson really is. . . .

(12 June 1859)

"A twitching regret" bothered him on leaving Farringford. "At present," he added, sadly, "I am doing little, but dimly walking on along the dusty twilight lanes of incomprehensible life. I wish you were married. I wish I were an egg and was going to be hatched." And then, years later, when Fortescue was married to Lady Waldegrave, Lear found himself reflecting on their afterlife:

Perhaps in the next eggzi stens you and I and My Lady may be able to sit for placid hours under a lotus tree a eating of ice creams and pelican pie, with our feet in a hazure coloured stream and with the birds and beasts of Paradise a sporting around us.

(16 August 1869)

It would be a mistake to look all the time for a deeper meaning in Lear's humor. Much of it is straightforward enough. One need only recall his account of his hunger after an illness: "Hunger! did you ever have a fever? No consideration of morality or sentiment or fear of punishment would prevent my devouring any small child who entered this room now. I have eaten everything in it but a wax-candle and a bad lemon." Then there is the wild account of Nice, with its play on words:

I never was in so dry a place in all my life. When the little children cry, they cry dust and not tears. There is some water in the sea, but not much:—all the wetnurses cease to be so immediately on arriving:—Dryden is the only book read:—the neighbourhood abounds with Dryads and Hammerdryads: and weterinary surgeons are quite unknown. . . .

(24 February 1865)

At the caves of Ipeica, on his Sicilian travels, Lear becomes "acquaint with a family of original Froglodytes: they are," he wrote, "very good creatures, mostly sitting on their hams, & feeding on lettuces & honey." When he has visited the monasteries of Athos, he decides:

More pleasing in the sight of the Almighty I really believe, & more like what Jesus Christ intended man to become, is an honest Turk with 6 wives, or a Jew working hard to feed his little old clo' babbies, than these muttering, miserable, mutton-hating, man-avoiding, misogynic, morose, & merriment-marring, monotoning, many-mule-making, mocking, mournful, minced-fish & marmalade masticating Monx.

(9 October 1856)

Yet this play on words is not the kind of humor we really expect of Lear. What we expect is his familiar nonsense. Sometimes we find it in a phrase, as when he describes the scenery of Gozo as "pomskizillious and gromphibberous"; but sometimes, to our delight, we recognize Lear's nonsense in extenso. Here and there in the letters we come across one of those "spongetanious" passages which only the inventor of the Jumblies could have written:

When the 300 [Tennyson] drawings are done, I shall sell them for £18,000: with which I shall buy a chocolate coloured carriage speckled with gold, and driven by a coachman in green vestments and silver spectacles,—wherein, sitting on a lofty cushion composed of muffins and volumes of the Apocrypha, I shall disport myself all about the London parks, to the general satisfaction of all pious people. . . .

(22 October 1880)

And then, on 6 September 1863, Lear makes a heartfelt request to Chichester Fortescue:

I want you to write to Lord Palmerston to ask him to ask the Queen to ask the King of Greece to give me a "place". As I never asked anything of you before, I think I may rely on your doing this for me. I wish the place to be created a-purpos for me, and the title to be Lord High Bosh and Nonsense Producer, with permission to wear a fool's cap (or mitre)—3 pounds of butter yearly and a little pig,—and a small donkey to ride on. Please don't forget all this, as I have set my heart on it.

And this remark is not so flippant as one might suppose. Lear wanted credit for his nonsense. "I wish," he wrote, "I could have all the credit due to me, small as that may be." And again: "If you are asked ever about that Book of Nonsense, remember I made *all* the verses." Lear took his nonsense in all seriousness. And beneath his nonsense verse, as beneath the nonsense in his letters, there is sometimes unexpected gravity and truth.

THE NONSENSE POET

As we have seen, it was during the 1830's, at Knowsley Hall, that someone had shown Lear the lines beginning: "There was an Old Man of Tobago." The greater part of the first *Book of Nonsense* was then, as he tells us, "struck off with a pen." It was in this verse form and the delight of Lord Derby's grandchildren that the nonsense poet discovered himself:

> There was an old Derry down Derry,
> Who loved to see little folks merry;
> So he made them a Book,
> And with laughter they shook,
> At the fun of that Derry down Derry.

That verse introduced the first *Book of Nonsense* in 1846. But the Derby children were not the only ones that Lear loved to amuse. In his *Mid-Victorian Memories*, R. E. Francillon, the son of a judge at Cheltenham, remembered:

We children were delighted eye-witnesses of some of the earliest poems of the first *Book of Nonsense*. We possessed a good share of the original drawings, made while we stood by the artist's knee, and their attendant limericks were household words, long before there was any thought of their publication.

But, whoever he wrote for, it is plain that Lear was doing more than amusing a young audience. He was escaping from reality, ridding himself of his worries and haunting inhibitions. Lear, understandably, found life hard, and society in general unsympathetic. "They" did not understand the sensitive, "they" did not appreciate the original and enterprising; and again and again in his limericks he lamented and ridiculed the philistine cruelty of the world:

> There was an Old Man of Whitehaven,
> Who danced a quadrille with a Raven;
> But they said—"It's absurd
>   To encourage this bird!"
> So they smashed that Old Man of Whitehaven.

> There was an Old Person of Chester,
> Whom several small children did pester;
> They threw some large stones,
>   Which broke most of his bones,
> And displeased that Old Person of Chester.

But Lear did more than ridicule the harshness of society. In his letters he writes about his uncertainty, his restlessness, his financial insecurity, and, above all, his ugliness. Again and again in his limericks, as a kind of release he jokes about the same things. He laughs at enormous beards, poor eyesight, excessively long legs, fatness, thinness. And, above all, because it is his own most obvious shortcoming, he makes fun of enormous noses:

> There was an Old Man in a Barge,
> Whose nose was exceedingly large;
> But in fishing by night, it supported a light,
> Which helped that Old Man in a Barge.

Holman Hunt tells us that Lear was terrified of dogs. And that, I think, is why the characters in Lear's limericks own dogs far larger than themselves; they are chased by horrible cows, virulent bulls, or—like the Young Lady of Clare—by a ferocious bear. Lear's laughter is a kind of nervous defiance.

Lear earned his hard living by landscape painting; but it is doubtful whether he cared more about his paintings than his nonsense. From the first moment he was delighted by the popularity of his nonsense verse. When the revised edition of his book appeared in 1861, he reminded Chichester Fortescue: "Tell me when you have seen the new *Book of Nonsense*. Please recommend it all you can. . . . Over five hundred copies have already been sold. Please do what you can to increase the sale by axing and talking about it. . . . " He was proud of the £125 he earned from the *Book of Nonsense*—it was almost all he earned from a book which went into nearly 30 editions even in his lifetime; and he was gratified by the eccentric in Corfu

who has taken a kind of monomaniac fancy to my Nonsense Book, and declares that he knew *personally* the Aunt of the Girl of Majorca!! I hear it is more than humanity can bear to hear him point out how exactly like she is—and how she used to jump the walls in Majorca with flying leaps.

(11 January 1863)

So far, Lear had only published limericks. He had not invented the form, but he had introduced it to general notice; henceforward it was to be associated par excellence with his name. Now his nonsense was to take other forms. At Cannes, in the winter of 1868, he met a little girl who inspired him with a masterpiece. Janet Symonds was three years old, the daughter of John Addington Symonds, the author of the *History of the Italian Renaissance* (1886). "Did I tell you how much we see of Mr. Lear?" Symonds asked a friend. "He comes here nearly every day, and nearly every day he brings Janet a fresh picture or poem—a portrait of the *Blue Bird* or the *Red Bird*. . . . " In these birds we can see distinct reminiscences of the salmon-crested cockatoo and the red and yellow macaws, wistfully distorted into nonsense birds with runcible names. It was for Janet Symonds that Lear invented the most famous bird in his aviary; for Symonds he recorded that "one original illustrated song about the Owl and the Pussy-cat who went to sea and got married, she is very fond of and has by heart":

> The Owl and the Pussy-Cat went to sea
>   In a beautiful pea-green boat,
>   They took some honey, and plenty of money,
>   Wrapped up in a five-pound note.

The Owl looked up to the stars above,
And sang to a small guitar,
"O lovely Pussy! O Pussy, my love,
What a beautiful Pussy you are,
You are,
You are!
What a beautiful Pussy you are!"

We owe much of Lear's nonsense to the children he knew; and the next child to inspire him was Hubert Congreve, the son of a former Rugby master living at San Remo. Congreve recalled his first meeting, in the early autumn of 1869, with this tall, bearded, bespectacled gentleman, who asked at once "if I knew who he was, and without waiting for a reply proceeded to tell me a long, nonsense name, compounded of all the languages he knew." From that day to his death, wrote Congreve, "Lear was my dearest and best friend of the older generation. . . . He was always full of interest in our doings, and a week seldom passed without his bringing us a drawing of some event in our lives or of some plant which had flowered in our gardens." And this, perhaps, was the origin of Lear's nonsense botany: of Manypeeplia Upsidownia, of Jinglia Tinkettlia and Nasticreechia Krorluppia. Occasionally the Congreves were invited to dine with him, and he always sent a nonsense menu. It was only natural that nonsense cooking should fascinate him too:

To make Gosky Patties. Take a Pig, 3 or 4 years of age, and tie him by the hind leg to a post. Place 5 pounds of currants, 3 of sugar, 2 pecks of peas, 18 roast chestnuts, a candle, and 6 bushels of turnips, within his reach; if he eats these, continually provide him with more. Then procure some cream, some slices of Cheshire cheese, four quires of foolscap paper, and a packet of black pins. Work the whole into a paste. . . . Visit the paste and beat the Pig alternately for some days, and ascertain if at the end of that period the whole is about to turn into Gosky Patties. If it does not then, it never will. . . .

In the summer of 1870, Lear went to stay at a hotel in the mountains near Turin to complete his *Nonsense Songs, Stories, Botany and Alphabets*. There he met Margaret Terry, the little daughter of an American artist. The child whispered to her mother that she would like to have Lear for an uncle. Lear, delighted, "glowed, bubbled and twinkled more than ever." He became the child's devoted friend and "adopty duncle"; they went for walks in the chestnut forests, where they kicked the chestnut burrs before them, the "yonghy-bonghy-bòs," as they called

them, and Lear sang "The Owl and the Pussycat" "to a funny little crooning tune of his own composition." He drew a complete nonsense alphabet for Margaret Terry, and every day she found a letter of it on her plate at luncheon. Lear's nonsense alphabets must have been a quite unforgettable way of learning reading: we should remember the letter D forever once we had seen "The Dolomphious Duck, who caught Spotted Frogs for her dinner with a Runcible Spoon"; we should know the letter F for all time, once we had met the Fizzgigious Fish.

It is strange that Lear should have chosen to call the chestnuts the "yonghy-bonghy-bòs." A year and more later, on Christmas Day 1871, when his third book, *More Nonsense*, had just appeared, he told Chichester Fortescue that he had just written a poem on the Yongy-Bonghy-Bò. It was the most significant poem he had put on paper. There had been glimpses of Lear himself in his limericks; but "The Courtship of the Yonghy-Bonghy-Bò" takes us much deeper into his private life. It was autobiography that he dared not express in serious writing. He had written the tale of the four little children who went round the world, with a cat and a Quangle-Wangle, for the four children of Lord Westbury, the lord chancellor; and Lord Westbury's unmarried daughter, Augusta Bethell, had inspired him with such affection that, for the only time in his life, he had seriously thought of marriage.

Augusta Bethell was, appropriately, a writer of children's books. She was extremely fond of Lear and would almost certainly have accepted him. But the need for decision made Lear all the more aware of his infirmities. He could not bring himself to propose to her. By some irony of fate, she married a Mr. Parker, who was completely paralyzed—a much more hopeless invalid than Lear himself. When she was widowed, a few years later, she and Lear met often, and with the greatest pleasure on both sides. In 1883, she came to San Remo, and when she had gone, he wrote: "I miss her horridly. So ends the very last possible chance of changing this life." Within a year of his death, he asked her to come again; she came, and he very nearly proposed. "But nothing occurred beyond her very decidedly showing me how much she cared for me. . . . This, I think, was the death of all hope":

"Lady Jingly! Lady Jingly!
Sitting where the pumpkins grow,
Will you come and be my wife?"

Said the Yonghy-Bonghy-Bò.
"I am tired of living singly,—
On this coast so wild and shingly,—
I'm a-weary of my life;
If you'll come and be my wife,
Quite serene would be my life!"—
Said the Yonghy-Bonghy-Bò,
Said the Yonghy-Bonghy-Bò.

. . .

Lady Jingly answered sadly,
And her tears began to flow,—
"Your proposal comes too late,
Mr. Yonghy-Bonghy-Bò!
I would be your wife most gladly!"
(Here she twirled her fingers madly)
"But in England I've a mate!
Yes! you've asked me far too late,
For in England I've a mate,
Mr. Yonghy-Bonghy-Bò!
Mr. Yonghy-Bonghy-Bò!"

. . .

From the Coast of Coromandel
Did that Lady never go;
On that heap of stones she mourns
For the Yonghy-Bonghy-Bò.
On that Coast of Coromandel,
In his jug without a handle,
Still she weeps and daily moans;
On that little heap of stones
To her Dorking Hens she moans
For the Yonghy-Bonghy-Bò,
For the Yonghy-Bonghy-Bò.

The poem appeared in 1877 in *Laughable Lyrics*. This was the fourth, and last, nonsense book to be published in Lear's lifetime, and it is not only an epitome of his art, it is also a pathetic commentary on a life of unhappiness and escape. The old man with his "purely original dress," set upon by children and animals, makes Lear's final comment on the cruelty of society. Mr. and Mrs. Discobbolos seek asylum on the top of a wall, for that is the only place where they are safe from trouble and sorrow. But, above all, it is clear from this book that Lear has now created a complete and self-contained nonsense world. The Quangle-Wangle who had once sailed round the world with the four little children now had a permanent home on the top of the Crumpetty Tree; and the hills of the Chankly Bore, which the Jumblies had once visited, the Great Gromboolian Plain, where the pelicans' daughter was living, were now inhabited by one of Lear's saddest creations. The Dong with a Luminous Nose is Lear himself, still

aware of his ugliness; the Dong, in his vain and constant search for his Jumbly girl, is Lear still dreaming of Augusta. This may be nonsense, but, once again, it is poetic nonsense. It is nonsense with a flavor of Tennyson, the friend whom Lear had consistently admired.

When awful darkness and silence reign
    Over the great Gromboolian plain,
        Through the long, long wintry nights:—
When the angry breakers roar,
As they beat on the rocky shore:—
        When storm-clouds brood on the towering heights
Of the Hills on the Chankly Bore:—

Then, through the vast and gloomy dark,
There moves what seems a fiery spark,
        A lonely spark with silvery rays
        Piercing the coal-black night,—
        A meteor strange and bright:—
Hither and thither the vision strays,
        A single lurid light.

Slowly it wanders,—pauses,—creeps,—
Anon it sparkles,—flashes and leaps;
And ever as onward it gleaming goes
A light on the Bong-tree stems it throws.
And those who watch at that midnight hour
From Hall or Terrace, or lofty Tower,
Cry, as the wild light passes along,—
        "The Dong!—the Dong!
    "The wandering Dong through the forest goes!
    "The Dong!—the Dong!
"The Dong with a luminous Nose!"

In March 1884, Lear fell very ill with pleurisy and inflammation of the lungs; it was May before he could leave San Remo, and even then his manservant had to lift him in and out of railway carriages, because his feet were too swollen for him to walk. Early in June, he sent Chichester Fortescue, now Lord Carlingford, "a few lines just to tell you how your aged friend goes on":

O my agèd Uncle Arly!
Sitting on a heap of Barley
Thro' the silent hours of night,—
Close beside a leafy thicket:—
On his nose there was a cricket,—
In his hat a Railway Ticket,—
(But his shoes were far too tight.)

"My Aged Uncle Arly," Lear told John Ruskin, was "the last Nonsense poem I shall write."

A manuscript copy of "My Aged Uncle Arly" had been sent to Ruskin in gratitude for his letter to the *Pall Mall* magazine. Asked to choose his favorite books, Ruskin had decided:

Surely the most beneficent and innocent of all books yet produced is the *Book of Nonsense*, with its corollary carols—inimitable and refreshing, and perfect in rhythm. I really don't know any author to whom I am half so grateful, for my idle self, as Edward Lear. I shall put him first of my hundred authors.

Lear was enchanted by Ruskin's praise; he was delighted when the *Spectator* called his verse "meloobious" and set examination questions on his work:

1. Comment, with illustrations, upon Mr. Lear's use of the following words: Runcible, dolomphious, borascible. . . .
2. Enumerate accurately all the animals who lived on the Quangle-Wangle's hat. . . .

In a life that was often unhappy, Lear did at least enjoy the beginnings of his immortality.

What is the secret of this immortality? Where is the charm of Lear? It lies (as it always does with poets) in his love of words: their cadences, their very look on the page, their mystery, their endless, exciting power of evocation. Lear played delightedly with language; and if at times he deliberately misused it (where else have we heard "a promiscuous oration"?), even his misuse seems to have a meaning. When the Queen's English proved to be restricting or inadequate, he simply invented a word for his purpose:

> There was an old person of Grange,
> Whose manners were scroobious and strange. . . .

Far be it from us to observe that Lear applies the identical epithet to a snake. Runcible is an adjective which is cheerfully accorded to a spoon, a raven, and a hat. But what does that matter? It is a word, like many others in Lear, which gives us unique, indescribable delight.

Lear coined a vocabulary, and he did so with gusto. I think it is in his gusto that he differs most from Lewis Carroll. One never feels with Lear that his nonsense is an intellectual recreation; one never has the sense of contrivance. We can almost hear him

pottering round his garden at San Remo, spontaneously christening his plants Sophtsluggia Glutinosa, or Minspysia Deliciosa. We can hear the limericks tossed off the moment the first line is given. And yet what art, deliberate or natural, lies behind those apparently casual verses. Lear is the master of the incompatible, the wildly impossible:

> There was an Old Man of Blackheath,
> Whose head was adorned with a wreath,
> Of lobsters and spice, pickled onions and mice,
> That uncommon Old Man of Blackheath.

He is master, too, of the totally unexpected: of the line which catches the reader unawares:

> There was an Old Man of Three Bridges,
> Whose mind was distracted by midges,
> He sate on a wheel, eating underdone veal,
> Which relieved that Old Man of Three Bridges.

Lear understands every kind of humor: the humor of words and the humor of situation; he can be dry, rumbustious, zany, slapstick, and, sometimes, macabre. Occasionally he anticipates and parodies in advance the "automatic writing," the irrational inspiration of the surrealists:

> Mrs. Jaypher found a wafer
> Which she stuck upon a note;
> This she took and gave the cook.
> Then she went and bought a boat
> Which she paddled down the stream
> Shouting: "Ice produces cream,
> Beer when churned produces butter!
> Henceforth all the words I utter
> Distant ages thus shall note—
> From the Jaypher Wisdom-Boat."

But the magic of Lear cannot really be analyzed. The wisest comment on it was made by a critic who, in his nursery days, had come face to face with Edward Lear himself. "As far as I can understand," wrote St. Loe Strachey, talking of *The Lear Coloured Bird Book for Children*,

the charm is due to the fact that in some incomprehensible way Lear has managed to get his personal feeling for childhood to run along the lines of his brush and into the hearts of children. . . .

The fact that remains is that children love Lear's pictures and that Lear meant them to love them, and that is enough.

Perhaps these remarks should also apply to Lear's written nonsense. But if as adults we seek further, we may learn more of Lear by a comparison. Lear is often compared with his contemporary in nonsense, Lewis Carroll; but a world divides them. Carroll approached his nonsense by way of logic and mathematics; Lear approached it through his paintings and through poetry and—which is most important— through life itself. Lear was intensely human—and his humanity, warm and honest and "spongetanious," cannot ever fail to be endearing.

SELECTED BIBLIOGRAPHY

I. BIBLIOGRAPHY. W. B. O. Field, *Edward Lear on My Shelves* (lim. ed., New York, 1933), privately printed, a biography, bibliography, and lists of original drawings, watercolors, lithographs, engravings, and woodcuts; many quotations from reviews and from Lear's diaries covering a period of 30 years.

II. COLLECTED WORKS. *Edward Lear's Nonsense Omnibus* (London, 1943), with intro. by E. Strachey, includes all the original pictures, verses, and stories of the *Book of Nonsense, More Nonsense,* and *Nonsense Songs, Stories, Botany and Alphabets;* R. L. Mégroz, ed., *The Lear Omnibus* (London, 1945); H. Jackson, ed., *The Complete Nonsense of Edward Lear* (London, 1947), with intro. by Jackson.

III. SELECTED WORKS. *Edward Lear's Nonsense Songs* (London, 1938), with the author's own illus.; R. L. Megróz, ed., *A Book of Lear* (London, 1939); B. Reade, *Edward Lear's Parrots* (London, 1949), with a foreword by E. L. Warre, a scholarly account of Lear's interest in natural history, includes 12 repros. of colored lithographs from *Psittacidae,* but they are poorly repro.; H. Van Thal, ed., *Edward Lear's Journals: A Selection* (London, 1952).

IV. SEPARATE WORKS. *Illustrations of the Family of Psittacidae, or Parrots* (London, 1832), contains 42 lithographic plates drawn from life and on stone, most of them figured for the first time; *Views in Rome and Its Environs* (London, 1841), drawn from nature and on stone; *Gleanings from the Menagerie and Aviary at Knowsley Hall* (Knowsley, 1846), printed for private distribution; *Illustrated Excursions in Italy,* 2 vols. (London, 1846); *A Book of Nonsense* (London, 1846), published under the pseudonym Derry Down Derry; *Journals of a Landscape Painter in Albania etc.* (London, 1851); *Journals of a Landscape Painter in Southern Calabria and the Kingdom of Naples* (London, 1852), repr. as *Edward Lear in Southern Italy: Journals of a Landscape Painter in Southern Calabria and the Kingdom of Naples* (London, 1964), with intro. by P. Quennell; *Views in the Seven Ionian Islands* (London, 1863); *Journal of a Landscape Painter in Corsica* (London, 1870); *Nonsense Songs, Stories, Botany and Alphabets* (London, 1871); *More Nonsense, Pictures, Rhymes, Botany* (London, 1872), published just before Christmas 1871 but dated 1872; J. de C. Sowerby, F. L. S., and E. Lear, *Tortoises, Terrapins and Turtles* (London, 1872), drawn from life; *Laughable Lyrics* (London, 1877), a fourth book of nonsense poems, songs, botany, and music; *Poems by Alfred, Lord Tennyson* (London, 1889), illus. by Lear.

Queery Leary Nonsense (London, 1911), with intro. by the earl of Cromer, some pieces, including 3 additional illus. for "The Owl and the Pussycat," appear for the first time, the bird plates are repro. from the drawings made by Lear for the eldest son of Lord Cromer; *The Lear Coloured Bird Book for Children* (London, 1912), with a foreword by J. St. Loe Strachey, originally contained in *Queery Leary Nonsense* but now published separately; *Lear in Sicily* (London, 1938), with intro. by G. Proby, 20 line drawings from a tour in 1847 with J. J. Proby, commentary taken from Lear's letters; A. Davidson and P. Hofer, eds., *Teapots and Quails* (London, 1953), with intro. by Davidson and Hofer, all material previously unpublished except for a few of the limericks, which appeared in W. B. O. Field's *Edward Lear on My Shelves* (1933); R. Murphy, ed., *Edward Lear's Indian Journal* (London, 1953), contains watercolors and extracts from his diary of 1873–1875; *Edward Lear in Greece: Journals of a Landscape Painter in Greece and Albania* (London, 1965); *Lear in the Original. Drawings and Limericks by Edward Lear for His "Book of Nonsense"* (New York–London, 1975), intro. by H. W. Liebert, here first published in facs. together with other unpublished nonsense drawings.

V. LETTERS. Lady Strachey, ed., *Letters of Edward Lear* (London, 1907), facs. ed., contains letters to Chichester Fortescue (Lord Carlingford) and Frances Countess Waldegrave; Lady Strachey, ed., *Later Letters of Edward Lear* (London, 1911), contains letters to Fortescue, Countess Waldegrave, and others; *Letters of Edward Lear,* 2 vols. (New York, 1976).

VI. BIOGRAPHICAL AND CRITICAL STUDIES. A. Davidson, *Edward Lear. Landscape Painter and Nonsense Poet (1812–1888)* (London, 1938; repr. 1950, 1968); E. Sewell, *The Field of Nonsense* (London, 1952), a general study of nonsense writing that draws comparisons and contrasts between Lear, Carroll, and others; P. Hofer, *Edward Lear as Landscape Draughtsman* (London–Cambridge, Mass., 1967), contains numerous repros. together with critical and bibliographical information; V. Noakes, *Edward Lear. The Life of a Wanderer* (London, 1968); J. Lehmann, *Edward Lear and His World* (New York–London, 1977); S. Hyman, *Edward Lear's Birds* (New York, 1980), illus., with intro. by P. Hofer.

ANTHONY TROLLOPE
(1815-1882)

Hugh Sykes Davies

I

ANTHONY TROLLOPE was born on 24 April 1815. His father was a barrister, learned in law, but of difficult temper and impractical in the management of his affairs. The first twenty years of his son's life were overshadowed by the gradual failure of the legal practice and by a series of ill-planned and worse-executed maneuvers to make money in other ways.

The ruin of the family was delayed, and at the last made less ruinous, by Anthony's mother, Frances Trollope. One of her husband's weirdest schemes was to set up a great bazaar in Cincinnati; and he dispatched his wife to America to supervise its building, in a striking medley of classical and oriental styles. Funds were exhausted before it could be stocked with goods, and Mrs. Trollope found herself in penury. She learned from this crisis not only that she must herself take on a great part of the task of supporting her family, but also a possible means of performing it. On her return to England, she wrote her first book, a racy and rather acid study of the American way of life. It was successful, and she went on at once to write novels and other travelogues. When her husband finally became bankrupt in 1834, she took the family to Belgium and supported them by her pen, never laying it aside for long, even while she saw to the housekeeping and tended the death-beds of her favorite son, her husband, and her youngest daughter. Her later days were happier and more prosperous, but she went on writing indefatigably when the financial need had passed. When she died, at the age of eighty-three, she had written forty-one books, and her annual rate of production had not been far below that achieved by Anthony himself. They were both late starters in literature: he was forty when his first book was published, and she fifty-two. For both of them the first conscious aim in writing was to make money; but once started, they both found that it satisfied in them needs much deeper than that of money.

Possibly Trollope inherited from his mother some qualities of mind and spirit that favored quick and copious writing, and certainly he had before him her example of what might be made of these qualities. But the deeper needs that writing came to satisfy were the unhappy by-product of his father's misfortunes. When he was seven, he went to Harrow as a day boy. At twelve, he was moved to his father's old school, Winchester, but taken away three years later because the bills had not been, and could not be, paid. Long before his departure, the other boys had known of the unpaid bills and had made use of their knowledge. "It is the nature of boys to be cruel," he mildly observed of their doings when he wrote of them in later life.[1] But worse was to follow, for he went back to Harrow again as a day boy. By this time his mother was in America, and he was living with his father, unkempt and uncouth, in a gloomy tumbledown farmhouse, from which he tramped twice a day through muddy lanes to sit among the well-fed and smartly dressed boarders. "The indignities I endured are not to be described," he wrote later.

But I was never able to overcome—or even attempt to overcome—the absolute isolation of my school position. Of the cricket-ground or racket-court I was allowed to know nothing. And yet I longed for these things with an exceeding great longing. I coveted popularity with a coveting which was almost mean. It seemed to me that there would be an Elysium in the intimacy of those very boys I was bound to hate because they hated me. Something of the disgrace of my school-days has clung to me all through life.
(vol. I, pp. 22–23)

He was removed from Harrow at last by the bankruptcy of his father and went with the rest of the family to Belgium, to become a useless and aimless witness of their successive deaths. At the age of nine-

[1]A. Trollope, *An Autobiography*, 2 vols. (London, 1883), vol. I, p. 12. All quotes from the autobiography are from this edition.

teen, however, he was wangled by family friends into the Post Office as a junior clerk, with competitive examinations to the civil service still to come. In later life he wrote and spoke vehemently against that mode of recruitment, on the grounds that it would certainly have excluded him and that the service would have lost a good official by his exclusion. Probably he was right on both points, yet it would not have been easy for any department to function with more than one or two Anthony Trollopes on its strength. He was unpunctual and insubordinate, and he got into "scrapes." Once, in an argument with the secretary, he banged a table so hard that it catapulted an inkwell into his chief's face; since the Post Office was at that time ruled by a retired colonel, he was lucky to have escaped dismissal or something worse. And one day the office was invaded by a lady under a vast bonnet, with a basket on her arm, crying loudly, "Anthony Trollope, when are you going to marry my daughter?" He did not have to marry the young lady, but he admitted that "these little incidents were all against me in the office."

This period of his life lasted for seven years, and it is the one period of which he has told us very little. He lived in poor lodgings, spent much time in bars, got into debt, and made his one and only acquaintance with a moneylender. He began, however, to make friends, and after the disgrace of his schooldays, it meant much to him that men of his own age were willing to like him, to talk with him, and to spend their weekends walking with him. In the office, he kept his place, largely because he turned out to be very good at writing letters, and in the end even his "scrapes" did him a backhanded service, for the ink-stained colonel recommended him for a job in Ireland, as the best way to be rid of him.

It was a very great service, however backhanded. Ireland accomplished a transformation in him hardly less dramatic than that which characterizes the life cycles of insects. Hitherto, his state had been dark and larval, or chrysalid at best, and his days had been spent in obscurity and lonely poverty. "From the day on which I set foot in Ireland," he wrote, "all these evils went away from me. Since that time who has had a happier life than mine?" The essence of the Irish magic was that for the first time he found himself among people who liked him, who did not regard him as a shameful and useless encumbrance. The work was not in an office under superiors, but in the open air on his own, riding up and down, making arrangements or putting disarrangements to rights.

He became good at the work itself, and passionately fond of riding. He took to hunting and found a hobby that was his only major addiction to the end of his life. After three years of this new life, he married, was promoted, and soon began to write his first novel.

He spent most of his time in Ireland until 1859, and remained in the Post Office until 1867. He rose from being an ill-reputed and difficult clerk to being an efficient but still rather difficult public servant, with a flair for negotiating with all kinds of people, of many nations. He had a fine eye for the practical—he was the inventor of the English pillar-box. Above all, he made himself useful to his department in ways that meant that he was kept on his travels, rather than in an office. He came to know many parts of Britain itself, and visited Egypt, America, and the West Indies on postal business. He hunted two days a week, and became a haunter of London clubs, partly for the sake of whist, partly because his acquaintance was now reaching up into higher circles of society and letters. And on top of all this, he wrote at the average rate of 1.7 books per annum and made money by them.

In middle life, he found all that he had missed as a boy—respect, friendship, and worldly success. And he enjoyed it all, hugely and noisily. He banged about the world, rode about Essex and other hunting counties, fell off his horse and lost his spectacles and laughed, dined at the club and laughed, dined at home or with his friends and laughed. In 1882, he was laughing at a comic book read aloud with his family after dinner when he had a stroke, from which he died a month later, on 6 December.

He had been successful and had valued his success all the more because of his early failures. "To be known as somebody,—" he wrote, "to be Anthony Trollope if it be no more,—is to me much." But to understand both the man and his work, it is necessary to set this beside that other verdict: "Something of the disgrace of my school-days has clung to me all through life."

II

THE above quotations are all from Trollope's *Autobiography*, written in 1875–1876, but not published until 1883, a year after his death. Its reputation has kept pace with the recent revival of respect for his novels, and it is now probably one of the most widely read of English autobiographies. This modest popularity it well deserves. As an account of his life, it is so complete and so just that his biographers have added little to its detail and less to its broad outline. It is in no sense a work of intimate self-revelation, and was not intended to be. It is rather a tour de force of self-description by a man who, sitting for his own portrait, drew it with that deceptive first appearance of prosaic fidelity that serves as the clue to the undermining irony of his male portraits (he is rarely ironic about women). To the serious business of self-regard he brought the same standards that inform his portraits of others, with results hardly less fictional.

Yet the self-portrait is a little uneven, clearly delineated where his habitual perceptions were strong, but fainter and more confused where they were weak. His strength lay in describing the manners and morals of the world in which he was so anxious to bear—and even more anxious to deserve—a good name; and in his account of his dealings with this world, he had a natural rightness and honesty that enabled him to behave well, and to describe clearly. His moral standards were not, perhaps, very profound or very subtle, but they were worthy and workable, and they made his conduct better than that of many men who were his superiors in moral perception. His weakness lay rather in his attitude to his own writing and to literature in general. Here he fell into confusions and distortions that have harmed his reputation and—what is worse—damaged his work.

The problem for him lay in a simple contradiction. On the one hand, he was trying to rise in the world by writing novels; on the other hand, the world into which he wished to rise did not have a high regard for novels, or for those who wrote them. "Thinking much," he said, "of my own daily labour and of its nature, I felt myself at first to be much afflicted and then to be deeply grieved by the opinion expressed by wise and thinking men as to the work done by novelists." To this problem, he found two possible answers. Very early in his career as a novelist he proposed to write a history of English prose fiction, which was to have "vindicated my own profession as a novelist" by demonstrating in the work of his predecessors and contemporaries "that high character which they may claim to have earned by their grace, their honesty, and good teaching." But this history was never written, though a few of its leading ideas are suggested briefly in chapters 12 and 13 of the *Autobiography*. The other possible answer, on the contrary, was given fully, loudly, and insistently throughout the book. It was that novel writing should be regarded as a profession like any other and that the object of the novelist, like that of every other professional man, was to make money for himself and his dependents. This object was not an unworthy nor a base one. He wrote:

But it is a mistake to suppose that a man is a better man because he despises money. Few do so, and those few in doing so suffer a defect. Who does not desire to be hospitable to his friends, generous to the poor, liberal to all, munificent to his children, and to be himself free from the carking fears which poverty creates?

(vol. I, p. 142)

This was the answer to which he committed himself, and it was elaborated in almost every account he gave of his dealings with publishers, up to the last page of the *Autobiography*, with its detailed financial statement of his earnings from each of his books, meticulously totaled to £68,939 17s. 5d.

It was, perhaps, the answer most likely to impress the world that he sought to impress. The men he met in the hunting field, or over the card table at his club, were more likely to accept it than that other argument about the good done by novelists in the moral education of their readers; and they were more likely to welcome among them a professional man just such as they were themselves—barristers, clergymen, engineers—who made no claim to be doing more than earning a good living. But though it was perhaps well fitted for this purpose, it was wrong, even perversely wrong. The novelist is not, of course, exempt from the common necessity of earning a living. But he earns it as a novelist, rather than as a barrister, a clergyman, an engineer, a politician, or a confidence trickster, because his tastes and abilities carry him to the novel rather than to any of these other lucrative activities. Yet although Trollope could not or would not see this, it is typical of him that he gave a faithful report of the manner in which his own tastes and abilities were turned in this direction. Writing of those disgraced schooldays, and of the hardly less-disgraced years as a clerk in the Post Office, he said:

I was always going about with some castles in the air firmly built within my mind. Nor were these efforts at architecture spasmodic or subject to constant change from day to day. For weeks, for months, if I remember rightly, from year to year, I would carry on the same tale, binding myself down to certain laws, to certain proportions. . . . Nothing impossible was ever introduced,—nor anything which, from outward circumstances, would seem to be violently improbable. . . . This had been the occupation of my life for six or seven years before I went to the Post Office, and was by no means abandoned when I commenced my work. There can, I imagine, hardly be a more dangerous mental practice; but I have often doubted whether, had it not been my practice, I should ever have written a novel. I learned in this way to maintain an interest in a fictitious story, to dwell on a work created by my own imagination, and to live in a world altogether outside the world of my own material life.

(vol. I, pp. 57–58)

It is here, and not in the passages on moneymaking, that Trollope describes his real impulse to write novels. He became a writer, not because of his need for money but because of his talent for imaginative daydreams. It was natural that he should have confused the need with the talent, for both drew their strength from the same source. The former was a conscious passion, almost an obsession, because it was the outward symbol of his desire to rise above those early outward troubles, and the latter also was passionate, but more obscurely, because it had been his hidden inner resource against them. The confusion was natural, but nonetheless unfortunate. At first it prevented him from discovering where his true gift lay, and even after this discovery, he underrated its value in himself. In deference to the standards of the hunting field and the club, he abused and exploited it by writing too much and too quickly, without waiting for his imagination to gather weight and depth. Like some of the more enterprising bankers of his time, he possessed genuine gold, but made it serve to support a recklessly diffuse paper circulation.

III

MISCONCEIVING both his own powers and the nature of fiction, Trollope fell an easy prey to the shallower notions of his age about the way novels should be written. It was his job, he supposed, as an honest professional man, to provide his customers with the commodity they expected; and what they expected, he was taught to believe, was "realism," slices of life faithfully observed and entertainingly told, with a few touches of wholesome morality. When he first resolved to write a novel, the life that lay under his eyes was that of Ireland, so he cut a few slices from it, observed them industriously, and wrote them down as best he could. His two Irish novels were failures, as they deserved to be. A historical novel followed, as dismally cluttered up with book learning as the Irish novels had been by unimaginative reporting. Then he tried his hand at a guidebook; but the publishers to whom specimens were sent omitted to read them, and the project was dropped.

He was turned from these false starts, from his conception of the novel as a mere animated guidebook, not by any growth of literary perception on his own part, but by a lucky accident of his official career. In 1851, he was given the task of organizing country posts in South West England, and for two happy years he rode up and down and about in six or seven counties, visiting many places, meeting many people, but always in a hurry. It was his first experience of England outside London, and its combination of variety and hurry was exactly what his imagination needed to work upon; the materials offered to it were extensive, but he moved too quickly to become bogged down anywhere. From these wanderings he got not another careful slice of life, but a hazy, rich impression of towns and villages, of churches and country houses, of clergy and laity, and of the quietly intricate patterns of their manners and social life. It was upon this impression that he based his first truly imaginative novel, *The Warden* (1855), the first of the Barsetshire series, which has come to be regarded as his highest achievement. The book was conceived one summer evening in Salisbury, but the Barchester of the novels was never merely Salisbury, nor was the county round it any one of the counties through which he had traveled. It was pieced together from memories of them all, and though it grew to be so clear in his head that he once drew a very detailed map of it, its air of convincing reality was imaginative, not geographical. In the same way, the clergy who were its main characters were not of his acquaintance. He tells us in the *Autobiography*:

I never lived in any cathedral city,—except London, never knew anything of any Close, and at that time had enjoyed no peculiar intimacy with any clergyman. My archdeacon, who has been said to be life-like, and for whom I confess I have all a parent's fond affection, was, I think, the simple result of an effort of my moral consciousness. . . . I had not then even spoken to an archdeacon.

(vol. I, p. 124)

Similarly, the great journalist Tom Towers was thought to be very like an eminent man of the staff of the *Times* (London), and the *Times* itself, in its review of *The Warden*, mildly rebuked the author for indulging in personalities. Trollope protests:

But at that time, living away in Ireland, I had not even heard the name of any gentleman connected with *The Times* newspaper, and could not have intended to represent any individual by Tom Towers. As I had created an archdeacon, so I had created a journalist. . . . my moral consciousness must again have been very powerful.

(vol. I, p. 133)

This gift for the imaginative creation of character by the use of his "moral consciousness" was revealed for the first time in *The Warden*, but it had been developed through those long years of daydreaming, and in its own rather unusual direction. His private fantasies had not been adventurous, nor had they conferred upon him glittering social status. "I never became a king," he tells us,

or a duke . . . a learned man, nor even a philosopher. But I was a very clever person, and beautiful young women used to be fond of me. And I strove to be kind of heart, and open of hand, and noble in thought, despising mean things; and altogether I was a very much better fellow than I have ever succeeded in being since.

(vol. I, pp. 57–58)

This passionate and genuinely imaginative concern with moral existence was the essence of his approach to the novel, from *The Warden* onward. Above all, it was his chief means of insight into character and its depiction. The physical characteristics of his personages are rarely made clearly visible, though they are often conscientiously described. It is their moral physiognomies that are sharply drawn, through what they do and say, what they are said to think and feel, and not seldom by direct comments upon them from their maker.

In the type of moral character chosen for portrayal, *The Warden* set the pattern to which he kept in nearly all his later novels. There was no villain, indeed no character much below the middle range of the moral scale, nor was there anyone conspicuously above it, save the Warden himself. Trollope became

exactly what he wished, the moral historian of men and women in the middle range, the usual run of humanity—"with no more of excellence, nor with exaggerated baseness—so that my readers might recognize human beings like to themselves, and not feel themselves to be carried away among gods or demons."

Finally, *The Warden* was typical of all the novels that were to follow in its disregard for plot. It would, indeed, have been incompatible with his choice of the middle range of characters to have involved them in sensational and complicated situations: ordinary people commonly lead ordinary lives. But apart from this, the elaboration of remarkable incident was quite irrelevant to his main purpose—the depiction of moral character. It mattered little to him how his creatures were set in motion, for once they were on the move they had so great a capacity for living their own lives. In *The Warden* itself, he posed them a problem about the proper use of church endowments, a contemporary, if not a burning, issue: just such a case had arisen in Winchester when he was at school there, and was still before the courts many years after he had written this book. But he himself had no clear view of its rights and wrongs, nor did he need one. All that he needed was the opportunity to let his imagination play upon its issues and cross-issues, as they would appear to differing modes and degrees of moral sensibility. And it was in the process of doing this that men and women—not issues—came alive under his hand.

IV

THE intense moral realization of his characters gave them, once created, a very tenacious hold upon his imagination: so tenacious that he was often unwilling, almost unable, to let them go. His two most notable creations in *The Warden* were of this kind, and they were carried on into *Barchester Towers* (1857), *Doctor Thorne* (1858), *Framley Parsonage* (1861), and *The Last Chronicle of Barset* (1867). Other characters were added, of course, and some of them obtained almost as close a grip on their author's affections. Many other novels were written in the same period. But Archdeacon Grantly and his father-in-law went on leading their lives in his imagination, growing older as he grew older, yet always themselves as he remained himself. Of the two, the archdeacon was the more prominent and active, and much more akin to Trollope. His father-in-law, who had been Warden in the first book, stood at the upper limit of Trollope's moral range, and once he had made his great decision in that first episode, there was little for him to do in the world but be gentle to his family and friends, play his cello, and take good care of the music in the cathedral. Yet he did all this in such a way that we are made to feel his virtue, his religion even, beyond any description that Trollope felt able to give. The archdeacon was coarser in grain, quick to anger, but quick to forget his anger, more worldly, but generous and warmhearted. The two existed side by side, as characters must often do in fiction, making a richer pattern by their contrasting qualities than they could ever have made separately. When the older man came to die, it was through the mouth of the archdeacon that Trollope expressed his estimate both of the dying man and of the archdeacon:

> "I feel sure that he never had an impure fancy in his mind, or a faulty wish in his heart. His tenderness has surpassed the tenderness of woman; and yet, when occasion came for showing it, he had all the spirit of a hero. I shall never forget his resignation of the hospital. . . . The fact is, he never was wrong. He couldn't go wrong. He lacked guile, and he feared God,—and a man who does both will never go far astray. I don't think he ever coveted aught in his life,—except a new case for his violoncello and somebody to listen to him when he played it." Then the archdeacon got up, and walked about the room in his enthusiasm; and, perhaps, as he walked some thoughts as to the sterner ambition of his own life passed through his mind. What things had he coveted? Had he lacked guile? He told himself that he had feared God,—but he was not sure that he was telling himself the truth even in that.
>
> (*The Last Chronicle of Barset*, ch. 81)

Nothing is more like Trollope himself than this moment of explosive self-perception. The archdeacon, like his creator, had standards by which to measure his fellow men, and he was tolerably sure of their general rightness. But when he came to ask how far he himself measured up to them, he had his awkward moments. He had coveted many things greatly: a bishopric, power, the ruin of his enemies, wealth, and, above all in his later days, the glory of his children. He had indeed done his best for them, and they had not done badly for him. His daughter was a marchioness, and though her husband the marquess was unquestionably a moron, she was still unques-

tionably a marchioness. His eldest son, Henry, had done well in the Indian Army, had won the Victoria Cross and a wife with a little money. The wife had died, leaving the young widower with a baby daughter, but Henry still had his fine record, some money of his own, and a handsome allowance from his father. He had retired from the army, and settled in Barsetshire as a country squire, with land and farms and horses and foxes of his own.

All this had been achieved by stern ambition, and not without guile; and whatever God might think about it, the archdeacon was usually well pleased with his achievements. In *The Last Chronicle of Barset*, he was sorely tried because Henry fell deeply in love with a young woman, the daughter of a cleric who was the very opposite of himself—pious, very poor, unworldly, and, to make the worst of an already bad job, awaiting his trial on a charge of stealing a check. So outrageous was Henry's choice that his father opposed this new marriage, even threatened to stop the allowance. The struggle between father and son was long and obstinate on both sides, and even the mother's intervention was not able to end it. It was brought to its climax, and at the same instant to its solution, in an interview between the archdeacon and the girl herself, which illustrates as comprehensively as any passage in Trollope both the emotional force of which he was capable and the moral standards that he accepted without question. The first part of the interview does her credit—more credit than the archdeacon had expected. She refers to her father's disgrace, and gives her promise that unless his name is cleared, she will marry nobody:

> The archdeacon had now left the rug, and advanced till he was almost close to the chair on which Grace was sitting. "My dear," he said, "what you say does you very much honour—very much honour indeed." Now that he was close to her, he could look into her eyes, and he could see the exact form of her features, and could understand—could not help understanding—the character of her countenance. It was a noble face, having in it nothing that was poor, nothing that was mean, nothing that was shapeless. It was a face that promised infinite beauty, with a promise that was on the very verge of fulfilment. There was a play about her mouth as she spoke, and a curl in her nostrils as the eager words came from her, which almost made the selfish father give way. Why had they not told him that she was such a one as this? Why had not Henry himself spoken of the speciality of her beauty? No man in England knew better than the archdeacon the difference between beauty of one kind and beauty of another kind in a woman's

face—the one beauty, which comes from health and youth and animal spirits, and which belongs to the miller's daughter, and the other beauty, which shows itself in fine lines and a noble spirit—the beauty which comes from breeding. "What you say does you very much honour indeed," said the archdeacon.

"I should not mind at all about being poor," said Grace.

"No; no; no," said the archdeacon.

"Poor as we are—and no clergyman, I think, ever was so poor—I should have done as your son asked me at once, if it had been only that—because I love him."

"If you love him you will not wish to injure him."

"I will not injure him. Sir, there is my promise." And now as she spoke she rose from her chair, and standing close to the archdeacon, laid her hand very lightly on the sleeve of his coat. "There is my promise. As long as people say that papa stole the money, I will never marry your son. There."

The archdeacon was still looking down at her, and feeling the slight touch of her fingers, raised his arm a little as though to welcome the pressure. He looked into her eyes, which were turned eagerly towards his, and when doing so he was sure that the promise would be kept. It would have been sacrilege—he felt that it would have been sacrilege—to doubt such a promise. He almost relented. His soft heart, which was never very well under his own control, gave way so far that he was nearly moved to tell her that, on his son's behalf, he acquitted her of the promise. . . . As he looked down upon her face two tears formed themselves in his eyes and gradually trickled down his old nose. "My dear," he said, "if this cloud passes away from you, you shall come to us and be my daughter." And thus he pledged himself. There was a dash of generosity about the man, in spite of his selfishness, which always made him desirous of giving largely to those who gave largely to him. He would fain that his gifts should be bigger, if it were possible. . . . He had contrived that her hand should fall from his arm into his grasp, and now for a moment he held it. "You are a good girl," he said—"a dear, dear, good girl. When this cloud has passed away, you shall come to us and be our daughter."

(*The Last Chronicle of Barset*, ch. 57)

It was thus that Trollope created the most solid of his male characters, by a temporary merging of his own personality in theirs: here, he has all but put himself into the archdeacon's shoes and gaiters. But the merging was never uncritical, because he was critical of himself; he was always capable of qualifying a virtue, of noting an unworthy doubt, and took frequent pleasure in slight backhanded ironies at the expense of their inner weaknesses, as he did at the expense of his own.

As for the girls, he was inclined to be in love with them in the same vicarious fashion. His contemporaries, we are informed by a review written in 1867, liked to make gentle jokes about his intimacy with the minds of his heroines: How, they asked, had he managed to "find it all out"? And shortly after Trollope's death, Henry James accurately noted the nature of his relation with them:

Trollope settled down steadily to the English girl; he took possession of her, and turned her inside out. He never made her the subject of heartless satire . . . he bestowed upon her the most serious, the most patient, the most tender, the most copious consideration. He is evidently always more or less in love with her. . . . But . . . if he was a lover, he was a paternal lover. . . .[2]

It was, indeed, the English girl who saved Trollope from the labor of devising plots. She was there to be loved, and love for her was enough to set in motion not only one or two young men, but their families too. For only if the love went hand in hand with an income large enough to support marriage—and marriage in the style to which both parties were accustomed—could it run smoothly. All that was needful, then, to produce a story with situations full of doubt and perplexity was to bring the power of love into conflict with the demands of property and social status. The ensuing confusion would involve not only the lovers, but their families and friends, and as wide a circle of acquaintance as might be needed to fill a three-volume novel. Trollope made this discovery early in the Barsetshire series, and thenceforward he never bothered his head with plots. "When I sit down to write a novel," he blandly observed, "I do not at all know, and I do not very much care, how it is to end." For this relief, he was almost entirely indebted to the English girl with her ability to inspire love, and to the Victorian sense of property with its inveterate tendency to make love injudicious. As the great tragic conflicts in French classical plays tend to arise from the opposition of love and honor, so Trollope's arose from love and property.

But it would be unjust to present him as becoming thus involved only with young lovers, or with characters on the whole amiable and admirable. Such was his involvement in any creation of his own that he was almost equally capable of becoming devoted to personages neither young nor amiable. In the Barsetshire novels, for example, the archdeacon's

---

[2]H. James, *Partial Portraits* (London, 1888), p. 127.

archenemy is Mrs. Proudie, wife of the bishop and mistress of the palace that the archdeacon had coveted so much, and that his father had held before him. Mrs. Proudie is probably the best-known virago in English fiction, above all for her achievements in henpecking her husband, yet even to her, Trollope developed a powerful attachment. The manner of her death was curious. One night at his club, he heard two clergymen criticizing him for carrying the same characters from novel to novel, and they were very hard on Mrs. Proudie. "I got up, and standing between them, I acknowledged myself to be the culprit. 'As to Mrs Proudie,' I said, 'I will go home and kill her before the week is over.' And so I did. . . . but I have never dissevered myself from Mrs Proudie, and still live much in company with her ghost" (vol. II, pp. 109–110).

V

THE Barsetshire novels have come to be regarded as Trollope's chief, if not his only, contribution to literature, both by the common reader and by the general run of critics and literary historians. They hold this position partly through their own merits of character and milieu, but partly because they can so easily be made to satisfy the common reader's most common weakness in his choice of fiction, his liking for some more or less adult fairyland where he can take a well-earned holiday from the tougher and duller realities of his own life. "Barset," J. B. Priestley has observed, "is a haven of rest." It is natural enough that novels whose main setting was rural England, and whose main characters were so often country clergy, should have been appreciated in this way. But it is an injustice to this series of novels to perceive in them no more than pleasant placidity, and it can easily lead to a still greater injustice in estimating Trollope's work. For the more solid qualities in this series are to be found in many of his other novels, where the milieu is less obviously fairylike, but where his central virtue of moral imagination shows itself both with greater depth and with wider range.

These qualities are nowhere more massively developed than in the linked series of novels that ran through his later life, much as the Barsetshire series had run through his earlier years, the "political" novels whose central characters are Plantagenet Palliser and his wife, Glencora: *Can You Forgive Her?* (1864–1865), *Phineas Finn* (1869), *The Eustace Diamonds* (1873), *Phineas Redux* (1874), *The Prime Minister* (1876), and *The Duke's Children* (1880).

The main setting has moved from Barsetshire to London, and the main characters are men of wealth and high social status, leaders in their professions and in the House of Commons. The general impression is one of greater "realism," at any rate insofar as this world is clearly more remote from any conceivable fairyland than Barsetshire had been. But, in following Trollope's achievement in this less idyllic milieu, it is even more necessary to realize how much it issued from his imagination. It had been the dread of his boyhood, as he walked to Harrow along the muddy lanes, that "mud and solitude and poverty" would be his lot through his whole life. "Those lads about me would go into Parliament, or become rectors and deans, or squires of parishes, or advocates thundering at the Bar," he supposed; and he told himself that he would never live among them. But with the success of his middle years, he had after all risen to live among them. He knew members of Parliament, thundering barristers, and the brother of his closest friend was dean of Ely. And in 1868, he tried to rise still higher, by standing as a candidate for Parliament himself, at Beverley. He was defeated, and both the fact and the manner of his defeat left a very sore place in his spirit. But if he could rise no further himself, his imagination could go where it liked, and its expeditions were the main impulse of the political novels. This was his own view of them, and as usual he saw himself with accuracy:

By no amount of description or asseveration could I succeed in making any reader understand how much these characters [Palliser and Lady Glencora] with their belongings have been to me in my later life; or how frequently I have used them for the expression of my political and social convictions. They have been as real to me as free trade was to Mr Cobden, or the dominion of a party to Mr Disraeli; and as I have not been able to speak from the benches of the House of Commons . . . they have served me as safety-valves by which to deliver my soul.

(vol. I, pp. 240–241)

In this way, his defeat at Beverley gave him a new imaginative impulse, and at the same time ensured that his imagination would not get itself bogged down in too much minute observation. His acquaintance with the political world, like his earlier survey of South West England, was both wide and vague enough to give him precisely the kind of rich but hazy impression that left his imagination neither starved nor shackled.

In the political novels, as in the earlier series, there is a vast array of characters, and most of them are set and kept in motion by Trollope's usual forces, love and property. But in the central character, Plantagenet Palliser, the chief interest is subtler and deeper. It is a long, full study of a conscience, delicate in itself, and even more perplexed because its owner has wealth, a dukedom, political power, and a very thin skin. The close of *The Prime Minister* is a good example of what Trollope's "moral consciousness" could make of this material. Palliser has been prime minister for three years, as head of a coalition government. When it falls, his old friend and ally, the duke of St. Bungay, expresses the hope that he will take some office in the next cabinet. "I don't think I could do that," Palliser told him, "Caesar could hardly lead a legion under Pompey." But when their talk was over, he found himself regretting "that apparently pompous speech by Caesar. . . . Who was he that he should class himself among the great ones of the world." In the days that followed, this moment of unintended arrogance irked him almost more than the end of his power and the formation of a new administration. A few weeks later, he was talking with his former chancellor of the exchequer, one of the few political allies he respected, and by him he was given this assurance:

"If the country is to lose your services for the long course of years during which you will probably sit in Parliament, then I shall think that the country has lost more than it has gained by the Coalition."

The Duke sat for a while silent, looking at the view, and, before answering Mr Monk,—while arranging his answer, —once or twice in a half-absent way called his companion's attention to the scene before him. But, during this time he was going through an act of painful repentance. He was condemning himself for a word or two that had been ill-spoken by himself, and which, since the moment of its utterance, he had never ceased to remember with shame. He told himself now, after his own secret fashion, that he must do penance for these words by the humiliation of a direct contradiction of them. He must declare that Caesar would at some future time be prepared to serve under Pompey. Then he made his answer.

(ch. 80)

This is a more interesting process of the moral life than any studied in the Barset novels, and the obser-vation is more penetrating: few moralists have noted so clearly the part that a small phrase, almost a chance phrase, can play in bringing the fluid confusions of the inner life to a point where they crystallize into decision.

But the fine conscience of Plantagenet Palliser is more than an individual study. It is also at the center of Trollope's political world, and he finds in it the explanation of a process of change in England that was otherwise mystifying. He was himself a Liberal, though with many touches of the Tory in his temperament. He approved in general of the slow process of amelioration that was going on in his day, the gradual spread of democracy and of education to wider sections of the population. He even approved of the extension of the franchise, but at the same time he wondered at the fact that some of the great Whigs, especially those of wealth and title, should be willing to use their political influence for its destruction, by encouraging it to pass into the hands of millions of men with votes to be cast in secret ballot. Palliser is that type of Whig, and in his exact and exacting conscience Trollope finds the explanation of this remarkable change. No other English novelist, and few historians, saw the problem so clearly and advanced so convincing a solution for it.

It is this extension of his "moral consciousness" to the whole pattern of English life that informs the political novels and justifies to the full the remarkable tribute that Henry James paid Trollope a few years after his death:

Trollope will remain one of the most trustworthy, though not one of the most eloquent, of writers who have helped the heart of man to know itself. . . . His natural rightness and purity are so real that the good things he projects must be real. A race is fortunate when it has a good deal of the sort of imagination—of imaginative feeling—that had fallen to the share of Anthony Trollope; and in this possession our English race is not poor.

(*Partial Portraits*, p. 133)

VI

TROLLOPE wrote forty-seven novels, and since few readers will wish to read them all, some answer is needed to the question, which are most worth reading? It is not easy to find one, for quite apart from the large number involved, there are few that fall markedly below his usual level, and perhaps even fewer that rise much above it.

The verdict of the common reader has always been that the Barset series should be regarded as his best and most typical work, and that there is little point in going much further with him. His more serious and persistent readers, however, generally believe that the "political" series is at least as good and very probably better. Beyond this, there is confusion. Are the other three dozen novels merely an extension of the Trollopian world over a wider area, a repetition of his favorite themes and his familiar types of character under new names and against slightly shifted scenery? Or do some of them present qualities not to be found anywhere in the two central series?

The second argument has been urged with much force in a study by A. O. J. Cockshut, which sets out to alter radically the accepted view of Trollope's whole work.[3] It contends that Trollope's outlook was, especially in the later part of his life, much less superficial than has usually been supposed, less orthodox, less bluffly optimistic, and more prone to question the assumptions of the age about morality and property. In the light of this contention, the emphasis of attention is changed both within the two main series and in the novels outside them. In the Barset novels, it falls above all on the lonely agony of Mr. Crawley, the clergyman wrongly accused of stealing a check, but not sure within himself that he is innocent. In the "political" series, it falls upon the madness of Mr. Kennedy in *Phineas Finn* and *Phineas Redux*, and the appalling loneliness of his wife, Lady Laura, who has married him for his money—or at least refused to marry the man she really loved because he had no money. And in *The Eustace Diamonds*, Cockshut finds Trollope's first decisive movement toward satire, and to a view of goods and chattels not wholeheartedly Victorian. With this alteration of emphasis in the better-known novels, there goes the claim that what is most important in them was often more fully developed elsewhere. The gloom and loneliness of the individual, for example, was explored most deeply in *He Knew He Was Right* (1869), which traces the degeneration of a husband from unreasonable jealousy of his wife into actual madness. The fullest development of satire is in *The Way We Live Now* (1875), and of the attack on property and inheritance in *Mr. Scarborough's Family*

(1883). These and other of the outlying novels Cockshut would place in the forefront of Trollope's work.

This study has been usefully done; it provokes a more careful reading of some perhaps unduly neglected novels in the later period and corrects some wrong impressions about those which have been widely read. Cockshut, moreover, has drawn together very skillfully the evidence of Trollope's passionate interest in certain situations and characters: the almost inevitably bad relations between fathers and sons, the "snarling intimacy of family life," the desperation of girls whose only future is marriage and whose labor in life is to entrap a suitably endowed husband. And yet the direction of the emphasis is wrong; it runs too directly against the main current of criticism. In his own day, Trollope's reviewers constantly stressed his choice of the middle range of humanity, of the ordinary man or woman, even of the commonplace; they only wondered at his power of making it interesting, without distortion and without much apparent imaginative heightening of color. Henry James's phrase succinctly comprehends the whole contemporary impression: "His great, his inestimable merit was a complete appreciation of the usual." The judgment is the more weighty because a writer's contemporaries very rarely mistake the nature of his merit, though they often misjudge its degree. In concentrating so much attention upon Trollope's handling of the unusual, the heterodox, Cockshut has indulged in an exaggeration, even if a useful one.

My own conviction is that all the essential qualities of Trollope are to be found in the two central series, and that there they are balanced in their right proportions. Outside them, only a few novels appear to me to have a really strong claim on the general reader.

The first is *The Way We Live Now*. It was written in 1873, and it savagely satirized the new power of financiers and speculators in English life. Trollope saw them compassing the ruin, or at least the degradation, of the landed gentry, literature, the press, social life, even the court itself. It is a magnificently sustained piece of anger, imaginatively realized and dramatically presented. The last act of its great villain, Augustus Melmotte, ruined, drunk, and defiant, trying to speak in Parliament, and glowering angrily but speechlessly round the House, has a force, both immediate and symbolic, beyond Trollope's usual range. In 1876 *The Prime Minister* ap-

---

[3]A. O. J. Cockshut, *Anthony Trollope: A Critical Study* (London, 1955).

peared, and in it the new corruption of finance was represented by a small-scale swindler, Lopez. Had Trollope but waited for his imagination to devise and select, he might have put the far greater figure of Melmotte in the same place. A novel in which Plantagenet Palliser was opposed to Melmotte, politically, morally, and imaginatively, would in all probability have been Trollope's unquestioned masterpiece, his most complete comment on the values of his age. That it did not get written is the heaviest single penalty he paid for his precipitation in covering the daily stint of paper. But even so, *The Way We Live Now* deserves to be read more widely and to be allowed a distinguished place beside the main political novels.

The second novel that I would specially commend is *The Claverings*, published in 1867. It is a work of a very different kind. It is short and has a concentration of effect unusual in Trollope. There is no subplot to distract the development of the central situation, and all the characters play real parts in it. The main problem it explores, the hesitations and weaknesses of a young man caught between a beautiful but poor young girl to whom he is engaged and an equally beautiful but rich widow whom he had loved before her marriage, is exactly of the kind to display at its best Trollope's ability to analyze the unheroic but not quite base man of common mold. But it is above all in its style that it is distinctive. For the most part, Trollope's manner of writing is adequate rather than eloquent, and so impersonal that one often feels it might have been practiced by almost anyone else in the same period: though it is remarkable how surely, in fact, a fair specimen of his work can be recognized for what it is. In *The Claverings*, however, more than in any other book, he showed what he could do when he was neither writing against the clock, nor merely "for length" (the dreadful phrase is his own). It is not merely that as a whole the book is better written than most of the others, but that it also shows some of his subtler qualities of style more clearly than the rest.

There is, for example, a turn of phrase almost peculiar to him, and very characteristic of his ironically intimate report of the inner life: it depends upon the addition of some slight qualification to a previous statement. An example has been given already from the archdeacon's reflections:

He told himself that he had feared God, —but he was not sure that he was telling himself the truth even in that.

Here are the others:

"If I were to name the class of men whose lives are spent with the most thorough enjoyment, I think I should name that of barristers who are in large practice and also in Parliament."
"Isn't it a great grind, sir?" asked Silverbridge.
"A very great grind, as you call it. And there may be the grind but not the success. But—" He had now got up from his seat at the table and was standing with his back against the chimney-piece, and as he went on with his lecture, —as the word "But" came from his lips—he struck the fingers of one hand lightly on the palm of the other as he had been known to do at some happy flight of oratory in the House of Commons. "But it is the grind that makes the happiness."

(*The Duke's Children*, ch. 25)

Colonel Osborne knew that his visit had been very innocent; but he did not like the feeling that even his innocence had been made the subject of observation.

(*He Knew He Was Right*, ch. 23)

It cannot be said of him that he did much thinking for himself;—but he thought that he thought.

(*The Prime Minister*, ch. 2)

In *The Claverings*, this characteristic Trollopian turn of phrase is used frequently, and especially in the depiction of the wavering hero. "He told himself that he was an ass, but still he went on being an ass." Thus he got himself into his trouble between the old love and the new, and in the midst of it, when he was being true to neither, Trollope concludes an address to the reader on the failings of his hero: "He should have been chivalric, manly, full of high duty. He should have been all this, and full also of love, and then he would have been a hero. But men as I see them are not often heroic."

Another of Trollope's characteristic devices is the repetition of a short phrase, at brief intervals but with such shifts of context, such exaggeration, that it acquires the ironic power conferred in the same manner on the phrase "honorable men" in Antony's speech in *Julius Caesar*. In *The Claverings* there are two fine examples of its use. One is in the twelfth chapter, describing the visit of the beautiful young widow to the splendid estate she had won by her loveless marriage, and the phrase woven through it is: "She had the price in her hands." It gathers weight continually through the chapter, which ends upon the final bitter variation: "She had the price in her hands, but she felt herself tempted to do as Judas did, to go out and hang herself." Five chapters later, the same device is put to more openly comic and hostile uses, when the best mode of wooing this same rich young widow is discussed by Captain Clavering and Captain Boodle, after dinner at their club:

"Well, now, Clavvy, I'll tell you what my ideas are. When a man's trying a young filly, his hands can't be too light. A touch too much will bring her on her haunches, and throw her out of step. She should hardly feel the iron in her mouth. But when I've got to do with a trained mare, I always choose that she shall know that I'm there! Do you understand me?"

"Yes; I understand you, Doodles."

"I always choose that she should know I'm there." And Captain Boodle, as he repeated these manly words with a firm voice, put out his hands as though he were handling the horse's rein.

(ch. 17)

After the phrase has been relished a further half-dozen times, Boodle leaves his friend alone to meditate upon it:

He sat the whole evening in the smoking-room, very silent, drinking slowly iced gin-and-water; and the more he drank the more assured he felt that he now understood the way in which he was to attempt the work before him. "Let her know I'm there," he said to himself, shaking his head gently, so that no one should observe him; "yes, let her know I'm there." Everything was contained in that precept. And he, with his hands before him on his knees, went through the process of steadying a horse with the snaffle-rein, just touching the curb, as he did so, for security. It was but a motion of his fingers and no one could see it, but it made him confident that he had learned his lesson.

(ch. 17)

And in this way the phrase is made to undermine these two men, to reveal all their coarseness, their monotony of mind, their pompous ineptitude.

An acquaintance with *The Claverings*, then, is worth making not only for its own sake; it is probably the readiest way for a reader to sensitize himself to the subtler aspects of Trollope's style, and above all to his characteristic modes of irony. Without this sensitivity, none of his novels can be read rightly, for even in his dealings with the characters he knew and loved best—indeed especially with them—this irony is never far away. But its quality is so quiet, its onset so unostentatious, that it can easily be missed.

For these reasons, then, these two novels seem to deserve attention. But it must at once be added that many of the others are as good and very possibly better. *Ralph the Heir* (1871), for example, has some fine political scenes and at least one character, Sir Thomas Underwood, profounder in conception than any in *The Way We Live Now. The Belton Estate* (1866) is comparable with *The Claverings* in its compression; it has a parallel theme, the hesitations of a young woman between two lovers, developed with all that power of creating a dramatic scene that has been illustrated above in the encounter between the archdeacon and Miss Crawley. Others of the lesser-known novels that certainly deserve to be much better known are *Orley Farm* (1862), *Sir Harry Hotspur of Humblethwaite* (1871), *Is He Popenjoy?* (1878), *Dr. Wortle's School* (1881), and *Ayala's Angel* (1881). But for the attention of American readers there is one novel that has special and powerful claims, *The American Senator* (1877). Its main plot hangs on visits to a typical piece of rural England by an inquiring and inquisitive American senator, with his reflections on what he sees and hears, often expressed in letters. These descriptions and comments offer very convenient and lively cover for some of Trollope's own tilts at some treasured British windmills, and his implied opinions on America are more tolerant and perceptive than those of his mother's first book. As an early example of fictional sociology it is well worth reading, but the main plot is soon nearly submerged in a powerful study of the struggle to entrap a husband waged by an aristocratic pauper. The bitterness of the battle and its ruthlessness are both explored with a horror and sympathy that are hardly matched anywhere else in Trollope's work, and not often equalled anywhere. The list could easily be made much longer, but the reader who wishes to explore these novels further has no lack of guides. If he is interested in the gloomier and less "usual" aspects in them, he cannot do better than follow Cockshut; if, on the other hand, he prefers a more orthodox and central view, he should consult the *Commentary* of Michael Sadleir, to whom this generation owes much for defending and explaining a writer who seemed on the very point of slipping into oblivion.

But whatever he may choose to read, he should guard against two misconceptions that can prevent him from giving both himself and Trollope a fair chance. He should not, under the impression of length and weight of circumstance, mistake what is before him for mere photography, and so miss the real, though unostentatious, imagination that has molded it; nor should he let the apparent uniformity and directness of the style lull him into a hypnotic automatism, insensitive to those subtler turns of phrase that are so characteristic an expression of Trollope's "moral consciousness," of his kindly but ironic perception of the gap between what we are and what we ought to be, wish to be, or believe ourselves to be.

SELECTED BIBLIOGRAPHY

I. BIBLIOGRAPHY. M. L. Irwin, *Anthony Trollope: A Bibliography* (New York, 1926), contains useful references to early reviews, articles in periodicals, etc.; M. Sadleir, *Trollope: A Bibliography* (London, 1928), based on the compiler's renowned collection now in the Parrish Collection in the Princeton University library: *Supplement* (1934), and additional material in Sadleir's *XIX Century Fiction* (1951), final authority on the works of Trollope themselves, with a fascinating section on the extent of their popularity, as measured by the book market; W. G. Gerould and J. T. Gerould, *A Guide to Trollope* (Princeton, N. J., 1948), contains bibliographical tables and a dictionary of characters, places, and events in the novels; D. Smalley, ed., "Trollope," in L. Stevenson, ed., *Victorian Fiction: A Guide to Research* (Cambridge, Mass., 1964); J. C. Olmsted and J. E. Welch, eds., *The Reputation of Trollope: An Annotated Bibliography 1925–1975* (New York, 1978).

II. COLLECTED WORKS. *Note:* There is no complete ed. of Trollope's works, and it now seems unlikely that there ever will be, for the Oxford University Press has been forced to discontinue *The Oxford Trollope* that was begun in 1948, at a point when it included only nine titles (in fifteen vols.). Many of the novels, along with the *Autobiography*, are published in the World's Classics series by the same publishers, and for most purposes this can be regarded as the standard, if not complete, ed. Several of the novels are also available in Everyman's Library and in Nelson's Classics. Several other reprints of the more popular novels have appeared under several imprints, such as Zodiac, Panther, Dover. Their choices have been influenced largely by the appearance of the novels on radio and television programs. While they have certainly helped to make Trollope more widely known and even read, they have created a severe problem for those who wish to find a particular passage. Page references, if given at all, would have to be given for seven or eight different eds., which might not include the one the reader might possess. If inclusive, they would be very cumbrous. It has seemed better, therefore, to give only references to chapters, which are generally uniform. To find a short passage it may be necessary to read through a whole chapter. But this is nearly always well worth doing.

F. Harrison, ed., *The Barsetshire Novels*, 8 vols. (London, 1906); M. Sadleir, ed., *The Barsetshire Novels*, 14 vols. (Oxford, 1929), Shakespeare Head ed.; M. Sadleir and F. Page, eds., *The Oxford Trollope*, 15 vols. (London, 1948–1954), includes the following: *Can You Forgive Her?* 2 vols. (1948); *Phineas Finn*, 2 vols. (1949); *The Eustace Diamonds*, 2 vols. (1950); *An Autobiography . . .* (1950); *Phineas Redux*, 2 vols. (1951); *The Prime Minister*, 2 vols. (1952); *The Warden* (1952); *Barchester Towers*, 2 vols. (1953); *The Duke's Children* (1954); B. A. Booth, ed., *The Letters of Anthony Trollope* (London, 1951), uniform with vols. of the Oxford ed.

III. SELECTIONS. E. C. Dunne and M. E. Dodd, eds., *The Trollope Reader* (New York, 1947), gives few of his dramatic scenes, but exemplifies very well his range of observation; J. Hampden, ed., *The Parson's Daughter and Other Stories* (London, 1949), includes *Katchen's Caprices*, not repr. since its first appearance in *Harper's Weekly* (1866–1867), and four other stories; L. O. Tingay, ed., *The Bedside Barsetshire* (London, 1940), has its uses, but proves very clearly that Trollope needs space and time to develop his effects; J. Hampden, ed., *Mary Gresley and Other Stories* (London, 1951), includes five stories.

IV. SEPARATE WORKS. *The MacDermots of Ballycloran*, 3 vols. (London, 1847), novel; *The Kellys and the O'Kellys: A Tale of Irish Life*, 3 vols. (London, 1848), novel; *La Vendée: An Historical Romance*, 3 vols. (London, 1850), historical novel; *The Warden* (London, 1855), Barsetshire novel, also with an intro. by A. O. J. Cockshut (London, 1955); *Barchester Towers*, 3 vols. (London, 1857), Barsetshire novel, also with an intro. by P. Hansford Johnson (London, 1952); *The Three Clerks*, 3 vols. (London, 1858), novel; *Doctor Thorne*, 3 vols. (London, 1858), Barsetshire novel; *The Bertrams*, 3 vols. (London, 1859), novel; *The West Indies and the Spanish Main* (London, 1859), travel.

Castle Richmond, 3 vols. (London, 1860), novel; *Tales of All Countries*, 2nd series (London, 1861–1863), short stories; *Framley Parsonage*, 3 vols. (London, 1861), Barsetshire novel; *Orley Farm*, 2 vols. (London, 1862), novel; *North America*, 2 vols. (London, 1862), travel, also in D. Smalley and B. A. Booth, eds. (New York, 1951); *Rachel Ray*, 2 vols. (London, 1863), novel; *The Small House at Allington*, 2 vols. (London, 1864), Barsetshire novel; *Can You Forgive Her?* 2 vols. (London, 1864–1865), political novel; *Miss Mackenzie*, 2 vols. (London, 1865), novel; *Hunting Sketches* (London, 1865), sketches, also in J. Boyd, ed. (London, 1934) and L. Edwards, ed. (London, 1952); *The Belton Estate*, 3 vols. (London, 1866), novel; *Travelling Sketches* (London, 1866), sketches; *Clergymen of the Church of England* (London, 1866), essays; *Nina Balatka: The Story of a Maiden of Prague*, 2 vols. (London, 1867), novel; *The Last Chronicle of Barset*, 2 vols. (London, 1867), Barsetshire novel; *The Claverings*, 2 vols. (London, 1867), novel; *Lotta Schmidt: and Other Stories*

(London, 1867), short stories; *Linda Tressel*, 2 vols. (London, 1868), novel; *Phineas Finn, the Irish Member*, 2 vols. (London, 1869), political novel; *He Knew He Was Right*, 2 vols. (London, 1869), novel; *Did He Steal It?* (London, 1869), drama, privately printed, an adaptation by Trollope from the central episode of *The Last Chronicle of Barset*, also in R. H. Taylor, ed. (Princeton, N. J., 1952).

The Vicar of Bullhampton, 2 vols. (London, 1870), novel; *An Editor's Tales* (London, 1870), short stories; *The Struggles of Brown, Jones and Robinson: By One of the Firm* (London, 1870), novel, a pirated ed., repr. from the *Cornhill* magazine, had appeared in the U. S. in 1862; *The Commentaries of Caesar* (London, 1870), translation; *Sir Harry Hotspur of Humblethwaite* (London, 1871), novel; *Ralph the Heir*, 3 vols. (London, 1871), novel; *The Golden Lion of Granpère* (London, 1872), novel; *The Eustace Diamonds*, 3 vols. (London, 1873), political novel; *Australia and New Zealand*, 2 vols. (London, 1873), travel; *Lady Anna*, 2 vols. (London, 1874), novel; *Phineas Redux*, 2 vols. (London, 1874), political novel, also in the Oxford Illustrated ed., 2 vols. (London, 1951); *Harry Heathcote of Gangoil: A Tale of Australian Bush Life* (London, 1874), novel; *The Way We Live Now*, 2 vols. (London, 1875), novel; *The Prime Minister*, 4 vols. (London, 1876), political novel; *The American Senator*, 3 vols. (London, 1877), novel; *Christmas at Thompson Hall* (New York, 1877), short story; *South Africa*, 2 vols. (London, 1878), travel; *Is He Popenjoy?* 3 vols. (London, 1878), novel; *The Lady of Launay* (New York, 1878), short story; *How the "Mastiffs" Went to Iceland* (London, 1878), travel, privately printed; *An Eye for an Eye*, 2 vols. (London, 1879), novel; *Thackeray* (London, 1879), criticism; *John Caldigate*, 3 vols. (London, 1879), novel; *Cousin Henry*, 2 vols. (London, 1879), novel.

The Duke's Children, 3 vols. (London, 1880), political novel; *The Life of Cicero*, 2 vols. (London, 1880), biography; *Dr. Wortle's School*, 2 vols. (London, 1881), novel; *Ayala's Angel*, 3 vols. (London, 1881), novel; *Why Frau Frohmann Raised Her Prices and Other Stories* (London, 1882), short stories; *Lord Palmerston* (London, 1882), biography; *The Fixed Period*, 2 vols. (London, 1882), novel; *Marion Fay*, 3 vols. (London, 1882), novel; *Kept in the Dark*, 2 vols. (London, 1882), novel; *Mr. Scarborough's Family*, 3 vols. (London, 1883), novel; *The Landleaguers*, 3 vols. (London, 1883), novel; *An Autobiography*, 2 vols. (London, 1883); *An Old Man's Love*, 2 vols. (London, 1883), novel.

M. Sadleir, ed., *The Noble Jilt: A Comedy* (London, 1923), drama, written in 1850 but never acted, used as the main plot of *Can You Forgive Her?* and mentioned in *The Eustace Diamonds*; M. Sadleir, ed., *London Tradesmen* (London, 1928), sketches, from the *Pall Mall Gazette* (1880); M. L. Parrish, ed., *Four Lectures* (London, 1938); B. A. Booth, ed., *The Tireless Traveller* (Cambridge, 1941), letters contributed to the *Liverpool Mercury* (1875);

J. Hampden, ed., *The Two Heroines of Plumplington* (London, 1953), short story.

V. Biographical and Critical Studies. E. Montégut, *Revue des Deux Mondes* (1855 and 1858), studies by a French critic who specialized in the interpretation of English literature. The first of these reviews contains a long study of *The Warden*, the second deals fully with *Barchester Towers* and *Doctor Thorne*. They illustrate very clearly the general superiority of the French critical approach to fiction over that of the English reviewers of the same period. It was this superiority in skill and seriousness that enabled Montégut to perceive Trollope as not simply a naive realist but a writer who imposed upon his report of life a pattern of his own, with a style of his own. Both reviews were repr. in the first vol. of his *Écrivains Modernes de l'Angleterre* (Paris, 1892); H. James, *Partial Portraits* (London, 1888), the most perceptive of the early estimates of Trollope's quality; F. Harrison, *Studies in Early Victorian Literature* (London, 1895), a short essay of special interest because it gives a firsthand impression of Trollope himself and of the surprise felt by the writer that such fine qualities should have happened to lodge in so bluff and noisy a man; G. Saintsbury, *Corrected Impressions* (London, 1895), the short discussion of Trollope in the essay "Three Mid-Century Novelists" is a shallow and contemptuous attempt to record his "comparative oblivion"; may be of some interest as marking the nadir of his reputation; in his "Trollope Revisited," in *Essays and Studies by Members of the English Association*, VI (1920), the same author copiously but indecisively admits that the oblivion had been, after all, only very comparative.

L. Stephen, *Studies of a Biographer*, vol. IV (London, 1902), the essay on Trollope is short and pleasantly nostalgic, and treats him as a pleasing record of a peaceful but bygone age, the earliest expression of this mode of appreciating him; G. S. Street, *A Book of Essays* (London, 1902), a short essay on Trollope claims for him a higher place than was usual at the time and discusses his "realism" with some penetration; T. H. S. Escott, *Anthony Trollope: His Work, Associates and Literary Originals* (London, 1913), the first full-length biography, many details were filled in by a writer who knew Trollope personally; M. E. Speare, *The Political Novel: Its Development in England and America* (New York, 1924), some interesting points are made about Trollope's treatment of politics, but the author is prevented from doing justice to him by his admiration of Disraeli, whom Trollope disliked both as a politician and as a novelist; S. van B. Nicholas, *The Significance of Anthony Trollope* (New York, 1925), only 490 copies of this booklet were printed, some of its literary judgments are too enthusiastic, but it contains one of the first attempts to draw a map of Barsetshire and to classify the novels; M. Sadleir, *Trollope: A Commentary* (London, 1927; rev. eds. 1945, 1961); H. Walpole, *Anthony Trollope* (London, 1929).

D. MacCarthy, *Portraits* (London, 1931); C. C. Koets, *Female Characters in the Works of Trollope* (Amsterdam, 1933); D. Cecil, *Early Victorian Novelists* (London, 1934), a judicious estimate of Trollope is given, containing some valuable comparisons between him and some of his contemporaries, especially Jane Austen, who was his favorite novelist in his youth; B. A. Booth, ed., *The Trollopian* (Los Angeles, 1945–1949), a quarterly, continued after 1949 as *Nineteenth Century Fiction*; L. P. Stebbins and R. P. Stebbins, *The Trollopes: The Chronicle of a Writing Family* (London, 1945), contains much biographical information about Trollope's mother and his eldest brother, Thomas Adolphus, one of the first attempts to emphasize the gloomier and less orthodox strains in Trollope himself; E. Bowen, *Trollope: A New Judgement* (Oxford, 1946); B. C. Brown, *Anthony Trollope* (London, 1950), a sympathetic attempt to define the "theme" common to the novels, some illuminating suggestions about the effect of civil service experience upon Trollope's approach to life and people; A. O. J. Cockshut, *Anthony Trollope: A Critical Study* (London, 1955); R. Helling, *A Century of Trollope Criticism* (Helsinki, 1956), a detailed survey of the ups and downs of Trollope's reputation from his own day to the present, with a good selection of quotations from the original reviews and a good bibliography of Trollope criticism; M. Praz, *The Hero in Eclipse in Victorian Fiction* (London, 1956), a long ch. on Trollope is perhaps the most favorable and discriminating judgment so far made by a writer neither English nor American; B. A. Booth, "Orley Farm: Artistry Manqué," in R. C. Rathburn and M. Steinmann, eds., *From Jane Austen to Joseph Conrad* (Oxford, 1958); A. Mizener, "Anthony Trollope: The Palliser Novels," in R. C. Rathburn and M. Steinmann, eds., *From Jane Austen to Joseph Conrad* (Oxford, 1958); B. A. Booth, *Anthony Trollope: Aspects of His Life and Work* (London, 1959), this very learned study is specially interesting on the social background and vagaries of Trollope's fame.

H. Sykes Davies, "Trollope and His Style," in *A Review of English Literature*, I, no. 4 (October 1960); R. Arnold, *The Whiston Matter* (London, 1961); R. J. Polhemus, *The Changing World of Anthony Trollope* (Berkeley, Calif., 1968); D. Smalley, ed., *Trollope: The Critical Heritage* (London, 1969); R. Roberts, *Trollope: Artist and Moralist* (London, 1971); J. P. Hennessy, *Anthony Trollope* (London, 1971; New York, 1972); D. Skilton, *Trollope and His Contemporaries* (London, 1972); J. W. Clark, *The Language and Style of Anthony Trollope* (London, 1975); J. Halperin, *Trollope and Politics: A Study of the Pallisers and Others* (London, 1977); R. Terry, *Anthony Trollope: The Artist in Hiding* (London, 1977); P. D. Edwards, *Anthony Trollope: His Art and Scope* (London, 1978); A. Pollard, *Anthony Trollope* (London, 1978); T. Bareham, ed., *Anthony Trollope* (London, 1980); N. J. Hall, *Trollope and His Illustrators* (London, 1980); G. Harvey, *The Art of Anthony Trollope* (London, 1980); W. M. Kendrick, *"Novel Machine": The Theory and Fiction of Anthony Trollope* (Baltimore, 1980).

THE BRONTËS
CHARLOTTE (1816-1855)
EMILY (1818-1848)
ANNE (1820-1849)

Winifred Gérin

INTRODUCTION

THE BRONTËS present a rare, almost a unique example in English literature of collective genius. Theirs was not only a partnership between relations, as was that of William and Dorothy Wordsworth, of Charles and Mary Lamb, and of Gabriel, Christina, and Michael Rossetti. It was not only a bond of the flesh but a union of the spirit that held them together, sprung as they were from identical circumstances and from a common soil—as the cascades and waterfalls of their native moorlands gush from the hillsides of their own momentum and plunge into deeps invisible at their source.

The preserved manuscripts of Charlotte and Branwell Brontë that date from their twelfth year attest to their extraordinary precocity; but precocity does not account for all. The children of the poet Robert Southey were also precocious, with as strong and as shared a creative urge as the little Brontës. Thanks to the Southeys' cousin and playfellow, Hartley Coleridge, the son of Samuel Taylor Coleridge, they invented as complete a dream kingdom—Eujuxria—as Branwell and Charlotte did with Angria, or Emily and Anne with Gondal. But nothing came of Eujuxria, and few people read Hartley's adult writings today. What distinguishes Branwell's three sisters is that as they grew they evolved, both as humans and writers, with the experience of life, and were able to transmute their experience into the abiding truth of art.

A close-knit family unit, the young Brontës were bound together by an intense affection that, begun as an emotional link between motherless children, became an intellectual fusion of like minds that eventually colored all their thoughts. This interconnection between adult minds, usually associated with twinship, was one effect of the peculiar upbringing the Brontës received at the hands of their widower father.

SHAPING INFLUENCES: THE FATHER

IT is a curious fact, and one central to the Brontës' intellectual development, that their father's clerical position was the least of the influences at work in making writers of them. However religiously they were brought up (and Charlotte's early knowledge of the Bible was phenomenal) and however deep and genuine were their later religious convictions, no word of religion enters into their voluminous juvenilia. The fact only further confirms the existing evidence of the absolute intellectual freedom of their home.

Patrick Brontë entered the church because it was the one career that offered to lift him out of his poor and Irish peasant background. He was born in a cottage at Emdale, County Down, on 17 March 1777. By slow degrees, as a teacher in a boys' school at Glascar, as tutor in a private family, and as teacher in the parish school at Drumballyroney, he made the grade and got a scholarship to St. John's College, Cambridge, in October 1802.

As a young boy Patrick Brontë had once worked for a blacksmith, and one day a gentleman, whose horse he held, noticed him and said aside to the smith: "Now, that boy standing here, though he is only six or seven years old, is what I call a gentleman by nature." The remark, overheard by Patrick, influenced his whole outlook and conduct, he later told one of his Haworth parishioners. It gave him hope as well as undefined ambition.

There was never any question in the minds of his sponsors and benefactors (the Irish Presbyterian minister Andrew Harshaw; the Reverend Thomas Tighe, John Wesley's friend; and Henry Thornton, William Wilberforce's friend) but that he should take orders on obtaining his B.A. degree. This he did in July 1806. From then on his course was traced out for him by way of successive curacies, in Essex (at Wethersfield), in Shropshire (at Wellington), and eventually in the West Riding of Yorkshire at Dewsbury, where he arrived in December 1809. From there he received successive promotions to the livings at Hartshead (1811–1815), Thornton (1815–1820), and finally to Haworth in 1820, where he remained until his death in 1861.

While nothing suggests that Patrick Brontë was a victim sacrificed to a fate that was not of his choosing, the whole bent of his nature and intellect was for another sort of life, of which he had intoxicating glimpses while at Cambridge. In the national emergency created by the presence of Napoleon's armies at Boulogne and the imminent threat of invasion, the undergraduates in residence formed themselves into a volunteer defense corps of which Patrick Brontë of St. John's was one of the most zealous recruits. Poor scholarship student that he was, his daily contacts with the young bloods of the university, like young Lord Palmerston, already committed to a career in politics, offered Patrick Brontë insights into the life of the governing classes that were as new as they were alluring. Years later, with the crisis provoked by the Luddite riots (1811–1812)—in which the role of the clergy in industrial districts became one of an active peacekeeping force—Patrick was among the first, and the few, to carry pistols in defense of his parishioners' property. From then on, in peaceful times as in turbulent, over the remaining fifty years of his life, he primed his pistols daily, discharged them every morning, and lived in a mental state of siege ended only by his death. His predicament, recognized for what it was by his daughter Charlotte, was related by her in the character of the Reverend Mathewson Helstone in *Shirley* (1849). The pistol-carrying old rector, expecting Luddites in ambush behind every hedgerow, was considered diabolical by his enemies. "He was not diabolical at all," commented Charlotte.

The evil simply was—he had missed his vocation: he should have been a soldier, and circumstances had made him a priest. For the rest, he was a conscientious, hardheaded hard-handed, brave, stern, implacable, faithful little man. . . . It seems to me, reader, that you cannot always cut out men to fit their profession, and that you ought not to curse them because that profession sometimes hangs on them ungracefully. . . .

(ch. 3)

Except for the epithet "little"—Mr. Brontë was immensely tall—that description fits him as his cassock did not.

He was thirty-five before he married. His bride, Maria Branwell, of a Methodist Penzance family, was as unworldly as he, and considered poverty a positive benefit to the soul. Despite—or because of—her complete involvement in religion, she had a fine, witty mind, an independent spirit rare in women of her day, and physical endurance that only her own children would rival. The marriage took place on 29 December 1812; six children were born of it: Maria in April 1814, Elizabeth in February 1815, Charlotte in April 1816, Patrick Branwell in June 1817, Emily Jane in July 1818, and Anne in January 1820. In the year following Anne's birth, Mrs. Brontë died of cancer on 15 September. She was thirty-eight.

Leaving no memory with her surviving children, not even with the clever five-year-old Charlotte, her part in the moral makeup of her daughters was yet primordial and lasting. Her love letters, written to Patrick during their engagement and read by Charlotte thirty-eight years later, drew from her daughter this tribute of understanding and love: "it was strange now to peruse, for the first time, the records of a mind whence my own sprang; and most strange, and at once sad and sweet, to find that mind of a truly fine, pure, and elevated order. . . . I wish she had lived and that I had known her. . . ." To anyone reading those letters today, the mother's intellectual legacy to the daughters is apparent: *Jane Eyre* (1847), written years before Charlotte had knowledge of her mother's letters, is the true product of her mother's mind.

To console himself for a missed military career, Patrick Brontë took to writing poetry—just as he consoled himself for the menial tasks of his boyhood by learning Milton by heart. Both before and immediately after his marriage he wrote a great deal. He was genuinely in love, but the only form of verse he could manage was the rhyming couplet; the only imagery he knew was that of the conventional eighteenth-century allegories, staled long since by use. Yet he had an observant eye and a true love of nature and animals. When these were his themes, he found something personal to say, as in his lines from "Winter" in his *The Rural Minstrel* (1813):

> Ye feathered songsters of the grove,
> Sweet philomel and cooing dove,
> Goldfinch, and linnet gray,
> And mellow thrush, and blackbird loud,
> And lark, shrill warbler, of the cloud,
> Where do ye pensive stray?
> The milk-white thorn, the leafy spray,
> The fragrant grove, and summer's day,
> Are seen by you, no more;
> Ah! may you light on friendly sheds,
> To hide your drooping, pensive heads,
> From winter's chilling roar.

The fact that he had known the delight of writing, regardless of the quality of what he wrote, was all-important to his children when their time came for writing "from morning till noon, and from noon till night" and was the first incentive in making them writers. The little volumes printed by the Halifax and Bradford booksellers, "embellished," as the jargon of the period had it, with engravings, just like the volumes of Thomas Gray and William Cowper that they knew, took on the significance of fetishes for them. If they could be copied even in their minutest detail, then the path to Parnassus was surely clear before them. To these locally printed volumes of their father's verse must be attributed the children's assumption of the diaeresis in spelling their name which, up to that time, Mr. Brontë had variously spelled with an acute or a grave accent and continued, for the most part, to do until his daughter Charlotte, like Nelson, made the name illustrious. The fact appears to be that the printer, not possessing either accent among his letters, substituted the diaeresis much in use then for the classical texts of his clerical clientele. The title pages of the little Brontës' first tiny books remain to illustrate the change of accent that this mere printer's error provoked.

With the death of Mrs. Brontë, the joy went out of scribbling for her widower, as of much else, and a fresh channel for his energies had to be sought. He found it by immersing himself in politics, in following with passion the reports of the parliamentary debates in the daily and weekly press with which the household was well supplied. The period was one of ferment and constitutional reform; the debates affecting the centuries-old legislature, such as those on the Catholic Emancipation Bill of 1829 and the Reform Bill of 1832, were conducted on a high dramatic level of eloquence that made kindling

reading to the former Cambridge colleague of the now illustrious Lord Palmerston. Brontë's high Tory frenzies were communicated undiminished to his children. How Charlotte, as a child of twelve, and her brother and sisters, were caught up in the passions of the hour, she herself described only a few days after the event in one of her earliest fragments, dated March 1829.

> Parliament was opened, and the great Catholic question was brought forward and the Duke's measures were disclosed, and all was slander violence, party-spirit, and confusion.
> . . . I remember the Sunday when the Intelligence extraordinary came with Mr Peels speech in it containing the terms on which the catholics were to be let in with what eagerness papa tore off the cover and how we all gathered round him and with what breathless anxiety we listened as one by one they were disclosed explained and argued upon so ably and so well and then when it was all out how aunt said she thought it was excellent and that the catholics [could] do no harm with such good security. . . . the Royal Dukes in their robes and the Great Duke in green sash and waistcoat the rising of all the peeresses when he rose the reading of his speech papa saying that his words were like precious gold and lastly the majority one to 4 in favour of the bill. . . .
>
> ("Tales of the Islanders," vol. II)[1]

The children knew all the issues at stake, all the personalities engaged in the opposing camps. Already the duke of Wellington was a household word among them; for as long as they could remember, their father had extolled him as the world's greatest military genius, the country's finest man. It needed no other incentive for Charlotte to adopt him as her very own great and special hero, who would figure at the center of all her tales for the next ten years to come, as Arthur Augustus Adrian, Duke of Zamorna and King of Angria.

EDUCATION

WITHOUT holding theories on education, like Maria Edgeworth's father, Brontë held one-sided views little in accordance with school curricula, even of those days. Provided his children were well-read in the classics, in literature, history, geography, and grammar—in all the subjects, in short, that appealed to

---

[1]"Tales of the Islanders" has been in the possession of the Berg Collection at the New York Public Library since 1940. It was composed from 12 March 1829 to 30 July 1830.

him and, in turn, appealed to them—he gave no thought to a systematic program of work or to the practical sides of education that his son at least would need if he were to be prepared for any profession except the church. But Brontë, like his wife before him, held the making of money as unimportant; what mattered was to encourage in each child its God-given gifts, and he proudly noted in his son a gift for drawing. Branwell's future was therefore assured. Since no gentleman could afford to be ignorant of the classics, he decided to teach Branwell Latin and Greek himself, confident that he could do so better than any tutor at a school. Branwell therefore never went to school, unless it were, as his friend Leyland later reported, for a few months in 1825 to the local grammar school, where his diminutive size and frail nerves stood him in poor stead. Certain it is that by 1826 he was at home, where he remained for the next nine years.

The tragic circumstances of the girls' short schooling at the Clergy Daughters' School at Cowan Bridge near Tunstall, Lancashire, in consequence of whose rigors the two elder girls, Maria and Elizabeth, died of tuberculosis at the ages of twelve and ten, had two lasting effects. The younger girls did not go to school again until they were in their teens, and Charlotte, aged eight when her sisters died, never regained either the health or the confidence of childhood.

The traumatic experience of Cowan Bridge left its mark on her for life, as Mrs. Gaskell noted twenty-five years later at their first meeting. "She is very little and very plain," she reported to Mrs. Froude; "her stunted person she ascribes to the scanty supply of food she had as a growing girl, when at that school of the Daughters of the Clergy. . ." (*The Letters of Mrs. Gaskell*, 25 August 1850).

When she came to write *The Life of Charlotte Brontë* (1857), Mrs. Gaskell also remarked on the absence of hope "which formed such a strong characteristic in Charlotte" and that she again ascribed among more physical causes "to the deep pang of losing her two elder sisters. . . ." And Ellen Nussey, who first met her seven years after the event, remembered how she spoke of those sisters: "Her love for them was most intense; a kind of adoration dwelt in her feelings which, as she conversed, almost imparted itself to her listeners. She described Maria as a little mother among the rest, super-human in goodness, and cleverness. . . ."[2] The

loss to Charlotte of Maria and Elizabeth, and the injustices and privations she suffered at the Clergy Daughters' School, were only fully exorcised when she came to write *Jane Eyre*. As all readers of the book well know, "Lowood" and "Helen Burns" are the lasting monument to that unforgettable landmark in Charlotte's life.

Upon Emily the school left no traceable effect: she was there only eight months. Anne, mercifully, was too young to go at all. The whole interlude lasted only ten months for Charlotte, from August 1824 to June 1825, when Brontë fetched her and Emily home.

At home they were taught by him for the next six years. This was no ill fortune for them, since he encouraged them to read all that was best in literature, biography, and history, of which he had a well-stocked library, and he laid no embargo on their choice. Brontë must have been one of the very few clergymen to own the whole poetic works of Lord Byron and to allow his children free access to them. At twelve, Charlotte was quoting from *Manfred* and *Cain* as familiar reading.

Brontë did better for his children still; conscious of their artistic temperaments, he engaged a music teacher for the girls and an art teacher for Branwell—with whom the girls also took lessons—and he became a founder-member of the neighboring Keighley Mechanics' Institute Library, so that they should never lack books. The contemporary catalog shows that there were more than 300 titles covering a wide range of subjects, from philosophy to natural history.

One-sided as their education might have been, their knowledge of public events was exceptional and would never have been obtained at any boarding school. They were kept abreast of the news not only by their father but by their reading of the political and literary journals of the day, *Blackwood's* magazine chiefly. It was *Blackwood's* with its wide range of critical, historical, and political matter that gave the Brontës the incentive and the prototype on which to base their own beginnings as writers.

THE BRONTË JUVENILIA

It is evident from a statement made later by Branwell that he and his sisters were reading *Blackwood's* magazine regularly from the year 1825 (the year their sisters died), when he was eight and Charlotte nine

---

[2]"Reminiscences of Charlotte Brontë," in *Scribner's Monthly*, May 1871; repr. in *Brontë Society Transactions*, 1899.

years old. To produce their own magazines in imitation of *Blackwood's,* with all the special features of the original, including the Ettrick Shepherd's column "Noctes Ambrosianae," became the children's main occupation for the next two years. From January 1829 to December 1830 Charlotte and Branwell produced fifteen numbers of *Branwell's Blackwood's* magazine, changed after three numbers to *Branwell's Young Men's* magazine. The issues included editorial comment, critical reviews of books especially dear to the children, like *Ossian's Poems,* original poems, riddles, serialized tales, comment on the news of the day, in attempted replica of the original magazine, but on a miniature scale, the volumes varying in size from number to number, from 4.75 cm. by 3.5 cm. to 6.4 cm. by 5.1 cm., each volume bound in packing paper and neatly stitched. The explanation of the size lies with another of the children's projects of the time, the dramatization in terms of a historical scenario of the imaginary deeds of a set of wooden soldiers, given to Branwell by his father, for whose reading the magazines were intended. The *Young Men,* as the children called them, under the assumed personalities of the duke of Wellington, Napoleon, Marshal Soult, the duke of York, and other public figures (which varied with the children's reading), were the protagonists of a succession of "Plays" and the subjects of a serialized epic into whose plot went ingredients from all the books that had most impressed them: *Aesop's Fables, The Arabian Nights,* the *Travels of Mungo Park,* the Arctic voyages of William Parry and Sir John Ross, the novels of Sir Walter Scott, the poetry of Byron, translations from François René de Chateaubriand's works, and the steady flow continuing in *Blackwood's* throughout the 1820's of the first memoirs of the Peninsular campaign written by some of the eyewitnesses, and Southey's instantly popular *History of the Peninsular War* (1823–1832). From that source in particular, since it appealed to their strong bent for heroics, the children derived the names of their semihistorical characters. Among these was Charlotte's Duke of Zamorna. The name was drawn from the town of Zamora on the Douro, the scene of one of Wellington's victories, after which he received the title Marquis of Douro. Modeled on the admired hero, Charlotte's character had much more of a Regency rake to him than the qualities of the Iron Duke. He was the romantic figure par excellence, a prey to his passions with the best of them, and with a love life rivaling Don Juan's. Here is an early sketch of him purporting to figure in an album:

Fire! Light! What have we here? Zamorna's self, blazing in the frontispiece like the sun on his own standard. De Lisle has given him to us in full regimentals—plumed, epauletted and sabred . . . he stands as if a thunderbolt could neither blast the light of his eyes nor dash the effrontery of his brow. Keen, glorious being! O Zamorna! What eyes those are glancing under the deep shadow of that raven crest! They bode no good. . . . All here is passion and fire unquenchable. Impetuous sin, stormy pride, diving and soaring enthusiasm, war and poetry, are kindling their fires in all his veins and his wild blood boils from his heart and back again like a torrent of new-sprung lava. Young Duke! Young demon!

("A Peep into a Picture Book," 1834)[3]

One of the side effects of the Brontës' close companionship with their outspoken father was their absolute freedom from conventional moral inhibitions. Patrick Brontë was a product of the Regency far more than of the Victorian era into which he lived so long. While the highest standards of truth and honor were inculcated into the children for their personal guidance, Brontë hid nothing of the facts of life from them, leaving them free to read the Elizabethan and Jacobean dramatists like another Bible. One of the first impressions of the family received by Charlotte's school friend, the fifteen-year-old Ellen Nussey, on her first visit to the parsonage, was of Brontë at the breakfast table relating

strange stories, which had been told to him by some of the oldest inhabitants of the parish, of the extraordinary lives and doings of the people who had resided in far-off, out-of-the-way places, but in continuity with Haworth—stories which made one shiver and shrink from hearing; but they were full of grim humour and interest to Mr Brontë and his children. . . .

("Reminiscences of Charlotte Brontë")

The interest attaching to Zamorna is that he did not remain a puppet but evolved into an individual over the years to find his final expression in the character of Rochester.

To see the list of Charlotte's and Branwell's childish manuscripts is to realize that the magazines were only a small part of their prodigious output of stories, dramas, dialogues, and poems. Both children had a habit of noting at the end of the day the number of words they had written—these were often two to three thousand a day.

[3]Reprinted in T. J. Wise and J. A. Symington, eds., *The Miscellaneous and Unpublished Writings of Charlotte Brontë and Patrick Branwell Brontë,* 2 vols. (Oxford, 1936–1938), vol. I, p. 361.

On 28 June 1830 Branwell noted of a tragedy he had written on Caractacus in 380 lines: "Begun June 26. Ended June 28, AD 1830. Therefore I have finished it in 2 days, Sunday, which happened between, being left out."

A striking feature of the Brontës' youthful collaboration (the part of Emily and Anne was inventive rather than written in those early years) was the gradual build-up from scattered fragments of a coherent plot relating the actions of a complete society with its own government, culture, and laws, peopled by a distinguished dramatis personae of politicians, military men, civil servants, writers, musicians, underlings, and beautiful hostesses, whose receptions in scintillating salons hung with diamond-drop chandeliers were the dream fulfillment of Charlotte's austere girlhood.

The characters in the Brontës' early stories and "Plays" (which appear to have been stories in action) did not make merely ephemeral appearances but were constant features of the plot, their idiosyncrasies becoming known to the reader and their motives and actions made reliably consistent from one incident to the next. They are the early witness to Charlotte's exceptional power for portraying character.

These social groups were settled in a specific geographical region, the African coast of Guinea, suggested by the voyages of Mungo Park, where they built themselves a magic capital city, the Great Glass Town or Verdopolis, as an outpost against the Ashantees, and whose distinguishing feature was its towering position above a shining river, in the likeness of Martin's vast Assyrian complexes.[4] Of Martin's pictures, Brontë had five engravings hanging on the walls of his study, *The Fall of Babylon* and *The Fall of Nineveh* among them, which can leave no doubt whence the children drew their inspiration for the magic city of their invention. Charlotte wrote of it in a story of 1829:

The City was lying in its splendour and magnificence surrounded by the broad stream of the Guadima. The palace was majestically towering in the midst of it, and all its pillars and battlements seemed in the light of the moon as if they were transformed into silver by the touch of a fairy's wand.

("The Search after Happiness")

[4]John Martin, a romantic artist famous for his paintings of grandiose biblical and historical scenes.

In another passage she wrote that

it bore the character of a dream of gorgeous fiction . . . few believed in its existence. It seemed as the cities of old: Nineveh and Babylon with the temples of their Gods.

("Albion & Marina," 1830)[5]

Because the plot of the Glass Town chronicles expanded to embrace every fresh element of interest in the Brontës' lives, they did not tire of it even after five years, when the Confederation of Glass Town States (by then Emily and Anne had each a Glass Town Province of her own called respectively after their special heroes, Parry's Glass Town and Ross's Glass Town) was enlarged by conquest to embrace the kingdom of Angria, under the triumphant Zamorna. The creation of his court and new capital city—Adrianopolis—the chronicle of his wars, the relation of his marriages and numerous amours was the happy, if interrupted, pursuit of Charlotte's next five years. By then she was a young woman in her twenties, frustrated in her writing by the painful necessity of earning her living by teaching. But what distinguishes the literature of Angria from the juvenilia of other writers was the lasting hold it had on its author's mind. How hard Charlotte found it to shake off the obsessional dream, even as a teacher in a foreign school, her later statements show.

THE MANUSCRIPTS OF GLASS TOWN AND ANGRIA
(ca. 1829–1839)

PRESERVED in scattered collections in English and American universities and libraries can still be seen today the manuscripts of the Brontë juvenilia, written in microscopic script imitating print, whose sheer quantity makes the student forget that it represents probably only a third of the original output, the rest having been lost or destroyed.

Branwell's major role, after his debut as editor of *Branwell's Blackwood's* magazine and sundry booklets of poems and commentaries, was as historian of the *Young Men* themselves, the wooden soldiers whose conquests and settlement in Africa he recorded, as a boy of thirteen, in a narration of 15,000 words, complete with Map of the Great Glass Town

[5]Reprinted in *The Miscellaneous and Unpublished Writings of Charlotte Brontë and Patrick Branwell Brontë*, vol. I, pp. 28–29.

Confederacy. This was followed by a work of greater scope relating the history of the "Foundation of the Kingdom of Angria" in 30,000 words, which was again followed by a "History of Angria" in ten parts, whose writing extended over two and a half years, and their sequel, the six-volume "Letters of an Englishman." His involvement in politics (it was the time of the Reform Bill agitation up and down the country) provided him with his material for the creation of the type of demagogue antihero needed for the plot as the opposition to the military dictatorship of Zamorna. The creation of the character of Alexander Percy, Viscount Elrington, later Earl of Northangerland, was a masterstroke on Branwell's part, for the character presented the perfect foil to Zamorna and introduced an element of intrigue and political chicanery, finally of rank rebellion, that kept the plot alive. Percy was adopted by Charlotte with all his blemishes intact and figured in her later Angrian tales as Zamorna's dangerous rival, treacherous foe, and, more dramatic still, as father of Zamorna's second wife, Mary Percy. Branwell wrote about government, provincial administration, transport, defense, taxation, communications, in an effortless style that aped the journalese of the provincial press. He worked out the exact distances between the imaginary provinces, established the timetables of mail coaches connecting them, calculated the finances of the country, and the exact strength of its armed forces.

These subjects were not attractive to Branwell's sisters, but they were a necessity if the plot were to be solidly based, and his contributions had the effect of giving it verisimilitude and a needed masculine touch. Branwell was so soaked in the military memoirs of the day that he could dash off a dispatch from the secretary of war to a defaulting officer as to the manner born.

Sir [he wrote at the outset of a new tale], you are requested without delay to join your company in the Twenty Ninth Regiment encamped at the Town of Wharton.
Signed   Chas Warner S.W.
War Office, Adrianopolis,
December 26th 1835
To Captain Hastings
Angrian Hotel,
Verdopolis[6]

[6]"The History of Angria"; repr. in *Miscellaneous and Unpublished Writings. . .*, vol. II, p. 112.

It is worth noting that the defaulting officer, Captain Hastings, who was increasingly beset with Branwell's own failing of disinclination to work, assumed the center of the stage in his later manuscripts and figured in a convincing novelette by Charlotte, as late as 1838–1839. This was how the brother and sister worked.

The juvenilia of Charlotte Brontë, after a period of pure fairy tales modeled on the pattern of *The Arabian Nights* and Sir Charles Morell's *Tales of the Genii* (1764), settled down into a series of sharply observed reviews of the social scene; these were all the more remarkable as she had no knowledge of society herself. While there was inevitably a strong element of Daisy Ashford[7] naiveté in them, her character drawing was striking from the outset. Her feeling for situation, for the interplay of personality, was innate. Her knowledge of the behavior, conversation, and dress of great ladies was derived solely from the social columns of the press and the fashionable *Annuals* whose tremendous vogue followed speedily on their introduction into England by the Swiss engraver Rudolph Akerman: such books soon became familiar even in the provinces. Charlotte possessed several copies of these charmingly produced little volumes, *The Keepsake* and *Friendship's Offering* in particular. Her drawings after the engravings in them show how closely she studied every detail of costume, attitude, and expression of the famous beauties portrayed and used them for the description of the heroines in her tales.[8]

The titles of some of her early fragments show how preoccupied she was with describing society: "High Life in Verdopolis," "Characters of the Great Men of the Present Time," "Visits in Verdopolis," "Passing Events," "A Peep into a Picture Book," "The Scrap Book," etc. All these character sketches and others derived from Finden's illustrations of the works of Byron[9] centered on the courts of Zamorna and on the lovely women who intrigued for his notice. Charlotte read from her thirteenth year about French novels in the literary journals, the detailed critical analyses of them in *Blackwood's* and *Fraser's* magazines, and she knew a great deal about

[7]Referring to *The Young Visiters* (1919), by the nine-year-old Daisy Ashford.
[8]See W. Gérin, *Charlotte Brontë* (Oxford, 1967), pp. 49–53.
[9]*Finden's Byron Beauties, or The Principal Female Characters in Lord Byron's Poems, Engraved from Original Paintings* (London, 1836).

irregular liaisons. She also knew from her early reading of Byron a great deal about the torments of love, which she was later to analyze so memorably in all her books. The sufferings of Jane Eyre, of Caroline Helstone in *Shirley,* and of Lucy Snowe in *Villette* (1853) would never have been so poignantly real if their author had not had early prevision of their pain and tried her apprentice hand at portraying it. Charlotte was a born romantic, and the poetry of Byron was, without comparison, the strongest single influence on her youth, the one that corresponded closest to her own extravagant desire. Too late she realized the threat to happiness of such dreams. One of her heroines, Caroline Vernon, in a novelette of 1839, is described as

fresh, naïve, romantic, really romantic, throwing her heart and soul into her dream, longing only for the opportunity . . . to die for somebody she loves . . . to give up heart, soul and sensation to one loved hero, to lose independent existence in the perfect adoption of her lover's being. . . .
("Caroline Vernon ")[10]

So too, Jane Eyre would feel and speak on the eve of her marriage:

My future husband was becoming to me my whole world; and more than the world; almost my hope of heaven. He stood between me and every thought of religion, as an eclipse intervenes between man and the broad sun. I could not, in those days, see God for His creature, of whom I had made an idol. . . .
(ch. 24)

Repeatedly in the juvenilia such foretastes of the mature novelist's thinking can be found. The novelettes of Charlotte Brontë written between her twentieth and twenty-third year have only recently been published; they repay reading. They remain to show that the juvenile writings of the Brontës were not the mere effect of a passing phase of childhood; they were the prelude to authorship, the proof of real creative powers. The protagonists of those early tales were not merely good practice for future character studies: they took such lasting hold of their authors' imaginations that some of them would become central to the plots of the mature works ahead. Not only Rochester and Jane in *Jane Eyre;* but Paul

Emmanuel and Paulina Hume in *Villette;* the Crimsworth brothers in *The Professor* (1857); Yorke Hunsdon, Hyram Yorke, and Mathewson Helstone in *Shirley;* and Blanche Ingram in *Jane Eyre* had all appeared in the juvenilia in recognizable form. It will be seen when the novels are analyzed how much they owed to the novice work of their author. As Charlotte herself recognized later, all this adolescent writing was no wasted effort but a true apprenticeship to her trade.

The drawback to the Brontës of such involvement in the life of their imaginary creations was that it made them unfit to come to terms with real life and people when they had to go out into the world. This was a source of great unhappiness to them—and a fatal handicap to Branwell in the attempt to earn his living. In childhood and early youth, they had too few contacts with other children or with styles of living other than their own to know how different their home was from that of the generality of families, especially the new rich living in the industrial West Riding towns, among whom it was to be the girls' ill fortune to find employment. Their inability to come to grips later with that alien world became one of the main themes of the novels of Charlotte and Anne, who had particular experience of it.

THE NATURAL ENVIRONMENT OF THE BRONTËS' HOME

BROUGHT up in such a close-knit family circle—with very few outside social contacts of any kind, save their father's parishioners in the village and in the moor farms—the Brontë children yet had one far greater outlet than the children of the West Riding towns about them in their luxurious homes with fine gardens: they had the absolute freedom of the moors that stretch for a radius of twenty miles round the hill village of Haworth. There ran that "little and a lone green lane" Emily wrote about later, "that opened on a common wide"; and there that view of

A distant, dreamy, dim blue chain
Of mountains circling every side;

and there

A heaven so clear, an earth so calm,
So sweet, so soft, so hushed an air,

---

[10]Reprinted in F. E. Ratchford, ed., *Legends of Angria* (New Haven, Conn., 1933), p. 260, and in W. Gérin, ed., *Five Novelettes by Charlotte Brontë* (London, 1971).

And, deepening still the dream-like charm,
Wild moor-sheep feeding everywhere—

That was the scene; I knew it well,
I knew the path-ways far and near,
That winding o'er the billowy swell
Marked out the tracks of wandering deer.
(Hatfield, 92)[11]

When Charlotte's friend Ellen Nussey first visited the Brontës in their early teens, what struck her most was the absolute self-assurance of Emily and Anne, generally so shy and withdrawn, when once out on the moors, acting as her guides; fording the stony becks, climbing the rocky slopes, philosophizing to the tadpoles in the clear mountain streams, dancing with sheer delight at the brightness of the day.

It was not a question of nature study for these nature-loving children, but of companionship. They knew and befriended every kind of creature, carrying the injured ones home, even to the untamable Merlin hawk "Hero" that Emily cherished and mourned when her aunt disposed of it. Emily was fearless of wild animals and knew all their haunts. The trait explains much in the character of the author of *Wuthering Heights* (1847). Without the moors for playground in childhood, and for inspiration in adolescence, it is doubtful if Emily would have written *Wuthering Heights* at all or ever been the poet and mystic she became.

The important fact about the moors to one of her shy and withdrawn nature was that they liberated her spirit. How literally, and how in a mystical sense, this became true, her poetry is there to attest; but to all the Brontës the moors gave a sense of freedom and independence, of which most other girls of their time were deprived. The moors about Haworth are not a flat tract of land seen at a glance (like the moors behind Whitby). They are deeply fretted with ravines and chequered with flowing rills that thread the heather and hurry to cascade over platforms of rocks into the stony hollows beneath. Emily described the scene and how it affected her in one of her earliest poems.

High wavering heather, 'neath stormy blasts bending,
Midnight and moonlight and bright shining stars;
Darkness and glory rejoicingly blending,
Earth rising to heaven and heaven descending,

Man's spirit away from its drear dungeon sending,
Bursting the fetters and breaking the bars.
(Hatfield, 5)

Everywhere on the moors is a hiding place for children, a stage for drama. The range and variety of scene, the continually changing prospects of sky and mountains were the source, not only of greatest joy for the Brontës, but a stimulus to invention. It was out on the moors that the essentially outdoor scenario of Gondal was conceived; that Emily and Anne played out in their own persons the fateful dramas affecting the outlaws, the exiles, the betrayed friends and lovers of Gondal's baleful Queen Augusta Geraldine Almeda—the regal counterpart of Charlotte's Duke of Zamorna. The role of nature in the conception of Gondal was primordial, as it was in Emily's life. To leave the moors for any other kind of region, for a disciplined, confined, restrictive mode of living, like a school, proved almost fatal to her when she was sent to school at fifteen. Her condition had to be recognized for the danger it was, and she had urgently to be sent home, where she perfectly recovered.

THE GONDAL LITERATURE

THE entire prose literature of Gondal has disappeared; only portions of the poetry of Gondal survive. From specimens of Emily's early longhand preserved in her diary papers, it could be argued that she wrote so badly that, self-critical as she was, she herself destroyed the early Gondal fragments. She gradually evolved a microscopic imitation of print that had the advantage of looking neat and was virtually illegible to anyone but herself. In this she wrote the poems. More difficult to explain is the destruction of the later Gondal prose of which we have evidence in the diary papers, written as late as 1845.

In those it was specifically stated that the girls' interest in the Gondals was as keen as ever and that they had every intention of "sticking by the rascals," as Emily called them. She was, according to Anne, busily engaged at that time in writing yet another Gondal script, the "Life of the Emperor Julius." Thanks to the preservation of the Gondal poems the Emperor Julius is well known to us, as are most of the other Gondal characters and situations referred to in the diary papers.

[11]C. W. Hatfield, ed., *The Complete Poems of Emily Brontë* (New York, 1941). References are to poem numbers as established by Hatfield.

Two lists of Gondal place names and characters, written by Anne, *ca.* 1832–1833, have been preserved. These confirm, or elucidate, the information contained in the poems, where the connection between the characters is mostly taken for granted by the authors. From these sources enough data can be pieced together to supply a framework for the lost prose Gondal fragments.

The list of place names was neatly, and alphabetically, inserted in the "Vocabulary of Proper Names" (otherwise the Index) to the children's old geography book, the Reverend J. Goldsmith's *A Grammar of General Geography*, dated 1823, which can still be seen in the Brontës' old home. From these insertions can be derived the fact that Gondal itself was "a large island situated in the North Pacific" with a capital city called Regina, and that its dependent colony, Gaaldine, was "a large island newly discovered in the South Pacific."

Islands had long been regular features of the Brontës' games (Charlotte recorded the inauguration of one such in 1827), and Emily's islands were the direct successors to, and an inherited piece of machinery from, a particular narrative of Charlotte's "Tales of the Islanders," on which Emily had collaborated in 1829–1830. Both Gondal and Gaaldine were divided into several kingdoms, of which the principal were Almedore and Exina, from which were drawn the reigning and rival families of Julius Brenzaida of Angora, King of Almedore,[12] and of Gerald Exina, King of Zalona, his cousin.

The dominant personality of the whole Gondal saga was Emily's heroine, Augusta Geraldine Almeda, of the reigning house of Almedore, as her name suggests.[13] The origin of the character whose uncontrollable passions, crimes, and eventual murder supply the drama of the Gondal poems derives inappropriately enough from Emily's early interest in the young Princess Victoria. Victoria had already figured in Charlotte's and Emily's joint production, "Tales of the Islanders." Victoria, it may be remembered, was to have been called Augusta but for the objection of her uncle George IV. Instead she was called Alexandrina, a name that occurs frequently in the Gondal literature. The idea of absolute sovereignty passing to a young girl near her in age obviously stimulated Emily's own growing sense of personal independence and adventure, and the éclat surrounding the preparations for Victoria's coronation launched her on a drama about kingship and rival claimants to the throne of Almedore, a treacherous rivalry that soon extended beyond the crown to the person of Augusta Geraldine Almeda herself. The plot of the evolving Gondal saga centered mainly on four persons: the capricious Queen and her rival lovers, Julius Brenzaida of Angora, Ferdinando de Samara, and Lord Alfred Aspin of Aspin Castle. The only interest for modern readers in these characters as distinct from the poems in which they figure is that they were the first foreshadowings of the triangle in *Wuthering Heights:* Cathy, Heathcliff, and Edgar Linton. They exhibit the same distinguishing traits as their ultimate prototypes—uncontrolled caprice in the woman, ruthless ambition in one man, and weakness in the other. From early adolescence, when Emily was sketching her Gondal characters, through the consummate achievement of *Wuthering Heights,* she was absorbed in working out this symbol of the soul's division between its conflicting elements.

The fragments—many of them without beginning and end—that constitute the poetry of Gondal were obviously intended as links in a coherent sequel; many of the poems in dialogue form bear the initials of the speaking characters (A.G.A. for Augusta, F.S. for Ferdinando de Samara, A.S. for Alfred Aspin, J.B. for Julius Brenzaida), as in a play. Emily's most famous lament, "Cold in the earth," mistakenly believed to represent a personal grief by its first publishers, was spoken over Julius Brenzaida's grave by yet another of his loves, Rosina Alcona (Hatfield, 187). That poem, written in 1845 when Emily was twenty-seven, shows the lasting hold that the Gondal framework had on her imagination. Because the total cycle contains such masterpieces as these, Gondal can never be considered as a merely juvenile recreation. Its initial conception was broad enough to contain the whole range of Emily's work, the philosopical poems and the single novel as well.

In this integration of her whole life's work within one wide unbroken vision, Emily differed from Anne. For Anne, Gondal represented conscious make-believe that, as her personal experience widened, she discarded in favor of realism.

Emily, too, made a superficial division later in

---

[12]The poems specifically dealing with Julius in the Hatfield edition of Emily's poems are nos. 40, 56, 77, 80, 81, 125, 150, 151, 156, 178, 182.

[13]The poems specifically dealing with Augusta in the Hatfield edition of Emily's poems are nos. 9, 16, 60, 61, 75, 85, 96, 100, 110, 133, 137, 143, 148, 158, 169, 171, 173, 180.

1844 between her philosophical poems and the Gondal poems, which she copied into separate notebooks with distinct titles: "Gondal Poems" for the one and "Poems by EJB" for the other, which can be seen in the British Museum. But one theme bound all her work together, and that was the influence of nature. She could no more eliminate the natural scene from the Gondal poems than from her heart. Some of her loveliest evocations of the earth about her appear in the Gondal poems.

The condition of the climate, of the season, the day and the night, were all-important to the drama she had in hand. Climate, indeed, was an integral feature of the Gondal invention, the two islands, Gondal and Gaaldine, differing fundamentally because of it. Gondal had an exotic vegetation and sky, conducive to soft living and love; Gaaldine, on the contrary, reflected the tempestuous skies of Haworth, and its people, the passionate, wild temperament of the Yorkshire hill folk.

To glance along the first lines of Emily's Gondal poems, as distinct from the descriptive philosophical poems, is to realize how pervasive is nature in all her writing:

> All blue and bright, in glorious light,
> The morn comes marching on;
> And now Zalona's steeples white
> Glow golden in the sun.
> (Hatfield, 156)

> Cold, clear, and blue, the morning heaven
> Expands its arch on high;
> Cold, clear, and blue, Lake Werna's water
> Reflects that winter's sky.
> (Hatfield, 1)

The famous poem,

> The linnet in the rocky dells,
> The moor-lark in the air,
> (Hatfield, 173)

with its exact evocation of the Haworth moors in summer, was in fact a threnody for the death of Augusta, murdered and buried in the heather.

One of the effects of the early partnership between Emily and Anne was the growth of the Gondal plot out of their natural surroundings and out of their early close knowledge of the moors. To assume the characters of their heroes and heroines was a game they played all their lives under the moors' liberating influence. Emily recorded the trait as late as her diary paper of 1845. In the following extract Anne is speaking as Alexander Hybernia, and the setting is all-important.

> "Zenobia, do you remember,
>   A little lonely spring
> Among Exina's woody hills
>   Where blackbirds used to sing?

> And when they ceased as daylight faded
>   From the dusky sky,
> The pensive nightingale began
>   Her matchless melody.

> Sweet bluebells used to flourish there
>   And tall trees waved on high,
> And through their ever-sounding leaves
>   The soft wind used to sigh."
> ("Alexander and Zenobia," 96–107)[14]

Anne was writing of the recognizable "oasis of emerald grass," a place on the moors the girls called the Meeting of the Waters, mentioned by Ellen Nussey as their favorite haunt.

As liberty was "the breath of Emily's nostrils" (as Charlotte said later), so the theme of freedom was central to the Gondal poems, with the conflicting issue of loss of freedom as a necessary corollary. The poems are mainly concerned with individuals in revolution, in conflict with the law. Poem after poem deals with strife, with the subject of exile, sometimes of victory, of alienation, of outlawry from loved surroundings.[15]

Second only to the sense of boundless space induced by the moors in Gondal is the incidence of prison scenes, of dungeon settings, of despair and death. These latter themes are not, however, present in the early poems; they increase in direct ratio as the authors themselves lost their freedom by enforced absences from home for school or governess life.

"In dungeons dark I cannot sing," wrote Emily after only a short experience in a Halifax school—

[14]From T. J. Wise and J. A. Symington, eds., *Poems of Emily and Anne Brontë* (Oxford, 1934). The poem was previously unpublished.
[15]See Hatfield, nos. 32, 33, 40, 75, 77, 104, 119, 125, 133, 141, 143, 151, 156, 164.

In sorrow's thrall 'tis hard to smile:
What bird can soar on broken wing?
What heart can bleed and joy the while?
(Hatfield, 77)

The despair induced by alien circumstances, such as absence from home in adolescence, became a universalized despair for a far less curable evil as Emily grew up: whether at home or abroad, the sense of being a spirit immured in walls of flesh with little hope of escape haunted her personal and her poetic life with a ceaseless yearning to break out.

It was only at rare moments that she could attain such a feeling of release coupled with a loss of personal identity. But it was this mystic condition of oneness, the supreme achievement of being, that she strained to bring about and that became the sole objective of her life: it is this experience that informs her finest poetry.

The simplest expression of the experience appears in the lines:

I'm happiest when most away
I can bear my soul from its home of clay
On a windy night when the moon is bright
And the eye can wander through worlds of light—

When I am not and none beside—
Nor earth nor sea nor cloudless sky—
But only spirit wandering wide
Through infinite immensity.

(Hatfield, 44)

All too often and too soon the experience is followed by returning consciousness of the limitation of earthly life, as in the supreme lines:

"Oh, dreadful is the check—intense the agony
When the ear begins to hear and the eye begins to see;
When the pulse begins to throb, the brain to think again,
The soul to feel the flesh and the flesh to feel the chain!"
(Hatfield, 190)

It is too often forgotten that these famous lines were written in the context of a Gondal prison scene: they reveal the degree of integration that Emily succeeded in achieving between her personal and her imaginary life, and to what extent Gondal was a forerunner of the adult work to come. What theme was more central to the great poems or to the single novel than this, of the soul's escape from its mortal condition?

THE BRONTËS' HOME LIFE

IT might appear paradoxical in a mystic poet like Emily that it was she, rather than any of the other Brontës, who made herself the guardian of the home as they all grew up; but so it was. Home life was a condition of health and happiness to her; she intensely loved not only the freedom of the moors but the austere daily round followed by the household inside the parsonage walls from year's end to year's end and was its careful chronicler. It would seem she found nothing constricting in its monotony and regularity.

It is mainly due to Emily's diary papers, written at regular intervals in conjunction with Anne, that the details of the Brontës' home life are known to us. Intended for no eyes but her own and Anne's, they yet contain a greater number of facts about the family's habits and home life than the hundreds of letters written by Charlotte to strangers. While Charlotte's letters were intensely personal, concerned with her immediate problems, Emily's home journals were objective statements of fact, noted without commentary, like the dialogue in a play. They cover every aspect of the domestic scene, and for outsiders to understand them they require some explanation.

Before quoting the two earliest in date, those of 1834 and 1837, it should be said that the model for keeping such records and the form in which Emily and Anne kept them seems to have been suggested to them by Lord Byron, whose boyish diary papers quoted in Thomas Moore's *Letters and Journals of Lord Byron*, published in 1830, had just been read by the Brontës. Byron's interest in his domestic pets, the weather, the time of day, and so on closely parallels the form Emily's papers took.

Of special interest in the first paper is the excellent dinner being prepared in the kitchen for the children's meal, which contradicts Mrs. Gaskell's reports of their poor food; the girls' casual unconcern over the tasks—bed making or piano practicing—that had been set for their day even when their teacher, Mr. Sunderland, was expected (he was organist of Keighley Parish Church); the interest in politics and the loan of newspapers from the local doctor; Tabby's admonitions to lazy girls; their aunt's correction of Anne's bad habit of sitting on her own feet; the week's washing going on in the scullery. Then, suddenly, in the midst of these domestic minutiae, the incursion of the Gondals as a matter of course. With the anticipated walk on the moors to crown the day, the family's doings are laid bare for all to see.

November the 24, 1834, Monday,
Emily Jane Brontë, Anne Brontë.
I fed Rainbow, Diamond Snowflake Jasper [Grasper?] Phaesant [alias?] this morning—Branwell went down to Mr Driver's & brought news that Sir Robert Peel was going to be invited to stand for [Leeds?] Anne and I have been peeling apples for Charlotte to make us an apple pudding and for aunt nuts and apples—Charlotte said she made puddings perfectly and she was of a quick but limited intellect . . . aunt has come into the kitchen just now and said where are your feet Anne—Anne answered on the floor aunt—papa opened the parlour door and gave Branwell a letter saying here Branwell read this and show it to your aunt and Charlotte—The Gondals are discovering the Interior of Gaaldine—Sally Mosley is washing in the back kitchen.

[end of first side][16]

Three years later, on the occasion of Branwell's twentieth birthday, Emily wrote a further record of home life (doubtless there had been others now lost written between). Though signed by both girls, the writing is Emily's and it is "embellished" by a sketch of them both sitting at a table littered with manuscripts.

The record is more concerned than the previous one with their Gondal writing; Anne's poem referred to here has been preserved; not so Emily's "Life of Augusta Almeda." It also shows a knowledge of the state of Angrian affairs reached by Charlotte and Branwell in their current writing. Zamorna is reported at Eversham (one of the capital cities of the Glass Town Confederation) and Northangerland in exile on Monkey's Isle, statements that corroborate the plot in the existing manuscripts. The incursion of real events in the allusion to Queen Victoria shows that Emily's early interest had not flagged. The debate over an evening walk shows also how the girls got into the "humour" for writing.

Monday evening June 26th 1837
A bit past 4 o'clock Charlotte working in Aunt's room, Branwell reading Eugene Aram to her—Anne and I writing in the drawing-room—Anne a poem beginning "Fair was the evening and brightly the sun"—I Augusta Almeda's life 1st v. 1–4th page from the last—fine rather coolish thin grey cloudy but sunny day   Aunt working in the little room the old nursery   Papa gone out   Tabby in the kitchen—The Emperors and Empresses of Gondal and Gaaldine preparing to depart from Gaaldine to Gondal to prepare

for the coronation which will be on the 12th July   Queen Vittoria ascended the throne this month   Northangerland in Monkey's Isle—Zamorna at Eversham. All tight and right in which condition it is to be hoped we shall all be this day 4 years at which time Charlotte will be 25 and 2 months—Branwell just 24 it being his birthday—myself 22 and 10 months and a piece Anne 21 and nearly a half   I wonder where we shall be and how we shall be and what kind of a day it will be then—let us hope for the best.

Emily Jane Brontë—Anne Brontë
I guess that this day 4 years we shall all be in this drawing-room comfortable I hope it may be so. Anne guesses we shall all be gone somewhere comfortable. We hope it may be so indeed.
[Obviously Miss Branwell put her head round the door.]
Aunt: Come Emily it's past 4 o'clock
Emily: Yes, Aunt   Exit Aunt
Anne: Well, do you intend to write in the evening
Emily: Well, what think you
(We agreed to go out 1st to make sure if we got into the humour. We may stay in—)

The first breakup of this close-knit family life occurred when Charlotte was fifteen and was sent for three terms (January 1831–June 1832) to a boarding school twenty miles from home, Roe Head at Mirfield Moor. It was an enlightened establishment, as different from the Clergy Daughters' School as could be, run on generous lines by its principal, Miss Margaret Wooler. Helped by two sisters, Miss Catherine and Miss Eliza, Miss Wooler provided as systematic an education as the fashion of the times required, enlarging the scope of Charlotte's very one-sided learning by a thorough grounding in modern languages and grammar. It was intended to fit Charlotte to earn her living eventually as a governess, and the expense of her schooling was borne by her godmother, Mrs. Atkinson, whose clerical husband was an old friend of Patrick Brontë's and had replaced him at nearby Hartshead. Charlotte was not unhappy and made three lasting friendships: that of Miss Wooler herself, and of two schoolfellows, Ellen Nussey and Mary Taylor. Her lifelong exchange of letters with these two forms the bulk of her preserved correspondence.

Charlotte's sisters were made the beneficiaries of her newfound learning; for the following three years (summer 1832–1835) she assumed their education, supplemented by the music and drawing lessons of teachers provided by their father. Meanwhile Branwell was given what was believed in the fond home circle to be an adequate art training to qualify him for entrance to the Academy Schools.

[16]From the Bonnell Collection; repr. in T. J. Wise and J. A. Symington, eds., *The Brontës, Their Lives, Friendships and Correspondence*, 4 vols. (Oxford, 1934), vol. I, p. 124.

The date coincided with other radical changes in his sisters' lives: Charlotte was offered a teacher's post by Miss Wooler and Emily offered free schooling there in part-payment for her services; Anne was to benefit by the same arrangement at a future date.

Charlotte wrote to her new friend Ellen Nussey on 2 July 1835:

> We are all about to divide, break up, separate. Emily is going to school, Branwell is going to London, and I am going to be a governess. This last determination I formed myself, knowing I should have to take the step sometime . . . and knowing also that papa would have enough to do with his limited income, should Branwell be placed at the Royal Academy and Emily go to Roe Head . . . I am going to teach in the very school where I was myself taught . . . and, in truth, since I must enter a situation, "My lines have fallen in pleasant places." I both love and respect Miss Wooler. . . .[17]

None of the arrangements fell out as anticipated. Emily was near to dying after only two months of school regimen and had to be hurried home while Anne took her place. Anne, who had been considered too delicate to leave home, gave proof of a surprising resolution of spirit in determining to earn her own living like the rest and bore with school life for the next two and a half years, ending as probably the best educated of the Brontës in consequence.

The deplorable outcome of Branwell's single incursion into the competitive world of the capital affected not only his own prospects forever, but marked the decline in his personal prestige in the family circle. From the humiliating experience of London his ego never recovered. Whatever gifts he had received from nature could only thrive in an atmosphere of adulation and easy success; he had none of the staying power of his sisters to overcome hardship nor, as he advanced in age, did he show any of the talents that had been so conspicuous in his boyhood. His tragedy indeed it was to be the only one not to fulfill the promise of childhood.

BRANWELL IN LONDON

BRANWELL himself related the circumstances of his London fiasco in a fictional narrative written in May

1836, some six months after the event. As a document it is extremely revealing, both for the insights it gives into Branwell's mental and emotional makeup, and for the fictional wrapping he chose to give what was after all no Angrian adventure but hard matter of fact. To escape from the implications of reality became an increasing necessity with him as circumstances failed to square up to the exorbitant expectations of his boyhood. As an Angrian adventure, indeed, he saw his own plight, and so presented it to his imaginary readers, giving it the title "Adventure of Charles Wentworth" that appears in the fifth volume of his "History of Angria."

What is recognizably true in his fictional account of his adventure is Branwell's state of mind. He had some gift for self-analysis and already at nineteen saw into the causes for his inability to act because nothing in real experience appeared to him worth an effort—nothing equaled his expectations of it. "He set forth on his journey of 300 miles," he tells us, "with plenty of letters of introduction . . ." but already at the outset he realized that this journey "to the mightiest city of the world, where he was to begin real life, and in a while, maybe, take a lead in it," did not give him half the pleasure he had always fancied it would. "Now this, thought he, was always looked to by me *as one of my* grand fountains of happiness . . . I was nearing the great spring where all my thirst would be gratified—" and he came to the conclusion, before even making trial of proof, that "*Happiness* consists in Anticipation. . . . He recollected his advisers had told him when they saw him in expectation of an ample fortune . . . give himself up to idleness and go about doing nothing and caring nothing but building air-castles for the adornment of his future life—'Now,' they said, '*you can never have real happiness without working for it. . . .*' My first argument leads me to the conclusion that I shall have nothing to reward my exertions. Then why should I labour? . . ." Arrived "in the mighty city of Africa" on the second day of his journey, he walked about his room at the hotel "in a pleasant sort of excitement, and then, as that ebbed off, longing for supper . . . " and was kept awake all night by his thoughts.

Next morning he reflected that he had not a relation in the city, which to him was a pleasant and delightful reflection. Then he examined his letters and put them up again, thought of his wealth and independence, took breakfast and sallied out into the streets with an outward appearance of remarkable dejection, and something very likely broken

[17]In T. J. Wise and J. A. Symington, *The Brontës: Their Lives, Friendships and Correspondence* (Oxford, 1934), vol. I, p. 129.

circumstances, but which really arose from constant *thinking*. . . . His mind was too restless to stop and fully examine anything.

In this mood he reached the embankment and leaning on the parapet watched the shipping come and go. His profound dejection brought tears to his eyes,

and a feeling like a wind seemed to pass across his spirits, because now he felt that not even the flashes of glory which these streets and buildings had struck from his soul, not even these feelings which he had reckoned on as something to supply years of dullness, could preserve his thoughts from aimless depression. . . . Next day found him still unknown and unvisited. . . . Nor was he bent studiously on ransacking the great libraries or studying in the picture galleries. He was restlessly, aimlessly . . . feeding his feeling with "little squibs of rum" as he called them to himself, since he was perfectly aware that they would only the more depress him afterwards. . . .[18]

Without presenting himself to the Secretary of the Academy Schools, without delivering any of his letters of introduction to the professors whose classes he would need to attend, without taking one step toward advancing the business that had brought him to London, he returned to Haworth a beaten man, conscious only of the fatal flaw in his character that made him incapable of action.

CHARLOTTE AS TEACHER

OVER a period of nine years, with intervals of unemployment, Charlotte Brontë was a teacher, first in her old school, then as private governess in two families, and finally as English teacher in a Brussels school. The cumulative experience of those years, while it greatly altered her character, never lessened her passion for writing or interrupted the steady flow of her invention.

As a family, the Brontës were unable to adapt themselves to strange surroundings, though all three girls made conscientious efforts to do so. Since they were paid to give their services, they scrupulously gave them, though it was with death in their souls. Each kept alive only by pursuing her dream existence: Charlotte in a continuous stream of Angrian narratives; Emily in a spate of Gondal poems; Anne alone took stock of her surroundings with a determination to come to grips with them, and noted their peculiarities with an eye to future reference.

Charlotte's manuscripts from the Roe Head period (1835–1838) were written on notepaper from home in the microscopic script she and Branwell had perfected. The sections were necessarily short because of the circumstances under which she wrote them—mostly while supervising the girls at their homework—and difficult to decipher because of her habit of writing with her eyes closed. These fragments have a value for us in revealing her methods of composition.

The visual quality of her mature writing must be apparent to all readers of her novels; it is perhaps the most distinguishing feature of her style. The intensity of the focus she brought to bear on any scene under description was the effect, so the Roe Head writings reveal, of an inner vision obtained not only by an exceptional power of imagination but by shutting the eyes on her surroundings. Her own descriptions of the processes of invention show that writing on any subject began by *seeing*; she had a sharpened inner vision that equaled the effect of drugs. There is no evidence that Charlotte took drugs, even when Branwell did, but the resultant dream condition was very similar. The following excerpts from her Roe Head fragments are chosen not only as showing her imagination at work but for their account of the deep frustration she suffered when the urge to write overmastered her. The bitterness of the experience informs all her writing of the time with a new language of revolt. She wrote one evening while supervising the girls at their homework:

I am just going to write because I cannot help it. Wiggins [Branwell] might indeed talk of scribble-mania if he were to see me just now—encompassed by bulls (query calves of Bashan) all wondering why I write with my eyes shut—staring, gaping long their astonishment. A C[oo]k on one side of me, E L[ister] on the other and Miss W[ooler] in the background, stupidity the atmosphere, school-books the employment, asses the society. What in all this is there to remind me of the divine, silent, unseen land of thought, dim now and indefinite as the dream of a dream, the shadow of a shade. There is a voice, there is an impulse that wakens up that dormant power which in its torpidity I sometimes think dead. That wind pouring in impetuous currents through the air, sounding wildly unremittingly from hour to hour, deepening its tone as the night ad-

---

[18]"The Adventure of Charles Wentworth" in "The History of Angria," vol. V; repr. in *Miscellaneous Writings and Unpublished Writings*. . . , vol. II, p. 181.

vances, coming not in gusts, but with a rapid gathering stormy swell, that wind I know is heard at this moment far away on the moors at Haworth. Branwell and Emily hear it and as it sweeps over our house down the church-yard and round the old church, they think perhaps of me and Anne.[19]

Another fragment dated 11 August 1836 and written, therefore, after she had been teaching for a year at Roe Head, tells the same tale of revolt at her circumstances, of mental agony at not being able to follow the impulsion of that "mighty phantasm"—the Angrian dream—though, as she significantly recorded, "it showed almost in the vivid light of reality the ongoings of the infernal world." These are strong words, but she would repeat their substance seven years later when in a Brussels boarding school, and their truth cannot be doubted:

All this day I have been in a dream half miserable and half ecstatic miserable because I could not follow it out uninterruptedly, and ecstatic because it showed almost in the vivid light of reality the ongoings of the infernal world. I had been toiling for nearly an hour with Miss Lister, Miss Marriott and Ellen Cook striving to teach them the distinction between an article and a substantive. The parsing lesson was completed, a dead silence had succeeded it in the school-room and I sat sinking from irritation and weariness into a kind of lethargy. . . . Must I from day to day sit chained to this chair prisoned within these four bare walls, while these glorious summer suns are burning in heaven and the year is revolving in its richest glow, and declaring at the close of every summer's day, the time I am losing, will never come again? Stung to the heart with this reflection I started up and mechanically walked to the window—a sweet August morning was smiling without . . . I shut the window and went back to my seat. Then came on me rushing impetuously all the mighty phantasm that we had conjured from nothing to a system strong as some religious creed. I felt as if I could have written gloriously—I longed to write. . . .

There follows her account of a brief leisure hour when she could at last give herself up to the dream. It is evident that composition was an almost unconscious process (there was nothing literary about it), a surrender to a panorama of images passing before her inward eye, whose meaning she had to interpret like any Sybil presented with a conundrum.
She describes how, after accompanying the girls

on their afternoon walk, she was free to go to her room. Charlotte

crept up to the bed-room to be alone for the first time that day. Delicious was the sensation I experienced as I laid down on the spare-bed and resigned myself to the luxury of twilight and solitude. The stream of thought, checked all day came flowing free and calm along its channel. My ideas were too shattered to form any defined picture as they would have done in such circumstances at home, but detached thoughts soothingly flitted round me and unconnected scenes occurred to me then vanished producing an effect certainly strange but to me very pleasing . . . the toil of the day succeeded by this moment of divine leisure had acted on me like opium and was coiling about me a disturbed but fascinating spell such as I never felt before. What I imagined grew morbidly vivid. I remember I quite seemed to see with my bodily eyes a lady standing in the hall of a gentleman's house as if waiting for someone. It was dusk and there was the dim outline of antlers with a hat and rough great-coat upon them. She had a flat candle-stick in her hand and seemed coming from the kitchen or some such place. She was very handsome it is not often we can form from pure idea faces so individually fine she had black curls hanging rather low in her neck a very blooming skin and dark anxious looking eyes.

The key to her processes of invention is in the final passage where she tells how she "works out the vision" and relates it to the Angrian saga—with its whole cast of "statesmen and Kings. . . ." The confession explains much of the sheer scale of Angria and its lasting hold on her imagination, since every new scene imagined is only fresh grist to that mill.

No more I have not time to work out the vision. A thousand things were connected with it, a whole country, statesmen and Kings, a Revolution, thrones and princedoms subverted and reinstated—meantime the tall man washing his bloody hands in a bason and the dark beauty standing by with a light remained pictured in my mind's eye with irksome and alarming distinctness. I grew frightened at the vivid glow of the candle at the reality of the lady's erect and symmetrical figure. . . . At last I became aware of feeling like a heavy weight lying across me. I knew I was wide awake and that it was dark and that moreover the ladies were now come into the room to get their curl-papers they perceived me lying on the bed and I heard them talking about me. . . . I must get up I thought and I did so with a start. I have had enough of morbidity vivid realisations—every advantage has its corresponding disadvantages—tea's ready Miss Wooler is impatient. . . .

A striking feature of these lucubrations is their swaggering tone—their assumption of masculine

---

[19] The Bonnell Collection; quoted in F. E. Ratchford, *The Brontës' Web of Childhood* (New York, 1941), pp. 109–110.

know-all, one is tempted to say, their vulgarity—and one has to remember that her model and partner up to that time had been her brother, Branwell (Branwell's failure in London had not yet undermined his standing as her collaborator). How much of a pose it was she could not hide for long. Her real feelings are ardently romantic, sensuously stirred by every sight of beauty, by every act of heroism. She is caught up in another narrative, watching an "exquisitely beautiful girl" move through ranks of admiring "patricians" in a grand salon:

I hear them speak as well as she does, I see distinctly their figures—and though alone, I experience all the feelings of one admitted for the first time into a grand circle of classic beings—recognising by tone, gesture and aspect hundreds whom I never saw before, but whom I have heard of many a time, and is not this enjoyment? I am not accustomed to such magnificence as surrounds me, to the gleam of such large mirrors, to the beauty of marble figures, to soft foreign carpets to long wide rooms and lofty gilded ceilings. I know nothing of people of rank and distinction, yet there they are before me. . . .

The degree of her involvement in her imaginary characters brings a sharp rejection of her actual surroundings, which she regards as obstacles to the dream life, surroundings that she hates but has to endure.

I now after a day of weary wandering, return to the ark which for me floats alone on the billows of this world's desolate and boundless deluge. . . . It is the still small voice always that comes to me at eventide that . . . which takes up my spirit and engrosses all my living feelings, all my energies which are not merely mechanical . . . Haworth and home wake sensations which lie dormant elsewhere. Last night I did indeed lean upon the thunder-waking wings of such a stormy blast as I have seldom heard below, and it whirled me away like heath . . . for five seconds of ecstasy, and I sat by myself in the dining-room while all the rest were at tea, the trance seemed to descend on a sudden. . . .

A long narration followed and she was in the boudoir of the Queen of Angria, her best-loved character, Mary Percy, Zamorna's wife, when the spell was broken. "While the apparition was before me the dining-room door opened and Miss Wooler came in with a plate of butter in her hand. 'A very stormy night, my dear,' she said. 'It is,' I said."

Charlotte reached her twentieth year (April 1836) with an embittered sense of unfulfillment; ". . . a thousand wishes rose . . . which must die with me for they will never be fulfilled . . ." she wrote. To her the company of these "transcendantly fair and inaccessible sacred beings," was a recourse as habit-forming as drug addiction; she resented every obstacle put in her way. Despite her hopeless prospects she was increasingly conscious of her powers and resolved to put her chances as writer to the test. Instigated by Branwell she wrote to the Poet Laureate, Southey, on 29 December 1836, during the Christmas holidays at Haworth. Branwell wrote to Wordsworth on the same occasion. She sent Southey specimens of her writing with so touching, yet at the same time so extravagant, a letter, that his opinion could not be anything but unfavorable. He has been blamed for not recognizing her gifts and for urging her to abandon authorship as a livelihood. She had asked him for his frank opinion, and he sent it on the evidence of the manuscripts in hand. What he perceived more clearly than any signs of ability in this young correspondent was her uncontrolled imagination, the fevered excitement in which she wrote, the extravagance of the scenes she described, the Byronic passions unleashed. Southey's reply was expressed with such kindness and good sense that it carried more weight with Charlotte than immediate encouragement. She bore the disappointment with exemplary courage and, what mattered more, with intelligence and the resolution to do differently in the future. From Southey's advice can be traced the sobering effects on her unbridled emotionalism and exorbitant dreams. He saw the great danger her imagination could be to her happiness in a workaday world. "There is a danger," he wrote her on Easter Monday 1837,

of which I would, with all kindness and all earnestness, warn you. The day dreams in which you habitually indulge are likely to induce a distempered state of mind and, in proportion as the ordinary uses of the world seem to you flat and unprofitable, you will be unfitted for them without becoming fitted for anything else . . . do not suppose that I disparage the gift which you possess, nor that I would discourage you from exercising it. I only exhort you so to think of it and so to use it, as to render it conducive to your own permanent good. . . . It is not because I have forgotten that I was once young myself . . . but because I remember it. . . .

Charlotte endorsed his letter, received after considerable delay: "Southey's advice to be kept for ever. My twenty-first birthday. Roe Head. April 21st, 1837."

The remaining manuscripts written during the two

following years, 1837–1839, show not only an enlargement of her powers, but growing self-criticism. The holidays at midsummer and Christmas allowed her to launch on longer narratives. Though still devoid of much sense of structure or plot, they already show in full measure a sense of character and great descriptive powers; her forte, then as later, was in the analysis of feeling. These qualities are all apparent in the five major novelettes written during this period. Written sporadically and mostly at great speed, not all have titles, and three of them are without ends; but for bibliographical purposes they have been cataloged as follows: "Passing Events," the first in date (it was so-called by Charlotte herself). She wrote it in eight days, during her Easter holidays in April 1836. Its quite disconnected successor "Julia" was finished on 29 June 1837. This was followed by "Mina Laury," written during the Christmas holidays of 1837–1838, dated by Charlotte 17 January 1838, the day she returned to Roe Head. "Captain Henry Hastings," a novelette in two parts, was written at great speed during February and March 1839. By then she had left Roe Head (May 1838) and was at home for a year. From June to August 1839 Charlotte was absent from home again as governess in a private family, the Benson-Sidgwicks, at Stonegappe in Lothersdale. In her holidays from this engagement she wrote "Caroline Vernon," finished in December 1839. Both these last tales are considerably longer than any attempted before, and are complete. The analysis of character, of motive, of feeling, while still Byronic in substance, shows a new ability in the author to *observe* people and portray them with truth. Gone are the dream figures of her earlier fantasies; gone too is the almost reverent approach to her heroes and heroines; she sees them now as faulty and suffering mortals, in whose fortunes she is no longer inextricably caught up; she is able now to stand aside, a compassionate witness to their folly.

These novelettes (there were others that she destroyed) contain in embryo many of the themes she would elaborate in her later, published novels, and are therefore of special interest in following her development as a writer. Without them, the student of her work would be left without any clues to the radical change in style and manner that divides her adolescent from her mature work. The author of the preface to *The Professor* (1846; published 1857), who declared as her principle for writing fiction, "I have said to myself that my hero should work his way through life, as I had seen real living men work theirs . . . " is barely recognizable as the writer of those frenzied Roe Head journals: she had discarded fantasy and accepted the limitations of life.

ANONYMOUS AUTHORSHIP: THE ASSUMPTION OF THE MALE IDENTITY

WHEN the Brontës published their first novels, under pseudonyms, it was not from mere expediency to overcome contemporary prejudice against women writers, but from a habit harking back to childhood when they acted out their imaginary "Plays" under assumed names. Nothing less than the most illustrious would satisfy them: Wellington for Charlotte, Bonaparte for Branwell, the explorer Sir Edward Parry and Sir John Ross for Emily and Anne. Patrick Brontë noted the trait when reporting later to Mrs. Gaskell: "When mere children, as soon as they could read and write, Charlotte and her brother and sisters used to invent and act little plays of their own, in which the Duke of Wellington, my daughter Charlotte's hero, was sure to come off conqueror; when a dispute would not infrequently arise amongst them regarding the comparative merit of him, Buonaparte, Hannibal and Caesar. . . ."[20] With the growth of a little more wisdom, they accepted secondary roles that permitted them greater freedom of movement than those of the heroes themselves; Charlotte adopted the identity of Wellington's son, Charles Wellesley, and Branwell that of Marshal Soult's son, Young Soult, under which to chronicle the doings of their superiors. Under the signature of Lord Charles Albert Florian Wellesley, Charlotte wrote the majority of her Angrian chronicles between 1830 and 1836. In that year, she changed it to Charles Townsend (variously spelled Townshend, which again was a transition from Charles Thunder, from the Greek $\beta\rho o\upsilon\tau\eta$ [Brontë] for thunder). Lord Charles Wellesley was distinguished as an "author" by certain recognizable Branwellian traits, which harked back to the time of closest collaboration between brother and sister; he was swaggering, inquisitive, bumptious, exaggerating, prying, mischief-making, sneaking (Branwell had once been called Sneaky), all

---

[20]In E. C. Gaskell, *The Life of Charlotte Brontë* (London, 1900), p. 58.

the qualities Charlotte had ascribed to her brother in a lively skit of 1834, "Patrick Benjamin Wiggins," when his growing self-assertiveness in dress, language, and pretensions began to make him a figure of fun to his sisters. It was in studying Branwell's absurdities that Charlotte found her sense of humor. It was a first step toward independence from him, and the second was her assumption of a new literary "identity" in the person of Charles Townsend.

Charlotte's collaboration with Branwell, however, begun when both were children editing *Branwell's Blackwood's* magazine and signing their editorials "U.T." (Us Two) and "W.T." (We Two), was more than a literary partnership: it was a fusion of minds, and she found it hard indeed to free herself from his dominion. Charles Townsend, though he "wrote" without any reference to a partner, was as like Branwell Brontë as two peas, and left his mark on two at least of the novelettes Charlotte wrote between 1836–1839, "Passing Events" and the far more professional "Captain Henry Hastings." The importance of Charles Townsend, however, does not rest for us today in his supposed authorship of the novelettes, but for his recognizable hand in *The Professor*, which, one has to remember, is the only one of Charlotte's published works ostensibly written by a man, by the hero William Crimsworth; and in this fact undoubtedly lay the book's early failure.

In her uneasy assumption of masculine characteristics, Charlotte always harked back to the coxcombical tone adopted from Branwell and developed under the mask of Charles Townsend, but her inconsistency in sustaining the part, and her frequent lapses into feminine reflexes as her own thoughts and feelings took control, undermine all credibility in the character. William Crimsworth's self-love and easily roused vanity are jarring notes in the perfectly observed vignettes of Belgian characters that take the stage as the plot unfolds and moves to its climax in the triumphant creation of Zoraide Reuter and the touching beauty of Frances Henri. In creating *them* Charlotte was using her own observation of people and real life and had no need of the mouthpiece of the fake reporter, Townsend. It was his last appearance, and from then on Currer Bell—or Charlotte Brontë, call herself as she would—having gained her freedom, could speak in her own character. It was not merely from Townsend that she was freeing herself, but from the far older and more enduring thralldom to her brother.

Among the five novelettes of the period 1836–1839, three already show Charlotte's new determination to write in her own character, or at least in that of her heroines: "Mina Laury," "Captain Henry Hastings," and "Caroline Vernon." They are essentially feminine productions and deal with a common theme, one that obsessed Charlotte for years and that she finally worked out when Jane Eyre rejected Rochester's proposals of illicit love; it might be called the *seduction theme*.

In "Mina Laury," Mina's fate has already been settled before the tale begins. She has been Zamorna's mistress for some years; was the devoted attendant of his illegitimate son (by another mistress) when the rebels murdered him in her arms. Her disinterested love for her "Master" (as Jane Eyre would also call Rochester), her unobtrusive understanding of his cares and needs, are touchingly described. She is prepared to sacrifice everything for love; her sacrifice is the greater as she has nothing further to hope for from the unfaithful Zamorna. She is no fool and can see her position clearly; but her passion is incurable. Her feelings, she admits,

> were so fervid, so glowing in their colour that they effaced everything else—I lost the power of properly appreciating the value of the world's opinion, of discerning the difference between right & wrong. Zamorna . . . was sometimes more to me than a human being—he superseded all things—all affections, all interests, all fears or hopes or principles—Unconnected with him my mind would be a blank . . . I know the extent of my own infatuation. . . .[21]

At twenty-one, without any actual experience of love, Charlotte Brontë was able to write like that by poetic intuition, by sheer imaginative prescience. It was a subject she had brooded on since childhood and under the spell of Byron.

In "Captain Henry Hastings" two subjects dominate the plot: the brother-and-sister relationship of Henry and Elizabeth Hastings, closely modeled on that of Branwell and Charlotte, with the brother falling into disgrace and danger of death (he has murdered his superior officer) and flying for shelter to the sister; and the secondary theme of the attempted seduction of Elizabeth by Sir William Percy. Elizabeth Hastings is no Mina Laury; she is an intelligent, reserved, strong-minded young woman who earns her

[21]The Bonnell Collection; repr. in *Legends of Angria*, p. 180, and in *Five Novelettes by Charlotte Brontë*.

living as a teacher; in appearance she is reported as resembling her brother (as Charlotte and Branwell resembled each other).

Neither were handsome, the man had wasted his vigour & his youth in vice—there was more to repel than charm in the dark fiery eye sunk far below the brow—an aspect marked with the various lines of suffering, passion & profligacy—yet there were the remnants of a strong and steady young frame. . . . His sister was almost as fair as he was dark—but she had little colour—her features could lay no claim to regularity—though they might to expression—yet she had handsome brown eyes—and a lady like & elegant turn of figure. had she dressed herself stylishly & curled her hair, no one would have called her plain—but in a brown silk frock—a simple collar & hair parted on her forehead in smooth braids—she was just an insignificant—unattractive young woman without the bloom . . . of beauty. . . .[22]

Elizabeth Hastings is as passionate at heart as Mina Laury and longs as greatly to be loved; but the man she loves has never noticed her. "There is no bitterness the human heart knows," commented Charlotte in describing her heroine's despair, "like that of being alone and despised, whilst around it hundreds are loved and idolized. . . ." The day comes when she is thrown by chance in Sir William's way and is tricked into admitting her love. Reckoning on an easy victory over her, he is startled at being firmly put in his place.

"Elizabeth, . . . your eyes betray you—they speak the language of a very ardent, very imaginative temperament—they confess not only that you love me, but that you cannot live without me . . . yield to your nature & let me claim you this moment as my own. . . ."
Miss Hastings was silent—but she was not going to yield —only the hard conflict of passionate love—with feelings that shrank horror-struck from the remotest shadow of infamy compelled her for a moment to silent agony. . . .

Like Jane Eyre, and unlike Mina Laury, her answer was in flight. Elizabeth Hastings' reaction to her brother's degradation is the more interesting because of the real situation existing at the time between Charlotte and her brother, who was already fast becoming an alcoholic and a drug addict.

It was very odd [Charlotte wrote of her heroine's feelings] but his sister did not think a pin the worse of him for

all his Dishonour—it is private mean-ness—not public infamy that degrade a man in the opinion of his relatives. . . . Miss Hastings heard him cursed by every mouth—saw him denounced in every newspaper, still he was the same brother to her he had always been—still she beheld his actions through a medium peculiar to herself—She saw him go away with a triumphant Hope . . . that his future actions would nobly blot out the calumnies of his ennemies—yet after all she knew he was an unredeemed villain—human nature is full of inconsistencies—natural affection is a thing never rooted out where it has once really existed. . . .

The latest in date of Charlotte's preserved novelettes, "Caroline Vernon," is at the same time a more ambitious tale with a wider range of scene and character than the preceding ones and with a more profound analysis of the devastations of love. It is the story of a young girl, Caroline, the illegitimate child of Alexander Percy and a Parisian actress, Louisa Vernon. She is brought up in retirement as Zamorna's ward. The situation, as readers of *Jane Eyre* can recognize, is a foreshadowing of that existing in Rochester's household at Thornfield Hall: the child Adèle brought up in her guardian's home out of the reach of her deplorable Parisian mother. The difference in the moral conception of the two situations is central to Charlotte's development as writer and moralist. In "Caroline Vernon" the emphasis is on the irresistible nature of passion, on the fatal power it has on a youthful heart. Caroline Vernon has no governess like Jane Eyre to teach her self-restraint and self-respect; she grows up a reckless creature who, at fifteen, throws herself at her guardian's head on the model of Claire Clairmont with Byron and is ruined by him. The analysis of her awakening feelings for the middle-aged amorist Zamorna has become as perceptive a character study as any Charlotte wrote at the height of her powers, but it is not a moral homily.
Caroline is described as " . . . fresh, naive, romantic, really romantic, throwing her heart and soul into her dream, longing only for the opportunity . . . to die for somebody she loves . . . to give up heart, soul and sensation to one loved hero, to lose independent existence in the perfect adoption of her lover's being. . . . " These are the very thoughts and feelings Charlotte herself had known since her ardent hero-worshiping girlhood, feelings that had been at the heart of her whole Angrian creation, built up as it had been around her romantic love for the imaginary Zamorna. Charlotte Brontë knew Caroline Vernon's dilemma because it was—and had long been—her

[22]The Widener Collection, Harvard University; repr. in *Five Novelettes by Charlotte Brontë.*

124

own; only by writing of it in this manner could she exorcise it.

> The young lady's feelings were not exactly painful, they were strange, new & startling—she was getting to the bottom of an unsounded sea, & lighting on rocks she had not guessed at. . . . Thus did Zamorna cease to be an abstract principle in her mind—thus did she discover that he was a man vicious like other men . . . with passions that sometimes controlled him—with propensities that were often stronger than his reason. . . .[23]

Since Charlotte knew nothing of seduction, her analysis of the seducer was, as she herself said, mere abstraction; but the feelings of the seducer's victim were vividly real to her. Having put herself into Zamorna's power, Caroline sees him with fresh eyes:

> His deep voice, as he uttered this—his high-featured face, & dark large eye, beaming bright with a spark from the depths of Gehenna, struck Caroline Vernon with a thrill of nameless dread—here he was—the man that Montmorency had described to her—all at once she knew him—Her Guardian was gone—Something terrible sat in his place. . . . She feared, she loved—Passion tempted, conscience warned her—But, in a mind like Miss Vernon's, Conscience was feeble . . . & when Zamorna kissed her & said in that voice of fatal sweetness which has instilled venom into many a heart "Will you go with me tomorrow, Caroline?" she looked up in his face with a kind of wild devoted enthusiasm & answered "Yes." . . .[24]

Southey's advice, apparent in the greater sobriety of language in the later novelettes, had not affected their matter: this was still the unashamed exploitation of the theme of romantic love.

Another year's reflection, however, and the result of a fresh approach to a professional writer to gain his advice—this time it was Hartley Coleridge—drew from Charlotte that solemn recantation of her past errors known as the "Farewell to Angria." She wrote to Hartley Coleridge in December 1840 and sent him a specimen novelette with a long covering letter signed "C.T." (Charles Townsend) that included this significant passage: "It is very edifying . . . to create a world out of one's own brain and people it with inhabitants who are like so many 'Melchise-

dics'—'without father, without mother'— . . . By conversing daily with such beings, and accustoming your eyes to their glaring attire and fantastic features—you acquire a tone of mind admirably calculated to enable you to cut a respectable figure in practical life. . . ." The ability to ridicule her own addiction and to acknowledge its uselessness in practical life was already a sign of Charlotte's amendment: Hartley's kind but firm condemnation of her style completed the cure. In the undated "Farewell to Angria" generally ascribed to this time she wrote:

> I have now written a great many books, and for a long time have dwelt on the same characters and scenes and subjects . . . but we must change, for the eye is tired of the picture so oft recurring and now so familiar. Yet do not urge me too fast, reader, it is no easy thing to dismiss from my imagination the images that have filled it so long; they were my friends and my intimate acquaintances. . . . When I depart from these I feel almost as if I stood on the threshold of a home and were bidding farewell to its inmates. . . .[25]

The resolution to write unemotionally, however much it might apply to *The Professor*, bears little relation in the end to the great novels to come; they spring in true line of succession from Angria. Charlotte Brontë's is a curious, perhaps an exceptional case of emotional perception *preceding experience*. It might indeed be doubted whether, without the invention of Angria, she would ever have known the kind of love she found in Brussels, a love that was *necessarily* unrequited.

When Harriet Martineau reviewed *Villette* on its publication, she did not hesitate to speak out her mind on what displeased her in a work whose overall greatness impressed her as it did all Currer Bell's admirers: this was what she called

> the prevalence of one tendency, or one idea, throughout the whole conception and action. All the female characters, in all their thoughts and lives, are full of one thing, or are regarded by the reader in the light of that one thought—love . . . so dominant is this idea—so incessant is the writer's tendency to describe the need of being loved, that the heroine . . . leaves the reader . . . under the uncomfortable impression of her having . . . entertained a double love, or allowed one to supersede another. . . . It is not thus in real life. . . .[26]

[23]The Widener Collection; repr. in *Legends of Angria*, pp. 267–268, and in *Five Novelettes by Charlotte Brontë*.
[24]The Widener Collection; repr. in *Legends of Angria*, pp. 304–305, and in *Five Novelettes*.

[25]The Bonnell Collection; repr. in *Legends of Angria*, p. 315.
[26]*Daily News*, 3 February 1853.

Harriet Martineau, while deeply wounding Charlotte, who by the time she wrote *Villette* wrote of love from personal experience, had nevertheless perceived what had from the beginning been Charlotte's source of inspiration: "the need of being loved." This need, felt at the core of all Charlotte's work, this sense of deprivation, these wounded feelings, natural in a child orphaned early of her mother, bereft while still a child of the sisters she passionately loved—found their outlet and early compensation in the creation of an imaginary life built to the measure of her unfulfilled desires. Without the long emotional apprenticeship of the Angrian chronicles culminating in the novelettes of her early twenties, who knows if Charlotte Brontë would ever have come to write the works for which she is remembered: *Jane Eyre*, *Shirley*, and *Villette*?

THE CREATIVE WORK

THE dispersal of the family in the summer of 1835, which sent the young Brontës each in pursuit of training away from home, kept them effectually apart for nearly ten years. The school holidays that brought them home twice a year were short ones in those days, and the separation between them became a psychological as well as a physical reality. They were all growing from adolescence into young man- and womanhood and taking the definitive turns that would shape their characters. The ties of childhood, peculiarly strong between Charlotte and Branwell, were irretrievably broken; they spoke a different language when next they lived together, and held opposite moral codes. The early union of heart and imagination that had bound Emily and Anne, on the other hand, was cemented into an enduring relationship. Neither girl is ever known to have sought outside friendships, as Charlotte did: each found sufficient companionship in the other, both at work and play. Insofar as Emily was ever known to confide in anyone, she confided in Anne.

The pattern of the intervening years is singular in that, despite varying experience, the children's objective remained constant: and for the girls it was to be reunited and achieve their independence—they had the idea of setting up a school together—and, as recompense for their pains, the "dream of authorship," never wholly abandoned even in the worst times of their drudgery.

EMILY BRONTË AS TEACHER AT HALIFAX

IN September 1837, Emily Brontë went as teacher to a girls' boarding school in the Halifax suburb of Southowram, kept by a Miss Elizabeth Patchett. To leave home voluntarily and take a situation in a school after the fiasco of her Roe Head venture was evidence of a new resolution on Emily's part and of an overriding domestic reason—the increasing need for the girls to earn their living as Branwell's prospects of doing so dwindled.

Emily's reactions to the alien life of a big establishment were exactly like Charlotte's at Roe Head: uncompromising hostility. Charlotte reported of her in a letter of 2 October 1837 to Ellen Nussey: "I have had one letter from her since her departure, it gives an appalling account of her duties—hard labour from six in the morning until near eleven at night, with only one half-hour of exercise between. This is slavery. I fear she will never stand it. . . ."

Emily stood it for at least six months—two of the then long terms—because she was too proud to fail again. Years later Charlotte described how, by "the mere force of resolution," Emily endured an even worse exile from home in a Brussels school: ". . . with inward remorse and shame she looked back on her former failure, and resolved to conquer in this second ordeal. She did conquer, but the victory cost her dear. . . ." In this respect, Emily's period at Law Hill must be regarded as an important character-forming experience.

Law Hill was a prosperous school patronized by rich mill owners who aimed at giving their daughters a coating of polish with foreign languages, music, riding, and the more expensive accomplishments of the day. Neither among the staff nor the pupils did Emily find congenial associates, so that she was driven in on herself as at Roe Head.

The result was not a deeper incursion into a make-believe world, but the awakening of a poetic impulse expressing itself in ever more powerful verse. The poetry written at Law Hill and immediately afterward was increasingly personal in substance and, even when Gondal in theme, dealt with personal problems. These were of an increasingly spiritual character as Emily evolved.

While the overall theme of the Law Hill poems is *alienation*, provoked by the writer's acute homesickness, a new and recurrent theme appears that marks the beginning of her visionary life; this theme is *spiritual escape*. The language in which she described these states of mind, these "visitations" of a liberating power, is the same in which she wrote of perfectly material occurrences: there can be no doubting their reality to her. The more so that the "Power" first manifested at Law Hill continued with Emily afterward, and stayed with her until a few months before her death.

LAW HILL: THE METAPHYSICAL EXPERIENCE

ONE speaks of a "Power," of a "Presence" that made itself felt—if not seen—in Emily Brontë's moments of extrasensory perception, because they are her own words for whatever liberating experience befell her, and upon whose return she waited as a prisoner in a dungeon awaits deliverance. She had many expressions for this "Visitant of air," and she called the awaited presence, over the years, her "Angel," her "Strange Power," her "darling pain," her "true friend," "herald of death," "vision," but the incident that marked its first manifestation, while she was at Law Hill, is both the most revealing of the propitious circumstances required and the most precise as to the Vision's consolatory power. The poem is no. 37 in Hatfield's edition.

> I'll come when thou art saddest,
> Laid alone in the darkened room;
> When the mad day's mirth has vanished,
> And the smile of joy is banished
> From evening's chilly gloom.
>
> I'll come when the heart's real feeling
> Has entire, unbiased sway,
> And my influence o'er thee stealing,
> Grief deepening, joy congealing,
> Shall bear thy soul away.
>
> Listen, 'tis just the hour,
> The awful time for thee;
> Dost thou not feel upon thy soul
> A flood of strange sensations roll,
> Forerunners of a sterner power,
> Heralds of me?

From that moment onward it is this metaphysical quality infused into her life that is present in all her greatest poems and in *Wuthering Heights*, and it became Emily Brontë's own distinguishing trait as a human being and as a writer. From then on she lived,

as it were, on two planes of existence, the material and the spiritual.

In judging the degree of *reality* accompanying such experiences, it has to be remembered that Emily's sister Charlotte described her own mental compositions as appearing to her in a sequence of visions, as clear to the inward eye as outward sights and scenes were to the physical eye; the family were endowed with unusual powers of imagination.

Two stages are clearly discernible by which Emily reached the "bodiless" state of her purely metaphysical verse: in the first the sharpness of her longing for home evokes the recognizable sights and scenes of home, which comfort her with their illusory presence for a while, and then vanish. Of a very different nature are the trancelike states that follow, in which it is not the familiar scenes of home that are displaced, but she herself who is liberated from the body into a state of bliss. How far Emily would go from *there*, the whole body of her work remains to tell. It would become her life's purpose to recapture those intimations of a life *outside of herself* that she first received at Halifax. The experience, common to many metaphysical poets in *childhood*—as with Henry Vaughan, Thomas Traherne, and Wordsworth—appeared in Emily's case only to intensify as she grew older; this makes the rarity of her case.

Among the nostalgic poems of the Halifax period are the following:

> Loud without the wind was roaring
>   Through the waned autumnal sky;
> Drenching wet, the cold rain pouring
>   Spoke of stormy winters nigh.
>
> . . .
>
> "It was spring, for the skylark was singing."
>   Those words, they awakened a spell—
> They unlocked a deep fountain whose springing
>   Nor absence nor distance can quell.
>
> In the gloom of a cloudy November,
>   They uttered the music of May;
> They kindled the perishing ember
>   Into fervour that could not decay. . . .
>
> (Hatfield, 91)
>
> A little while, a little while,
>   The noisy crowd are barred away;
> And I can sing and I can smile
> A little while I've holyday!
>
> . . .

Yes, as I mused, the naked room,
The flickering firelight died away
And from the midst of cheerless gloom
I passed to bright, unclouded day—

A little and a lone green lane
That opened on a common wide;
A distant, dreamy, dim blue chain
Of mountains circling every side;

A heaven so clear, an earth so calm,
So sweet, so soft, so hushed an air
And, deepening still the dream-like charm,
Wild moor-sheep feeding everywhere—

That was the scene; I knew it well,
I knew the path-ways far and near
That winding o'er each billowy swell
Marked out the tracks of wandering deer.

. . .

Even as I stood with raptured eye
Absorbed in bliss so deep and dear,
My hour of rest had fleeted by
And given me back to weary care.

(Hatfield, 92)

LAW HILL AND WUTHERING HEIGHTS

It was during her time at Law Hill that Emily heard the story of the builder and original owner of the house, Jack Sharp, whose career so resembled Heathcliff's that its direct bearing on the plot of *Wuthering Heights* cannot be doubted. Jack Sharp belonged to a highly respected local family, the Walkers of Walterclough Hall, an Elizabethan house lying just below the school and visible from its windows, which in Emily's time was still in the possession of a cousin of Sharp's, a Miss Caroline Walker. She had kept a retrospective diary covering sixty years of her family's fortunes, beginning in 1772, in which she recorded the systematic ruin brought on her father and brother by the machinations of Sharp. He had been adopted by his uncle and owed everything to him, just as Heathcliff did to Mr. Earnshaw. Not content with getting the property into his hands, he set about degrading the children of the second generation, as Heathcliff did with Hareton. Jack Sharp's case differed from Heathcliff's in that the Walkers succeeded in ousting him from their old home, when he revenged himself on them by building Law Hill on the brow of the moor above them, to be a perpetual thorn in their flesh; from there he inveigled the younger generation of the family over to play cards for high stakes till they were penniless and in his power. Many details and incidents in the Walker diaries find echoes in *Wuthering Heights*, even to the name of the family manservant, Joseph; but it was presumably not from the diaries that Emily learned these facts, but from Miss Patchett, who had bought Law Hill only some twenty years after Sharp's death in London. However it reached her, the tale was common knowledge to the residents in the district at the time Emily was there.

Another evident connection with *Wuthering Heights* that can be linked with Emily's stay in the district is High Sunderland Hall, the massive stone mansion that lay under Beacon Hill only a mile and a half from Miss Patchett's, and whose dominating position made it a notable landmark throughout the district. The immense façade was ornamented, like the front of Wuthering Heights, with "grotesque carvings lavished over the front, and especially about the principal door above which, among a wilderness of crumbling griffins, and shameless little boys," the date was inset. The interior of High Sunderland went back, with modifications, to the thirteenth century and bore no resemblance to the interior of Wuthering Heights. This, as all visitors to the Haworth district know, was modeled on the paneled interior of Ponden Hall, the home of the Heaton family and well known to the young Brontës.

Whatever benefits—or injuries—Emily's experience at Law Hill brought her, it strengthened and confirmed the bent of her nature toward independence and solitude. From then on she lived more to herself alone than either of her sisters did, and sought fulfillment in the absorbing spiritual life that is the substance of her poems and one novel.

ANNE BRONTË AS GOVERNESS AT BLAKE HALL

After two and a half years of schooling at Roe Head, Anne Brontë took a post as governess with the Ingham family of Blake Hall, Mirfield, some twenty miles from home. The move was against her family's wishes because of her delicate health. From childhood she suffered from chronic asthma and left school after what appeared to be an attack of neglected bronchitis, but which was evidently, in the light of later developments, the first indication of tuberculosis. Anne was, however, quite determined to earn her own living and at nineteen set out on her first bid for independence with high hopes. "Poor Child!" wrote Charlotte of her departure on 15 April 1839,

she left us last Monday; no one went with her; it was her own wish that she might be allowed to go alone, as she thought she could manage better and summon more courage if thrown entirely upon her own resources. We have had one letter from her since she went. She expresses herself very well satisfied and says that Mrs. Ingham is extremely kind. You would be astonished what a sensible, clever letter she writes; it is only the talking part that I fear. But I do seriously apprehend that Mrs. Ingham will sometimes conclude that she has a natural impediment in her speech. . . .

Anne's nervous stutter had from childhood been a matter of mirth to her brother and sisters; in alien surroundings it might, as Charlotte feared, become a problem.

Agnes Grey

Anne's experiences at Blake Hall are very exactly reproduced in the incidents relating to the Bloomfield family in *Agnes Grey* (1847). The circumstances of her heroine are barely transposed from her own: Agnes Grey, like Anne Brontë, is the daughter of a clergyman of limited means who goes out to earn her living as governess to young children. Her tribulations are Anne's own, arising partly from her own youth and inexperience and partly from the utter disregard shown by her employers to her comfort.

Modern readers who find it hard to credit the humiliations to which a young governess could be exposed at the time are referred to the witness of Lady Amberley (the wife of John Russell, Viscount Amberley, and daughter-in-law of the prime minister), who wrote in her personal journal of 1868: ". . . read *Agnes Grey*, one of the Brontës', and should like to give it to every family with a governess and shall read it through again when I have a governess to remind me to be human. . . ." If such a noted humanitarian as Lady Amberley needed *reminding* to treat the governess with consideration, Anne Brontë's witness to her own treatment need not be doubted; it is the quality of truthfulness in *Agnes Grey* that makes its lasting appeal. The quality of reliability in the telling makes *Agnes Grey* more than

a work of fiction; it gives it the character of personal experience that, for the modern reader, has the value of a social document. Anne's evidence about the snobbery of the period as exemplified by her employers' attitude toward the governess, and about the worldliness of the higher clergy as portrayed in the Reverend Mr. Hatfield, is evidence received at first hand that is all the more convincing in that it is given with a certain dry humor. Humor is not usually associated with the work of the Brontës, but it would be difficult to miss in *Agnes Grey*.

George Moore rated *Agnes Grey* very high.[27] He claimed that it "was the most perfect prose narrative in English literature . . . simple and beautiful as a muslin dress . . . the one story in English literature in which style, characters and subject are in perfect keeping. . . ." Without necessarily going the whole way with George Moore, a great deal more can be claimed for *Agnes Grey* than has generally been conceded. The denigration stems, in the first place, from the book's essential difference from the rest of the Brontë works, with which it is invariably and unfavorably compared. There is no common denominator between the objective, classically reserved, spare style of Anne's book and the subjective romantic moodiness that characterizes her sisters' work. Anne's unexaggerated, plain narration relates her work far more to the habits of thought of the late eighteenth-century novelists Maria Edgeworth, John Galt, and, in certain flashes of wit, to Jane Austen.

Anne Brontë's own life is so associated with sorrow that it is forgotten or overlooked that she could be as witty at times as Jane Austen. Take the following traits of character in *Agnes Grey*:

Mr. Bloomfield [Agnes' pupils' father] was a retired tradesman who had realized a very comfortable fortune, but could not be prevailed upon to give a greater salary than £25 to the instructress of his children. . . .

(ch. 1)

The grandmother of the family, old Mrs. Bloomfield, alternately patronized and ignored Agnes Grey; she could on occasions be chatty, but when she began making covert criticisms of her daughter-in-law's injudicious spoiling of her children, Agnes saw the danger of such communications.

With humor she studied the querulous master of the house and the incompetent mistress, but the

[27]See *Conversations in Ebury Street* (London, 1924).

savagery of the children both within and without doors put her beyond patience. Constantly her employer complained of the children's worsening manners and declared they put him "quite beyond his patience (banging the door). 'It puts *me* quite beyond my patience, too!' muttered I."

Agnes Grey's only comfort was in thinking that time *must* amend the children:

every month would contribute to make them some little wiser, and consequently, more manageable—for a child of nine or ten as frantic and ungovernable as these at six and seven would be a maniac. . . .

(ch. 3)

Agnes Grey was not written immediately after Anne's experience at Blake Hall but was begun during her next engagement as governess with the Robinson family of Thorp Green, near York. Its original title was *Passages in the Life of an Individual.* Her engagement lasted four years (1841–1845) and contributed a very different knowledge of life from the background of home.

To its disadvantage, *Agnes Grey* falls into two parts, the second of which, written after the embittering experiences of Thorp Green, reduces the pace and lowers the vitality of a tale that had started with so elastic a tread. Anne did not attempt in *Agnes Grey* to create the social scene of Thorp Green; she only lightly sketched the likenesses of the elder Robinson girls and their mother in the vignettes of the Murray family; the worldly outlook of the elder and the stable manners of the younger afford the only light relief to the low spirits prevalent in the latter part of the book. By the time she came to write it she had suffered "some very unpleasant and undreamt-of experiences of human nature" at Thorp Green, as she recorded in her diary paper of July 1845. This, combined with the disaster overtaking Branwell when he joined her as tutor there, supplied the material of her second and controversial novel, *The Tenant of Wildfell Hall* (1848).

It could be argued with justice that her work lacks invention; its chief failing, especially when compared with her sisters' work, is that it lacks atmosphere—the pervasive scenic and emotional atmosphere that lies at the center of all their work. Hers is not a literature of escape, but a faithful reportage of things seen and suffered. She would, one suspects, have made a scrupulous diarist and, in our day, an intrepid journalist. Without her experiences

as governess among strangers, it may be doubted whether she would have written fiction at all; the true bent of her talent was toward poetry, for which she had both the sense of rhythm and a musical ear. Like her prose, her verse was not of her period and was strongly influenced by the models of the Wesleyan hymns.

CHARLOTTE BRONTË IN BRUSSELS

WHILE real experience would supply the basic material for Charlotte Brontë's novels, the passionate intensity of her feelings and the visionary power of her imagination would transform ordinary incidents and characters into heroic proportions, which give an element of greatness to all she wrote. Thus, the most fruitful single experience of her life came when she and Emily went, in February 1842, to a Brussels school on a pupil-teacher basis. The intention was to perfect their languages so as to permit them eventually to open a school of their own, on the model of Miss Wooler's very successful one. They stayed in Brussels until the end of the year, when the sudden death of their aunt obliged their return home. In January 1843, Charlotte returned alone to Brussels while Emily took her aunt's place as their father's housekeeper. Charlotte stayed another full year in Belgium, returning finally in January 1844.

During that year she came into close contact with the husband of the *directrice* of the *pensionnat*, M. Heger, to whom she gave English lessons in exchange for individual coaching in French. He was, as she later said, "a man of power as to mind," whose cultural attainments and strong personality were precisely calculated to fire her ardent nature and fill her obsessional need of love. Without revealing her feelings to him, or even without admitting the thought to herself, she fell tragically in love with him, a man who was neither free nor inclined to return her feelings. The situation, however, was clearly assessed by the shrewd Mme. Heger, who hastened Charlotte's return home in 1844.

While Emily's experience in Brussels left no traceable impress whatever on her work, on Charlotte's intellectual and emotional development it left a lasting imprint that found its ultimate expression in *Villette.* It did not matter that her experience was limited to school and governess life; it sufficed to stimulate the latent creative urge that had struggled for outlet since girlhood. The Brontës needed no wide area of human experience to build a world upon; they worked in depth, like well-sinkers boring for a spring; and the discoveries they made into the nature of the human spirit and its place in the universe are as refreshing today as a draught of mountain water.

FIRST PUBLICATIONS

By midsummer 1845, the Brontës' experience of the life of their time, their contacts with the world, were virtually over. Charlotte alone of the four young people would know a short reemergence into society when her meteoric rise to fame drew her briefly onto the stage of literary London under the aegis of her publisher, George Smith, of the firm of Smith, Elder & Co., after 1849. How little she was suited by temperament and character to such notoriety, her unhappiness on such occasions plainly showed. The recognition in which she and Branwell in particular had always believed, came too late to bring any satisfaction to her, since she was the only one of the family left to receive it; all the others died before recognition came.

Poems by Currer, Ellis and Acton Bell

The reunion to which all four young Brontës had so ardently looked forward during their years of separation as the lodestar of their endeavors brought them none of the expected happiness. Charlotte returned from Brussels in January 1844, shattered in health and embittered in mind and heart. Anne and Branwell returned for good from their posts as tutor and governess in the Robinson family in June 1845 under the shadow of Branwell's disgrace. He was dismissed on an unspecified charge, about which Branwell himself was less reticent than his employer: he boasted for all to hear that he had been the lover of Mrs. Robinson, who, according to him, had given him every encouragement and to whom he considered himself bound by sacred vows until the expected death of her invalid husband should free her to marry him. Meanwhile, the shock of the discovery of the affair and the enforced separation from Mrs. Robinson completed the mental ruin begun through drink and drugs, and he became a helpless burden on the home. Emily alone of the once ardent and active quartet had found her objective in life and

was writing poetry of high philosophic thought in great contentment of mind. It was Charlotte's discovery of the manuscript notebooks of Emily's poetry written during the previous two years that prompted their design to attempt publication.

Emily's poetic genius had come into full flower following her return from Brussels in the winter of 1842 while she lived alone with her father. Between that time and the midsummer of 1845, she wrote all the masterpieces for which she is lastingly known; and, as would shortly appear, to that period also belonged the beginnings of *Wuthering Heights*.

Much against Emily's inclinations, Charlotte contacted successive publishers with a view to bringing out a joint volume of verse to which all three sisters could contribute a selection of their work. Finally, a small firm that specialized in religious verse, Aylott & Jones of Paternoster Row, consented to take the proffered manuscript at the authors' expense. In May 1846, they brought out the volume of 165 pages, priced 4s., at a cost to them of £31 10s. There were sixty-one poems in all: nineteen titles by Charlotte and twenty-one each by Emily and Anne.

The sudden incursion into print, prompted as much by Charlotte's deep disillusionment of the last years and the heartbreak of her unrequited love for M. Heger as by their "honourable ambition," as she called it, found the inexperienced authors out of their depths on many counts. They had hurriedly to decide on pseudonyms; "by a sort of conscientious scruple" not liking positively to assume masculine pseudonyms, yet fearing the effects of prejudice against women writers, they "veiled their own names under those of Currer, Ellis and Acton Bell," as Charlotte later revealed in her "Biographical Notice of Ellis and Acton Bell." Her own contributions to the book were insignificant; she was no poet and was the first to acknowledge it. Reading them in later years she found them "crude and rhapsodical." But writing poetry had been a true solace to her, and in verse she could vent her wounded feelings and portray the figure of the man she loved, and the scenes where she had met him. Thus, in the poem "Gilbert," she describes the *pensionnat* garden in the midst of the city,

> Where flowers and orchard-trees were fenced
> With lofty walls around:
> . . .
> This garden, in a city-heart,
> Lay still as houseless wild,

> Though many-windowed mansion fronts
> Were round it closely piled;
>
>   . . .
>
> The city's many-mingled sounds
> Rose like the hum of ocean. . . .[28]

It was the scene over which she lingered again and again in both *The Professor* and *Villette*. In another poem, "The Letter," in a first sketch for the finished portrait in *Villette*, is the recognizable likeness of M. Heger:

> A stalwart form, a massive head,
> A firm, determined face.
>
> Black Spanish locks, a sunburnt cheek,
> A brow high, broad, and white,
> Where every furrow seems to speak
> Of mind and moral might.

Poems that the author later interpolated into the text of *The Professor*, like the poem "Frances" ("Unloved—I love, unwept—I weep") and the poem of strongest accusation against M. Heger for his blindness to her suffering, "He saw my heart's woe," were written in this period.

However pedestrian was Charlotte's contribution to the volume of poems, she had provided the impetus and impulse, the initiative to publish, without which her sisters would, in all probability, never have attempted professional authorship. In this respect, the *Poems* were of importance in bringing their names before the public. Individually, Charlotte and Anne could not have stood alone as poets.

Anne Brontë had, nevertheless, a genuinely lyrical and very personal talent that perfectly voiced the heartache and homesickness she suffered in her long years as governess among uncongenial strangers. She confessed in *Agnes Grey* to the feelings that first prompted her to write poetry, feelings further awakened by her own unhappy love for her father's curate, the Reverend William Weightman, who died of cholera in 1842 while she was away from home.

> When we are harassed by sorrows or anxieties, or long oppressed by any powerful feelings which we must keep to ourselves, for which we can obtain and seek no sympathy from any living creature, and which yet we cannot, or will not wholly crush, we often naturally seek relief in poetry —and often find it, too—whether in the effusions of others, . . . or in our own attempts to give utterance to those thoughts and feelings . . . more appropriate . . . for the time . . . to unburden the oppressed and swollen heart. . . .
>
> (ch. 17)

From such springs of emotion were born her best poems of love and loss. Their elegiac tone, simple sincerity, and unexaggerated expression hold the same kind of appeal for readers today that Anne's own personality seemed to hold for the few persons who met her in life; like George Smith, the publisher, who, on the only occasion of their meeting, said of her: "She was a gentle, quiet, rather subdued person, by no means pretty, yet of a pleasing appearance. . . . Her manner was curiously expressive of a wish for protection and encouragement, a kind of constant appeal, which invited sympathy. . . ."[29]

The very titles of her poems convey this character as described by George Smith: "Appeal," "Severed and Gone," "Farewell to Thee," "The Captive Dove," "Oh, they have robbed me of the hope," "If this be all," "Despondency," "Home," "Memory," "The Consolation." She sought and found her consolation in religion and in nature, and in the strength of her affections for her family. In a mood of rare exhilaration she wrote of the scene about her home:

> My soul is awakened, my spirit is soaring
> And carried aloft on the wings of the breeze;
> For above and around me the wild wind is roaring,
> Arousing to rapture the earth and the seas.
>
> The long withered grass in the sunshine is glancing,
> The bare trees are tossing their branches on high;
> The dead leaves, beneath them, are merrily dancing,
> The white clouds are scudding across the blue sky.
>
> I wish I could see how the ocean is lashing
> The foam of its billows to whirlwinds of spray;
> I wish I could see how its proud waves are dashing,
> And hear the wild roar of their thunder to-day!
>   ("Lines Composed in a Wood on a Windy Day")[30]

What the 1846 selection of Brontë poems clearly achieved for Emily, as distinct from her sisters, was

[28]C. K. Shorter and C. W. Hatfield, eds., *The Complete Poems of Charlotte Brontë* (London, 1923).

[29]*Cornhill* magazine (December 1900).
[30]C. K. Shorter, ed., *The Complete Poems of Anne Brontë* (London, 1921).

to demonstrate once and forever the superiority of her work to theirs. This the contemporary critics recognized at once. For us latter-day readers, moreover, it proves the total integration of Gondal into the body of her work. There, in the 1846 edition, where the original Gondal stage directions, attributions, and signposts were removed and all traces of the Gondal inspiration obliterated, the spiritual fusion between Gondal and the philosophic and personal poems was so complete as to preclude all suspicion in contemporary readers' minds of any distinct and separate source of inspiration. (This confusion, in the long run, could only be damaging to author and subject matter alike, as will be noticed below.) Without going the whole, or even the greater part, of the way with Fannie Ratchford, who claimed that the *whole* body of Emily Brontë's work was Gondal inspired,[31] it is evident to all students of the poems that Gondal themes pervade even the greatest of the philosophical poems—as, for instance, the poem of Gondal drama, "Julian M. & A. G. Rochelle" (Hatfield, 190), which contains one of the most specific statements of Emily's metaphysical experience. What has to be admitted is that, while the poetry of Gondal was the earliest of Emily's compositions (deriving from her adolescent years) and despite Emily's striding development as a poet, she never "outgrew" Gondal and it remained an essential part of her artistic apparatus to the end.

So much admitted, it has become evident ever since the publication of C. W. Hatfield's masterly edition of the *Complete Poems of Emily Bront*ë in 1941 that the correct attribution of the specifically Gondal poems is essential to any judgment of Emily Brontë's work.

The confusion caused in the 1846 and subsequent editions of the poems as to the "reality" of the experiences described could not but be damaging to the poetry and the author alike. To delete the Gondal references—title, dramatis personae—from such a poem as "Cold in the earth" (Hatfield, 182) was not merely to obliterate the Gondal source of the poem's inspiration, but to falsify its character, with the unfortunate result that it was for many years believed to be the expression of a personal sorrow suffered by the author.

Of all the selections of Emily Brontë's poems, the 1846 volume was undoubtedly the worst. The initial

subterfuge resorted to by the author to preserve the secret of Gondal had the very contrary effect of what she desired in the end. Not until Hatfield's editing of the poems from the original manuscripts in 1941 could the public see Emily Brontë's poetry *whole and in perspective*. The importance of Hatfield's work cannot be exaggerated. Never before could Emily's stature as a poet be estimated. To her misfortune, and the public's loss, her work had previously been known merely through the anthologies that, even in the generous selection made by A. C. Benson in his edition, *Brontë Poems* (1915), repeated many of the editorial errors of the 1846 edition and of Charlotte's even more falsified text in the posthumous 1850 selection of her sister's work.

While it has to be remembered that much of Emily's work has *not* been preserved—only 193 poems and fragments remain—the publication of Hatfield's edition has made it generally known, and her reputation now stands unchallenged and alone. The quality is, admittedly, uneven, but the tone is always elevated and original. Partial glories abound throughout; individual verses and lines are memorable and haunting, even when the impetus lacks thereafter. This apparent flagging in the performance was the inevitable result of the visionary—and hence transitory—nature of Emily's inspiration. Note the opening lines of nos. 5, 7, 9, 35, 79, 91, 108 in Hatfield's edition, which arrest the reader at once with their precision of setting and sentiment.

Because of the personal quality of everything Emily Brontë wrote, every reader will find his or her own masterpieces, but those that have received universal recognition are nos. 37, 85, 140, 146, 157, 170, 173, 174, 176, 181–185, 190, 191 in the Hatfield edition. These poems, whether Gondal in inspiration or of purely personal experience (like "Stars" or 'The Night Wind," nos. 184 and 140), hold the essence of what Emily believed in and pursued. They are the counterpart of *Wuthering Heights* in verse, the legacy of a profoundly pessimistic writer who found her only compensation in moral values (courage especially) and in spiritual escape from her material condition. They are the record of a positive metaphysical experience that is almost unique in English literature.

So much being said as to the quality of the content of Emily Brontë's poetry, it has to be admitted that the style is often disappointingly derivative. There is nothing original in her prosody; she was content to accept the forms that came most easily to her hand:

---

[31]See her *Gondal's Queen* (London, 1955).

the meter and vocabulary of the Wesleyan hymns (a potent influence in her evangelical home), the lyrical language of Byron—and even of Tom Moore (so apparent in such poems as "Cold in the earth")—and the sober simplicity of Wordsworth (see "The Old Church Tower and the garden wall," "The blue bell is the sweetest flower," nos. 94 and 31 in the Hatfield edition). Like Shakespeare before her, Emily Brontë was of her time and, while pursuing eternal verities, spoke the language of her contemporaries.

Inevitably, it was Emily's contribution to the *Poems* that took the critics' attention. Of Ellis Bell they predicted that his verse would "yet find an audience in the outer world. A fine quaint spirit has the latter, which may have things to speak that men will be glad to hear—and an evident power of wing that may reach heights not here attempted . . ." (*Athenaeum*, 4 July 1846). The reviewer in the *Critic* also recognized the rare quality of Ellis Bell and gave a long extract from "The Philosopher": "They in whose hearts are chords strung by Nature to sympathize with the beautiful and the true, will recognize in these compositions the presence of more genius than it was supposed this utilitarian age had devoted to the loftier exercises of the intellect . . ." (4 July 1846).

Though only two copies of the book sold in the first year, the critics' notices were incentive enough to spur the authors onward to fresh attempts: "The mere effort to succeed had given a wonderful zest to existence," wrote Charlotte later; ". . . it must be pursued. . . ." Before even the *Poems* were published, Charlotte was contacting other publishers about the manuscripts of "three distinct and unconnected tales of prose fiction" that she and her sisters had finished or were in the process of finishing, the first drafts of *Agnes Grey, The Professor,* and *Wuthering Heights,* which, despite initial rebuffs, would all be published in the end.

THE NOVELS

THE "three distinct and unconnected tales" first mentioned by Charlotte in her approach to publishers on 6 April 1846, even before the appearance of the *Poems,* mark the split-up of the literary partnership that had linked the Brontës' work from childhood and had persisted even into the joint volume of poems with which they first came before the public.

The tales had been written without reference to each other and as a result of the authors' quite separate experience of life away from home. *Agnes Grey,* as already mentioned, was the outcome of Anne Brontë's six years as governess in two different posts; *The Professor* (originally called *The Master*), as the title indicates, was the fruit of Charlotte's two years in a foreign school and of her insights into the masculine world of a large boys' school; and *Wuthering Heights* was the natural outcome of Emily's withdrawn and unworldly existence, first at Law Hill and then in her father's parsonage on the Yorkshire moors, the culmination of years of intense spiritual experience in which the visionary world of her daydreams became as present to her imagination as the material one did to her eyes.

Composition and Characteristics

Despite their thematic differences, the first Brontë novels had one overriding characteristic in common: they were the expression of a strong personal compulsion, of a need for compensation for loss—loss of liberty, loss of companionship, loss of love. They were written as an outlet for fervent imaginations and wounded feelings, in isolation and among inimical surroundings, as a refuge from the limitations of their lot. They followed no fashion and showed very little worldly experience; they were not written for publication in the first place, nor to make money, and therefore they subscribed to none of the fashionable requirements of the lending libraries. What they had was a disquieting honesty of vision, a deeply moral sense (something more than social morality), and a scale of poetic values that enlarged the seeming limits of fiction so as to include the role of nature in determining the destinies of men, something very fresh at the time.

As Charlotte recorded later,[32] they had "very early cherished the dream of one day becoming authors." The novels, like the poems, were the logical sequence of a lifelong passion. It was their timing that provoked their publication. With a first book of poems in print, there was a sudden incentive to complete the novels and send them out into the world that particular summer. The need for the stimulus of professional recognition was paramount with Charlotte at the time, and she was strong enough to carry her sisters along with her.

[32]"Biographical Notice of Ellis and Acton Bell," 1850.

Agnes Grey, begun at Thorp Green and finished at Haworth in the autumn of 1845, was probably the first of the novels to be completed. *Wuthering Heights*, begun by Emily during her sisters' absence from home, and continued during the winter 1845–1846, was the next to be finished; and *The Professor*, written wholly after Charlotte's return from Belgium, was completed on 27 June 1846, a month after the *Poems* were published. The parcel containing the three manuscripts was posted to Henry Colburn, the publisher, on 4 July 1846, showing that its dispatch had only awaited the completion of *The Professor*. The tribulations accompanying the Brontës' attempts at publication are too well known to be repeated yet again; suffice it to say here that the manuscripts were rejected by six successive firms and that when at last acceptance came, after a full year, it was for *Wuthering Heights* and *Agnes Grey*, not for *The Professor*, which never found a publisher in Charlotte Brontë's lifetime. This blow to her hopes was, however, palliated by the triumphant reception given to her second novel, *Jane Eyre*, written entirely in the space of the intervening year, and published on 16 October 1847. *Jane Eyre* thus overtook *Wuthering Heights* and *Agnes Grey*, which, while accepted in August 1847, did not appear finally until mid-December 1847. They were published together as a three-volume novel, two months behind *Jane Eyre*, yet close enough for their joint impact to be simultaneously felt by the public and critics alike.

The Professor

Though not published until two years after its author's death (it appeared on 6 June 1857), *The Professor* can in no way be considered Charlotte's final statement, but rather a work of her apprentice years to which, both in substance and manner, it so closely relates. Written in the two years immediately following her return from Brussels, the book was yet too close to that experience to give an undistorted view of what had most deeply and closely affected the author. Instead, she approached it once removed, from behind a mask as it were, through the medium of the old familiar formula of her adolescent writings. She transposed her own experience once again into the narration of a male protagonist, William Crimsworth.

William Crimsworth was in direct line of succession to Charles Townsend, alias Lord Charles Florian Wellesley, the narrator of Charlotte's adolescent Angrian tales, and the pseudonym under which she was pleased to disguise her own personality. William Crimsworth of *The Professor* is very little more evolved, civilized, and sophisticated than his crude predecessors in the role, who last made their appearance in the novelettes written in 1839–1840. He suffers from the affiliation to the earlier characters, who had begun as immature, half-humorous, half-irritated caricatures of the author's brother, Branwell Brontë. His only usefulness was that he was a ready-made mouthpiece and at hand. In addition to William Crimsworth, the plot of *The Professor* is burdened with a further legacy from the juvenilia in the theme of the inimical brothers, Edward and William Crimsworth, who retain even the Christian names of their predecessors in the field, Edward and William Percy, last seen in the novelette "Captain Henry Hastings."[33] The rival brothers was a theme that can be traced back to Charlotte Brontë's earliest writings, dating from her thirteenth year, in which the sons of the duke of Wellington, Arthur and Charles Wellesley, figured in tale after tale as dramatic foils to each other: the elder, evolving from the insipid virtue of his beginnings in "Tales of the Islanders" (1829), "High Life in Verdopolis," "The Tragedy and the Essay," and others, into the Byronic Zamorna; and the younger, into the brash, mischief-making, meddling, inquisitive personage of Charles Townsend, the gleeful reporter of his brother's countless love affairs. The uneasy cynicism of Townsend, carried over into the character of William Crimsworth, might well account for *The Professor*'s initial failure with the publishers. He was a misfit in an otherwise naturalistic tale. Happily the book has great and distinct qualities that save it from its affiliation to the juvenilia.

What is entirely new in *The Professor* are the closely observed scenes and characters, derived from the author's Belgian experiences, which mark a leap forward in judgment and mastery of her medium. The Belgian section of *The Professor* is a mature work with at least two finely observed and integrated characters: the heroine, Frances Henri, and the anti-heroine, Zoraide Reuter, the *directrice* of the girls' school in which William Crimsworth is engaged to teach English. It was a situation that allowed Charlotte to record her deeply felt personal tribulations as a teacher in a foreign land, even if she touched as yet only lightly on the subject of frus-

[33]See W. Gérin, ed., *Five Novelettes*.

trated love, which was to be at the heart of *Villette*. The school scenes have an authentic ring that only firsthand knowledge could supply and are shot through with more humor than are their somber parallels in *Villette*. The portrayal of Mlle. Reuter is all the more admirable and subtle in that the deception practiced on the susceptible (and not a little foppish) Crimsworth is equally carried out on the reader, who sees her through his eyes and is beguiled by her for just as long—and no longer—as he is. The character is penetratingly observed, as first shown in the ambiance of the classrooms (ch. 12).

The sketches of the two old ladies, the respective mothers of M. Pelet and Mlle. Reuter, are among the raciest observations of human nature ever made by Charlotte Brontë; they are far better observed, for example, than the group of socialites in *Jane Eyre*, the Ingram family and their hangers-on.

Pelet's house was kept and his kitchen managed by his mother, a real old Frenchwoman; she had been handsome—at least she told me so—and I strove to believe her; she was now ugly, as only Continental old women can be; perhaps, though, her style of dress made her look uglier than she really was. . . .

(ch. 8)

Mme. Pelet's crony, the aged Mme. Reuter, is sketched with an equal lightness of touch; she

was as fat and as rubicond as Madame Pelet was meagre and yellow; her attire was likewise very fine, and spring flowers of different hues circled in a bright wreath the crown of her violet-coloured velvet bonnet. . . . In general the Continental, or at least the Belgian, old women permit themselves a licence of manners, speech, and aspect, from which our venerable granddames would recoil as absolutely disreputable, and Madame Reuter's jolly face bore evidence that she was no exception to the rule of her country. . . .

(ch. 8)

One of the earliest and longest-lived fallacies relative to *The Professor* is that it was an early sketch for *Villette*. It cannot be denied that, had *The Professor* found a publisher in its author's lifetime, Charlotte might have hesitated to write yet another tale set in Brussels. As it was, at least six years elapsed between the writing of *The Professor* and work on *Villette*, a book that cost its author heart-searching agonies and repeated breakdowns before it made its appearance in January 1853. What is important to note is that the two books are wholly distinct tales whose Brussels setting does not disguise the Yorkshire source of inspiration of *The Professor*, nor its direct affiliation to the novelettes of Charlotte's juvenilia. One superficial difference noticeable to all readers of the two books is that while the names of places and persons were not disguised in *The Professor*, they were in *Villette*, where even the name of the capital city had to be concealed. There were to be no compromising revelations made in *The Professor* as in *Villette*. The reader has only to compare the treatment of the main characters in the two tales—M. Pelet and Mlle. Reuter, Crimsworth and Frances Henri in the one, and Paul Emmanuel and Mme. Beck, Lucy Snowe and Dr. John in the other—to realize the difference. The observation in the first book is at once more diffused and far more superficial; the sense of destiny that shapes the emotional climate of *Villette* is wholly absent in the more sunny earlier work. The characters and incidents have not the same portentous significance; they do not make the same wounding impact on each other (though Zoraide does her best to wreck Frances' hopes) that every interchange between the protagonists in *Villette* creates. The differences, in short, are of such an emotional quality as to be fundamental.

While both books derive from a common experience, *Villette* had the advantage of ten years' maturing reflection, the author's growing mastery of her medium, and the further scarifying influence of the early deaths of her sisters and only brother to give perspective to the once all-important experience of Brussels. By that time the trauma of her unrequited love was so far healed as to be capable of analysis, and M. Heger was seen not in relation to herself alone but as an independent and complete human being. The creation of Paul Emmanuel, one of the greatest characters in fiction, would have been impossible for the writer of *The Professor* so soon after the events themselves. Charlotte Brontë was already too much of an artist to attempt it. The same inhibition prevented any attempt to portray Mme. Heger in Zoraide Reuter; except for the basic deceitfulness of both women, the resemblances are insignificant, whereas the differences in their situations are firmly underlined. Zoraide is unmarried and very conscious of her attractions; the matronly Mme. Beck, with her nursery full of children, was a direct identification with Mme. Heger.

The mistaken and surprising identification of M. Heger with M. Pelet was long ago disproved by irrefutable evidence[34] and the real prototype of Pelet identified in the person of the French director of the *Athénée Royal* of Brussels, Joachim-Joseph Lebel (note the similarity of names), a man whose character and conduct were notoriously like those of the fictional Pelet and well known to Charlotte Brontë. M. Lebel was called in at times to teach the young ladies of the *pensionnat* Heger, where he was on friendly if not intimate terms with the household and teaching staff. Skeptical and amoral, pleasure-loving and unattached, M. Lebel had none of the characteristics or qualities of the ascetic M. Heger. Charlotte Brontë's portrait of M. Lebel in *The Professor* apparently so closely resembled the original as to provoke instant recognition among her first Brussels readers. Mrs. Gaskell's categorical denial of Pelet's identification with M. Heger further confirmed this view.[35]

Of Frances Henri, the charming heroine of *The Professor*, much could be said in praise. She is one of Charlotte Brontë's happiest creations, with a quality of inner stillness that neither Jane Eyre nor Caroline Helstone quite attain. What she has in common with them, and with all the women with whom Charlotte identified herself, is a capacity for suffering that is spiritualized. The scene in the Brussels cemetery when Crimsworth rediscovers Frances sitting by a new-made grave (that of her only relative), after an agonized interval of separation, conveys this quality of perceptive stillness that invests the whole character. She is no less finely attuned to the inner harmonies of joy as to sorrow; the scene of the lovers' reunion is pervaded by nothing so blatant as noisy jubilation; Frances leads Crimsworth back to her frugal lodging and offers him tea while the storm spends itself outside. He notices at once the empty grate and realizes that she cannot afford a fire.

I knew she read at once the sort of inward truth and pitying pain which the chill vacancy of that hearth stirred in my soul; quick to penetrate, quick to determine, and quicker to put in practice, she had in a moment tied a holland apron round her waist; then she disappeared, and reappeared with a basket; it had a cover; she opened it, and produced wood and coal; deftly and compactly she arranged them.

. . . "It is her whole stock, and she will exhaust it out of hospitality," thought I.

(ch. 19)

By such scenes of genre painting Charlotte Brontë could already convey the emotional content of a scene as much by selective detail as by dialogue, here wholly absent. Indeed, the dialogue is weak; it falls far behind the book's descriptive power, and far behind the revealing verbal exchanges of *Jane Eyre*, which was so shortly to follow it.

Jane Eyre

The character of Charlotte's Brontë's second novel, *Jane Eyre*, was advertised from the outset by its subtitle, "An Autobiography," and was received as such by its first critics. *Blackwood's* reviewer (October 1848) said that it was "a pathetic tale, so like the truth that it is difficult to avoid believing that many of the characters and incidents are taken from life." G. H. Lewes found the same thing: "Reality—deep significant reality, is the characteristic of this book. . . ."[36]

In *Jane Eyre* the author gathered together not merely the recent experiences of her adult years, but the unobliterated recollections of childhood at the Clergy Daughters' School at Cowan Bridge. Confined as that experience had in reality been to a period of ten months in the author's ninth year, it is given a duration and a prominence in the novel that cast its shadow over all the subsequent action. Jane Eyre, the heroine, is essentially a "deprived child," a penniless orphan whose isolation in an inimical world makes her doubly vulnerable to its indifference and cruelty. It also makes her doubly responsive to the least proffer of friendship and love. At the orphanage the child forms a passionate attachment to an older and precociously intelligent girl, Helen Burns (whose prototype was Charlotte's own eldest sister, Maria, who died of tuberculosis at thirteen), because Helen is good to her. It is also so with the school superintendent, Miss Evans, who treats Jane with justice and confidence in her ability to make good. Normal human relationships based on mutual trust and humanity take a disproportionate place in Jane's affections, because of the traumatic experiences of her childhood. This point is made manifestly clear by the author before engaging her heroine in the vortex of her love for her employer, Mr. Rochester.

[34]See M. H. Spielmann, "Charlotte Brontë in Brussels," in B. Wood, ed., *Charlotte Brontë, 1816–1916: A Centenary Memorial* (London, 1917).
[35]Letter to Emily Shaen, 8 September 1856, in J. A. V. Chapple and A. Pollard, eds., *The Letters of Mrs. Gaskell* (London, 1966).
[36]*Fraser's* magazine (December 1847).

With the figure of the master/lover, Edward Rochester, Charlotte reached the parting of the ways between the early obsessive dream creation of her Angrian chronicles and the experience of real life. Rochester is invested with the conflicting attributes of the real-life Belgian professor, Constantin Heger, whom Charlotte had loved, and much of the Byronic swagger of the imaginary Zamorna. With Rochester, Zamorna makes his last appearance in Charlotte Brontë's writing, and it is a notable one. The romantic ideal of Zamorna, conceived in girlhood and evolved for over ten years throughout a voluminous literary output, died hard with its author just *because* of her unrealized love for her Belgian professor. Zamorna was *there*, ever present, in her mind, in compensation for the deprivation of her lot.

For two-thirds of *Jane Eyre* it is Zamorna/Rochester who sustains the plot; without the strong element of Zamorna in the character, which accounts for his French liaisons and his illegitimate daughter (just as in "Caroline Vernon," where the selfsame situation exists), there could have been no attempted seduction of the innocent Jane Eyre and the tale would have lost both its drama and its moral significance, which rests on her rejection of dishonor.

The seduction theme had figured twice before in Charlotte's novelettes, written in her early twenties, and had been treated there in two conflicting ways. Caroline Vernon, barely sixteen, was shown as succumbing with rapture to seduction by Zamorna and being ruined in consequence. The far more mature Elizabeth Hastings[37] is shown as rejecting the dishonorable proposals of Sir William Percy. The fact that she loved him and had no alternative prospect in life but hard work and loneliness turned her rejection into a moral victory. At no age was Charlotte Brontë a moral prig (especially not in her early twenties) and the reasons she gave for Elizabeth's decision were *not*, she made abundantly clear, so much out of virtue as out of self-respect. "I'll never be your mistress," she answers Sir William, "I could not without incurring the miseries of self-hatred. . . ."

It is for the selfsame motive that Jane Eyre rejects the solicitations of Rochester and by so doing takes the first decisive step in English literature since Clarissa Harlowe toward redressing the inequality between the sexes. A good woman, according to

[37]See "Captain Henry Hastings," in W. Gérin, ed., *Five Novelettes.*

Richardson, could not survive the loss of her virtue. Charlotte Brontë declared that a good woman, like any decent man, could not live without self-respect. Urged by Rochester with the most compelling arguments not to abandon him because of the existence of his maniac wife, Jane withstands his fire throughout the hours of a thundering night, the storm outside reflecting the tempest in the lovers' minds. Reminded by Rochester that she has no one to be injured or offended by any act of hers, since she is alone in the world—"Who in the world cares for *you?* or who will be injured by what you do?" he pleads. "*I* care for myself," answers Jane. "The more solitary, the more friendless, the more unsustained I am, the more I will respect myself . . ." (ch. 27).

With that reply Rochester's attempted seduction crumbles; he has no argument to oppose it. He is answered by an equal in judgment and a superior in honor. It is the second time in the book that the author claims equality for her heroine with her hero. The first incident occurs when Jane anticipates Rochester's declaration of love by avowing her own feelings for him. It was so novel a departure from the conventional canons of fiction that it shocked and startled the literary establishment and the book's first readers. It was considered a grossly coarse thing for a woman to declare her love for a man—and for an author to describe it—even a reputedly male author like Currer Bell. Jane Eyre commits two faults against Victorian female delicacy when she declares her love—as yet unsolicited—for one man and rejects another, later in the book, on the score of *not* loving him. Such statements were tantamount to admitting a knowledge of the passion of love not permissible in a decent woman. Hence the savage comment by Elizabeth Rigby who, reviewing *Jane Eyre* in the *Quarterly Review* (December 1848), expressed the opinion that if the unknown author of *Jane Eyre* were a woman, as some suspected, then "she was one who must have forfeited the society of her own sex."

What Currer Bell had done, and what many of her female contemporaries could not forgive her for, was to place truth before propriety and to recognize the equality of the sexes where passion was concerned. Without being in any way "a feminist" in the militant sense of the word, Charlotte Brontë felt deeply about the oppressed status of women in her time, especially women endowed with intelligence but devoid of fortune or looks, like herself. She made *their* predicament her own when she chose to write a novel about a governess with a mind infinitely superior to her employer's. Admittedly, William Makepeace Thackeray, Charlotte's greatly admired contemporary, was doing the same thing in the same year when he created Becky Sharp; but Becky is first and foremost an adventuress, and only a governess by expediency. Jane Eyre's situation as governess is inherent in the conception of the character and in the conduct of the plot. Her unprotected subordinate position is necessary to point the contrast with her independence of mind, her strong moral sense, her superiority over her "Master." For such a girl the expectations of happiness were remote, her right to be loved nil. It is in Jane Eyre's proud declaration of her rights as a human being that the novelty lay and that a new voice was heard for the first time in fiction. Believing Rochester to be on the eve of marrying Blanche Ingram, the rich and fashionable beauty, Jane decides to leave her post, and tells him so. Purposely obtuse to the meaning of her visible grief, Rochester asks her if she is sorry to go:

The vehemence of emotion, stirred by grief and love within me, was claiming mastery, and struggling for full sway, and *asserting a right to predominate, to overcome, to live, rise, and reign at last; yes, and to speak. . . .* "I grieve to leave Thornfield . . . I love it, because I have lived in it a full and delightful life—momentarily at least. I have not been trampled on, I have not been petrified. I have not been buried with inferior minds, and excluded from every glimpse of communion with what I reverence, with what I delight in—with an original, a vigorous and expanded mind. I have known you, Mr Rochester; and it strikes me with terror and anguish to feel I absolutely must be torn from you for ever. I see the necessity of departure; and it is like looking at the necessity of death."

(ch. 23)

Pressed by him to stay, she cries:

"I tell you I must go! Do you think I can stay to become nothing to you? Do you think I am an automaton?—a machine without feelings? and can bear to have my morsel of bread snatched from my lips, and my drop of living water dashed from my cup? Do you think, because I am poor, obscure, plain and little, I am soulless and heartless? You think wrong!—I have as much soul as you—and full as much heart! And if God had gifted me with some beauty and much wealth, I should have made it as hard for you to leave me, as it is now for me to leave you. I am not talking to you now through the medium of custom, conventionalities nor even of mortal flesh: it is my spirit that addresses your spirit; just as if both had passed through the grave, and we stood at God's feet, equal—as we are!"

The true value of the declaration lay, as the author well knew, not in Jane's reaping material good by it, but in her voluntary renunciation of her claim, once made. Urged by Rochester to remain with him and to cease struggling "like a wild, frantic bird," she replies: "I am no bird; and no net ensnares me; I am a free human being with an independent will, which I now exert to leave you."

The emotional truth of that scene, perceptible to any reader even without knowing the circumstances of Charlotte Brontë's life, gains still in power and pity when it is compared with the words she actually wrote to M. Heger after leaving Brussels. The same similes occur in describing the spiritual starvation she suffers when deprived of his friendship.

Monsieur [she wrote in the penultimate letter of the series], the poor have not need of much to sustain them—they ask only for the crumbs that fall from the rich man's table. But if they are refused the crumbs, they die of hunger. Nor do I, either, need much affection from those I love. . . . you showed me of yore a *little* interest, when I was your pupil in Brussels, and I hold on to the maintenance of that *little* interest—I hold on to it as I would hold on to life.

(letter of 9 January 1845)

What *Jane Eyre* proclaims is the triumph of spiritual values over material ones. This was the leitmotif of all the Brontë novels. Rochester has finally to admit: "it is you, spirit—with will and energy, and virtue and purity—that I want, not alone your brittle frame . . . ," and in saying so sheds the dross of his nature and attains to Jane's fine quality (ch. 27).

While exacting of her heroine the selfsame sacrifice that she had exacted of herself in leaving M. Heger, Charlotte laid a heavy burden on her personal faith. The large place given to religion in *Jane Eyre* is the necessary corollary of the perpetual spiritual contests into which the protagonists are thrown. Religion meant too much to Charlotte Brontë for her *not* to resent intensely the false image of it presented to the defenseless child she had once been at the Clergy Daughters' School by the tyrants and hypocrites who administered the school; or to dread the sort of "premature death" that the sectarian missionary, St. John Rivers, offered Jane when proposing a loveless marriage. The character of St. John was essentially conceived as a foil to Rochester; even the language that describes the two men is charged with the kind of temperature they spread around them. Rochester is constantly seen in the red glow of a fire-lit room, while all the imagery of frost is reserved to describe St. John. "Reader," asks Jane, "do you know what terror these cold people can put into the ice of their questions? How much of the fall of the avalanche is in their anger? of the breaking up of the frozen seas in their displeasure?" (ch. 35).

Despite the carping of the moralists, *Jane Eyre* received general and critical acclaim overnight. It ran into three editions in its first winter and the lending libraries were besieged for copies by their subscribers. Thackeray's encomiums crowned its success and gave the author her most intensely felt satisfaction. "It interested me so much," wrote Thackeray to the publisher,

that I have lost (or won if you like) a whole day in reading it. . . . Who the author can be I can't guess, if a woman she knows her language better than most ladies do, or has had "classical" education. It is a fine book, the man and woman capital, the style very generous and upright, so to speak. . . . Give my respects and thanks to the author, whose novel is the first English one (and the French are only romances now) that I've been able to read for many a day.[38]

While Thackeray conceded the book's excitement, what commended it to him was the quality of the writing, the clear, forceful, unartificial writing, so different from the usual productions of the lady contributors to the fashionable journals. The other quality he especially noticed, the book's "upright" character, is of its essence. Rectitude was a basic Brontë quality: the importance of what people are and believe in, as opposed to their sense of self-interest. Applied to fiction, it contributed a new dimension to popular literature. All unconsciously Currer Bell, with her scrupulous regard for truth and critical self-analysis, had advanced the novel by half a century.

The notoriety of *Jane Eyre* roused intense curiosity about the unknown Currer Bell. Who was he—or she? Nobody, least of all the publishers, could answer the question. The mystification was intensified by the almost simultaneous publication of *Wuthering Heights* and *Agnes Grey* (mid-December 1847) under the pseudonyms of Ellis and Acton Bell.

[38]Letter to W. S. Williams (23 October 1847), in G. N. Ray, ed., *The Letters and Private Papers of W. M. Thackeray* (London, 1947), vol. II, pp. 318–319.

A full year later Lockhart, the editor of the *Quarterly Review*, was still mystified: "I know nothing of the writers," he told Miss Rigby of his staff, "but the common rumour is that they are brothers of the weaving order in some Lancashire town. . . . If you have any friend about Manchester it would, I suppose, be easy to learn accurately as to the position of these men" (13 November 1848).

The Tenant of Wildfell Hall

Even before the manuscripts of *Wuthering Heights* and *Agnes Grey* were accepted for publication by the London firm T. C. Newby, of Mortimer Street, Cavendish Square, in August 1847, Anne Brontë began writing a second novel, *The Tenant of Wildfell Hall*, published in June 1848. Unlike *Agnes Grey*, it was a full-length three-volume novel. The measure of the Bells' success so far can be judged by the improved conditions given the author; instead of paying for publication, Anne Brontë was to receive £25 on publication and further payments of £25 on the sale of 250 copies. *The Tenant* was an immediate success with the public, and helped by the popularity of *Jane Eyre*, Newby set about securing the American rights by announcing it to the New York firm of Harper Bros. as the new work of the best-selling Currer Bell. From America the echoes of this transaction reached Currer Bell's own publishers, Smith, Elder & Co., who were understandably annoyed at this apparent breach of contract by the author, who had undertaken to give *them* her next work. The confusion occasioned by the Bell pseudonyms had therefore to be clarified and their separate identities revealed. During a three-day visit to London, Charlotte and Anne made themselves known to their respective publishers, and Newby was fittingly exposed. Emily neither joined them nor consented that her identity be revealed. Her insistence on complete anonymity and repugnance to all forms of publicity were so pronounced as to deter her, it would seem, from further authorship. While her intention to write a second novel may be inferred from a letter addressed to Ellis Bell by Newby in February 1848 (prior to the exposure of his fraud), no trace of such a work remained after her death, and it must be supposed that either she herself, or Charlotte on her instructions, destroyed the manuscript. Only one poem written later than January 1846 was preserved after her death.

The Tenant of Wildfell Hall, which achieved considerable success in its own day, has not stayed the course like the rest of the Brontë novels. It was written too obviously as a work of propaganda, a treatise against drunkenness, to qualify as a work of art. Nevertheless, there are whole scenes and sections that are strongly written and truthfully seen. Nothing Anne Brontë wrote could be trivial or uncompromising. Her forthright determination to expose what she thought needed exposure is never less than admirable, and her compassion is a very vital quality. Unhappily, the book's inception and realization were the outcome not of a creative urge but of a bitter sense of duty toward the innocent victims of a debauched society of which she, in her four years as governess in the Robinson family, had some "very unpleasant and undreamt-of experience." The victims whose ruin she lamented, her own brother Branwell, and to some extent, herself, who had gone out into the world too ignorant to avoid its bitter lessons, must be made a warning to save others from the same fate.

She set out to show the effect of Branwell's moral degradation carried to its ultimate limits; how the overthrow of his mind had led to drink and drugs, and must, inevitably, lead to death. Branwell lived for three years in the family home, a broken man, incapable of any work, a complete burden on his sisters, and it was the daily spectacle of his misery that spurred her to attempt to rescue others from a similar fate.

The objective was naive, but the absolute singleness of purpose that drove her was not without its effect. She neither flinched from portraying scenes of orgy nor from analyzing the feelings of revulsion with which the heroine, Helen Huntingdon, reacted to her drunken husband's embraces. Here is no dutiful Victorian wife submitting to her marital duties; Helen Huntingdon slams her bedroom door in the face of her besotted husband, and locks it firmly against him. Perfectly unaware of the amazed incredulity with which the first readers of *Wildfell Hall* would react to such scenes, Acton Bell defended her right to treat of *any* theme, even so controversial a one as a married woman's rights, so long as it was true and so long as it needed to be exposed. Once again, as in *Jane Eyre*, the Brontë heroine acts with immense spirit and does not allow herself to be crushed by the weight of social conventions. The right of a woman to think and act according to her own conscience, unsupported by the law of the land, was a new one in English fiction. (In France these matters had long been debated, thanks to Georges Sand, and had not failed to rouse the moral reprobation of the literary establishment.)

The Tenant of Wildfell Hall was condemned on the score of its "coarseness" and brutality and for the "morbid revelling in scenes of debauchery"—but it sold like wildfire for its excitement and startling plot. It achieved a veritable succès de scandale contrary to all the expectations of its modest author.

It seems incredible to us today that Anne Brontë, who is chiefly remembered for her piety and resignation to her own sufferings and early death, should ever have been regarded as a dangerous and immoral firebrand—but such was the state of middle-class opinion in the mid-nineteenth century. In an admirable preface to the second edition of the book, Acton Bell answered her critics with true Brontë spirit:

My object in writing the following pages is not simply to amuse the Reader. I wished to tell the truth, for truth always conveys its own moral to those who are able to receive it. . . . Let it not be imagined, however, that I consider myself competent to reform the errors and abuses of society, but only that I would fain contribute my humble quota to so good an aim.[39]

Answering those critics who doubly condemned the book on the suspicion that it was written by a woman, she wrote:

As to whether the name be real or fictitious, it cannot greatly signify. . . . As little . . . can it matter whether the writer . . . is a man, or a woman . . . because, in my own mind, I am satisfied that if the book is a good one, it is so whatever the sex of the author. . . . All novels are, or should be, written for both men and women to read, and I am at a loss to conceive how a man should permit himself to write anything that would be wholly disgraceful to a woman, or why a woman should be censured for writing anything that would be proper and becoming for a man.

Wuthering Heights

While *Agnes Grey*, *Jane Eyre*, and *The Tenant of Wildfell Hall* are novels with a contemporary interest, Ellis Bell's single novel, *Wuthering Heights*, is of a totally different character. Concerned with eternal principles of life, death, love, and immortality, it has a timeless quality that puts it closer to such a

---

[39]*The Shakespeare Head Brontë.* Subsequent quotations from *Wuthering Heights, Shirley,* and *Villette* are from this edition.

work as *The Faerie Queen* than to any contemporary Victorian novel. It has no concern for social questions, but is an expression of primitive passions, of the elemental forces in man and nature that the author shows as connecting all creation. Hers is a cosmic vision that has little to do with nineteenth-century materialism. At the same time the narrative is firmly set in the soil. The chronological framework of the plot is precise; the seasonal changes meticulously noted, but rather as might be done by men in space who are removed from the world's orbit. The people moving in the spacious panorama of the moorlands are seen with the sharp focus of the dreamer who notes all the details of his dream but cannot account for them. No one questions the action of *Wuthering Heights*; it is far too compelling to be explained and is invested throughout with the unequivocal nature of supernatural vision, the same that informs Emily's poetry. Yet the houses and the interiors are as homely as a Dutch painting. Nothing could be less fey than Emily Brontë's Yorkshire kitchens, cobbled stable-yards, laboring servants. It is the *naturalness* of *Wuthering Heights* that heightens its dreamlike quality (for everyone knows that dreams are deceptively realistic in detail) and that makes its spiritual daring unique. In this respect the book is the perfect mirror of its author's mind, since it reflects her own exceptional ability to live on two planes of consciousness at one and the same time.

For the reader who finds *Wuthering Heights* a perplexing book to understand, it is useless to recommend critical commentary or analysis of its elusive pattern; the only key to its secret lies in the poetry Emily Brontë was writing immediately before and during the composition of the novel. The poems, both in substance and manner, are a running commentary, as it were, on the theme of the novel. Both art forms capture the echoes, fleeting shadows, dissolving images of the author's explorations into "the shadowy regions," as she called them, the unknown territories of the soul. While the poems reflect the immediate impact of the mystical visions, almost as they occurred (see "Night Wind," "A Day Dream," "Stars"), the novel is an attempt to rationalize those occurrences into terms of human experience. The quest of the poetic protagonists, whether they are Gondal heroes or the author herself, is for a state of spiritual union, either with the loved one or with an immaterial essence (as in "The Prisoner"). Universal Oneness is the central theme of the poems as of *Wuthering Heights*. It is a state, as the poet gradually discovered, that could only be achieved by liberation from the shackles of life (hence the repeated imagery of the captive in the dungeon released from her chains), by oblivion, finally by loss of identity, the essential prelude to eternal life, the goal perpetually shining before the poet's eyes.

Emily Brontë was writing poetry of high philosophic content for at least four years (1841–1845) before embarking on her single novel. The step by step advance in the poems into surer assumptions and less speculative formulas can be understood by comparing the perfect clarity of the philosophy of the novel with the poems that went before. By the time she came to write *Wuthering Heights* she had reached the certainty that death alone was the door to life, a revelation first glimpsed in the poem "A Day Dream" and treated in countless subsequent poems.

> "Let Grief distract the sufferer's breast,
> And Night obscure his way;
> They hasten him to endless rest,
> And everlasting day. . . .
>
> And could we lift the veil and give
> One brief glimpse to thine eye,
> Thou would'st rejoice for those that live,
> Because they live to die."
>
> (Hatfield, 170)

Such a vision explains the irresistible force of the death wish in Catherine and Heathcliff, who are separated in life by every mortal impediment their enemies can devise and their own cruel natures create.

The very substance of the plot of *Wuthering Heights*, a triangle of human relationships between two men and a woman, Heathcliff, Linton, and Catherine, was already present in the poetry of Gondal years before the inception of the novel, in the persons of Augusta, the gentle Lord Alfred, and the demonic Fernando. But while the poems were visibly the immediate progenitors of the novel, it had other and much earlier sources of inspiration in the poetry of Byron and Gothic novels such as the *Confessions of a Justified Sinner* by James Hogg, *The Bridegroom of Barna* by Bartholomew Simmonds, Hoffmann's *The Devil's Elixir*, Mary Shelley's *Valperga*, to which Emily Brontë had access in the literary journals of the day, *Blackwood's* and *Fraser's* in particular. From

142

these multiple sources stemmed the original conception of Heathcliff, both as a character and as a principle of evil, much as Charlotte's parallel figure of Zamorna had done. The young Brontës had read *Manfred* and *Cain* very early, even if not *Paradise Lost*, and the satanic element present in Byron's heroes, with their defiance of all order, cosmic or social, their personal sense of grandeur, their lust for power, influenced the Brontës' conceptions of a superman just as it did the writers of the Gothic novels. Quite evidently Heathcliff derived from the Gothic poetry and fiction on which Emily Brontë had been nourished, the "novels of evil-possession," as they might be called. She lays much emphasis on his savage, not to say animal, nature: his "cannibal teeth," his "basilisk eyes"; "He is not a human being and has no claim on my charity," says his wife, Isabella, of him. "A tiger or a venomous serpent could not rouse terror in me equal to that which he wakens"; and on another occasion she speaks of "the fiend that usually looks out of his eyes." In his rages he foams at the mouth, "like a mad dog." In grief he is described as "lifting up his eyes and howling not like a man, but like a savage beast."

The importance of these descriptions lies not in their truth to the character, but in their revelation of the poverty of mind of the speaker, the vain Isabella and the simple Nelly Dean, who are thus exposed by their author as incapable of comprehending such a man as Heathcliff. Catherine's love for him appears all the rarer by comparison with *their* credulity and ignorance. Her love-hate relationship to him is built upon the perception of their essential resemblance to one another, that ungenerous form of love that is still a pursuit of self. Catherine's misery is shown as proceeding from this: she will not sacrifice anything for Heathcliff, though she is fully conscious of her affinity to him. She is shown as far more guilty of treachery in marrying another man whom she does not love than is Heathcliff in destroying the whole family of his erstwhile benefactors.

The morality of *Wuthering Heights*, as one might expect from such an author, is not the conventional morality of established religion and human law, but the revealed morality of natural law and divine justice. Having pursued with his hatred the family of his enemies into the second generation, Heathcliff is shown as sated with his revenge and arrested before the final gesture by a quite different and wholly compelling longing: to reach Catherine, dead these twenty years. By *willing* his own death, his last action is

shown as no longer one of hate, but of love. Here, in the urgency of the soul to seek, and attain, its release, Emily Brontë speaks as one to whom the experience had, in fact, come. One has only to compare her lines

"Then dawns the Invisible, the Unseen its truth reveals;
My outward sense is gone, my inward essence feels—
Its wings are almost free, its home, its harbour found;
Measuring the gulf it stoops and dares the final
   bound!"

(Hatfield, 190)

with the description of the death of Heathcliff to realize the vital truth they carried for her. "I have a single wish," he says, "and my whole being and faculties are yearning to attain it. They have yearned towards it so long, and so unwaveringly, that I'm convinced it *will* be reached—and *soon*—because it has devoured my existence: I am swallowed up in the anticipation of its fulfilment."

The laws of nature, as revealed in the elements of earth, fire, wind, and water, are the all-powerful agents of this tale. Never before in English fiction (and only once in Shakespeare) had the elements been made the agents of a human drama. From the opening chapters, when the blizzard drives the narrator to shelter overnight at the Heights and he wakens to the plaint of the ghost-child at the window—"Let me in! Let me in!"—to the disinterring of Cathy in the snowbound churchyard, and on to the end where the halcyon evening sheds peace round the graves of the united lovers, every incident in the story is played out before the background of nature. So essential is the mood of nature to Emily Brontë's view of life that no aspect of the seasons or time of day was unimportant to her purposes. Each scene is ushered in not so much by a direct description as by a reflection of its feeling in the natural scene. Hareton Earnshaw's birth comes at midsummer:

"On the morning of a fine June day, my first bonny little nursling, and the last of the ancient Earnshaw stock was born. We were busy with the hay in a far away field, when the girl that usually brought our breakfasts, came running an hour too soon, across the meadow and up the lane, calling me as she ran."

(ch. 8)

The presence of nature is constantly realized for the reader by a choice of simile: young Catherine, her nurse recalls, "grew like a larch and could walk and talk, too, in her own way, before the heath bloomed a second time over Mrs. Linton's dust" (ch. 18).

Predominant as is the book's atmosphere of storm and darkness, no feature of the passing year is unobserved by the author. The demi-seasons are as keenly noted as the high peaks of summer or winter. One senses a suspension of the human drama in such scenes as the following, placed in the dead season of the year.

On an afternoon in October, or the beginning of November—a fresh watery afternoon, when the turf and paths were rustling with moist, withered leaves, and the cold, blue sky was half hidden by clouds—dark grey streamers, rapidly mounting from the west, and boding abundant rain—I requested my young lady to forego her ramble. . . . In summer, Miss Catherine delighted to climb among these trunks, and sit in the branches, swinging twenty feet above the ground. . . . From dinner to tea she would lie in her breeze-rocked cradle, doing nothing except singing old songs—my nursery lore—to herself, or watching the birds, joint tenants, feed and entice their young ones to fly: or nestling with closed lids, half thinking, half dreaming, happier than words can express.

(ch. 22)

Thomas Hardy, whose Wessex novels came considerably later than *Wuthering Heights* and give as primordial a place to the environment in the human drama, did not share Emily Brontë's metaphysical flights. What he had, and she had *not*, was the historian's sense of the presence of the Past lying just below the surface of the Present. What *she* had to a unique degree was the perception of a spirit world just beyond sight. That she frequently penetrated its barriers the whole range of her poetry attests. So do such passages in *Wuthering Heights* as the already quoted passage of the death of Heathcliff. So does the death of Catherine. Victorian fiction, so prolific in deathbed scenes, has nothing comparable to offer. After months of illness and on the eve of giving birth to her daughter, Catherine is sinking fast, watched by the faithful Nelly. Catherine says:

"The thing that irks me most is this shattered prison, after all. I'm tired of being enclosed here. I'm wearying to escape into that glorious world, and to be always there: not seeing it dimly through tears, and yearning for it through the walls of an aching heart; but really with it, and in it. Nelly, you think you are better and more fortunate than I; in full health and strength: you are sorry for me—very

soon that will be altered. I shall be sorry for *you.* I shall be incomparably beyond and above you all."

(ch. 15)

To the contemporaries of Emily Brontë who had not read even the small selection of her poems contained in the joint volume published with her sisters, the light that their lines shed on her novel was as yet denied. An almost total incomprehension met the book on its first appearance. The reviewer in the *Atlas* wrote: "We know nothing in the whole range of our fictitious literature which presents such shocking pictures of the worst forms of humanity. . . . It is a sprawling story, carrying us, with no mitigation of anguish, through two generations of sufferers—though one presiding evil genius sheds a grim shadow over the whole, and imparts a singleness of malignity to the somewhat disjointed whole. A more natural unnatural story we do not remember to have read."

It is open to question whether the grudging praise that reviewers occasionally meted out to the book would be more acceptable to the author than their outright condemnation, so little understanding did they bring to it. *Douglas Jerrold's Weekly* commented that "There seems to us great power in this book, but it is a purposeless power, which we feel a great desire to see turned to better account." The critic of *Britannia* complained that the author's creations "all have the angularity of misshapen growth, and form in this respect a striking contrast to those regular forms we are accustomed to meet in English fiction." The characters were "so new, so grotesque, so entirely without art, that they strike us as proceeding from a mind of limited experience but of original energy and of a singular and distinctive cast." The single contemporary critic, Sydney Dobell, in the *Palladium* (September 1850), who recognized the quality of the book and paid tribute to the author's genius (though he believed the author to be Currer Bell), came too late to be read by Emily. She had been dead nearly two years by then. Dobell's comments are as valid today, when the whole climate of criticism has been revolutionized, as in 1850. "There are passages in this book," he wrote,

of which any novelist, past or present, might be proud. Open the first volume at the fourteenth page, and read to the sixty-first. There are few things in modern prose to surpass these pages for native power. We cannot praise too highly the brave simplicity, the unaffected air of intense belief, the admirable combination of extreme likelihood with the rarest originality, the nice provision of the possible even in the highest effects of the supernatural. . . . The thinking-out of some of these pages—is the masterpiece of a poet, rather than the hybrid creation of the novelist.

Emily Brontë was criticized for using the device of the triple narratives—that of Lockwood, of the child Cathy in her journal, and that of Nelly Dean—which was regarded as a clumsy and inexpert formula. This is to overlook its utility in acting like successive curtains raised upon the scene which give the unfolding tale not only sustained excitement, but a sense of expanding time that is needed by the author to convey the passage of twenty years. The evolution of taste has justified Emily Brontë in her handling of a tale that is among the leading best-sellers in the world and has proved to us today that she knew very well what she was about.

Shirley

Shirley is the one Brontë novel begun in a time of promise and awaited with impatience by its publishers. The enduring success of *Jane Eyre* spread an atmosphere of euphoria over the anticipated new novel by Currer Bell. Whatever she chose to write would be welcome to her readers and publishers alike. Letters of encouragement flowed from the London office of Smith, Elder & Co. Since their encounter over the American rights fraud, Currer Bell and her publishers were on the best of terms. The zest with which she set to work on the new novel is apparent in the opening scenes, and sadly absent in what follows. The book was marred halfway through by the fatal arrest in the writing caused by the illness and successive deaths of the author's two sisters and brother, who all died within the space of nine months. Branwell was the first to go, on 24 September 1848; Emily followed him on 19 December 1848; and Anne in the following May at Scarborough. All died of tuberculosis, in conditions inconceivable to us today; all went without medical treatment except Anne. In fact Emily did not even concede herself to be ill. Branwell alone took to his bed for one day before he died. Charlotte's life was affected by the disaster—which she compared to the effects of an earthquake—throughout the few years left to her, which she devoted to her stricken father. The work of that period was indelibly marked with the tragedy. The two novels undertaken in the last six years of her life were painfully conceived and laboriously produced, but they established her fame at home and a high reputation abroad.

Shirley, which began as a high-spirited comedy of Yorkshire life set in the time of the Luddites, written with relish and a strong smattering of Yorkshire dialect, covers a far larger canvas than *Jane Eyre*, though it never matches the intensity of feeling and interest of the earlier novel. The ludicrous incongruities of the presence in that predominantly evangelical region of High Church curates, the conflict between obstinate mill owners and rebelling mill hands, the clash between "High Tories" like old Helstone and Radicals like Hyram Yorke, are painted with broad strokes of consummate humor. Currer Bell showed she could be as objective in marshaling her crowd scenes, her portrayal of men at work, her meetings of parochial church councils, as she had been subjective in analyzing the feelings of Jane Eyre. The book set off at a rattling good pace and promised once again to be both original and true and penetrated with profound psychological insights. Caroline Helstone remains one of the most charming heroines not in Brontë fiction alone, but in all Victorian fiction.

It was the book's major misfortune that work on it had to be suspended in the middle, at chapter 24, for the author to nurse her dying sisters. Resumed after months of interruption and grief, it never recovered its original impetus. What had started off as a vigorous record of active, predominantly masculine life finished as a low-toned analysis of unrequited love. It was as though Charlotte, having briefly cast off the oppression of a lifetime's disappointments with the success of *Jane Eyre*, and allowing herself to view the future through rose-tinted spectacles, were plunged into a gloom greater than that of her frustrated youth.

With nothing left to hope for from her own life, she sought, and found, her only consolation in creative work. It is lastingly to her credit as an artist that she never allowed her terrible need of happiness to create a false world of happiness in her fiction. She painted life as she found it, implacably hard toward some. It is also to her credit that she showed no envy toward the more fortunate. There is a fine passage in *Villette* (ch. 37) on this subject. "Without any colouring of romance or any exaggeration of fancy," she wrote there, "some real lives do . . . actually anticipate the happiness of Heaven; and, I believe that if such perfect happiness is once felt by good people . . . its sweet effect is never wholly lost."

Perhaps because of the tragic circumstances under which *Shirley* was finished, the love interest reverts to Charlotte's own frustrated love for M. Heger. Robert Moore, the prosperous cloth manufacturer hit by the anti-Napoleonic "Orders in Council," his brother Louis, and their sister Hortense are half-Belgian (by one of those international marriages of which Charlotte met examples abroad) and on several occasions the dialogue breaks into French. Robert is loved by his little cousin Caroline Helstone and he in turn courts the enchanting Shirley Keeldar, whose fresh arrival in the district sparks off as much match-making as in an Austen novel. The fact that Shirley is an heiress places her beyond the reach of the male population of Briarfield, though one audacious curate does not think so. Shirley has, however, lost her heart to another man before coming into the district, a man who turns out to be Robert's brother Louis, engaged as tutor in the family of Shirley's uncle. Louis, having neither place nor fortune of his own, is too much of a man of honor to betray his love to Shirley. The two pairs of frustrated lovers are thus at variance in a situation that promises to be insoluble.

It is not the plot of *Shirley*, however, that provides the book's chief interest, but the characters, of which there is a rich assortment, and the atmosphere, which is always fresh with a North-country directness of speech and honesty of mind that match the open country of the setting—Birstall and Gomersal, Hartshead and Mirfield—as Charlotte Brontë knew it in the 1830's.

The best of the characters are those in the secondary parts: old Mathewson Helstone, the High Tory cleric, who is more at ease handling firearms than a prayerbook; Hyram Yorke, the irate Radical, always thirsting for social upheaval and preaching the principles of the French Revolution. They are vitally alive and full of idiosyncrasies and racy talk. The story does not, however, depend on them, and all they can do is to provide a convincing background before which the principals can perform.

The principals remain unrealized. The Moore brothers present an unsatisfactory duplication of the Heger prototype, and their relations with the two heroines, Shirley and Caroline, offer only another aspect of the master/pupil theme, with nothing of the passion that swept through *Jane Eyre*. While Caroline is touchingly portrayed and her disappointed love analyzed with all the author's peculiar understanding of the case, she is rather a Frances Henri than a Jane Eyre, a passive victim, not the arbiter of her own destiny. Caroline's plea for fresh opportunities for women (ch. 22) is a theme very close to the author's heart. "I feel there is something wrong somewhere," she reflects,

I believe single women could have more to do—better chances of interesting and profitable occupations than they now possess. . . . The brothers of these girls are every one in business or in professions; they have something to do; their sisters have no earthly employment, but household work or sewing; no earthly pleasure but an unprofitable visiting; and no hope, in all their life to come, of anything better. This stagnant state of things makes them decline in health. . . . The great wish—the sole aim of everyone of them—is to be married, but the majority will never marry; they will die as they now live.

In 1849 that claim made on women's behalf was as novel as it was rousing; it gained Currer Bell the friendship of such pioneers for women's advancement as Harriet Martineau.

As a whole, the book lacks a central plot and compelling interest. There are too many characters for whom the prototypes were readily identified by the first readers; Charlotte was writing too close to her models to see them through the aerial perspective of art. Helstone was found to have countless resemblances to Patrick Brontë; he, too, was a military man at heart. The whole Yorke family was identified as Charlotte's friends at Gomersal, the Taylor family; the Moores, as noted, were copies of originals who still overshadowed them. Only in the brilliant realization of Hortense Moore did Charlotte produce both a startling resemblance to an original and a fully integrated character in fiction. Hortense Moore, with her self-satisfied complacency, her immersion in household tasks, her skirmishes with her servant, her moralizings, her culinary recipes, her vanity, her benevolence, is a hugely successful comic creation. She was also so startlingly like the prototype on whom Charlotte modeled her, Mlle. Haussé of the *pensionnat* Heger in Brussels, that English fellow pupils, the Wheelwright girls, reading the book on its first appearance, immediately recognized the portrait. It was the means of further discovering Charlotte, with whom they had lost touch, under the mask of Currer Bell.

Of the character of Shirley herself, the intended heroine of the book, much fault could be found with the finished portrait, and much praise for the component parts. It was Shirley's misfortune that she had been cast as an idealized portrait of Emily Brontë, whose daring nature, love of poetry, of animals, of nature she is shown as sharing to an extent incompatible with the rest of her attributes—her society manners, her assurance, her elegance, beauty, and wealth. Such an evocation was doomed to failure from the outset. Emily was neither an approachable person nor an explicable one; her silences were not the stuff of which fictional dialogue is made. As the central character in a novel, such an elusive woman was out of place.

The book's want of a central character and of a sufficient plot is felt throughout. The author's uncertainty in proceeding was evident in her hesitation over the title: she intended originally to call it *Hollow's Mill* (the home of Robert Moore) to emphasize the Yorkshire and rural setting of the tale. George Smith did not like the title for his metropolitan public, and urged a change; for want of a better, Charlotte settled for *Shirley*, a character who did not hold the book together, as indisputably as did Jane Eyre. The weakness of *Shirley* seems to lie in the author's inability to cast off her moorings and sail for the high seas. Such liberation from former models did not come until the achievement of *Villette*.

Villette

The publication of *Shirley* (December 1849) brought Currer Bell the friendship of Mrs. Gaskell, Harriet Martineau, Thackeray, and many other fellow writers, and the entry into the literary coteries of London. Her publishers' attempts to lionize her on the few occasions she consented to stay in the capital were a fiasco; so was Thackeray's proffered hospitality. Currer Bell was unable to communicate in company and suffered acutely from the sense of her inadequacy. Hers was a genius that needed solitude—or a few trusted companions like Mrs. Gaskell—in which to expand. It was in the almost total seclusion of Mrs. Gaskell's home that she wrote *Villette* (1853) in the three years following *Shirley*, her last novel and her best, the richest and most completely integrated of all her work, a masterpiece of sustained imagination and style.

In *Villette* Charlotte Brontë gathered together themes previously touched upon in the earlier works but not fully realized, and those incidents of her own life that had shaped its course, with a deeper insight than ever before into their significance. The destiny of Lucy Snowe, the heroine of *Villette*, is seen with

far greater pessimism than was that of Jane Eyre and seen as *inevitable*. In comparison with *Villette*, *Jane Eyre* indeed appears a tale buoyant with hope.

Lucy Snowe's isolation is even more complete than Jane Eyre's, who had at least an aunt and cousins, inimical as they were. There is no one to care what happens to Lucy Snowe as she embarks on the Ostend packet with £16 in her pocket and no certain destination at her journey's end. There is an element of desperation in Lucy's movements that was not present in the previous novels, a newly acquired sense of destiny that Jane Eyre and Caroline Helstone had only glimpsed before. It is present in all the decisive turnings in the plot, as when Lucy takes the resolution to leave England and look for work abroad. It is typical of the Brontës' response to natural phenomena, of their affinity to the moods of nature, that such climaxes in the plot are received by Lucy as revelations of a supernatural power. Having consulted in vain an old servant of the family on what course to take, Lucy leaves her in greater perplexity than before.

> I left her about twilight; a walk of two miles lay before me. . . . In spite of my solitude, my poverty, and my perplexity, my heart, nourished and nerved with the vigour of a youth that had not yet counted twenty-three summers, beat light and not feebly. Not feebly, I am sure, or I should have trembled in that lonely walk, which lay through still fields, and passed neither village nor farmhouse, nor cottage; I should have quailed in the absence of moonlight, for it was by the leading of stars only I traced the dim path; I should have quailed still more in the unwonted presence of that which to-night shone in the north, a moving mystery—the Aurora Borealis. But this solemn stranger influenced me otherwise than through my fears. Some new power it seemed to bring. I drew in energy with the keen, low breeze that blew on its path. A bold thought was sent to my mind; my mind was made strong to receive it.
>
> "Leave this wilderness," it said to me, "and go out hence."
>
> "Where?" was the query.
>
> I had not far to look . . . I mentally saw within reach what I had never beheld with my bodily eyes; I saw London.
>
> (ch. 5)

In London she hears of the opportunities for English women to teach abroad and decides to go to Brussels.

The change of scene to Belgium (ch. 7), where the rest of the story is set, is thus quite naturally brought about, and the plot firmly planted in the now familiar Brussels ground. Here is the same school, the same walled garden, the same boys' school next door, the same teachers, even the same pupils—but *not* the same principals. In the characters of M. Paul Emmanuel and Mme. Beck, Charlotte has cast off the disguises she employed in the earlier novel of Brussels life; she has abandoned the stand-in figures of Pelet and Mlle. Reuter, and presents the complete full-length portraits, not merely of the characters' prototypes, but of two perfectly conceived and realized human beings who surpass the actuality of their living originals as much as art surpasses reality.

Charlotte had at last had time in which to see her Brussels experience in perspective, to see her own past sufferings from the vantage point of accrued wisdom and the sense of proportion that further suffering gives. She had grown in the interval to derive from the whole destructive episode of Brussels a philosophy of suffering with which to face not only her own future, but to see the past with all its implications as part of a plan. Above all, she could see it now through the medium of re-created feeling and high imagination. Despite the intensity of feeling that burns on every page of the book, it is a work "recollected in tranquillity." Unlike *Jane Eyre*, *Villette* was not written in the heat of the battle, but when the battle was lost and won and there was an end of strife. Also an end of hope.

So much being admitted, not the least miracle about the book's quality is the zest with which it is written, the humor of some of its greatest scenes, a humor almost totally absent from *Jane Eyre*. Lucy Snowe can perfectly love her irascible little Belgian professor and laugh at him at the same time. This is where art replaces life.

While *Villette* is reckoned to be one of the most autobiographical novels in the English language, it is also one of the most highly imagined. Though the incidents are related with the most scrupulous regard for verisimilitude, they are charged with mystery. Given the circumstances in which Lucy Snowe finds herself—above all, given her highly wrought temperament—the reader accepts that these things could have happened to her; but they did not happen to Charlotte Brontë. And therein she shows that she has emerged from her long apprenticeship to writing as a consummate artist, drawing more from an experience than what actually happened.

Villette is a novel packed with characters and incidents, with tense drama, with profound reflections on life, with uncanny penetration into human motives and conduct; above all, it is charged with atmosphere, an atmosphere so palpable at times as to make acceptable to the reader the intrusion of seemingly supernatural incidents.

There is a last point of comparison to note with *The Professor*. In *The Professor*, the names of places and persons are given without disguise—because the author had nothing to hide in her objective picture of Belgian life—and the Rue d'Isabelle and its exact position at the foot of the stairs running down from the statue of General Beliard could be given correctly. In *Villette*, all the place-names are disguised—the country becomes Labassecour, its capital Villette, the Rue d'Isabelle becomes the Rue Fossette (derived from its emplacement over the royal kennels once situated in the moat or fosse by the city walls)—because in *Villette* Charlotte Brontë had set out to write of persons and incidents so revealingly as to be easily recognized. How afraid she was that the book might come into the hands of M. and Mme. Heger can be judged by the fact that she laid an embargo on any French edition being published in her lifetime. She could not foresee that in the very year of her death, which occurred only two years after the publication of *Villette*, a piratical French firm would get hold of a copy and publish it without reference to the English publishers. In 1857 no international copyright laws existed, as Dickens found to his cost over the piratical American practices. The deep offense taken by Mme. Heger at the portrayal of herself as Mme. Beck had a lasting effect; she would not see Mrs. Gaskell when the biographer of Currer Bell called to gather data for her work—thus depriving posterity of much firsthand information about Charlotte's former life in Brussels.

The fact that the parallel portrait of M. Heger as Paul Emmanuel was not only brilliantly but sympathetically treated by the author only confirmed Mme. Heger's worst suspicions that her former English teacher had indeed been in love with her husband.

While little of the book's succès de scandale abroad was suspected in England, it was recognized from the outset as a roman à clef—to which the key was missing until 1913 when the son of M. Heger, Dr. Paul Heger, donated to the British Museum the letters of Charlotte Brontë to his father. The letters, while explaining the emotion in which *Villette* was conceived, provide also the measure of the gulf that separates reality from art. Without the anguish that dictated those letters, *Villette* would, admittedly, never have been written; but the book was far more than the sum of its parts and stands alone, outside the experience that begat it.

The Brussels episode in Charlotte Brontë's life provided only one theme in the complex pattern that makes up the finished book; there are two, if not three, other recognizable strands in its design, derived from quite other sources. There is the "Dr. John" theme, given such prominence in the first twenty-six chapters that its eventual submersion to the "Paul Emmanuel" theme was held a blemish by the first critics. Dr. John Bretton and his notable mother, Lucy Snowe's godmother, were so recognizably based on the characters of Charlotte Brontë's publisher George Smith and his mother, with whom Charlotte stayed on her London visits, that she herself feared giving offense when first submitting the manuscript to him. The likenesses were not altogether flattering nor wholly acceptable to the originals, and the text as we know it carries modifications and excisions from the first draft. Charlotte Brontë stayed with the Smiths in January 1853 to correct the sheets as they were actually coming from the printers.

To the first readers of *Villette* there was no adequate explanation for the switch in interest from Dr. John to Paul Emmanuel, except that they had to recognize that he runs away with the book; the author's personal commitment to the prototype of the character was unknown to them. Among the few to penetrate the mystery was Mrs. Gaskell's friend Catherine Winkworth, who hazarded the guess, on hearing of Charlotte Brontë's engagement to Mr. Nichols: "one can fancy her much more really happy with such a man than with one who might have made her more in love, and I am sure she will be really good to him. But I *guess* the true love was Paul Emmanuel after all, and is dead; but I don't know, and I don't think that Lily [Mrs. Gaskell] knows."[40]

Paul Emmanuel is generally admitted to be not only one of the most vital and convincing characters in fiction but also one of the most original. He is superbly realized, with all his faults, his petty vanities, his tyrannies, his tempers, his integrity, his immense generosity. Rarely can the likeness of a greatly loved person have been so unsentimentally portrayed.

The place of the character of Paul Emmanuel in the evolution of the Brontë hero is not only paramount, but final. In him there remain no traces of the Byronic, Angrian ideal of the all-conquering Zamorna that had served the author throughout her adolescent writings and echoes of which still persisted into the characters of Rochester and Robert Moore. Despite the hold Rochester has upon the reader, he is not a wholly integrated character, not an individual in the sense that Paul Emmanuel is, created from life; and Robert Moore is seldom more than the shadow of a shade.

The character of Mme. Beck is always triumphantly witty, achieved with no trace of the author's personal rancor toward the prototype until the last scenes.

In *Villette* we see the work of Charlotte Brontë come full circle, with the creations of her beginnings, the Angrian themes and characters, set to serve a final purpose here. How tenacious she could be of certain themes and situations, of particular key characters, has already been noticed with the brothers in *The Professor* and *Shirley*; it is apparent again in *Villette* in the character of Paulina Mary Hume, the foil to Lucy Snowe, her fortunate rival in love and life; and in the incident of the death of Miss Marchmont's lover.

To speak of the latter first: it is briefly related (ch. 4) by Miss Marchmont herself on her deathbed as a faraway grief of her young womanhood, when she stood in winter dusk at the windows of her home expecting the arrival of her fiancé. She heard the sound of his horse's hoofs, saw his approach through the gloaming up the drive toward the house door; but he had been thrown, become inextricably entangled in his horse's reins, trampled on, dragged, and fatally injured. The servants brought him in to die in her arms. A similar incident had figured in a tale of Charlotte's juvenilia, "Mina Laury,"[41] in which the Duchess of Zamorna's carriage is overturned and herself thrown out in the drive before the portal of Hawkescliffe Lodge, where the duke hides his mistress, Mina Laury. Brought into the house in a fainting condition, the Duchess is tended by Mina Laury herself, each woman penetrating the identity of the other but revealing nothing to her rival, until the inopportune arrival of the duke himself precipitates a comedy ending. The differences in treatment and at-

---

[40]See M. J. Shaen, ed., *Memorials of Two Sisters, Susanna and Catherine Winkworth* (London, 1908).

[41]See W. Gérin, ed., *Five Novelettes.*

mosphere of the two versions of the incident exemplify the way in which Charlotte Brontë made repeated use of old material when she felt that the maximum effect had not been drawn from it.

This is not quite the case with Paulina Mary Hume, the child "Polly" in *Villette* and one of Charlotte Brontë's most exquisite studies of childhood, who yet had figured in the juvenilia, as the child-wife of Zamorna, Marion Hume, who in turn gave place to the fuller portrait of Mary Percy, Duchess of Zamorna, Queen of Angria. The early sketches of the character carried the same characteristics as the completed portrait in *Villette,* of a fair, frail creature of exquisite sensibilities and profound capacity for love, whose good fortune in attracting—and fixing—the love of those she loved was a sunshine theme that had a lifelong fascination for Charlotte Brontë—chiefly, it could be argued, because of her own totally different lot in life.

Her own place in her fiction, as in life, was always in the shade, in the roles variously taken by Frances Henri, Jane Eyre, Caroline Helstone, Lucy Snowe—heroines whose predominant traits and attributes were indeed shaped in the heroic mold, victims of fate, yet one and all rising above their fate with the supreme Brontë quality of courage.

CONCLUSION

In the year following the publication of *Villette,* Charlotte Brontë married her father's curate, the Reverend Arthur Bell Nichols, on 29 June 1854. This was not a love match on her part, but it turned out to be surprisingly happy. Her health, already undermined by incipient tuberculosis, could not, however, stand up to the strain of pregnancy, and she died only ten months after her marriage, on 31 March 1855. Had she lived another month, she would have reached the age of forty, the only one of the Brontë children to do so.

Her widower remained faithful to his promise not to desert her father, who survived her by six years, dying at the age of eighty-four on 7 June 1861. Nichols, who had carried out all of Brontë's parochial duties until the latter's death, was not confirmed in the living and returned to his native Ireland in October 1861, where he settled in his former home at Banagher, King's County, and eventually married

a cousin, Mary Bell. He lived to a great age, dying at Banagher on 2 December 1906.

Destination of the Brontë Manuscripts
As residuary legatee of his wife's property, including the manuscripts of Emily and Anne's unpublished works, Nichols inherited the copyright of all the Brontë works, published and unpublished. He was very loath to make either publicity or profit from any of them and only with great reluctance was persuaded by George Smith and Mrs. Gaskell to sanction the posthumous publication of *The Professor* (on 6 June 1857). The residue of Brontë manuscripts was taken by him to Ireland where, in 1895, he was visited by Clement Shorter on behalf of T. J. Wise, the notorious collector, and persuaded greatly against his wish to part with the Brontë copyright and much of his collection of manuscripts for a derisory sum. Out of this collection Wise, after publishing edited extracts with the aid of Shorter, made a fortune selling the manuscripts to American collectors and libraries in whose hands they remain to this day. On the death of the second Mrs. Nichols in 1914, the remaining Brontë manuscripts were sold in London salerooms, when many were acquired by the British Museum (notably the two notebooks of Emily Brontë's poems, and juvenilia by Charlotte and Branwell). The manuscripts of Charlotte Brontë's novels published by Smith, Elder & Co. were bequeathed to the British Museum on the death of Smith's daughter, Mrs. Reginald Smith.

Thanks to the great generosity of the late Mrs. H. H. Bonnell, the widow of the chief single collector of Brontë manuscripts in the United States, a large proportion of Brontë manuscripts is now back in England, on permanent loan to the Brontë Parsonage Museum at Haworth.

SELECTED BIBLIOGRAPHY

GENERAL

I. BIBLIOGRAPHY. J. A. Symington, ed., *Catalogue of the [Parsonage] Museum and Library [at Haworth],* The Brontë Society (Haworth, 1927); T. J. Wise, ed., *A Brontë Library: A Catalogue of Printed Books, Manuscripts and Autograph Letters by the Members of the Brontë Family* (London, 1929), a separate catalog of the Bonnell Collection in the Haworth Museum was published at Haworth in 1932; L. Hanson and E. M. Hanson, eds., *The Four Brontës* (London, 1949); M. G. Christian, ed., "The Brontës:

Bibliographies and Manuscripts," in L. Stevenson, ed., *Victorian Fiction, A Guide to Research* (Oxford–Cambridge, Mass., 1964), see also *The Shakespeare Head Brontë* and *Brontë Society Transactions* (vols. I, VI, IX).

II. COLLECTED WORKS. Mrs. H. Ward and C. K. Shorter, eds., *The Life and Works of Charlotte Brontë and Her Sisters*, 7 vols. (London, 1899–1900), Haworth ed., contains valuable critical intros.; A. C. Benson, ed., *Brontë Poems* (London, 1915); T. J. Wise and J. A. Symington, eds., *The Shakespeare Head Brontë*, 19 vols. (Oxford, 1931–1938), contains the novels (11 vols.), life and letters (4 vols.), miscellaneous and unpublished writings (2 vols.), poems (2 vols.), and bibliography; M. Lane, ed., *Novels by Charlotte and Emily Brontë* (London, 1964), Everyman's Library; J. Jack and M. Smith, eds., *The Works of the Brontës* (London, 1969–   ), Clarendon ed. in progress, contains to date: J. Jack and M. Smith, eds., *Jane Eyre*; H. Marden and I. Jack, eds., *Wuthering Heights*; H. Rosengarten and M. Smith, eds., *Shirley*.

III. LETTERS. C. K. Shorter, *Charlotte Brontë and Her Circle* (London, 1896), a new ed. titled *The Brontës and Their Circle* (London, 1914) includes the Heger letters; C. K. Shorter, *The Brontës: Life and Letters*, 2 vols. (London, 1908), reliable, though incomplete; T. J. Wise and J. A. Symington, eds., *The Brontës: Their Lives, Friendships and Correspondence*, 4 vols. (Oxford, 1934), in *The Shakespeare Head Brontë*, also incomplete and less correct than the Shorter ed.; J. A. V. Chapple and A. Pollard, eds., *The Letters of Mrs. Gaskell* (Manchester, 1966), has frequent bearing on the Brontës; J. Stevens, ed., *Mary Taylor, Friend of Charlotte Brontë: Letters from New Zealand and Elsewhere* (Wellington, 1973), makes available facets of Charlotte's life incompletely known before.

IV. JUVENILIA. C. Brontë, *The Twelve Adventurers and Other Stories*, C. W. Hatfield, ed. (London, 1925); C. Brontë, *The Spell: An Extravaganza*, G. E. Maclean, ed. (Oxford, 1931); *The Miscellaneous and Unpublished Writings of Charlotte and Patrick Branwell Brontë*, 2 vols. (Oxford, 1936–1938), in *The Shakespeare Head Brontë*; C. Brontë, *Tales from Angria*, P. Bentley, ed. (London, 1954), published in 1 vol. with *The Professor . . . Emma: A Fragment, with a Selection of Poems by Charlotte, Emily and Anne Brontë*, with an intro. and biography; C. Brontë, *Five Novelettes*, W. Gérin, ed. (London, 1971), transcribed from the original MSS, novelettes written in her twenties: "Passing Events," "Julia," "Mina Laury," "Captain Henry Hastings," "Caroline Vernon."

V. POEMS. *Poems by Currer, Ellis and Acton Bell* (London, 1846), the unsold sheets were reiss. in 1848 by Smith, Elder & Co.

VI. GENERAL BIOGRAPHICAL AND CRITICAL STUDIES. E. C. Gaskell, *Life of Charlotte Brontë*, 2 vols. (London, 1857); F. H. Grundy, *Pictures of the Past: Memories of Men I Have Met and Places I Have Seen* (London, 1879); A. M. Mackay, *The Brontës: Fact and Fiction* (London, 1897); E. Dimnet, *Les Soeurs Brontë* (Paris, 1910), trans. by L. M.

Sill (1927); M. Sinclair, *The Three Brontës* (London, 1912); E. Chadwick, *In the Footsteps of the Brontës* (London, 1914), in collecting her material, the author was still in contact with survivors of the Brontë circle; I. C. Willis, *The Brontës* (London, 1933); D. Cecil, *Early Victorian Novelists* (London, 1934), contains the essays "Charlotte Brontë" and "Emily Brontë and *Wuthering Heights*"; F. E. Ratchford, *The Brontës' Web of Childhood* (New York, 1941), a pioneer work on the earliest MSS; P. Bentley, *The Brontës* (London, 1947); G. E. Harrison, *The Clue to the Brontës* (London, 1948), discusses the influence of Methodism on the Brontës; E. Raymond, *In the Steps of the Brontës* (London, 1948); L. Hanson and E. M. Hanson, *The Four Brontës: The Lives and Works of Charlotte, Branwell, Emily and Anne Brontë* (London, 1949); M. Lane, *The Brontë Story: A Reconsideration of Mrs. Gaskell's Life of Charlotte Brontë* (London, 1953); I.-S. Ewbank, *Their Proper Sphere: A Study of the Brontë Sisters as Early Victorian Female Novelists* (London, 1966); W. Craik, *The Brontë Novels* (London, 1968); J. O'Neill, ed., *Critics on Charlotte and Emily Brontë* (London, 1968); P. Bentley, *The Brontës and Their World* (London, 1969), their lives in illustration; N. Sherry, *The Brontë Sisters: Charlotte and Emily* (London, 1969); I. Gregor, ed., *The Brontës: A Collection of Critical Essays* (Englewood Cliffs, N. J., 1970); T. Winnifrith, *The Brontës and Their Background* (London, 1973); M. Allott, ed., *The Brontës: The Critical Heritage* (London, 1974); G. Leeming, ed., *Who's Who in Jane Austen and The Brontës* (London, 1974); E. M. Delafield, ed., *The Brontës: Their Lives Recorded by Their Contemporaries* (London, 1979).

VII. TOPOGRAPHICAL WORKS. J. H. Turner, *Haworth Past and Present* (Brighouse, 1879); W. Keighley, *Keighley Past and Present* (Keighley, 1879); J. A. Erskine Stuart, *The Brontë Country: Its Topography, Antiquities and History* (London, 1888); W. Scruton, *Thornton and the Brontës* (Bradford, 1898).

THE REVEREND PATRICK BRONTË

I. SEPARATE AND COLLECTED WORKS. *Cottage Poems* (Halifax, 1811); *The Rural Minstrel* (Halifax, 1813); *The Cottage in the Wood* (Bradford, 1815), story and poems; *The Maid of Killarney* (London, 1818), story; J. H. Turner, ed., *Bronteana: Collected Works and Life* (Bingley, 1898).

II. BIOGRAPHICAL STUDIES. W. Wright, *The Brontës in Ireland, or Facts Stranger than Fiction* (London, 1893); W. W. Yates, *The Father of the Brontës: His Life and Work at Dewsbury and Hartshead* (Leeds, 1897); A. B. Hopkins, *The Father of the Brontës* (Baltimore, 1958); J. Lock and W. T. Dixon, *A Man of Sorrow: The Life, Letters and Times of the Rev. Patrick Brontë, 1777–1861* (London, 1965), comprehensive study.

CHARLOTTE BRONTË (pseudonym Currer Bell)

I. SEPARATE AND COLLECTED WORKS. Currer Bell, ed., *Jane Eyre, An Autobiography*, 3 vols. (London, 1847), repr. 1848 as "By Currer Bell," with preface; J. L. Davies, ed., *Jane Eyre* (New York, 1950), also repr. in World's Classics, Zodiac, Penguin, Signet, and Pan eds.; *Shirley: A Tale*, 3 vols. (London, 1849), also repr. in World's Classics, New English Library, and Penguin eds.; *Villette*, 3 vols. (London, 1853), repr. in World's Classics, Zodiac, and Pan eds.; *The Professor: A Tale*, 2 vols. (London, 1857), repr. (1860) with *Emma*, a fragment of a novel, first published in *Cornhill* magazine (1860); C. K. Shorter and C. W. Hatfield, eds., *The Complete Poems of Charlotte Brontë* (London, 1923), with bibliography and notes; R. Hartill, ed., *Poems* (London, 1973).

II. BIOGRAPHICAL AND CRITICAL STUDIES. E. C. Gaskell, *The Life of Charlotte Brontë*, 2 vols. (London, 1857), the 3rd ed. (1857) of this standard biography was "revised and corrected" and has since been repr. many times; "Reminiscences of Charlotte Brontë" by A Schoolfellow [Ellen Nussey], *Scribner's Monthly* (May 1871), repr. in *Brontë Society Transactions* (1899); Sir T. Wemyss-Reid, *Charlotte Brontë: A Monograph* (London, 1877); A. Birrell, *Life of Charlotte Brontë* (London, 1887); Mrs. G. M. Smith, ed., *George Smith: A Memoir* [by S. Lee] (London, 1902); C. K. Shorter, *Charlotte Brontë and Her Sisters* (London, 1905); F. Macdonald, *The Secret of Charlotte Brontë, Followed by Some Reminiscences of the Real Monsieur and Madame Heger* (London, 1914), evidence of a later pupil at the *pensionnat* Heger; B. Wood, ed., *Charlotte Brontë, 1816–1916: A Centenary Memorial* (London, 1917), Brontë Society symposium, containing several interesting essays; M. H. Spielmann, *The Inner History of the Brontë-Heger Letters* (London, 1919), lim. ed., repr. from the *Fortnightly Review* (April 1919); L. Huxley, *The House of Smith Elder* (London, 1923); E. F. Benson, *Charlotte Brontë* (London, 1932); L. Hinkley, *The Brontës: Charlotte and Emily* (London, 1947); M. H. Scargill, "All Passion Spent," *University of Toronto Quarterly*, 19 (1950); K. Tillotson, *Novels of the 1840's* (London, 1954), includes *Jane Eyre*; M. Crompton, *Passionate Search: A Life of Charlotte Brontë* (London, 1955); E. P. Shannon, "The Present Tense in Jane Eyre," in *Nineteenth Century Fiction*, 10 (1956); R. B. Heilman, "Charlotte Brontë's New Gothic," in R. C. Rathburn and M. Steinmann, eds., *From Jane Austen to Joseph Conrad* (Minneapolis, 1958); R. Pascal, "The Autobiographical Novel," *Essays in Criticism*, 9 (1959), discusses *Villette*; R. B. Martin, *The Accents of Persuasion: Charlotte Brontë's Novels* (London, 1966); W. Gérin, *Charlotte Brontë: The Evolution of Genius* (Oxford, 1967); M. Allott, ed., *Charlotte Brontë: Jane Eyre and Villette, A Casebook* (London, 1973); C. Burkhart, *Charlotte Brontë: A Psycho-sexual Study* (London, 1973); M. Peters, *Style in the Novel: Charlotte Brontë* (London, 1973); M. H. Blom, *Charlotte Brontë* (London, 1977); C. A. Linder, *Romantic Imagery in the Novels of Charlotte Brontë* (London, 1979).

EMILY JANE BRONTË (pseudonym Ellis Bell)

I. SEPARATE AND COLLECTED WORKS. *Wuthering Heights: A Novel*, 3 vols. (London, 1847), Anne Brontë's novel *Agnes Grey* occupies vol. 3; H. W. Garrod, ed., *Wuthering Heights* (London, 1930), World's Classics, repr. 1950; also, M. Schorer, ed. (New York, 1950), W. M. Sale, ed. (New York, 1963), and T. Crehan, ed. (London, 1965); C. K. Shorter and C. W. Hatfield, eds., *Complete Poems* (London, 1923); H. Brown and J. Mott, eds., *Gondal Poems* [from the MS in the British Museum] (Oxford, 1938); C. W. Hatfield, ed., *The Complete Poems* (New York, 1941); N. Lewis, ed., *A Peculiar Music: Poems for Young Readers* (London, 1971).

II. BIOGRAPHICAL AND CRITICAL STUDIES. "C. Bell," "Memoir of Ellis Bell," in *Wuthering Heights and Agnes Grey*, by Ellis and Acton Bell (London, 1850); A. M. F. Robinson [Mme. Duclaux], *Emily Brontë* (London, 1883); M. Maeterlinck, *La Sagesse et la Destinée* (Paris, 1898), trans. into English as *Wisdom and Destiny*, by A. Sutro (1898).

C. K. Shorter, *Charlotte Brontë and Her Sisters* (London, 1905); V. Woolf, *The Common Reader* (London, 1925), contains an essay, "Jane Eyre and Wuthering Heights"; C. P. Sanger, *The Structure of "Wuthering Heights"* (London, 1926); C. Simpson, *Emily Brontë* (London, 1929); G. E. Harrison, *Methodist Good Companions* (London, 1935); I. C. Willis, *The Authorship of Wuthering Heights* (London, 1936); F. S. Dry, *The Sources of "Wuthering Heights"* (Cambridge, 1937); G. E. Harrison, *Haworth Parsonage: A Study of Wesley and the Brontës* (London, 1937); H. Brown, "The Influence of Byron on Emily Brontë," *Modern Language Review* (July 1939).

C. Morgan, *Reflections in a Mirror*, 2nd ser. (London, 1944–1946); L. Hinkley, *The Brontës: Charlotte and Emily* (London, 1947); G. D. Klingopoulos, "Wuthering Heights," *Scrutiny*, 16 (1947); D. A. Traversi, "Wuthering Heights After 100 Years," *Dublin Review*, 222 (1947); J. Debu-Bridel, *Le Secret d'Emily Brontë* (Paris, 1950); F. R. Leavis, "Reality and Sincerity: Notes in the Analysis of Poetry," *Scrutiny*, 19 (Winter 1952–1953), examines "Cold in the earth"; M. Spark and D. Stanford, *Emily Brontë: Her Life and Work* (London, 1953); J. Blondel, *Emily Brontë: Experience spirituelle et création poétique* (Paris, 1955); F. Ratchford, *Gondal's Queen* (London, 1955); M. Visick, *The Genesis of Wuthering Heights* (Hong Kong, 1958); W. D. Paden, *An Investigation of Gondal* (New York, 1958).

J. Blondel, "Nouveaux regards sur Emily Brontë," *Annales de la Faculté des Lettres d'Aix*, 35 (1961); J. H. Miller, "Emily Brontë," in *The Disappearance of God* (London–Cambridge, Mass., 1963); J. F. Goodridge, *Emily Brontë: Wuthering Heights* (London, 1964); P. Drew, "Charlotte Brontë as a Critic of *Wuthering Heights*," in *Nineteenth Century Fiction*, 17 (1964); J. Hagan, "The Control of Sympathy in *Wuthering Heights*," in *Nineteenth Century Fiction*, 21 (1967); J. Hewish, *Emily Brontë: A Critical and Biographical Study* (London, 1969); Q. D. Leavis, "A Fresh Approach to *Wuthering Heights*," in Q. D. Leavis and F. R. Leavis, *Lectures in America* (London, 1969); M. Allott, ed., *Emily Brontë: Wuthering Heights, A Casebook* (London, 1970); W. Gérin, *Emily Brontë: A Biography* (Oxford, 1971); H. Dingle, *The Mind of Emily Brontë* (London, 1974); A. Smith, ed., *The Art of Emily Brontë* (London, 1976).

ANNE BRONTË (pseudonym Acton Bell)

I. Separate and Collected Works. *Agnes Grey: A Novel* (London, 1847), first published as vol. 3 of Emily Brontë's *Wuthering Heights; The Tenant of Wildfell Hall*, 3 vols. (London, 1848), repr. with a preface (1850); C. K. Shorter, ed., *Complete Poems* (London, 1921), with a bibliographical intro. by C. W. Hatfield; E. Chitham, ed., *Poems of Anne Brontë* (London, 1979).

II. Biographical Studies. "C. Bell," "Memoir of Acton Bell," in *Wuthering Heights and Agnes Grey*, by Ellis and Acton Bell (London, 1850); G. Moore, *Conversations in Ebury Street* (London, 1924); W. T. Hale, *Anne Brontë: Her Life and Writings* (Bloomington, Ind., 1929); W. Gérin, *Anne Brontë* (Edinburgh, 1959), biography; A. M. Harrison and D. Stanford, *Anne Brontë: Her Life and Work* (London, 1959).

PATRICK BRANWELL BRONTË

I. Separate Works. J. Drinkwater, ed., *The Odes of Horace—First Book, Translated by Branwell Brontë* (London, 1923); J. A. Symington and C. W. Hatfield, eds., *"And the Weary Are at Rest"* (London, 1924), privately printed, see also *The Shakespeare Head Brontë*.

II. Biographical Studies. F. A. Leyland, *The Brontë Family: With Special Reference to Patrick Branwell Brontë*, 2 vols. (London, 1886); M. Oliphant, *Annals of a Publishing House*, 3 vols. (Edinburgh–London, 1897–1898), vol. 2 has relevance to Branwell Brontë; A. Law, *Patrick Branwell Brontë* (London, 1924); D. du Maurier, *The Infernal World of Branwell Brontë* (London, 1960); W. Gérin, *Branwell Brontë* (London, 1961), a biography. *Note: The Brontë Society Transactions*, Bradford, etc., 1895–   , published annually, provide up-to-date criticism and comment on Brontë studies.

ARTHUR HUGH CLOUGH

(1819-1861)

Isobel Armstrong

INTRODUCTION

CLOUGH has until recently been regarded as a marginal and eccentric poet. Yet he is in no sense a peripheral writer. His work is unique in Victorian poetry, and he developed a remarkably individual idiom.

Even a new reader of Clough soon learns to recognize his characteristic tones and manners of approach:

So that the whole great wicked artificial civilised fabric—
All its unfinished houses, lots for sale, and railway
  outworks—
Seems reaccepted, resumed . . .[1]
  ("The Bothie of Tober-na-Vuolich," pt. 9, 105–107)

> Thou shalt have one God only; who
> Would be at the expense of two?
>   . . .
> Thou shalt not kill; but needst not strive
> Officiously to keep alive. . . .
>   ("The Latest Decalogue," 1–2; 11–12)

Tibur is beautiful too, and the orchard slopes, and the
  Anio
Falling, falling yet, to the ancient lyrical cadence.
          ("Amours de Voyage," canto 3, 214–215)

Many of the qualities most distinctive of Clough's work are suggested here: he assumed that the familiar details of Victorian daily life could be valid material for poetry; he used ironic wit and epigram for his most serious purposes and managed it with adroit sharpness; he extracted lyricism from the sober ordinariness of language; and he manipulated the cadences of conversational speech so as to

achieve an apparently casual, understated eloquence. All these qualities are typical of Clough, but hardly typical of Victorian poetry. They make his work unorthodox, inventive, sophisticated, and self-conscious. Experiment and strong intelligence mark all that he wrote. One cannot claim that he is a major poet; but his unusual and individual achievement makes him among the most exciting and rewarding of Victorian minor poets.

The 1869 volume of Clough's poetry was reprinted fourteen times before the end of Victoria's reign; but in the twentieth century, interest in his work declined. Perhaps Clough did not live long enough to achieve the status of a Great Victorian: he was born in 1819 and died in 1861, when he was only 42. He achieved little in public life, a failure constantly regretted by his friends, who had expected much. His life is nevertheless full of interest. His formative experiences were those of many mid-nineteenth-century intellectuals, but he responded to them with exceptional sensitivity. These experiences are germane to an understanding of his poetry and of his surprising eclipse.

The first important phase in Clough's life began in 1829, when he went to Rugby School. Until this time his life had been unusual; his father, a moderately wealthy middle-class cotton merchant, had moved from Liverpool to Charleston, South Carolina, when Clough was only four, and Clough did not return to England until 1828. Yet neither Charleston nor his family were important influences; from the time he went to Rugby until his entry to Balliol College, Oxford, in 1837, he was dominated by Dr. Thomas Arnold, the headmaster. "This was practically the end of Arthur's childhood," his sister said of Clough's return to England; justifiably, for after this he was forced to develop precociously under the pressure of the moral and intellectual responsibilities Rugby imposed on him. The discipline of his Rugby training, and the strain he experienced in acquiring it, affected him throughout his life.

---

[1]All quotations of poems are from H. F. Lowry, A. L. P. Norrington, and F. L. Mulhauser, eds., *The Poems* (Oxford, 1951), the definitive ed.

155

Dr. Arnold, whose ideas were to revolutionize the English public school system, found Clough an ideal pupil not only for his academic brilliance, but because he was responsive to the new concepts of boarding-school life that Arnold introduced at Rugby. Clough, with his almost obsessive loyalty to the place, and his efforts, especially in the senior form, to be a moral example to the rest of the school, was an illustration of Arnold's belief that education and moral training were inseparable. Even Clough's early letters are full of self-important piety redolent of Rugby's earnestness—"Here is a bit of a hymn for you Georgy," he wrote in a postscript to his younger brother. By the time he was in the senior form he spoke about the school with intense reverence.

I verily believe my whole being is regularly soaked through with the wishing and hoping and striving to do the School good . . .[2]

(20 January 1836)

Clough never lost the moral scrupulousness fundamental to a Rugby training, even though in the ten years after leaving the school he rejected almost all the particular intellectual positions he had held so unquestioningly while there. Like so many mid-nineteenth-century intellectuals, he went through a crisis in religious belief and a period of intense disillusionment with the values of his society. In the long poems written during this time, *The Bothie of Tober-na-Vuolich* (1848), *Amours de Voyage* (1849), and *Dipsychus* (1849–1850), the evidence of mental and emotional strain is increasingly obvious.

Clough's period of anxiety began when he was plunged into the theological controversy of the Oxford or Tractarian movement that was at its height at the time he went up to Oxford in 1837. Dr. Arnold was bitterly opposed to the ideas of John Henry Newman, the leader of the Oxford movement (which attempted to bring the Anglican church closer to the Catholic tradition, emphasizing accordingly the authority of the church and the importance of dogma, rather than the Protestant ideas of the responsibility of the individual conscience and private judgment in spiritual matters), and Clough was drawn into the controversy "like a straw drawn up the draught of a chimney." The effect of this intensive intellectual upheaval and preoccupation

with fundamental religious questions was eventually to undermine *all* his beliefs. To the end of his life, Clough felt the need, a need made more acute by his sensitive Rugby conscience, to analyze and rethink every position, in any sphere, religious, political, or social. In religion this habit was particularly strong. In his essay on Clough, Walter Bagehot, who knew him, described his temperament in this way:

If you offer them any known religion they "won't have that"; if you offer them no religion they will not have that either; if you ask them to accept a new and as yet unrecognised religion, they altogether refuse to do so. They seem not only to believe in an "unknown God," but in a God whom no man can ever know.[3]

Clough's academic achievement also suffered from the distractions of theology, and he did not get the first class degree expected of him. ("I have failed," he said dramatically to Dr. Arnold after walking from Oxford to Rugby on this occasion.) He redeemed himself, however, by winning a fellowship to Oriel College in 1842.

Clough's time at Oxford was not happy: toward the end of his undergraduate career, his father's business began to fail; in June 1842 Dr. Arnold died; his brother George and his father died shortly afterward; and in October 1848 he voluntarily ended his term at Oxford by resigning his fellowship on the grounds that he could no longer make the subscription to the Thirty-Nine Articles required by university statutes. Oxford, nevertheless, was a time of freedom in comparison with his later experiences. At Oxford, he consolidated a lasting friendship with Thomas and Matthew Arnold (particularly with Matthew, the poet), sons of Dr. Arnold. He was an active member of the Decade, an intimate debating club, and in the long vacations he went on reading parties to the Lake District or Scotland. These carefree occasions gave him material for his first long poem, *The Bothie of Tober-na-Vuolich*.

After he left Oxford, Clough's life was unsettled until he married Blanche Smith, a cousin of Florence Nightingale, in 1854. He spent a brief and lonely time in London from 1849 to 1852 when he was in charge of University Hall, a residential hall for students of University College, London. This period was the nadir of his life. "He shut himself up and went

[2]F. L. Mulhauser, ed., *Correspondence of A. H. Clough*, 2 vols. (London, 1957), vol. I, p. 35.

[3]*Literary Studies* (London, 1879), vol. II, p. 304.

through his life in silence," his wife wrote of him. Finally, he left University Hall because of difficulties with the authorities over religious observance there, and emigrated to America in 1852, intending to live by writing and teaching in Cambridge, Massachusetts. This was not easy (his largest commission was the drudging task of revising that translation of Plutarch's *Lives* known as John Dryden's), so he returned to England in 1853, and his friends found him a minor post in the Education Office. This post enabled him to marry, but even then he was overwhelmed by work, and with astonishing selflessness he voluntarily increased the strain on his health by assisting his exacting cousin, Florence Nightingale, in her charitable work. Travel abroad in the last year of his life did not restore his health, and he died in Florence in 1861.

The detailed record of Clough's life might at first suggest that he was dogged by misfortune. Yet in spite of the considerable information that exists, and Clough's extensive correspondence, it is difficult to be certain that he was radically damaged by his misfortunes, for his personality is an enigma. His letters, for instance, are in the main so impersonal and toneless that disappointingly little emerges from them (he is exceptionally evasive, for example, about the true nature of his religious problems, and even his love letters are outstanding only for their uncompromising reserve). Though there are letters to a great number of important literary and intellectual figures—Matthew Arnold, Thomas Carlyle, Ralph Waldo Emerson, James Froude, Charles Eliot Norton, Benjamin Jowett, Charles Kingsley—it is difficult to deduce from them why he should have been so highly respected by these men.

Even his contemporaries were puzzled by him. This description by Thomas Arnold in the journal *Nineteenth Century* (1898) is hardly informative. It is hesitant, as if Arnold were aware that he had not completely understood Clough's personality:

His clear black eyes, under a broad, full and lofty forehead, were often partly closed as if through the pressure of thought; but when the problem occupying him was solved a glorious flash would break from his eyes, expressive of an inner joy and sudden illumination. . . . His mouth was beautifully formed, but both it and the chin were characterised by some lack of determination and firmness. This deficiency, however, so far as it existed, was harmful only to himself; those who sought his counsel or help found him the wisest of advisers, the steadiest and kindest of friends.

In the absence of convincing accounts of Clough's personality, conjecture is inevitable. Until recently, the picture of him has been unfortunate and oversimplified, and this may well have discouraged the reading of his poetry. He has been caricatured as the first and quintessential product of the English public school system (for example, by Lytton Strachey in *Eminent Victorians*); certainly to be mentioned in *Tom Brown's Schooldays*, that naively pious schoolboys' epic of Rugby life under Dr. Arnold, as "our own Rugby poet," is almost enough to justify such a picture. Alternatively, critics have followed the account of Clough presented in "Thyrsis," Matthew Arnold's elegy on him. "Thyrsis," while epitomizing Clough as the Victorian intellectual defeated by the dilemmas of his generation, has been far too influential:

> Some life of men unblest
> He knew, which made him droop, and fill'd his head.
>   He went; his piping took a troubled sound
>   Of storms that rage outside our happy ground;
> He could not wait their passing, he is dead.
>
> (46–50)

"Thyrsis," as even Arnold admitted, is a highly selective account of Clough. Yet his portrait of Clough as the poet of a kind of low seriousness, radically unsettled by anxiety, nagging inconclusively at intellectual problems, has prevailed. Arnold's criticisms have some relevance, but they are exaggerated; the neurotic Clough of "Thyrsis" needs to be modified. Fortunately, this corrective is to be found in an analysis of Clough's poetry by his contemporary, R. H. Hutton. Hutton usefully compares Clough's poetry with that of Matthew Arnold. Hutton recognizes that Clough could be overintrospective, but:

With all his intellectual precision, there is a something of the boyishness, of the simplicity, of the vascular Saxon breadth of Chaucer's poetry in Clough. . . . There are both flesh and spirit, as well as emotion and speculation. . . . Clough's is the tenderness of earthly sympathy. . . . Both [Arnold and Clough] fill half their poems with the most subtle intellectual meditations; but Clough leaves the problems he touches on all but where they were, reproaching himself for mooning over them so long. . . . Finally, when they both reach their highest poetical point, Mr. Arnold is found painting lucidly in a region of pure and exquisite sentiment, Clough singing a sort of paean of buoyant and exultant strength.[4]

---

[4]*Essays, Theological and Literary* (London, 1877), vol. II, p. 256.

The "buoyant and exultant strength" described by Hutton has to be constantly invoked to balance the melancholy threnody of "Thyrsis," for Clough's poetry has firmly positive qualities; it is at once sensitive and sturdy; a strong poetry, permeated with humane objectivity and realism. It is often broadly humorous, brilliantly witty, and ironic.

An examination of two of Clough's poems, "O land of Empire, art and love!" and "Say not the struggle nought availeth," will show how assessments of Clough's work as widely apart as those of Arnold and Hutton were possible. It will also serve as an introduction to a general discussion of his work.

TWO POEMS

"O land of Empire, art and love!" is ostensibly a satire on overdelicacy, but the purpose of the satire is to develop by implication a social theory of art that is deliberately unsentimental and antiromantic, and that, as will become clear, defends the whole range and subject matter of Clough's poetry. The opening at once establishes the poet's firm common sense and lack of squeamishness. With uninhibited irony, it satirizes the uneasy English tourist in Italy, who is alarmed to find that his aesthetic enjoyment of Italian art and culture is spoiled by the squalor of their setting. Clough mocks the tourist's accents:

> Yet, boy, that nuisance why commit
>   On this Corinthian column?
>
>   . . .
>
> Are these the fixed condition
> On which may Northern pilgrim come
> To imbibe thine ether-air, and sum
>   Thy store of old tradition?
> Must we be chill, if clean, and stand
> Foot-deep in dirt in classic land?
> (33–42)

As the poem proceeds, the Corinthian column described in the introduction is seen to be the symbol for a work of art, and the physical squalor represents the whole life—sordid and crude as well as refined—of the society that produces a work of art. By using a further analogy between art and a growing flower (thereby bringing in the ideas of vitality and nourishment), Clough makes it clear that art and society must have a symbiotic relation one with another. A healthy art can develop only when it draws upon the whole life of its environment, just as a flower draws upon the earth.

> From homely roots unseen below
>
>   . . .
>
> The stem that bears the ethereal flower
> Derives that emanative power;
> From mixtures fetid foul and sour
> Draws juices that those petals fill.
> (45–50)

Matthew Arnold was to say that poetry is "at bottom a criticism of life." In this poem Clough forestalled him and went even further by saying that poetry is primarily a criticism of *everyday* life and society also. It must accept the whole of life and be firmly related to the solid facts of day-to-day existence. When in 1853 he wrote his *Review of some poems by Alexander Smith and Matthew Arnold*, Clough urgently demanded a new realism, a poetry dealing "with general wants, ordinary feelings, the obvious rather than the rare facts of human nature," and with "positive matters of fact." His own poetry fulfills these demands. In the poetic form particularly suited to describing the domestic affairs of everyday life, the verse novel, he dealt sanely and frankly with love, sex, personal relations. In his poems appear the "obvious" surroundings and situations of contemporary life: reading parties in Scotland (*The Bothie*), tourism in Europe (*Amours de Voyage*). His theory plainly committed him to write of contemporary problems—social, political, and religious—and accordingly he wrote of the siege of Rome in 1849, Chartist ideas, equality, the relation of rich and poor, David Friedrich Strauss and German biblical criticism. Arnold was particularly disturbed by Clough's willingness to discuss contemporary problems, because he felt that it would increase the tendency to morbid intellectuality that, as "Thyrsis" shows, he considered the flaw of Clough's poetry; but Clough's theory was based on a firm and realistic acceptance of things. It is not surprising that in the review just quoted, he stated a preference for the "real flesh and blood" of the minor poet Alexander Smith, in comparison with the fastidiousness of his friend Matthew Arnold.

"Say not the struggle nought availeth" is Clough's most famous poem.

> Say not the struggle nought availeth,
>   The labour and the wounds are vain,

The enemy faints not, nor faileth,
    And as things have been, things remain.

If hopes were dupes, fears may be liars;
    It may be, in yon smoke concealed,
Your comrades chase e'en now the fliers,
    And, but for you, possess the field.

For while the tired waves, vainly breaking,
    Seem here no painful inch to gain,
Far back through creeks and inlets making
    Came, silent, flooding in, the main,

And not by eastern windows only,
    When daylight comes, comes in the light,
In front the sun climbs slow, how slowly,
    But westward, look, the land is bright.
                                        (1–16)

The rejection of defeatism is Clough's most insistent theme. For all his commitment to facts, he was determined never to be defeated by them. The old, well-worn metaphor of battle could easily lead to facile optimism and superficial heroics, but there are none here. Instead, with a peculiarly firm diffidence, he states that fear, just as much as hope, can be deceptive. The very structure of the lines reflects an empirical balance in the thought and precludes attitudinizing—"If hopes were dupes, fears may be liars." "Say not" is Clough's celebration of a heroic ideal, and yet is rooted in commonsense reality. Its strength is that it holds the two moods in equipoise. There is a tension between the sense of achievement and certain triumph, and the weariness of dogged, tired effort—"For while the tired waves, vainly breaking, . . ." The emotional force of this image is just prevented from dominating the whole poem. It does not counteract the equally powerful rejection of defeat.

This finely adjusted balance is not always achieved in Clough's poetry, and therefore the criticisms in "Thyrsis," overstated as they are, cannot altogether be displaced by Hutton's "buoyant and exultant strength." Bagehot felt that Dr. Arnold's pupils suffered from "a fatigued way of looking at great subjects"; certainly, some poems ("Easter Day II" among the short poems and *Dipsychus* among the long poems) state the intellectual meaning that it is worth "going on," and yet the general mood of the poems suggests that it is not.

The order in which Clough wrote his poems is not the order in which they were published. Therefore, before discussing *Ambarvalia*, his earliest work, it is convenient to give a brief chronology in order of publication (omitting the occasional prose pieces, the most important of which were published in *The Poems and Prose Remains of A. H. Clough*, 1869, and which are only of relevance insofar as they bear upon his poetry). *The Bothie of Tober-na-Vuolich* appeared in 1848. *Ambarvalia*, a joint production of Clough and Thomas Burbidge,[5] was published in 1849, though the poems in it were written before *The Bothie*. *Amours de Voyage* first appeared in the Boston *Atlantic Monthly* in 1858, though it was written during 1849. *Dipsychus*, published posthumously in 1865, belongs to the same period of composition as *Amours de Voyage*. *Mari Magno*, Clough's last poem, a succession of brief, linked narratives, was composed in 1861 and first appeared in a cut version in 1862. There are a number of shorter poems and the unfinished *Mystery of the Fall*, belonging to the same period as *Amours de Voyage* and *Dipsychus*.

AMBARVALIA

"Why should I say I see the things I see not?"

THE title of this volume of poems, *Ambarvalia*, refers to the annual festival in ancient Rome during which the fields and boundaries were purified. It seems to have been chosen as a gesture of modesty, for the festival had homely, agricultural associations. Yet Clough's contributions to the volume have none of the parochialism the title was meant to imply. In comparison with Burbidge's poems, Clough's (written for the most part during his time at Oxford) have an intellectual grip and maturity that are unusual. Burbidge's pieces are capable enough—mild, gentlemanly productions, carefully worked out and sincerely felt—but Clough's are imaginatively and intellectually superior because they possess that "buoyant and exultant strength" that was with him from the beginning.

Beside me—in the car—she sat,
    She spake not, no, nor looked to me:
From her to me, from me to her,
    What passed so subtly stealthily?

[5]Thomas Burbidge (1816–1892) was a poet and clergyman. Clough's friendship with him began at Rugby School.

> . . . Yet owned we, fused in one,
>   The Power which e'en in stones and earths
> By blind elections felt, in forms
>   Organic breeds to myriad births;
> By lichen small on granite wall
>   Approved, its faintest feeblest stir
> Slow-spreading, strengthening long, at last
>   Vibrated full in me and her.
>   ("Natura Naturans," 1–4; 41–48)

There is an exhilarating response here to those ordinary facts of human life that were already important to Clough. The poet simply meets a girl on a train. With joyful frankness Clough celebrates the physical awareness between them, and then, in a sudden and imaginative enlargement of vision, he shows that the experience gave him insight into the significance of evolution. The slow generation of species culminated in human love and love is the energy working in creation. The muscular strength of the alliteration conveys a sense of fecundity.

> Flashed flickering forth fantastic flies,
> Big bees their burly bodies swung
>   · · ·
> The leopard lithe in Indian glade,
> And dolphin, brightening tropic seas,
> In us were living, leapt and played.
>   ("Natura Naturans," 57–64)

All the poems in *Ambarvalia* manifest Clough's strength; his expressions of moral responsibility have a firmness, a quiet integrity, and eloquence. There is the sober, urgent dignity of "Qui laborat orat," in which Clough says that genuine prayer expresses itself as action in practical life, an early statement of a habitual theme. Or there is the poised gravity of "Qua cursum ventus":

> To veer, how vain! On, onward strain,
>   Brave barks! In light, in darkness too,
> Through winds and tides one compass guides—
>   To that, and your own selves, be true.
>   (17–20)

Something more distinguishes Clough's poems—a theme. The aggressive "Why should I say I see the things I see not?" is a key line. The poems defend intellectual honesty; implicitly or explicitly they claim the right to question, the right to be skeptical, demanding inquiry and analysis in every sphere. There is the iconoclastic poem on duty, in which

Clough attacks social convention because it restricts intellectual and moral freedom:

> Ready money of affection
>   Pay, whoever drew the bill.
> With the form conforming duly,
> Senseless what it meaneth truly,
> Go to church—the world require you,
>   To balls—the world require you too
>   · · ·
> Duty—'tis to take on trust
>   What things are good, and right, and just.
>   ("Duty—that's to say complying," 11–20)

In another poem on religion he examines the possibility of belief or nonbelief alike with conscientious distrust, and reiterates an honest skepticism rather than the honest doubt that Tennyson later professed in *In Memoriam*:

> Receive it not, but leave it not,
>   And wait it out, O Man!
>   ("When Israel came out of Egypt," 11–12)

In this constant intellectual analysis, Clough transferred his Rugby scrupulousness to all areas of experience. He once wrote that he wanted to escape "the vortex of Philosophism" at Oxford, yet philosophism is germane to these poems. In the more mature longer poems he turned it to further artistic advantage and evolved a highly successful technique for presenting philosophism in verse.

THE LONG POEMS

Myself my own experiment

". . . but you know you are a mere d——d depth hunter in poetry," Arnold wrote to Clough in a letter of 24 May 1848, shortly before the publication of *The Bothie of Tober-na-Vuolich*. He was objecting to the predominance of "thinking aloud" in Clough's poetry, but in accusing him of trying to "solve the universe" and in interpreting this as a sign of weakness, Arnold underrated Clough's self-consciousness and intelligence, failing to grasp that in these poems, reasoning is not only a procedure but a theme. All these poems, though they otherwise differ, have a common theme—that of the intellectual temperament itself.

In *Ambarvalia* Clough insisted on the primacy of analysis and inquiry, but he understood its dangers. He early recognized his own tendency to what he called in a letter of 26 August 1837 to J. N. Simpkinson "double-mindedness," a faculty for analyzing problems so minutely and fairly that what started as a discipline in empirical honesty ended as vacillating inconclusiveness. Asserting his pragmatic commitment to "positive matters of fact" in the long poems, he satirized any kind of gratuitous theorizing (whether it took the form of abstract speculation or introspection). The long poems are brilliant studies in the psychology of intellectuals.

Clough regarded the overanalytic temperament seriously enough to make it the crux of the unfinished *Mystery of the Fall*, where it is the salient characteristic of fallen man. Adam exults in reasoning and self-analysis because the "curious seething process" of introspection makes him intellectually autonomous—"myself my own experiment." But Eve condemns the interminable "thinkings and cross-thinkings" that began with self-consciousness. These "thinkings and cross-thinkings" are dramatized in the long poems. The hero of *The Bothie*, Philip, is the victim of his own overimpulsive theorizing. Claude, the hero of *Amours de Voyage*, is betrayed by his fastidious introspections, and the hero of *Dipsychus* has an almost pathological conscientiousness.

Though Arnold and Clough seem to be diametrically opposed as to poetic principles, their diagnosis of the vitiating intellectual habit of the nineteenth century was the same; they agree that this habit was a morbid "dialogue of the mind with itself," as Arnold called it in the preface to his own poems of 1853. Arnold tried to eradicate it altogether from his poetry; Clough deliberately explored it. In doing so he avoided morbidity (two of the poems are straightforward comedies) by means of presenting the psychology of the analytic mind dramatically; ". . . it is both critically best and morally safest to dramatize [sic] your feelings, where they are of private personal character," he wrote to J. P. Pell in a letter of 7 July 1838, early in his poetic career. In the three long poems, Clough greatly developed the "dramaticizing" method, and the dramaticizing technique creates the effect of impersonal, objective presentation. Further, the dramatic presentation allows him to pack these poems with energy and life, because his intellectuals soliloquize in a concrete, vividly delineated environment, surrounded by characters as much individualized as themselves. The sense of locality is so strong that the characters never become detached from their contexts. In *Amours de Voyage*, which is set in Rome, the topography of Rome and its surroundings is never allowed to become indistinct:

> Ye, too, Ye marvellous Twain, that erect on Monte Cavallo
> Stand by your rearing steeds in the grace of your motionless movement,
> Stand with your upstretched arms and tranquil regardant faces,
> Stand as instinct with life in the might of immutable manhood,—
>
> (canto 1, 186–189)

These long poems are Clough's major achievement and culminate in the tour de force of *Dipsychus*, where Clough treated the theme of the intellectual with more seriousness, if with more pessimism, than in the other poems.

INTELLECTUALS EBULLIENT: THE BOTHIE *AND* AMOURS DE VOYAGE

THESE two poems, both verse novels written in hexameters, are predominantly comic studies of intellectuals. *The Bothie* is a mock-heroic account of an undergraduate reading party or vacation study group in Scotland. Philip, the hero, is full of unrealistic radical and egalitarian ideas that lead him particularly to sentimentalize working-class women. Slipping away from his companions while on a walking tour, he has an eminently rash flirtation with a servant girl, Katie. His disappointment over this affair drives him to the other extreme, and he has an equally unsuccessful flirtation with an heiress, Lady Maria. His friends and tutor hear rumors of his activities with suspense and puzzlement shared by the reader. Finally, he falls genuinely in love with Elspie, a poor Highland girl, daughter of the owner of the "bothie," or hut, named in the title of the poem. As he achieves emotional maturity and a sense of responsibility in personal relationships, so he begins to hold his political ideas with more realism. The two processes are interdependent.

Amours de Voyage is in letter form. Claude, the hero, happens to visit Rome during Mazzini's defense of the Roman republic when the French besieged Rome in 1849. He is thrown into the company of the Trevellyns, an English family also traveling. He loses the opportunity to propose to their daughter, Mary, who loves him, by examining his state of mind so lengthily that she leaves Rome before he has completed his self-analysis. Claude can make up his mind about nothing; "Il doutait de tout, même de l'amour," runs one of the epigraphs to the poem.

In each poem the intellectual and his characteristics emerge fully from the narrative. Wit is an almost obligatory part of the intellectual's equipment, and Clough exploited the intellectual's wit and wrote from within its own terms—its jokes, epigrams, aphorisms, its ebullient delight in sheer sophisticated cleverness, or its effervescent, extravagant indulgence in undergraduate humor. The humor of these poems is always the humor of the educated. Clough understood the humor of the intellectual mentality so well that he reproduced with remarkable authenticity the educated voice, speaking from the intellectual's exclusive world of assured knowledge and easy, almost negligent intelligence. When the undergraduates of *The Bothie* decide to abandon their studies temporarily, they dismiss the classics with an absurd, exhilarated mock-rhetorical apostrophe that only a knowledge of the classics could have allowed them to make:

> Slumber in Liddell-and-Scott, O musical chaff of old
> Athens,
> Dishes, and fishes, bird, beast, and sesquipedalian
> blackguard!
> Sleep, weary ghosts, be at peace and abide in your
> lexicon-limbo!
>
> (pt. 2, 222–224)

Claude, the hero of *Amours de Voyage*, analyzes Italian art and culture in knowledgeable, elegant arabesques of wit as he wanders in Rome. "Rome disappoints me much," he says. "*Rubbishy* seems the word that most exactly would suit it."

> What do I find in the Forum? An archway and two or
> three pillars.
> Well, but St. Peter's? Alas, Bernini has filled it with
> sculpture!
> . . .
> Yet of solidity much, but of splendour little is extant:
> "Brickwork I found thee, and marble I left thee!"
> their Emperor vaunted:
> "Marble I thought thee, and brickwork I find thee!"
> the Tourist may answer.
>
> (canto 1, 43–44; 48–50)

All the freedom of comment, irreverence, and iconoclastic allusion in these poems is achieved by exploiting the voice of the intellectual.

The dramatic situations of *The Bothie* and *Amours de Voyage* are the same—the intellectual in love—and yet the two poems are very different. *The Bothie*, despite its searching criticism of Philip's ideals, is a young man's idyll, while *Amours de Voyage* is a mature and highly finished satire. Accordingly, in *Amours de Voyage* elegant verbal sharpness supersedes the boisterous mock-heroic verse of *The Bothie*. Yet the boisterousness of *The Bothie* gives the poem its distinctive "buoyant and exultant" energy. Clough parodies epic description with exuberance; he makes one young man dress for dinner in the "waistcoat work of a lady" and another in a "shirt as of crochet of women" as if they were elaborately arming for battle. The best swimmer in the company becomes heroically "the Glory of Headers." And yet this mocking syntax, which sounds like a pedantically literal translation, moves easily into the lyrical phrasing of "perfection of water" when Clough describes the pool used by the group for bathing:

> where beads of foam uprising
> Mingle their clouds of white with the delicate hue of
> the stillness.
>
> (pt. 3, 39–40)

Clough never allows the poem to lose buoyancy. The grave advice of the young man's tutor, Adam, is juxtaposed with a flippant discussion of women put into the terminology of Gothic architecture—the "sculliony stumpy-columnar," the "Modern-Florid, modern-fine-lady." When Philip laments over Katie, feeling that he has deserted her too brutally, his sad reiterations—"Would I were dead, I keep saying, that so I could go and uphold her!"—are followed immediately by a gay account of a Highland reel, "swinging and flinging, and stamping and tramping, and grasping and clasping."

The gaiety of *The Bothie* is mitigated in *Amours de Voyage*. Here Clough presents the fastidious introspections of Claude, the overly self-conscious intellectual, with particularly cutting satire. Claude is so intellectually scrupulous, witty, sensitive, cleverly cruel that he reduces all experience to bathos. When he exclaims, "Hang this thinking!" he inadvertently defines his own weakness. His habit of analysis is a defense against what he calls "the factitious." He is so afraid of the factitious that he cannot believe even in his own emotion.

> I am in love, you say: I do not think so, exactly.
> (canto 2, 265)

The line—a lingering half-denial followed by a half-retraction—is the epitome of equivocation. In the comedy of the statement, with its scrupulous phraseology, and the final outrageous pseudoprecision of "exactly," Clough does not disguise Claude's chronic inability to commit himself.

As a self-conscious study in self-consciousness, *Amours de Voyage* is a kind of nineteenth-century "Love Song of J. Alfred Prufrock." In both poems, the mixture of wit and poignancy, comedy and pain comes from the protagonists' never quite successful attempt to control emotions by reducing their importance. Claude's intellectual posturings and defensive detachment are shared by T. S. Eliot's hero. The protagonists of both poems have a faculty for dismissing themselves with self-deprecating irony, a sort of supercilious verbal shrug.

> I grow old . . . I grow old . . .
> I shall wear the bottoms of my trousers rolled.
> (T. S. Eliot, "Prufrock")

> After all, perhaps there was something factitious about it;
> I have had pain, it is true; have wept; and so have the actors.
> (*Amours de Voyage*, canto 5, 164–165)

Amours de Voyage, however cutting its satire, is not a harsh poem. It is constantly lightened by the brilliant verbal extravagance of Claude himself: "After endeavouring idly to minister balm to the trembling Quinquagenarian fears of two lone British spinsters"—thus he describes his gallantry during the siege. Clough broadens the poem by presenting other characters besides Claude, and by treating Mary's feelings with genuine sympathy. Mary's typically Victorian family, naive middle-class tourists who create their unmistakably British ethos with complete assurance wherever they go, are refreshingly normal. Her sister, Georgina, engaged to the "tender domestic" Vernon, is particularly appealing, chattering her way through Rome with artless superficiality:

> Rome is a wonderful place . . .
> Not very gay, however; the English are mostly at
>   Naples;
> There are the A.'s, we hear, and most of the W. party.
> (canto 1, 56–58)

Mary herself ends the poem, determining to forget Claude in sad but sane resignation. "You have heard nothing [of Claude]; of course, I know you can have heard nothing," she writes to a friend. Her resignation puts the action of the poem in proportion, a proportion provided also by the short lyrics that head each canto. These, recalling in warm and tender lyricism the ancient Rome of gods and heroes that "lives in the exquisite grace of column disjointed and single," are set against the tensions of the siege and the emotional problems of the central characters.

> Over the great windy waters, and over the clear-crested
>   summits,
>   Unto the sun and the sky, and unto the perfecter
>   earth,
> Come, let us go,—to a land wherein gods of the
>   old time wandered
>   Where every breath even now changes to ether
>   divine.
> (canto 1, 1–4)

DIPSYCHUS—*THE INTELLECTUAL AGONISTES*

Dipsychus is set in Venice and consists of a series of soliloquies and dialogues between Dipsychus and a character designated as "Spirit," as they wander through Venice. "Dipsychus" translated means "double-minded," and the double-mindedness of Dipsychus is of the moral sort. "Now the over-tender conscience will, of course, exaggerate the wickedness of the world," Clough wrote in the epilogue to *Dipsychus*. Dipsychus is divided against himself because his moral scruples prevent him from deciding on any course of action in the morally degenerate society (as he interprets it) in which he lives. The Spirit, always in opposition to Dipsychus, represents this materialist society, the society of mid-nineteenth-century Europe.

"I could have gone cracked . . ." was Clough's comment on his state of mind during the time he composed *Dipsychus*, and the poem has none of the free assurance behind *The Bothie* and *Amours de Voyage*. Its equivalent to their wit is a tone of corroding mockery and tragic cynicism:

> I dreamt a dream; till morning light
> A bell rang in my head all night,
> Tinkling and tinkling first, and then
> Tolling; and tinkling; tolling again.
> So brisk and gay, and then so slow!

O joy, and terror! mirth, and woe!
Ting, ting, there is no God; ting, ting—
Dong, there is no God; dong,
There is no God; dong, dong!

(sc. 5, 7–15)

Dipsychus is a study of the mental and spiritual crisis of the contemporary Victorian intellectual, and voices the sense of loss—loss of belief, loss of confidence in the values of society—that fills so much of Victorian poetry. The intellectual's dilemma in *Dipsychus* is that his values run counter to the values of society, so that he is in moral isolation. He is able to diagnose but not to remedy the limitations of his society, and the predicament is demoralizing. Since it has this wide reference, *Dipsychus* is more ambitious than the other long poems, though it was never finished.

The opposition between the intellectual and his society is displayed by means of counterpoint. Throughout the poem Dipsychus' despair of society and the Spirit's cynical acceptance of it create a counterpoint of moods and attitudes. Deep emotion alternates with callousness, just as in the elegy quoted above, which alternates lightness and resonance.

Ting, ting, there is no God; ting, ting—
Dong, there is no God, dong . . .

Clough allows the Spirit to voice among other things the materialist attitudes that he particularly wanted to attack; and the Spirit, a cheerfully insensitive philistine, subjects all major questions—sex, class, religion—to a coarse irony:

Once in a fortnight say, by lucky chance
Of happier-tempered coffee, gain (Great Heaven!)
A pious rapture.

(sc. 10, 124–126)

Why, as to feelings of devotion, —
I interdict all vague emotion.

(sc. 8, 67–68)

They may talk as they please about what they call pelf,
And how one ought never to think of one's self,
And how pleasures of thought surpass eating and
    drinking—
My pleasure of thought is the pleasure of thinking
  How pleasant it is to have money, heigh ho!
  How pleasant it is to have money.

(sc. 4, 190–195)

This satire is a continuation of Clough's attacks on commercial values begun in *The Bothie* and extended in short poems such as "In the Great Metropolis," with its savage jiglike refrain "The devil take the hind most, O!" (Clough was radical enough to be addressed by his friends as "Citizen Clough.") In *Dipsychus* the satire is deepened and supplemented by the profounder despairing commentary of Dipsychus himself. He cannot share the common sense of the Spirit, who will recognize a vague and ill-defined God when distress or trouble forces him to take refuge in belief.

And almost every one when age,
Disease, or sorrows strike him,
Inclines to think there is a God,
Or something very like Him.

(sc. 5, 182–185)

Dipsychus feels too intensely the loss of firm Christian morality and religious feeling.

O pretty girl who trippest along,
Come to my bed—it isn't wrong.
Uncork the bottle, sing the song!
Ting, ting, a ding: dong, dong.
Wine has dregs; the song an end;
A silly girl is a poor friend
And age and weakness who shall mend?
Dong, there is no God; Dong!

(sc. 5, 19–26)

Dipsychus' statements have a dramatic immediacy because of their directly topical implications, yet their seriousness gives the poem more than topical relevance.

The antagonism between Dipsychus and the Spirit represents more than the antagonism between the intellectual and his society. The satire in the poem has a double focus, and the opposition between the two characters serves a further purpose. It represents the conflict of an oversensitive conscience (Dipsychus might have been a product of Dr. Arnold's Rugby) with instinct and impulse, the animal side of man that Dipsychus regards with unnecessary dread and timidity. In this sense the poem is a dialogue between soul and body, taking place within Dipsychus himself. However superficial the Spirit's morality, he has the reasonableness of the natural man eminently lacking in Dipsychus. His flippant Gilbertian rhymes and neat satiric couplets embody some precise and acute comment, and he speaks the most energetic verse in the poem:

These juicy meats, this flashing wine,
May be an unreal mere appearance;
Only—for my inside, in fine,
They have a singular coherence.

This lovely creature's glowing charms
Are gross illusion, I don't doubt that;
But when I pressed her in my arms
I somehow didn't think about that.
                    (sc. 4, 106–113)

Thus life we see is wondrous odd,
And so, we argue, may be God.
At any rate, this rationalistic
Half-puritano-semitheistic
Cross of Neologist and Mystic
Is, of all doctrines, the least reasonable—
                    (sc. 7, 53–58)

The spirit emphasizes that Dipsychus makes his problems more acute by being intellectually and morally effete. Fastidiously afraid of being contaminated by the vices of "the world," he is too much inhibited by moral scruples, as Claude was by intellectual scruples. "It's all Arnold's doing; he spoilt the public schools," grumbles the supposed uncle of the author who discusses the poem with him in the engaging epilogue to Dipsychus. He echoes a friend's criticism of Rugby boys—"They're all so pious"; the situation of Dipsychus makes his comment almost justifiable.

Dipsychus is the only one of Clough's poems to which the criticisms in "Thyrsis" are applicable. The "feeling of depression, the feeling of ennui," which Arnold described as the dominating mood of his generation, are to be found in Dipsychus, because it is infused with the self-pity it tries to objectify. Dipsychus opens with a specific reference to an earlier poem, "Easter Day," an elegy on the general loss of Christian morality and religious feeling. The literal occurrence of the Resurrection in the past, Clough says there, is of minor importance compared with the necessity to practice Christian morality in the present:

Weep not beside the Tomb
    Ye women . . .
Go to your homes, your living children tend,
    Your earthly spouses love;
Set your affections not on things above . . .
("Easter Day, Naples, 1849," 95–96; 104–106)

This shows signs of the influence of Carlyle, whose early essays, with their doctrine of work ("Do the Duty which lies nearest to thee") Clough read enthusiastically as an undergraduate. Clough's confidence in these ideas had lessened by the time he wrote Dipsychus. Perhaps as Bagehot suggests, those "terrible notions of duty" (Amours de Voyage) instilled by Dr. Arnold proved too exhausting. The poem has some of that drudging weariness that is just controlled in "Say not." Though Dipsychus takes up the words of "Easter Day" in the opening elegy—"Christ is not risen"—it has none of the implicit confidence asserted by the resonant phrasing of "Easter Day." In "Easter Day" Clough rejected Christian myth but maintained hope in Christian morality, and, therefore, there is a certain stoical grandeur in his rejection of the Resurrection, a grandeur lacking in Dipsychus, in spite of the profoundly elegiac quality of Dipsychus' laments and the vigor of the Spirit's verse:

Through the great sinful streets of Naples as I past,
With fiercer heat than flamed above my head
My heart was hot within me; till at last
My brain was lightened, when my tongue had said
Christ is not risen!

Christ is not risen, no,
He lies and moulders low;
    Christ is not risen.
                ("Easter Day, Naples, 1849," 1–8)

ALLEGORY OF THE COMMONPLACE
IN THE LONG POEMS

ARNOLD was too much of a purist fully to appreciate Clough's work. He wished to remove poetry as far as possible from the commonplace—a position exactly the opposite of Clough's. The essentials of poetry, Arnold wrote in 1853 (in the preface to his own volume of poetry), were "great actions, calculated powerfully and delightfully to affect what is permanent in the human soul." The actions of Clough's poems—all local, topical, and domestic—seemed to him to fall short of these essentials. Yet Arnold was led to misread Clough. All Clough's long poems transcend a narrowly contemporary significance. To understand why, it is necessary to return again to his emphasis on "positive matters of fact"; the reiterated theme of those long poems is the importance of the commonplace. They all assert that life has to be lived actively and creatively in and through the commonplace. This is the equivalent of the "great actions" proposed by Arnold. In Clough's poems the "permanent" things are the commonplace emotions and activities of ordinary experience and practical life. Taken together, these poems are a protest against the devaluation of ordinary experience, and this is the permanently relevant theme of Clough's poetry.

The long poems repeatedly show the fallacy of departing from "positive matters of fact" (fact is a key word in them), and whatever the subject under discussion—love, religion, social criticism, politics—it is always checked against solid reality. Clough's imaginative perception of the possibilities of ordinary experience shows itself particularly when he uses a group of symbolic situations and images that he relates firmly to the commonplace facts of everyday life—battle, marriage, building, growing things. These gather significance as they are explored in the poems, sometimes appearing as metaphors; or literal situations in the poems may be simultaneously real and allegorical. Battle is one of the most significant symbols, and as in "Say not," Clough revivifies this well-worn image by giving it a precise application, particularly in *The Bothie* and *Amours de Voyage*, and exploring it with his customary sanity.

The battle symbol was particularly suitable for Clough's purpose; it implies a practical struggle in exacting circumstances, and he used it to show that the actuality of the commonplace must be accepted with similar action and vigor. Such an acceptance of the facts was to him a great and demanding exercise, and the heroic associations of battle endorse this idea—an idea condensed in "Say not the struggle nought availeth." In *The Bothie*, just as in "Say not," the battle image is used to renounce defeatism. At the end of *The Bothie*, Philip, whose love for Elspie has given him new hopes and a new sense of responsibility, decides to give his social ideals a practical application. He regains vigor and energy, asking, "Where is the battle!"

> O where is the battle!
> Neither battle I see, nor arraying, nor king in Israel,
> Only infinite jumble and mess and dislocation,
> Backed by a solemn appeal, "For God's sake do
>   not stir, there!"
>
> (pt. 9, 62–65)

The decision to fight the "infinite jumble" of society is supported by two metaphors of hope, the tide turning and daylight gradually illuminating a drab town.

> As at return of tide the total weight of ocean,
> Drawn by moon and sun from Labrador and
>   Greenland,
> Sets-in amain, in the open space betwixt Mull and
>   Scarba,
> Heaving, swelling, spreading, the might of the mighty
>   Atlantic;
> There into cranny and slit of the rocky, cavernous
>   bottom
> Settles down, and with dimples huge the smooth
>   sea-surface
> Eddies, coils, and whirls; by dangerous
>   Corryvreckan:
> So in my soul of souls through its cells and secret
>   recesses,
> Comes back, swelling and spreading, the old
>   democratic fervour.
> But as the light of day enters some populous city,
> Shaming away, ere it come, by the chilly day-streak
>   signal,
> High and low, the misusers of night, shaming out the
>   gas lamps—
> All the great empty streets are flooded with
>   broadening clearness,
> Which, withal, by inscrutable simultaneous access
> Permeates far and pierces to the very cellars lying in
> Narrow high back-lane, and court, and alley of
>   alleys
>   . . .
> —Such—in me, and to me, and on me the love of
>   Elspie!
>
> (pt. 9, 73–88; 108)

This passage, where the hexameters gather a magnificent energy, is one of the finest sustained pieces Clough ever wrote. The images of battle, sea, and daylight are parallel with those used in "Say not," and they have identical implications.

In *Amours de Voyage* the actual battle during the siege of Rome takes on a symbolic meaning, and it is used to expose Claude's habit of devaluating all important experience, particularly the common experience of falling in love. When Rome is besieged by the French, he asks of the Italians, "Will they fight?" Will he himself fight? "Am I prepared to lay down my life for the British female?" he asks, wondering whether he will assist the English women during the siege, and the parodying tone immediately reduces an ethical question to one of ironic good manners. By fighting against the French in an unequal struggle, the Italians attempt on the public, social level what Claude fails to attempt on the personal level when he retreats from the responsibilities of his love affair. Claude's literal refusal "to lay down my life for the British female" is also a metaphorical rejection of effort and action not only in the sphere of personal relationships but in all spheres of experience, a refusal to fight the symbolic battle of *The Bothie* and "Say not." The battle in Clough's poetry always stands for commitment to experience and actuality. Clough's battle symbol contrasts sharply with Arnold's. His armies are not the "ignorant armies" that "clash by night" in Arnold's "Dover Beach."

"GROTESQUE" STYLE AND "HURRY SCURRY ANAPAESTS"

ARNOLD wrote, complaining of Clough's style, of "a growing sense of the deficiency of the beautiful in your poems" (24 February 1848). He complained thus well before the publication of *Ambarvalia*; when Clough adopted the hexameter, Arnold was generally unsympathetic. Much later he described elements of Clough's style as "grotesque," and Clough's use of the hexameter must have seemed to him gratuitously inelegant.

> On the whole, we conclude the Romans won't do it, and I shan't.
> *(Amours de Voyage*, canto 2, 49)

Certainly, on first inspection the elements of Clough's style seem unpromising; the lines are built up by a simple grammar full of slack construction, relying on long series of unconnected adjectives, and on the simple connective expedient of "and"; this ramifying grammar supports cumbersome words; the lines abound in repetition. Clough had his own conception of "the beautiful," resting on the axiom that almost any word or expression, however ordinary or however grotesque, has potential poetic value, just as he recognized that almost any situation is capable of poetic treatment. From this basis he created an idiom of extraordinary sensitivity and expressiveness.

By far his most frequent poetic device is repetition—repetition of words, of phrases, repetition in the form of synonymous expressions. Yet it never becomes monotonous. In the following passage it creates a literal, understated lyricism, emerging unassumingly with sober beauty from the most ordinary details of description and from the most ordinary words:

> . . . where over a ledge of granite
> Into a granite basin the amber torrent descended;
> Beautiful, very, to gaze-in ere plunging; beautiful also,
> Perfect as picture, as vision entrancing that comes to the sightless,
> Through the great granite jambs the stream, the glen, and the mountain,
> Beautiful, seen by snatches at intervals of dressing,
> Morn after morn, unsought for, recurring; . . .
> *(The Bothie of Tober-na-Vuolich*, pt. 5, 21–27)

The most controversial element in Clough's poetry is his hexameter. The hexameter is a six-stress line that, when it is unrhymed, can be used even more freely than blank verse, and Clough realized that he could create with it a supple line, full of modulations of phrasing. His hexameters are used to achieve informal, naturalistic speech rhythms. They sound casual, yet they demand as much technical skill as the disciplined satiric couplets spoken by the Spirit in *Dipsychus*. In the Prologue to *Dipsychus*, the supposed uncle of the author attacks his nephew's "hurry scurry anapaests," and objects that there can be "three or four ways of reading" every line, "each as good and as much intended as the other." But the author defends his refusal to keep to the metrical stress of the line and shows that the deviation is deliberate. And this calculated deviation is justified by the verse, for by it Clough achieved subtle shifts of emphasis, pauses, and delicate rhythmic effects. Such flexible irregularities make his hexameter a precise instrument. It can record the fussy volubility of Georgina, Mary Trevellyn's sister, in *Amours de Voyage:*

> Dear, I must really stop, for the carriage, they tell me, is waiting.
> (canto 1, 60)

Or it can realize the slow movement of pauses and recommencements as in the cadences of the following line. By its sheer phrasing, lyrically embodying Claude's involuntary enchantment with Mary Trevellyn, it achieves "the beautiful":

She goes,—therefore I go; she moves,—I move, not to
lose her.

(canto 2, 291)

MARI MAGNO—*ON THE GREAT SEA*

Mari Magno, resembling in structure Chaucer's
Canterbury Tales, is a series of tales told by strangers
traveling to America on a liner. The tales themselves
are all of travel—in England and Scotland, on the
continent, to the colonies. Travel is indeed related to
the main theme of *Mari Magno.* All the stories are
about love and marriage: the success or failure of
personal relations; the physical travel and movement that the characters have to undertake represents the demands of changing experience. Clough
used the tales in *Mari Magno* to ask: What is love?
Does it work out in experience? How far is it dependent on circumstances? These are the questions
behind his examination of adolescent love (The
Lawyer's First Tale, The Clergyman's First Tale);
love, marriage, and sexual infidelity (The Clergyman's Second Tale); love, marriage, and class (The
Lawyer's Second Tale); love and chance, love and
expedience (The American's Tale, The Mate's
Story). Clough had also used travel with a semisym-
bolic sense in the other poems; in *Amours de Voyage,* for instance, Claude decides to travel to Egypt,
and his aimless travel reflects his vacillating
temperament. Yet the travel motif is more dominant
in *Mari Magno* because the poem is particularly concerned with the challenge of change.

Hutton's remark, "Clough's is the tenderness of
earthly sympathy," is particularly relevant to *Mari
Magno.* A realistic tenderness and a kind of humane
poignancy are the poem's shaping moods. These
moods are not common in the long poems, though
they emerge in short lyrics such as "Les Vaches," a
poem at once exquisite and sturdy, the reverie of a
peasant girl as she drives the cows home and
wonders how she and her lover will stand the test of
time:

> Ah dear, and where is he, a year agone
> Who stepped beside and cheered us on and on?
> My sweetheart wanders far away from me,
> In foreign land or o'er a foreign sea.
> Home, Rose, and home, Provence and La Palie.
>
> . . .
>
> Or shall he find before his term be sped,
> Some comelier maid that he shall wish to wed?

> (Home, Rose, and home, Provence and La Palie.)
> For weary is work, and weary day by day
> To have your comfort miles on miles away.

("Les Vaches," 6–10; 30–34)

With the same sensitive realism that underlies "Les
Vaches," Clough writes in *Mari Magno* of adultery,
seduction, illegitimacy, the force of sexual desire.
Mari Magno is distinguished from the other long
poems by its subtle treatment of the emotions. This
passage in the Clergyman's First Tale, where an
adolescent boy first becomes aware of adult feeling,
is characteristic of the poem:

> "Emma," he called,—then knew that he was wrong,
> Knew that her name to him did not belong.
> Half was the colour mounted on her face,
> Her tardy movement had an adult grace.
> Her look and manner proved his feeling true,—
> A child no more, her womanhood she knew.
> Vexed with himself, and shamed, he felt
>
> . . .
>
> Something there was that from this date began,
> Within their bloods a common feeling ran.

(13–19; 22–23)

The new tenderness in *Mari Magno* does not entirely compensate for the loss of other qualities. It is a
retrospective poem. Habitual themes and situations
reappear—an Oxford don falls in love with a Highland girl, a young man is unable to make up his mind
about his feelings—and there is a loss of immediacy
in the repetition. *Mari Magno* is deficient in comedy;
though the lyric of the *Conducteur* (who cannot put
love behind him in spite of middle age) in "My Tale"
is wryly humorous, the ebullient wit and iconoclasm
of the early poems is absent. All in all, *Mari Magno*
does not equal the achievement of the earlier long
poems. Clough abandoned the "dramaticizing"
technique, and the poem lacks the vitality of the
other poems because the characters no longer speak
for themselves. He replaced the hexameter either
with octosyllabic or heroic couplets, and by keeping
strictly to the metrical stress he eliminated some of
the elements that give life to his verse—variety of
cadence, idiomatic tones. The plainness of the
language is often flat, without its customary suc-
cinctness. It is as if he were determined that no
device of style, no image or linguistic detail, should
get between the reader and the reality of the human
situations he describes. His desire for "positive matters of fact" defeats the poetry in *Mari Magno* by
making it factual.

It is difficult to assess Clough's work with any finality because of the paradoxes within it. He is in some ways a precursor of twentieth-century poetry, yet some aspects of his work make it possible to discuss him as a poet within the eighteenth-century tradition who found himself living in the nineteenth century. He has a special minor place in English poetry, since he is a Janus-like poet, both retrospective and revolutionary.

By temperament empirical and pragmatic, eminently concerned with fact, objectivity, and common sense, Clough might seem emotionally and intellectually of the eighteenth century. His poetry is intelligent, witty, and satiric; it is concerned with society as well as the poet's individual imagination; it has formal and verbal affinities with eighteenth-century poetry. On the other hand, Clough was disturbed by a consciousness of disequilibrium and instability, and these have to be emphasized when he is considered as a precursor of modern poetry.

> . . . I see . . .
> Only infinite jumble and mess and dislocation.

The frustration with which the isolated intellectual views his society is the phenomenon of modern poetry; so is his response to this condition—analysis, the "dialogue of the mind with itself"—and Clough acknowledged and responded to the modern situation in this way. In content, the inclusiveness and realism he demanded anticipated the modern poetry of the city, the urban and industrial environment; in technique, his hexameter achieved some of the rhythmical freedom of modern verse.

That Clough's poetry can be analyzed in two ways points to the complexities of his work, its peculiar blend of sensitive common sense, sturdiness, and sophistication. If these qualities are puzzling, they make for endurance. Clough's work is still important and relevant. He was one of the first poets to write about the intellectual; the searching, buoyant sanity he brought to problems still familiar will always be refreshing. He was one of the few Victorian poets to be witty without writing comic verse, and he is not only witty but serious without being heavy, moving without being melodramatic. His most enduring quality proves to be what his wife called, rather anxiously, "honest coarse strength and perception." Though she added, "can there not be strength without losing delicacy?" Clough's "coarse strength" vindicates his poetry by giving it energy. Even Arnold, always Clough's most persistent critic, allowed him on this account the finest praise. Though he was writing about *The Bothie*, his remark applies to a great deal in Clough's work as a whole; it gives the reader, he said, "the sense of having, within short limits of time, a large portion of human life presented to him, instead of a small portion."

SELECTED BIBLIOGRAPHY

I. Bibliography. T. G. Ehrsam and R. H. Deily, *Bibliographies of Twelve Victorian Authors* (New York, 1936), records only books and articles about Clough, supp. by J. G. Fucilla in *Modern Philology*, 37 (1939); F. E. Faverty, ed., *The Victorian Poets, A Guide to Research* (Cambridge, Mass., 1956); W. E. Houghton, "Prose Works of Clough: A Check List and Calendar," in the *Bulletin of the New York Public Library*, 64 (1960), part of a general bibliography published later. *Note:* The bulk of the Clough MSS are in the Bodleian Library, Oxford, presented in 1959 by B. A. Clough and K. Duff. Other documents are at Balliol College, Oxford, Oriel College, Oxford, and Dr. Williams Library, London. American collections are in the Houghton Library, Harvard University, and Honnold Library, Claremont College, California. See Lowry et al., eds., *The Poems* (Oxford, 1951), for particulars of Clough's MS notebooks and papers.

II. Collected Works. *Rugby* magazine, 2 vols. (1835–1837), Clough edited six of eight issues of the magazine, articles and poems by him are signed variously "T. Y. C.," "Z," and "A. V."

Poems in the *Rugby* magazine assumed to be Clough's (references are to vol. and pp.): "The Poacher of Dead Man's Corner," I:35; "The Warrior's Last Fight," I:62; "Count Egmont," I:160; "Sonnet 4," I:173,175; "I watched them from the window," I:308; "Song of the Hyperborean Maidens," I:309; "To ———, on going to India," I:320; "The old man of Athens," I:399; "The Exordium of a very long Poem," I:404; "Lines," II:74; "An Answer to Memory," II:132; "An Incident," II:135; "Epilogue to the Sonnets," II:284; "Verses from the School House," II:346; "Rosabel's Dream," II:361; "To a Crab Tree," II:397.

Prose in the *Rugby* magazine assumed to be Clough's: "Introductory," I:9–14; "Ten Minutes before Locking Up," I:91–95; "Macaulay's Battle of Ivry," I:123–132; "October," I:199–205; "School Society," I:207–215; "A Long Talk," I:311–319; "Henry Sinclair or, 'Tis Six Years Ago," II:56–61; "May it please Your Royal Majesty," II:103–104; "The Rugby Register," II:105–111; "A

Peripateticographical Article," II:223–234; "Sonnets in the Abstract," II:270–274; "Two Autumn Days in Athens," II:345–358; "Address of Leave-Taking," II:398–400.

III. COLLECTED EDITIONS. *Poems* (London, 1862; 2nd ed., enl., 1863), with a memoir by F. T. Palgrave, ed. by the poet's wife, also in C. Whibley, ed. (London, 1913); *Letters and Remains* (London, 1865), privately printed, contains first complete version of *Dipsychus; The Poems and Prose Remains*, 2 vols. (London, 1869), ed. by Clough's wife with J. A. Symonds, the prose remains repr. separately (1888); *The Poetical Works: With a Memoir by F. T. Palgrave* (London, 1906), in the Muses' Library; H. F. Lowry, A. L. P. Norrington, and F. L. Mulhauser, eds., *The Poems* (Oxford, 1951), the definitive ed., Oxford English Texts.

IV. LETTERS. H. F. Lowry and R. L. Rusk, eds., *Emerson-Clough Letters* (Cleveland, Ohio, 1932); F. L. Mulhauser, ed., *Correspondence*, 2 vols. (London, 1957).

V. SELECTED WORKS. *Selections from the Poems of A. H. Clough* (London, 1894), in the Golden Treasury series; E. Rhys, ed., *The Bothie and Other Poems* (London, 1896); H. S. Milford, ed., *Poems* (London, 1910), including *Ambarvalia*, both versions of *The Bothie, Amours de Voyage*, etc., the ed.'s preface contains the best account of Clough's hexameters.

VI. SEPARATE WORKS. *The Longest Day: A Poem Written at Rugby School* (London, 1836); W. Smith, *Dictionary of Greek and Roman Biography and Myth*, 3 vols. (London, 1844–1849), Clough contributed 77 short biographies to the first two vols., each signed "A. H. C."; *Illustrations of Latin Lyrical Metres*, Classical Museum, 4, (1846), see G. Tillotson, "New Verses by Clough," in the *Times Literary Supplement* (18 June 1954); *The Bothie of Toper-na-Fuosich: A Long Vacation Pastoral* (Oxford, 1848), Clough later changed title to "Tober-na-Vuolich" and a rev. version appeared in *Poems* (1863); *Ambarvalia: Poems by T. Burbidge and A. H. Clough* (London, 1849), Clough's contributions issued in separate vol. in 1850; *Amours de Voyage* (Boston, 1858), first published in the *Atlantic Monthly*, first printed as a whole in *Poems* (1862); "Poems and Ballads of Goethe," review of a translation, in *Fraser's* magazine, 59 (1859); *Greek History from Themistocles to Alexander in a series of Lives from Plutarch. Revised and arranged (with a Preface) by A. H. Clough* (London, 1860); *Plutarch's Lives. The translation called Dryden's, corrected from the Greek and revised (with an introduction) by A. H. Clough*, 5 vols. (Boston, 1864, 1874, 1876, 1902), also in E. Rhys, ed., 3 vols. (London, 1910), the Everyman's Library.

VII. BIOGRAPHICAL AND CRITICAL STUDIES. A. P. Stanley, *The Life and Correspondence of Thomas Arnold, D.D., late Headmaster of Rugby School*, 2 vols. (London, 1844); T. Hughes, *Tom Brown's Schooldays* (London, 1857); C. Kingsley, "Review of the Bothie of Toper-na-Fuosich," in *Fraser's* magazine, 39 (1849); W. M. Rossetti, "Review of the Bothie of Toper-na-Fuosich," in the *Germ*,

1 (1850); M. Arnold, *On Translating Homer* (London, 1861), contains illuminating asides on *The Bothie*; D. Masson, "Clough's Poems," in *Macmillan's* magazine, 6 (1862); F. T. Palgrave, "Arthur Hugh Clough," in *Fraser's* magazine, 65 (1862); J. A. Symonds, "Arthur Hugh Clough," in *Fortnightly Review*, n.s. 4 (1868); J. Dowden, "Arthur Hugh Clough," in *Contemporary Review*, 12 (1869); J. C. Shairp, "Balliol Scholars: A Remembrance," in *Macmillan's* magazine, 7 (1873), a poem that begins with a description of Clough very like M. Arnold's "Thyrsis"; R. H. Hutton, *Essays, Theological and Literary*, vol. II (London, 1877), contains commentary on Clough; W. Bagehot, *Literary Studies*, vol. II (London, 1879), contains a perceptive and sympathetic study of Clough; S. Waddington, *Arthur Hugh Clough: A Monograph* (London, 1883), the first full-length study; R. H. Hutton, *Literary Essays* (London, 1888); J. C. Shairp, *Portraits of Friends* (London, 1889), contains Shairp's contribution to the memoir prefixed to *Poems and Prose Remains*; W. H. Hudson, *Studies in Interpretation* (London, 1896); B. A. Clough, *A Memoir of Anne Jemima Clough* (London, 1897), extracts from Anne's early journal, many concerned with Clough; J. M. Robertson, *New Essays Towards a Critical Method* (London, 1897); R. A. Armstrong, *Faith and Doubt in the Century's Poets* (London, 1898); T. Arnold, "Arthur Hugh Clough: A Sketch," in *Nineteenth Century* (1898).

C. H. Herford, *English Tales in Verse* (London, 1902); H. Sidgwick, *Miscellaneous Essays and Addresses* (London, 1904); R. H. Hutton, *Brief Literary Criticisms* (London, 1906); E. M. Chapman, *English Literature in Account with Religion* (London, 1910); S. A. Brooke, *Four Poets: Clough, Arnold, Rossetti, Morris* (London, 1913); E. Guyot, *Essai sur la Formation Philosophique due Poète Clough: Pragmatism et Intellectualisme* (Paris, 1913); L. Strachey, *Eminent Victorians* (London, 1918), contains some satirical remarks on Clough; J. I. Osborne, *Arthur Hugh Clough* (London, 1920); S. T. Williams, *Studies in Victorian Literature* (New York, 1923); A. M. Turner, "A Study of Clough's Mari Magno," in *PMLA*, 94 (1929); M. Kent, "A Balliol Scholar," in *Criterion* (July 1930); F. L. Lucas, *Eight Victorian Poets* (London, 1930); W. H. Garrod, *Poetry and the Criticism of Life* (London, 1931); D. MacCarthy, *Portraits* (London, 1931); J. Drinkwater, ed., *The Eighteen Sixties* (London, 1932), contains essay on Clough by H. Wolfe, who develops a new approach to Clough and finds him a satirical poet; H. F. Lowry, *The Letters of Matthew Arnold to Arthur Hugh Clough* (London, 1932), invaluable for Arnold's view of Clough's poetry, still the best case against Clough; T. Scudder, *The Lonely Wayfaring Man* (London, 1936); G. Levy, *Arthur Hugh Clough* (London, 1938); L. Trilling, *Matthew Arnold* (London, 1939).

F. W. Palmer, "Was Clough a Failure?" in *Philological Quarterly*, 22 (1943); F. W. Palmer, "The Bearing of Science on the Thought of Arthur Hugh Clough," in

PMLA, 59 (1944); F. L. Mulhauser, "Clough's Love and Reason," in *Modern Philology*, 42 (1945); E. Underwood, "A. H. Clough," in *Times Literary Supplement* (8 September 1945); J. Heath-Stubbs, *The Darkling Plain* (London, 1950); I. Macdonald, "Victorian Verse Novels," in the *Listener* (16 March 1950); C. B. Tinker and H. F. Lowry, eds., *The Poetry of Matthew Arnold* (London, 1950); K. Badger, "Clough as Dipsychus," in *Modern Language Quarterly*, 12 (1951); G. P. Johari, "Clough at Oriel and at University Hall," in *PMLA*, 66 (1951); D. N. Dalglish, "Clough: The Shorter Poems," in *Essays in Criticism*, 2 (1952); J. D. Jump, "Clough's Amours de Voyage," in *English*, 9 (1953); V. S. Pritchett, *Books in General* (London, 1953); F. J. Woodward, *The Doctor's Disciples* (London, 1954); P. Veyriras, "Un Regain d'intérêt pour Arthur Hugh Clough," in *Etudes Anglaises*, 11 (1958); R. Gollin, "Arthur Hugh Clough's Formative Years: 1819–1841," in *Dissertation Abstracts*, 20 (1959); M. Timko, "Arthur Hugh Clough: A Portrait Retouched," in *Victorian News Letter*, 15 (1959); M. Timko, "The 'True Creed' of Arthur Hugh Clough," in *Modern Language Quarterly*, 21 (1960); M. Timko, "Amours de Voyage: Substance or Smoke?" in *English*, 13 (1960); W. E. Houghton, "Arthur Hugh Clough: A Hundred Years of Disparagement," in *English Studies*, 1 (1961); K. Chorley, *Arthur Hugh Clough: The Uncommitted Mind* (Oxford, 1962), an authoritative biography, the most sensitive and sympathetic discussion of Clough's work to date.

JOHN RUSKIN

(1819-1900)

Peter Quennell

I

OF all the great Victorian writers, not excluding Thomas Carlyle, John Ruskin is probably the least read. This may seem a melancholy admission with which to set forth upon a study of his life's work; but Ruskin's decline during the twentieth century has been very largely caused by the peculiar character of his literary temperament. The origins of his unpopularity, therefore, deserve some thought if we are to allow his genius its right value.

First, the modern reader is apt to associate Ruskin with a particularly unprofitable period in the history of English taste; his name recalls the worst excesses of the Victorian neo-Gothic architect. We think of polychromatic brick, Venetian-Gothic balconies, swags of sculptured ivy leaves, nowadays rimmed with soot and wreathed around the portals of railway station, hotel, or public library. Such phenomena we attribute to Ruskin's influence, but it must not be forgotten that Ruskin himself felt that the effect of his teachings on many of his disciples had been almost wholly bad. "I would rather, for my own part," he wrote in his preface to the third edition of *The Stones of Venice,*

that no architects had ever condescended to adopt one of the views suggested in this book, than that any should have made the partial use of it which has mottled our manufactory chimneys with black and red brick, dignified our banks and drapers' shops with Venetian tracery, and pinched our parish churches into dark and slippery arrangements for the advertisement of cheap coloured glass and pantiles.[1]

In the second place, Ruskin was a prophet with a decidedly dictatorial turn, and neither prophets nor dictators are much respected at the present day. The habit of prophesying grew upon Ruskin. As his need to prophesy increased and his sense of the corruption of the age he lived in became more and more oppressive, so did his literary control decline, with the result that some of his later productions are extraordinarily diffuse and incoherent. This tendency was aggravated by a kind of personal willfulness. Although apparently the most dogmatic of men, like Keats he did not believe that an artist's or a critic's mind should ever be finally made up. Indeed, he gloried in his inconsistencies; and to justify his practice of contradicting himself, he evolved a characteristic theory. He called it the theory of "polygonal truth." Ruskin at the time was still a zealous, if somewhat anxious and perplexed, student of the Old and New Testaments. One text in Holy Writ, he had observed, often appeared to contradict another. But he also observed, or professed to observe, that by examining the Bible with sufficient care he could usually discover an intermediate statement; and that, just as Mont Blanc was "set between opposite fan-shaped strata," so two groups of opposing texts supported and upheld a third, the central proposition from which the divine author intended we should take comfort. Never an unduly modest man, Ruskin considered that in his own writings he could afford to allow himself a similar latitude; and presently he went so far as to announce that he intended henceforward to "put my self-contradictions in short sentences and direct terms, in order to save sagacious persons the trouble of looking for them." In fact, he had determined to write as he pleased, as his "progressions of discovery," changes of mood, and "oscillations of temper" happened to direct his pen. The course that it followed was singularly erratic; and to trace any single line through his prophetic utterances is often a bewildering and exhausting task.

Finally, there is the problem of his private

[1] *The Stones of Venice,* vol. I, in E. T. Cook and A. D. O. Wedderburn, eds., *The Works of John Ruskin,* 39 vols. (London, 1902–1912), vol. IX, p. 11. All citations from Ruskin's works are from this edition.

character. Both from the hints conveyed by his books and his letters and from the portraits drawn in a series of twentieth-century biographies, we have gained a disquieting and discouraging impression of the prophet's personal temperament. Others he saved; himself he could not save. There is an aura of frustration and bitterness about much of Ruskin's later writing. We are aware of a painful struggle being conducted just beneath the surface—a struggle never resolved in art, a fact that constantly impeded and confused him, provoking, it is true, some splendid flashes of eloquence, yet often fatally interrupting the orderly presentation of the writer's ideas. Thus, Ruskin may seem to be triply suspect—an art critic whose influence was bad; a social prophet whose theories were confused and contradictory; a literary craftsman whose achievement was flawed by the unresolved conflicts of his private career. How, then, can he be described as a man of genius? Why should Marcel Proust have recognized him as an intercessory guardian spirit, one of the angels of literature, under the shadow of whose protecting wings his own genius had gradually expanded? The explanation is to be found in every book that Ruskin published, even in such perplexing works as *Fors Clavigera* (1871–1884) or *The Queen of the Air* (1869). The cross-grained moralist and petulant theorist was also a poetic visionary with a passionate, instinctive love of life, deeply enamored of the beauty of the visible world and capable of translating that passion into superbly expressive and melodious language.

Ruskin's strength and his weakness alike evidently had their source in the circumstances of his childhood. Born on 8 February 1819, he was the son of a prosperous sherry merchant, James Ruskin, who had early migrated from Scotland to London, and his wife, Margaret, four years older than himself, whom he had married, after a long engagement, when she had reached the age of thirty-seven. Mr. Ruskin was an old-fashioned merchant, upright, industrious, opinionated, with an interest in the liberal arts. Mrs. Ruskin, wrote her son, was in her youth a "tall, handsome, and very finely made girl"; an excellent household manager, high-minded, pious, and charitable; and a "natural, essential, unassailable, yet inoffensive, prude."[2] "My father," Ruskin

declared, "chose his wife much with the same kind of serenity and decision" as that with which he chose his clerks (*Praeterita*, vol. I, p. 126). John was their only child. Under their guidance he learned "peace, obedience, faith," but he was denied the companionship of other children. He grew up, carefully protected and disciplined, to "lead a very small, perky, contented, conceited, Cock-Robinson-Crusoe sort of life," traveling around England in his parents' carriage, while his father called on provincial wine merchants and visited the castles and country houses for which he had a romantic taste, or writing and designing in his lonely nursery (*Praeterita*, vol. I, p. 37). When he was six, he composed his first book, inspired by Maria Edgeworth's cautionary tales, Byron's *Manfred*, and Joyce's *Scientific Dialogues*[3]—a strange combination that was indicative, he later remarked, of the "interwoven temper of my mind, at the beginning of days, just as much as at their end . . ." (*Praeterita*, vol. I, p. 56).

The great disadvantages, however, of this mode of education, despite the intense solicitude with which his father and mother perpetually watched and guarded him, were a certain "lack of love" and the almost complete absence of any real freedom. His judgments of right and wrong, he complained, "were left entirely undeveloped; because the bridle and blinkers were never taken off me" (*Praeterita*, vol. I, p. 46). He grew up, in short, hopelessly unprepared for adult experience, with the result that when he developed a schoolboy passion for the schoolgirl daughter of his father's partner, the cosmopolitan M. Domecq, its effects on his mind were so unaccountably violent that they threatened to produce a physical and nervous breakdown. To assist his recovery, his parents took him abroad. The Ruskins' journeys in search of the picturesque had now been extended across the Channel. John Ruskin was becoming familiar with the Alps and learning to admire the architecture of France, Italy, and Germany. At the same time, he succumbed to the fascination of the greatest of living English artists. James Ruskin marked his son's twenty-first birthday by presenting him with one of J. M. W. Turner's sketches.

---

[2]*Praeterita*, vol. I, in *The Works*, vol. XXXV, p. 122.

[3]Jeremiah Joyce (1763–1816), a Unitarian minister of advanced political views, for which he had been prosecuted at the hands of Pitt's government, was the author of many popular scientific treatises, including *Scientific Dialogues, Dialogues in Chemistry,* and *The Arithmetic of Real Life and Business.*

II

FROM Ruskin's youthful devotion to Turner sprang the ambitious work that at once gave him an established place among modern English art critics. The opening volume of *Modern Painters*, subtitled *Their Superiority in the Art of Landscape Painting to All the Ancient Masters Proved by Examples of the True, the Beautiful, and the Intellectual from the Works of Modern Artists, Especially from Those of J. M. W. Turner, Esq., R.A.*, was published during the spring of 1843, when its author was just twenty-four. Its publication marked the beginning of his first great period of creative activity. This was a period when he wrote in the grand manner—in a rich and decorative style that he afterward learned to despise, and for which he substituted a far simpler and more didactic mode of expression. Yet both the style of his youth and the style of his middle age are based ultimately on the lessons he had received in youth. During childhood, his literary taste had been formed: "I had Walter Scott's novels, and the *Iliad* (Pope's translation) for constant reading . . . on week-days; on Sunday, their effect was tempered by *Robinson Crusoe* and the *Pilgrim's Progress . . .* " (*Praeterita*, vol. I, p. 13). Naturally—the Ruskins were a pious household—he had learned the Bible at his mother's knee:

. . . once knowing the 32nd of Deuteronomy, the 119th Psalm, the 15th of the 1st Corinthians, the Sermon on the Mount, and most of the Apocalypse, every syllable by heart, and having always a way of thinking with myself what words meant, it was not possible for me, even in the foolishest times of youth, to write entirely superficial or formal English. . . .

(*Praeterita*, vol. I, in *The Works*, vol. XXXV, p. 14)

Notwithstanding the maturity of his style, many of the theories advanced in the first volume of *Modern Painters* have failed to stand the test of time. The author is concerned to prove that Turner's paintings are vastly superior to those of the great majority of the Old Masters, whether French, Flemish, or Dutch—the masters of the Italian schools were still generally outside Ruskin's field—because Turner had made a scientific study of the formation of clouds and the stratification of rocks. Turner was "sincere": most of his rivals were ingenious mannerists. Moreover, the technical side of an artist's achievement must not be allowed excessive value:

". . . all those excellences which are peculiar to the painter . . . are merely what rhythm, melody, precision and force are in the words of the orator and poet, necessary to their greatness, but not the test of their greatness."[4] It was the artist's "thought" that counted, rather than his method of expressing it. Hence he devotes an eloquent passage to a canvas by Edwin Landseer, called *The Old Shepherd's Chief Mourner*, in which the delicacy and accuracy of the painter's brushstrokes enable him to tell a useful and pathetic story—the story of a humble and harmless life, which has now reached a quiet and lonely end, symbolized by the attitude of the shepherd's dog and by the old man's spectacles marking his place in a well-worn volume of the Holy Scriptures. Here Ruskin's point of view is essentially moralistic; but, thanks to the "interwoven temper of his mind," it does not dominate the whole work. Particularly instructive is his conception of art as a "universal language"—not a tongue merely to be spoken in the studios and drawing rooms, but a means of communicating to mankind at large the noblest aspirations of the creative spirit. We must study a work of art in relation to its time, must regard it as one aspect of a far larger intellectual process, closely connected with the products of the other arts and with the general development of human affairs.

More important still was the pervasive influence of the writer's sensibility. Ruskin was one of the earliest critics to treat criticism as a record of personal adventure, not only among the masterpieces of art but among the transcendent beauties of the natural world. No reader who turned to his description of clouds—differentiated so painstakingly and minutely, and yet with such intense poetic feeling: the colossal mountains of gray cumulus, through whose shadowed sides a sunbeam strikes; the "quiet multitudes of the white, soft, silent cirrus"; those "mighty watch-towers of vapour" whence "waving curtains of opaque rain are let down into the valleys, swinging . . . in black bending fringes, or pacing in pale columns along the lake level, grazing its surface into foam as they go"—could doubt that he had heard a new voice, which heralded the beginning of a new epoch in the history of critical and imaginative literature.

Although *Modern Painters* was not completed un-

---

[4]*Modern Painters*, vol. I, in *The Works*, vol. III, pp. 87–88.

til 1860 by the addition of its last belated volume, Ruskin's opening phase may be said to have extended from 1843 to 1854. The second volume of *Modern Painters* was followed, after a short interval, by *The Seven Lamps of Architecture*, which itself was followed, early in 1852, by his most famous book, *The Stones of Venice*. His Venetian studies marked the climax of the first period of Ruskin's creative career. Half handbook to the antiquities of a city that he believed to be falling into a rapid decline, half imaginative disquisition on his own imaginative adventures and aesthetic ideals, it is a book to be skipped through rather than studied at length—for Ruskin's prejudice against the Renaissance involves him in many erratic judgments; yet even as we skip, we are continually arrested by some brilliant stroke of thought or fancy. His essay on "The Nature of Gothic" may be partial and misguided. But given the author's standpoint, it is a masterly feat of presentation. Ruskin sees the variegated surface of Europe through the eyes of a migratory bird:

We know that gentians grow on the Alps, and olives on the Apennines; but we do not enough conceive for ourselves that variegated mosaic of the world's surface which a bird sees in its migration, that difference between the district of the gentian and of the olive which the stork and the swallow see far off, as they lean upon the sirocco wind. Let us, for a moment, try to raise ourselves even above the level of their flight, and imagine the Mediterranean lying beneath us like an irregular lake, and all its ancient promontories sleeping in the sun: here and there an angry spot of thunder, a grey stain of storm, moving upon the burning field; and here and there a fixed wreath of white volcano smoke, surrounded by its circle of ashes; but for the most part a great peacefulness, of light, Syria and Greece, Italy and Spain, laid like pieces of a golden pavement into the sea-blue, chased, as we stoop nearer to them, with bossy beaten work of mountain chains, and glowing softly with terraced gardens, and flowers heavy with frankincense, mixed among masses of laurel, and orange, and plumy palm, that abate with their grey-green shadows the burning of the marble rocks, and of the ledges of porphyry, sloping under lucent sand. Then let us pass farther toward the north, until we see the orient colours change gradually into a vast belt of rainy green, where the pastures of Switzerland, and poplar valleys of France, and dark forests of the Danube and Carpathians stretch from the mouths of the Loire to those of the Volga, seen through clefts in grey swirls of rain-cloud and flaky veils of the mist of the brooks, spreading low along the pasture lands: and then, farther north still, to see the earth heave into mighty masses of leaden rock and heathy moor, bordering with a broad waste of gloomy purple that belt of field and wood, and splintering into irregular and grisly islands amidst the northern seas, beaten by storm, and chilled by ice-drift, and tormented by furious pulses of contending tide, until the roots of the last forests fail from among the hill ravines, and the hunger of the north wind bites their peaks into barrenness; and, at last, the wall of ice, durable like iron, sets, deathlike, its white teeth against us out of the polar twilight.

(*The Stones of Venice*, in vol. X, pp. 186–187)

This was the homeland of Gothic architecture— "not only the best, but the *only rational* architecture, as being that which can fit itself most easily to all services, vulgar or noble"; and Ruskin then proceeds to distinguish, with beguiling eloquence, though with doubtful accuracy, between the static quality of classical buildings and the restless, dynamic spirit that he detects in Gothic ornament:

It is that strange *disquietude* of the Gothic spirit that is its greatness; that restlessness of the dreaming mind, that wanders hither and thither among the niches, and flickers feverishly around the pinnacles, and frets and fades in labyrinthine knots and shadows along wall and roof, and yet is not satisfied, nor shall be satisfied. The Greek could stay in his triglyph furrow, and be at peace; but the work of the Gothic art is fretwork still, and it can neither rest in, nor from, its labour, but must pass on, sleeplessly, until its love of change shall be pacified for ever in the change that must come alike on them that wake and them that sleep.

(vol. X, p. 214)

As the reader may already have noted, Ruskin, though never unmindful of his early lessons in the writing of English—the structure of his elaborate sentences is orderly: every word that he employs does exactly what he intends it to do—aimed at producing a kind of orchestral effect, both by contrasting the images he introduced and by invoking all the melodious resources of his very large vocabulary. One of his most successful efforts in this style embellishes the second volume of *The Stones of Venice*. He begs his readers to imagine that they have just examined the west front of an English cathedral and walked around the cathedral close,

where nothing goes in but the carts of the tradesmen who supply the bishop and the chapter, and where there are little shaven grass-plots . . . before old-fashioned groups of somewhat diminutive and excessively trim houses, with little oriel and bay windows jutting out here and there, and deep wooden cornices and eaves painted cream colour and white, and small porches to their doors in the shape of cockleshells. . . .

(vol. X, pp. 78–79)

Overhead rises the bulk of the cathedral itself—a

great mouldering wall of rugged sculpture and confused arcades, shattered and grey, and grisly with the heads of dragons and mocking fiends, worn by the rain and swirling winds into yet unseemlier shape, and coloured on their stony scales by the deep russet-orange lichen, melancholy gold. . . .

(vol. X, p. 79)

About the "bleak towers" that crown the edifice circle the cathedral jackdaws, "a drift of eddying black points, now closing, now scattering, and now settling suddenly into invisible places among the bosses and flowers," filling the "whole square with that strange clangour of theirs, so harsh and yet so soothing, like the cries of birds on a solitary coast between the cliffs and sea."

We have now been prepared for the vision of St. Mark's:

five great vaulted porches, ceiled with fair mosaic, and beset with sculpture of alabaster, clear as amber and delicate as ivory,—sculpture fantastic and involved, of palm leaves and lilies, and grapes and pomegranates, and birds clinging and fluttering among the branches, all twined together into an endless network of buds and plumes; and in the midst of it, the solemn forms of angels . . .

(vol. X, p. 82)

while, high above,

the breasts of the Greek horses are seen blazing in their breadth of golden strength, and the St. Mark's lion, lifted on a blue field covered with stars, until at last, as if in ecstasy, the crests of the arches break into a golden foam, and toss themselves far into the blue sky in flashes and wreaths of sculptured spray. . . .

(vol. X, p. 83)

But the last theme is probably the most poignant; for accompanying Ruskin's exquisite sense of beauty was a sense of omnipresent evil:

And what effect has this splendour on those who pass beneath it? You may walk from sunrise to sunset, to and fro, before the gateway of St. Mark's, and you will not see an eye lifted to it, nor a countenance brightened by it.

Priest and layman, soldier and civilian, rich and poor, pass by it alike regardlessly. Up to the very recesses of the porches, the meanest tradesmen of the city push their counters; nay, the foundations of its pillars are themselves the seats—not "of them that sell doves" for sacrifice, but of the vendors of toys and caricatures. Round the whole square in front of the church there is almost a continuous line of cafés, where the idle Venetians of the middle classes lounge, and read empty journals; in its centre the Austrian bands play during the time of vespers, their martial music jarring with the organ notes—the march drowning the miserere, and the sullen crowd thickening round them—a crowd, which, if it had its will, would stiletto every soldier that pipes to it. And in the recesses of the porches, all day long, knots of men of the lowest classes, unemployed and listless, lie basking in the sun like lizards; and unregarded children—every heavy glance of their young eyes full of desperation and stony depravity, and their throats hoarse with cursing—gamble, and fight, and snarl, and sleep, hour after hour, clashing their bruised centesimi upon the marble ledges of the church porch.

(vol. X, pp. 84–85)

III

RUSKIN's sense of evil had developed gradually; and to understand its source and the havoc it produced, we must turn once again to the curious circumstances of his private life. In 1848, he had elected to marry, his choice having fallen on an attractive, well-meaning, commonplace young girl named Euphemia, or Effie, Gray. During his courtship he had written her passionate letters—it was by no means true that, as he afterward declared, he had married simply in order to please his parents—but once married, he showed himself an absent-minded and neglectful husband. The marriage was never consummated: Ruskin apparently suffered from some form of psychological impotence. His wife left him and obtained a divorce; and, deeply disappointed and embittered, Ruskin retreated to his parents' house on Denmark Hill, where they continued to watch over him with apprehensive pride and love. It seems possible that Ruskin's failure in marriage may have had some connection with the experiences of his boyhood. He had been a lonely child; and in a letter to a woman friend, written at a considerably later stage, he speaks of a resemblance between himself and Jean Jacques Rousseau and of the "evil" that had poisoned his existence until he finally conquered it.

Sexual happiness, at least, was beyond his reach; but the impulses he could not satisfy were never completely overcome, and the resultant conflict helped to produce a strain of rabid puritanism, perpetually warring against the more voluptuous, indeed some of the more generous, aspects of his private character. Everything was wrong with the world, including his own existence and the pampered and privileged position that he occupied in his parents' household. What right had he to be secure and prosperous? And as the years went by, Ruskin became increasingly concerned with the practical betterment of mankind, now embarking on some grandiose scheme of improvement, now turning his attention to some minor project, such as a plan for cleansing the London streets or adding to the beauty of an Oxfordshire lane.

Among the reformer's more important activities was the delivery of a series of lectures to the recently founded Working Men's College. Armed with exhibits from his own collection—thirteenth-century illuminated manuscripts, Dürer engravings, rare mineral specimens, and the skins of West Indian birds—he did his best to open his audience's eyes to an unknown world of beauty. Nor were his efforts entirely unsuccessful: it is clear that he enjoyed a personal triumph. But at the same time, he lectured his listeners severely, even mercilessly, about the limitations of their political views. Ruskin was no egalitarian: the liberal tendency of his period he never ceased to distrust and despise. Parliamentary reform he considered a doubtful blessing: the workingman's life would not be better and happier merely because he had secured the right to vote. Nevertheless (he remarked to his students) he supposed that they were "all agape . . . for this mighty privilege of having your opinions represented in Parliament?" Well,

the concession might be desirable . . . if only it were quite certain you had got any opinions to represent. But have you? Are you agreed on anything you systematically want? Less work and more wages, of course; but how much lessening of work do you suppose is possible? . . . Have you planned the permanent state which you wish England to hold? Do you want her to be nothing but a large workshop and forge? . . . Or would you like to keep some of your lords and landed gentry still, and a few green fields and trees? . . . Your voices are not worth a rat's squeak . . . till you have some ideas to utter with them.

(Letter III, *Legislation*, in *The Works*, vol. XVII, pp. 325–326)

Ruskin's other activities between 1854 and 1860 included the production of a series of *Academy Notes*, in which he periodically examined the achievement of contemporary artists, the cataloging of Turner's sketches—he had become Turner's executor after the old man's death—and the part that he played in the erection of a new museum at Oxford. While his friends the Pre-Raphaelites were frescoing the Union, the club of the university debating society, Ruskin strove to make the museum the kind of edifice of which he had always dreamed. Gothic architecture should be harnessed to modern requirements: nineteenth-century stonemasons should revive the spiritual inspiration of the great thirteenth-century cathedral builders. In his prosecution of this splendid plan, he was unsparing of his advice and money. The architect, Benjamin Woodward, seemed appropriately grateful for the help he received; and Ruskin soon described him as one of his "truest and most loving friends" and "one of the most earnest souls that ever gave itself to the arts." Yet, as happened with so many of the prophet's dreams, the realization of his project somehow failed to satisfy him. Woodward and his attendant stonemasons, the Pre-Raphaelite artists who, at Ruskin's direction, had supplied elaborate designs for capitals and cornices (incorporating "flower and beast borders—crocodiles and various vermin," angels and children and "field mice nibbling wheatears") had certainly given of their best and allowed their imagination free rein. But, in the end, as he confessed at a later period, the structure that arose "failed signally of being what he hoped." His glorious medieval vision had gradually dissolved, leaving him face to face with the bleak realities of nineteenth-century commercial life.

Simultaneously, in the sphere of personal experience, he was undergoing an important crisis. Ruskin had been brought up as an Evangelical Christian, and during the summer of 1854, he had enjoyed a rich renewal of his early faith and had received what he described as his "third call from God." It came, "in answer to much distressful prayer," while he ascended the slopes of a Swiss mountain. Confronting "the Jungfrau and the two Eigers . . . clear and soft in the intense mountain light," and looking down across a "field of silver cloud," which "filled the valley above the lake of Brienz," he was overwhelmed by a feeling of hope and joy, and "stood long, praying that these happy hours and holy sights might be of more use to me than they have been, and might be remembered by me in hours of temptation or mortification." But his faith thus strengthened and reaffirmed began to falter as he approached the end of the decade, when, with characteristic and disarming honesty, he first admitted the existence of a very different set of values. Were purity and unselfishness infallible guides? It was a curious fact (he noted in a letter of 1858) that,

whenever I work selfishly—buy pictures that I like, stay in places that I like, study what I like, and so on—I am happy and well; but when I deny myself, and give all my money away, and work at what seems useful, I get miserable and unwell. The things I most regret in my past life are great pieces of virtuous and quite heroical self-denial; which have issued in all kinds of catastrophe and disappointment, instead of victory. Everything that has turned out well I've done merely to please myself, and it upsets all one's moral principles. Mine are going I don't know where.

Worse still from the moralist's standpoint, moral purity did not always prove to be the basis of creative power. In 1858, when he happened to be staying in Turin, he wrote a letter to an American correspondent, drawing a dramatic contrast between a ridiculous young English clergyman, a "little squeaking idiot," to whose sermon he had listened at the Protestant Chapel, and the superb Venetian artist, Paolo Veronese, whose frescoed representation of the Queen of Sheba he had spent the previous day examining. Must he believe that "this mighty Paolo Veronese . . . within whose brain all the pomp of humanity floats in a marshalled glory" was a "servant of the devil," condemned to the everlasting bonfire; while the "poor little wretch in a tidy black tie . . . expounding Nothing with a twang" was the representative of Eternal Truth? He would go further. The early religious painters, Fra Angelico and his school, whom Ruskin had hoped to be able to prefer, by comparison with those "Vagabonds of Venetians" were but "poor weak creatures." Whereas he had asserted in his ingenuous youth that the ideal artist was a man of ascetic life and deep religious feeling, he now decided that the greatest had all of them been "boldly Animal," and that "to be a first-rate painter—you mustn't be pious; but rather a little wicked, and entirely a man of the world." "A good, stout, self-commanding, magnificent Animality [he concluded] is the make for poets and artists"—adding, somewhat pathetically: "I don't understand it; one would have thought purity gave strength, but it doesn't."

The diminution of Ruskin's religious faith was accompanied by a general revolt against his parents' influence. Not only did they stand for the orthodox Christian beliefs that he was slowly casting off, but their household represented the tyranny of the existing political and social scheme. James Ruskin was a highly successful merchant; and the commercial practice of nineteenth-century England was bound up with the doctrine of laissez-faire, as propounded and propagated by the Manchester Economists, who spoke of an unalterable law of supply and demand, and declared that any attempt to raise wages or to regulate the supply of labor would precipitate the whole kingdom into economic anarchy. During the summer of 1860, Ruskin struck his first blow, preparing for the newly founded *Cornhill* magazine, then edited by Thackeray, a series of controversial essays with the general title *Unto This Last*.[5] His basic thesis was extremely simple—human beings cannot be considered as mere economic units, whom the employer is authorized to hire at the lowest wage he can persuade them to accept, thus securing the "greatest benefit to the community, and through the community, by reversion, to the servant himself." The laborer (he announced) is no machine activated by "steam, magnetism, gravitation, or any other agent of calculable force": his "motive power is a Soul," and the "force of this peculiar agent . . . enters into all the political economist's equations, without his knowledge, and falsifies every one of their results."[6] The employer must recognize his employee as a *man* and in that capacity must learn to respect and even, so far as he can, to love him. Affection and respect alone could bridge the intolerable gulf between the classes.

In retrospect, the assertion seems harmless enough; but at the time it produced a wild explosion of journalistic acrimony. The world, exclaimed one angry journalist, did not intend to allow itself to be "preached to death by a mad governess." Ruskin's essays were "eruptions of windy hysterics," a farrago of "utter imbecility." "The way in which Mr Ruskin writes of the relations of rich and poor" was a positive incitement to revolutionary violence. And so clamorous were the protests of his critics that Thackeray lost his nerve and refused to print the fifth installment. Afterward reprinted in book form, the

[5]"I will give unto this last, even as unto thee." Matthew 20: 14.
[6]"The Roots of Honour," *Unto This Last*, in *The Works*, vol. XVII, p. 29.

series, nevertheless, was very widely read and discussed. It is said, in later years, to have been Mahatma Gandhi's favorite volume, and to have contributed more than any other book of its kind to the formation of the British Labour Party.

IV

VIEWED as a work of literature, *Unto This Last*, which opens the second period of Ruskin's literary career, possesses outstanding merits. It is written in a plain, unornamented style, very unlike the rich and involved prose of *Modern Painters* and *The Stones of Venice*. No "pretty passages," such as had once caused old Mr. Ruskin to shed admiring tears, impede the smooth flow of the writer's argument. But he still remembered his valuable early training: every sentence is well proportioned and every word is put to its proper use:

Among the delusions which at different periods have possessed themselves of the minds of large masses of the human race, perhaps the most curious—certainly the least creditable—is the modern *soi-disant* science of political economy, based on the idea that an advantageous code of social action may be determined irrespectively of the influence of social affection.

Of course, as in the instances of alchemy, astrology, witchcraft, and other such popular creeds, political economy has a plausible idea at the root of it. "The social affections," say the economists, "are accidental and disturbing elements in human nature; but avarice and the desire of progress are constant elements. Let us eliminate the inconstants, and, considering the human being merely as a covetous machine, examine by what laws of labour, purchase, and sale, the greatest accumulative result in wealth is obtainable. Those laws once determined, it will be for each individual afterwards to introduce as much of the disturbing affectionate element as he chooses, and to determine for himself the result on the new conditions supposed."

("The Roots of Honour," *Unto This Last*, in *The Works*, vol. XVII, p. 25)

The effect is weighty, incisive, masculine; and had Ruskin continued in this vein, he might have become one of the ablest controversial writers in the English language. Alas, a personal problem arose to frustrate the design. The breakdown of Ruskin's marriage had not stifled his emotional nature or extinguished his longing to lead a normally harmonious life. He was still capable of falling in love. But,

unfortunately, the human beings who stirred his emotions were almost always those least calculated to bring him any solid happiness. Since his experience of adult love had left such bitter memories, he was increasingly attracted toward the beauty of the very young; and during the course of 1858, just before his "unconversion," he first set eyes upon Rose La Touche, an attractive, precociously sensitive and intelligent little girl, who at the time was only nine years old. Ruskin himself was forty; and at the outset, their relationship was merely that of an affectionate, middle-aged scholar and his clever, impressionable pupil. But soon deeper and more dangerous feelings began to complicate the scholar's attitude. He dreamed of marrying his delightful protégée once she had become a woman; her mother and father, he believed—Mrs. La Touche was a keen admirer of Ruskin's genius—were prepared to give the union their blessings; and for seventeen feverishly unhappy years—until Rose, who, as she developed, grew more and more unstable, died in 1875—he continued to pursue this delusive image, which, at the very moment when he seemed to be grasping it, never failed to melt away. Poor Rose, with her morbid piety and her precocious sensibility, aggravated the mood of frustration and confusion that was to culminate in mental shipwreck.

Meanwhile he did not desist from his patient efforts to improve society. In a study of this length, it is impossible to provide a detailed account of the works of Ruskin's middle period. Their subject matter is astonishingly various—among the subjects treated in *The Two Paths*, *Sesame and Lilies*, *The Ethics of the Dust*, *The Cestus of Aglaia*, and *The Queen of the Air*, all published between 1859 and 1869, are the application of design to modern manufacture, female education, the laws of art, crystallography, and Greek mythology, together with some strange excursions into the symbolism of the animal world; and the author's method of treatment, as his mysterious titles suggest, is usually very far from straightforward. The sternly didactic prophet was also a poetic visionary; and, like certain poets of the present day, Ruskin is apt to follow a tenuous thread of private meaning through long series of loosely connected images. Thus, in *The Cestus of Aglaia*, which purports to consist of "Nine Papers on the Laws of Art," he allows the legend of the Patient Griselda to introduce memories of an Alpine waterfall; the cataract to lead him to Swiss history and a mention of the "Grey League"; the word "grey" to evoke a line by Tennyson and, lastly, recall the color of the paper used by Turner for his preliminary sketches. One is not surprised that many of Ruskin's readers should have found his message hard to grasp. Yet each of the books listed above contains flashes of the old fire. Often his poetic eloquence bursts out where it is least expected, generally provoked by some hidden strain of passionate feeling. With Ruskin's adoration of natural beauty coexisted a secret horror of the flesh; he was both puritanical and deeply sensuous; and the conflict gave a distinctive coloring to his vision of the everyday world. Thus the serpent, as an emblem of sexual desire, must be considered, he had now come to believe, a symbol of "permitted evil"; while the bird, wandering freely through the heavens, symbolized the life of the spirit.

We will take the bird first. It is little more than a drift of the air brought into form by plumes; the air is in all its quills, it breathes through its whole frame and flesh, and glows with air in its flying, like a blown flame: its rest upon the air, subdues it, surpasses it, outraces it;—*is* the air, conscious of itself, conquering itself, ruling itself.

("Athena Keramitis," *The Queen of the Air*, in *The Works*, vol. XIX, p. 360)

As for the serpent:

it is the very omnipotence of the earth. That rivulet of smooth silver—how does it flow, think you? It literally rows on the earth, with every scale for an oar; it bites the dust with the ridges of its body. Watch it, when it moves slowly:—A wave, but without wind! a current, but with no fall! all the body moving at the same instant, yet some of it to one side, some to another, or some forward, and the rest of the coil backwards; but all with the same calm will and equal way—no contraction, no extension; one soundless, causeless, march of sequent rings, and spectral procession of spotted dust, with dissolution in its fangs, dislocation in its coils. Startle it;—the winding stream will become a twisted arrow;—the wave of poisoned life will lash through the grass like a cast lance. It scarcely breathes with its one lung (the other shrivelled and abortive); it is passive to the sun and shade, and it is cold or hot like a stone; yet "it can outclimb the monkey, outswim the fish, outleap the jerboa, outwrestle the athlete, and crush the tiger." It is a divine hieroglyph of the demoniac power of the earth—of the entire earthly nature. As the bird is the clothed power of the air, so this is the clothed power of the dust; as the bird the symbol of the spirit of life, so this of the grasp and sting of death.

(*The Queen of the Air*, in *The Works*, vol. XIX, pp. 362–363)

The Queen of the Air was published in 1869; and in 1871 Ruskin began the publication of the extraordinary work called *Fors Clavigera*, a succession of open letters addressed "to the workingmen and labourers of Great Britain," in which, besides discoursing on social and economic problems, he allowed himself many autobiographical asides— descriptions of his childhood and youth and appreciations of the pictures he loved, diversified with references to his passion for Rose La Touche and vivid thumbnail sketches of people and places that had caught his fancy. Reading *Fors Clavigera*, declared Cardinal Manning, was like listening to the "beating of one's heart in a nightmare." Ruskin's view of life, indeed, was becoming gradually more and more nightmarish, as his sense of evil increased and his hold on reality grew progressively weaker. His plight was intensified, moreover, by a sense of personal isolation. His father, the dominant influence of his youth, had died in 1864; Margaret Ruskin, to whose household he had returned after James's death, followed her husband in December 1872. Rose La Touche, already lost to him, finally disappeared in 1875; and Ruskin, having communicated the news of her death not only to his old friend Thomas Carlyle but to the workingmen of Great Britain, settled down to an existence of solitary, unceasing work. He continued to work until 1878, when, heralded by a sequence of vivid and fantastic dreams, the complete breakdown, with which he had long been threatened, suddenly overwhelmed his mental faculties. In a few months Ruskin had regained his balance, but henceforward the shadow of insanity was never very far removed.

V

IN 1885, he was obliged to resign the Slade Professorship of Fine Art at Oxford, to which he had been elected in 1869 and which had inspired him with high hopes of educating contemporary taste. Thereafter, breakdown succeeded breakdown; and by 1888 it was clear to his friends that his active life must be abandoned. Nor did the writer himself demur. Secluded at his house in the Lake District, where he was nursed and watched over by a devoted relation, Joan Severn, surrounded by his pictures and plants and his rare and precious mineral specimens, he became a lonely, remote, impressive figure, whom enthusiastic young lovers of art occasionally visited to pay their homage. But, having ceased to vex his spirit with the problems of the future or mourn over the ugliness of the present day, his imagination slipped back toward the experiences of his own past. His third, and culminating, period was brief but brilliant. Ruskin's unfinished autobiography, which he called *Praeterita*, occupied him intermittently from 1885 to 1889. The most enjoyable book that he had ever produced, and in some respects the best written, it tells the story of his childhood and education and of the gradual unfolding and flowering of an artist's sensibility. The style is limpid and smooth—at least, until he reaches the final passages, where his control begins to slacken; but, despite the comparative plainness of his style and the endearing simplicity with which he approaches the reader, he can still accomplish, if his theme demands it, a long and magnificently descriptive flight. To *Praeterita*, for example, we owe this celebrated description of the sources of the Rhone:

> For all other rivers there is a surface, and an underneath, and a vaguely displeasing idea of the bottom. But the Rhone flows like one lambent jewel; its surface is nowhere, its ethereal self is everywhere, the iridescent rush and translucent strength of it blue to the shore, and radiant to the depth.
>
> Fifteen feet thick, of not flowing, but flying water; not water, neither—melted glacier, rather, one should call it; the force of the ice is with it, and the wreathing of the clouds, the gladness of the sky, and the continuance of Time.
>
> Waves of clear sea are, indeed, lovely to watch, but they are always coming or gone, never in any taken shape to be seen for a second. But here was one mighty wave that was always itself, and every fluted swirl of it, constant as the wreathing of a shell. No wasting away of the fallen foam, no pause for gathering of power, no helpless ebb of discouraged recoil; but alike through bright day and lulling night, the never-pausing plunge, and never-fading flash, and never-hushing whisper, and, while the sun was up, the ever-answering glow of unearthly aquamarine, ultramarine, violet-blue, gentian-blue, peacock-blue, river-of-paradise blue, glass of a painted window melted in the sun, and the witch of the Alps flinging the spun tresses of it for ever from her snow.

(*Praeterita*, vol. II, in *The Works*, vol. XXXV, pp. 326–327)

There the thread of memories was abruptly snapped off. Ruskin was never able to resume the writing of *Praeterita*; for, although he lived on until 1900, the smallest literary task—even the composi-

tion of a brief informal letter—was soon utterly beyond his strength. A bearded patriarch, silent and abstracted, he had retired into a private universe of reveries and dreams.

Himself he believed that his lifework had failed; and, from some points of view, a critic is bound to agree that his pessimism was not ill-founded. None of his schemes of reform had resulted in much practical benefit; some, indeed, like the Guild of St. George[7]—his attempt to establish, on rigidly authoritarian lines, the nucleus of a new society—had dwindled and decayed many years before the prophet's death. He had impressed his contemporaries, but he had not influenced them; he had entertained, but he had not enlightened; industrial civilization continued to go its way, enriching, blighting, and transfiguring Europe. Nor could his admirers claim that Ruskin's utterances, apart from the hatred he expressed of ugliness in all its forms, revealed any consistent line of thought. The "interwoven temper of his mind" colored even his prophetic writings; and although it was evident that he worshiped beauty and order, and believed passionately in social justice, he seemed often strangely uncertain as to the methods by which beauty and justice might at length be brought back. He was, in different moods, a "Tory of the sternest sort," a militant Socialist, a Communist. Only on one point was he perfectly clear: in no circumstances, and under no degree of pressure, did he ever intend to become a Liberal. He was a furious "Illiberal," he exclaimed, and proud of it; and when the case of Governor Edward John Eyre (who was alleged to have put down riots in Jamaica with unnecessary harshness) led to the formation of a Liberal "Jamaica Committee," headed by John Stuart Mill, Herbert Spencer, and T. H. Huxley, Ruskin joined the opposite camp, which included Carlyle, Tennyson, and Dickens.

We should also recollect that he was an ardent Imperialist, whose first lecture as Slade Professor at Oxford envisaged a scheme of imperial expansion, organized on military—one might almost say on

---

[7]Ruskin himself had promised to contribute a tenth of his possessions. The plan, founded on his study of Plato's *Laws* and *Republic*, aimed at the creation of a hierarchical society, of which Ruskin would be the acknowledged Master. Discipline was sternly insisted on. As a small beginning, the guild was to acquire and cultivate small plots of land, build or repair cottages, and found local museums and picture galleries. Agriculture was to be encouraged; commerce and industry would be repressed.

Fascist—principles. His attitude toward the English laboring classes was almost equally ambiguous. As we have seen, he did not wholeheartedly approve of the idea of universal suffrage and never lost his belief in the value of a graded social hierarchy, embracing a majority of those who were prepared to obey and a chosen minority that had learned to rule. He attacked the frivolity of the spending and governing class and admitted that there were times when he felt ashamed of being styled a gentleman: "We live, we gentlemen, on delicatest prey, after the manner of weasels; that is to say, we keep a certain number of clowns digging and ditching . . . in order that we . . . may have all the thinking and feeling to ourselves." Yet, at the same time, he exalted the aristocratic ideal, observing in a lecture at Oxford that

a highly-bred and highly-trained English, French, Austrian or Italian gentleman (much more a lady) is a great production; a better production than most statues; being beautifully colored as well as shaped . . . a glorious thing to look at, a wonderful thing to talk to; and you cannot have it . . . but by sacrifice of much contributed life.

Similarly protean were his religious convictions. His early faith, which he had begun to lose about 1858, had completely vanished by 1869, when he definitely renounced his belief in Christianity and the doctrine of an Eternal Father. Later, under the influence of Spiritualism, he slowly groped his way back toward the religion of his childhood.

VI

So much for the negative side of the portrait; it remains to estimate his positive achievement. Here Proust's tribute deserves recapitulation. Ruskin (he declared) was an aesthete who dedicated his life—or the better part of it—to an unswerving cult of Beauty. But a significant reservation must at once be made:

This Beauty, to which he elected to consecrate his life, was not conceived as a means of embellishing and sweetening existence, but as a reality infinitely more important than life itself, to which, indeed, he would have sacrificed his own. From this idea, as you will see, Ruskin's whole aesthetic system springs.[8]

[8]"John Ruskin," in *Gazette des Beaux-Arts*, no. 514 (April 1900), p. 315.

One phrase seems particularly helpful—"a reality infinitely more important than life itself." Wildly though he plunged into other activities, patiently though he planned to reform the world, tragic as was his dissipation of spiritual and intellectual energies that, at an earlier period and in happier circumstances, he might have devoted to creative work, Ruskin remained an impassioned artist, for whom art was still the crown of life. But his conception of an artist's role was lofty and exacting. Since art with Ruskin was a form of religion—an expression of man's highest needs—he could not believe that it should remain shut up within the temple of connoisseurship: that it should be permitted to enter some departments of life and be rigorously excluded from many others. Its universal language should be heard everywhere—in the streets as well as in the gallery, in the factory and workshop as well as in the artist's studio. Nor could the student of art afford to avert his eyes either from the contemporary world around him or from the history of past ages; works of art were not produced in the void, but originated in the spiritual experience of an entire generation. They had endless references to the existence of mankind—past, present, and future. Every masterpiece was a crystallization of the noblest human thoughts and feelings.

Such was the starting point that Ruskin adopted in all his major critical essays; and although as a theorist he may have been misguided—he refused to admit, for example, that Renaissance painting, which he adored, and Renaissance architecture, which he detested and reviled, sprang ultimately from the same source—he helped to revolutionize the practice of criticism by raising it, in his own books, to the level of imaginative literature. This he did with the help of an admirable style and a preternaturally acute vision. Few English writers are more exquisitely observant, or have managed to translate their observations into more precise and moving terms. Whether he is writing of mountains and clouds, of seashells on a Mediterranean beach or the petals of a cyclamen beneath a tree, of St. Ursula in Carpaccio's fresco or a sunburned Italian beggar girl sprawled across a heap of sand, he describes the scene and the response that it awakes in him with equal vividness and equal delicacy. Even the conflict that clouded his middle period did not deprive him of the power to feel and see; and when the conflict had finally burned itself out and he was entering on his last stage, the genius that had made its first appearance in the opening volumes of *Modern Painters* reemerged triumphantly in the pages of *Praeterita.* Between those two books he had traveled far; but the end of his journey was close to the beginning. Ruskin's mental pilgrimage is one of the most dramatic—perhaps one of the most pathetic—in the whole history of English letters.

SELECTED BIBLIOGRAPHY

I. BIBLIOGRAPHY. T. J. Wise and J. P. Smart, *A Bibliography of the Writings in Prose and Verse,* 19 parts (London, 1889–1893), privately printed, important for its detailed descriptions of the early eds.; E. T. Cook and A. D. O. Wedderburn, eds., *The Works,* vol. XXXVIII (London, 1912), the standard bibliography, but with references only to the full bibliographies of separate books in earlier vols. of *The Works;* J. Carter and G. Pollard, *An Enquiry into the Nature of Certain Nineteenth-Century Pamphlets* (London, 1934), in this inquiry into the Wise forgeries eight pamphlets by Ruskin are scrutinized; K. H. Beetz, ed., *John Ruskin: A Bibliography (1900–1974)* (London, 1977).

II. COLLECTED WORKS. *Collected Works,* 11 vols. (Keston-Orpington, 1871–1880); A. D. O. Wedderburn, ed., *On the Old Road,* 2 vols. (Orpington, 1885; rev. ed., 3 vols., 1899), a collection of miscellaneous essays, pamphlets, etc., published 1834–1885; W. G. Collingwood, ed., *The Poems,* 2 vols. (Orpington, 1891); *Collected Works,* 22 vols. (New York, 1891–1892), the Brantwood ed., with intros. by C. E. Norton, the first authorized in America, where many of Ruskin's books had been printed; E. T. Cook and A. D. O. Wedderburn, eds., *The Works,* 39 vols. (London, 1902–1912), the definitive ed., including hitherto unpublished material; *Poems* (London, 1906), with an essay on the author by G. K. Chesterton; *The Ruskin House Edition,* 4 vols. (London, 1907).

III. SELECTIONS. W. S. Williams, ed., *Selections from the Writings* (London, 1861); W. G. Collingwood, ed., *Selections from the Writings,* 2 vols. (Orpington, 1893); A. M. Wakefield, ed., *Ruskin on Music* (Orpington, 1894); W. Jolly, ed., *Ruskin on Education* (Orpington, 1894); W. G. Collingwood, ed., *The Ruskin Reader* (Orpington, 1895); F. Widmore, ed., *Turner and Ruskin,* 2 vols. (London, 1900); E. T. Cook, ed., *Ruskin on Pictures* (London, 1902), a collection of criticism not before printed; A. C. Benson, ed., *Selections from Ruskin* (Cambridge, 1923); E. A. Parker, ed., *Selections from "The Stones of Venice"* (London, 1925); A. H. R. Ball, ed., *Ruskin as a Literary Critic* (Cambridge, 1928); P. Quennell, ed., *Selected Writings* (London, 1952); J. Evans, ed., *The Lamp of Beauty* (London, 1959), a selection of Ruskin's writings on

art; K. Clark, ed., *Ruskin Today,* chosen and annotated by Clark (London, 1964); J. D. Rosenberg, ed., *The Genius of John Ruskin* (London, 1964), with an intro. by Rosenberg.

IV. SEPARATE WORKS. *Salsette and Elephanta* (Oxford, 1839), the Newdigate Prize Poem; *Modern Painters,* vol. I (London, 1843), vol. II (1846), vols. III and IV (1856), vol. V (1860); *The Seven Lamps of Architecture* (London, 1849); *Poems* (London, 1850), privately printed; *The King of the Golden River; or the Black Brothers: A Legend of Syria* (London, 1851), illus. by R. Doyle; *The Stones of Venice,* vol. I (London, 1852), vols. II and III (1853); *Notes on the Construction of Sheep-Folds* (London, 1851); *Pre-Raphaelitism* (London, 1851); *Lectures on Architecture and Paintings* (London, 1854); *Notes on Some of the Principal Pictures Exhibited in the Rooms of the Royal Academy* (London, 1855); *Notes on the Turner Gallery at Marlborough House* (London, 1856); *The Elements of Drawing* (London, 1857), illus. by Ruskin; *The Political Economy of Art* (London, 1857); *The Two Paths* (London, 1859); *The Elements of Perspective* (London, 1859); *Unto This Last* (London, 1862); *Sesame and Lilies* (London, 1865); *The Ethics of the Dust* (London, 1866); *The Crown of Wild Olive* (London, 1866); *Time and Tide by Weare and Tyne* (London, 1867); *The Queen of the Air* (London, 1869); *Lectures on Art* (Oxford, 1870); *Fors Clavigera,* 8 vols. (London, 1871–1884); *Munera Pulveris* (Keston, 1872), this and the following five works were first printed in *Collected Works* (1871–1880); *Aratra Pentelici* (Keston, 1872); *The Relation Between Michael Angelo and Tintoret* (Keston, 1872); *The Eagle's Nest* (Keston, 1872); *Val D'Arno* (Orpington, 1874); *Ariadne Florentina* (Orpington, 1876); *Praeterita,* vol. I (Orpington, 1886), vol. II (1887), vol. III, 4 pts. (1885–1889), the 1949 ed. has a valuable intro. by K. Clark, also in J. Murray, ed. (London, 1964); *Dilecta,* 3 pts. (Orpington, 1886–1900), contains correspondence, diary, notes, etc., illus. *Praeterita; The Cestus of Aglaia* (Orpington, 1905), Ruskin's papers on art written in 1865–1866; J. R. Tutin, ed., *A Walk in Chamounix and Other Poems* (Hull, 1908); J. Evans and J. H. Whitehouse, eds., *The Diaries of John Ruskin,* 3 vols. (Oxford, 1957–1959).

V. LETTERS. T. J. Wise, ed., *Letters from John Ruskin to William Ward,* 2 vols. (London, 1893), privately printed; T. J. Wise, ed., *Letters to the Rev. F. J. Faunthorpe,* 2 vols. (London, 1895–1896), privately printed, T. J. Wise privately printed eds. of several other groups of Ruskin's letters; *Letters to M. G. and H. G.* [Mary and Helen Gladstone] (Edinburgh, 1903), privately printed, with a preface by G. Wyndham; C. E. Norton, ed., *The Letters of John Ruskin to C. E. Norton,* 2 vols. (Boston, 1903); J. H. Waterhouse, *The Solitary Warrior: New Letters by Ruskin* (London, 1929); R. Unwin, ed., *The Gulf of Years* (London, 1953), letters from Ruskin to Kathleen Olander; R. Skelton, ed., *John Ruskin: The Final Years* (London, 1955), selections with commentary from unpublished letters in the John

Rylands Library, Manchester; J. L. Bradley, ed., *Ruskin's Letters from Venice, 1851–2* (New Haven, Conn., 1956); V. A. Burd, ed., *The Correspondence of John James Ruskin, His Wife and Their Son, 1801–1843*, 2 vols. (Ithaca, N. Y., 1973); V. Surtees, ed., *Reflections of a Friendship: John Ruskin's Letters to Pauline Trevelyan* (London, 1979). *Note:* There is an extensive collection of unpublished Ruskin letters in the Pierpont Morgan Library, New York City.

VI. Biographical and Critical Studies. J. Milsand, *L'Ésthétique Anglaise, Étude sur M. John Ruskin* (Paris, 1864); B. H. Green, *Mr. Ruskin: His Opinions and Comparisons of Painters* (London, 1869); R. B. Walker, *John Ruskin* (Manchester, 1879); E. J. Baillie, *John Ruskin: Aspects of His Thought and Teaching* (Orpington, 1882); J. M. Mather, *Life and Teaching of John Ruskin* (Manchester, 1883); W. G. Collingwood, *John Ruskin: A Biographical Outline* (London, 1889); E. T. Cook, *Studies in Ruskin* (Orpington, 1890); R. P. Downes, *John Ruskin: A Study* (London, 1890); W. G. Collingwood, *The Art Teaching of John Ruskin* (London, 1891); W. G. Collingwood, *The Life and Work of John Ruskin*, 2 vols. (London, 1893; rev. ed., 1900); C. Waldstein [Walston], *The Work of John Ruskin* (London, 1894); R. de la Sizeranne, *Ruskin et la Religion de la Beauté* (Paris, 1897), trans. 1899, with two app. by G. Allen; J. A. Hobson, *John Ruskin, Social Reformer* (London, 1898); W. M. Rossetti, *Ruskin, Rossetti and Pre-Raphaelitism* (London, 1899); A. A. Isaacs, *The Fountain of Siena: An Episode in the Life of John Ruskin* (London, 1900); M. H. Spielmann, *John Ruskin: A Sketch of His Life, His Work and His Opinions; with Personal Reminiscences* (London, 1900); H. D. Rawnsley, *Ruskin and the English Lakes* (Glasgow, 1901); W. H. Shaw, *John Ruskin, Ethical and Religious Teacher* (Oxford, 1901); C. R. Ashbee, *An Endeavour Towards the Teaching of John Ruskin and William Morris* (London, 1901), an account of the work of the *Guild of Handicraft in the East End of London;* F. Harrison, *John Ruskin* (London, 1902), in the English Men of Letters series; W. G. Collingwood, *Ruskin Relics* (London, 1903); F. W. Farrar, *Ruskin as a Religious Teacher* (London, 1904); F. Y. Powell, *John Ruskin and Thoughts on Democracy* (London, 1905); C. Earland, *Ruskin and His Circle* (London, 1910); A. Wingate, *Life of John Ruskin* (London, 1910); A. C. Benson, *Ruskin: A Study in Personality* (London, 1911); E. T. Cook, *The Life of John Ruskin* (London, 1911); E. T. Cook, *Homes and Haunts of John Ruskin* (London, 1912); J. Burdon, *Reminiscences of Ruskin* (London, 1919); J. H. Whitehouse, *Ruskin Centenary Addresses* (London, 1919); J. H. Whitehouse, *Ruskin the Prophet* (London, 1920); J. W. Graham, *The Harvest of Ruskin* (London, 1920); R. G. Collingwood, *Ruskin's Philosophy* (London, 1920); F. W. Roe, *The Social Philosophy of Carlyle and Ruskin* (New York, 1922); A. W. Ellis, *The Tragedy of John Ruskin* (London, 1928); J. Bardoux, *John Ruskin, Poète, Artiste, Apôtre* (London, 1931); E. H. Scott, *Ruskin's Guild of St. George* (London, 1931); H. Ladd, *The Victorian Morality of Art, An Analysis of Ruskin's Aesthetic* (New York, 1932); D. Larg, *John Ruskin* (London, 1932); R. H. Wilenski, *John Ruskin* (London, 1933); J. H. Whitehouse et al., *To the Memory of Ruskin* (Cambridge, 1935); G. Crow, *Ruskin* (London, 1936); J. H. Whitehouse, *Ruskin the Painter and His Works at Bembridge* (London, 1938); G. H. B. Hugstotz, *The Educational Theories of John Ruskin* (London, 1942); J. H. Whitehouse, *Ruskin's Influence Today* (London, 1945); R. Livingstone, *Ruskin* (London, 1945), a lecture before the British Academy; W. James, *The Order of Release* (London, 1947), the story of Ruskin, Effie Gray, and J. E. Millais, see also J. H. Whitehouse, *Vindication of Ruskin* (London, 1950), an answer to *The Order of Release;* P. Quennell, *John Ruskin: The Portrait of a Prophet* (London, 1949); D. Leon, *Ruskin the Great Victorian* (London, 1949); J. Evans, *John Ruskin* (London, 1952); J. D. Rosenberg, *The Darkening Glass: A Portrait of Ruskin's Genius* (London, 1960); Q. Bell, *Ruskin* (London, 1963); M. Lutyens, *Millais and the Ruskins* (London, 1967); M. Lutyens, *The Ruskins and the Grays* (London, 1972); J. C. Sherburne, *John Ruskin, or The Ambiguities of Abundance: A Study in Social and Economic Criticism* (Cambridge, Mass., 1973); K. O. Garrigan, *Ruskin on Architecture: His Thought and His Influence* (Madison, Wis., 1974); R. Hewison, *John Ruskin: The Argument and the Eye* (London, 1976); R. Hewison, *Ruskin and Venice* (London, 1978); P. Conner, *Savage Ruskin* (London, 1979); J. D. Rosenberg, *The Genius of John Ruskin* (London, 1979); V. A. Burd, ed., *John Ruskin and Rose La Touche: Her Unpublished Diaries of 1861 and 1867* (London, 1980).

GEORGE ELIOT

(1819-1880)

Lettice Cooper

MARIAN EVANS

In the Midlands of England, between the manufacturing towns of Coventry and Nuneaton in Warwickshire, lies a stretch of level country, undramatic, without mountain or river. The soil is rich, it is farmers' country, but even in the first half of the nineteenth century, when one coach a day linked Coventry with Nuneaton, it was partly industrial. The manor house looked across the green plain to the colliery tip; the villager, who wove cloth on the handloom in his cottage, carried it to be finished at the neighboring mill. But it was mostly rural, with Shakespeare's birthplace only a few miles away, a countryside of red brick farms, of cowslips and cuckoos, of wide skies reflected in canal waters. In this country, on 22 November 1819, Mary Ann, or Marian, Evans, later to be George Eliot, was born.

Her father, Robert Evans, Welsh by descent, was the son of a builder and carpenter. He started his working life as a farmer but later became agent for the estate of Arbury, the property of a local landowner. Evans was known and respected throughout the county, both for his upright character and for his wide knowledge of the whole fabric of country life. He could give sound advice about house or farm buildings, about timber, mining, soil, land valuation, stock, or crops. He was traditional in his opinions, a lifelong supporter of the Church of England and the Tory party. Marian was his youngest child, the third child of his second marriage, to the daughter of a yeoman farmer. When Marian was born, the two children of the first marriage were nearly grown, and they soon moved out into the world. Her parents, her sister Christiana, and her brother Isaac made up her home.

The youngest child in such a family sometimes feels anxiously that there is no one left for her. Father and mother have each other, brother and sister are already allies. The passionate longing for someone of her own, someone to put her first, was to run all through George Eliot's life, and it was not until she found it in George Henry Lewes that her genius was to flower. The child Marian craved above all for the whole love of her brother. Naturally she was disappointed, for Isaac at eight years old went to school, returning only for the holidays from the world of boys and men to pet and patronize the little sister with whom he was often impatient. She could not walk far enough nor climb high enough, she cried too easily, and her devouring affection set up the inevitable resistance. There was plenty of kindness in the family for Marian; her father was especially fond of her, but there was no one to be hers alone. The high-powered child in the household of ordinary people suffered the disproportionate agonies of her kind.

There were minor troubles. Marian was plain and untidy; her sister Chrissey was pretty and neat. Chrissey was the favorite with the grown-up people, a good girl, useful in the house and approved by their mother; while Marian was often in disgrace for slouching over a book instead of helping, and for her unmanageable mane of hair. Not that she was always unhappy. It was a good life for a child in the red brick house at Griff, with its farm buildings, garden, and pond, and with the freedom of wood and field all round. Her father often took her with him as he drove about the Arbury estate. Standing between his knees in farm or cottage as he sat and discussed the tenants' problems, Marian absorbed a great deal about country people and their lives. Those years of childhood, she said in one of her unremarkable poems, were "seed to all my good," and she speaks of "blest hours of infantine content." She was, in fact, like most children, sometimes unhappy and sometimes happy, but both with more intensity than most children. She was a woman on a grand scale in the making.

Mrs. Evans was delicate, and to relieve her the two

girls were sent away early to school, first to a small school at Attleborough in Warwickshire, where Marian suffered from the cold and from night terrors, then to a larger school at Nuneaton. Miss Lewis, the first mistress there, became Marian's great friend, and later it was to her that the girl wrote those ponderous, priggish, pathetic letters that were her chief outlet between the ages of seventeen and twenty-five. Miss Lewis was caught up in the full tide of the evangelical movement, which in its later stages was to break away from the established Church of England into nonconformity, but in its early stages was a movement within the established church and did much to reanimate a more personal and vital faith. Marian in adolescence was strongly influenced by Miss Lewis. Her temperament was deeply religious, and goodness was always to be her predominant interest in life. When Marian was fifteen, her mother died, and soon afterward Chrissey married. Marian left school and took charge of the house and of her father and brother. She also visited the poor and did her share of work at the clothing clubs and other charities of the neighborhood. The solemn sixteen-year-old went gravely through these boring duties with the older women, secretly panting for a richer life and for a chance to use the full powers of which she was conscious. "You may try, but you cannot imagine what it is to have a man's force of genius in you, yet to suffer the slavery of being a girl."

Some life of her own she did have. She took lessons in Italian, German, and music. She read, as always, greedily, but there was no one to whom she could talk about books and ideas. Miss Lewis by post was her nearest approach to congenial company. Her deep-rooted sense of duty and the strong puritanism that in early life exalted the value of self-sacrifice prevented Marian from contemplating any change. Her father lived at Griff, and it was her duty to look after her father. No doubt there were many afternoons when she walked alone by the canal and saw her life as an interminable round of duty and self-sacrifice. Years afterward, when asked if she would ever write her autobiography, she said of that time: "The only thing that I should care to dwell on would be the absolute despair I suffered of ever being able to achieve anything." At this time in her life she was not even able to enjoy an occasional holiday, for when at nineteen she paid a first visit to London with her brother Isaac, she refused to go to a theater and wrote austerely to Miss Lewis, "I was not at all

delighted with the stir of the Great Babel." Miss Lewis' evangelicalism had done its work. Just before her nineteenth birthday, Marian wrote, "May I seek to be sanctified wholly!" A provincial young prig? Yes, but a chrysalis in whom life and color and winged power were the more closely folded because the colors were unusually bright and the wings strong. They were soon to begin breaking their sheath.

To a great many artists who have struggled out of a society indifferent to the arts, the first congenial friendship has been the opening of the new world. When Marian was twenty-two, Isaac married and took over from his father both the agency for the Arbury estate and the agent's house at Griff. She and her father moved to a semidetached house in Foleshill Road, Coventry. Coventry was then a small town, but it was the country girl's first entry into the great world. Here for the first time she made friends who shared her own interests: Charles Bray, whose book *The Philosophy of Necessity* was published in that year, and his wife, formerly Caroline Hennell, whose brother Charles had written *An Inquiry Concerning the Origin of Christianity*, which Marian had already read. It must have been delightful to the bookish girl to meet authors in the flesh, to go for the first time to a house where free discussion of abstract ideas was the natural climate. To the new friends Marian seemed a gentle, modest girl who surprised them by the wide range of her reading and by everything that distinguished her from the more commonplace young women of the neighborhood. She was not pretty. Her head was large, her face heavy; she had no self-confidence, believing herself to be plainer than she really was, for her eyes were beautiful, and there was great sweetness in her voice and smile. She had no surface charm and was not easy to know, but there was a warmth and sincerity in her that made her lovable to anyone who could break the barrier of diffidence.

The evangelical Miss Lewis must have felt that she was losing her hold on her pupil, who had been questioning the tenets of orthodox religion for some time, even before she met the Brays. Stimulated by the constant discussion in their house and encouraged by their moral support, Marian dramatically and solemnly renounced her faith. It was a shattering blow to her father, who even threatened to sell the house and go and live alone in a cottage. Marian accepted the challenge. She would take lodgings in Coventry and earn her living by teaching. She went away for a few weeks. Common sense and the discovery that he was very uncomfortable without her prevailed with Robert Evans. He agreed to take her back, and she compromised by accompanying him to church on Sundays. She remained with him until he died, when she was thirty years old.

During this time she achieved her first piece of writing apart from her voluminous and, it must be admitted, tedious letters. She translated David Friedrich Strauss's *Das Leben Jesu* (1846). It took her two years and often bored her, but probably it helped to form the habit of sticking to a long piece of work that is so necessary for the writer of even the most inspired novel. This was a miserable time in her life, only relieved by her friendship with the Brays and the Hennells. Her father, in his failing health, often could not bear to be left alone for an hour. Her own health suffered from the confined life and from the day-long frustration of her urgent spirit, which had not yet found its proper channels. She loved her father deeply, and his feebleness and approaching death tore her heart. "What shall I be without my father? It will seem as if a part of my moral nature was gone!" Clearly if she was to develop her full powers she needed more freedom to develop in her own way, and her friends must have been relieved for her when after his long illness he died. The Brays were just going abroad for a holiday. They took Marian with them and left her in a pension at Geneva, where she spent a peaceful eight months readjusting and resting.

When she came back to England, she met at the Brays's house John Chapman, who had just become editor of the *Westminster Review.* He gave her some books to review. A little later on he bought the paper and offered her the post of honorary assistant editor. She was to be paid for her contributions, and she had a small income of her own. She came up to London in 1851, lodged with the Chapmans, and settled in to work on the paper.

The work delighted her but there was soon trouble at home. Chapman's wife grew jealous of her. His relationship with Marian was warm, based on shared interests and touched with enough feeling to make it extremely stimulating to both of them. Chapman was at that time having an affair with the children's governess, a pretty, silly girl, who also lived in the house and whom Mrs. Chapman seems to have tolerated. Wife and mistress combined to drive out Marian. Indignant, she returned to Coventry, and the *Westminster Review* immediately fell in-

to disorder without her energy and ability. Chapman went after her and persuaded his wife and mistress to agree that she should come back. Surprisingly, she came. She had already traveled a long way from the evangelical girl at Griff. She lived two years in Chapman's house, and in the constant stir of work and interesting society, the three women managed somehow to live together in comparative peace, while Chapman no doubt enjoyed the best of all three worlds.

Marian was now in the full tide of London literary life. She met Charles Dickens, James Froude, T. H. Huxley, Harriet Martineau, George Grote, and J. S. Mill. She became a great friend of the philosopher Herbert Spencer. He was near her own age, handsome and distinguished, sharing all her interests. It was one of those friendships that everybody expected to ripen into marriage, but it never happened. Spencer had theories about marriage; he thought the legal bond between two people was incompatible with perfect happiness. Probably he was rationalizing a deep-rooted fear, but his views may have influenced Marian and prepared the way for her union with George Lewes. Spencer's influence was very important in another way, for it was he who first suggested to her that she might try her hand at fiction.

Herbert Spencer introduced Lewes to Marian. Lewes was at that time editing the *Leader*, the first critical weekly to appear in England. He was an ugly, lively, genial, amusing, warm-hearted man, a very high-class journalist, who did not hesitate to tackle any subject and had something stimulating if not profound to say about most of them. He was a brilliant editor, the kind of man who promotes good work in other people. He was unhappily married; his young wife had been seduced by Thornton Hunt, son of Leigh Hunt. Thornton Hunt was the father of four of the children who bore the name of Lewes. Under the law as it then stood, Lewes could not get a divorce. He made his wife and the children an allowance and lived apart from them.

Marian and Lewes fell deeply in love, and she had to make a choice on which her whole life was to depend. Her father's strict piety, her mother's yeoman pride, her country and small town respectability, even her friends at Coventry, who a few years ago had seemed so daring, were on the side of self-denial, and she had grown up with self-denial as a religion. All her past was against an illegal union with Lewes, but life and love and the future were on his side. She agreed to live with him as his unmarried wife. In the summer of 1854, they went abroad together for what was a honeymoon in all but name.

It was not as she would have chosen it to be. She was sensitive to the good opinion of her friends and family; she had qualms then and afterward. But at last she had a full emotional life, someone who needed her as she needed him, someone with whom she came first. Lewes's love and admiration were a continual reassurance against her diffidence. She was no longer lonely. From the fulfillment of her nature came the release of her pen. Marian, who would have preferred to be Marian Lewes, was still Marian Evans, but she was to have a new name that would obliterate both. Soon after they returned to England, she began her career as a novelist under the pen name George Eliot.

GEORGE ELIOT

Scenes of Clerical Life

Marian and George Lewes settled down in a small house at Richmond. It was necessary for both to go on working, for there were Lewes's wife and children to provide for as well as themselves. Marian had often dreamed of writing a novel. Now, under the stimulus of happy love and discriminating encouragement the idea came to birth. She began with a long short story, "Amos Barton," which appeared in *Blackwood's* magazine in 1857 under the pen name George Eliot, chosen because George was the name of her beloved and because she liked the sound of Eliot. *Blackwood's* also published the two stories that followed, "Mr. Gilfil's Love Story" and "Janet's Repentance." The three appeared together in 1858 in book form under the title *Scenes of Clerical Life.* Even while the stories were appearing separately, they arrested attention and were at once recognized by Dickens and Thackeray, among others, as the work of a new writer of importance.

It was the heyday of Victorian fiction. Thackeray's *The Virginians* was running in serial form, as well as Dickens' *Little Dorrit*; and *A Tale of Two Cities* was to appear in 1859. It was ten years since the publication of *Wuthering Heights*, and Charlotte Brontë's *Villette* had appeared in 1853. Dickens, Thackeray, the Brontës, all were novelists of heightened tone and color. By comparison with them George Eliot was sober, rooted in everyday life. She used for her three scenes the three back-grounds of her youth and childhood—the country parish, with its village and surrounding farms; the great country house that she knew so well from her father's long connection with Arbury; the country town, like Nuneaton, which served as a setting for the clash between the new evangelical movement and traditional religion.

George Eliot came late to her vocation. She was thirty-eight when she wrote *Scenes of Clerical Life*, and the substance of nearly all her novels was to be memory, worked upon by her creative imagination. She always turned back for her material to the scenes of her first thirty years, and except for some parts of her last novel, *Daniel Deronda*, she wrote almost always about provincial life.

Her memory for the speech of the countryside was particularly acute. The vicar Amos Barton, struggling to keep wife and children on a miserably inadequate income, is presented to the reader by village gossip. The village sees that the simple, stupid man is deluded by the pinchbeck charms of the "countess," and that her stay at the vicarage is an imposition that is going to prove the last straw to Milly Barton, who is worn out by her exertions and is pregnant with yet another child. The village recognizes and exaggerates the spark of romantic feeling for the countess, which appears to Amos himself to be no more than good will toward a friend in trouble. Both the hard judgment of the vicar's deluded innocence and the practical kindness shown when Milly is on her deathbed are of the very essence of village life.

Milly herself is the first of George Eliot's notable women. Indeed the central figure in each scene of *Clerical Life* is a woman. Mr. Gilfil is there only to tell the story, and his being a clergyman presumably provides a link with the other two tales. Any honest young lover and mourning husband would have done as well. It is Caterina's story. Caterina, the Italian-born adopted child of the great house, is the young Marian Evans, the girl whose intensity of feeling could find no adequate response in the more phlegmatic people round her. Caterina is separated from her surroundings by not being English, as Marian had felt herself isolated by a greater capacity for passion and suffering.

"Amos Barton" and "Mr. Gilfil's Love Story," although fairly long, are real short stories, given unity by one theme. "Janet's Repentance" shows that already George Eliot is moving toward the form of the novel, for it is made up of two interweaving strands. Janet's miserable relationship with her husband, the deterioration of her character under the strain, and her redemption through the influence of the good, evangelical clergyman, Mr. Tryan, is the main theme, but Mr. Tryan's struggle against the ill-will and suspicion of the conservative townspeople is also important. The evangelical movement, the clash between the old and new ways of ministry and worship in the church, had always interested George Eliot. She had remarked in one of her earlier letters that it was a pity that English novelists neglected this subject, which lay ready to their hand, and she continued to be interested in it long after she herself had abandoned any form of worship. Her admiration for the saintly characters that the movement produced colors especially her early novels, and Miss Lewis, even if she mourned for the pupil who had slipped away from her, must, if she was worldly enough to read novels at all, have realized that she had left her mark. Indeed it was so deep a mark that George Eliot could never handle her good evangelicals quite dispassionately. Mr. Tryan, and later Dinah Morris in *Adam Bede*, seems a little too good to be true. He is even a trifle mawkish, and the sentimentality with which George Eliot handles him is the weakness of "Janet's Repentance."

Its strength, as in the other two stories, is in the woman, in Janet herself. She is one of those women of great possibilities only partly realized, whom George Eliot was to develop in her later novels. Janet, brutally treated by her husband, drinks to escape from her sorrows. Such a heroine was a new departure in fiction. It is impossible to imagine Dickens or Thackeray allowing one of their good young women even to think of such a failing. Their good women were good and their bad women were bad, but George Eliot was already emerging from this tradition. "If," she wrote, "the ethics of art do not permit the truthful presentation of a character essentially noble, yet liable to great error that is anguish to its own nobleness, then it seems to me that the ethics of art are too narrow." For her, and through her for the novel, such ethics were already widening. Caterina, who could contemplate murder, and Janet, who could take refuge from her sorrows in drunkenness, belong to the modern novel, which, it has lately been recognized, owes so much to George Eliot.

Henry James remarked that for George Eliot the novel was "not primarily a picture of life but a moralized fable." It is true that the problem of goodness, of how far people manage to live up to the best that is in them, gives an underlying urgency to all her work. But the picture of life is also there and emerges in these stories in a hundred touches of insight and descriptive power, even though parts of the stories are sentimentalized. It was clear to the readers of *Blackwood's* that here was a new author of great gifts. "It is a long time," Blackwood wrote to his unknown contributor, "since I have read anything so fresh, so humorous, so touching." Always diffident, George Eliot throve on encouragement. Her first full-length novel, *Adam Bede,* appeared in 1859, only a year after *Scenes of Clerical Life* was published in book form.

Adam Bede

Dickens was one of the first to recognize that the new novelist was a woman, and by the time *Adam Bede* was published, the authorship was no longer a secret, although George Eliot continued to write under her pen name. The germ of *Adam Bede* was a story that she once heard from a Methodist aunt who had accompanied a condemned girl to the place of her execution. From this sprang the idea of Hetty Sorrel, condemned to death for the murder of her illegitimate child, and of Dinah Morris, the Methodist preacher who comforted Hetty in prison and went with her on her way to the scaffold. As in "Janet's Repentance," George Eliot still sees evangelicalism through the haze of her adolescent romance, and Dinah Morris, like Mr. Tryan, is an idealized character, completely flawless. She is less irritating than Mr. Tryan because, as with all her good women, George Eliot is very successful in giving an impression of real sweetness. Dinah is someone impossible to accept wholly, but also impossible to dislike. She may have been half-unconsciously modeled on Miss Lewis, but probably she had in her a good deal of the quality of her author.

The seed of the plot fell into rich soil. George Eliot told her publishers that her first full-length novel would be "full of the breath of cows and the scent of hay." The real substance of *Adam Bede* is all the early background of her family. The Poysers' farm is in the center of the canvas, presided over by Mrs. Poyser, a figure whose earthy and homely reality makes Dinah Morris appear thin. Mrs. Poyser was probably Marian's own mother, the daughter of a yeoman farmer, fragile of body, intrepid of spirit, with her shrewd tongue and her kind heart. Adam Bede himself derives from Marian's father, Robert Evans, the upright workman, self-respecting and generally respected for character and capacity. Adam suffers a little, like Dinah, from excess of virtue, although he is conscious of a hardness in himself that finally breaks down when he holds out his arm to Hetty in court. The reader turns with some relief to the imperfect characters, to the pretty, vain, childish Hetty and to her seducer, the squire's son, Arthur Donnithorne, who is not a deliberate villain but a spoiled young man brought up to expect things to go easily for him and who is appalled at the result of his pleasant dalliance.

The weakness of the book, besides the excessive virtue of Dinah, is, as with so many Victorian novels, the sacrifice of probability to plot and the tidiness of the ending. George Eliot was moving toward a new kind of novel in which representation of life was to be more important than the resolution of a plot, but she was still partly bound by the old convention. Hetty's pardon, so dramatically and improbably brought to the place of execution by Arthur Donnithorne, is an artificial device to spare the reader. In the relationship between Hetty and Arthur, and in all that grows out of it, there is a sense of destiny that is falsified by this resolution. Again, although Adam's love for Hetty is utterly convincing and brings him most to life as a human being, his final marriage to Dinah has none of that inevitability, but seems like a mechanical device to round off the story.

But these are the flaws in a rich tapestry of rural life of the time—the farm, the cottage, the workshop, the rectory, the great house. It is a picture of a society based on the land, a society still stable, a hierarchy in which each order has its own rights. The scene in which Mrs. Poyser routs the old squire, who has come to propose a deal in farm property that would be unfair to the Poysers, has all the sturdy quality of an English folk song:

"You may run away from my words, sir, and you may go spinnin' underhand ways o' doing us a mischief—for you've got Old Harry to your friend, though nobody else is—but I tell you for once as we're not dumb creatures to be abused and made money on by them as ha' got the lash i' their hands, for want o' knowing how t' undo the tackle. An' if I'm th' only one as speaks my mind, there's plenty o' the same way o' thinking i' this parish and the next to 't; for your name's no better than a brimstone match in everybody's nose—if it isna two-three old folks as you think o' saving your soul by giving 'em a bit o' flannel and a drop o' porridge. An' you may be right i' thinking it'll take but little

to save your soul, for it'll be the smallest savin' y' iver made, wi' all your scrapin'!"[1]

(bk. IV, ch. 32)

Such was the speech—witty, pungent, and colored with homely images—that George Eliot heard in her childhood, and that was a great part of her training as a writer.

The Mill on the Floss

The life that Marian and George Lewes led together, at first in the house at Richmond, later in London in a house near Regent's Park, was one, as he recorded in his diary, of "deep wedded happiness." The stepsons were devoted to Marian, and she to them. Both Marian and Lewes worked hard and were always interested in each other's work, although inevitably, as her books appeared and her reputation soared, hers became the first consideration. Lewes was born to be an unselfish prince consort. Marian found in him the wholehearted devotion that she had always yearned for. He cherished her, cheered her melancholy, encouraged her diffidence, spared her the practical difficulties of life, entertained the people who came to their house, leaving Marian free for the only kind of social pleasure she liked, serious conversation with one or at most a few real friends. He even kept from her the few unfavorable reviews of her novels. It seems strange that a woman of her fiber should have allowed such a thing to happen, but she was abnormally sensitive and prone to melancholy and self-distrust. Except for these dark moods, and for bad headaches and other minor ailments that often troubled her, and except for a certain amount of anxiety about Lewes's never robust health, their life was extremely happy. George Eliot's career moved steadily from success to success as her great talent expanded. There is little to tell of the life that ran so smoothly, and George Eliot's history is the history of her novels from the time that she joined George Lewes, up to his death.

Her second long novel, *The Mill on the Floss*, was published in 1860, only a year after *Adam Bede*. It is the book in which she drew most directly on her own early life. Maggie Tulliver, the sensitive, passionate child of a stolid family, craving for her brother's love; the ardent girl growing up in a narrow world with a thirst for life, beauty, and knowledge is the

[1]All quotations from the novels are from *The Works*, 21 vols. (London, 1908–1911).

young Marian Evans herself, transmuted into fiction. Maggie repeats her author's childish troubles, for she is often in disgrace, considered plain and tiresome, compared unfavorably with her pretty, docile cousin Lucy, as Marian had been with Chrissey. With Maggie as with her creator the strongest need is the need of being loved, the second the need for more scope than her surroundings provide. Somewhere in herself she feels possibilities that might be realized in a world of less rigid conventions and narrow judgments; she knows instinctively that there must be somewhere a world of different values in which her qualities would not be despised and, when she runs away to the gypsies, it is in the hope of finding such a world, less cramping to the fullness of her own instinctive life.

With Maggie's adoration of her brother Tom and her sense of inferiority as a mere girl who can only share his amusements on sufferance, there is also a feeling of superiority, for Maggie is quicker than the stupid Tom and knows it, even while she reveres him for the things that she cannot do and craves his approval. It is because Tom, disapproving, threatens to tell their father, whose health is failing, that Maggie gives up the stolen meetings with Philip Wakem that are the only break in her restricted life. Later, when Maggie is spending a holiday with Lucy and half-unconsciously steals the love of Lucy's recognized admirer, Stephen Guest, the worst of her punishment for the abortive elopement is Tom's anger. The climax of the book is the reconciliation between brother and sister at the moment of death, when both are swept down together by a mass of wreckage in the flooded river. It does not make any difference that Tom is stupid, self-righteous, and uncomprehending. He remains to the end the pivot of Maggie's world, exercising that power over her which the lesser but more fully integrated personality so often wields over the character with much greater potentialities but still disorganized.

The Mill on the Floss has both the strength and the weakness of an autobiographical novel. There is no more vivid picture in English fiction of the sorrows and sufferings of a child. The world of those early chapters is the world as seen through the eyes of a child. George Eliot used, with some adaptation of course, the surroundings of her own home, and visitors to the house at Griff can still see the mill and the Red Deeps where Maggie had the stolen interviews with Philip. By the time that George Eliot wrote *The Mill on the Floss*, she had abandoned her girlish belief that happiness was wrong and renunciation good for its own sake. Her very life as a writer had depended on her being able to abandon it, but in her portrait of the young Maggie she allows no mature nor objective judgment to qualify the identification. The portrait gains in freshness and intensity as much as it loses in proportion.

The second half of *The Mill on the Floss* is less closely autobiographical. Stephen Guest has often been criticized as unworthy of Maggie and unlikely to attract her love. Certainly he is seen only from outside and is a local dandy, a vain, complacent, trivial young man; but Maggie, like so many people with greater powers of feeling, is slow in coming to emotional maturity. She has led a starved life teaching in a girls' school. Stephen is young, exuberant, and handsome. George Eliot does convey, although it was impossible for a novelist in Victorian England to say it, that what sprang up between them was sexual feeling. Maggie, like her creator, is avid for love. Less fortunate than her creator, she moves in a world where there is no one of her own caliber. She loves the most attractive man she knows, as soon as he breaks down her resistance by showing a preference for her. A novelist writing today would probably be aware that there must have been some satisfaction as well as other feelings in taking Stephen from Lucy, the girl who had been held up to Maggie as a model in her childhood, as Chrissey had to Marian. George Eliot's high-mindedness and the comparative innocence of the period leave these undercurrents unexplored. Maggie is all remorse about Lucy; Lucy all gentle forgiveness. Lucy is an idealized portrait but, as with Dinah Morris, George Eliot succeeds in giving to what might have been simply an intolerable prig a sweetness that makes her bearable.

The Mill on the Floss does not depend only on Maggie and her story. It has a superb setting of English family life, narrated as always by George Eliot with humor and shrewd observation. Mrs. Tulliver is a woman in herself of little personality, but as the representative of the Dodson family, she has an authority that the more lively Mr. Tulliver resents but cannot always resist. Aunt Glegg is the embodiment of these always right Dodsons. Bullying her husband and her sisters, exacting the full measure of respect due her from younger relatives, touchy, arrogant, quick tempered, she refuses to receive Mr. Tulliver when he offends her, but is resolute in leaving her will unaltered, for people must not be able to say after she is dead that she did not do right by her sister's children. She is the harshest critic of Maggie as she grows up, but when Maggie is disgraced in the eyes of their world, it is Aunt Glegg who offers her a home. Not that she needs to, for in this crisis the flabby, poor-spirited Mrs. Tulliver stands by her child. The central religion of the Dodson family is that blood is thicker than water. The Dodsons are the very marrow of the English middle class of the last century, a tradition that still survives.

A Dodson would not be taxed with the omission of anything that was becoming, or that belonged to that eternal fitness of things which was plainly indicated in the practice of the most substantial parishioners and in the family tradition,—such as obedience to parents, faithfulness to kindred, industry, rigid honesty, thrift, the thorough scouring of wooden and copper utensils, the hoarding of coin likely to disappear from the currency, the production of first-rate commodities for the market, and the general preference for whatever was home-made.

(bk. IV, ch. 1)

Silas Marner

Adam Bede and *The Mill on the Floss* are novels filled with their author's early experience. Her father and mother, her own childhood, the aspirations of her youth, her relationship with her brother, her devotion to Miss Lewis provided a good deal of the material, translated, of course, since she was always a novelist, into fiction. In her last three novels she was to move further away from immediate experience and to create in the truth of that experience different worlds. Between the early novels and the later ones come two interim books, very different from each other, both marking an extension of imagination. They are *Silas Marner* and her only historical novel, *Romola*.

Silas Marner (1861), the shortest and in form the most perfect of George Eliot's novels, is really a fairy tale expressed in everyday village life. As in so many fairy tales, the focal point is gold, the gold that Marner, the old, epileptic weaver, hoards under the stone in his cottage and which is stolen from him by Dunstan Cass, the squire's dissolute son. On Christmas Eve, the very season of magic gifts, while the whole neighborhood is dancing and feasting at the squire's house, the solitary, half-blind weaver, recovering from one of his fits, sees something on the stone floor of his cottage that may be his lost gold come back to him. Still partly dazed from the epileptic attack, he puts out his hand and touches the living gold of a child's hair. There follows the redemption by love. Silas, whose feelings have atrophied while his only object was to make money and save it, now begins a new life as the father of an adopted child.

The child is the link with the other half of the story, the fortunes of the Cass family. Dunstan's bones whiten undiscovered in the Stone Pit. Godfrey is set free on that Christmas Eve to court and marry Nancy Lammeter, free from the burden of a young man's rash marriage, for the child who wandered into Silas Marner's hut had not come there alone, but had tottered toward the light of his fire from the side of a woman who was found lying dead at his doorway in the snow.

Silas Marner is so complete a work of art that the reader feels no incongruity between the romantic tale and its realistic setting. Is it probable that even a nearsighted man would mistake gold hair for gold coins? It does not much matter. This most charming of George Eliot's novels has the quality of a legend, the kind of story that would be handed down in the village for years afterward. It is the perfect Christmas story. The conversation of the men in the Rainbow Inn has often been admired for its veracity and liveliness. The weaknesses of the two Cass brothers are admirably described. Nancy Lammeter is another of those young women whose prettiness George Eliot conveys so vividly—although it has been said of her that she is often hard on them. She, who had no doubt suffered a good deal from believing herself ugly, had an acute sense of feminine beauty. There is a fairy tale quality again in the preparations for the party in the squire's house, the dresses of silvery twilled silk lifted from the clean, rustling paper, the necklace of coral clasped round Miss Nancy's white neck. It is not a fairy tale that ends in complete happiness all round, for Godfrey has to continue to suffer his childlessness, the penalty for distrusting Nancy's generosity and for disowning his child for eighteen years. Perhaps *Silas Marner* is the best introduction to George Eliot, certainly for a young reader, and it is the most shapely of all her novels.

Romola

Silas Marner, for all its real picture of village life, is an excursion into fantasy. *Romola* (1863), also a spring away from memories of George Eliot's youth, goes to a world that she could only know from books and by the patient reconstruction of a learned and historically conscious traveler. It is a full, elaborately documented story of Florence in the time of Savonarola. "It is," says F. R. Leavis, "the work of a gifted mind but of a mind misusing itself." To most of her admirers it is the least readable of all her novels. The characters, weighed down by their historical trappings, too deliberately and carefully established in their period, move heavily and have much less vitality than her men and women of the English Midlands. George Eliot put more work into *Romola* than into any other novel. She herself said that she began the book a young woman and finished it an old one.

Romola, the noble and beautiful Florentine girl, is, like Maggie Tulliver, a self-portrait, in some ways more like her author, for she is the only one of her notable women to whom George Eliot attempted to give her own intellectual equipment. Tito, the Greek, who marries Romola and afterward turns against her, is another and meaner version of Arthur Donnithorne. He has deceived Tessa, an ignorant young *contadina*, with a ceremony of mock marriage, and she innocently believes the children whom she bears him to be legitimate, one day to be publicly acknowledged by their father, whose secret appearances and disappearances she hardly dreams of questioning. When Tito has succumbed to the avenger, who has been dogging him throughout the book, Romola, who has no child, takes in Tessa and the children and shelters them. The story is played out against the full historical background, the arrival of the French under Charles VIII, the struggle between the followers of the Medici and the popular party, the trial and execution of Savonarola.

Perhaps one of the things that makes *Romola* so much less lively and readable than George Eliot's other novels is that she is denying herself the use of one of her greatest gifts, her use of ordinary conversation. Her men and women of the English Midlands live by the pungency and vitality of their speech, whereas Romola and Tito use a carefully manufactured dialogue, meant to represent the speech of their time. Yet even though many admirers of George Eliot find *Romola* difficult to read and have no desire to reread it, it is still recognizably the work of a great novelist in scope and breadth, in humanity and compassion.

Felix Holt

Sometimes a book on which the writer spends great care and labor with only partly successful results acts as a springboard for the imagination. Certainly after

Romola George Eliot wrote her three greatest novels. It may be that the historical perspective of *Romola* turned her mind toward the history of her own time. *Felix Holt* (1866) is a political novel, although the politics are not the best part of it. It is an uneven book, the plot is involved, depending on legal complications in the inheritance of the Transome estate. The legal business is both tedious and unconvincing; there is something of an outworn tradition in all the farrago of the missing heir and the interloper turned out. There is a lively and vigorous picture of an election in a country town, but the great strength of the novel lies in the emotional drama of the Transome family.

Mrs. Transome, hardened by her unhappy secret; Harold Transome, with his carefully planned life and his always realizable ambitions, his good-tempered selfishness; Jermyn, the coarse-fibered rascal who is also a good and affectionate husband and father, misusing his trust for the welfare of his family—all these are drawn with the hand of a master. We are skillfully and gradually made aware of the likeness between Harold and Jermyn. The commonplace egotism of Jermyn, tempered by Mrs. Transome's keen-edged personality, becomes in their son a hardness veiled by natural geniality. All that is greedy and unprincipled in Jermyn is also greedy and unprincipled in the son, although a different nurture and a wider experience have put a finer glaze on the surface. Mrs. Transome, the bitter old woman, realizes that she will get no more real tenderness from her son than from her former lover. Her tragedy is not only that she has implicated both with herself in an impossible situation, but that she is necessary to neither.

Felix Holt is meant to be the foil to Harold and Jermyn. He is the idealized "working man" of his time, the high-principled reformer who cares nothing for personal advantage and is willing to give his life to the cause of the oppressed. He is determined not to rise out of his own class but to remain in it as a manual worker and to devote his spare energies to educating the children of his fellow workers. George Eliot was no revolutionary in politics. A gradual improvement in conditions and nurture was her idea of a revolution. She had nothing like the inside knowledge of the hardships of poverty that Mrs. Gaskell showed in *Mary Barton*. Perhaps the reason was that the poor whom she really knew were all country people, and poverty is always less bearable in a city. Felix Holt remains an embodiment of an idea, and an idea perceived intellectually from outside, rather than a living person. He is most alive in his relationship with the lovely, lively Esther Lyon. The early scenes between the two when they are falling reluctantly in love and want to conceal it from themselves by sparring are very good indeed. Esther softens into love and tenderness, and although she appreciates luxury and position and is delighted to find herself able to be at home in the Transome world, she throws it all away for Felix's sake.

As always the novel is remarkable not only for the main theme, but for the humor and veracity of the minor characters. No English novelist, not Dickens himself, is more at home in the public house and the marketplace. Some of the characters recall those of the earlier novels: Rufus Lyon is, again like Dinah Morris and Mr. Tryan, the saintly evangelical; Felix Holt's grumbling but devoted mother recalls Lizbeth Bede; but Esther is no longer a heroine drawn from her author's own self-portrait; and Mrs. Transome, Harold, and Jermyn are genuine creations. There is nothing in George Eliot's work more powerful than the tragedy of Mrs. Transome. The destiny whose seed was sown so long ago is worked out in the course of the novel with the inevitability of a Greek drama. *Felix Holt* is not one of the best-known or most widely read of George Eliot's novels, probably because the political novel is not popular with English readers, but it is certainly one most worth reading.

Middlemarch

Middlemarch (1871–1872) is now generally recognized as not only the full flower of George Eliot's genius but as one of the finest novels in the English language. Its subtitle is *A Study of Provincial Life.* Its scene is a country town in the Midlands, and the big houses around the town. Its theme, as Gerald Bullett has said in his *George Eliot: Her Life and Books* (1948), is "the diversity of provincial manners and the significance of ordinary lives."

Its several strands are connected by the slight and apparently casual threads that link up human lives. As in nearly every great novel, there is more than one story. There is the story of Dorothea Brooke, an ardent girl unsatisfied by the idle country house life in which she has been brought up. Like Maggie Tulliver, like the young Marian Evans, she is conscious of powers yearning for development and of an intensity that sets her apart from her sister Celia, the natural young woman who is half afraid of Dorothea's superiority and half amused at "Dodo's no-

tions." It is inevitable that Celia, whose lighter personality has matured earlier, should marry the robust and conventional Sir James Chettam, while Dorothea marries the elderly scholar Casaubon. She dreams of devoting her life to helping him with his work, only to discover that this great work is an occupation that offers him a retreat from life, a dreary hotch-potch of other men's ideas, endlessly compiled for a book that will never be written and could have no value if it were. Apart from the disillusionment about Casaubon's work, Dorothea suffers the natural disappointment of a vigorous young woman married to a man prematurely old in whom feeling has long since atrophied, although he has enough jealousy to see before Dorothea is aware of it the dawning love between her and his cousin, the artist Will Ladislaw.

Ladislaw is one of the links with the story of Lydgate, the young doctor who comes to Middlemarch full of faith in himself and in the work, scientific and practical, that he means to do. He is a parallel with Dorothea, for he too marries somebody who is the negation to all his aspirations. Rosamund Vincy, the daughter of a comfortable, unpretentious family, has been educated out of homeliness and into gentility. Completely self-centered, she is hardly aware of Lydgate as a person; she sees him as an opportunity of climbing out of the tradesmen's world in which she was born, into professional and county society. Her values are incomprehensible to him as his are to her, but her blinkered obstinacy prevails, and his ambitions are caught up in a net of debts incurred to satisfy his wife's idea of happiness. He loses the fine edge of his integrity and incurs suspicion of deep disgrace from which he is never wholly cleared, except in the opinion of his nearest friends. He leaves Middlemarch to make what life he can, a successful one, since he is an able man, but with an incompatible wife and disappointed hopes.

It is easier to sympathize with him in his tragic self-betrayal than with Bulstrode, whose ostentatious virtue and high reputation in Middlemarch are based on a shabby fraud at the expense of a widow and her child. Yet Bulstrode, because he is handled with profound compassion, moves the reader. One of the most poignant passages in the book is the account of his wife's discovery that the husband whom she has always revered has cheated over his first wife's estate, and that his disgrace is known in Middlemarch. It is the end of all her happiness and pride. Obeying an instinct that she cannot articulate, she lingers in her bedroom, taking off her ornaments and changing her elaborate hairdressing for a plain one, putting on a black dress, mourning for the life of respect and importance she has shared with him. Going downstairs at last she sees him in his chair, looking withered and shrunken. She puts a hand on his shoulder, saying gently, "Look up, Nicholas" so that he bursts into tears and without question or answer they weep side by side.

George Eliot's novels have abounded in the saints of the evangelical movement, but in Bulstrode she presents another of the characters whom the movement seemed to foster, the man who combines a steady and not always scrupulous pursuit of profit and success with a religion that is always on his lips but in a separate compartment of his heart. "It was a principle with Mr. Bulstrode to gain as much power as possible that he might use it for the glory of God. He went through a great deal of spiritual conflict and inward argument in order to adjust his motives and make clear to himself what God's glory required."

In contrast to Lydgate and Bulstrode, the man of unshakable integrity is Caleb Garth, the land agent, another version of George Eliot's father, an older and more human Adam Bede. His daughter Mary, with her sturdy sense and loyalty, is the one hope of stability for Fred Vincy, who is spoiled like his sister Rosamond but not ruined, because unlike her he has a warm heart. Fred has been nearly destroyed by vain expectations. Another plot, which might almost be the plot of a detective novel, is focused on Stone Court, where the rich, old Featherstone lies dying, watched faithfully by Mary Garth, and hungrily by all those who could hope to benefit by his death.

All these strands are woven into a pattern of that varied scene of provincial life that George Eliot knew so much better than any other woman writer of her century. She was at ease in the billiard room of the public house, in the rectory parlor, at the committee meeting, and in the drawing room of the country house. Dorothea Brooke is a woman, like her creator, of exceptional quality, but everyone else in the book is of average stature. They are people of moderate gifts and mixed faults and virtues, to whom George Eliot has given significance by her respect for them as human beings and by her profound sympathy and compassion. Even when she is writing of how Rosamond Vincy's shallow egotism destroys her husband, she sees the disappointing marriage, too, through Rosamond's eyes, and shows that she, too, in her limited way, is a feeling and suf-

fering human being. Fred Vincy is an unsatisfactory young scapegoat to such judges as Mrs. Garth and his father, but how sympathetically and humorously George Eliot draws his own young impatience with the people who grudge him a bit of fun and are forever "at him" about the serious purposes of life.

Deeply concerned, as all George Eliot's novels are, with the serious purposes of life, *Middlemarch* is also enlivened all the time by humor. It is the funniest of all her books. Even Dorothea, with whom she obviously identifies herself, she sees sometimes through the amused eyes of Celia.

Occasionally the humor fails, as in some of the scenes between Dorothea and Will Ladislaw, the only character in the book who never for an instant comes to life. But everywhere it provides the savor in this long, sober chronicle of ordinary life, which leaves the reader with the conviction that lives after all are never ordinary when presented by an author who feels them deeply and can discern at least a part of their pattern.

Daniel Deronda

Daniel Deronda (1874–1876), George Eliot's last novel, draws much less on her early knowledge of farm and village. Its scene is laid in country houses, in London, and abroad.

There are two main stories: the story of Gwendolen Harleth, a brilliantly pretty, spirited, self-absorbed girl, with a doting mother and subdued half sisters, and the story of a young Jewess, Mirah, who comes to England to find her long-lost mother and brother. Mirah, gentle and affectionate, is a complete foil for Gwendolen.

The link between the two stories is Daniel Deronda himself, the adopted son of an English country gentleman, Sir Hugo Mallinger, who has brought him up in ignorance of his parentage. Daniel supposes himself and is supposed to be Sir Hugo's illegitimate son. He is a serious young man with great integrity and with a natural authority that affects most of those who come near him.

Gwendolen's fortunes are linked with Deronda in the dramatic opening scene, when he is idly watching the gambling in the casino at a French resort and notices a beautiful girl who stakes her last guinea and loses. Next morning Deronda happens to see her going into a pawn shop. When she has come out, he enters and buys the turquoise necklace that she has just sold. He returns it to her with an unsigned note of gentle reproach. Gwendolen finds out who wrote the note, and from that day Daniel Deronda becomes in her mind a mentor whose approval she craves.

At their home of Offendene in England Gwendolen's mother and half sisters are facing ruin from the failure of their investments. Before going abroad Gwendolen had refused an offer of marriage from Grandcourt, the great man of the neighborhood. She did not love him, but he could have given her much that she wanted; she would probably have accepted him, but she discovered that he already had four children by a woman whom he had promised to marry.

When Gwendolen returns to Offendene, Grandcourt again proposes to her. She has to choose between this splendid marriage and a humble post as a governess. She knows that Grandcourt is hard and selfish, but, confident in her young beauty, she believes that she will easily manage him. When she discovers that Grandcourt's inbuilt egotism is too much for her, she turns for comfort to Deronda, whom she often meets in London society. Grandcourt perceives what Gwendolen does not know—that she is in love with Deronda—and sweeps her off on a Mediterranean yachting cruise.

Deronda's life is moving in another direction, toward Mirah, whom he saves from suicide, and toward her brother Ezra Mordecai, who turns out to be a man of great emotional and intellectual power, but who is dying of consumption. He implores Deronda to carry on his work and to help restore the Jews to their own country.

Sir Hugo sends Deronda out to Genoa to see his dying mother, who proves to have been a famous Jewish singer and who reveals to him that his father was a Jew. Gwendolen and Grandcourt are also in Genoa. She is miserable, having discovered on this holiday the full extent of her husband's sadism. When they are out sailing, Grandcourt is swept overboard. Gwendolen, paralyzed by shock and conflict of feeling, is slow in throwing the rope to him. A minute later she desperately jumps in and tries to save him. She is rescued, but Grandcourt is drowned. To Deronda she confesses that she feels herself a murderess. She was too late with the rope because "I saw my wish outside me."

Deronda tries to comfort her, but the discovery of his Jewish birth turns him finally toward Mirah and the service of his own people. Gwendolen is left desolate with nothing but the hope that she may in time become the kind of woman that Deronda would wish her to be.

Nothing that George Eliot wrote is more powerful than this study of Gwendolen Harleth. The change from the willful, glowing girl into the bullied wife is superbly handled. George Eliot does not attempt to disguise Gwendolen's murderous feelings toward Grandcourt. That cry—"I saw my wish outside me"—ushers in the changed attitude toward human nature that divides the novels of this century from those of the last. *Daniel Deronda* is a great novel that combines the modern sense of complexity of character with the fullness and richness of Victorian fiction.

CONCLUSION

Daniel Deronda was George Eliot's last novel. It is by her novels alone that she lives. She wrote a number of short stories, of which the most remarkable is "The Lifted Veil," a good deal of pedestrian poetry, including a long dramatic poem, *The Spanish Gypsy* (1868), and a book of satirical essays called *Impressions of Theophrastus Such* (1879). All her work was written during the twenty-three years of her life with George Lewes. In 1878, two years after the publication of *Daniel Deronda*, Lewes died.

It was a mortal blow to George Eliot, who lived only two years after him. The end of her story is a strange one. For weeks after Lewes's death she shut herself up and remained in a stupor of despair, seeing no one. The first friend she did care to see was John Walter Cross, the son of a London merchant, one of the many intelligent young men who had frequented the house near Regent's Park. Cross was at that time thirty-nine, and George Eliot sixty. He had just lost his mother, to whom he was devoted, and no doubt he turned unconsciously to George Eliot to fill her place, as she turned to him in a desperate search for comfort. They were constantly together, and on 6 May 1880 they were married.

George Eliot called the astonishing marriage "a blessing falling to me beyond my share." It has been conjectured that it was a relief to her conscience to find herself at last a married woman. It seems more likely that she, for whom George Lewes's love had been life itself, was snatching desperately at any comfort to relieve the agony of loneliness and deprivation. There was no time to see how the strange marriage would work. Cross seems to have been devoted to Marian. After her death he compiled the first biography from her letters and journals. No doubt his affection and his company gave Marian Evans some comfort. Her nature was deeply loving, and it had become a necessity to her to have someone to love, and to be protected and cherished. But the loss of Lewes had been a blow too deep for recovery. In December 1880, six months after her marriage, she died.

In a review of *Felix Holt* published soon after its appearance, Henry James spoke of George Eliot's "closely wedded talents and foibles." He found her plots "artificial" and her conclusions "weak," but he also found that:

In compensation for these defects, we have the broad array of those rich accomplishments. . . . First . . . the firm and elaborate delineation of individual character. . . . Then comes that extensive human sympathy, that easy understanding of character at large, that familiarity with man, from which a novelist draws his real inspiration, . . . to which he owes it that, firm locked in the . . . most rigid prose, he is still more or less of a poet. George Eliot's humanity colours all her other gifts.[2]

She was not a writer who in her lifetime had to struggle for recognition. From the publication of her first book, she was acknowledged by her peers, including Dickens and Thackeray. Her career was one of unbroken success, and in spite of her moods of diffidence and self-distrust, she knew herself to be an important novelist.

After her death her reputation seemed for a time to be obscured. No one really interested in the English novel could ignore her, but many people who did not read her had an idea of her as a governessy bluestocking, a turgid, out-of-date Victorian. Lately a more general interest in her work has revived, and the sound and affectionate studies by Gerald Bullett and by Joan Bennett, F. R. Leavis' critical estimate, T. W. J. Harvey's study as well as Gordon Haight's full biography, and the television versions of her novels have stimulated a more just and also a more general appreciation of her superb gifts.

It is now more than a hundred years since the publication of *Scenes of Clerical Life*. During that time a change has taken place in the attitude of both novelists and their readers to the characters in a novel. To say that moral judgment in the novelist and in the reader has disappeared would be an exag-

geration, for there is no one civilized enough to read a book who has not some moral standard to which he expects himself, and still more other people, to conform, and even if he does not know it, he applies this in fiction as in life. Moreover, those standards in Western civilization are impregnated with the Christian tradition and with values accepted over hundreds of years. But moral judgment, although nearly always there, is in the background, often unacknowledged, and depends far more on individual taste in life than on agreed standards.

What has very nearly departed from the novel and from its readers is moral concern. The modern novelist wishes to present a picture of life from some angle. The reader wishes to see what that particular facet of life is like. He does not feel distressed if the characters in a novel behave badly. His great interest is to see how and why they behave badly. On the whole neither the writer nor the reader feels moral concern for the characters; they both feel a more objective interest. Moral concern for her characters was the very essence of George Eliot. "Is he, or she, going to manage to be noble or not?" is the real plot of her novels. Sometimes her ideas of nobility are unacceptable to one kind of modern reader, who has learned that unselfishness can be a masochism and sometimes forgets that it can also be love, who is more afraid of priggishness than of homicide, insanity, or perversion. But the choice between living by one's own best or second-best values is still universal. It is the urgency of that choice that creates the tension in George Eliot's work, and without tension there is no great novel.

There is no doubt whatever that George Eliot is a great novelist. Her awareness of life is both wide and deep. She is one of the most intellectual of English novelists, but with her intellectual power goes no tinge of contempt, nothing that dries up her sympathy with average men and women. She uses a mind nourished by philosophy and learning to express the significance of ordinary lives. With that "firm and elaborate delineation of individual character," of which Henry James spoke, is combined a genius for bringing each character to life, not only as an individual but as part of the social pattern. Her vision is whole. For her there is no division between the inner and outer life, between the profound emotion, the agonizing spiritual conflict, and the bargain in the lawyer's office, the election brawl, the gossip in farm kitchen or tap room. All is unified by her deep-rooted love of humanity. Beneath all her faithful and often humorous rendering of its mean-

[2]H. James, *Notes and Reviews* (Freeport, N. Y., 1968), pp. 200–201.

nesses and absurdities lies her sense of its potential grandeur.

She is vividly aware of its humor. Infinitely pompous and solemn in her private correspondence, she shows in all her novels the shrewd and racy humor of an old countrywoman, which only breaks down when she is handling one of her idealized characters or one of those too closely identified with herself. Her dialogue is nearly always masterly. The tirades of her vigorous older women, the talk of men idling or working together, have the veracity of simple poetry and reveal the nature of the speakers more effectively than any description.

George Eliot's particular contribution to the English novel is that she left it aware of character on a very much deeper level. Her analysis of motive is penetrating, and she has more understanding than any English novelist writing before Freud of the undercurrents of mind and heart. Because her human beings are more complicated and more mixed than those of the novelists who preceded her, they are nearer to the truth of human nature. This penetration is not only of the intellect, it is born of a harmony between mind and feeling, illuminated by compassion and love for humanity. In her best work there is a depth and reality that no English novelist has surpassed, nor can any of them surpass her in her power of taking the reader into her created world.

SELECTED BIBLIOGRAPHY

I. Bibliography. P. H. Muir, "A Bibliography of the First Editions of Books of George Eliot," contributed to the *Bookman's Journal*, Supplement (1927–1928); M. L. Parrish, *Victorian Lady Novelists: George Eliot* (New York, 1933), first eds. of George Eliot formerly in the library of M. L. Parrish and now in Princeton University, expertly described and annotated by their late owner.

II. Collected Editions. *The Novels*, 6 vols. (Edinburgh, 1867–1878); *The Works*, 20 vols. (Edinburgh, 1878–1880), the Cabinet ed.; *The Complete Poetical Works* (New York, 1888); M. Browne, ed., *The Complete Poems* (Boston, 1888); *The Works*, 12 vols. (Edinburgh, 1901–1903), the Warwick ed.; *The Works*, 21 vols. (London, 1908–1911).

III. Separate Works. D. F. Strauss, *The Life of Jesus Critically Examined*, trans. from the fourth German ed. by Marian Evans, 3 vols. (London, 1846); L. Feuerbach, *The Essence of Christianity*, trans. from the second German ed. by Marian Evans (London, 1854); *Scenes of Clerical Life*, 2 vols. (Edinburgh, 1858), novel; *Adam Bede*, 3 vols. (Edinburgh, 1859), novel; *The Mill on the Floss*, 3 vols. (Edinburgh, 1860), novel; *Silas Marner, The Weaver of Raveloe* (Edinburgh, 1861), novel; *Romola*, 3 vols. (London, 1863), novel; *Felix Holt, the Radical*, 3 vols. (Edinburgh, 1866), novel; *The Spanish Gypsy: A Poem* (Edinburgh, 1868); *How Lisa Loved the King* (Boston, 1869), verse; *Middlemarch: A Study of Provincial Life*, 4 vols. (Edinburgh, 1871–1872), novel; *The Legend of Jubal, and Other Poems* (Edinburgh, 1874); *Daniel Deronda*, 4 vols. (Edinburgh, 1876), novel; *Impressions of Theophrastus Such* (Edinburgh, 1879), essays; C. L. Lewes, ed., *Essays and Leaves from a Note-book* (Edinburgh, 1884); *Early Essays* (London, 1919), privately printed.

IV. Letters. J. W. Cross, ed., *George Eliot's Life as Related in Her Letters and Journals*, 3 vols. (Edinburgh, 1885); R. Stuart, ed., *Letters to Elma Stuart, 1872–80* (London, 1909); R. B. Johnson, ed., *Letters* (London, 1926); A. Paterson, *George Eliot's Family Life and Letters* (London, 1928); G. S. Haight, ed., *The George Eliot Letters*, 9 vols. (London–New Haven, Conn., 1954–1979).

V. Biographical and Critical Studies. G. Roslyn [Joshua Hatton], *George Eliot in Derbyshire* (London, 1876); D. Kaufmann, *George Eliot and Judaism* (Edinburgh, 1877); J. C. Brown, *The Ethics of George Eliot's Works* (Edinburgh, 1879); W. Morgan, *George Eliot* (London, 1881); M. Blind, *George Eliot* (London, 1883); G. W. Cooke, *George Eliot: A Critical Study of Her Life, Writings and Philosophy* (London, 1883); R. E. Cleveland, *George Eliot's Poetry and Other Studies* (London, 1885); M. Lonsdale, *George Eliot: Thoughts upon Her Life, Her Books and Herself* (London, 1886); O. Browning, *Life of George Eliot* (London, 1890); C. L. Thomson, *George Eliot* (London, 1901); L. Stephen, *George Eliot* (London, 1902), in the English Men of Letters series; C. S. Olcott, *George Eliot: Scenes and People in Her Novels* (New York, 1910); C. Gardner, *The Inner Life of George Eliot* (London, 1912); M. H. Deakin, *The Early Life of George Eliot* (Manchester, 1913); L. W. Berle, *George Eliot and Thomas Hardy* (New York, 1917); A. J. C., *Notes on the Influence of Sir Walter Scott on George Eliot* (Edinburgh, 1923); I. G. Mudge and M. E. Sears, *A George Eliot Dictionary* (New York, 1924); V. Woolf, *The Common Reader* (London, 1925), contains an essay on George Eliot; A. L. Summers, *The Homes of George Eliot: An Appreciative Commentary on Her Characteristics and Philosophy* (London, 1926); E. S. Haldane, *George Eliot and Her Times: A Victorian Study* (London, 1927); A. Paterson, *George Eliot's Family Life and Letters* (London, 1928); J. L. May, *George Eliot* (London, 1930); E. and G. Romieu, *La Vie de George Eliot* (Paris, 1930), trans. by B. W. Downs (London, 1932); A. T. Kitchel, *George Lewes and George Eliot* (New York, 1933); Lord David Cecil, *Early Victorian Novelists* (London, 1934), contains an essay on George Eliot; B. C. Williams, *George Eliot: A Biography* (New York, 1936); S. Dewes, *Marian: The Life of George Eliot* (London, 1939); G. Bullett, *George Eliot:*

Her Life and Books (London, 1947); J. Bennett, *George Eliot: Her Mind and Her Art* (Cambridge, 1948); F. R. Leavis, *The Great Tradition* (London, 1948), contains an important critical study of George Eliot; B. Willey, *Nineteenth Century Studies* (London, 1949), contains a section on George Eliot; J. Holloway, *The Victorian Sage: Studies in Argument* (London, 1953), includes a ch. on George Eliot; R. Speaight, *George Eliot* (London, 1954; new ed. 1968); B. Hardy, *The Novels of George Eliot: A Study in Form* (London, 1959); R. Stump, *Movement and Vision in George Eliot's Novels* (Seattle, 1959); J. Thale, *The Novels of George Eliot* (New York, 1959); M. Crompton, *George Eliot the Woman* (London, 1960); T. W. J. Harvey, *The Art of George Eliot* (London, 1961); J. Beaty, *Middlemarch from Notebook to Novel: A Study of George Eliot's Creative Method* (Urbana, Ill., 1961); K. A. McKenzie, *Edith Simcox and George Eliot* (Oxford, 1961); D. Van Ghent, *English Novel: Form and Function* (London, 1961); C. B. Cox, *The Free Spirit: A Study of Liberal Humanism in the Work of George Eliot* (London, 1963); W. Allen, *George Eliot* (London, 1965); G. S. Haight, ed., *A Century of George Eliot Criticism* (Boston, 1965); J. Holmstrom and L. Lerner, eds., *George Eliot and Her Readers* (London, 1966); L. Lerner, *The Truthtellers: Jane Austen, George Eliot, D. H. Lawrence* (London, 1967); J. P. Couch, *George Eliot in France: A French Appraisal of George Eliot's Writings, 1858–1960* (Chapel Hill, N. C., 1967); G. S. Haight, *George Eliot: A Biography* (Oxford, 1968); R. Sprague, *George Eliot: A Biography* (Philadelphia–London, 1968); I. Adam, *George Eliot* (London, 1969); B. Hardy, ed., *Critical Essays on George Eliot* (London, 1970); A. E. S. Viner, ed., *George Eliot* (London, 1970); G. R. Creeger, ed., *George Eliot: A Collection of Critical Essays* (London–Englewood Cliffs, N. J., 1970); G. S. Haight, *George Eliot and John Chapman* (London, 1970); R. T. Jones, *George Eliot* (Cambridge, 1970), the British Authors series; D. R. Carroll, ed., *George Eliot: The Critical Heritage* (London, 1971); W. Kroeber, *Styles in Fictional Structures: The Art of Jane Austen, Charlotte Brontë, George Eliot* (Princeton, N. J., 1971); C. Bedient, *Architects of Self: George Eliot, D. H. Lawrence, E. M. Forster* (Berkeley, 1972); M. Laski, *George Eliot and Her World* (London, 1973), the Pictorial Biography series; D. F. Strauss, *George Eliot's Translation of the Life of Jesus Critically Examined* (London, 1973); N. Roberts, *George Eliot: Her Beliefs and Her Art* (London, 1975); R. Levitt, *George Eliot: The Jewish Connection* (Jerusalem, 1975); C. M. Fulmer, ed., *George Eliot: A Reference Guide* (London, 1977); H. S. Kakar, *The Persistent Self: An Approach to Middlemarch* (Delhi, 1977); R. Liddell, *The Novels of George Eliot* (London, 1978); A. Mintz, *George Eliot and the Novel Vocation* (Cambridge, Mass., 1978); H. Witemeyer, *George Eliot and the Visual Arts* (New Haven, Conn., 1979).

MATTHEW ARNOLD
(1822-1888)

Kenneth Allott

I

IF anyone asks what is central in Matthew Arnold's achievement—a question easily prompted by the volume of his work and the range of its interests—one of two replies is probable, in accordance with what is momentarily uppermost in our minds. It may be the missionary nature of Arnold's activities:

Therefore to thee it was given
Many to save with thyself
(no. 87, 140–141)[1]

he wrote approvingly of his father, Dr. Thomas Arnold, in "Rugby Chapel"—in which case we are likely to say that what is central, in the sense of being nearly omnipresent, is the moral and social passion that is the mainspring of such books as *Culture and Anarchy* and *Literature and Dogma* and a sizable element in the poems and literary criticism. Alternatively, at a tangent to this, we may be thinking of what is distinctive, what most gives the taste of Arnold in Arnold's works, in which case we shall be found paying attention to a handful of poems and some selected pages of literary criticism that embody insights with an economical freshness and liveliness, and arguing that they are central in the sense that nobody else could have written them. In this manner a looseness in the original question brings forward two main aspects of Arnold's genius that cannot always be easily separated in his writings. On the one hand, there is the disinterestedness with which objects, ideas, and experiences may be viewed by him ("to see the object as in itself it really is"): the roll call of examples includes such a poem as "Growing Old," the splendid pages on the "ways of handling nature" in *On the Study of Celtic Literature*, Arnold's opinion that the onlooker sees most of the game and that the critic should always remain a little remote from practice. On the other hand, there is the impulse to catechize and instruct, which involves him in judging ideas and even works of art partly by their relevance to apparent social needs: culture, Arnold insists, is a poor thing if it is self-regarding and, in a balanced view, "moves by the force . . . of the moral and social passion for doing good." Something is here left out. Over prose work representing both of these aspects (but not over his verse) Arnold's wit plays at times, aerating its seriousness and preventing its moderation from becoming insipid. If wit is not quite at the center of his achievement, it is an attractive accompaniment of some very characteristic writing. Max Müller speaks of Arnold's Olympian manners at Oxford. It would take a dull dog not to find endearing the Olympian impudence with which he begins an apology to Mr. Wright, a translator of the *Iliad:* "One cannot always be studying one's own works, and I was really under the impression, till I saw Mr. Wright's complaint, that I had spoken of him with all respect. . . ."[2]

Ideally, detachment and zeal are the two sides of a single responsibility: the critic (using the term in the convenient Arnoldian sense to cover social commentator as well as literary critic) is loyal to the whole truth, but his judgment of what the public needs at a particular moment causes him to floodlight one fragment of it rather than another. Practically, however, there are sometimes two distinct responsibilities, and an awkward strain may be set up in the critic who is trying to do justice to both of them. Some confusions

[1] All references for poems are to M. Allott, ed., *The Poems of Matthew Arnold,* 2nd ed. (London, 1979), which has a slightly modernized text. The text reprinted here is that of the 1885 edition. Poem numbers are submitted for titles where appropriate.

[2] Preface to *Essays in Criticism* (London, 1865), vol. III, p. 286. Quotations of prose works are from R. H. Super, ed., *The Complete Prose Works of Matthew Arnold,* 11 vols. (Ann Arbor, Mich., 1960–1977). Volume numbers and page numbers are given.

and peculiarities of emphasis in Arnold's prose—occasionally in the literary criticism, but more often elsewhere—show this clearly enough. There is some truth in the generalization that in the best of Arnold's poetry and literary criticism, insight is preferred to missionary zeal and that an inverse order holds for the social and religious essays, but at best this is a rule with many exceptions. It may give us a reason for echoing the common opinion that Arnold's literary criticism and some of his poems[3] ought to be read first, or, to put it another way, that he is first and most importantly a poetic critic. But we should not in consequence think of the missionary aspect of Arnold's personality simply as a source of weakness. It was a source of both weakness and strength. It saved him from the typical solipsistic pedantries of the ivory tower critic. It seems to have supplied the motive-force for his devotion to his literary vocation: we think of Arnold rising earlier than the servants to read and write before the busy working day of a school inspector, and we recall that temperamentally by his own confession a life of fly-fishing and reading the newspapers would have made him happy. And it may be connected with the common sense that ballasts his other qualities, preventing his intelligence from feeding too much on abstractions and his finesse from becoming too ethereally fine.

"From time to time, every hundred years or so, it is desirable that some critic shall appear to review the past of our literature, and set the poets and the poems in a new order . . . Dryden, Johnson and Arnold have each performed the task as well as human frailty will allow," T. S. Eliot has said (and today we may complete this short list with his own name). There are other poet-critics—Ben Jonson, Shelley, Coleridge (for many purposes the greatest of all English critics)—but, within the exact scope of Eliot's intended meaning, only three of the highest rank before the twentieth century. They are easily recognized. Each one in his own time singles himself out from his fellow-poets by a highly developed civic sense on all matters touching the health of literature. Each, too, shows something of the flair of a public relations officer, so that he is readily accepted as the reigning king of the Sacred Wood, who personifies the unquestioned (because apparently self-evident) literary assumptions of the age. The relationship of a

poet-critic to his immediate predecessor may be admiring, but it must be murderous (see Sir James Frazer's *The Golden Bough*): it has been noted that Eliot, while striving to be just, always has an edge in his voice when he speaks of Matthew Arnold. (F. O. Matthiessen calls it "deft, if inconspicuous sniping, kept up over quite a few years.") In this context Eliot's admission of the importance of Arnold's historical role is as handsome as it is convincing.

Matthew Arnold's appearance in the Victorian age at one remove from the present makes his importance much more than historical. He is nearer to us in time than other critics, and this in itself suggests that his criticism may still carry a "live" charge, but the nearness is not simply a matter of chronology: it depends on a similarity between the Victorian age and our own, which underlies all the superficial differences, and it implies the existence of a real watershed between ancient and modern somewhere in the neighborhood of Coleridge's *Biographia Literaria* (1817)—to put it as far back as possible. All great critics have their *aperçus* (to adopt Arnold's expression), which are timeless, but it is also the critic's function to organize these perceptions, to see how they best hang together in a pattern (the *ordo concatenatioque veri* is Arnold's name for it), and in the end much of every pattern is outmoded. An effort at translation from a dead tongue is needed when we consider the treatment of some of the classical questions of criticism in a seventeenth- or eighteenth-century critic, whereas Arnold's treatment is still in the vernacular in spite of the period flavor of a few of his usages. Equally important to our appreciation of him as a "living" critic is a self-conscious approach that engages our natural sympathies. He performs and is the first spectator of his own performance, and this watchfulness smoothly dilates the reader's understanding of the meaning of critical activity:

. . . judging is often spoken of as the critic's one business; and so in some sense it is; but the judgement which almost insensibly forms itself in a fair and clear mind, along with fresh knowledge, is the valuable one; and thus knowledge, and ever fresh knowledge, must be the critic's great concern for himself; and it is by communicating fresh knowledge, and letting his own judgement pass along with it,—but insensibly, and in the second place not the first, as a sort of companion and clue, not as an abstract lawgiver,—that he will generally do most good to his readers. Sometimes, no doubt, for the sake of establishing an author's place in literature, and his relation to a central standard (and if this is not done, how are we to get at our

---

[3]Some only, for in many pieces—notably the sonnets of *New Poems* (1867)—the "willed" or missionary element is uncomfortably strong.

best in the world?), criticism may have to deal with a subject-matter so familiar that fresh knowledge is out of the question, and then it must be all judgement; an enunciation and detailed application of principles. Here the great safeguard is never to let oneself become abstract, always to retain an intimate and lively consciousness of the truth of what one is saying, and, the moment this fails us, to be sure that something is wrong.

("The Function of Criticism at the Present Time," in *Essays in Criticism*, vol. III, p. 283)

This is so true that in becoming obvious it has almost ceased to seem valuable, but it would not have crossed Dr. Johnson's mind to study himself so curiously or to explain himself in quite this way. It is a post-Coleridgean note.

Again, rightly considered, Arnold's tendency to stray from literary criticism into social and religious comment links him with Eliot and others among our contemporaries and distinguishes him from earlier critics—indeed, the tendency to stray seems to be a peculiar professional hazard in and after the romantic period. To seek the reason would take us far, but I suppose it to be connected with the withering of customary certainties in literary criticism (for example, the obsolescence of "kinds"), and this withering is part of a wider skepticism. When most questions are open questions, a critic may be hard put to it to deal with the propriety of a lyric's diction without raising the ghosts of moral and social issues. In Arnold and Eliot, and in a few capable modern critics on a smaller scale than either, the tendency to range widely marks the seriousness of the attention brought to bear on literature. They shoulder the same sort of burden because they belong to the same cultural phase of the European mind.

Even an incomplete description of the variety of Arnold's attachments to the present must include one further illustration. For two generations or more now, critics have discussed the dilemma of the serious writer in a democracy that is for the most part complacently unaware that the education of taste lags hopelessly behind literacy. The problem, though smaller then, existed for some Victorians. "You see before you, gentlemen," Arnold told the income tax commissioners at Edgware in 1870, "what you have often heard of, *an unpopular author*." It was more than a joke. He did not avoid public acclaim—on the contrary he wrote delightedly to his mother when he saw men with sandwich boards in Regent Street advertising his essay on Marcus Aurelius—but he soberly realized how little ex-

cellence could mean to a mass audience. "Excellence dwells among rocks hardly accessible," he declared, "and a man must almost wear his heart out before he can reach her" (the easy, popular view that excellence was abundant had been taken by a lady from Ohio who sent Arnold a volume on American writers). He knew that his fastidiousness would appear to many both arrogant and lymphatic, but this did not deflect him from his course.[4] He also knew (sometimes with a jealous tincture) that his poetry would have to make its way slowly: general applause is perfunctory for verse that illustrates, in Henry James's words, "a slight abuse of meagreness for distinction's sake." Arnold's is an unobtrusive example of a literary integrity that a degree of isolation neither weakens nor sours: ". . . no one knows better than I do how little of a popular author I am," he writes equally to a sister in 1874, "but the thing is, I gradually produce a real effect, and the public acquires a kind of obscure interest in me as this gets to be perceived."[5]

It would have meant something to Arnold that Walter Bagehot liked his poems (and took them with him on his honeymoon), or that Gerard Manley Hopkins sprang to his defense against the more conventional Robert Bridges ("I do not like to hear you calling Matthew Arnold Mr. Kidglove Cocksure . . . I am sure he is a rare genius and a great critic"), but it never disturbed him not to be the "people's candidate." The knowledge that the Victorian public was tepid about Arnold's gifts may have helped to keep his head above water when the high tide of disapproval of Victorianism rolled in during and after World War I: more upholstered reputations sank waterlogged.

Matthew Arnold is certainly not a neglected "great Victorian" in the present decade, but in one respect his reputation as a literary critic is less settled than it was a generation ago. This is a promising fact, for it is another indication that his influence is live, and at this interval from Eliot's accession to the kingship of

---

[4]"It is true that the critic has many temptations to go with the stream, to make one of the party of movement, one of these *terrae filii*; it seems ungracious to refuse to be a *terrae filius*, when so many excellent people are; but the critic's duty is to refuse, or, if resistance is vain, at least to cry with Obermann: *'Périssons en résistant.'*" ("The Function of Criticism at the Present Time," *Essays in Criticism*, vol. III).

[5]G. W. E. Russell, ed., *The Letters of Matthew Arnold, 1848–1888* (London, 1895), vol. II, p. 117.

the Sacred Wood, it is becoming easier to see and acknowledge it. Arnold's historical position is disputed by nobody: he is a distinguished poet and a major critic, some of whose poems and literary essays are already secure English classics. What is disputed is the extent to which he can influence usefully the practice of criticism in our time. Now that Eliot's earlier critical work is in turn becoming historical, and we are less dazzled by the immediacy of his achievement as a poet and critic, Arnold's usefulness may be given broader limits and his authority may be expected to grow. This is fortunate. No two English critics complement each other so well in the whole of their critical performance; no other English critic has succeeded half so well as either in discovering the tone and temper most exactly suited to the handling of literary subjects.

II

ARNOLD's writings have an inner logic shaped by personality and events. There need be nothing puzzling in the variety of subject matter, style, and intention found in such works as *Empedocles on Etna, A French Eton,* and *Friendship's Garland* if we keep in mind the main stages of his career; and the tug-of-war of purposes in a particular essay makes sense more rapidly when we recognize that duality haunts Arnold's thinking (Hellenism and Hebraism, Celt and Teuton, "natural magic" and "high seriousness," and so on) and expresses something in his nature. Arnold's own diagnosis of this something cannot be disregarded.

> Ah! two desires toss about
> The poet's feverish blood.
> One drives him to the world without,
> And one to solitude . . .
> ("Stanzas in Memory of the Author
> of 'Obermann,'" no. 39, 93–96)

he tells us (in a stanza that illuminates the distinction between detachment and missionary zeal made in the previous section). He is also the inventor of that striking phrase "the dialogue of the mind with itself." Certainly he did not think of his own nature as monolithic: "I am fragments," he admitted to his

favorite sister, Jane,[6] in 1853. Since the change from poetry to prose and the tendency to branch out from literary criticism into social and theological comment are both intimately connected with the development of Arnold's personality, something more must be said on this subject (even at the risk of oversimplification) when we have outlined his career.

Matthew Arnold was born on Christmas Eve 1822 at Laleham-on-Thames, and died at the Dingle, Liverpool, on 15 April 1888. He went to school at Winchester and Rugby and ended his Oxford years by election to an Oriel Fellowship (1845). In 1851 he wanted to marry and obtained through Lord Lansdowne, whose secretary he had been, the position of school inspector, which he held continuously until he retired in 1886. Various attempts to find a more congenial post all ended in frustration, and when his friend John Duke Coleridge was appointed lord chief justice of common pleas in 1873, Arnold joked about the servants' hall being the right place for him if he paid a visit. He was a Balliol man, he declared sardonically, who had not "got on." A civil list pension at sixty was the only official recognition of his talents. Unlike Alfred Tennyson or Robert Browning, he had to make time for his literary work after dreary rounds of school visits and interminable report writing.

Here is my programme for this afternoon: Avalanches, the Steam Engine, the Thames, Indian Rubber, Bricks, the Battle of Poictiers, Subtraction, the Reindeer, the Gunpowder Plot, the Jordan. Alluring is it not? Twenty minutes each, and the days of one's life are only three score years and ten.
(*Letters of Matthew Arnold, 1848–1888,* vol. I, p. 281)

He was a sympathetic rather than a stringent inspector, and some of his colleagues thought of him as an amateur even after a lifetime of service. To put it euphemistically, there were jobs that would have suited him better. But against the suggestion of waste must be set whatever is valuable in the argument of *Culture and Anarchy* or *Friendship's Garland:* without Arnold's enforced intimacy with dissent in the persons of nonconformist school-managers and teachers, his portrait of the middle class would not have been a speaking likeness. His experiences as a school inspector helped to turn him into a critic of society.

[6]Known to the family as "K."

The relief in the irksomely monotonous landscape of Arnold's official career comes from his tenure of the Oxford Chair of Poetry (1857–1867),[7] which he held along with his bread-and-butter appointment, three educational missions to the continent (which sometimes allowed him to feel pleasantly ambassadorial), and a six-month lecture-tour to America in 1883–1884. His regular "anti-attrition" was in a most affectionate family life, a diversity of friendships, solitary fishing, holidays abroad, favorite cats and dogs, including the superb Atossa—

> So Tiberius might have sat,
> Had Tiberius been a cat,
> ("Poor Mathias," 41–42)

the Athenaeum, a little botanizing, tireless letter-writing, country house visits, and wide reading in six languages. Most of the poetry was written before 1857, almost all the prose after. The late 1860's and the 1870's were the years in which Arnold was most concerned in his writings with society and religion. Obvious trigger-causes were the troubles at the time of the second Reform Act (1867) and the "crisis of belief" in the early 1870's.

The man behind this brief dossier was tall and solidly built, and affected a certain dandyism of manner which does not quite sort with the strength of his face—he inherited a "Cornish" nose from his mother's side of the family—or its tinge of melancholy. As a young man he was thought handsome, and he long kept a youthful appearance and energy —it is not very fanciful to see a connection between his luxuriant black hair, hardly touched with gray in his late forties, and what Eneas Sweetland Dallas calls "the intense juvenility—a boy-power to the *nth*" of his more ebullient prose. But this confident and youthfully energetic man had had an inauspicious childhood, which included the early wearing of iron leg-braces, a succession of illnesses and accidents, and a loved and admired father's undisguised suspicion that he was lazy and irresponsible. Arnold's later wish to be "papa's continuator" is rooted in the fact of Dr. Arnold's death before his son had done anything to "justify" himself.

Probably Arnold's gaiety and fecklessness are best looked on as protective clothing for a genuine but never too sturdy poetic gift which he feared to expose to the onslaught of his father's earnestness. If so, it was also a highly effective piece of camouflage, for few of Arnold's intimates seem to have expected the seriousness of his first book of poems in 1849. Of course, they may have been shortsighted: in 1846 George Sand was not deceived and described Arnold's appearance at Nohant as that of "*un Milton jeune et voyageant.*" It is proper to assume that there was always an earnestness in the poet's nature which responded sympathetically to Dr. Arnold's fervor, but that he hid both it and his poetic seriousness behind a mask of frivolity in order to feel free enough and private enough to be a poet. This makes Dr. Arnold a more significant figure in the story of his son's development than anyone else—than even Arthur Clough, or "K," or the shadowy Marguerite.

It is interesting to notice the places that were loved by Matthew Arnold. In England, he was fondest of the Thames valley, the city of Oxford with the surrounding "scholar-gipsy" countryside, Loughrigg and the fells overlooking "Fox How," the family home by the shallow Rotha on the outskirts of Ambleside (the clear running water that was Arnold's passion belongs to all three places and escapes into much of his characteristic poetic imagery). Abroad, he was always happy in France, and a small part of Switzerland glowed in his mind. Oxford and Thun[8] are more than place-names: they are mnemonics for recalling states of happiness associated with his fullest experience of feeling before settling down.

> And yet what days were those, Parmenides!
> When we were young, when we could number friends
> In all the Italian cities like ourselves . . .
> ("Empedocles on Etna," 235–237)

Few poets have ever been so miserably aware of the passage of time ("How life rushes away, and youth. One has dawdled and scrupled and fiddle-faddled— and it is all over")[9] and the reiterated scoring in his notebooks of the phrase "*les saines habitudes de la maturité*" shows with what an effort at self-mastery he tried to welcome the bleakness of responsibility. Here again we seem to be close to Arnold's "secret."

---

[7]Arnold was the first professor to lecture in English instead of Latin. He drew enthusiastic audiences.

[8]Thun is the scene of the love affair with the French girl known in the Switzerland poems as Marguerite. It is simplest to say that we know nothing about it.

[9]H. F. Lowry, ed., *The Letters of Matthew Arnold to Arthur Hugh Clough* (Oxford, 1932), no. 37, p. 120.

The divergent impulses that determine the dichotomies of his literary and social analysis exist because he is in two minds between wholeheartedly accepting maturity (and Dr. Arnold's mission) and the partial rejection implied by an agonized regret for youth and poetry and irresponsibility (which is the other face of detachment). At Thun in 1849 Arnold had two books with him, Béranger and Epictetus, and we find him writing to Clough that Béranger appealed to him less than formerly. It comes almost too pat to symbolize the victory of Stoic self-mastery over pleasure and poetry, a victory that governs Arnold's later development in the years of prose. But if poetry died, the poet in Arnold did not. He lived on to ensure the delicacy of the literary critic's insight, the social critic's unfailing contempt for optimistic claptrap. If Arnold is a good critic, it is because regret kept open a line of communication with his poetic past, because "character" was never quite free from the promptings of "temperament." When he tells us that the work of the nineteenth century in literature is work for the "imaginative reason," he is asserting that a control that is never imperiled is likely to become obtuse. Even a fifth column may be useful in keeping a government on its toes.

"They went forth to battle and they always fell," Arnold quotes in speaking of the Celts, and in the opposition he establishes between Celt and Teuton we have another avatar of the conflict between poetic temperament and moral character. "Natural magic" is Celtic and a happiness of poetic style, whereas Teutons have no sense of style in spite of being worthy, forthright, and necessary. "I have a great *penchant* for the Celtic races, with their melancholy and unprogressiveness," Arnold wrote to Lady de Rothschild, and it is curious how emphatically in this instance he repudiated any suggestion that Dr. Arnold might have shared his sentiments.[10] The Celt strained against "the despotism of fact" as the poet in Arnold's makeup struggled against accepting maturity. When Arnold insisted that his father had not really understood the Celts, he was insisting that his father had not understood him. He was also saying obliquely what he once said openly: "My dear father had many virtues, but he was not a poet." Several critics have noticed that Sohrab's death in the poem at the hands of his father, Rustum, is a type of Arnold's sacrifice of the poetic temperament so that he may identify himself more closely with his father's

moral earnestness. What is also to be remarked if we are to do full justice to the situation is Sohrab's profound admiration and affection for Rustum and the poignancy of his regret for the final loss of

> . . . youth, and bloom, and this delightful world.
> ("Sohrab and Rustum," 856)

Matthew Arnold, as W. H. Auden said, "thrust his gift in prison till it died," but he did it out of love. Perhaps this explains why his maturity is so little cross-grained, and why he is almost incapable of a false note when he sings of renunciation and unwished necessity.

In his finest short story, "The Point of It," E. M. Forster pessimistically argues that "everyone grows hard or soft as he grows old," and Arnold himself did not have many illusions about the irony of the "gifts reserved for age." There are, I think, a few signs of hardening in the later Arnold (far fewer than in most of his contemporaries): a crotchetiness about the Irish question in the 1880's, which found fuel in his old antipathy to Gladstone; traces of personal agitation when he accuses the French of worshiping the goddess Lubricity; an ill-natured stiffness in one or two remarks about John Keats and Percy Bysshe Shelley (with the connotation of an almost reflex disapproval of sexuality); some absurdity in his ducking respect for German "higher critics of the Bible."[11] But these signs do not add up to much, and it is pleasanter to stress how open to fresh impressions, how "ondoyant et divers" as a critic, he remained to the end. He conquered regret without turning his heart into a stone, and the last pages of his letters show us a man who deserves admiration—shrewd, capable, deeply affectionate, still interested in everything about him, and honorably civilized.

III

Matthew Arnold had written some verse before he went to school at Winchester, and a few pieces (including some "animal" poems and the frigid "West-

---

[10]*Letters of Mathew Arnold, 1848–1888*, vol. I, p. 279.

[11]Contrast Arnold's blithe impatience with them as a younger man. In May 1850 he writes to Clough about F. W. Newman's *Phases of Faith*: "One would think to read him that enquiries into articles, biblical inspiration, etc., etc., were as much the natural functions of a man as to eat and copulate. This sort of man is only possible in Great Britain and North Germany, thanks be to God for it" (*Arnold to Clough*, no. 34, p. 115).

minster Abbey") belong to the 1880's. But almost all the work by which he is still known was produced between 1845 and 1867. Indeed, *New Poems* of the latter year contained such a thin harvest for the second decade that it had to be filled out with "Empedocles on Etna," reprinted for the first time since 1852 at the request—as Arnold was careful to tell his readers —of a "man-of-genius, Mr. Robert Browning." But if few poems were composed between 1857 and 1867, certain of them were among Arnold's most finished work, notably "Thyrsis," considered by some to be his poetic masterpiece. It is part of Arnold's "tragedy" as a poet that he reached his fullest command of expressive power when his creative impulse was already failing—a fact noticed with laconic bitterness in "The Progress of Poesy." Arnold's first two volumes were *The Strayed Reveller* (1849) and *Empedocles on Etna* (1852). The various collections issued between 1853 and *New Poems* lean heavily on the two early books, both of which had been published pseudonymously. For example, *Poems* (1853) contains lyrics from both volumes, as well as the famous preface defending the suppression of "Empedocles on Etna," "Sohrab and Rustum" (written to illustrate—in the words of the preface—"that the action itself, its selection and construction, . . . is . . . all-important"), "The Scholar-Gipsy," and various other new pieces that are less well known. Arnold liked to play with his poems when he was unable to write many new ones, suppressing and reviving now one and now another, and tinkering with their order in different collections, so that the makeup of his successive books of verse is confusing; but these changes hardly affect our estimate of him as a poet.

It is clear from *The Strayed Reveller* that a naked ethical intention intrudes into Arnold's poems from the beginning and often does them injury. "Intrude" may seem to be an odd word in connection with an intention so typical of Arnold and so usually present in his work, but I use it advisedly to suggest that his truest note as a poet depends on qualities of feeling at war with ethical impulse. This is evident in Arnold's response to his own poems. "Empedocles on Etna" is rejected for reasons that may be summarized by saying that Arnold thought his poetic drama would dispirit rather than fortify (though we may well think him wrong in his judgment of its probable effect). There is another weak aesthetic choice for "heroic" moral reasons in a letter to Clough: "I am glad you like the Gipsy Scholar—but what does it *do* for you . . . in its poor way I think Sohrab and Rustum *animates*—the Gipsy Scholar at best awakes

a pleasing melancholy. But this is not what we want."[12] Arnold was quite wrong. What his readers have always wanted from him is more poems like "The Scholar-Gipsy" or the Cadmus and Harmonia episode from "Empedocles on Etna," that is to say, more pieces in which he realizes his poetic vocation without interference. Caught faithless between two worlds and "wavering between the profit and the loss," his vocation was to sing of melancholy and indecision, to express the sad confusion of desires that find no sufficient object, to create for us the self-conscious animal whose thinking runs ahead and undermines his present experience of happiness. The best poetry is a time-haunted, dimly lit *campagna* of regret, for all Arnold's wish that it should be something different. Not that the regret is simple and unmixed. The bracing of moral intention is never completely absent from the pieces I have in mind, but in them it appears inoffensively and always as a minor constituent, to make the regret stoically tight-lipped, to produce an effect that I can describe only as one of ravaged composure. The best poetry, then, is written by a "Celt" and pierces by its understatement. When the "Teuton" shoulders aside the "Celt," and morality takes charge, we get the priggish artificiality of "East London" or "The Second Best":

> Not here, O Apollo!
> Are haunts meet for thee . . .
> ("Empedocles," 421–422)

while in other poems, undoubtedly superior but still liable to worry us, it is impossible to say whether "Teuton" or "Celt" has gained the upper hand. "Palladium" may be cited as an example. A final class consists of poems innocent of a conscious moral intention but into whose conception too strong a willed element has entered, and we have then the blameless nullities of *Merope* and "Balder Dead."[13] "Sohrab and Rustum" is another "willed" poem, but, as I have already indicated, it managed to attach itself to Arnold's emotional life without his knowledge, and it draws whatever effectiveness it has from this source. In this brief account of the poetry it is fair to say that Arnold's deepest poetic intuition is of

---

[12]*Arnold to Clough*, no. 51, p. 146.
[13]This conjunction is perhaps a little unfair. *Merope* is virtually unreadable, whereas "Balder Dead" has many of the secondary poetic virtues and even some emotional vitality in the exchanges between Hermod and Balder toward the end of part 3.

The something that infects the world
("Resignation," 278)

and that he never makes us anxious for him as an artist when he writes of it (for instance, in "The Sick King in Bokhara"), or nostalgically of loss, or—at his most positive—of fortitude and resignation. On the other hand, his attempts to whistle up a simple cheerfulness are invariably poetic failures—even the modified optimism at the end of "Obermann Once More" has a counterfeit ring.

When Arnold discovered how dark were his gifts as a poet, he stopped writing poetry—an action for which we are prepared after the rejection of "Empedocles on Etna." In his letters the pathos of his middle-aged regret for the loss of his Ariel, whom he had handed over to perpetual confinement in the charge of a moralist, is real and moving. But as a poet he had then done what it was in him to do. In "Empedocles on Etna," "Resignation," and "The Sick King in Bokhara," in passages from "Sohrab and Rustum" and the unequal "Tristram and Iseult," in many of the shorter lyrics, and in almost all the elegiac pieces (including "Thyrsis" and "The Scholar-Gipsy"), we have his most genuine note. "Arnold is more intimate with us than Browning, more intimate than Tennyson ever is except at moments," Eliot observes justly, and it must be of some of these pieces that he is thinking. Henry James certainly had them in mind when he spoke with his customary exactitude of Arnold's "minor magic" and of his sensitive touching of "the particular ache, or regret, or conjecture, to which poetry is supposed to address itself." In a number of these successes it must be admitted that Arnold incurs the censure that he himself pronounced on those who substitute "thinking aloud" in poetry for "making something"—in his view a tendency encouraged by Wordsworth. A too casual thinking aloud seems to be the fault of "The Future," "The Buried Life," and "The Youth of Man," which are ramshackle in structure. (We recognize the support that the pastoral convention gave Arnold in "Thyrsis" and the advantages that he found in a well-defined subject in "A Southern Night" and "Stanzas from the Grande Chartreuse.") But these structural faults weaken without disabling the poems in which they occur, and it may be claimed for these pieces, as perhaps on behalf of the greater number of Arnold's poems, that they are more satisfying at the tenth than at the first reading, and more endearing than many Victorian poems that wear their too obvious hearts on gaudier sleeves. Let us set down here a typical penny-plain passage of Arnold's verse:

> Rais'd are the dripping oars,
> Silent the boat! the lake,
> Lovely and soft as a dream,
> Swims in the sheen of the moon.
> The mountains stand at its head
> Clear in the pure June-night,
> But the valleys are flooded with haze,
> Rydal and Fairfield are there;
> In the shadows Wordsworth lies dead.
> So it is, so it will be for aye.
> Nature is fresh as of old,
> Is lovely; a mortal is dead.
> ("The Youth of Nature," 1–12)

These verses chosen at random are in a quiet way impressive. There is no Keats in them and little Wordsworth. The vocabulary is simple, the moonlight and water are among Arnold's most pleasing stage properties, even the hint of a mechanical quality in the rhythm (which seems to be accepted as if to slight any charge of extravagance) is, I think, effective, and the whole verse paragraph lucidly projects the constraint put upon emotion. A reader may not be attracted by these unassuming lines and still find it possible to admire "Thyrsis" or "Dover Beach," but I do not think he can be said to have understood Arnold's poetic character unless they engage his sympathies.

Clearly an informed appreciation of Arnold as a poet must recognize the severe limitations of his gift. He has little poetic *élan* (the possession of which he envied Byron), slight ease, rare incandescence, no prodigality in phrase or metaphor: he spends his poetic income thriftily. He makes too much of excellence of subject, and one has unhappy memories of Benjamin Haydon's historical paintings and the old recipes for an epic—this is not to deny the significance of his protest against the overvaluing of the poetic "moment" and poetic frills by the "spasmodic" admirers of Keats in Arnold's own day. He is completely undramatic—the banality of the dialogue in the second part of "Tristram and Iseult" is disconcerting—and lack of dramatic sense narrows his scope as a narrative poet. He is uninventive in verse forms, limited in color and vocabulary in all but a very few pieces, repetitive in theme and situation, too often seriously insensitive to the sound of his poems. Such a line as the following in a poem that is something of a showpiece—

But when the moon their hollows lights
("To Marguerite—Continued," 7)

—is far from unusual; Tennyson would have shuddered at it. Yet Arnold triumphs over his maladroitness and unobtrusively creates a presumption in his own favor by the time we are ready to sit down in judgment. He is like a handicapped man whom his disabilities have taught a distinctive spryness and resource, and for whom we are prepared to make allowances. He triumphs by a feeling for poetic decorum in which many other Victorians were exasperatingly deficient, by his intelligent command of tone and temper, by an intimidating kind of honesty, for he steadily refuses to varnish his unease. He is an unfinished Giacomo Leopardi, comfortless in the Victorian Canaan. We understand at once what Hopkins means when he says that sometimes Arnold's poems "seem to have all the ingredients of poetry without quite being it," and we agree with him again when he continues, ". . . still they do not leave off of being, as the French say, very beautiful." When the devil's advocate has done his worst, "Empedocles on Etna" remains perhaps the best long poem by a Victorian, while in "Thyrsis," "The Scholar-Gipsy," and three or four shorter pieces (which do not include the overpraised and rather vapid "Requiescat") Arnold's poetry is no longer hobbled, and he escapes from his limitations, as a stutterer may escape in dreams, into speech of unimpeded fluency.

Arnold argued that his poetry represented "the main line of modern development" in his day and that this would finally recommend it to attention. He was prepared to await his turn. There is certainly a level of approach at which we can link many of Arnold's poems with Clough's "Dipsychus" and Herman Melville's "Clarel" under the heading of Victorian "poetry of doubt"—it may be useful to think of his influence on A. E. Housman and Edwin Arlington Robinson—but I have here preferred to suggest that his complaint against

. . . this strange disease of modern life
With its sick hurry, its divided aims . . .
("The Scholar-Gipsy," no. 78, 203–204)

betrays a more fundamental discontent. As a poet he is always, it seems to me, the romantic Celt struggling against the "despotism of fact." His muted nostalgia is for a wholeness and simplicity of experience that never was. By any normal system of

moral bookkeeping it may be reprehensible, and clearly the more robust comment on experience is "if you don't like it, you can lump it," but any man who has not buried his youth too deeply can understand Arnold. What evidence there is points to his being found more congenial today than any other mid-Victorian poet.

IV

In May 1853, Matthew Arnold wrote to Clough:

I catch myself desiring now at times political life, and this and that; and I say to myself—you do not desire these things because you are really adapted to them, and therefore the desire for them is merely contemptible—and it is so.

(*Arnold to Clough*, no. 44, p. 135)

Ten years later we find him writing to his mother:

It is very animating to think that one at last has a chance of getting at the English public. Such a public as it is and such a work as one wants to do with it.
(*Letters of Matthew Arnold, 1848–1888*, vol. I, pp. 233–34)

It is the gap between the self-regarding ethic of the first statement and the eager wish to interfere of the second that explains the plausibility of the late Professor E. K. Brown's *Matthew Arnold: A Study in Conflict*, the most acute study yet of Arnold as a prose writer, critic, and controversialist, in which it is argued that the objectivity of Arnold's criticism is flawed by his wish to be a moral leader, and that in the social essays detachment is often most flagrantly only a wraithlike appearance. In many places in Arnold's prose, Professor Brown held, it is proper to talk of a "strategy of disinterestedness," for the apparent candor and urbanity are almost exclusively at the service of an "interested disposition."

Once or twice already I have expressed reservations about this view. Evidently the poet speaks in the first letter quoted above, the son of Dr. Arnold in the second. But to agree with many other commentators that there is a conflict in Arnold, and that it casts a shadow over his writings, need not lead us to assume with Professor Brown that a crusading impulse is incompatible with a local and particular objectivity: if this were really so, one would expect Arnold's criticism to have some of the polemical extravagance of Ruskin's or the later Carlyle's. This view also fails to recognize how much of Arnold's most "detached" literary criticism we may owe to his missionary impulse. To put this naively, Arnold might very well have kept his *aperçus* to himself if he had not felt them to be useful when he began at the call of duty "to pull out a few more stops in that powerful but at present somewhat narrow-toned organ, the modern Englishman."

Arnold's prose works in the incomplete Macmillan collected edition run to ten volumes—this disregards his letters, and there are uncollected papers to fill two volumes more—and, within the confines of the present essay, I can hardly even signal the inclusiveness and authority of Arnold's interpretation of his age, or hope to submit Professor Brown's thesis to the examination that it deserves: instead I must say that in my opinion Arnold ordinarily succeeds in finding a third way between a limiting involvement in practical issues and a lack of interest in the social implications of his ideas. His "detachment" is more than a confidence-man's patter. If a "strategy of disinterestedness" exists in Arnold's wish to speak calmly and without rancor, the wish is in no sense Jesuitical: it stands both for the respect with which the writer approaches the truth and for the power of his writings to charm an audience. To a dispassionate reader "The Function of Criticism at the Present Time" in *Essays in Criticism* (1865) is quite explicit on the double need for disinterestedness and moral engagement. It tells us what Arnold thought he was doing and, in nine cases out of ten, it is what he was doing.

At this point it is obvious that limited space must enforce a paralyzing generality on any attempt to survey Arnold's prose. I propose to escape from this difficulty by indicating the motivation of Arnold's criticism as a whole, selecting a few topics, mostly in the literary criticism, for a rapid closer look. Such a bias may be justified because the literary criticism is in fact more often studied than the social and religious writings, and because it is superior to them in freshness, confidence, and ease—this is more especially true of the earlier critical essays. To come to *On Translating Homer* (1861) or *On the Study of Celtic Literature* (1867) straight from the poetry, or to turn back to them after being immersed in *Literature and Dogma* (1873) or *Last Essays on Church and Religion* (1877), is to find oneself in an atmosphere with an exhilaratingly high proportion of oxygen. This mood of the early criticism (with the exception perhaps of the valuable but partly perverse 1853

preface) exhibits publicly the excitement at discovering an unexpected second vocation that is characteristic of so many of Arnold's private letters to Clough—a correspondence third only to Keats's letters and Hopkins' letters on English literature for its sharp insights and its fascinating glimpse at the elliptical gamboling of a free intelligence. A famous passage in Sainte-Beuve's *Portraits Contemporains*, in which he speaks of a critical vocation often being concealed in youth by poetry and of criticism as "*un pis-aller honourable*," apparently came to Arnold—increasingly aware that his talent, though distinguished, was stinted—with the force of a revelation.

The most general motive of Arnold's criticism is ethical. He is almost without metaphysical passion, which may be the fundamental reason for F. H. Bradley's dislike of the religious writings, but his ethical passion is unmistakable. To Arnold metaphysical reasoning was simply methodical self-bewilderment, but he had as strongly as George Eliot the conviction that the moral law exists and speaks unequivocally in experience. On the one side, then, religion was ceremonial practices, which he supported *because* they were absurd—much as Walter Bagehot defended the decorative elements in the English constitution as "social cement." On the other side, religion was morality, which religious feeling could light up and transform into a driving force. The rest was overbelief (*Aberglaube*). In the eyes of orthodox churchmen, Arnold was "widening the rat-hole in the Temple," but he saw himself as a conservative. Miracles did not occur, theology was a pseudoscience, and literary tact discerned that theologians had done enormous violence to the loose figurative language of the Bible, language never meant to be precise, but thrown out at objects of consciousness not fully grasped. If the philosopher F. H. Bradley could tartly describe the God of Arnold's writings as no more than "an hypostasized copy-book heading," Arnold was quite sure that the traditional idea of God arose from a failure to distinguish the scientific and poetic uses of language. Arnold believed that he was defending religion by surrendering its untenable outposts, but we are more likely to feel that he was attempting—in an adaptation of Hartley Coleridge's phrase about Wordsworth—to smuggle Spinoza into the pulpit in a curate's ragged surplice.

What made Arnold so keen to save religion from its friends was his conviction of its social importance. Numerous impulses (including the religious one), he argued, must be met for man's harmonious development:

Money-making is not enough by itself. Industry is not enough by itself. Seriousness is not enough by itself. . . . The need in man for intellect and knowledge, his desire for beauty, his instinct for society, and for pleasurable and graceful forms of society, require to have their stimulus felt also, felt and satisfied.

("A Liverpool Address," vol. X, p. 83)

This is the master thought of Arnold's social writings. His experiences as a school inspector had made him peculiarly aware that social and political influence was passing into the hands of the middle class, which was quite unready for power and even unsuited to it. He could not turn hopefully from the Philistines to the old aristocracy. With a cool eye for a real lord and no faith in the Carlylean alternative of an industrial nobility, he confided in an ideal of democratic state action, and the state's first responsibility was to be in the field of education. The matter was urgent. The upper classes were materialized, the middle class was vulgarized, the lower classes were brutalized (the famous division into Barbarians, Philistines, and Populace). The state was the only possible source of national unity, but for a combination of reasons it was regarded with deep suspicion, and this made Arnold overemphatic and something less than disinterested in certain pages of *Culture and Anarchy* (1869).[14] The battle cry of Hebraism and Hellenism was important for all Englishmen, most important for the Philistines. Hebraism characterized the narrow life of that typical Philistine, the thrifty, earnest Dissenter who divided his time between countinghouse and chapel, sure of his solvency in this world and salvation in the next. He stood sadly in need of Hellenization; culture might woo

him from his dreary tea-meetings and temperance lectures (with lantern slides), his hymnal and his balance sheets. Culture might induce him to reexamine his stock notions and habits, might broaden his religious sympathies, might ultimately shame him into dissatisfaction with a "dismal, illiberal life" in Sheffield or Camberwell. In Arnold's opinion, culture spoke most persuasively through literature.[15]

This explanation of the main motive of Arnold's social thinking does not bring in all his important social ideas—it omits, for example, his stress on equality, the subject of an essay in 1878—but it is enough to show the link between the social and the literary criticism. In "The Function of Criticism at the Present Time," the failure of the romantic poets in spite of their prodigious creative talent is ascribed to a weakness in the surrounding cultural atmosphere. For a great creative epoch "two powers must concur, the power of the man and the power of the moment." Arnold sees a critical effort in his own generation as the necessary spadework for a new creative age. It is the critic's job by making available "the best that is known and thought in the world" to produce a "current of fresh and true ideas" in society. If he fails, the poet is unable to realize all his gifts or to produce work of the first order. The critic, then, is much more than a judge. At one and the same time he is a kind of midwife to artistic genius and the mediator between the artist and the general public.

Nothing takes precedence of the critic's function to supply fresh knowledge, and in speaking of this Arnold is a European.

But, after all, the criticism I am really concerned with . . . is a criticism which regards Europe as being, for intellectual and spiritual purposes, one great confederation, bound to a joint action and working to a common result; and whose members have, for their proper outfit, a knowledge of Greek, Roman, and Eastern antiquity, and of one another.

("The Function of Criticism at the Present Time," in *Essays in Criticism*, vol. III, p. 284)

Occasionally scholars have regretted the essays on minor figures of foreign literature (Joseph Joubert, Henri-Frédéric Amiel, et al.) as if they were a frivolous turning aside from the truly important, but Arnold has a ready answer. He is bringing to light comparatively unknown excellence, and while he is

---

[14]The appeal to find in the state a collective representation of the "best self" in every man has been supposed by some writers to have dangerous Hegelian overtones, but it was really no more than a political application of the religious idea of "dying to the old Adam." The state was to charge itself with supporting the "disinterested" ethical self of which every person was capable. It is quite wrong to suppose that Arnold had a sneaking weakness for authoritarianism; he came to look on Carlyle as a "moral desperado," and he was one of the few literary men who had no patience with the rowdy defense of Governor Eyre. Arnold had much the same view of the state as Dr. Arnold, and both looked back to Edmund Burke.

[15]*Culture and Anarchy* (1869), *Mixed Essays* (1879), and the satirical extravaganza *Friendship's Garland* (1871) are the most valuable of the social writings.

so engaged he avoids a very real danger: he runs no risk of interesting readers in his treatment of the subject at the expense of the subject itself (how much modern criticism of Shakespeare or Milton is X's judgment of Y's opinion of Z's remarks). Arnold thought the critic should explore widely and "welcome everything that is good," but this did not blur for him the distinctions between "excellent and inferior, sound and unsound and only half-sound." These distinctions were of "paramount importance." Arnold's severity can be measured by his remarks on the limiting effects of Milton's temper on his genius, or his disquiet when faced with the uneven copiousness of Shakespeare's style.

Two of the three most significant aspects that identify Arnold's critical practice have now been mentioned—namely, the concern with fresh information and the need to discriminate between what is excellent and what is less good while welcoming positive excellence even in unusual or subordinate "kinds." The third aspect has to do with his wholesome sense of the difficulty of criticism. His preference for the judgment that forms itself insensibly in the critic's mind (with its corollary that for the reader the critic's opinion should appear simply to make explicit what is implicit in the accompanying information) is clearly connected with his awareness of the delicacy of the critical act.

To handle these matters properly there is needed a poise so perfect that the least overweight in any direction tends to destroy the balance. . . . To press to the sense of the thing itself with which one is dealing, not to go off on some collateral issue about the thing, is the hardest matter in the world. The "thing itself" with which one is here dealing, the critical perception of poetic truth, is of all things the most volatile, elusive, and evanescent; by even pressing too impetuously after it, one runs the risk of losing it. The critic of poetry should have the finest tact, the nicest moderation, the most free, flexible, and elastic spirit imaginable; he should be indeed the "ondoyant et divers," the *undulating and diverse* being of Montaigne.

("On Translating Homer: Last Words," vol. I, p. 174)

Again, the care to reach the truth exemplified in this passage is certainly not unrelated to Arnold's desire to charm. To charm meant to investigate his subject in such a way that the reader's own prejudices should not be interposed between him and what the critic had taken so much trouble to say.

Around this just and comprehensive understanding of the critic's task, the counters of Arnold's criticism—"high seriousness," "natural magic," "the grand style," "*Architectonicè*"—group themselves, not as precise meanings, but as instruments he found useful in obtaining a view of the truth and in creating for his readers an intimate sense of his critical adequacy. Arnold's prose style should be noticed in a study of his technique of persuasion. It has several modes, including the lyrical and the willfully impertinent—both are illustrated in the preface to the second edition of *Essays in Criticism* (1869)—but the usual middle style resembles Newman's prose in its subtle vitality. Perhaps the similarity is more than stylistic, and it may be right to be reminded of Newman's psychological account of what we do when we reason or believe, as we read Arnold's description of what constitutes the critical act.

In what has been said, there is a basis of justification for calling Arnold a great critic. The argument would need to be completed in a fuller discussion by an analysis of his remarks on Homer, Dante, Shakespeare, Milton, Voltaire, Thomas Gray, Dr. Johnson, Leopardi, Heinrich Heine, and the English romantic poets—to mention only a few of those to whom he paid attention. In some instances the necessary assembling of scattered references has yet to be attempted; and perhaps some modern critics have been overhasty in giving us Arnold's opinion on a particular topic without making a real effort to discover what it was. It is possible that on many of these subjects we might not express ourselves exactly as he did, but this is unimportant. Occasionally—for example, in discussing Byron as a man of feeling—I think that he misses the point, but quite often he comes very close to a reputable contemporary opinion: I would cite in evidence his parenthetic observation that Shelley's "natural magic" is almost entirely in his rhythm and hardly at all in his language; or, again, the several judgments on Goethe, which add up to a very respectable whole view (and what a triumph of detachment, in its Victorian context, his reserved attitude to *Wilhelm Meister* represents). Such successes more than cancel his too much paraded critical howlers, some of which are susceptible of a kind of defense. For example, Arnold's opinion that Dryden and Pope are "classics of our prose" shows that he failed to appreciate the Augustan achievement in poetry, but it pithily expresses that turning down of the imaginative lamps that any reader must feel as he moves from a study of the great Renaissance poets to the poetic literature of the late seventeenth and early eighteenth centuries.

In estimating Arnold's special importance as a critic today, debate about the supersession of this or that opinion is unhelpful. What matters is his example of serious critical responsibility. Literary criticism was not a matter of self-expression for Arnold. He directs attention at his subject and away from his own dexterity. He does his best to steer clear of aesthetics and general theories of literature (which fascinated Coleridge certainly but are usually the infatuation of lesser men). He commits himself unambiguously and in an unpedantic language, and he makes no secret of the relationship between his literary opinions and his views on the great questions of life and society. His candor is never ill-humored. In all these respects, T. S. Eliot is his only rival. I have already said that these two major critics complement each other in a variety of ways. No better exercise for sharpening the wits can be imagined than the setting up of one against the other on any topic on which they overlap. For several decades now we have used Eliot to correct Matthew Arnold. It is useful to remember that the process can run in reverse.

SELECTED BIBLIOGRAPHY

I. BIBLIOGRAPHIES. T. B. Smart, *The Bibliography of Matthew Arnold* (London, 1892), revised and expanded, in *The Works*, vol. XV (London, 1904); T. J. Wise, *Catalogue of the Ashley Library*, vol. I (London, 1922); T. G. Ehrsam, R. H. Deily, and R. M. Smith, *Bibliographies of Twelve Victorian Authors* (London, 1936); V. L. Tollers, ed., *A Bibliography of Matthew Arnold 1932-1970* (University Park, Pa., 1974).

II. CONCORDANCE. S. M. Parrish, ed., *A Concordance of the Poems of Matthew Arnold* (Ithaca, N.Y., 1959).

III. COLLECTED EDITIONS. G. W. E. Russell, ed., *The Works of Matthew Arnold*, 15 vols. (London, 1903-1904), contains the poems (vols. I and II), the prose works (vols. III-XII), and the letters (vols. XIII-XV), but omits various uncollected essays.

IV. POETRY. *Poems: A New and Complete Edition* (Boston, 1856); *Poems*, 2 vols. (London, 1869), contains narrative and elegiac poems (vol. I), dramatic and lyric poems (vol. II); *Poems. New and Complete Edition*, 2 vols. (London, 1877), contains early poems, narrative poems, and sonnets (vol. I), and lyric, dramatic, and elegiac poems (vol. II); *Poems*, 3 vols. (London, 1885), contains early poems, narrative poems, and sonnets (vol. I), lyric and elegiac poems (vol. II), dramatic and later poems (vol. III); the first comprehensive ed. and the last ed. supervised by Arnold; *The Poetical Works* (London, 1890), the Globe ed.; H. S. M.[ilford], ed., *The Poems, 1840-1867* (Oxford, 1909), intro. by A. T. Quiller-Couch, repr. seven times until 1940, reiss. as *The Poetical Works* (Oxford, 1942; repr. 1945), with poems written after 1867; C. B. Tinker and H. F. Lowry, eds., *Poetical Works* (London, 1950), with critical apparatus; K. Allott, ed., *The Poems of Matthew Arnold* (London, 1965), contains material omitted from *Poetical Works* (1950) and is fully annotated, 2nd ed. by M. Allott (London, 1979), among the new poems not included in the 1965 ed. are two pieces later found by K. Allott and some seven youthful poems written in the period 1836-1841, included by the second editor; other emendations include the reordering of some poems because of the first editor's fresh weighing of evidence and their dates of composition, and additional variant readings for certain poems based on the renewed study of manuscript material; K. Allott and M. Allott, eds., *Poems* (London, 1979), the Annotated English Poets series.

V. PROSE. *Works*, 10 vols. (1883-1903), the Smith, Elder & Co. "Popular" ed., contains all the important prose vols. except *Essays in Criticism*, First and Second Series, and *Discourses in America*; *Essays by Matthew Arnold* (Oxford, 1914), contains *Essays in Criticism*, First Series, *On Translating Homer* (with F. W. Newman's reply), *On Translating Homer: Last Words*, and five essays "hitherto uncollected" in Great Britain, four of these essays had already appeared in the American *Essays in Criticism*, Third Series (see below); R. H. Super, ed., *Complete Prose Works*, 11 vols. (Ann Arbor, Mich., 1960-1977), in chronological order with textual notes and explanatory commentary, contains *On the Classical Tradition* (vol. I), *Democratic Education* (vol. II), *Lectures and Essays in Criticism* (vol. III), *Schools and Universities on the Continent* (vol. IV), *Culture and Anarchy with Friendship's Garland and Some Literary Essays* (vol. V), *Dissent and Dogma* (vol. VI), *God and the Bible* (vol. VII), *Essays Religious and Mixed* (vol. VIII), *English Literature and Irish Politics* (vol. IX), *Philistinism in England and America* (vol. X), *The Last Word* (vol. XI).

VI. SELECTIONS. *Selected Poems* (London, 1878), selected by Arnold himself; W. Buckler, ed., *Passages from the Prose Writings of Matthew Arnold* (London, 1880), selected by Arnold himself; L. Trilling, ed., *The Portable Matthew Arnold* (New York-London, 1949); J. Bryson, ed., *Matthew Arnold: Poetry and Prose* (London, 1954), the Reynard Library ed., a comprehensive selection that includes some of Arnold's letters; A. D. Culler, ed., *Poetry and Criticism of Matthew Arnold* (Boston, 1961), the Riverside ed.; C. Ricks, ed., *Selected Criticism* (New York, 1972), the Signet Classics series; G. Sutherland, ed., *Arnold on Education* (London, 1977); M. Allott, ed., *Selected Poems and Prose* (London, 1978). *Note:* Verse and prose selections are numerous. Selections from the verse have appeared in the Temple Classics, the World's Classics, the Muses' Library, Everyman's Library. Among prose selections the following should be noted: L. E. Gates, ed., *Selections from the Prose Writings (New York, 1898); D. C. Somervell, ed., Selections from Matthew Arnold's Prose (London, 1924); E. K. Brown, ed., Representative Essays of Matthew Arnold (Toronto, 1936), which contains some reprinted passages from early eds.

VII. SEPARATE WORKS. Alaric at Rome: A Prize Poem, Recited in Rugby School (Rugby, 1840), a facs. was privately printed by T. J. Wise (London, 1893); Cromwell: A Prize Poem, Recited in the Theatre, Oxford (Oxford, 1843); The Strayed Reveller, and Other Poems, by "A" (London, 1849); Empedocles on Etna, and Other Poems, by "A" (London, 1852); Poems, new ed. (London, 1853), repr. poems from 1849 and 1852, includes a critical preface and, among the new poems, "Sohrab and Rustum" and "The Scholar-Gipsy"; Poems, 2nd ed. (London, 1854), without five poems included in the 1st ed. but with "A Farewell," first published in 1852, and a further brief preface; Poems, Second Series (London, 1855), repr. poems from 1849 and 1852, includes "Balder Dead" and one other new poem; Poems, 3rd ed. (London, 1857), repr. of the 1854 collection with a new piece in the "Switzerland" group; Merope: A Tragedy (London, 1858), verse with a preface, also annotated in J. C. Collins, ed. (Oxford, 1906); England and the Italian Question (London, 1859), also in M. Bevington, ed., with "Matthew Arnold and the Italian Question" by J. Fitzjames Stephen (Durham, N.C., 1953); The Popular Education of France with Notices of that of Holland and Switzerland (London, 1861); On Translating Homer: Three Lectures Given at Oxford (London, 1861), also in W. H. D. Rouse, ed. (London, 1905); On Translating Homer: Last Words: A Lecture Given at Oxford (London, 1862); A French Eton; or, Middle Class Education and the State (London, 1864); Essays in Criticism (London, 1865), known as "First Series," the 2nd ed. (1869) has a condensed preface, the 3rd ed. contains an additional essay "A Persian Passion Play," also usefully annotated in C. A. Miles and L. Smith, eds. (Oxford, 1918); On the Study of Celtic Literature (London, 1867), also in A. Nutt, ed. (London, 1910), repr. in Everyman's Library (London, 1977); New Poems (London, 1867), includes "Empedocles on Etna," repr. for the first time since 1852, and six other pieces that had already appeared in a collection; Schools and Universities on the Continent (London, 1868); Culture and Anarchy: An Essay in Political and Social Criticism (London, 1869), also in J. D. Wilson, ed. (Cambridge, 1932).

St. Paul and Protestantism: With an Introduction on Puritanism and the Church of England (London, 1870), the Popular ed. of 1887 contains a new preface and "A Comment on Christmas"; Friendship's Garland: Being the Conversations, Letters, and Opinions of the Late Arminius, Baron Von Thunder-Ten-Tronckh. Collected and Edited, with a Dedicatory Letter to Adolescens Leo, Esq., of "The Daily Telegraph" (London, 1871); Literature and Dogma: An Essay Towards a Better Apprehension of the Bible (London, 1873), the Popular ed. of 1883 is condensed;

Higher Schools and Universities in Germany (London, 1874), repr. of the German chapters of Schools and Universities on the Continent; God and the Bible: A Review of Objections to "Literature and Dogma" (London, 1875), the Popular ed. of 1884 is condensed; Last Essays on Church and Religion (London, 1877); Mixed Essays (London, 1879); Irish Essays and Others (London, 1882); Discourses in America (London, 1885); Education Department: Special Report on Certain Points Connected with Elementary Education in Germany, Switzerland, and France (London, 1886), repr. by the Education Reform League with a brief prefatory note (London, 1888); General Grant: An Estimate (Boston, 1887), the two parts of this essay have not appeared as a book or been included in any collection of Arnold's essays in Great Britain; Essays in Criticism, Second Series (London, 1888); Civilization in the United States: First and Last Impressions (Boston, 1888), contains General Grant and three essays on America; F. Sandford, ed., Reports on Elementary Schools, 1852–1882 (London, 1889), also in F. S. Marvin, ed. (London, 1908).

Matthew Arnold's Notebooks (London, 1902), preface by the Hon. Mrs. Wodehouse, a brief selection; Essays in Criticism, Third Series (Boston, 1910), the essays on Renan and Tauler have not been collected in Great Britain; B. Matthews, ed., Letters of an Old Playgoer (New York, 1919), these letters appear in The Works, vol. IV (London, 1904); H. F. Lowry, K. Young, and W. H. Dunn, eds., The Note-Books of Matthew Arnold (London, 1952), the literary contents of Arnold's notebooks and his reading lists, essential for students; K. Allott, ed., Five Uncollected Essays of Matthew Arnold (Liverpool, 1953), contains Arnold's three essays on America, an uncollected essay on Sainte-Beuve, and "A Liverpool Address"; F. Neiman, ed., Essays, Letters, and Reviews by Matthew Arnold (Cambridge, Mass., 1960), collects and annotates uncollected pieces by Arnold, including some anonymous items recently identified, essential for students. Note: For works arranged and edited by Arnold or containing contributions by him, see Smart's Bibliography, pp. 37–42.

VIII. LETTERS. G. W. E. Russell, ed., Letters of Matthew Arnold, 1848–1888, 2 vols. (London, 1895), censored by Arnold's family and the arranger, has no index; A. Whitridge, ed., Unpublished Letters of Matthew Arnold (New Haven, Conn., 1923); H. F. Lowry, ed., The Letters of Matthew Arnold to Arthur Hugh Clough (Oxford, 1932), contains two valuable introductory chapters; W. E. Buckler, ed., Matthew Arnold's Books: Toward a Publishing Diary (Paris–Geneva, 1958), includes numerous extracts from Arnold's letters to his publishers between 1860 and 1888, with introductory chapter and brief notes; A. K. Davis, Jr., ed., Matthew Arnold's Letters: A Descriptive Checklist (Charlottesville, Va., 1968), lists 2,658 letters—more than half of them unpublished—and 2,506 different correspondents.

IX. BIOGRAPHICAL AND CRITICAL STUDIES. W. Rossetti,

review of *The Strayed Reveller* in the *Germ: Thoughts Towards Nature in Poetry, Literature, and Art*, no. 2 (February 1850); *The Poems and Prose Remains of A. H. Clough* (London, 1869), vol. I contains a review (1853) of Arnold's early poetry; A. C. Swinburne, *Essays and Studies* (London, 1857), includes a good essay on Arnold's *New Poems* (1867); F. H. Bradley, *Ethical Studies* (London, 1876), contains a merciless dissection of Arnold's religious views in a clever parody of his style; W. H. Mallock, *The New Republic . . .* (London, 1877), "Mr. Luke" is a satirical portrait of Arnold; R. H. Hutton, *Literary Essays*, 2nd ed. (London, 1877), includes an essay on Arnold's poetry; F. Harrison, *The Choice of Books* (London, 1886), contains "Culture: A Dialogue" (1867); J. M. Robertson, *Modern Humanists* (London, 1891), contains a useful study of Arnold, *Modern Humanists Reconsidered* appeared in 1927; A. Birrell, *Res Judicatae* (London, 1892), includes a short study of Arnold; J. G. Fitch, *Thomas and Matthew Arnold and Their Influence on English Education* (London, 1897); L. Stephen, *Studies of a Biographer* (London, 1898), vol. II contains a study of Arnold; G. Saintsbury, *Matthew Arnold* (London, 1899).

T. Arnold, *Passages in a Wandering Life* (London, 1900), an important source for Matthew Arnold's early life; A. G. Butler, *The Three Friends: A Story of Rugby in the Forties* (Oxford, 1900), contains an agreeable description of Arnold in his "dandy" phase; W. C. Brownell, *Victorian Prose Masters* (New York, 1901); H. W. Paul, *Matthew Arnold* (London, 1902), English Men of Letters series; G. W. E. Russell, *Matthew Arnold* (London, 1904); E. H. Coleridge, *Life and Correspondence of John Duke Coleridge* (London, 1904), includes some interesting letters by Arnold; W. H. Dawson, *Matthew Arnold and His Relation to the Thought of Our Time* (London, 1904); H. James, *Views and Reviews* (London, 1908), includes a review (1865) of *Essays in Criticism*, First Series, see also the essay by James in the *English Illustrated Magazine*, vol. I (January 1884); A. P. Kelso, *Matthew Arnold on Continental Life and Literature* (Oxford, 1914); Mrs. Humphrey Ward, *A Writer's Recollections* (London, 1918), by Arnold's niece, the author of *Robert Elsmere* (London, 1888).

H. J. C. Grierson, *Lord Byron: Arnold and Swinburne* (London, 1921), the Warton Lecture on English Poetry for the British Academy, repr. in *The Background of English Literature . . .* (London, 1934); W. P. Ker, *The Art of Poetry* (London, 1923); W. Raleigh, *Some Authors* (Oxford, 1923); R. E. C. Houghton, *The Influence of the Classics on the Poetry of Matthew Arnold* (Oxford, 1923); J. M. Murry, *Discoveries* (London, 1924); H. Kingsmill, *Matthew Arnold* (London, 1928); A. Whitridge, *Dr. Arnold of Rugby* (New York, 1928); J. B. Orrick, *Matthew Arnold and Goethe* (London, 1928), publication of the English Goethe Society, n.s., vol. IV; H. W. Garrod, *Poetry and the Criticism of Life* (Oxford, 1931), includes three lectures on Arnold; C. H. Harvey, *Matthew Arnold* (London, 1931); E. Chambers, *Matthew Arnold* (London, 1932), the Warton Lecture on English Poetry for the British Academy; T. S. Eliot, *Selected Essays* (London, 1932), contains "Arnold and Pater" (1930); T. S. Eliot, *The Use of Poetry and the Use of Criticism* (London, 1933), contains a brilliant, unsympathetic account of Arnold; F. J. C. Hearnshaw, ed., *The Social and Political Ideas of the Victorian Age* (London, 1933), includes "Matthew Arnold and the Educationists," a valuable essay on Arnold's social thinking by J. D. Wilson; F. W. Bateson, *English Poetry and the English Language* (Oxford, 1934), contains interesting remarks on Arnold's poetic diction; E. K. Brown, *Studies in the Text of Matthew Arnold's Prose Works* (Paris, 1935); I. E. Sells, *Matthew Arnold and France* (Cambridge, 1935), explores the influence of Senancour and includes an unpublished early poem by Arnold; F. R. Leavis, *Revaluation* (London, 1936), contains a note on Arnold's poetry, see also Leavis' "Arnold as Critic," in *Scrutiny* (December 1938); C. Stanley, *Matthew Arnold* (Toronto, 1938); L. Trilling, *Matthew Arnold* (London, 1939), a sympathetic and penetrating study of Arnold's ideas by a liberal critic; B. Groom, *On the Diction of Tennyson, Browning and Arnold* (Oxford, 1939), S. P. E. Tract, no. 53, useful.

C. B. Tinker and H. F. Lowry, *The Poetry of Matthew Arnold: A Commentary* (London, 1940), still essential for the student but now to be used with caution; G. H. Ford, *Keats and the Victorians . . .* (New Haven, Conn., 1945), pt. 2 is a sensitive examination of Keats's influence on Arnold; E. K. Chambers, *Matthew Arnold* (Oxford, 1947); L. Bonnerot, *Matthew Arnold, Poète* (Paris, 1947), scholarly and formidably detailed, an app. contains Arnold's letters to Sainte-Beuve, includes excellent bibliography; E. K. Brown, *Matthew Arnold: A Study in Conflict* (Chicago, 1948), stimulating; I. Macdonald, *The Buried Self: A Background to the Poems of Matthew Arnold, 1848–1851* (London, 1949), fiction but interestingly documented; W. F. Connell, *The Educational Thought and Influence of Matthew Arnold* (London, 1950), a scholarly survey; F. E. Faverty, *Matthew Arnold the Ethnologist* (Evanston, Ill., 1951); G. Tillotson, *Criticism and the Nineteenth Century* (London, 1951), contains three valuable essays on Arnold; E. D. H. Johnson, *The Alien Vision of Victorian Poetry* (Princeton, N.J., 1952), contains a section on Arnold's poetry; J. Holloway, *The Victorian Sage: Studies in Argument* (London, 1953), includes an interesting discussion of Arnold's techniques of persuasion; N. Wymer, *Dr. Arnold of Rugby* (London, 1953), makes use of much unpublished material, including an early poem by Arnold; F. J. Woodward, *The Doctor's Disciples* (London, 1954); J. D. Jump, *Matthew Arnold* (London, 1955); K. Tillotson, *Matthew Arnold and Carlyle* (London, 1956), the Warton Lecture on English Poetry for the British Academy, scholarly and stimulating; F. L. Mulhauser, ed., *The Correspondence of Arthur Hugh Clough* (Oxford, 1957), contains many new references to Arnold; J. H. Raleigh, *Matthew Arnold and American Culture* (Berkeley–Los Angeles, 1957), of particular interest to readers outside America; W. A. Jamison, *Arnold and the Romantics* (Copenhagen, 1958); P. F. Baum, *Ten Studies in the Poetry of Matthew Arnold* (Durham, N.C.,1958); V. Buckley, *Poetry and Morality: Studies in the Criticism of Matthew Arnold, T. S. Eliot and F. R. Leavis* (London, 1959); W. Robbins, *The Ethical Idealism of Matthew Arnold* (London, 1959).

T. W. Bamford, *Thomas Arnold* (London, 1960); W. S. Johnson, *The Voices of Matthew Arnold* (New Haven, Conn., 1961); D. G. James, *Matthew Arnold and the Decline of English Romanticism* (Oxford, 1961), a hostile look at Arnold as a critic; G. T. Fairclough, *A Fugitive and Gracious Light: The Relation of Joseph Joubert to Matthew Arnold's Thought*, University of Nebraska Studies, n.s., no. 23 (Lincoln, Nebr., 1961); H. C. Duffin, *Arnold the Poet* (London, 1962); L. Gottfried, *Matthew Arnold and the Romantics* (London, 1963), the best study of this subject; A. O. J. Cockshut, *The Unbelievers* (London, 1964); P. W. Day, *Matthew Arnold and the Philosophy of Vice* (Auckland, 1964); P. J. McCarthy, *Matthew Arnold and The Three Classes* (London, 1964); F. J. W. Harding, *Matthew Arnold the Critic and France* (Geneva, 1964); E. Alexander, *Matthew Arnold and John Stuart Mill* (London, 1965); W. D. Anderson, *Matthew Arnold and the Classical Tradition* (Ann Arbor, Mich., 1965); D. J. DeLaura, *Matthew Arnold and John Henry Newman*, University of Texas Studies in Literature and Language, vol. VI (Austin, Tex.,1965); G. Tillotson and K. Tillotson, *Mid-Victorian Studies* (London, 1965); E. Frykman, *"Bitter Knowledge" and "Unconquerable Hope": A Thematic Study of Attitudes Towards Life in Matthew Arnold's Poetry 1849–1853* (Gothenberg, 1966); A. D. Culler, *Imaginative Reason: The Poetry of Matthew Arnold* (New Haven, Conn., 1966), intelligent and lively, but sometimes fanciful in interpretation; J. Bertram, ed., *New Zealand Letters of Thomas Arnold the Younger* (London, 1966), contains many references to Matthew Arnold and the family circle at Fox How; G. R. Strange, *Matthew Arnold: The Poet as Humanist* (Princeton, N. J., 1967); W. A. Madden, *Matthew Arnold: A Study of the Aesthetic Temperament in Victorian England* (Bloomington, Ind., 1967), discusses the poetry and, more summarily, the prose; S. Potter, ed., *Essays and Studies* (London, 1968), contains a study of Arnold's "Empedocles on Etna"; F. R. Leavis, "Arnold as Critic," in *A Selection from Scrutiny* (Cambridge, 1968); C. Dawson, ed., *Matthew Arnold: The Critical Heritage* (London, 1973); K. Allott, ed., *Matthew Arnold: A Symposium* (London, 1975), includes F. Newman, "A Reader's Guide to Arnold," W. Madden, "Arnold the Poet: Lyric and Elegiac Poems," K. Allott and M. Allott, "Arnold the Poet: Narrative and Dramatic Poems," D. J. DeLaura, "Arnold and Literary Criticism: Critical Ideas," R. H. Super, "Arnold and Literary Criticism: Critical Practice," J. Bertram, "Arnold and Clough," P. Keating, "Arnold's Social and Political Thought," B. Willey, "Arnold and Religion," W. Anderson, "Arnold and the Classics," J. Simpson, "Arnold and Goethe"; W. Robbins, *The Ethical Idealism of Matthew Arnold: A Study of the Nature and Sources of His Religious Ideas* (Toronto, 1975); L. Trilling, *Matthew Arnold* (London, 1976); A. L. Rowse, *Matthew Arnold: Poet and Prophet* (London, 1976); M. Allott, ed., *Matthew Arnold* (London, 1978); J. Simpson, *Matthew Arnold and Goethe* (London, 1979); C. Dawson and J. Pfordresher, eds., *Matthew Arnold, Prose Writings: The Critical Heritage* (London, 1979); P. Horan, *Matthew Arnold* (London, 1979).

GEORGE MEREDITH
(1828-1909)

Phyllis Bartlett

I

GEORGE MEREDITH was by preference a poet, by profession a novelist. Inadvertently, he wrote the most famous English essay on comedy. A recent historian of the English novel aptly quoted a sentence from Meredith's admirer Robert Louis Stevenson to sum up much that is best in Meredith's work: "To me these things are the good; beauty, touched with sex and laughter; beauty with God's earth for the background." Meredith would have added mind to Stevenson's creed, for without intelligence at work, sex degenerates into sensualism, and man is incapable of comic laughter. Meredith leads his readers past the morbid emotions, which he well knew how to dissect, into a healthy, intelligent, luminous world. As the poet Siegfried Sassoon said at the end of his book on Meredith, "the idea of Meredith means a sense of being fully alive. To be at one's best is to be Meredithian."

Born at Portsmouth on 12 February 1828, Meredith was privately educated. The most advanced schooling that Meredith ever had was when from the age of fourteen to sixteen he attended a school conducted by the Moravian Brothers at Neuwied on the Rhine, and these two years evidently led him to the abiding belief that the good life included international involvement: travel, a daily study of foreign as well as domestic politics, and a detailed knowledge of European history and literature. Among his earliest exercises in verse were translations from German poets, and late in life he wrote that "the noble Goethe" had been "the most enduring of the formative readings of his youth."[1] His favorite vacations were spent walking in the Tyrolean and Italian Alps or in the south of France, and he felt that he understood Austrians, Italians, and Frenchmen as well as he understood Germans. But among all these sympathies, his final affiliation was France. Beginning with an absorbed interest in the long poem *Mirèio* (1859) of Frédéric Mistral and the problem of translating the Provençal dialect into English, his interest in French literature led him to become a profound scholar of the France of Molière and of the history of modern France. His self-education in classical as well as in English and European literature is impressive. Meredith spontaneously practiced what his contemporary Matthew Arnold preached as the main business of criticism: he tried "to know the best that is known and thought in the world."

II

MEREDITH found poetry easier to write than prose fiction, and since he started his long career by writing poems, he will be introduced as poet before he is shown as novelist. When he was twenty-three he published at his own expense a volume that he could ill afford, starkly titled *Poems* (1851). The publication was premature, as he soon realized, but the variety of the book's contents forecast his future range. It contained poems with classical subjects, pastorals, a sociological study of "London by Lamplight," the first celebration of his lifelong passion for the southwest wind, and many songs. It also contained a sketch of "Love in the Valley," a fascinatingly sensuous diary of young love, unrivaled in English, that he rewrote and expanded more than a quarter of a century later. The poem begins:

> Under yonder beech-tree single on the green-sward,
>   Couched with her arms behind her golden head,
> Knees and tresses folded to slip and ripple idly,
>   Lies my young love sleeping in the shade.

[1] W. Allen, *The English Novel, A Short Critical History* (London, 1954), p. 227.

Had I the heart to slide an arm beneath her,
  Press her parting lips as her waist I gather slow,
Waking in amazement she could not but embrace me:
  Then would she hold me and never let me go?[2]

This is the later version, but the sight of the sleeping girl had been the inspiration for his first manuscript draft.

Meredith dedicated this volume to his father-in-law, Thomas Love Peacock, the poet and satirical novelist who had been a good friend of Percy Bysshe Shelley. In 1849, Meredith had married Peacock's daughter, Mary, a widow several years older than he: beautiful, clever, and erratic. After eight years this marriage collapsed; Mary left him for another man, a liaison that did not last long, and in 1861 she died.[3] What Meredith learned of jealousy and the analysis of heartbreaking emotions through this ordeal went into the making of a kind of love poem totally different from "Love in the Valley"—"Modern Love," the poem that gave his second volume of poetry its main title: *Modern Love, and Poems of the English Roadside, with Poems and Ballads* (1862).

Modern Love, composed of fifty sixteen-line sonnets, is Meredith's poetic masterpiece in the tragic mode, but it contains the wisdom that led him out of emotional disaster into the common sense of common day. It was a poem that shocked most reviewers because it was such an open analysis of an unhappy marriage. The first sentence alone, with its perfect snake imagery, is naked in its intimacy:

> By this he knew she wept with waking eyes:
> That, at his hand's light quiver by her head,
> The strange low sobs that shook their common bed
> Were called into her with a sharp surprise,
> And strangled mute, like little gaping snakes,
> Dreadfully venomous to him. . . .
>
>   (I, p. 133)

Toward the end of the poem the wife makes an attempt to be sexually kind to her husband, but the next morning by the seashore, the intense image of the waves and sand perfectly expresses to him the quality of their experience:

Mark where the pressing wind shoots javelin-like,
Its skeleton shadow on the broad-backed wave!
Here is a fitting spot to dig Love's grave;
Here where the ponderous breakers plunge and strike,
And dart their hissing tongues high up the sand:
In hearing of the ocean, and in sight
Of those ribbed wind-streaks running into white.
If I the death of Love had deeply planned,
I never could have made it half so sure,
As by the unblest kisses which upbraid
The full-waked sense; or failing that, degrade!
'Tis morning: but no morning can restore
What we have forfeited. I see no sin:
The wrong is mixed. In tragic life, God wot,
No villain need be! Passions spin the plot:
We are betrayed by what is false within.
              (XLIII, p. 152)

The last two sentences of this sonnet have been much quoted, and they are indeed a key to much of Meredith's poetry as well as to his novels. They are one of the "great, flashing, transfigured platitudes," in which, according to C. Day Lewis, Meredith spoke his wisdom, as did Shakespeare.[4] Another great platitude occurs in the last sonnet when the poet tries to sum up what fundamentally had gone wrong with this highly sensitive husband and wife. Not content with the present, they had examined the past too much:

> Then each applied to each that fatal knife,
> Deep questioning, which probes to endless dole.
> Ah, what a dusty answer gets the soul
> When hot for certainties in this our life!—
>   (L, p. 155)

The *Poems of the English Roadside* alluded to in the title of the *Modern Love* volume are "Juggling Jerry," "The Old Chartist," and "The Beggar's Soliloquy." They are colloquial, thoughtful monologues, indicating the respect the poet felt for the characters he would stop and talk with on his country walks.

Meredith did not publish another volume of poems for twenty-one years, very likely because he could not afford to. Soon after purging himself with "Modern Love," he had married again, a sweet, stable woman of French extraction, and he had three children to support, one by his first wife and two by his second. He published eight novels during this

[2]*The Poetical Works of George Meredith,* with some notes by G. M. Trevelyan (London–New York, 1912), p. 230. The first version (1851) is on p. 573. All poems are cited from this edition.
[3]See J. I. M. Stewart, "Thomas Love Peacock," in *British Writers,* vol. IV (New York, 1981).

[4]Introduction to *Modern Love* (London, 1948), p. xxvi.

long interval, earned a steady income by a boring job as reader for Chapman and Hall, and sold poems to good periodicals. A number of these poems have for their subject mythological or historical characters. Perhaps the most arresting of these is "The Nuptials of Attila," a long poem in swift rhythm, with refrains, that tells of the Hun's mysterious death in his bride's bed.

It was in *Poems and Lyrics of the Joy of Earth* (1883) and *A Reading of Earth* (1888) that Meredith emerged as a philosophical nature poet, a position he holds in any study of nineteenth-century English thought about nature and man.[5]

The volume of 1883 opens with a difficult poem, "The Woods of Westermain," and the adjuration:

> Enter these enchanted woods,
> You who dare.
>
> (I, p. 193)

Woods, immemorially emblematic of life's experiences, are in this poem the woods of nature, which will be frightening to those who fear her, benign to those who do not. Early in the poem is a striking reflection on what the sight of oxen ruminating suggests: the evolution of man, the emergence of Earth from water, and a time when matter had not consolidated into the heavenly bodies:

> . . . where old-eyed oxen chew
> Speculation with the cud,
> Read their pool of vision through,
> Back to hours when mind was mud:
> Nigh the knot, which did untwine
> Timelessly to drowsy suns;
> Seeing Earth a slimy spine,
> Heaven a space for winging tons.
>
> (III, p. 195)

In this one sentence, occurring in a list of nature's bounties, Meredith expresses his acceptance of the most up-to-date science. Never a man with an orthodox religion to be shaken by scientific discoveries, he welcomed whatever knowledge came his way. Bonamy Dobrée has well remarked that Meredith did not make an effort to understand evolution intellectual-

ly; rather "he allowed it to act upon him till it became part of his intuition. Far from avoiding evolution, he translated it altogether out of the region of science, properly speaking. For him evolution was a series of steps from earth to mind, and thence to spirit. . . ."[6] Meredith was a genuine evolutionary meliorist, but, like Shelley, another poet infused with scientific discoveries, he thought that the processes of nature could be helped along by human endeavor. Thus, he explains in "The Woods of Westermain" that the dragon of the woods is self, by which he means an inflated belief in the importance of one's own personality. Even this great human weakness is subject to change:

> Him shall Change, transforming late,
> Wonderously renovate.
> Hug himself the creature may:
> What he hugs is loathed decay.
> Crying, slip the scales, and slough!
>
> (IV, p. 199)

Self can be remade into a useful servant of society; Norman Kelvin has accurately named the theory "social Lamarckism."[7]

A lovely poem in the same volume as "The Woods of Westermain," "The Lark Ascending," after describing at length the skylark's song, contrasts it to man's, which can never be so sweet because:

> Our wisdom speaks from failing blood,
> Our passion is too full in flood,
> We want the key of this wild note
> Of truthful in a tuneful throat,
> The song seraphically free
> Of taint of personality,
>
> (IV, p. 223)

And yet, Meredith qualifies, there are men among the dead and the living who have yielded "substance," done work, sweet enough "For song our highest heaven to greet" because of their love of Earth and their "self-forgetfulness divine." This is one of Meredith's great themes.

His specific against the dominance of self is the perfect union of blood, brain, and spirit. If one attains this union in maturity, he will not need to fear

---

[5]See, for instance, J. W. Beach, *The Concept of Nature in Nineteenth Century Poetry* (New York, 1936), and G. Roppen, *Evolution and Poetic Belief, A Study in Some Victorian and Modern Writers* (Oslo, 1956).

[6]B. Dobrée, *The Broken Cistern: The Clark Lectures, 1952–53* (London, 1954), p. 94.

[7]N. Kelvin, *A Troubled Eden, Nature and Society in the Works of George Meredith* (Edinburgh, 1961), p. 117.

the failure of blood (health and animal vitality) in old age, for he can regard with pleasure this joyous triad in those younger than himself. This belief is impressively expressed in an ode, "Youth in Memory," by an image of old trees by the stream of life:

> They now bared roots beside the river bent;
> Whose privilege themselves to see:
> Their place in yonder tideway know;
> The current glass peruse;
> The depths intently sound;
> And sapped by each returning flood,
> Accept for monitory nourishment,
> Those worn roped features under crust of mud,
> Reflected in the silvery smooth around:
> Not less the branching and high singing tree,
> A home of nests, a landmark and a tent,
> Until their hour for losing hold on ground.
>
> (IV, pp. 404–405)

It follows that there should be no mourning when the tree loses its hold on ground; yet Meredith's faith in the rightness of the natural life cycle was badly shaken when his beloved wife was dying slowly of cancer in 1885. He wrote noble poems during these months: "The Thrush in February," "A Faith on Trial," and "Hymn to Colour." In the allegorical "Hymn to Colour":

> Love took my hand when hidden stood the sun
> To fling his robe on shoulder-heights of snow.
> Then said: There lie they, Life and Death in one.
> Whichever is, the other is: but know,
> It is thy craving self that thou dost see,
>   Not in them seeing me.
>
> (IV, p. 362)

It is true that Earth is a slayer "whom no cry can melt," but love again comes to the poet's rescue in "The Thrush in February," a poem that concludes:

> Love born of knowledge, love that gains
> Vitality as Earth it mates,
> The meaning of the Pleasures, Pains,
> The Life, the Death, illuminates.
>
> For love we Earth, then serve we all;
> Her mystic secret then is ours:
> We fall, or view our treasures fall,
> Unclouded, as beholds her flowers.
>
> Earth, from a night of frosty wreck,
> Enrobed in morning's mounted fire,

> When lowly, with a broken neck,
> The crocus lays her cheek to mire.
>
> (IV, p. 331)

The most difficult concept to grasp in Meredith's ideal triad of blood, brain, and spirit is that of spirit, and there has been animated controversy on whether spirit in Meredith's thinking is simply an irradiated intelligence, the mind of common sense—that he certainly always worshiped—or whether it is the "Wisdom and Spirit of the Universe," unforgettably invoked by William Wordsworth. The difficulty arises from the multiplicity of Meredith's philosophical statements, expressed in verse and prose over the decades. In later life he was conspicuously more willing to refer to God than he had been earlier, and perhaps a straight didactic passage from a late poem, "The Test of Manhood," may throw some light on the role of spirit:

> In manhood must he find his competence;
> In his clear mind the spiritual food:
> God being there while he his fight maintains;
> Throughout his mind the Master Mind being there,
> While he rejects the suicide despair;
> Accepts the spur of explicable pains
> Obedient to Nature, not her slave:
> Her lord, if to her rigid laws he bows;
> Her dust, if with his conscience he plays knave,
> And bids the Passions on the Pleasures browse:—
>
> (IV, pp. 543–544)

At his best, man must find his "spiritual food" in his own mind where is also God, the master mind that has also given nature her "rigid laws." If man lets his senses (blood) dominate, he is lost. Meredith wrote to Mrs. J. B. Gilman on 16 March 1888:

I have written always with the perception that there is no life but of the spirit; that the concrete is really the shadowy; yet that the way to spiritual life lies in the complete unfolding of the creature, not to the nipping of his passions. An outrage to Nature helps to extinguish his light. To the flourishing of the spirit, then, through the healthy exercise of the senses.[8]

Readers indifferent to Meredith's positivist thinking will nevertheless like his nature poetry for its precise rendering of sights and sounds. For instance,

[8]C. L. Cline, ed., The Collected Letters of George Meredith, 3 vols. (Oxford, 1970), vol. II, p. 910.

in "The Lark Ascending" he gives us the "chirrup, whistle, slur and shake" of the bird's song, as well as abundant figures of speech for its joyousness. In "Night of Frost in May," nightingales make their appearance. With no diminution of their traditionally romantic appeal, their song is so closely noted that anyone who has heard it can recapture it in memory. First:

> The ear conceived a severing cry,
> Almost it let the sound elude,
> When chuckles three, a warble shy,
> From hazels of the garden came,
> Near by the crimson-windowed farm.
> They laid the trance on breath and frame,
> A prelude of the passion-charm.
>
> Then soon was heard, not sooner heard
> Than answered, doubled, trebled, more,
> Voice of an Eden in the bird
> Renewing with his pipe of four
> The sob: a troubled Eden, rich
> In throb of heart: unnumbered throats
> Flung upward at a fountain's pitch
> The fervour of the four long notes,
> That on the fountain's pool subside,
> Exult and ruffle and upspring:
> Endless the crossing multiplied
> Of silver and of golden string.
> There chimed a bubbled underbrew
> With witch-wild spray of vocal dew.
>
> (IV, p. 325)

"Tardy Spring" and "The South-Wester" are buoyant observations of the coming of spring and the cloudscapes of one day.

Unfortunately, in Meredith's later years his long poems grew more turgid, elliptical, and harsh. The volume that contains the lovely "Night of Frost in May" takes its title, *The Empty Purse* (1892), from a long "Sermon to our Later Prodigal Son," who is considered lucky to have run through his inheritance because he can now do something useful, like enter politics, eschewing demagogues and working for the changing and better times:

> *Keep the young generation in hail,*
> *And bequeath them no tumbled house!*
> (IV, p. 453)

Later, Meredith admitted that "this was not poetry. But I had to convey certain ideas that could not find place in the novels."

In the late 1890's he put intense passion and many months of hard work into composing three *Odes in Contribution to the Song of French History* (1898), a subject he had long studied. The metaphors and symbols in these odes are so elusive that the labored poems mean little to one who is not a specialist in the subject.[9] With these odes he also reprinted "France, December 1870," an ode that he had written during the month when the Germans had surrounded Paris. As his letters, particularly to his friend John Morley, show, the Franco-Prussian War had thrown him into great emotional perturbation, for he had always been a friend to the two nations; but out of his pain he had conceived this ode that, with all its criticism of post-Revolutionary France, expressed the hope that her earlier ideal faith in reason would again light not only the spirit of the French people but the rest of what we would now call the "free world":

> Now is Humanity on trial in thee:
> Now mayst thou gather humankind in fee;
> Now prove that Reason is a quenchless scroll;
> Make of calamity thine aureole,
> And bleeding head us through the troubles of the sea.
> (IV, p. 504)

This earliest is by far the best of the four odes. The volume sold well and increased the number of Frenchmen who came to pay their respects to the sage of Flint Cottage, Box Hill, Dorking (now owned by the National Trust).

With all the poet's necessary insistence on the importance of reason, it is good to be able to note that the purely lyrical voice of Meredith is here and there raised even in old age, as witness the faultless "Song in the Songless":

> They have no song, the sedges dry,
>   And still they sing.
> It is within my breast they sing,
>   As I pass by.
> Within my breast they touch a string,
>   They wake a sigh.
> There is but sound of sedges dry;
>   In me they sing.
>
> (IV, p. 548)

Ears tuned to English may have noticed in the preceding quotations something of Meredith's vari-

---

[9]The best guides are the historian G. M. Trevelyan's notes in his edition of Meredith's *Poetical Works* (London–New York, 1912), and M. E. Mackay, *Meredith et la France* (Paris, 1937).

ety. He was as zealous a student of versification as A. C. Swinburne and Rudyard Kipling and, indeed, in 1870, wrote a friend that he hoped "to write some papers on poetry and versification." He scanned the measures of "Phoebus with Admetus" and "Melampus," and explained the meter of "Love in the Valley" in notes at the end of *Poems and Lyrics of the Joy of Earth*. He subtitled his poem "Phaèthôn," "Attempted in the Galliambic Measure," adding to *Ballads and Poems of Tragic Life* (1887) an especially learned note on this measure. He thought light verse an excellent exercise, and many of his letters contain such verses. He was a careful student of the translation of Homer and contributed to this art various passages from the *Iliad* in English hexameter verse. His sonnets, other than those of "Modern Love," are imitative of Wordsworth, whom he considered the greatest English practitioner of the Italian form. His many exhortations on the subject of verse may be summed up in a sentence from a letter: "I beg of you to learn to love the instrument, not merely certain tunes."

III

On 1 February 1877 Meredith delivered his only public lecture, addressing the London Institution for the Advancement of Literature and the Diffusion of Useful Knowledge on "The Idea of Comedy and the Uses of the Comic Spirit." First published in the *New Quarterly* magazine (April 1877), then in book form 1897, this essay has subsequently been studied in all English-speaking countries as a classic contribution to the study of comedy. It is the one overt display of Meredith's self-education. Yet he wore his robe of erudition easily, as a believer in the comic spirit should, and lightened his literary criticism with anecdotes from real life to illustrate his theme. As indicated by the title, the essay is in two parts.

"The Idea of Comedy" starts with an assessment of comedy in England. Meredith finds English literature rich in comic elements but poor in number of comedies. He explains in his second paragraph that for a great comic poet to flourish, "A society of cultivated men and women is required, wherein ideas are current, and the perceptions quick, that he may be supplied with matter and an audience."[10] The presence

[10]G. Meredith, *An Essay on Comedy and the Uses of the Comic Spirit*, L. Cooper, ed. (Ithaca, N. Y., 1956), p. 75.

of women in this sentence is a vital part of Meredith's thesis. The primary gift for a comic poet is immediately declared as "subtle delicacy." "He must be subtle to penetrate." This poet's foes are Puritanical nonlaughers, Bacchanalian excessive laughers, and sentimentalists. With the one exception of William Congreve's *The Way of the World* (1700), Meredith finds the English comedy of manners coarse, stereotyped, and better forgotten; the French are better at "stately comedy," because "they know men and women more accurately than we do." He explains briefly that although Shakespeare "is a well-spring of characters which are saturated with the comic spirit," he does not fit into the subject of this essay because his characters are enlarged "by great poetic imagination" and "are subjects of a special study in the poetically comic."

It is Molière who is Meredith's idea of the "Idea of Comedy." He studies Molière's career and explains the success of his best plays, made possible by the "quick-witted" bourgeoisie of Paris. "Cultivated men and women who do not skim the cream of life, and are attached to the duties, yet escape the harsher blows, make acute and balanced observers. Molière is their poet." Even Congreve's *The Way of the World*, exceptional in its brilliant writing and the character of Millamant, is inferior to *Le Misanthrope* because it has no idea in it. In a letter written nine years after this essay Meredith said, "Molière is the sole writer of pure Comedy, so rare is it."

He closes the first part of his essay by reasserting that the "laugh of men and women in concert" is essential to pure comedy. Because of the position of women in German society, Germany has not yet attained spiritual laughter, and it is completely impossible in such an Eastern culture as the Arabian, which, though "intensely susceptible to laughter," keeps women behind the veil: "the comic Muse" is one of the best friends of cultivated women.

The second part of this essay, "The Uses of the Comic Spirit," starts with the argument that the comic spirit is needed to offset Folly, to correct dullness, and to throw light on public affairs. Meredith maintains that Folly takes many "shapes in a society possessed of wealth and leisure," and that plain common sense without the comic spirit is too angry, contempt too inhumane, and the defensive operation of "the heavily armed man of science and the writer of the leading article or elaborate essay" too slow to combat Folly successfully. "O for a breath of Aristophanes, Rabelais, Voltaire, Cervantes, Fielding, Molière! These are the spirits that, if you know them well, will come when you do call." Dullness and boredom can only be banished by the comic spirit which blows away the "vapours of unreason and sentimentalism." Meredith argues that the spirit of Aristophanes is needed in England's public affairs, and he gives an excellent sketch of the Greek poet's relationship with the public life of Athens.

After his analysis of the general uses of the comic spirit, Meredith turns to the English: "They have the basis of the comic in them—an esteem for common sense"; even so, they lack the comic spirit, perhaps because they are not yet used to living in society, a point that Meredith illustrates by a number of anecdotes. Although he names Fielding, Goldsmith, Jane Austen, and John Galt as delightful comic writers in prose, he contends that the English genius in general tends to satire and humor. He then distinguishes the comic from satire, irony, and humor, illustrating his distinctions. Meredith is now ready to try to describe the comic poet, his "narrow field" and "still narrower" audience. Comic laughter is impersonal and polite, "often no more than a smile. It laughs through the mind, for the mind directs it; and it might be called the humour of the mind."

In the most eloquent rhetoric of the whole essay, Meredith personifies the comic spirit as looking down on men with brows of a sage and lips of a faun.

Men's future upon earth does not attract it; their honesty and shapeliness in the present does; and whenever they wax out of proportion, overblown, affected, pretentious, bombastical, hypocritical, pedantic, fantastically delicate; whenever it sees them self-deceived or hoodwinked, given to run riot in idolatries, drifting into vanities, congregating in absurdities, planning short-sightedly, plotting dementedly; whenever they are at variance with their professions, and violate the unwritten but perceptible laws binding them in consideration one to another; whenever they offend sound reason, fair justice; are false in humility or mined with conceit, individually, or in the bulk; the Spirit overhead will look humanely malign and cast an oblique light on them, followed by volleys of silvery laughter.

(p. 142)

Meredith might well have ended his essay with this dazzling sentence, but the rest of the essay reads as if he could scarcely bear to close. He adds to the benefits the comic spirit brings, redescribes the quality of comic laughter, gives examples of what deplorable things happen to men when the comic idea is absent, again insists on the necessity of talking with women as equals, and explains the advantages of enclosing the comic idea in the dramatic form.

IV

MEREDITH's first works of prose fiction were fantastic amalgamations of supernaturalism and common sense, written with the misguided hope that they would pay his bills. The intensive student of Meredith finds many of his maturing ideas in *The Shaving of Shagpat* (1855), if not in *Farina* (1857), the anticlimax of which is the invention of eau de cologne. Neither of these entertainments has general appeal.

Meredith's first real novel was *The Ordeal of Richard Feverel* (1859), and it is important, before contemplating it, to place all of his novels correctly in the history of the novel. Because of his various romantic characters and the elaborations of his prose style, some critics have been misled into calling him a romantic novelist, but he is not. All of his primarily romantic or chivalric characters come to a poor, if not a downright catastrophic, end. Yet he hated the novels of Zola, feeling dragged into the gutter by them; equally he hated "happy tales of mystery." Writing metaphorically, as was his way when dealing with concepts, he best described his position in an aside to the reader of *Beauchamp's Career* (1876):

My way is like a Rhone island in the summer drought, stony, unattractive and difficult between the two forceful streams of the unreal and the over-real, which delight mankind—honour to the conjurors! My people conquer nothing, win none; they are actual, yet uncommon. It is the clock-work of the brain that they are directed to set in motion, and . . . the conscience residing in thoughtfulness which they would appeal to; and if you are there impervious to them, we are lost.[11]

His realism, then, is the realism of intelligent thinking, not of the gutter or sweatshop. Ramon Fernandez, a French philosophical critic who wrote unforgettably about Meredith in the 1920's, made a just statement:

[11]All quotations from the novels are from the *Memorial Edition*, 27 vols. (London, 1909–1911).

Meredith is the first to have shown that in the order of life a romantic or decadent judgement is always a false judgement, because it is not formed in conditions necessary to all true thought. He beheaded romanticism. We can still feel its twinges and shudderings: we are no longer entitled to mistake these for thoughts.[12]

In matters of style, Meredith felt that a novelist should please himself. A character spoke for him in *Sandra Belloni* (1886):

The point to be considered is, whether fiction demands a perfectly smooth surface. Undoubtedly a scientific work does, and a philosophical treatise should. When we ask for facts simply, we feel the intrusion of a style. Of fiction it is a part. In the one case the classical robe, in the other any medieval phantasy of clothing. . . . In poetry we are rich enough; but in prose we owe everything to the license our poets have taken in the teeth of critics.

"Poetic rashness," to use his own phrase, is the mark of Meredith's prose. It has been much reproached, but so fine a reader and writer as Virginia Woolf found to her surprise, rather late in life, that she liked it. In her diary of 27 March 1937, she wrote: "I began *Lord Ormont and His Aminta* and found it so rich, so knotted, so alive, and muscular after the pale little fiction I'm used to, that, alas, it made me wish to write fiction again. . . . I like his effort to escape plain prose."[13]

The escape from plain prose and the havoc that a romantic hero can wreak upon himself and others are both apparent in Meredith's first novel. The plot of *Richard Feverel* resembles that of Shakespeare's *Romeo and Juliet;* the theme is the education of a boy into manhood; but, apart from the traditional plot and theme, *Richard Feverel* was something new on the literary scene. It was at once ironic, clever, psychologically analytic, and poetic, so bold in its expression of extramarital sexual passion that it was banned from Mudie's lending library to the detriment of its sales. In spite of this mishap, Meredith did not cut any of the offending matter when he revised the novel in 1885. By condensing the first four chapters into one, he did, however, create obscurities in the subsequent narration. Ideally one should read the text of the first edition.

[12]R. Fernandez, *Messages*, M. Belgion, trans. (New York, 1927), p. 190.
[13]V. Woolf, *A Writer's Diary* (London, 1953), pp. 279–80.

The irony in this extraordinary novel is pervasive. It even hovers over the oft-quoted two first love scenes between Richard and Lucy: "Ferdinand and Miranda" and "A Diversion Played on a Penny-Whistle." Richard had been reared on a system by his domineering father, Sir Austin Feverel, and he was supposed to marry an upper-class girl, but he fell in love at first sight with a girl from a Roman Catholic farming family. After setting the frame of their meeting in the context of Shakespeare's *The Tempest*, Meredith observes of the fair young pair: "If these two were Ferdinand and Miranda, Sir Austin was not Prospero, and was not present, or their fates might have been different." Passages from the scene when they first kiss will illustrate both the poetic prose of the nature scenes and the irony of human encounter:

Golden lie the meadows: golden run the streams: red gold is on the pine-stems. The Sun is coming down to Earth, and walks the fields and waters.

The Sun is coming down to Earth, and the fields and the waters shout to him golden shouts. He comes, and his heralds run before him, and touch the leaves of the oaks, and planes, and beeches, lucid green, and the pine-stems redder gold; leaving brightest foot-prints upon thickly weeded banks, where the foxglove's last upper-bells incline, and bramble-shoots wander amid moist rich herbage. The plumes of the woodland are alight; and beyond them, over the open, 'tis a race with the long-thrown shadows; a race across the heaths and up the hills, till, at the farthest bourne of mounted eastern cloud, the heralds of the sun lay rosy fingers and rest.

. . .

He calls her by her name, Lucy: and she, blushing at her great boldness, has called him by his, Richard. Those two names are the key-notes of the wonderful harmonies the angels sing aloft.

"Lucy! my beloved!"

"O Richard!" . . .

Out in the world there, on the skirts of the wood-land, a sheep-boy pipes to meditative Eve on a penny-whistle.

Love's musical Instrument is as old, and as poor; it has but two stops; and yet, you see, the Cunning Musician does thus much with it!

(ch. 19)

The perceptive reader knows that these innocents need more than two stops to their accompaniment. Richard's chivalric education is corrupted to wrong purposes after his secret marriage, and the final irony is the death of Lucy instead of Richard after he has fought an unnecessary duel in defense of her honor.

Throughout Meredith's career he was criticized pejoratively for his cleverness. In *Richard Feverel* his cleverness, or wit, is manifest in two ways: the bright talk of "the wise youth," Adrian Harley, Richard's tutor, and the book of aphorisms that Sir Austin had written before the time of the action of the novel. His "Pilgrim's Scrip," often quoted in the novel, is particularly rich in cynical comments about women and was undoubtedly a means by which Meredith unloaded some of his bitterness about his first wife's desertion. It was the first of several such tutelary books, means that Meredith devised for displaying his talent in the art of epigrammatic utterances. "The Book of Egoism" is quoted in *The Egoist* (1879); *Diana of the Crossways* (1885) is introduced by excerpts from "Diaries and Diarists touching the Heroine"; and a book written by the father of the heroine of *The Amazing Marriage* (1895), called "Maxims for Men," sets a standard for the behavior of the heroine.

Evan Harrington (1861), appearing two years after *Richard Feverel*, is a lighthearted novel, notable for its sketch of Meredith's famous tailor-grandfather, Melchizedek Meredith, a naval outfitter of Portsmouth, who seems to have been the first tailor in English history to have comported himself as an equal with his social superiors. The Great Mel's daughter, the Countess de Saldar, whose main purpose in life is to conceal her family background, is an unforgettable comic character.

An enchanting singer is the heroine of *Emilia in England* (1864), later called *Sandra Belloni,* and of *Vittoria* (1867). In *Sandra Belloni,* as in *Evan Harrington,* the comic spirit darts its gibes at social pretentiousness, especially at the sentimentality of the upper-class Pole family that befriends the lowly Emilia. The unmasking of sentimentalists was one of Meredith's favorite operations. He comes straight to the point in the first chapter of *Sandra Belloni:*

Sentimentalists are a perfectly natural growth of a fat soil. Wealthy communities must engender them. If with attentive minds we mark the origin of classes, we shall discern that the Nice Feelings and the Fine Shades play a principal part in our human development and social history, I dare not say that civilized man is to be studied with the eye of a naturalist; but my vulgar meaning might almost be twisted to convey that our sentimentalists are a variety owing their existence to a certain prolonged term of comfortable feeding.

But the novel is not, as might be expected, high comedy. A great scene halfway through is titled "Suggests that the Comic Mask has some Kinship with a Skull"; it starts the falling action in which Emilia loses her voice for a long time and almost dies, apparently ruined by the flat refusal of Mr. Pole to allow his son to marry her.

Vittoria[14] is a historical novel of epic action. Emilia, the first of several Meredithian heroines who learn from tragic experience and recover, had regained her voice by the end of *Sandra Belloni* and is now, with the name Vittoria, cantatrice at La Scala in Milan and a leader of the 1848 Italian uprising against Austria. The novel is intricately plotted because it deals with plots. The historian G. M. Trevelyan wrote of it:

Meredith's *Vittoria* is not only a great prose poem on an epic moment in human affairs, but a detailed and accurate analysis of a people and of a period. . . . The character of the revolution in the plain of Po, which alone made the movement in the Peninsula a serious fact, is better studied in *Vittoria* than in any history.[15]

The Chief, who is introduced in chapter 2, is Mazzini. Trevelyan described this characterization as:

an example of perfect historical portraiture inspired by the highest poetic gift. Compared to Meredith, with his profound and subtle analysis and all-embracing vision of the man, every other writer, whether historian or poet, has merely played with the subject of Mazzini's personality.[16]

Meredith knew personally both Austrian officers and Italian patriots and said that he thought he had done justice to both sides. Vittoria made her debut as a prima donna in an opera named *Camilla,* which Meredith sketched in full as an opera of Young Italy. Camilla's dying lines were intended to express the heart of Mazzini's creed:

> Our life is but a little holding, lent
> To do a mighty labour: we are one
> With heaven and the stars when it is spent
> To serve God's name: else die we with the sun.

[14]Between the two Emilia-Sandra-Vittoria novels appeared *Rhoda Fleming* (1865), a somber treatment of the then popular theme of the fallen woman.

[15]G. M. Trevelyan, "Englishmen and Italians," *Proceedings of the British Academy* (London, 1919–20), pp. 100–1.

[16]G. M. Trevelyan's introduction to *English Songs of Italian Freedom* (London, 1911), pp. xx–xxi.

Meredith cherished this quatrain, and it is spread on an open book as the headstone to his grave in Dorking cemetery.

He wrote only one more historical novel, *The Tragic Comedians* (1880). As the title indicates, this novel is of a mixed dramatic genre; it concentrates on a single plot, the story of Ferdinand Lasalle, one of the founders of German socialism, and Hélène von Donniges, Princess von Racowitza. German readers may be attracted to this story, as they are likely to be to *The Adventures of Harry Richmond* (1871).

In *Harry Richmond* Meredith wrote for the only time in his career a novel in the first person, the person of Harry, a boy who must outgrow the spells of a completely irrational and romantic father. In the course of his adventures, Harry wanders into Germany and meets a German princess, Ottilia, whom he later very nearly marries. Princess Ottilia has been brought up by her professor to worship reason, and she has a good mind, good enough for her tutor to wish to bring her up to the degree of Doctor of Laws. She lectures Harry on the subject of England:

You have such wealth! You embrace half the world: you are such a little island! All this is wonderful. The bitterness is, you are such a mindless people—I do but quote to explain my Professor's ideas. "Mindless," he says, "and arrogant, and neither in the material nor in the spiritual kingdom of noble or gracious stature, and ceasing to have a brave aspect." He calls you squat Goths.

(vol. I, ch. 28)

Ottilia counters the influence in Harry of his flamboyant father, who calls himself Richmond Roy and thinks that he is the son of a king and that the government in time will recognize his claims. He is so preposterous and gaudy that for some readers he steals the role of hero from his son, but Meredith did not intend him to be taken this way. Harry moves from rapt, unconsidered admiration for his astonishing father to pity for him. Before his "Adventures" are three-quarters of the way through, he has begun to see his father clearly. Harry by now could reason and analyze the "endless worry" he felt about his father, who had ceased to amuse him.

I know . . . that to the rest of the world he was a progressive comedy: and the knowledge made him seem more tragic still. He clearly could not learn from misfortune. . . . I chafed at his unteachable spirit, surely one of the most tragical things in life.

(vol. II, ch. 47)

Beauchamp's Career is considered one of Meredith's finest novels. The historian G. M. Young aptly wrote:

Beauchamp's Career is best read, and best understood, as a political study, with three, if not four love stories weaving themselves in and out of the central theme, the Southampton election of 1868 when Meredith's friend, Commander Maxse, stood as a Radical and was beaten.[17]

Meredith had gone to Southampton to assist Frederick Augustus Maxse in this campaign, and although immediately after Maxse's defeat he considered the experience a waste of time, he picked up a knowledge of the practical working of politics that made a solid, informative basis for one of the best of English political novels. Although the first four chapters are difficult for readers uninformed about English politics, they are worth mastering for the sake of the light that they throw on a period of English history. The gentry's feeling against trade—the middle-class belief in free trade and self-interest was derisively alluded to as "Manchester"—is matched by their inflated pride over England's achievements in the Crimean War. The publication of the novel took place after Gladstone's first defeat (1874), at a time when the Conservatives were in the ascendance and there were rumblings of radical dissatisfaction throughout the country. The social and historical background once understood, the reader will find the rest of the novel swift-moving and exciting.

Within the political context of the novel there are four chief protagonists. Beauchamp's uncle, Everard Romfrey, is a conservative whose political views are limited to the fear that the game laws (the protection of wild game for the pleasure of country gentlemen) were threatened by the protests of the hungry poor. Blackburn Tuckham, a lawyer in charge of another country gentleman's properties, is a rational, fairminded conservative. Dr. Shrapnel is the gentlehearted demagogue, a type of idealistic radical reformer. And the central character of the novel, Nevil Beauchamp, is the devoted disciple of Dr. Shrapnel. All of the other English characters in the novel, except the sodden, unidealistically drawn poor people of the town in which Beauchamp runs for election, are Tory-minded. The novel is primarily a novel of ideas, as Meredith states in the first chapter:

[17]Introduction to *Beauchamp's Career* (London, 1950), the World's Classics edition.

228

This day, this hour, this life, and even politics, the centre and throbbing heart of it . . . , must be treated of: men, and the ideas of men, which are—it is policy to be emphatic upon truisms—are actually the motives of men in a greater degree than their appetites: these are my theme.

In characterizing the hero of this novel of ideas, Nevil Beauchamp, Meredith as usual plays with his cards on the table.[18] In the fourth chapter Beauchamp is sharply sketched. His stamp of mind is "the obverse of Byronism":

For Beauchamp will not even look at happiness to mourn its absence; melodious lamentations, demoniacal scorn, are quite alien to him. His faith is in working and fighting. . . . The simple truth has to be told: how he loved his country, and for another and a broader love, growing out of his first passion, fought it; and being small by comparison, and finding no giant of the Philistines disposed to receive a stone in his foreskull, pummelled the obtumescent mass, to the confusion of a conceivable epic.

Beauchamp is also handsome, courageous, and impatient. Having been thwarted by his poacher-stalking uncle, Everard Romfrey, in his desire for a formal education, he was sent to sea at fourteen and shaped his young thinking from a devout reading of Thomas Carlyle's *On Heroes, Hero-Worship, and the Heroic in History* (1841). He speaks for Meredith's lifetime conviction that England should be better prepared to meet her enemies, that a defensive navy and voluntary enlistment were not sufficient to meet her needs.

A good sample of political discussion in the novel is a conversation between Beauchamp and two Tories, his young cousin Tuckham and the middle-aged Seymour Austin, the senior Tory member for Bevisham in the House of Commons. Beauchamp wants to establish a radical newspaper, and Tuckham protests that the annual outlay that Beauchamp plans for it is too low in consideration of the libels it will incur. Tuckham asks:

"It's to be a penny journal?"
"Yes, a penny. I'd make it a farthing——"
"Pay to have it read?"
"Willingly."
Tuckham did some mental arithmetic, quaintly, with rapidly blinking eyelids and open mouth. "You may count it at the cost of two paying mines," he said firmly. "That is, if it's to be a consistently Radical Journal, at law with

[18]E. M. Forster, *Aspects of the Novel* (London, 1927), p. 123.

everybody all round the year. And by the time it has won a reputation, it will be undermined by a radicaller Radical Journal. . . . And what on earth are you contending for?"
"Freedom of thought, for one thing."
"We have quite enough free-thinking."
"There's not enough if there's not perfect freedom."
"Dangerous!" quoth Mr. Austin.
"But it's that danger which makes men, sir; and it's fear of the danger that makes our modern Englishman."
(vol. II, ch. 45)

After trying to persuade Beauchamp that he is too idealistic in thinking that he can hire good writers, Tuckham remarks that, anyway, his writers would not be writing for intelligent people.

"There's the old charge against the people."
"But they're not. You can madden, you can't elevate them by writing and writing. Defend us from the uneducated English! The common English are doltish; except in the North, where you won't do much with them. Compare them with the Yankees for shrewdness, the Spaniards for sobriety, the French for ingenuity, the Germans for enlightenment, the Italians in the Arts; yes, the Russians for good-humour and obedience—where are they? They're only worth something when they're led. They fight well; there's good stuff in them."
"I've heard all that before," returned Beauchamp, unruffled. "You don't know them. I mean to educate them by giving them an interest in their country. At present they have next to none. Our governing class is decidedly unintelligent, in my opinion brutish, for it's indifferent. My paper shall render your traders justice for what they do, and justice for what they don't do."
"My traders, as you call them, are the soundest foundation for a civilized state that the world has yet seen."
(vol. II, ch. 45)

Listening to this conversation, Cecilia Halkett blushes when she hears that Beauchamp's paper is to be called *The Dawn*, because she is in love with him and knows that marriage with him would mean a new life for her and also that her wealth could support such a paper. In such ways, Meredith, with the greatest truth to human nature, interplays ideas and emotions. Cecilia is not one of his witty heroines, but she is a pure, intelligent, English beauty; in breed, they are perfectly suitable; in disposition, they are not. Meredith not only shows how Beauchamp unwittingly subjugates her heart but how he troubles her established opinions.

The well-born Cecilia is balanced against Beauchamp's equally well-born first love, a Frenchwoman, Renée, who is first seen at the age of seventeen, fanning her invalided brother, Beauchamp's friend from the Crimean War, in a gondola in Venice.

> She chattered snatches of Venetian caught from the gondoliers, she was like a delicate cup of crystal brimming with the beauty of the place . . . thought flew, tongue followed, and the flash of meaning quivered over [her features] like night-lightning.
>
> (vol. I, ch. 5)

This girl was affianced, in the continental fashion, to a marquis much older than herself.

Three-fourths of the way through the novel Renée surprises Beauchamp by suddenly arriving in London, dreaming that he would run off with her, away from her dismal marriage. In this crucial "trial," Meredith's hero, however passionate, is unromantic and is also easily routed by Renée in a test of wit.

> Beauchamp . . . bent above her: "You have come to me, for the love of me, to give yourself to me, and for ever, for good, till death? Speak, my beloved Renée."
>
> Her eyes were raised to his: "You see me here. It is for you to speak."
>
> "I do. There's nothing I ask for now—if the step can't be retrieved."
>
> "The step retrieved, my friend? There is no step backward in life."
>
> "I am thinking of you, Renée."
>
> "Yes, I know," she answered hurriedly.
>
> "If we discover that the step is a wrong one?" he pursued: "why is there no step backward?"
>
> "I am talking of women," said Renée.
>
> "Why not for women?"
>
> "Honourable women, I mean," said Renée.
>
> Beauchamp inclined to forget his position in finding matter to contest.
>
> Yet it is beyond contest that there is no step backward in life. She spoke well; better than he, and she won his deference by it. Not only she spoke better: she was truer, distincter, braver: and a man ever on the look-out for superior qualities, and ready to bow to them, could not refuse her homage.
>
> (vol. II, ch. 40)

Beautiful, grown courageous, quick-witted, Renée is one of Meredith's most alluring heroines, and his creation of her is one reason why, when he was asked late in life which of his novels he liked best, he named *Beauchamp's Career*. He liked it for its "breezy, human interest" and consistent, logical

plot: "Then, a thing that weighs with me, the French critics liked it; they said that Renée is true to life."[19]

On the subject of plot Meredith is paradoxical. In the same passage in which he sketches Beauchamp's character he forewarns "readers of this history that there is no plot in it," and in a letter of 14 September 1887, he writes that he does not make a plot: "If my characters, as I have them by heart before I begin on them, were boxed in a plot, they would soon lose their features" (*Letters*, vol. II, p. 888). Yet, in retrospect, he realized that in some novels he had plotted better than he intended, and it is for his excellence in plot making that E. M. Forster praised him, while deriding, it would seem unfairly,[20] his representation of social values.

Usually, Meredith's fine plots are evolved from his tragicomic view of his characters. In *Beauchamp's Career*, for example, the hero has a tragic flaw: he does not understand himself, other men, and—particularly—women. On the subject of the parliamentary campaign, Beauchamp says to the intelligent young woman whom he was ultimately to marry, partly because of his failures of nerve with Renée and Cecilia:

> "It's only a skirmish lost, and that counts for nothing in a battle without end: it must be incessant."
>
> "But does incessant battling keep the intellect clear?" was her memorable answer.

Beauchamp attributed this answer to the influence of masculine minds upon her: "Could a sweet-faced girl, the nearest to Renée in grace of manner and in feature of all women known to him, originate a sentence that would set him reflecting?" In this novel, it is Beauchamp's political rival, Seymour Austin, who is a great believer in the intelligence of women and the public roles that they were destined to fill.

Between *Beauchamp's Career* and Meredith's renowned next novel, *The Egoist*, two tales of long short-story length, *The House on the Beach* and *The Case of General Ople and Lady Camper*, appeared in the *New Quarterly* magazine (1877). They have simple, almost farcical plots. *The House on the Beach* explores lightly one of Meredith's favorite themes, social climbing, and forecasts the main involvement

---

[19]L. Stevenson, *The Ordeal of George Meredith, A Biography* (New York, 1953), p. 199.

[20]See O. Sitwell, "The Novels of George Meredith and some Notes on the English Novel," the English Association Presidential Address, 1947.

of *The Egoist*, an inexperienced young girl's engagement to an egoist. *General Ople and Lady Camper* has more subtle facets. The egoist has been a brave soldier who retired too early out of what he thinks is modesty and what the lady thinks is irresponsibility. He is a good man, and the trials that the witty and realistic caricaturist Lady Camper puts him through in order to focus his attention on his daughter's need for financial independence very nearly drive him insane. But the malignity of the comic spirit, it must be remembered, is also humane, and the intelligent, eccentric lady rescues the general in time. Although her cartoons seared him, they revealed himself to himself, and the plot is resolved quickly by showing that a simple man if told by a woman that she uses rouge will also accept her statement that she is seventy when she is really forty-one. The story is instructive on the difference in language between middle-class and aristocratic English of the period. The lady forbids the general to use the terms: "a gentlemanly residence" or a "bijou" for his small estate, a "gentlemanly appearance" for himself, "thanks" for "thank you," "female" as an adjective,"quite so," and "lady-friend."[21]

A brief prelude to *The Egoist* introduced the essence of Meredith's ideas on the comic spirit to a wider audience than would have read the "Essay on Comedy" in the *New Quarterly* two years before. *Beauchamp's Career* and *The Egoist* mark the turning point in his reputation; critical opinion veered in his favor, and the educated public followed. Today, because it illustrates the famous essay and is a beautifully constructed novel in the high comic mode, *The Egoist* is generally considered to be Meredith's finest novel.

Sir Willoughby Patterne, the egoist, in every outward way has much to recommend him. Not only is he handsome, physically fit, and impeccably dressed, but he can be an entertaining conversationalist and a wittily ironic correspondent. He deeply believes in his own virtues: fidelity and generosity (to those persons who worship him). Like Beauchamp, he is sentimental in his concept of "woman." Meredith writes ironically that "he was anything but obtuse"; his penetration of other people went just so far as to mirror their favorable responses to himself. Thus, when his first spirited betrothed jilted him, he soon rationalized the blow into a release which he, as

a man of honor, could never have effected. He rebuilt his ego by paying attention to his devoted tenant, the clever, poetic, and portionless Laetitia Dale, and by building a laboratory and declaring himself dedicated to science; then he startled the county by a sudden three-year absence on a trip around the world. When he returned, Laetitia was the first friend he met:

He sprang to the ground and seized her hand. "Laetitia Dale!" he said. He panted. "Your name is sweet English music! And you are well?" The anxious question permitted him to read deeply in her eyes. He found the man he sought there, squeezed him passionately, and let her go.

(vol. I, ch. 4)

The central action of the novel is set at Patterne Hall, Sir Willoughby's estate, in a house-party situation, a perfect high comedy background. Clara Middleton, who had "money and health and beauty, the triune of perfect starriness, which makes all men astronomers," had consented to an engagement with Willoughby for the simple reason that she was not in love with anyone else and was overwhelmed by his whirlwind wooing. As a Darwinian, Willoughby regards this match as a triumph for the species and an assurance of the survival of the Patternes. Clara and her scholarly father visit Sir Willoughby. An inmate of the house is Vernon Whitford, the egoist's cousin, an essayist of modest means who helps manage the estate. Vernon, in turn, has taken as his protegé and pupil another cousin of Willoughby, a boy, Crossjay Patterne, one of the many children of an impoverished and brave marine. Vernon resolves early in the novel that his benefactor's impending marriage is a good time to make a move: for him to try to make his living by his pen in London and for Crossjay to be sent to a school that will qualify him to enter the navy, the boy's greatest ambition. Sir Willoughby brings up Vernon's inexplicable decision with his betrothed so "that she might be taught to look to him and act for him." He says to her of Vernon:

"I want him here; and, supposing he goes, he offends me; he loses a friend; and it will not be the first time a friend has tried me too far; but, if he offends me, he is extinct."

"Is what?" cried Clara, with a look of fright.

"He becomes to me at once as if he had never been. He is extinct."

"In spite of your affection?"

"On account of it, I might say. Our nature is mysterious, and mine as much so as any. Whatever my regrets, he goes

[21]In 1877 the *New Quarterly* magazine printed Meredith's only tragic tale, *Chloe*, a morality story of eighteenth-century Bath under the dictatorship of Beau Nash.

out. This is not a language I talk to the world. I do the man no harm; I am not to be named unchristian. But . . . !"

(vol. I, ch. 10)

This brief passage reveals the essence of Sir Willoughby, who, in the same chapter, while describing another man, jocularly warns Clara against marrying an egoist.

In the course of the novel we watch Clara grow from an ignorant, although well-educated, girl into a young woman who passionately imagines what it would mean to be married to a man who has become both morally and physically repulsive to her. Willoughby has stated that he is to be all the world to her, but she wants more of the world than she could ever have if she were totally possessed by this sentimental gentleman. Her lonely fight to break her engagement is made all the more difficult because her father, bemused by his host's excellent port, is entirely on Willoughby's side and demands that she do her duty. Clara, however, has acquired a sophisticated concept of what is involved in this "duty," and she is fortified in her rebellion by her growing love for the rational man of nature, Vernon Whitford.

When Clara finally wins her freedom, Sir Willoughby has already covered his failure by proposing to the constant Laetitia. In fact, he exhausts her for a whole night with his entreaties. But she is by now enlightened; there is no longer the glorious image of the man in her eyes, and before she consents she is determined in his presence to enlighten his adoring aunts.

"Dear ladies," Laetitia said to them . . . , "I am going to wound you, and I grieve to do it: but rather now than later, if I am to be your housemate. He asks me for a hand that cannot carry a heart, because mine is dead. I repeat it. I used to think the heart a woman's marriage portion for her husband. I see now that she may consent, and he accept her, without one. But it is right that you should know what I am when I consent. I was once a foolish romantic girl; now I am a sickly woman, all illusions vanished. . . . I can endeavour to respect him, I cannot venerate."

"Dear child!" the ladies gently remonstrated.

Willoughby motioned to them.

"If we are to live together, and I could very happily live with you," Laetitia continued to address them, "you must not be ignorant of me. . . . I have a hard detective eye. I see many faults."

"Have we not all of us faults, dear child?"

"Not such as he has; though the excuses of a gentleman nurtured in idolatry may be pleaded. But he should know that they are seen by her he asks to be his wife, that no

misunderstanding may exist, and while it is yet time he may consult his feelings. He worships himself."

(vol. II, ch. 49)

He is nothing daunted; he must have her; he must save face; and, what is more, he will forever believe that she has always been his one true love. "'I salute my wife,' said Willoughby, making her hand his own, and warming to his possession as he performed the act." He now "had the lady with brains! He had: and he was to learn the nature of that possession in the woman who is our wife."

In his last four novels, *Diana of the Crossways* (1885), *One of Our Conquerors* (1891), *Lord Ormont and His Aminta* (1894), and *The Amazing Marriage* (1895), Meredith continued to explore masculine egotism and feminine courage, and there are always sensible men around to support the women. His prose style grows more involved in these novels and his metaphorical approach more difficult. The plots and the richly conceived characters from which the plots spring are evidence of his unflagging inventiveness.

Diana of the Crossways is the story of a witty woman who early in the novel leaves an insufferable husband and who makes her living by writing fiction. Diana is one of the first "career women" in fiction, and for several decades was to be a favorite among newly emerging emancipated women and their male supporters. Since Meredith tells in his opening chapter of his heroine's charm and wit, it is his responsibility to illustrate this wit. For instance, Diana says:

Of romance: "The young who avoid that region escape the title of Fool at the cost of a celestial crown."

Of sentimentalists: that they "fiddle harmonics on the strings of sensualism."

Of oratory: "It is always the more impressive for the spice of temper which renders it untrustworthy."

Of women: "We live alone and do not much feel it till we are visited."

Of herself: "I thank God I'm at war with myself."

Of such "lapidary sentences" as she herself makes: that they "have the value of chalk-eggs, which lure the thinker to sit."

(ch. 1)

Meredith's novels abound in such aphorisms, voiced in his own person, if the characters are not endowed with the wit to phrase them.

Because she is living beyond her means, Diana sells a political secret, the importance of which she underestimates, and when fully aware of her perfidy she nearly dies and is only brought back to life by the power of touch (later a D. H. Lawrence concept) of her beloved friend Emma Dunstane.

For a correspondent unable to assimilate the content of *One of Our Conquerors*, Meredith's daughter quoted him as saying that the conqueror "is a man of rapid circulation, a prompt assimilation, a benevolent nature, and a loose morality. Such men are sure to conquer and come to naught." Victor Radnor is a successful financier. Although Meredith disapproved of everything about Radnor except his financial ability, he drew the character with enough kindliness to make credible the fact that he had persuaded the lovely woman Nataly to live with him as his wife out of wedlock after he had abandoned the wealthy, older woman whom he had married in his youth. Nataly's courageous unconventionality surpasses even the courage of Clara Middleton and Diana Warwick. The close of Radnor's and Nataly's lives is tragic, for they are "betrayed by what is false within": Radnor's shallow optimism and Nataly's having to keep her heart disease secret by "the wearing of the mask to keep her mate inspirited." Never does Meredith blame them for their illicit union. They "had kept faith with Nature," and left behind them a brave, intelligent daughter.

In the title *Lord Ormont and His Aminta* the possessive pronoun is telltale to anyone who has followed Meredith's concepts of marriage. Lord Ormont is one of his egregious egoists, a cavalry general, a savior of India, a sexagenarian, sentimentally worshiped by young Aminta. He takes her for his own in a doubtful sort of marriage, but although she is now "his Aminta," he will not introduce her to London society. As usual with Meredith's heroines, Aminta grew into an informed woman with the courage to break her marriage and flee with the sweetheart of her schooldays to found a coeducational school in Switzerland. The problem of education is second only to that of marriage in this attractive novel. The schoolmaster Matey Weyburn's program, clearly a radical one in the 1890's, was to separate the two sexes "as little as possible."

All the—*passez-moi le mot*—devilry between the sexes begins at their separation. They're foreigners when they meet; and their alliances are not always binding. The chief object in life, if happiness be their aim, and the growing better than we are, is to teach men and women how to be one; for if they're not, then each is a morsel for the other to prey on.

(ch. 24)

Meredith's final novel, *The Amazing Marriage*, is no advance on *One of Our Conquerors* or *Lord Ormont and His Aminta* in construction or concept. It had been long in the making and reflects the uncertainty of interrupted design. It was a source of amazement to its contemporary readers as well as to us today how the arrogant Lord Fleetwood managed to beget a child of his innocent Carinthian bride, Carinthia, since immediately after the marriage ceremony he took her to a prize fight and then left her at an inn. (Answer, far from apparent, is that he climbed into her inn bedroom by ladder the night of their marriage.) But the chief matter of concern in the novel is the maturing of Carinthia to the point where she no longer doggedly and devotedly tries to make the egoistical Fleetwood acknowledge their marriage. When her lord finally repents and wants her, she will have none of him and goes off with her brother to work as a nurse during the Carlist uprising in Spain. Among the characters in this vividly written novel is Fleetwood's friend, Gower Woodseer, a natural philosopher, modeled from Robert Louis Stevenson.

Meredith's fiction, as well as his poetry, is so various in design and type as to make impossible a neat summing-up. The ideas in all of his writing join forces; he worked with a passionate interest in his art and the lessons he wanted to proffer to intelligent men and women. At the end of *One of Our Conquerors*, the young heroine Nesta, happy in her marriage, is made even happier when she hears that she has helped another woman "know what is actually meant by the good living of a shapely life." This phrase is perhaps the best epigraph to the total work of George Meredith.

SELECTED BIBLIOGRAPHY

I. BIBLIOGRAPHY. M. B. Forman, *A Bibliography of the Writings in Prose and Verse* (London, 1922), considered the standard bibliography, supplement *Meredithiana* issued in 1924; B. Coolidge, *A Catalogue of the Altschul Collection of George Meredith in the Yale University Library* (New Haven, Conn., 1931), also supplement in *Yale University Gazette* 22, 1948; H. L. Sawin, *George Meredith: A Bibliography of Meredithiana, 1920–1953*, Bulletin of Bibliography 21 (1955–1956); J. C. Olmsted and J. E. Welch, eds., *An Annotated Bibliography of George Meredith, 1925–1975* (New York, 1978).

II. COLLECTED WORKS. *Edition Deluxe*, 34 vols. (London, 1896–1898 and 1910–1911); *New Popular Edition*, 18 vols. (London, 1897–1898 and 1902–1905); *Memorial Edition*, 27 vols. (London, 1909–1911), vol. XXVII contains a bibliography by A. J. K. Esdaile, considered a most useful ed.; *The Poetical Works* (London–New York, 1912), notes by G. M. Trevelyan; *Standard Edition*, 15 vols. (London, 1914–1920); Mickleham ed., 18 vols. (London, 1922–1924), the most complete ed.; P. Bartlett, ed., *Poems*, 2 vols. (New Haven, Conn., 1969; repr. 1978).

III. Selected Works. G. Hough, ed., *Selected Poems* (London, 1980).

IV. Separate Works. *Poems* (London, 1851); *The Shaving of Shagpat. An Arabian Entertainment* (London, 1855), fiction; *Farina: A Legend of Cologne* (London, 1857), fiction; *The Ordeal of Richard Feverel. A History of Father and Son*, 3 vols. (London, 1859; rev. ed. London, 1885), novel; *Evan Harrington*, 3 vols. (London, 1861), novel; *Modern Love, and Poems of the English Roadside, with Poems and Ballads* (London, 1862), *Modern Love* also published separately with intro. by C. Day Lewis (London, 1948); *Emilia in England*, 3 vols. (London, 1864), novel, repr. as *Sandra Belloni* (London, 1886); *Rhoda Fleming*, 3 vols. (London, 1865), novel; *Vittoria*, 3 vols. (London, 1867), novel; *The Adventures of Harry Richmond*, 3 vols. (London, 1871), novel; *Beauchamp's Career*, 3 vols. (London, 1876), novel, repr. in the World's Classics (London, 1950); *The House on the Beach. A Realistic Tale* (New York, 1877), fiction; "On the Idea of Comedy and the Uses of the Comic Spirit," in *New Quarterly* magazine (April 1877), lecture at the London Institute, 1 February 1877, published separately as *An Essay on Comedy and the Uses of the Comic Spirit* (London, 1897); *The Egoist. A Comedy in Narrative*, 3 vols. (London, 1879), novel, repr. in the World's Classics (London, 1947); *The Tragic Comedians, a Study in a Well-Known Story*, 2 vols. (London, 1880), fiction; *Poems and Lyrics of the Joy of Earth* (London, 1883); *Diana of the Crossways*, 3 vols. (London, 1885), novel; *Ballads and Poems of Tragic Life* (London, 1887); *A Reading of Earth* (London, 1888), verse; *Jump-to-Glory Jane. A Poem* (London, 1889), privately printed, also in H. Quilter, ed. (London, 1892); *The Case of General Ople and Lady Camper* (New York, 1890), fiction; *The Tale of Chloe: An Episode in the History of Beau Beamish* (New York, 1890), fiction, also published with *The House on the Beach* and *The Case of General Ople and Lady Camper* in one vol. (London, 1894); *One of Our Conquerors*, 3 vols. (London, 1891), novel; *Poems. The Empty Purse. With Odes on the Comic Spirit, Youth and Memory, and Verses* (London, 1892); *Lord Ormont and His Aminta*, 3 vols. (London, 1894), novel; *The Amazing Marriage*, 2 vols. (London, 1895), novel; *Odes in Contribution to the Song of French History* (London, 1898); *A Reading of Life and Other Poems* (London, 1901); *Milton* (London, 1908), verse; *Last Poems* (London, 1909); *Celt and Saxon* (London, 1910), fiction; *Up to Midnight. A Series of Dialogues* (Boston, 1913), fiction.

V. Letters. *Letters to Alice Meynell with Annotations* (London, 1923), a few copies were privately printed for T. J. Wise of some letters from Meredith to E. Clodd and C. K. Shorter (London, 1913), and for M. B. Forman of some letters from Meredith to R. N. Horne (London, 1919), to Swinburne and Watts-Dunton (London, 1922), and various correspondents (London, 1922); C. L. Cline, ed., *The Letters of George Meredith*, 3 vols. (Oxford, 1970).

VI. Biographical and Critical Studies. R. Le Gallienne, *George Meredith: Some Characteristics* (London, 1890), includes some notes on Meredith in America by W. M. Fullerton; G. M. Trevelyan, *The Poetry and Philosophy of George Meredith* (London, 1906); T. S. Short, *On Some of the Characteristics of George Meredith's Prose Writing* (London, 1907); R. H. P. Curle, *Aspects of George Meredith* (London, 1908); J. M. Barrie, *George Meredith* (London, 1909); M. B. Forman, *George Meredith: Some Early Appreciations* (London, 1909); J. Moffatt, *George Meredith: A Primer to the Novels* (London, 1909); E. J. Bailey, *The Novels of George Meredith* (New York, 1910); C. Photiadès, *George Meredith: Sa Vie—Son Imagination—Son Art—Sa Doctrine* (Paris, 1910), English trans. (London, 1913); J. W. Beach, *The Comic Spirit in George Meredith, An Interpretation* (London, 1911); H. Bedford, *The Heroines of George Meredith* (London, 1914); J. H. E. Crees, *George Meredith: A Study of His Works and Personality* (Oxford, 1918); A. M. Butcher, *Memories of George Meredith* (London, 1919); S. M. Ellis, *George Meredith: His Life and Friends* (London, 1919); J. H. E. Crees, *Meredith Revisited* (London, 1921); R. Galland, *George Meredith: Les Cinquante Premières Années* (Paris, 1923); W. Chislett, *George Meredith: A Study and an Appraisal* (London, 1925); J. T. Milnes, *Meredith and the Comic Spirit* (London, 1925); J. B. Priestley, *George Meredith* (London, 1926); M. S. Henderson, *The Writings and Life of George Meredith* (London, 1926); R. E. Sencourt, *The Life of George Meredith* (London, 1929); M. E. Mackay, *Meredith et la France* (Paris, 1937); A. Woods, *George Meredith as Champion of Women and Progressive Education* (Oxford, 1937); G. B. Petter, *Meredith and His German Critics* (London, 1939); S. Sassoon, *Meredith* (London, 1948), considered a notable treatment of the poetry; O. Sitwell, *The Novels of Meredith and Some Notes on the English Novel* (Oxford, 1948); L. Stevenson, *The Ordeal of George Meredith* (New York, 1953), considered the best biography; W. F. Wright, *Art and Substance in George Meredith, a Study in Narrating* (Lincoln, Nebr., 1953); B. Dobrée, *The Broken Cistern: The Clark Lectures, 1952–53* (London, 1954); J. Lindsay, *George Meredith, His Life and Work* (London, 1956); N. Kelvin, *A Troubled Eden, Nature and Society in the Works of George Meredith* (Edinburgh, 1961); G. Beer, *Meredith: A Change of Masks* (London, 1970); V. S. Pritchett, *George Meredith and English Comedy* (London, 1970), the Clark Lectures; D. Williams, *George Meredith: His Life and Lost Love* (London, 1977).

DANTE GABRIEL ROSSETTI
(1828-1882)

Oswald Doughty

I

ROSSETTI, like William Blake, whose works he edited in later life, achieved the rare distinction of eminence in both painting and poetry. And as with Blake, both arts are, for Rossetti, a means of expressing fundamental intellectual and emotional dispositions. He was born in London on 12 May 1828, not far from Oxford Circus, into what his contemporaries would have called "genteel poverty." His father, an Italian political exile turned teacher of Italian in London, later became a professor at King's College there. His mother, seventeen years younger than her husband, was an Anglo-Italian governess. Rossetti's brother, William Michael, and his two sisters, Maria Francesca and the poet Christina Georgina, completed the family.

From King's College School and a private art school, Rossetti passed in 1845 to the Antique School of the Royal Academy, an indifferent, contemptuous, and rebellious student in all. Impatient of academic methods and discipline, he soon drifted away to join two other students, William Holman Hunt and John Everett Millais, in founding the famous Pre-Raphaelite Brotherhood, shortly afterward completed by the accession of two more young painters, James Collinson and Frederic Stephens; a young sculptor, Thomas Woolner; and Rossetti's devoted brother, William, employed in the Excise Office. About these there quickly gathered a small circle of friends and sympathizers practically indistinguishable from the original Brotherhood.

Although united in revolt against the art schools and fashionable art of the day, the Brotherhood differed considerably in other respects. Hunt's dissent was primarily moral. In place of the superficial, trivial, and insincere, he demanded seriousness, morality, nobility. Art must copy "Nature" closely; be "a handmaid in the cause of justice and truth." Millais was at heart indifferent and skeptical. Rosset-

ti thought a revolt against the academicians would be exciting, a good lark. The rest, except as "good companions," scarcely counted. In practice the more obvious revolutionary qualities of the Brotherhood were a more natural way of painting, greater attention to detail, and naturalistic lighting. Hunt's aim of "modernity," of stark realism as a moral influence, was seldom attempted by the others. Admiration for the medieval murals in the Campo Santo at Pisa (almost entirely destroyed in World War II), as reproduced in a book of Lasinio's mediocre engravings, strengthened the Brotherhood's dislike of the conventional "Raphaelism" of the time; hence they named their society "The Pre-Raphaelite Brotherhood."

The leadership of Hunt as first founder of the Brotherhood quickly passed to Rossetti, by accident rather than design. The impress of Rossetti's dominating personality and initiative, of his literary and pictorial talent influenced by acquaintance with Italian art and letters, and of his superior intellectual grasp, imposed upon the Brotherhood and their painting whatever of unity they displayed. Thus the leadership soon publicly accorded to Rossetti by John Ruskin, and angrily denied by Hunt, was essentially justified. Equally so were Rossetti's denials, long afterward, that he had ever been a Pre-Raphaelite at all in the sense of Hunt's "Pre-Raphaelitism," which, in fact, Rossetti's influence unconsciously destroyed. In addition, not only did Rossetti give the Pre-Raphaelites their greatest publicity by founding a propagandist magazine, the *Germ*, but in doing so he extended their influence beyond painting into literature.

Although the *Germ*, which appeared in January 1850 and died the following May, failed to clarify or exemplify the supposed principles of Pre-Raphaelitism beyond a vague assertion of adherence to "Nature," it gave Rossetti the opportunity he desired to publish his writings, both poetry and prose. His contributions—the prose tale "Hand and Soul" and several poems, including "The Blessed Damozel" —and those of his sister Christina are almost all of value that the *Germ* contains. In painting Rossetti was also active, exhibiting his *Girlhood of Mary Virgin* in 1849 and his *Ecce Ancilla Domini!* in 1850. At the same time, Hunt and Millais were exhibiting at the Royal Academy. And on all their canvases, as Rossetti had suggested for the fun of it, there appeared the sign of the Brotherhood, the mysterious initials "P.R.B."

This was the Pre-Raphaelites' undoing. For two years rumors of a secret Brotherhood, in aesthetic and probably political revolt, had accumulated. Whatever political interest the group had shown was in general much less than their interest in art and letters, but it was what would now be called "leftist," as the sympathies of young and impecunious artists tend to be. Formed in the year of revolution, 1848, suspected of secret subversive aims, aesthetic, political, and religious—the destruction of the Royal Academy, the propagation of Chartism, and "Popery"—the Brotherhood invited attack from traditionalists in art, politics, and religion. And indeed the onslaught now made upon it would have been fatal but for the timely aid of Ruskin, who in two letters to the *Times* in May 1851 came to their rescue. Nevertheless, divergent interests and needs soon disrupted the Brotherhood. In 1852, Woolner set out for Australia to find gold; the next year Millais was elected to the once despised academy; and in 1854, Hunt went off to Palestine to paint biblical subjects. William Rossetti and Stephens, failing as painters, turned art critics and by their writings did much to advance Pre-Raphaelitism and Rossetti.

The attack upon the Brotherhood in 1850 marks the opening of the most important formative period in Rossetti's early life. For it was now that he met and fell in love with the golden-haired milliner Elizabeth Siddal, who ten years later became his wife. Into this first love there entered all the idealism Rossetti had absorbed from the Platonic works in his father's study, as well as from the poetry of Dante and the medieval troubadours, which he was himself translating into verse. Almost as strong an influence was that of his devout, quiet, self-controlled mother, so unlike her excitable, visionary, and somewhat eccentric husband. The mother's high Anglicanism stimulated Rossetti's asceticism and moral idealism at this time, and soon became an important element in the internal conflict that disturbed his young manhood and in some degree continued into later years.

In November 1852 Rossetti left home to live at 14 Chatham Place, in rooms overlooking the Thames and Blackfriars Bridge. His mood at this time, reflected in some of his poems, was often uncertain and unhappy. The failure of the *Germ*, of the Brotherhood, of his love for Elizabeth Siddal—a love increasingly difficult as the years passed without marriage, and she herself lost health and beauty—all increased Rossetti's permanent sense of frustration occasioned by the rival claims of poetry and painting upon his time and attention. Temporarily abandoning his attempts to paint in oils, he now turned to watercolors, and during these years produced in this medium many small paintings on Dantesque and Arthurian subjects, now recognized as his best pictorial work.

In 1855, the poverty of the lovers was relieved by Ruskin, who, to assist their marriage, granted them a pension and agreed to buy all their paintings. For by this time, "Lizzie" Siddal was also painting, encouraged by Rossetti, who soon believed her a better artist than himself. Two years later Pre-Raphaelitism entered a new phase, still more remote from Hunt's aims, when Rossetti gathered new admirers at Oxford, including William Morris and Edward Burne-Jones, to paint the walls of the debating hall of the Union Society. Although owing to ignorance of the technique of mural painting, the work quickly faded, it attracted great attention and enthusiasm, and brought Rossetti and Pre-Raphaelitism once again—but this time happily—into the limelight. More insistently than before, it associated the movement with poetry, for Morris and his friend Algernon Swinburne, a fellow undergraduate, soon began to appear as leading poets of the day. Henceforth, this new Pre-Raphaelitism, often "advanced," even "daring" in the eyes of contemporaries, became a fashionable cult, with Rossetti its almost unchallenged leader.

Three years later, in 1860, Rossetti married Miss Siddal. The influence of a vulgar but beautiful model, Fanny, had darkened the friendship between Elizabeth and Rossetti during recent years, and continued to affect their married life, which was saddened in time by the stillbirth of a daughter and by young Mrs. Rossetti's mental overstrain. On 10 February 1862, Elizabeth was found unconscious and dying of an overdose of laudanum. Despite the coroner's verdict of accidental death, Rossetti was haunted for the remainder of his life by suspicions of suicide and by remorse for both real and imaginary wrongs done to her. Overwhelmed with grief and contrition, he impulsively buried in her coffin the book of original poetry he was about to publish, declaring that it had diverted his attention from her sickness and suffering.

Unable to remain where everything spoke of loss, Rossetti soon removed to the fine old house at 16 Cheyne Walk, Chelsea, overlooking the river and close to Battersea Bridge. There Fanny joined him as housekeeper. The house remained his home for the next twenty years, until his death.

II

ROSSETTI's entry, as a widower, into 16 Cheyne Walk, opens the final period in his career. The twenty years that lay before him were to establish his reputation as a leading poet and painter, who nevertheless refused to exhibit his paintings and restricted his social life to a small circle of friends. From watercolors he now turned with increasing skill to oils, and from his former Dantesque and Arthurian subjects to portraits of beautiful women, often representing mythological or fanciful conceptions. "Women and flowers," a friend of Rossetti's contemptuously labeled these paintings, for the change in his art reflected an unhappy change in his way of life.

Disappointment and cynicism had begun to displace Rossetti's former idealism. In poetry he had for many years been almost completely silent. Inspiration had passed with the passing of his first rapture for Elizabeth Siddal. Not until the sonnets "Soul's Beauty" in 1866 and "Body's Beauty" in 1867, written for two of his paintings, did Rossetti reveal his revulsion from cynicism, and a return to his former Dantesque and Platonic idealism. In "Body's Beauty" he laments the power of a disintegrating, soulless passion; in "Soul's Beauty" he exalts one that satisfies imagination and intellect as well as sense; ideal beauty

> ... which can draw,
> By sea or sky or woman, to one law,
> The allotted bondman of her palm and wreath.

> This is that Lady Beauty, in whose praise
>> Thy voice and hand shake still, —long known to thee
>> By flying hair and fluttering hem, —the beat
>> Following her daily of thy heart and feet,

> How passionately and irretrievably,
> In what fond flight, how many ways and days![1]
>> ("Sibylla Palmifera," 6–14)

F. R. Leavis has dismissed this sonnet as mere pretense, despite the evident sincerity of the possibly transient emotion that inspired it. It was in fact the expression of an attitude early and deeply absorbed, which retains its emotional sincerity long after it has been intellectually rejected: an attitude revived in Rossetti at this time by a new experience in love.

During his prolonged stay in Oxford when painting there in 1857, Rossetti had made the acquaintance of Jane Burden, with whom he was said to have fallen in love. But for his long friendship with Elizabeth Siddal they would have married. Instead Jane, much admired by the Oxford Pre-Raphaelites, married the devoted Morris. For some years the Morrises lived in the country; but about this time they returned to London, and soon Rossetti was painting Jane's portrait. It was a period of crisis in Rossetti's own development. Solitary retrospection, ill health, insomnia (with chloral and alcohol an increasing but unavailing remedy for the last) had induced a depression so deep as to approach melancholia. In many a sonnet of *The House of Life* we glimpse the nights of sleepless misery, of vain questioning of the past and the future, that Rossetti experienced during these years in Cheyne Walk.

In those sonnets too we find regret for years in "Willowwood," where parted lovers wander, lost and unhappy, lamenting the frustrated past or the lonely, forbidding future. But in *The House of Life* we also find a new love, "regenerate rapture," as Rossetti calls it, but secret, clandestine. And the portraits of Mrs. Morris now multiply, far beyond those of all other models, to the close of Rossetti's life. Regenerate rapture also brings a poetic revival and inspires the greater part of Rossetti's long sonnet sequence, *The House of Life*. With it Rossetti's poetic ambitions, temporarily buried with the poems in his wife's grave, revive also, and ultimately he allows a persuasive friend to obtain them for him. In some of the sonnets of *The House of Life*, Rossetti asks how it is that a new love can displace the memory of an old one. For *The House of Life* is a record unique in English poetry; unique in its Latin frankness and emotionalism, in its combination of realism and idealism, in its freedom from self-consciousness, and

---

[1]All quotations from the poems are taken from O. Doughty, ed., *Poems* (London, 1961), the Everyman's Library.

in its absorption in its central theme of love. This was recognized and sternly rebuked by a critic in the *Spectator* as late as 1904, with the remark: "Love, his controlling theme, is not an English obsession. We love in the intervals of other business."

Rossetti, having recovered the buried poems, proceeded with their publication, and in 1870 his first volume of original verse appeared, entitled simply *Poems*. Nine years before, his translation of Dante's *Vita Nuova* and the poetry of the troubadours had appeared and received little notice. No such fate befell *Poems*. The critics, sincerely appreciative for the most part, many of them personal friends of the poet, led a chorus of praise, and Rossetti's reputation as a poet-painter was firmly established.

Early in 1871, he became joint tenant with William Morris of the charming old manor house Kelmscott, near Oxford. Morris at this time was seldom there, but his wife and two daughters lived there with Rossetti until the close of the year. In October a vulgar, virulent, and dishonest attack was made upon Rossetti and his poems by a jealous journalist, Robert Buchanan, in the *Contemporary Review*. Shortly afterward it reappeared, enlarged into a pamphlet entitled *The Fleshly School of Poetry*, at that time a damning indictment that could deprive Rossetti not only of his success as a poet, but by frightening away patrons, also of his means of livelihood as a painter. The shock brought a nervous breakdown, and Rossetti attempted suicide by laudanum, the drug that had killed his wife. Three months in Scotland largely restored his mental balance, and an immediate return to Kelmscott and Janey almost completed the cure. Poetry and painting were resumed, but fits of nervousness and suspicion also occurred at times; and a sudden, unprovoked attack by Rossetti upon a party of anglers who, he mistakenly believed, had laughed at him in passing, brought a final departure from Kelmscott and his return to Cheyne Walk in July 1874.

Over the last years of Rossetti's life we need not linger. The "chloralized years," his brother called them. Increasing insomnia and physical decline, increasing recourse to the fatal remedy, such is the main course of Rossetti's life henceforth until the end. Nor was this all. Increasing solitude, increasing debts despite the large sums his works now realized, and consequent slavery at his easel in sickness and in health to meet his obligations were additional burdens. Although he still chiefly painted women, the flowers gradually disappeared, and in harmony with his existence these female subjects become in time symbols of melancholy, of mystery, as in the brooding *Pandora* and *Proserpine*, the cruel and sinister *Astarte Syriaca*, painted amidst much physical and mental anguish. Astarte Syriaca

> . . . of Love's all penetrative spell
> Amulet, talisman, and oracle,—
> Betwixt the sun and moon a mystery.
> (12–14)

After a year or two of "regenerate rapture," Rossetti's poetic inspiration had again subsided, but the last two years of his life witnessed something of a revival. Few of the poems he now wrote were self-expressive. His sonnets on the leading romantic poets were academic in their emotional detachment, probably exercises undertaken in vain attempts to combat insomnia. Similarly detached were the three long "ballads" of these later years, "Rose Mary," "The White Ship," and "The King's Tragedy." On his deathbed Rossetti resumed and completed the macabre *Ballad of Jan Van Hunks*, begun many years before.

Most of Rossetti's later verse was published in 1881 in two volumes, *Ballads and Sonnets* and *Poems*. The poems previously published in 1870 were redistributed, with new ones, throughout the two volumes, the first of which, *Ballads and Sonnets*, included the now completed *House of Life*.

After a visit to the Lake District in the autumn of 1881 in a vain search for restored health, Rossetti returned to London and remained in Cheyne Walk until ordered into the country by his doctor. Reluctantly he went to Birchington, where a friend had placed a large bungalow at his service. There he lingered with fading strength until his death on Easter Day, 9 April 1882.

III

So closely was Rossetti's painting associated with his poetry that it was frequently called by his contemporaries "the painted poetry of Rossetti." We need not doubt the story that tells how the painter James McNeil Whistler, recognizing this quality in a picture on Rossetti's easel one day, a picture that, like many of Rossetti's, had inspired a descriptive sonnet, cried: "Rossetti, take down the picture and frame the sonnet!" Nevertheless, our business here is with Rossetti's poetry alone.

Although Rossetti is generally remembered for one or two well-known poems, such as "The Blessed Damozel" and "Sister Helen," these by no means suggest the measure and variety of his achievement in verse. Nor would even the addition of *The House of Life* make the selection adequately representative. Rossetti's poetry reflects many facets of his own rich, complex personality, and his most significant experiences as well. This largely explains, in a poet who wrote comparatively little, the surprising variety of his verse in both form and content.

In his earliest poetry, an adolescent confusion of temperamental tendencies and parental and literary influences is often evident. The medievalism and Dantesquerie of his father, the high Anglican devotionalism of his mother and sisters, his own instinctive aestheticism, pictorial, colorful, and decorative, all combine and culminate in that unconscious symbol and revelation of the poet's ego in youth, "The Blessed Damozel," who, still longing for her lover on earth,

> . . . leaned out
> From the gold bar of Heaven;
> Her eyes were deeper than the depth
> Of waters stilled at even;
> She had three lilies in her hand,
> And the stars in her hair were seven.
> (1–6)

"My Sister's Sleep," which tells of a girl's death on Christmas Eve, is far more effective in its realism, its severe emotional restraint, than the decorative and sentimental "Blessed Damozel," despite evident traces of immaturity. The tale is told in stark and moving simplicity and economy; it presents indeed a Pre-Raphaelite picture:

> Without, there was a cold moon up,
> Of winter radiance sheer and thin;
> The hollow halo it was in
> Was like an icy crystal cup.
>
> Through the small room, with subtle sound
> Of flame, by vents the fireshine drove
> And reddened. In its dim alcove
> The mirror shed a clearness round.
> . . .
> Twelve struck. That sound, by dwindling years
> Heard in each hour, crept off; and then
> The ruffled silence spread again,
> Like water that a pebble stirs.

> Our mother rose from where she sat:
> Her needles, as she laid them down,
> Met lightly, and her silken gown
> Settled: no other noise than that.
>
> "Glory unto the Newly Born!"
> So, as said angels, she did say,
> Because we were in Christmas Day,
> Though it would still be long till morn.
>
> Just then in the room over us
> There was a pushing back of chairs,
> As some who had sat unawares
> So late, now heard the hour, and rose.
>
> With anxious softly-stepping haste
> Our mother went where Margaret lay,
> Fearing the sounds o'erhead—should they
> Have broken her long watched-for rest!
>
> She stopped an instant, calm, and turned;
> But suddenly turned back again;
> And all her features seemed in pain
> With woe, and her eyes gazed and yearned.
>
> For my part, I but hid my face,
> And held my breath, and spoke no word:
> There was none spoken; but I heard
> The silence for a little space.
>
> Our mother bowed herself and wept:
> And both my arms fell, and I said,
> "God knows I knew that she was dead."
> And there, all white, my sister slept.
>
> Then kneeling, upon Christmas morn
> A little after twelve o'clock,
> We said, ere the first quarter struck,
> "Christ's blessing on the newly born!"
> (13–20; 25–60)

In this poem, incidentally, we have not only one of the earliest but also one of the most impressive examples of Rossetti's extraordinary power to create a sense of silence, and to use it with dramatic effect.

Never again were Rossetti's creative powers so variously active as from the age of nineteen to twenty-six. Besides sonnets and lyrics, he also wrote during these years the "ballads" "Dennis Shand," "Sister Helen," and the most balladlike of all in form, the humorous "Stratton Water." Now too he began many of his longer, best-known poems, later revised and completed, such as "Dante at Verona," "The Portrait," "The Bride's Prelude" (never finished),

"Jenny," "A Last Confession," "The Burden of Nineveh," "The Staff and Scrip."

All these poems are inspired by Rossetti's early diverse experiences, interests, and enthusiasms. Although his Dante in "Dante at Verona" is no more the real Dante than his Blessed Damozel is the Beatrice of the *Paradiso*, their common origin in the *Vita Nuova* and the *Divina Commedia* is more evident than Rossetti's supposed derivation of his Damozel from Poe's "The Raven." Rossetti's imagination was, like his poetic language, too earthy, too physical to re-create Dante's Beatrice; but the Damozel at least suggests for Beatrice a more substantial, somewhat glamorized half-cousin, who has abandoned St. Thomas Aquinas for the Oxford movement. This same inability to create the delicate controls of a purely spiritual relationship similarly affects Rossetti's Dante, who becomes indeed the young Rossetti himself at this time, influenced as he then was by the high moral and ascetic standards of his home. The Dante

> Of the soul's quest whose stern avow
> For years had made him haggard now.
> ("Dante at Verona," 23–24)

recalls Hunt's similar description and portrait of Rossetti in these early years. Nor is this the sole resemblance in the poem; Dante's controlling ideal in Beatrice is also the reflection of Rossetti's own idealism.

Both "The Bride's Prelude" and "The Staff and Scrip" are inspired by Rossetti's enthusiasm for the spirit and physical pomp of romanticized medievalism with the scope it gave him for the expression of passion, of courtly love, of delight in color and decoration. "The Bride's Prelude" also presents a theme that came to have an almost morbid fascination for Rossetti: clandestine passion and its punishment. Already the unblessed damozel who was to appear from time to time in Rossetti's art and life has emerged. Despite its somewhat tedious tale, the poem is notable for its Pre-Raphaelite, colorful, decorative, descriptive detail, and its creation of an atmosphere as tense, as silent, and as real as that in "My Sister's Sleep," a sense of heat and silence as pervasive as that of silence and cold in the other poem:

> Within the window's heaped recess
> The light was counterchanged
> In blent reflexes manifold

> From perfume-caskets of wrought gold
> And gems the bride's hair could not hold
>   . . .
> The room lay still in dusty glare,
>   Having no sound through it
> Except the chirp of a caged bird
> That came and ceased: and if she stirred,
> Amelotte's raiment could be heard.
> (21–25; 96–100)

In a poem of sentimentalized pseudochivalry, "The Staff and Scrip," the hero perishes in the devoted service of a lady he has hardly seen. She continuously mourns his death, very pathetically, until her own demise many years later.

"Jenny," like "The Last Confession," reminds us of Hunt's Pre-Raphaelite principle of the "modern" picture, which must admonish vice, as in his "Awakened Conscience." But with Rossetti admonition yields to sympathy with human suffering and misery. Rossetti's treatment of "Jenny," another unblessed damozel, is, however, weakened by an unconvincingly pious sensuality and by the conventional sentimentality of the period in any literary or pictorial reference to prostitution. When in later years "Jenny" was completed, Fanny became the model, as she was too for the picture and related sonnet "Found," in which Rossetti presented a similar theme.

Although the influences of Robert Browning and of Tennysonian blank verse obviously unite at times in "A Last Confession," the poem retains its originality. As with Rossetti's "Guineveres" and "Astarte Syriaca," the "heroine" of "A Last Confession" (another unblessed damozel) becomes also a femme fatale. The dying Italian patriot, wounded mortally by the Austrians, confesses to a priest that he has murdered the woman he loves:

>   I told you how
> She scorned my parting gift and laughed. And yet
> A woman's laugh's another thing sometimes:
> I think they laugh in Heaven. I know last night
> I dreamed I saw into the garden of God,
> Where women walked whose painted images
> I have seen with candles round them in the church.
> They bent this way and that, one to another,
> Playing: and over the long golden hair
> Of each there floated like a ring of fire
> Which when she stooped, stooped with her, and
>   when she rose
> Rose with her. Then a breeze flew in among them,

As if a window had been opened in heaven
For God to give his blessing from, before
This world of ours should set; (for in my dream
I thought our world was setting, and the sun
Flared, a spent taper;) and beneath that gust
The rings of light quivered like forest-leaves.
Then all the blessed maidens who were there
Stood up together, as it were a voice
That called them; and they threw their tresses back,
And smote their palms, and all laughed up at once,
For the strong heavenly joy they had in them
To hear God bless the world. Wherewith I woke:
And looking round, I saw as usual
That she was standing there with her long locks
Pressed to her side; and her laugh ended theirs.

(110–136)

Impressive, despite its many weaknesses of immaturity, interesting in its revelation of the power over Rossetti's imagination, even in the least likely places, of the *Paradiso*, this poem also reminds us that for Rossetti the blessed damozels were never far from the unblessed.

IV

LIKE all the romantic poets, Rossetti was very conscious of the mystery of human existence. It found expression in his last days in the drawing "The Sphinx," and in two mediocre, still unpublished sonnets, similarly entitled. He was impressed too by the apparently endless flight of absolute time, the passing of epochs, the rise and fall of civilizations. These thoughts and feelings found expression in one of Rossetti's best poems on this theme, "The Burden of Nineveh," suggested by the arrival at the British Museum of a huge stone idol, "A wingèd beast from Nineveh," which symbolizes for Rossetti the insoluble mystery, the apparently endless deceptions of humanity by fate, the futility of human beliefs, the apparent meaninglessness of the universe from a human standpoint.

On London stones our sun anew
The beast's recovered shadow threw.
(No shade that plague of darkness knew,
No light, no shade, while older grew
By ages the old earth and sea.)
Lo thou! could all thy priests have shown
Such proof to make thy godhead known?

From their dead Past thou liv'st alone;
And still thy shadow is thine own,
Even as of yore in Nineveh.
. . .
For as that Bull-god once did stand
And watched the burial clouds of sand,
Till these at last without a hand
Rose o'er his eyes, another land,
And blinded him with destiny:—
So may he stand again; till now,
In ships of unknown sail and prow,
Some tribe of the Australian plough
Bear him afar,—a relic now
Of London, not of Nineveh!

(41–50; 171–180)

A similar mood informs "The Sea Limits," where rhythm and word-music move to a deeper, characteristically sonorous note, suited to both the sea imagery and the serious thought and emotion it embodies: the moan of the sea swell as an eternal measure of the endless lapse of absolute time. Anton Chekhov expressed the same idea in his exquisite little story "The Lady with the Dog," and T. S. Eliot (who found Rossetti's poetry "very important" to himself "at an early phase of his development") in *The Dry Salvages*. For Rossetti the sea is indeed symbolic of the basic mystery of the universe:

Consider the sea's listless chime:
Time's self it is, made audible,—
The murmur of the earth's own shell.
Secret continuance sublime
Is the sea's end: our sight may pass
No furlong further. Since Time was,
This sound hath told the lapse of Time.
. . .
Gather a shell from the strown beach
And listen at its lips: they sigh
The same desire and mystery,
The echo of the whole sea's speech.
And all mankind is thus at heart
Not anything but what thou art:
And Earth, Sea, Man, are all in each.

(1–7; 22–28)

Some of the poems of Rossetti's adolescence appear to have been inspired by his love for Elizabeth Siddal and the joys, sorrows, and complexities it brought into his life. Such are some nine sonnets (later included in *The House of Life*), two excellent lyrics, "Sudden Light" and "The Woodspurge," and the long lyrical poem "Love's Nocturn." One of these sonnets, "The Birth-Bond," reveals his exalted, Dantesque Platonism:

> Have you not noted, in some family
>   Where two were born of a first marriage-bed,
>   How still they own their gracious bond, though fed
> And nursed on the forgotten breast and knee?—
> How to their father's children they shall be
>   In act and thought of one goodwill; but each
>   Shall for the other have, in silence speech,
> And in a word complete community?
>
> Even so, when first I saw you, seemed it, love,
>   That among souls allied to mine was yet
> One nearer kindred than life hinted of.
>   O born with me somewhere that men forget,
>   And though in years of sight and sound unmet,
> Known for my soul's birth-partner well enough!

"Sudden Light," one of the loveliest of Rossetti's lyrics, gives exquisite expression to the sense of the timeless and repetitive that haunted his most profound emotional experience. The poem closes with a hint of love's decay, a foreboding found elsewhere also in Rossetti's verse.

> I have been here before,
>   But when or how I cannot tell:
> I know the grass beyond the door,
>   The sweet keen smell,
> The sighing sound, the lights around the shore.
>
> You have been mine before,—
>   How long ago I may not know:
> But just when at that swallow's soar
>   Your neck turned so,
> Some veil did fall,—I knew it all of yore.
>
> Has this been thus before?
>   And shall not thus Time's eddying flight
> Still with our lives our love restore
>   In death's despite,
> And day and night yield one delight once more?

As in this final stanza, the two polarities of love and death were ever associated in Rossetti's thought. They run, a twofold thread, through *The House of Life*.

In darker mood two years after "Sudden Light," Rossetti wrote "The Woodspurge," technically one of his best lyrics:

> The wind flapped loose, the wind was still,
> Shaken out dead from tree and hill:

> I had walked on at the wind's will,—
> I sat now, for the wind was still.
>
> Between my knees my forehead was,—
> My lips drawn in, said not Alas!
> My hair was over in the grass,
> My naked ears heard the day pass.
>
> My eyes, wide open, had the run
> Of some ten weeds to fix upon;
> Among those few, out of the sun,
> The woodspurge flowered, three cups in one.
>
> From perfect grief there need not be
> Wisdom or even memory:
> One thing then learnt remains to me,—
> The woodspurge has a cup of three.

Here again we have the realism, the pictorial quality, the admirable economy of words and emotional expression earlier revealed in "My Sister's Sleep."

"The Woodspurge" was written in 1856 at a time of tension, when Rossetti's continual postponement of marriage to Elizabeth had alienated the lovers. Three years later, when the rift had widened, Rossetti wrote three little lyrics of fading love: "Even So," "A Little While," and "A New Year's Burden," lamenting "The love once ours, but ours long hours ago." "Even So," again by verbal economy and emotional control admirably suited to its particular lyric form, is an outstanding poem:

> So it is, my dear,
> All such things touch secret strings
>   For heavy hearts to hear.
> So it is, my dear.
>
> Very like indeed:
> Sea and sky, afar, on high,
>   Sand and strewn seaweed,—
> Very like indeed.
>
> But the sea stands spread
> As one wall with the flat skies,
> Where the lean black craft like flies
>   Seem well nigh stagnated,
>   Soon to drop off dead.
>
> Seemed it so to us
> When I was thine and thou wast mine,
>   And all these things were thus,
>   But all our world in us?
>
> Could we be so now?
> Not if all beneath heaven's pall
>   Lay dead but I and thou,
>   Could we be so now!

DANTE GABRIEL ROSSETTI

The next year was the year of Rossetti's marriage, when Elizabeth Siddal appeared to be dying. It is also the year of the inferior but emotional "Song of the Bower," a passionate outburst at the fear of separation from Fanny, which, however, did not occur. The sonnet "Dantis Tenebrae" was written in memory of his father. The next poem, "Lost Days," is one of conscience-stricken regret. Written shortly after his wife's death, it is one of Rossetti's most powerful sonnets:

> The lost days of my life until to-day,
>   What were they, could I see them on the street
>   Lie as they fell? Would they be ears of wheat
> Sown once for food but trodden into clay?
> Or golden coins squandered and still to pay?
>   Or drops of blood dabbling the guilty feet?
>   Or such spilt water as in dreams must cheat
> The throats of men in Hell, who thirst alway?
>
> I do not see them here, but after death
>   God knows I know the faces I shall see,
> Each one a murdered self, with low last breath.
>   "I am thyself,—what hast thou done to me?"
> "And I—and I—thyself," (lo! each one saith,)
>   "And thou thyself to all eternity!"

V

THAT Rossetti's works present only two slight and casual pieces of verse written during the four bohemian years that followed his wife's death surely suggests the superficiality of his way of life at that time and the essential sincerity of his poetry. Not until a new and profound passion revitalized him and his imagination did he recover his creative power and find expression in an extraordinary outburst of love poetry, unique in English literature as the work of a man forty years of age. In the four "Willowwood" sonnets he wrote in 1868, the year in which he painted a portrait of Janey Morris in Cheyne Walk, he described in Dantesque symbolism the mutual admission of a long-suppressed passion:

> I sat with Love upon a woodside well,
>   Leaning across the water, I and he;
>   Nor ever did he speak nor looked at me,
> But touched his lute wherein was audible
> The certain secret thing he had to tell:
>   Only our mirrored eyes met silently
>   In the low wave; and that sound came to be
> The passionate voice I knew; and my tears fell.

> And at their fall, his eyes beneath grew hers;
> And with his foot and with his wing-feathers
>   He swept the spring that watered my heart's drouth.
> Then the dark ripples spread to waving hair,
> And as I stooped, her own lips rising there
>   Bubbled with brimming kisses at my mouth.
>
> ("Willowwood" I)

As already said, *The House of Life* records all the phases, the intellectual and emotional experiences, of Rossetti's "regenerate rapture," his belief in an integrating passion that would compensate for the sorrows and frustrations of the past.

Inevitably there are differences of quality among the hundred and two sonnets of the complete *House of Life*,[2] but a high average is maintained throughout. Several sonnets indeed were written earlier; some are not love sonnets at all. And it must be admitted that Dante Gabriel often approaches his brother's tendency to write lines that are much more easily read than spoken. Sometimes, indeed, the physical difficulty of speaking a line approaches impossibility. Nevertheless, if only as a leader in the sonnet revival of his day—and he is much more than that—Rossetti deserves a leading place among the sonneteers of English poetry. His last love sonnet, "Ardour and Memory," written as late as 1879, is a sonnet of saddened retrospection in the absence of the beloved:

> The cuckoo-throb, the heartbeat of the Spring;
>   The rosebud's blush that leaves it as it grows
>   Into the full-eyed fair unblushing rose;
> The summer clouds that visit every wing
> With fires of sunrise and of sunsetting;
>   The furtive flickering streams to light re-born
>   'Mid airs new-fledged and valorous lusts of morn,
> While all the daughters of the daybreak sing:—
>
> These ardour loves, and memory: and when flown
>   All joys, and through dark forest-boughs in flight
>   The wind swoops onward brandishing the light,
> Even yet the rose-tree's verdure left alone
> Will flush all ruddy though the rose be gone;
>   With ditties and with dirges infinite.

Like so many of Rossetti's sonnets after his residence in the country, at Kelmscott, "Ardour and Memory" is full of images drawn from nature. Few if any think

---

[2]Several that obviously are out of place there were inserted regretfully by Rossetti, to fill gaps caused by the refusal of Mrs. Morris to allow some of the love sonnets—thus lost to us—to appear.

of Rossetti as a poet of nature, nor can we, in the sense of a Wordsworthian depth and delight in the contemplation of natural phenomena; but the extent to which Rossetti's poetry is permeated with natural imagery, generally overlooked, is surprising.

This is not the place for an examination or discussion of the so-called ballads written during Rossetti's last years. Long narrative poems rather than ballads, extravagantly praised in their own day when such verse was popular, they suggest to the modern reader little reason why they should be in verse rather than in prose. In the grimly comic *Ballad of Jan Van Hunks,* however, form and content are integrated, and the surrender of the poetic form would entail loss. In "Rose Mary," the first of the three "ballads" in his late volume *Ballads and Sonnets,* Rossetti combined two favorite themes: the supernatural, and clandestine passion and its punishment. The extravagant praise once bestowed upon the poem by established critics (a poem doubtless written to beguile many sleepless nights and bearing obvious signs of Rossetti's poetic decline) is unlikely to be repeated today. Both "The White Ship" and "The King's Tragedy" are based upon well-known historical incidents. The first describes the shipwreck and drowning of Prince William, son of Henry I. The second tells of the murder of King James I of Scotland, and how Kate Barlass tried to bar the door against his murderers. Both poems have a certain dramatic vitality, but lack subtlety of both characterization and versification. The reader who turns to them for essential poetry will be disappointed.

VI

Rossetti was not a poet to form a pedantic theory of poetry; yet he has sometimes been treated as such. From time to time, for particular reasons, he made casual remarks about poetry in his correspondence. Some of these have been seized upon as if they were carefully considered, definite, and permanent principles: particularly his so necessary injunction to Hall Caine to remember the importance of "fundamental brainwork." Yet even in saying this, Rossetti implicitly denied the importance of formal principles in verse, when he added: "A Shakespeare sonnet is better than the most perfect in form because Shakespeare wrote it." There was some truth in everything Rossetti said about art, and he was too

much of an artist to fear apparent inconsistencies. Thus, writing of William Blake, he declared: "Colour and metre, these are the true patents of nobility in painting and poetry, taking precedence of all intellectual claims." In saying this Rossetti was not blind to the importance of intellect, which he had rightly stressed to Caine, but he also knew that the greatest lyrics could seldom if ever claim profound intellectual content; and for Rossetti, as for those of the later aesthetic movement who followed him, lyric was the essence of poetry. Where intellectual analysis or even comprehension failed, he would wisely follow his own aesthetic intuitions. "The truth is," he wrote of Blake's "My Spectre," "I do not understand it a bit better than anybody else, only I know better than some may know, that it has claims as poetry, apart from the question of understanding it." In this too his attitude was certainly "modern."

For Rossetti as for most of the romantic poets, intellect was closely integrated with emotion. "My opinion is this," wrote Samuel Coleridge, "that deep thinking is attainable only by a man of deep feeling, and that all truth is a species of revelation." That was essentially the romantics' attitude, and it was Rossetti's. For him, therefore, emotion was a basic element of poetry, the most essential of all. Poetry, he declared, was "best where most impassioned, as all poetry must be." This is certainly true of Rossetti's verse, particularly when the emotion is held in restraint, as it usually is verbally, by avoidance of rhetoric, pathos, and self-conscious sentimentality. From these Rossetti is saved, even in *The House of Life,* by the sincerity of his experience and the frankness and realism of his expression. Difficult and dangerous for poetry as is the theme of *The House of Life,* Rossetti for these reasons seldom if ever falls into the unconscious vulgarity that occasionally touches another sonnet sequence of unhappy love then being written, George Meredith's *Modern Love.*

Nearly all the essential poetry Rossetti wrote is intensely personal, subjective in essence, though by no means lacking in objectivity. Woman and love are its chief inspiration, a traditional source of lyric inspiration. His verse is sensuous and passionate but also sincere, profound, and intellectual. He not only thinks through the senses like his romantic predecessors, he also thinks intellectually of his love experiences, relating them to Dantesque and Platonic, or rather Neo-Platonic, idealism. It is an aspect of his work not only overlooked in his own day by his shocked antagonists and enthusiastic supporters—concentrating in affirmation or denial upon his supposed "fleshliness"—it has received inadequate recognition even to the present time.

In a sense, Rossetti was an amateur in both the arts he practiced. He could not endure, much less delight in, mastering the difficulties of technique in either painting or poetry. And poetry, although preferred as "my true mistress," largely because of its freedom from the compulsions attendant upon painting as a means of livelihood, inevitably experienced the disadvantages as well as the advantages of a vocation that through force of circumstance had become an avocation. But though an amateur, Rossetti was an amateur of genius. He was also a great personality in an age of great personalities. "What a supreme man is Rossetti!" exclaimed the poet Philip Marston. "Why is he not some great exiled king, that we might give our lives in trying to restore him to his kingdom?" And to a would-be denigrator of the poet, "You mustn't say anything against Rossetti," was the reply of Whistler. "Rossetti was a king!"

SELECTED BIBLIOGRAPHY

I. Bibliography. W. M. Rossetti, *Bibliography of the Works of Dante Gabriel Rossetti* (London, 1905); W. M. Rossetti, *Dante Gabriel Rossetti: Classified Lists of His Writings* (London, 1906); T. J. Wise, *The Ashley Library Catalogue*, 11 vols. (London, 1922–1936), vols. IV, VIII, IX, and X have particular reference to Rossetti MSS and printed items, the Ashley Library was purchased by the British Museum in 1938; P. F. Baum, ed., *Dante Gabriel Rossetti* (Durham, N. C., 1931), an analytical list of MSS in the Duke University Library with hitherto unpublished verse and prose; T. G. Ehrsam, R. H. Deily, and R. M. Smith, *Bibliographies of Twelve Victorian Authors* (New York, 1936).

II. Collected Works. W. M. Rossetti, ed., *Collected Works*, 2 vols. (London, 1886); W. M. Rossetti, ed., *Poetical Works* (London, 1895), contains poems not published in Rossetti's lifetime; W. M. Rossetti, ed., *The Works* (London, 1911); O. Doughty, ed., *Poems* (London, 1957), also in Everyman's Library (London, 1961).

III. Separate Works. *The Early Italian Poets* (London, 1861), translations, in 1 vol. of 2 pts. (1874), also in the Temple Classics (London, 1904) and the Muses' Library (London, 1905); *Poems* (London, 1870), new ed. with additional poems (London, 1881); *Poems* (Leipzig, 1873), Tauchnitz ed.; *Dante and His Circle: With the Italian Poets Preceding Him* (London, 1874), pt. 2 with Italian text (Lon-

don, 1908), a rev. and rearr. ed. of *The Early Italian Poets*; *Ballads and Sonnets* (London, 1881); *The Ballad of Jan Van Hunks* (London, 1929), first published posthumously, intro. by M. Bell, also a text from original MSS by J. R. Wahl, ed. (New York, 1952).

IV. Selections. E. G. Gardner, ed., *Poems and Translations* (London, 1912), the Everyman's Library; *Poems and Translations, 1850–1870* (Oxford, 1914), in the World's Classics; *Poems and Translations 1850–1870* (London, 1926), in the Oxford Standard Poets; *The House of Life* (Cambridge, Mass., 1928), intro. and notes by P. F. Baum; F. L. Lucas, ed., *Dante Gabriel Rossetti* (London, 1933), an anthology; J. C. Troxell, ed., *Sister Helen* (New Haven, Conn., 1939); J. R. Wahl, ed., *The Kelmscott Love Sonnets of Dante Gabriel Rossetti* (Cape Town, 1954), with intro. essay.

V. Letters. W. M. Rossetti, *D. G. Rossetti's Family Letters, With a Memoir*, 2 vols. (London, 1895); G. B. Hill, ed., *Letters of Dante Gabriel Rossetti to William Allingham, 1854–70* (London, 1897); W. M. Rossetti, ed., *Ruskin: Rossetti: Pre-Raphaelitism* (London, 1899); W. M. Rossetti, ed., *Pre-Raphaelite Diaries and Letters* (London, 1900); W. M. Rossetti, ed., *Rossetti Papers, 1862–70* (London, 1903); W. M. Rossetti, ed., *Family Letters of Christina Rossetti* (London, 1908); O. Doughty, ed., *Letters of Dante Gabriel Rossetti to His Publisher, F. S. Ellis* (London, 1928), with intro. and notes; J. Purves, ed., "Dante Gabriel Rossetti: Letters to Miss Alice Boyd," in the *Fortnightly Review* (May 1928); H. G. Wright, ed., "Unpublished Letters from Theodore Watts-Dunton to Swinburne," in the *Review of English Studies* (April 1934); J. C. Troxell, ed., *Three Rossettis* (Cambridge, Mass., 1937), unpubl. letters to and from Dante Gabriel, Christina, and William; P. F. Baum, ed., *Dante Gabriel Rossetti's Letters to Fanny Cornforth* (Baltimore, 1940); A. Asrian, "The Browning-Rossetti Friendship," in *Publications of the Modern Language Association* (December 1958); O. Doughty and J. R. Wahl, eds., *Letters of Dante Gabriel Rossetti*, vol. I: *1835–1860* and vol. II: *1861–1870* (Oxford, 1965); vol. III: *1871–1876* and vol. IV: *1877–1882* (Oxford, 1967); J. Bryson and J. Troxell, eds., *Dante Gabriel Rossetti and Jane Morris: Their Correspondence* (Oxford, 1976).

VI. Biographical and Critical Studies. R. Buchanan, *The Fleshly School of Poetry* (London, 1872); T. H. Caine, *Recollections of Dante Gabriel Rossetti* (London, 1882), repr. with additions and omissions in 1928; W. Sharp, *Dante Gabriel Rossetti* (London, 1882); W. Hamilton, *The Aesthetic School in England* (London, 1882); P. W. Nicholson, *Dante Gabriel Rossetti, Poet and Painter* (Edinburgh, 1886), in the Round Table series; J. Knight, *Life of Dante Gabriel Rossetti* (London, 1887); W. M. Rossetti, *Dante Gabriel Rossetti as Designer and Writer* (London, 1889); W. H. Pater, "Dante Gabriel Rossetti," in *Appreciations* (London, 1889); H. V. Marillier, *Dante Gabriel Rossetti* (London, 1899; 2nd ed., abr. and rev., 1901).

F. M. Hueffer, *Rossetti. A Critical Essay on His Art*

(London, 1902); H. T. Dunn, *Recollections of Dante Gabriel Rossetti and His Circle* (London, 1904); A. C. Benson, *Rossetti* (London, 1906), in the English Men of Letters series; W. M. Rossetti, *Some Reminiscences*, 2 vols. (London, 1906); F. G. Stephens, "D. G. Rossetti," in the *Preraphaelite* (London, 1908), a repr. of the original study publ. in *Portfolio Monographs* (1894); F. Rutter, *D. G. Rossetti* (London, 1908).

L. A. Willoughby, *Dante Gabriel Rossetti and German Literature* (Oxford, 1912); H. Jackson, *The Eighteen Nineties* (London, 1913); H. Dupré, *Un Italien d'Angleterre* (Paris, 1921); M. Beerbohm, *Rossetti and His Circle* (London, 1922), caricatures; R. L. Megroz, *Dante Gabriel Rossetti* (London, 1928); E. Waugh, *Rossetti, His Life and Works* (London, 1928).

R. D. Waller, *The Rossetti Family (1824–54)* (Manchester, 1932); F. Winwar, *The Rossettis and Their Circle* (London, 1934); E. R. Vincent, *Gabriele Rossetti in England* (Oxford, 1936); W. Gaunt, *The Pre-Raphaelite Tragedy* (London, 1942); N. Gray, *Rossetti, Dante, and Ourselves* (London, 1947); R. Ironside, *Pre-Raphaelite Painters* (London, 1948); O. Doughty, *A Victorian Romantic: D. G. Rossetti* (London, 1949; 2nd ed., 1960); G. Hough, *The Last Romantics* (London, 1949).

P. Henderson, ed., *The Letters of William Morris* (London, 1950); J. Heath-Stubbs, *The Darkling Plain* (London, 1950); O. Doughty, "Rossetti's Conception of the 'Poetic' in Poetry and Painting," in *Essays by Divers Hands*, Transactions of the Royal Society of Literature, vol. XXVI (Oxford, 1953); O. Doughty, "D. G. Rossetti as a Translator," in *Theoria* (Pietermaritzburg, 1953); G. C. Leroy, *Perplexed Prophets* (Philadelphia, 1953); P. Lautor, "The Narrator of 'The Blessed Damozel,'" in *Modern Language Notes* (May 1958); W. B. Todd, "Notes on Rossetti's 'Early Italian Poets,'" in the *Book Collector* (London, 1960); A. J. Sambrook, "D. G. Rossetti and R. W. Dixon," in *Études Anglaises*, 14 (1961); "Rossetti's 'Willow-Wood' Sonnets and the Structure of 'The House of Life,'" in *Victorian Newsletter*, 22 (1961); J. Savarit, *Tendances mystiques et esotériques chez Danté-Gabriel Rossetti* (Paris, 1961).

CHRISTINA ROSSETTI

(1830-1894)

Georgina Battiscombe

I

CHRISTINA ROSSETTI was born in London on 5 December 1830, the fourth and youngest child of Gabriele Rossetti and his wife, Frances. Both as a person and as a poet Christina was to be so greatly influenced by her family that any study of her life and works must go into the family background in some detail.

Like his elder son and his younger daughter, Gabriele Rossetti was a poet. He had held the position of curator of antique bronzes and marbles in the museum at Naples, but his clearly expressed liberal opinions made him objectionable to the government of King Ferdinand and he was obliged to flee the country. Arriving in England in 1824, he settled in London and maintained himself by teaching Italian, later becoming professor of Italian at King's College, London University. In 1826, he married Frances Polidori, a girl seventeen years younger than himself, of part-Italian descent. Her father, Gaetano Polidori, was, like Rossetti, an Italian refugee and a man of letters. He was married to an Englishwoman, Anna Maria Pierce, by whom he had eight children. One of their sons, John, became traveling physician to Lord Byron, with whom he soon quarreled, afterward committing suicide. From her Polidori relations Christina is said to have inherited her good looks and also what D. M. Stuart describes as "that indefinable and indelible air of good-breeding remembered by all who knew her." The Polidori home was at Holmer Green in Buckinghamshire, and here as a child Christina spent many happy holidays, learning the love of flowers, small animals, and insects that is a marked characteristic of her writings.

At home in London, the atmosphere of the Rossetti family circle was essentially an intellectual one. "I always had a passion for intellect," said Mrs. Rossetti, "and my wish was that my husband should be distinguished for intellect, and my children too." The wish came true, so much so that the poor lady was also heard to remark that she could have done with a little less intellect in her family and a little more common sense. Of the four children—Maria Francesca, Gabriel Charles Dante (usually known as Dante Gabriel), William Michael, and Christina Georgina—Christina was rated in her childhood the least intellectual. In temperament she was nearest to Dante Gabriel, they being called the "storms" of the family, while Maria and William were the "calms." Christina was both pretty and passionate; in old age she told her niece that on one occasion, when scolded by her mother, she seized a pair of scissors and ripped up her own arm. But such outbreaks were rare, and on the whole her childhood was a very happy one. The four children were devoted to one another and to their parents. All four drew, painted, wrote stories and verses, read avidly; "as they shared the same tastes no one was bored or left out, frustrated or underprivileged."[1] Money was not plentiful, but the Rossettis had no extravagant tastes, and in these early days there was always enough for their simple, unworldly needs.

The tradition of life in the Rossetti home in Hallam Street was Italian rather than English, even down to the food served at meals. Gabriele Rossetti kept open house for Italian refugees of all sorts, from the great Giuseppe Mazzini to a passing organ grinder. Though English was Christina's mother tongue, she spoke it with the carefully exquisite intonation usually characteristic of the well-educated foreigner. She spoke and wrote Italian with such ease that in later years she composed poems in the language that were described by an Italian critic as "not undeserving of commendation." It is typical of her dual cultural inheritance that as a child Christina's two favorite books were *The Arabian Nights* and the plays of Pietro Metastasio. The Rossetti children reveled in

[1] R. G. Grylls, *Portrait of Rossetti* (London, 1964), p. 15.

the "horrific" romances of Ann Radcliffe, Monk Lewis, and Charles Maturin, and their favorite poets were George Crabbe, Samuel Taylor Coleridge, Percy Bysshe Shelley, and, above all, John Keats. Gabriele Rossetti was a devoted Dante scholar and, although when they were very young the children not unnaturally rebelled against the idea of reading Dante, they certainly did not escape that all-pervading influence.

Beside this Italian tradition must be set the intelligent, respectable, ladylike, essentially English outlook that the Polidori sisters had inherited from their Pierce ancestry. Frances Rossetti was English rather than Italian in her attitude toward life, and she was also a convinced and practicing member of the Church of England. Though nominally a Roman Catholic, Gabriele was in fact an agnostic, but he allowed all the children to be brought up in their mother's faith. According to Christina's brother William, love of her family and devotion to religion were the twin motive-powers in Christina's life, and the importance to her of this Anglican upbringing cannot be overestimated. It was Anglicanism of a special kind, the intensely serious, sober religion of the early years of the Oxford movement, the religion of John Keble and Hurrell Froude and the young John Henry Newman, austere, even ascetic, and very rigid, yet at the same time glowing with the fire of the romantic revival. Christina was in her early teens when the Rossetti family first began to attend services at Christ Church, Albany Street, where the vicar, William Dodsworth, was a well-known figure in the Oxford movement, and it was at this church that Christina learned the teaching and practices of what was afterward to be known as Anglo-Catholicism.

At home, the secular as well as the religious education of the two girls was entirely in the hands of their mother. But formal education was perhaps the least important factor in the upbringing of these children, living as they did in a circle so peculiarly alive to everything of intellectual or artistic interest. Christina in particular was much influenced by her brilliant brother, Dante Gabriel, who enlivened the boredom of conventional schooling by discovering for himself the writings of William Shakespeare, Sir Walter Scott, William Blake, and, among contemporary poets, Alfred Tennyson, Robert Browning, and the now forgotten Ebenezer Jones. But although he had written poems and plays from earliest childhood, Dante Gabriel was determined that he would be primarily a painter. He always remained convinced that Christina too had artistic gifts, and he may well have been right, to judge from a very able portrait-sketch of him that she made when she was only seventeen.

Christina, however, chose poetry. At the age of five, she composed her first couplet, and from twelve onward she was forever scribbling verses, although she was so shy that she never allowed her family to catch her in the act of composition. In 1847, her grandfather Polidori collected the best of these early poems and printed a small volume of them at his private press.

By this date, when Christina was in her seventeenth year, troubles were gathering thickly round the Rossetti family. In 1843, Gabriele had fallen ill. Being also threatened with blindness, he was obliged to abandon his teaching post, and the responsibility for maintaining the family now fell entirely on his wife. Dante Gabriel had already determined on an artistic career and was therefore useless as a breadwinner, but Maria took work as a governess and William at the age of fifteen became a government clerk. Christina was also intended to be a governess, but her health made this impossible. During the nine years from 1843 to 1852 she was frequently ill with what at one time was thought to be angina, at another, tuberculosis. These early and apparently very serious illnesses had a great effect upon her outlook and therefore upon her poetry; William Rossetti says of her that "she was compelled, even if not naturally disposed, to regard this world as a 'valley of the shadow of death.'"

In order to support her family, Frances Rossetti turned to teaching, taking in pupils and later starting a day school, where Christina helped as far as her health allowed. She also made herself useful in a very different way, sitting for Dante Gabriel as a model for the head of the Blessed Virgin in his two pictures *The Girlhood of Mary Virgin* and *Ecce Ancilla Domini.* Disapproving of the unimaginative teaching at the Academy School of Art, Dante Gabriel had persuaded the painter Ford Madox Brown to take him as a pupil. Now, in 1848, he founded the famous Pre-Raphaelite Brotherhood, consisting of seven young men: Dante Gabriel himself, W. Holman Hunt, John Millais, William Rossetti, Thomas Woolner, Frederick George Stephens, and James Collinson, with Madox Brown as a benevolent father figure. The aims of "the P.R.B." were never clearly defined:

Mainly it was Anti: against the enervating influence of Raphael's followers down to contemporary Academicians with their trivial sentimentality and glossy surfaces; against the neglect of moral subject-matter and whatever obscured primary colours and definite outline on the canvas. . . . In technique they believed in painting with a bold free-hand sweep of the brush, at the same time demanding minute attention to detail.[2]

But if their aims were indefinite, their paintings were clearly very different from the productions of the average academician, and in 1849 the exhibition of *The Girlhood of Mary Virgin* and pictures by Hunt and Millais marked the beginning of a new movement in the world of art.

Christina of course made acquaintance with the members of the P.R.B. and identified herself with their interests and enthusiasms. Of them all, the one who chanced to fall in love with her was the somnolent and not very exciting James Collinson, then regarded as a painter of some promise. He proposed to her in 1848 and was rejected on the ground that he had recently become a convert to Roman Catholicism; whereupon he reverted to his original Anglicanism and proposed once more. This time he was accepted. Two years later, however, he once again joined the Church of Rome, and Christina broke off the engagement. William Rossetti describes Collinson as "a well-meaning man, of timorous conscience." Christina had probably been less in love with him than with love itself but, nevertheless, to quote William Rossetti again, "he had struck a staggering blow at her peace of mind on the very threshold of womanly life, and a blow from which she did not fully recover for years."

Late in 1849 or early in 1850, Dante Gabriel met a beautiful golden-haired girl, a milliner's apprentice named Elizabeth "Lizzie" Siddall, with whom he fell violently in love. One of Christina's sonnets, "In an Artist's Studio," well describes his infatuation with this lovely but ineffectual creature:

> One face looks out from all his canvases,
>   One selfsame figure sits or walks or leans:
>   We found her hidden just behind those screens,
> That mirror gave back all her loveliness.
> A queen in opal or in ruby dress,
>   A nameless girl in freshest summer-greens,
>   A saint, an angel—every canvas means
> The same one meaning, neither more nor less.

He feeds upon her face by day and night,
  And she with true kind eyes looks back on him,
Fair as the moon and joyful as the light:
  Not wan with waiting, not with sorrow dim;
  Not as she is, but was when hope shone bright;
  Not as she is, but as she fills his dream.[3]

Lizzie sat as Dante Gabriel's model for innumerable paintings and drawings; he wrote poems to her, spent himself in devotion to her, but she remained aloof. William described her talk as being "like the speech of a person who wanted to turn off the conversation and leave matters as they were before," and as she was in conversation so she was in love. She could not bring herself either to marry Dante Gabriel or, it seems, to become his mistress, but neither could she let him go. Meanwhile, her health went from bad to worse, and the Rossetti family, who had naturally never been enthusiastic about the marriage, became more and more averse to any such idea.

January 1850 saw the publication of a Pre-Raphaelite periodical, somewhat inelegantly entitled the *Germ*, which only survived for four monthly issues. To this paper Christina contributed seven poems. Except for the privately printed volume of juvenilia, the only poem of hers yet to appear in print had been "Heart's Chill Between," published two years previously in the *Athenaeum*.

In the spring of 1853, Mrs. Rossetti at last abandoned her unsuccessful attempts to run a day school in London and removed with her husband and Christina to Frome in Somerset, where they started yet another school, which in its turn proved a failure. This stay at Frome was for Christina a period of most uncongenial exile, but it lasted only a year, for in 1854 William, whose prospects had considerably improved, brought the whole family back to London to live with him in Albany Street. Hardly had they settled into their new home when Gabriele died. Christina now took to doing such hack work as articles for dictionaries and Italian translations in order to make a little money, but she seldom succeeded in earning as much as ten pounds a year. Meanwhile she was writing some of her best poetry, including "Young Love Lies Sleeping," "Remember Me When I Am Gone Away," and "When I Am Dead, My Dearest." In 1854, there was talk of producing a volume of her

[2]*Ibid.*, p. 26.

[3]All verse quotations are taken from W. M. Rossetti, ed., *The Poetical Works of Christina Georgina Rossetti* (London, 1904).

verses with illustrations by Lizzie Siddall, but the idea came to nothing, and it was not until 1861 that, with the help and encouragement of Dante Gabriel, she set about preparing her poems for publication.

The book was to be called *Goblin Market*, after the long poem, which is perhaps the best-known of all Christina Rossetti's works. The book was published in 1862 and proved an immediate triumph, the first popular success achieved by the Pre-Raphaelites. Christina, said Algernon Charles Swinburne, was a Pre-Raphaelite Jael leading her hosts to victory. A second volume, *The Prince's Progress*, which appeared in 1866, was almost as great a success as the first one. Christina had now "arrived" in the literary world; she had become what the Victorians termed a "lion," and she was invited to meet other lions, such as Browning and Tennyson. But she would not take her place in the intellectual and literary society of the day; her religion taught her to flee the snares of the world and to shun all praise and applause. She was also inhibited by her paralyzing shyness. At the height of her fame, she went to stay with Mrs. Alexander Gilchrist, widow of Blake's biographer and an intimate friend of the Rossetti family. When Christina did not appear for supper her hostess went up to her room and found her "waiting in some trepidation, too shy to venture down alone, or to be formally announced by the servant, into the expectant group in the drawing room."[4] On the rare occasions when she could be persuaded to attend a party her behavior could be rather disconcerting:

Mrs. Tebbs herself told me that one day she was at a party when suddenly there uprose from a chair a little woman dressed in black, who announced solemnly, "I am Christina Rossetti!" and having so said returned to her chair.[5]

In spite of Christina's rise to fame the 1860's were not happy years for the Rossetti family. In 1860, Dante Gabriel had at last married his Lizzie, but in 1862 she died of an overdose of laudanum in circumstances pointing strongly to suicide. In the first onset of his grief Dante Gabriel sought comfort in the family home with his mother and Christina, but in time he decided to settle at Tudor House, Cheyne Walk. It

was here that Christina was to meet so many of the famous writers and painters of the day, including Swinburne, always a great admirer of her poetry, George Meredith, and William Morris. It was also at Tudor House that she renewed acquaintance with an old pupil of her father's, Charles Bagot Cayley, a scholar and linguist who translated Aeschylus, Homer, Dante, Petrarch, and the Hebrew psalms, and even supervised a translation of the New Testament into the Iroquois language.

Christina fell in love with this gentle, abstracted scholar, and he with her, although he seems to have been a singularly ineffectual lover. In an affectionate but slightly exasperated poem, Christina likens him to a buzzard and a mole:

> My blindest buzzard that I know,
>   My special mole, when will you see?
>   Oh no, you must not look at me,
> There's nothing hid for me to show.
> I might show facts as plain as day:
> But, since your eyes are blind, you'd say,
>   "Where? What?" and turn away.
>   ("A Sketch," 14–20)

In 1866, Cayley proposed marriage, and Christina rejected him as she had rejected Collinson, solely on religious grounds. He had been brought up in the Church of England, but apparently was no longer a strict, believing Christian. The matter touched Christina much more deeply than her youthful engagement to Collinson had, for there is little doubt that she was deeply in love with Cayley. He remained her faithful friend until his death in 1883, writing her stilted little letters and sending her such curious presents as a sea mouse preserved in spirits.

The 1860's also saw Christina's first visit to her paternal homeland of Italy, an experience that awakened some deep racial memory:

> To see no more the country half my own,
>   Nor hear the half familiar speech,
>   Amen, I say; I turn to that bleak North
>   Whence I came forth—
> The South lies out of reach.
>
> But when our swallows fly back to the South,
>   To the sweet South, to the sweet South,
> The tears may come again into my eyes
>   On the old wise,
> And the sweet name to my mouth.
>   ("*Italia, Io Ti Saluto*")

[4]M. F. Sandars, *The Life of Christina Rossetti* (London, 1930), p. 134.
[5]*Ibid.*, p. 130.

Other holidays were spent with her friends the Bell Scotts at Penkill Castle in Ayrshire, home of Alice Boyd, a great patron of Pre-Raphaelitism in the North.

In 1871, Dante Gabriel became co-tenant of Kelmscott Manor, near Lechlade, the other tenant being William Morris, with whose wife, Janey, Dante Gabriel was already deeply in love. Christina was a frequent visitor to Kelmscott whenever her health allowed, but this same year she was smitten with Graves's disease and remained an invalid for several years. She bore her suffering and, what was even more trying, the physical disfigurement incidental to this disease, with the greatest bravery and cheerfulness. During her illness she wrote little or no poetry, but in 1872 she published *Sing-Song*, an attractive book of verses for children.

The early 1870's saw the breakup of Christina's home circle, for in 1873 Maria became an Anglican nun, and two years later William married Ford Madox Brown's daughter, Lucy. For the first two years of their married life, William and Lucy shared a house with Mrs. Rossetti and Christina, but in 1876 it was thought best to separate, Mrs. Rossetti and Christina making their home with the Polidori aunts in Torrington Square. Maria, who had found great happiness during her brief life as a nun, died this same year. She was a stern character whose view of religion was even more literal minded than Christina's. We are told that "she shrank from entering the Mummy Room at the British Museum under a vivid realization of how the general resurrection might occur, even as one stood among those solemn corpses turned into a sight for sightseers."[6] But according to Dante Gabriel, Maria was "the cheeriest of us all," and the two sisters had dearly loved one another. It was of Maria that Christina wrote in a moving poem:

> My love whose heart is tender said to me,
> "A moon lacks light unless her sun befriend her.
> Let us keep tryst in Heaven, dear Friend," said she,
> My love whose heart is tender.
>
> From such a loftiness no words could bend her;
> Yet still she spoke of "us," and spoke as "we,"
> Her hope substantial, whilst my hope grew slender.

[6]L. M. Packer, *Christina Rossetti* (Cambridge–New York, 1963), p. 312.

> Now keeps she tryst beyond earth's utmost sea,
> Wholly at rest, tho' storms should toss and rend her;
> And still she keeps my heart and keeps its key,
> My love whose heart is tender.
>   (Untitled, from "Songs for Strangers and Pilgrims")

Another tragic sorrow was Dante Gabriel's physical and mental deterioration. For some years he had been obliged to take chloral to combat his insomnia, and now, with ill health and troubles of many sorts coming upon him, he had increasing recourse to chloral and whiskey. Through these sad years Christina continued to write poetry, and she also gave much time to writing books in prose for the Society for Promoting Christian Knowledge, work that she regarded as her duty. In 1881, she published *A Pageant and Other Poems*, including with other good things the sonnet sequence "Monna Innominata." In 1882, Dante Gabriel's long and painful decline ended. He had gone down to Birchington in Kent, the doctors hoping that he might benefit by the sea air; and Mrs. Rossetti and Christina went there to keep him company and help with the nursing. He died on Easter Day. A year later Charles Cayley also died, leaving Christina as his literary executor. In 1886 came the worst loss of all, the death of old Mrs. Rossetti. Christina had always put her mother first in her affections, and she expressed her love in a charming series of valentines, the last one, written in the year of Mrs. Rossetti's death, ending with the lines:

> But blest be any weather which finds us still together,
> My pleasure and my treasure, O blessed Mother mine.

Christina now devoted herself to the care of her two old aunts until they also died. She published no more poetry, although she continued to write poems, which were not printed until after her death. In 1892, she was operated on for cancer. She recovered and lived for another two years, more or less an invalid, but by August 1894 it was clear that she was dying. For a while her mind was clouded by spiritual terror and distress, but at the end peace returned; and she died quietly on the morning of 29 December 1894. Her last poem was a curiously appropriate one:

> Sleeping at last, the trouble and tumult over,
> Sleeping at last, the struggle and horror past,
> Cold and white, out of sight of friends and of lover,
> Sleeping at last.

No more a tired heart downcast or overcast,
No more pangs that wring or shifting fears that hover,
Sleeping at last in a dreamless sleep locked fast.

Fast asleep. Singing birds in their leafy cover
Cannot wake her, nor shake her the gusty blast.
Under the purple thyme and the purple clover
Sleeping at last.
("Sleeping at Last")

II

CHRISTINA ROSSETTI was influenced on the one hand by Pre-Raphaelitism, on the other by the Oxford movement. Of these two forces, Pre-Raphaelitism was by far the most powerful where her poetry was concerned, but the Oxford movement had the greater effect upon her life and character. It is strange to see her passionate Italian side disciplined into a correct Church of England mold: the sister of Dante Gabriel Rossetti trying to behave like the typical heroine of that most respectable and ladylike of novelists, Charlotte Mary Yonge. In character Christina was retiring and reserved—it should be remembered that John Keble, the model poet of the Oxford movement, regarded reserve not merely as a Christian virtue but as a basis for a complete and reasoned *Ars Poetica*. Christina had taught herself to practice asceticism, neither needing nor demanding superfluities. Before her illness in 1871 she was a singularly good-looking woman, but she was always a hard mistress to her own beauty. Her clothes were ugly and unfashionable; Max Beerbohm drew a cartoon showing Dante Gabriel remonstrating with his sister: "Well, Christina, your heart may be like a singing-bird, but why do you dress like a pew-opener?"

In her poetry, however, the opposite strain in Christina Rossetti's nature came uppermost. Here is no sign of the reserve inculcated so carefully by the prophets of the Oxford movement, no vestige of that dislike of emotional exposure so characteristic of the British temperament. In fact, no English poet lays bare personal emotion more unashamedly than Christina Rossetti does in the best of her lyrics. Here is nothing ascetic, but rather an intense awareness and delight in the beauties of this world. Her poetry is not sensual as Dante Gabriel's poetry and pictures are sensual—that infamous jibe about "the fleshly school of poetry" hurt his spirit so much because it

came just a little too near the mark—but it is certainly sensuous. Her poems are as full of color and detail as a Pre-Raphaelite picture; she crams them with jewels and flowers, with rich fabrics and tapestries, with beautiful things to see and touch and smell and taste:

Raise me a dais of silk and down;
    Hang it with vair and purple dyes;
Carve it in doves and pomegranates,
    And peacocks with a hundred eyes;
Work it in gold and silver grapes,
    In leaves and silver fleurs-de-lys;
Because the birthday of my life
    Is come, my love is come to me.
("A Birthday," 9–16)

It should be remarked that this is the only one of Christina's better-known poems—possibly it would be correct to say it is the only one of all her poems—to deal with a happy fulfillment to love. The chief themes of her poetry are love and death, but the love is either unrequited or cut short. She writes of this tragic unfulfilled love in a tone that is curiously personal. Speaking of the poem that begins, "I took my heart in my hand," Maurice Bowra says, "No woman could write with this terrible directness if she did not to some degree know the experience which she described." The question is, to what degree did Christina actually know this experience for herself, and to what degree did she imagine it or deduce it from the experience of those around her?

Christina had a lively and sympathetic imagination. We know that she could write convincingly about an unhappy love before she had experienced love of any sort: the twin poems "Death's Chill Between" and "Heart's Chill Between" were written when she was only sixteen. It would be a great mistake to suppose that because Christina's love poems are so personal they are necessarily written to or about any particular person; it is a worse mistake to use the contents or chronology of her poems as evidence to support a theory about the nature of her love life. Unfortunately, Lona Mosk Packer, the most scholarly of Christina's biographers, has fallen into just this error. She believes that the love of Christina's life was neither Collinson nor Cayley but the painter-poet William Bell Scott, who was a married man; hence the sense of guilt and horror that characterizes some—but by no means most—of her love poetry. Christina certainly had a special liking for Bell Scott—William Rossetti tells us that he was "a man whom she viewed with great predilection"— but there is no evidence to suggest that she viewed him with love, and in the absence of such evidence the best that can be said for Mrs. Packer's theory is the Scottish verdict of "not proven."

Against this theory, on the other hand, must be set the fact that no breath of family tradition or whisper of gossip hints at any such passion on Christina's part. Moreover, it seems impossible that she could have used her love for Cayley merely as a stalking-horse to conceal a far greater love for Bell Scott; that upright and truthful man, William Rossetti, states deliberately and explicitly that "no woman ever loved a man more deeply or more constantly," adding that Christina loved Cayley "to the last day of his life, and the last day of her own."

It could be argued in favor of the Bell Scott hypothesis that if in fact Christina loved Cayley so deeply she could not possibly have refused to marry him on such inadequate grounds. Cayley was not an unbeliever in any very militant sense; he was, indeed, a nominal member of Christina's own church, and as far as religious differences were concerned their position would have been similar to the position of Christina's parents, who had enjoyed a very happy, united married life, although one of them was a convinced Anglican and the other in name a Roman Catholic but in fact an agnostic. But to maintain that Christina's reasons were inadequate is to misunderstand the whole ethos of her period and setting. Some of her contemporaries, in fact as well as in fiction, refused to marry their lovers for the very same reason that made Christina refuse Cayley. Isobel Bateman, at one time leading lady to the famous actor Henry Irving and later mother-general of an Anglican order of nuns, refused a young man whom she loved because he was an unbeliever. That intrepid traveler Isabella Bird Bishop had an aunt who "refused a clerical suitor on a doctrinal scruple and pined away,"[7] a martyrlike fate that also overtook Caroline Lydell, a character in Miss Yonge's story *The Two Guardians* who had broken off her engagement to a rich and eligible young man for a similar reason. (Incidentally, Miss Yonge is the most reliable guide we possess to the emotions and actions of young ladies such as Christina Rossetti, who were brought up under the influence of the Oxford movement.)

The real trouble, of course, is Cayley's own inadequacy. He is but a weak prop on which to hang such love poetry as Christina's. Her imagination, however, could make bricks out of the poorest straw. Moreover, there is no necessity to suppose that she loved Cayley with the intense devotion that Elizabeth Barrett had for Robert Browning or Dante Gabriel for his Lizzie; she was perfectly capable of making a very little experience of emotion go a long way poetically. Unfulfilled love was all round and about Christina; it was the only form of love that earnest Pre-Raphaelites regarded as the genuine article, and it was a major theme in Pre-Raphaelite painting and poetry. The story of Dante and Beatrice was the archetypal myth of the movement, and the Rossetti family in particular had been, in Christina's own phrase, "sucked into the Dante vortex": both their father and Maria were Dante scholars of the first order.[8]

Possibly Christina did not really expect any true lovers "to live happily ever after." Not only in theory but also in practice the loves of the Pre-Raphaelites were apt to go unrequited. The hot-blooded Dante Gabriel, who certainly had much experience of sexual love, waited ten years for Lizzie without, in all probability, making her his mistress, and it is uncertain whether his still more passionate affair with Janey Morris ever went as far as sexual intercourse. Christina did not have to look far to find material that she could use to heighten and elaborate her own rather tenuous experiences of love and renunciation with Collinson and Cayley.

But the real explanation of Christina's refusal of love, her constant insistence on its sadness rather than on its sweets, is something far more fundamental than the Pre-Raphaelite preoccupation with the Dante-Beatrice theme, far more serious than poor Charles Cayley's inability to attain to the complexities of belief demanded of the adherents of the Oxford movement. As early as 1857, several years before the Cayley episode, Christina wrote a long poem entitled 'The Heart Knoweth Its Own Bitterness.' It should be read in full, because here, if anywhere, is the key to her secret. Maurice Bowra, referring to her love for Cayley, writes: "Surely this refusal to marry sprang from something very deep in her nature, something which made her shrink from the demands of the flesh." The poem makes clear

[7]D. Middleton, *Victorian Lady Travellers* (London–New York, 1965), p. 20.

[8]Maria Rossetti's book *A Shadow of Dante* (London, 1871) is still regarded as one of the best introductions to him.

that this shrinking was no commonplace horror of
sexual intimacy; it was not the nature but the inadequacy of the demands of the flesh that made her turn
away to another love:

> You scratch my surface with your pin,
>   You stroke me smooth with hushing breath:—
> Nay pierce, nay probe, nay dig within,
>   Probe my quick core and sound my depth.
> You call me with a puny call,
>   You talk, you smile, you nothing do:
>   How should I spend my heart on you,
> My heart that so outweighs you all?
>
> (33–40)

The last line shows that the pronoun "you" is
meant to be taken in the plural; Christina is not addressing the inadequate Cayley or the sleepy Collinson but the whole breed of human lovers. To quote
Bowra again: "Only in God could she find a finally
satisfying object for the abounding love that was the
mainspring of her character." And so indeed Christina herself saw the matter:

> Not in this world of hope deferred,
>   This world of perishable stuff:—
> Eye hath not seen nor ear hath heard
>   Nor heart conceived that full "enough";
> Here moans the separating sea,
>   Here harvests fail, here breaks the heart:
>   There God shall join and no man part,
> I full of Christ and Christ of me.
>
> (49–56)

But for all her dedication to the divine lover,
Christina Rossetti was no mystic if we take that word
in what Archbishop William Temple calls "the proper sense, as signifying a direct apprehension of God
by the human mind." She has often been described as
akin to the Caroline metaphysical poets; if so, her
kinship is with George Herbert rather than with
Henry Vaughan the mystic. On this point it is interesting to compare her with another Victorian
woman poet, Emily Brontë. Christina was a Christian without being a mystic; Emily was a mystic, but
not necessarily a Christian one. Nowhere in Christina Rossetti's writing is there any account of a moment of direct apprehension such as Emily gives us in
the poem usually known as "The Prisoner":

> Then dawns the Invisible; the Unseen its truth reveals;
> My outward sense is gone, my inward essence feels;

> Its wings are almost free—its home, its harbour found,
> Measuring the gulf, it stoops, and dares the final bound.

From this mystical experience, Emily Brontë distilled
the essence of the experience of human love between
man and woman, an emotion that was to her unknown. No sensible person would look for factual
counterparts to Catherine and Heathcliff; *Wuthering Heights* is a book about human love that draws
its inspiration from an experience of what we can
only call divine love. But just as Emily Brontë uses
her apprehension of *agape,* divine love, to help her
to an understanding of *eros,* human love, so
Christina Rossetti uses her understanding of *eros* to
help her to an apprehension (though not a direct one)
of *agape.*

For Christina there was no deep division between
eros and *agape;* she saw the two loves as very closely
akin. There is a curious and touching purity in her
eros; there is passion in her conception of *agape:*

> Oh, my soul, spread wings of love to fly,
>   Wings of dove that soars on home-bound wing;
> Love trusts Love, till Love shall justify
>
> ("Everything."[9])

With the change of the one word "soul," who
could say whether that verse referred to love sacred
or profane? As she herself wrote of St. John the
Evangelist, her love of God was "human-eyed":

> I have no wit, no words, no tears;
>   My heart within me like a stone
> Is numbed too much for hopes or fears.
>   Look right, look left, I dwell alone;
> I lift mine eyes, but dimmed with grief
>   No everlasting hills I see;
> My life is in the falling leaf:
>   O Jesus, quicken me.
>
> ("A Better Resurrection," 1–8)

The cry is one of such purely human anguish that the
last line strikes the reader with a sense of shock.
Christina did not attain to the divine love easily. Her
poetry is full of tensions—the tension between her
two nationalities, English and Italian; the tension
between the sensuousness of Pre-Raphaelitism and
the asceticism of the Oxford movement; above all,
and by far the most important, the tension between

[9]Untitled poem from *Songs for Strangers and Pilgrims,* beginning
"Everything that is born must die."

love human and divine. As Bowra says, "It was this conflict between her human self and her divine calling which created her most characteristic poetry."

Side by side with the thought of love is the thought of death. These two great themes haunt all Christina Rossetti's writing; they even occur in her verses for children. A poem beginning "A baby's cradle with no baby in it, / A baby's grave where Autumn leaves drop sere" is not perhaps to be accounted very unusual reading for Victorian infants, but no one would expect to come across in any collection of poems for children this little song of love and death and farewell:

> "Good-bye in fear, good-bye in sorrow,
>   Good-bye, and all in vain,
> Never to meet again, my dear"—
>   "Never to part again."
> "Good-bye today, good-bye tomorrow,
>   Good-bye till earth shall wane,
> Never to meet again, my dear"—
>   "Never to part again."
>   (Untitled, from *Sing-Song*)

Somewhere in the course of her religious education Christina Rossetti must have been taught, just as other good little Anglo-Catholics are taught in Sunday school, that the church is divided into three parts: the church militant, expectant, and triumphant. Only this division between expectant and triumphant can explain the apparently contradictory nature of her view of life after death. In poem after poem, she speaks of the dead as asleep, their affections faded, their memories dimmed:

> Unmindful of the roses,
>   Unmindful of the thorn,
> A reaper tired reposes
>   Among his gathered corn;
>   So might I, till the morn!
>   ("One Sea-side Grave," 1–5)

But another, equally characteristic series of poems deals very precisely with that triumphant "morn." The sleeping dead are only waiting "in darkness for beatitude to be." No other English poet has written so often or so vividly of the joys of heaven. In spite of her love of children and childhood, Christina never looks back, as Wordsworth and Vaughan look back, to a heaven that lies about us in our infancy, "that shady city of palm-trees"; her gaze is always forward toward "the city luminous," the city that can only be entered through the gate of death. Heaven, and no other, is the country of her poetic imagining:

> Oh what is that country
>   And where can it be,
> Not mine own country,
>   But dearer far to me?
> Yet mine own country,
>   If I one day may see
> Its spices and cedars,
>   Its gold and ivory.
>
> As I lie dreaming,
>   It rises, that land;
> There rises before me
>   Its green golden strand,
> With the bowing cedars
>   And the shining sand;
> It sparkles and flashes
>   Like a shaken brand.
>   ("Mother Country,"
>   1–16)

She knows its trees and flowers, its beasts and birds:

> Golden-winged, silver-winged,
>   Winged with flashing flame,
> Such a flight of birds I saw,
>   Birds without a name:
> Singing songs in their own tongue—
>   Song of songs—they came.
>   . . .
> They flashed and they darted
>   Awhile before mine eyes,
> Mounting, mounting, mounting still,
>   In haste to scale the skies,
> Birds without a nest on earth,
>   Birds of Paradise.
>   ("Birds of Paradise," 1–6; 19–24)

Sometimes she breaks into the rhythm of a victory march in her effort to express the triumphant nature of her vision:

> Hark! the Alleluias of the great salvation,
>   Still beginning, never ending, still begin,
> The thunder of an endless adoration:
> Open ye the gates, that the righteous nation
>   Which have kept the truth may enter in.
>   ("All Saints: Martyrs," 25–29)

And again still more clearly comes the tramp of the feet of the blessed:

What are these that glow from afar,
These that lean over the golden bar,
Strong as the lion, pure as the dove,
With open arms and hearts of love?
They the blessed ones gone before,
They the blessed for evermore.
Out of great tribulation they went
Home to their home of Heaven-content;
Through flood, or blood, or furnace-fire,
To the rest that fulfils desire.
                    ("Martyrs' Song," 7–16)

Sometimes, however, Christina would write of death in a way that was neither peaceful nor triumphant nor in fact Christian at all. She was fascinated by ghosts and ghost stories, a taste that may date back to her childhood reading of the Gothic extravaganzas of such authors as Ann Radcliffe. Of her ghost poems, two of the best are "The Hour and the Ghost," a macabre colloquy between a bridegroom, a bride, and her ghostly lover, and a spine-chilling little fragment entitled "A Nightmare":

I have a friend in ghostland,—
Early found, ah me how early lost!—
Blood-red seaweeds drip along that coastland
    By the strong sea wrenched and tost.

If I wake he hunts me like a nightmare:
    I feel my hair stand up, my body creep:
Without light I see a blasting sight there,
    See a secret I must keep.

With these "occult" poems might be classed a curious and not altogether successful poem, "My Dream," describing a dream about a crocodile which is reminiscent of Thomas De Quincey's crocodile visions. Christina's verse is peopled with grotesque and slightly sinister creatures, like her goblins of "Goblin Market," ratels and wombats, serpents and lizards. In spite of her preoccupation with love and death, she was not invariably a serious writer; she could be sharp and witty and even nonsensical, kin to Lewis Carroll and to Edward Lear. This side of her nature has been precisely and exquisitely described by Virginia Woolf:

Death, oblivion, and rest lap round your songs with their dark wave. And, then, incongruously, a sound of scurrying and laughter is heard. There is a patter of animals' feet and the odd guttural notes of rooks and the snufflings of obtuse furry animals grunting and nosing. For you were not a pure saint by any means. You pulled legs;

you tweaked noses. You were at war with all humbug and pretence.

This odd, wry humor appears in her colloquial poems, including "No, Thank You John," and "Winter, My Secret":

I tell my secret? No indeed, not I:
Perhaps some day, who knows?
But not today; it froze, and blows, and snows,
And you're too curious: fie!
You want to hear it? well:
Only, my secret's mine, and I won't tell.
                                    (1–6)

Part of the success of her colloquial verse is due to her extraordinary mastery of meter. Metrically she is not so much an innovator as a very able manipulator of existing forms, which she shapes and alters to suit her individual turn of thought and expression. She has two gifts invaluable to any singer, be they poet or musician, a clear, pure tone and a very acute ear. "Your instinct was so sure, so direct, so intense," writes Virginia Woolf again, "that it produced poems that sing like music in one's ears—like a melody by Mozart or an air by Gluck."

This sure command of technique marks Christina Rossetti's early poems as clearly as her later ones. D. M. Stuart writes of her: "she has no earlier and no later style"; and Virginia Woolf makes the same point: "I doubt if you developed very much. . . . You were an instinctive poet." Technically, the most interesting of her poems is "Goblin Market." Bowra speaks of "her command of a rippling meter," but sometimes she ripples so much as to approach perilously near to a Gilbert and Sullivan patter song, especially when she overindulges her taste for feminine rhymes:

It suffices, What suffices?
All suffices, reckoned rightly:
    Spring shall bloom where now the ice is.
                            ("Amen," 11–13)

In "Goblin Market," however, this short, tripping meter exactly suits the fairy tale subject, and Christina uses and varies it with a skill that amounts almost to genius:

"Come buy, come buy:
Our grapes fresh from the vine,
Pomegranates full and fine,

Dates and sharp bullaces,
Rare pears and greengages,
Damsons and bilberries,
Taste them and try:
Currants and gooseberries,
Bright fire-like barberries,
Figs to fill your mouth,
Citrons from the South,
Sweet to tongue and sound to eye;
Come buy, come buy."

(19–31)

"Goblin Market" has been much praised by the critics; it is perhaps the best known and most admired of all Christina's poems. And with good reason, for "Goblin Market" is that rare thing, a wholly satisfactory narrative poem. Christina's poetic invention never flags; she manages to hold our attention from beginning to end. The story is a fairy tale with overtones. Day after day two sisters, Laura and Lizzie, hear the goblins crying their wares. Lizzie flees from temptation, but Laura is less prudent. One evening she buys the goblin fruit with a curl from her golden head and eats her fill. When she returns home Lizzie gently upbraids her:

"Dear, you should not stay so late,
Twilight is not good for maidens;
Should not loiter in the glen
In the haunts of goblin men.
Do you not remember Jeanie,
How she met them in the moonlight,
Took their gifts both choice and many,
Ate their fruits and wore their flowers
Plucked from bowers
Where summer ripens at all hours?
But ever in the noonlight
She pined and pined away;
Sought them by night and day,
Found them no more but dwindled and grew grey;
Then fell with the first snow. . . .

(43–57)

Laura now begins to pine away, as Jeanie had pined, craving the magic fruit that no one may taste twice. Those who have fallen victims to the goblins' wiles can never again buy their wares, never again hear them calling. But Lizzie hears them:

Beside the brook, along the glen,
She heard the tramp of goblin men,
The voice and stir
Poor Laura could not hear;

Longed to buy fruit to comfort her,
But feared to pay too dear.

(306–311)

At length Lizzie masters her fear and seeks out the goblins, begging them to sell her their fruit so that she can take it back to Laura. This they refuse to do unless she herself first tastes it and, when she refuses, they set upon her:

Their tones waxed loud,
Their looks were evil.
Lashing their tails
They trod and hustled her,
Elbowed and jostled her,
Clawed with their nails,
Barking, mewing, hissing, mocking,
Tore her gown and soiled her stocking,
Twitched her hair out by the roots,
Stamped upon her tender feet,
Held her hands and squeezed their fruits
Against her mouth to make her eat.

(396–407)

But she is not to be moved:

White and golden Lizzie stood,
Like a lily in a flood, —
Like a rock of blue-veined stone
Lashed by tides obstreperously, —
Like a beacon left alone
In a hoary, roaring sea,
Sending up a golden fire. . . .

(408–414)

At last the goblins tire of teasing her and vanish. Her face covered with fruit pulp and running with juice, she hurries home to Laura and cries to her to make haste:

"Hug me, kiss me, suck my juices
Squeezed from goblin fruits for you,
Goblin pulp and goblin dew.
Eat me, drink me, love me;
Laura, make much of me;
For your sake I have braved the glen
And had to do with goblin merchant-men."

(468–474)

Laura is saved by Lizzie's self-sacrifice; she will never forget how "her sister stood,/In deadly peril to do her good,/And win the fiery antidote."

The moral of the fable must not be pressed too far; Christina herself said that in her own intention

"Goblin Market" was no allegory at all. But if not an allegory it is some sort of a parable, possibly connected with the story of Eve, mother of all living. Here is the forbidden fruit, whose taste in the end brings death, and here is salvation brought by someone who loves, and deliberately chooses to risk and to suffer. The theme of Eve recurs often in Christina's poetry, in "An Afterthought," for instance, and "Bird and Beast." One of her most quoted poems is in fact entitled "Eve." Here, as in "Goblin Market," she uses the short, irregular meter that is particularly her own:

> "How have Eden bowers grown
> Without Adam to bend them?
> How have Eden flowers blown,
> Squandering their sweet breath,
> Without me to tend them?
> The Tree of Life was ours,
> Tree twelvefold-fruited,
> Most lofty tree that flowers,
> Most deeply rooted:
> I chose the Tree of Death."
>
> (8–17)

Christina's other fairy tale narrative poem, "The Prince's Progress," is not as successful as "Goblin Market." It tells the story of a prince who sets out on a journey to claim his betrothed princess. Ensnared by various tempters, he dallies by the way and, when at last he arrives in sight of the princess' palace, he is too late:

> What is this that comes through the door,
> The face covered, the feet before?
>   This that coming takes his breath;
> This Bride not seen, to be seen no more
>   Save of Bridegroom Death?
>
> (472–476)

"The Prince's Progress" contains some fine passages, such as the description of the prince's climb up a towering mountain:

> Up he went where the goat scarce clings,
> Up where the eagle folds her wings,
> Past the green line of living things,
>   Where the sun cannot warm the cold, —
> Up he went as a flame enrings
>   Where there seems no hold.
>
> (311–316)

As a whole the poem only just fails of excellence, but fail it does. There is a certain monotony about it; Christina does not vary the length of line, as she does in "Goblin Market," to suit the varying mood of the story. Only at the very end, when the meter changes altogether as "the bride-chant rises steadier than the torches' flame," does she touch the level of her own best poetry with the well-known song beginning "Too late for love, too late for joy, /Too late, too late."

Christina took four years, from 1861 to 1865, to complete "The Prince's Progress." Meanwhile she was writing a much shorter, less famous poem, a variation upon the same theme, entitled "Songs in a Cornfield." A party of girls are reaping in a cornfield and singing as they reap, all except Marian, who cannot sing because her lover has gone away:

> Where is he gone to
>   That he comes not home?
> To-day or to-morrow
>   He surely will come.
> Let him haste to joy,
>   Lest he lag for sorrow,
> For one weeps today
>   Who'll not weep to-morrow.
>
> (19–26)

The girls first sing of a faithless love, and then of the migrating swallows:

> There went the swallow—
> Too late to follow:
>   Lost our note of way,
>   Lost our chance to-day;
> Goodbye, swallow, sunny swallow, wise swallow.
>
> (76–80)

At last Marian breaks her silence with a tragic little song, and then the poem closes on a note that echoes its beginning:

> If he comes to-day,
>   He will find her weeping;
> If he comes to-morrow,
>   He will find her sleeping;
> If he comes the next day,
>   He'll not find her at all—
> He may tear his curling hair,
> Beat his breast, and call.
>
> (110–117)

In these early years of the 1860's, Christina herself was in love with the imperceptive Cayley, "the blindest buzzard that I know," who "sees not what's within his reach," and it was natural that her mind should be preoccupied with the theme of a dilatory lover who would not, until it was too late, reach out to grasp what had once been his for the taking. But the whole atmosphere of "The Prince's Progress," perhaps the most typically Pre-Raphaelite of all Christina's poems, inevitably suggests not so much Christina's own love for Cayley as the tragic love affair of her brother Dante Gabriel and Elizabeth Siddall, which came to its catastrophic ending in February 1862. Delay and hesitation on the part of both these lovers had led to their final undoing. Christina's description of the prince, with "his curly black beard like silk," and his careless physical prowess as opposed to his moral weakness—

> He was strong to do and dare . . .
>   In his lusty youth and his pride,
>   Tough to grapple but weak to snare, —

calls to mind the young Dante Gabriel in the days before drink, drugs, and unhappiness had marred his looks and stolen away his strength.

Although there are echoes in her writings from poets as far apart as Richard Crashaw and Arthur Hugh Clough, the poet who influenced Christina most was this same brother, Dante Gabriel; not that there is much likeness between her poems and his except a certain similarity of subject matter. He was, however, her chief critic, but some of the critical advice he gave her was very bad, as when he insisted that she should insert an episode dealing with an alchemist into "The Prince's Progress." As a general rule, Christina deferred to her brother's judgment, but occasionally she stood up to him boldly, refusing, for instance, to burden "The Prince's Progress" still further with an irrelevant tournament.

From Dante Gabriel she may well have learned her liking for the ballad form (good examples of her ballads are "Love from the North," "Husband and Wife," "Sister Maude") and also possibly for the sonnet. But her sonnets have a freshness and an originality entirely her own, very different from the loaded richness of Dante Gabriel's sonnet series, *The House of Life.* In that series are four linked sonnets entitled "Willowwood." With these poems in mind, Christina wrote a sonnet of her own that she called "An Echo from Willowwood." If the first of Dante Gabriel's "Willowwood" sonnets is put beside Christina's similar poem the notes of difference— and also the less striking similarities—in the writing of brother and sister can be seen very clearly. Here is Dante Gabriel's sonnet:

> I sat with Love upon a woodside well,
>   Leaning across the water, I and he;
>   Nor ever did he speak nor looked at me,
> But touched his lute wherein was audible
> The certain secret thing he had to tell:
>   Only our mirrored eyes met silently
>   In the low wave; and that sound came to be
> The passionate voice I knew; and my tears fell.
> And at their fall, his eyes beneath grew hers;
> And with his foot and with his wing-feathers
>   He swept the spring that watered my heart's drouth.
> Then the dark ripples spread to waving hair,
> And as I stooped, her own lips rising there
>   Bubbled with brimming kisses at my mouth.

And here is Christina's—slighter, much less mannered, less sensual, telling the same tale in terms of a real-life occurrence, and yet alive with the same passion:

> Two gazed into a pool, he gazed and she,
>   Not hand in hand, yet heart in heart, I think,
>   Pale and reluctant on the water's brink,
> As on the brink of parting which must be.
> Each eyed the other's aspect, she and he,
>   Each felt one hungering heart leap up and sink,
>   Each tasted bitterness which both must drink,
> There on the brink of life's dividing sea.
> Lilies upon the surface, deep below
>   Two wistful faces craving each for each,
>   Resolute and reluctant without speech:—
> A sudden ripple made the faces flow,
>   One moment joined, to vanish out of reach:
> So these hearts joined and ah, were parted so.

Conventional verse forms such as the sonnet seem to have held a great attraction for Christina. She wrote, for instance, many poems in rondeau form, a sixteenth-century style that enjoyed a short return to fashion toward the end of the nineteenth century, popularized by such writers as Swinburne, William Ernest Henley, and Austin Dobson. The rondeau is a poem with two rhymes only, the opening words recurring twice as a refrain. Christina's version usually has eleven lines; a good example is her last poem, "Sleeping at Last," which has already been quoted. Hers was a poetry of concentration rather than development and therefore particularly adapted to this form with its repetition both of phrase and rhyme, the meter as it were folding inward upon the central idea of the poem. Such effortless, instinctive fusion of form and subject is always the mark of the genuine artist, and Christina Rossetti was certainly a genuine poet—some critics would even dare to call her a great one.

SELECTED BIBLIOGRAPHY

I. BIBLIOGRAPHY. T. G. Ehrsam and R. H. Deily, *Bibliographies of Twelve Victorian Authors* (New York, 1936), supplement by J. G. Fucilla in *Modern Philology*, 37 (1939); W. E. Fredeman, *Pre-Raphaelitism, A Biblio-Critical Study* (Cambridge, Mass., 1965); R. W. Crump, *Christina Rossetti, A Reference Guide* (Boston, 1976).

II. COLLECTED WORKS. W. M. Rossetti, ed., *The Poetical Works of Christina Georgina Rossetti* (London, 1904), with a memoir and notes; R. W. Crump, ed., *The Complete Poems*, vol. I (Baton Rouge, 1979), a variorum ed., in progress.

III. SELECTED WORKS. W. M. Rossetti, ed., *New Poems Hitherto Unpublished or Uncollected* (London, 1896); W. M. Rossetti, ed., *Selections* (London, 1904), in the Golden Treasury series; A. Meynell, ed., *Selected Poems* (London, 1910); W. de la Mare, ed., *Selected Poems* (Newtown, 1930), a lim. ed. from the Gregynog Press.

IV. SEPARATE WORKS. *To My Mother on the Anniversary of Her Birth, April 27, 1842* (London, 1842), a single-sheet poem privately printed by her maternal grandfather, G. Polidori; *Verses* (London, 1847), dedicated to her mother, written between the ages of twelve and sixteen, privately printed by G. Polidori, repr. by J. D. Symon (1906); *Goblin Market and Other Poems* (London, 1862); *The Prince's Progress and Other Poems* (London, 1866); *Consider* (New York, 1866), verse, a single sheet printed as a text for illuminating; *Commonplace and Other Short Stories* (London, 1870), prose, but "Hero" contains the poem repr. in *The Poetical Works* as "Father and Lover"; *Sing-Song. A Nursery Rhyme Book* (London, 1872), 1893 ed. adds five poems; *Annus Domini: A Prayer for Each Day of the Year* (London, 1874), includes the poem later repr. with an extra stanza as "Wrestling"; *Speaking Likenesses* (London, 1874), prose; *Goblin Market, The Prince's Progress, and Other Poems* (London, 1875), two poems omitted and two titles changed from *Goblin Market* (1862), two poems also omitted and two titles changed from *The Prince's Progress* (1866), thirty-seven new pieces added; *Seek and Find, A Double Series of Short Studies of the Benedicite* (London, 1879); *A Pageant and Other Poems* (London, 1881); *Called to Be Saints: The Minor Festivals Devotionally Studied* (London, 1881), prose with thirteen poems; *Letter and Spirit: Notes on the Commandments* (London, 1883); *Time Flies: A Reading Diary* (London, 1885), verse and prose, 130 poems; *Poems* (London, 1890), a repr. of the 1875 ed. of *Goblin Market*, adding the 1881 ed. of *A Pageant*, and thirteen new poems; *The Face of the Deep: A Devotional Commentary of the Apocalypse* (London, 1892), prose, but contains over 200 poems and verse fragments; *Verses Reprinted from Called to Be Saints, Time Flies, The Face of the Deep* (London, 1893), some of the poems are modified or given new titles and a few pieces are added, the eighth and last section is the series of poems "Songs for Strangers and Pilgrims"; W. M. Rossetti, ed., *New Poems Hitherto Unpublished or Uncollected* (London, 1896); *Maude, A Story for Girls* (London, 1897), with an intro. by W. M. Rossetti, prose with six poems, two printed for the first time.

V. LETTERS. W. M. Rossetti, ed., *Rossetti Papers* (London, 1903), contains letters of Christina Rossetti; W. M. Rossetti, ed., *The Family Letters of Christina Georgina Rossetti* (London, 1908); J. C. Troxell, ed., *Three Rossettis: Unpublished Letters to and from Dante Gabriel, Christina, William* (Cambridge, Mass., 1937); L. M. Packer, ed., *The Rossetti-Macmillan Letters* (Cambridge, 1963).

VI. BIOGRAPHICAL AND CRITICAL STUDIES. W. B. Scott, *Autobiographical and Critical Notes* (London, 1892); E. A Proctor, *A Brief Memoir of Christina G. Rossetti* (London, 1895); H. T. M. Bell, *Christina Rossetti, A Biographical and Critical Study* (London, 1898), with a bibliographical checklist by J. P. Anderson; W. M. Rossetti, ed., *The Poems of Dante Gabriel Rossetti with Illustrations from His Own Pictures and Designs* (London, 1904), 2 vols.; W. M. Rossetti, *Some Reminiscences* (London, 1906); F. M. Ford, *Memories and Impressions* (London, 1911); M. F. Sandars, *The Life of Christina Rossetti* (London, 1930); D. M. Stuart, *Christina Rossetti* (London, 1930), in the English Men of Letters series; R. D. Waller, *The Rossetti Family, 1824–1854* (Manchester, 1932); V. Woolf, "I Am Christina Rossetti," in *The Common Reader*, 2nd ser. (London, 1932); W. Gaunt, *The Pre-Raphaelite Tragedy* (London, 1942); C. M. Bowra, *The Romantic Imagination* (Oxford, 1950), contains an essay on Rossetti; H. House, *All in Due Time* (London, 1955); M. Sawtell, *Christina Rossetti, Her Life and Religion* (London, 1955); L. M. Packer, *Christina Rossetti* (Cambridge–New York, 1963); R. G. Grylls, *Portrait of Rossetti* (London, 1964); R. Trevelyan, *A Pre-Raphaelite Circle* (London, 1975); R. W. Crump, ed., *Christina Rossetti: A Reference Guide* (London, 1976); O. Bornand, *Diary of William Rossetti* (Oxford, 1977); A. Jimenez, ed., *The Bible and the Poetry of Christina Rossetti* (London, 1979); G. Battiscombe, *Christina Rossetti: A Divided Life* (London–New York, 1981).

LEWIS CARROLL

(1832-1898)

Derek Hudson

INTRODUCTION

THE story of Charles Lutwidge Dodgson (Lewis Carroll) is one of the most curious in Victorian literature. It is paralleled in certain respects by that of his younger contemporary Gerard Manley Hopkins. The poems of Hopkins and the fantasies of Carroll were written in the heart of the Victorian era by bachelor clergymen who led academic, ascetic, restricted, intensely religious lives. Both were fascinated by the study of words. Both were painstaking amateur draftsmen of minor merit whose artistic preoccupations influenced their writings. For different reasons, neither was anxious publicly to acknowledge his creative work during his lifetime: Dodgson took refuge in a pseudonym; Hopkins died unknown to fame, his startlingly original poems remaining unpublished until thirty years after his death. With divergent religious views and many differences in personal character and taste, these quiet, withdrawn men had in common the creation of unique and lasting masterpieces that transcended their contemporary world, and indeed ran strangely counter to Victorian conventions.

The comparison cannot be pressed further. Hopkins wrote for an adult audience (incidentally, neither he nor Gladstone enjoyed *Alice in Wonderland*). Dodgson, like William Makepeace Thackeray with *The Rose and the Ring*, wrote the *Alice* books primarily for children, though in language that only adults can fully appreciate.

It has taken time to establish the status of both writers. Although, in contrast with Hopkins, Lewis Carroll's *Alice* books were well known and thoroughly enjoyed while he lived, there was a period after his death during which public interest in him slackened, and his permanent standing was in doubt. World War I turned many readers back to *Alice*; henceforth the sale values of Lewis Carroll's manuscripts and first editions increased steadily un-til they reached a climax in 1928, when Dr. A. S. W. Rosenbach paid £15,400 at Sotheby's for the manuscript of the original version of *Alice's Adventures in Wonderland*. A year later he resold it to an American, Eldridge R. Johnson, for nearly double that sum. The generosity of Johnson and of other American sympathizers brought the manuscript to the British Museum in 1948, as a gesture of appreciation of Great Britain's part in World War II.

The respect shown to the *Alice* manuscript, coupled with the remarkable tributes paid to Lewis Carroll's memory at the centenary of his birth in 1932, settled him unequivocally among the immortals. Quotations from his books have long been commonplaces of journalism and conversation. His characters are a part of national folklore and mythology. The Mad Hatter and the Ugly Duchess are as well known and indispensable to Englishmen as Falstaff or Sherlock Holmes.

Two Victorians, Lewis Carroll and Edward Lear, carried the art of nonsense to the highest point that it has so far touched, or is likely to touch. It is no accident that both were Englishmen. I would say that, after William Shakespeare, there is no English author more deserving of study by a foreigner intent on exploring English character and English humor than Lewis Carroll. Although his work has long been available in translation in most of the languages of the world, and although increasing attention has been paid to it in Europe (especially in France) within the last several decades, foreign readers may still find him hard to appreciate.

Nonsense was not a Victorian invention, but there is no tradition of nonsense in European literature comparable to the strong nonsensical element in Shakespeare, sustained even in the rational eighteenth century by Samuel Foote's well-known lines "So she went into the garden to cut a cabbage-leaf," and continued into the nineteenth century by the superb fooleries of Sydney Smith. "To say that a bishop deserved to be preached to death by wild curates," remarked G. K. Chesterton, "is not merely satire; it is a satisfaction of the fancy." Nonsense has proved a refreshing bypath of literature, a kind of detached comedy, an unengaged view of life. It reached its full flower in England, as Emile Cammaerts pointed out, in the wake of the romantic movement, as a reaction to Lord Byron and Percy Bysshe Shelley:

The association of the names of Lear and Carroll with those of Ruskin and Tennyson seems at first almost paradoxical, but there is nevertheless a certain connection between the attitude of mind of the old and modern Romanticists and that of Nonsense writers. . . . Nonsense stands, with regard to Romanticism, very much in the same position as Satire and Epigram, with regard to Classicism.[1]

It is equally important to realize that Lewis Carroll exemplified what G. M. Young has called a "new, unpietistic handling of childhood." There is throughout *Alice's Adventures in Wonderland* (1865) and *Through the Looking-Glass* (1871) a strongly marked reaction to the edifying, moralizing nursery literature typical of the early nineteenth century. Alice herself, in the fantastic adventures of her dream world, is witness to the virtues of innocence, of level-headed common sense, of patrician courage and dignity; but there is nothing goody-goody in the treatment of her adventures, which, it is essential to remember, were primarily intended to be told to and to give pleasure to children.

EARLY LIFE

ONE of the many farfetched theories about Lewis Carroll that must finally be abandoned is that he was a split personality, a sort of literary Jekyll and Hyde, divided between a prim and pedantic mathematician named C. L. Dodgson and a delightful writer of children's stories called Lewis Carroll. True, he chose for his own convenience to publish his serious mathematical and logical books under his own name and to issue his fanciful creative work under a pseudonym, but there is no more justification for the theory of split personality than this. In fact, apart

[1]E. Cammaerts, *The Poetry of Nonsense* (London, 1925), p. 85.

from the unpredictability of genius, the outlines of his personality were foreshadowed in his heredity and are clearly recognizable in him as a child. It almost appears that his intimations of Wonderland were, one might say, photographed in his mind before he was fourteen and remained to be developed long afterward, when he was outwardly cast in the mold of the Victorian don. Only thus, perhaps, can we explain the curiously similar freshness of outlook, the same combination of would-be sophistication and complete innocence that we recognize both in *The Young Visiters* by the child author Daisy Ashford and in *Alice in Wonderland.* The former suggests a remarkable fusion of precocity and inspiration; the latter represents a precocious emotion recollected in tranquility for the benefit of other children.

Charles Lutwidge Dodgson, born at Daresbury parsonage, Cheshire, on 27 January 1832, was descended from two ancient north-country families, and inherited from the Dodgsons a tradition of service to the church and from the Lutwidges a tradition of service to the state. His father, the Reverend Charles Dodgson, a distinguished classical scholar with a special interest in mathematical studies, combined personal generosity with a certain puritanical austerity, and yet enjoyed a rich vein of nonsensical humor. His mother, Frances Jane Lutwidge, a first cousin of his father, was a woman of unusually sweet and gentle character. The qualities of his parents descended to their son. No father, perhaps, ever sent his son a more direct invitation to devote himself to nonsense than did Canon Dodgson when he wrote to Charles at the age of eight:

I will not forget your commission. As soon as I get to Leeds I shall scream out in the middle of the street, *Iron-mongers—Ironmongers*—Six hundred men will rush out of their shops in a moment—fly, fly, in all directions—ring the bells, call the constables—set the town on fire. I *will* have a file & a screw-driver, & a ring, & if they are not brought directly, in forty seconds I will leave nothing but one small cat alive in the whole town of Leeds, & I shall only leave that, because I am afraid I shall not have time to kill it.

Then what a bawling & a tearing of hair there will be! Pigs & babies, camels & butterflies, rolling in the gutter together—old women rushing up the chimneys & cows after them—ducks hiding themselves in coffee cups, & fat geese trying to squeeze themselves into pencil cases—at last the Mayor of Leeds will be found in a soup plate covered up with custard & stuck full of almonds to make him look like a sponge cake that he may escape the dreadful destruction of the Town. . . . [2]

To find young Dodgson brought up on parental fantasies of this kind is significant. In *Alice in Wonderland* he sent Bill the Lizard down the chimney and put the Dormouse into the teapot; and though he refined his nonsense into a sensitive art, there is conspicuous in it an element of ruthlessness that may have been inherited from his father. During childhood his character developed on lines that it followed consistently throughout his life. When the family moved to Croft Rectory near Darlington in 1843, Charles Dodgson set out to entertain his brothers and sisters with elaborate games in the big garden, with poems and stories, with humorous drawings, and with a series of illustrated manuscript magazines, of which the first, *Useful and Instructive Poetry*, produced at the age of thirteen, contains remarkable anticipations of Humpty Dumpty and of the Mouse's tale in *Alice*. A collection of treasures hidden under the nursery floor at Croft in 1843 included a small thimble, a child's white glove, and a child's "left-hand shoe"—objects that had their individual significance for the Dodo, the White Rabbit, and the White Knight. There was also a block of wood with these words scribbled on it in Charles's hand:

> And we'll wander through
> the wide world
> and chase the buffalo. [3]

Lewis Carroll may have had a subconscious longing to escape into Wonderland, but, despite the handicap of a stammer that never left him, his was a happy and active childhood. He displayed a precocious talent for mathematics, for parody, for diverting his brothers and sisters. His handwriting at the age of twelve has been described by an expert analyst as "outstanding in maturity, tenderness and sensitivity." Yet by the time he was twenty he was writing a careful round hand that seems to show him decidedly introverted and rigidly set in his ways.

What was it that disturbed his development and narrowed his outlook? He had, no doubt, advanced prematurely and suffered proportionately in adolescence; but it was the miserable years he spent at Rugby School and the untimely loss of his beloved mother that most affected him. His diligence as an Oxford undergraduate was rewarded by a double first in mathematics and by a Christ Church Studentship. Yet at twenty-one he could write:

> I'd give all wealth that years have piled,
>   The slow result of Life's decay,
> To be once more a little child
>   For one bright summer-day. [4]

Although this deep sense of nostalgia was to remain a dominant influence throughout his life, Lewis Carroll's character was so complex and original, his interests so varied, that he found much to offset his recurrent melancholy. He was by instinct a graphic and visual artist who never abandoned the struggle to draw, and who regularly visited art exhibitions and the studios of artists. Realizing that he lacked the talent to become a professional artist, he turned to the new art of photography and made himself the best photographer of children in the nineteenth century. Long before his pseudonym Lewis Carroll—derived by transposition from the names Charles Lutwidge—had become famous, he was known to John Ruskin, Alfred Tennyson, George Macdonald, W. Holman Hunt, and many other well-known people as a student of art and an ardent amateur photographer. Allied to his interest in art, a love of the theater became a lasting passion. Literature, science, and medicine all attracted him; his devotion to children proved lifelong. Nevertheless, his life had its mainspring in religion. At the age of twenty-nine he was ordained deacon of the Church of England. This was a necessary step if he was to retain a Christ Church Studentship; his conscience approved; yet, even had he been able sufficiently to overcome his stammer, it is unlikely that he would have found parochial work congenial to his temperament. He did not proceed to priest's orders, and in later life he considered himself "practically a layman."

All this varied activity lay outside the sphere that he had specially chosen for himself—the sphere of mathematical and logical studies. "I always feel that

---

[2]D. Hudson, *Lewis Carroll* (London, 1954), pp. 23–24.
[3]I am indebted to Winifred Mansbridge for the suggestion that this is a misquotation of a line from the song "The Buffalo," dating from the early eighteenth century: "We'll wander through the wild woods and we'll chase the buffalo," from W. A. Barrett, ed., *English Folk-Songs* (London, 1891).

[4]"Solitude," in *The Complete Works of Lewis Carroll* (New York, 1937; London, 1939), p. 959. The poem is dated 16 March 1853. Hereafter citations are page references.

a sermon is worth the preaching," he once wrote, "if it has given *some* help to even *one* soul in the puzzle of Life." The choice of words is significant, for Dodgson indeed viewed life as a great puzzle, or series of puzzles. Much of his energy went to the solving and devising of puzzles, whether the official problems of academic research or the amateur conundrums that he propounded to his child-friends. As a mathematician, his work was useful, up to a point, notably in Euclid, but has not proved sufficiently distinctive to interest his posterity. Yet, though lasting success in pure mathematics eluded him, his knowledge of mathematics and logic provided an essential element in Lewis Carroll's literary achievement. Never before had such a humorist, such a lover of children, such an artist, such a precise student of language, possessed Dodgson's equipment as mathematician and logician. The rich glow of fantasy was controlled by a scientific, analytical mind; the paradoxes were shaped and refined until they formed the inimitable crystal.

THE ORIGINS OF ALICE

For all his academic success and inborn love of teaching, Dodgson's early experience as lecturer in mathematics at Christ Church—he began his duties in 1855—showed that he lacked a natural gift of communicating to an assembled class.

His lectures, it seems, were dull and uninspiringly delivered. A part-time engagement to teach the boys at St. Aldate's School proved no more successful. "School class again noisy and troublesome—I have not yet acquired the arts of keeping order," runs a diary entry of 1856.[5] Dodgson's shyness and his stammer told heavily against him.

It soon became clear, therefore, that Dodgson's main contribution to the academic life of Oxford would lie in the sphere of research and publication. He conscientiously delivered himself of some thirty works, large and small, on mathematical and logical subjects, which appeared under his own name. But with the possible exception of *Euclid and His Modern Rivals* (1879)—Falconer Madan has described this as "an outstanding example of serious

argument cast in an amusing style"—our interest in him as a writer does not derive from the publications of Charles L. Dodgson, M.A., Student and Mathematical Lecturer of Christ Church, Oxford. It is the boy and the man who entertained children with his fantasy, parody, and humor whom we love and honor.

Nothing could be more mistaken than to imagine that the first publication of *Alice's Adventures in Wonderland* in 1865 was solely the fruit of a sudden unexpected inspiration. It is true that its origin must be attributed to one particular event—a trip upriver from Oxford with three little girls in 1862—but Dodgson had been unconsciously preparing himself for *Alice in Wonderland* and its sequel *Through the Looking-Glass* for twenty years. We have seen that drawings in his *Useful and Instructive Poetry*, written in 1845, foreshadowed Humpty Dumpty and the Mouse's tale, while a Shakespearean skit in that same little book touched upon dreams and visions and the half-state between sleeping and waking, setting them aside, as it were, for future reference. We see him here, and in his later manuscript scrapbooks, *The Rectory Umbrella and Mischmasch*, absorbed in parody and fantasy and preoccupied by their pictorial illustration. Dr. Thomas Fowler, a fellow member with Dodgson of a mathematical reading party at Whitby in 1854, remembered that he "used to sit on a rock on the beach, telling stories to a circle of eager young listeners of both sexes" and believed that "it was there that 'Alice' was incubated." Certainly the poem "She's all my fancy painted him," which formed the basis of the White Rabbit's "evidence" at the trial of the Knave of Hearts, was composed in 1854; but it is unlikely that other ingredients of *Alice* derive from this early date. The importance of the Whitby visit lies in the knowledge that, while he was there, Dodgson was establishing his character as a raconteur and as a free-lance humorous journalist in the pages of the *Whitby Gazette*. Gradually he began to give literary shape (though not always in writing) to some of those whimsical intimations and impressions that had haunted him since childhood, fantasies that belonged (as we now know) to the Wonderland country and to the other side of the Looking-Glass. For the *Alice* books were in some degree an autobiographical miscellany, woven together with uncanny skill.

In 1855, when he was twenty-three, Dodgson wrote a four-line stanza in parody of Anglo-Saxon poetry that has become extremely famous:

---

[5] R. L. Green, ed., *The Diaries of Lewis Carroll*, 2 vols. (London, 1953; New York, 1954), vol. I, p. 77.

Twas bryllyg, and ye slythy toves
Did gyre and gymble in ye wabe:
All mimsy were ye borogroves;
And ye mome raths outgrabe.

We know these lines now as the opening stanza of "Jabberwocky"[6] in *Through the Looking-Glass*. The spelling was slightly altered, and Dodgson's original explanations of the words differ considerably from those provided by Humpty Dumpty:

"That's enough to begin with," Humpty Dumpty interrupted: "there are plenty of hard words there. '*Brillig*' means four o'clock in the afternoon—the time when you begin *broiling* things for dinner."

"That'll do very well," said Alice: "and '*slithy*'?"

"Well, '*slithy*' means 'lithe and slimy.' '*Lithe*' is the same as 'active.' You see it's like a portmanteau—there are two meanings packed up into one word."

"I see it now," Alice remarked thoughtfully: "and what are '*toves*'?"

"Well, '*toves*' are something like badgers—they're something like lizards—and they're something like corkscrews."

"They must be very curious-looking creatures."

"They are that," said Humpty Dumpty; "also they make their nests under sun-dials—also they live on cheese."

"And what's to '*gyre*' and to '*gimble*'?"

"To '*gyre*' is to go round and round like a gyroscope. To '*gimble*' is to make holes like a gimlet."

"And '*the wabe*' is the grass plot round a sun-dial, I suppose?" said Alice, surprised at her own ingenuity.

"Of course it is. It's called '*wabe*' you know, because it goes a long way before it, and a long way behind it—"

"And a long way beyond it on each side," Alice added.

"Exactly so. Well then, '*mimsy*' is 'flimsy and miserable' (there's another portmanteau for you). And a '*borogrove*' is a thin shabby-looking bird with its feathers sticking out all round—something like a live mop."

"And then '*mome raths*'?" said Alice. "I'm afraid I'm giving you a great deal of trouble."

"Well, a '*rath*' is a sort of green pig: but '*mome*' I'm not certain about. I think it's short for 'from home'—meaning that they'd lost their way, you know."

"And what does '*outgrabe*' mean?"

"Well, '*outgribing*' is something between bellowing and whistling, with a kind of sneeze in the middle. . . . "

(pp. 215–217)

[6]Roger Lancelyn Green has shown that there is a strong probability that the rest of the poem was influenced by "The Shepherd of the Giant Mountains," a translation by Menella Smedley from the German of Fouqué (*Times Literary Supplement*, 1 March 1957).

In 1856, Dodgson contributed to the *Train* a parody of William Wordsworth called "Upon the Lonely Moor," which eventually formed the basis of the White Knight's song. And in his diary of 9 February 1856 we find the entry—

Query: when we are dreaming and, as often happens, have a dim consciousness of the fact and try to wake, do we not say and do things which in waking life would be insane? May we not then sometimes define insanity as an inability to distinguish which is the waking and which the sleeping life?

—a remark that suggests the Cheshire Cat's "We're all mad here."

Enough has been said—more perhaps might be said if the diaries of 1858–1862 were not missing—to show that, when he wrote *Alice in Wonderland* and its sequel, Lewis Carroll gathered together loose ends of fancy and experience that stretched back many years. Much of this hoarded material appears in the *Alice* books in the form of humorous verse, especially parody, for Dodgson had made himself proficient in the genre since his childhood. As he developed, he also began to write serious romantic poems that were less successful, being conventional exercises lacking originality and inspiration. Yet many of the prose passages and situations in the *Alice* books could not have been realized without the help of an instinctive and insistent vein of poetry, associated perhaps with that "*very* rebellious mind" that a graphologist has detected in his adolescent handwriting.

We cannot say with any certainty that Dodgson ever fell in love in the adult sense, although we know that his sister believed he was in love with the famous actress Ellen Terry when she was about seventeen. It is unlikely that he ever declared his love, if it existed, or that he ever seriously contemplated marriage with Ellen Terry, for she was then already married (though unhappily). From his early youth, however, he had sought the society of little girls, thus compensating himself in part for his inability to form friendships with women of his own age. Children were an escape from sex rather than any sort of conscious satisfaction of it, but they gave him the affection he needed and helped him to fulfill the Platonic and protective love that was characteristic of his nature. His ordeal as a stammerer may largely explain his development; for he found—as others similarly afflicted have found—that he could talk freely and naturally with children and was happiest in their company.

In 1864, before *Alice in Wonderland* was published, he was writing to George Macdonald's daughter, Mary, letters full of delightful nonsense in no way inferior to those in *Alice*. Although his letters, like the *Alice* books, can only be fully appreciated by adults, they are additional proof that he wrote his nonsense primarily to give pleasure to children. And as for *Alice in Wonderland* itself, there is no doubt of his source of inspiration. She was Alice Liddell, one of the daughters of Dr. H. G. Liddell, the formidable dean of Christ Church. Dodgson apparently first met her on 25 April 1856, when she was not quite four years old, and he added to his diary entry a comment he reserved for outstanding occasions: "I mark this day with a white stone."

THE *ALICE* BOOKS

DODGSON's friendship with the Liddell children flourished, though their mother could be difficult and obstructive on occasions, and he was never on the best of terms with their father. To this serious-minded, high-principled, conscientious young man the association became increasingly important, implying as it did a release of spirit that he found nowhere else. Harry and Lorina, the older children, shared his affection with Edith, the youngest, but Alice—a pretty child with an oval face, dark hair, and shy fawnlike eyes—became his favorite.

He had told them all many stories before the famous day, 4 July 1862, on which he and his friend Robinson Duckworth of Trinity took Lorina (aged thirteen), Alice (aged ten), and Edith (aged eight) on a trip upriver to Godstow. It was during that afternoon that he began the story that was later developed into *Alice's Adventures in Wonderland*. A suggestion of wild impromptu still clings to the opening chapters describing the fall down the rabbit hole and the little door into the garden. The episode of the pool of tears is a reminiscence of another expedition he had made with the three Liddells to Nuneham on a rainy day a fortnight earlier.

In the six months that followed, Dodgson wrote out his story, at Alice's special request, under the title *Alice's Adventures Under Ground*. The drawings with which he illustrated it are not without merit. They have a private anguish that is more moving than amusing, and the earnestness of the amateur occasionally rises in them to a weird frenzy almost Blake-like in its intensity. The original manuscript consists of only 18,000 words, but on George Macdonald's recommendation Dodgson determined to revise it for publication, and in the course of so doing he enlarged it to 35,000 words. John Tenniel, the *Punch* artist who had made his name as a book illustrator with his decorations for *Aesop's Fables*, and who was particularly skilled at drawing animals, consented to illustrate. His drawings were remarkably successful, though there is little doubt that they betray the strong influence of the French artist J. J. Grandville.[7] Dodgson interested himself in their progress at every stage.

A comparison between the first manuscript version of *Alice in Wonderland*, now in the British Museum, and the printed book shows that the general tendency, as might be expected, is away from parochial allusions and mere child's play toward more advanced and reasoned ingenuity. The most important additions are the chapters "Pig and Pepper" and "A Mad Tea-party" and the trial scene, but such favorite parodies as "Speak roughly to your little boy," "Twinkle, twinkle, little bat," "'Tis the voice of the Lobster," and "Will you walk a little faster" do not appear in the first version. Many local allusions remain, some of them probably derived from the famous expedition to Godstow. Dodgson himself was the Dodo (perhaps a reproduction of his stammer as he pronounced his own name); Duckworth was the Duck, Lorina the Lory, Edith the Eaglet—and Alice, of course, was Alice. The three little girls in the Dormouse's story, Elsie, Lacie, and Tillie, are only the three Liddells in another disguise: Elsie stands for L. C., the initials of Lorina Charlotte; Lacie is an anagram for Alice; and Matilda (Tillie) is a family nickname for Edith.

It is difficult to put oneself in the place of someone who reads *Alice in Wonderland* for the first time, but not difficult to say why it immediately appealed, and still appeals, to children. This is an extraordinary world of fantasy, where Alice can shrink almost to insect size or grow to the dimensions of a giant; where she can talk to a caterpillar on a mushroom; where a cat can exist merely as a grin; where there are Mock Turtles instead of real turtles; where playing cards become persons. The animals and the jokes about lessons are easy for children to understand;

7See M. Mespoulet, *Creators of Wonderland* (New York, 1934). I am grateful to Bryan Montagu for drawing my attention to this convincing study.

the Caucus-race, the tea-party, the game of croquet, the lobster quadrille—all are based on facts of every-day experience suddenly turned topsy-turvy and made startlingly entertaining. Much of the play with language and many of the parodies are only fully appreciated by grownups, but the source of

> Twinkle, twinkle, little bat!
> How I wonder what you're at!
> (p. 79)

can hardly be missed even nowadays ("You know the song, perhaps?" asks the Mad Hatter), while Isaac Watts's "'Tis the voice of the sluggard" still sounds recognizably behind

> "'Tis the voice of the Lobster: I heard him declare
> You have baked me too brown, I must sugar my hair."
> (p. 111)

For the rest, a limpid prose that holds the attention of grownups is that most likely to retain the affection of children, as Kenneth Grahame and Beatrix Potter have proved, though the mixture must be infinitely subtle. Lewis Carroll was a notable master of dialogue. Consider the counterpoint of this passage from the trial scene:

"What do you know about this business?" the King said to Alice.

"Nothing," said Alice.

"Nothing whatever?" persisted the King.

"Nothing whatever," said Alice.

"That's very important," the King said, turning to the jury. They were just beginning to write this down on their slates, when the White Rabbit interrupted: "Unimportant, your Majesty means, of course," he said, in a very respectful tone, but frowning and making faces at him as he spoke.

"Unimportant, of course, I meant," the King hastily said, and went on to himself in an undertone, "important— unimportant—unimportant—important—" as if he were trying which word sounded best.

Some of the jury wrote it down "important," and some "unimportant." Alice could see this, as she was near enough to look over their slates; "but it doesn't matter a bit," she thought to herself.

At this moment the King, who had been for some time busily writing in his note-book, called out "Silence!" and read out from his book "Rule Forty-two. All persons more than a mile high to leave the court."

Everybody looked at Alice.

"I'm not a mile high," said Alice.

"You are," said the King.

"Nearly two miles high," added the Queen.

"Well, I sha'n't go, at any rate," said Alice; "besides, that's not a regular rule: you invented it just now."

"It's the oldest rule in the book," said the King.

"Then it ought to be Number One," said Alice.

(pp. 124–125)

The story of the withdrawal of the first edition of *Alice in Wonderland* in August 1865, owing to supposed deficiencies in the printing of the illustrations, and its reissue later in the same year, makes a bibliographical adventure too complicated to be described here. The success of the "funny pretty book," as Christina Rossetti called it, was immediate, though the advance of its sales proved gradual rather than spectacular. Time was needed for the general acceptance of the revolution in children's literature implied by *Alice in Wonderland*; for this was not the goody-goody book conventionally familiar to Victorians, but handled childhood freshly and without sententiousness.

Alice's Adventures in Wonderland (to give the book its full title once more) is best thought of in conjunction with its equally famous sequel *Through the Looking-Glass and What Alice Found There*, which was published in time for Christmas 1871, again illustrated by Tenniel. As early as August 1866, Lewis Carroll told his publisher, Macmillan, that he had "a floating idea of writing a sort of sequel to *Alice*"; but he did not seriously start work on it until two years later. He had much material ready to his hand, including the poem "Jabberwocky" and the parody of Wordsworth, "Upon the Lonely Moor," while he drew on Halliwell-Phillips' collection of nursery rhymes for "Tweedledum" and "Tweedledee," "The Lion and the Unicorn," and several similar ingredients. Alice Liddell and her sisters remained the inspiration for the second book as they had been for the first, although this time their influence cannot be so exactly documented. We know that Dodgson had told them many stories about chessmen, at a time when they were learning to play chess; and since *Through the Looking-Glass* was based roughly on a game of chess, some of these stories naturally took their place in the new book, along with other reminiscences of the Liddells (Dinah was a recollection of Alice's cat). The idea of going through the looking-glass into a mysterious country beyond seems to have derived, however, from a meeting between Dodgson and another Alice, his little cousin Alice Raikes. Dodgson gave her an orange and asked her in which hand she was holding it. When she said, "The right," he invited her to stand before a mirror and tell him in which hand the girl in the looking-glass held the orange. "The left hand," came the puzzled reply. "Exactly," agreed Dodgson, "and how do you explain that?" "If I was on the *other* side of the glass," said Alice Raikes, "wouldn't the orange still be in my right hand?" "Well done, little Alice," replied Dodgson, "the best answer I've had yet."[8]

Lewis Carroll achieved the rare distinction of writing a worthy sequel to a masterpiece. The *Looking-Glass* world is a land where things go the wrong way round, where flowers talk, where the characters of popular rhymes come to life, where chessmen are humanized. *Through the Looking-Glass* is to some tastes an improvement on its predecessor and has certainly impressed itself equally on the national consciousness. It was the White Queen whose rule was "jam tomorrow and jam yesterday—but never jam today." It was the Anglo-Saxon Messenger with the "Anglo-Saxon attitudes" who called Alice "as large as life, and twice as natural!" In the White Knight, Carroll parodied his own passion for small inventions. And if we must choose a representative poem, or a typical stanza of Carrollian verse, it is to "The Walrus and the Carpenter" that we turn:

> "The time has come," the Walrus said,
>   "To talk of many things:
> Of shoes—and ships—and sealing wax—
>   Of cabbages—and kings—
> And why the sea is boiling hot—
>   And whether pigs have wings."
>
>   (p. 186)

Many readers make no marked distinction between the two books, considering them as parts of the same story; Alice herself is the unifying factor, the rational being in a mad world, the Victorian child with courage, dignity, and common sense. As Walter de la Mare said, "She wends serenely on like a quiet moon in a chequered sky." If there are times when she seems a bit of a prig, she is not the less convincing on that account, and always she is kind, courteous, and considerate. She likes the Walrus "because he was a *little* sorry for the poor oysters"; she is afraid that the Red King will catch cold from lying on the damp grass, being "a very thoughtful lit-

tle girl." Though her predicament is continually alarming, though the argument invariably goes against her, she has the resource to change the subject and hold on to her courage and common sense. I am not sure that *Alice* did not do more for the character of Victorian girlhood than Queen Victoria; yet even the Queen could not say this time that she was "not amused."

The combined *Alice* is a work of supreme originality. Carroll was clearly influenced by Lear's nonsense verses; conceivably he was slightly influenced by Charles Kingsley's *The Water Babies;* I have a personal theory that he may have got some hints from chapter 11 of George Eliot's *The Mill on the Floss*—"Maggie Tries to Run Away from her Shadow." But that is the most that can be said. Written in the heart of the Victorian era—and by a man who in other respects was held fast to his period— *Alice* is timeless in its appeal. The outstanding achievement is the creation of a dream world that is never for one moment unacceptable. Walter de la Mare has compared its atmosphere not only to that of Blake's *Songs of Innocence* and Thomas Traherne's *Meditations,* but to the medieval descriptions of paradise and the gemlike Italian pictures of the seventeenth century. To those who deny Lewis Carroll's poetry, we can answer with de la Mare:

> . . . what of the visionary light, the colour, the scenery; that wonderful landscape, for example, in *The Walrus and the Carpenter,* as wide as Milton's in *Il Penseroso*—the quality of its sea, its sands, its space and distances? What of the exquisite transition from one setting on to another in a serene seductive discontinuity in—for but one example—the chapter entitled "Wool and Water"?[9]

Carroll's art is so well concealed, his prose so limpid that we may fail to realize how carefully the stories are organized. And there is a sense of purpose in them that lies beneath the surface entertainment and marks the philosopher. Baffled at first in the mad world of her dream, the child learns to speak up for herself, to live with eccentricity on her own terms, and finally to sympathize. The old copybook moralizing has been mocked, but something has been taught nevertheless; the adventures of Wonderland have given spiritual encouragement to a child in

---

[8]Alice Wilson Fox, letter to the editor of the *Times* (London), 15 January 1932, p. 8.

[9]W. de la Mare, "Lewis Carroll," in W. de la Mare, ed., *The Eighteen-Eighties* (Cambridge, 1930), p. 254.

the real world; the lesson has been as strange and unexpected as the book itself.

Besides this curious and almost unconscious lesson in character, *Alice* conveys only one further message that could possibly be termed didactic, and it is a message that came naturally from a student of language and logic: "Pay attention to what you are saying!"

Alice asks the Cheshire Cat, "Would you tell me, please, which way I ought to go from here?"

"That depends a good deal on where you want to get to," said the Cat.

"I don't much care where—" said Alice.

"Then it doesn't matter which way you go," said the Cat.

"—so long as I get *somewhere*," Alice added as an explanation.

"Oh, you're sure to do that," said the Cat, "if you only walk long enough."

(p. 72)

No child can read *Alice* without gaining an increased understanding of the importance of words. Inspired wordplay, mixed with judicious slapstick, and set within the framework of an idiosyncratic view of the human situation, is the essence of *Alice*. Lewis Carroll added at least two words to the English language—"chortle" and "galumph"—and he revived a number of forgotten words, among them "whiffling," "burbled," "beamish," and "slithy." For the nearest parallel to his humorous method we must turn to the cinema—to the Marx Brothers, whose dialogue not only has many verbal similarities with his, but who also, like him, assert one grand false proposition at the outset and so persuade their audiences to accept anything as possible.

LATER VERSE

THE success of the *Alice* books made little difference to the life of their author. For the fame that came to him as Lewis Carroll, and for any sort of "lionizing," he showed a marked distaste. His daily round was exceedingly methodical, not to say persnickety. He gave some of his time to a painstakingly matter-of-fact diary. From 1861 onward he kept a register of all his correspondence, which at his death had reached about 100,000 items. He pursued his mathematical studies, the more important of which concerned Euclid, with extreme conscientiousness. He performed occasional minor duties in the church as a deacon (emerging as an earnestly effective preacher at the end of his life). The theater continued to remain a passionate interest; he still studied drawing with a stubborn though despairing determination; and up to 1880 he pursed his hobby of photography with remarkable distinction. He went abroad only once, on a trip to Russia with Dr. H. P. Liddon, and he found his physical relaxation in long walks in the countryside around Oxford and Guildford (where he made a home for his sisters in 1868) or in holidays at south coast resorts, of which Eastbourne became his favorite. For mental relaxation, he enjoyed nothing more than the devising of puzzles and games; and if crosswords had been known in his time, he would certainly have been an addict.

To picture him as an uncommunicative recluse would, however, be misleading. He visited his artistic, literary, and theatrical friends in London and was ready to make other friends besides—particularly among the parents of young daughters. He had admitted that children were "three-fourths of my life," and like another Victorian clergyman, the diarist Francis Kilvert, he became increasingly preoccupied with little girls. Half in play and half in earnest, these friendships could grow rather intense, but he conducted them always with a most scrupulous regard for the proprieties and with a tender concern for the happiness of his child-friends.

In college affairs Dodgson was one of those "difficult" characters not uncommonly found in such societies. He took an uncompromising line in domestic politics, and several of his humorous satires ridicule the reforms sponsored by Dean Liddell and the Governing Body. For ten years he held the onerous post of Curator of the Senior Common Room at Christ Church, a sort of housekeeper to a men's club, in which capacity he showed himself not only efficient but, it must be admitted, on occasion testy and small-minded. There was no end to his complaints against the college servants. He took little interest in the activities of the undergraduates and was himself the target for a lively satire, *Cakeless*, written by one of their number. Yet the sum total of Christ Church opinion would not have been hostile to Dodgson; for it would have had to reckon with genuine modesty and courtesy, wit and kindness, and with a quite remarkable generosity to good causes that appealed to him.

An analysis of this complex character—at once self-centered and unselfish, richly endowed emotionally but at the same time emotionally immature—suggests that he suffered much nervous tension, which he had disciplined himself to control but which showed itself in occasional outbursts of irritability. A paradox himself, the dichotomy of his character is revealed in the subtle changes of significance and abrupt reversal of statements in *Alice*. He followed a lonely bachelor existence with stoic courage. "College life is by no means unmixed misery," he wrote, "though married life has no doubt many charms to which I am a stranger." Essentially ambivalent, one feels that he instinctively avoided problems of adult love and intimacy because he knew that in any close relationship something compelled him to seek distance and detachment. Several writers, notably A. L. Taylor, have argued that he was actually in love with Alice Liddell in an adult sense; yet when his nephew and biographer S. D. Collingwood hinted at "the shadow of some disappointment" in his life, it was to Ellen Terry that he referred, and it is difficult to see his love for Alice as anything but fundamentally Platonic and protective. After she had outgrown her childhood Dodgson saw relatively little of her.

Nevertheless, it is to Alice Liddell's inspiration that we owe the two *Alice* books, and among his child-friends she held a very special place. Only once again, after Alice Liddell's influence had passed, did Lewis Carroll write an admitted masterpiece. This was *The Hunting of the Snark*, the longest and best sustained nonsense poem in the English language. The last line came into his mind while he was walking in Guildford in July 1874; the poem was not ready for publication until 1876.

The Hunting of the Snark describes the expedition of the Bellman and his ill-assorted crew in search of that fabulous creature, which proves on discovery to be a particularly dangerous variety, the Boojum. The details of the *Snark* were "hammered out" by a craftsman of light verse; but, like the best modern art, the poem is both obscurely instinctive and sharply intellectual. Once again, he found inspiration in a little girl, this time Gertrude Chataway; once again, there was method in his madness; the strange odyssey was carefully organized and gains cumulative effect from its telling, until the final verses reach a climax that is not negligible poetry:

> They hunted till darkness came on, but they found
> Not a button, or feather, or mark,

> By which they could tell that they stood on the ground
> Where the Baker had met with the Snark.

> In the midst of the word he was trying to say,
> In the midst of his laughter and glee,
> He had softly and suddenly vanished away—
> For the Snark *was* a Boojum, you see.

> (p. 778)

Lewis Carroll's verse was collected during his lifetime in *Phantasmagoria* (1869) and *Rhyme? and Reason?* (1883), which included *The Hunting of the Snark*, while the volume of *Collected Verse* (1932) brings together nearly all the verse that he wrote in widely differing contexts. This entertaining book displays him as a master of parody and places him in the English tradition of light verse between Edward Lear and C. S. Calverley.[10] Even his few serious poems—melancholy and romantic in feeling—and his affectionate occasional trifles belong to this tradition; but, as with other masters of light verse, they do not show him at his best. Living in a world of lost summers, his wistful nostalgia could become over-lush:

> Ever drifting down the stream—
> Lingering in the golden gleam—
> Life, what is it but a dream?
> (p. 272)

Yet, in the context of the *Alice* books at least, verse and prose are so perfectly dovetailed that we do not want anything altered; even the supplementary occasional pieces become tolerable.

As an innovator of nonsense verse he remained effective to the last. Amid the disappointment of *Sylvie and Bruno* (1889) he gave us the original verse epigram that has been called the "Waterford":

> He thought he saw a Banker's Clerk,
> Descending from a bus:
> He looked again, and found it was
> A Hippopotamus:
> "If this should stay to dine," he said,
> "There won't be much for us."
> (p. 334)

[10]John Galsworthy, in 1889, at the age of twenty-two, described Lewis Carroll as his "favourite poet" in the confession album of one of his cousins, which was published in H. V. Marrot, *The Life and Letters of John Galsworthy* (London, 1935).

SYLVIE AND BRUNO

For the general reader, the humorous verse scattered throughout the two volumes of *Sylvie and Bruno* may be its chief attraction. But for the student of Lewis Carroll, this elaborate failure, which occupied him on and off for twenty years of his life, demands a little more attention. Even the least successful productions of genius have an interest above the ordinary; the confused patchwork of *Sylvie and Bruno* conceals what was in some ways a strikingly original experiment, though one beyond his powers.

The nucleus of *Sylvie and Bruno* is to be found in a short tale, "Bruno's Revenge," contributed by Dodgson to *Aunt Judy's* magazine, edited by Margaret Gatty, in 1867. This fairy tale forms the greater part of chapters 14 and 15 of the book. He told more chapters of it to the children at Hatfield on visits to Lord Salisbury in 1873 and 1875. By the following year he was looking for an illustrator to succeed Tenniel. "I should much like to write one more children's book," he informed Macmillan, "before all writing-power leaves me."

Unfortunately, that supremely lucid "writing-power" of Dodgson's did begin to disintegrate rather rapidly as he became increasingly absorbed by college business and by his miscellaneous scientific and artistic interests. *Sylvie and Bruno* was compiled from a mass of material accumulated over many years. Dodgson determined to break away from the pattern of his previous dream tales, but had no clear idea of how to do it. Unlike the *Alice* books, *Sylvie and Bruno* never advanced systematically. Failure could have been predicted.

The most serious fault, besides its shapelessness, is that in *Sylvie and Bruno* Dodgson the didactic moralist overwhelmed Dodgson the artist. When he allowed himself to follow the course of his fairy tale, or to pursue some entertaining byway of fantasy in prose or verse, he was still recognizably the Lewis Carroll of former days; but the attempt to display his old talent within the setting of a conventionally "uplifting" society novel proved fatal to the book as a whole. Harry Furniss' illustrations faithfully reflected this dilemma. Worse still, the boy Bruno spoke in a deplorable convention of baby talk that had been happily avoided in *Alice*. And the book grew impossibly long. The publication of *Sylvie and Bruno* in 1889 was not the end. In 1893 came *Sylvie and Bruno Concluded*, and each volume ran to four hundred pages. Moreover, they were both prefaced by rambling apologetic addresses such as a clergyman might make from the steps of the chancel, involving good works and moral reflections of every kind.

It is possible, then, to pick out the interpolated songs and poems, or to read the fantastic passages on the "Outlandish Watch" or the visit to Dogland, with pleasure; it requires an unusually patient and sympathetic reader to follow the story from beginning to end. Yet the strangely incoherent compilation is somehow symbolic of the hidden conflicts of Dodgson and of the Victorian era in which he lived. The element of experiment in the construction of the book has its place in literary history. Dodgson introduced his "fairies" into human situations and postulated that man may go through three stages in relation to the supernatural—the ordinary state of "no consciousness"; the mixed or "eerie" state, in which he is conscious both of his own surroundings and of supernatural presences; and a form of trance or dream state. His attempt to sustain a narrative on these distinct planes is, not surprisingly, difficult to follow. Maurice Maeterlinck and J. M. Barrie later handled similar material more successfully in the theater with musical assistance; and perhaps the work of Dorothy Richardson, James Joyce, and Virginia Woolf sometimes suggests the same line of experiment explored with different methods.

Sylvie and Bruno was Carroll's last attempt at imaginative literature on a large scale. He was greatly occupied with games and puzzles toward the close of his life. His last book, part I of *Symbolic Logic*, appeared in 1896; it is pleasant to record that it went through four editions within a year. The exploitation of the *Alice* books in their various guises, translations, and adaptations, still kept him busy, and he made a number of small verbal changes for a new edition in 1897.[11] During his later years he suffered from intermittent ill health; he was feeling the effect of cumulative strain, brought on by the rigorous discipline of his life and by continual overwork. At Christmas 1897, he was busily engaged on part II of *Symbolic Logic* when he caught a feverish chill that turned to bronchitis. He died at "The Chestnuts," his sisters' detached red brick house near the Castle at Guildford, on 14 January 1898.

[11]Stanley Godman is apparently the first to have noted these, in the *Times* (London), 27 July 1957.

CONCLUSION

WHEN Lewis Carroll was very small, he approached his father with a book of logarithms and asked for an explanation. Although he was told he was too young, he persisted, "*But*, please explain!" It is not enough nowadays that the *Alice* books should be enjoyed; they too must be "explained"—and to some people the psychoanalytic methods of Freud have provided a tempting line of investigation. I believe that it is misguided to apply this method to a work of imaginative literature, and that, so far from heightening appreciation, the clinical dissection of an author's mind may tend to belittle his creation and impair enjoyment.

Of course from the medical standpoint the study is legitimate. "When a superior intellect and a psychopathic temperament coalesce in the same individual," said William James, "we have the best possible condition for the kind of effective genius that gets into the biographical dictionaries." "Genius," said Cesare Lombroso, going a little further, "is a symptom of hereditary degeneration of the epileptoid variety." Any work of genius, then, is fruitful ground for psychoanalysis; the more spontaneous the fantasy, as in Samuel Coleridge's "Kubla Khan" or the early chapters of *Alice in Wonderland*, the greater the opportunity for discovering sexual symbolism. There is a psychoanalytic theory that the pool of tears in *Alice* represents the amniotic fluid, and that all this part of the book is an allegory of the birth trauma (though in plain fact the pool of tears was a reference to an earlier outing with the three Liddells, on a wet day a fortnight before the famous expedition to Godstow). Viewed in this light, the gayest of books can become a nightmare of neurosis—much in the same way that a student of Eric Partridge's *Dictionary of Slang* finds, after reading a few pages, that his ordinary talk is inevitably full of obscenity. We might remember what Lewis Carroll wrote to Mary Macdonald: "Don't be in such a hurry to believe next time—I'll tell you why—If you set to work to believe everything, you will tire out the muscles of your mind, and then you'll be so weak you won't be able to believe the simplest things."

Attempts have also been made to identify characters in the *Alice* books with actual individuals. Many contemporary references that might have amused the Liddells are undoubtedly preserved in the books, but it is dangerous to read too many allusions and hidden meanings into them, for Carroll did not construct his characters from observation, except in the most general sense; as he himself said, his ideas were wont to "come of themselves." Similarly, with alleged references to religious controversy or to contemporary politics, Carroll's care to change the passionflower to a tiger lily in *Through the Looking-Glass*, because of "the sacred origin of the name," is proof enough of his view that adult susceptibilities were not the concern of a fairy story. A. L. Taylor has been more successful in suggesting the mathematical and logical influences behind Carroll's work; but in general I believe that Carroll has been the victim of misplaced ingenuity from critics who have taken not only themselves but the *Alice* books far too seriously. Tweedledee's "Contrariwise" may be the best answer: "if it was so, it might be; and if it were so, it would be; but as it isn't, it ain't."

Charles Dodgson never really outgrew his childhood and remained, in the modern jargon, "fixated" to his early years—that I believe to be true. It was at once his weakness and his strength, for it explains the unique quality of his writing for children. He was remarkably mature and sensitive at twelve and thirteen; his father encouraged nonsense; *Useful and Instructive Poetry* contains many curious anticipations of his later work. The painful years at Rugby and the death of his beloved mother drove all this underground into his subconscious, to be recaptured in *Alice* when he was past thirty and set in donnish ways.

He was always happiest, as a stammerer, in the company of children. He wrote to please them, and they drew out of him first his nonsense letters (the psychoanalysts have yet to tackle these), then his immortal books. His precise care of words as a logician and his leaning toward a mathematician's philosophy gave his writing the inimitable quality that has tantalized and delighted grownups. Nevertheless, but for his love of children, the *Alice* books would never have been written. He did not send Alice down the rabbit hole on a summer's afternoon for the benefit of a future generation of Freudians but rather for the present pleasure of three Victorian children.

When he was asked what "he meant" by *The Hunting of the Snark*, Lewis Carroll replied: "I'm very much afraid I didn't mean anything but nonsense! Still, you know, words mean more than we mean to express when we use them; so a whole book ought to mean a great deal more than the writer means. So, whatever good meanings are in the book,

I'm glad to accept as the meaning of the book." These words, and especially the phrase "good meanings," deserve to be pondered.

Never perhaps has a writer turned his repressions to such healthy uses as Lewis Carroll. He triumphed over his dilemma, and though his own life was not entirely happy, he has given pleasure to millions. He belongs neither to the highbrow nor to the psychoanalyst; he belongs to the children and all who have the gift of laughter, anywhere in the world.

SELECTED BIBLIOGRAPHY

I. BIBLIOGRAPHY. S. H. Williams, *A Bibliography of the Writings of Lewis Carroll [Charles Lutwidge Dodgson, M.A.]* (London, 1924), the pioneer bibliography, still of value; M. L. Parrish, coll., *A List of the Writings of Lewis Carroll . . .* (Philadelphia, 1928), privately printed, catalog of the collection of M. L. Parrish of Philadelphia, now in the Princeton University Library; S. J. Williams and F. Madan, *A Handbook of the Literature of the Rev. C. L. Dodgson [Lewis Carroll]* (London, 1931), for thirty years the standard bibliography, a supplement was issued in 1935; F. V. Livingston, *The Harcourt Amory Collection of Lewis Carroll in the Harvard College Library* (Cambridge, Mass., 1932), privately printed; R. L. Green, "Lewis Carroll's Periodical Publications," *Notes and Queries* (March 1954); R. L. Green, *The Lewis Carroll Handbook* (London, 1962), a new version of the Williams and Madan, rev., augmented, and brought up to date, further rev. by D. Crutch (Folkestone, 1979).

II. COLLECTED EDITIONS. *The Collected Verse of Lewis Carroll* (London, 1932), with illus. by Sir J. Tenniel, A. B. Frost, H. Holiday, H. Furniss, and the author; *The Complete Works of Lewis Carroll* (New York, 1937; London, 1939), with an intro. by A. Woollcott and illus. by J. Tenniel, incomplete but useful; R. L. Green, ed., *The Works of Lewis Carroll* (London, 1965), with an intro. by Green, more comprehensive than the preceding; J. Fisher, ed., *The Magic of Lewis Carroll* (London, 1973), compendium of games, puzzles, etc.

III. SELECTIONS. S. D. Collingwood, ed., *The Lewis Carroll Picture Book* (London, 1899), an entertaining miscellany, the subtitle reads "A Selection from the Unpublished Writings and Drawings of Lewis Carroll, together with Reprints from Scarce and Unacknowledged Works," includes some of his photographs and letters, and reminiscences of him, reiss. as a paperback under the title *Diversions and Digressions of Lewis Carroll* (London, 1961); L. Reed, ed., *Further Nonsense Verse and Prose*, illus. by H. M. Bateman (London, 1926), a sequel (hence the mis-leading title) to L. Reed, ed., *Nonsense Verse: An Anthology; Alice in Wonderland, Through the Looking-Glass, Etc.* (London, 1929), with intro. by E. Rhys, useful selection of the works, including *Phantasmagoria, A Tangled Tale, The Hunting of the Snark,* and Carroll's own illus. to *Alice; For The Train* (London, 1932), Lewis Carroll's contributions to the *Train,* 1856–1857, preface by H. J. Schonfield, contains excerpts from his other writings on the subject of trains; J. F. McDermott, ed., *The Russian Journal and Other Selections* (New York, 1935); J. E. Morpurgo, ed., *The Humorous Verses of Lewis Carroll,* with illus. by J. Tenniel (London, 1950).

IV. SEPARATE WORKS—JUVENILIA. *The Rectory Umbrella and Mischmasch* (London, 1932), the last two of Lewis Carroll's MS magazines, published in full with a foreword by F. Milner; *Useful and Instructive Poetry [1845]* (London, 1954), the earliest of the MS scrapbooks, with an intro. by D. Hudson; *The Rectory Magazine* (Austin, 1975), with an intro. by J. Bump, facs. of the second of the MS magazines.

V. SEPARATE WORKS (UNDER THE PSEUDONYM LEWIS CARROLL). *Alice's Adventures in Wonderland* (London, 1865), with forty-two illus. by J. Tenniel, the author stopped the publication of the first ed. because he was dissatisfied with its production, and in consequence barely more than a dozen copies have survived; there was a 2nd ed. in 1866; apart from the Bible, few books have been more widely translated in whole or in part; only French, Italian, German, and Danish complete translations appeared in the author's lifetime; *Phantasmagoria and Other Poems* (London, 1869); *Through the Looking-Glass and What Alice Found There* (London, 1872), with fifty illus. by J. Tenniel, translated into German in 1923, and French in 1949; *Some Popular Fallacies About Vivisection* (Oxford, 1875); *The Hunting of the Snark* (London, 1876), with nine illus. by H. Holiday, translated into French by Louis Aragon (1929); *An Easter Greeting to Every Child Who Loves "Alice"* (Oxford, 1876); *Doublets: A Word-Puzzle* (London, 1879).

Rhyme? and Reason? (London, 1883), with sixty-five illus. by A. B. Frost and nine by H. Holiday; *A Tangled Tale* (London, 1885), with six illus. by A. B. Frost; *Alice's Adventures Under Ground* (London, 1886), a facs. of the original MS book (now in the British Museum) afterward developed into *Alice's Adventures in Wonderland,* with thirty-seven illus. by the author, reiss. 1965; *The Game of Logic* (London, 1886); *The Nursery "Alice"* (London, 1889), contains twenty colored enlargements from Tenniel's illus. with the text "adapted to nursery readers," a delightful effort, too little known; *Sylvie and Bruno* (London, 1889), with forty-six illus. by H. Furniss; *Circular Billiards for Two Players* (London, 1890); *Eight or Nine Wise Words about Letter-Writing* (London, 1890), issued with the "Wonderful Stamp Case" in a pink envelope containing both; *Sylvie and Bruno Concluded* (London, 1893), with forty-six illus. by H. Furniss; *Syzygies and Lanrick: A*

Word-Puzzle and a Game for Two Players (London, 1893); *Symbolic Logic: Part I. Elementary* (London, 1896); *Three Sunsets and Other Poems* (London, 1898), with twelve drawings by E. G. Thomson; *Feeding the Mind* (London, 1907), lecture delivered in October 1884, with a prefatory note by W. H. Draper; *The Wasp in a Wig* (New York, 1977), with preface, intro., and notes by Martin Gardner, first publication of galley proofs of an episode omitted from *Through the Looking-Glass*.

VI. SEPARATE WORKS (BY C. L. DODGSON). *A Syllabus of Plain Algebraical Geometry* (Oxford, 1860); *The Formulae of Plane Trigonometry* (Oxford, 1861); *A Guide to the Mathematical Student: Part I, Pure Mathematics* (Oxford, 1864); *Condensation of Determinants* (London, 1866); *An Elementary Treatise on Determinants* (London, 1867); *The Fifth Book of Euclid* (Oxford–London, 1868); *Euclid, Book V* (Oxford, 1874); *Euclid and His Modern Rivals* (London, 1879); Charles L. Dodgson, M.A., ed., *Euclid, Books I and II* (London, 1882); *Lawn Tennis Tournaments* (London, 1883); *The Principles of Parliamentary Representation* (London, 1884); *Supplement to "Euclid and His Modern Rivals"* (London, 1885); *Suggestions as to the Election of Proctors* (Oxford, 1886); *Curiosa Mathematica Part I. A New Theory of Parallels* (London, 1888); *Curiosa Mathematica Part II. Pillow-Problems* (London, 1893).

VII. SEPARATE WORKS (ANONYMOUS). *Rules for Court Circular: (A New Game of Cards for Two or More Players)* (n.p., 1860); *An Index to "In Memoriam"* (London, 1862), suggested and ed. by Dodgson but chiefly compiled by one or more of his sisters; *Croquet Castles* (n.p., 1863), an elaborate variation of the game of croquet for five players; *The New Method of Evaluation as Applied to π* (Oxford, 1865); *The Dynamics of a Particle* (Oxford, 1865); *Castle-Croquet* (Oxford, 1866), a rev. of *Croquet Castles* for four players; *The Elections to the Hebdomadal Council* (Oxford, 1866); *The Deserted Parks* (Oxford, 1867), a parody of Goldsmith's *The Deserted Village*, attacking a proposal that the University Parks at Oxford. should be used in part for college cricket grounds, the proposal was rejected; *The Offer of the Clarendon Trustees* (Oxford, 1868), an amusing jeu d'esprit on the subject of providing opportunities at the New Museum for mathematical calculations; *The New Belfry of Christ Church* (Oxford, 1872); *The Vision of the Three T's* (Oxford, 1873), these two items are both skits on proposals for architectural alterations at Christ Church; *The Blank Cheque* (Oxford, 1874), a clever fable, with the university as Mrs. Nivers, based on a proposal to authorize the building of the new Examination Schools before any plan or estimate had been prepared; *Notes by an Oxford Chiel* (Oxford, 1874), repr. of six of Dodgson's anonymous Oxford pieces; *Word-Links* (Oxford, 1878), a word game; *Mischmasch* (Oxford, 1882), a word game; *Twelve Months in a Curatorship: By One Who Has Tried It* (Oxford, 1884); *Supplement to "Twelve Months in a Curatorship"* (Oxford, 1884); *Three*

Years in a Curatorship: By One Whom It Has Tried (Oxford, 1886); *A Postal Problem* (n.p., 1891); *Curiosissima Curatoria* (Oxford, 1892).

VIII. DIARIES AND LETTERS. *Tour in 1867 by C. L. Dodgson* (Philadelphia, 1928), privately printed, the diary of a trip to Russia in 1867 with Dr. H. P. Liddon, from the MS in the Parrish Collection; E. M. Hatch, ed., *A Selection from the Letters of Lewis Carroll to His Child-Friends* (London, 1933); R. L. Green, ed., *The Diaries of Lewis Carroll*, 2 vols. (London, 1953; New York, 1954); M. N. Cohen, ed., *The Letters of Lewis Carroll*, 2 vols. (London, 1979). *Note:* The originals of Dodgson's numerous letters to his publisher, Macmillan, were sold in London in 1957 and are now in the U. S.

IX. BIOGRAPHICAL AND CRITICAL STUDIES. S. D. Collingwood, *The Life and Letters of Lewis Carroll (Rev. C. L. Dodgson)* (London, 1898); I. Bowman, *The Story of Lewis Carroll* (London, 1899); H. Furniss, *Confessions of a Caricaturist*, 2 vols. (London, 1901); E. Cammaerts, *The Poetry of Nonsense* (London, 1925); W. de la Mare, "Lewis Carroll" (London, 1932), this essay originally appeared in W. de la Mare, ed., *The Eighteen-Eighties* (Cambridge, 1930); C. Hargreaves, "Alice's Recollections of Carrollian Days," in the *Cornhill* magazine (July 1932); L. Reed, *The Life of Lewis Carroll* (London, 1932); F. Madan, ed., *The Lewis Carroll Centenary in London 1932* (London, 1932); A. M. E. Goldschmidt, "Alice in Wonderland Psycho-Analysed," in the *New Oxford Outlook* (May 1933); W. Empson, *Some Versions of Pastoral* (London, 1935), contains the essay "Alice in Wonderland: The Child as Swain."

W. Weaver, *Lewis Carroll: Correspondence Numbers* (New York, 1940); C. Morgan, *The House of Macmillan (1843–1943)* (London, 1943); F. B. Lennon, *Lewis Carroll* (London, 1947; rev. ed., 1962); R. L. Green, *The Story of Lewis Carroll* (London, 1949); H. Gernsheim, *Lewis Carroll: Photographer* (London, 1950); D. H. Munro, *Argument of Laughter* (Melbourne, 1951); P. Alexander, *Logic and the Humour of Lewis Carroll* (Leeds, 1951), repr. from the *Proceedings of the Leeds Philosophical Society*, VI, pt. 8, pp. 551–556; E. Sewell, *The Field of Nonsense* (London, 1952); A. L. Taylor, *The White Knight: A Study of C. L. Dodgson (Lewis Carroll)* (London, 1952); H. Parisot, *Lewis Carroll (Poètes d'Aujourd'hui)* (Paris, 1952); E. Wilson, *The Shores of Light* (London, 1952), contains an estimate of Lewis Carroll; G. K. Chesterton, *A Handful of Authors* (London, 1953), contains an estimate of Lewis Carroll; R. L. Green, "The Real Lewis Carroll," in the *Quarterly Review* (January 1954); D. Hudson, *Lewis Carroll* (London, 1954; reiss. 1976); R. L. Green, "The Griffin and the Jabberwock," in the *Times Literary Supplement* (1 March 1957); S. Godman, "Lewis Carroll at the Seaside," in the *Times* (London) (27 July 1957); R. L. Green, "Lewis Carroll's First Publication," in the *Times Literary Supplement* (13 September 1957).

R. L. Green, *Lewis Carroll* (London, 1960); A. Liede,

Dichtung Als Spiel, 2 vols. (Berlin, 1963), contains studies of Edward Lear and Lewis Carroll; M. Gardner, ed., *The Annotated Alice* (London, 1964); W. Weaver, *Alice in Many Tongues: The Translations of "Alice in Wonderland"* (London, 1964), a first-class pioneering work; C. H. Carruthers, *Alicia in Terra Mirabili* (London, 1964); C. H. Carruthers, *Aliciae Per Speculum Transitus* (London, 1966), fluent Latin translations of *Alice's Adventures in Wonderland* and *Through the Looking-Glass*; R. Phillips, ed., *Aspects of Alice* (London, 1972), critical essays; J. Gattegno, *Lewis Carroll: Fragments of a Looking-Glass* (London, 1977), trans. of *Lewis Carroll: une vie* (Paris, 1974); A. Clark, *Lewis Carroll: A Biography* (London, 1979); M. Batey, *Alice's Adventures in Oxford* (London, 1980).

LESLIE STEPHEN
(1832-1904)

Phyllis Grosskurth

I

It is amusing to speculate whether Lytton Strachey considered including Leslie Stephen in his gallery of eminent Victorians. Certainly Stephen had characteristics that openly elicited Strachey's contempt, notably his reluctance, so typical of his period, to come to grips with the business of literary criticism. A further consequence of this attitude, namely Stephen's concentration on the moral values of the artist, would undoubtedly have provoked Strachey's irritation, as exemplifying the absurd earnestness of the previous generation. Yet, apart from a natural reluctance to offend a family with whom he had close affinities, there were reasons why Strachey would have hesitated to mete out the sort of ridicule that reduced Dr. Thomas Arnold to a bandy-legged pomposity. Stephen's ironical attitude toward pretension, his loathing of cant, and above all his uncompromising honesty were attributes that Strachey not only admired but would have regarded as generally uncharacteristic of the Victorians.

Stephen's dates place him unquestionably in the heart of the Victorian period. His background, education, connections, and interests all link him with that profoundly influential group of upper-middle-class intellectuals who contributed so much to their time. He was also a product of a certain non-conformist strain in the Victorian pattern—namely the earnest Clapham sect, whose piety found practical expression in fighting the slave trade with indefatigable vigor. James Stephen, an efficient and respected public servant who was later knighted for his services, with the aid of his gentle wife, Jane Venn (daughter of the rector of Clapham), instilled in his five children a conviction of the importance of moral rectitude, which they never relinquished. "My father was a living categorical imperative," Stephen later said of him. Despite the austerity, there was a sweetness and simplicity that was very much a part of the family atmosphere, a tempering gentleness that offset the nervous, highly strung temperament that Leslie perhaps inherited from his father's branch of the family. The period of bigoted rigidity associated in some degree with the Evangelical movement belonged to the earlier generation of Leslie's grandfather and his great friend and brother-in-law, William Wilberforce. James, through his political career and his literary connections as a writer for the *Edinburgh Review*, contributed to his Kensington household a modified worldliness that would have been impossible even a generation earlier.

Sir James's decision in 1842 to send Leslie and his older brother Fitzjames to Eton as day boys was characteristic of his unorthodox independence. Fitzjames, tough and stubborn, hated the school but later doggedly defended its bracing effect on the character. Leslie, sickly and shy, nursed a bitterness toward Eton for the rest of his life. According to his first biographer, F. W. Maitland, "One of the most Cantabrigian of Cambridge men, he was the least Etonian of Eton men."[1] The child who had spent rapturous hours in Kensington Gardens, who had responded so ardently to poetry that the doctor forbade it because of its unsettling effect on him, found nothing to satisfy him in his new environment. As a day boy he was the ignominious butt of the boarders, and after four miserable years his father, recognizing that the experiment had been a mistake, abruptly decided to withdraw him.

For the next few years Leslie's health was a constant anxiety to his family. As a result, the remainder of his schooling was desultory, including a year of sporadic attendance at lectures at King's College, London. In 1850, Sir James was appointed Regius Professor of Modern History at Cambridge, and Les-

[1]F. W. Maitland, *The Life and Letters of Leslie Stephen* (London, 1906), p. 35.

277

lie entered Trinity Hall, his father's old college. At this period he was a tall, lanky youth who was conscientiously using a chest expander, but the experience at Cambridge proved decisive in developing him both physically and intellectually. It was such an extraordinarily happy time in his life that a long section of *Some Early Impressions,* written in 1903, is devoted to the Cambridge years, while his earlier memories are dismissed somewhat cursorily.

There were the inevitable disappointments and frustrations that were the consequence of following an extremely confident brother. To Leslie's great chagrin he was not elected to the Apostles, the highly coveted and select society of which Alfred Tennyson had been one of the founding members. He found compensation in the friendship of other seriously inclined young men, and it was the relationships that developed from intellectual discussions that Stephen particularly cherished. Somewhat reserved, he made few close friends apart from Henry Fawcett, the future politician, whose radical views Stephen shared. While at Cambridge, Fawcett was blinded in a hunting accident, and Stephen's tender devotion to him after his mishap was recalled by many of his contemporaries.

With some misgivings about his health, Stephen's parents had allowed him to read for an honors degree in mathematics. Much to their astonishment he actually flourished under the grueling ordeal of preparing for the tripos. In a group of particularly brilliant men he stood twentieth out of one hundred and forty-three contenders. That his achievement never completely satisfied him, that it was always connected in his mind with his opinion of himself as a second-rater, seems evident from his lifelong veneration of any senior wrangler. Throughout his writings, even in the most unexpected contexts, he records his admiration for this exalted class of men.

At Cambridge, Stephen began to develop his remarkable capacity for physical endurance. Rowing became an obsession, and he has gone down in history as one of the great coaches. His most satisfying memory of Cambridge was of running along the banks of the Cam exhorting his men to greater and greater efforts. At Cambridge too he began his marathon walking tours: a brisk stroll to London in twelve hours to attend a dinner of the Alpine Club was always recalled with immense pleasure.

A practical, incisive mind such as Stephen inherited from his father was particularly receptive to the intellectual climate of Cambridge. How Stephen would have developed had he been at Oxford raises an unanswerable question: Cambridge and Stephen were so congenial to each other that it is inconceivable to think of him anywhere else. In his later writings Stephen repeatedly emphasized that Cambridge, unlike Oxford, did not respond fervently to prophets or idols. Naturally skeptical, Stephen cast a wary eye on John Henry Newman and Benjamin Jowett and their luminous-eyed devotees. Cambridge, with its firm hold on the concrete, smiled scornfully at such extravagant nonsense. A man like Jowett was particularly dangerous; his vague Hegelianism, in which a concept could at the same time embrace both its positive and negative qualities, encouraged fuzzy thinking and emotionalism. "It was," Stephen remarked with satisfaction, "one of the great advantages of Cambridge that there was no such person in the place."

Cambridge might have been the home of hard-headed realists, but it could not altogether escape the turbulent upheavals of the time. "We were in one of the periods at which a crust of conventional dogma has formed, like the paleocrystic ice of the polar sea, upon the surface of opinion." Stephen recalled in later years:

The accepted formulas are being complacently repeated in all good faith by the respectable authorities. And yet new currents are everywhere moving beneath, and the superincumbent layer of official dogma is no longer conformable to the substratum of genuine belief. Then a sudden cataclysm begins to break up the crust, and to sweep away the temporary bridging of the abyss which superficial observers had mistaken for solid earth.

(*Some Early Impressions,* pp. 52–53)

Leslie Stephen spent twelve years at Cambridge, and in those years he lost his faith, not through any sudden cataclysm such as James Anthony Froude experienced, nor through the anguished introspection of an Arthur Hugh Clough; his conversion was gradual, unemotional, matter-of-fact. Upon becoming a fellow of his college in 1855, he was ordained as a matter of course, but by 1862 he realized that he could no longer conscientiously conduct the chapel services. To his restrained delight he found that he did not view the decision as separating him from a cherished security, but rather as the lifting of an onerous weight of insincerity and doubt. Never a man to fall under the heady spell of another, Stephen was not influenced by a latter-day Voltaire or

William Godwin. However, Charles Darwin's *Origin of Species* (1859) undoubtedly left a strong imprint on his mind, and he had also been reading John Stuart Mill's *System of Logic* attentively. When he later came to write *The English Utilitarians* (1900), he remarked that the inexorable logic of Mill's position could lead his supporters only to agnosticism.

II

CURIOUSLY, Stephen lingered on at Cambridge for two more years, his position steadily becoming more untenable. When he finally moved to London, he was unable to explain why he had taken so long to make the definitive break; habit, especially the habit of pleasant routine and surroundings, is the most exigent of tyrants. However, once the separation was effected, Stephen again experienced a sense of relief, this time of emerging from a hothouse atmosphere into the larger air of the London literary world.

As on a number of other occasions during his life, his brother Fitzjames had already established a position there. This connection provided Stephen with an entrée, but at the same time his brother's ceaseless success discouraged in the younger man any real ambition toward the development of his own powers. An ironical detachment toward his own work became a habitual mode of defense with Stephen, which he retained long after an impressive array of books lay behind him. When Fitzjames had become a distinguished jurist, Leslie still regarded himself as the plodding hack.

His literary career was launched with an introduction to the editor of the *Saturday Review*, J. D. Cook. Although Stephen disapproved of its mild liberalism, he was delighted to be accepted as a contributor of two articles a week, ranging over a vast area of subjects from the metaphysical to the mundane. This was the great era of literary journalism; the periodicals provided a sounding board for every controversial subject of the day, and Stephen entered enthusiastically into the fray. Soon he was also writing for the newly founded *Pall Mall Gazette*, the *Cornhill*, the New York *Nation*, and, most enthusiastically of all, for the *Fortnightly*, edited by his friend and fellow radical John Morley. Following a visit to the United States, he attained considerable notoriety from the publication of a pamphlet attacking the *Times* (London) for its at-

titude toward the northern position in the Civil War. Stephen always retained a warm affection for the Yankees and formed close friendships with Charles Eliot Norton and James Russell Lowell.

During these early years in London, Stephen was introduced to the two daughters of Thackeray. Gawky, reticent, and ill at ease with women, Stephen forced himself to propose to Minnie; and in 1867, they set up house with the other ebullient sister, Annie, a minor novelist. The arrangement worked surprisingly well, and the family bond became even closer when Stephen accepted the editorship of the *Cornhill*, Thackeray's old magazine, in 1871.

Stephen made an extremely able if not a great editor. He instituted no revolutionary changes, and the mixture continued much as before with serialized novels, assorted articles, and usually one of Stephen's essays, later incorporated into *Hours in a Library* (1874–1879). While he did not take credit for discovering any unknown geniuses, he congratulated himself on not passing up one; and the creditable tone of the *Cornhill* was maintained by contributions from Robert Louis Stevenson, John Addington Symonds, George Meredith, Henry James, and Thomas Hardy. While Stephen sometimes distinguished between his feelings as a man and his responsibility as an editor, his views in fact accorded closely with the prevailing canons of Victorian taste. The *Cornhill* had been founded as a family magazine in 1860, and Stephen was determined not to publish anything that might bring a blush to a young lady's cheek. Hardy had particular difficulty with Stephen in this respect. Repeatedly he was advised to excise or modify what now appear the most innocuous of expressions; eventually, in 1877, his contributions to the magazine came to an end when Stephen objected vociferously to the opening situation of *The Return of the Native*. Unusually independent in most respects, during his tenure of the *Cornhill* Stephen was extraordinarily conscious of the presence of Mrs. Grundy at his shoulder.

While a devoted nucleus of subscribers continued to patronize the *Cornhill*, the more venturesome journals lured many of its readers away. Taste was changing, and Stephen had not kept pace with it. People were no longer interested in interminably long serialized novels or earnest essays on the relationship between art and morality. When in 1882 the publisher George Smith broke the somber news to him that under his editorship the circulation had slipped from 25,000 to 12,000, Stephen realized that he had no alternative but to resign. The blow was a hard one, but Smith did not leave Stephen much time to smart over the humiliation. Almost immediately, on the strength of the prestige attached to Stephen's name as a result of the publication of the *History of English Thought in the Eighteenth Century* (1876), Smith offered Stephen the editorship of the *Dictionary of National Biography*, which he was about to launch.

III

FOR a time there seemed a possibility that Stephen might have followed his friend Henry Fawcett into politics, had he not been diverted into literary work; and by 1885 he was writing to John Morley, "You have soared into a political empyrean, while I am knee-deep in dictionary and drudgery."

From a scholar's point of view, the *Dictionary of National Biography* remains Stephen's greatest achievement. While it is essential that it should be continually revised and brought up to date, the sixty-six volumes are still a storehouse of invaluable information for the biographer, the historian, and the interested reader. For the biographer particularly, a footnote that might otherwise require days of laborious research can be reduced to a few minutes of work. That biography has changed from a vague impressionistic narrative to a precise, detailed exercise in careful scholarship is due in no small measure to the aid and influence of the *Dictionary of National Biography*.

When Stephen accepted the editorship, he was faced with a colossal task, for no compilation of so comprehensive a nature had yet been attempted. The first problem was to decide upon a limited number of specific criteria for those who could be admitted to its pages. Certain rigid demands must be met or the task would never be completed. A general rule was enunciated that only those who had done something worthy of commemoration would be listed; if one included a man who had simply written an obscure book several centuries before, the biography would soon become a bibliography, and its original plan would be submerged. As Stephen conceived it,

A dictionary ought, in the first place, to supply you with a sufficient indication of all that has been written upon the

subject; it should state briefly the result of the last researches; explain what appears to be the present opinion among the most qualified experts, and what are the points which seem still to be open; and, above all, should give a full reference to all the best and most original sources of information.

(*Studies of a Biographer*, vol. I, p. 19)

The organization of the vast quantity of material was solely the responsibility of Stephen, who had a single able assistant, Sidney Lee. The various subjects were distributed to appropriate scholars, and Stephen believed it wise to assign Oxford men to Oxford scholars, Catholics to Catholics, although contributors were advised to curb eulogistic excesses. Precision and concision were prescribed; articles must be submitted within six months; otherwise, contributors were given a free rein. While the impersonal tone of a handbook was avoided, the uneven approach and emphasis of articles by divers hands brought inevitable criticism; but in the circumstances no other result was possible. The general tone of the dictionary was undoubtedly as Stephen wished it to be, for he viewed the work not simply as a series of handbooks for the scholar, but as a "confidential friend" who could provide an element of entertainment beyond dry-as-dust information.

But there was little entertainment for the editor in the compilation of the material. Twice a year a list of proposed names for inclusion appeared in the *Athenaeum* with an accompanying request for additional suggestions. Stephen and Lee were inundated with the names of the obscure and the bizarre, sometimes accompanied by threats and cajolery from interested parties. And always there were never-ending lists of nominees whose qualifications had to be checked meticulously. Stephen was speaking from the heart when he later told an audience, "Much of the work to be done was uninteresting, if not absolutely repulsive." Great sighs of irritation were rent from him as he slashed out unnecessary verbiage and scribbled minute spidery marginalia over the contributors' manuscripts. By and large his relations were cordial with his contributors, with the exception of the historian E. A. Freeman, who resigned huffily when Stephen refused to accept his use of initial diphthongs for the spelling of Athelstan and other Anglo-Saxon names.

Stephen edited the first twenty-one volumes himself, five jointly with Sidney Lee, and contributed three hundred and eighty-seven articles to all the volumes except three. The wonder is that he was able to stay the course as long as he did. The sickly boy had developed into a wiry, energetic man as a result of his vigorous walking tours and growing obsession for mountain climbing. Nevertheless the strain of overwork brought on several attacks of influenza, which finally convinced him that all the determination in the world would not compensate for his failing powers. Stephen shared the Victorian admiration of "character," and he set himself standards of behavior and achievement that could be surrendered only by a clear-eyed recognition of hard facts. The decision to resign from the editorship in 1891 was facilitated by the knowledge that he left the completion of the task to a capable lieutenant. But the initiation of the gigantic effort, its organization, and its general character bear the inimitable stamp of Leslie Stephen. Stephen himself never appreciated the extent and importance of his achievement. His attitude is revealed in his comments on Dr. Johnson's dictionary. It was, he wrote,

the highest kind of work to which a literary journeyman could be set, but it was still work for a journeyman, not for an artist. He was not adding to literature, but providing a useful implement for future men of letters.

(*Samuel Johnson*, p. 39)

IV

THE months following his resignation were a difficult period in Leslie Stephen's life, and it is doubtful how successfully he would have endured them without the help of his beloved second wife. In 1875, Minnie had died very suddenly on a trip to Switzerland, a blow from which Stephen never fully recovered. The taciturn, moody man had come to rely on Minnie's gentle love, and the emptiness of an existence without her plunged him into grim despair. During three lonely years, his only source of comfort was an old family friend and neighbor, Julia Duckworth, a strikingly beautiful young widow. Gradually she began to grow more necessary to him, and in 1878 they were married.

Of this union, four extraordinarily interesting children were born: Vanessa (Bell), Thoby, Virginia (Woolf), and Adrian. Leslie Stephen may have been aloof with strangers, but he was the most devoted of family men. Virginia Woolf has described his

delightfully easy way with children, whom he would entertain with ingenious drawings and cutouts of animals; and how he would spend every evening reading aloud to them from the Waverley novels or half reclining, with eyes closed, would recite "The Scholar-Gypsy" or some of his other favorite poems. There were other moods of monumental depression and discouragement, in large measure sincere, in some measure staged for the benefit of a loving and sympathetic wife. In *To the Lighthouse* (1927) Virginia Woolf portrays the pathetic comedy of the Stephens' married life in the relationship of the Ramsays: she manages to capture both the absurdity and the integrity of a man who jealously guarded his inner self from the eyes of an inquisitive world. Scornful of public introspection, Stephen wrote at the beginning of his curiously impersonal reminiscences, *Some Early Impressions:*

Clearly I am not qualified for autobiography, nor, to say the truth, do I regret the circumstance. I have no reason to think that the story of my "inner life" would be in the least interesting, and, were it interesting, I should still prefer to keep it to myself.

(p. 9)

Mr. Ramsay, storming up and down the lawn, would have spoken such sentiments from a raging self-pity that the world had failed to appreciate him. On Leslie Stephen's printed page, irony served as sufficient defense.

Only his wife knew how bitterly he reacted to a holiday in Switzerland in 1891 when, in precarious health, he could only look wistfully up at the coveted peaks; and it was after the visit ended in a frightening bout of influenza that she persuaded him to resign the editorship of the *Dictionary of National Biography.* Stephen possessed a temperament that tended to be suspicious of emotionalism, and he felt particular contempt for religious fanaticism; yet at the same time he was a man of deeply turbulent emotions, all the more troublesome because his code of behavior forced him to keep them under rigid control. In only one area of his life did he relax his habitual self-discipline—namely, in his passionate enjoyment of mountain climbing.

While he frequently recorded his appreciation of the beauty of the Alps, essentially their fascination for him lay in the challenge they offered as a test of character. Moreover, the test demanded qualities that Stephen possessed in an eminent degree. As a writer he was well aware that his capacities were not of the kind that make a great artist. He was not a man dominated by a driving imagination. Therefore he would never rise above the production of literary history or criticism—a role he always depreciated somewhat contemptuously. But mountain climbing required practicality, perseverance, tenacity. His companions noted the dogged silence with which he attacked the challenge rearing above him. This same brisk attitude was evident in his administration of the Sunday Tramps, a walking club he founded and which he led out in all weathers with a set goal of so many miles to be covered within so many hours. Humorless as his attitude might appear to some, Stephen thoroughly enjoyed this sort of activity because here he was presented with difficulties that he knew he was capable of surmounting.

Victorian travelers flocked to what Stephen called "The Playground of Europe" in such numbers that there was no self-respecting tourist who could not distinguish between the charms of Mürren and those of Zermatt. The Alps seemed to provide the Victorians with a release from the physical and mental conventions of life at home. Many another writer echoed Stephen's opinion that the Alps

are places of refuge where we may escape from ourselves and from our neighbours. There we may breathe air that has not passed through a million pairs of lungs; and drink water in which the acutest philosophers cannot discover the germs of indescribable diseases. . . . The rocks and the glaciers have a character of their own, and are not undergoing the wearisome process of civilisation. . . . Human society has been adapted to the scenery, and has not forced the scenery to wear its livery.

(*The Playground of Europe*, pp. 68–69)

The middle of the century saw the beginning of the vogue for mountain climbing, stimulated by the formation of the Alpine Club in 1857. An enthusiastic member, Stephen scaled a number of impressive peaks, and his greatest achievement was the right to boast that he was the first man to conquer the Schreckhorn. With his long, lanky build and legs that were often compared to compasses, he scrambled about crag and precipice with the nimbleness of a mountain goat.

His supreme sense of ease on the peaks is revealed in the picture of him smoking a pipe contentedly on the top of the Eiger-Joch. John Ruskin was appalled at the sacrilege, and while Stephen acknowledged

that it was Ruskin who had first opened his eyes to the sublimity of the Alps through the pages of *Modern Painters* (1843–1860), he pointed out that the Alps had conquered him so completely that he had not moved beyond them to the beauties of the Venetian painters. For the remainder of his life he remained abysmally ignorant of the fine arts, an indifference he viewed with unshakable complacency.

This does not suggest that mountain climbing appealed to Stephen simply as a solution for suppressed psychological problems. "I love everything in the shape of a mountain," he wrote, "from Mont Blanc down to Hampstead Hill." Though he did not declaim aloud to his mountaineering companions, his aesthetic reactions were recorded in prose unusually fervent for Stephen, in essays such as "Sunset on Mont Blanc" and "The Alps in Winter" in *The Playground of Europe*. Mont Blanc he describes as

the most solitary of all mountains, rising, Saul-like, a head and shoulders above the crowd of attendant peaks, and yet within that single mass there is greater prodigality of the sublimest scenery than in whole mountain districts of inferior elevation. The sternest and most massive of cliffs, the wildest spires of distorted rock, bounding torrents of shattered ice, snowfields polished and even as a sea-shell, are combined into a whole of infinite variety and yet of artistic unity. One might wander for days, were such wandering made possible by other conditions, amongst his crowning snows, and every day would present new combinations of unsuspected grandeur.

(p. 259)

Here Stephen paid homage to an aspect of nature that he would never accord to a human being. Significantly, Shelley's intense feeling about the Alps provided the only bond of sympathy that Stephen could establish with a poet whom he found inimical in every other respect. The gulf between him and his brother Fitzjames is indicated by an episode, later grimly recounted by Stephen, on the only occasion when they went climbing together. Fitzjames talked of nothing but the *Saturday Review* all the way to the top and back.

V

So intense was Stephen's love of the Alps that he could declare that "the love of mountains is intimately connected with all that is noblest in human nature.

If no formal demonstration of that truth be possible, our faith in it will be not the less firm." He makes no attempt to explain the statement, nor does he consider it necessary to elaborate. To systematize, to force intuitions into formalized propositions, is to erect a tenuous house of cards out of man's inexpressible longings for the infinite.

In his most famous essay, "A Bad Five Minutes in the Alps," included in *Freethinking and Plainspeaking*, Stephen considers the various ways in which men have chosen to fortify themselves in the face of death. He constructs an allegory from an imaginary experience in which he loses his footing on a mountain expedition and, clinging precariously to a ledge, tries to find some spiritual consolation in the seemingly inevitable fate that awaits him. Looking back on the world as he has known it, he reflects that he had always viewed it as a pretty fair sort of place, certainly not Newman's vale of woe where mankind seemed implicated in some terrible aboriginal calamity. In turn he then rejects any comfort that a materialist, a pantheist, or a positivist might proffer him. He cannot find comfort in the possibility of his toenails being absorbed into the general totality of nature, nor can he contemplate with satisfaction a world lacking his presence yet nevertheless presenting a noble vista of social science associations proliferating over the face of the earth.

Eventually he discovers that solid ground lies unexpectedly only a few feet below him. None of the avenues that he has explored have provided him with any acceptable image of an afterlife. All that remains is to get back to the business of living.

Stephen abandoned the pretense of faith when he realized that he could not accept the chimeras men told each other they believed in the name of religion. When many of his contemporaries found refuge in the liberalism of the Broad Church, Stephen accused them of double-dealing in their lip service to a *legal* imposition such as the Thirty-Nine Articles, while they privately disagreed with its enunciated doctrines. The Thirty-Nine Articles, he wrote in the essay "The Broad Church," should be recognized for what they were: "an expression of the views about theology current . . . in the sixteenth century; . . . the best available compromise" that could be effected at the time from the mass of undigested dogmas that had accumulated through the centuries. Clergymen might be very much surprised to discover that the world could survive the demise of Anglicanism; indeed, they might discover that it would be better off for discarding outworn beliefs. In any event, "Whatever happens, the religious instincts of mankind will survive and will find some mode of expression."

Certainly the worst possible answer to the mood of perplexity that most thinking men were experiencing was an escape into ritualism, "surely the most vapid form of sacerdotalism ever imposed upon effeminate natures." Stephen was one of the few men of the time who remained absolutely impervious even to the beauty of Newman's character, and on frequent occasions he finds as many harsh things to say of him as he does of Charles Kingsley. The Oxford movement was an anachronism in Stephen's view, a flight from reality; always Stephen ranged himself with the forces of the present, with man accepting and adapting himself to the world in which he found himself. Thus he sneered at any form of revivalism whether in religion, architecture, or poetry, because each represented a conscious imitation of the past, a pose substituting for actuality. "The passionate and deep emotions, to which the highest art is owing, must burst forth in spontaneous and original expression."

Neither the Broad Church nor the ritualistic movement satisfied Stephen because each represented a compromise with truth. Not that he could not sympathize with those who, despite their misgivings, were reluctant to face up to the logic of their situation. He was fully aware that it cost many a bitter pang to part with what had been a beautiful fancy, but children must grow up, and fairy tales must be discarded in the colder light of the adult world.

Stephen's position is perhaps made clearer if one considers Matthew Arnold's dilemma concerning Bishop John William Colenso. Arnold may well have been in intellectual agreement with Colenso's doubts about the historical validity of the Scriptures, yet he criticizes him for giving voice to his views, lest he unsettle the faith of the credulous working classes. To some degree Stephen shared Arnold's misgivings as to the effect of devastating revelations about Noah's flood on the morality and "lofty sentiment" of the masses of the people, and the solution he proposed was, as we shall see, a strong reiteration of the necessity to preserve a firmly based "science of ethics." Facing realistic truths was seldom easy, Stephen admitted, but there was no reason why life should be made easy for us. "Did you ever know your father to do a thing because it was pleasant?" his mother had once asked his brother Fitzjames. The same sense of integrity informed Stephen's break with conventional religion. Even at the risk of unsettling others, "We ought not to tell lies, or to countenance the telling of lies."

As a young clergyman, he had intrepidly faced up to the fact that his belief rested on no solid basis. There was no alternative but to resign his fellowship; and in 1875, when the law had finally made it possible to renounce his Holy Orders as well, Hardy witnessed the deed of renunciation in a private but very dramatic little scene. It has often been remarked that Stephen was scrupulous about not unsettling the faith of others while thinking through his own doubts before he discarded what he described as the choking neckcloth. But he could not continue in the role of one who deluded both himself and others with rationalizations that his intellect was forced to reject. F. D. Maurice became a bête noire with Stephen, who shuddered over his "fatuous" efforts to force new truth into old molds. Similarly, while he admired Jowett's power as a teacher, the Master of Balliol's fondness for sitting on the fence aroused his scornful indignation. Jowett had no philosophy to which he adhered, no fixed principles, nothing to offer the young except a cowardly ambiguity of belief.

VI

As Stephen makes clear in the essay "Darwin and Divinity," he was profoundly aware that men possessed a religious sense, a craving for the expression of wonderment when confronted with the mystery of human existence. But he could not rest satisfied with the conventional objects of worship. Man had outgrown the present shabby concepts and had not yet found adequate replacements.

While not prepared to suggest any new formulas, Stephen held out a measure of hope for man in the doctrine of evolution. In Darwin's "general stream of tendency" he detected a spiritual nature, the meaning and end of which lay in impenetrable mystery, but which seemed to promise a progressive movement for the future of man. Such a belief has obvious affinities with George Bernard Shaw's concept of the "Life Force," according to which certain gifted individuals act as instruments for the realization of the potentialities of the race. In his forthright way, Stephen would probably have pooh-poohed such ideas as absurdly mystical, yet although he might

dismiss the supernatural and the divine, the fact remains that when he asks in "An Apology for Plainspeaking," "Why stand we gazing into heaven when we have but to look round to catch the contagion of noble enthusiasm from men of our own race?" he is unwittingly postulating a larger-than-human dimension.

Stephen's open-minded attitude in matters of belief is one thing; his attitude in matters of ethics is another. In the Leslie Stephen lecture of 1937, Desmond MacCarthy spoke of "that close alliance between Agnosticism and Puritanism" that characterized both Stephen and Thomas Huxley. It is not surprising that the most vehement attack against Algernon Swinburne's prurience should have come from the pen of a fellow agnostic, John Morley. Stephen spoke of the "hypertrophy of the conscience" that afflicted those who had come under Dr. Arnold's influence, but it was a phrase equally applicable to himself. As in the case of so many other nineteenth-century skeptics, Stephen went to great pains to prove that an absence of belief in the supernatural did not in any sense diminish the importance of morality. Indeed, a concentration on the here and now intensified the necessity for formulating a workable ethical code both for the development of the individual character and for the clarification of his obligations toward society.

Stephen spent six years in the preparation of *The Science of Ethics* (1882), and it always remained his favorite among his books. Since it meant so much to him, Stephen was hurt when it was ignored by the public and treated slightingly by contemporary moral philosophers such as Henry Sidgwick. According to Noel Annan, the work is "worthless *as ethics*; it is simply an expression of opinion about a scientific process related to ethics by crude biological analogies."[2] What Stephen attempted to do was to trace the origin and evolution of ethics as a mode of conduct adapting itself to a changing environment. A viable morality is essential if a community is to continue in a process of growth; all the basic moral virtues are necessary to the well-being of society. Responsible conduct, for Stephen, is fundamentally an obligation to be exercised in the world of men. As Annan implies, Stephen, like Herbert Spencer, equated evolution with progress: the passage of time brings inevitable advancement. How could Stephen justify his rejection of the belief in immortality if he

[2]N. G. Annan, *Leslie Stephen: His Thought and Character in Relation to His Time* (London, 1951), p. 217.

could not view this present life as providing cause for hope?

Annan describes Stephen as "an amateur who has blundered into a profession which demands rigorous training" (p. 215). The glaring omission in *The Science of Ethics* is Stephen's failure to come to grips with the perennial problem of the individual faced with alternatives of action: How does he distinguish the morally right decision from the morally wrong? Morality consists in behaving in conformity with the prevailing spirit of progress, Stephen suggests. But then, a more rigorous ethical philosopher like Henry Sidgwick might ask, what sort of guide is this slipshod criterion as an aid to individual conduct?

Stephen possessed a firm conviction of a *type* of the upright man of integrity, but he was not prepared to draw up codes of behavior enunciating principles of guidance. A perusal of his comments on the men whom he admired is almost the only way of finding some indication of the qualities he esteemed.

Repeatedly Stephen emphasized the dangers of excessive veneration of great men and women. Nevertheless he shared, more than he recognized, the Victorian tendency to turn to the lives of noble individuals as objects of emulation as the old connection between religion and morality broke down. If Stephen came close to adulation of any individual, that man was Darwin. Darwin's candor, patience, and sagacity Stephen found extraordinarily attractive. Yet he has nothing to say about Darwin's nervous refusal to comment on the conclusions that could not fail to be drawn from his postulations.

The fact that Darwin's hesitation did not disturb Stephen is curious, because it was his habit to expect men to follow their speculations to their logical conclusions. Thus his contempt for Tennyson is evident in his remarks on *In Memoriam*. Here he views the poet as "a man clinging to a spar left floating after a shipwreck, knowing that it will not support him, and yet never able to make up his mind to strike out and take his chance of sinking or swimming." Such indecisiveness vitiates any consolatory strength that he may seek to provide, for it is impossible to turn to him for guidance or moral sustenance. Those who assumed the role of teacher—and it is apparent that Stephen believes this to be one function of the poet—must commit themselves decisively to belief or unbelief. Men like Tennyson, Jowett, and F. D. Maurice are not only cowardly but positively dangerous for the unsettling effect they have on the young.

A positive or courageous attitude toward life Stephen describes by his favorite word, "masculine." While it is apparent that Stephen always felt something of the resentment of a younger brother against the dominating influence of Fitzjames, clearly when it came to writing his life Stephen venerated him for the strong impression of integrated personality with which he faced the world. Similarly, while Stephen's attitude to Thomas Carlyle is somewhat mixed, by and large he admits

And yet, though I cannot think without pity of the man of genius who felt so keenly and thought so gloomily of the evils around us, I feel infinitely more respect for his frame of mind than for that of the man who, sharing, verbally at least, this opinion, can let it calmly lie in his mind without the least danger to his personal comfort.

(*Hours in a Library*, vol. III, p. 305)

Stephen recoiled from Carlyle's political philosophy, and he shuddered when he heard Fitzjames echoing Carlyle's antidemocratic tirades; but at least Carlyle adhered tenaciously to his convictions. Arnold's praise of Montaigne as *ondoyant et divers* would be little to Stephen's taste.

Stephen's analysis of Arnold's thought in the second volume of *Studies of a Biographer* displays a curious mixture of genuine admiration for the author of "The Scholar-Gypsy" with an undisguised disapproval of Arnold's "morbid" tendency. Arnold's sympathy for the nineteenth-century Amiels and Obermanns ("excellent but surely effeminate persons") reveals an unmanly indulgence in self-pity. Stephen reacted with irritation to those who wandered aimlessly "between two worlds, one dead, / The other powerless to be born." He could not take seriously the cries of aggrieved lamentation with which they greeted the threats to cherished illusions. Sturdy common sense, the ability to look unflinchingly at facts, a defiant absence of sentimentality, these were the qualities Stephen demanded of men and of artists. Such equipment may have provided him with admirable tools for living, but they were hardly adequate for literary criticism.

VII

As we have seen, Stephen became a literary critic by accident through the countless books that were thrust on him for reviewing. His emphasis is on exposition rather than analysis; his tastes are predictable, and his judgments are based largely upon his esteem for various authors as men. In 1937, Desmond MacCarthy described Stephen as "the least aesthetic of noteworthy critics," only to bring down the wrath of Mrs. Q. D. Leavis, who claimed that in the last resort all literary judgments must be moral judgments and that Stephen should be cherished for elevating value above response.

What Stephen would have liked criticism to be is indicated in his essay on Charlotte Brontë, in which he discusses Swinburne's proclivity for extravagant praise and blame:

After all, though criticism cannot boast of being a science, it ought to aim at something like a scientific basis, or at least to proceed in a scientific spirit. The critic, therefore, before abandoning himself to the oratorical impulse, should endeavour to classify the phenomena with which he is dealing as calmly as if he were ticketing a fossil in a museum.

(*Hours in a Library*, vol. III, p. 272)

But did Stephen really have a clear idea of what a scientific method was? And, if so, would he have been willing to treat literature in such a manner? The quintessential scientific approach of that period is to be found in Zola's *Le Roman expérimental*, in which he declared that, artistically treated, man should be subject to the same laws as the stone on the road. Such a view precludes any such preconceptions as moral standards or value judgments.

How far removed Stephen was from such detachment is indicated in the essay "Art and Morality," which appeared in the *Cornhill* in 1875. "Art," he declares, "is the means by which the men who feel most strongly and think most powerfully appeal to the passions of their weaker brethren." The word "passions" suggests that art may be a two-edged instrument, one that must be handled with particular discretion. Immediately Stephen goes on to assert that it is impossible to maintain that art can have no bearing upon behavior; on the contrary, unobtrusive though its means may appear, the very emotion with which it has been conceived is communicated to the reader. Here Stephen, the consistent advocate of reason, recognizes the undeniable pull of the passions. "People think me cold and sarcastic," he once wrote to Mrs. Herbert Fisher, "and yet you know that I have some feeling; only it does not get easily to the surface. . . ."

Stephen's concern for the possible ill effects of art is not confined solely to the individual. Society is composed of a group of interacting individuals, each of whom could spread contagion to the community at large. Accordingly, in the interests of society there are certain emotions that it is unwise to portray in art. Only by suppressing the baser emotions can we move steadily upward away from the beast. Like so many other Victorian critics Stephen contends that the ultimate value of art depends upon the moral qualities of the artist.

In the case of William Shakespeare and John Keats, Stephen realizes that he is confronted with situations that are not very easily defined. How can one extract the morality from either poet? How is one to justify a creation like Falstaff? Here Stephen has no alternative but to admit that there are instances when one cannot deny that art in itself is neither good nor bad. "It may be a poison or a medicine. Its action depends upon the condition of the patient."

This is a curious *volte-face*, and Stephen has to shift his ground with a peculiar sidestepping motion. Responsibility is now removed in some degree from the individual artist to society as a whole. Stephen has been forced to adopt the Ruskinian position that only a thoroughly moral community can hope to produce healthy works of art. Society bears much of the responsibility for the art it produces; the artist in turn has a debt to society to preserve its integrity.

In "Thoughts on Criticism, by a Critic," another essay that appeared in the *Cornhill* in 1876, he lays down as a first rule of criticism that you must have "the rare courage of admitting your own feelings." In effect this is the first and last rule. Stephen explains that literary judgments are formed empirically into a body of doctrine comparable to the case law of the jurists. Yet this body of doctrine has little substance or abstract validity since human judgments are capricious and conflicting. Consequently, all a critic can do is to record his own judgment with some regard for the opinion of the authorities of the past, being always concerned with the necessity of speaking out against vice, vulgarity, or stupidity.

So frequently does Stephen voice the conviction that morality is as intricately connected with art as with life that he seems to be setting up something more than a straw man. Walter Pater's *Studies in the History of the Renaissance* had appeared in 1873; in the famous conclusion, the manifesto of the art for art's sake movement, Pater had declared that "art comes to you proposing frankly to give nothing but the highest quality to your moments as they pass, and simply for those moments' sake." Although Stephen never mentions Pater by name, such an ideal of art would have appeared criminally irresponsible to him; but Pater's concept of the aesthetic critic as one who possesses "a certain kind of temperament, the power of being deeply moved by the presence of beautiful objects" is a principle that Stephen tacitly assumes. Like Pater, he is distrustful of system and formula. In the end, while he may equate absence of heat with detachment, in actuality he is only describing the approach favored by a temperament such as his own, and the compendium of his criticism remains the record of his responses, his particular power of being moved by works of art. "Whoever thinks for himself, and says plainly what he thinks, has some merit as a critic," he says in his study of Dr. Johnson. The expression is blunter, the style more commonplace, but is the subjective position not precisely that of Pater? All that is lacking is the power of being moved in a profound way.

VIII

STEPHEN collected the bulk of his literary criticism into two series of essays, *Hours in a Library* and *Studies of a Biographer* (1898–1902). One dominant feature emerges from these essays, which range through Stephen's wide and eclectic taste: his preoccupation with the man rather than with the writer. He liked criticism to be mingled with biography in the sort of amalgam Dr. Johnson achieved in *Lives of the Poets*. Stephen wrote in an era that was untroubled by the fear of concentrating on the peripheral or of committing the "biographical heresy." "Now I confess," he writes quite unashamedly in "Shakespeare as a Man,"

> that to me one main interest in reading is always the communion with the author. *Paradise Lost* gives me a sense of intercourse with Milton, and the Waverley Novels bring me a greeting from Scott. . . . I may study Darwin's *Origin of Species* to clear my views upon natural selection; but as a book it interests me even through the defects of style by the occult personal charm of the candid, sagacious patient seeker for truth.
>
> (*Studies of a Biographer*, vol. IV, pp. 3–4)

He could feel no sympathy for Robert Browning's view that if Shakespeare unlocked his heart in the sonnets, "the less Shakespeare he."

As I have emphasized, Stephen's value judgments are based primarily upon ethical considerations. James Anthony Froude and Henry Fielding were admired for their "masculinity," despite shortcomings that he glosses over. Yet such a bias did not restrict him unduly; that he could like both Mill and Carlyle significantly indicates the breadth of his sympathy. There were, of course, unconcealed favorites, Dr. Johnson heading the pantheon. His study of the Great Cham reveals that his love was compounded with gratitude for Johnson's example of endurance amid a sea of troubles. Like Arnold, Stephen regarded the greatest literature as capable of uplifting and rejoicing, and it is for this quality that he holds William Wordsworth in such reverence. During the bitter days after his first wife's death, Wordsworth was the only poet he was able to read; here was a case of what Mill called Wordsworth's attraction for prosaic minds. As Dover Wilson says, Stephen was "instinctively and passionately of Wordsworth's mind" in "his passion for truth as he saw it, in his almost stark integrity of mind, and above all in his profound moral sense."[3]

When Wordsworth rises to the heights of imaginative insight inspired by an incident such as crossing the Simplon, Stephen is left far behind. The most valuable element in his poetry for Stephen is the philosophy that can be extracted from it. Significantly, his own essay on the poet is entitled "Wordsworth's Ethics," just as he discusses "Pope as a Moralist." In proportion to the body of his complete works, Stephen's writings on poetry comprise an extremely small part of the whole. The selection of poets whom he chose to write about is revealing— Alexander Pope, George Crabbe, Samuel Taylor Coleridge, Wordsworth, Tennyson, Arnold—and almost always attention is directed to the ideas embodied in the poetry. If the aesthetic worth of the poetry is ever considered, Stephen seems much more at ease in discussing poetic prose such as Thomas De Quincey's. The romantics and the metaphysicals lay completely outside his range, and Stephen was not reluctant to say so.

He shook his head in bewilderment when Matthew Arnold attempted to analyze the Celtic elements in English poetry; his prosaic mind, he confessed, was not adapted for discriminating "those exquisite essences." His own feeling for poetry was

[3] J. D. Wilson, *Leslie Stephen and Matthew Arnold as Critics of Wordsworth* (London, 1939), p. 12.

intense, but it lacked any appreciation of its musical quality. His emotional response remained on a fairly simple level, and the only canon he ever establishes for the estimation of great poetry is its "adhesiveness"—that is, its capacity for being retained by the memory. Perhaps in practice this principle is not so very dissimilar from Arnold's "touchstones," although Stephen never considers the qualities that poetry must possess to make it unforgettable.

Stephen's best essays are those in which he discusses the impact of one individual on another: Godwin on Shelley, Coleridge on Carlyle, or Carlyle on Ruskin. He is perceptive in drawing analogies, bringing out affinities, illustrating subtle differences. He is also skillful at extracting the strength and the weakness of a writer like Daniel Defoe, whose cast of mind he could understand, or in differentiating between the types of realism to be found in Defoe, Jane Austen, Honoré de Balzac, or Charlotte Brontë. In the final analysis, we might say that Stephen's interests are not primarily "literary." Basically he is interested in individuals. Even in tracing currents of thought, he is concerned with ideas as they originate with men and as they affect men.

IX

If Stephen came close to creating a masterpiece, it is his *History of English Thought in the Eighteenth Century*. Stephen was unique among the Victorians in his understanding and appreciation of the despised neoclassicists. When he looked back at the various periods of history, he felt confident that he would have been most at home among the Augustans, with their emphasis on rationality, common sense, and decorum. Yet there was further reason why Stephen found it satisfying to turn to this period in the years following his loss of faith.

Stephen believed that man marks out a path of inevitable progress, but that his advance is halted periodically by the forces of obscurantism. As Stephen traces the controversies of the deists, the empiricists, and the utilitarians, he either explicitly or implicitly compares analogous situations in his own century. The history of ideas forms a continuum, he suggests, and the problems and uncertainties of one century are the outcome of earlier failures to come to terms with unpalatable realities:

The hollowness in theory and the impotence in practice of English speculation in the last half of the century, is but the natural consequence of the faint-heartedness which prevented English thinkers from looking facts in the face. The huge development of hypocrisy, of sham beliefs, and indolent scepticism, is the penalty which we have had to pay for our not daring to meet the doubts openly expressed by Hume, and by Hume alone.

(*History of English Thought in the Eighteenth Century*, vol. I, p. 315)

Even Mill, whom Stephen admired in so many ways, was fallible enough to try to extract some tenuous thread of orthodoxy from the pages of Hume's treatises.

It is in this work, too, when Stephen discusses the poets of the period, that he reveals his real attitudes toward poetry. The romantics were reaching out beyond solid ground to penetrate the vast mysteries of the unknowable; in their brooding upon the enigmas of the universe, they were following the same will-o'-the-wisp as those who clung to outmoded religious beliefs with their faith in the supernatural. Mysteries never tempted Stephen. Augustan poets are more to his taste because they are sensible enough to realize that they would be presumptuous to aspire beyond the tangible. "Knowledge of human nature, as it actually presented itself in the shifting scene before them, and a vivid appreciation of the importance of the moral law, are the staple of the best literature of the time," Stephen notes approvingly. In other words, they made splendid agnostics.

In *The English Utilitarians* Stephen added a sequel to the *History of English Thought in the Eighteenth Century*. This work he found particularly congenial, as he had always been in fundamental agreement with the tenets of the school. The group originally attracted him by its obvious sincerity and by its refusal to pay lip service to either the insubstantial or the illogical. Nothing less than solid fact would satisfy them. Yet, humanist as he was above all else, Stephen recoiled from the assumption that facts can be extracted from handbooks and statistics. In a discussion of James Mill's *History of British India* (1817), Stephen commented, "Some facts require imagination and sympathy to be appreciated, and there Mill was deficient." Much as he respected John Stuart Mill, certain aspects of his character left him slightly uneasy. Mill took himself a trifle too seriously; at heart he preferred a prig (Stephen had a loathing of prigs), and he never seems fully to appreciate the force of human passions; he fancies that the emotions which stir men to their depths can be controlled by instilling a few moral maxims or pointing out considerations of utility.

(*The English Utilitarians*, vol. III, p. 71)

Stephen was no cold-blooded rationalist. He recognized the power and persuasiveness of the passions; admittedly, they must be controlled and directed by the intellect, but their absence made a man less than a human being.

X

TOWARD the end of his life Stephen expressed the belief that he had dissipated himself on too many projects—"a jack of all trades," he called himself—and he did not believe that he would deserve more than a passing footnote in the history of nineteenth-century thought. In his capacity for hard work, in his curiosity and willingness to undertake a wide variety of subjects, he was undoubtedly characteristic of his period. He was also an interesting representative of a vigorous intellectual strain that has been overlooked to some extent in the current estimate of the Victorians. While many other worried individuals shared Arthur Hugh Clough's tormented anxieties, there were those, such as Sidgwick, T. H. Huxley, and Stephen himself, who faced up to their doubts with "masculine" determination.

Stephen's contemporary reputation as one of the foremost critics of his time has not been sustained. He left behind him a great mass of critical essays, none of them startlingly original or intuitive, but nevertheless filled with sensible, well-informed observations. He is not remembered by posterity as a great stylist like Newman or Pater; or as having Arnold's gift of striking off an incisive "adhesive" phrase. But he did possess a delightfully mordant streak of irony, particularly when aroused by sanctimoniousness. "I often wished," he once wrote, "that I too had a little sweetness and light that I might be able to say such nasty things of my enemies." At the same time he was acute enough to realize the probable justice of Arnold's opinion of *him*:

Had Arnold been called upon to pronounce judgment upon me, he must, however reluctantly, have set me down as a Philistine. It is a word which I dislike; but I cannot deny that, in his phraseology, it would be indisputably appropriate.

(*Studies of a Biographer*, vol. II, p. 79)

The *Dictionary of National Biography* was his supreme achievement. Yet the remainder of his work is not inconsiderable: *The Playground of Europe* is a most enchanting account of a prolonged love affair; *Essays in Freethinking and Plainspeaking* and *An Agnostic's Apology* are among the most cogent statements of the nineteenth-century agnostic position. The *History of English Thought in the Eighteenth Century* and *The English Utilitarians* are still regarded as unexcelled in their field.

A dissipation of effort? Possibly; but that was the man Leslie Stephen—an inquiring amateur, not too serious about himself or his work, one who realized his ambition to "live and die a gentleman."

SELECTED BIBLIOGRAPHY

I. COLLECTED WORKS. *Collected Essays,* 10 vols. (London, 1907); *Men, Books and Mountains: Essays Collected* (London, 1956), also in S. Ullman, ed. (London, 1978). *Note:* There is no complete collected ed. of Stephen's writings.

II. SELECTIONS. N. Annan, ed., *Selected Writings in British Intellectual History* (Chicago, 1979).

III. SEPARATE WORKS. *The Poll Degree from a Third Point of View* (London, 1863); *Sketches from Cambridge, by a Don* (London, 1865), repr. from the *Pall Mall Gazette*; [L. S.], *"The Times" on the American War; an Historical Survey* (London, 1865); *The Playground of Europe* (London, 1871); *Essays on Freethinking and Plainspeaking* (London, 1873), a newer ed. (1907) contains essays on Stephen by J. Bryce and H. Paul; *Hours in a Library*, 3rd ser. (London, 1874–1879), new ed. with additions (1892), repr. in 4 vols. for *Collected Essays* (1907); *History of English Thought in the Eighteenth Century*, 2 vols. (London, 1876); J. Morley, ed., *Samuel Johnson* (London, 1878), English Men of Letters series, other vols. contributed by Stephen to this series are *Alexander Pope* (1880), *Jonathan Swift* (1882), *George Eliot* (1902), and *Thomas Hobbes* (1904); *The Science of Ethics* (London, 1882); *The Life of Henry Fawcett* (London, 1885); *An Agnostic's Apology and Other Essays* (London, 1893); *The Life of Sir James Fitzjames Stephen* (London, 1895; repr. 1971); *Social Rights and Duties*, 2 vols. (London, 1896); *Studies of a Biographer*, 4 vols. (1898–1902); *The English Utilitarians*, 3 vols. (London, 1900; repr. 1970); L. Stephen and S. Lee, *Lives of the 'Lustrious: A Dictionary of Irrational Biography* (London, 1901); *Robert Louis Stevenson. An Essay* (London, 1903); *English Literature and Society in the Eighteenth Century* (London, 1904), Ford lectures, 1903; *Some Early Impressions* (London, 1924), repr. from the *National Review*.

IV. Works Edited by Leslie Stephen. *Brighton Election Reporter*, nos. 1–6, 10–25 (February 1864); *Alpine Journal*, vols. IV and V (November 1868–May 1872); *Cornhill* (1871–1882); *The Works of Henry Fielding* (London, 1882), with biographical essay; *Dictionary of National Biography*, 66 vols. (London, 1885–1900), Stephen was editor from 1885 to 1891 and edited twenty-one vols. himself and five vols. with Sidney Lee, his coeditor and successor.

V. Introductions, Memoirs, and Articles. F. Galton, ed., *Vacation Tourists and Notes on Travel in 1860* (London, 1861), contains "The Ascent of the Allalein Horn"; E. S. Kennedy, ed., *Peaks, Passes and Glaciers*, vol. II, 2nd ser. (London, 1862), contains "The Ascent of the Schreckhorn" and "The Passage of Eiger Joch"; J. D. Campbell, *Samuel Taylor Coleridge*, 2nd ed. (London, 1896), contains memoir of the author; O. W. Holmes, *The Autocrat of the Breakfast Table* (London, 1903), contains an intro.; E. Legouis, *The Early Life of William Wordsworth* (London, 1897), J. W. Matthews, trans., with prefatory note by Stephen; *The Works of Samuel Richardson* (London, 1882), with prefatory ch. of biographical criticism; "Belief and Evidence" (London, 1877), a paper read before the Metaphysical Society; "The Uniformity of Nature" (London, 1879), a paper read before the Metaphysical Society; "What Is Materialism? A Discourse" (London, 1886), South Place Ethical Society publication; *The Works of William Makepeace Thackeray*, 48 vols. (London, 1879), edition deluxe, vol. XLVIII contains "The Writings of W. M. Thackeray"; J. Payn, *The Backwater of Life* (London, 1899), contains an intro.

VI. Biographical and Critical Studies. F. W. Maitland, *Life and Letters of Leslie Stephen* (London, 1906), the standard biography until superseded by Annan's; J. Morley, *Recollections*, 2 vols. (London, 1918), personal reminiscences by a close friend; F. Thompson, *Leslie Stephen as Biographer* (London, 1915); E. Gosse, *Silhouettes* (London, 1925), contains an appreciative essay on Stephen; D. MacCarthy, *Leslie Stephen* (London, 1937), in this lecture MacCarthy discusses Stephen's inability to treat literature from an aesthetic point of view; Q. D. Leavis, "Leslie Stephen, Cambridge Critic," *Scrutiny*, VII (March 1939), Mrs. Leavis defends Stephen against MacCarthy's objections; J. D. Wilson, *Leslie Stephen and Matthew Arnold as Critics of Wordsworth* (London, 1939); M. M. Bevington, *The Saturday Review, 1858–68* (New York, 1941); J. W. Robertson Scott, *The Story of the Pall Mall Gazette* (London, 1950); V. Woolf, *The Captain's Death Bed* (London, 1950), contains "Leslie Stephen," a daughter's affectionate memories; N. Annan, *Leslie Stephen: His Thought and Character in Relation to His Time* (London, 1951), admirable definitive biography, with much critical material; L. Woolf, *Sowing* (London, 1961), brief recollections by Stephen's son-in-law, husband of Virginia Woolf; Q. Bell, "The Mausoleum Book," *Review of English Literature*, VI (January 1965), a fascinating account of the long private letter about his life that Stephen wrote to his children; C. Himmelfarb, *Victorian Minds* (New York, 1968), contains a perceptive essay on Stephen.

WILLIAM MORRIS

(1834-1896)

Philip Henderson

THE upper Thames above Radcot Bridge meanders through some of the oldest, sleepiest country in England. It is bordered by water meadows, and the villages are built of orange-gray Cotswold stone in a native Gothic style that survived in this part of the country well into the seventeenth century. The churches of Bampton, Lechlade, and Fairford date from the days when the Cotswolds were a wool center. Fairford has some famous medieval glass, nearby Faringdon has the tomb of Sir Henry Unton, ambassador to Paris in the reign of Queen Elizabeth I, and in the churchyard of Kelmscott is the grave of William Morris—a solid, unpretentious affair designed by his friend Philip Webb in the local Cotswold tradition. Morris was carried to the grave on 6 October 1896 on a farm wagon with a yellow body and bright red wheels, wreathed with vine and strewn with willow boughs—"the only funeral," remarked W. R. Lethaby, "I have ever seen that did not make me ashamed to have to be buried."[1]

With the death of William Morris, poet, designer, typographer, and Socialist, the nineteenth century came to a symbolic end, and England lost one of her greatest men. For Morris, with his rare combination of qualities, his largeness of nature, his sweetness and idealism, his solidity, his immense practical energy, exemplifies the sharply paradoxical qualities that the English genius can accommodate. Yet he had nothing in common with the commercial, scientific, industrial society of his (or our own) day. He turned away from what he called "the dull squalor of civilization" to romance, myth, and epic. In this, of course, he was at one with many poets and artists of the nineteenth century—Alfred Tennyson, Robert Browning, Matthew Arnold, Edward Burne-Jones, Dante Gabriel Rossetti, and Richard Wagner. But Morris, though his work is not free from nostalgia,

compared with that of his friends Rossetti, Algernon Swinburne, and Burne-Jones, is unusually wholesome. His rejection of his age was more fundamental than that of either Thomas Carlyle or John Ruskin; and though he fell under the influence of Karl Marx when he became a Socialist, his attack upon capitalist society went beyond Marx in its rejection of the whole fabric of industrial civilization. He was not interested in organizing men more efficiently into units of production: he had seen what machinery had made of the cities of England already, and he saw what machinery was making of men. Art for him included everything made by the hands of man, and with Ruskin he defined beauty in art as the result of man's pleasure in the thing made. Reduce man's working day to a round of soul-destroying labor, make him a machine-minder, house him in a hovel, one of thousands of hovels exactly alike spreading across the face of the country like a disease, and what he produces will inevitably bear the imprint of such conditions. As Morris said in his lecture 'The Lesser Arts": "Unless people care about carrying on their business without making the world hideous, how can they care about art?" So, when he came to write his utopia, *News from Nowhere* (1890), he projected the outward conditions of Geoffrey Chaucer's England into the future—anticipating, as has been rather unkindly remarked, the garden suburb. In the nature of things, frustration and sadness are implicit in such a vision. No man can deny his age with impunity, or without sentimentalism, and some of this sentimentalism infected Morris' poetry, his prose romances, his book designs, and his tapestries.

A rich man, he lived partly at Kelmscott, a haven of gray gables and rook-haunted elms, with sometimes "a sense of the place being too beautiful to live in," and partly at Hammersmith, in a fine Georgian house on the banks of the lower Thames. As a Socialist, he worked for the future, but his heart was in the past. He advocated revolution and founded the Soci-

---

[1] W. R. Lethaby, *Philip Webb and His Work* (London, 1935), p. 195.

ety for the Protection of Ancient Buildings. He said: "What business have we with art at all unless all can share it?" Yet only the rich could afford the sumptuous productions of Morris & Co. and the Kelmscott Press. Theoretically Morris despised luxury in art, yet his goods were the last word in luxury. He was quite aware of these contradictions himself, and they were, to some extent, forced upon him by conditions beyond his control. But they made him furious. While at work on the interior decorations of Rounton Grange, Northallerton, in 1876, he was heard striding about one of its empty rooms and talking to himself excitedly. Asked if anything was the matter, he replied: "It is only that I spend my life in ministering to the swinish luxury of the rich." In compensation, much of his time in later life was given to touring the grim industrial areas of northern England and Scotland to spread the gospel of socialism. But as he traveled by train he carried his notebook with him, translating Homer or writing romances that are visions of a regenerated mankind living close to nature in harmony and simplicity.

William Morris was born at Elm House, Walthamstow, on 24 March 1834, one of a family of nine of Welsh descent. Today Walthamstow is geographically an extension of east London, but when Morris was a child the village stood in pleasant Essex country overlooking the valley of the Lea, within a mile or so of Epping Forest. It was a favorite residence of "City men," who drove up daily to London in the stagecoach. Morris' father was a bill broker with offices in Lombard Street; he was well-to-do and soon to be made rich by the steep rise in the price of copper shares. The family moved three times during Morris' childhood, but they always remained in the neighborhood of Epping Forest. From Woodford Hall, to which they moved when Morris was six, the course of the Lea might be traced winding through the marshes, with white and ruddy-brown sails moving among the cornfields and pastures. In his later romances, Morris often returned in imagination to this scene of his boyhood—"the wide green sea of Essex marshland, with the great domed line of the sky, and the sun shining down in one flood of peaceful light over the long distance." There was something Flemish in the landscape, and it was to the art of Flanders that Morris was drawn by natural inclination.

It is important to stress Morris' different environments, whether during the early years in Essex or the middle and later years in Oxfordshire (in both cases it was an environment of river and marsh), because his mind reflected things with the clarity of water; his eye was so sharp and accurate and his memory so retentive that anything that once impressed him was remembered in its minutest detail and liable to appear in his work years later. "A man careless of metaphysics and religion," so he described himself, "as well as of scientific analysis, but with a deep love of the earth and the life on it, and a passion for the history of the past of mankind."

At school at Marlborough, Morris tells us that he learned nothing at all, but he spent much of his time exploring the strange bare Wiltshire country with its ancient British ruins of Avebury and Stonehenge. In 1853, he went up to Exeter College, Oxford, where he formed friendships, destined to be for life, with Burne-Jones, Charles Faulkner, Cormell Price, and Philip Webb. Webb he met after he had given up all idea of a clerical career (for which his family had originally intended him) and was working in the Oxford office of George Edmund Street, the Gothic Revival architect.

Oxford, at that time, was still in its main aspects a medieval city—"a vision of grey-roofed houses, a long street, and the sound of many bells." The Anglo-Catholic Tractarian movement was still in the air, and Morris and his friends were so much affected by it that they formed a brotherhood to launch "a crusade and holy war against the age." But gambling in railway shares had proved more exciting than theological controversy, and the growth of the Great Western Railway really finished off Tractarianism, as far as the outside world was concerned. Once the railway reached Oxford, it was the end of the Middle Ages. But, within the cloistered walls of their colleges, Morris and his friends were enthusiastically discovering Carlyle's *Past and Present*, Charles Kingsley, Tennyson, Browning, and above all Thomas Malory's *Morte d'Arthur* and Ruskin's *Stones of Venice*. It is not too much to say that Ruskin's book, with its chapter "On the Nature of Gothic," came with the force of a revelation and set Morris on the path he was to follow for the rest of his life. In the minds of these young men the Gothic Revival had already become a Gothic Renaissance. When, in the long vacation of 1854, Morris and Burne-Jones visited Belgium and northern France, they saw for the first time the painting of Hans Memling and Jan van Eyck and the cathedrals of Amiens, Beauvais, and Rouen. On his return Morris wrote in the *Oxford and Cambridge Magazine*: "I think those same churches of North France the grandest, the most beautiful, the kindest and most loving of all the buildings that the earth has ever borne."[2] This visit confirmed his decision to be an architect and inspired perhaps the finest description of Amiens that has ever been written.

The spirit of the rather lush perfervid tales Morris was writing at this time comes out in the description of the garden in "The Story of the Unknown Church":

in the garden were trellises covered over with roses and convolvulus, and the great-leaved fiery nasturtium; and specially all along by the poplar trees were there trellises, but on these nothing grew but deep crimson roses; and hollyhocks too were all in blossom at that time, great spires of pink, and orange and red, and white, with their soft, downy leaves. I said that nothing grew on the trellises by the poplars but crimson roses, but I was not quite right, for in many places the wild flowers had crept into the garden from without; lush green briony, with green-white blossoms, that grows so fast, one could almost think that we see it grow, and deadly nightshade, La bella donna, O! so beautiful; red berry, and purple, yellow-spiked flower, and deadly, cruel-looking, dark green leaf. . . .

(vol. I, p. 151)

Remarkable and typical of Morris is the intense feeling for primary colors, the sense of texture, the physical feel of the flowers, and the striving for meticulous accuracy of vision. Already he is looking at the world with a craftsman's eye.

If in the early tales everything is inclined to be too "beautiful"—the word itself recurs rather too often—that cannot be said for the poems he was also writing and which appeared in *The Defence of Guenevere* (1858). Some of these have all the savagery as well as the color and pageantry of the Middle Ages: suggesting rather the vigor of thirteenth-century stained glass than the dreaminess of Burne-Jones and the claustrophobic atmosphere of Rossetti. In his medievalism Morris was always much nearer to the real thing than any of the other Pre-Raphaelites, though it is true that there is a close parallel between some of these poems and some of Rossetti's watercolors done about this time—*Ar-*

thur's Tomb, for example. *The Defence of Guenevere* is nearer to the abrupt colloquialism of Browning than to the silver-tongued mellifluence of Tennyson. The title poem, with the passionate figure of Guenevere defending her adulterous love for Lancelot—"My face made beautiful with my young blood"; "King Arthur's Tomb," with the last anguished meeting of the lovers, separated by the body (or effigy) of the dead king; "Concerning Geffray Teste Noir," with the knights cutting down the townsfolk of Beauvais; and, above all, "The Haystack in the Floods," the most tragic poem in the book, telling of how Jehane and her Robert are overtaken by the tyrant Godmar, from whom they are fleeing, and of how Robert is bound and butchered before her eyes—these should have convinced readers at the time that here was no sentimental medievalist.

> With a start
> Up Godmar rose, thrust them apart;
> From Robert's throat he loosed the bands
> Of silk and mail; with empty hands
> Held out, she stood and gazed, and saw,
> The long bright blade without a flaw
> Glide out from Godmar's sheath, his hand
> In Robert's hair; she saw him bend
> Back Robert's head; she saw him send
> The thin steel down; the blow told well,
> Right backward the knight Robert fell,
> And moan'd as dogs do, being half dead,
> Unwitting, as I deem: so then
> Godmar turn'd grinning to his men,
> Who ran, some five or six, and beat
> His head to pieces at their feet.
>
> . . .
>
> This was the parting that they had
> Beside the haystack in the floods.

(vol. I, p. 128)

But the book, where it was noticed at all, was attacked as affected and effeminate and of Rossetti's school. Nor did work in Street's office involve the building of cathedrals. Indeed, much of it involved the "restoration" of old churches, a practice that Morris was later to found a society to prevent. He remained with Street less than a year, and in the autumn of 1856 went with him on his second visit to the Low Countries. It was after this visit that he adapted van Eyck's motto *Als ich Kanne* for his own, in the French form *Si je puis*. In this year also he first met Rossetti, who persuaded him to give up archi-

[2]"The Churches of Northern France," *The Collected Works of William Morris*, with introductions by his daughter May Morris, 24 vols. (London, 1910–1915), vol. I, p. 349. All quotations from Morris' writing are from this edition, unless otherwise noted.

tecture and become a painter. Believing that the high-water mark of English romantic poetry had been reached by John Keats, romantic painting was, in Rossetti's view, a virgin field. "If a man has any poetry in him," he declared, "he should paint, for it has all been said and written, and they have scarcely begun to paint it."

Morris became an ardent admirer and pupil of the Pre-Raphaelite school, and got to know Holman Hunt and Ford Madox Brown. At that year's Royal Academy exhibition he saw, "fell in love with," and bought Arthur Hughes's *April Love*. This painting, considered the very height of exquisite sentiment, represents a girl in a violet dress standing by an ivy-covered summer house; her face is averted with a tearful smile from a shadowy lover, who is partly seen weeping against a windowsill in the background. At the same exhibition Morris saw Holman Hunt's *Scapegoat*, Sir John Millais' *Autumn Leaves*, and Henry Wallis' *Death of Chatterton*, which is still one of the most popular pictures in the Tate Gallery.

"The long battle between the Palladian and Gothic styles for the new University Museum had been at last decided by the Oxford authorities in favour of the latter," writes J. W. Mackail in his *Life of William Morris* (1899). "Woodward's plans, in a style of mixed Rhenish and Venetian Gothic, had been accepted. . . ." Besides his work on the museum, Benjamin Woodward was building a debating hall for the Union Society in 1858. Above a gallery, which ran round its inside walls, was a broad belt of wall divided into bays, pierced by twenty six-foil circular windows, surmounted by an open timber roof. It was arranged that Rossetti, who was a friend of Woodward, should fill the blank spaces with frescoes, and to this end he enrolled his friends, among them Morris, Burne-Jones, and Arthur Hughes. The ten paintings were to be a series of scenes from that bible of the later Pre-Raphaelites, the *Morte d'Arthur*. For his subject Morris chose a strangely prophetic one—prophetic, that is, as far as his own future domestic life was concerned, "How Sir Palomydes loved La Belle Iseult with an exceeding great love, and how she loved not him again, but rather Sir Tristram." The subject, Mackail remarks, was one for which Morris felt "a singular and almost morbid attraction, that of the unsuccessful man and despised lover." Burne-Jones has left a delightful account of the proceedings in the Union debating hall during its decoration by this band of zealots.

For the purposes of our drawing we often needed armour, and of a date and design so remote that no example existed for our use. Therefore Morris, whose knowledge of all these things seemed to have been born in him, and who never at any time needed books of reference for anything, set to work to make designs for an ancient kind of helmet called a basinet, and for a great surcoat of ringed mail with a hood of mail and the skirt coming below the knees. These were made for him by a stout little smith who had a forge near the Castle. Morris's visits to the forge were daily, but what scenes happened there we shall never know; the encounters between these two workmen were always stubborn and angry as far as I could see. One afternoon when I was working high up at my picture, I heard a strange bellowing in the building, and turning round to find the cause, saw an unwonted sight. The basinet was tried on, but the visor, for some reason, would not lift, and I saw Morris embedded in iron, dancing with rage, and roaring inside. The mail coat came in due time, and was so satisfactory to its designer that the first day it came he chose to dine in it. It became him well; he looked splendid.[3]

The episode is typical of Morris, with his firm grasp of practical details and his determination to bring the Middle Ages right into the present to the extent of dining in chain mail. There is also his sudden uncontrollable rage when thwarted by intractable inanimate objects. These rages passed as soon as they came, leaving him humble and repentant. In fact, Morris was always too ready to blame himself and was known to deal his own head resounding blows with his fists in self-punishment. When he was bored he would stand rubbing his back against the wall like a sheep. Such endearing habits naturally made him the butt of his friends, who delighted to "set him off" by all kinds of practical jokes. Burne-Jones, for instance, would send a letter to Morris & Co. in indecipherable handwriting, or a bulky parcel that consisted entirely of layers of wrappings. This habit of teasing Morris persisted among his friends long after they had all left Oxford.

Unfortunately, the knowledge of tempera painting had died out in England, and the paint was applied directly to the damp plaster of the walls of the Union over a coat of whitewash, with the result that within a year all the frescoes had faded to ghosts of themselves. Of Morris' painting, William Bell Scott reported that in 1858 little remained but Tristram's head over a row of sunflowers. Since then, however,

[3] J. W. Mackail, *The Life of William Morris*, 2 vols. (London, 1899; repr. London–New York, 1968), vol. I, pp. 120–121.

all the frescoes have been restored by Professor Tristram, the expert on medieval wall paintings.

When this work was going forward in the autumn of 1857, Morris met La Belle Iseult in the flesh. Her real name was Jane Burden, and she was the daughter of a livery stable keeper—or "groom," as he is described in the marriage register—of Holywell. As a matter of fact, it was Rossetti who saw her first and invited her to pose for them. Both Morris and Rossetti fell in love with her. Morris painted her as Guinevere,[4] and his shy, passionate adoration appears in his poem "Praise of my Lady." And after his wife's death in 1862, Rossetti never ceased to draw and paint Jane Morris, her image becoming more and more romantically distorted and surrounded in picture after picture with a sultry, brooding sexuality. The portrait which is said to be the best likeness is the *Proserpine*, of which several copies exist. Henry James, who visited the Morrises at Queen Square in 1869, wrote of another of Rossetti's paintings of Mrs. Morris "that if you hadn't seen her you'd pronounce it a distempered vision, but in fact it was an extremely good likeness." Morris had married Jane Burden in April 1859, and from then on she became a cult among these later Pre-Raphaelites and their friends, just as Elizabeth Siddal had been for the original Pre-Raphaelite Brotherhood. But Jane Morris remains a shadowy figure in the background of her husband's life, suffering from a succession of nervous ailments. To Henry James she was:

an apparition of fearful and wonderful intensity. . . . Imagine a tall lean woman in a long dress of some dead purple stuff, guiltless of hoops . . . with a mass of crisp black hair heaped into great wavy projections on each side of her temples, a thin pale face, a pair of strange sad, deep, dark, Swinburnian eyes, with great thick black oblique brows, joined in the middle and tucking themselves away under her hair, a mouth like "Oriana" in our illustrated Tennyson, a long neck without any collar, in lieu thereof some dozen strings of outlandish beads. . . .[5]

In fine, Jane Morris was the first and most famous product of Morris & Co. Very different is James's account of Morris.

He impressed me very agreeably. He is short, burly, corpulent, very careless and unfinished in his dress. . . . He

has a very loud voice and a nervous restless manner and a perfectly unaffected and business-like address. His talk indeed is wonderfully to the point and remarkable for clear good sense. . . . He is an extraordinary example, in short, of a delicate sensitive genius and taste, saved by a perfectly healthy body and temper.

(vol. I, pp. 18–19)

With the building of Red House, Bexley Heath, a new period began in Morris' life. He had discussed the plans of the house with Webb during a holiday in France in the autumn of 1858, as they rowed down the Seine together from Paris to Le Havre, and he moved into it with his wife in 1860. Built among the apple orchards of Kent, with its steep tiled roof and deep Gothic porches, Red House was of superficially medieval design: in all essentials it was a modern house—the first modern house—because here construction was frankly shown and stucco was rejected in favor of plain brick. In all respects the exterior design was an expression of its inside requirements. Out of the furnishing of this house grew Morris & Co. "To my mind," Morris said in one of his lectures, "it is only here and there (out of the kitchen) that you can find in a well-to-do house things that are of any use at all." So, in furnishing his own house, he began by making a clean sweep of Victorian knick-knacks, and would have nothing that was not both useful and pleasant to look at. "Upon entering the porch," writes a contemporary, "the hall appeared to one accustomed to the narrow ugliness of the usual middle-class dwelling of those days as being grand and severely simple." "The walls were bare, and the floors," writes Lady Burne-Jones,

nor could Morris have endured any chair, table, sofa or bed, nor any hanging such as were then in existence. . . . For the walls of other rooms than the drawing-room [which had frescoes by Burne-Jones] Morris designed flower-patterns, which his wife worked in wool on a dark ground.[6]

Morris had his own ideas about gardens; these, too, were given a medieval flavor. The garden at Red House was "spaced formally into four little square gardens making a big square together; each of the smaller squares had a wattled fence round it, with an opening by which one entered, and all over the fence roses grew thickly." Each enclosure in the garden

---

[4]This painting, *Queen Guinevere*, was presented to the Tate Gallery in London by May Harris in 1938.

[5]P. Lubbock, ed., *The Letters of Henry James*, 2 vols. (New York, 1920), vol. I, pp. 17–18.

[6]Georgiana Burne-Jones, *Memorials of Edward Burne-Jones*, 2 vols. (New York, 1904), vol. I, p. 213.

had its own particular show of flowers; on one side was a bowling alley, on the other orchard walks. At the back of the house was a small well-court, formed by the two sides of the house and rose trellises. "This little court," says Lady Burne-Jones, "with its beautiful high-roofed brick well in the centre summed up the feeling of the whole place." It was the kind of house a prosperous Flemish burgher might have had in the fifteenth century. Good cheer flowed in abundance as the friends—Rossetti, Burne-Jones, Madox Brown, Swinburne, Valentine Prinsep, and others—met for the weekend. "It was the most beautiful sight," writes one, "to see Morris coming up from the cellar before dinner, beaming with joy, with his hands full of bottles of wine and others tucked under his arms."

But Morris' income, derived from the same Devonshire copper mine that had made his father rich, began to dwindle fast, and "the idea came to him," writes Burne-Jones,

> of beginning a manufactory of all things necessary for decoration of a house. Webb had already designed some beautiful table glass . . . metal candlesticks, and tables for Red House, and I had already designed several windows for churches, so the idea grew of putting our experiences together for the service of the public.
>
> (*Memorials*, vol. I, p. 213)

In 1861, the firm of Morris, Marshall, Faulkner & Co., Fine Art Workmen in Painting, Carving, Furniture and the Metals, was founded. It included, besides Morris, Rossetti, Burne-Jones, and Webb, Ford Madox Brown, Arthur Hughes, P. P. Marshall, and C. J. Faulkner, who, for a time, gave up his post as a mathematical don at Oxford to keep the firm's books. Most of the capital was provided by Morris (who, as time went on, also did most of the work), and the others took out twenty shares of £1 each. From the early days of the firm, with its offices in Red Lion Square,[7] dates the cabinet designed by Webb and painted by Morris with the legend of St. George (the interior was deep crimson—"dragon's blood") now in the Victoria and Albert Museum. Wallpapers by Morris followed: the Trellis was the first in 1862, the subject probably taken from the

rose trellises at Red House; then the Daisy paper, which was actually issued first, and the germ of this, Mackail tells us, is to be found in a Jean Froissart manuscript in the British Museum—though this particular motif is common enough both on monumental brasses and in the borders of medieval stained glass windows. For their other designs the firm made good use of the South Kensington Museum. They produced anything from glass drinking vessels to wrought iron bedsteads and stained glass windows, for private houses as well as churches. Both in his wallpapers and his textiles, Morris shows himself as probably the greatest pattern designer England has ever had—"the great classical designer of his age," as Peter Floud calls him—while his experiments with vegetable dyes, as distinct from the crude colors produced by the aniline dyes then commonly in use, were triumphantly successful. As Lethaby remarks: "Morris' colour-work glows from within, something happened to the several items in association, as when bells chime" (*Philip Webb*, p. 45).

Burne-Jones's work is hardly to everybody's taste today, though there can be no doubt that he, too, was a very gifted designer. Superficially, nothing could be less like the very solid, downright Morris than the work of his closest friend. But, looking deeper, one sees that there is much in common between the inner worlds of these two men. After *The Defence of Guenevere*, Morris moved steadily away from his earlier dramatic style to the tranced dreamworld of *The Life and Death of Jason* (1867) and *The Earthly Paradise* (1868–1870), where the decorative element smooths away and dilutes all painful emotion. But, as suggested earlier, his dreamworld has none of the unwholesomeness of Burne-Jones's, which, even at its finest in the Perseus and Briar-Rose sequences, is diffused with a peculiar phantasmal effulgence, like the light from an underworld. Morris never leaves the earth's surface or the light of day. The main difference between them is that Burne-Jones is reported to have said that he would like to forget the world and live inside a picture.

Morris' poetry and his designs can be studied together with some advantage. "If his poems were too like wallpapers," as G. K. Chesterton remarked, "it was because he really could make wallpapers." Morris took a good deal of trouble to get over what his age regarded as the defects of his early poetry, its violence and abruptness, and in *Jason* and *The Earthly Paradise* he achieved a quiet refinement. In fact, all that is most interesting in his personality is

[7]In 1865 Morris & Co. moved to 26 Queen Square, Bloomsbury; in 1875 the firm was reorganized under Morris' sole control; and in 1881 it moved to Merton Abbey, Surrey, with showrooms in Oxford Street.

excluded from this excessively good-mannered and anemic poetry. One suspects that it increasingly became a soporific and that he worked to forget personal unhappiness and frustration. He had, it seems, deliberately to deaden his emotions with diffuseness and overelaboration to achieve the desired tapestry effect. The result is not great poetry, but it has great charm, taken in small doses; and it was enormously popular in its time. Morris rejected any idea of inspiration in his poetry and said it was merely a matter of craftsmanship. One would not wish to contradict him.

The best parts of *The Earthly Paradise* are the short poems on the months, which introduce each day of storytelling: poems, Mackail tells us, in which may be found "an autobiography so delicate and so outspoken that it must be left to speak for itself." They breathe an elegiac lyricism peculiarly English, and have a clarity, sweetness, and simplicity peculiar to Morris. Thus he writes of April:

> When Summer brings the lily and the rose,
> She brings us fear; her very death she brings
> Hid in her anxious heart, the forge of woes;
> And, dull with fear, no more the mavis sings.
> But thou! thou diest not, but thy fresh life clings
> About the fainting autumn's sweet decay,
> When in the earth the hopeful seed they lay.

> Ah! life of all the year, why yet do I
> Amid thy snowy blossoms' fragrant drift,
> Still long for that which never draweth nigh,
> Striving my pleasure from my pain to sift,
> Some weight from off my fluttering mirth to lift?
> Now, when far bells are ringing, "Come again,
> Come back, past years! why will ye pass in vain?"
> (vol. III, p. 169, ll. 8–21)

In the verse on September, Morris writes of himself as:

> Like a new-wakened man thou art, who tries
> To dream again the dream that made him glad
> When in his arms his loving love he had.
> (vol. V, p. 1, ll. 19–21)

But most revealing of all, because they give us a glimpse of the strange, baffled relationship between Morris and his wife, are the lines on January:

> From this dull rainy undersky and low,
> This murky ending of a leaden day,

> That never knew the sun, this half-thawed snow,
> These tossing black boughs faint against the grey
> Of gathering night, thou turnest, dear, away
> Silent, but with thy scarce-seen kindly smile
> Sent through the dusk my longing to beguile.

> There, the lights gleam, and all is dark without!
> And in the sudden change our eyes meet dazed—
> O look, love, look again! the veil of doubt
> Just for one flash, past counting, then was raised!
> O eyes of heaven, as clear thy sweet soul blazed
> On mine a moment! O come back again
> Strange rest and dear amid the long dull pain!
> (vol. VI, p. 65, ll. 1–14)

Morris began to write the verse stories that form *Jason* and *The Earthly Paradise* in the middle 1860's in their original and more vigorous form as "Scenes from the Fall of Troy," the drafts for which are preserved in the British Museum. It was for him a period of great emotional stress, the reason for which can only be guessed in the light of the recurrent theme of his poetry—the transience and bitterness of love. His abandoned novel also dealt with the love of two brothers for one woman. Doubtless one would not be far from the mark in supposing Rossetti cast for the role of one of the brothers. Mackail had, as he confessed, to use much tact in dealing with these years in his biography of Morris.[8]

The scheme of *The Earthly Paradise* is set forth in the argument at the beginning of the prologue.

Certain Gentlemen and mariners of Norway, having considered all they had heard of the Earthly Paradise, set sail to find it, and after many troubles and the lapse of many years came old men to some Western land, of which they had never before heard: there they died, when they had dwelt there certain years, much honoured of the strange people.

These travelers, who had left Europe to escape the Black Death—for the poem is set in the time of Chaucer—include a Swabian scholar, a Breton, and a Scandinavian born in Byzantium, where his father

[8]"Of course, my difficulties over the work itself were great, especially in the constant need for what is called 'tact,' which is a quality unpleasantly near untruthfulness often; and especially I feel that my account of all those stormy years of *The Earthly Paradise* time and the time following it must be excessively flat owing to the amount of tact that had to be exercised right and left" (from an unpublished letter of J. W. Mackail to Mrs. Coronio, 12 May 1899). See also in this context Oswald Doughty's *A Victorian Romantic: Dante Gabriel Rossetti*, 2nd ed. (London, 1960).

was a member of the bodyguard of the Greek emperor. They do not find the earthly paradise, though they sail steadily west till they reach a far outpost of surviving ancient Greek civilization. Here they are hospitably entertained by the elders of the city, to whom they relate stories at intervals during the year, and are entertained in the same way by their hosts. Twelve of the stories are from medieval sources and twelve from classical sources. The conclusion we are invited to draw is that the only earthly paradise is the world of art, where the agony and strife of human hearts are caught and stilled in a strange blending of dream and reality.

By addressing him in the medieval manner as "mine own master dear," Morris directly challenges comparison with Chaucer. But how different is the languor of his autumnal world from the springtime vigor with which the Canterbury pilgrims set out, with the young sun in the sign of the ram, sap rising in the flowers, and the birds making love in the trees all night—the eternal enchanted springtime of the medieval imagination. Morris gives the impression of writing with an aching heart, Chaucer with a smile on his lips. Morris aimed at the direct simplicity of his master, but gone are the sly humor, the earthiness, and in their place is a gentle archaism. Among Morris' pilgrims there is no young Squire, certainly no Wife of Bath. Everything is pitched in a key that suggests a pale reflection of the Knight's tale: Chaucer's style has suffered a strange sea-change in its passage to the nineteenth century. As Oliver Elton remarks: "The mood is that of sad old men telling old stories to other sad old men," and many pages of *The Earthly Paradise* have the true medieval touch of ennui.

The story of *Jason*, originally intended for *The Earthly Paradise*, grew to such proportions—it is an epic romance of seventeen books—that it had to be published first, and with its publication Morris suddenly achieved popularity as a poet. *Jason* proved to be one of the most widely read poems of the nineteenth century, and its vogue did not abate till the 1914 war, the date at which the Victorian era really ended. It is a poem carried through in a spirit of happy craftsmanship, and it satisfies by the very perfection with which the poet realizes his aim. Its effect is essentially pictorial. "The pictures are clear and chaste, sweet and lucid, as early Italian work," wrote Swinburne on its appearance.

There are crowds and processions, battle-pieces, and merry-makings, worthy of Benozzo and Carpaccio, single figures or groups of lovers, in flowery watery land, worthy of Sandro or Filippino. The seapieces are like the younger Lippi's. . . . Rarely but in ballad and romance periods has such poetry been written, so broad and sad and simple.[9]

Though somewhat exaggerated in tone, Swinburne's tribute gives a better idea of Morris' achievements than the sour strictures of modern critics, who are in any case out of sympathy with his aims. For it has become the fashion to ignore the romantic narrative poetry of the nineteenth century, in spite of the fact that it forms a large and important part of the English tradition. Morris aimed in his poetry quite frankly at entertainment; he meant for us to enjoy it. This may seem strange in an "age of anxiety," which takes its subjects from the trivial and the drab, but it is a worthy aim and one that has a respectable ancestry going back to Homer.

> Forget six counties overhung with smoke,
> Forget the snorting steam and piston stroke,
> Forget the spreading of the hideous town;
> Think rather of the pack-horse on the down,
> And dream of London, small and white and clean,
> The clear Thames bordered by its gardens green. . . .
>
> (vol. III, p. 3, ll. 1–6)

Such is the famous opening of the prologue of *The Earthly Paradise*. But, in grafting classical tales onto a medieval setting in the manner of Chaucer, Morris was writing at a treble removed from his subject, so that what emotion comes through to us is like an image refracted from a succession of mirrors, or, as he says himself, "like an old dream, dreamed in another dream." May Morris tells us that the story which gave her father the greatest trouble, and the one for which the largest number of early drafts exists, is "The Hill of Venus," which retells the Tannhäuser legend. As Morris tells it, it has affinities with "La Belle Dame Sans Merci": it is Tannhäuser without the Venusberg, for the Burne-Jonesian figure of Love which appears offers a very "shadowy bliss" indeed. Once more it is the tale of a man awakening from a dream of love to shiver in the cold winds of reality.

Swinburne was by no means so enthusiastic about *The Earthly Paradise*, writing to Rossetti on 10 December 1869:

his Muse is like Homer's Trojan women . . . drags her robes as she walks; I really think a Muse (when she is

---

[9]Reprinted in "Morris's *Life and Death of Jason*," in *Essays and Studies* (London, 1875), pp. 118, 121.

neither resting nor flying) ought to tighten her girdle, tuck up her skirts, and step out. It is better than Tennyson's short-winded and artificial concision—but there is such a thing as a swift and spontaneous style. Top's [the name that Morris' friends gave him on account of his mop of curly hair] is spontaneous and slow; and, especially my ear hungers for more force and variety of sound in the verse. It looks as if he purposely avoided all strenuous emotion or strength of music in thought and word; and so when set by other work as good his seems hardly done in earnest.[10]

The fact is that Morris gave no more than a small part of himself to poetry, which remained for him the recreation of a man busy in other ways. The extraordinary thing is that he produced so much of it. But his opinion of Swinburne was no more complimentary. Soon after the publication of Swinburne's *Tristram of Lyonesse* in 1882, he wrote:

But to confess and be hanged, you know I never could really sympathise with Swinburne's work; it always seemed to me to be founded on literature, not on nature. . . . In these days the issue between art, that is, the god-like part of man, and mere bestiality is so momentous, and the surroundings of life are so stern and unplayful, that nothing can take serious hold of people, or should do so, but that which is rooted deepest in reality and is quite at first hand; there is no room for anything which is not forced out of a man of deep feeling, because of its innate strength and vision.[11]

This was written when Morris was preparing to plunge into revolutionary politics and is evidence of the growing contradiction between Morris the Marxist and Morris the poet. Unfortunately, it disposes of most of his own poetry no less than Swinburne's. Also it ignores that craving for romance that was so conspicuous a feature of the nineteenth century— and that Morris & Co. was founded to satisfy— when England had become "the workshop of the world" at the price of vulgar and tasteless comfort on the one hand and, on the other, the spread of poverty and squalor and degradation.

In the same year (1871) that Morris took Kelmscott Manor jointly with Rossetti, he paid his first visit to Iceland. The joint tenancy was never a success from the beginning, and Rossetti finally left Kelmscott four years later. Like all the chief events of Morris' life, the Iceland journey has its own symbolic significance: for it coincided with a turning away from romance and all that Rossetti's influence had meant, and a growing appeal for him of the grim and stoical world of the sagas.[12] Indeed, Rossetti's influence had been so powerful that it was natural that Morris should now react against it. Other things, too, contributed to bring their friendship to an end. Morris had been studying Icelandic for some years previously with Eirikr Magnusson: together they had produced a prose version of the *Volsunga Saga* and some translations of the Eddas. Magnusson did the actual translation, and then Morris rewrote it in his own words. Morris was to visit Iceland again in 1873, but during his first visit he kept a journal into which he put some of his finest descriptive writing. The Iceland journal of 1871 is, indeed, more vivid than the epic *Sigurd the Volsung* (1876), for which Morris drew upon both the Icelandic *Volsunga Saga* and the German *Nibelungenlied*, and which he considered, with good reason, to be the crown of his achievement as a poet. To some extent, *Sigurd* is a weakening and romancing of the saga material. Morris' version is artistically more complete. He leaves out the gaps and ragged edges and makes a neat finish, but he does not present anything like the striking power and force of the original.[13] One is conscious of a massive effort, but the starkness and simplicity are gone, in spite of the fact that Morris was himself deeply moved by these very qualities in the saga itself, writing to Charles Eliot Norton in 1869:

the scene of the last interview between Sigurd and the despairing and terrible Brynhild touches me more than anything I have ever met with in literature: there is nothing wanting in it, nothing forgotten, nothing repeated, nothing overstrained; all tenderness shown without the use of a tender word, all misery and despair, without a word of raving, complete beauty without an ornament, and all this in two pages of moderate print.

(21 December 1869)

The hexameters of *Sigurd* run on to 345 pages of what one might call immoderate print, as rhetorical,

[10]C. Y. Lang, ed., *The Swinburne Letters,* 6 vols. (New Haven, Conn., 1959–1962).

[11]P. Henderson, ed., *The Letters of William Morris* (London, 1950), p. 158. All quotations from the letters are from this edition.

[12]The later prose romances are definitely northern in feeling, too, and designed to show the superiority of the free northern tribes to Roman civilization. On his return from Iceland, Morris wrote *Love Is Enough* (1872), a poignantly lyrical work which, with its elaborate structure of a play within a play, is removed as far as possible from reality. In its search for a dream-mistress it is also a clear case of sublimation.

[13]D. M. Hoare, *The Works of Morris and Yeats in Relation to Early Saga Literature* (London, 1937), p. 69.

in fact, as Swinburne's *Tristram* itself, though one can certainly say that this is a poem "forced out of a man of deep feeling, because of its innate strength and vision." For into *Sigurd*, Morris put all his passionate feeling for the landscape of Iceland and its literature. His admiration for the stoical courage of the saga heroes was such that he now began to model himself upon them—and certainly he looked the part! He would have nothing to do with Wagner, though both founded their greatest works on the same material. In 1873, Buxton Forman sent him his brother's translation of part of the text of *The Ring*. In thanking him for it, Morris wrote:

I have not had time to read it yet: nor to say the truth am I much interested in anything Wagner does, as his theories on musical matters seem to me as an artist and non-musical man perfectly abominable; besides I look upon it as nothing short of desecration to bring such a tremendous and world-wide subject under the gaslights of an opera: the most rococo and degraded of all forms of art—the idea of a sandy-haired German tenor tweedledeeing over the unspeakable woes of Sigurd, which even the simplest words are not typical enough to express! Excuse my heat: but I wish to see Wagner uprooted. . . .

(12 November 1873)

A curious opinion, especially as there is no evidence that Morris had ever listened to a note of *The Ring*! Wagner, on his side, was much interested in Morris' work, and, on his visit to England in 1877, tried to meet him through the conductor Edward Danreuther. Morris, however, came to dinner straight from his workshop, dressed in his oldest clothes and determined to be disagreeable, and it is fortunate, perhaps, that the meeting did not take place, Wagner being detained by rehearsals. There is, nevertheless, a strong Wagnerian element in *Sigurd*, as in such lines:

> But forth by dale and lealand doth the son of Sigmund
> wend,
> Till far away lies Lymdale and the folk of the forest's
> end;
> And he rides a heath unpeopled and holds the
> westward way,
> Till a long way off before him come up the mountains
> grey;
> Grey, huge beyond all telling, and the host of the
> heapèd clouds,
> The black and the white together, on that rock-wall's
> coping crowds;

> But whiles are rents athwart them, and the hot sun
> pierceth through;
> And there glow the angry cloud-caves 'gainst the
> everlasting blue,
> And the changeless snow amidst it; but down from
> that cloudy head
> The scars of fires that have been show grim and
> dusky-red. . . .

(vol. XII, pp. 150–151)

Sigurd has a gray and baffled splendor, a resigned nobility, and none of the glory of *The Ring* music, but there is nothing quite like it in all English literature. Nothing, of course, could well be further from contemporary taste in poetry, with its precise, deadpan statements—or, for that matter, from the grim brevity of the sagas themselves.

But one cannot think of any poet today capable of sustaining such a large-scale work. Once we have taken the plunge, the surge and roll of the verse carries us forward with the true epic impetus.

Turning to the Iceland journal of 1871, one can see what Morris really felt:

I confess I shuddered at my first sight of a really northern land. . . . (The Faroes seemed to me such a gentle sweet place when we saw them again after Iceland.) The hills are not high, especially on one side as they sloped beachless into the clear but grey water; the grass was grey between greyer ledges of stone that divided the hills in regular steps: it was not savage but mournfully empty and barren, the grey clouds dragging over the hill-tops or lying in the hollows being the only thing that varied the grass, stone, and sea. . . .

(vol. VIII, p. 11)

It was hard and even dangerous traveling. Morris, Magnusson, and Faulkner spent all day in the saddle and sometimes slept out at night. From Lithend, the site of Gunnar's hall, they went up the valley down which the Markfleet comes roaring from the glaciers. The journal continues:

. . . past this the cliffs were much higher . . . and most unimaginably strange: they overhung in some places much more than seemed possible; they had caves in them just like the hell-mouths in 13th century illuminations; or great straight pillars were rent from them with quite flat tops of grass and a sheep or two feeding on it, however the devil they got there: two or three tail-ends of a glacier too dribbled over them hereabouts, and we turned out of our way to go up to one: it seemed to fill up a kind of cleft in the rock wall, which indeed I suppose it had broken down; one could see its spiky white waves against the blue sky as we came up to it. . . . The great mountain-wall which closes up the valley, with its jagged outlying teeth, was right before us . . . often the wall would be cleft, and you would see a horrible winding street, with stupendous straight rocks for houses on either side: the bottom of the cleft quite level, but with a white glacier stream running out of it, and the whole blocked up at the end by the straight line of the master-mountain.

(vol. VIII, pp. 52–53)

It is a pity that Morris did not write more of such direct and vivid prose; his later romances, except for *A Dream of John Ball* (1888) and *News from Nowhere*, are cast in such an archaic idiom as to seem strangely affected, though when they were written they delighted many people and provided Morris with a much-needed avenue of escape for his imagination when his hopes for a new world had come to a dead end. W. B. Yeats has described the enchantment of these romances in *Ideas of Good and Evil* and wrote later that they were "the only books I was ever to read slowly that I might not come too quickly to the end."[14] More recently C. S. Lewis has also paid tribute to their peculiar spell of "northernness." To a rationalist like George Bernard Shaw they seemed merely an attempt to rewrite Don Quixote's destroyed library.

Vividness and strength are always apparent in Morris' writing when he is wrestling with the world about him, describing actual things or the events of history, instead of escaping into myth and legend, into woods beyond the world, or to wells at the end of it. It is there in his last long poem, *Pilgrims of Hope* (1886), so different from all his other poetry, in which he returned once more to his own private misery in a setting of the Paris Commune.[15] It is in all the lectures he began to give at the end of the 1870's. These lectures, Morris tells us, gave him more trouble than anything else he ever wrote, for here he was wrestling with a problem that has occupied us very much since his time—the relationship of art to society. It was mainly through this channel that, like Ruskin before him, Morris approached socialism. As he wrote in 1883:

Both my historical studies and my practical conflict with the philistinism of modern society have *forced* on me the

conviction that art cannot have a real life and growth under the present system of commercialism and profit-mongering. I have tried to develop this view, which is in fact Socialism seen through the eyes of an artist, in various lectures, the first of which I delivered in 1878.

This was the lecture "The Lesser Arts," into which Morris put the whole of his aesthetic philosophy. It was actually given in 1877, the year that also saw the foundation of the Society for the Protection of Ancient Buildings (S. P. A. B.) and the opening of Morris & Co.'s showrooms in Oxford Street.

Morris' desire to protect old buildings from restoration is one aspect of his love of the past, his desire for an unchanging order, which came into conflict at this time with his socialism. In the manifesto which he wrote for the S.P.A.B., after complaining that the last fifty years of tampering with ancient buildings "have done more for their destruction than all the foregoing centuries of revolution, violence, and comtempt," he goes on:

For Architecture, long decaying, died out, as a popular art at least, just as the knowledge of mediaeval art was born. So that the civilized world of the nineteenth century has no style of its own amidst its wide knowledge of the styles of other centuries. From this lack and this gain arose in men's minds the strange idea of the Restoration of ancient buildings; and a most strange and most fatal idea, which by its very name implies that it is possible to strip from a building this, that, and the other part of its history—of its life, that is—and then to stay the hand at some arbitrary point, and leave it still historical, living, and even as it once was.[16]

In spite of the amount of time Morris gave to speaking at street corners and touring industrial areas, he was always very much more than a politician. During the 1880's the study of Marx had become a driving force in his life; but by the end of the 1880's he was already becoming disillusioned and as disgusted with his Socialist and anarchist comrades as he had been earlier with the liberals and radicals during his activity in the Eastern Question Association of the 1870's. Writing to Lady (then Mrs.) Burne-Jones in May 1885, in one of those letters that give us the man more than anything else he wrote, he says:

---

[14]W. B. Yeats, *Autobiographies* (London, 1926), p. 174.
[15]The hero of the poem shows great generosity and forbearance toward his best friend, who has secretly become his wife's lover.

[16]M. Morris, *William Morris, Artist, Writer, Socialist*, 2 vols. (Oxford, 1936), vol. I, pp. 109–110.

On Sunday I went a-preaching Stepney way. My visit intensely depressed me, as these Eastwards visits always do: the mere stretch of houses, the vast mass of utter shabbiness and uneventfulness, sits upon one like a nightmare: of course what slums there are one doesn't see. You would perhaps have smiled at my congregation: some twenty people in a little room, as dirty as convenient, and stinking a good deal. It took the fire out of my fine periods, I can tell you: it is a great drawback that I can't *talk* to them roughly and unaffectedly. Also I would like to know what amount of real feeling underlies their bombastic revolutionary talk. . . .

(27 May 1885)

In July 1888 he writes to the same correspondent:

Whatever might be said about the reception of ideal Socialism or Communism, towards this State Socialism things are certainly tending, and swiftly too. But then in all the wearisome shilly-shally of parliamentary politics I should be absolutely useless: and the immediate end to be gained, the pushing things just a trifle nearer to State Socialism, which when realized seems to me but a dull goal—all this quite sickens me. . . . Yet on the other hand I sometimes vex myself by thinking that perhaps I am not doing the most I can merely for the sake of a piece of "preciousness."

(29 July 1888)

This "preciousness" was, presumably, his "ministering to the swinish luxury of the rich" by the productions of Morris & Co.

By 1888 Morris was becoming increasingly interested in typography. With Emery Walker, he supervised the printing of his romances *A Tale of the House of the Wolfings* (1888) and *The Roots of the Mountains* (1889), for which he used a special type modeled on an old Basel font. Out of this interest came the founding of the Kelmscott Press in 1891. Morris had always been keenly interested in book production, and twenty years earlier had abandoned a scheme for an illustrated edition of *The Earthly Paradise* after Burne-Jones had made more than a hundred designs for the blocks. His main difficulty as a typographer lay in the fact that printing was a craft born on the threshold of the Renaissance, a period that was for him the root of all evils. He was bound, therefore, like the earliest printers, to treat book production as an extension of manuscript. As far as possible, in the Kelmscott books Morris reproduced by type and woodblock all the characteristics of the illuminated manuscripts of the Middle Ages, and since the decoration was in black and white in-stead of in color this meant that, in the more lavish productions, the page became too black and heavy. The Chaucer, printed in Gothic type, its borders encrusted with foliage, its decorated initials and its eighty-seven woodcuts by Burne-Jones, radiates its own peculiar splendor. The projected Froissart would have been even more magnificent. But the majority of books printed at the Kelmscott Press were not on this scale and were very much simpler and plainer. Morris designed two new fonts of type: Troy type, of which the Chaucer is a smaller variant, a Gothic font; and Golden type, a roman font. Troy was modeled on the early German printers; Golden, on the Venetian printers of the fifteenth century.

The impetus that Morris gave to fine printing by his example at the Kelmscott Press was immense. Though his own taste was for decorated books, he admitted the value of "books whose only ornament is the necessary and essential beauty which arises out of the fitness of a piece of craftsmanship for the use for which it is made." Fitness for use was a revolutionary principle in the nineteenth century and out of it the whole modern movement of architecture and design has grown. In this, and in his recognition that the future of the arts is bound up with architecture, lies Morris' influence as a craftsman. He did not, as is often said, want to return to the Middle Ages and stay there: but he felt that in design, as in literature, the true English tradition had been lost since the sixteenth century, and that it was necessary to return to it if the arts were to be set on the right road again.

A Dream of John Ball and *News from Nowhere* stand apart from the other romances in that they are based upon history and located in a recognizable England. They were both written for the pages of the *Commonweal,* the journal of Morris' Socialist League, but into them he put his deepest thoughts on life and human destiny. The first is set in the time of the Peasants' Revolt, in Kent in the fourteenth century, and its archaisms strike one as a natural part of the subject. Otherwise, the language is idiomatic and of great purity and simplicity. John Ball, the priest who leads the revolt against feudalism, preaches from the village cross on the text that fellowship is heaven and lack of fellowship hell. His sermon is not unlike the later sermons of Hugh Latimer.

"Forsooth, he that waketh in hell and feeleth his heart fail him, shall have memory of the merry days of earth, and how that when his heart failed him there, he cried on his fellow, were it his wife or his son or his brother or his gossip or his brother sworn in arms, and how that his fellow heard him and came and they mourned together under the sun, till again they laughed together and were but half sorry between them. This shall he think on in hell, and cry on his fellow to help him, and shall find that therein is no help because there is no fellowship, but every man for himself. Therefore, I tell you that the proud, despiteous rich man, though he knoweth it not, is in hell already, because he hath no fellow; and he that hath so hardy a heart that in sorrow he thinketh of fellowship, his sorrow is soon but a story of sorrow—a little change in the life that knows not ill."

(vol. XVI, pp. 230–231)

In the clear brilliance of its pictures of the Middle Ages, *John Ball* recaptures the vividness of *The Defence of Guenevere*. But the magic of the tale is in the second part, where the dreamer (who is, of course, Morris himself in the habit and likeness of Chaucer) sits talking with the priest all night in the moonlit church. The atmosphere is still that of "The Unknown Church" of the early Oxford days, but it is deepened and restrained by all the historical knowledge and experience acquired since. John Ball has suspected all along that this elderly man in the habit of Chaucer is "a sending from another time," and in the church he questions him about things to come. With the dawn, the dreamer wakes in his bedroom at Hammersmith, with the dreary sound of the early morning steam whistles in his ears calling the workmen to the factories. The concluding page gives us a sudden and revealing picture of Morris himself.

The historical survey of the five hundred years lying between John Ball and the dreamer should be read in conjunction with the prophetic survey in the historical chapters of *News from Nowhere*. Both are implicitly Marxist and should be pondered by those who think of Morris as an unpractical dreamer. Though he regarded *News from Nowhere* as a trifle, it appears now more like his masterpiece, for into it he put not only his social philosophy and hopes for the future, but also his love of the earth and its seasons, his tenderness, his humanity, and his wisdom.

The enchanting simplicity of its style is one with the fundamentally childlike nature of the man himself. Once more the tale is given the framework of medieval allegory. The writer comes home at night after "a brisk conversational discussion up at the League as to what would happen on the Morrow of the Revolution," at the conclusion of which he

"finished by roaring out very loud, and damning all the rest as fools." Next morning he wakes up in the twenty-first century. The revolution has taken place and the people of England have been living for about a hundred and fifty years in a state of ideal communism. Machinery has not been abolished entirely, but it is nowhere in evidence, and one has the impression that production has reverted again to handicraft: at any rate, whatever industry there is has not been allowed to spoil either the town or the country. Towns have once more taken on a medieval aspect, money has fallen into disuse, and everyone lives in a condition of sophisticated simplicity.

Perhaps it is all too "trim and clean and orderly and bright," and everybody too uniformly good-humored, but one must remember that it is utopia, where there are no laws except enlightened public opinion, where economics are left delightfully vague, and dustmen dress as troubadours. Familiar places like Hammersmith, Piccadilly (now an arcaded shopping street reminiscent of Padua), Trafalgar Square (an orchard), the British Museum, and Hampton Court have been assimilated easily and delightfully into the future. The Houses of Parliament are still in use, but as a storage place for manure—an instance of Morris' schoolboyish sense of humor. In fact, the only thing that "dates" in *News from Nowhere* is the rather trying camaraderie, which is evidently based on the behavior of Morris' immediate circle. Writing in 1890, Morris chose 1952 as the great revolutionary year in English history, the first year of the civil war that marked the changeover from the remnants of degenerate capitalism to communism:

". . . the world was being brought to its second birth [says old Hammond, the antiquarian who relates how the change came about] how could that take place without a tragedy? Moreover, think of it. The spirit of the new days, of our days, was to be delight in the life of the world. . . . In times past, indeed, men were told to love their kind, to believe in the religion of humanity and so forth. But look you, just in the degree that a man had elevation of mind and refinement enough to be able to value this idea, was he repelled by the obvious aspect of the individuals composing the mass which he was to worship; and he could only evade that repulsion by making a conventional abstraction of mankind that had little actual or historical relation to the race; which to his eyes was divided into blind tyrants on the one hand and apathetic degraded slaves on the other. But now, where is the difficulty in accepting the religion of humanity, when the men and women who go to make up humanity are free, happy, and energetic at least, and most commonly beautiful of body also, and surrounded by beautiful things of their own fashioning, and a nature bettered and not worsened by contact with mankind? This is what this age of the world has reserved for us."

(vol. XVI, pp. 132–133)

Significantly, the word *art* has died out, "because it has become a necessary part of the labor of every man who produces." The historical account of the actual changeover and the years leading up to it, as given by Hammond, is most real and convincing, and here Morris' political experience stood him in good stead—not, of course, that he really supposed that London would ever appear as he imagines it. But he did think that once the towns had lost their importance as commercial and manufacturing centers, the people would naturally return to the country and simplicity of life. Needless to say, everyone in *News from Nowhere* works only at what interests him, for no one is any longer obliged to earn the right to live. And since work has once more become a pleasure instead of a drudgery for the majority of people, it is natural that their surroundings should have also once more become pleasant. The long account of the river trip up the Thames from Hammersmith to Kelmscott, through the enchanted countryside, is a re-creation of a similar journey Morris made with his family and friends in the summer of 1880. The final chapters are set at Kelmscott itself.

News from Nowhere is a picture of life as Morris would have had it, not as he thought it would ever be—another earthly paradise in fact—and the saddest part about it is its title. In the end it all fades as a dream in which we have been impossibly happy and in which all complexities and conflicts are resolved into a golden harmony. Yet when the dreamer wakes once more in "dingy Hammersmith," it is not altogether with despair, for he still hears the voice of Ellen coming to him from that nowhere of the future:

Go back again, now that you have seen us, and your outward eyes have learned that in spite of all the infallible maxims of your day there is yet a time of rest in store for the world, when mastery has changed into fellowship—but not before. Go back again, then, and while you live you will see all round you people engaged in making others live lives which are not their own, while they themselves care nothing for their own real lives—men who hate life though they fear death. Go back and be happier for having seen us, for having added a little hope to your struggle. Go on living while you may, striving, with whatsoever pain and labour

needs must be, to build up little by little the new day of fellowship, and rest, and happiness.

(vol. XVI, pp. 210–211)

It is in such passages that we see the essential greatness of William Morris.

The volume of Morris' literary work was immense, but it is only a small part of his total achievement. His influence has lived on in spheres other than literature, but as a poet it was immediately felt by the young W. B. Yeats. Yeats was then living with his father in the new red-brick suburb of Bedford Park, built by Norman Shaw on Morris principles (with even a pub called The Tabard, after Chaucer), and he has written of how Morris stopped him one day in Holborn and said: "'You write my sort of poetry,'" and "would have said more had not he caught sight of a new ornamental cast-iron lamppost and got very heated on the subject" (*Autobiographies*, pp. 180–181). Again, Morris' direct influence may be seen in the early poems of Ezra Pound, in "Near Perigord," for instance, though Pre-Raphaelite medievalism, with its roots in Rossetti, Morris, and Swinburne, was pervasive over a large area of English poetry up to the beginning of World War I, at least.

It is, perhaps, doubtful if anyone now reads *Sigurd*, which, Shaw tells us, Morris used to chant, "rocking from one foot to the other like an elephant"; but *Jason* and some of the stories of *The Earthly Paradise*, with their beautiful introductory poems on the months, are probably more accessible to readers today. To Yeats, Morris seemed "the happiest of poets" because he did everything with "an unheard of ease." But at the heart of his poetry there are sadness and loss.

This sadness and sense of loss he sought in the longer poems to smother beneath an abundance of descriptive detail, such as we find in Flemish tapestries. Much of Morris' poetry is not only like tapestry, he also wrote verses for the fabrics woven at Merton Abbey. The "Vine" tapestry bears this inscription:

> I draw the blood from out the earth;
> I store the sun for winter mirth.[17]

and into the "Orange Tree" were woven the lines:

[17]Reprinted as "Tapestry Trees," *Collected Works*, vol. IX, p. 194, ll. 15–16.

Amidst the greenness of my night,
My odorous lamps hang round and bright.

(ll. 17–18)

Apart from the isolated peak of *Sigurd*, Morris is often seen at his best in occasional verses such as these and in the charming lines he wrote to be embroidered on the hangings round the great Elizabethan four-poster bed in which he slept at Kelmscott and which can still be seen there:

> The wind's on the world
> And the night is a-cold,
> And Thames runs chill
> Twixt mead and hill,
> But kind and dear
> Is the old house here,
> And my heart is warm
> Midst winter's harm.
> Rest, then and rest,
> And think of the best
> Twixt summer and spring
> When all birds sing
> In the town of the tree,
> And ye lie in me
> And scarce dare move
> Lest earth and its love
> Should fade away
> Ere the full of the day.
>
> I am old and have seen
> Many things that have been,
> Both grief and peace,
> And wane and increase.
> No tale I tell
> Of ill or well,
> But this I say,
> Night treadeth on day,
> And for worst and best
> Right good is rest.

Morris' last words, as he lay dying, were: "I want to get mumbo-jumbo out of the world." He had spent his life fighting mumbo-jumbo in its various forms and some of the things he fought for have been achieved; others have come about in a form in which he would hardly recognize them; and many things that he loathed have since grown to monstrous proportions, so that simplicity, harmony, and fellowship, and the healing influences of nature in our lives, seem to be further away than ever. One might say of Morris' achievement, with John Ball: "men fight and lose the battle, and the thing they fought for comes about in spite of their defeat, and when it comes turns out to be not what they meant." As Bernard Shaw has observed, Morris grows in stature the further we draw away from him in time. His greatness lies not so much in anything he did, for he never fully expressed himself in any one activity: his greatness is in his vision and in what he was.

SELECTED BIBLIOGRAPHY

I. Bibliography. H. B. Forman, *The Books of William Morris, with Some Account of His Doings in Literature and the Allied Arts* (London, 1897), contains a list of Morris' contributions to *Justice,* the *Commonweal,* and other periodicals, illus. with facs.; S. C. Cockerell, *A Note By William Morris on His Aims in Founding the Kelmscott Press, Together with a Short History of the Press* (London, 1898); S. C. Cockerell, *An Annotated List of all the Books Printed at the Kelmscott Press* (London, 1898); T. Scott, *Bibliography of the Works of William Morris* (London, 1899); *A Catalogue of MSS. and Early Printed Books from the Libraries of William Morris,* 4 vols. (New York, 1906–1907), in the J. P. Morgan Library.

II. Collected Works. M. Morris, ed., *The Collected Works of William Morris,* 24 vols. (London, 1910–1915), the intros. to each vol. contain photographs, repros., and much biographical material; M. Morris, *William Morris, Artist, Writer, Socialist,* 2 vols. (Oxford, 1936), contains juvenilia and other work repr. from MSS or from periodicals, letters, lectures, the review of Rossetti's *Poems,* and G. B. Shaw's "William Morris as I Knew Him"; *Lectures,* 5 vols. (London, 1898–1901).

III. Selected Works. G. D. H. Cole, ed., *Stories in Prose, Stories in Verse, Shorter Poems, Lectures and Essays* (London, 1934); *On Art and Socialism* (London, 1947), intro. by H. Jackson, a selection of Morris' lectures; P. Henderson, ed., *The Letters of William Morris to His Family and Friends* (London, 1950), contains facs., prospectus of Morris & Co., and *Unjust War: An Address to the Working-men of England; Unpublished Letters of William Morris* (to Dr. John Glasse, 1886–1895) (London, 1951), intro. by R. P. Arnot; *Morris & Company 1861–1940. A Commemorative Centenary Exhibition* (London, 1961), catalog contains repros. in black and white of wallpapers, textiles, stained glass, painted furniture, and other products of Morris' firm; A. Briggs, ed., *William Morris: Selected Writings and Designs* (London, 1962), contains a supp. by G. Shankland, "William Morris, Designer," and repros. of Morris' designs for wallpapers, textiles, stained glass, books, and examples of interior decoration; G. Grigson, ed., *William Morris: Choice of Verse* (London, 1969); P. Faulkner, ed., *Early Romances in Prose and Verse* (London, 1973), the Everyman's Library.

IV. Separate Works. *The Defence of Guenevere* (London, 1858), verse, also the Kelmscott Press ed. (London, 1892); *The Life and Death of Jason* (London, 1867), verse, also the Kelmscott Press ed. (London, 1895); *The Earthly Paradise*, 4 vols. (London, 1868–1870), verse, also the Kelmscott Press ed. (London, 1896–1897); *The Story of Grettir the Strong*, trans. from Icelandic with E. Magnusson (London, 1869), prose romance; *The Story of the Volsungs and Niblungs, with Certain Songs from the Elder Edda*, trans. from Icelandic with E. Magnusson (London, 1870), prose and verse; *Love Is Enough, or the Freeing of Pharamond, A Morality* (London, 1872), drama, also the Kelmscott Press ed. (London, 1897); *Three Northern Love Stories*, trans. from Icelandic with E. Magnusson (London, 1875), prose romance; *The Aeneids of Virgil, Done into English Verse* (London, 1875), verse; *The Story of Sigurd the Volsung and the Fall of the Niblungs* (London, 1876), verse, also the Kelmscott Press ed. (London, 1898); *Hopes and Fears for Art* (London, 1882), prose, five lectures delivered in Birmingham, London, and Nottingham, 1878–1881; *Chants for Socialists* (London, 1884), verse, repr. from *Justice* and the *Commonweal*; *Pilgrims of Hope* (London, 1886), a poem in thirteen books, repr. from the *Commonweal*; *The Odyssey of Homer, done into English Verse* (London, 1887); *Signs of Change* (London, 1888), prose, seven lectures; *A Dream of John Ball and a King's Lesson* (London, 1888), prose romance, repr. from the *Commonweal*; *A Tale of the House of the Wolfings* (London, 1888), prose and verse; *The Tables Turned, or Nupkins Awakened* (London, 1889), drama, a Socialist interlude; *The Roots of the Mountains* (London, 1889), prose and verse; *News from Nowhere, or an Epoch of Rest* (Boston, 1890), prose romance, repr. from the *Commonweal*, frontispiece by W. Crane, first London ed. (1891), also the Kelmscott Press ed. (London, 1892); *The Story of the Glittering Plain* (London, 1891), prose romance, the first book printed at the Kelmscott Press; *Poems by the Way* (London, 1891), the Kelmscott Press ed.; *The Saga Library*, trans. from Icelandic with E. Magnusson, vols. I–IV (London, 1891–1895), prose romance; *Gothic Architecture* (London, 1893), the Kelmscott Press ed.; *Socialism: Its Growth and Outcome*, with E. B. Bax (London, 1893), sociology; *Of the Friendship of Amis and Amilie, Done into English* (London, 1894), prose romance; *The Wood Beyond the World* (London, 1894), prose romance; *The Tale of Beowulf, Done out of the Old English Tongue*, with A. J. Wyatt (London, 1895), verse; *Child Christopher and Goldilind the Fair*, 2 vols. (London, 1895), prose romance, the Kelmscott Press ed.; *Old French Romances, Done into English* (London, 1896), prose romance; *The Well at the World's End* (London, 1896), prose romance; *The Water of the Wondrous Isles* (London, 1897), prose romance, the Kelmscott Press ed.; *The Story of the Sundering Flood* (London, 1897), prose romance, the Kelmscott Press ed.; *The Churches of Northern France, No. 1* (Portland, Me., 1901), essay, repr. from the *Oxford and Cambridge Magazine*; *Architecture, Industry and Wealth* (London, 1902), miscellaneous prose, collected papers.

V. BIOGRAPHICAL AND CRITICAL STUDIES. W. Pater, *Appreciations* (London, 1889), the ch. "Aesthetic Poetry," which was devoted to Morris, was removed from the 1890 and later eds.; A. Vallance, *William Morris: His Art, His Writings and His Public Life, A Record*, 2nd ed. (London, 1898); J. W. Mackail, *The Life of William Morris*, 2 vols. (London, 1899; repr. London–New York, 1968), the standard biography, World's Classics ed. (London, 1950), with intro. by Sir S. Cockerell; W. B. Yeats, *Ideas of Good and Evil* (London, 1903), contains the ch. "The Happiest of Poets," see also Yeats's *Autobiographies* (London, 1926); G. Burne-Jones, *Memorials of Edward Burne-Jones*, 2 vols. (London, 1904); W. Allingham, *A Diary* (London, 1907); A. Noyes, *William Morris* (London, 1908), in the English Men of Letters series; H. Jackson, *William Morris: Craftsman-Socialist* (London, 1908; rev. and enl. 1926); W. Crane, *William Morris to Whistler* (London, 1911); F. M. Ford, *Memories and Impressions* (London, 1911); J. Drinkwater, *William Morris, A Critical Study* (London, 1912); A. Compton-Rickett, *William Morris: A Study in Personality* (London, 1913), intro. by R. B. C. Graham; H. Jackson, *The Eighteen Nineties: A Review of Art and Ideas at the Close of the Nineteenth Century* (London, 1913; 1927); A. C. Brock, *William Morris: His Work and Influence* (London, 1914), in the Home University Library; J. B. Glasier, *William Morris and the Early Days of the Socialist Movement* (London, 1921); O. Elton, *A Survey of English Literature 1830–1880* (London, 1921), includes a ch. on Morris; W. S. Blunt, *My Diaries, 1888–1896* (London, 1922); H. H. Sparling, *The Kelmscott Press and William Morris, Master-Craftsman* (London, 1924); J. W. Mackail, *Studies in English Poets* (London, 1926), includes a ch. on Morris; K. C. Marillier, *History of the Merton Abbey Tapestry Works* (London, 1927); F. L. Lucas, *Eight Victorian Poets* (London, 1930), includes a ch. on Morris; H. J. Massingham and H. Massingham, eds., *The Great Victorians* (London, 1932), includes an essay on Morris by J. M. Murray; B. I. Evans, *English Poetry in the Later Nineteenth Century* (London, 1933), includes a ch. on Morris; M. Weekly, *William Morris* (London, 1934), in the Great Lives series; P. Bloomfield, *William Morris* (London, 1934); R. P. Arnot, *William Morris: A Vindication* (London, 1934), a Marxist interpretation; G. H. Crow, *William Morris: Designer* (London, 1934), *The Studio* suppl., contains repros. in color and black and white of wallpapers, chintzes, tapestries, furniture, stained glass, drawings, designs, and other related material; W. R. Lethaby, *Philip Webb and His Work* (London, 1935); N. Pevsner, *Pioneers of the Modern Movement from William Morris to Walter Gropius* (London, 1936), the first real evaluation of Morris' influence on architecture; D. M. Hoare, *The Works of Morris and Yeats in Relation to Early Saga Literature* (London, 1937); C. S. Lewis, *Rehabilitations* (London, 1938), includes a ch. on Morris' prose romances; W. Gaunt, *The Pre-Raphaelite Tragedy* (London, 1942), an entertaining biographical study of Morris and his associates; G. Hough, *The Last Romantics* (London, 1949); G. B. Shaw, *Pen Portraits and Reviews* (London, 1949), includes a review of Mackail's *Life of William Morris;* H. R. Angeli, *Dante Gabriel Rossetti: His Friends and Enemies* (London, 1949), an account of Morris' friendship with Rossetti with which to correct Mackail's version; O. Doughty, *A Victorian Romantic: Dante Gabriel Rossetti* (London, 1949; 2nd ed., 1960), the first attempt to penetrate the mystery surrounding Morris' private life; R. D. Macleod, *Morris without Mackail (As Seen by His Contemporaries)* (Glasgow, 1954); E. P. Thompson, *William Morris: Romantic to Revolutionary* (London, 1955), a study of Morris' political activities, with a perceptive ch. on his poetry, ranks in value with Mackail and M. Morris; R. P. Arnot, "Bernard Shaw and William Morris," in *Transactions of the William Morris Society* (1957); R. F. Jordan, "The Medieval Vision of William Morris," in *Transactions of the William Morris Society* (1960); P. Floud, "The Wallpaper Designs of William Morris," in *Penrose Annual,* vol. 54 (1960); G. D. H. Cole, "William Morris as a Socialist," in *Trans-actions of the William Morris Society* (1960); R. C. H. Briggs, "A Handlist of the Public Addresses of William Morris," in *Transactions of the William Morris Society* (1960); J. Lindsay, "William Morris, Writer," in *Transactions of the William Morris Society* (1961); P. Faulkner, *William Morris and W. B. Yeats* (London, 1962); J. Purkis, "The Icelandic Jaunt: A Study of the Expeditions Made by Morris to Iceland in 1871 and 1873," in *Transactions of the William Morris Society* (1962); R. C. H. Briggs, "The Work of William Morris," in *Transactions of the William Morris Society* (1962); H. Bushell, ed., *The Icelandic Journals of William Morris* (London, 1963), see also *The Journal* of the William Morris Society, published biannually; E. Godwin and S. Godwin, *Warrior Bard: The Life of William Morris* (London, 1972); P. Faulkner, ed., *William Morris: The Critical Heritage* (London, 1973); W. M. Bax and E. B. Bax, *Socialism: Its Growth and Outcome* (London, 1974); F. Clark, ed., *William Morris: Wallpapers and Chintzes* (London, 1974); A. C. Sewter, *The Stained Glass of William Morris and His Circle* (New Haven, Conn., 1974); P. Meier, *William Morris, the Marxist Dreamer,* 2 vols. (Hassocks–Atlantic Heights, N.J., 1978), trans. from the French by F. Gubb.

ALGERNON CHARLES SWINBURNE

(1837-1909)

Ian Fletcher

I

SWINBURNE is not a Victorian curiosity, but a highly original poet, an exhilarating metrist; his poetry explores unusual areas of experience, and his lyricism, at its best, is rich and haunting. Yet till very lately he was a notorious critical "case," a synonym almost for a literary disease. In his own lifetime, a German journalist could place him definitively as a "higher degenerate," one of the symptoms being the poet's love of repetition, "echolalia."

And if Swinburne's later fortunes were singular, so was his contemporary reception. His first volume was virtually ignored; his second made him famous; his third was attacked on all sides and the publisher cowed into withdrawing it. *Poems and Ballads* (1866) had violated that high Victorian decorum, the tacit assumption that poetry represented an extension of ethics by other means, its subject matter only what was well above the girdle. Swinburne's earlier lyrics are a breviary of Freudian insights. He gives voice to the dark underside of the Victorian psyche, writing of the aggressive, the cruel, even the demonic aspects of sexual love, and of the suppression or perversion of human instincts by social and religious tyrannies. And in *Atalanta in Calydon* (1865), that great dramatic poem, he arrives at the notion of "the death of the family," the contention that this institution is by nature oppressive and must be superseded by more flexible social forms. Swinburne surely intended to shock his public by anti-Christian gestures and erotic polemics, although such were certainly not the limits of his aims; yet his own succès de scandale engulfed him. Readers were dazzled or repulsed by the violent rhythms or topics of his verse.

Swinburne has also suffered from the familiar slump of reputation in the years succeeding an author's death—the fate of George Bernard Shaw offers an obvious parallel. And before his fortunes could recover he became involved in the diffused attack of the 1920's on Victorianism in general. They were further soured by the critical propaganda for an autonomous "modern" movement in poetry, which was conducted largely by the "modern" poets themselves. T. S. Eliot and Ezra Pound, for example, were understandably anxious to secure themselves an audience, and that meant displacing their immediate predecessors. As Harold Bloom puts it, the poet *creates* his predecessors (by constructing fictions of literary history), but "the relation of . . . the new poet to his predecessors cannot be cleansed of polemics or rivalry," and this rivalry stems from anxiety about poetic identity.

Such a strategy was intended to mask the fact that Eliot was himself a deeply romantic poet, and to suggest that his poetry had more in common with the seventeenth-century metaphysical poets, with their wit and word-play, than with the allegedly decaying romanticism of the late nineteenth century (the French, Charles Baudelaire and the symbolists, were absolvable). This involved the creation of a canon: Eliot called it "the main stream." Eliot was to describe his early essays as "a by-product of my private poetry-workshop; or a prolongation of the thinking that went on to the formation of my own verse," and this late candor sanctioned the admission of some of the poets who had been formerly excluded from "the main stream." In America a race of literary journalists and "new," close-reading, and not infrequently neo-Christian, critics arose, and since it had already been agreed that word-play, complexity, and ambiguity were not to be found in Swinburne, he was largely absent from their searching analyses. In England, F. R. Leavis and his adepts had their version of literary history. The one great poet of the later Victorian period, greater than Alfred Lord Tennyson or Robert Browning, was Gerard Manley Hopkins, and had not Hopkins himself, with the clairvoyance of genius, said the last but one word on Swinburne: "a perfect style must be of its age. In virtue of this archaism and on other grounds [Swinburne] must rank with the medievalists," and did not Swinburne suffer also from the defect of having "no real understanding of rhythm"? Paradoxically Hopkins and Swinburne now appear as the most extreme of the Victorian poets, though extreme in radically different ways. But by a further paradox, Hopkins' response to the "pied" particularity of things extends that stroking in of details so frequent in Tennyson, Browning, and Dante Gabriel Rossetti. Hopkins is, indeed, as one critic has suggested, more Victorian than the Victorians in his inspired clutter of detail. Swinburne, however, moves toward music and symbolist dream in attempting to create a closed world, without objects, through language. This point was made in Eliot's casuistical defense of Swinburne:

The poetry [of *Poems and Ballads*] is not morbid, it is not erotic, it is not destructive. These are adjectives which can be applied to the material, the human feelings, which in Swinburne's case do not exist. The morbidity is not of human feeling but of language. Language in a healthy state presents the object, is so close to the object that the two are identified.

(*The Sacred Wood*, p. 149)

For Eliot, Swinburne's verse is sui generis. But his description does not take account of its characteristic tension between *subject matter* and *surface*, which is the outcome of a moral horror different in quality but not in kind from that of Baudelaire, nor does it admit that word-play and complexity are to be encountered in Swinburne.

The comparison with Baudelaire is crucial, because of the French poet's influence. There are affinities: woman as emblem of the unattainable; the "quarrel with God"; the inversions of *Les Litanies de Satan*, recalling a common use of litanies of supplication, worship, and terror in contexts of disgust and revolt. There is a shared distrust of overt morality as falsifying experience, a shared awareness of ennui as the human condition. The distinctions, however, are sharp. Unlike Swinburne, Baudelaire possessed a gift for luminous concision, and his ennui is counterpointed by an energy that is by no means always frenetic. Baudelaire is also more aware of the tang and resonance of objects, and this enables him to correlate outer and inner landscapes. This particularly enriches his interpretations of the modern city, with its workmen, prostitutes, and the numerous lives momentarily and obliquely touching his consciousness. William Wordsworth had presented London as an infernal carnival in the sixth book of *The Prelude*. Baudelaire's Paris is infernal also, but Wordsworth's healing image of the blind beggar is replaced by the procession of seven old men through the dirty fog, who mysteriously embody the intimate nightmare of the outer world. To this nothing in Swinburne corresponds. If on one occasion at least he evokes an industrial landscape,[1] the human figures evade him. The great Italian poet Gabriele D'Annunzio was to be influenced by Swinburne and himself creates a largely linguistic world. Objects, though "things," in D'Annunzio's best work possess an intense sensual presence, as it were, momentary incarnations of some panic energy in nature. D'Annunzio too can marvelously use older forms and masters; but, unlike Swinburne, he has a huge vocabulary and can be the subtler metrist.

There is, of course, an indictment for his admirers to answer. If Swinburne radiates some of the signs of genius—energy, abundance, and a powerful literary identity—his range of subject seems slender. The metrical effects, surprising, stunning even at first, gradually dull the response by reliance on anapests and iambs; the initial effect of wildness is eventually tamed by patterns of expectation; unlike Baudelaire, Swinburne did not dislocate his meters, while his alliterations were continuous, brash, and self-indulgent. The poet has a harem of words to which he remains depressingly faithful: his vocabulary is often heavily biblical, with a manneristic profusion of God, hell, serpents, stings, rods, flames, and thunders, a surprising characteristic in one who was so determinedly a hammer of the Christians. Swinburne's muse is indeed a kind of inverted Balaam: he curses God in the tones of an Old Testament prophet out of a job, or one perhaps resisting the burdens of office. And the subjects of Swinburne's verse seem to melt into one subject. Whether he is exploring a pungent sado-masochistic psychology or the sea as mother figure; extolling the liberation of Italy as emblem of man's liberation from all tyrannies, religious or political; or sounding the bracing moral

---

[1]Such nights as these in England, the small town
Chatters and scrawls its purpose out in brown,
Searing with steam the hill's dead naked shape;
By juts of hurt impatience, let's escape
Quick sighs of fire from chimnied engine-works.
(Unpublished fragment)

suasions of the Navy League: it makes little difference. The noxious rhythms, the vocabulary, blurred and generalized, persist, so that we can barely tell if we are meant to admire a battleship or a breast. A. E. Housman, one of Swinburne's best and wittiest critics, sums it up: "The sea, like babies and liberty, went into the sausage machine into which he crammed anything and everything, round goes the handle and out of the other end comes . . . noise." Housman admired some of the poems, but considered that

there is no reason why they should begin where they do or end where they do; there is no reason why the middle should be in the middle; there is hardly a reason why, having once begun, they should ever end at all; and it would be possible to rearrange the stanzas which compose them in several different orders without lessening their coherency or impairing their effect.

But Tennyson's comment has an equal aptness: "He is a reed through which all things blow into music."

The most serious charge against Swinburne is that his insights seem always to move toward the peripheral, the immature. His work resounds with echoes from his wide reading. Besides the Bible, there are the classics, Jacobean drama, the continental literatures, the border ballads. But literature fashioned out of other literature is finite. Swinburne was sometimes a deliberate, often highly accomplished pasticheur; he was also a clever parodist. His pastiche and his parody can be readily enjoyed, but what of involuntary parody? Too often the poetry he proffers as original reads like self-parody or self-echo. In displaying such "Alexandrian" symptoms, he is not, of course, alone. Much Victorian poetry is self-consciously literary, abstracted even from the more formalized gestures of Victorian communication. But there is no poet whose style is so deliberate a literary mosaic. Even when Swinburne seems to speak most directly and feelingly to his reader, as in this passage from "The Triumph of Time," he feels in quotation marks:

> "What should such fellows as I do?" Nay,
> My part were worse if I chose to play;
> For the worst is this after all; if they knew me,
> Not a soul on earth would pity me.[2]
>
> (st. 3)

[2]All quotations from the works are from *The Complete Works*, 20 vols. (London, 1925–1927).

Understanding of one's state and acceptance of humiliation should not, incidentally, be confused with self-pity.

II

SWINBURNE is one of England's relatively few upper-class poets. His father, younger son of Sir John Swinburne (the baronetcy went back to 1660), was to achieve the rank of admiral in the British navy; his mother was the fourth daughter of the third earl of Ashburnham. A cousin vividly describes Algernon's first appearance at Eton.

. . . he stood there between his father and mother, with his wondering eyes fixed upon me! Under his arm he hugged his Bowdler's Shakespeare, a very precious treasure, bound in brown leather. . . . He was strangely tiny. His limbs were small and delicate; and his sloping shoulders looked far too weak to carry his great head, the size of which was exaggerated by the tousled mass of red hair standing almost at right angles to it.[3]

His actual size seems to have been about five feet. The cousin softens this description by referring to Swinburne's voice as "exquisitely soft . . . with a rather sing-song intonation," evidently the vatic, romantic reading voice, which was common to Wordsworth (according to Tom Moore's journal), to Tennyson, and to William Butler Yeats—as the last two have been preserved on record. Other accounts speak of Swinburne's voice rising to an eldritch shrillness, of his dancing steps and continuous vivid movements.

Swinburne's bohemianism, republicanism, and war with God can be viewed as a patrician individualism. This would have seemed less odd two generations earlier, in the regency period. It was mid-Victorian middle-class evangelical values that intensified its provocative qualities. Swinburne located (like Yeats) some of his most deeply felt values under the aristocratic notions of courage, honor, and chivalry. Of his own courage, moral and physical, there can be no doubt: fearless on a horse, he was a passionate swimmer in dangerous seas. Undoubtedly his small size led to a compensatory need

[3]Edmund Gosse, *The Life of Algernon Charles Swinburne* (London, 1917), p. 319.

to prove himself "manly"—hence his stoical endurance of beatings at Eton, his drinking with the bunch, and his close association with vigorous male personalities.

Much of Swinburne's childhood was spent on the Isle of Wight and at his grandfather's family seat, Capheaton, in Northumberland, a county on the Scots border. Northumberland's bleak spaces, its wildness in sea and wind, its legends and traditional ballads strongly attracted him. Of these last, Swinburne made many imitations, capturing directness, dialect, brutality, and anonymous narrative qualities with assured skill. The softer landscapes of the Isle of Wight passed also into his work. Close to the Swinburne house on that island lived his mother's sister Lady Mary Gordon and her husband, Sir Henry, the admiral's first cousin. Their daughter, Mary Gordon, a tomboyish girl (like Swinburne she rode well), with some gift for literature, was the close companion of his earlier years, probably the central personality in his emotional life, and certainly a muse figure. The two were so closely interrelated that marriage would have been considered dangerous, and Swinburne's physical oddity must have constituted a warning eugenic emblem.

Algernon's wide and intense reading had been initiated by acquiring French and Italian from his mother, but he also read enthusiastically at Capheaton in his grandfather's large library, which contained many French works. His education continued at Eton, to which he was sent in 1849 at the age of twelve. He seems to have become difficult, and after four years left school for three years of private tutoring, going up to Benjamin Jowett's Balliol College, Oxford, in 1856. Swinburne was soon involved with a club called Old Mortality, whose later members were to include Walter Pater and J. A. Symonds.

In 1857 he encountered the manic exuberance of Rossetti, William Morris, and Edward Burne-Jones, who were busy with mural painting at the Oxford Union debating hall. The meeting was decisive in several ways. It confirmed Swinburne's devotion to literature and art. The imagery of the murals was Arthurian, and Swinburne was soon composing Arthurian verse in the naive idiom of Morris' *The Defense of Guenevere* (1858). Like numerous undergraduate groups, Old Mortality then proceeded to a magazine, *Undergraduate Papers*, to which Swinburne with characteristic versatility contributed poetry, an essay on his favorite Elizabethan and Jacobean dramatists, and an amusing mock-review. Jowett, who liked his young men to get along (and on) in the world, tended to disapprove of Swinburne's dedication to poetry. In 1858 and 1859, Swinburne was busy with writing and revising his *Rosamond*, a distinctly Pre-Raphaelite closet play, achieving a second class in moderations, working at a prize poem on the life and death of Sir John Franklin, and experimenting with devout pastiches of Francis Beaumont and John Fletcher, full of their witty sexual perversities as well as his own flagellant fantasias. *Laugh and Lie Down* (1859) plays with the theme of homosexuality, and this was to be repeated in later work. Swinburne's sexual life has been much discussed, the conclusions veering between sado-masochism and homosexuality. Discounting natural tendencies to the homoerotic, latent or displayed in many men, one must distinguish that, to quote Matthew Arnold, from any "descent to the realm of immediate practice." Possibly Swinburne had a playful relationship of this order with Simeon Solomon (whose tastes were unequivocal), and he was undoubtedly attracted to physically strong men. He was fascinated by Theodore Watts-Dunton's seven-year-old nephew in later life and on happier terms with his mother than with his father. Both of his known relationships with women were inconclusive.

With Jowett, Swinburne's later relationship was affectionate enough, but it is probable that the master was involved in Swinburne's departure from Oxford in November 1860. The publication that year of two plays, *The Queen-Mother* and *Rosamond*, may have confirmed Jowett's dubieties. In the following year, Swinburne met a more dangerous mentor: Richard Monckton Milnes, politician, man about town, dim poet, and collector of erotica. It was Milnes who introduced to Swinburne another of his formative influences, the marquis de Sade. In 1862 Swinburne published poetry and criticism in the *Spectator*, including his pioneering article on Baudelaire. In London he acquired a reputation as a delphic talker, a genius. To an American observer he appeared as "a tropical bird, high-crested, long-beaked, quick-moving, with rapid utterance and screams of humour, quite unlike any English lark or nightingale." For a time he joined Rossetti in that bizarre ménage at 16 Cheyne Walk, with its menagerie and artists' models. The mythologizing of Rossetti and his associates was already beginning, but the story of Solomon and Swinburne sliding naked down the banisters and Rossetti roaring at them for disturbing his painting has at least a typical truth. Rossetti's relationship to Swinburne was partly that of master to disciple, and they shared memories of Rossetti's wife, Lizzie, who had committed suicide in 1862 and to whom Swinburne had been chivalrously devoted. In a friendly way, however, Rossetti soon indicated that he wished to terminate the cotenancy.

Between 1862 and 1865, Swinburne was perfecting *Poems and Ballads*. His main models were the meters of Greek poetry, Percy Bysshe Shelley, Baudelaire, William Blake, and a discovery that he probably owed to Rossetti and greeted with the same levity and admiration he accorded to the "divine" marquis. This was the doctor from Georgia in the American "old South," Thomas Holley Chivers, transcendentalist friend of Edgar Allan Poe, from whose poems those of Chivers are sometimes indistinguishable. Chivers' headlong meters are to be found in volumes of strange title, such as *Eonchs of Ruby* and *Nacoochee*. Very close to the note almost of burlesque in Swinburne's "Dolores":

> Cold eyelids that hide like a jewel
>> Hard eyes that grow soft for an hour;
> The heavy white limbs, and the cruel
>> Red mouth like a venomous flower;
>>> (st. 1)

is this from Chivers' "Lily Adair":

> Her eyes, lily-lidded, were azure,
>> Cerulean, celestial, divine—
> Suffused with the soul-light of pleasure,
>> Which drew all the soul out of mine.

even if Swinburne could barely emulate those languid rhyming vowels of the southern states.

In 1863 Swinburne completed *Chastelard*, the first part of a trilogy devoted to his admired Mary Stuart, though the play was not to be published for another two years. In the autumn of that year, he was staying with the Gordons on the Isle of Wight, helping Mary write her *Children of the Chapel*, a romance full of flagellation scenes, and at work on his masterpiece, *Atalanta in Calydon*. From the same year dates what is probably the finest of his lyrical pieces, "The Triumph of Time." It was now perhaps that Swinburne realized there was to be no intimate future with Mary, that he was condemned to being, as he put it in the words of Mary Stuart's rival, Elizabeth, "but barren stock." Mary Gordon was married two

years later to a middle-aged military man, who lived in the north of Scotland. There were no meetings and no surviving letters for another twenty-five years. Already Swinburne had begun his brilliant study of Blake, concluded a version of his novel *Love's Cross Currents*, and proceeded some way with another novel, *Lesbia Brandon*, but he had also begun to drink excessively.

Of *The Queen-Mother* and *Rosamond*, two notices only have been traced, both unfavorable; but with the publication of *Atalanta in Calydon* in 1865, Swinburne achieved immediate fame. Milnes is supposed to have engineered a program for publicizing the book, made more attractive by Rossetti's subtle and original binding, with its asymmetrical Celtic and Greek decorative forms. The following year Swinburne published *Poems and Ballads* (the contents of which were mostly earlier than *Atalanta*). One or two reviewers defended Swinburne's outspokenness, but even John Morley, later a friend, who was free from the familiar Victorian notion that art should idealize the actual to promote public and domestic pieties, described the poet as "the libidinous laureate of a pack of satyrs" and asked "whether there is really nothing in woman worth singing about except 'quivering flanks' . . . 'splendid supple thighs' . . . 'stinging and biting'?" Rossetti, concerned that Swinburne was without normal sexual experience with women, paid Adah Isaacs Menken, burly, busty circus-rider and writer of Whitmanesque verse, the sum of ten pounds to seduce the poet. Menken was honest enough to return the money with a complaint that echoed Morley's: "I can't make him understand that biting's no use." However, a change of direction in Swinburne's art, though not in his life, soon occurred. Early in 1867 Swinburne had completed a longish political poem, *A Song of Italy*, and in that same year he had written his "Ode on the Insurrection at Candia." In the following year, he published "Siena," one of those poems that were to form his volume on the liberation of Italy, *Songs Before Sunrise*. An amusing, probably apocryphal story, told by Edmund Gosse, relates how a meeting of Swinburne's friends and associates, including Jowett, Karl Blind, and Giuseppe Mazzini, was convened to discuss "what could be done *with* and *for* Algernon." That there were meetings of family and friends we need not doubt. Swinburne was prepared to transfer his devotions to a lady as exacting as, but nobler than, Dolores, Our Lady of Pain. Or, as Edward Thomas puts it, "Freedom or Liberty was a safer object of worship than Man, because she could never be embodied, though too easily personified." Embodied, however, in the person of Mazzini, she was.

In 1868 appeared *William Blake,* Swinburne's greatest work in prose, in 1871 *Songs Before Sunrise,* and in 1874 his "double-length chronicle play" *Bothwell;* 1876 saw his second essay on Greek tragic poetry, *Erechtheus,* and 1878 the second series of *Poems and Ballads,* which comprised such cardinal pieces as his elegy on Baudelaire, "Ave Atque Vale," and "A Forsaken Garden." The last two were of all Swinburne's volumes the most indulgently reviewed.

Yet now, if we except *Tristram of Lyonesse,* published in 1882 but begun early in the 1870's, a dozen or so poems, and some criticism, his good work was finished, though he was to live for a further thirty-one years. In the 1870's the alcoholic collapses became more frequent. After each crisis Swinburne would rapidly recover in the family home, but on his return to his London rooms the cycle of crisis, collapse, and recovery would recommence. He was becoming lonely. The most serious separation was from Rossetti, whose feelings of guilt, followed by his unhappy affair with Jane Morris and the attacks on the "fleshliness" of his poetry, had finally brought him to attempted suicide. Rossetti's brother advised Swinburne not to approach his old friend and mentor. From 1872 to the time of Rossetti's death in April 1882, there was neither direct communication nor meeting. Increasingly Swinburne became dependent on the last of his father-figures, Theodore Watts (later Watts-Dunton), a solicitor with literary interests, who already had been usefully involved with Rossetti's affairs. In 1879, Watts was sanctioned by the Swinburne family to take Algernon into care: the poet was by then forty-two and for the next thirty years Watts acted as his guardian. Points can be made against Watts: he was probably jealous of Swinburne's old associates and tended to treat the poet as his own property. Swinburne clearly became dependent on him and made no attempt to break out of the suburban prison at The Pines, 2 Putney Hill. Watts also influenced Swinburne in the direction of conformism. The poet's moral tone improved; he foamed at Parnell when in earlier days he had pleaded for the Fenians; he sonorously slanged the Boers and rhapsodized over the jubilee of the Divine Victoria. Extravagantly loyal to friends, he had, however, exhibited moral inflexibility even before The Pines closed round him: in 1873, for example, when Simeon Solomon had been charged with an act of homosexual indecency, Swinburne's reaction had been one of panic-stricken prudery.

Each morning Swinburne would take a long, healthy walk across Putney to the Rose and Crown public house at Wimbledon, South West London, for his single bottle of beer, crooning a rune over every pram he encountered on the outward and return journeys. Indoors, on occasions of celebration, a little wine might be drunk: if the demon poetry had been domesticated, the demon drink had been tamed. Increasing deafness cut off Swinburne still more radically from the outer world, perhaps in the end even from the other inhabitants of The Pines. Inwardly he seems to have been happy; his old friends he may have lost; he had his books. In April of 1909, there came first influenza, then pneumonia, then death.

III

IN 1876 when a new edition of *Poems and Ballads* was proposed, their author suggested to his publishers that some poems might be transferred to a volume of earlier work, including also *The Queen-Mother, Rosamond,* and various unpublished poems. His proposal, which was not taken up, would have clarified the central themes and tones of *Poems and Ballads.*

That earlier work mostly betrayed Pre-Raphaelite influence: Morris' juxtaposition of dream and violence, in Walter Pater's phrase "the desire of beauty quickened by the sense of death," and, more important, Rossetti's juxtaposition of realism and the supernatural. Rossetti, Jerome J. McGann has convincingly argued, deliberately manipulates Christian imagery in such a way as to exclude traditional responses. By emptying such imagery of its inherited content, Rossetti enables us to experience physical detail "in a new and wholly sensational way," and this relates to his belief in eros rather than agape; that is, in sexual affection exalted as the highest known value (though arguably Rossetti's final position involves, like Swinburne's, the sublimation of the self through art). In Rossetti's poem "The Woodspurge," perfect grief leaves the speaker simply with the irreducible: "The woodspurge has a cup of three." It reads like a failed emblem in the tradition of the seventeenth-century poem of meditation, in which all natural objects lead the mind to a Creator who is also immanent within creation. But here the flower is no easy symbol of Trinitarian hope; what remains to the speaker is "the enormous relevance of the flower's nonsymbolic fact. At that time and in that place the speaker gained a measure of relief from the simple act of observation . . . the poem hints at the mystery . . . in the mere fact of sensory observation." If we compare Rossetti's "The Woodspurge" with Swinburne's "Sundew," we may perceive some distinction between the two poets. Swinburne's poem opens:

> A little marsh-plant, yellow green,
>   And pricked at lip with tender red.
> Tread close, and either way you tread
> Some faint black water jets between
> Lest you should bruise the curious head. . . .
>
> (st. 1)

and ends by rejecting the flower because it does not recall the woman whom the speaker loves. The sundew is actually carnivorous, its tentacles extended in a rosette of leaves. The appearance of precision here misleads, and there is no triumphant conclusion in the sufficiency of sensuous experience. Rossetti's attitude to the Christian associations he undercuts is in general decorous; similarly, Swinburne in "A Christmas Carol," suggested by one of Rossetti's drawings, captures all the solemn candor of the form. "The Two Knights," an early poem omitted from *Poems and Ballads*, altogether capitulates to "The Blessed Damozel," but "The Leper" interestingly marks the transition to Swinburne's personal style. This dramatic lyric, somewhat reminiscent of Morris' early manner, is spoken by a medieval clerk whose love has a masochistic tinge. He panders for the girl he hopelessly loves by bringing the knight she desires to her bedroom in secret. She thanks her "sweet friend" for preserving her from scandal. Then she becomes afflicted with leprosy. All, including

> . . . he inside whose grasp all night
>   Her fervent body leapt or lay,
> Stained with sharp kisses red and white,
>   Found her a plague to spurn away.
>
> (st. 17)

The clerk hides her in a "wattled" house and tends her:

> Six months, and I sit still and hold
>   In two cold palms her cold two feet.
> Her hair, half grey half ruined gold,
>   Thrills me and burns me in kissing it.

> Love bites and stings me through, to see
>   Her keen face made of sunken bones.
> Her worn-off eyelids madden me,
>   That were shot through with purple once.
>
> (st. 26–27)

Baudelaire's "Une Charogne" is a source, though the tone is distinct. "The Leper" ends with a moral casuistry that echoes Browning's "Porphyria's Lover."

> It may be now she hath in sight
> Some better knowledge; still there clings
>   The old question. Will not God do right?
>
> (st. 35)

The subdued metaphor throughout is "the body of love": communion. The speaker, searching still for total communion, empathizes happily: he is necrophiliac, sacrilegious, vampiristic. These are acts that violate taboo. Taboo's function is to expel the violence of the "sacred," those fierce experiences that unify the self with a higher ground of being and whose violence leads them to be proscribed by society. Taboo inspires both fear and religio-erotic fascination, even adoration. "Invading the sacred" through erotic desire, the Swinburnean hero, as Chris Snodgrass has pointed out, himself becomes a sanctified figure, and paradoxically by such erotic and "perverse" acts reconstitutes and makes once more immediately present the sacred "center." In "The Leper" Swinburne glimpsed the dialectic of "spiralling contraries": he was partly to realize that dialectic in his art, though not in his life.

Swinburne tops up the poem with a mock-source for this fictive tale in his best Renaissance French. Identity begins to be established here by parody and caricature, stylistic and iconographical, used by the poet to transcend his source: the hair, profuse sexual symbol among the Pre-Raphaelites, is not "dim" merely, as it becomes in Morris' "Old Love," but rancid, "half grey half ruined gold," while Pre-Raphaelite archaism is also mocked. Through such ironic mockery of his sources, Swinburne, like Donne, protects his tone from absurdity or bathos.

IV

THOSE early poems were probably written before the "moment of truth" between Swinburne and Mary Gordon; the cousins' situation certainly underlay the remainder. Mary and Algernon had shared a private world; part of their mythology was Mary's fictional role as Swinburne's younger brother at school, sympathetically involved in his experiences of flogging. The relationship was so independent of sexual distinction that the shock was more profound when it became apparent they must separate; Mary must marry. For this "fall" from a world of unity the family was directly responsible, and, behind the family, society, and the power, "God," which both expressed. This power, sensed only as cruelty and violation, had been responsible for the peculiarities of Swinburne's personality (and physique).

In his analysis of *Poems and Ballads*, Morse Peckham distinguishes between "self" and "personality," which "is simply something that is given . . . is, in a strange but true sense, entirely alien to oneself," and in Swinburne's case, with the capacity to humiliate the self. Personality is hell and can only be understood and accommodated to as far as possible. Swinburne's insights into his own psychology and his need to aestheticize the self, a transformation of concrete situation into artifice, result in peculiarities of style and negation of development. As Peckham puts it: "from the meaningless chaos of experiences, the self creates through art a world of order and value. Style offers a stance, an orientation, safely to experience that chaos . . . the selfhood of each poet of the past redeems the other as model. The artist can achieve impersonality, make a unique use of tradition which will give him an individuality or selfhood." In a late, self-conscious, Alexandrian or silver Latin age of culture, it is necessary, in Harold Bloom's phrase, "to become one with the redemptive imagination of the precursor." This is a dialectic not of imitation of external characteristics but of impersonation, parody, caricature sometimes of the precursor. Peckham describes Swinburne's style in *Poems and Ballads* as one of "non-expressive aesthetic"; that is to say, with a surface beauty that arrests penetration into the painful depths of content. This surface is won by Swinburne's control over the styles of many writers, and by numerous forms, including many modulations of rhymed stanzas, some distinctly unusual. It becomes fused by continuous usage of alliterations, assonances, patterns of repeated vowel noises, repeated syntactical patterns. That Swinburne intended this highly glazed reflexive surface, there can be no doubt. Often he strews epithets, simply for sound, as decor; tepid words such as "sweet," found four times in a

single stanza of "A Ballad of Death," "sad," "pale," "fair," "bright," all contributing to the nonexpressive surface. Sometimes as many as four epithets (which may be internally rhymed) exhaust their substantive. Such are not emotional shorthand merely, but analogous rather to the many unaccented articles, conjunctions, and prepositions, which are designed to assure a glancing rapidity of reading. But the reader must be alert. "As bones of men under the deep sharp sea"; that second epithet is witty, not decorative. Criticism has justly observed that the diction of *Poems and Ballads* is rarely ornate. Dismissed as overlush and decadent, Swinburne is, on the contrary, according to John Rosenberg, the most *austere* among the greatly gifted poets of the nineteenth century:

> Oh yet would God this flesh of mine might be
> Where air might wash and long leaves cover me,
> Where tides of grass break into foam of flowers,
> Or where the winds' feet shine along the sea.
> ("Laus Veneris," st. 14)

A master of monosyllables; he is indeed "the supreme master in English of the bleak beauty of little words."

"The structure of the book," Swinburne himself commented, "has been as carefully considered and arranged as I could make it." And in a pamphlet defending himself against the reviewers, he wrote that

> the book is dramatic, many-faced, multifarious; and no utterance of enjoyment or despair, belief or unbelief, can properly be assumed as the assertion of its author's personal feeling or faith.
> (*Notes on Poems and Reviews*, para. 4)

This is not necessarily history. But we may believe that Swinburne made some attempt to distance the personal, and he was obviously familiar with Baudelaire's ordering of *Les Fleurs du Mal* into sections representing possible avenues of escape from a modern *accidie*. The effect of *Poems and Ballads*, however, is rather that of a continuous monologue that resounds through a number of masks.

Swinburne rationalized the "fall" in terms of his mentors Sade, Blake, and Baudelaire, and so furnished for the speaker of *Poems and Ballads* an intellectual program that has been brilliantly analyzed for us by Julian Baird. While Swinburne respected Sade as theologian, he was less impressed by Sade as artist. But even as theologian Swinburne probably considered Sade inferior to Blake, for Sade persisted in the Christian dualism that distinguished between body and spirit. According to him the body is fulfilled only in filth, misery, and cruelty, by means of which the individual consciousness is engulfed in unity with another. In spite of Sade's anti-Christian polemics, his was mere despairing mortification of the flesh, not pagan freedom. Blake, according to Swinburne's reading, realized that body and spirit were indivisible, "body" should never be "bruised to pleasure soul"; "above all gods of creation and division, [Blake] beheld by faith in a perfect man a supreme God." There was neither divine person nor divine thing but the human. But this insight needs to be won from a "fallen" world of custom and restraint in which Christian immanence has retracted, but nature's divinity is not admitted; rather, a transcendent and cruel creator is postulated. Against this "new" nature and this "new Nature's god," man must rebel and himself become God:

God is man, and man God; as neither of himself the greater, so neither of himself the less: but as God is the unfallen part of man, man the fallen part of God, God must needs be (not more than man, but assuredly) more than the qualities of man. . . . The other "God" . . . who created the sexual and separate body of man did but cleave in twain the "divine humanity," which becoming reunited shall redeem man without price and without covenant and without law; . . . meantime, the Creator is a divine daemon, liable to error, subduable by and through this very created nature of his invention, which he for the present imprisons and torments.

(*William Blake*, 1868 ed., pp. 155–156)

The ideal of *Poems and Ballads* is therefore a species of gnosticism. It institutes an attempt to transcend the dualism of spirit and matter and return to hermaphrodite unity, through a series of variations on the dominant theme of love, heterosexual, homosexual, oral-genital, and sado-masochistic, a dialogue between the poems themselves.

The volume opens with two imitations of early sixteenth-century court ballads, "A Ballad of Life" corresponding to a Blakean state of innocence, which "the poet-dreamer can appreciate as beautiful, but from which he is separated by intervening years and which he does not fully understand." "A Ballad of Death" represents Blake's state of experience, "a sorrowful waking state which takes full cognizance of the death of innocent physical love in a world which

accepts laws for the flesh" (Baird). Both poems are addressed to Lucrezia Borgia: the first celebrates her as the divinity of matter,[4] the second laments her death "as a vesture with new dyes, / The body that was clothed with love of old." The allusion is to that notion of sacred and profane love, best known through Titian's famous painting, where sacred love has been interpreted as the naked, profane love as the clothed, lady: shame comes with the "fall."[5] Lucrezia, in legend, had committed incest with father and brother, but here she is seen as representing purified nature, the love that must be distinguished behind the lineaments of lust. Emblem of unity, of Renaissance paganism, she becomes the first in a series of emblematic ladies, all of whom are judged in the light of the living Lucrezia. Figures such as Faustine and Dolores (no less than the "nightmare life-in-death" of Samuel Taylor Coleridge, and Shelley's Medusa) mark the reappearance in romantic poetry of those dazzling witches of romantic epic: Alcina, Acrasia, and Armida. The Swinburne female represents the familiar, paradoxical attempt to reconcile the romantic antinomies: pleasure–pain; mystery–knowledge; coition–death; and to preserve essence in a world of flickering phenomena. Essentially passive, she is both victim and victress: though the poet sacrifices himself to her, her gaze (like that of Yeats's ladies on unicorns, in "Meditations in Time of Civil War"), is turned inwards, in an act of self-worship that becomes masochistic precisely because she has taken herself as object. Swinburne uses other literary commonplaces, but always in a strictly personalized manner: the sexual, for example, as emblem of cosmic disorder. The varieties of love are symbolized by Venus as popular or heterosexual love, as homoerotic, as sapphic, and as Venus Anadyomene. In this last the sea is represented as sexual "Mother and lover," older than history, beyond family and society, with whom one can intensify identity and yet be, as with other lovers one cannot, totally mingled, and whose embraces are at once more fatal and sexually keen than those of others.

"A Ballad of Death" concludes with a journey and a return:

---

[4] This is presumably the origin of Lucrezia's puzzling appearance as Madame Hulé in the thirtieth of Ezra Pound's *Cantos*.
[5] See "Sacred and Profane Love," in E. Wind, *Pagan Mysteries in the Renaissance*, 2nd and rev. ed. (London, 1967), for the complex history of interpretation.

. . . it may be
That when thy feet return at evening
Death shall come in with thee.

Even the proposed revision of the volume would not have assured that subtle placing and cogent unfolding of poem after poem in dialogue with one another that we find in the maturity of Yeats. Yet a broad narrative line can be traced in *Poems and Ballads.* The end of "A Ballad of Death" leads naturally on to "Laus Veneris." This poem relates the poet Tannhäuser's fruitless journey to Rome for absolution by the pope from the sin of his service to Venus under the Venusberg.[6] The pope refuses absolution and Tannhäuser returns to Venus. Originally a medieval legend, this tale had been retold several times in the nineteenth century, by Heinrich Heine, Ludwig Tieck, in Richard Wagner's opera (1849), and in Baudelaire's defense of the work twelve years later, while the subject became popular in England particularly in the fin de siècle.[7] The medieval setting recalls Heine's theory that the pagan gods after the triumph of Christianity either enlisted in the new religion or became demons.

In Swinburne's poem, written in a stricter variation of the meter used by Edward FitzGerald in his *Rubáiyát* (1859), we meet further literary commonplaces creatively distorted. The Venusberg, in its heat and aridity, resembles one of those false secondary gardens of Eden that are found in Renaissance epic. "The scented dusty daylight burns the air." Just as temptation *creates* Edmund Spenser's Bower of Bliss (though the reader remains informed by imagery no less than by comment that it *is* illusion, infernal not paradisal), so Tannhäuser recreates Venus as succuba, notwithstanding his choice of her in place of Christ. In Julian Baird's reading, the situation is that of "A Ballad of Life" inverted. In that poem the lover could distinguish the

gold of love under the dusty overlayer of lust. For Tannhäuser, who believes in duality of body and spirit, love and lust remain the same, but individuated still. Thus as knight he believes in Christ, but as lover in Venus: here there is no epiphany of feminine purity, as in some versions of the Tannhäuser story. In the traditional false earthly paradise the lover sleeps, while the insatiate succuba wakes. Here Venus sleeps with the lineaments of satisfied desire; the only sign of life is "a purple speck / Wherein the pained blood falters and goes out." But Tannhäuser desires final death and judgment, associating Venus with the great harlot of Revelation.

> For till the thunder in the trumpet be,
> Soul may divide from body, but not we
>   One from another; . . .
>
> I seal myself upon thee with my might,
> Abiding always out of all men's sight
>   Until God loosen over sea and land
> The thunder of the trumpets of the night.
>   (st. 105–106)

This is the longing for confirmation of damnation experienced by the inverted Christian who cannot transcend what he hates and loves. The poem conforms also to the traditional romantic theme of the quest, and Tannhäuser's return journey mirrors the aesthetic pilgrim's penitential reversal.

Next in order there follows a fragment of dialogue between Phaedra and Hippolytus with choric interventions. If Tannhäuser remains strangely passive in love, Phaedra is aggressive, a woman obsessed with desire for her stepson, the victim of an unknown god who, like Death, cannot be appeased with gifts, or rather can only be appeased by the death of both Phaedra and Hippolytus. Phaedra's madness communicates itself through images of bestiality. The mother–son relationship precisely inverts that in *Atalanta in Calydon:* Hippolytus sacrifices himself to the false "god" of custom and restraint. This is followed by three poems associated by Swinburne and bearing directly on the autobiographical situation.

In "The Triumph of Time," half allegory, half narrative, Swinburne speaks in his own voice. The poem is at once rapid in movement and long in proportion to its intellectual content, that length suggesting the processional rite of the "triumph" form as practiced by poets from Petrarch to Shelley. The theme is the

---

[6]The mountain that became the refuge of Venus after the defeat of the pagan gods by Christianity. Burne-Jones's lost watercolor of 1861 on the topic probably influenced Swinburne. A larger version of the theme in oil of 1873–1878 has a Venus who was aptly described by a contemporary as "wan and death-like, eaten up and gnawn away by disappointment and desire." Its iridescent colors, "shot" reds and golds, also connect with Swinburne's imagery.

[7]See, for example, John Davidson's "A New Ballad of Tannhäuser" in *New Ballads* (London-New York, 1897); Herbert E. Clarke's *Tannhäuser and Other Poems* (1896); Walter Pater's allusions in the unpublished portions of *Gaston de Latour* (1896); and Aubrey Beardsley's *Venus and Tannhäuser* (1896).

conspiracy of fates, gods, and Time, again a love which is imaged sacramentally: "This wild new growth of the corn and vine"; but the speaker learns that communion will be impossible; he is alone. Time, in traditional mode, acts as both destroyer of his love and revealer of his true situation.

The hermaphrodite image of innocent primitive unity, two bodies and souls, is invoked:

> Twain halves of a perfect heart, made fast
> Soul to soul while the years fell past;
>
> . . .
>
> But now, you are twain, you are cloven apart;
> Flesh of his flesh, but heart of my heart;
> And deep in one is the bitter root,
> And sweet for one is the lifelong flower.
>
> (st. 6 and 13)

And so, to the marine Venus:

> O fair green-girdled mother of mine,
> Sea, that art clothed with the sun and the rain,
> Thy sweet hard kisses are strong like wine,
> Thy large embraces are keen like pain.
> Save me and hide me with all thy waves,
> Find me one grave of thy thousand graves,
> Those pure cold populous graves of thine,
> Wrought without hand in a world without stain.
>
> (st. 34)

Late in the poem, to generalize the adolescent fantasy of dying for the loved one, Swinburne recalls the troubadour Rudel, who fell in love with the Princess of Tripoli, set out for her duchy, saw her, and died in her smile.

> There lived a singer in France of old,
> By the tideless dolorous midland sea.
> In a land of sand and ruin and gold
> There shone one woman, and none but she.

(The troubadours were viewed in the nineteenth century as the originators of romantic love.)

The second poem, "Les Noyades," presents a similar strategy; this is a rapid balladish version of an incident from the French Revolution that had been vividly reported by Thomas Carlyle. Carrier, an agent of the Revolution, is sent to suppress a revolt in Nantes. To dispose of the numerous prisoners he adopts a "final solution," having many supporters of the *ancien régime* placed on board ships on the Loire, which are then sunk: "daylight . . . witnesses Noyades: women and men are tied together, feet and feet, hands and hands; and flung in: this they call *Mariage Républicain*." In Swinburne, though nowhere else, Carrier appears as a destructive androgyne: "A queen of men, with helmeted hair." A young worker and a noble "maiden, wonderful, white" are bound together and the young man exults in this consummation through death. The speaker in the poem breaks away from the past into the present and imagines himself and his lost love being driven down from the Loire to the sea:

> We should yield, go down, locked hands and feet,
> Die, drown together, and breath catch breath;
>
> (st. 19)

but the poem twists at the end:

> But you would have felt my soul in a kiss,
>
> . . .
>
> And I would have given my soul for this
> To burn for ever in burning hell.

The last poem of this trilogy, "A Leave-Taking," is ceremoniously controlled, but concludes with the same wish, dissolution in the sea. The theme of incest and sacrifice is pursued in "Itylus." "Anactoria," which follows, is a monologue of the Lesbian poet Sappho modeled on the tirades of Ovid's "Sappho to Phaon" and Alexander Pope's baroque "Eloisa to Abelard." The couplets often fall into an Augustan mode, in which the balanced phrases are underscored by alliteration:

> Bade sink the spirit and the flesh aspire,
> Pain animate the dust of dead desire,
>
> (179–180)

Sappho's obsession with Anactoria's image is mimed in the recurring rhymes of some couplets that fracture Augustan decorum. Sappho represents the most frenetic example of the desire to restore primitive unity by means of a violent mingling with the beloved, but love turns to the wish to violate what is loved, as in the witty couplet that transforms sterile love into art:

> Take thy limbs living, and new-mould with these
> A lyre of many faultless agonies?
>
> (139–140)

But art too is as sterile as love, its emblem for Anactoria. Sappho's hatred extends to "the mute melancholy lust of heaven" and God: "Him would I reach, him smite, him desecrate." Finally, self-violation ensues, and Sappho hurls herself into the "insuperable" sea. "Anactoria" had touched on the failure of immortality through art; death and immortality are the themes of the "Hymn to Proserpine," a monologue spoken by a pagan at the close of the ancient world, who is caught between worlds.

In "Hermaphroditus" Swinburne exploits a Pre-Raphaelite derangement of a tradition, that of lyrics and sonnets closely related to the visual arts.[8] Like Rossetti, Swinburne does not use the genre merely to exalt art over nature, or to argue a hierarchy of arts, or make a "picturesque" attempt to reproduce visual effects in language. Rossetti, for example, invariably *interprets* the image, relating his poem to a particular work of art, considered as capturing "a moment's monument." "Hermaphroditus" is based on a statue in the Louvre with female breasts and male genitals, reclining on a couch in ambiguous posture. The literary source is Ovid's recounting of the tale of Salmacis and Hermaphroditus, who blend into one androgynous being in water. Rossetti had described picture and poem as bearing "the same relation to each other as beauty does in man and woman: the point of meeting where the two are identical is the supreme perfection." The "beauty" of the picture is reciprocated by the "identical"—if superficially dissimilar—"beauty" of the poem, resulting in an indivisible ideal unity, comparable only to the state of love. In Rossetti's sonnets for pictures of women, the metaphor is actualized as an encounter between observer-poet and portrait-beloved. Swinburne's own prose interpretation connects "Hermaphroditus" with art and the artist. Of his friend Simeon Solomon's painting *My Soul and I*, Swinburne wrote: "[It] contains both the idea of the separation of male and female qualities and their union as body and soul. . . . " And of Solomon's iconography in general, "In almost all of these there is perceptible the same profound suggestion of . . . the identity of contraries." (Swinburne's "Erotion" originated in a picture of Solomon's.) The Pre-Raphaelite hermaphrodite stems from the male-female union of the epiphany of the woman soul to the young painter in Rossetti's "Hand and Soul."[9] Swinburne's response is

poised between the optimism and pessimism that the hermaphrodite image generated in the nineteenth century:

> A strong desire begot on great despair,
> A great despair cast out by strong desire.
>> (st. 1)

"Fragoletta" or "little strawberry" prolongs the same theme and is followed by two poems that introduce the tyrannies of the religion of law: "A Litany" presents an Old Testament God who speaks a threatening first antiphon and the human response slavishly echoes both syntax and rhyme. "Faustine," a tour de force of forty-one stanzas, pivoting on the proper name at the end of each, is another critical presentation of the fatal woman: the transformation of a contemporary into the Empress Faustine, beautiful and vicious in legend. Like all fatal women, continuously reincarnated, she becomes victim of men's images of her. In his notes Swinburne refers to her as "doomed as though by accident from the first to all evil and no good, through many ages and forms, but clad always in the same type of fleshly beauty." This is followed by another poem for a painting, "Before the Mirror," designed to accompany James MacNeil Whistler's *The Little White Girl*, which shows a girl in profile leaning on a mantelpiece while her reflection in three-quarter view in the mirror reveals a pensive, perhaps suffering expression. The elegy for Walter Savage Landor and the ode to one of Swinburne's constant heroes, Victor Hugo, celebrate two figures who championed private and public liberty and so extend the concept of freedom from the religious to the social and political plane. At this climactic stage of *Poems and Ballads* we encounter three closely interrelated poems: "Dolores," "The Garden of Proserpine," and "Hesperia."

"Dolores" is the most notorious poem of the volume, a lyric of frenzied negations devoted to the madonna of sado-masochism, a parody almost of the fatal woman theme: Medusa's or Lamia's head has become suspiciously similar to that of Mr. Dick's King Charles in *David Copperfield*. In "Faustine," "Les Noyades," or "Laus Veneris" we witness the transformation by guilt of woman from either past or present into *femme fatale*. In "Dolores" the image in itself is convoked. Each individual stanza is possessed by that rhythm of tumescence and detumescence that flows and ebbs through "Anactoria." His letters indicate that Swinburne sometimes

---

[8]The genre goes back to Homer's Shield of Achilles, the sixteenth book of the Greek Anthology, and to Renaissance "gallery" poems. Typically, Swinburne parodies Rossetti's sonnets for pictures.

[9]Another source is Théophile Gautier's *Mademoiselle de Maupin* (Paris, 1835).

considered "Dolores" as a "black" joke: "Thy skin changes country and color, / And shrivels or swells to a snake's." The poem ends with the promise that death will bring "the joys of thee seventy times seven, / Our Lady of Pain," regardless of any belief or blankness about immortality, hell, or heaven. The conclusion of "Anactoria" is parodied. The coda is exhaustion, but also purgation. In "The Garden of Proserpine," Thanatos, a severe Greek angel, is welcome after Eros in all his wilder shapes:

> Pale, beyond porch and portal,
>   Crowned with calm leaves, she stands
> Who gathers all things mortal
>   With cold immortal hands;
>   . . .
> She waits for each and other,
>   She waits for all men born;
>   . . .
> From too much love of living,
>   From hope and fear set free,
> We thank with brief thanksgiving
>   Whatever Gods may be
> That no life lives for ever;
> That dead men rise up never;
> That even the weariest river
>   Winds somewhere safe to sea.
>
> (st. 7, 8, and 11)

"Hesperia" alludes to that land in the west of the fortunate dead and pleasant memories, reigned over by Proserpine. The poem's rhythms contrast with its two predecessors by slow authority, as of sea music, the second short half of every first and third line finishing with an inflexing feminine rhyme, the breaking wave. After the feral interiors of "Dolores" and the windless void of Proserpine's garden, the reascent from the experiences recorded in the whole volume is marked now by memories of wind and the sea, of wild riding, and, associated with the healing presence of the Venus Anadyomene, of the one woman who underlay all images of loss, hatred, and compensation,

> Thee I behold as a bird borne in with the wind from
>   the west,
>   Straight from the sunset, across white waves whence
>   rose as a daughter
>   Venus thy mother, in years when the world was a
>   water at rest.
>
> (10–12)

transfigured now synesthetically into a muse: "Thy silence as music, thy voice as an odour that fades in a flame." The speaker hopes that the loved woman will understand and pity, but not love; for love, he has proved, is "As the cross that a wild nun clasps till the edge of it bruises her bosom" (validating the comparison of "Anactoria" with "Eloisa and Abelard"). Dolores is transcended and the poem concludes with a memory of Swinburne's reckless horse-riding with Mary, creating a future of its own.

The two translated love songs that follow are of appropriate lightness; "Félise," a dramatic monologue, is spoken by a young man to a somewhat older woman, after a year's absence from one another. Swinburne commented that he had expressed their story "Plainly and 'cynically' enough! Last year I loved you Félise and you were puzzled, and didn't love me—quite." The poem affects the reader—as other diffused poems do not—as overelongated, though the young man is playing rather cruelly. The intention is to present a new "mask," one of control over the personality, but the drift into a familiar antitheism undercuts the objectivity. "Hendecasyllabics"—following "An Interlude" of spring—has art, winter, and endurance as its themes and, like its companion piece, "Sapphics," the stress on exercise indicates distance and control. "Sapphics" also "corrects" "Anactoria" in its ritual, chastened version of Sappho's death:

> By the grey sea-side, unassuaged, unheard of,
> Unbeloved, unseen in the ebb of twilight,
> Ghosts of outcast women return lamenting,
>   Purged not in Lethe.
>
> (st. 19)

The loose progression of the volume is continued with the ballads whose subject foreshadows that of Swinburne's next major work, *Atalanta in Calydon,* in particular that of "The Bloody Son," a tale of fratricide and exile. The new work centers on the tyranny (and death) of the family.

V

To write a play in the style of the Greek tragic poets was not unusual in nineteenth-century England; but the form was often used to evade the realities of the contemporary scene. Swinburne, however, used it to confront, if obliquely, his own age. The principal sources for *Atalanta in Calydon* are Homer, Ovid's *Metamorphoses,* and the extant fragments of Euripides' *Meleager*. The legend runs: Althaea, Queen of Calydon, pregnant with her first child, Meleager, dreams that she has given birth to a firebrand. The three Fates attend his birth and prophesy that he will be strong and fortunate and will live as long as a brand, at that time in the fire. His mother plucks out the brand and guards it. While Meleager is away with Jason's Argonauts, his father, King Oeneus, sacrifices to all the gods but Artemis. In revenge Artemis stirs up various tribes to fight against the Calydonians, and becomes still more angry when Oeneus defeats his enemies. She then sends a wild boar to Calydon that ravages the land, killing many who attempt to hunt it down. Men come from all over Greece to try their hand at destroying this beast. With them comes Atalanta, a virgin, who is highly favored by Artemis. For Atalanta's sake Artemis allows the boar to be killed. Atalanta pierces the beast with her spear and then Meleager kills it, presenting its carcass to Atalanta, with whom he has fallen in love. Althaea's brothers, Toxeus and Plexippus, who have already grumbled hugely about Atalanta's presence on the hunt, attempt to take the spoil from her, but Meleager protects Atalanta and kills the pair of them. On hearing this Althaea in a frenzy of rage takes the brand and throws it into the fire. As the brand (clearly connected with sexual identity) is consumed, so Meleager wastes away and dies and his mother dies soon after him, broken with grief, though in Swinburne's play she suffers a "symbolic" death only.

Atalanta can be structurally related to the formal design of Greek tragedy: prologos, parodos, episode, stasimon, exodos. Of the three extant tragic poets, Swinburne apparently most admired Aeschylus; but to detect Aeschylus as model is difficult. Swinburne does not use the chorus to carry portions of the narrative, nor does he attempt any Aeschylean reconciliation of human and divine order. At the close of the *Oresteia*, moreover, the old goddesses, the Furies, are persuaded to yield by new patriarchal gods; in *Atalanta* the female principle triumphs, nominally Artemis, though there must be doubt as to her precise nature, while the symbolic destruction of Althaea qualifies the triumph. Some have proffered unconvincing Sophoclean readings of the play as asserting a "golden mean" that Althaea, Atalanta, and Meleager all violate: but this would deny the work any modern element and in any case this is a reading of Sophocles no competent commentator would now wish to maintain: those who advise

moderation or *sophrosyne* (Ismene in the *Antigone*, Chrysothemis in the *Electra*) are shown to be morally inferior to the absolutists. Swinburne is closer to Euripides in sometimes using the chorus as lyrical refreshment or mirror of the action. The chorus beginning, "O that I now, I too were / By deep wells and water-floods" clearly recalls the famous chorus in the *Hippolytus:* "Would that I might hide in the secret hollows of the mountains," representing a similar moment of evasion. There is, however, no *deus ex machina* in *Atalanta*. More broadly, Swinburne's moral tone is often as mysterious as that of Euripides.[10]

The choric odes are not merely Greekish but often susceptible to precise Greek metrical analysis. Swinburne makes extensive use of what are now called the aeolic meters, whose nucleus is the choriamb: -uu-, with or without variables on either side. He was probably thinking of anapests rather than dactyls, perhaps unfortunately, since he considered that anapests were as natural in English as dactyls were alien.

In *Atalanta* the chorus sometimes gives a lyrical formulation to the inner feelings of the protagonists. They begin with the innocently hopeful "When the hounds of spring are on winter's traces," chanted at dawn: if light follows dark, spring, winter—the boar must surely be killed. This motif is counterpointed immediately by Althaea's assertion of a determined cycle of pain and pleasure to which men's lives are confined. But even in the opening chorus, the implication of such a cycle troubles the imagery: "scare / The wolf that follows, the fawn that flies," resolved by Althaea's "Night, a black hound, follows the white fawn day." Criticism has remarked a further structural element: the conflict between the dialectic public world of the iambic meter and the Dionysiac world of the choric. The chorus' exuberance dwindles finally to a curt, bleak utterance: the lords of life, whoever they may be, have a kingdom of "strong hands," reflecting on the pitiful manly strength of Meleager and the brothers (and perhaps on the pitiful diminutiveness of Swinburne himself).

This larger structural device is supported by iterative imagery. Swinburne has as usual been accused here of infatuation with certain words, but the repetitions are deliberate and regulated: night/day; spring/winter; male/female; flower/blossom/bud;

---

[10]Oddly enough, as Swinburne detested that "Zola of the fifth century."

hard/soft; and, at the play's onset, are invoked in the persons of Artemis and Apollo, moon and sun. Contrapuntal words that dominate are "fire," associated with Althaea, and "snow" and "whiteness," Atalanta's properties as surrogate of Artemis. But these images are not polarized merely; they are also ambiguous in the play's plural world. Fire is alluded to as purging disease—the boar is to be "consumed"; but fire also destroys life, Meleager's life. Atalanta is a snowy *rose*. In terms of character, Althaea is passionate and unforgiving; Atalanta, for all her desolating purity, is at the end still capable of pity.

> Hail thou: but I with heavy face and feet
> Turn homeward and am gone out of thine eyes.
> (2310–2311)

The simplest reading of the play is to isolate Althaea as agent in a *Sons and Lovers* situation. Swinburne was fascinated by matriarchal, aristocratic figures subtly controlling their families. Althaea is a tragic version of the ruthless antiromantic Lady Midhurst of *Love's Cross Currents*. But among Swinburne's aims in *Atalanta* was that of excluding the overtly modern and discursive. To achieve this he had to subdue the autobiographical and the amusement of attacking the Christian God under veil of complaint about the Greek pantheon. To be sure, Althaea and Meleager are pivotal figures: Althaea is both passionately and intensely stoical, distrustful of the gods. For her, life has "much to be endured and little to be enjoyed." One must be wary, attempt to sustain patterns of civility, kingdom, and family, our only refuge in a cruel world: the Victorian parallels are clear. Althaea belongs with those who practice restraint and distrust nature. Her husband, King Oeneus, plays an oddly muted part. A compromiser, past his best, he attempts to mediate with "soft obstetric hand" between Meleager and Althaea:

> Nor thee I praise, who art fain to undo things done:
> Nor thee, who art swift to esteem them overmuch.
> (627–628)

These well-meaning banalities are futile. Althaea's two brothers are presented rather as rugby club hearties, thrusting their virility at everyone. On Atalanta their genial comment is that the only justification for virgins is that their throats can be cut for purposes of sacrifice. Such beefy conservatism strongly contrasts with the intelligent conservatism of Althaea. Swinburne was not one of those arrogant radicals who assume that all reactionaries are by definition stupid.

Atalanta herself has all the passivity of the fatal woman: she does not tempt Meleager, though it is through her that Althaea and Artemis destroy him. Indeed, Althaea cooperates with Meleager in creating Atalanta's fatal woman aspect:

> She the strange woman, she the flower, the sword,
> Red from spilt blood, a mortal flower to men,
> Adorable, detestable—even she
> Saw with strange eyes and with strange lips rejoiced.
> (1692–1695)

Does Althaea detect some numinous tinge about Atalanta? She fears her because Atalanta is literally a stranger, a foreigner, outside the warm structure of family and kingdom but, more profoundly, strange as a virgin by vocation, one who lives in the white shadow of Artemis. Atalanta has evaded the roles that give woman social identity: she does not weave and breed as do other women: she hunts with men. But Althaea is also distrustful of romantic love as such; it is, by Greek tradition, a disaster; its strict correlative, pain, so the chorus chants: "For an evil blossom is born / Of sea-foam and the frothing of blood," alluding apparently to Aphrodite's birth (and Atalanta's effect on Meleager) but with dramatic irony defining Althaea: "For they knew thee for mother of love, / And knew thee not mother of death."

What of Meleager's attitudes? A plausible suggestion is that he anticipates the aestheticism so eloquently expressed in Pater's "Conclusion" to *Studies in the History of the Renaissance* (1873). Meleager too recognizes the inevitability of a pleasure-pain cycle, that life becomes more flame-like from the fact that "each man, dying, is earth and shadow; the nothing sinks into nothingness," to cite the fragment from Euripides' *Meleager* that Swinburne prefixed to his play. Meleager's response is that the individual must seize on the good moment before the cycle returns to pain. He embodies the Dionysiac reverberation of the opening chorus: not to lay hold of joy "on this short day of frost and sun," is "to sleep before evening." But that seizure precisely brings Meleager to sleep before evening; it is the dim Oeneus who survives. Yet Meleager chooses joy, love, and, it has been suggested, in Paterian mode, art. At the close of the Greek play that *Atalanta* most resembles, the *Hippolytus* of Euripides, as the virgin Artemis leaves the dying hero, he addresses her as a Madonna come to witness his *pietà:* "thou leavest me now, blessed virgin," but Artemis is void of power to ease his pain; she can say only that if gods could weep, she would. Hippolytus asks the human auditors to cover his face with his cloak that he may retain dignity in the last anguish. Atalanta, a mortal, though Artemis' double, can feel pity and more. Meleager asks her:

> But thou, dear, hide my body with thy veil,
> And with thy raiment cover foot and head,
> And stretch thyself upon me and touch hands
> With hands and lips with lips. . . .
>
> (2298–2301)

It is a traditional orgasm-as-death passage (very close to a similar passage in Torquato Tasso's *Aminta,* but also to Wagner's *Tristan*). Meleager does not die alone; this is communion, a life-enhancing ritual moment; life measured not by length but intensity; life as the end of life, in this mime of the sexual act, a ghostly Eros. Pater is again relevant: "With this sense of the splendour of our experience and of its awful brevity, gathering all we are into one desperate effort to see and touch." Such insight brings Meleager joy and death. He forgives Althaea, recognizing that she can only act out the antinomies of her role:

> . . . thou too, queen,
> The source and end, the sower and the scythe,
> The rain that ripens and the drought that slays . . .
>
> . . .
>
> To make me and unmake me—thou, I say,
> Althaea, since my father's ploughshare, drawn
> Through fatal seedbed of a female field
> Furrowed thy body . . . I
>
> . . .
>
> Hail thee as holy and worship thee as just
> Who art unjust and unholy . . .
>
> . . .
>
> . . . me too thou hast loved, and I
> Thee; but this death was mixed with all my life,
> Mine end with my beginning.
>
> (2210–2212; 2214–2217; 2221–2222; 2237–2239)

Althaea in destroying Meleager destroys her role and herself: "I am severed from myself, my name is gone," and employs for the last time the image of fire: "My name that was a healing, it is changed, / My name is a consuming. / From this time . . . / My lips shall not unfasten till I die." So she has no words for Meleager's last speech. As L. Wymer observes, she suffers a death-in-life that epiphanizes her past life and role. Ironically she has become her own image of Atalanta: a stranger to herself and her son. The play, indeed, abounds with the words "division," "cleave": in Meleager's dying speech, for example, "I sprang and cleft the closure of thy womb."

The ancient form acts as challenge and discipline: Swinburne achieved in *Atalanta in Calydon* an effect paralleled by *Samson Agonistes.* In either case the poet, without violating the Greek norms, arrives at a highly personal tragic insight. Just as Milton's blindness gives acuity to his drama of temptation, so Swinburne's peculiar psychology enables him to realize the price that a weak-bodied aesthete must pay in a world without gods or personal immortality.

VI

MANY nineteenth-century poets were deeply involved in romantic politics. Reacting from the Enlightenment and its instrument, the internationalist French Revolution, there emerged a nationalism of the "sacred soil," of ancestors "who stemmed with their own bodies" the invader. Nations were defined by wars of independence, first in Germany, then on that most sacred soil of all, the Greek. Byron's effort and death for Hellenism became profoundly symbolic. The "Young Ireland" group of poets and politicians and the Italian *Risorgimento* form part of this same vivid movement. The first phase of the *Risorgimento,* or "resurrection," associated with Swinburne's master Mazzini, was, however, strongly tinged with notions from the Enlightenment. But by the later 1860's, when Swinburne was composing most of his *Songs Before Sunrise,* the Italian struggle had mutated into a more narrow nationalism.

Songs Before Sunrise is Swinburne's celebration of the *Risorgimento* as it moved toward its climax in the loss by "Pius Iscariot" (so Swinburne called Pius IX) of the Patrimony of Peter to the kingdom of Italy. The models are Walt Whitman and Hugo's *Les Châtiments.* Swinburne's republican zeal can be detected as early as 1852, the date of his first surviving political poem. The strategy of *Songs Before Sunrise* is to appropriate the rhetoric of ecclesiastical tyranny, of typology also, to dignify Italy and republicanism. Despite the political reality, the *Risorgimento* is presented here as part of a world process, in which man creates himself God through aggregation to a perfect society: "Love, the beloved republic." These notions were widespread among "advanced" men of letters. As one of Swinburne's contemporaries put it:

Every great poet of the last half century is loud in this demand for liberty of passion and liberty of action—freedom of the individual will. But if the individual be thus free, what guarantee is there that he will not injure his neighbour and reduce society to chaos? The answer is that love is the harmonizer of the passions, and that large idea of friendship—the universal brotherhood of democracy—the harmonizer of human action.[11]

Italy becomes Madonna, the people Christ; the republic, a Christ in the tomb. This rhetoric (its polemics have interesting connections with those of Blake) functions sometimes successfully, sometimes with results as grotesque as those of Richard Crashaw's deliberate confusions of spiritual and physical: in "Blessed Among Women" we learn that Italy is "four times blest, / At whose most holy breast / Four times a godlike soldier-savior hung."

The contents fall into three broad categories, the weakest celebrating topical events in the war for liberty. "The Ride from Milan" veers toward doggerel; the odes are tumid merely. But the quasi-philosophic poems such as "Genesis," "Mater Triumphalis," and "Hertha," which combine evolutionary themes with a mystical pantheism, are surprisingly impressive. "Hertha," for example, asserts the mother-creative principle against the false creator-god of Blake, who seeks to limit men, by imposing on them the identity of servants. Yet it is when all large abstractions melt into some sense of the sacred actualities of Italy, as in "Siena" (evoking St. Catherine of Siena's voluptuous trances of a vicarious suffering, no less than her public role as rebuker of great men and mentor of popes); or in the inevitable but still piercing comparison of Italy with Israel in bondage, "Super Flumina Babylonis," that Swinburne remains most moving. In "Christmas Antiphones," he appropriates the Christian form of the carol with a conspicuous success. And the rhythms are subtle still, as

[11]John Todhunter, Reading University (England), MS 202/4/3/1.

in this stylized grief, some peasant woman released by the wordless rocking of the body:

Who is this that sits by the way, by the wild wayside,
In a rent stained garment, the robe of a cast-off bride,
In the dust, in the rainfall sitting, with soiled feet bare,
With the night for a garment upon her, with torn wet hair?
She is fairer of face than the daughters of men, and her eyes,
Worn through with her tears are deep as the depth of skies.
("Mater Dolorosa," st. 1)

Swinburne perhaps had reservations about Mazzini's practical failure: his distrust of materialism (and so of material means). There is a curious episode in *Lesbia Brandon* involving Mazzini's surrogate, Attilio Mariani. Of Mariani we read that "even the sublime vanity of martyrs has its weak side," and on his death he bequeaths the hero two books, whose titles point to contradictions in Mazzini's personality: the memoirs of Felice Orsini and Stendhal's *La Chartreuse de Parme*.

VII

FEW people think of Swinburne as the author of prose fiction, yet he published one striking novella, *Love's Cross Currents*, while two substantial fragments, *Lucretia Borgia: The Chronicle of Tebaldeo Tebaldei* and *Lesbia Brandon*, have since been edited from manuscript. . There is also a short story, "Dead Love," in Morris' early manner; a considerable fragment of a novel in French, and two shorter, highly amusing French burlesques: *La Fille du Policeman*, a tale, and an unfinished play, *La Soeur de la Reine*.

Written early in the 1860's, *Love's Cross Currents* appeared in serial (and abbreviated) form in 1877 under the pseudonym of Mrs. Horace Manners, possibly on account of its situations representing a refinement of those played out on the Isle of Wight between Swinburnes and Gordons. *Love's Cross Currents* offers us an aristocratic family group, complexly interrelated with violent emotions of hate and affinity, but with its members necessarily united against the bourgeois world. After a prologue detailing the web of relationships, the narrative is unfolded through letters in the manner made popular in the eighteenth century. The two principal figures are Lady Midhurst, now in her early sixties, ruthless, intelligent, patrician heir of the Enlightenment, and

Mrs. Clara Radworth, in her later twenties, less intelligent, more passionate, married to a dull husband and impatient of the family game. These two ladies conduct a struggle over one of Lady Midhurst's grandchildren, Reginald Harewood (a character who bears some resemblance to the author). Reginald, responding to some not too veiled encouragement, has fallen in love with Clara. Lady Midhurst wishes to break up this relationship, partly because it threatens family stability, partly because she is fond of Reginald. That the affair is so far technically innocent is irrelevant: it may provoke a scandal. Moreover the role of lap-dog barely suits Redgie's style: it makes him much less amusing. Lady Midhurst's other problem is her granddaughter, Reginald's half-sister, who has married Clara's cousin, Lord Cheyne (with whom Clara has herself been in love). Amicia, a dim, glimmering creature of Pre-Raphaelite aspect, possibly echoes Rossetti's wife, Lizzie Siddall. She and Clara's brother, Frank, had once loved one another, meet again, have an affair. The plot becomes as tortuous as any Restoration comedy of intrigue and is drastically resolved. Lord Cheyne is drowned and Frank inherits the great house and title. Clara believes she has triumphed doubly over Lady Midhurst. But Lady Midhurst then discloses that Amicia is pregnant, actually by Frank, who, though all the family become aware of the child's true father, loses by his own precipitancy both house and title. A suavely bullying Lady Midhurst now dissolves her other problem by threatening to show Redgie some letters written by Clara when infatuated with a Frenchman. These will conflict with the image Clara has imposed on her admirer. Clara is forced to send Redgie about his business in cold terms.

Though the tone of *Love's Cross Currents* is French rather than English, its social ambiance is immediately convincing: Swinburne really knew those country houses. Finely characterized though Mrs. Radworth is, Lady Midhurst, with her tart brilliance, is among the most pungent characters in the Victorian novel, sustaining comparison with the Countess de Saldar, Mrs. Brookenham, or even Becky Sharp. Swinburne evokes her in rich phrase: "she worried him with dexterous feline mouth" (Lady Midhurst at the dinner table). A character in *Lesbia Brandon* (in which Lady Midhurst also appears) mistakenly opines that "she is nothing now but husks and fangs." Clara is equally overconfident and mistaken when she observes that Lady Midhurst has "fallen into a sort of hashed style, between a French *portière* and a Dickens nurse," for Lady Midhurst is always stylish, even when, after Cheyne's death, she gives her tepid granddaughter stoical advice. We may believe that Swinburne endorses every pagan word: "All slavishness, whether of body or spirit, leaves a taint where it touches. It is as bad to be servile to God as it is to be servile to man. Accept what you must accept, and obey where you must obey, but make no pretense of a free-will offering." More characteristic is the radiant malice in her dismissal of Clara, whom she not merely triumphs over by letter, but actually visits to enjoy the aesthetics of a visible defeat.

To use her own style, she is *dead beat*, and quite safe; viciously resigned. . . . She would have me racked if she could, no doubt, but received me smiling from the tips of her teeth outwards, and with a soft dry pressure of the fingers. Not a hint of anything kept back. . . . I have no doubt she will set all her wits to work and punish him for her failure. She will hardly get up a serious affair again, or it might be a charity to throw her some small animal by way of lighter food. It would not surprise me if she fell to philanthropic labour, or took some devotional drug by way of stimulant. The *bureau d'amourettes* is a bankrupt concern, you see: her sensation-shop is closed for good. I prophesy she will turn a decent worrying wife of the simpler Anglican breed; home-keeping, sharp-edged, earnestly petty and drily energetic. Negro-worship now, or foreign missions, will be about her mark; perhaps too a dash and sprinkle of religious feeling, with the chill just off; with a mild pinch of the old Platonic mixture now and then to flavour and leaven her dead lump of life. . . . Pity she had not more stock in hand to start with.

(ch. 30)

The success of *Love's Cross Currents* owes much to the dry clarity enforced on it by the epistolary form: the "avenging buds of the birch" barely emerge, and Swinburne's perpetual awareness of the inbreeding subject is muted and comically modulated. He preserves all the immediacy of the novel in letters, though the range of characters is sufficient to evade the implausibities inherent in the form that troubled the eighteenth-century practitioners. Among mid-Victorian fiction it remains unique: a welcome alternative to the prevailing idealism or didacticism; a relief from the heavy "aesthetic teaching" of a George Eliot.

Lesbia Brandon is a more ambitious work, but too fragmentary to grasp as a whole. Swinburne is inconsistent about dates, and dates are important here, while the family interrelationships have become still more dramatically intricate: Denham, the tutor, in himself an interesting creation, in love with Lady Wariston, after some years somewhat implausibly becomes her lover, and the aged, sadistic Linley (a male counterpart of Lady Midhurst without her affections) reveals that Denham is Lady Wariston's half-brother, a disclosure quite in the mode of contemporary "sensation" novelists such as Mary Elizabeth Braddon. There is a distinct sense of *déjà vu:* this cerebral androgyne, this sadistic tutor, the sexual play of sister with pretty younger brother—all have been met before, expressed with more authority, in *Poems and Ballads*. But *Lesbia Brandon* reads well. Lady Midhurst makes a subordinate but vivid appearance; the lengthy fragment is full of a sharp and detailed eloquence of landscape and psychological casuistry: Linley with his "horrible delicacy of ear"; Denham, frustrated in his love, beating Lady Wariston's young brother with additional savagery because of the haunting difference between Herbert and his sister. Herbert's dream is a brilliant adolescent case study:

He saw the star of Venus, white and flower-like as he had always seen it, turn into a white rose and come down out of heaven, with a reddening centre that grew as it descended liker and liker a living mouth; but instead of desire he felt horror and sickness at the sight of it, and averted his lips with an effort to utter some prayer or exorcism; vainly, for the dreadful mouth only laughed, and came closer. And cheek or chin, eyebrow or eye, there was none; only this mouth. . . .

(ch. 7)

Was Swinburne an important novelist *manqué?* Possibly the more objective form of the novel might have distanced the aggressively autobiographical had he persisted. Could he have achieved a *bildungsroman?* I incline to doubt it, though we must regret that the impossibility of an audience constrained him finally to abandon *Lesbia Brandon,* which is best regarded as the brilliant detritus of the poetry of the middle 1860's. When that poetry was written, there was little need for the novel, yet one would surely be content to exchange most of Swinburne's later verse for an achieved *Lesbia Brandon.*

VIII

THAT later verse can be summarily discussed. The second series of *Poems and Ballads* is a good miscellaneous volume: some pieces, such as "Ave Atque Vale," a dreamily eloquent memorial poem on Baudelaire whose theme reverses that of "Laus Veneris," were written in the middle 1860's. Another admirable poem, "A Forsaken Garden," has been well described as "symbolizing a total world beyond death and time realized through art alone": first of a kind of ideal autobiographical musing over those earlier years when Swinburne's emotional life had been most intense: "What lies before me is my past." In such a vein, he nearly always writes commandingly: "Thalassius" and "On the Cliffs" in later collections. This volume contains also a distinguished group of translations from François Villon, though Swinburne discreetly replaced certain lines by asterisks in his published version of "La Belle Heaulmière." His finest translation from Villon did not appear until 1964 in "The Ballad of Villon and Fat Madge," where the earthier and exuberantly comic aspects of Swinburne's genius, too often muted, are at last released:

When all's made up she drops me a windy word,
　　Bloat like a beetle, puffed and poisonous:
Grins, thumps my pate, and calls me dickey-bird,
　　And cuffs me with a fist that's ponderous.
　　We sleep like logs, being drunken both of us;
Then when we wake her womb begins to stir;
To save her seed she gets me under her
　　Wheezing and whining flat as planks are laid:
And thus she spoils me as whoremonger
　　Inside this brothel where we drive our trade.
(*New Writings by Swinburne*, pp. 13–14)

The grimly wry and direct confessional note is brilliantly caught.

Four years later appeared the last major volume, *Tristram of Lyonesse and Other Poems*. In the title poem, Swinburne outdoes Tennyson's "Idylls of the Prince Consort," particularly "The Last Tournament" (1871), where Tristram and Iseult, as servants of Tennyson's cautionary tale against adultery, become coarse echoes of Launcelot and Guenevere: emblems of the autumnal moment of Arthur's court. By contrast, Swinburne presents them as guiltless, absolute for love, and wins a nice debating point by recounting how Modred is the fruit of Arthur's adultery with Morgause. Tennyson's presentation of Mark is nastily effective; Swinburne presents the King sympathetically, so intensifying the love-hate role of Iseult of Brittany. The architectonic of *Tristram of Lyonesse* depends on a cyclic rhythm of months and the larger rhythms of the sea acting out a tragic determinism. The repetition of certain words and phrases has been not inaptly compared with the leitmotifs of Wagner's luscious opera: "sea," "rose," "flame," "molten," "melting," and the image of unity through the four lips of the lovers becoming, at the close of the first canto, "one burning mouth" and "one silent mouth" at the last. Orgasm and death are associated, but with more tragic authority than in *Poems and Ballads*. The poem is too long: the third canto and the interspersed lyrics are mediocre, and the diction is not always satisfying. Still, despite all "languors and ardours," a strong and rapid narrative line remains; the meter acts like a funnel; the pace of the language carries one along and, for once, physical love is fulfillment. This prolonged hymn to erotic consummation remains the last irradiation of Swinburne's youth. From then on, though often skillful, Swinburne has increasingly less to say. Occasionally he hits on a new theme. It has been noted that he adds to the image of Pan so popular in the second half of the nineteenth century. In the three later poems devoted to the god, "A Nympholept," "Pan and Thalassius," and "The Palace of Pan," the goat-foot becomes ambiguous, close to Pater's presentation of Dionysus and Apollo. In Swinburne's version of him, Pan brings both terror and ecstasy, good and evil—so evading any sentimentalizing of nature. Recent criticism has with some justice pointed to the neglected achievements of Swinburne's later verse. It can hardly be denied that among the sad flux of the poetry after 1882 one can find impressive poems that have not been sufficiently remarked. "By the North Sea," for example, is one of the poet's most splendid offerings. Here, metrical brilliance is exercised in the evocation of a brooding underworld landscape that has only to be read once to haunt the memory.

IX

MOST of the great English critics have been practicing poets; immediate examples comprise Ben Jonson, John Dryden, Samuel Johnson, Wordsworth, Coleridge, John Keats, Matthew Arnold, and Yeats. To this select group, Swinburne belongs, though important rather than great in his criticism. T. S. Eliot has aptly summarized its virtues: Swinburne had read widely and discriminatingly. And with the great critics, he has this in common: one senses that the whole European literary tradition is for him a continuous presence. His value judgments are firm and lasting. Eliot has pointed also to Swinburne's

defects: his language, sometimes suggesting falsetto parody of his verse; hectic alliteration tangling with florid insult and rapture; his impatience with carrying through analysis; his refusal to focus rigorously on individual lines or images to make general points.

Such limitations partly rise from Swinburne's canons of criticism, which are both neoclassic and romantic. Neoclassic in that he believed in critical justice; in treating a work as a whole and in conversing with the reader by stating the pervasive general truth. This saves him from the disjunctive approach to Elizabethan drama of Charles Lamb and other earlier romantic critics, with their distillation of "specimens" and "beauties." Like Lamb, however, Swinburne is rarely aware that his texts are documents of the theater, created mostly under conditions of actual staging, not in some Parnassian airpump. In his later criticism particularly, Swinburne assumed the mannerism of Augustan prose with its pomp of periphrasis. His romantic aspect appears in an open-mindedness to originality, innovation, and difficulty. He was an enthusiast for George Chapman, Charlotte and Emily Brontë, Whitman—authors not precisely fashionable in the mid-nineteenth century. He was alert also to what was best (and worst) in his older and immediate contemporaries; but after 1879 he not merely failed to respond to younger contemporaries, he revoked some of his former generosities.

In the earlier criticism, he is sinuous in his sympathies. A devoted classicist, Swinburne found Shakespeare's *Troilus and Cressida* repulsive; he acutely senses that all the characters (with the possible exception of Ulysses) are flawed, even though he tends to identify Thersites' point of view with that of the author. Yet he can still refer to "this . . . mysterious and magnificent monster . . . one of the most admirable of all Shakespeare's works" at a time when few nineteenth-century critics could bring themselves even to discuss the play. In *A Study of Shakespeare* (1880), he takes a pioneering glance at the earlier quarto of *Hamlet*. About multiple authorship of the plays in the Shakespeare Folio, he is cautious: he finds that *Henry VIII* is Shakespeare's absolutely, and he refuses to enlarge the canon to admit the agreeable, anonymous *Edward III*, in a stylistic analysis of some length. His attacks on the New Shakespeare Society and on the yet wilder logic of certain German scholars are still funny and apposite. Himself an inspired amateur, Swinburne tended to have a low opinion of professional scholars. He knew as much, if not more than they, and the poetry was the thing. The oddity of his prose style often veils a luminous common sense about literary matters.

His dramatic criticism, is, however, less rewarding than his earlier essays on art and literature. The "Notes on Designs of the Old Masters at Florence" and the *Notes on the Royal Academy Exhibition, 1868,* with their lingering cadences and troubled images, influenced Pater (though Rossetti's prose is the archetype). Such evocations of works of art belong to a tradition of "impressionist" criticism that includes the aesthete and poisoner T. G. Wainewright, William Hazlitt, and Théophile Gautier. In this tradition, impressions could be both subject and aesthetic object simultaneously. If we compare Swinburne's evocations of particular artifacts with those of Pater, we discover that, while both remain eloquent and suggestive, Pater more frequently intuits elements in the picture or the sculpture apparently not available from the historical record or within the limits of the observer's temperament.

Of the literary essays, we may note that on *Les Fleurs du Mal,* contributed in 1862 to the *Spectator,* in which Swinburne recognizes that "those who will look for them may find moralities in plenty behind every poem of M. Baudelaire." But in what is a very early though not simple-minded statement of the "art for art's sake" position in England, he urges that it is not the business of art to teach *directly.* If an artist is scrupulous in matters of art, his work will involve a corresponding moral scrupulousness. The *William Blake* essay contains the mature exposition of Swinburne's "art for art's sake" views. We may conclude with this quotation: "Art is not like fire or water, a good servant and a bad master; rather the reverse. . . . Handmaid of religion, exponent of duty, servant of fact, pioneer of morality, she cannot in any way become. . . . Her business is not to do good on other grounds, but do good on her own: all is well with her while she sticks fast to that."

Swinburne's essay on Byron begins by praising the third and fourth cantos of *Childe Harold,* but then sharply insists that the great Byron is only to be found in the satires, broadly the modern view. The polemical *Notes on Poems and Reviews* (1866) and *Under the Microscope* (1872), Swinburne's contribution to the "fleshly school" controversy around Rossetti, are written in the avowedly biased tradition of the pamphlet and still make trenchant reading.

His *William Blake* is not merely essential for an understanding of Swinburne's work in the 1860's; it remains one of the major documents of nineteenth-century criticism. An intensely difficult author is sympathetically and intelligently handled. Swinburne dismisses at once the widely held contemporary opinion that the obscurity of Blake's writing and the eccentricity of his opinions originate in his madness. Introducing a commentary on the prophetic books, Swinburne did not succeed, perhaps hardly wished to, in uncovering their dark mythological scheme. He was handicapped also by not being aware of the *Four Zoas,* which would have provided something of a key. But he does analyze searchingly such a work as *The Marriage of Heaven and Hell,* which he considered to be Blake's greatest. But the heart of the volume lies in the first two sections: the "Life and Designs" and the "Lyrical Poems." His Blake is of course made in Swinburne's image; as Harold Bloom puts it: "an uneasy blend of Rousseau and De Sade, at once somehow an heroic naturalist and an erotic rebel straining against even the limits of nature in his vitalism." Swinburne seizes on any opportunity to stress pagan joy in Blake and recounts the oral report that Blake had suggested the introduction of a second wife into his household. Failure to grasp that, for Blake, nature and imagination were antithetical lies at the heart of Swinburne's fruitful misunderstanding of Blake. For Swinburne the antinatural was generally limited to the anticonventional. Morality for him remains polarized with art for art's sake; there is no middle view, no alternative. As one critic observes, he is "hamstrung by the very puritan tradition he is trying to shake off." Consequently he anticipates Yeats in making a gnostic of Blake, a sexual (but not ascetic) antinomian, for whom the erotic is demonic illusion. As the extract already quoted shows, the demiurge who

created the sexual and separate body of man did but cleave in twain "the divine humanity" . . . is a divine daemon, liable to error, subduable by and through this very created nature of his invention, which he for the present imprisons and torments. *His* law is the law of Moses, which according to the Manichean heresy Christ came to reverse as diabolic.
(*William Blake,* 1868 ed., pp. 155–156)

It is perhaps less that Swinburne misunderstands than that he diminishes Blake by imprisoning him in this simple dualism of preference for desire and energy over reason and restraint. Swinburne brilliantly but falsely interprets *The Marriage of Heaven and Hell* as an inversion of accepted values, not sensing that the "spiralling contraries" of that mélange of prose and verse are both necessary. Missing the two meanings of "hell" in "The Marriage," he actually invents two meanings of "nature" in *Jerusalem* and *Milton*, because his neo-Sadian theology requires that. Wonderful book though it is, the *William Blake* could have been a different, perhaps better work if Swinburne had not as usual paused at the point of moving beyond a Blake necessary for himself. He recognizes, for example, that the *Songs of Innocence and of Experience* are counterpointed, but does not proceed with the insight; and after one piece of actual exegesis of the prophetic books that is now generally accepted, Swinburne hastily flinches, "Lest, however, we be found unawares on the side of those hapless angels and baboons, we will abstain with all due care from any not indispensable analysis." Yet what Yeats was to term "the great procession of symbols" was surely indispensable.

X

SWINBURNE was a pertinacious author of poetic dramas. For this activity, the nineteenth century was barely auspicious. To isolate any single cause is difficult: there was the evangelical assault on the play and the player and the tyranny of Shakespeare, while English prose drama was itself in eclipse (painfully recovering in the 1860's with the work of Tom Taylor and Thomas Robertson). The English scene, moreover, had been unusually barren of good dramatic criticism. Although there were actor-managers ready to encourage poets, Tennyson and Browning achieved no more than moderate success. But Shelley and Thomas Beddoes, who wrote for private reading rather than performance, were more successful—could at least challenge the later Jacobeans. Swinburne follows their practice (we noted how in his own dramatic criticism he took little account of stage conditions).

His two early plays, *The Queen-Mother* and *Rosamond*, reveal Jacobean influence crossed with Pre-Raphaelitism. In either case, a strong matriarch, queens Catherine and Eleanor, destroys other women. The character of Denise, maid-in-waiting and devoted mistress to Henry III of France, is a triumph. *The Queen-Mother* pivots on her role as

the Queen's pawn in bringing on the King's involvement with the Bartholomew massacre and her reactions on realizing she has been misled. *Chastelard*, first of the Mary Stuart trilogy, is closely tuned with *Poems and Ballads*. Mary at once enjoys and detests her role as fatal woman; Chastelard himself is one who finds erotic consummation in death; but it is difficult for the reader to involve his emotions with either. The exposition is competent, the verse often striking, and the scene where Chastelard induces Mary to kiss him on the neck at the spot where he knows the axe will fall is luridly memorable. In *Bothwell* (1874) and *Mary Stuart* (1881), Swinburne perceptibly becomes more constrained by historical sources and more sympathetic to Mary, but in these plays her character is comparatively weakly projected. The later plays sometimes display routine skill in exploiting situation; but few of them now hold their interest. *The Sisters* (1892), however, has unusual qualities. Set ostensibly in 1816, it involves once more the close aristocratic world of *Love's Cross Currents* and is deeply autobiographical—the last reworking of the Mary Gordon story. The blank verse is relaxed:

Anne: April again, and not a word of war.
Last year, and not a year ago, it was
That we sat wondering when good news
would come.

Mabel: And had not heard or learnt in lesson-books
If such a place there was as Waterloo.

. . .

Reginald: We are lucky. There's the old laboratory,
made
It seems for our stage purpose, where you
know
Sir Edward kept his chemicals and things—
Collections of the uncanniest odds and
ends. . . .

(I.i; III.i)

That last epithet has a casual 1890's note. Swinburne should have realized that his general idiom was suitable for comedy or tragi-farce, but not for tragedy. Anne, the jealous, murdering sister, deviates into high blank verse and the play reaches a faltering climax through a holocaust, which, although set in a nineteenth-century drawing room, is worthy of Jacobean tragedy.

XI

SWINBURNE discovered his poetic identity through the distinction between personality and "self" trapped within personality, in his case an absurd body, without access to women. His solution was to transmute concrete being into artifice by imitation, parody, and caricature. In other words, he tried to release identity by remolding the styles of the past into an integrity that was of the surface only, and thus to achieve selfhood with the aid of tradition. But the price was negation of development; the quest for unity of being was broken off at a stage of precarious balance. This disequilibrium begins with *Songs Before Sunrise*, where the self is unlocated, is operatically merely voice. Such failure of the redemptive imagination in the middle years has precedents in romantic poetry; in, for example, Wordsworth and Coleridge, though both these poets were able to transfer loss into triumph. But Wordsworth, however unlike Swinburne in most respects, furnishes a model of genius mutating into low-keyed talent. Swinburne found no means of living out a mythology, or rather the self-mythology he could live by proved self-defeating. As a consequence Swinburne was not able to take up history and nation into the self-drama. He belonged to a dying class; there was no idea or group with which he could fruitfully identify, and this explains the abstractions and inconsistencies of his political attitudes. The price of negating development was that his work finally became pure surface over void. Those strict forms of rondeau and sonnet by which he sought to chasten an imagined abundance merely emphasized poverty. Fixed at the level of tension between personality and self, Swinburne failed to arrive at a notion of antiself "filling up all that the self fell short in." As a consequence the self was never reborn. Had Swinburne correctly read *The Marriage of Heaven and Hell*, he would have grasped that the dialectic of poetic development lay through "spiralling contraries."

SELECTED BIBLIOGRAPHY

I. BIBLIOGRAPHY. T. J. Wise, *A Bibliography of the Writings in Prose and Verse of A. C. Swinburne*, 2 vols. (London, 1919–1920); T. J. Wise, ed., *The Ashley Library: A Catalogue of Printed Books, Manuscripts and Autograph Letters*, 11 vols. (London, 1922–1936), vols. VI–X (1925–1930) contain Swinburne entries; T. J. Wise, *A Swinburne Library* (London, 1925), a repr. of vol. VI, privately printed, limited ed.; C. J. Hyder, *Swinburne's Literary Career and Fame* (Durham, N. C., 1933); J. Carter and H. G. Pollard, *An Enquiry Into the Nature of Certain Nineteenth-Century Pamphlets* (London, 1934), exposes Wise's forgeries of eds. of Swinburne; T. G. Ehrsam, R. H. Deily, and R. M. Smith, *Bibliographies of Twelve Victorian Authors* (New York, 1936); W. Partington, *Forging Ahead* (New York, 1939), enl. ed. titled *Thomas J. Wise in the Original Cloth* (London, 1946); J. Carter and H. G. Pollard, *The Firm of Charles Ottley, Landon & Co.: Footnote to An Enquiry* (London, 1948); F. E. Faverty, ed., *The Victorian Poets: A Guide to Research* (Cambridge, Mass., 1956; rev. ed. 1968), Swinburne studies are discussed by C. K. Hyder; W. B. Todd, "Swinburne Manuscripts at Texas," in *Texas Quarterly*, 2 (Autumn 1959), essays by J. Carter, H. G. Pollard, W. B. Todd; W. E. Fredeman, *Pre-Raphaelitism: A Bibliocritical Study* (Cambridge, Mass., 1965).

II. COLLECTED WORKS. *The Poetical Works* (New York, 1884), also includes some dramas: *The Queen-Mother, Rosamond, Chastelard, Atalanta in Calydon, Bothwell,* and *Erechtheus; The Poems*, 6 vols. (London, 1904); *The Tragedies*, 5 vols. (London, 1905); *Poems and Tragedies*, 2 vols. (Philadelphia, 1910); *The Golden Pine Edition*, 7 vols. (London, 1917–1925); *Collected Poetical Works*, 2 vols. (London, 1924); *The Complete Works*, 20 vols. (London, 1925–1927), the Bonchurch ed., vols. I–X contain the poetry and dramas; C. Y. Lang, ed., *The Swinburne Letters*, 6 vols. (New Haven, Conn., 1959–1962).

III. SELECTED WORKS. R. H. Stoddard, ed., *Selections* (New York, 1884); *Selections* (London, 1887); W. Sharp, ed., *Lyrical Poems* (Leipzig, 1901), the Tauchnitz ed.; *Dead Love and Other Inedited Pieces* (Portland, Me., 1901); W. M. Payne, ed., *Selected Poems* (Boston, 1905); *Selected Lyrical Poems* (New York, 1906); A. Beatty, ed., *Poems* (New York, 1906); A. Beatty, ed., *Dramas* (New York, 1909), selected by the ed.; *A Pilgrimage of Pleasure, Essays and Studies* (Boston, 1913), contains *A Pilgrimage of Pleasure, Dead Love, Les Fleurs du Mal, Charles Dickens,* and some reviews, also a bibliography of the works of Swinburne by E. J. O'Brien; E. Gosse, ed., *The Springtide of Life: Poems of Childhood* (London, 1918); E. Rhys, ed., *Poems* (New York, 1919), Modern Library ed.; E. Gosse and T. J. Wise, eds., *Selections* (London, 1919); E. H. Blakeney, ed., *A Golden Book of Swinburne's Lyrics* (London, 1922); G. S. Viereck, ed., *The Triumph of Time and Other Poems* (Girard, Kans., 1925); W. O. Raymond, ed., *Selections* (New York, 1925); H. M. Burton, ed., *Selections* (Cambridge, 1927); H. Wolfe, ed., *Selected Poems* (London, 1928); C. K. Hyder and L. Chase, eds., *The Best of Swinburne* (New York, 1937); L. Binyon, ed., *Selected Poems* (London, 1939), World's Classics ed.; R. Church, ed., *Poems and Prose* (London, 1940), Everyman

Library ed.; H. Treece, ed., *Selected Poems* (London, 1948); H. Hare, ed., *Selected Poems* (London, 1950); E. Shanks, ed., *Selected Poems* (London, 1950); K. Foss, ed., *A Swinburne Anthology: Verse, Drama, Prose, Criticism* (London, 1955); E. Sitwell, ed., *Swinburne: A Selection* (London, 1960); B. Dobrée, ed., *Poems* (London, 1961); C. V. Lang, ed., *New Writings by Swinburne: A Medley of Poems, Critical Essays, Hoaxes and Burlesques* (Syracuse, 1964); J. D. Rosenberg, ed., *Selected Poetry and Prose* (New York, 1968); M. Peckham, ed., *Poems and Ballads and Atalanta in Calydon* (New York, 1970); C. K. Hyder, *Swinburne as Critic* (London–Boston, 1972).

IV. SEPARATE WORKS. J. F. Waller, ed., "William Congreve," in *Imperial Dictionary of Universal Biography*, 3 vols. (London, 1857), repr. in *Pericles and Other Studies* (London, 1914); *Laugh and Lie Down* (London, 1859); *The Queen-Mother; Rosamond: Two Plays* (London, 1860); "Dead Love," in *Once a Week* (October 1862), short story, repr. ca. 1888 in a forged first ed. (1864; facs. ed., 1904); "The Sundew," in *Spectator* (26 July 1862), a rev. version appears in *Poems and Ballads* (London, 1866); "The Pilgrimage of Pleasure," in M. Gordon, *Children of the Chapel* (London, 1864), a morality play included as ch. 5; *Atalanta in Calydon: A Tragedy* (London, 1865; facs. repr., Oxford, 1930); *Chastelard: A Tragedy* (London, 1865); *Poems and Ballads* (London, 1866), issued first by Moxon, then by Hotten; *Notes on Poems and Reviews* (London, 1866), Swinburne's reply to his critics, repr. in C. K. Hyder, ed., *Swinburne Replies* (Syracuse, N.Y., 1966); "Preface," in *A Selection from the Works of Lord Byron* (London, 1866), an excellent essay on Byron; "Cleopatra," in *Cornhill* (September 1866), poem written to illus. a drawing by F. Sandys, repr. ca. 1887 in a forged ed. dated 1866; *An Appeal to England* (London, 1867), verse, for clemency to the Fenian rebels, publ. simultaneously in the *Morning Star* (22 November 1867) and as a broadside; "Regret," in *Fortnightly Review* (September 1867), verse, repr. in rev. form in *Poems and Ballads: Second Series* (London, 1878); *A Song of Italy* (London, 1867); *William Blake: A Critical Essay* (London, 1868), seems to have been available in December 1867; *Notes on the Royal Academy Exhibition, 1868* (London, 1868), repr. with omissions in *Essays and Studies* (London, 1875); "Siena," in *Lippincott's* (June 1868), separately printed the same year in Philadelphia and London; "Introduction," in *Christabel and the Lyrical and Imaginative Poems of S. T. Coleridge* (London, 1869).

Ode on the Proclamation of the French Republic (London, 1870); "Tristram and Iseult: Prelude of an Unfinished Poem," in [J. Friswell, ed.], *Pleasure: A Holiday Book of Prose and Verse* (London, 1871), rev. in *Tristram of Lyonesse* (London, 1882); *Songs Before Sunrise* (London, 1871); *Bothwell, Act One* (London, 1871), privately printed; *Under the Microscope* (London, 1872), a masterly, ironic prose pamphlet directed against the philistine critics of Rossetti and himself; [A. Lemerre, ed.], *Le*

Tombeau de Théophile Gautier (Paris, 1873), poems by various authors on the death of Gautier, those by Swinburne in four languages, two in English, two in French, one in Latin, one in Greek; *Bothwell: A Tragedy* (London, 1874); "Introduction," in *The Works of George Chapman* (London, 1874–1875), also separately printed the same year; *Songs of Two Nations* (London, 1875); "The Devil's Due," in *Examiner* (11 December 1875), published under the pseudonym "Thomas Maitland," a privately printed ed., dated 1875, appeared ca. 1896 and is probably forged; *Essays and Studies* (London, 1875); "Francis Beaumont" and "John Fletcher," in *Encyclopaedia Britannica* (London, 1875); *Notes of an English Republican on the Muscovite Crusade* (London, 1876); "Introduction," in C. J. Wells, *Joseph and His Brethren: A Dramatic Poem* (London, 1876), I have suspected that Swinburne may have been more actively concerned with the revision; *Erechtheus: A Tragedy* (London, 1876); *Lesbia Brandon* (London, 1877), novel, only galley proofs printed, used by R. Hughes in his 1952 ed.; *A Note on Charlotte Brontë* (London, 1877); "William Congreve," in *Encyclopaedia Britannica* (London, 1877); *Poems and Ballads: Second Series* (London, 1878); *An Election* (London, 1879), verse, a lithographed pamphlet; "Frank Fane: A Ballad," in *Pearl*, 1 (1879), an unsigned contribution to an "underground" magazine.

Songs of the Springtides (London, 1880); *Specimens of Modern Poets: The Heptalogia, or The Seven Against Sense* (London, 1880), a vol. of parodies; *Studies in Song* (London, 1880); *A Study of Shakespeare* (London, 1880); *Mary Stuart: A Tragedy* (London, 1881); *Tristram of Lyonesse and Other Poems* (London, 1882); *A Century of Roundels* (London, 1883), the strict form adopted by Swinburne to chasten his fluency, an object not achieved; "Dolorida," in A. Moore, ed., *Walnuts and Wine* (London, 1883), verses in French; "Introduction," in *Les Cenci* (Paris, 1883), intro. in French to T. Dorian's trans. of Shelley's play; "Christopher Marlowe," in *Encyclopaedia Britannica* (London, 1883); "Mary Queen of Scots," in *Encyclopaedia Britannica* (London, 1883); "Wordsworth and Byron," in *Nineteenth Century* (April–May 1884); *A Midsummer Holiday and Other Poems* (London, 1884); *Marino Faliero: A Tragedy* (London, 1885); *The Commonweal: A Song for Unionists* (London, 1886), repr. from the *Times* (London) (1 July 1886); *Miscellanies* (London, 1886), a collection of previously printed periodical and encyclopedia articles; *A Study of Victor Hugo* (London, 1886); "Introduction," in H. Ellis, ed., *Thomas Middleton* (London, 1887), the Mermaid ed.; *A Word for the Navy* (London, 1887), verse, privately printed; *The Whippingham Papers* (London, 1888), privately printed, about half the vol. written by Swinburne; "Cyril Tourneur," in *Encyclopaedia Britannica* (London, 1889); *A Study of Ben Jonson* (London, 1889); *Poems and Ballads: Third Series* (London, 1889); *The Ballad of Dead Men's Bay* (London, 1889); "A Logical Ballad of Home Rule," in *St. James's Gazette* (2 March 1889).

A Sequence of Sonnets on the Death of Robert Browning (London, 1890), privately printed; "Preface," in R. Herrick, *The Hesperides and Noble Numbers* (London, 1891), the Muses' Library ed.; *Music: An Ode* (London, 1892); *The Sisters: A Tragedy* (London, 1892); *Grace Darling* (London, 1893), verse, privately printed; *Astrophel and Other Poems* (London, 1894); *Studies in Prose and Poetry* (London, 1894); *Robert Burns: A Poem* (Edinburgh, 1896), privately printed and pirated; *The Tale of Balen* (London, 1896), verse; "Introduction," in E. B. Browning, *Aurora Leigh* (London, 1898); *A Channel Passage* (London, 1899); *Rosamond, Queen of the Lombards: A Tragedy* (London, 1899); "Victor Hugo," in *Encyclopaedia Britannica* (London, 1902); *Percy Bysshe Shelley* (Philadelphia, 1903), also publ. in *Chambers Cyclopaedia of English Literature* (London, 1903); *A Channel Passage and Other Poems* (London, 1904), includes numerous poems previously published only in periodicals; *Love's Cross Currents: A Year's Letters* (London, 1905), novel, first published in installments in the *Tatler* (25 August–29 December 1877), pirated in an ed. from Portland, Me. (1901), and publ. in a fuller version in 1905; "Introduction," in *Pericles* (London, 1907), vol. XIII of Lee's ed. of Shakespeare (London, 1906–1909); *The Duke of Gandia* (London, 1908), drama, reads like an early work; *The Age of Shakespeare* (London, 1908); *M. Prudhomme at the International Exhibition* (London, 1909), privately printed; *Of Liberty and Loyalty* (London, 1909), privately printed; *The Saviour of Society* (London, 1909), verse, privately printed; *The Portrait* (London, 1909), verse, privately printed; *The Marriage of Monna Lisa* (London, 1909), privately printed; *The Chronicle of Queen Fredegond* (London, 1909), privately printed; *In the Twilight: A Poem* (London, 1909), privately printed; *Lord Scales: A Ballad by a Borderer* (London, 1909), privately printed; *Lord Soulis: A Ballad by a Borderer* (London, 1909), privately printed; *The Worm of Spindlestonheugh: A Ballad by a Borderer* (London, 1909), privately printed; *Border Ballads* (London, 1909), privately printed, contains "Earl Robert," "Duriesdyke," "Westland Well"; *Ode to Mazzini* (London, 1909), privately printed; *Shakespeare* (London, 1909).

A Criminal Case: A Sketch (London, 1910), privately printed; *A Record of Friendship* (London, 1910), privately printed, Swinburne's account of his relationship with Rossetti and Lizzie Rossetti written in 1882 after Rossetti's death; *The Ballade of Truthful Charles and Other Poems* (London, 1910), privately printed; *Les Fleurs du Mal, and Other Studies* (London, 1913), privately printed; *Charles Dickens* (London, 1913), repr. in part from *Quarterly Review* (July 1902); E. Gosse, ed., *A Study of Victor Hugo's "Les Misérables"* (London, 1914), privately printed, the first and fifth essays not by Swinburne; *Pericles and Other Studies* (London, 1914), privately printed, reprs. *Pericles* with essays and articles not separately published elsewhere; *Thomas Nabbes: A Critical Monograph* (London, 1914), privately printed;

Christopher Marlowe in Relation to Greene, Peele and Lodge (London, 1914), privately printed; E. Gosse, ed., *Théophile* (London, 1915), privately printed; *Lady Maisie's Bairn, and Other Poems* (London, 1915), privately printed; *Poems from Villon, and Other Fragments* (London, 1916); *The Death of Sir John Franklin* (London, 1916), privately printed, an undergraduate poem; E. Gosse, ed., *The Triumph of Gloriana* (London, 1916), privately printed; *Poetical Fragments* (London, 1916), privately printed; E. Gosse, ed., *A Vision of Bags* (London, 1916), burlesque, privately printed; *Wearieswa': A Ballad* (London, 1917), privately printed; E. Gosse and T. J. Wise, eds., *The Posthumous Poems* (London, 1917); *Rondeaux Parisiens* (London, 1917), privately printed; *The Italian Mother, and Other Poems* (London, 1918), privately printed; *The Ride from Milan, and Other Poems* (London, 1918), privately printed; *The Two Knights, and Other Poems* (London, 1918), privately printed; *A Lay of Lilies, and Other Poems* (London, 1918), privately printed; *Queen Yseult: A Poem in Six Cantos* (London, 1918), privately printed; *Undergraduate Sonnets* (London, 1918), privately printed; *Lancelot, The Death of Rudel, and Other Poems* (London, 1918), privately printed; *The Character and Opinions of Dr. Johnson* (London, 1918), privately printed; E. Gosse and T. J. Wise, eds., *Contemporaries of Shakespeare* (London, 1919); *The Queen's Tragedy* (London, 1919), privately printed; *French Lyrics* (London, 1919), privately printed.

W. A. MacInnes, ed., *Ballads of the English Border* (London, 1925), includes all known previously publ. and unpubl. ballads; G. Lafourcade, ed., *Swinburne's Hyperion, and Other Poems* (London, 1928); R. Hughes, ed., *Lucretia Borgia: The Chronicle of Tebaldeo Tebaldei* (London, 1942); C. K. Hyder, ed., "Swinburne: 'Changes of Aspect' and 'Short Notes,'" *PMLA*, 58 (March 1943); *A Roundel of Retreat* [Washington, D. C., 1950], privately printed, the imprint reading "London, Charles Ottley, Landon & Co., 1950," clearly a joke; R. Hughes, ed., *Pasiphaë: A Poem* (London, 1950), an extremely interesting fragment dated approximately 1866; *Will Drew and Phil Crewe and Frank Fane by a Great English Literary Figure* [1962?], privately printed; *Le Prince Prolétaire* (Bethesda, Md., 1963), privately printed; *The Influence of the Roman Censorship on the Morals of the People* (Brooklyn, 1964), privately printed; C. Y. Lang, ed., *New Writings by Swinburne* (Syracuse, N. Y., 1964), includes some uncollected poems, the early burlesques *La Soeur de la Reine* and *La Fille du Policeman*, with extensive annotations; C. K. Hyder, ed., *Swinburne Replies* (Syracuse, N. Y., 1966), repr. *Notes on Poems and Reviews*, *Under the Microscope*, and the *Dedicating Epistle to the Collection of 1899*, with an intro. and notes; J. S. Mayfield, ed., *Shelley* (Worcester, Mass., 1973); F. J. Sypher, ed., *A Year's Letters* (New York, 1974), reedited from British Library MS Ashley 5073 and MS in J. A. Symington Collection, Rutgers University Library; J. S. Mayfield, ed.,

Hide and Seek (London, 1975), with notes, an early unpublished poem in the meter of Meredith's *Love in the Valley*; E. P. Schuldt, ed., "Some Unpublished Balliol Essays of A. C. Swinburne," in *Review of English Studies*, 27 (November 1976).

Letters from Swinburne have been published in the following issues of *Notes and Queries*: 19 (February 1972); 20 (February 1974); 21 (June 1974); 22 (October 1975); 23 (February 1976); 26 (August 1979); and 27 (June 1980).

Note: There are numerous MSS extant. Particularly important are those in the Ashley collection in the British Museum.

V. BIOGRAPHICAL AND CRITICAL STUDIES. Baron Houghton [R. M. Milnes], "Swinburne's *Atalanta in Calydon*," in *Edinburgh Review*, 122:249 (July 1865); Baron Houghton [R. M. Milnes], "Mr. Swinburne's *Chastelard*," in *Fortnightly Review*, 4:23 (15 April 1866); R. W. Buchanan, review of *Poems and Ballads*, in *Athenaeum*, 2 (1866); R. W. Buchanan, "Immortality in Authorship," in *Fortnightly Review*, 6:33 (15 September 1866); [J. M. Morley], "Mr. Swinburne's New Poems," in *Saturday Review*, 22 (4 August 1866); W. M. Rossetti, *Swinburne's Poems and Ballads: A Criticism* (London, 1866); J. Thomson, "The Swinburne Controversy," in *National Reformer* (23 December 1866), repr. in his *Satires and Profanities* (London, 1884); M. D. Conway, review of *William Blake*, in *Fortnightly Review*, n.s. 3:14 (1 February 1868); A. Austin, "The Poetry of the Period: Mr. Swinburne," in *Temple Bar*, 26 (July 1869), repr. in his *The Poetry of the Period* (London, 1870).

R. W. Buchanan, *The Fleshly School of Poetry* (London, 1872); W. J. Courthorpe, "The Latest Development of Literary Poetry: Swinburne, Rossetti, Morris," in *Quarterly Review*, 132:263 (January 1872); W. K. Clifford, "Cosmic Emotion," in *Nineteenth Century*, 2 (October 1877), repr. in his *Lectures and Essays* (London, 1879); V. de l'Isle Adam, *Histoires Insolites* (Paris, 1888), contains "Le Sadisme Anglais."

O. Wilde, review of *Poems and Ballads: Third Series*, in *Pall Mall Gazette* (27 June 1889), repr. in his *Reviews*, vol. II (London, 1910); O. Elton, *Modern Studies* (London, 1907); E. Thomas, *Algernon Charles Swinburne: A Critical Study* (London, 1912); Sotheby, Wilkinson, and Hodge, *Catalogue of the Library of Swinburne* (London, 19–21 June 1916); E. Gosse, *The Life of Algernon Charles Swinburne* (London, 1917), repr. in Bonchurch ed., vol. XIX; M. C. J. Leith, *The Boyhood of Swinburne* (London, 1917); A. Symons, "Swinburne," in *Fortnightly Review* n.s. 101:605 (May 1917); E. Gosse, "The First Draft of Swinburne's *Anactoria*," in *Modern Language Review*, 14 (July 1919), also privately printed, n.d., and repr. in his *Aspects and Impressions* (London, 1922).

T. S. Eliot, *The Sacred Wood* (London, 1920), contains essays "Swinburne as Critic" and "Swinburne as Poet"; C. Watts-Dunton, *The Home Life of Swinburne* (London, 1922); G. Lafourcade, "Swinburne et Baudelaire," in

Revue Anglo-Américaine, 1 (February 1924); G. Lafourcade, *Atalanta in Calydon:* le manuscrit, les sources," in *Revue Anglo-Américaine*, 3 (October–December 1925); T. E. Welby, *A Study of Swinburne* (London, 1926); H. Nicolson, *Swinburne* (London, 1926); G. Lafourcade, "Swinburne and Whitman," in *Modern Language Review*, 22 (January 1927), rev. version in *Revue Anglo-Américaine*, 9 (October 1931); G. Lafourcade, *La Jeunesse de Swinburne, 1837–1876*, 2 vols. (Paris, 1928); C. K. Hyder, "*Laus Veneris* and the Tannhäuser Legend," *PMLA*, 45 (December 1930); M. Praz, *La Carne, la Morte e il Diavolo nella Letteratura Romantica* (Florence, 1930), trans. as *The Romantic Agony* (Oxford, 1933), a pathography of romantic literature; C. K. Hyder, "The Medieval Background in 'The Leper,'" in *PMLA*, 46 (December 1931); C. K. Hyder, *Swinburne's Literary Career and Fame* (Durham, N. C., 1931); G. Lafourcade, *Swinburne: A Literary Biography* (London, 1932); C. K. Hyder, "Swinburne and the Popular Ballad," in *PMLA*, 49 (March 1934); G. Lafourcade, "L'Algolagnie et Swinburne," in *Hippocrate* (March–April 1935); G. Lafourcade, "Le Triomphe du Temps: ou la réputation de Swinburne," in *Études Anglaises*, 1 (March 1937); R. C. Child, "Swinburne's Mature Standards of Criticism," *PMLA*, 52 (September 1937).

R. Hughes, "Unpublished Swinburne," in *Life and Letters*, 56 (January 1948); C. Dahl, "Swinburne's Loyalty to the House of Stuart," in *Studies in Philology*, 46 (July 1949); J. A. Cassidy, "Robert Buchanan and the Fleshly Controversy," in *PMLA*, 67 (March 1952); J. K. Robinson, "A Neglected Phase of the Aesthetic Movement: English Parnassianism," in *PMLA*, 68 (September 1953), relates Swinburne's experiments in Old French forms to similar work by Lang, Gosse, Dobson, etc.; J. S. Mayfield, *Swinburne's Boo* (Bethesda, Md., 1953), privately printed, repr. in *English Miscellany*, 4 (Rome, 1953), separately bound and privately reiss. (Washington, D. C., 1954); C. Y. Lang, "The First Chorus of *Atalanta*," in *Yale University Library Gazette*, 27 (January 1953); R. Z. Temple, *The Critic's Alchemy* (New York, 1953), on Swinburne as critic and interpreter of French literature; C. Y. Lang, "Some Swinburne Manuscripts," in *Journal of Rutgers University Library*, 18 (Autumn 1954); A. W. Henry [Ehrenpreis], "A Reconstructed Swinburne Ballad," in *Harvard Library Bulletin*, 12 (Autumn 1958); P. R. Baum, "The Fitzwilliam Manuscript of Swinburne's *Atalanta*, Verses 1,038–1,204," in *Modern Language Review*, 54 (1959).

C. Y. Lang, "*Atalanta* in Manuscript," in *Yale University Library Gazette*, 37 (July 1962); T. E. Connolly, *Swinburne's Theory of Poetry* (Albany, N. Y., 1964); R. L. Peters, *The Crowns of Apollo: Swinburne's Principles of Literature and Art* (Detroit, 1965); J. D. Rosenberg, "Swinburne," in *Victorian Studies*, 11:2 (December 1967); "A Rare Find," in *American Book Collector*, 17 (6 March 1967), two missing pages of *Lesbia Brandon*; R. E. Lougy, "Swinburne's Poetry and Twentieth-Century Criticism," in *Dalhousie Review*, 48 (Autumn 1968); K. McSweeney, "The Structure of Swinburne's *Tristram of Lyonesse*," in *Queen's Quarterly*, 75:iv (Winter 1968); J. O. Fuller, *Swinburne: A Critical Biography* (London, 1968), useful, if somewhat highlighted; R. L. Peters, "A. C. Swinburne's 'Hymn to Proserpine': The Work Sheets," *PMLA*, 83 (October 1968).

C. K. Hyder, ed., *Swinburne: The Critical Heritage* (London, 1970), a useful anthology of views of Swinburne's work and personality up to the period before WW I; M. Peckham, *Victorian Revolutionaries: Speculations on Some Heroes of a Culture Crisis* (New York, 1970); C. Y. Lang, ed., *Victorian Poetry*, 9:i–ii (Spring–Summer 1971), a special issue devoted to Swinburne, contains some of the finest criticism to date, particularly essays by T. L. Wymar and R. Mathews on *Atalanta*, by J. Baird on "Swinburne, Sade and Blake," by D. A. Cook on "Anactoria," and by J. J. McGann on "Ave Atque Vale"; K. McSweeney, "Swinburne's *Poems and Ballads* (1866)," in *Studies in English Literature*, 11 (Autumn 1971); M. Panter-Downes, *At the Pines: Swinburne and Watts-Dunton in Putney* (London–New York, 1971); M. Raymond, *Swinburne's Poetics* (The Hague, 1971); J. J. McGann, *Swinburne: An Experiment in Criticism* (Chicago, 1972); W. D. Jenkins, "Swinburne, Robert Buchanan, W. S. Gilbert," in *Studies in Philology*, 79:iii (1972), suggests that reflections of Swinburne's sado-masochism appear in some of the choric passages in *Patience* and relates the character of Grosvenor in *Patience* to Buchanan; B. F. Fisher IV, "Swinburne's *Tristram of Lyonesse* in Process," in *Texas Studies in Literature*, 14:3 (Fall 1972); J. O. Jordan, "The Sweet Face of Mothers: Psychological Patterns in *Atalanta in Calydon*," in *Victorian Studies*, 11:2 (Summer 1973); J. S. Mayfield, *Swinburneiana: A Gallimaufry of Bits and Pieces About Algernon Charles Swinburne* (Gaithersbury–London, 1974); P.

Henderson, *Swinburne: The Portrait of a Poet* (London, 1974); R. C. Murfin, "Athens Unbound: The Unity of Swinburne's *Erechtheus*," in *Victorian Poetry*, 12:3 (Autumn 1974); J. Forces, "Two Flagellation Poems by Swinburne," in *Notes and Queries*, 22 (October 1975), attributes to Swinburne two poems found in the pornographic periodical *Pearl*: "Frank Fane, a Ballad" and "Charlie Collingwood's Flogging"; I. Frieke and D. C. Frieke, eds., "The Proserpine Figure in Swinburne's *Poems and Ballads, I*," in *Aeolian Harps* (Bowling Green, Ohio, 1976); D. C. Frick, "The Idea of Love in Swinburne's *The Sundew*," in *English Language Notes*, 13 (March 1976); T. L. Meyers, "Shelley's Influence on *Atalanta in Calydon*," in *Victorian Poetry*, 14:2 (Summer 1976); R. A. Greenberg, "Swinburne and the Re-Definition of Classical Myth," in *Victorian Poetry*, 14:3 (Autumn 1976); R. Trevelyan, *A Pre-Raphaelite Circle* (London, 1978), material on Swinburne's relations with the Trevelyan family; R. C. Murfin, *Swinburne, Hardy, Lawrence and the Burden of Belief* (Chicago, 1978); G. M. Ridenour, "Time and Eternity in Swinburne: Minute Particulars in Five Poems," in *English Literary History*, 45 (Spring 1978); D. G. Riede, *Swinburne: A Study of Romantic Mythmaking* (Charlottesville, Va., 1978); D. Thomas, *Swinburne: The Poet in His World* (Oxford, 1979); J. W. Rosenbaum, "Of Hunts and Hunters: *Atalanta in Calydon*," in *The Pre-Raphaelite Review*, 3 (November 1979).

A. H. Harrison, "Love Strong as Death and Valour Strong as Love: Swinburne and Courtly Love," in *Victorian Poetry*, 181 (Spring 1980); C. W. Morley, "Swinburne as Art Critic," in *Journal of Pre-Raphaelite Studies*, 1: 2 (May 1981); K. McSweeney, *Tennyson and Swinburne as Romantic Naturalists* (Toronto–London, 1981), a brave attempt to rehabilitate the later Swinburne.; "The Poetry of Swinburne," in W. E. Buckler, *The Victorian Imagination* (Brighton, 1981).

WALTER HORATIO PATER
(1839-1894)

Ian Fletcher

PATER's reputation was at its height in the twenty years after his death. Lately there has been an intensified interest in his work, although with reservations. Prejudice and fashion are to blame. The very name "Pater" has come to be associated with an undisciplined impressionistic criticism, and one or two rather uncharacteristic passages, such as the prose poem on the Mona Lisa, are assumed to be broadly representative. The modern critic is often suspicious of any work that falls outside fairly strict categories: how can he compare such works with others and "place" them with a suitable conviction? This difficulty applies to Pater with peculiar force. His work seems to lie in a twilight of categories between criticism and creation; between art and literary criticism, *belles-lettres*, classical scholarship, the *journal intime*, and the philosophic novel. Few readers are sufficiently catholic to judge him, not simply as a critic of art or of literature, but as something at once more or less than these things. Pater's work represents above all the triumphs and failures of a temperament. It records, in his own words, "a prolonged quarrel with himself." As in most domestic arguments, there is a good deal of repetition: personal isolation, the means of transcending it, the good life as tension between moral rigor and culture, and the final defeat of isolation through ritual, sympathy, and the sacrifice of personality—topics like these are worried over, established, developed, qualified, reinterpreted. Under many disguises Pater is a self-explorer, honest and severe, who touches, in the process, on interests central to his own time. His style, though mannered, is one of the most individual and hypnotically satisfying in English: the faithful counterpart of that exhausting backward and forward struggle with himself. For Pater was incapable of renunciation: he lived in a world where "we must needs make the most of things," even of things incompatible or dangerous. What unites these interests and evasions?

MUCH of Pater's work is transposed and distanced autobiography. In a short "imaginary portrait," "The Child in the House," Pater attempts to reshape the past as it might have been relived by his adult self. Here he examines scrupulously his own sensuous education and strives to account for the richness and oddity of his temperament. Like Pater, the child is precociously aware of isolation and a close association of pain and beauty:

> . . . an almost diseased sensibility to the spectacle of suffering, and . . . the rapid growth of a certain capacity of fascination by bright colour and choice form . . . marking early the activity in him of a more than customary sensuousness, "the lust of the eye," . . . which might lead him, one day, how far! Could he have foreseen the weariness of the way!

The weariness belongs to the priest of art, who did not so much make as have imposed upon him "the sacrifice of a thousand possible sympathies." For sharply though he responded to the beauty of colors and forms, Pater was himself singularly plain and timid.

In "The Child in the House," Pater regards home—an experience for the child, a symbol for the adult—as a sanctuary from spiritual wandering. Adult life is equated with exile, and in several of Pater's experiments in ruminative fiction, men come back to die at home with a sense of fulfillment. The child is seen as a conventional animal, prizing even the restraints laid upon him as reassurance. Childhood routine provides the source of Pater's lifelong concern with ritual as the most efficacious of man's instruments for spiritual communication: ritual provides life with a set of ideal symbols, and at the level of ritual the otherwise frightening and destructive experiences of beauty and terror can be related, however fraily, to daily habit.

Pater's personal history, whatever the raw excitements of the inner life, had none of the squalor and excitement of some of his contemporaries'. His father died while he was still an infant, his mother while he was at boarding school, and his two sisters were sent to complete their education abroad: these events must have accented his sense of isolation. In 1858 he went up to Oxford. There he joined an undergraduate society of a radical cast, Old Mortality, whose other members included the philosopher T. H. Green and the poet Algernon Charles Swinburne. Pater read several papers to the society which, as one contemporary recorded, made "the lamps burn blue." The most famous of these papers, though its text has not survived, defended the Comtian notion of "subjective immortality": we live on, not in bodily form or as spirits "behind the veil," but in the minds and emotions of our friends, and through them become part of the culture. After taking a second class in *Litterae Humaniores*, and tutoring privately for a year or two, Pater was elected in 1864 a fellow of Brasenose College. The remainder of his life, with the exception of some years spent partially in London, was passed quietly in Oxford, where his sisters kept house for him.

In his youth Pater had been attracted toward at least the outer shows of Christianity. By the time of his election, however, he had become strongly influenced by the popular and plausible notions of Auguste Comte. Both in conversation and in writing he was now known as a lover of irony and smoothly destructive paradox. In the most important of his early essays, that on Samuel Taylor Coleridge as philosopher (1866), there are overt anti-Christian implications and confident asperities of tone: implications and asperities carefully toned down in the revised version published in *Appreciations* (1889). In spite of such skepticism, Pater persisted for some time in attempting to take holy orders, an attempt that seems to have crystallized under John Keble's influence, and may have determined Pater's view that beliefs are transmitted by temperament.

The 1860's in England were a period of crisis in opinion. In periodicals such as the *Fortnightly Review*, the troubled English mind struggled with competing loyalties to science and religion, to authority and "the free play of mind," reaching a remarkably articulate stage of self-consciousness. Pater was an avid reader of the more intellectual magazines of the time, and for him, as for others, they provided something essential, an insight not only into his own personal doubts, but into the spirit of the age. This uneasy movement of the English mind underlies all Pater's earlier writing, and as the uneasiness was never wholly resolved, he cannot be said to have arrived at a "settled position." It was in such magazines as the *Fortnightly* that Pater published most of the essays contained in his first book, *Studies in the History of the Renaissance* (1873), itself a glancing contribution to the problem of evolving a new ethic to replace partially discredited traditional beliefs.

By the middle of the 1870's, though he had now a distinct place in the world of letters, Pater's mild academic ambitions remained unsatisfied. He seems to have been a conscientious but not conspicuously successful tutor, though his pupils, Gerard Manley Hopkins among them, remembered him with affection. "Don't suppose," Field Marshal Douglas Haig, visiting Oxford after World War I, is reputed to have remarked in his blunt, laconic fashion, "there's a man called Pater still here? Taught me something about the writing of English." Pater's administrative powers were slender; he was not a good committee man, and there are many amusing stories about his vagueness at college meetings. But more decisive reasons accounted for Pater's failure to exercise an influence on Oxford life commensurate with his abilities. *The Renaissance* had alarmed the Master of Balliol College, the most powerful single personality in the university, Benjamin Jowett. And Oxford's ingratitude to Pater, both during his lifetime and after his death, is, on wider grounds, not surprising. Neither in his gifts nor in his eccentricities was Pater a typical Oxford man. He was not an exact scholar; he was not in large companies a ready or amusing talker. He owed his fellowship partly to his gifts as a stylist, but even his style was not in the main Victorian tradition of Oxford prose. It was not the innocently luminous style of John Henry Newman, of Henry Mansel, or, with a little more of professional mannerism, of Matthew Arnold—the style that is like the perfection of common room conversation. Pater's style, with its elaborate and refined cadences, appeals to the inner rather than the outer ear. The reader must construe as he reads. Yet that prose of Pater's, many felt, with all its artifice, could be profoundly subversive. He could be seen as "a corruptor of youth."

Already in the early 1870's, Pater had begun to modify some of the more extreme positions adopted in *The Renaissance*. His mood was shifting with the shifting tides of the time. The forces of tradition (some would have said of reaction) were being rallied by the new Oxford Idealism. But there were deeper sources of change within Pater himself. Over the years he had begun to feel the limitations of a self-regarding ethic that sought the meaning of life in the intensity of highly charged moments of experience. He had proclaimed that creed in the conclusion to *The Renaissance*, with a confidence which, as so often in Pater, already marked disquiet; in the second edition he suppressed the conclusion altogether, restoring it with careful modifications in the third. This timidity sprang from the very popularity of the book, especially with the younger generation, whose general misunderstanding of *The Renaissance* was to Pater as painful as it was surprising.

Such innocence and isolation point to Pater's uncertainty about an audience, about his own private self and his public role as writer, further emphasized by the fact that in some moods he saw his art as essentially "private." In his disciples, Pater's uncertainties were disconcertingly resolved: "Is this then what I am?" Oscar Wilde, the most systematic (and most dangerous) vulgarizer of his ideas, might well have been writing a parable of the master's relationship with his younger admirers in *The Picture of Dorian Gray* (1890), where the hero's double, the portrait, changes while his own face remains a beautiful *tabula rasa*.

In 1883 Pater resigned his position as a tutor at Brasenose, though not his fellowship, and devoted the next two years to the arduous composition of *Marius the Epicurean* (1885). This was a work on a much larger scale than anything he had previously attempted; designed to expand and rectify the deliberately elliptical statements of the conclusion, and to place them in a concrete historical setting and in the context of an imagined life story. For Marius, Pater's hero, the wistful quest with which the book is concerned does arrive at some sort of goal. Marius, at the end of the tale, is on the threshold of Christian belief, having transcended isolation through the sympathy that leads to action and self-sacrifice. But Marius also transcends isolation through the sense of at last belonging, again wistfully and on the outer fringes, to a society of like-minded souls, the society of the primitive Christian church, for which Pater's miniature emblem, in *Marius the Epicurean*, is the decorous beauty of the household of Cecilia.

Most of Pater's later writing in some sense supplements *Marius*. In 1887 he collected together four essays in ruminative fiction, *Imaginary Portraits*, and in 1889 published a rather miscellaneous collection of critical studies, *Appreciations*. This includes the famous essay "Style," the outcome of a crisis personal no less than aesthetic. *Plato and Platonism* (1893) was the last book published in his lifetime. Pater presents Plato as an impressionist philosopher, as tentative in judgment as the author of *Marius* himself. The book is also interesting as one of the earliest clear statements in English of the position of historical relativism. Pater feels it is not the business of a lecturer on Plato to abstract certain doctrines as typically Platonic, and to decide whether they are true, false, or meaningless; it is rather to grasp Plato as a man, and to grasp the world in which Plato moved, and to try to show how natural it is that such a man in such a world should have such ideas. *Plato and Platonism* was Pater's own favorite among his books; perhaps because it was based on lectures, it is written in an unusually relaxed style.

When he wrote *The Renaissance*, the young Pater thought of religion as merely one of several high passions: but there seems to be evidence that his later response was not merely to the beauty of outward Christian observance but to the moral beauty of the Christian life. And his last, unfinished essay deals sympathetically with Blaise Pascal as an example of "the inversion of . . . the aesthetic life." Pater was a devout attendant at the services in Brasenose chapel; and in the "friary" of St. Austin's, a small Anglo-Catholic chapel lost in the slums of Southeast London, he may have found a living and contemporary image of the primitive Christian community. His interest in it, together with eight years of spending his vacations in London, reflects the effort made in his last years to subdue the sense of isolation by identifying himself with some dedicated group, however marginal. Pater may have thought that the literary world of London would offer him a more lively and admiring social ambience than Oxford. Writers, mostly much younger men, such as George Moore, Arthur Symons, William Sharp, and Lionel Johnson, looked up to Pater as a master; but he seems to have mixed little with them socially, nor does he figure as a person in classic works of literary reminiscence of the 1880's and 1890's, such as William Butler Yeats's *Autobiographies*. London, in the end, proved perhaps as much a desert for Pater as Oxford: like the Desert Fathers he remained (however unwillingly) a hermit to the end.

Pater's own kindness to and interest in other people were plain and effortless. But prizing, as he did, his own personality above everything else—it was, for him, the only certain element in experience— Pater lacked that final requisite of all personal relationships, the ability to surrender personality. Much of Pater's writing consists of a deliberate mythologizing of his friends, as though, in T. S. Eliot's words, he were constantly seeking through personal relationships something beyond them. In his *Imaginary Portraits*, he created ideal types, such as Emerald Uthwart, based in some of their traits on friends, but so acutely idealized that they become in effect incarnations of everything that Pater wished to be himself. Pater's isolation was also an inevitable function of his vocation. Like Gustave Flaubert, he was the martyr of an ideal of style. Like Flaubert, his life was unified, not by the sequence of the ordinary human passions—romantic love, family responsibility, worldly ambition—but by the single purpose of creating high literature. For Pater art no less than life was ritual: a total discipline which involved, in that poignant phrase of his already quoted, "the sacrifice of a thousand possible sympathies." Even though a collection of his letters has been published, Pater's "mystery" remains as opaque as ever. His natural costiveness, unlike the exuberance of Henry James, made him a grudging letter writer, while his life was given some stability by the continued presence of his two sisters, one of them a woman of considerable intelligence. He had no need to search desperately for friends. The materials for an adequate biography are perhaps no longer available. The outer man so largely eluding us, we must seek the inner man in the books; books that both hide and reveal those secrets of personality where, in considering this strangely reserved and yet almost indiscreetly candid writer, the critic must begin and end.

III

PATER's earlier essays are dominated by a group of related ideas: human isolation within the "flux" (a flux of which human personality is itself part), the relativist spirit of the modern world, and the impor-

tance of temperament, which Pater opposes to the rigidity of "character." Such a picture of an unstable, ungraspable world is colored by Pater's sense of personal isolation, but reflects also the troubled intellectual climate of the 1850's and 1860's.

Newman's conversion to Catholicism in 1845 had robbed the Anglican church of its moral and intellectual center. The shift among some of the more intellectual Oxford divines toward latitudinarianism is reflected in the famous *Essays and Reviews* (1860). These "modernists" subordinated religion to the "verifying faculty" of scientific law, and suggested that the church should exist in a fluid state, without fixed principles. Even a man of the Right, like Dean Mansel, whom Pater much admired, tended to undercut skepticism with skepticism. Newman was to prolong this line of argument in his *Grammar of Assent* (1870), appealing to the limits of positive knowledge, the unbearableness of uncertainty, and to the impracticability of basing fundamental assents on merely syllogistic arguments. His appeal, on behalf of faith, was to the sense of awe and the convergences of probability. In *The Development of Christian Doctrine* (1846), which he wrote, standing up, on the verge of conversion, in agony and tears, Newman had hit upon the notion of evolution that was beginning to transform science and historical theory. It was the dissolvent, rather than the defensive, element in such daring Christian thinkers that most profoundly attracted the young Pater. What the prevailing skepticism implied for him was not a weapon against crude free thought; it was rather a personal liberation from the constraints of dogma; it offered the possibility of dallying unashamedly with a self-pleasing ethic, without sacrificing the sensuous aspects of religion.

This dissolvent element pervades Pater's essay on Coleridge—the main theme is not Coleridge's poetry or his criticism but his metaphysics. Pater attacks Coleridge for his aspiration toward the Absolute, which he sees as an expression of mental sickliness in revolt against the patient tentativeness of scientific method (in a lecture to his students, Pater was once to create a mild furor by describing monastic religion as resembling "a beautiful disease"). Knowledge, for Pater, is essentially a matter of the specific, and Coleridge is to be blamed for tamely accepting the conclusions of traditional Christianity and seeking to justify them in a new and abstruse manner, instead of applying his fine critical spirit to the sources through which it is claimed that Revelation has been made. Moreover, "urbanity" for Pater, as for Arnold, is one of the requisites of culture. One should be able to survey the dilapidation of a cherished theory into picturesque ruin with a condoning smile. This urbanity Coleridge, according to Pater, lacks: and the consequent roughness of form of most of his prose works and his excess of seriousness—"a seriousness arising not from any moral principle, but from a misconception of the perfect manner"—are his typical defects. Pater then proceeds to show how irrelevant metaphysics is to the spirit of the nineteenth century:

Modern thought is distinguished from ancient by its cultivation of the "relative" spirit in place of the "absolute." . . . To the modern spirit nothing is, or can be rightly known, except relatively and under conditions. The philosophical conception of the relative has been developed in modern times through the influence of the sciences of observation. Those sciences reveal types of life evanescing into each other by inexpressible refinements of change. Things pass into their opposites by accumulation of undefinable quantities. . . . The faculty for truth is recognized as a power of distinguishing and fixing delicate and fugitive detail. The moral world is ever in contact with the physical, and the relative spirit has invaded philosophy from the ground of the inductive sciences. There it has started a new analysis of the relations of body and mind, good and evil, freedom and necessity. Hard and abstract moralities are yielding to a more exact estimate of the subtlety and complexity of our life. Always, as an organism increases in perfection, the conditions of its life become more complex. Man is the most complex of the products of nature. Character merges into temperament: the nervous system refines itself into intellect. Man's physical organism is played upon not only by the physical conditions about it, but by remote laws of inheritance, the vibration of long-past acts reaching him in the midst of the new order of things in which he lives. When we have estimated these conditions he is still not yet simple and isolated; for the mind of the race, the character of the age, sway him this way or that through the medium of language and current ideas.

("Coleridge," *Appreciations*, pp. 65–66)[1]

Thus, for Pater, the morality of his own age was necessarily more complex and flexible than that of a writer like Coleridge, who, for all his speculative, roving genius, still believed wholeheartedly in "hard and abstract moralities" (in, say, the Ten Command-

ments): whereas for Pater all moral problems tended to become special cases. (This, indeed, is what led him, as early as 1874, to write an admirable essay on *Measure for Measure*.) The *Studies in the History of the Renaissance* is his earliest attempt to organize the tentative method over a fairly wide range of instances, though within a definable context; to organize a search for fixed points within the bewildering flux of the modern world.

IV

The Renaissance was intended as a prolegomenon to a new age: an age whose choicer spirits might achieve oneness with themselves through aesthetic contemplation. The topics dealt with range from the thirteenth to the eighteenth centuries. For Pater, the Renaissance was not a phenomenon confined narrowly to one place or period, but a widespread, discontinuous, and prolonged movement of the European spirit; its essence, the vivid and disruptive impact of the values of Greek life, thought, and art on the jaded or one-sided local traditions of European culture. Pater thought of these jaded and one-sided traditions as mainly those of the Christian Middle Ages, but not wholly so; for he saw Johann Winckelmann, the eighteenth-century German Hellenist, and the subject of one of his best essays, as reacting not against Christianity, but against the decadence of early Humanism itself, against a sterile neoclassical eighteenth-century orthodoxy, and as seeking out the reality, rather than the conventional picture, of ancient Greece. Yet Winckelmann is a little set apart from Pater's other Renaissance types. They all, painters and poets, had the sense of discovering in the classical world something *new,* and the possibility of renewed creation. Winckelmann, their belated descendant, had the sense, rather, of recovering something *lost.* The Hellenistic past, for Winckelmann, becomes the starting point of a mode of contemplation rather than of creation. He anticipates the critical attitude that, for Pater, was the attitude of the nineteenth-century mind at its best.

To the historians of the eighteenth century, the Renaissance suggested mainly the reacquisition of classical learning, the new taste for Roman (rather than Greek) antiquities that marks the fifteenth and sixteenth centuries, first in Italy, and then through the other civilized parts of Europe. It meant the rise

[1] All quotations from *Appreciations* are taken from the second edition (1890).

of the Humanists and the fall of the Schoolmen. But Pater's own century had acquired a more subtle, vivid, and objectively defined historical sense. The Renaissance was now seen as the rebirth of man, a rebirth of individuality, the beginning, in fact, of the modern world. In Pater's own age, this wistfulness about a past, now for the first time so sharply conceived by historians that it could be explored, in imagination, as the present can be conceived, combined with a typical Victorian unease. This led many to project an "ideal moment" into the past. But the views of writers who romantically idealized selected portions of the past were often quite unrelated to historical actualities; Pater wrote as a scholar, if a somewhat vagrant one.

Pater's method, in *The Renaissance*, of exploring not so much a period as a movement of history through selected individuals, places him in line with Jules Michelet, with the German romantic historians, and in a sense even with Thomas Carlyle. History for him has both a dramatic interest and a practical bearing. In Jakob Burckhardt's famous *Civilization of the Renaissance in Italy* (1860) Pater was to see a way of concentrating on sudden luminous moments of a period, of a movement, rather than attempting to draw a flat systematic map of it. This approach had an obvious attraction for a writer who believed passionately both in the fruitfulness of the tentative approach and in the isolation of all individuals within the "flux." There is, however, one important difference between Burckhardt and Pater. Burckhardt tended to insist oversharply on distinctions between "historical periods," periods that, we are more and more realizing, are less realities than conveniences of the historian. Pater emphasized the essential continuity of the Renaissance with the Middle Ages on the one hand, and with modern times on the other, and in this he is in line with present historical research. He also differed from the leading historians of his time in the special nature of his interest in the individual. For Pater, as for Charles Augustin Sainte-Beuve, it is rather the man behind a work of art or literature (rather than, for instance, the "style of an age") that gives a work unity. Art, for him, existed for personality's sake; and he saw the shaping of personality, through the creation and appreciation of art, as, in a sense, the highest kind of art. It is here that he is fundamentally a moralist, not a mere (or pure) critic of literature or art.

The preface summarizes Pater's critical method. Pater begins with Arnold's definition of the critic's first duty as being "to see the object as in itself it really is," but significantly adds, "in aesthetic criticism the first step towards seeing one's object as it really is, is to know one's own impression as it really is." For Pater, the impression is our sole contact with anything external to ourselves. Pater parts company from Arnold in stressing Hellenism and muting Hebraism. Whereas both Pater and Arnold use literature as the basis for a theory of life, Pater follows much more consistently the corollary of culture as an inward process. Arnold is too glib when he relates the instinct for the good life to literature as represented by the submission to "the best that has been thought and said" and to the problem of the good life in relation to others. For Pater this is not possible, believing as he does that man is fundamentally isolated and that the senses are all that men have in common. Culture at this stage appears only as a harmony of sensations in the individual life, and for this reason he extends Arnold's concern with literature (Arnold was indifferent to the other arts) to painting and sculpture.

Pater's method of great receptivity and intensification of personality through contemplation of the work of art is an ideal for the few, not the many, in his own age; and in its insistence on the appreciative approach it offers a consumer's rather than a producer's view of art. Here is a typical passage:

> The aesthetic critic, then, regards all the objects with which he has to do, all works of art and the fairer forms of nature and human life, as powers or forces, producing pleasurable sensations, each of a more or less peculiar . . . kind. This influence he feels, and wishes to explain, analysing it, and reducing it to its elements. To him, the picture, the landscape, the engaging personality in life or in a book, La Gioconda, the hills of Carrara, Pico of Mirandula, are valuable for their virtues, as we say in speaking of a herb, a wine, a gem; for the property each has of affecting one with a special, a unique impression of pleasure. Education grows in proportion as one's susceptibility to these impressions increases in depth and variety.
>
> (preface to *The Renaissance*, p. ix)[2]

A certain looseness in the texture of his argument is typical of Pater. He tends to use abstract concepts decoratively, to isolate ideas rather than to relate them; and when he ascribes so much to the "fineness of truth" of the single word, he often treats it, or

---

[2]All quotations from *The Renaissance* are taken from the first edition (1873).

other fragments or details of larger wholes (a piece of decorative or symbolic detail in a painting, say), as if it were an aesthetic sufficiency. Yet the apparent want of discrimination between the different levels of pleasure therein gives a misleading impression of Pater's total attitude. The mention of *persons* as well as *things* must involve the moral dimension, since the aesthetic critic is contemplating what is *responsive*. The impressions, also, received from even the simplest objects of contemplation that Pater lists here—a herb, a wine, a gem—are, in fact, complex. The "unique" impression is the uniqueness of a complex whole, whose elements, or some of them, may be broadly or closely similar to elements of other complex wholes. By not adverting to this point, Pater seems to leave out from the critic's function the task of comparison, and grading, of broadly or partly similar wholes, and the notion of a hierarchy or different kinds of wholes.

The chief qualifications of the aesthetic critic are, for Pater, alertness, openness, a clear notion of what he is trying to isolate. But Pater was not primarily concerned with pure aesthetic theory; he is a practical critic: he feels that the man who "experiences impressions strongly, and drives directly at the analysis and discrimination of them, has no need to trouble himself with the abstract question of what beauty is in itself or what is its exact relation to truth or experience." Yet, though he appears to isolate beauty in an uncompromising art-for-art's-sake fashion, Pater had to admit that the perfection of oneself in relation to beautiful objects must at least indirectly involve the moral perfection of oneself in relation to others, for among "the objects with which criticism deals" are "artistic and accomplished forms of human life."

The single essay in *The Renaissance* which deals most directly with "artistic and accomplished forms of human life" is that on Winckelmann, with whom Pater felt a profound personal sympathy. Winckelmann grew up in eighteenth-century Germany without any advantages, was largely self-taught, and dedicated himself passionately to the study of Greek antiquity. His example was the foundation of Johann Wolfgang von Goethe's struggle to acquire a classical balance between breadth of culture and intensity of feeling: "One *learns* nothing from him, but one *becomes* something." And in this sense Winckelmann is the supreme example of the transmission of culture through temperament. Pater saw in Winckelmann's story the example of a life full of "distin-

guishing intensity," a life of rich being, not of mere doing. As an art critic, also, Pater admired Winckelmann for his feeling for the concrete, his lack of shame in handling the sensuous side of Greek art. For the spectator, Pater noted approvingly, the intellectual and the spiritual are properly merged in the sensuous. Yet from the example of Winckelmann, Pater realized the sacrifice involved in the aesthetic life.

From this stringent ideal of the cultivated man as receptive spectator rather than violent originator, Pater arrives at the theory of the conduct of life he inculcates in the conclusion to *The Renaissance*. This is a highly compressed, evocative document. Pater gives, first, his own version of David Hume's and John Stuart Mill's phenomenalism. The sole unit of experience is "the impression." All that is actual is a single, sharp moment, gone before it can be said to be. Yet there lingers inexplicably within that moment the relic, more or less fugitive, of other such moments gone by. These moments are in perpetual flight, but their onset can be "multiplied," and their impact made more vivid by "the high passions." As the moment is isolated by analysis from its context, so the observer is abstracted from his social frame: he is cut off alike from the solidity of the world and from social solidarity:

> Experience, already reduced to a swarm of impressions, is ringed round for each one of us by that thick wall of personality through which no real voice has ever pierced on its way to us, or from us to that which we can only conjecture to be without. Every one of those impressions is the impression of the individual in his isolation, each mind keeping as a solitary prisoner its own dream of a world.
>
> (p. 209)

The price to be paid for the freedom of the human sensibility to seek first and foremost the heightening of its sensations is a high one. The solid world, the social world, even the vague assurance of something beyond the veil, all go. The purpose of such language, with its melancholy emphasis on dissolution and isolation, is to set the stage for the real message of the conclusion. This is that we should multiply and intensify our sensations at all cost; that not the wisdom of experience, but the excitement of experiencing, is the one thing necessary:

> Not to discriminate every moment some passionate attitude in those about us, and in the brilliance of their gifts some tragic dividing of forces on their ways is, on this short day of frost and sun, to sleep before evening. . . . We have

an interval, and then our place knows us no more. . . . Our one chance lies in expanding that interval, in getting as many pulsations as possible into the given time. High passions give us this quickened sense of life, ecstasy and sorrow of love, political or religious enthusiasm, or the "enthusiasm of humanity." . . . Of this wisdom, the poetic passion, the desire of beauty, the love of art for art's sake, has most; for art comes to you professing frankly to give nothing but the highest quality to your moments as they pass, and simply for those moments' sake.

(pp. 211–213)

This is not, however, the mere creed of art for art's sake: it is art for the sake of a specially conceived morality. For Pater, as Frank Kermode has pointed out, "art is what is significant in life, and so sensibility or insight, corruptible as it is, is the organ of moral knowledge, and art, for all its refusal to worship the idols of vulgar morality, is the only true morality; indeed it is nothing less than life itself."[3] Intensities, for Pater, were not all in one narrowly monotonous key, the key, for instance, of sublimated or tantalized sexuality: making love was an intense experience; so was a mystic's vision; so were the overtones of "a chorus-ending in Euripides." (For all his talk about intensifying and multiplying sensations, he does not quite cultivate them for their own sake: he seeks through them rather the unification of personality.) Yet after Pater wrote, it was impossible for critics and artists to continue in the naively moralistic view of art that had marked even a great critic like John Ruskin or a painter of genuine integrity like William Holman Hunt.

V

The Renaissance possesses distinct unity of tone; but its total effect remains somewhat baffling. This partly derives from its being a federation of periodical essays, published over a period when Pater's thought was in rapid evolution. Pater was himself probably aware of the resulting inconsistencies, but he may have accepted these as records of his mental history, and the preface and the conclusion clearly represented attempts at a final blend. The culminating essay, that on Winckelmann, was the earliest composed and recalls the skepticisms of the Coleridge essay. The essay on the French proto-Renaissance, "Two Early French Stories," and "Joachim du

[3]*Romantic Image* (London, 1957).

Bellay" had appeared in 1872, five years after "Winckelmann" and a year before *The Renaissance* was published. These two essays gesture toward a shadowy theme: a cyclic movement in the Renaissance itself from twelfth- and thirteenth-century France to the France of the Pléiade.

Other themes may be distinguished. We are made aware, for example, of preparations for the emergence by the end of the book of that culture hero of the nineteenth century, Goethe. In the first essay, phrases limit the vivid rebelliousness of the French Middle Ages; its openness to the return of the pagan Venus, its intellectual curiosity, the free play of its human affections: "the perfection of culture," Pater tells us, "is not rebellion but peace"; its end, a "deep moral stillness." And such perfection finds its most complete embodiment in Goethe. In the preface Pater associates beauty in landscape, painting, and the fair forms of human life, whereas the latter becomes tranposed in the conclusion into " the face of one's friend." At times he lingers over what is virtually some Platonic belief in the body's beauty as vehicle of the soul, index of an inward harmony and completeness. Pico della Mirandola, for example, retains a medieval chivalry of intellect, a readiness to encounter the most mysterious and uncouth ideas in the belief that "nothing which has ever interested living men and women can wholly lose its vitality." Pico, like Pater himself, evades renunciations: the old gods survive the flame of his conversion, and Pico furnishes too an example of that transmission of culture by beauty of form and personality.

"The fair face of one's friend": Pater discreetly alludes to "the vague and wayward loves" of Michelangelo and Leonardo da Vinci, to the passionate male friendships of Winckelmann. But such are later corrected by the intense but chaste relationship of Marius with Flavian and with Cornelius. Even in the earlier book, the ideal is less the homosexual than the Platonic, the androgynous— that point where the beauty of male and of female dissolves in a higher accordance, though the androgyne, as so often in the later nineteenth century, can be other than healing. In one of Michelangelo's works we meet that "face of doubtful sex, set in the shadow of its own hair." The image of the androgyne, of an untroubled centrality, one might argue, is related itself to an idea that persists through *The Renaissance*: the tendency of the individual arts to transcend their formal limits and aspire to the condition of music, most nondiscursive of all arts. Personality itself, at its fairest, most developed, has precisely such an aspiration, associated with the ideal of transpicuousness we encounter in Pater's first surviving prose work, "Diaphanéité," and later found by Pater in the moral sexlessness of Greek sculpture. But that triumph of form over matter remains associated in a manner almost mystical with death; like the swoon of Leda in Yeats's sonnet "Leda and the Swan," "only the abstract lines remain, in a great indifference." The Pléiade, Pater tells us, were insatiable of music and in du Bellay's most famous poem, the "Hymn to the Winds," "matter itself becomes almost nothing; the form almost everything." The theme is resumed in the Giorgione essay, where Pater describes Giorgione's school as refining on that "feverish, tumultuously coloured world of the old citizens of Venice—exquisite pauses in time, in which, arrested thus, we seem to be spectators of all the fullness of existence, and which are like some consummate extract or quintessence of life." Here Pater involves us in a Keatsian dying-into-life. We have the profile of a *symboliste* theory of art; the essay on Giorgione has been seen, too, as anticipating Clive Bell's notion of "significant form."

Art critics have indeed been milder to Pater than have the literary critics, though his descriptions of paintings share the expressive qualities of his discussion of literary texts. The method is to mime the emotional effect of a work of art through the tone and cadence of his prose, and (like Ruskin, in this field his master) he extends the spatial effects of an art work into the temporal. Pater was contemporary with the first scientific historians of art in Germany and occasionally embodies their findings (not always fortunately; he limits Giorgione's canon to one painting); but he remains distinctly light on technical as opposed to dramatic or meditative description and was no haunter of archives. Yet art historians of severe method, such as Bernard Berenson and Herbert Horne, have put on record their debt to Pater.

At his best, Pater allows the reader sufficient plain visual data to share in, or to resist, his interpretation of the work of art. In describing Botticelli's *Birth of Venus*, for example, he intuitively remarks the slender, unripe, Gothic idiom of the goddess' body. And this insight is followed by a sensitive record of the painting's faintly menacing detail:

An emblematical figure of the wind blows hard across the grey water, moving forward the dainty-lipped shell on which she sails, the sea "showing his teeth" as it moves in thin lines of foam, and sucking in one by one the falling roses, each severe in outline, plucked off short at the stalk, but embrowned a little, as Botticelli's flowers always are. Botticelli meant all that imagery to be altogether pleasurable; and it was partly an incompleteness of resources, inseparable from the art of that time, that subdued and chilled it; but his predilection for minor tones counts also; and what is unmistakable is the sadness with which he has conceived the goddess of pleasure, as the depositary of a great power over the lives of men.

("Sandro Botticelli," *The Renaissance*, p. 49)

This "quotation" from Botticelli can indeed be applied to much of the master's work, even if Pater consistently underestimates the achievements of the Florentine Renaissance, describing it as "in many things, great rather by what it designed than by what it achieved."

VI

If the Botticelli passage is a triumph, there may be reservations about the second most famous passage in Pater: his evocation of Leonardo's famous portrait of a lady, *La Gioconda*, or the "Mona Lisa." This lady has a smiling mouth and is set, not in a domestic background, but, as Pater puts it, "in that cirque of fantastic rocks, as in some faint light under sea."

The presence that thus so strangely rose beside the waters is expressive of what in the ways of a thousand years man had come to desire. Hers is the head upon which all "the ends of the world are come," and the eyelids are a little weary. It is a beauty wrought out from within upon the flesh, the deposit, little cell by cell, of strange thoughts and fantastic reveries and exquisite passions. Set it for a moment beside one of those white Greek goddesses or beautiful women of antiquity, and how would they be troubled by this beauty, into which the soul with all its maladies has passed? All the thoughts and experience of the world have etched and moulded there, in that which they have of power to refine and make expressive the outward form, the animalism of Greece, the lust of Rome, the reverie of the Middle Age with its spiritual ambition and imaginative loves, the return of the Pagan world, the sins of the Borgias.

("Leonardo Da Vinci," *The Renaissance*, p. 118)

There follows the passage that Yeats printed as free verse in his *Oxford Book of Modern Verse*, followed by two sentences of summary:

She is older than the rocks among which she sits; like the vampire, she has been dead many times, and learned the secrets of the grave; and has been a diver in deep seas, and keeps their fallen day about her; and trafficked for strange webs with Eastern merchants; and, as Leda, was the mother of Helen of Troy, and, as Saint Anne, the mother of Mary; and all this has been to her but as the sound of lyres and flutes, and lives only in the delicacy with which it has moulded the changing lineaments and tinged the eyelids and the hands. The fancy of a perpetual life, sweeping together ten thousand experiences, is an old one; and modern thought has conceived the idea of humanity as wrought upon by, and summing up in itself, all modes of thought and life. Certainly Lady Lisa might stand as the embodiment of the old fancy, the symbol of the modern idea.

(pp. 118–119)

The Mona Lisa as the embodiment of the old fancy. Even there Pater attributes more to the painting than is readily legible. There are clear embarrassments in attempting to discover verbal equivalents for visual experience, and Pater is not writing scientific art criticism. The passage represents a reverie on the painting as on Leonardo's work in general; but it remains more than self-indulgent fantasy. First, we may note that the passage occurs in the middle of the Leonardo essay, at the center of *The Renaissance*, and its significance radiates backward and forward, back to what is embodied in history, forward to what is as yet only symbolized, or prescribed. The description collects phrases which Pater uses of the master's other works, for Mona Lisa's face is the final embodiment of an image that obsessed Leonardo; that same face impressing itself on the icons of Saint John, Saint Anne, and the Madonna, and, as may be gathered from a copy of the now lost painting, of Leda and the swan. To take one example of phrases recollected, as in some trance, from other parts of the essay, we can cite that "diver in deep seas," reflecting the earlier "faint light under sea" which on the literal level could be the varnish that both preserves and distorts the painting. Laid over paint first as preservative, later to lend some mellow, speciously antique patina, it chills the spring of color, but adds mystery. The painting has also ripened through time in the sense of being interpreted and reinterpreted, each analysis thickening the varnish that lies over Leonardo's original paintwork.

Pater's account assumes into itself much of the history of that interpretation. For Giorgio Vasari, in the sixteenth century, Lisa's smile is pleasing; the painting preeminently lifelike; Leonardo is seen as one who controls nature by making a perfect model of it, as in primitive magic. The romantic critics shift to the notion of portraiture as bodying forth the subjectivity of the sitter, so the smile and landscape that the sixteenth century may have seen as unfinished or formalized become willed and significantly related.

Pater associates landscape and face more firmly than his predecessors, and Sir Kenneth Clark concludes that he is right: the rocky backgrounds of Leonardo's portraits show a real understanding of the forces that led to their structure; but there are also landscapes of fantasy, projections not of Lisa's but Leonardo's inner world. With Luigi Lanzi in the eighteenth and through to William Hazlitt and Stendhal in the early nineteenth century, interpretation of the haunting smile proceeds from gaiety to equivocation: the smile belongs equally to mistress and to saint. Michelet, who sees Leonardo as prophet and type, interprets the smile as delight at scientific "forbidden knowledge" mingled with irony at the expense of an old world that is passing: Leonardo as the first modern man, though the smile is nervous, troubled. Pater takes Michelet into the regions of myth, and French critics writing immediately before Pater provide him with vocabulary; the smile is now satanic, sibylline, voluptuous, caught in mystery of the half-light, and Théophile Gautier, touching on Leonardo's obsessive faces, provides the final touches:

We have seen their faces, but not upon this earth; in some previous existence perhaps; through the subtle modeling we divine the beginnings of fatigue . . . a spirit entirely modern . . . beneath the form expressed, one feels a thought which is vague, infinite, inexpressible, like a musical idea . . . images already seen. . . .

Vasari's "jesters and singers" whom rumor suggested Leonardo had employed to "protract the subtle expression," Pater finally modulates into the "flutes and lyres" of Algernon Charles Swinburne's *Laus Veneris*. (Swinburne's description of some heads of Michelangelo, written in 1868, had a considerable effect on Pater's style of this period.)

Pater's Mona Lisa has assumed by now the lineaments of the romantic fatal woman, who enters men's lives from beyond history and is an indication of the autonomy of images that live their life independently of the minds to which they give themselves. She resolves the painful antinomies of pleasure-pain; knowledge-mystery; orgasm-death. Leonardo is oracle; not victim, but victor over his image. That image sums up all the forces that lay behind the Renaissance of which Leonardo made a model, but the image now needs remastering.

Anthony Ward[4] has persuasively argued that Pater's own image of the Lady Lisa is intended as a model for the future, a model that will enable him in the determinist nightmare of the Darwinian world to "go on writing." Ward reminds us of Pater's distinction, in the essay "Style," that the "masculine," the "controlling, rational, forming power" of the artist, is exerted on the "feminine," the brute amorphous mass of the artist's experience, which constitutes "soul" as opposed to "mind," a related distinction. Organization achieved by mind is the design made on the web of the artist's experience; in Pater's case, what he knew of reality as he had been taught to see it by Charles Darwin. Man was merely "the most complex of the products of nature." The tissues of his brain were indeed "modified by every ray of light and sound"; he was under the influence of "natural law" or, in Pater's own despairing term, "necessity."

To continue paraphrasing Ward, Darwin also taught Pater that though man's consciousness, his being, was fragmented into moments that changed even as they were being formed, these fragments bore in them "the central forces of the world." In Pater's view an organic development involved the notion that though the organism was in constant change, at each moment in its development it vestigially contained, legible upon it, a sort of synoptic history of development. This "web" is reflected by submitting it to the controlling power of design. Insofar as an artist can reduce the incoherent flux of experience to design, he will be able to emancipate himself from that incoherence. To the extent that the power of design affects the artist's own response to the incoherence and determinism of the nightmare, it will establish his freedom from it, and the type of such a design is the Mona Lisa. As Ward puts it: "The modern, [Friedrich Wilhelm Joseph] Schelling said, must create his own mythology out of the material given to the intelligence of his age." In the "Mona Lisa," we may see Pater struggling to evolve the myth, or artistic model, which would locate and give expression to that material. "He was intent on . . . making the ideas he wished to express saturate and

become identical with the vessel made to contain them." He wished to define the image on the female "fabric of his dreams." And he wished the fabric of dreams to be legible upon the image.

In Leonardo's picture *The Daughters of Herodias*, the characters, Pater says, are: "clairvoyants, through whom, as through delicate instruments, one becomes aware of the subtler forces of nature, and the modes of their action, all that is magnetic in it." They are significant examples in which we actually see those forces at work on human flesh. Pater was trying to create an image or model, a design, into which he could pour all the female fluid matter of his understanding of the world so as to locate it there and make it legible. Mona Lisa contains each of the three particulars Ward has defined, and she satisfies at the same time the masculine demands Pater was making in that she reduces the three particulars to a design. Man "in the ways of a thousand years" can be translated into Walter Pater himself. The Lady Lisa is expressive of what he himself desires, and "the ways of a thousand years" does not only function legitimately as a liturgical gesture: it is also an attempt to give universality and authority to the image.

The Mona Lisa is a "head," a single entry upon which "all the ends of the world are come," concentrating in a single finite image all man's relation to the objects about him, his sense of their "tyranny." "Wrought out from within upon the flesh, the deposit, little cell by cell." The image, that is to say, is a changing one. It develops as it is conceived. The flux enters into it but is controlled, and the phrase, deposited "little cell by cell," clearly shows knowledge of the doctrine of organic development. We are also told of the accumulative nature of the image, since from Leonardo's childhood, we have seen it "defining itself on the fabric of his dreams." In the moment of our apprehension of her face we may see all history vestigially legible, "all the thoughts and experience of the world. . . ." She contains a synoptic history of the development of civilization, such as "the animalism of Greece."

Evolution introduced a new conception of time into English consciousness. In a moment there were concentrated " ten thousand experiences." In the notion of carbon, Pater says there was both the notion of coal and of the diamond. The artist's role was thus to collapse the growth of a thing into one of his moments of vision, and to contradict temporal development. He was to make the moment "wholly concrete."

[4]In *Walter Pater: The Idea in Nature* (London, 1966).

The image of the Mona Lisa represents, in the words of the Giorgione essay,"an exquisite pause in time . . . in which we seem to be spectators of the fullness of all existence." And in such moments, man was free from the world's deliquescence. And the Mona Lisa is also free, spectator of all existence, yet although detached from her experience she has still organized it into her design and so is able to free herself from it; but freed from the experience, that experience cannot be denied and must be expressed. She at once resists and so gives expression to the "magnetic nightmare." She shows the action of mind on soul, shows man dealing with his experience so as to control it, thus giving him back his sense of freedom. She is at once the realization and the suggestion of an artistic idea. And to Ward's invocation of Darwin, we can add contemporary biological theory, particularly that of Rudolf Virchow, who posits in his *Cellular Pathologie* of 1858 "an eternal law of continuous development" in terms of cells, which recalls not merely the "Mona Lisa" but the phraseology of the early essay on Coleridge.

The Renaissance and the earlier essays are dense with the language of contemporary science, echoing verbally essays in the *Westminster Review* of the late 1860's. It is such vocabulary that underlies Pater's most striking metaphor of the gem-like flame, a notion that fuses stillness and motion, transparency and heat, and which first appears in the brief essay "Diaphanéité," first read as a paper to Old Mortality. Later essays elaborate the image: "the fine edge of light, where the elements of our moral nature refine themselves to burning point" (*Miscellaneous Studies*, 1895, pp. 247–248), where "the rays in themselves impotent begin to unite and burn" (*The Renaissance*, p. 214). The essay "Diaphanéité," the portrait of an ideal type of self-transparency, of spirit and matter fused, is a mode for Pater's later historical and mythic heroes. The essay has been plausibly related to Johann Gottlieb Fichte's lectures on "The Nature of the Scholar." Here, the philosopher states that the Divine Idea "lies concealed beyond all natural appearances" and that

a certain part of the meaning of this Divine Idea of the world is accessible to, and conceivable by, the cultivated mind. . . . In every age, that kind of education and spiritual culture by means of which the age hopes to lead mankind to the knowledge of the ascertained part of the Divine Idea, is the Learned Culture of the age; and every man who partakes in this culture is the scholar of the age.

Fichte's insights appear to suggest some actuality beyond the flux, behind the veil. But Pater, even though he made the same insights the starting point for explorations of his own culture, would not simply usurp another man's insights; that would be to deny the changing and growing nature of truth. Fusion, union, is not stasis; it is also transmutation, new harmony, and it is the "diaphanes" who become the heralds of rebirth in the culture: "a majority of such would be the regeneration of the world" (*Miscellaneous Studies*, p. 254).

The more we examine this so-called purple panel, the more we find that it is dense with meaning.

VII

In *The Renaissance* Pater had been trying to fix the secret individual experiences of a few personalities who in his scheme of values mattered supremely, by attempting to define in them some central quality, some fixed point in the flux. That fixed point was best illustrated in Michelangelo by the Biblical phrase "Out of the strong came forth sweetness." In Leonardo the fixed point was the conflict between the scientist's curiosity and the artist's love of beauty; and so on. But there was one great objection to making ideal types out of actual historical personages. Anybody who has actually existed remains, even after his death, subject to the flux. New scholarly discoveries have altered, for instance, since Pater's time, our view of Giorgione, of whom Pater accepted only one picture as proven authentic; and even where there has not been this type of development, we cannot help seeing Pater's Leonardo or his Botticelli as doubly distant in time from us; as presented to us through the subtly distorting medium of Pater's own late nineteenth-century sensibility (and our view of that sensibility is itself a subtly distorted mid-twentieth-century view).

It was Pater's awareness of this fundamental flaw in the notion of making art out of history that turned him from writing about historical figures, idealized into types, and toward writing, as in *Imaginary Portraits* and *Marius the Epicurean*, about imaginary figures who could be, without possibility of reduction, ideal types. He decided to create characters who had no historical existence, who could still, like the characters in *The Renaissance*, be incarnations of the unending development of culture, but who could be fixed, like works of art. There are likely to be no such shifts in our evaluations of Pater's purely imaginary characters. What they have in common is that they are all gifted or dedicated natures, born out of due time. Duke Carl is the herald of a serene neoclassicism in a Germany desolated by religious wars; Sebastian van Storck is torn between the life of feeling and the passion for metaphysics, and chilled by the abstractions of Spinozan philosophy. In other such stories (some of them were published posthumously), we find buried Hellenism irrupting into the Gothic twilight. Brother Apollyon is really Apollo in exile, while Denys of Auxerre reenacts the ritual of Dionysus as Lord of Misrule, so playing out Pater's notion that ritual remains, while beliefs falter. All the subjects of Pater's *Imaginary Portraits* are destroyed by the age in which they live, but remain unchanged at the center; portents of change, they are themselves unchanging; all of them die unreasonably and almost casually, drastically, yet in a way that seems irrelevant to their life-patterns. The effect of these imaginary portraits is curiously cold, though impressive. We do not feel our way into these stories; rather we reflect on them from a distance. Perhaps we are supposed to have heard them before (as in the case of Dionysus and Apollo, with their harsh cycles, we certainly have) but told in another tone of voice. They reflect Pater's own predicament; images of himself projected into history, full of the sense of exile, never communicating directly, but, like gods, dying to be reborn in the soil and through their newly vivified culture.

VIII

Marius the Epicurean, Pater's central work, an extended imaginary portrait, makes sense on two levels: first, as a scholarly, imaginative re-creation of second-century Antonine Rome; second, as a subtle, trenchant, and indirect analysis of high Victorian England. Pater was quite open in a letter to a friend about the contemporary bearing of the book:

> I regard this . . . matter as a sort of duty. For, you know, I think that there is a . . . sort of religious phase possible for the modern mind . . . the conditions of which phase it is the main object of my design to convey.
>
> (*Letters of Walter Pater*, p. 52)

Certain obvious affinities existed between Pater's England and Marcus Aurelius' Rome. Both were centers of vast empires; both governments were internally stable; both were intermittently at war with other races on the frontier. More profoundly, both provided an intellectual climate in which a bewildering number of competing faiths and philosophies were able to flourish. The Antonine period represented for Pater the ripe autumn of the Graeco-Roman world, and one of the implications of *Marius* is that in Victorian England the almost overripe fruit of civilization is also hanging heavy on the bough.

From the broad church historians, like Thomas Arnold or Arthur Stanley, Pater may well have derived the notion that societies pass through the same life-cycles as individuals and that God's providence is constantly active, thus disrupting the determined patterns of history. For the broad church historians, Rome provided the model of a finished civilization, while their own was, on a higher level, still pursuing its course. God's providence intervened largely through the process of religion accommodating itself to progress, and it is this principle of accommodation that Pater seems to have in mind when he refers to "a religious phase possible to the modern mind," one which will take into account the "flux" and by so doing will transcend it. Another indication of the manner in which providence asserted itself through history was furnished by ritual. When Pater attended mass at a high Anglican church such as St. Alban's, Holborn, he could not fail to notice that the celebrant was wearing the formal evening dress of a Roman gentleman of the second century. Myth, on the other hand, to Pater, as to Arnold, expressed something fluid, though some myths no longer religiously responded to seemed to possess a permanent poetic value. It is, therefore, in ritual, rather than in the abstract moral and metaphysical appeal of religion or in naked mysticism that Pater is interested:

> Players and painted stage took all my love,
> And not those things that they were emblems of.
> (W. B. Yeats, "The Circus Animals' Desertion")

But the deeper significance of *Marius* is that it explores Pater's inner life more coherently than the scattered brilliances of *The Renaissance* were able to do. Marius is essentially Pater himself with a personal beauty that he never had, seeking and finding a life of communion and sacrifice for which Pater only wistfully longed.

The structure of *Marius* resembles that of Pater's other imaginary portraits. Character is genuinely evoked, but at a distance. The people in *Marius* never make a brutal impact on one another; they never converse. Their ideas reach us through diaries, lectures, and Platonic fable. This is partly tact on Pater's part, for he knew he had none of the ordinary novelist's gifts. It is partly also a deliberate method of indicating the essential isolation of the central figure and of embodying character, as Pater's own character in life was essentially embodied, through the artistic presentation of the emotional impact of ideas.

The book opens with a sensitive account of the old, simple Roman religion of the household gods of hearth and field; a rustic religion of "usages and sentiments" rather than dogma, of "natural piety." Perhaps this is comparable to the old high-and-dry Anglicanism of Pater's childhood. Marius, the child-priest, is soon orphaned, leaves the security of his childhood home, and loses his attachment to the old pagan religion. In Pisa, he meets the young esthete Flavian, whose physical beauty and moral corruption are epitomes of the decaying pagan world. Flavian has literary ambitions and his "euphuism"— here seen as art without morality—has, for Pater, obvious topical relevance to the creed of art for art's sake. The first part of *Marius* ends with the death of Flavian, still struggling to finish his masterpiece, the *Pervigilium Veneris.*

Marius, though not infected by Flavian's corrupt sophistication, is deeply moved by his death. He realizes that for the pagan there is no consolation in the face of death. It is the first of several emotional crises, which also become moral and intellectual crises, and which are all concerned with the gulf between the living and the dead and man's bafflement, awe, or horror in the face of death. Rejecting the philosophy of "flux," Marius learns from Aristippus of Cyrene to concern himself less with troubling thoughts than with the happy ordering of the feelings, "life as the end of life." This is not a crude hedonism, but a method of tactful discrimination. Marius then proceeds to Rome to become Marcus Aurelius' secretary, and the pointed contrast between the refined egoism of his own Epicureanism and the stern disinterestedness of the emperor's Stoicism has its effect. He now begins to think of Epicureanism as an essentially adolescent philoso-phy. From a discourse of Cornelius Fronto, a teacher of rhetoric at Rome, Marius conceives the notion that morality may indeed be a kind of artistic ordering of life, but comparable to the ordering Fronto finds in the universe itself, that of a single great polity.

But to Marius, Fronto's metaphysics also seems painfully abstract. He admires much more the practical discipline which Aurelius has made of the Stoic philosophy, but his admiration cools when he realizes that the emperor's love of humanity is rather abstract, too. And this disillusionment is reinforced by the spectacle of Aurelius' helpless grief at the death of his child. Stoicism cannot meet the test of death. At this time Marius has a spiritual experience of supreme importance. Riding among the Sabine Hills, he senses, behind the veil of matter, an unseen friend or guide, and so arrives at the notion of a personal creator, utterly different from the vague principle of cosmic order of the Stoics. Even through his early Cyrenaicism, Marius had preserved a certain austerity of temperament, and at the time when, through a knightly young figure, Cornelius, he meets a community of Christians, he is already preparing himself, though unconsciously, for his own sacrificial death.

In Christianity Marius is to find all that he found good in paganism: the sense of communion; humble acceptance of the good things of the earth (unlike Aurelius' proud rejection of them); the heightened response to life of a refined Cyrenaicism; the moral dignity of Stoicism itself—but all transcended, not rejected. The inclusion of paganism in its noblest forms in Christianity is symbolized for Marius by "the fragments of older architecture, the mosaics, the spiral columns" that compose the architecture of the Christian catacomb in Cecilia's house. And Marius' development toward Christianity is by way of culture, not self-denial: not by the sacrifice of any one of the aspects of the self but by the "harmonious development of all the parts of human nature, in just proportion to one another." (All this is very plausible, but not particularly Christian.) For the church under the Antonines radiates the full beauty of holiness through its poetry and music, establishing a tradition that was to last to Pater's own day.

Marius' first contact with Christianity is, typically, through death, through the catacomb. At the graves of the Christian martyrs, he learns that death can be joy; but he is also initiated into life, into natural love, when the family of the gracious Cecilia becomes for him an emblem of the heavenly family of the church itself. And witnessing the eucharistic celebration, he feels that he has at last found something to hold by, dimly sensing there a redemptive cyclic movement: "There was here a veritable consecration, hopeful and animating, of the earth's gifts, of old dead and dark matter itself, now in some way redeemed at last, of all that we can touch and see . . . and in strong contrast to the wise emperor's renunciant and impassive attitude towards them."

For Marius, this is a new "spirit" investing old rites, not a new "matter": ritual as ever remains the fixed element in religion, though myth changes. Marius' own hope for the future now rests mainly on his friendship with Cornelius. In this friendship, he seems to reach out in imagination to a happier and holier future, and it is in this spirit that Marius sacrifices himself for Cornelius' safety, dying, consoled by Christian rites, in a Christian household. "His death, according to their generous view in this matter [being] of the nature of a martyrdom; and martyrdom, as the Church has always said, a kind of sacrament with plenary grace." Christian by nature, not grace, poor Marius, and it is pleasant to think that his relics, in later years, may have been venerated as those of an early martyr; but the conclusion of the book has its subdued ironies. Marius' end seems weariness rather than exaltation: Marius the spectator has become Marius the actor, having overcome the "endless dialogue of the mind with itself," and commitment leads only to self-destruction.

As a work of art, *Marius* has a dense and logical structure, based on a series of contrasts, dialectical or ironic. Flavian placed over against the rather unreal figure of Cornelius; the severe beauty of Cecilia juxtaposed with the "malign" beauty of the empress Faustina; the Roman games with the martyrs, "athletes of God." But minor incidents are easily overlooked. Marius' visit to his own family catacomb, as the last of his race, lends an added poignancy to the feeling that he can identify himself with "the coming world," through his friendship with Cornelius, who is to marry Cecilia. Even the much criticized insertion of a translation of Apuleius' "Cupid and Psyche" has complete relevance to Marius' developing philosophy: it serves "to combine many lines of meditation, already familiar to Marius, into the ideal of a perfect imaginative love, centred upon a type of beauty entirely flawless and clean . . . in contrast with that ideal . . . men's actual loves . . . might ap-

pear to him . . . somewhat mean and sordid." And Pater would have known the tradition of allegorizing the fable as the soul's desire for union with God.

IX

SURPRISINGLY little of Pater's criticism is directed toward English literature as distinct from subjects derived from painting, sculpture, or antiquity. The essay on *Measure for Measure* retains some interest; but apart from one or two major pieces, this aspect of his work is not rewarding.

The essay on William Wordsworth in *Appreciations*, originally published in 1874, strongly counterpoints the conclusion to *The Renaissance* and remains a cardinal example both of Pater's *finesse* and his failings as a literary critic. It appeared some years before Arnold's fine essay on Wordsworth, at a time when, for various reasons, Wordsworth was beginning to lose the hold he had once had, especially on younger readers. Pater was, therefore, drawing attention to a poet recognized as great but beginning, partly because of the bulk and unevenness of his performance, to be a little neglected. He had already in *The Renaissance* strikingly isolated what was for him Wordsworth's greatest virtue, meditative pathos. Perhaps the gravest defect of this essay (it is inherent in the "appreciative" method as such, which will always pay more attention to texture than to structure, to moments of intensity than to the background they arise from) is the failure to see that the "alien element . . . something tedious and prosaic . . ." in Wordsworth is not only inseparable from, but often serves to heighten, Wordsworth's moments of grand concentration. Pater's essay conjures up a spectral Wordsworth, purged of all that is "alien" and "prosaic," but purged also of his large craggy individuality. He scales the great poet down to something smaller, sweeter, smoother than life-size:

His life of eighty years is divided by no very profoundly felt incidents: its changes are almost wholly inward, and it falls into broad, untroubled, perhaps somewhat monotonous spaces. What it most resembles is the life of one of those early Italian or Flemish painters, who, just because their minds were full of heavenly visions, passed, some of them, the better part of sixty years in quiet, systematic industry. This placid life matured a quite unusual sensibility, really innate in him, to the sights and sounds of the natural world. . . . The poem of *Resolution and Independence* is a storehouse of such records: for its fulness of imagery it may be compared to Keats's *Saint Agnes' Eve.*

("Wordsworth," *Appreciations*, pp. 42–43)

Pater would not have known about Annette Vallon, but he ought to have noticed that the French Revolution, for Wordsworth, was "a profoundly felt incident"; and he ought to have noticed that a line in the poem he is mentioning, "Resolution and Independence," "And mighty poets in their misery dead," does not reflect anything at all like this Flemish placidity. But it is acute of him to isolate "Resolution and Independence" for its "fulness of imagery," though at the same time when he compares it with "The Eve of St. Agnes," he again shows the limitations of his method. "Resolution and Independence" is a poem with a tough underlying moral structure of self-discovery and self-rebuke, an underlying, almost didactic structure that would have appealed to, say, Alexander Pope or Samuel Johnson; whereas "The Eve of St. Agnes" is self-indulgent erotic fantasy distanced miraculously into art. But Pater is extremely effective when he deals more generally with Wordsworth's qualities:

Clear and delicate at once, as he is in the outlining of visible imagery, he is more clear and delicate still, and finely scrupulous, in the noting of sounds; so that he conceives of noble sound as even moulding the human countenance to nobler types, and as something actually "profaned" by colour, by visible form, or image. . . .

(p. 43)

And in the following passage he rises to the full height of his subject, though even here, as we follow the mannered cadences, we may have a slight uneasy sense that Pater's Wordsworth is a little too much like the young Marius, a little too self-consciously appreciating the simple ritual dignities of the Roman religion of the boundaries and the soil:

Religious sentiment, consecrating the affections and natural regrets of the human heart, above all, that pitiful awe and care for the perishing human clay, of which relic-worship is but the corruption, has always had much to do with localities, with the thoughts which attach themselves to actual scenes and places. Now what is true of it everywhere, is truest of it in those secluded valleys where one generation after another maintains the same abiding-place; and it was on this side, that Wordsworth apprehended religion most strongly. Consisting, as it did so much, in

the recognition of local sanctities, in the habit of connecting the stones and trees of a particular spot of earth with the great events of life, till the low walls, the green mounds, the half-obliterated epitaphs seemed full of voices, and a sort of natural oracle, the very religion of these people of the dales appeared but as another link between them and the earth, and was literally a religion of nature. It tranquillized them by bringing them under the placid rule of traditional and narrowly localized observances. "Grave livers," they seemed to him, under this aspect, with stately speech, and something of that natural dignity of manners, which underlies the highest courtesy.

(pp. 48–49)

It is perhaps easiest to "place" Pater as a critic by comparing him with his rather older contemporary Matthew Arnold. He has neither Arnold's flair—sometimes also a weakness—for the ambitious generalization nor Arnold's uncanny gift, sometimes (as in his treatment of Pope and John Dryden) unscrupulously used, for picking on the very quotation that will appear to prove his point. Pater tries to focus on what might be called the sensuous aspects of literature, aspects that seem to him to have an almost physical resonance, rather than, like Arnold, on literature as "a criticism of life." Partly because of this, he is a humbler critic than Arnold. Arnold is always arrogantly sure that he is right, even in the quite numerous instances where his successors have almost unanimously decided that he is crashingly wrong. Pater shows a sounder general taste in what for him is more or less contemporary literature than Arnold. Arnold makes a great fuss about a very minor pair, Maurice and Eugénie de Guérin, and about one of the world's great bores, Etienne Sénancour. Pater mentions with praise, in passing, Stendhal, William Blake, Flaubert, none of them "safe" or fashionable authors in his time. Again, Pater is always a scholar as Arnold quite strikingly is not one. Furthermore, Pater is perhaps the first English critic of importance to have the historical sense very profoundly developed. It is that sense which makes him, on the whole, avoid too arrogant "placing" or absolute judgments. He wishes to *see* a work of literature or art as vividly as possible in its historical setting, rather than to rap its knuckles in a schoolmasterly way for not conforming to the moral and social standards of Dr. Arnold's Rugby. He is less superficial than Arnold about, for instance, the Greeks; Arnold saw them as bathed perpetually in a white Apollonian light; Pater knew about the dark, earthy side of Greek religion. But against all this there has to be set the fact that Arnold, unlike Pater, could occasionally speak of poetry with the authority which only a good practicing poet possesses; and that Arnold, as a critic, even when he is most wrongheaded, speaks always with moral urgency, a concern about the social function of the arts, which was not Pater's *métier*. Perhaps those who know both writers find in Pater more that is gently suggestive and stimulating; in Arnold, more to excite, more to admire, and more to dislike.

X

ONE comes back, again and again, in discussing Pater, to the idea of style; style as a mode of perception, a total responsive gesture of the whole personality rather than—for all Pater's own very notable stylistic mannerism—a mere way of arranging words. Pater's essay "Style," an expansion of a review of Flaubert's *Correspondence*, was published toward the end of his life and from its unusual firmness of statement may constitute something of an aesthetic credo. Pater begins by remarking that the distinction between poetry and prose has been pushed too far and, following Hazlitt and anticipating Eliot, stresses that poetry should possess the virtues of good prose. Following Arnold, Pater believes that prose is "the special and opportune art of the modern world," its flexibility enabling it to deal, far better than Victorian verse, with modern life's complexities. He makes Thomas De Quincey's distinction between the literature of power and that of knowledge: the literature of knowledge has as its criterion truth of fact only; but imaginative prose is to be judged for its fineness of truth, the writer's personal sense of fact, exactness of transposition of the inner vision.

It is natural for a writer to shape the pattern of his attention to fact to his ingrained flair for fitness. But human beings are infinitely various, and the quality of a given piece of literature will depend not on mere transposition of fact, but on fact in its infinite variety as experienced by a specific personality. The writer must have a scholar's tact, for his material, language, is as much a "given" thing as the raw material of the sculptor. The liberties he takes will show his recognition of the expanding potentialities of language as well as its agreed civilized limits; just the degree to which he oversteps these limits will be an

index to the balance of his imagination and his taste. The notion of the flux applies also, with an especially moving pungency, to language. Words slip, slide, flatten out under excessive pressures. The artist-scholar will be acutely aware both of the root-meanings of words and of the constant shifts of their actual meanings in changing contexts; he will aspire to a purged and yet ranging vocabulary, including elements of both the racy and the recondite. He must be aware of developments in philosophy and science —how to tame, for example, ferocious words like "transcend," "ideal," "phenomenon," breaking into the language about this time, so that literature will not be shut out of the expanding vocabulary of the modern scientific intellectual.

But all such requisites of style are subdued to the architectonic quality that reveals the shaping presence of "mind," guaranteeing the tact of the writer's omissions. All the laws of good writing aim, thus, at an identity almost of word with object, so that word, phrase, sentence, sequence of cadences seems almost to *become* what it presents. (Compare the remark, in the Giorgione essay which I earlier quoted, about all the arts aspiring to the condition of music, since in music the distinction between matter and form is as far as possible annihilated.)

This doctrine of confluence of matter and form leads Pater on to Flaubert's notion of the *mot juste*. But he is forced to reject Flaubert's insistence on the artist's impersonality, since, for Pater, style essentially mirrors the uniqueness of temperament, "is the man."

One seems to detect the influence of a philosophic idea . . . of a natural economy, of some pre-existent adaptation, between a relative, somewhere in the world of thought, and its correlative, somewhere in the world of language—both alike, rather, somewhere in the mind of the artist. . . .

("Style," *Appreciations*, p. 27)

Flaubert seems to believe that we know what we are thinking in a purely nonverbal way. For Pater, the process is not so much that of an existent idea in search of expression as of the clarification of the thought itself. In the moment of difficulty for a good writer, it is not the "exact" word that is wanting; what is wrong is some tangle in the actual thinking itself. The problem of style is, fundamentally, one of self-transparency, of supple self-reflection.

Even if the architectonic ideal of "mind" in style is

satisfied, this does not imply that great as opposed to good literature will result. For Pater concludes his essay by telling us that greatness in literature depends not on form, but matter, not on handling, but substance; on the range and depth of the human interest of its theme.

> Given the conditions I have tried to explain as constituting good art;—then, if it be devoted further to the increase of men's happiness, to the redemption of the oppressed, or the enlargement of our sympathies with each other, or to such presentment of new or old truth about ourselves and our relation to the world as may ennoble and fortify us in our sojourn here, or immediately, as with Dante, to the glory of God, it will be also great art . . . it [will have] something of the soul of humanity . . . and find its logical, its architectural place, in the great structure of human life.
>
> (p. 36)

This argument undercuts not merely the ideal of unified matter and form, but the whole of Pater's earlier insights into the nature of literary art. Pater had, indeed, already recognized the limitations of his intellectualist ideal, by admitting the presence of a further element in style, that of "soul," exhibited mainly in devotional literature of a highly personal type. If the quotation above is to be taken as his final position, then Pater has renounced aestheticism and submitted to a simple Christian humanitarianism.

But the issue is not so plain. In his writings after "Style" we find little practical outcome, and in "Style" itself, the architectonic ideal itself is not observed. The aesthetic unit, for Pater, remains fixed at the sentence, if necessary a sentence extended by parenthesis, distinction, and qualification to paragraph length. That style is a matter of *perception*, not of cadence or euphony, is the principle laid down in the essay; but one finds so often in Pater the isolated cadence or sentence making its impact by itself; one must pause after every sentence to adjust oneself to a new rhythm (not a new turn of argument). In "Style" itself, the plea for a flexible prose and the rejection of Flaubert are only loosely connected. We must read "Style," with its jagged transitions, as a set of related perceptions, or set, even, of ultimately isolated perceptions, held together only by their occurrence within a common periphery. A typical passage of argument may make this clearer:

> Music and prose literature are, *in one sense*, the opposite terms of art. . . . *If* music be the ideal of all art whatever,

precisely because in music it is impossible to distinguish the form from the substance . . . then, literature, by finding its specific excellence in the absolute correspondence of the term to its import, will be but fulfilling the condition of all artistic quality in things everywhere, of all good art.

> (p. 35)

It is rather like a proportion sum: let *a* be *b*. Pater attempts first to disarm us by that qualifying phrase "in one sense," and once we are off guard the innocent word "if" is used to establish as an axiom what has been proposed entirely without empirical justification. In such a passage Pater is modulating logic aesthetically, subjecting our pleasure in seeing an argument properly worked out to our pleasure in what I. A. Richards has called "a music of ideas."

Pater's ideal vocabulary is purged and ranging, scholarly but adventurous; but his actual vocabulary, even at its most mature and discriminating in the finally revised *Marius* of 1892 (the relation of this to "Style" has been acutely analyzed by Edmund Chandler), consists of many words that are either precious, intensive, or cloudy. His vocabulary is purged and scholarly, but very narrow; that of a special, even an intensely private, personality. And though Pater asserts that literature is great through the dignity of its broad human interests, what, as Chandler asks, are we to make of this passage:

> . . . not only scholars, but all disinterested lovers of books, will always look to [literature], as to all other fine art, for . . . a sort of cloistral refuge, from a certain vulgarity in the actual world. A poem like *Lycidas*, a perfect fiction like *Esmond*, perfect handling of a theory like Newman's *Idea of a University*, has for them something of the uses of a religious "retreat."
>
> ("Style," *Appreciations*, p. 14)

The assumption here still seems to be that art is closed, finished, perfect, while life has an indefinitely open texture. Art is the moral object, intrinsically superior to everyday reality, not a means of encountering experience with greater openness and alertness. So Pater's actual criticism remains fixed always upon the work of art as a thing in itself, and does not move beyond the work of art to its wider or deeper human relevance. He comes back always to his private sensibility, and the immediate modifications a work of art has produced in that; all wider ranges of interest are left out of consideration. "Style" perhaps represents an honest awareness of the limitations of his own attitudes to art and life, and his own inability at a late stage of development to transcend these. For the scholar-artist, as opposed to the creative artist, art is not liberation, the escape from involvement or emotion through an apparently self-dependent world, but a kind of short-circuiting of emotion, from the work of art back to the work of art.

XI

PATER's reputation falls into four broad phases, the first lasting till 1885, the year of the publication of *Marius*. Early critics were baffled both by the method and the manner of *Studies in the History of the Renaissance* despite the frame of the preface and the conclusion. The challenge of a new type of criticism proved too much; it raised the unanswered question as to whether Pater was scholar or dilettante; irresponsible apologist for an amoral aestheticism or serious moralist. Until the publication of *Marius*, then, it proved difficult to control an image of so controversial, yet so obscure, a figure as the quiet tutor of Brasenose. The almost uniformly suspicious, sometimes patronizing, almost always crass reviews of *The Renaissance* gave way to a more respectful response to *Marius*, yet even then reviewers tended to regard *Marius* as a clarification, rather than as a radical reordering of the insights contained in the conclusion. Still, from 1885 on, Pater was increasingly treated as a writer of extreme originality, and sometimes, indeed, as a literary saint. *Appreciations* and *Plato and Platonism*, in particular, led critics to evolve an antithesis between the difficult "brilliances" of *The Renaissance* and the "friendliness" of the later prose. By the end of the century, Pater's reputation had been established as stylist, as creative critic, as the propagandist of aestheticism (associated with Dante Gabriel Rossetti, Swinburne, and Edward Burne-Jones), and even by some as a genius. Edward Thomas' study of 1913 sets out and partially succeeds in diminishing the stylist. The loss of innocence by so many in World War I, the gray rather than red 1930's, were hardly periods in which Pater could comfortably survive. His alma mater found him an embarrassing shade, so near a parody of an actual Oxford that he had to be dismissed through gossip or with an elegant sneer. More astringent sneers proceeded from Cambridge, F. R. Leavis observing that D. G. Rossetti no more burned with "a hard gem-like flame" than did Pater. And there the matter rested until the work of Graham Hough and Kermode.

Pater's one indisputably great disciple, W. B. Yeats, began to lead scholars back to the master. In particular, the close relation of Pater to the twentieth century began to be explored. In the 1960's, Pater attracted much criticism, both precise and imaginative, chiefly from the United States. *Marius* and *Imaginary Portraits* became the focus of attention. The old naturalist and realist criteria for fiction have now been abandoned and the boundaries between prose and poetry can be defined far less rigidly than before. A new image of Pater as a myth-maker of considerable power began to emerge, while other scholars began to relate Pater more and more to the central concerns of his age. This approach, though, tended to mute somewhat the sharply individualized nature of Pater's work.

What can the general reader profitably gather from Pater's work? He will probably find *The Renaissance*, *Marius*, and *Imaginary Portraits* (including "Apollo in Picardy") more rewarding than other volumes. But the sustaining interest of reading Pater will be less the impetus, the sense of design, than the sudden recurring felicity of image or cadence; a cadence as evocative, it may be, as "the legend of Leda, the delight of the world breaking from the egg of a bird"; an epiphany such as this from the essay on du Bellay:

A sudden light transfigures a trivial thing, a weathervane, a wind-mill, a winnowing flail, the dust in the barn door; a moment—and the thing has vanished, because it was pure effect; but it leaves a relish behind it, a longing that the accident may happen again.

(*The Renaissance*, p. 145)

Or an image, complete, precise, yet mysterious as this of the effeminate, menacing Dionysus:

He will become, as always in later art and poetry, of dazzling whiteness; no longer dark with the air and sun, but like one . . . brought up under the shade of Eastern porticoes or pavilions, or in the light that has only reached him softened through the texture of green leaves; honey-pale, like the delicate people of the city, like the flesh of women, as those old-vase-painters conceive of it, who leave their hands and faces untouched with the pencil on the white clay.

(*Greek Studies*, p. 35)

Or this description of the paintings of Watteau, the sense of an ending indeed:

> The storm is always brooding through the massy splendour of the trees, above those sun-dried glades, or lawns, where delicate children may be trusted, thinly clad; and the secular trees themselves will hardly outlast another generation.

> (*Imaginary Portraits*, 1964 ed., p. 34)

We read Pater not because we expect to be dominated by him, but because we enjoy being surprised by him. And like many unmethodical writers, who depend on disconnected intuition, he has a gift of chiming in through his intuitions with the more organized perceptions of some writers who have succeeded him: much of the highly methodized aesthetics of Yeats exist in a kind of evasive or tangential state in Pater. Pater's place as an influential writer in a diffused sense has yet to be explored: historical relativism; the symbolical energies of English poetry from Yeats onward; the spirit of tactful accommodation of cultural skepticism to spiritual inwardness; the sense of the inner life's sanctities; all these directions have some of their roots in Pater. He remains the classic example of a type of temperament in whom we can recognize certain subdued and almost inexpressible moments of the self, its moments of wistfulness and hesitation and its partial triumphs of perception; and more than Marius, or any of those shadowy half-created characters in *Imaginary Portraits*, he has created himself for us in his oeuvre as a permanently significant symbolical figure: the most complete example, the least trivial, of the aesthetic man.

SELECTED BIBLIOGRAPHY

I. BIBLIOGRAPHY. G. d'Hangest, Walter Pater: *L'Homme et l'oeuvre* (Paris, 1961); J. Sparrow, "Walter Horatio Pater," in *New Cambridge Bibliography of English Literature* (London, 1970), gives an excellent listing up to 1965; S. Wright, *Bibliography of the Writings of Walter Pater* (Folkestone, 1975); F. E. Court, *Walter Pater. An Annotated Bibliography of Writings About Him* (DeKalb, Ill., 1980); R. M. Seiler, "Walter Pater Studies: 1970–1980," in P. Dodd, ed. *Walter Pater: An Imaginative Sense of Fact* (London, 1981).

II. COLLECTED WORKS. *Collected Works*, 9 vols. (London, 1900–1901); *The Works*, 10 vols. (London, 1910; repr. New York, 1967), New Library ed., not complete. A new ed. of the works, collected, uncollected, and unpublished, is in preparation; L. Evans, ed., *The Letters of Walter Pater* (Oxford, 1970), approximately 275 letters, with highly informative notes. Further letters appear in *Notes and Queries*, n.s. 22, 10 (October 1975) and *Notes and Queries*, n.s. 25, 4 (August 1978).

III. SELECTED WORKS. E. E. Hale, Jr., ed., *Prose Selections* (New York, 1901); A. L. F. Snell, ed., *Selections* (New York, 1924); H. G. Rawlinson, ed., *Selected Essays* (London, 1927); R. Aldington, ed., *Selected Works* (London, 1948); D. Patmore, ed., *Selected Prose* (London, 1949); J. Uglow, ed., *Walter Pater: Essays on Literature and Art* (London, 1973); H. Bloom, ed., *Selected Writings of Walter Pater* (New York–London, 1974).

IV. SEPARATE WORKS. *Studies in the History of the Renaissance* (London, 1873); 2nd ed. (London, 1877) entitled *The Renaissance: Studies in Art and Poetry*, with the conclusion omitted and the essay on Giorgione added; 3rd ed. (London, 1888), with the conclusion modified and restored; later eds. by L. Kronenberger (New York–Ontario, 1959), by K. Clark (London, 1961), with an excellent intro., by L. Evans (New York–London, 1977), repr. of the 1922 ed., which was based on the 1893 text, the last to have Pater's supervision, by D. L. Hill (Berkeley–Los Angeles–London, 1980), the most scholarly ed., giving the 1893 text, recording all variant readings along with elaborate critical and explanatory notes, elucidating the history of composition, publication, and reception of each essay, and with an essay on the book as a whole; also repr. book reviews of S. Colvin's *Children in Italian and English Design* (1872) and J. A. Symonds' *The Renaissance in Italy: The Age of the Despots* (1875); *Marius the Epicurean: His Sensations and Ideas,* 2 vols. (London, 1885); 2nd ed. (London, 1885) has as the main change the suppression of a brief, morbid episode in ch. 20; 3rd ed. (London, 1892) has extensive changes; later eds. by A. K. Tuell (New York, 1926), with many notes relating in particular to the sources, by J. C. Squire in 2 vols. (London, 1929), by A. K. Tuell (New York, 1929), by O. Burdett (London, 1934), by J. Sagmaster (New York, 1935), and by H. Bloom (New York–Toronto, 1970), with an intro. that is sensitive and informed; *Imaginary Portraits* (London, 1887), ed., with an intro., by E. J. Brzenk (New York–Evanston–London, 1964), a useful selection including, along with the four original portraits, "Diaphanéité," "Apollo in Picardy," and "An English Poet," French trans. by G. Khnopff, with an intro. by A. Symons (London, 1899), by E. Coppinger (Paris, 1922), and by P. Neel (Paris, 1930), Italian trans. by M. Praz (Rome, 1944); *Appreciations* (London, 1889), 2nd ed. (London, 1890) omits the essay "Aesthetic Poetry" (a condensed version of an earlier essay on the poetry of William Morris, which had furnished part of the conclusion to *Studies in the History of the Renaissance*) and substitutes a review of Octave Feuillet's novel *La Morte; Plato and Platonism: A Series of Lectures* (London, 1893), French trans. by S. Jankelevitch (Paris, 1923); "Note on F. W.

Bussell," in W. Rothstein, *Oxford Characters: A Series of Lithographs*, 6th ser. (London, 1893), lim. ed.; *An Imaginary Portrait* (Oxford, 1894), is "The Child in the House" repr. from *Macmillan's* magazine (August 1878) and not included in *Imaginary Portraits* of 1887, privately printed in an ed. of 250 copies at the Daniel Press, repr. again in *Miscellaneous Studies* of 1899; *Greek Studies: A Series of Lectures* (London, 1895), prepared for the press by C. L. Shadwell, Pater's literary executor; *Miscellaneous Studies: A Series of Essays* (London, 1895; 1899), prepared for the press by C. L. Shadwell; *Gaston de Latour: An Unfinished Romance* (London, 1896), prepared for the press by C. L. Shadwell; *Essays From "The Guardian"* (London, 1896), privately printed, with a preface by E. Gosse; *Essays From "The Guardian"* (Portland, Maine, 1897; London, 1901); *Uncollected Essays* (Portland, Maine, 1901); *Sketches and Reviews* (New York, 1919), includes "Aesthetic Poetry" and the text of the early essay on Coleridge; *The Chant of the Celestial Sailors: An Unpublished Poem* (Winchester, 1926), an early poem printed by E. H. Blakeney in an ed. of 30 copies; M. Ottley, ed., "An English Poet," in the *Fortnightly Review* (April 1931).

V. MANUSCRIPT MATERIAL. Some of Pater's early poems are extant, chiefly in the collection of J. Sparrow, which also includes lengthy and important unedited portions of *Gaston de Latour* and the MS of *Demeter and Persephone*. It seems that *Gaston* was to have been of a length similar to *Marius*. The MS of "Diaphanéité" is at King's School, Canterbury, and that of "Pascal" in the Bodleian Library (Don 84) at Oxford University. An important collection of MSS in the Harvard College Library (6MS. Eng. 1150) is in the process of being edited by S. Bassett. One of these MSS is discussed by L. Brake, "A Commentary on Arezzo: An Unpublished Manuscript by Walter Pater," in *Review of English Studies*, 27 (1976). Lists of books that Pater borrowed from the Taylorian and Bodleian libraries survive. Falconer Madan's diary at Brasenose College Library, Oxford, gives some details of Pater's attendance and voting at college meetings. There is a comic and probably apocryphal section on Pater in Sir E. Trelawney Blackhouse's MS memoirs in the Bodleian Library.

VI. BIOGRAPHICAL AND CRITICAL STUDIES. J. J. Morley, "Mr. Pater's Essays," in the *Fortnightly Review* (April 1873), a review of *Studies in the History of the Renaissance*; M. Pattison, review of *Studies in the History of the Renaissance*, in the *Westminster Review*, 43 (1873); J. A. Symonds, review of *Studies in the History of the Renaissance*, in the *Academy* (15 March 1873); G. Saintsbury, "Modern English Prose," in the *Fortnightly Review* (February 1876); W. H. Mallock, *The New Republic* (London, 1877), Pater is satirized sharply, amusingly, not altogether fairly as Mr. Rose, the aesthete with a taste in scatology; Mrs. H. Ward, review of *Marius the Epicurean*, in *Macmillan's* magazine (June 1885); O. Wilde, review of *Imaginary Portraits*, in the *Pall Mall Gazette* (11 June 1887); G. Moore, *Confessions of a Young Man* (London, 1888), later

eds. from 1904 contain a preface with reminiscences of Pater along with a letter.

O. Wilde, review of *Appreciations*, in the *Speaker* (22 March 1890), repr. in *Reviews* (London, 1908) and in *A Critic in Pall Mall* (London, 1919); B. Bosanquet, *A History of Aesthetic* (London, 1892); L. Johnson, "Mr. Pater Upon Plato," in the *Westminster Gazette* (2 March 1893); L. Johnson, "The Spirit of Plato," in the *Speaker* (28 October 1893); L. Johnson, "The Work of Mr. Pater," in the *Fortnightly Review* (September 1894), all three last-named articles repr. with revs. in *Post Liminium* (London, 1911); E. Gosse, "Pater: A Portrait," in the *Contemporary Review* (December 1894), repr. in Gosse's *Critical Kit-Kats* (London, 1896); F. W. Bussell, "In Memoriam: W. H. Pater," in the *Oxford* magazine, 13 (1894); H. von Hofmannsthal, "Walter Pater," in *Die Zeit* (Vienna) (1894), repr. in *Gesammelte Werke in Einzelausgaben*, Prosa 1 (Frankfurt, 1950); E. Gosse, "Walter Horatio Pater," in *Dictionary of National Biography* (London, 1895; rev. ed., 1909); M. Beerbohm, "Be It Cosiness," in the *Pageant* (1 December 1895), repr. as "Diminuendo" in *Works* (London, 1908), an essay that deals with Pater in both senses of the word; T. S. H. Escott, "Some Oxford Memories of the Pre-Aesthetic Age," in the *National Review* (October 1895); R. Le Gallienne, *Retrospective Reviews: A Literary Log* (London, 1896), has three articles on Pater; W. A. Knight, *Memoir of John Nichol* (Glasgow, 1896), gives some account of "Old Mortality"; L. Johnson, "A Note Upon Mr. Pater," in the *Academy* (16 January 1897), repr. with revs. in *Post Liminium* (London, 1911); A Symons, *Studies in Two Literatures* (London, 1897), the essay on Pater was repr. in *Studies in Prose and Verse* (London, 1904) and rev. as *A Study of Pater* (London, 1932); "F" [author], "In Pater's Rooms," in the *Speaker* (26 August 1899), a brief description of the rooms, followed by an account of a conversation with Pater that ranges over the composition of prose, contemporary architecture, and Newman.

L. Johnson, "For a Little Clan," in the *Academy* (13 October 1900), rev. and repr. in *Post Liminium* (London, 1911); E. Newman, *Studies in Music* (London, 1901), contains "Pater on Music"; I. Zangwill, *Without Prejudice* (London, 1902), contains "Pater and Prose"; F. Greenslet, *Walter Pater* (New York, 1903); G. Moore, "Avowals VI: Pater," in the *Pall Mall* magazine (August 1904), repr. with revs. in *Avowals* (London, 1919); A. E. M. Foster, *The Sensitive, and Other Pieces* (London, 1905), contains essay on Pater; A. C. Benson, *Walter Pater* (London, 1906), in the English Men of Letters series; E. Manson, "Recollections of Walter Pater," in the *Oxford* magazine (7 November 1906); G. Saintsbury, "Walter Pater," in the *Oxford* magazine (7 November 1906); G. Saintsbury, "Walter Pater," in the *Bookman* (1906); T. Wright, *The Life of Walter Pater*, 2 vols. (London, 1907), one of the (unintentionally) comic masterpieces of English literature, not authorized by the Misses Pater, some acrimonious correspondence from them is contained in the collection of the University of Indiana; Wright had access to the papers of three of Pater's friends, R. McQueen, Richard Jackson, and William Sharp; some of McQueen's correspondence with Wright is also at the University of Indiana, Bloomington; *Brasenose College Quatercentenary Monographs*, 3 pt. (Oxford, 1909), contains an essay on Pater by J. Buchan and T. H. Ward's "Reminiscences Brasenose 1864–1872"; A. Cecil, *Six Oxford Thinkers* (London, 1909), contains essay on Pater.

E. Sharp, *William Sharp: A Memoir* (London, 1910), contains memories of Pater and texts of six of his letters; E. Dowden, *Essays, Modern and Elizabethan* (London, 1910), contains essay on Pater; G. Saintsbury, *History of English Criticism* (London, 1911); G. Saintsbury, *History of English Prose Rhythm* (London, 1912), contains a close analysis of Pater's rhythms, pointing out how he preserves the cadences of prose; *Selected Writings of William Sharp* (London, 1912), vol. III, *Papers Critical and Reminiscent*, contains two essays, one on *Marius the Epicurean*, one on Pater as a personality, repr. from the *Atlantic Monthly* (December 1894); F. Wedmore, *Memories* (London, 1912); E. Thomas, *Walter Pater: A Critical Study* (London, 1913), contains some acute, not always sympathetic, close criticism; R. Mobbs, *Études Comparées de Jugements de Mrs. Humphrey Ward, de Matthew Arnold et de Walter Pater sur le Journal Intime de H. F. Amiel* (Geneva, 1913); E. J. Bock, *Walter Pater's Einfluss auf Oscar Wilde* (Bonn, 1913); J. H. Huneker, *The Pathos of Distance* (New York, 1913), contains "Pater Re-read"; A. Ransome, *Portraits and Speculations* (London, 1913), contains essay on Pater; S. C. Chew, "Pater's Quotations," in the *Nation* (New York, October 1914); E. Mason, *A Book of Preferences in Literature* (London, 1915), contains "Walter Pater, and Some Phases of Development"; B. Fehr, "Walter Pater und Hegel," in *Englische Studien*, 50, no. 2 (1916); A. Symons, *Figures of Several Centuries* (London, 1916), contains essay on Pater; H. Proesler, *Walter Pater und Sein Verhältnis zur Deutschen Literatur* (Fribourg, 1917); W. W. Jackson, *Ingram Bywater: The Memoir of an Oxford Scholar* (Oxford, 1918); Mrs. H. Ward, *A Writer's Recollections* (London, 1918); R. Michaud, *Mystiques et Réalistes Anglo-Saxons d'Emerson Bernard Shaw* (Paris, 1918), contains "Un Paien Mystique, Walter Pater"; F. Harris, *Contemporary Portraits* (New York, 1919), contains "Walter Pater," entertaining but to be taken with suspicion.

W. H. Mallock, *Memoirs of Life and Literature* (London, 1920); St. J. Lucas, "Pater and the Army," in *Blackwood's* magazine (March 1921); F. Duthuit, *Le Rose et le Noir: de Pater à Oscar Wilde* (Paris, 1923); J. S. Harrison, "Pater, Heine and the Old Gods of Greece," in *Publications of the Modern Language Association*, 39 (1924), examines the relation between some of the *Imaginary Portraits* and Heine's *Gods in Exile*, showing how Pater has medievalized incidents in the legends of Dionysus and Apollo; M. Du-

claux, "Souvenirs sur Pater," in *Revue de Paris* (15 January 1925); F. Staub, *Das Imaginäre Porträt Walter Paters* (Zurich, 1926); L. P. Smith, "On Re-Reading Pater," in the *Dial*, 83 (1927), repr. in *Reperusals and Re-Collections* (London, 1936); H. A. L. Fisher, *James Bryce*, 2 vols. (London, 1927), contains a complete list of members of Old Mortality; Z. E. Chandler, *An Analysis of the Stylistic Technique of Addison, Johnson, Hazlitt and Pater* (Iowa City, 1928); R. A. Scott-James, *The Making of Literature: Some Principles of Criticism* (London, 1928), ch. 25 deals with Pater, repr. in 1948 with additions; C. Wright, "Out of Harm's Way: Some Notes on the Esthetic Movement of the 'Nineties,'" in the *Bookman* (November 1929); Z. Grabowski, *Walter Pater, Zycie, Dzielo, Styl* (Poznan, 1929).

C. Du Bos, *Approximations* (Paris, 1930), contains "Sur Marius 1 Épicurien de Pater"; W. de la Mare, ed., *The Eighteen-Eighties* (Cambridge, 1930), contains "The Place of Pater" by T. S. Eliot; A. Beyer, *Walter Paters Beziehungen zur Französischen Literatur und Kultur* (Halle, 1931); A. J. Farmer, *Walter Pater as a Critic of English Literature: A Study of "Appreciations"* (Grenoble, 1931); J. Schaffer, *Walter Pater und Sein Bildungsideal* (Vienna, 1931); L. Rosenblatt, *L'Idée de l'art pour l'art dans la littérature Anglaise pendant la période Victorienne* (Paris, 1931), ch. 5 deals with Pater; E. B. Burgum, "Pater and the Good Life," in *Sewanee Review*, 40 (1932); B. Newman, "Pater: A Revaluation," in *Nineteenth Century* (May 1932); K. Molenda, *Walter Pater und Sein Verhaltnis sur Französischen Kritik der 18 Jahrhunderts* (Vienna, 1932); J. G. Eaker, *Pater: A Study in Methods and Effects* (Iowa City, 1933); H. H. Young, *The Writings of Pater: A Reflection of British Philosophical Opinion from 1860 to 1890* (Lancaster, Pa., 1933); "Michael Field" [K. H. Bradley and E. E. Cooper], *Works and Days* (London, 1933), selections from the voluminous diaries of the authors, containing a number of allusions to Pater; L. F. Farnell, *An Oxonian Looks Back: An Autobiography* (London, 1934), alludes to Pater; S. Bailey, ed., *Letters and Diaries of J. C. Bailey, Edited by His Wife* (London, 1935); "Marius l'Épicurien de Pater et ses points de départ Français," in *Revue de Littérature Comparée*, 15 (1935); L. Cattan, *Essai sur Walter Pater* (Paris, 1936); T. Wright, *An Autobiography* (London, 1936), contains amusing anecdotes about Pater and an account of Wright's quarrel with the Misses Pater; *Vernon Lee's Letters, with a Preface by Her Executor* [I. Cooper Willis] (London, 1937), privately printed; R. C. Child, "Is Walter Pater an Impressionistic Critic?" in *Publications of the Modern Language Association*, 53 (1938); F. Olivero, *Il Pensiero Religioso ed Estetico di Pater* (Turin, 1939).

M. Gutscher, *Henry James und Walter Pater* (Vienna, 1940); M. Schoen, "Pater on the Place of Music among the Arts," in the *Journal of Aesthetics and Art Criticism*, 6 (1942); H. H. Law, "Pater's Use of Greek Quotations," in *Modern Language Notes*, 58 (December 1943); R. Ironside,

"Walter Pater," in the *Cornhill* magazine, 161 (1944); R. C. Child, *The Aesthetic of Pater* (New York, 1946); J. Pick, "Divergent Disciples of Pater," in *Thought*, 23 (1948); D. F. Hoppé, "Walter Pater on Plato's Aesthetics," in *Modern Language Quarterly*, 18 (1948); G. G. Hough, *The Last Romantics* (London, 1949), contains an excellent essay on Pater; M. Sadleir, *Michael Ernest Sadleir* (London, 1949), has a brief, memorable image of Pater among undergraduates.

J. H. Buckley, "Pater and the Suppressed Conclusion," in *Modern Language Notes*, 56 (1950); F. E. Peters, "Pater's Lacedaemon," in the *Classical Bulletin*, 27 (1950); R. V. Osbourn, "*Marius the Epicurean*," in *Essays in Criticism*, 1, (1951); W. Vollrath, *Verschwiegenes Oxford: Matthew Arnold, Goethe und Pater, Fellow of Brasenose* (Heidelberg, 1951); G. Tillotson, *Criticism and the Nineteenth Century* (London, 1951), touches on Pater as art critic, with useful comments on Pater's relation to Arnold; M. Millhauser, "Pater and the Flux," in the *Journal of Aesthetics and Art Criticism*, 12 (1953); W. Blissett, "Pater and Eliot," in *University of Toronto Quarterly*, 22 (1953); R. V. Johnson, "Pater and the Victorian Anti-Romantics," in *Essays in Criticism*, 4 (1954); J. Hafley, "Walter Pater's *Marius* and the Techniques of Modern Fiction," in *Modern Fiction Studies*, 3 (1957); F. Kermode, *Romantic Image* (London, 1957), demonstrates passim the importance of Pater as a source for the assumptions behind modern expectations of poetry; E. J. Brzenk, "Pater and Apuleius," in *Comparative Literature*, 10 (1958), see also *Victorian Studies*, 3 (1960) and 4 (1961), for replies to this article; E. Chandler, "Pater on Style," in *Anglistica* (Copenhagen), 20 (1958), discusses the revisions for the 3rd ed. of *Marius* (1892), in the light of Pater's criteria in "Style"; R. Wellek, *A History of Modern Criticism, 1750–1950* (London, 1955–1966), vol. IV (1966) contains a ch. on Pater's literary theory and criticism; I. Fletcher, "Why Not Take Pater Seriously?", in *Essays in Criticism*, 9 (1959); E. J. Brzenk, "The Unique Fictional World of Pater," in *Nineteenth Century Fiction*, 13 (1959); P. Appleman et al., *1859: Entering a Year of Crisis* (Bloomington, Ind., 1959), contains "Darwin, Pater, and a Crisis in Criticism" by Appleman.

B. Duffey, "The Religion of Pater's Marius," in *Texas Studies in Literature and Language*, 2 (1960); W. Iser, *Pater: Die Autonomie des Aesthetischen* (Tübingen, 1960); R. Ellmann, ed., *Edwardians and Late Victorians* (New York, 1960), includes "The Ivory Tower as Lighthouse" by R. Temple; G. d'Hangest, *Walter Pater: L'Homme et l'Oeuvre*, 2 vols. (Paris, 1961), Études Anglaises, no. 7, contains an excellent bibliography; R. T. Lenaghan, "Pattern in Pater's Fiction," in *Studies in Philology*, 58 (1961); U. C. Knoepflmacher, "Pater's Religion of Sanity: *Plato and Platonism* as a Document of Victorian Unbelief," in *Victorian Studies*, 6 (1962); R. V. Johnson, *Pater as Critic: His Critical Practice Considered in Relation to His Theories of Life and Art* (Melbourne, 1962); B. A. Inman, "The Organic Structure of *Marius the Epicurean*," in

Philological Quarterly, 41 (1962); L. M. Rosenblatt, "The Genesis of Pater's *Marius the Epicurean*," in *Comparative Literature*, 14, no. 3 (Summer 1962); R. V. Johnson, *Aestheticism* (London, 1963); V. M. Vogeler, "The Religious Meaning of *Marius the Epicurean*," in *Nineteenth Century Fiction*, 19 (1964); D. J. de Laura, "Pater and Eliot: The Origin of the 'Objective Correlative,'" in *Modern Language Quarterly*, 26 (1964); B. Charlesworth, *Dark Passages: The Decadent Consciousness in Victorian Literature* (Madison, Wis., 1965); U. C. Knoepflmacher, *Religious Humanism and the Victorian Novel* (Princeton, N. J., 1965), has a long section on *Marius*; J. J. Duffy, "From Essay to Portrait: Walter Pater After *The Renaissance*," in *Toth*, 6 (1965); F. X. Roellinger, "Intimations of Winckelmann in Pater's 'Diaphanéité,'" in *English Language Notes*, 2 (1965); R. C. Pierle, "Walter Pater and Epicureanism," in *Southern Quarterly*, 7 (1965); A. Ward, *Walter Pater: The Idea in Nature* (London, 1966), mainly concerned with Pater's relation to Hegel, includes a long analysis of the "Gioconda" passage; J. J. Duffy, Walter Pater's Prose Style: An Essay in Theory and Analysis," in *Style*, 1 (1967); G. C. Monsman, *Pater's Portraits: Mythic Patterns in the Fiction of Walter Pater* (Baltimore, 1967); M. Shmiefsky, "A Study in Aesthetic Relativism: Pater's Poetics," in *Victorian Poetry*, 6 (1967); G. MacKenzie, *The Literary Character of Walter Pater* (Berkeley, 1967); F. E. Court, "Change and Suffering in Pater's Fictional Heroes," in *Modern Fiction Studies* (1967–1968); J. B. Gordon, "The Beginnings of Pater's Pilgrimage: A Reading of 'The Child in the House,'" in *Tennessee Studies in Literature*, 13 (1968); J. B. Gordon, "The *Imaginary Portraits*: Walter Pater's Aesthetic Pilgrimage," in *University Review* (Kansas City, Mo.), 35 (1968); G. Levine and W. Madden, eds., *The Art of Victorian Prose* (London, 1968), contains useful essays by G. S. Fraser on "Walter Pater: His Theory of Style, His Style in Practice, His Influence" and by G. R. Stange on "Art Criticism as a Prose Genre"; J. B. Gordon, "Pater's Gioconda Smile: A Reading of 'Emerald Uthwart,'" in *Studies in Short Fiction*, 6 (1969); D. J. de Laura, *Hebrew and Hellene in Victorian England: Newman, Arnold and Pater* (Austin, Tex., 1969).

R. Crinkley, *Walter Pater: Humanist* (Lexington, Ky., 1970); "The Art of the High Wire," in the *Times Literary Supplement* (26 February 1971), a review of the *Letters*, both wide-ranging and incisive; S. Wright, "Richard Charles Jackson," *Antigonish Review*, 1, no. 4 (1971); W. Shuter, "History as Palingenesis in Pater and Hegel," in *Publications of the Modern Language Association*, 86, no. 3 (May 1971); I. C. Small, "Plato and Pater: Fin-de-Siècle Aesthetics," both in *British Journal of Aesthetics*, 12 (1972); D. A. Downes, *The Temper of Victorian Belief* (London, 1972), studies of Pater, Newman, and Kingsley, has an interesting chapter on Marius; C. Dahl, "Pater's '*Marius* and Historical Novels in early Christian Times," in *Nineteenth Century Fiction*, 86 (1973); R. Wollheim, *On Art and the Mind* (London, 1973), includes excellent essay on Pater and metaphysics; B. A. Inman, "Pater's Conception of the Renaissance: From Sources to Personal Ideal," in *Victorian Newsletter* (1975); G. Monsman, "Pater and his Younger Contemporaries," in *Victorian Newsletter* (1975); R. McMullen, *Mona Lisa: The Picture and the Myth* (Boston, 1975); B. A. Inman, "Sebastian Van Storck: Pater's Exploration into Nihilism" in R. Bizot, "Pater and Yeats," in *English Literary History*, 43, no. 3 (Fall 1976); M. Ryan, "Narcissus Autobiographer, *Marius the Epicurean*," in *English Literary History*, 43, no. 2 (Summer 1976); P. Dale, *The Victorian Critic and the Idea of History* (Cambridge, Mass., 1977), Pater is the fixed point of this volume: his historicism derives from an admixture of romantic attitude and positivist ideas; C. Ricks, "Pater, Arnold and misquotation," in the *Times Literary Supplement* (25 November 1977); G. Monsman, *Walter Pater* (Boston, 1977), a splendid general study; I. Small, "The Vocabulary of Pater's Criticism and the Psychology of Aesthetics," in *British Journal of Aesthetics*, 18 (1978), relates preface and conclusion of *The Renaissance* to the debate about the physiology and psychology of aesthetics among Herbert Spencer, Alexander Bain, and James Sully between 1860 and 1876; O. C. Ayers "*Marius the Epicurean*, The Dialectic as a Form of Truth," in *Studies in English Literature*, 18 (Autumn 1978); R. Wollheim, "The Artistic Temperament" in the *Times Literary Supplement* (22 September 1978); I. C. Small, "The Sources for Pater's Spinoza and 'Sebastian van Storck,'" in *Notes and Queries*, 25 (1978); M. Levey, *The Case of Walter Pater* (New York–London 1978), a curiously lackluster performance, but with much useful detail about Pater's family and earlier life; B. Bullen, "Walter Pater's *Renaissance* and Leonardo da Vinci's Reputation in the Nineteenth Century," in *Modern Language Review*, 74 (December 1979); F. Court, *Walter Pater* (De Kalb, Ill., 1979); G. Monsman, "*Gaston de Latour* and Pater's Art of Autobiography," in *Nineteenth Century Fiction*, 33, no. 4 (March 1979).

P. Meisel, *The Absent Father: Virginia Woolf and Walter Pater* (New Haven, Conn., 1980); R. Seiler, *Walter Pater: The Critical Heritage* (Boston, 1980), a profile of Pater's reputation between 1873 and 1908; G. Monsman, *Walter Pater's Art of Autobiography* (New Haven, Conn., 1980); L. M. Johnson, *The Metaphor of Painting: Essays on Baudelaire, Ruskin, Proust and Pater* (Ann Arbor, Mich., 1980); P. Dodd, ed., *Walter Pater: An Imaginative Sense of Fact* (London, 1981); B. A. Inman, *Walter Pater's Reading: An Annotated Bibliography of His Library* (New York–London, 1981), lists Pater's borrowings from Queen's College Library, the Bodleian Library, the Brasenose College Library, and the Taylor Institution, Oxford, between 1860 and 1894, the books in Pater's library are also listed; F. M. Turner, *The Greek Heritage in Victorian Britain* (New Haven, Conn.–London, 1981), by far the best book on the topic, though Pater is not treated at great length.

GERARD MANLEY HOPKINS

(1844-1889)

Graham Storey

INTRODUCTION AND EARLY POEMS

JUDGED by the lives of most English nineteenth-century poets, Gerard Manley Hopkins' life was outwardly uneventful. He was born on 28 July 1844 into a prosperous and cultivated home near London and spent his boyhood in Hampstead. He received a conventional middle-class education that culminated in four, mainly very happy, years at Balliol College, Oxford, where he took first classes in classics. His conversion to Roman Catholicism in 1866 was much more of a crisis to his family, teachers, and friends than it would be today. Two years later he entered the Society of Jesus, and after the rigorous Jesuit training, he spent the remainder of his relatively short life (he died on 8 June 1889) carrying out the mission and teaching duties of a Jesuit priest.

This outward life—much of it inevitably isolated—conceals the remarkable intensity of his inner life, of his solitary experience, an intensity that, transmuted into poetry, has moved and excited a vast number of twentieth-century readers. Hopkins' admirers are, I think, most impressed by his remarkable technical originality, by his constant innovations in language, rhythm, and syntax, and by the exhilarating sense of freedom such experimenting brings. For this, they are fully willing to face the linguistic difficulties that inevitably arise. They are impressed too by his energy, both aesthetic and intellectual; by the fineness and self-exactingness of his mind; by his remarkable sensitivity to detail, to the minutiae of nature (a sensitivity that he shares particularly with Samuel Taylor Coleridge); and by his power to express extremes of feeling, uncharted—or not so courageously charted—by other Victorian poets. Few poets have communicated so strongly both excitement at natural beauty and its opposite, intimate knowledge of the terrors of despair. Hopkins above all communicates the mystery of self-hood, both of the experiencing self and of the objects experienced. All of his poetry is religious; but it appeals strongly to an immense number of readers who do not share his faith.

The canon of Hopkins' mature poems is small: between the end of 1875, the year of "The Wreck of the Deutschland," his first great mature poem, and his death in 1889, he wrote only forty-nine finished poems. The poems and fragments that he wrote as an undergraduate, following a few as a schoolboy, are in fact more numerous, but their chief interest now is in showing how excitedly he responded to other poets, particularly to the young John Keats. Hopkins' three earliest known poems, "The Escorial," which won a school prize when he was only fifteen, "A Vision of the Mermaids" (which he illustrated with a pen-and-ink drawing), and "Winter with the Gulf Stream" (published in *Once a Week* on 14 February 1863, when he was eighteen—one of the few poems published in his lifetime), all show his absorption of Keats. It is Keatsian color that enriches the envisioned mermaids:

> clouds of violet glow'd
> On prankèd scale; or threads of carmine, shot
> Thro' silver, gloom'd to a blood-vivid clot.[1]

Later undergraduate poems chart the religious doubts that led to the crisis of his conversion; and many of these poems again draw for their tone on accepted Victorian models: Christina Rossetti, John Henry Cardinal Newman, Matthew Arnold. Such absorption—or, in some cases, clear imitation—makes the totally new and original voice of "The Wreck" all the more remarkable. Two of the early poems, of 1865 and 1866, are particularly interesting

---

[1]All poems are quoted from W. H. Gardner and N. H. MacKenzie, eds., *Poems of Gerard Manley Hopkins*, 4th ed. (Oxford, 1967).

for the light they throw on Hopkins' inner conflicts and hopes. Both the symbolism of "The Alchemist in the City" and the alchemist's sense of isolation and wasted effort point to a similar sense of separateness and failure in Hopkins himself. "The Habit of Perfection" ("Elected Silence, sing to me") asks for a total denial of the senses, but it expresses the senses, in their imagined denial, with a sensuousness that is still Keatsian:

> O feel-of-primrose hands, O feet
> That want the yield of plushy sward. . . .

That sharp clash of sensuousness (with its intimate grasp on nature) and asceticism is perhaps the most striking characteristic of the young Hopkins' temperament.

Some of Hopkins' undergraduate essays—in particular, the longest of them, "On the Origin of Beauty: A Platonic Dialogue" (1865), which owes much to John Ruskin—show how consciously he was now searching for an aesthetic of his own. "The Probable Future of Metaphysics," written two years later, goes beyond both Ruskin and Walter Pater (who had been his tutor): a belief in Platonic "Ideal Forms" behind every form in nature is now the only alternative to "a philosophy of flux." Hopkins was now moving to the two famous terms he coined the following year in some notes on the early Greek philosopher Parmenides: "inscape" and "instress." Their importance for him was both philosophical and aesthetic; they pointed again to Plato's Ideal Forms; and they provided the objective criteria for both the beauty and reality that he was seeking. "Inscape" he used to denote the distinctive pattern that expresses an object's inner form, gives it its selfhood. "Instress" he used in two senses: (1) for the energy that "upholds" an object's inscape, gives it its essential being, and (2) for the force that the inscape exerts on the perceiver. How important these concepts were for his mature poetry a letter to his friend Robert Bridges of 15 February 1879 shows explicitly:

But as air, melody, is what strikes me most of all in music and design in painting, so design, pattern or what I am in the habit of calling "inscape" is what I above all aim at in poetry.[2]

Not only do his poems aim at "catching" the inscapes of things ("I caught this morning morning's minion . . ."), but the individual poem itself is an inscape; a pattern of sound and shape as well as of meaning.

Ironically (as it must seem to us now), while Hopkins was developing his all-important poetic criteria, he was writing no poetry. In May 1868, the month in which he made his decision to become a Jesuit, he decided both to burn the poems he had already written ("Slaughter of the innocents" is his 11 May journal entry)[3] and to write no more, "as not belonging to my profession" (as he later told Canon Richard Watson Dixon). Little now unknown was probably destroyed, but his self-imposed poetic silence was kept for over seven years. Instead, his powers of minute observation, his constant search for distinctive beauty, went into the journal he kept faithfully from 1866 to 1875. The journal is in a great many ways a workshop for the poems that were to follow it.

But to persuade himself that the writing of poetry would not interfere with his vocation as a priest, Hopkins needed far more than aesthetic justification. He needed a spiritual fiat, a conviction that, as a poet, he could serve God. It was this that the *Spiritual Exercises* of St. Ignatius Loyola, the meditations that are the central study and practice of every Jesuit, undoubtedly provided. We know what a profound effect they had on him. His most important spiritual writing was the beginning of a commentary on them; its opening, the celebration of selfhood, is his finest piece of sustained prose. Ignatius' favorite image, of the Jesuit as Christ's dedicated soldier, pervades many of his poems. The opening section of "The Wreck of the Deutschland" was inspired by his first experience of the *Exercises* as a novice seven years before. And, for Hopkins, they gave the most compelling of all reasons to rededicate himself as a poet. "Man was created to praise," the *Spiritual Exercises* open; in "Further Notes" on that opening Foundation Exercise, Hopkins wrote: "This world then is word, expression, views of God. . . . the world, man, should after its own manner give God being in return for the being he has given it." The poet, then, has his own place in this sacramental view of nature: the "being" he renders back to God is

---

[2]All letters to Robert Bridges are quoted from C. C. Abbott, ed., *The Letters of Gerard Manley Hopkins to Robert Bridges*, rev. ed. (London, 1955).

[3]See H. House, ed., *The Journals and Papers of Gerard Manley Hopkins*, 2nd ed., completed by G. Storey (London, 1959), pp. 537–539. All quotations from the journals are taken from this ed.

not only himself but the poem he has created, in its distinctive form another of God's works.

Moreover, in August 1872, while studying philosophy at Stonyhurst, Hopkins discovered the thirteenth-century Franciscan philosopher John Duns Scotus.

At this time, I had first begun to get hold of the copy of Scotus on the Sentences in the Baddely library and was flush with a new stroke of enthusiasm. It may come to nothing or it may be a mercy from God. But just then when I took in any inscape of the sky or sea I thought of Scotus.
(journal, August 1872)

Hopkins' enthusiasm was justified. Duns Scotus believed in the "principle of individuation," that the mind could come to know the universal (the *summum* of all medieval philosophy) through apprehending an individual object's "this-ness" (*haecceitas*) and that such apprehensions ultimately reveal God. Hopkins had intuitively believed this earlier, as a famous journal entry shows:

I do not think I have ever seen anything more beautiful than the bluebell I have been looking at. I know the beauty of our Lord by it. It[s inscape] is [mixed of][4] strength and grace.
(journal, 18 May 1870)

Duns Scotus gave philosophical and, above all, religious support for Hopkins' own theories of inscape and instress. It is not surprising that several of the mature poems show Duns Scotus' strong influence and that one, "Duns Scotus's Oxford" (1879), is a deeply felt tribute to him.

"THE WRECK OF THE DEUTSCHLAND"

IN December 1875, when Hopkins read the account of the wreck of the *Deutschland* and the Rector of St. Beuno's, with whom he was studying theology, told him that "he wished someone would write a poem on the subject," he was ready to break his seven years' poetic silence. What is remarkable is that the poem he wrote should be so utterly different from all the poems he had written before—in language, rhythm,

and structure. "The Wreck of the Deutschland" displays all his technical innovations, already in their most sustained form. Of these, the best-documented is his use of "sprung rhythm," of which, explaining the origins of "The Wreck" to Canon Dixon on 5 October 1878, he wrote: "I had long had haunting my ear the echo of a new rhythm which now I realized on paper."[5] But he had been equally concerned over the past two years with poetic language and, above all, its attainment of stress and emphasis: this had been the main subject of lectures on rhetoric he had given, as part of his training, at Manresa House, Roehampton, in 1873–1874. And the excitement of being sent to St. Beuno's, of learning Welsh, and of reading Welsh classical poetry undoubtedly played its part. In the letter to Dixon already quoted, he went on to mention "certain chimes suggested by the Welsh poetry I had been reading (what they call *cynghanedd*)." So an extraordinary confidence in a quite new poetic technique came together with a conviction that he now had a spiritual fiat for writing poetry again, and the result was one of the great religious poems in the English language.

"The Wreck of the Deutschland," Hopkins' longest and, for many, his greatest work, is at once an occasional poem—the central stanzas follow very closely the reports of the wreck in the *Times* (London), 8–13 December 1875—a religious ode, celebrating God's mastery and mercy; and a deeply personal spiritual autobiography: "What refers to myself in the poem is all strictly and literally true and did all occur," Hopkins told Bridges; "nothing is added for poetical padding." It is a complex and difficult poem, and a brief summary may help toward the understanding necessary for its great rewards.

Part I (stanzas 1–10) gives us Hopkins' own spiritual crisis: first, the agony of his own "shipwreck," as he submits to God's mastery ("Thou mastering me/God!"), then the grace of God's mercy, mediated to him through Christ's presence in the Communion (the second half of stanza 3). God's mastery and mercy are developed now almost as in a fugue: first, experienced personally in stanzas 4 ("I am soft sift/In an hourglass") and 5 ("I kiss my

---

[4]Hopkins' brackets.

[5]All letters to Canon Dixon are quoted from C. C. Abbott, ed., *The Correspondence of Gerard Manley Hopkins and R. W. Dixon*, rev. ed. (London, 1965).

hand/To the stars"), then as the paradox of Christ's Incarnation and Passion (stanzas 6 and 7), which demands our acceptance in the striking image of a ripe sloe bursting in our mouths. Stanzas 9 and 10 bring the two qualities together:

> Make mercy in all of us, out of us all
> Mastery, but be adored, but be adored King.

In their asking for "wrecking" and "storm," the fulfillment of God's double purpose, they link up with part II.

Part II (stanza 11 to the end) gives us the narrative of the shipwreck and of "the tall nun," introduced by stanza 11, proclaiming the inevitability of death ("The sour scythe cringe, and the blear share come") and ending with a prayer to Christ that completes and deepens the theme of part I. The sailing of the *Deutschland* from Bremen, the storm, and the wreck of the ship on the Kentish Knock occupy only six stanzas (12–17); the tall nun is dramatically introduced at the end of stanza 17 ("a lioness arose breasting the babble"); and after four stanzas (20–23) describing the nuns' exile and their dedication to the martyred St. Francis, we reach the center of the poem in stanza 24, the tall nun's cry, "'O Christ, Christ, come quickly.'" In the next three stanzas Hopkins puts forward, only to reject, possible motives for her cry. It was not that she wished to become more like "her lover" Christ, nor that she wanted a martyr's crown in heaven, nor even that she was driven to ask for ease by the "electrical horror" of the storm. No, it was the daily burden of a life of constant self-sacrifice ("The jading and jar of the cart,/Time's tasking") that made her cry out (stanza 27). Stanza 28, the climax of the poem, gives us the true meaning of the nun's cry: the ellipses ("But how shall I . . . make me room there . . .") show that it is all but inexpressible. The nun has *seen* Christ himself walking across the water. He will take her to him. Stanza 29 praises her for her understanding. In uttering the cry, the word kept within her, she has, as it were, given Christ a new birth: hence the significance of this night being the eve of the feast of the Immaculate Conception (stanza 30). There is yet a further miracle: the nun's cry has providently startled the lost sheep, the other passengers, the "Comfortless unconfessed," back to the fold—is not "the shipwrack then a harvest?" (stanza 31). The next two stanzas renew Hopkins' praise of God's mastery and mercy, the theme of part I, and the poem ends with two prayers. The first is to Christ, to "burn" anew,

having "royally" reclaimed "his own," and the second is to the tall nun, "Dame, at our door/ Drowned," to intercede in heaven for the return of Christ to England.

What gives such a poem, written in two formal parts and thirty-five eight-line stanzas, its compelling sense of unity is, above all, its symbolism. The suffering of the tall nun in the shipwreck (part II) mirrors Hopkins' own spiritual suffering in *his* "shipwreck" (part I); both ultimately mirror Christ's suffering and Crucifixion, so that the poem ends as a paean of praise to Christ himself. T. K. Bender, in *Gerard Manley Hopkins: The Classical Background* (1966), went further and, claiming that Hopkins wrote in the tradition of Pindar, the greatest of the Greek writers of odes, saw him, like Pindar, as holding the poem together through the power of an unstated but key image. The image he sees as unifying the poem is that of water, with its double powers of healing and destruction. The destruction, in a shipwreck poem, we expect, but few poets have given to the sea the almost apocalyptic power that Hopkins gives to it here:

> And the sea flint-flake, black-backed in the regular blow,
> Sitting Eastnortheast, in cursed quarter, the wind;
>   Wiry and white-fiery and whirlwind-swivellèd snow
> Spins to the widow-making unchilding unfathering deeps.
>
> (st. 13)

Yet, at the same time, the sea brings the five martyred nuns to their salvation; they

> Are sisterly sealed in wild waters,
>   To bathe in his fall-gold mercies, to breathe in his all-fire glances.
>
> (st. 23)

Throughout the rest of the poem, water, the flushing of liquid, melting are images of divine mercy and help:

> Stroke and a stress that stars and storms deliver,
>   That guilt is hushed by, hearts are flushed by and melt—
>
> (st. 6)

And, in the great vision of Christ's return to earth, in the penultimate stanza, the analogy is again with water, a refreshing shower:

Not a dooms-day dazzle in his coming nor dark as
    he came;
      Kind, but royally reclaiming his own;
A released shower, let flash[6] to the shire, not a
    lightning of fire hard-hurled.

                                (st. 34)

The image of water, then, as Bender says, seems to be a key symbol that points to the poem's ultimate subject, the paradox of suffering.

But, if such use of imagery was traditional, Hopkins' use of language and sprung rhythm was daringly experimental. The sprung rhythm shocked his friend Robert Bridges, an orthodox prosodist ("the dragon in the gate," he later called "The Wreck" in his edition of Hopkins' poems); and it was too much for Fr. Henry Coleridge, editor of the Jesuit journal *The Month*, who, as Hopkins said, "dared not publish" the poem. Sprung rhythm, in fact, was vital to what Hopkins was trying to do in poetry by employing speech rhythms to give the words their maximum sound-impact and stress. He explained it to Canon Dixon very simply: "To speak shortly, it consists in scanning by accents or stresses alone, without any account of the number of syllables, so that a foot may be one strong syllable or it may be many light and one strong" (5 October 1878). In a later letter (27 February 1879) he was simpler still: "This then is the essence of sprung rhythm: *one stress makes one foot*, no matter how many or few the syllables."

The stressing throughout "The Wreck" is the same except that in part I the first line of each stanza has two stresses and in part II three; thereafter the number of stresses in each stanza is 3–4–3–5–5–4–6. As Harold Whitehall showed convincingly in an essay in *The Kenyon Critics* (1937), most of Hopkins' distinctive poetic devices—alliteration, internal rhyming, "chiming" of consonants—all that he defended as achieving "more brilliancy, starriness, quain, margaretting," help us to know which are the strong stresses (Whitehall suggested that this was in fact their main purpose). We quickly see how, as Hopkins intended, they both "fetch out" the meaning (his own phrase) and intensify it. The stressing of stanza 2, for example, is an integral part of the spiritual crisis as Hopkins reexperiences it:

             I did say yes
      O at lightning and lashed rod;
  Thou heardst me truer than tongue confess

[6]Here in its meaning "as a rush of water."

         Thy terror, O Christ, O God;
  Thou knowest the walls, altar and hour and night:
    The swoon of a heart that the sweep and the
      hurl of thee trod
        Hard down with a horror of height:
And the midriff astrain with leaning of, laced with fire
    of stress.

The terror of that is strongly physical too: "a heart . . . trod/Hard down," "the midriff astrain": the strong stresses reenact the violence, and they almost compel us to read the words aloud as Hopkins pleaded to Bridges again and again to do: "Take breath and read it with the ears, as I always wish to be read, and my verse becomes all right." For Hopkins, poetry, like every art, had to have its proper "performance." As he wrote much later (1885) to his youngest brother Everard: "poetry, the darling child of speech, of lips and spoken utterance . . . must be spoken; *till it is spoken it is not performed*, it does not perform, it is not itself."

The shock of "The Wreck" to Bridges, and no doubt to Fr. Coleridge, too, was not only its new rhythm but its language. Hopkins was equally aware of what he was aiming to do here. He wrote to Bridges on 14 August 1879:

For it seems to me that the poetical language of an age shd. be the current language heightened, to any degree heightened and unlike itself, but not (I mean normally: passing freaks and graces are another thing) an obsolete one. This is Shakespeare's and Milton's practice and the want of it will be fatal to Tennyson's Idylls and plays, to Swinburne, and perhaps to Morris.

The reference to Shakespeare is as important as the comment on his contemporaries. From "The Wreck" onward, Hopkins' use of language *is* Shakespearean: he employs the resources of words to their utmost, makes them work urgently and physically. The words, as he claimed, are "current"; they are also, as he allowed, too, "to any degree heightened" to make their dramatic effect.

For Milton, and particularly for Milton's prosody, Hopkins had the highest possible admiration. "His achievements are quite beyond any other English poet's, perhaps any modern poet's," he wrote to Bridges on 3 April 1877; and to Dixon the following year (5 October): "His verse as one reads it seems something necessary and eternal. . . . I have paid a good deal of attention to Milton's versification and collected his later rhythms. . . . I found his most advanced effects in the *Paradise Regained* and, lyrically, in the *Agonistes*." Milton's verse remained a constant subject in Hopkins' letters to both Bridges and Dixon; and it is clear that, as a highly conscious innovator himself, he derived immense encouragement from the poet he saw as the greatest innovator in English prosody.

In stanza 27 of "The Wreck," Hopkins finds, after several attempts, the true reason for the tall nun's cry of "O Christ, Christ, come quickly":

> No, but it was not these.
> The jading and jar of the cart,
> Time's tasking, it is fathers that asking for
>   ease
>   Of the sodden-with-its-sorrowing
>   heart,
> Not danger, electrical horror; then further it finds
> The appealing of the Passion is tenderer in prayer
>   apart:
>   Other, I gather, in measure her mind's
> Burden, in wind's burly and beat of endragonèd seas.

The key words here were, and are, in current use (though "electrical" was audacious in 1875); the alliteration and assonance of "jading and jar," "Time's tasking," and "sodden-with-its-sorrowing" heighten and deepen an experience, grounded in the difficulties of a life of constant self-sacrifice, that Hopkins knew only too well.

Rhythm, language, and the inner relationship between the two parts of the poem give "The Wreck" its sense of unity. But critics have been worried by two apparent digressions: stanzas 20–23, describing the birthplace of the five nuns and their relationship to St. Francis, and the final stanza, asking the drowned nun to pray for the conversion (or reconversion) of England to Rome. "The Wreck of the Deutschland" is both a profoundly Catholic and a daringly apocalyptic poem. The exile of the nuns from Germany under the anti-Catholic Falck Laws, their martyrdom in the wreck, even their number, five, mirroring St. Francis' five stigmata, are all central to the poem's true subject, the paradox that suffering brings salvation. The final stanza extends the miracle of the tall nun's vision to the prayed-for miracle of England's conversion. It was Elisabeth Schneider, in *"The Wreck of the Deutschland*: A New Reading" (1966), who first claimed that, for Hopkins, the tall nun actually *saw* Christ as a miraculous presence—hence the virtual impossibility of expressing her experience at the poem's climax:

> But how shall I . . . make me room there:
>   Reach me a . . . Fancy, come faster—
> Strike you the sight of it? look at it loom there,
>   Thing that she . . . There then! the Master,
> *Ipse*, the only one, Christ, King, Head:
>   He was to cure the extremity where he had cast her;
>   Do, deal, lord it with living and dead;
> Let him ride, her pride, in his triumph, despatch and have
>   done with his doom there.
>
> (st. 28)

Christ has come to the tall nun at the climax of the storm; the poem's ultimate prayer—made through her intercession—is that this should prophesy his second coming, to restore England to his flock. The worship of Christ in the magnificently chiming and interlocking final two lines completes His dominant presence throughout the whole poem:

> Pride, rose, prince, hero of us, high-priest,
> Our hearts' charity's hearth's fire, our thoughts' chivalry's
>   throng's Lord.
>
> (st. 35)

POEMS, 1877–1882

HOPKINS followed "The Wreck of the Deutschland" with ten sonnets, all written in Wales ("Always to me a mother of Muses") during 1877, his final year at St. Beuno's, leading up to his ordination that September. They include some of his best-known and best-loved poems: "God's Grandeur," "The Starlight Night," "The Windhover," "Hurrahing in Harvest." A stanza from part I of "The Wreck," "I Kiss my hand/To the stars" (stanza 5), provides the key to the most exultant of them: the finding, "instressing," of God's mystery in the wonders of nature. In a sense, then, these are poems of meditation, celebrating the created world in all its beauty and wildness—and in all its detailed texture and color—as embodying God; and Louis Martz, in *The Poetry of Meditation* (1954), has claimed that Hopkins belongs to that great seventeenth-century tradition. What is peculiar to Hopkins is the astonishing energy with which, time and again, the meditation is made to lead to a call for spiritual action.

"The Starlight Night," the second of these sonnets (dated 24 February 1877), embodies just this pattern. The octet gives us all the beauty of the star world, its order ("bright boroughs," "circle-citadels"), mystery, and movement (like rippling leaves or doves in flight). It also insists on the excitement with which we should experience it:

> Look at the stars! look, look up at the skies!
> O look at all the fire-folk sitting in the air!

There is an excitement intensified by the imperatives and exclamations and by the use of a sprung line:

> Look at the|stars!|look, look|up at the skies!

Then the sestet insists on the action we must take to make all this beauty our own:

> Buy then! bid then!—What?—Prayer, patience, alms, vows.

The reward, moreover, is even higher—"within-doors house/The shocks [the sheaves of the harvest]" . . . "Christ and his mother" and all the saints.

"God's Grandeur," the sonnet written the day before, introduces a new note, the shaming contrast between the beauty of nature and man's sin or ugliness. The sonnet begins exultantly:

> The world is charged with the grandeur of God.

It moves to one of Hopkins' most intimate, movingly vulnerable apprehensions of nature's secret life:

> There lives the dearest freshness deep down things.

But in between there is the cry against man's instinct to spoil (it loses none of its strength by going back to William Blake and William Wordsworth), emphasized by the lines' repetition and assonance:

> Generations have trod, have trod, have trod;
> And all is seared with trade; bleared, smeared with toil;
> And wears man's smudge and shares man's smell: the soil
> Is bare now, nor can foot feel, being shod.

It is a note we hear in several more poems: in another of this group of sonnets, "The Sea and The Skylark," written at Rhyl, the North Welsh sea resort, the lark's pure and fresh song shames "this shallow and frail town"; in "Duns Scotus's Oxford," Oxford's "base and brickish skirt" confounds "Rural rural keeping—folk, flocks, and flowers"; and in "Ribblesdale" (1882), industrialist man, "heir/To his own selfbent so bound," thoughtlessly spoils "Thy lovely dale."

In "Pied Beauty" ("Glory be to God for dappled things—") Hopkins brings together all the "dappled" distinctive life he so loved—particularly the multitudinous detail of color, texture, and shape:

> For skies of couple-colour as a brinded cow;
> For rose-moles all in stipple upon trout that swim;
> Fresh-firecoal chestnut-falls; finches' wings;

then in the final two lines he puts them in their proper created order and calls for the action that, alone for him, can save his and our souls:

> He fathers-forth whose beauty is past change:
> Praise him.

Such an ending points to the inadequacy of T. S. Eliot's description of Hopkins as essentially a "nature-poet."

The two most exultant of these sonnets of 1877 are "The Windhover," written in May, and "Hurrahing in Harvest," written the following September, three weeks before his ordination. Hopkins later described "The Windhover" to Bridges as "the best thing I ever wrote." Despite the controversies about its meaning, almost all readers of Hopkins have agreed on its poetic greatness. The octet wonderfully catches every movement of the kestrel in his soaring and gliding flight; sprung rhythm and imagery (the riding-school, the "skate's heel") add to his beauty and power. But the dedication "To Christ our Lord," added by Hopkins, is all-important. "I caught," the sonnet's opening words—"I caught this morning morning's minion"—shows Hopkins seizing the inscape of the kestrel; but the images from chivalry ("minion," "kingdom," "dauphin"), taken from the great meditation on the kingdom of Christ in the *Spiritual Exercises*, make it clear that he sees too the presence of Christ in the bird's beauty and mastery, the "achieve of, the mastery of the thing!"

The meaning of the sestet and of "My heart in hiding" from the end of the octet (line 7) has aroused continuing controversy. Some critics, notably I. A. Richards and William Empson, have seen "My heart in hiding" as a cry of envy for the sensuous life symbolized by the kestrel; and they interpret the whole poem as one of inner friction, a subconscious conflict between priest and poet. Conflict there must certainly be in any life of self-sacrifice, and "The Wreck of the Deutschland" shows how intensely Hopkins had dedicated himself to that life. But he never wavered in his vocation, and an unforgettable phrase he used to his agnostic friend Alexander Baillie on 10 April 1871 shows what the Jesuit life meant to him: "this life here [at Stonyhurst] though it is hard is God's will for me as I most intimately know, which is more than violets knee-deep."[7] Hopkins had dedicated himself to the "hidden life"; and the two key images of the sonnet's final three lines stress ("No wonder of it") that the heart dedicated to such service ultimately shines brightest. The "shéer plód" (Hopkins' own stress marks) of the horse makes the ploughshare shine down the furrow ("sillion"); and the "blue-bleak embers" of a dying fire, as they split apart, blaze out gold and orange-red. The final line, "Fall, gall themselves, and gash gold-vermilion," suggests strongly Christ's three crises on His way to the Crucifixion.

This still leaves the sonnet's crux, the meaning of "Buckle" in the second line of the sestet:

> Brute beauty and valour and act, oh, air, pride, plume, here
> Buckle! AND the fire that breaks from thee then, a billion
> Times told lovelier, more dangerous, O my chevalier!

Acceptance of the life of self-sacrifice must support its commonest meaning of "collapse, give way under strain"; and the "AND" (thus capitalized) points to the paradox that, though the kestrel's plumage apparently crumples as it swoops down, the light that flashes from it is then at its loveliest. *This* is the paradox of sacrifice. But, as several critics have pointed out, the kestrel's wings do *not* in fact crumple as it dives. "Buckle" has in fact two other meanings: (a) "fasten, buckle on" (*transitive*) and (b) "grapple, prepare for action" (*intransitive*). If either of these was intended, the mood of "buckle" is imperative. In (a) the cry is to Christ, to buckle on to his heart ("here"—stressed in the line) the kestrel's beauty and power; in (b) the cry is to the kestrel's qualities themselves, to come to his heart and prepare themselves for action. It is part of the richness and tension of the poem that no one of these meanings totally and certainly excludes the other two.

"Hurrahing in Harvest" was the outcome, Hopkins wrote to Bridges, "of half an hour of extreme enthusiasm as I walked alone one day from fishing in

the Elwy." Hopkins' rapture is intense but precise; the vision is of "our Saviour" Himself, present in the cornfields. Such a presence needs one of his most daring and original images to express it—"as a stallion stalwart, very-violet-sweet!" (we remember the "violets knee-deep" of his letter to Baillie); and its force on him, the beholder, a final, most striking image of immense physical and spiritual energy:

> The heart réars wíngs bold and bolder
> And hurls for him, O half hurls earth for him off under his feet.

The moment of understanding, the experience's "instress," has been transformed into pure, visionary activity.

"Spring," written in May 1877, shows us another of nature's "inscapes" that most moved Hopkins, its "wildness and wet," as he called it in the later poem "Inversnaid." Here we have

> When weeds, in wheels, shoot long and lovely and lush . . .

("wheels," in particular, is exact—their coiling shape—and exuberant). But the sestet first questions the scene's meaning:

> "What is all this juice and all this joy?"

And then, characteristically, Hopkins transforms it to innocent human beauty—"Innocent mind and Mayday in girl and boy"—and sees it as threatened:

> . . . Have, get, before it cloy,
> Before it cloud, Christ, lord, and sour with sinning.

This feeling for innocence threatened by corruption is the major theme of a group of poems inspired by Hopkins' experiences as a priest: "The Handsome Heart" and "The Bugler's First Communion," both written at Oxford in 1879 when he was serving at St. Aloysius' Church; and "Brothers," based on a scene that touched him at Mount St. Mary's College, Chesterfield (where he was "sub-minister" in 1877–1878), but not completed until 1880. With "Felix Randal," written in April 1880 at Liverpool, where he was priest at St. Francis Xavier's, these are almost his only poems describing incidents in his relations with others. Poetically, the first three seem to have obvious weaknesses; if some readers have been drawn to their delicacy and pathos, others have dismissed

---

[7]C. C. Abbott, ed., *Further Letters of Gerard Manley Hopkins* (London, 1938).

them as indulgent and sentimental. And the main reason for such reservations, if we share them, is that, in terms of what we are accustomed to from Hopkins, the incidents they recount—a boy's "gracious answer," a bugler's first Communion, a man's response to his younger brother's acting— seem too simple; we miss the urgency and complexity of the poems about himself. But we cannot miss the ardor of the prayers that end the first two:

> . . . Only . . . On that path you pace
> Run all your race, O brace sterner that strain!
> ("The Handsome Heart")

Recorded only, I have put my lips on pleas
Would brandle[8] adamantine heaven with ride and jar,
    did Prayer go disregarded:
Forward-like, but however, and like[9] favourable heaven
    heard these.
> ("The Bugler's First Communion")

Nor the sudden, happy recognition of the goodness of human nature that ends "Brothers":

> There dearly thén, deárly,
> Dearly thou canst be kind.

The sonnet "Felix Randal" ("Felix Randal the farrier, O is he dead then? my duty all ended") is a far greater poem; to many it is one of Hopkins' most memorable. More powerfully than in any of his other poems, it brings together priest and poet. It is concerned with an adult, not children—a blacksmith, one of his Liverpool flock, who has just died. It is an elegy but the strong feeling it contains goes both ways. Hopkins' ministrations have comforted Felix, but the blacksmith's need of them has equally comforted Hopkins:

This seeing the sick endears them to us, us too it endears.

Hopkins makes Felix's attraction for him quite clear ("his mould of man, big-boned and hardy-handsome"); and as this becomes the accepted love of and for the priest at the sickbed, the poet can address Felix directly and through his imagination conjure up Felix's marvelously boisterous life in the past:

How far from then forethought of, all thy more boisterous
    years,

8Shake.
9Most likely.

When thou at the random grim forge, powerful amidst
    peers,
Didst fettle for the great grey drayhorse his bright and
    battering sandal!

Meanwhile, the year before, at Mount St. Mary's College, Hopkins had written his second long narrative poem, "The Loss of the Eurydice." Like "The Wreck of the Deutschland," it is an occasional poem: the *Eurydice* had just foundered off the Isle of Wight and many details of the disaster are taken from reports in the *Times* (London), 25–27 March 1878. Like "The Wreck," it is an explicitly religious poem; Hopkins sees the wreck, with its loss of three hundred young lives, as an analogy for England's lapse from Roman Catholicism. But there the resemblances end. It is a much simpler poem than "The Wreck," with none of the urgency or complexity of his own close spiritual involvement. This lack of complexity is underlined by the far simpler prosodic structure: four-line stanzas, each line bearing three stresses. "The scanning runs on without break to the end of the stanza, so that each stanza is rather one long line rhymed in passage than four lines with rhymes at the end," runs a note Hopkins added to his manuscript. But the rhymes "in passage" make, at times, considerable demands on us:

> Some asleep unawakened, all un-
> warned, eleven fathoms fallen
> (st. 1)

> But what black Boreas wrecked her? he
> Came equipped, deadly-electric
> (st. 6)

There is not the powerful symbolism of "The Wreck" to give "The Eurydice" that kind of unity. But the description of the storm itself—the sudden quickening of the language, the alliteration, the stresses of the sprung rhythm—suggests an apocalyptic violence:

> A beetling baldbright cloud thorough England
> Riding: there did storms not mingle? and
>   Hailropes hustle and grind their
> Heavengravel? wolfsnow, worlds of it, wind there?
> (st. 7)

The picture of the young drowned sailor is as good as anything Hopkins did in its kind:

Look, foot to forelock, how all things suit! he
Is strung by duty, is strained to beauty,
   And brown-as-dawning-skinned
With brine and shine and whirling wind.
(st. 20)

And stanzas 22–26, in which he contemplates the loss of young life and equates it with England's lapse from Rome, show, movingly, Hopkins' real concern:

Only the breathing temple and fleet
Life, this wildworth blown so sweet,
   These daredeaths, ay this crew, in
Unchrist, all rolled in ruin—
(st. 24)

The prayer that ends the poem—like that which ends "The Wreck" and so many of the poems of this period—shows how intensely Hopkins hopes, through his poetry, to awaken men to God's providence:

But to Christ lord of thunder
Crouch; lay knee by earth low under:
(st. 28)

Oxford, where Hopkins was a priest at St. Aloysius' Church from December 1878 to October 1879, proved an exceptionally fruitful place and time for his poetry. In all, he wrote nine poems there—besides the two already discussed, "Binsey Poplars," "Duns Scotus's Oxford," "Henry Purcell," "The Candle Indoors," "Morning, Midday, and Evening Sacrifice," "Andromeda," and "Peace." Of these, many would claim "Henry Purcell" to be among his finest—if most difficult—sonnets. Both it and, expectedly, "Duns Scotus's Oxford," owe a great deal to Scotus. The latter poem is more than a tribute; in its celebration of the distinctiveness of Oxford, its *haecceitas* ("Towery city and branchy between towers"), it follows Scotist principles; hence the despair that Scotus' own city, where he traditionally both studied and taught, should have betrayed its past beauty:

Thou hast a base and brickish skirt there, sours
That neighbour-nature thy grey beauty is grounded
Best in; . . .

Yet, for Hopkins, Scotus' presence still haunts Oxford; and the sonnet ends with a moving and heartfelt acknowledgment of what he owes to him:

Yet ah! this air I gather and I release
He lived on; these weeds and waters, these walls are what
He haunted who of all men most sways my spirits to peace;

Of reality the rarest-veinèd unraveller . . .

That last phrase, in its giving to Scotus true insight into the reality of things, links closely with "Henry Purcell," written the following month, and particularly with the important epitaph Hopkins gave to it: that Purcell's music has "uttered in notes the very make and species of man as created both in him and in all men generally."

"Henry Purcell," then, again both explores and celebrates distinctiveness; not only of the genius of Purcell's music but, ultimately through that music, of "the very make and species of man," of selfhood itself:

It is the forgèd feature finds me; it is the rehearsal
Of own, of abrúpt sélf there so thrusts on, so
   throngs the ear.

This is the essence of Purcell's music: "forgèd" has the force of being beaten out on the anvil, beaten to the right shape, to utter Purcell's "abrúpt sélf" (the stress marks are Hopkins' own). The sestet then seeks to find an exact analogy in nature to bring this insight home, and Hopkins finds it in one of his boldest and most majestic images, that of the "great stormfowl":

. . . so some great stormfowl, whenever he has walked
   his while

The thunder-purple seabeach, plùmed purple-of-
   thunder,
If a wuthering of his palmy snow-pinions scatter a
   colossal smile
Off him, but meaning motion fans fresh our wits with
   wonder.

The image is difficult, as Robert Bridges found the whole sonnet. But, because of that, Hopkins explained the meaning of almost every phrase in letters to him; and, as he showed, the analogy between Purcell and the "great stormfowl" is an exact one: "It is as when a bird thinking only of soaring spreads its wings: a beholder may happen then to have his attention drawn by the act to the plumage displayed" (4 January 1883). In the same way, Purcell, in his music, shows us unawares its distinctive ("archespecial") beauty. It is one of the poems Hopkins most liked himself ("one of my very best pieces," he told Bridges); and its richness and complexity (especially of the final image) fully justify the prosodic innovation he made in it: it is his first sonnet in alexandrines, six-feet lines with a stress to each foot—a meter to which he returned in "Felix Randal."

A third sonnet, "As kingfishers catch fire," given neither title nor date by Hopkins, is an even stronger expression of the belief he shared with Duns Scotus in the fulfilling of individuality. The striking similarity of its imagery to a passage from his December 1881 commentary on the *Spiritual Exercises* suggests that Hopkins may have written it at Roehampton, during his tertianship, a period of renewal after the horrors of his missions in Liverpool and Glasgow. It is a very much simpler sonnet than "Henry Purcell"; but its simplicity is that of absolute confidence, as he moves from the "selving" (his own word) of animate and even inanimate objects—kingfishers, dragonflies, stones, bells—to the "selving" of "the just man" who, by fulfilling himself, becomes, through grace, another Christ:

> Acts in God's eye what in God's eye he is—
> Chríst. For Christ plays in ten thousand places,
> Lovely in limbs, and lovely in eyes not his
> To the Father through the features of men's faces.

But another note enters increasingly the poems he wrote, after his ten months at Oxford, in Lancashire, either in Liverpool, while serving at St. Francis Xavier's, or at Stonyhurst, where he taught classics for two years, 1882–1884. It is a strong sense of transience, a conviction that the beauty he so loved in the world would pass, however cherished. Almost ten years earlier, on 17 April 1873, when an ash tree was felled in the garden at Stonyhurst, he had recorded in his journal:

... there came at that moment a great pang and I wished to die and not to see the inscapes of the world destroyed any more.

It is this feeling of wretchedness at the loss of natural beauty that gives such poignancy to "Binsey Poplars"—felled while he was in Oxford in 1879, a poignancy transmuted by the musical repetitions:

> Ten or twelve, only ten or twelve
> Strokes of havoc únselve
>   The sweet especial scene,
>   Rural scene, a rural scene,
>   Sweet especial rural scene.

During this period, Hopkins was beginning to write music, mostly airs to his own, Bridges', and Canon Dixon's poems.[10] To some degree, as in this poem, the clear musical concern, while seeming to intensify the feeling, also serves to transmute it, to make it more bearable. This is certainly the effect of the first part of "The Leaden Echo and the Golden Echo," the Maidens' song from his projected verse drama "St. Winefred's Well," written at Stonyhurst in October 1882, of which he wrote to Dixon on 23 October 1886: "I never did anything more musical." Both parts employ musical repetition more than any other poem Hopkins wrote. "The Leaden Echo" ends on the key word "despair" conjured up by the passing of beauty, but its repetition again seems to transmute, to distance it; while "The Golden Echo," although finding the only answer, for Hopkins, to mortal beauty's loss:

> Give beauty back, beauty, beauty, beauty, back
> to God, beauty's self and beauty's giver,

still has two lines that face personal feelings head on, in words and rhythm that seem frighteningly undistanced:

> O then, weary then whý should we tread? O why are we
> so haggard at the heart, so care-coiled, care killed,
> so fagged, so flashed, so cogged, so cumbered,
> When the thing we freely fórfeit is kept with fonder a
> care. . . .

Those two lines alone of the comparatively few poems of 1880–1882 seem to look forward uncompromisingly to the later poems of desolation. But almost all of them have some sense of loss, of blight, of "unselving" (to use Hopkins' own word from "Binsey Poplars"), even though that is far from the total—or even major—tone of the poem. Much the most delicate and subtle of them—indeed one of the most delicate and subtle of all Hopkins' poems—is "Spring and Fall," addressed to a young child ("Márgarét, are you grieving/Over Goldengrove unleaving?"), composed on his way back from Lydiate, in Lancashire, to Liverpool, in September 1880. The sharp but gentle questioning goes to the roots of all sorrow; and one phrase in particular shows Hopkins' skill in using the full resources of words:

[10]For a full account of Hopkins as musician, see H. House and G. Storey, eds., *The Journals and Papers of Gerard Manley Hopkins* (Oxford, 1959), pp. 457–497.

Though worlds of wanwood leafmeal lie;

where "wan" fuses both "dismal" and, as an obsolete prefix, "deficient" or "lost." The end of the poem is perhaps the finest expression we have of Hopkins' belief in the true wisdom of the heart and the spirit ("ghost"):

> Nor mouth had, no nor mind, expressed
> What heart heard of, ghost guessed:
> It ís the blight man was born for,
> It is Margaret you mourn for.

Two other poems, written in the autumns of 1881 and 1882, are, at first sight and sound, celebrations, though in very different moods, of the countryside Hopkins so loved—"Inversnaid" of the Scottish Highlands, "Ribblesdale" of the Lancashire dale in which Stonyhurst College lies. But each ends with a warning not to destroy such inscapes. "Inversnaid" describes the movement of the Scottish burn so happily and excitedly that we might miss the sudden menace of the whirlpool:

> Of a pool so pitchblack, féll-frówning,
> It rounds and rounds Despair to drowning.

And no one can miss Hopkins' cry in the final stanzas:

> What would the world be, once bereft
> Of wet and of wildness? Let them be left,
> O let them be left, wildness and wet;
> Long live the weeds and the wilderness yet.

just as no one can miss Hopkins' fear, in the sestet of "Ribblesdale," that man, "the heir/To his own self-bent so bound," will despoil "Thy lovely dale."

POEMS OF DESOLATION, 1884–1885

THE very intensity of the six "terrible sonnets" (as Bridges called them) of 1885—one of them, as Hopkins told Bridges, "written in blood" (17 May 1885)—has led many to believe that the entire five years of Hopkins' time in Dublin—from February 1884, when he took up his appointment as Professor of Greek at University College and Fellow of the Royal University of Ireland, to his death on 8 June 1889 from typhoid—were years of unrelieved wretchedness. This is not confirmed by the other poems he wrote in Ireland: the other two sonnets of 1885—"To what serves Mortal Beauty?" and "The Soldier"—and most of the varied poems, some unfinished, he wrote from 1887 to within six weeks of his death. Nor is it shown by Hopkins' other remarkably wide-ranging signs of intellectual energy, including his projected books on Homer and on "the Dorian Measure or on Rhythm in general" (of which virtually nothing, sadly, remains); letters to Bridges on prosody and John Milton; to R. W. Dixon, on Dixon's own poems and on poetry in general; to Coventry Patmore, giving him detailed criticism for a new edition of his *Collected Poems*; and to his old friend Alexander Baillie on possible early relations between Egypt and Greece. In addition, he was writing a lot of music, and in the year before his death, he began drawing again.

But there can be no doubt of the paralyzing desolation that Hopkins felt in the winter of 1884 (to which the first drafts of "Spelt from Sybil's Leaves" belong) and for more than a year afterward. The "terrible sonnets" themselves document his feelings of isolation, of intense inner struggle, and, paradoxically (since they are, to many readers, his finest sonnets), of frustration at his inability to create. Many factors certainly contributed to such feelings: bad health and nervous depression, increased by the strain on his eyes of almost continuous reading of examination papers; his sense of being an exile, exacerbated by the Irish nationalism he detested. And, perhaps, there were less conscious conflicts: the residual, and perhaps for him, inevitable conflict between priest and poet; the suppression of strong, possibly homosexual, feelings; and, most likely, the exaggeration, in his search for sanctity, of the distinction between his "affective" will, his love of beauty (including poetic beauty), and his "elective will," his desire for duty and holiness (an explanation put forward very convincingly by Fr. Christopher Devlin in *The Sermons and Devotional Writings of Gerard Manley Hopkins*, 1959).

"Spelt from Sybil's Leaves," to which Hopkins returned during the first six months of 1885, shows his powers at their finest. It is the only one of his sonnets to use an eight-stress line (marked by a strong caesura after four stresses); he described it to Bridges as "the longest sonnet ever made" and wrote to him on 11 December 1886:

Of this long sonnet above all remember what applies to all my verse, that it is, as living art should be, made for performance and that its performance is not reading with the eye but loud, leisurely, poetical (not rhetorical) recitation, with long rests, long dwells on the rhyme and other marked syllables, and so on. This sonnet shd. be almost sung: it is most carefully timed in *tempo rubato* [irregular rhythm].

It is a poem of prophecy, of warning, drawing its title from both Vergil's Cumaean Sybil, who guided Aeneas to the underworld (*Aeneid* 6), and the *Dies irae*, "The Day of Wrath," of the Roman Catholic Burial Mass: "As David and the Sybil testify . . . what terror shall affright the soul when the judge comes."[11] In the terrible description of the war within, with which it ends:

> . . . a rack
> Where, selfwrung, selfstrung, sheathe-\|and shelterless,\|
> thóughts agaínst thoughts ín groans grínd,

it prophesies the major theme of the six "terrible sonnets"; but its warning is much more comprehensive. The analogy of the haunting picture of the descent of night, in the first half of the sonnet, is the ending of all "selving," of all the "dappled things" Hopkins loved, of all distinctiveness:

> For earth\|her being was unbound; her
> dapple is at an end, as-
> tray or aswarm, all throughther, in throngs;\|self ín self
> steepèd and páshed—qúite
> Disremembering, dísmémbering\|áll now. . . .

What is deeply impressive in the poem is not only the power of each analogy, each set of images, but the felt exactitude of their parallelism. The straining of evening to be night *becomes* the total blanketing-out of earth's individual features, now lit only by the last rays of the dying sun ("Her fond yellow horn-light wound to the west"); the loss of each object's true shape and meaning, its inscape ("self ín self steepèd and páshed") *becomes*—the warning is in line 7 ("Heart, you round me right/With")—the nightmare alternative, where the trees have the shape of dragons and the "bleak light" the texture of a Damascene-worked sword. And this again is "Óur tale," the dire prophecy of the poem's title: once we let earth's multiplicity go—her "once skéined stained véined varíety"—once we attempt to reduce life to absolute moral judgment—"black, white;\|right, wrong"—we shall experience the self-torturing, self-wringing rack of the poem's last line. But the final analogy carries the direst warning: "párt, pen, páck" refers to Christ's separation of the sheep from the goats at the Last Judgment (Matt. 25: 31–33). On one level, fear of this judgment lies behind the image in the final line of unprotected conscience on the rack, from which there can be no escape.

Hopkins' description of "Sibyl's Leaves" to Bridges as "living art . . . made for performance"—his totally justified pride in it as a sonnet—must strongly modify our sense of its apparently bleak pessimism. "To what serves Mortal Beauty?" written during a retreat at Clongowes on 23 August 1885—very near in time to the final draft of "Sibyl's Leaves"—shows how gracefully and relaxedly Hopkins could treat the conflict that Fr. Christopher Devlin has suggested is central to the desolate sonnets of this year, his "affective will," his love of beauty, versus his "elective will," his duty to God. The famous story of Pope Gregory the Great sending Augustine to convert England, after seeing the handsome English slaves ("*Non Angli sed Angeli*"),[12] is one example of the higher use of mortal beauty:

> Those lovely lads once, wet-fresh\|windfalls of war's storm,
> How then should Gregory, a father,\|have gleanèd else from
> swarm-
> èd Rome? But God to a nation\|dealt that day's dear chance.

The sonnet's ending, the hope to "Merely meet" mortal beauty and to wish for it, as for all outward beauty, spiritual beauty, "God's better beauty, grace," presents the Christian "use" of beauty and does so with no sign of conflict or strain.

A sense of strain is dominant in the six desolate (although in differing degrees) sonnets that, insofar as we can date them, were written in 1885, the strain, above all, of isolation, of feeling deserted by God, of being certain that his creative capacity was dead. But we cannot miss either the energy, the determination to resist despair, or the authenticity, the equal determination to be utterly true to his own feelings, however self-tortured and self-torturing. Formally, these sonnets are the antitheses of "Spelt from Sybil's Leaves": the language is stark, bare, stripped, to ex-

---

[11]Paul L. Mariani has also shown how close the poem is to some of Hopkins' Retreat notes for the meditation on Hell from the *Spiritual Exercises* (*A Commentary on the Complete Poems of Gerard Manley Hopkins* [Ithaca, N. Y., 1970], pp. 199 ff.).

[12]"Not Angles, but Angels."

press the essentials of the experience recorded, the resultant pitch of concentration a powerful new rhetoric.

Our only keys to dating them are letters and retreat notes. We know Hopkins' state of mind in the spring of 1885 from a letter to Alexander Baillie: his constitutional melancholy, he wrote, was becoming

. . . more distributed, constant, and crippling. . . . when I am at the worst, though my judgment is never affected, my state is much like madness.

But two letters to Bridges help us to identify and date the sonnets themselves. In May 1885 Hopkins wrote to him, "I have after long silence written two sonnets, which I am touching: if ever anything was written in blood one of these was." And in September of the same year, "I shall shortly have some sonnets to send you, five or more. Four of these came like inspirations unbidden and against my will." Bridges thought the sonnet "written in blood" was "Carrion Comfort"; the more desolate "No worst, there is none," written on the same manuscript page as a revised version of "Carrion Comfort," seems more likely.[13] There can be little doubt that the "five or more" sonnets mentioned in the September letter—neither these nor the one "written in blood" were in fact sent to Bridges—were the "terrible sonnets" and thus very probably written in 1885.

"Carrion Comfort" has the greatest energy of these sonnets. It is generated at once in the opening line, in the refusal to "feast" on despair:

Not, I'll not, carrion comfort, Despair, not feast on thee;

(there are three more repeated "nots" in the first quatrain). The energy is increased by all the physical images of wrestling, and it is felt strongly again in the successive questions Hopkins asks of his terrible and mysterious adversary. The "underthought" of the sonnet (Hopkins' own word for the "often only half realised" source of a poem's images) combines the Book of Job with Gen. 32: 24–30, Jacob's wrestling with God; but, in turn, the adversary becomes Christ the winnower and finally Christ the Master. By kissing His rod and hand, Hopkins seems to have recovered: "my heart lo! lapped strength, stole joy,

[13]Norman MacKenzie has recently argued for "I wake and feel" as being the most likely in *A Reader's Guide to G. M. Hopkins* (London, 1981), pp. 171–172.

would laugh, chéer." But the sonnet ends on an agonizedly questioning note: the only certainty now is that the initial struggle with despair has become a wrestling bout with God Himself, scrupulously and bitterly documented:

That night, that year
Of now done darkness I wretch lay wrestling with (my God!) my God.

The poem "No worst, there is none" creates—or re-creates—an extraordinarily intense sense of physical and mental pain, mainly through imagery, sound, and rhythm, but also through an "underthought" that combines the most intense works of suffering, all of which Hopkins knew intimately: the Book of Job (the "whirlwind"), Aeschylus' *Prometheus Bound* (Prometheus chained to his mountain), *King Lear* (the sonnet's final two lines). In the very first line, "Pitched past pitch of grief" suggests an inexpressible degree of pain; "More pangs . . . schooled at forepangs, wilder wring" turns the grief into something horrifyingly active. The image of the lowing herd of cattle turns the pain into sorrow; but the anvil wincing and singing and Fury's shrieking force the sense of physical pain on us again and turn the screw tighter. Throughout the octet, repetitions and sound accentuate the experience; a mark that Hopkins made in his manuscript connecting "sorrow" with "an" in line 6, thus putting four of the line's five stresses on "áge-old anvil wince and sing," shows how sprung rhythm could "fetch out" his meaning.

The sestet begins with one of Hopkins' most striking images, painfully relevant to the states of near-madness he described in his letters:

O the mind, mind has mountains; cliffs of fall Frightful, sheer, no-man-fathomed. Hold them cheap May who ne'er hung there. . . .

It ends with clear references to the Book of Job, *King Lear*, and *Macbeth* that not only deepen the experience but universalize it. After the intense pain of the sonnet, the resigned acceptance of the final line seems the only course left open:

all
Life death does end and each day dies with sleep.

"To seem the stranger lies my lot" records both Hopkins' loneliness as a Roman Catholic in Ireland

and his conviction that he can no longer create. The power of the first ten lines is that of direct, simple statement: his grief is poignant, but restrained. That restraint makes the clotted movement of lines 11–13, mirroring his bewildered frustration, the more powerful:

> . . . Only what word
> Wisest my heart breeds dark heaven's baffling ban
> Bars or hell's spell thwarts. . . .

Many years ago F. R. Leavis compared these lines to Macbeth's speech, "My thought, whose murder yet is but fantastical," as a "rendering of the very movement of consciousness";[14] and the judgment still holds. Hopkins' bafflement is at his inability to create (seen, as so often in this period, as a natural sexual process: "my heart breeds"); and, as we know from his letters, this sense of frustration extended to all his activities, musical and scholarly as well as poetic. Whether we read the sonnet's last sad phrase, "a lonely began," as a verb following an omitted relative pronoun or as a coined noun, its economy and poignancy fit perfectly the tone of the whole sonnet; its honesty demands our respect.

"I wake and feel the fell of dark" is, for most readers, probably the most desolate of these sonnets. The multiple meanings of the opening image, "the fell of dark" ("animal hide," "fierce," and "having fallen" are perhaps the key ones), dominate the octet.[15] All of them powerfully suggest the physical oppressiveness of the night's experience and carry that oppressiveness back, as the "black hoürs" "mean years, mean life." The image of "dead" (i.e., undelivered) letters sent to an unhearing God completes the sense of total lostness.

The sestet adds physical nausea to Hopkins' state: "gall" is poison as well as bitterness. In line 11 the bones, blood, and flesh that he praised God for binding in him in the first stanza of "The Wreck of the Deutschland" are now part of God's curse on him:

> Bones built in me, flesh filled, blood brimmed the curse.

There are two ambiguities in the sonnet's last three lines. Either "selfyeast" or "a dull dough" can be the subject of "Selfyeast of spirit a dull dough sours":

either way, the right, healthy process—the leavening of body by spirit—has been soured, perverted. The second ambiguity should not be there: both theology and the syntax of the final two lines assert that the agonies of the damned in hell must be worse than his. Yet the doubt persists: "but worse" *could* mean that his torments were worse than theirs. The possibility of that is an index of the sonnet's authenticity:

> With witness I speak this.

We believe Hopkins is at his lowest ebb; and in the final two of these Dublin sonnets, "Patience, hard thing!" and "My own heart let me more have pity on," we can readily believe that at last some light has dawned for him. In each he seeks a way out of his misery; but in neither does he belittle the difficulties. The prayer for patience is totally realistic; it means he must continue to endure, to accept "war" and "wounds" and, worse still, the inner conflicts, the grating and bruising of his heart on itself. But patience offers consolations absent from the more tormented sonnets. Like ivy, "Natural heart's ivy," she "masks / Our ruins of wrecked past purpose" (the "beginnings of things, ever so many, which it seems to me might well have been done, ruins and wrecks," as Hopkins described his many unfinished projects in a letter to Baillie); and there, in an image of ivy's purple berries and liquid-green leaves, at once precise and hauntingly beautiful,

> . . . she basks
> Purple eyes and seas of liquid leaves all day.
> ("Patience, hard thing!")

But the final emblem of patience is God Himself. It is He who distills kindness, as a bee distills honey, and fills His honeycomb with it, "and that comes those ways we know."

The description of his own state in the octet of "My own heart let me more have pity on" is more complex and superbly, if difficultly, rendered. Hopkins knows that his torment is self-caused and at that stage is sure that there is no way out. The dense syntax and imagery perfectly mirror his bewilderment:

> I cast for comfort I can no more get
> By groping round my comfortless, than blind
> Eyes in their dark can day or thirst can find
> Thirst's all-in-all in all a world of wet.

---

[14]*New Bearings in English Poetry* (London, 1932), p. 170.
[15]Norman MacKenzie has discussed the many possible meanings of "fell" in *Hopkins* (Edinburgh, 1968), pp. 88–90.

We have to understand "world" after "comfortless," so as to parallel "dark" in the next line, and to appreciate that thirst itself seeks water (as the Ancient Mariner did, surrounded by the sea) just as blindness seeks light. As with Shakespeare and the seventeenth-century metaphysical poets, the effort forces us to share the writer's experience.

But the tone of the sestet, like that of the sonnet's first two lines, is self-reproaching, more relaxed, has even a touch of humor:

> Soul, self; come, poor Jackself, I do advise
> You, jaded, let be . . .

Bewilderment has now become self-exhortation: "leave comfort root-room" (let it expand like a plant); "let joy size" (let it grow—at God's will); trust unpredictable moments of happiness. The final coined verb ("as skies/Betweenpie mountains": as patches of sky seen between them dapple the mountains) suggests, in its very idiosyncrasy, at least a momentary restoration of Hopkins' faith in his own creativity.

FINAL POEMS, 1887–1889

MOST of the poems that Hopkins wrote in the last two years of his life—including the unfinished "Epithalamion"—show, despite his often harrowing letters, how poetically alive he was until his final illness. They also show his constant technical experimentation. Of his three extended sonnets with codas, only one, "Tom's Garland" (September 1887), his one attempt to write a political poem "upon the Unemployed," did not work as he had hoped: he had to confess to Bridges that it was "in point of execution very highly wrought, too much so, I am afraid"; and most modern readers have agreed with him. Each of the other two, "Harry Ploughman" and "That Nature is a Heraclitean Fire," totally justifies, in its own individual way, Hopkins' experimenting. But during the same period he was also deliberately reverting almost to the opposite style, to the "Miltonic plainness and severity" that he told Bridges he had aimed at in "Andromeda," written almost ten years earlier at Oxford. It is this experiment in style, his admiration for John Dryden, "the most masculine of our poets" as he put it, and his hope "to be more intelligible, smoother, and less

singular" (letter to Bridges, 25 September 1888) that lie behind the other sonnets of these two years, however different their concerns: "St. Alphonsus Rodriguez," "Thou art indeed just, Lord," and "To R.B.," his last poem, written six weeks before his death and addressed to Bridges. The fourth of these sonnets, "The Shepherd's Brow" (3 April 1889), Bridges excluded from the canon as "thrown off one day in a cynical mood." It is in fact the last of five full drafts; but a note of something near hysteria in its despair makes it, as a poem, much less impressive than either the earlier desolate sonnets or the three "plainer" sonnets of Hopkins' last year.

On 6 November 1887 Hopkins wrote to Bridges of "Harry Ploughman," written at Dromore two months before: "I want Harry Ploughman to be a vivid figure before the mind's eye; if he is not that the sonnet fails." On 11 October, he had written to Bridges that the sonnet was "altogether for recital not for perusal" and its rhythm was "very highly studied." He also thought that the sonnet was a "very good one." It is in fact an astonishingly vivid picture of a ploughman in action, "fetched out" by the sprung rhythm (in one of the two manuscripts Hopkins gives seven "reading-marks" to help the reader)[16] and by the five extra "burden-lines" (which Hopkins thought might be recited by a chorus). The octet—increased to eleven lines by the three "burden-lines"—gives us Harry himself, as Hopkins saw or imagined him in his strength and almost sculptured handsomeness:

> Hard as hurdle arms, with a broth of goldish flue,
> Breathed round; the rack of ribs; the scooped flank . . .

The bodily details accumulate; but they form a unity, the vital inscape of a man ready for action, all his limbs perfectly disciplined:

> By a grey eye's head steered well, one crew, fall to;
> Stand at stress. . . .

Hence the dominant images of the serving sailor or soldier: "one crew," "as at a rollcall, rank," "His sinew-service."

In the sestet the ploughing itself takes over; and now plough and ploughman, his curls lifted and laced by the wind, his feet racing behind the plough-

---

[16]Reproduced in *The Poems of Gerard Manley Hopkins*, 4th ed., p. 293.

share and the upturned shining earth, form a new unity, the inscape of work well done. Ploughing as a symbol of work has a long history, both pagan and Christian; and Hopkins greatly admired one contemporary painting of it, Frederick Walker's *The Plough* (Royal Academy, 1870), which he thought "a divine work" (letter to Dixon, 30 June 1886).[17]

The poem's syntax throughout is difficult, as Hopkins himself confessed to Bridges, and words are used in unusual senses, demanding a leap of understanding from the reader, to make—as they do—the maximum impact. The two word-coinages in line 16, "Churlsgrace, too, child of Amansstrength" (the first from "churl," peasant), sum up the two qualities, grace and strength, that have combined to create this powerfully active figure.

"That Nature is a Heraclitean Fire and of the Comfort of the Resurrection" was written on 26 July 1888, near Dublin, "one windy bright day between floods," Hopkins told Dixon. Both technically and imaginatively it is one of his finest sonnets, fully justifying its great length (it is in alexandrines and has three codas). Hopkins was pleased with what he called its distillation of "early Greek philosophical thought," but prouder of its originality: "The effect of studying masterpieces is to make me admire and do otherwise," he wrote to Bridges two months after its composition.

Heraclitus (*ca.* 535 B.C.–*ca.* 475 B.C.) believed that all nature would ultimately resolve itself into fire. Everything was in a state of flux; not even man's body or soul could escape destruction. This relentless process is the subject of the central section of the sonnet's three sections, lines 10–16. But before this, the sonnet's opening section, lines 1–9, gives us one of Hopkins' most dynamic, excited pictures of nature in movement: racing clouds, light, and boisterous wind play together in apparent abandon:"Heaven-roysterers, in gay gangs⏐they throng." Then, suddenly, Hopkins sees them as part of the Heraclitean process; the wind turns the floods into earth and ooze; then all, as in Heraclitus, becomes fire:

> . . . Million-fuelèd,⏐nature's bonfire burns on.

But man's toiling footprints have been obliterated, too, leading Hopkins to the dramatic change of tone in the second section, as he contemplates the loss of man's mind and soul, communicated in three highly expressive word-coinages: man's "firedint," the spark his being gives out; his "Manshape," his inscape or essence; his "disseveral" being, his individual selfhood. All these "death blots black out"; all traces of his precious individuality "vastness blurs and time⏐beats level."

But the change of tone in the final section is more dramatic still. "Enough! the Resurrection" is, for Hopkins, a complete answer to Heraclitus. There is no balking of man's frailties and almost comic inadequacies: he is still "This Jack, joke, poor potsherd,⏐patch, matchwood," but Christ has promised his ultimate survival; he is therefore, too, "immortal diamond." The echo of the last short line makes certainty, for Hopkins, more certain.

"Epithalamion," Hopkins' unfinished ode for his youngest brother Everard's wedding in April 1888, deserves to be better known. It was only a collection of fragments that Bridges, with the greatest skill, put together; and there is little success in the faltering attempt at the end to make the scene, of the boys bathing, apply allegorically to marriage—or indeed in the rather absurd picture of the "listless stranger" (Hopkins himself?) undressing and taking off his boots. But there are marvelous lines that communicate to the full Hopkins' joy in re-creating such a remembered scene and his technical skills in doing so. Of the boys bathing:

> With dare and with downdolphinry and bellbright bodies
>   huddling out,
> Are earthworld, airworld, waterworld thorough hurled,
>   all by turn and turn about;

of the pool, surrounded by his favorite trees:

> Fairyland; silk-beech, scrolled ash, packed sycamore, wild
>   wychelm, hornbeam fretty overstood
> By. Rafts and rafts of flake leaves light, dealt so, painted
>   on the air, . . .

And of the strangely shaped rocks that we know, from his journal and some of his drawings, he was so fond of:

> . . . a coffer, burly all of blocks
> Built of chancequarrièd, selfquainèd, hoar-huskèd
>   rocks
> And the water warbles over into, filleted⏐with glassy
>   grassy quicksilvery shivès and shoots. . . .

---

[17]It is reproduced in R. K. R. Thornton, ed., *All My Eyes See: The Visual World of G. M. Hopkins* (Sunderland, 1975), p. 105.

However diverse the concern, of the three "plain" sonnets written in Ireland during his last year, they share certain new qualities of tone. They are, in form and meter, a return to tradition after the long, experimental sonnets they follow. Letters to Bridges, sending him earlier, finally rejected drafts of "St. Alphonsus Rodriguez," show how deliberate this return was; and one comment on it, however ironically framed, shows how desperate he was to be understood: "The sonnet (I say it snorting) aims at being understood." He called its sestet "both pregnant and exact"; the near-classical claim is justified by all three sonnets. They are also, all three, very personal, related intimately to his spiritual trials and, above all, to what he felt keenly—and, as the poems themselves show, wrongly—as poetic sterility. And to objectify that personal tone, to give it a new, quiet dignity, they have, each of them in different ways, a near-ironic self-awareness.[18]

"St. Alphonsus Rodriguez" was "written to order" in autumn 1888 in honor of a recently canonized sixteenth-century Jesuit hall porter in Majorca. The quiet irony comes from the clear identification of his own state in Dublin, apparently fruitless and inactive, with that of Alphonsus. The sonnet celebrates "the war within" as against the outward martyrdom of "exploit," the inner trials Alphonsus suffered:

> Those years and years . . . of world without event
> That in Majorca Alfonso watched the door.

The God "who, with trickling increment, / Veins violets," is the God he trusts, despite his sense of aridity, to bring him slowly but firmly to fulfillment.

In "Thou art indeed just, Lord" (17 March 1889), that trust is sorely tried. The epigraph, from Jer. 12: 1, "Why do the ways of the wicked prosper?" partly paraphrased in the sonnet's opening three lines, is bitter enough: Hopkins' tone, emphasized by the repeated "Sir," turns it into a dignified plea. The poignant picture of returning spring in the sestet— "fretty chervil," "fresh wind," and nesting birds— contrasted with his own sense of sterility reinforces the personal bitterness: the image of the straining eunuch comes in both a letter to Bridges and a private retreat-note of the same year. But the prayer of the final line,

[18]Paul L. Mariani, in his *Commentary on the Complete Poems*, stresses the irony (including "The Shepherd's Brow" in his discussion) and claims that "these last sonnets amount to a new direction in lyrical poetry" (pp. 299, 316).

> Mine, O thou lord of life, send my roots rain

in which the "Mine" must surely govern both "lord of life" and "roots," both reacknowledges God's power over him and at least posits a new intimacy between them. The cry of sterility has produced one of his most beautifully structured and tonally delicate sonnets.

Hopkins' last poem, "To R.B.," dated 22 April 1889, six weeks before his death, and sent to Bridges with his last letter to him, again laments his flagging inspiration. But bitterness is now muted. What we have instead is a confident control of the Conception and birth image in the octet and the perfect mirroring of the explanation of his "un-creativity" in the movement and sound of the last four lines:

> O then if in my lagging lines you miss

> The roll, the rise, the carol, the creation,
> My winter world, that scarcely breathes that bliss
> Now, yields you, with some sighs, our explanation.

JOURNAL AND LETTERS

HOPKINS kept a journal from May 1866, his third year at Oxford, to February 1875, six months after he had begun studying theology at St. Beuno's College in North Wales. It has been of great use to biographers in giving details of outward events— and some more inward events—in Hopkins' life: the exact day, so far as he could record it, of his conversion; his feelings about the various Jesuit institutions in which he lived during his training; two occasions on which he broke down when hearing passages from the lives of Catholics read aloud; the first time he read Duns Scotus and its effect on him.

But its greatest interest is that it covers all but the last ten months of his seven years' "poetic silence," for it was Hopkins' journal that became the outlet for his remarkable powers of observation and for his hypersensitive response to the minutiae of nature. Its most vivid writing is therefore a splendid gloss on the mature poems that were to follow: the trees, skies, clouds, mountains, rushing water, rocks, flowers that were to become the subjects and images of so many of the poems are all recorded here. The journal is full of "wildness and wet," "the weeds and the wilderness." It is also full of unusual words—dialect, archaic, sometimes coined—which he sought out, as in his poems, to express the inscapes that gave him such delight: "brindled and hatched," "knopped," "pelleted," "ruddled" (of clouds); "dappled with big laps and flowers-in-damask" (of the sun in rain); "They look like little gay jugs by shape when they walk, strutting and jod-jodding with their heads" (of pigeons), to cite only a few. It is in the journal that we have almost all the explicit examples of "inscape" and "instress," used for objects in nature, paintings, even buildings, from 1868 onward: "Query has not Giotto the instress of loveliness" (27 June 1868, on a visit to the National Gallery) is the first; "Swiss trees are, like English, well inscaped—in quains [coigns, wedge-shaped blocks]" (7 July 1868, in Switzerland), the second.

The comments on contemporary paintings in the journal are extremely interesting.[19] Like Ruskin, Hopkins made notes on the exhibitions he visited: during the nine years covered by the journal he went whenever he could to the main exhibitions of the Royal Academy, the National Gallery, and the Society of Painters in Water-Colours, as well as to two special loan exhibitions of National Portraits. On all these he made notes, sometimes only jottings, as well as commenting on them in letters. As we might expect, a great many paintings are judged in terms of their inscape (or instress) or lack of it. As an undergraduate, he had greatly admired the Pre-Raphaelites; the painters in whom he took the most delight or critical interest during these years were Sir John Everett Millais, Frederick Leighton, Frederick Walker, Sir Lawrence Alma-Tadema, and the sculptor Sir Hamo Thornycroft. In 1863, as an undergraduate, he had described Millais as "the greatest English painter, one of the greatest of the world." At the Royal Academy exhibition in May and June 1874 he is more critical, but still highly appreciative:

Millais—*Scotch Firs*; "*The silence that is in the lonely woods*"—No such thing, instress absent, firtrunks ungrouped, four or so pairing but not markedly, true bold realism but quite a casual install of woodland with casual heathertufts, broom with black beanpods and so on, but the master shewn in the slouch and toss-up of the firtree-head in near background, in the tufts of fir-needles, and in everything. So too *Winter Fuel*: "*Bare ruined choirs*" etc—almost no sorrow of autumn; a rawness (though I felt this

less the second time), unvelvety papery colouring, especially in raw silver and purple birchstems, crude rusty cart-wheels, aimless mess or minglemangle of cut underwood in under-your-nose foreground; aimlessly posed truthful child on shaft of cart; but then most masterly Turner-like outline of craggy hill, silver-streaked with birchtrees, which fielded in an equally masterly rust-coloured young oak, with strong curl and seizure in the dead leaves.

(journal, 23 May 1874)

Such a passage illustrates well the vigor, observation, and freshness of the best of Hopkins' journal-writing; it also shows the search for significant detail and for the unusual word in which to capture it that will play such a part in his mature poems.

Hopkins' letters fill three volumes, all edited by C. C. Abbott. There are letters to his undergraduate friends, including the famous letter to Alexander Baillie of 10 September 1864 on the "three kinds" of poetic language; much later letters to Baillie on possible early relations between Egypt and Greece; letters to his family, mainly to his mother; both sides of his correspondence with two fellow poets, Canon R. W. Dixon and Coventry Patmore; and letters to his most intimate friend, the future poet laureate, Robert Bridges. These three contemporary poets, however much they may have lacked understanding of Hopkins' own poetry—and particularly of his technical innovations—were his only regular readers in his lifetime: his "public," as he called Bridges. The letters to Dixon and Patmore are mainly interesting for the detailed comments on poetry utterly different from Hopkins' own: they show what a meticulous and sympathetic critic Hopkins was. And it is in his letters to Dixon that we find the explanation for Hopkins' seven years' poetic silence, when he became a Jesuit; the account of how "The Wreck of the Deutschland" came to be written; the clearest explanation of sprung rhythm; and his antipathy after the Jesuit *Month*'s rejection of both "The Wreck" and "The Loss of the Eurydice" toward further attempts at publication.

But it is the letters to Bridges that reveal most of Hopkins as a man and add considerably to his stature both as a poet and as a critic, perhaps almost as much as the letters of Keats, whom Hopkins so persistently admired, add to his stature. Dixon was twelve years older than Hopkins, Patmore twenty-two: in a Victorian ambience, that gap made the letters between them necessarily formal. Hopkins and Bridges were the same age, undergraduates at Oxford together, and by 1865 close friends. Despite

---

[19]They are the subject of a chapter by Norman White in *All My Eyes See: The Visual World of G. M. Hopkins*, pp. 89–106, that reproduces many of the paintings that particularly interested Hopkins.

Bridges' dislike of Roman Catholicism and his lack of sympathy with Hopkins' poetic experiments, they remained close friends to the end of Hopkins' life. For Hopkins, the friendship was vital. After he had become a Jesuit, they met only about a dozen times. Hence the reliance on letters: there are 172 (including a few cards) of Hopkins'; Bridges destroyed his own letters after his friend's death.

Hopkins' letters make wonderful reading. The best of them are vivid, candid, spontaneous, and often sharply comic. They show his capacity to laugh at himself, which we would hardly have expected from the poems. A great many of them, as we would expect, discuss in detail his own and Bridges' poems. Frequently under attack for "obscurities" and "eccentricities," Hopkins is often on the defensive: but the line-by-line explanations he consequently gave Bridges provide the best running commentary we have on his poetry (a commentary often used in earlier sections of this essay). It is to Bridges' questioning of individual effects that we owe some of Hopkins' best-known defenses of both his practice and poetic beliefs:

Why do I employ sprung rhythm at all? Because it is the nearest to the rhythm of prose, that is the native and natural rhythm of speech, the least forced, the most rhetorical and emphatic of all possible rhythms. . . .

(21 August 1877)

The above letter was written after Bridges had called the verse of "The Wreck of the Deutschland" "presumptious [sic] jugglery."

To do the Eurydice any kind of justice you must not slovenly read it with the eyes but with your ears, as if the paper were declaiming it at you. For instance the line "she had come from a cruise training seamen" read without stress and declaim is mere Lloyd's Shipping Intelligence; properly read it is quite a different thing. Stress is the life of it.

(21 May 1878)

He answered Bridges' charge of "queerness" against the first three lines of the sestet of "The Lantern out of Doors."

. . . as air, melody, is what strikes me most of all in music and design in painting, so design, pattern or what I am in the habit of calling "inscape" is what I above all aim at in poetry. Now it is the virtue of design, pattern, or inscape to

be distinctive and it is the vice of distinctiveness, to become queer. This vice I cannot have escaped.

(15 February 1879)

This leads me to say that a kind of touchstone of the highest or most living art is seriousness; not gravity but the being in earnest with your subject—reality.

(1 June 1886)

In his criticism of Bridges' own poems, so unlike his own, Hopkins is generous, meticulous, exact in both praise and dispraise. He can be sharp when he wants to be:

"Disillusion" does exist, as typhus exists and the Protestant religion. The same "brutes" say "disillusion" as say "standpoint" and "preventative" and "equally as well" and "to whomsoever shall ask."

(26 January 1881)

And his affection never blurs what he sees as blemishes in character:

You seem to want to be told over again that you have genius and are a poet and your verses beautiful. . . . You want perhaps to be told more in particular. I am not the best to tell you, being biassed by love, and yet I am too. . . . If I were not your friend I should wish to be the friend of the man who wrote your poems.

(22 October 1879)

But there is a great deal more than criticism of each other's poetry in these letters. The two friends shared many other interests: the classics, Milton, music, language, prosody, contemporary writers and painters. Hopkins writes on all of them, sharply and individually. Above all, he can write of his feelings when he most needed a confidant in his last five difficult years in Dublin.

Bridges has been much criticized: for his delay of thirty years in publishing the poems (which he scrupulously kept); for the charges of obscurity and lapses of taste he leveled at some of them in his preface, when he finally edited them in 1918; and for his often tactlessly expressed dislike of Hopkins' Roman Catholicism. Almost all modern readers and critics, with one or two noted exceptions (recorded in the bibliography), are firmly on Hopkins' side. What these letters show, besides the remarkable distinctiveness of a far-ranging mind fully engaged in whatever it touched, is how essential Bridges was to Hopkins' emotional stability; and how important poetry, the other "vocation," remained to the dedicated Jesuit priest.

A final point must be made. Hopkins could never have been accepted as a major poet by his own contemporaries: his innovations were too extreme, his aims—to the temper of his time—too independent. Only comparatively few readers were ready for him in 1918: Bridges' edition of his poems (750 copies only) took twelve years to sell. He has had no obvious followers. But from the 1930's onward his impact has been immense in many countries of the world. His technical innovations in rhythm and language have been endlessly debated and almost universally admired. The challenge he offers appeals strongly to the twentieth-century reader. In this important regard, the thirty years' delay in publication of his poems has in fact worked in Hopkins' favor.

SELECTED BIBLIOGRAPHY

I. BIBLIOGRAPHY. The Kenyon Critics, *Gerard Manley Hopkins: A Critical Symposium* (Norfolk, Conn., 1945; repr. New York, 1975), contains a bibliography; M. Charney, "A Bibliographical Study of Hopkins Criticism, 1918-1949," *Thought*, 25 (June 1950), 297-326; E. H. Cohen, *Works and Criticism of Gerard Manley Hopkins: A Comprehensive Bibliography* (Washington, D. C., 1969); G. Watson, ed., *The New Cambridge Bibliography of English Literature*, vol. III (Cambridge, 1969), entry for Hopkins by G. Storey; T. Dunne, *Gerard Manley Hopkins: A Comprehensive Bibliography* (Oxford, 1976). *Note: The Hopkins Research Bulletin* carried annual bibliographies, 1970-1976.

II. COLLECTED WORKS. R. Bridges, ed., *Poems of Gerard Manley Hopkins* (Oxford, 1918), with preface and notes; C. Williams, ed., *Poems of Gerard Manley Hopkins*, 2nd ed. (Oxford, 1930), with additional poems and a critical intro.; W. H. Gardner, ed., *Poems of Gerard Manley Hopkins*, 3rd ed. (Oxford, 1948), with notes and a biographical intro.; W. H. Gardner and N. H. MacKenzie, eds., *Poems of Gerard Manley Hopkins*, 4th ed. (Oxford, 1967; repr. 1970), with additional notes, a foreword on the revised text, and a new biographical and critical intro., the authoritative ed., incorporating all known poems and fragments.

III. LETTERS AND JOURNALS. C. C. Abbott, ed., *The Letters of Gerard Manley Hopkins to Robert Bridges* (Oxford, 1935; rev. ed., 1955); C. C. Abbott, ed., *The Correspondence of Gerard Manley Hopkins and R. W. Dixon* (Oxford, 1935; rev. ed. London, 1955); H. House, ed., *The Note-Books and Papers of Gerard Manley Hopkins* (Oxford, 1937), with notes and a preface by House, the first

publication of Hopkins' early notebooks and journal, with a selection of devotional writings and drawings; C. C. Abbott, ed., *Further Letters of Gerard Manley Hopkins* (Oxford, 1938; enl. 2nd ed., 1956), contains letters to Hopkins' family and friends, and his correspondence with Coventry Patmore; H. House, ed., *The Journals and Papers of Gerard Manley Hopkins*, 2nd ed., rev. and enl., and completed by G. Storey (Oxford, 1959), contains Hopkins' full journal, music, and a large selection of his drawings; C. Devlin, S.J., ed., *The Sermons and Devotional Writings of Gerard Manley Hopkins* (Oxford, 1959), contains all of Hopkins' known spiritual writings with Fr. Devlin's intros.

IV. SEPARATE WORKS. "Winter with the Gulf Stream," in *Once a Week*, 8 (14 February 1863), p. 210; "Barnfloor and Winepress," in *Union Review*, 3 (1865), p. 579; A. H. Miles, ed., *The Poems and the Poetry of the Century* (London, 1893), vol. VIII contains eleven poems by Hopkins (including a partial text of "A Vision of the Mermaids"), with a short intro. by R. Bridges; H. C. Beeching, sel. and arr., *Lyra Sacra* (London, 1895), contains five poems by Hopkins; R. Bridges, ed., *The Spirit of Man* (London, 1916), contains six poems by Hopkins (including partial texts of "Spring and Fall" and "The Habit of Perfection" and stanza 1 of "The Wreck of the Deutschland," as amended by Bridges).

V. SELECTED WORKS. W. H. Gardner, ed., *Poems and Prose of Gerard Manley Hopkins* (London, 1953; rev. ed., 1969); J. Pick, ed., *A Hopkins Reader* (Oxford, 1953; rev. and enl. ed., Garden City, N. Y., 1966); J. Reeves, ed., *Selected Poems of Gerard Manley Hopkins* (London, 1953; ppbk. ed., 1967); G. Storey, ed., *Hopkins: Selections* (Oxford, 1967); N. H. MacKenzie, ed., *Poems by Gerard Manley Hopkins* (London, 1974), Folio Society.

VI. BIOGRAPHICAL AND CRITICAL STUDIES. K. Brégy, "Gerard Hopkins: An Epitaph and an Appreciation," in *Catholic World*, 88 (January 1909), pp. 433-447, one of the first critical essays written from a strong Catholic viewpoint; J. Keating, "Impressions of Father Gerard Hopkins, S.J.," in the *Month*, 114 (July, August, and September 1909), pp. 59-68, 151-160, and 246-258, early biographical essays; I. A. Richards, "Gerard Hopkins," in the *Dial* (New York), 81 (September 1926), pp. 195-203, highly influential early critical essay; W. Empson, *Seven Types of Ambiguity* (London, 1930), contains two important sections on Hopkins; G. F. Lahey, S.J., *Gerard Manley Hopkins* (Oxford, 1930), the first biography; F. R. Leavis, *New Bearings in English Poetry* (London, 1932; repr. 1950), contains an important and appreciative chapter on Hopkins; E. Phare, *The Poetry of Gerard Manley Hopkins* (Cambridge, 1933); B. Kelly, *The Mind and Poetry of Gerard Manley Hopkins* (Ditchling, 1935; repr. New York, 1971); *New Verse*, 14 (April, 1935), contains essays on Hopkins by A. Bremond, C. Devlin, L. W. Griffith, G. Grigson, H. House, L. MacNeice, and C. Madge.

D. Daiches, *Poetry and the Modern World* (Chicago,

1940), contains a section on Hopkins; J. Pick, *Gerard Manley Hopkins: Priest and Poet* (Oxford, 1942; rev. ppbk. ed., 1966); W. H. Gardner, *Gerard Manley Hopkins (1844–1889): A Study of Poetic Idiosyncrasy in Relation to Poetic Tradition*, 2 vols. (London, 1944 and 1949; rev. ed., Oxford, 1966), the fullest, if discursive, critical study of Hopkins as a poet; The Kenyon Critics, *Gerard Manley Hopkins: A Critical Symposium* (Norfolk, Conn., 1945; repr. New York, 1973), contains essays by M. McLuhan, H. Whitehall, J. Miles, A. Warren, R. Lowell, and A. Mizener; M. M. Holloway, *The Prosodic Theory of Gerard Manley Hopkins* (Washington, D. C., 1947); W. A. M. Peters, S.J., *Gerard Manley Hopkins: A Critical Essay Towards the Understanding of his Poetry* (Oxford, 1948; repr. 1970), stresses the effects on Hopkins' poetry of his theories of inscape; N. Weyand, S.J., and R. V. Schoder, S.J., eds., *Immortal Diamond* (London, 1949), contains essays by twelve Jesuit critics; F. R. Leavis, *The Common Pursuit* (London, 1952), contains an influential ch. on Hopkins; D. Davie, *Purity of Diction in English Verse* (London, 1952; 2nd ed., 1967), contains "Hopkins as a Decadent Critic," including some strictures on his language; G. H. Hartman, *The Unmediated Vision* (New Haven, Conn., 1954), contains an essay on Hopkins; L. L. Martz, *The Poetry of Meditation* (New Haven, Conn., 1954; rev. ed., 1962), shows Hopkins' debt to this tradition; G. Grigson, *Gerard Manley Hopkins* (London, 1955), for the British Council, Writers and their Work, no. 59 (rev. ed., 1962), a particularly perceptive study on Hopkins as a nature-poet; A. Heuser, *The Shaping Vision of Gerard Manley Hopkins* (Oxford, 1958).

D. A. Downes, *Gerard Manley Hopkins: A Study of His Ignatian Spirit* (London, 1960), stresses the sacramental nature of Hopkins' poetry; J.-G. Ritz, *Robert Bridges and Gerard Hopkins, 1863–1889: A Literary Friendship* (Oxford, 1960); R. Boyle, S.J., *Metaphor in Hopkins* (Chapel Hill, N. C., 1961), includes a detailed analysis of "The Windhover"; Y. Winters, *The Function of Criticism* (London, 1962), repr. his well-known attack on Hopkins from the *Hudson Review* (1949); T. K. Bender, *Gerard Manley Hopkins: The Classical Background and Critical Reputation of His Work* (Baltimore, 1966); G. H. Hartman, ed., *Hopkins: A Collection of Critical Essays* (Englewood Cliffs, N. J., 1966), includes essays by M. McLuhan, J. Wain, F. R. Leavis, F. O. Matthiessen, A. Warren, W. J. Ong, and others; F. N. Lees, *Gerard Manley Hopkins* (New York, 1966); E. W. Schneider, "The Wreck of the Deutschland: A New Reading," in *PMLA* (March 1966), 110–122; D. McChesney, *A Hopkins Commentary* (London, 1968), detailed commentary on the main poems; N. H. MacKenzie, *Hopkins* (Edinburgh, 1968), Writers and Critics series, an excellent general intro.; E. W. Schneider, *The Dragon in the Gate: Studies in the Poetry of G. M. Hopkins* (Berkeley, 1968); A. Thomas, S.J., *Hopkins the Jesuit: The Years of Training* (Oxford, 1969), based on Jesuit archives, contains a previously unpublished journal kept by Hopkins while he was a Jesuit novice.

P. L. Mariani, *A Commentary on the Complete Poems of Gerard Manley Hopkins* (Ithaca, N. Y., 1970); P. M. Ball, *The Science of Aspects: The Changing Role of Fact in the Work of Coleridge, Ruskin and Hopkins* (London, 1971); A. G. Sulloway, *Gerard Manley Hopkins and the Victorian Temper* (London, 1972); H. W. Fulweiler, *Letters from the Darkling Plain: Language and the Grounds of Knowledge in the Poetry of Arnold and Hopkins* (Columbia, Missouri, 1972); R. K. R. Thornton, *Gerard Manley Hopkins: The Poems* (London, 1973), a short, helpful intro. in the Studies in English Literature series; M. Bottrall, ed., *Gerard Manley Hopkins: Poems—A Casebook* (London, 1975), contains essays by H. Read, T. S. Eliot, H. House, G. Grigson, E. Jennings, P. A. Wolfe, and others; P. Milward, S.J. (text), and R. V. Schoder, S.J. (photographs), *Landscape and Inscape: Vision and Inspiration in Hopkins's Poetry* (London, 1975); R. K. R. Thornton, ed., *All My Eyes See: The Visual World of G. M. Hopkins* (Sunderland, 1975), examines the visual aspect of Hopkins' life, illus. by his own, his brothers', and his contemporaries' work; P. Milward, S.J., and R. V. Schoder, S.J., eds., *Readings of "The Wreck": Essays in Commemoration of the Centenary of G. M. Hopkins' "The Wreck of the Deutschland"* (Chicago, 1976); B. Bergonzi, *Gerard Manley Hopkins* (London, 1977), an up-to-date, succinct biography in the Masters of World Literature series; J. Milroy, *The Language of Gerard Manley Hopkins* (London, 1977); J. Robinson, *In Extremity: A Study of Gerard Manley Hopkins* (Cambridge, 1978); N. H. MacKenzie, *A Reader's Guide to G. M. Hopkins* (London, 1981). Note: Periodicals containing valuable regular contributions about Hopkins include *The Hopkins Research Bulletin*, 1970–1976, and *The Hopkins Quarterly*, 1974–   , Guelph, Ontario. The Hopkins Society Annual Lectures, 1970–   , are distributed to its members by the Society.

ROBERT LOUIS STEVENSON

(1850-1894)

G. B. Stern

ROBERT LOUIS STEVENSON was born on 13 November 1850; he died in 1894. His stepdaughter remembers a note he wrote his wife bidding her not delay too long with his biography after his death, for "my fame will not last more than four years." By this modest and perfectly sincere estimate, we can imagine how astonished he would have been in 1935 at a set of Samoan stamps showing his grave on the crest of Mount Vaea and his house, Vailima; and another, rarer issue in 1939 commemorating the twenty-fifth anniversary of the Australian landing on the island at the outbreak of the 1914–1918 war, somewhat irrelevantly pictured with a head of Robert Louis Stevenson. Even more amazed would he have been by the centenary in 1950 that in print and on the air honored his name and proclaimed a longer life than even a hundred years for *Treasure Island* (1883), *The Strange Case of Dr. Jekyll and Mr. Hyde* (1886), and the two brief verses of "Requiem" (1887), if for no other of his writings.

It is hardly possible now to open a newspaper or a magazine without seeing "Jekyll and Hyde" quoted either as a caption or in illustration of some debatable point of modern schizophrenia. "Home is the sailor, home from the sea" is quoted nearly as often; in fact, at moments it becomes quite a struggle not to quote it. And the films have given *Treasure Island* as vivid a resurrection as any nineteenth-century writer could have desired who unconsciously employed such an excellent film technique as Stevenson; he said himself that he visualized his novels in a series of small, bright, restless pictures; "Thus with imagined wing our swift scene flies / In motion . . ." says the Chorus in Shakespeare's *Henry V.* And *The Wrecker* (1892), for instance, employing the speed, energy, and facility of the camera "on location," might certainly have been originally planned in terms of celluloid.

The Wrecker, however, is not to be listed among his books that have survived in equal popularity with *Treasure Island* and *Jekyll and Hyde.* Survival and popularity, as we are all aware, are capricious matters and play tricks that no one can ever foresee. Without doubt, his finest work was poured into the first few chapters of *Weir of Hermiston* (1896), *Kidnapped* (1886), two-thirds of *The Master of Ballantrae* (1888), a half-dozen of his short stories, about three poems, a generous handful of the letters he wrote spontaneously from all over the world to his friends and family, and one immortal letter that he sent to be published with the title *An Open Letter to the Revd. Dr. Hyde in Defence of Father Damien* (1890).

The London in which Stevenson pretended to have set the drama of *Jekyll and Hyde*, had it been called Timbuktu or Athens, would even then have been clearly recognizable as his native Edinburgh. G. K. Chesterton was probably the first to stress the significance of this, noticing how strangely Stevenson always produced his most vital work under the stimulus of banishment—strangely, because creative artists are said to draw constant nourishment from the soil where their roots are deeply planted and to wilt in exile—yet if we except *Treasure Island*, Stevenson was not dominated by an urgent need to write stories of Scotland till he left it behind him for good. And in comic proof that his nostalgia was reversible, *Treasure Island*, an aching for adventure in the fierce tropical heat of the Caribbean, was mostly written in the mists and gray cold of Braemar. Certainly when he conceived *Kidnapped* and *Jekyll and Hyde* in Bournemouth, his exile from Scotland was not yet such a histrionic affair as it would be in future years, when a sudden view from his high, snowy hut at Saranac was so poignantly to remind him of the Solway shore that straightway he began to write *The Master of Ballantrae*. It was a masterpiece even though he kept the scene at Durrisdeer—the enemy brothers fighting their duel by candlelight "in a windless stricture of frost" provides one of those unforgettable scenes of literature which have been far too often overlooked, to be classed with that other tremendous fight in *Kidnapped*, when Alan Breck and David Balfour defend themselves against a crew of fifteen in the roundhouse of the brig *Covenant:*

The sword in his hand flashed like quicksilver into the huddle of our fleeing enemies. . . . "And O, man," he cried in a kind of ecstasy, "am I no a bonny fighter?"[1]

The Master of Ballantrae can be read as a story of a dual personality less obviously confined in one body than Jekyll and Hyde. Two brothers stand for good and bad, love and hate. And in the course of time, hate wins. Henry, the gentle and the kind, is justified in hating James, incarnation of fascinating evil, if hate were ever justified. But James grows no less wicked while we have to watch Henry, a slave to his obsession, gradually drained of all good . . . till in the end, Henry and James are the same—and again Hyde has conquered Jekyll. Sir Arthur Quiller-Couch was later to develop that sinister idea in a novel called *Foe-Farrell,* which may well have been inspired by *The Master of Ballantrae;* for Quiller-Couch was one of Stevenson's ardent disciples; he it was who exclaimed for all the band of younger writers, on hearing of the death of Stevenson: "Now there's no one left to write for!" And to him was entrusted the task of finishing Stevenson's *St. Ives* (1897), the book which started with a breathtaking narrative of a French prisoner's escape from Edinburgh Castle.

"Inspiration": the act of drawing air into the lungs. So says the dictionary. Thus a vivid memory of Edinburgh, its force and impact, its authentic speech, character, and flavor, was enough of inspiration for those magnificent scenes in *Weir of Hermiston* between the stern old Justice-Clerk and his rebellious only son. It may truthfully be said of Stevenson that all his days were brave, but that in his early youth they were also days of bravado; and it had taken him more than twenty years to realize how his own father had suffered in the clash of opinions with a headstrong only son. In that one scene of *Weir,* Thomas Stevenson, engineer to the Commissioners of Northern Lights, stern Puritan and deeply loving father, was at last triumphantly understood.

And in the same book, the pure moorland air up by the Praying Weaver's Stone at Cauldstaneslap, where Archie Weir and Christina Elliot discover and confess their love, put an end to a notion that Stevenson could not write a great love scene. Indeed, his special genius may be described as this useful power of identification with each of his characters; "A Lodging for the Night,"[2] where François Villon, after assisting in a brutal tavern murder, stumbles in terrified flight through the snow-covered streets of medieval Paris, does not merit our praise for its virtuosity alone, nor for its strict economy of phrase and adjective, but because the same man who at the end of his life could plunder the soul of Adam Weir, here, fairly near the beginning of his career, could also by inspiration—identification—what you will!—enter fully into the motives, philosophy, and rationalizations of a fifteenth-century poet and scamp. And Villon's sardonic reactions to normal good treatment, displayed in argument with his courteous host, the Seigneur de Brisetout, are as exciting as the pace and action of the earlier half of the story.

One can find many similar examples of Stevenson's uncanny coalition with villainy. All the people in *The Ebb-Tide* (1894) are horrible—one does not so much read the last few chapters as feel them crawling up one's spine; and Long John Silver, James Durie of Ballantrae, or Jekyll's schizophrenic double, Hyde, might really cause readers to wonder whether he could present Brother Good without Sister Dull as an inevitable companion . . . till David Balfour, Jim Hawkins, Kirstie and her enchanting niece Christina join the procession of his living characters. In *Notes on Novelists* (1914) Henry James said of Stevenson, "he belongs to the class who have both matter and manner, whom life carries swiftly before it, and who communicate and signal as they go." He very rarely "communicated" in poetry, and when he did he wrote his verses literally like an amateur; that is to say, like an impetuous fellow in love; not, as when he wrote prose, with the severe self-discipline of a professional unremittingly engaged in a life-and-death struggle with style. Which is probably why critics are rather apt to underrate the stature, or rather the depth, of an occasional poem embodying his creed.

---

[1] *The Works of Robert Louis Stevenson,* Tusitala ed., 35 vols. (London, 1923–1924), vol. VI, p. 67. All references are to this edition unless otherwise noted.

[2] Appeared originally in *Temple Bar,* October 1877; included in *New Arabian Nights,* 2 vols. (London, 1882), vol. I.

To thrill with the joy of girded men
To go on for ever and fail and go on again,
And be mauled to the earth and arise,
And contend for the shade of a word and a thing not
    seen with the eyes:
With the half of a broken hope for a pillow at night
That somehow the right is the right
And the smooth shall bloom from the rough:
Lord, if that were enough?[3]

To browse through any of the several uniform editions of Stevenson's works must bring the conclusion that there is nothing uniform about them except their bindings. As we race through the titles, it emerges clearly, however, that to dismiss him as the author of "no more than a handful of stories for boys" is not only a fallacy, but a fallacy so preposterous that only Stevenson himself could be forgiven for such a statement, spoken once to his stepson, Lloyd Osbourne, in a mood of weariness shortly before his death. True that when he had grown to be a celebrity in a big way, a midshipman from H.M.S. *Curaçao*, hospitably made free of the library at Vailima, suddenly exclaimed, "Good Lord, I never realized! *He's* the josser who wrote *Treasure Island*." True, also, that elderly men gulped down *Treasure Island*, unashamed to have become boys for a spell; though when it was reported to the author how William Gladstone read it through in a night, he merely remarked coldly that Gladstone would have done better to have attended to the business of the Empire. For Stevenson was by nature a hero-worshiper, a passionate champion of lost causes, and he could not forgive the prime minister responsible for General Charles Gordon's death on the steps of the Residency at Khartoum.

But setting aside *Treasure Island* and *Kidnapped*, nobody in his senses would benevolently produce *The Ebb-Tide* as suitable literature for juveniles; nor, with all its promising title, *The Wrecker*; nor the tale of what happened on the Beach of Falesà; nor *The Master of Ballantrae*; nor *Weir of Hermiston*; nor *Jekyll and Hyde*; nor *Father Damien*. In short, and after a brief biographical sequence of events and dates, one could draw up a fairly adequate survey of the life and works of Robert Louis Stevenson by investigating and if necessary clearing away every fallacy that has grown up to surround and obscure the truth.

[3]From "If This Were Faith," poem no. 24 of *Songs of Travel* in *Works*, vol. XXII, p. 147.

But first the sequence.

His father, Thomas, was a son of Robert Stevenson, founder of the family of lighthouse engineers who built Skerryvore, Bell Rock, and other famous towers round the rocky coast of Scotland. His mother was Margaret, youngest daughter of the Reverend Lewis Balfour, minister at Colinton. A French strain in the Balfours became evident in the appearance of Robert Louis Stevenson and in his gaiety and resilience that conflicted with the Scottish strain of melancholy, integrity, and forthrightness inherited from the Stevenson side. He was a delicate only child, adored by his parents and "Cummy," his devoted nurse, a strongly religious woman with a dramatic vein, from whose fund of stories about the Covenanters he drew his passionate interest in that dour portion of his country's history. To her he dedicated *A Child's Garden of Verses* (1885): ". . . From the sick child now well and old"—but the sick child was rarely to be well and never old. It is strange that the Stevensons remained so long in 8 Howard Place, the gloomy, sunless house where Louis was born; much mischief had been done by the time he was three and they moved to Inverleith Terrace, and four years later to 17 Heriot Row. Thomas Stevenson had no rigid ideas about education; he was a delightful playmate, content that Louis' attendance at school should be irregular and undistinguished. Sometimes his mother took him abroad for his health and hers, and often he stayed with a throng of cousins at Colinton Manse, holidays happily commemorated in *A Child's Garden of Verses*. Several of his essays, notably "A Penny Plain and Twopence Coloured" and "The Lantern Bearers," would never have been written had he not played enthusiastically with a toy theater or joined other boy adventurers with evil-smelling lanterns strapped under their coats.

When Louis was seventeen, his father bought Swanston Cottage in the Pentland Hills near Edinburgh. Louis loved Swanston, loved his long rambles with his father or alone over the slopes of Allermuir, Caerketton, and Halkerside—his "hills of home." Thomas Stevenson took it for granted that presently he would enter the family profession, but Louis soon showed that he was temperamentally and physically unsuited for superintending the construction of harbors and lighthouses on the bleak windswept coast of Fife; so he was allowed to go to Edinburgh University on condition that he study law and leave writing to be a sideline. The young man idled, loafed, took up with the wrong companions, and caused serious anxiety at home and grimly disapproving looks from the "unco' guid" citizens of Edinburgh by his wayward, extravagant behavior; he did eventually obtain his law degree and, surprisingly, even a Silver Medal from the Royal Scottish Society of Arts for reading a paper on a new form of intermittent light.

Violent quarrels with his father on conduct and religion led to their tragic estrangement; and seriously affected by the unhappiness and misunderstandings that surrounded him, Louis fell ill. He was sent for convalescence to some cousins in Suffolk. Here, in 1873, he met Mrs. Sitwell, who, until he married, was to be the strongest influence in his life. Mrs. Sitwell made him consult a lung specialist. "Ordered South" was the verdict, and he stayed for several months in the south of France, writing and slowly recuperating. But before he went, she introduced him to Sidney Colvin, and they encouraged young Stevenson to become a professional writer. Through Colvin's good offices, he succeeded in getting his first essay, "Roads," published in *The Portfolio* (vol. 4, November 1873), using the initials that were to become his signature tune: R.L.S.

Back again from the Riviera, some of his essays were accepted by the *Cornhill* magazine; and he was taken by the editor, Leslie Stephen, to see another contributor, William Ernest Henley, who was having treatment under Dr. Joseph Lister at the Edinburgh Infirmary. A memorable friendship sprang up; and when Henley was appointed to the editorship of the *London* magazine, R.L.S. contributed the *New Arabian Nights*. This, however, did not immediately follow their first encounter; for in 1876, R.L.S. joined his cousin R. A. M. "Bob" Stevenson in a long, careless sojourn with the artists' colony at Barbizon. From a canoe trip through the canals, waterways, and rivers of northern France, he gained material for his first book, *An Inland Voyage* (1878). On his return to the Forest of Fontainebleau, he saw and fell in love with Fanny Osbourne, a beautiful married woman from Indiana, staying at the inn at Grez with her two children, Isobel and Lloyd. The next two years he spent his summers with her in France, his winters in Edinburgh, and established a growing reputation as a writer, mainly with essays on a variety of literary subjects. In 1878, Fanny Osbourne felt she had to return to her husband in California, and R.L.S. went on his lonely travels with a donkey in the Cevennes (Modestine was chosen by several children in a centenary competi-

tion for an essay on Stevenson's most bewitching character!).

A year later, hearing that Fanny, ill and unhappy, was starting divorce proceedings, Stevenson wrenched himself from his home, his parents, and his potential career, and against the strong advice of all his friends (Henley's went beyond all reason), followed her to California. He chose to travel steerage to New York and again fell dangerously ill from the further drastic experience of crossing the plains of America in the emigrant train. Twice he nearly died, first at Monterey and then in San Francisco, where he struggled through conditions of stark poverty to maintain himself by his writing without appealing for help from home. Finally, gaunt as a wolf and hardly able to stand, he married Fanny. The doctor told her he could not live more than a few months; she kept him alive and creative for fourteen years. After their honeymoon in the California mountains, where he wrote *The Silverado Squatters* (1883), a longed-for reconciliation with his parents drew him back again to Scotland, bringing his wife and his stepson, Lloyd Osbourne. Mr. and Mrs. Thomas Stevenson soon became tenderly attached to Fanny; and she and Louis alternated between summers spent with them at Pitlochry and Braemar, and winters in Davos, Switzerland. On a rainy day in the Highlands, Stevenson began writing *Treasure Island* to amuse Lloyd—and himself. He finished it at Davos in 1882, and it ran as a serial in *Young Folks,* where it was oddly unsuccessful with its juvenile readers. His lungs could not stand the climate of Scotland, and three times they had to go on those weary pilgrimages to the Swiss mountains; but in whatever state of bad health, except when he was nearly dying, he could not afford to let up on his writing. Besides finishing *Treasure Island* at Davos, he produced a first-class biography: the "Memoir" of Fleeming Jenkin (1887), tribute of gratitude to a dead friend, the university professor who had had the perception to stand by him in "the coiled perplexities of youth," during his wild odyssey through the taverns and brothels of Edinburgh.

In 1882, he and Fanny moved to the South of France. Châlet la Solitude at Hyères was their first home together and he said of it, years afterward, in a letter, "I've only been happy once, at Hyères." There he wrote *Prince Otto* (1885) and exultantly put on record that he received a hundred guineas from Cassells for the publishing rights of *Treasure Island*, which seemed to him then a very large sum.

A dangerous hemorrhage brought him to the state

of lying in a dark room, forbidden to speak, his arm strapped to his side; rendered incapable of sterner efforts as a wage earner, he scribbled a great many letters, a lot of gay nonsense, and most of *A Child's Garden of Verses*. On receiving news that Thomas Stevenson was failing, they returned and settled down at Bournemouth in a house his father bought for Fanny, which Louis chose to call Skerryvore.

During most of their three years in Bournemouth, Stevenson was confined to his detested bed, an apparently incurable invalid. *Kidnapped* brought him an unsensational meed of fame; but there was the desperate nightmare of perpetually needing money that probably evoked the actual nightmare, which was to find it. *The Strange Case of Dr Jekyll and Mr Hyde* leapt at once into amazingly big sales; it was pirated in America, where its popularity brought Stevenson his first experience, half astonished, half amused, as an idol of the public. For in 1887, after his father's death, he crossed the Atlantic on board the *Ludgate Hill*, with his mother, Fanny, Lloyd, and a merry cargo of apes and stallions.

In New York he soon had enough of adulation; his health collapsed once more, and he was banished to Saranac, the American equivalent of Davos, a small health resort high in the Adirondacks. Here was born *The Master of Ballantrae*, and, in collaboration with young Lloyd Osbourne, a gorgeous piece of buffoonery, *The Wrong Box* (1889).

After a biting winter in the snows, his American publisher, Scribners, commissioned a volume on the South Seas. Stevenson used his patrimony to charter a luxury yacht in San Francisco, and, still accompanied by his family, sailed on the *Casco* for the Marquesas, Tahiti, and the Sandwich (Hawaiian) Islands, a voyage that was a significant success from every point of view except the book itself; commissioned work never suited him, for the results were always labored, overly scrupulous, and disappointing, and he then had to cope with misgivings as to whether in honesty he should return the advances and cancel the contracts.

Once at sea, his health and activities were always miraculous to those who had hitherto only known him as an invalid on land. He struck up enduring friendships with native kings, dark warriors and princesses, traders and sailors and missionaries of all nations, and with a touching group of lepers, old men and children, whom he encountered on his visit to the island of Molokai. In 1889, he paid off the *Casco*, Mrs. Thomas Stevenson returned to Scotland, and he stayed on with Fanny and Lloyd for

nearly six months at Honolulu, where he finished *The Master of Ballantrae* and *The Wrong Box*. Then he went on a further exploration of the more uncharted archipelagos of the South Pacific, finally making harbor at Apia, on Opolu, one of the Samoan Islands (the sequence of Robert Louis Stevenson's addresses is a horror to any conscientious biographer). They were so delighted with the climate and the beauty of the place that they bought an estate halfway up Mount Vaea, where he and Fanny proposed to build a house in which to spend their winters. It fell out, however, that another serious hemorrhage at Sydney, on their way home in 1890, caused him to be forbidden on pain of death ever to revisit Europe or any temperate zone; the tropics were his only chance. So with what grace he could muster—and to accept misfortune with good grace was among his happier talents—he built Vailima; sent Lloyd back to Edinburgh and Bournemouth to collect their furniture; and joined by his mother and Fanny's daughter, Isobel Strong, with her little son Austin, settled in Samoa till his death. During this last fruitful period he wrote *Catriona* (1893), *The Wrecker*, *The Ebb-Tide*, *Records of a Family of Engineers* (1912), *St. Ives*, several poems and ballads, four striking South Sea tales to be published as *Island Nights' Entertainments* (1893), and those immortal chapters of *Weir of Hermiston* published posthumously in 1896. His stepdaughter, Belle, to whom he dictated them, relates how instinctively he found the right word, the right sentence, and the right incident, as though he had written it all before and only had to reel it off from memory.

At Vailima he lived as a sort of chieftain, visited by pilgrims and friends from all over the world. His native staff were devoted to him, and he had all the generous instincts of a Scottish clansman in his abundant hospitality toward his own kin, friends, and strangers—"distance no object." In the troubled politics and wars of Samoa, the weaker side as usual claimed his quixotic support; and he could not bear to remain a mere spectator at the defeat and banishment of the rebel King Mataafa whom he knew to be "the one man of governing capacity among the native chiefs, and whom, in the interest alike of whites and natives, he had desired to see the Powers not crush, but conciliate."

It would be literally true to say that since 1888, Stevenson's friends and readers had lost sight of him; which must mean that a man is either forgotten or becomes a legend while he is still alive. The spate and vitality of his intimate letters made it impossible that he should be forgotten, and his situation contributed to a tuppence-colored legend that he would have repudiated with real exasperation, for it was alien to his nature to assume importance. John Steinbeck relates an incident heard from an old woman who in her childhood had had an encounter with R.L.S. at Monterey. "It's not bad fun," he remarked, after the little girl had cheated him over a sale of blueberries, "it's not bad fun, to be made a fool of for ten cents!"

But the man was overstrained and overworked, and his friends' project for an Edinburgh collected edition failed to reassure him that he might now safely take a rest for a while. On 3 December 1894, he was struck down by a cerebral hemorrhage and died within two hours.

Certain men have provocative personalities: H. G. Wells once remarked a little sadly, "I don't know how it is, but whenever [a famous contemporary's] name is mentioned, there's a respectful hush, but when it's mine, there's a dog-fight!" The remark would be as true of Stevenson as of Wells; mention his name, and still, where anything is known about him at all, the result will not be indifference or calm, high hymns of praise, but a dog-fight; for his centenary revealed that far from being moribund, a casual reference to Robert Louis Stevenson will cause as much red blood to spurt as made the decks slippery on board the brig *Covenant*.

Jekyll and Hyde was his first huge selling success in England and America; he wrote it as a shilling shocker, and it became popular at once and ever after as a symbolic portrayal of the dual nature of man, with the moral inverted: not to impress us by the victory of good over evil, but to warn us of the strength and ultimate triumph of evil over good once sin is suffered to enter human habitation. Yet neither was Jekyll intended as a simple personification of good, but as good trying to keep up appearances, good wishing to maintain its prestige while it stealthily enjoys "going to the bad"; the author obviously regarded him as a contemptible Quisling who failed to put up any resistance movement against the invader. He once remarked to Andrew Lang, with admirable brevity: "I want to write about a fellow who was two fellows"; and in a letter discussing the interdependence of Jekyll and Hyde, he admitted to an old dingdong battle which perpetually preoccupies the disreputable human soul: "the only thing I feel dreadful about is that damned old business of the war in the members." It cannot be denied that he was inordinately fond of sermoniz-

ing—"I shall preach on my death-bed"—but he always found a more vivid medium in fiction, through narrative and character, than when he indulged himself with composing half-hour sermons for an imaginary pulpit.

It is well known how he originally dreamed "this fine bogey tale" and finished it in three days of furious writing, and then burned the draft and rewrote it in another three days, deferring to his wife's objection that he had left out the allegory. Long afterward, Stevenson alluded to the book, casually, as the worst thing he had ever done; he never harbored pretty illusions about his own work. Although rueful and ashamed that his own angel always seemed to put up such a poor show, he was no hypocritical weakling like Jekyll; and whatever enemy he carried within him, it utterly lacked the callous cruelty of Hyde.

"The legend goes" is a scornful phrase used with conviction by both sides in a battle; for nearly every biography will reveal a small but willful partiality, an almost invisible pendulum swing toward this pile of evidence or that: "Codlin's the friend, not Short." . . . And where the matter rests upon surmise, the subconscious has to choose between a discreet and somewhat irritating type of biographical softpedaling—"we need touch but lightly on"—or an inevitable swing over to the brutal realism of the Debunking School, which has found a peculiar satisfaction in stressing the early swashbuckling period of an author whom they considered had received more than his share of sentimental idolatry. Stevenson's fellow Scot, James M. Barrie, referred to "R.L.S., these familiar initials . . . the best beloved in recent literature"; and this has helped toward an odd notion that to think of Stevenson by his surname, not by his initials, made all the difference between a realistic approach or an attitude of whimsical tenderness—which seems to indicate that every biography of George Bernard Shaw referring to him as G.B.S. must necessarily mean that we are dandling him in our arms!

Probably Robert Louis Stevenson signed his earlier essays with his initials for the sake of convenience and brevity; he could hardly have known that after his death they would be condemned as a culpable form of petting party. On the other hand, the pro-Stevenson brigade often damage their own cause by reproducing portraits of a picturesque invalid with untidy hair lapping his shoulders and a smile of ineffable sweetness. (It must have been one of those that the little Samoan boy Pola threw on the floor when, directly after Tusitala's[4] death, he begged for his "sun-shadow." "'I will not have that!' he cried. 'It is pig-faced. It is not the shadow of our chief.' He leaned against the door and wept.") That long hair of Stevenson's has become the favorite object of ridicule for the scornful. He may have started it in a period of youthful folly, from the desire to be unconventional; and later, while he lived in a northern climate, in perpetual danger of tuberculosis, his doctors would not allow him out for fear of cold. But every portrait extant from the South Seas during the four years before his death shows the fallacy of still considering this fantastically thin man as an invalid: his hair was short, his clothes as normal as comfort and the tropical climate permitted; he spent hours every day in the saddle without fatigue, galloping over rough country; and he spent days and weeks at sea on a tramp steamer, never noticing the lack of amenities in the questionable jollity of thrashing through typhoon and hurricane.

Gardening in its herbaceous-border sense had never appealed to him at Bournemouth, but at Vailima this feeble dilettante hacked down trees and tore up masses of jungle growth before he even settled down to his morning's professional work. He laughed when threatened with expatriation by the furious German officials at Apia, but there was no laughter in his reaction to the news that Mataafa's warriors were being foully treated in prison. Everyone was afraid to interfere till Stevenson went storming down to the rescue in one of his crusading rages, bringing his men loaded with food, setting them to light the great ovens and clean out the stinking cells, attending to the victims who had been flogged through the streets, bringing the doctor to attend to them (and paying for it), and finally shaming the officials till they could no longer look the other way while these monstrous abuses were not only denounced but remedied by that troublesome writer who so maddeningly refused to mind his own business and remain writing nice books in his nice home halfway up a mountain.

For at all instances of cruelty or injustice to the oppressed, he flared up in a moment. From his childhood he had wanted to be a soldier; he loved fighting, but, he said, hated people to be angry with him—"the uncomfortable effect of fighting"—shrewdly laying his finger on the weak spot. And

should one appear to dwell overlong on Stevenson's personality at the expense of concentrating on his work—or works—it would only be a false detachment to allot him a final place in literature without an attempt to understand that what he was, and why, must include so much of what he did and how. Writers like Byron or Robert Burns, Percy Bysshe Shelley or Stevenson are handicapped through the possession of a certain exciting quality in their makeup and the involuntary drama of their death. Neither was he at all the type conveyed in that nauseating phrase, "a man with the heart of a boy"; his faults were essentially those of an adult male: a strong, hot temper with frequent use of strong, hot language; inconsiderate on a really grand scale (despite all his natural kindness) as regards the physical comfort of those around him, having himself no use for physical comfort; improvident in his generosity; wildly extravagant, and then given to moods of deep melancholy at the resulting state of his affairs.

When we encounter Henley's "assassin" review in the *Pall Mall* magazine, eight years after Stevenson's death, his lament for a lost friend whose genius had (apparently) been thwarted, hampered, enslaved, intimidated, deluded, badgered, and forced into mere wage earning by the gloomy, respectable, material-minded woman with whom he had been press-ganged into marriage, we are up against another fallacy of such controversial proportions that it would take several volumes to go into the matter thoroughly and sift delusion from fact. Fanny Stevenson's place has often been in the doghouse; but Colvin left behind, for the guidance of "all future biographers of R.L.S.," a round authoritative statement beginning:

With reference to the causes of estrangement and in the actual quarrel, between Stevenson's widow and sometime old friend William Ernest Henley, it ought to be publicly known that the wife had ample and just cause for regarding the friendship as one that entailed risks to Louis's health and should be discouraged accordingly.

As we are most concerned with the indictment that his wife ruined his writing for the sake of material gain, let us point out that Stevenson certainly did write many promising essays before he married, and also *Travels with a Donkey* (1879), *An Inland Voyage*, *New Arabian Nights* (1882), *The Amateur Emigrant* (1895), and *Across the Plains* (1892). But

---

[4]Tusitala was the Samoan name for Stevenson.

after he married Fanny Osbourne, besides the best of his short stories, he wrote *Treasure Island, Kidnapped, Catriona, Jekyll and Hyde, The Master of Ballantrae, Father Damien, The Ebb-Tide,* and *Weir of Hermiston*—titles that speak for themselves. As for deploring her continual wary eye on the main chance, letters extant show that it was Colvin, not Fanny, who tried to hold him back from publishing *The Ebb-Tide*, a grim, squalid, powerful tale which might easily have spoiled his sales as a purveyor of juvenile fiction. And when Stevenson flamed out into his *Open Letter in Defence of Father Damien* and read it to his family, gravely warning them that its publication might result in a libel action and the loss of all they had, she was the first to cry in a white heat of enthusiasm, "Print it! Publish it!" In the dedication to *Weir of Hermiston*, he set down what may surely be taken for fair corroboration of his wife's influence.

> Take thou the writing; thine it is. For who
> Burnished the sword, blew on the drowsy coal,
> Held still the target higher . . . who but thou?
> (*Works*, vol. XVI, p. xxi)

Another absurd fallacy has been that he hated his father, whom, nevertheless, he speaks of in a letter as "ever my dearest"; and in an essay of wonderful tenderness and perception, from *Memories and Portraits* (1887), he pays him a tribute of which any father might be proud. For undoubtedly R.L.S. honors the sound achievement of the "Lighthouse Stevensons" far beyond his own as an author.

> Say not of me that weakly I declined
> The labours of my sires and fled the sea,
> The towers we founded and the lamps we lit,
> To play at home with paper like a child.[5]

His summing-up of Lord Justice Weir—"steadfastly mounting the great bare staircase of his duty, uncheered and undepressed"—betrays again that no man could hope to win Stevenson by flamboyant exploits; he may have created Alan Breck for our delight, but we cannot suppose he thought him a character to emulate. Furthermore, in a letter to Henry James, he underlines his steady preference: "The world must return some day to the word 'duty,'

[5]Poem no. 38 from *Underwoods*, book I, in *Works*, vol. XXII, p. 95.

and be done with the word 'reward.' There are no rewards, and plenty duties."

And that he was never, in the responsible sense of the phrase, the breadwinner and head of his own household is a fallacy so damaging to his good repute that it should still be examined, contradicted, and once and for all thrown away. A hundred quotations from published letters, as well as from those not intended for publication, endorse his despair when illness tore gaps in his financial independence and corroborate his passionate desire, at whatever expense of sweat and toil, to stand on his own feet and support a family without having to appeal for money to a wealthy father. Curious that the swashbuckling author of *Treasure Island* should have been in essence "a family man"; he liked having his family always around him—his mother, his wife, his two stepchildren, Lloyd and Belle, and Belle's little son Austin; liked to gather them under his roof-tree, declaring that they alone made exile bearable. His native staff looked up to Tusitala with more reverence as a father and a wise man than as a teller of tales; and as a father, he took trouble to make them see the ethics of why certain things may not be done: when any of them was caught out in wrongdoing, he held a formal court of justice to make sure of the full truth before inventing a mild punishment to fit the crime. The collection of prayers he wrote, so often derided as merely fit for the nursery, were indeed deliberately written for the nursery; that is, for the clear understanding of those native converts to Christianity. This aspect of the white man's burden, combined with running a large estate, local politics, entertaining recklessly, and writing for a living, make it the more remarkable that he should have remained all his life so passionately preoccupied with the campaign for upholding literary style.

There are those who often contemptuously dismiss Stevenson as "a mere stylist"; as though a talent that was in the highest degree competent and fastidious counted for no more than a prinking among words, stepping daintily along an imitation pergola, a sort of picot edging to the silk. When he was young he scribbled that fatal phrase, "I have played the sedulous ape"; Sir Max Beerbohm, with his nonchalant gift for hitting the nail on the head, supposed that this must be "permanently kept in type in the journalistic offices . . . so frequently is it quoted against him." Yet a neophyte who was later to develop into a magnificent stylist could ill afford *not* to play the sedulous ape; it meant no more than that he did not tumble into style as a child tumbles into water, but studied it more consciously and conscientiously than young writers usually do, by examining the technique of his great masters in craftsmanship. Speaking of himself as "a working man," he assumed a title which he thoroughly deserved; he treated words courteously, not mangling them, though he confessed that his chief temptation was always "to cut the flesh off the bones." An old lady, Miss Adelaide Boodle, to whom he gave lessons in style when she was a girl and who was persona grata at their house in Bournemouth, wrote a delightful book about the Stevensons, where the very voice of R.L.S. can be heard teaching her how to write and breaking her heart twenty times on every page: *"Never let a long sentence get out of hand,"* he said to her. Did he ever think to say it to his friend Henry James?

The friendship between Stevenson and Henry James, those unlikely bedfellows in literature, is brilliantly discussed in *A Record of Friendship and Criticism,* published in 1948 by Janet Adam Smith. Both these writers cared intensely about style, and believed in the future of literature as warriors go on believing in a cause that might sometimes look as though it were already lost. Stevenson's amusing piece of doggerel, "The Pirate and the Apothecary," might well stand for their prototypes; for it would be difficult to find a greater contrast than the pirate in his characteristic mood of courage and laughing despair, and the apothecary, meticulously weighing out his scruples and his sentences, tasting, measuring, conscientiously concerned as to their exact effect. This volume should rate high among the first half-dozen of a vast Stevenson bibliography, revealing how in their too rare conversation pieces as well as in their voluminous correspondence both men recognized that a work of imagination must live by its own laws and only take so much from life as serves its purpose. Apothecaries do not, however, always dose themselves, and James's own style is a fairly potent reason why one would be more likely to choose G. K. Chesterton's estimate of Stevenson as a stylist.

The real defect of Stevenson as a writer, so far from being a sort of silken trifling and superficial or superfluous embroidery, was that he simplified so much that he lost some of the complexity of real life. He treated everything with an economy of detail and a suppression of irrelevance which had at last something about it stark and unnatural. He is to be commended among authors for sticking to the point; but real people do not stick quite so stubbornly to

the point as that. . . . Though he may seem to describe his subject in detail, he describes it to be done with it; and he does not return to the subject. He never says anything needlessly; above all, he never says anything twice.[6]

Nevertheless, and after all this, it must be admitted that, for some perplexing reason, Stevenson is not always *readable;* he demands an effort—no, fairer to say an initial effort; humor is not lacking, nor irony, nor the element of surprise, nor a plentitude of swift, exciting action; and the characters are sometimes disconcertingly alive—look at Alan Breck. The fault may be in our laziness to take trouble over an author already removed from contemporary interest, but not yet dead so long that we can surrender our reluctance to be rushed back from the present into the past.

But these strictures do not apply to his letters, which are undated in both senses of the word and wholly delightful, excepting only a batch published separately as *Vailima Letters* (1895), containing densely packed descriptions of his existence in Samoa, the scenery, climate, manners, customs, politics, flora, and fauna of the place. Not having time to waste in writing of these twice over, he suggested to Sidney Colvin that they should be kept and docketed for publication after his death and thus help provide for his family. But the hundreds of his other letters were intimate and spontaneous, not deliberately produced; they have been miscalled the letters of an egoist—again a fallacy; certainly they show a healthy—we underline the word—a *healthy* interest in himself and his mental processes, in his changes of heart as well as his actual doings, but nothing to compare with their vital interest in his friends, displayed in a fury of questions as to their affairs and their work; delight in their successes, compassion for their personal news, indignation over wrongs done to them, eagerness to help at any cost to himself. Surely here is no record of egoism? And surely no egoist had friends as he had friends?

Friendship is a keepsake word, but it must form an essential feature of a writer's biography if we are to understand the different influences at different times of his life. Thus without his friend Henley, Stevenson might never have wasted his small reserve of nervous energy on writing plays, very bad, very rumbustious plays. Or he might have written better

[6]G. K. Chesterton, *Robert Louis Stevenson* (London, 1927; repr. New York, 1955), pp. 127–128, 131.

plays, for he was fundamentally a dramatist; all the most famous scenes of his novels and tales could be acted with hardly any change. Henley has contributed generously and far more than a small share toward Stevenson's growth as a writer, but little to the Stevenson biography except that one mysterious ill-judged attack in the *Pall Mall* and one heart-broken poem: "When we that were dear are all too near / With the thick of the world between us. . . ." His nostalgic longing that one day they may "lie in the peace of the Great Release as once in the grass together" quickens our glimpses of two young men idly sprawling on a slope of the Pentlands, talking and talking of the wonderful things they were to achieve. Yet still one cannot write a biography of either without feeling that their war is not over. Final and visible causes for quarrel are always a little obscure; they begin many years before their protagonists are aware of them, and if we say heaven only knows when and where they end, it is in the hope that heaven at least does know. Kinder, meanwhile, to remember how Henley, after reading the posthumous fragment of *Weir of Hermiston*, wrote to Colvin a triumphant "I have found my Lewis [*sic*] again and in all his glory."

On the whole, even in his profligate youth, Stevenson chose friends to match his strength, not his weakness; they make quite an impressive roll call headed by Colvin, Fleeming Jenkin, Henley, Will Low (the American artist), and Charles Baxter (writer to the signet).[7] Henry James and Edmund Gosse came later. The last published letter of Stevenson's—it may be the last he ever penned—was written to Gosse in deep affection and sadness.

It is all very well to talk of renunciation, and of course it has to be done. But, for my part, give me a roaring toothache. . . . I have very little use for either watching or meditation. I was not born for age.

(*Works*, vol. XXXV, pp. 183, 184)

Henry James included in *Notes on Novelists* a highly perceptive review of Stevenson's letters:

He had incurred great charges, he sailed a ship loaded to the brim, so that the strain under which he sailed and wrought was immense; but the very grimness of it all is sunny, slangy, funny, familiar; there is as little of the florid in

his flashes of melancholy as of the really grey under the stress of his wisdom. . . . He has . . . a soundness all liberal and easy and born of the manly experience, that it is a luxury to touch.

(p. 17)

A solemn young Scots writer called J. M. Barrie once hauled him over the coals for his want of proper seriousness, in a somewhat impertinent essay published in *An Edinburgh Eleven:*

Mr. Stevenson has reached the critical point in his career, and one would like to see him back at Bournemouth, writing within high walls. We want that big book; we think he is capable of it, and so we cannot afford to let him drift into the seaweed.

(p. 103)

Three years afterward, Stevenson wrote to him from Samoa in a spirit to serve as example to all famous writers of how to take with humorous good nature the attacks of their lofty-minded juniors:

. . . I have been off my work for some time, and re-read the *Edinburgh Eleven*, and had a great mind to write a parody and give you all your sauce back again, and see how you would like it yourself.

(*Works*, vol. XXXIV, p. 273)

Another letter warmly praises Barrie's *A Window in Thrums* ("There are two of us now who the Shirra might have patted on the head!"—the Shirra was, of course, Sir Walter Scott, their hero) and ensured that Barrie, being human, became Stevenson's adoring, uncritical "pen friend"; and we hear no more in his former lofty vein.

Andrew Lang, who frankly preferred the books to the man, wrote an introduction to the Swanston edition, which should be read by the discriminate for its unbiased discrimination:

Many circumstances caused Stevenson, when at his best, to be a historical novelist, and he is, since Scott and Thackeray, the best historical novelist whom we have.

Add to all this his notable eminence in tales of shorter scope; in essays, whether on life or literature, so various and original, so graceful and strong; add the fantasies of his fables, and remember that almost all he did is good. . . . With his faith, whatever its tenets may have been, was implicated his uneasily active conscience; his sense of duty. This appears to have directed his life; and was practically

---

[7]A lawyer who conducts cases before the court of sessions.

the same thing as his sense of honour. Honour, I conceive, is, in a phrase of Aristotle's, duty "with a bloom on it."[8]

Sidney Colvin handed over his literary executor's privilege of writing the official *Life of Stevenson* (1901) to Graham Balfour, a cousin on the distaff side, who had stayed a year with Stevenson at Vailima. He did, however, himself edit the *Letters* with notes and introduction. J. A. Steuart's *Life of Stevenson* (1924), without overstressing those "revelations" so dear to the Debunking School, has certainly freed itself from the affectionate partisan spirit of kinsman or personal friend. Rosaline Masson, too, has written a *Life* (1923) which is almost free from it; the Masson family knew him personally, for her father was a distinguished professor at Edinburgh University at the same time as young Stevenson was cutting lectures and painting the town red. She wrote with authority and knowledge of her subject, rather than with intimacy; possibly she had not been allowed much intercourse with such a ne'er-do-well. She also edited a volume to which she gave the somewhat too sentimental title *I Can Remember Robert Louis Stevenson* (1922), containing nevertheless a variety of interesting matter that otherwise would have slipped through the grating and been swirled away; such as his comment, too wise not to be sad, to a servant eager to escape blame: "Hush. . . . You know when one tries to justify oneself, one puts someone else in the wrong—and life is not possible under those conditions."

For any student lost and bewildered by the multitude of Stevensoniana, a collection actually called *Stevensoniana* (1903), by Sir John Hammerton, a notable beachcomber in the quest of contemporary material, ought not to be missed. But the "sideline" biographies, with something of innocence—or shall we say naiveté—in their treatment, unprofessional and uncritical, with no literary "approach," not out to "refute" anything, nor swayed by post-mortem "research," are often the most revealing provided they are written with integrity, free from the sweetness of marshmallow. In our selection, therefore, of the Hundred Best Books on Stevenson, we should include *A Chronicle of Friendships* (1908), by Will Low, delightfully covering the Barbizon and Grez

period; and Lloyd Osbourne's prefaces to the Tusitala edition; *This Life I've Loved* (1937), by Isobel Field; *The Life of Mrs. Robert Louis Stevenson* (1920), by Nellie Sanchez (Fanny's sister); *R.L.S. and His Sine Qua Non*, by Adelaide Boodle (especially recommended); and *Memories of Vailima* (1902), by both his stepchildren.

The most distinguished contributions to Stevensoniana produced by the centenary year were a localized study by Moray MacLaren on *Stevenson and Edinburgh* (1950); a preface by John Hampden to *The Stevenson Companion*, felicitous title to a summing-up that is often shrewd and always courteous to the best companion in the world; and preeminently the *Collected Poems* (1950), edited by Janet Adam Smith, with an introduction and notes.

But the best assessment of Stevenson remains G. K. Chesterton's biography, written in 1927. Chesterton's appreciation of Stevenson every now and then might be comically inverted and read as Stevenson's appreciation of Chesterton, for they are extraordinarily similar in their outlook and aims: ". . . why should he be treated as a liar," Chesterton asks, "because he was not ashamed to be a story-teller?"

He had often said he wanted to be buried on top of Mount Vaea, but no way existed through the impenetrable tangle of scrub and undergrowth; so on the night of his death, Lloyd Osbourne summoned the chieftains and told them Tusitala was dead, and what he had wished. With the first light of dawn, the stronger men set themselves to hew a track up the steep slope. By noon it was ready, and a long procession of mourners set out to climb the mountain road in the blazing heat, following the coffin carried shoulder-high on the spears of Samoan warriors.

The other road was opened only a couple of months before his death: until then, there had been no more than a path up to Vailima, branching off the main road which crossed the island. But when Mataafa's men were released from prison, they chose to remain behind, instead of returning straight to their homes and families, and replace the path by a connecting road sixty feet wide, themselves paying for all the necessary materials and maintenance while they built it. Then they set up a board with an inscription:

Considering the great love of Tusitala in his loving care of us in our distress in the prison, we have therefore prepared a splendid gift. It shall never be muddy, it shall endure for ever, this road that we have dug.

---

[8] *The Works of Robert Louis Stevenson*, Swanston ed., 25 vols. (London, 1911–1912), with an introduction by Andrew Lang, vol. I., pp. lii, liii–liv.

Two roads. Two letters. Ori, sub-chief of the island of Tautira, had grown to love "Rui" like a brother, and after Stevenson's departure in the *Casco*, he wrote:

I make you to know my great affection . . . you looked from that ship, and I looked at you on the ship with great grief until you had raised the anchor and hoisted the sails. When the ship started, I ran along the beach to see you still. . . . I did not sleep that night, thinking continually of you, my very dear friend, until the morning. . . . Afterwards I looked into your rooms; they did not please me as they used to do. . . . I will not forget you in my memory. Here is the thought: I desire to meet you again. . . . It must be that your body and my body shall eat together at our table; there is what would make my heart content.

The second letter, a torn-off scrap written to Fanny in December 1894, needs no explanation:

Dear Madam: Many thousands mourn the death of Robert Louis Stevenson, but none more than the blind leper of Molokai.

The final item for this random collection appeared in the *Reader's Digest*. The author was telling of his unregenerate boyhood in Chillicothe, Missouri. The little town had no public library, so the boy and his gang read nothing but forbidden dime novels, shockers from the book-and-stationery shop.

One day when I went into the shop to select a new Nick Carter, Mr. McIllwrath spoke to me in a lowered voice. "You like to read exciting stories, don't you?" he said, and his eyes narrowed behind their smeared spectacles.

"Why, yes, sir," I said.

"All right, I'm going to tell you something I wouldn't tell just anybody. Back in the store here, I've got the most exciting dime novel you ever read." He led me to the rear of the store. "This book will cost you five times as much as a Buffalo Bill, but there's five times as much reading in it and it's about five times as exciting. Pirates, murder, hidden treasure—everything."

He took from a shelf a cheap red, clothbound book and slapped it affectionately. I read the title—*Treasure Island.*[9]

The rest is quickly told; the whole of the gang came under the spell of Long John Silver and Jim Hawkins; they were converted; they learned to read. But they kept *Treasure Island* hidden from the

[9]Clyde Brion Davis, *The Age of Indiscretion*, condensed in the *Reader's Digest*, vol. 57, August 1950, pp. 162–164.

adults, quaintly assuming that any exciting story would be considered bad.

". . . don't let your mother or sisters catch you with it. They might look inside and then there'd be a big stink and Mr. McIllwrath would get in trouble."

. . . It was with astonishment that I learned some years later that *Treasure Island* actually was a respectable book which could be read openly, and that some even regarded it as a classic.

Mr. McIllwrath later sold us *Kidnapped*. . . . I suspect the sour-faced old man was deliberately trying to develop a taste for literature in us.

(pp. 163–164)

There must be hundreds of Old Chillicothians and their like who could contribute similar experiences. Perhaps, after all, Stevenson sometimes wrote books for boys.

If any of these gestures were merely bogus, acts of nothingness that viewed from here and now would seem as impotent as a radio playing in an empty room, then one would have no reply to those of Stevenson's critics who maintain that he was little more than a pseudoromantic. But on the contrary, they are in a true romantic tradition we have met before, of unselfconscious service to the human race (memory may set up the names of Chinese Gordon and Lawrence of Arabia), a tradition that appears to be founded on solid sense. Providing the right nourishment for a boy's mind makes sense; and to inspire a road to materialize where no road was before. And Stevenson's address to the chiefs on the opening of the Road of Gratitude in 1894, can surely be read and reread for its contemporary message that begins with an echo from Ecclesiastes.

For there is a time to fight and a time to dig. You Samoans may fight, you may conquer twenty times, and thirty times, and all will be in vain. There is but one way to defend Samoa. Hear it before it is too late. It is to make roads, and gardens, and care for your trees, and sell their produce wisely, and, in one word, to occupy and use your country. If you do not, others will.

. . . because all things in a country hang together like the links of the anchor cable, one by another: but the anchor itself is industry.

(*Works*, vol. XXXV, pp. 191, 193)

Probably in another hundred years, if the conduct of the world has not changed beyond recognition, it may still be as relevant.

ROBERT LOUIS STEVENSON

SELECTED BIBLIOGRAPHY

I. Bibliography. W. F. Prideaux, *A Bibliography of the Works of Robert Louis Stevenson* (London, 1903), a new ed., rev., ed., and supplemented by Mrs. L. S. Livingstone (London, 1917), is a standard work—only the specialist in Stevensonian bibliography will need to consult, in addition, the important catalogs of the Widener and Beinecke collections (see below); *A Catalogue of the Books and Manuscripts of Robert Louis Stevenson in the Library of the Late H. E. Widener* (Philadelphia, 1913), with a memoir by A. S. W. Rosenbach; G. L. McKay, ed., *A Stevenson Library* (New Haven, Conn., 1951–1964), catalog of a collection of writings by and about Stevenson, formed by E. J. Beinecke, 6 vols., vols. I and II: printed books, pamphlets, broadsides, etc.; vol III: autograph letters by Stevenson and his wife; vol. IV: letters to and about R.L.S.; vol. V: MSS by R.L.S. and others; vol. VI: addenda and corrigenda, the catalog describes in detail the comprehensive collection of Stevenson's writings and Stevensoniana presented to Yale University on and since its 250th anniversary, indispensable for the specialist.

II. Collected Editions. S. Colvin, ed., *Works*, 28 vols. (London, 1894–1898), the first collected ed., known as the Edinburgh ed.; S. Colvin, ed., *A Stevenson Medley* (London, 1899); *Novels and Tales*, 26 vols. (New York, 1902), the Thistle ed., issued to subscribers only; *Essays and Criticisms* (Boston, 1903); *Tales and Fantasies* (London, 1905); *Essays of Travel* (London, 1905); *Essays in the Art of Writing* (London, 1905); *Works*, 20 vols. (London, 1906–1907), with bibliographical notes by E. Gosse, the Pentland ed., Gosse's biographical and bibliographical notes were issued separately in a 1908 privately printed ed.; *Works*, 25 vols. (London, 1911–1912), the Swanston ed., with an intro. by A. Lang; *Poems and Ballads* (New York, 1913), complete ed.; *Complete Poems* (New York, 1923), includes reprs. of the three collections of poems privately printed for members of the Bibliophile Society, Boston (2 vols., 1916; 1 vol., 1923), for an account of the fate of Stevenson's poetical MSS after his death see introduction to *Collected Poems* (London, 1950); F. van de Grift Stevenson and Lloyd Osbourne, eds., *Works*, 26 vols. (New York, 1921–1923; London, 1922–1923), the Vailima ed., with prefatory notes by F. van de Grift Stevenson, and portraits, limited ed. of 2,000 copies; *Works*, 35 vols. (London, 1923–1924), the Tusitala ed., the best and most complete ed., fully annotated; *Works*, 30 vols. (London, 1924–1926), the Skerryvore ed.; *Works*, 21 vols. (London, 1926–1927), the Lothian ed.; J. Adam Smith, ed., *Complete Poems* (London, 1950), with intro. and notes, the definitive ed., valuable notes; J. Hampden, ed., *The Stevenson Companion* (London, 1950), with an intro., contains *Weir of Hermiston* and a large selection of Stevenson's work; G. B. Stern, ed., *R.L.S., An Omnibus* (London, 1950); G. B. Stern, ed., *Selected Poems* (London, 1950); G. B. Stern, ed., *Tales and Essays* (London, 1950).

III. Separate Works. *The Pentland Rising: A Page of History, 1666* (Edinburgh, 1866), essay; *A New Form of Intermittent Light for Lighthouses* (Edinburgh, 1871), essay, first printed in the Transactions of the Royal Scottish Society of Arts, vol. VIII (1871); *On the Thermal Influence of Forests* (Edinburgh, 1873), essay, first printed in Proceedings of the Royal Society of Edinburgh, vol. VIII (1873); *An Appeal to the Clergy of the Church of Scotland* (London, 1875), essay; *An Inland Voyage* (London, 1878), travel; *Edinburgh: Picturesque Notes* (London, 1879), essays; *Travels with a Donkey in the Cevennes* (London, 1879), travel.

Virginibus Puerisque and Other Papers (London, 1881), twelve essays repr., with one exception, from magazines; *Familiar Studies of Men and Books* (London, 1882), nine essays repr. from magazines; *New Arabian Nights*, 2 vols. (London, 1882), fiction, vol. I: "The Suicide Club," "The Rajah's Diamond"; vol. II: "The Pavilion on the Links," "A Lodging for the Night," "The Sire de Maletroit's Door," "Providence and the Guitar"; all these stories had previously appeared in magazines; *The Silverado Squatters: Sketches from a Californian Mountain* (London, 1883), travel, originally published in *Century* magazine (November–December 1883); *Treasure Island* (London, 1883), fiction, originally published as by "Captain George North" in *Young Folks* (1882), also in Scribner Illustrated Classics series (New York, 1911; reiss. 1981); *Prince Otto: A Romance* (London, 1885), fiction, originally published in *Longman's* magazine (April–October 1885); *A Child's Garden of Verses* (London, 1885), more than half of the text had previously appeared in a trial ed. with the title *Penny Whistles; More New Arabian Nights: The Dynamiter* [in collaboration with F. van de Grift Stevenson] (London, 1885), fiction, Stevenson's wife was the sole author of "The Destroying Angel" and "The Fair Cuban."

The Strange Case of Dr. Jekyll and Mr. Hyde (London, 1886), fiction; *Kidnapped: Being Memoirs of the Adventures of David Balfour in the year 1751 &c.* (London, 1886), fiction, originally published in *Young Folks*, May–July 1886; *The Merry Men, and Other Tales and Fables* (London, 1887), fiction, includes "The Merry Men," "Will O' the Mill," "Markheim," "Thrawn Janet," "Olalla," "The Treasure of Franchard," all these stories had previously appeared in magazines; *Thomas Stevenson, Civil Engineer* (London, 1887), essay, privately printed, also in the *Contemporary Review* (June 1887); S. Colvin, ed., *Papers Literary and Scientific by the Late Fleeming Jenkin*, 2 vols. (London, 1887), contains Stevenson's "Memoir," published separately in New York (1887); *Memories and Portraits* (London, 1887), sixteen essays, mostly repr. from magazines, and including "Thomas Stevenson, Civil Engineer" and the "Memoir" from *The Papers of H. Fleeming Jenkin; Underwoods* (London, 1887), contains poems in English and Scots; *Ticonderoga: A Poem* (Edinburgh, 1887), privately printed, originally published in *Scribner's* magazine (December 1887), repr. in *Ballads* (London,

1890); *The Misadventures of John Nicholson: A Christmas Story* (New York, 1887), fiction, piratically repr. from *Cassell's Christmas Annual* (1887); *The Black Arrow: A Tale of the Two Roses* (London, 1888), fiction, originally published as by "Captain George North" in *Young Folks* (1883); *The Master of Ballantrae: A Winter's Tale* (London, 1889), fiction, originally published in *Scribner's* magazine (November 1888–October 1889); *The Wrong Box* [in collaboration with Lloyd Osbourne] (London, 1889), fiction.

Father Damien: An Open Letter to the Revd. Dr. Hyde of Honolulu (London, 1890), essay, originally published in the *Scots Observer* (May 1890) and privately printed in the same year in Sydney and Edinburgh; *Ballads* (London, 1890), verse, includes "The Song of Rahero," "The Feast of Famine," "Ticonderoga," "Heather Ale," "Christmas at Sea"; *Across the Plains, with Other Memories and Essays* (London, 1892), twelve essays repr. from magazines; *The Wrecker* [in collaboration with Lloyd Osbourne] (London, 1892), fiction, originally published in *Scribner's* magazine (August 1891–July 1892); *A Footnote to History: Eight Years of Trouble in Samoa* (London, 1892), essay; *War in Samoa* (London, 1893), privately printed essay, originally published in the *Pall Mall Gazette* (September 1893); *Island Nights' Entertainments* (London, 1893), fiction, includes "The Beach of Falesá," "The Bottle Imp," "The Isle of Voices," preceded by publication in periodicals from 1891 to 1892, and by a privately printed ed.; *Catriona: A sequel to Kidnapped, being the Memoirs of the Further Adventures of David Balfour at Home and Abroad, &c.* (London, 1893), fiction, originally published as "David Balfour" in *Atlanta* (1892); *The Ebb-Tide: A Trio and Quartette* [in collaboration with Lloyd Osbourne] (London, 1894), fiction, originally published in *To-Day* (November 1893–January 1894); *The Body Snatcher* (New York, 1895), fiction, originally published in *Pall Mall* (Christmas 1894); *The Amateur Emigrant: From the Clyde to Sandy Hook* (Chicago, 1895), travel, originally published in vol. III of the Edinburgh ed. of Stevenson's works.

Four Plays [in collaboration with W. E. Henley] (London, 1896), drama, contains *Deacon Brodie, Beau Austin, Admiral Guinea, Robert Macaire*, each play was originally issued separately in a small privately printed ed. in 1880, 1884, 1884, 1885, respectively, the first three were published together as *Three Plays* (London, 1892); *The Strange Case of Dr. Jekyll and Mr. Hyde, with Other Fables* (London, 1896), the *Fables* were originally published in *Longman's* magazine (August–September 1895) and first published separately (New York, 1895); *Weir of Hermiston: An Unfinished Romance* (London, 1896), fiction, originally published in *Cosmopolis* (January–April 1896); *A Mountain Town in France: A Fragment* (London–New York, 1896), essay; S. Colvin, ed., *Songs of Travel and Other Verses* (London, 1896), originally published in vol. XIV of the Edinburgh ed. of Stevenson's works; *St. Ives: Being the Adventures of a French Prisoner in England*

[completed by A. T. Quiller-Couch] (New York, 1897; London, 1898), fiction, the first thirty chapters, by Stevenson, were originally published in the *Pall Mall* magazine.

Prayers Written at Vailima (New York, 1904; London, 1905), with an intro. by Mrs. Stevenson, originally published in vol. XXI of the Edinburgh ed. of Stevenson's works; *Lay Morals and Other Papers* (London, 1911), ten essays originally published in magazines; *Memoirs of Himself* (Philadelphia, 1912), biography, privately printed from the original MS in the possession of H. E. Widener; *Records of a Family of Engineers* (London, 1912), essays; *The Hanging Judge: A Drama in Three Acts and Six Tableaux* [in collaboration with F. van de Grift Stevenson] (London, 1914), drama, privately printed, with an intro. by E. Gosse; *The Waif Woman* (London, 1916), fiction, originally published in *Scribner's* magazine (December 1914); *On the Choice of a Profession* (London, 1916), essay, originally published in *Scribner's* magazine (January 1915); *New Poems and Variant Readings* (London, 1918), unedited repr. of the two carelessly compiled vols. issued in 1916 to members of the Bibliophile Society, Boston; for a severe but justified stricture on this compilation and its sequel, see introduction to *Collected Poems* (London, 1950); J. C. Bay, ed., *The Manuscripts of Robert Louis Stevenson's Records of a Family of Engineers: The Unfinished Chapters* (Chicago, 1930), with an intro. *Note:* The above list does not include many of the authorized privately printed eds. in which some of Stevenson's stories, essays, and poems first appeared, among them the pamphlets printed on a hand press at Davos, 1881–1882, by Lloyd Osbourne, then a schoolboy; or a number of "manufactured rarities" for the collectors' market, consisting of small, privately printed eds. of occasional pieces of verse and prose from private collections in the United States.

IV. LETTERS. *Vailima Letters: Being Correspondence Addressed by Robert Louis Stevenson to Sidney Colvin, November 1890–October 1894* (London, 1895); *In the South Seas* (New York, 1896; London, 1900), an account of experiences and observations in the Marquesas, Paumotus, and Gilbert Islands in the course of two cruises, on the yacht *Casco*, 1888, and the schooner *Equator*, 1889, originally published in the *New York Sun* (1891) and privately printed in part in *The South Seas* (London, 1890); S. Colvin, ed., *Letters to His Family and Friends*, 2 vols. (London, 1899), with an intro. and notes, a new ed. (London, 1911), rearranged in 4 vols., has 150 new letters; L. Osbourne, ed., *Some Letters* (London, 1914); *Autograph Letters, Original Mss., Books, Portraits and Curios from the Library of the Late R. L. Stevenson*, 3 vols. (New York, 1914–1916), catalog of the sale of the Anderson Galleries, by Isobel Strong, of her stepfather's literary property; one of the consequences of this sale was the unauthorized and ill-considered production of the "manufactured rarities" referred to in the *Note* above; J. A. Smith, ed., *Henry James and Robert Louis Stevenson: A Record of Friendship and Criticism* (London, 1948), with an intro.; D. Ferguson and M. Waingrow, eds., *RLS: Stevenson's Letters to Charles Baxter* (New Haven, Conn., 1956).

V. Biographical and Critical Studies. W. Raleigh, *Robert Louis Stevenson* (London, 1895), lecture given at the Royal Institution, 1895, with additions; M. Fraser, *In Stevenson's Samoa* (London, 1895); M. Armour, *The Home and Early Haunts of Robert Louis Stevenson* (Edinburgh, 1895); J. Geddie, *The Home Country of R. L. Stevenson* (Edinburgh, 1898); E. B. Simpson, *Robert Louis Stevenson's Edinburgh Days* (London, 1898); M. M. Black, *Robert Louis Stevenson* (Edinburgh, 1898), *Famous Scots* series; L. C. Cornford, *Robert Louis Stevenson* (Edinburgh, 1899), Modern English Writers series.

H. B. Baildon, *Robert Louis Stevenson: A Life Study in Criticism* (London, 1901); Sir G. Balfour, *The Life of Robert Louis Stevenson*, 2 vols. (London, 1901); I. Strong and L. Osbourne, *Memories of Vailima* (New York, 1902; London, 1903), by Stevenson's stepchildren; W. R. Nicoll and G. K. Chesterton, *Robert Louis Stevenson* (London, 1902), *The Bookman* booklet no. 2; J. A. Hammerton, ed., *Stevensoniana* (London, 1903), new and revised ed. (Edinburgh, 1907), uniform with the Pentland ed. of Stevenson's works; Sir L. Stephen, *Robert Louis Stevenson: An Essay* (New York–London, 1903); A. W. Pinero, *Robert Louis Stevenson: The Dramatist* (London, 1903); L. Stubbs, *Stevenson's Shrine: A Record of a Pilgrimage* (London, 1903); A. H. Japp, *Robert Louis Stevenson: A Record, an Estimate, and a Memorial—with Hitherto Unpublished Letters from R. L. Stevenson in facsimile* (London, 1905); A. Johnstone, *Recollections of Robert Louis Stevenson in the Pacific* (London, 1905); E. B. Simpson, *Robert Louis Stevenson* (London, 1906); H. J. Moors, *With Stevenson in Samoa* (Boston, 1910; London, 1911).

K. D. Osbourne, *Robert Louis Stevenson in California* (Chicago, 1911); I. Strong, *Robert Louis Stevenson* (London, 1911), Little Books on Great Writers series; E. B. Simpson, *The Robert Louis Stevenson Originals* (London–Edinburgh, 1912); W. H. Low, *A Chronicle of Friendships, 1873–1900* (London, 1908), with illus. by the author; A. Webster, *R. L. Stevenson and Henry Drummond* (London, 1912); *Robert Louis Stevenson: The Man and His Work* (London, 1913), extra number of *The Bookman*, includes repros. of many portraits; F. Watt, *R.L.S.* (London, 1913); R. O. Masson, *Robert Louis Stevenson* (London, 1914), rev. ed. in People's Books series (London, 1920); F. Swinnerton, *R. L. Stevenson: A Critical Study* (London, 1914); A. W. Pinero, *Robert Louis Stevenson as a Dramatist* (New York, 1914), lecture ed. by C. Hamilton; C. Hamilton, *In the Trail of Stevenson* (London, 1916); C. Eaton, *A Last Memory of Robert Louis Stevenson* (New York, 1916); S. Chalmers, *The Penny Piper of Saranac: An Episode in Stevenson's Life* (Boston–New York, 1916); E. Brown, *A Book of R.L.S.: Works, Travels, Friends and Commentators* (London, 1919).

C. J. Guthrie [Lord Guthrie], *Robert Louis Stevenson: Some Personal Reflections and Recollections* (Edinburgh,

1920); H. H. Harper, *Robert Louis Stevenson: An Appreciation* (Boston, 1920); N. van de G. Sanchez, *The Life of Mrs. Robert Louis Stevenson* (London, 1920); C. Eaton, *Stevenson at Manasquan* (Chicago, 1921), with a note on the fate of the yacht *Casco*, by F. Dickie, and six portraits from Stevenson (in verse) by G. S. Seymour; M. Balfour [later Stevenson], *Stevenson's Baby Book: Being the Record of the Sayings and Doings of Robert Louis Balfour Stevenson*, K. D. Osbourne, ed. (San Francisco, 1922); R. O. Masson, ed., *I Can Remember Robert Louis Stevenson* (Edinburgh–London, 1922), enlarged ed. containing approximately 100 short articles by as many contributors (1925); R. O. Masson, *The Life of Robert Louis Stevenson* (Edinburgh–London, 1923); C. Sarolea, *Robert Louis Stevenson and France* (Edinburgh, 1923); L. Osbourne, *An Intimate Portrait of R.L.S.* (New York, 1924); A. St. John Adcock, ed., *Robert Louis Stevenson: His Work and His Personality* (London, 1924), essays by Adcock, H. C. Beeching, S. Colvin, S. R. Crockett, A. Gordon, E. Gosse, J. A. Hammerton, C. Lowe, I. MacLaren, N. Munro, W. Robertson Nicoll, A. Noyes, L. Osbourne, E. B. Simpson, Y. Y. (R. Lynd); J. A. Steuart, *Robert Louis Stevenson: Man and Writer, A Critical Biography* (London, 2 vols., 1924; 1 vol., 1926); G. Hellman, *The True Stevenson: A Study in Clarification* (Boston, 1925), with portraits and facs.; A. A. Boodle, *R.L.S. and His Sine Qua Non* [i.e., Stevenson and his wife]: *Flashlights from Skerryvore* (London, 1926); A. Cunningham, *Cummy's Diary*, R. T. Skinner, ed. (London, 1926), diary kept by Stevenson's nurse while traveling with him on the Continent during 1863, with preface and notes; J. A. MacCulloch, *R. L. Stevenson and the Bridge of Allan, with Other Stevenson Essays* (Glasgow, 1927); G. K. Chesterton, *Robert Louis Stevenson* (London, 1927; repr. New York, 1955); D. B. Morris, *Robert Louis Stevenson and the Scottish Highlanders* (Stirling, 1929).

H. D. MacPherson, *R. L. Stevenson: A Study in French Influence* (New York, 1930); L. E. Chrétien, *La Vocation de Robert-Louis Stevenson: Étude de psychologie littéraire* (Paris, 1930); S. Dark, *Robert Louis Stevenson* (London, 1931); F. Fabre, *Un Ami de la France: R. L. Stevenson dans le Velay* (Clermont-Ferrand, 1932), étude, suivie des Lettres écrites du Monastier en 1878; W. G. Lockett, *Robert Louis Stevenson at Davos* (London, 1934); T. M. MacCallum, *Adrift in the South Seas: Including Adventures with Robert Louis Stevenson* (Los Angeles, 1934); C. MacLean, *La France dans l'Oeuvre de R. L. Stevenson* (Paris, 1936); J. A. Smith, *R. L. Stevenson* (London, 1937); I. Field, *This Life I've Loved* (London, 1937); D. N. Dalglish, *Presbyterian Pirate: A Portrait of Stevenson* (London, 1937); S. Gwynn, *Robert Louis Stevenson* (London, 1939), English Men of Letters series; A. R. Issler, *Stevenson at Silverado* (Caldwell, Ida., 1939).

H. J. Cowell, *Robert Louis Stevenson: An Englishman's Re-Study, After Fifty Years, of R.L.S. the Man* (London, 1945); L. U. Cooper, *Robert Louis Stevenson* (London,

1947); D. Daiches, *Robert Louis Stevenson* (Glasgow, 1947); J. A. Smith, *A Record of Friendship* (London, 1948), discusses Stevenson's friendship with Henry James; *Essays Mainly on the Nineteenth Century* (London, 1948), presented to Sir Humphrey Milford, contains the essay "The Poetry of R. L. Stevenson" by H. W. Garrod; J. Bowman, *Robert Louis Stevenson* (London, 1949).

M. Elwin, *The Strange Case of Robert Louis Stevenson* (London, 1950); M. S. Lawson, *On the Bat's Back: The Story of Robert Louis Stevenson* (London, 1950); M. MacLaren, *Stevenson and Edinburgh: A Centenary Study* (London, 1950); A. R. Issler, *Our Mountain Heritage: Silverado and Robert Louis Stevenson* (Stanford, Calif., 1950); D. Daiches, *Stevenson and the Art of Fiction* (New York, 1951), privately printed, Frances Bergen memorial lecture, Yale University, May 1951; J. C. Furnas, *Voyage to Windward: The Life of Robert Louis Stevenson* (London, 1952), contains interesting, authoritative matter only recently discovered, and sets forth in a clear, dispassionate style that carries conviction a point of view defending Mrs. R. L. Stevenson in considered opposition to her detractors; R. Aldington, *Portrait of a Rebel: The Life and Work of R. L. Stevenson* (London, 1957); G. L. MacKay, *Some Notes on Robert Louis Stevenson, His Finances and His Agents and Publishers* (New Haven, Conn., 1958).

E. N. Caldwell, *Last Witness for Robert Louis Stevenson* (Norman, Okla., 1960); R. Kiely, *Robert Louis Stevenson and the Fiction of Adventure* (Cambridge, Mass., 1964); A. Nakajima, *Light, Wind and Dreams: An interpretation of the life and mind of Robert Louis Stevenson* (Tokyo, 1965); D. Butts, *R. L. Stevenson* (London, 1966); J. D. Hart *R.L.S.* (San Francisco, 1966); E. M. Eigner, *Robert Louis Stevenson and the Romantic Tradition* (Princeton, N.J., 1966); E. M. Compton Mackenzie, *Robert Louis Stevenson* (London, 1968); M. M. MacKay, *Island Boy: Robert Louis Stevenson and His Step-Grandson* [i.e., Austin Strong] *in Samoa* (London, 1969); L. U. Cooper, *Robert Louis Stevenson* (London, 1969); D. Daiches, *Robert Louis Stevenson and His World* (London, 1973); P. Binding, *Robert Louis Stevenson* (London, 1974); J. Pope-Hennessy, *Robert Louis Stevenson* (London, 1974); M. McGaw, *Stevenson in Hawaii* (Westport, Conn., 1978); J. Calder, ed., *A Robert Louis Stevenson Companion* (London, 1980).

OSCAR WILDE
(1845-1900)

John Stokes

To reveal art and conceal the artist is art's aim.

No artist desires to prove anything. Even things that are true can be proved.

No artist is ever morbid. The artist can express everything.
(From the preface to *The Picture of Dorian Gray*)

I

THE liberating potential of art that is extolled in these epigrams was Oscar Wilde's most constant theme, and it is as the high priest of aesthetic freedom that he has found his place in cultural histories. In his own life, however, Wilde was a consciously professional writer whose literary ideas were expressed within a particular situation, whose art was effectively a mediation between hopes and possibilities. Wilde's belief that his art could save him from his times turned out to be a disastrous error of judgment, but he was surely close to the truth when he announced that "to be premature is to be perfect," an ironical boast that was to become an established creed with avant-garde artists in general.

If Wilde's devotion to an ideal future served to justify his pose at the time, it now invites us to consider his ideas in their historical moment. By prolonging the tradition of the nineteenth-century dandy and developing the doctrine of the mask, he was, after all, only acting in accordance with his own evaluation of his period. As he wrote in 1894:

To the world I seem, by intention on my part, a dilettante and dandy merely—it is not wise to show one's heart to the world—and as seriousness of manner is the disguise of the fool, folly in its exquisite modes of triviality and indifference and lack of care is the robe of the wise man. In so vulgar an age as this we all need masks.
(*Letters of Oscar Wilde*, p. 353)

This response to the age was entirely characteristic of the Decadent movement to which Wilde belonged.

Self-disguise coupled with an active nostalgia offered the Decadent a shelter from the facile optimism that he felt surrounded him. His conviction that he was living through a period of transition not only provided an ironical perspective on history but encouraged him to invoke the styles of the past in his writing. Although his field of operation was the modern city, the Decadent's language was often archaic, his images grotesque and macabre, and he favored episodic techniques suitable for rendering discontinuous dreamlike experience.

To these tendencies Wilde brought his own unfailing zest for wit and paradox, his dramatic way of throwing into relief the ideas with which he was most seriously engaged. Consequently, even in its most Decadent phases, Wilde's career continued to be an ingenious solution to the problems of being a professional writer, and his essential concerns—integrity, the creation of an audience, and the function of art—did not change, even when they appeared to him, as to others, to be thoroughly compromised by social circumstance. Wilde's answer to circumstance, self-dramatization, was an implicit attack upon the widespread belief that there was some natural contract between the artist and his audience, and a challenge to the utilitarian notion that likened the relationship to the one between a manufacturer and his market. In his refusal to issue moral edicts, Wilde exposed the myth that art performs a simple social service, disdaining to prove in his narrative conclusions of which his audience was already persuaded.

At the same time Wilde could not rest with the kind of pessimism that actually took comfort from alienation. A writer, he chose to become an entertainer, thereby granting himself the freedom to claim the attention of his audience without sharing its pious expectations. An inevitable condition of this choice was that he should seem to remove himself from commitment to any definite social program.

Oscar Wilde was a one-man band, his art a public show in which he played all the instruments and more often than not was one of the spectators too. His versatility depended in part upon shameless plagiarism; but we should view him now as we do a period anthology, remembering that its form and content have been shaped as much by the preferences of the compiler as by the age that it tries to represent. A careful reading of the texts allows us to see more of Wilde than he wanted us to and more perhaps than he could see of himself. For all his professed delight in his own escapades, he was at heart a most reluctant product of his age.

II

OSCAR FINGAL O'FLAHERTIE WILLS WILDE was born in Dublin on 16 October 1854. His father, Sir William Wilde, was a distinguished surgeon, author of several books on the history and topography of Ireland, and, incidentally, a notorious seducer of women. Oscar's mother was also remarkable: deeply versed in Irish literary traditions, she achieved fame through her own writings, in particular for *Jacta Alea Est*, a patriotic outburst written in 1848 that exhorted the Young Ireland Movement to active rebellion against English oppression. His older brother, known as Willie, later became a London journalist and something of a reprobate. A younger sister, Isola Francesca, died when still a child, causing Oscar much grief. His moving poem "Requiescat" is in her memory.

The Wilde household was an eccentric, sometimes scandalous, but unquestionably learned milieu in which to grow up. At this period Dublin, as so often throughout its history, was a city whose cultural interests were a mixture of the cosmopolitan and the parochial. Wilde benefited from the best that Irish education had to offer: he attended the famous Protestant public school Portora Royal and Trinity College, Dublin, to which he won a scholarship in 1871.

At Trinity he quickly established himself as a brilliant student, attracting the attention of two outstanding classical scholars, Robert Yelverton Tyrrell and John Pentland Mahaffy. When Mahaffy published his pioneering and influential book *Social Life in Greece from Homer to Menander* (1874), he acknowledged the advice given to him by his instructive pupil. Precocity, a quality that the mature Wilde was always to hold in the greatest esteem, was something for which he had himself been acclaimed.

Wilde left Trinity laden with honors, among them the prestigious Berkeley Gold Medal for Greek, and in the autumn of 1874 he took up a classical scholarship at Magdalen College, Oxford. Oxford gave him his formative years. It was there that he was impressed by powerful minds such as John Ruskin, Walter Pater, and Benjamin Jowett, whose classical studies attempted to reconcile Socratic method with Christianity and with modern philosophy.

In the essays and lectures that Wilde wrote after leaving Oxford, Ruskin tends to be offered as a precursor. The austere, at times strident, moralism of the professor of fine art could hardly be accommodated within Wilde's glamorous Aestheticism, and as early as 1882 he was announcing that "the younger school" had departed from Ruskin in its "love of art for art's sake." The connection between art and work, however, the pivot of Ruskin's beliefs, was one that Wilde was never entirely to lose sight of.

A considerably more dominant influence was Walter Pater, whom Wilde revered as a father figure yet is sometimes said to have betrayed. The truth is that Pater, who never allowed himself to become a spokesman for others and was unwilling even to speak directly for himself, played the Ghost to Wilde's Hamlet, and was as much a realization of the son's own needs as a distinct presence. Of all the echoes in Wilde's work, the insistent cadences of the conclusion to Pater's *Studies in the History of the Renaissance* (1873) are by far the most pervasive:

High passions give one this quickened sense of life, ecstasy and sorrow of love, political or religious enthusiasm, or the "enthusiasm of humanity." Only, be sure it is passion, that it does yield you this fruit of a quickened, multiplied consciousness. Of this wisdom, the poetic passion, the desire of beauty, the love of art for art's sake has most; for art comes to you professing frankly to give nothing but the highest quality to your moments as they pass, and simply for those moments' sake.

(pp. 212–213)

Pater deals in injunctions so tentative and yet so intensely felt that he bestows on his readers the pleasant sensation that they are hearing their own inner promptings voiced through another. Reading Pater's prose Wilde discovered himself.

Pater's basic concerns, of course, were as typically Victorian as those of Ruskin, Matthew Arnold, or the other sages: progress, community, belief. His nervous attempt to reestablish the interdependence of aesthetics and conduct was to be seen as a premonition of the need for a "New Hellenism," a progressive slogan that denoted the reunion of the spiritual life with its natural roots and a revival of a classical vision unburdened by the moral hypocrisy, sexual puritanism, and aesthetic philistinism of nineteenth-century England. (A related phrase, sometimes used by Wilde, the "New Hedonism," expressed a more individualistic and scientifically based version of the same idea.)

At Oxford, Wilde made contact with two other trends with which Paterian aestheticism was somewhat uneasily associated. One was a practical application of sensibility to life-style, the burgeoning Aesthetic movement, which embraced Japanese art, blue-and-white china, and William Morris furnishings. The other was the homoerotic cult, sometimes known as "uranianism," which celebrated romantic attachments between men and boys.

As an undergraduate Wilde led an extremely full life. In the spring of 1877 he embarked on a tour of Italy and Greece with Mahaffy, his old Trinity tutor, and in 1878 he was awarded the Newdigate Prize for "Ravenna," a long poem inspired by the trip. In the following year he submitted for the Chancellor's English Essay Prize "The Rise of Historical Criticism," a repetitious piece that nevertheless demonstrates a remarkable breadth of knowledge and a precocious ease with abstract ideas that Wilde was later to distill into epigram. The essay displays his wide reading in the classics and is liberally scattered with references to modern thinkers such as Johann Fichte, Georg Hegel, Alexis de Tocqueville, and Herbert Spencer. Its most impressive qualities are its concern with the relationships between art and history, its implicit admiration of relativistic thought and its commitment to the idea of progress.

Surprisingly Wilde did not win the essay prize nor, in spite of a first-class degree, was he invited to become a fellow of his college. He transferred his attention to London.

Conquest of the capital was by no means immediate, and Wilde seems at first to have been somewhat vague about his future plans. He set up a male household off the Strand with the artist Frank Miles and began to cultivate that fringe of high society then operating between the court, as represented by the rakish Prince of Wales, and the theater, where Wilde's expansive charm endeared him to the actress Lily Langtry and other prominent personalities of

the day. And of course he wrote—a play, entitled *Vera; or, The Nihilists* (1880); journalism, which he had taken up even before leaving Oxford, with accounts of exhibitions at the fashionable Grosvenor Gallery; and poetry.

In 1881 he brought out a collection simply entitled *Poems*. Despite, or perhaps because of, energetic promotion by its author, the volume met with an extremely mixed reception. The most common, and not inaccurate, complaint was that the poems were scandalously derivative—though one of the most powerful resonances came not from other poetry but from Pater's prose. No more than others could Wilde resist transforming the "poetic passion" into the poetry of passion, and the facility with which he adapted Pater's most famous phrases is enough to make one wonder afresh what Pater himself really meant by them.

In the opening poem, "Hélas," the attractions of hedonism are opposed to an "ancient wisdom and austere control," which might stand for either the Christian or the pagan ideal, either the poet's Celtic inheritance or his responsibilities as a writer; while a later phrase, "the honey of romance," links hedonism with moral susceptibility. In Wilde's poetry even political options mirror the indecisiveness of the self. In "Sonnet to Liberty," for instance, the appeal of young revolutionaries resides in their passion rather than in their cause, and the call they make upon the unruly emotions of the poet has to be suppressed. The sonnet ends in melodrama: "These Christs that die upon the barricades, / God knows it I am with them, in some things."

"The Garden of Eros" is Wilde's most frankly Aesthetic poem, honoring, in the kind of reconstructive word-painting that the Victorians much admired, the leaders of the romantic tradition as an Aesthete might conceive of them: John Keats (Wilde's favorite poet), Percy Bysshe Shelley, Morris, Dante Gabriel Rossetti, and Algernon Swinburne. But the mood is listlessly elegiac, suggesting that these revered artists have fought a losing battle in the face of the modern world, and the poet concludes that to evoke beauty is necessarily to court transience and failure.

In the other long poems, "Panthea," "Humanitad," and "The Burden of Itys," the endeavor would seem to be to answer the modern nightmare vision of a universe lacking all purpose (borrowed in part from Alfred Tennyson) with a vague mystical pantheism that is largely derived from Shelley and

William Wordsworth, but is sometimes expressed in purely sensual terms. In "Humanitad" the Greek ideal of perfect form ("Which curbs the passion of that level line / Of marble youths, who with untroubled eyes / And chastened limbs ride round Athena's shrine / And mirror her divine economies") is opposed to Christian immanence ("Where we behold, as one who in a glass / Sees his own face, self-slain Humanity"). The hope is that man will transcend the image of suffering that he has created out of his own self-division and that, in a favorite formula taken from Johann Wolfgang von Goethe, he will "make the Body and the Spirit one."

In his early poetry Wilde mines the romantic tradition and looks to nature and to art for images that reciprocate his inner confusion. *Poems* is a deliberately portentous volume, which can be seen as Wilde's way of viewing his own situation in the light of the achievements of others to the point where plagiarism becomes a species of narcissism. One cannot even claim for him that faculty of creative borrowing for which T. S. Eliot or more recently Harold Bloom has professed an admiration, because for the most part Wilde's self-dramatization remains at the level of mimicry. His eclecticism sometimes causes him to lose control of his ideas and even his syntax: he is an inflationary poet who devalues what he takes. An indiscriminate proliferation of the first person pronoun, endless relative clauses, and continual qualification mark this as the poetry of an indecisiveness that goes beyond the professed options of Christianity or paganism, asceticism or sensuality, to a more basic uncertainty about emotion itself. For all the talk of conquest and submission the reader has little sense of passion actually experienced. Interestingly enough, that absence of reliable feeling is a sign of Decadent attitudes to come. Each one of the vital principles that Wilde attempts to espouse—art, religion, politics, and love—turns out to be already infected with its own failure.

The influence of the fine arts is always in evidence in Wilde's poetry, from a Pre-Raphaelite obsession with natural detail in "The Garden of Eros," through the exercises in classical archaeology that imitate painters such as Lord Leighton and Alma-Tadema, to the Whistlerian or Japanesque "impressions" that mark a later stage in Aesthetic taste. Wilde also frequently employs "the comparison of the arts," a familiar topic in the late nineteenth century. In the hands of the Aesthetes, adjudication between the competing claims of the different arts became a way of justifying art as a whole. Each art could be said to manifest superiority in a particular mode of representation: sculpture because its permanence conveys essence; painting because it faithfully reflects the color, detail, and rhythms of natural perception; poetry because language is tied to thought; music because it is least bound to the representation of a flawed reality; drama because it includes all the other arts. The permutations could be juggled continually, and Wilde expressed alternative preferences at various times. But in the lectures that he gave in the 1880's he followed a powerful direction in Aesthetic thought, and saw the decorative arts as offering an example that all the other arts should emulate.

III

"I'VE put my genius into my life; I've put only my talent into my works," runs Wilde's famous remark to André Gide. Even today opinion polls frequently make him the guest that most people would like to encounter at a dinner party. But some of his contemporaries were affronted by his dominating presence. The mature Wilde had no qualms about declaiming his own prose-poems at the table, and some of his best-known epigrams are sharp reversals of polite exchanges that rebuke the dull and presumptuous. Accosted by a persistent journalist, he is said to have excused himself with: "You will pardon me: I remember your name, but I can't recall your face." In the 1890's Laurence Housman noted "a certain decorative solemnity, in excess of what the occasion required," but later marveled at Wilde's "smooth-flowing utterance, sedate and self-possessed, oracular in tone, whimsical in substance, carried on without halt, or hesitation, or change of word." Much of Wilde's apparently impromptu wit has this same extravagant quality which, by playing manner off against meaning, turns common speech into drama. A glassy, self-regarding creation, Wilde's social personality was to develop according to the opportunities of the moment.

In the metropolitan world through which he sailed in the early 1880's, style and appearance certainly did much to create identity. To be seen was as important as to produce, and Wilde was always conscious of the relation between the two. And he was seen in several guises: affable country-house guest, happy, indeed eager to join in the weekend sport; top-hatted man-about-town at a private view or public reception; and, more daring but now socially recognizable, languorous, velveted Aesthete. It was this last role that was to offer him some immediate financial reward.

Although Wilde did not invent the Aesthetic movement, it is true to say that for a time he allowed it to invent him. The manner in which this occurred was essentially satirical. The cartoonist George du Maurier had begun a series in *Punch* featuring a comic Aesthete called Postlethwaite, who, as the series continued, came to bear an increasing resemblance to Wilde. At about the same time the actor Herbert Beerbohm Tree adapted some of his performances to mimic Wilde's well-known gestures and expressions. The climax of this satirical process was reached in 1881 with Gilbert and Sullivan's *Patience,* and its outrageous Aesthete, Bunthorne. It was thanks to the great popular success of *Patience* that Wilde was invited to lecture in the United States in 1882. This tour, which took him from coast to coast, had a considerable impact. For the most part a bemused America matched his condescending posture with rambunctious parodies in popular songs and cartoons, but he was granted an interview with the laureate of the democratic self, Walt Whitman, and a minority evidently took him very solemnly indeed. "I am an *intense lover* of the *beautiful,*" wrote one earnest admirer, "and have spent much time and thought over it." "Let me thank you sincerely for your fructifying lecture," wrote another. "I call it fructifying because it teaches a gospel hitherto not heard here, and one which I believe will have a better effect than the foundation of a cotton factory—a compliment which may sound ambiguous to you but it is the highest I can pay in this place enamoured of cotton factories."[1] Self-conscious, precious, and occasionally homoerotic in tone, Wilde's fan letters show the stirrings of an American Aestheticism that was to feed into the culture as a whole. His American manner, a calculated mix of European sensitivity and brash individualism, had obvious attractions for that perennial American type: the cultural exile.

The lectures that Wilde delivered in America were unsystematic and partly extemporized, hasty oracles that often emerged as oppositions, each set leading to the next by way of historical or intellectual contingency. In the most developed of the lectures, "The

[1]From letters housed in the William Andrews Clark Memorial Library, Los Angeles.

English Renaissance of Art," he maintains the common nineteenth-century distinction between the Hellenic and medieval spirits—aesthetic repose against mysterious vision—and proposes that these two currents have been synthesized in modern romanticism, which is characterized by *individualism*—community and history felt through the isolated consciousness—and *relativism*—the belief that all perceptions, emotions, and ideas are constantly evolving and can be understood only by reference to each other and to temporal change. The most celebrated locus for the concept of relativism—a vitally important one in the middle and late nineteenth century—is the opening passage of Pater's essay on Samuel Taylor Coleridge: "Modern thought is distinguished from ancient by its cultivation of the 'relative' spirit in the place of the 'absolute.' . . . To the modern spirit nothing is, or can be rightly known, except relatively and under conditions." Behind Pater's summing up lay influences with which Wilde too had become familiar—Darwinian science and Hegelian metaphysics. "In the work produced under the modern romantic spirit," declared Wilde in his lecture, "it is no longer the permanent, the essential truths of life that are treated of, it is the momentary situation of the one, the momentary aspect of the other that art seeks to render," and he linked this ambition with democratic aspirations: the desire felt by every man since the French Revolution to express himself according to his mood and the moment. In the survey of English romantic poetry that follows, Wilde tends to dismiss Shelley for being overanxious to escape from the circumstances of life, preferring William Blake for his belief that art must be specific and Keats for pursuing the perfection of beauty. Blake and Keats were revolutionary poets because their work reflected the influence of intellectual change upon art, and their immediate descendants are the Pre-Raphaelites and the members of the Aesthetic movement.

Wilde goes on to say that the artist's individualistic dedication to beauty has led inevitably to his estrangement from a public that no longer perceives the revolutionary origins of his art. The artist, moreover, has been obliged to make use of new techniques and new conditions, to reexamine his own creative activities. The emerging proposition, —which borders upon paradox—is that the spontaneous production of art can only be preserved by self-consciousness on the part of the artist. At this point we might seem to have come some way from the revolutionary spirit that Wilde originally projected as the source of the romantic movement, and we move on to what might initially look like an entirely different matter: the elevation of form over feeling, cornerstone of "art for art's sake." This shift is signaled by the mention of Théophile Gautier and Charles Baudelaire. Yet Wilde's argument is not inconsistent: art is a product of the imagination, not simply of the passions, and the artist is distinguished from the rest of mankind by his imaginative capacity to produce inspiring forms. The dicta that follow, that painting is merely "a beautifully colored surface," for example, stem from the precept that the artist must first of all respect his own imagination and his material if he is to avoid the public demand for consumption, for trivial meanings and conventional morality. Only by so doing will he ultimately be of any real value to that public.

Within Wilde's argument there lie many ironies, of which the most profound is the way in which he has rescued idealism from the implacable forces of relativism with which he began. Not only has he moved from society as a whole to individualism and then back again, but in the course of his purposive meanderings he has lit upon several aesthetic formulas, few of them his own invention, which he will repeat again and again throughout his career. "To most of us the real life is the life we do not lead"—this is because the life we do not lead is the life that we desire. The poet can express this desired life by becoming "the spectator of all time and of all existence." Hence the distinctive responsibilities of the critic, who must teach the public "the spirit in which they are to approach all artistic work." Yet art does have its interactions with life: in the drama, for instance, we discover "the meeting-place of art and life." Although "one should never talk of a moral or an immoral poem—poems are either well written or badly written, that is all" (here Wilde is translating directly from Gautier), there is crucially "la consolation des arts" (also taken from Gautier), which makes life endurable.

IV

IN 1883, soon after his return from America, Wilde spent three months in Paris, working on poems and plays and discussing literature with Stéphane Mallarmé, Paul Verlaine, and other members of the symbolist and Decadent schools. On his return he devoted his energies to consolidating his position as a writer. In 1884 he married Constance Lloyd, who came from a family of Dublin lawyers, had a moderate inheritance, and was interested in Aesthetic furnishings and fashions. Wilde described her as "quite young, very grave and mystical, with wonderful eyes, and dark brown coils of hair." The following year they moved into a house in Tite Street, Chelsea, decorated for them with dramatic simplicity by the Aesthetic architect E. W. Godwin. The Wildes had two sons in quick succession: Cyril, born in 1885, and Vyvyan in 1886, and they seem, at least to start with, to have led a happy and not unconventional domestic life. Yet W. B. Yeats's memory of the Wilde household in his *Autobiographies* (1926) suggests something more troubling, as if an effort of will were involved in the creation of an ideal environment: "It was perhaps too perfect in its unity, his past of a few years before had gone too completely, and I remember thinking that the perfect harmony of his life there, with his beautiful wife and his two young children, suggested some deliberate artistic composition."

Wilde's professional life—that of a tolerably industrious and versatile free-lance writer and journalist—was altogether less ordered. In 1887 he became editor of *The Woman's World*, a magazine that supported such progressive movements as Rational Dress; and elsewhere he reviewed books on many subjects. A combination of financial pressure and professional expediency obliged him to reconsider his métier, and it is with his changing ambitions in mind that we should assess the diversity of writings that belong to this period in his career. The tone of his work, too, had begun to change and some critics have suggested that this may have had to do with his initiation—or reinitiation—into the homosexual world.

He started producing short stories about survival in Victorian London, with its glamor, its squalor, its public opportunities, and its secret lives. It is an eerie world, where decay and expansion, plenitude and suffering exist side by side. Although Wilde's theme is success in fashionable orbits, an edgy interplay between style and concealment mirrors the larger duplicities of society as a whole. Many of his characters are possessed by a divided consciousness, but division is also implicit in the way that his narrative tone exploits the gulf between the lives that they lead and the beliefs that they profess to hold. As a general rule the survivors are those who have an ironic awareness of social hypocrisy, but that by no means guarantees their moral blamelessness.

The hero of "Lord Arthur Savile's Crime" (first published in periodical form in 1887) is told by a fortune-teller that he is destined to commit murder. This prophecy puts him in an alien state of mind in which he perceives, for the first time, terrifying discrepancies between the self and its roles. Concluding that the world is beyond his rational understanding, he resolves to act according to superstition, and fulfills and assuages the augury by killing the fortune-teller. Luckily for Lord Arthur, "Life to him meant action, rather than thought. He had that rarest of things, common sense." Had he possessed a superior mind—the mind of Hamlet, say, Wilde's favorite comparison—and confined himself to thought, the potential for self-destruction might have been greater. It was perhaps with his own disquieting sense of the imbalance between thought and action that Wilde proceeded with his secret life.

In the essays that Wilde wrote in the 1880's, the distinction between ideas and morality becomes an adjunct to a more immediate concern: the artist's realization of his own personality in a repressive and philistine society. The concepts of art and personality become almost, but not quite, synonymous; together they take priority over all other considerations and maybe justify all means. An increased stress upon antinomian, even illegal, behavior no doubt derived from his involvement with Verlaine, his continuing study of Baudelaire, and the stresses of his own sexual life.

In 1886 he delivered a lecture on Thomas Chatterton, doomed boy poet and literary forger, which was never published, and in 1889, "Pen, Pencil and Poison," an account of Thomas Wainewright, author and murderer. Both men became ironical models of the artistic personality: the forger Chatterton because he "claimed for the artist freedom of mood. He saw the realm of the imagination differed from the realm of fact,"[2] and the murderer Wainewright because in the pursuit of a fulfilling identity he flouted the most basic of social taboos. Wilde was exploring a theoretical paradox, which, although easy to summarize, was put to many uses. The artist is either congenitally unlike other people or is obliged to become unlike them because of his special

[2] From manuscript notes in the William Andrews Clark Memorial Library.

needs: "he is lacking in wholeness and completeness of nature," and he can fulfill himself only in his art. Yet to estimate fulfillment in terms of production alone would be to act like the philistine, the governor of the society from which he is estranged; and so it turns out that the artist, by extending his art into life, finds his true completion in style, in his very refusal to produce. He seeks to "be somebody, rather than to do something"; Wilde's modification of the Paterian emphasis on "being" joins Baudelaire's idea of the dandy to supply a definition of the artist that scorns the three major shibboleths of the philistine: fixed morality, material production, and innovation as the measure of social progress.

In Wilde's interpretation Chatterton and Wainewright subvert the rules of society first by concealing their activities and later by flaunting them. The fact that these were fictionalized portraits with no claim to precise historical accuracy helped him to manipulate an ambiguity between "crime" in the sense of evil deeds and crime as simply that which the law forbids. There was a parallel ambiguity in his use of the word "sin," which might denote either a theological or a social offense. Either way the association of such words with art places the artist outside a society that in Wilde's view flattered itself with the belief that civil and moral laws were largely in coincidence. As we shall see, society's willful myopia on that score had particular significance for homosexuals, and in Wilde's next experiment with fiction, homosexual undertones became much more audible.

"The Portrait of Mr. W.H. " (1889) opens a series of narrative Chinese boxes worthy of the Argentine writer Jorge Luis Borges. A brilliant exposition of a developing aesthetic theory, a credible hypothesis conceived within a fiction that is itself based upon a forgery, the story propounds the idea that it was the actor Willie Hughes who provided Shakespeare with his major inspiration. In their researches Wilde's spokesmen encounter many aesthetic riddles, of which the most important is the notion that just as Shakespeare found in the actor a living projection of his own aspirations as an artist, an incarnation of the multiple possibilities of his art, so it is true for all sensitive men that "consciousness, indeed, is quite inadequate to explain the contents of personality. It is art, and art only, that reveals us to ourselves." The playwright creates the forms that the actor embodies; the actor provides the playwright with inspiration. In the objective or "impersonal" forms of literature, in a theatrical role, for example, the artistic personality is made visible. Thus the impersonal turns out to be an aspect of the personality: the paradox is explicit, but in Wilde's theory, to which he was to remain faithful, the impersonal and the personal continue to confront each other in a perplexing series of exchanges where art is both the means and the end.

The sexual implications of theatrical metamorphosis are to be seen in an extreme form in the case of Elizabethan boy actors, who were of course required to portray women. Wilde's story suggests that sexual encounters parallel the creative interchange, most pertinently perhaps in homosexual relationships, where, it is sometimes said, since both partners are of the same sex, the subject might more easily rediscover itself in the object of its desire.

One curious feature of "The Portrait of Mr. W.H.," which Wilde may not have fully admitted to himself, is that these potent sexual myths run the risk of being undermined by the very flexibility of the aesthetic theory. The objective ideal may be a necessary fiction, opposed to those dull or misleadingly verifiable facts that confine the personality to restrictive circumstance, yet to locate that ideal in a mirroring object who is also another person is not simply to practice solipsism but to court ultimate fragmentation of the self: other people are themselves prone to treacherous shifts of personality, and none more so than actors, who are called upon to embody a wide range of personalities. Fortunately the art of the theater incorporates the element of illusion that accompanies this psychological truth, when it returns its participants and its spectators to mutable experience.

That early remark, "To most of us the real life is the life we do not lead," offers a clue to the importance of fantasy in Wilde's thought; and in his fairy tales, as in his murder, mystery, and ghost stories, Wilde found that fantasy and parable could combine—though his method was to take the reader to the brink of a moral insight without quite introducing him to it. Wilde used the fantastic modes as a means of projecting his own concerns upon readers whose responses were already engaged by familiar literary conventions.

The first audience for the fairy tales was probably Wilde's own sons. Children are of all people the most bound up with their own behavior, yet the most oblivious to what is expected of them, and in that respect alone, as Wilde liked to point out, they are father to the man. His stories take the consciousness of a child as their subject but in a thoroughly unpatronizing way: these are sophisticated works, attractive to all generations, and they have recently been submitted to rigorous critical analysis. Some of the stories have to do with dreams of a return to a primeval universe and the difficulties in isolating a pure motive, others with the mixed blessings of self-awareness and the illusions that follow any attempt to preserve a mirror relationship with the natural world. These are the problems of what Wilde calls the "soul," and although they are normally resolved with a wry acceptance of the dualities of human life, the specific problem of aesthetic experience remains intransigent within them.

"The Young King" (first published in periodical form in 1881) is an Aesthete who gains his greatest pleasure from contact with beautiful things; he finds in them an "anodyne to pain." In his dreams he discovers the unsettling truth that beautiful objects are made by the poor for the rich. Yet when he acts upon this revelation and dresses as a beggar he is resented by his people; and it is only when he is transfigured after gazing at an image of Christ that they recognize his saintliness. In "The Happy Prince" (1888) a swallow and a statue renounce material beauty to satisfy their charitable impulses. The statue loses his gilded surface, the swallow forgoes the sensuality of Egypt, yet when they die the pair are rewarded with permanent residence in an Aesthetic paradise, a city of gold, where the swallow, like one of Yeats's mechanical birds, will sing forever more.

In these stories Wilde outlines two realms of beauty: the transient and the permanent, the meretricious and the meritorious, but he gives no indication that noble deeds will bring forth any reward other than the embodiment of a higher Aesthetic ideal. The progression is rather from an innate capacity to appreciate beautiful things to an awareness of what the creation of that beauty involves in human terms, to a final point, reached only after suffering and sacrifice, when a transcendent beauty is attained. The fairy tales tell of the refinement of Aesthetic principle; the beauties of the moral life, which in themselves compensate for nothing, are only discovered when Aesthetic indulgence has been transformed. This makes Wilde's parabolic fantasies simultaneously liberating and repressive. His Aesthete-martyrs achieve their transcendence only after partial confrontation with repressed knowledge—the knowledge of "cost." If satisfaction is at first unwittingly at the expense of others—their labor and suffering—in its later moral phase it is at the expense of the Aesthete himself—the renunciation of beauty. Finally, in the dream of art and sympathy reconciled, transcendence becomes collaborative, since the Aesthete's charity is rewarded by admiring love, and the quality of beauty is attributed to his personality. Whether the Aesthete should ever forgo that admiration and beauty, the remaining demands of his voracious individualism, was an issue that was so sensitive as to be entrusted only to the wisdom of children.

The problematic reciprocity between the Aesthete and his fellow men mirrors the relationship between an artist and his audience, the inevitability of which Wilde was obliged to point out in his dealings with the painter James McNeill Whistler. Early in his career Wilde had borrowed from Whistler the principle that beauty lies in appearance as it is rendered by an artist and is not an essential quality of the subject, but when the two men quarreled in the mid-1880's—largely in fact over Wilde's supposed plagiarism—it was Wilde who showed himself to have advanced to the more complex position. Whistler's claim, heard at its most provocative in the famous "Ten O'Clock Lecture" of 1885, was that "the master stands in no relationship to the moment at which he occurs—a moment of isolation—hinting at sadness—having no part in the progress of his fellow men." In reviewing the lecture Wilde pointed out that the artist could not escape his conditions quite so easily:

An artist is not an isolated fact; he is the resultant of a certain *milieu* and a certain *entourage*, and can no more be born of a nation that is devoid of any sense of beauty than a fig can grow from a thorn or a rose blossom from a thistle.[3]

As we consider Wilde's extended critical statements we find that they are all concerned with the problems that result when an emergent formalism (the belief that the artist has complete freedom to transform the appearance of the world in his art) is juxtaposed with an equal conviction that art cannot be disengaged from the circumstances of its production, including of course the circumstances of the artist himself.

[3]From "Mr. Whistler's Ten O'Clock," in the *Pall Mall Gazette* (21 February 1885).

V

FOR his two major investigations into aesthetic theory Wilde fittingly chose a dialogue form. "The Decay of Lying" (1889) features "Cyril" and "Vivian" (the names of Wilde's sons); "The Critic as Artist," "Ernest" and "Gilbert." Both were printed first in periodicals and then in a volume called *Intentions* (1891), along with "Pen, Pencil and Poison" and an uncharacteristic essay on the "archaeological" method of staging, "Shakespeare and Stage Costume," now known as "The Truth of Masks." Dialogue serves a double purpose: it dramatizes a pedagogic method on Socratic lines, and it places the reader in the role of eavesdropper instead of addressing him directly. The title *Intentions* suggests that the dialogues are in some sense unfulfilled, and, as we shall see, they both end in paradox and not in formal resolution. Although Wilde leaves himself free to express an internal dialectic (so that the speakers together compose Wilde himself), there is still a clear division into master and pupil. The "pupil" (Cyril or Ernest) expresses conventional wisdom, the tedious consistency of public opinion (or more specifically of the edicts of its intellectual leaders), which the "master" (Vivian or Gilbert) exposes and replaces. At the same time Wilde protects himself from the dangers of proposing a new orthodoxy because the dialogue as a whole retains its literary autonomy: it is a "mask" that confesses "intentions" as yet unrealized.

"The Decay of Lying" is primarily an attack against the principles of realism on the ground that they assume a collusion between the artist and his audience that is socially and imaginatively inhibiting. Wilde's aim is to free art from the constraints of a previously conditioned audience, but in order to do so he has to give art an independent value; he has to resort yet again to "the ideal," although he remains opposed to the kind of social attitudes that idealize present knowledge. First of all he refutes the critical position that appeals to nature as the basis for art. Nature, says Vivian, presents us with a dull uniformity, whereas the human imagination is capable of an infinite variety. A lie is an expression of this variety because it spurns external evidence, and art is like a lie because it too refuses to be subjected to empirical proof, and need not be explained by reference to an affective or utilitarian function. Life can only benefit when it follows the variety of art rather than the monotony of nature.

Art remains in advance of life: consequently life imitates art more than art imitates life. We have reached the central paradox, the hinge of the dialogue.

The argument grows more obscure when we arrive a little later at its formal justification, and the pronouncement that "scientifically speaking, the basis of life—the energy of life as Aristotle would call it—is simply the desire for expression, and Art is always presenting various forms through which the expression can be attained." A page or so later we read that "art never expresses anything but itself." All this seems very muddling unless we are prepared to accept a perfect circularity: art is the source, the means, and the end of its own energy, and it develops by converting everything into itself, forever inventing new forms. The conclusion to "The Decay of Lying" seems to suggest a slight qualification of that extreme position, however, for there Vivian tells Cyril that "the self-conscious aim of life is to find expression."

The second dialogue, "The Critic as Artist," takes the problems of "self-consciousness," "expression," and "development" as far as they will go, blithely replacing Arnold's maxim that it is the aim of criticism to "see the object as in itself it really is" with an assertion that "the primary aim of the critic is to see the object as in itself it really is not." What Wilde means by this paradox is that it is the function of the critic to see the object as it might be, as other people fail to see it, especially when they conceive of themselves as a homogeneous mass. The critic is the ideal audience because he is independent of his time, free from the coercions of popular taste, and therefore supremely individual. Yet on a biological model he is a perfect specimen, summing up within himself the inherited wisdom of the past and projecting it into the future. Moreover he is an embodiment of the principle by which relativism leads to the ideal, since his subjective freedom multiplies the meanings of art through imaginative associations. The more complex, indeed the more contradictory, his impressions, the more complex and vital art will be seen to be.

Furthermore Gilbert is adamant that the realization of art takes place not in action but in contemplation. The critic does not implement his impressions, he does not forcibly apply them to any aspect of life outside the experience of art. (Although we might recall that according to "The Decay of Lying" the appearance, if nothing else, of life will be changed by exposure to art.) Nor does the critic make the fatal mistake of judging art by moral values, even if his very passivity, "being" rather than "doing," does allow an inner progression—"becoming."

Wilde adds several more twists to an already mazy pattern. The view that by "intensifying" his "impressions" within his "personality" by means of his "curiosity" (the vocabulary is Pater's but exaggerated), the critic increases the mystery of art, allows for the reintroduction of "sin," "an essential element of progress," which carries the argument to the point where it issues forth in the most notorious of all Wilde's pronouncements, "All art is immoral." Just as the meaning of "sin" hovers between the theological and the secular, so "immortal" can equally be taken to mean "amoral," that is, oblivious to socially validated codes, and "imagination" can be substituted for "art." Yet Wilde himself admits the interaction between art, ideas, and value, for Gilbert is soon to announce, as he draws into his closing movement, that the imagination is "simply concentrated race-experience." It is through their ever increasing consciousness of themselves, fed by their contemplation of art, their ability to turn first the objective into the subjective (from "art" to "impression") and then the subjective back into the objective (the "mask"), that the critical spirits are able to express within themselves the gropings toward the ideal that less developed intelligences still search for in a consensus response to art. "The Critical and the World Spirit are one": now in the very final moments comes the Hegelian transfiguration of the Aesthetic critic, the dreamer who has as his punishment and his reward that "he sees the dawn before the rest of the world."

Despite the undoubted circularity of Wilde's system we are still free to enjoy the manner of its exposition. The most interesting questions relate to Wilde's need to perform in this way. Why should a writer of such incisive intelligence get himself in such a tangle? There is a general answer to that question. We have seen that Wilde never attempts to distinguish art from what is not art, nor does he examine the reference of the word "beauty," though he does on occasion lend it to what was not generally thought to be beautiful. Both "art" and "beauty" are, in a word, *absolutes*, whose meaning exists apart from their application. The philosophical problem here—the relationship between word and thing—is as old as aesthetics itself, but it had become acute in the later part of the nineteenth century as the romantic tradition confronted a world in which both the

408

nature of production and the very appearance of human surroundings had radically altered. Wilde's nominalism no less than his satirical tactics was a brilliantly evasive reaction to this changed environment, and his vision of a world that is fit for critics to live in is utopian. But then "England will never be civilised till she has added Utopia to her dominions." In "The Soul of Man Under Socialism" (1891) he was a little more precise about where it might lie.

On this single occasion Wilde entered the public arena wearing no other mask than his subversive wit. "The Soul of Man" is prescriptive in the manner of someone who is making his own polemical contribution to a general debate. This after all was the period of the Fabian Society lectures, to which George Bernard Shaw contributed, and of William Morris' *News from Nowhere*.[4] The essay opens with a few smacks at favorite targets: bogus altruism, charity, and all the false virtues that try "to solve the problem of poverty . . . by keeping the poor alive"; as well as at "a very advanced school" who try to solve the problem "by amusing the poor" (possibly a reference to the People's Palace, a philanthropic organization in the East End of London whose aim was to bring culture to the working classes; Wilde had himself applied for the post of secretary in 1886).

Probably influenced by the anarchist tradition, Wilde strongly attacks private property, conceding only that under present circumstances the prophetic freedom of the individualist-aesthete is likely to depend upon his creating the material conditions that will help him to realize his "beautiful and intellectual life." Wilde's system proposes a progression from the individualism of the few to socialism, which is the individualism of the many. This was a common enough idea at the time, although just how it might come about always remained obscure: individualism would have to be a motive force for change in itself. In "The Critic as Artist" Wilde had referred to "the just rancour of the criminal classes"; in "The Soul of Man" he compares the virtuous poor, so degraded that they accept their state, with the criminal classes, who have reached that point of self-awareness where rebellion sets in. (Elsewhere Wilde equated the "criminal" and the working classes in a rather crude way, largely because he considered the law to be exclusively a repressor of freedom and not, even in a

class-dominated society, as guarantor of certain minimal liberties. Already he may have had one particular piece of legislation in mind: the Criminal Law Amendment Act of 1885, which penalized public and private indecencies between adult males.)

"The Soul of Man" endorses the complete individualist, who, like an artist, stands apart from life, adapting it to his own expression, and who, like a criminal, is opposed to the ordering principles of his society. The most perfect embodiment of this type is Christ, yet even he should be seen as transitional, since suffering and pity will disappear altogether from the future ideal society. As a final flourish proclaims, "The new Individualism is the new Hellenism."

VI

BEGUN in Oxford, almost completed in Paris in 1883 but not published until 1894, when it appeared in a superb edition with illustrations by Charles Ricketts, Wilde's long poem *The Sphinx* straddles this crucial period in his life, and we should not look to it for tight formal coherence. Rather, the poem anthologizes the images of Decadence with which he had familiarized himself by reading French literature, and frames them with a structure taken from Edgar Allan Poe's *The Raven*.

The Sphinx is a riddling *imago*, half-woman and half-beast, who, as Wilde described her elsewhere, is "as old as the world itself, and lives in the desert, and knows everything." Wilde's talent for improvisation enables him to sustain an interminable litany of images that conjure up the ancient wisdom, images that are culled from many sources, of which Baudelaire is the most obvious. The rampant inventiveness of the poet's imagination responds to the monstrous sexual energy of the Sphinx, with sacrificial invocations to fecundity of the kind that are associated with primitive sacrificial rites. A roll call of talismanic proper names and increasingly excited apostrophe mesmerize the will of poet and reader alike in authentic symbolist fashion. When the permutations are finally cut short with a return from pagan to Christian images, we are as disappointed as we are skeptical, for the power of myth to displace so thoroughly the controlling mind of the poet suggests some unspoken ground shared between him and the reader: Yeats's *Anima Mundi* perhaps or, in another vocabulary, the "unconscious."

[4]R. Shewan, *Oscar Wilde. Art and Egoism* (London, 1977), a study of Wilde's unpublished commonplace book, also shows the important influence of the essays and lectures of W. K. Clifford.

But the Sphinx keeps her secrets, and the poet must keep his too—which is that he alone might know what the secret is. A similar use of symbolist techniques to convey mysterious temptations is to be found in "The Harlot's House," also written in Paris (and first published in the *Dramatic Review*, April 1885). Here the occupants of a brothel appear to the poet like puppets in some ghastly tableau, shadowy figures whose mechanical dance of death flaunts the power of lust to destroy the individual will. When confessional fantasy manifests itself in poetry in this way, the motivation remains a secret that lies between the writer and his text, explicable only to the reader who keeps himself at one remove. A comparable approach must operate in a reading of Wilde's only novel, *The Picture of Dorian Gray* (1891).

VII

Dorian Gray comes to us obscured by a scandal that was largely of Wilde's own making. The novel was first serialized in *Lippincott's* magazine in 1890 and then revised (probably to remove overt homosexual emphases) before it reached hard covers. Nevertheless the book was greeted on publication with a storm of protest against the supposed immorality of the story and, even more, of Wilde's preface to it. Indeed the preface has attracted so much attention over the years that the story has sometimes been taken as merely a demonstration of its precepts. However, as a novel, much of the interest of *Dorian Gray* resides in its narrative method. It should be read obliquely, with a ready eye for collusion and disparity between author and character.

Wilde uses the first person very rarely, and by far the greater part is recounted in a third-person narration, which appears to be distanced from the characters yet knowingly at ease with their world. Even so the central consciousness of the novel is Dorian's: he is the most important, the most interesting, and probably the most intelligent of the characters. In contrast to Basil Hallward and Lord Henry Wotton, moral idealist and amoral cynic respectively, both condemned to failure and regret, Dorian alone has the capacity for growth through change. As Wilde himself confessed: "Basil Hallward is what I think I am: Lord Henry what the world thinks me: Dorian what I would like to be—in other ages, perhaps." Dorian, though not an artist, is deeply interested in art. His great mistake, of which he is at least inter-

mittently aware, is to abuse both art and life by forestalling their potential in order to preserve the present. That Dorian should ultimately fail to halt the process of aging in himself is biologically inevitable, but the problematic relationship of art to the processes of change is more difficult to understand; indeed it might not appear as a problem had not Wilde already made it one. In his critical essays Wilde retains a commitment to the absolute value of art, while affirming that it is an organic expression of the mood of its maker. He tries to explain subsequent difficulties with the theory that the meaning of a work is realized only within the changing consciousness of the person who views it. Dorian reverses this idea when he renounces change in himself and transfers that potential to a picture, although he finds that he cannot help but retain some of the feelings that initiate and accompany change. His experiment thus paradoxically reveals the problems within his author's aesthetic theory, and the maxims that Wilde put forward in his preface act as a kind of smokescreen to the honorable confusions within the novel. Where the preface plays with intellectual divisions, the novel restores their interrelatedness. "There is no such thing as a moral or an immoral book," says the preface, separating art from the terms of life; Dorian encounters the illogicality of an Aesthetic life—life as art—that does not encompass moral choice, which, as Pater conventionally pointed out in his review of the book, is an essential part of man's higher function. Dorian's discoveries about art are very pertinent indeed to his author's speculations.

Let us take a single example. Dorian falls in love with an innocent young actress who commits suicide when later he brutally rejects her. He explains his response to her death to Basil Hallward in this way:

"And besides, my dear old Basil, if you really want to console me, teach me rather to forget what has happened, or to see it from the proper artistic point of view. Was it not Gautier who used to write about *la consolation des arts?* I remember picking up a little vellum-covered book in your studio one day and chancing on that delightful phrase. Well, I am not like that young man you told me of when we were down at Marlow together, the young man who used to say that yellow satin could console one for all the miseries of life. I love beautiful things that one can touch and handle. . . . But the artistic temperament that they create, or at any rate reveal, is still more to me. To become the spectator of one's own life, as Harry says, is to escape the suffering of life."

(ch. IX)

It is possible to read that passage as a symposium of opinions, so organized that the authority for voicing them is continually being shifted. Dorian might have been thinking of Gautier's comment about his own poems that "l'art est ce qui console le mieux de vivre" ("art is the greatest consolation for living"), or perhaps of Gautier's observation in his highly consequential preface to Baudelaire's *Les Fleurs du Mal* (1857) about certain phrases that seem, like music, "chuchoter des consolations pour les douleurs inavouées et les irrémédiables désespoirs" ("to whisper consolations for unacknowledged sorrows and despairs without remedy"). Certainly Dorian would also have found in Gautier's preface, as Pater and Wilde no doubt did, an account of a crucial stage in Baudelaire's development: the discovery of his own estrangement from human life, when he becomes "the spectator of life," when "every sensation becomes subject to analysis," and when he "divides" ("se dédouble") and begins to "spy upon" himself.

The novel identifies Dorian as the modern type represented in Gautier's image of Baudelaire. But at the same time Dorian's entreaties to Hallward suggest that he is reaching toward a more advanced version of the idea of the "spectator," for his language also evokes Pater. The astute reader will spot ironies that lie beyond the consciousness of the character. In conversation with Hallward, Dorian outlines his development as he perceives it: his progression from the consolations of the confident "art for art's sake" that Gautier found in Baudelaire, the self-analyzing modern poet, to the restless position of the modern critic as defined by Pater, deeply engrossed with the creative personality that works of art bring into view, and the age of which that personality is a summing up. Dorian seems to aspire to the condition of the ideal critic as Pater described him in *Studies in the Renaissance*, who possessed "the power of being deeply moved by the presence of beautiful objects. . . . The question he asks is always: In whom did the stir, the genius, the sentiment of the period find itself!" In Pater's later book *Marius the Epicurean* (1885), however, the hero progresses from youthful curiosity ("even in his most enthusiastic participation . . . still essentially but a spectator") to a mature wisdom in which the capacities of the observer encompass the magnitude of the world: "the vision of men and things, actually revealed to him on his way through the world, had developed, with a wonderful largeness, the faculties to which it addressed itself, his general capacity of vision." Wilde's novel represents this Paterian striving only by reducing it to the complacent figure of Lord Henry, who observes the world without self-development. Sadly Dorian can do little more than execute Lord Henry's abused and incomplete version of the Paterian ideal.

There is a complex of ideas at work here: an initial proposition that art will console the sensitive man for the suffering in the world, that he can retreat from life and view himself as an object; and there is the larger idea that because art reveals the artist, the man who appreciates art will become a participant in life—the ultimate consolation. The problem for Wilde lay in finding empirical justification for the shift from one vision to the other, when the life that surrounded him appeared fraught with deception and threats to the self. In order to shock his public and to make it aware of its own illusions, he would sometimes exalt the first, concealing his failure to master the second.

Dorian is very like the young Marius, but he is trapped in a transitional moment, a moment that Wilde could perceive but not resolve. Phrases such as "la consolation des arts" and "the spectator of life" are part of the repertoire that Wilde deployed throughout his career, and noting their interchange here helps us to grasp the ironies of the novel and the ways in which the thoughts of its central consciousness enact the impasse of its author. None of Wilde's literary mentors, neither Gautier nor Pater, could solve the immediate historical problem of participation for him, not even by offering him the consolation of ideas.

VIII

THE drama is "the meeting-place of art and life," as Wilde had defined it early on; in later versions he added the rider "where art returns to life." In the 1890's the theater offered him a daring means of self-projection: an immediate involvement with the audience coupled with limitless opportunity for disguise. In the years from 1892 to 1895 Wilde replaced the pose of the Aesthete with a new and triumphant public role: monarch of the West End theater, dandy supreme, impresario of his times. But in other respects his hold on life was far from sure.

In 1891 he had met Lord Alfred Douglas, a sulkily beautiful youth, petulant and unstable, whose father, the marquess of Queensberry, was renowned for the violence of his temper and for the eccentricity of his attitudes to sex, which he saw as directly connected with heredity and purity of the line. Wilde became infatuated with Douglas, and although he continued, in fact increased, his contacts with the London homosexual underground, the two men became extremely dependent upon each other.

In 1892 *Lady Windermere's Fan* opened at the St. James's Theatre to enthusiastic notices, and in the same year a very different kind of play was put into rehearsal, though it was not to reach the stage: *Salomé*. Both plays show Wilde to be as intent as ever on his search for an appropriate form even though the medium had changed, and *Salomé* is Wilde's most extreme and personal expression of Decadent feeling.

"Death," claimed the poet Wallace Stevens, "is the mother of beauty," catching in a phrase a romantic and symbolist obsession; but for the Decadent there was an equal truth to be found in a converse speculation: might not beauty, he wondered, be the mother of death, might not there be some remorseless progression from the kind of life that art demanded to the ignominious and unresolved oblivion that would follow it? The Decadent's concern with his own demise was precipitated by uncertainties about the nature of the artistic life, and it is these that *Salomé* explores.

Notwithstanding the wealth of contextual material to be found in Mario Praz's *Romantic Agony* (1933) and the many insights in Frank Kermode's *Romantic Image* (1957), it may still be hard for us to respond to Wilde's play seriously, knowing of the several rival treatments of the theme, and perhaps concurring with the opinion that in the hands of Richard Strauss an overwritten drama became a powerful opera. Thanks in part to Aubrey Beardsley, who provided a famous set of illustrations to the published text, and to the busy imaginations of set designers, *Salomé* comes to us as the epitome of kitsch. But there can be no doubt that Wilde himself took his play with the utmost seriousness. Whatever the precise influences upon him (and scholars are still divided on the question) his choice of subject was not simply opportunist; nor was his choice of language—he wrote the play in French—a mere whim. Wilde deliberately sought the kind of hieratic cadence and monotonous simplicity most satisfactorily achieved in French symbolist poetry and drama. His belief in the artistic integrity of the play was ironically confirmed when the English censor forebade its perform-

ance in London on the ground of sacrilege, even though rehearsals were already underway with Sarah Bernhardt in the title role. Wilde's threat to leave the country in protest was not entirely empty.

When *Salomé* was published in French in 1893 (an English translation did not appear until the following year), the reviewers greeted it as an entirely representative product of Decadence. "It belongs indeed to the black art," wrote Richard Le Gallienne, then a gauche but ambitious young literary man. "Its motives are monstrous, its colour is evil, its language is lovely and accursed, the very harlotry of language. . . ." Le Gallienne continued in facetious vein with a summary of plot and character. Herodias is an unimaginative worldly creature. The moon is like the moon, that's all, she says. . . . And amid all the various interests comes the refrain of Jokanaan's voice from his pit proclaiming the day of the Lord. Herod inquires as to who this Son of Man is, and is told of the miracles at Cana and Capernaum and of his raising the dead. Mr. Wilde is amusing here. Herod exclaims that he has no objection to Christ's changing water into wine, and healing the blind—on the whole they are meritorious actions—but he cannot allow him to raise the dead. It would be terrible if the dead were to return!

To this account Wilde replied with some stern, fatherly rebukes:

Why is it that you describe the chill, sceptical, rationalistic Herodias as an "unimaginative worldly creature"? She is far more than that—she is reason in its tragic raiment—reason with its tragic end—and oh! Richard, why say that I am amusing, when Herod hears that in his royaume there is one who can make the dead come to life and filled with the terror at so hideous a prospect says in his insolence and his fear "that I do not allow." "It would be terrible if the dead came back."[5]

Wilde's placing of Herodias helps us to see why he thought of his play as a religious drama whose overall subject includes a clash between rational and imaginative modes of perception.

That is partly expressed in the dialogue, which plays constantly upon the different meanings of the word "look": "You would fancy she was looking for dead things"; "She has a strange look"; "He is look-

---

[5]From an unpublished letter in the William Andrews Clark Memorial Library. Le Gallienne's review appeared in the *Star* (22 February 1893).

ing at something." In *Salomé* characters are defined by the way they "look." In the major confrontation between Iokanaan and Salomé, two kinds of creative perception meet: the prophetic—aesthetics as an aspect of morality—and the imaginative—aesthetics as an aspect of sensuality. Iokanaan, the ascetic male, renounces and is destroyed; Salomé, the libidinous female, destroys, consummates, and is herself destroyed. We can interpret them as the spiritual consciousness, which attempts to transcend the call of the moment, replacing it with an apocalyptic trust in the future, and the aesthetic consciousness, whose passionate desire to capture the present negates it in the process. But an additional irony suggests the interaction of the two modes, for Salomé is associated, proleptically, with the sterile white moon, and Iokanaan is burning with a passionate black rage. The inclusive antinomies are expressed theatrically in typically symbolist fashion by continual reference to mysterious external phenomena, the moon and the wings of the angel of death. Thus the whole drama—character, decor, and language—is infused with the same set of meanings.

Although death awaits both main characters, the most benighted of all are Herod and Herodias, who are so morally and aesthetically primitive that they dare not pursue the implications of either mode of consciousness. This couple, the clumsy provokers of the action, rely upon empiricism to conceal themselves from themselves. Allowing nothing beyond their immediate needs, they deny their own possibilities, ignoring the fact that others will see in them qualities they prefer not to see in themselves. They are, in short, a pair of pragmatic philistines: Herod, a superstitious and comic voyeur who tries to control everything but his own lust; Herodias, a rationalist who mixes jealousy with self-serving politics. Far less tragic, although they are also "onlookers," are the young Syrian who sacrifices himself for Salomé, naively apostrophizing her as an image of purity, and the page who, with a possibly homosexual motive, attempts to protect the Syrian from involvement.

Which is not to suggest that this is all the play contains. *Salomé* has always attracted commentary, and convincing arguments have been put forward that it is a compromised expression of homosexual guilt, a manipulation of the incest taboo, and Wilde's attempt to expiate the opposing influences of Ruskin and Pater. As a Decadent text, however, the play is characteristic, in that art and sex become all the more compelling, and all the closer to each other, when contemplated in a mood of deathly foreboding. As Le Gallienne remarked, more wisely this time, "To those who talk of the immorality of the theme, Mr. Wilde might well ask: Is it not a virtuous act to transform evil things to beauty? Doesn't one thus, so to say, *redeem* them?" Finding beauty in ugliness was certainly a Decadent achievement, and so too was Wilde's discovery in religious and dramatic ritual of a perverse means of dramatizing his own state.

When Aubrey Beardsley provided illustrations for the play he included within them caricatures of Wilde himself—as jester and as Herod; most pertinently he turned the round moon into a cypher for the playwright's artful face. Beardsley's purpose was probably malicious, and Wilde was displeased by the illustrations; but a point had been made, and it was one that incriminated Wilde in his work in a way that he should surely have been prepared to admit. The symbolist approach aspired to an overall impersonality that would rid the drama of intrusive moral bias. If *Salomé* represents the destructive impulses of the Decadent artist, the mode of the play in which she appears aspires to a symbolic wholeness that will appease the artist's hellish solipsism. No wonder then that Wilde took his play seriously. It was his final attempt to become a dramatic writer on his own terms, that is to say, to dominate his audience by transforming the conditions of the theater. But in "The Soul of Man" he had already acknowledged that the theater is inescapably a matter of conditions, and in his four major prose dramas he was to adapt himself to its requirements.

Like Shaw's *Mrs. Warren's Profession* (1893), *Lady Windermere's Fan* relates to a topical genre exemplified by Arthur Wing Pinero's *The Second Mrs. Tanqueray* (1893), the problem play that concerns itself with the sexual morality of women. The play's originality does not lie in its plot nor, though there is much witty dialogue, in wit alone. What gives it its distinctive character is the way in which wit is seen as a part of the moral problem—an interest that links Wilde with the Restoration playwrights. Although it is customary for plays of this type to contain indolent observers (Cayley Drummle in *Mrs. Tanqueray*, Praed in *Mrs. Warren*), Wilde makes more of them than is usually the case and aligns them more generally with other characters. In *Lady Windermere's Fan* the life-style of the dandy, Lord Darlington, becomes a practical option: "If you pretend to be good," he says, "the world takes you very seriously. If you pretend to be bad, it doesn't." This sense of the witty deceit that escapes the hypocrisy of society is shared by almost everyone in the play except the puritanical heroine Lady Windermere, and indeed in Wilde's plays many of the characters sound like Wilde himself. In the dramatic rendering of social convention, the spoils logically go to the person who manipulates his role with the greatest ingenuity, who dupes all the other role-players. Wit is an aspect of this role-playing because it disengages the speaker from the responsibilities of his own identity, and exploits the naive view that upholds the value of sincerity. Yet the play undeniably contains melodramatic and sentimental passages where wit is most noticeable by its absence, and even Darlington is soon arguing, admittedly while attempting to seduce Lady Windermere, that the opinion of the world is of less importance than love. In its final reversals the play is equivocal. Mrs. Erlynne, a woman who has atoned for her dubious past with an act of noble self-sacrifice, chooses to suppress her true feelings behind a brittle façade—a wise person knows that being good means allowing society to think you bad—and Lady Windermere comes to realize that concealment and compromise, if not actual dissembling, are sometimes morally inevitable. She emerges somewhat more tolerant and correspondingly advanced.

In Wilde's next play, *A Woman of No Importance* (1894), we have another dandy, Lord Illingworth; another puritanical young woman, Hester Worsley; and a genuine fallen woman, Mrs. Arbuthnot, whose son, Gerald, is the focus of the drama. In the space of a single day Gerald is offered a position as Lord Illingworth's companion-secretary and discovers that his would-be employer is not only his father but is also attempting to seduce Hester, with whom Gerald is in love. These main characters are surrounded by a bevy of society ladies whose subversive wit confirms the difficulty of performing an authentic act. If Gerald is to reach maturity his only hope is to renounce the cynicism of Lord Illingworth and the society that admires it, without sacrificing his intelligence and gaiety. Guided by his mother, who refuses Lord Illingworth's belated offer of marriage, Gerald opts for morality, but on the basis of experience rather than of innocence.

Gerald's potential might appear to be realized in *An Ideal Husband* (1899) by Lord Goring, a dandy who comes to the aid of his friend Robert Chiltern, a rising young politician. Chiltern is being blackmailed about his past connections with the late Baron Arnheim, an unscrupulous financier; and Chiltern's wife, yet another idealistic puritan, insists that he make a public confession. In conversation with Goring, Chiltern cannot bring himself to deny the fascination that Arnheim's career still holds for him. Indeed he describes their relationship in terms that are reminiscent of that between Lord Henry Wotton and Dorian Gray. But whereas Lord Henry preached "the New Hedonism," the cultivation of sensual pleasure, Baron Arnheim had seduced the young Chiltern with a doctrine based upon the accumulation of power and money. This has acquired heroic proportions in Chiltern's memory. (One is reminded of the financial overreaching of Bernick in Henrik Ibsen's *The Pillars of Society* [1877]: Wilde probably wanted his audience to recognize the type with all its sinister attractions.) Chiltern is torn between lingering admiration for the courage of the ambitious rule-breaker and pitiful attempts to redeem his past through beneficent political acts. Either way, as Goring points out, he is allowing himself to be defined by the rules of society. Goring calls Arnheim's creed "thoroughly shallow"; nevertheless he realizes that the Chilterns must be rescued, and he carries this mission out successfully despite the risks to his own reputation.

Goring's altruism is enough to make one wonder if he should be counted among the dandies at all. He is supremely sensitive to the fluctuations of his own behavior and unswerving in his conviction that it is deference to the idealistic pretensions of public opinion that destroys personal integrity, but he represents a considerable departure from Lord Illingworth. Wilde's initial stage direction—"He is fond of being misunderstood. It gives him a point of vantage"—although carrying the familiar ring of dandyism, is virtually contradicted at a later stage when Goring himself remarks: "I am always saying what I shouldn't say. In fact, I usually say what I really think. A great mistake nowadays. It makes one so liable to be understood."

At the close of the play the Chiltern marriage has been saved, and Goring's own marriage is imminent. Chiltern will continue in politics, a chastened though not necessarily changed man, for he has recanted only his deeds and not the principles upon which they were based. Private values have been restored without any major disturbance to the public system.

What has changed is Wilde's sense of the dandy's

scope. At the very end Goring's fiancée offers him the freedom to "be what he chooses." But we already know that Goring's chosen role is to be a drastically limited one. In reply to his father's remonstrances at his lack of career he has replied, "I prefer it domestic" (an ironical echo of the claim that Wilde had made about *The Sphinx*, that it would "destroy domesticity"). Goring is the most attractive, alternately the most brilliant and the most candid, of all Wilde's surrogates. But this candor is achieved only by presuming a sentimental connection between the realms of human value (love) and public achievement (the great career). The dandy has been driven into a corner; he has triumphed over the moment but now he must retire; his function is fulfilled, and unfortunately it is left to the morally feeble Chilterns to lead society into the future.

An Ideal Husband is quite as eager to expose the "claims of the ideal" as any of Ibsen's plays—at least as they had been interpreted by Shaw—and quite as critical of the coercion that social ambitions exercise upon those people who are misguided enough to respect them. But exposure is as far as Wilde will allow himself to go. Those critics who have variously suggested that Goring fulfills the individualistic ethic foretold in "The Soul of Man," or that he has no need to develop, underestimate the significance of his disappearing act. Goring, wise and honorable man though he is, can have only a marginal claim on our admiration: secure in his inherited rank, sustained by his private income, cushioned by a tolerant wife and understanding valet, he passes into the land of dreams, a smile of sweet insouciance upon his face.

IX

COMEDY is like ignorance as defined by Lady Bracknell: "a delicate exotic fruit; touch it and the bloom is gone." Critics have always claimed, with something like relief, that Wilde's last and greatest play, *The Importance of Being Earnest* (1899), achieves the summit of comic form without the vestigial blemishes of moralism and sentimentality that had marred the earlier plays—a perfection so complete that comment is almost unnecessary. And it is certainly true that the plot precisely fits the traditional requirements of comedy: there is a lost heir miraculously recovered, there is pairing (cousins and brothers), there is a pastoral interlude, there is con-

tinual misidentity. But the presence of these elements proves little in itself—most can also be found in Dion Boucicault's *London Assurance* (1841), for instance, which Wilde may well have had in mind. At the same time critics have enjoyed pointing out that aspects of the play can be related to its author's own activities: that Jack's habit of "Bunburying," for example—avoiding family duties on the pretext of visiting a sick friend—matches the double life that Wilde himself had been living. This makes the play a fantasy about a fantasy: Jack is discovered, as Wilde was to be, but unlike Wilde he survives. The optimism of *The Importance* embraces the dream that duplicity will go unpunished, that everybody's best interests will finally coincide, that reconciliation is the natural order of things. Here pessimism is an attitude that belongs exclusively to the lower orders, who nevertheless obey their masters.

But the secret meanings have never interfered with the play's popularity: it has an immediate reference that gives it distinction within the genre. The miraculous symmetry holds more than a merely personal relationship to the world as Wilde knew it. For Wilde it was "a fanciful, absurd comedy," "so trivial, so irresponsible," but *The Importance* is trivial only in the sense that it laughs at irreducible problems, and absurd in the classic fashion, in that it turns the world upside down. The play is structured as a gigantic paradox in which Wilde's hierarchy of types finds itself the right way up. The dandies are now the true creators of society, who drag even the puritans and the cliché-mongers (Chasuble and Prism) behind them. They invent a world that matches their own needs, and reality obligingly concedes to their demands. But the needs are real enough: from first to last they are financial. Money is an obsessive concern in this play, and it is only when the need for money coincides with its availability that we achieve the ideal state. (By a natural irony this fantasy of solvency was being contradicted by the reality of Wilde's own life even as he wrote, for he was grossly overspending.) Money actually changes the way things look, so that Lady Bracknell's reaction on being told of Cecily's fortune is entirely to the point: "Miss Cardew seems to me a most attractive young lady, now that I look at her. Few girls of the present day have any really solid qualities that last, and improve with time." Inherited investments can of course be waylaid by marriage, which is an investment in heredity and in how people look. But money also changes the way things are, and sometimes things really are the way they look, as Cecily may be beginning to learn:

Chasuble: I suppose you know all about the relations between Capital and Labour. . . .

Cecily: I am afraid that I am not learned at all. All I know is about the relations between Capital and Idleness—and that is merely from observation. So I don't suppose that it is true.

Miss Prism: Cecily, that sounds like Socialism! And I suppose that you know where Socialism leads to?

Cecily: Oh, yes! That leads to Rational Dress, Miss Prism. And I suppose that when a woman is dressed rationally, she is treated rationally—She certainly deserves to be.

(Act II)[6]

But Cecily's innocent wisdom (based on some of Wilde's past enthusiasms) must be contrasted with Gwendolen's wily aesthetic ambition. Gwendolen, the girl who intends "to develop in many directions," quotes her author too: "In matters of grave importance, style, not sincerity, is the vital thing." When Wilde invokes his own past, it is in order to trick his audience into an appreciation of his own contrariness. *The Importance* delights in its display of a comic world in which appearance and reality are continually in exchange with one another; and it seems to suggest that in dealing with that world the mores of the aristocracy offer us, absurdly, the best example.

So the play gratifies a peculiarly English fantasy: it proffers an aristocratic style that successfully derides the pressing worries of the bourgeois life, demoting them to vulgar irritants. Debts are magically paid, relatives ("a sort of aggravated form of the public") are pacified, solicitors are insulted, and women are appeased. On the sunlit Hertfordshire lawns, male eccentricity is the norm, elegance an ultimate and effective defense. Riposte is all. If the nineteenth-century dandy is the bourgeois imagining himself as an aristocrat, then the aristocratic dandy redoubles the fantasy, making it all but impregnable. When Wilde subtitled his play "a serious comedy for trivial people" he was honoring us with an invitation to join a blessed company. Yet to say all this and to enthuse that *The Importance* disarms criticism is to deny it

the highest compliment—a final paradox remains for us to appreciate, a paradox within a paradox, a grave truth about the upside-down world. As Wilde's best interpreters, such as Sir John Gielgud, have realized, these people are not finally likeable. They are childish, greedy, often insulting—they are simple. The fantasy world is inhumane, only a callous snob would wish to live in it, and despite everything Wilde was not really a snob—that label among others must be reserved for the solicitor-general who, at Wilde's trial for homosexual indecency in May 1895, asked him, "What pleasure could you find in the society of boys much beneath you in social position?"

X

WE come now to the events that were to change Wilde's life utterly and that have inevitably determined the ways in which he has been remembered. *The Importance* opened on 14 January 1895 and on this, the night of Wilde's most resounding success, the marquess of Queensberry deposited a bouquet of vegetables at the theater. Soon afterward he delivered a card at Wilde's club with the misspelt message: "For Oscar Wilde posing somdomite." Wilde's answer was to sue the marquess for libel, but he lost his case when, during a remorseless cross-examination, it emerged that he had associated with well-known homosexual prostitutes. Almost immediately after the verdict was pronounced, Wilde was arrested and charged with committing indecent acts. Two trials resulted: at the first the jury failed to agree; at the second he was found guilty of several acts of gross indecency with young men and sentenced to two years' imprisonment with hard labor. The belief, on both sides, that Wilde was being tried as much for his aesthetic attitudes as for his sexual activities was greatly reinforced by the considerable use made by the prosecution of his published writings.

At first Wilde was held in London prisons, but he was soon moved to Reading, where, in spite of his friends' efforts to have his sentence commuted, he served the full term. When he emerged from the gates of Reading Gaol in May 1897 he carried with him a long handwritten letter to Douglas, which, for complicated reasons, Douglas probably never read in full. (The complete text was not in fact made public until 1962.) Later known as *De Profundis* (1905), this

[6]From the original four-act text, available in the ed. of S. A. Dickson (New York, 1956). The play is usually performed now in a reduced three-act version.

extraordinary document—which reads more like a manifesto than a personal communication—is by turns acrimonious and maudlin, nostalgic and portentous, despairing and aggressive. Although its ostensible purpose is to confront Douglas with much of the blame for the catastrophe, its psychological origin lies in Wilde's need to confront himself, and in that respect it is, alas, only partially successful. For reasons that are still not entirely clear, Wilde had taken great offense at Douglas' attempts to rally support in France, which, either by accident or design, had tended to center upon the publication of his own poems and of some of Wilde's more fulsome letters.

But it must be stressed that not once in *De Profundis* does Wilde make homosexuality per se the cause of his suffering, and the attack on Douglas refers less to his sexual conduct than to his inherited temperament: "decadence" in its simpler sense of indolence and triviality. Douglas becomes not only Wilde's evil genius but a frightening example of waste and a nightmare reflection of Wilde's own admittedly ironical "cult of idleness"—a thing, a fatal puppet whose purpose is nil, quite literally mindless. "The supreme vice is shallowness," Wilde bewails over and over; "everything that is realised is right," smothering in a Hegelian pun his old belief that only in self-consciousness does the creative act reach fruition. "To be entirely free, and at the same time entirely dominated by law, is the eternal paradox of human life that we realise at every moment," continues that same idea in an attempt to make universal, vatic, what may seem to us merely an expression of fin de siècle anguish or, more narrowly, an epitaph for Wilde's own situation. "I was a man who stood in symbolic relations to the art and culture of my age"; by turning himself into a symbol, Wilde retains yet another concept in the form that he had always known it: the symbol as multifaceted prism that, by refracting the views cast upon it, displays the ideal. So although Wilde is, as he says, "the child of my age," in his life and work he can still claim to transform the forces that have made him what he is. But *De Profundis* exposes these earlier principles to the harsh light of a prison cell.

In the preface to *Dorian Gray* Wilde had claimed that, as an artist, he could express everything. In *De Profundis* he fails to assimilate the contradictory lesson of the novel itself: expression depends upon experience, and experience is limited and affective, changing the artist even as he expresses it. All that Wilde can offer now is change as a transcendent cy-

cle, apotheosis rather than development. As for the artist, Wilde maintains that a gospel of suffering will have to replace the old gospel of hedonism, so that a universal joy can eventually be attained in some ideal future. The sacrificial model, superseded in fact, is Christ. Wilde's final prose mask is a pathetic absurdity, and one can only regret that the comedy of his self-identification is not more fully "realized." It is this protective ambivalence toward himself—passive egocentricity, epigrammatic piety—that makes Wilde's prison letter not revelation but gossip, at first embarrassing, then disappointing.

In prison Wilde endured the most extreme mental and physical discomfort. On his release he was unwilling to admit the extent of the psychological damage, but it was soon to become only too apparent. He made a brief stop in London, then journeyed to France, and the final phase began. It was to take him from Dieppe to Naples, to Rome, to Switzerland, finally to Paris. These last years present an unappealing spectacle. Wilde was plagued by financial worries, his relationship with Douglas went through a series of death throes interspersed with short periods of ecstatic reunion, he became paranoid about his friends' loyalty, and he was forever haunted by his loss of the one talent that had never previously let him down: his ability to write wittily, swiftly, fluently. For Wilde the final consolations lay not in art but in alcohol, boys, and—on his deathbed in a seedy hotel room in 1900—the Roman Catholic church. Yet it is possible to find some dignity in what he wrote after 1895: however lacrimose and distracted, the need for historical self-knowledge persisted.

The only completed piece of writing from these last years is *The Ballad of Reading Gaol* (1898). Critics have habitually complained that the poem alternates between an elegy of the human condition and a protest against the inhumanity of man-made laws. It is as if Wilde had lost his usually deft control over the transactions between actor and spectator and the multiple personality had become all but unmanageable. As the poem declares, "For he who lives more lives than one / More deaths than one must die." In his efforts to place himself in some appropriate relationship to a condemned man, Wilde suppresses the knowledge that the man's crime—murder—is of a radically different kind from his own alleged offenses. It would not be surprising, given his extreme misery, if Wilde had lost sight of ethical and legal distinctions, may perhaps even have wished to forget them. We have already noticed how, in *De Profundis*, he makes indulgence and betrayal, and not homosexuality, his crimes against himself.

Two especially puzzling stanzas seem to claim that sympathy with the criminal means identifying with the crime and hence repeating it:

> But there were those amongst us all
>   Who walked with downcast head,
> And knew that, had each got his due,
>   They should have died instead:
> He had but killed the thing that lived,
>   Whilst they had killed the dead.
>
> For he who sins a second time
>   Wakes a dead soul to pain,
> And draws it from its spotted shroud,
>   And makes it bleed again,
> And makes it bleed great gouts of blood,
>   And makes it bleed in vain!
> (*The Ballad of Reading Gaol*, pt. 4, 25–36)

The moral point here is obscure, suggesting perhaps a deeper level of sensibility than that of corporate guilt, as if Wilde were desperate to increase his alienation from the commonplace maxims, or perhaps to push beyond the comforts of vicarious emotions to the harsher realities of physical sacrifice exemplified by the crucifixion. In Wilde's work sympathy had always been a deceptive virtue that easily turned itself into a means of possession through emotional patronage, and sacrifice had already been retained for the superior man. In his final writings it is as if Wilde had to identify himself with Christ because with no other example could he do himself justice. Alternatively, in a mockery at such pretension, he would sometimes offer himself as a clumsy anomaly, "like ape or clown." On the seesaw of personality there was no longer any chance of poise, only an endless sickening alternation of roles. One section of *The Ballad* echoes *The Harlot's House*, reconvening the images of the dance of death in order to present the prison as a deterministic hell in which the structure of a microcosmic social life takes on the patterned finality of a doomed universe.

The emotional vertigo of Wilde's last poem is counterbalanced by two letters that he wrote to the *Daily Chronicle* protesting against prison conditions: these are full of a passionate common sense. Although it may have been inevitable that in the process of dramatizing his own isolation he turned sympathy into a deadly thing, in his daily practice Wilde,

paradoxical to the end, was too spontaneous a man ever to carry the principle through, too scrupulously aware of the fortunate discrepancies between the possibilities of art and the more pressing claims of life. Our own sympathetic response, prompted by the lasting power of its refrain—"each man kills the thing he loves"—must be to say that *The Ballad* reproduces the perplexities born of moral desperation.

Yet it is more than sympathy that Oscar Wilde inspires in us today; it is gratitude. In any optimistic reckoning of the way we live now there is a considerable debt to be paid to him. At a time when it seemed to many that a creative life could be lived only by the individual artist cut off from his audience, Wilde's literary strategies, for all their contradictions, their lingering idealism, and their tendency to take refuge in mere antithesis, were a bold response to intolerable options. History may yet confirm the prediction for Wilde that an American poet recently ascribed to Walt Whitman:

> Maybe yours will be an essential life—
>   one needing *to have been lived*![7]

SELECTED BIBLIOGRAPHY

I. Bibliography. "Stuart Mason" [C. S. Millard], *A Bibliography of the Poems* (London, 1907); *Two Hundred Books from the Library of Richard Butler Glaenzer* (New York, 1911); "Stuart Mason" [C. S. Millard], *Bibliography* (London, 1914), reprinted (London, 1967) with intro. by T. d'A. Smith, still the standard bibliography; *A Collection of the Original Manuscripts, Letters and Books of Oscar Wilde* (London, 1928), catalog of Dulau and Co., Booksellers, lists material from the collections of Robert Ross, C. S. Millard, and Vyvyan Holland; *Catalogue of an Exhibition of Books and Manuscripts in Commemoration of the Centenary of the Birth of Oscar Wilde* (Dublin, 1954); A. Horodisch, *Oscar Wilde's "Ballad of Reading Gaol": A Bibliographical Study* (New York, 1954); J. C. Finzi, *Oscar Wilde and His Literary Circle. A Catalog of Manuscripts and Letters in the William Andrews Clark Memorial Library* (Berkeley and Los Angeles, 1957), supersedes an earlier catalog, *The Library of William Andrews Clark, Wilde and Wildeana* (1922); *Wilde and the 90s* (Princeton, N. J., 1966), exhibition catalog; R. J. Finneran,

---

[7]From R. Howard, "Wild Flowers," in his *Two-Part Inventions* (New York, 1974).

ed., *Anglo-Irish Literature. A Review of Research* (New York, 1976), contains an extensive bibliographical essay by I. Fletcher and J. Stokes, a suppl. is in progress; E. H. Mikhail, *Oscar Wilde. An Annotated Bibliography of Criticism* (London, 1978), the most complete bibliography of secondary material.

II. COLLECTED EDITIONS. *The Writings of Oscar Wilde*, 15 vols. (New York, 1907); R. B. Ross, ed., *The Works of Oscar Wilde*, 14 vols. (London, 1908), an additional vol. containing the apocryphal *For the Love of the King* published in 1922; *The Works of Oscar Wilde*, 12 vols. (New York, 1923), individual vols. contain intros. by W. B. Yeats, A. Symons, and others; G. F. Maine, ed., *The Works of Oscar Wilde* (London and Glasgow, 1948); *Complete Works of Oscar Wilde*, with intro. by V. Holland, new ed. (London–Glasgow, 1966).

III. SELECTED WORKS. *Oscariana: Epigrams* (London, 1895), aphorisms supposedly chosen by Mrs. Wilde; R. B. Ross, ed., *Selected Poems* (London, 1911); R. B. Ross, ed., *Selected Prose* (London, 1914); H. Pearson, ed., *Plays, Prose Writings and Poems* (London, 1930); G. de Saix, ed., *Les Songes Merveilleux du Dormeur Éveillé. Le Chant du Cygne: Contes parlés d'Oscar Wilde* (Paris, 1942; New York, 1979), stories, prose poems, etc., reputedly told by Wilde; R. Aldington, ed., *Selected Works* (London, 1946); H. Pearson, ed., *Essays* (London, 1950); K. Amis, ed., *Poems and Essays* (London, 1956); R. Ellmann, ed., *Selected Writings* (London, 1961); R. Ellmann, ed., *The Artist as Critic* (London, 1968), the major critical essays together with a selection of little-known reviews; S. Weintraub, ed., *The Literary Criticism of Oscar Wilde* (Lincoln, Neb., 1968), a selection of Wilde's reviews; I. Murray, ed., *Plays, Prose Writings and Poems* (London, 1975); R. Gasson, ed., *The Illustrated Oscar Wilde* (London, 1977); I. Murray, ed., *Complete Shorter Fiction* (London, 1979).

IV. SEPARATE WORKS. *Newdigate Prize Poem: "Ravenna"* (Oxford, 1878); *Vera; or, The Nihilists* (London, 1880), drama; *Poems* (London, 1881); *The Duchess of Padua* (London, 1883), drama, first published in Paris (1905), repr. 1908; *The Happy Prince and Other Tales* (London, 1888); *Intentions* (London, 1891), essays; *The Picture of Dorian Gray* (London, 1891), novel, originally appeared in a different version in *Lippincott's Monthly* magazine (July 1890); *Lord Arthur Savile's Crime, and Other Stories* (London, 1891); *A House of Pomegranates* (London, 1891), story; *Lady Windermere's Fan* (London, 1893), drama, produced 1892, also in I. Small, ed. (London, 1980), annotated with an important intro. and cross-references to various versions; *Salomé* (Paris, 1893), drama, English trans. by Lord A. Douglas (London, 1894); *The Sphinx* (London, 1894), verse; *A Woman of No Importance* (London, 1894), drama, produced 1893; *The Soul of Man* (London, 1895), essay, privately printed, originally published as "The Soul of Man Under Socialism" in *Fortnightly Review* (February 1891); *The Ballad of Reading Gaol*, by "C.3.3" (London, 1898), verse; *The Importance of Being Earnest*, three-act version (London, 1899), drama, produced 1895, also in R. Jackson, ed. (London, 1980), annotated ed. of 1899 text with an important intro. and cross-references to various other versions; *An Ideal Husband* (London, 1899), drama, produced 1895.

Essays, Criticisms, and Reviews (London, 1901), privately printed; *De Profundis* (London, 1905), autobiography, an incomplete text, a supposedly complete and accurate version edited and introduced by V. Holland appeared in 1949, but the only reliable text is printed by R. Hart-Davis in *The Letters* (1962); *The Harlot's House* (London, 1905), poem; *The Rise of Historical Criticism* (Hartford, Conn., 1905), essay; R. B. Glaenzer, ed., *Decorative Art in America: A Lecture* (New York, 1906), criticism; "Stuart Mason" [C. S. Millard], ed., *Impressions of America* (Sunderland, 1906); *Constance*, intro. by G. de Saix, in *Les Oeuvres Libres*, no. 101 (Paris, 1954), a play based on Wilde's scenario; *Mr. and Mrs. Daventry*, by F. Harris, intro. by H. Montgomery Hyde (London, 1956), a play based on Wilde's scenario; S. A. Dickson, ed., *The Importance of Being Earnest*, 2 vols. (New York, 1956), four-act version, with facs. of the original MS; *The Portrait of Mr. W. H.* (London, 1958), story, complete version with intro. by V. Holland, originally published 1889; M. Ewing, ed., *Remorse: A Study in Saffron* (Los Angeles, 1961); W. Edener, ed., *The Picture of Dorian Gray* (Nürnberg, 1964), the *Lippincott's* text with variorum notes; *Irish Poets and the Poetry of the Nineteenth Century* (San Francisco, 1972), an 1882 lecture reconstructed by R. D. Pepper; "The House Beautiful: A Reconstruction of Oscar Wilde's American Lecture," by K. H. F. O'Brien, *Victorian Studies* 17 (June 1974); I. Murray, ed., *The Picture of Dorian Gray* (London, 1974), with informative intro. and textual notes; *Some Early Poems and Fragments* (Edinburgh, 1974).

V. LETTERS. *Wilde v. Whistler* (London, 1906), their published exchanges; R. Hart-Davis, ed., *The Letters of Oscar Wilde* (London, 1962), masterly ed., the most important source for all aspects of Wilde's life and work, supersedes all previous selections of the letters, except when they contain significant intros.; R. Hart-Davis, ed., *Selected Letters of Oscar Wilde* (London, 1979).

VI. BIOGRAPHICAL AND CRITICAL STUDIES. R. H. Sherard, *Oscar Wilde: The Story of an Unhappy Friendship* (London, 1902, 1905); F. Blei, ed., *In Memoriam Oscar Wilde* (Leipzig, 1905), contains essays by E. La-Jeunesse, A. Symons, and F. Blei; R. H. Sherard, *The Life of Oscar Wilde* (London, 1906); *Recollections of Oscar Wilde* (Boston-London, 1906), trans. and intro. by P. Pollard, a variation of *In Memoriam Oscar Wilde*; L. C. Ingleby, *Oscar Wilde* (London, 1907), see also Ingleby's *Oscar Wilde: Some Reminiscences* (London, 1922); St. J. Hankin, "The Collected Plays of Oscar Wilde," in *Fortnightly Review*, n.s. 83 (May 1908).

R. Laurent, *Études Anglaises* (Paris, 1910), contains essay on Wilde; Anna, comtesse de Brémont, *Oscar Wilde and His Mother: A Memoir* (London, 1911); "Stuart

Mason" [C. S. Millard], *Oscar Wilde: Art and Morality* (London, 1912), newspaper correspondence and other material relating to *Dorian Gray;* A. Ransome, *Oscar Wilde: A Critical Study* (London, 1922); "Stuart Mason" [C. S. Millard], *Oscar Wilde: Three Times Tried* (London, 1912); W. W. Kenilworth, *A Study of Oscar Wilde* (New York, 1912); R. T. Hopkins, *Oscar Wilde: A Study of the Man and His Work* (London, 1913); E. Bendz, *The Influence of Pater and Matthew Arnold in the Prose Writings of Oscar Wilde* (Göteburg, 1914); A. Douglas, *Oscar Wilde and Myself* (London, 1914); A. Wood, "Oscar Wilde as Critic," in *North American Review* 202 (December 1915); F. Harris, *Oscar Wilde: His Life and Confessions* (New York, 1916), entertaining but unreliable account of Harris' dealings with Wilde, later eds. include a comment by G. B. Shaw; E. Saltus, *Oscar Wilde: An Idler's Impression* (Chicago, 1917); R. H. Sherard, *The Real Oscar Wilde* (London, 1917).

"Stuart Mason" [C. S. Millard], *Oscar Wilde and the Aesthetic Movement* (Dublin, 1920); E. Bendz, *Oscar Wilde: A Retrospect* (Vienna, 1921); L. Housman, *Echo de Paris. A Study from Life* (London, 1923), contains a convincing evocation of Wilde's manner of speech; L. F. Choisy, *Oscar Wilde* (Paris, 1927); H. Davray, *Oscar Wilde: La Tragédie finale* (Paris, 1928); *The Autobiography of Lord Alfred Douglas* (London, 1929).

P. Braybrooke, *Oscar Wilde: A Study* (London, 1930); A. Symons, *A Study of Oscar Wilde* (London, 1930); L. Lemonnier, *La Vie d'Oscar Wilde* (Paris, 1931); A. J. Farmer, *Le Mouvement Esthétique et "Décadent" en Angleterre 1873–1900* (Paris, 1931); L. Lemonnier, "La Condamnation de Oscar Wilde et l'opinion française," in *Revue Mondiale* 102 (January 1931); "J. P. Raymond" and C. S. Ricketts, *Oscar Wilde: Recollections* (London, 1932); M. Praz, *Romantic Agony* (London, 1933; 2nd ed., 1951), repr. with new forward by F. Kermode (1970); G. J. Renier, *Oscar Wilde* (London, 1933); K. Hartley, *Oscar Wilde: L'Influence française dans son oeuvre* (Paris, 1935); M. L. Cazamian, *Le Roman et les idées en Angleterre* (Paris, 1935), has good discussion of *Dorian Gray;* J. Charbonnier, "L'Intellectualisme d'Oscar Wilde," in *Revue Anglo-Américaine* 12 (August 1935); V. O'Sullivan, *Aspects of Wilde* (London, 1936); L. Lewis and J. Smith, *Oscar Wilde Discovers America* (New York, 1936), still the best account of the U.S. tours; L. Lemonnier, *Oscar Wilde* (Paris, 1938); B. Brasol, *Oscar Wilde: The Man—The Artist* (London, 1938); Lord A. Douglas, *Without Apology* (London, 1938).

F. Winwar, *Oscar Wilde and the Yellow Nineties* (London, 1940); Lord A. Douglas, *Oscar Wilde. A Summing Up* (London, 1940); H. Pearson, *The Life of Oscar Wilde* (London, 1946), one of the better biographies; E. Roditi, *Oscar Wilde* (Norfolk, Conn., 1947); R. Merle, *Oscar Wilde* (Paris, 1948); H. Montgomery Hyde, *The Trials of Oscar Wilde* (London, 1948; new and enl. ed., 1962, repr. 1973),

still the classic treatment of the trials; G. Woodcock, *The Paradox of Oscar Wilde* (London, 1948); G. Hough, *The Last Romantics* (London, 1949); A. Gide, *Oscar Wilde* (London, 1949), collects in translation Gide's various discussions of Wilde; the marquess of Queensberry and P. Colson, *Oscar Wilde and the Black Douglas* (London, 1949).

H. Montgomery Hyde, *Cases that Changed the Law* (London, 1951); St. J. Ervine, *Oscar Wilde: A Present Time Appraisal* (London, 1951); G. C. Leroy, *Perplexed Prophets* (Philadelphia, 1953), contains section on Wilde; A. Ojala, "Aestheticism and Oscar Wilde," in *Annales Academiae Scientarum Finnicae*, 2 vols. (Helsinki, 1954–1955); V. Holland, *Son of Oscar Wilde* (London, 1954); *Adam* 22 (1954), special Oscar Wilde issue; A. Harris, "Oscar Wilde as Playwright: A Centenary Review," in *Adelphi* 30 (May 1954); R. Merle, *Oscar Wilde; ou la "Destinée" de l'homosexuel* (Paris, 1955); A. Wilson, "Oscar Wilde," in *London* magazine 2 (February 1955), searching investigation of Wilde's personality and sense of comedy; J. D. Thomas, "Oscar Wilde's Prose and Poetry," *Rice Institute Pamphlet* no. 42 (October 1955); O. Reinert, "Satiric Strategy in *The Importance of Being Earnest*," in *College English* 18 (October 1956); M. Peckham, "What Did Lady Windermere Learn?" in *College English* 18 (October 1956); R. Foster, "Wilde as Parodist: A Second Look at *The Importance of Being Earnest*," in *College English* 18 (October 1956); F. Kermode, *Romantic Image* (New York, 1957; ppbk ed., 1961); A. West, *The Mountain and the Sunlight* (London, 1958), contains a perceptive ch. on Wilde; B. Ford, ed., *The Penguin Guide to English Literature* 6 (London, 1958), contains "The Last Phase" by A. E. Rodway, which has sensible comments on Wilde's poetry; V. O'Sullivan, *Opinions* (London, 1959).

V. Holland, *Oscar Wilde: A Pictorial Biography* (London, 1960); T. R. Spivey, "Damnation and Salvation in *The Picture of Dorian Gray*," in *Boston University Studies in English* 4 (Autumn 1960); A. Ganz, "The Divided Self in the Society Comedies of Oscar Wilde," in *Modern Drama* 3 (May 1960); E. B. Partridge, "The Importance of Not Being Earnest," in *Bucknell Review* 9 (May 1960); R. Croft-Cooke, *Bosie: The Story of Lord Alfred Douglas* (London, 1963); H. Montgomery Hyde, *Oscar Wilde: The Aftermath* (London, 1963); V. Wyndham, *The Sphinx and Her Circle. A Memoir of Ada Leverson* (London, 1963); B. Charlesworth, *Dark Passages: The Decadent Consciousness in Victorian Literature* (Madison–Milwaukee, 1965), contains ch. on Wilde; H. Schiff, "Nature and Art in Oscar Wilde's *Decay of Lying*," in *English Studies* 18 (1965); J. D. Thomas, "*The Soul of Man Under Socialism*: An Essay in Context," in *Rice University Studies* 51 (Winter 1965); S. Sontag, *Against Interpretation* (New York, 1966), contains her essay "Notes on Camp"; I. Gregor, "Comedy and Oscar Wilde," in *Sewanee Review* 74 (April–June 1966), perhaps the best single essay on the plays; B. Borelius,

"Oscar Wilde, Whistler and Colours," in *Scripta Minora* 3 (1966–1967); E. San Juan, *The Art of Oscar Wilde* (Princeton, N. J., 1967); R. Ellmann, *Eminent Domain* (London, 1967), contains a subtle exploration of Wilde's influence on Yeats; T. de V. White, *The Parents of Oscar Wilde* (London, 1967), largely supersedes earlier books on the Wilde family; J. B. Gordon, "'Parody as Initiation': The Sad Education of Dorian Gray," in *Criticism* 9 (Fall 1967), first of Gordon's several discussions of the novel; J. Korg, "The Rage of Caliban," in *University of Toronto Quarterly* 37 (1967), on *Dorian Gray*; J. Lester, *Journey through Despair* (Princeton, N.J., 1968), contains discussion of Wilde; A. J. A. Symons, *Essays and Biographies* (London, 1969), contains three chs. on Wilde; P. Jullian, *Oscar Wilde* (London, 1969), an unreliable, gossipy biography; R. Ellmann, ed., *Oscar Wilde: A Collection of Critical Essays* (Englewood Cliffs, N. J., 1969); J. D. Thomas, "The Intentional Strategy in Oscar Wilde's Dialogues," in *English Literature in Transition* 12 (1969).

K. Beckson, ed., *Oscar Wilde: The Critical Heritage* (London, 1970), good selection of contemporary reviews; J. A. Ware, "Algernon's Appetite: Oscar Wilde's Hero as a Restoration Dandy," in *English Literature in Transition* 13 (1970); P. Rieff, "The Impossible Culture: Oscar Wilde and the Charisma of the Artist," in *Encounter* 35 (September 1970); L. J. Poteet, "Romantic Aesthetics in Oscar Wilde's *Mr. W. H.*," in *Studies in Short Fiction* 7 (Summer 1970); R. J. Jordan, "Satire and Fantasy in Wilde's *The Importance of Being Earnest*," in *Ariel* 1 (July 1970); J. B. Gordon, "Wilde and Newman: The Confessional Mode," in *Renascence* 22 (Summer 1970), the best analysis of *De Profundis*; W. V. Harris, "Arnold, Pater and Wilde and the Object As in Themselves They See It," in *Studies in English Literature, 1500–1900* 11 (Autumn 1971); K. Richards and P. Thomson, eds., *Nineteenth Century Drama* (London, 1971), contains J. W. Donohue, Jr., "The First Production of *The Importance of Being Earnest*: A Proposal for a Reconstructive Study"; R. Croft-Cooke, *The Unrecorded Life of Oscar Wilde* (London, 1972); J. E. Chamberlin, "Oscar Wilde and the Importance of Doing Nothing," in *Hudson Review* 25 (Summer 1972); N. Joost and F. E. Court, "*Salomé*, the Moon and Oscar Wilde's Aesthetics: A Reading of the Play," in *Papers on Language and Literature* 8, suppl. (Fall 1972); I. Murray, "Some Elements in the Composition of *The Picture of Dorian Gray*," in *Durham University Journal* 64 (June 1972), compares the 1890 and 1891 texts.

R. Ellmann, *Golden Codgers* (London, 1973), important essays on *Salomé*, Wilde as critic, and Wilde and Gide; M. Fido, *Oscar Wilde* (London, 1973); H. Sussman, "Criticism as Art: Form in Oscar Wilde's Critical Writings," in *Studies in Philology* 70 (January 1973); R. J. Green, "Oscar Wilde's *Intentions*: An Early Modernist Manifesto," in *British Journal of Aesthetics* 13 (Autumn 1973); C. Nassaar, *Into the Demon Universe* (New Haven, Conn.–London, 1974), has

useful insights despite an overstrained thesis; D. Parker, "Oscar Wilde's Great Farce: *The Importance of Being Earnest*," in *Modern Language Quarterly* 35 (June 1974); A. Gardner, "Oscar Wilde's Swansong," in *Dalhousie Review* 55 (Spring 1974), reading of *The Ballad of Reading Gaol*; H. Montgomery Hyde, *Oscar Wilde. A Biography* (London, 1975), the most detailed and trustworthy life so far; J. de Langlade, *Oscar Wilde, écrivain français* (Paris, 1975), Wilde's influence on French writers.

S. Morley, *Oscar Wilde* (London, 1976); E. Bentley, "The Homosexual Question," in *Canadian Theatre Review* 12 (Fall 1976), argues that the condemnation of Wilde was ideologically motivated; D. J. Spininger, "Profiles and Principles: The Sense of the Absurd in *The Importance of Being Earnest*," in *Papers on Language and Literature* 12 (Winter 1976); G. Stone, "Serious Bunburyism: The Logic of *The Importance of Being Earnest*," in *Essays in Criticism* 26 (January 1976); J. Meyers, *Homosexuality and Literature 1890–1930* (London, 1977), contains ch. on *Dorian Gray*; R. Shewan, *Oscar Wilde. Art and Egoism* (London, 1977), ingenious criticism and diligent new research; R. Ellmann and J. Espey, *Oscar Wilde. Two Approaches* (Los Angeles, 1977); A. Bird, *The Plays of Oscar Wilde* (London, 1977), surveys the complete dramatic output; J. E. Chamberlin, *Ripe Was the Drowsy Hour: The Age of Oscar Wilde* (New York, 1977), stimulating attempt to discuss the aesthetic and historical implications of Wilde's ideas; D. Lodge, *The Modes of Modern Writing* (London, 1977), contains an unusual reading of *The Ballad of Reading Gaol*; D. H. Eriksen, *Oscar Wilde* (New York, 1977), critical biography; B. Bashford, "Oscar Wilde, His Criticism and His Critics," in *English Literature in Transition* 20 (1977); P. K. Cohen, *The Moral Vision of Oscar Wilde* (Cranbury, N.J., 1978), fairly conventional literary criticism; K. Worth, *The Irish Drama of Europe from Yeats to Beckett* (London, 1978), has an interesting ch. on *Salomé*; M. S. Helfand and P. E. Smith, "Anarchy and Culture. The Evolutionary Turn of Cultural Criticism in the Work of Oscar Wilde," in *Texas Studies in Literature and Language* 20 (Summer 1978), makes use of Wilde's unpublished notebooks; E. Bentley, "Lord Alfred's Lover," in *Canadian Theatre Review* 18 (Spring 1978), a play; K. Powell, "Oscar Wilde 'Acting': The Medium as Message in *The Picture of Dorian Gray*," in *Dalhousie Review* 58 (1978–1979); B. Bashford, "Oscar Wilde and Subjectivist Criticism," in *English Literature in Transition* 21 (1978).

E. H. Mikhail, ed., *Oscar Wilde. Interviews and Recollections*, 2 vols. (London, 1979); T. Wratislaw, *Oscar Wilde, A Memoir* (London, 1979), with an apt intro. and notes by K. Beckson; J. McCormack, "Masks Without Faces: The Personalities of Oscar Wilde," in *English Literature in Transition* 22 (1979); R. K. Martin, "Oscar Wilde and the Fairy Tale: 'The Happy Prince' as Self-Dramatization," in *Studies in Short Fiction* 16 (Winter 1979); B. Fong, "Oscar Wilde: Five Fugitive Pieces," in

English Literature in Transition 22 (1979); H. Kail, "The Other Half of the Garden: Oscar Wilde's *De Profundis* and the Confessional Tradition," in *Prose Studies 1800–1900* 2 (1979); M. C. Kotzin, "'The Selfish Giant' as Literary Fairy Tale," in *Studies in Short Fiction* 16 (Fall 1979); N. Kohl, *Oscar Wilde. Das Literarische Werk zwischen Provokation und Anpassung* (Heidelberg, 1980), immense survey of Wilde's works with copious references to other critics; K. Powell, "Hawthorne, Arlo Bates and *The Picture of Dorian Gray*," in *Papers on Language and Literature* 16 (1980), intriguing source material; L. Dowling, "Imposture and Absence in Wilde's 'Portrait of Mr. W. H.,'" in *Victorian Newsletter* 58 (Fall 1980), an outstanding piece of "deconstructive" criticism; J. C. Oates, "*The Picture of Dorian Gray*: Wilde's Parable of the Fall," *Critical Inquiry* 7 (Winter 1980); M. Nichols, *The Importance of Being Oscar* (London, 1981), biographical narrative based upon Wilde's witticisms.

GEORGE GISSING

(1857-1903)

A. C. Ward

"WHO are the men that *do* things?" cries Captain Shotover in Bernard Shaw's *Heartbreak House,* and answers his own question: "The husbands of the shrew and of the drunkard, the men with the thorn in the flesh."

No thought of George Gissing is at all likely to have been in Shaw's mind when he made that generalization, yet it is exactly applicable to Gissing. He was the husband of a drunkard and, twice, of a shrew, and the thorn of poverty was his almost lifelong torment. But though the story of Gissing's life lends itself to use as a cautionary tale with an adjustable moral, those who have wished it other than it was have been moved by considerations unrelated to literature. Since his death in 1903 he has been the object of commiseration and condemnation alike: moralists attribute his miseries to his own faults and follies; others ascribe them to injustices of the social system.

Students of literature, however, grow accustomed to the necessity of accepting each and every author as the creature he is—saint or sinner or whatever grade of human character between those extremes. If we proceed to ethical judgment, we must conclude that, for example, Lord Byron and Percy Bysshe Shelley were scoundrels, and be horrified because Sir Thomas Malory—purveyor of the Arthurian stories that have occasioned high spiritual aspirations in many during the past five centuries—was guilty of murder, rape, sacrilege, and repeated robbery with violence. Appreciation of an author's writings does not usually depend upon familiarity with his personal life story, yet no writer is able to make a complete separation between his creative impulses and his individual experience of living: there is inevitable, if not obtruded, interaction. With George Gissing there was more than interaction, there was the closest interweaving. Although there is certainly no need for morbid dwelling on the facts that in early life he was a convicted thief and in his last years a bigamist, his deeds and his daily experiences were aspects of his character and determined the nature of his work. Despite theft and bigamy, Gissing was no scoundrel: both of these offenses were committed in the service of respectability—the respectability of others.

Gissing was, intellectually, a man of inflexible high principle, but he was constantly at odds with himself. Inhabiting the present, he was nevertheless homesick for the past; in theory a socialist, he was in fact a born and unchanging individualist; goaded by an urgent desire for companionship, he was yet thwarted by an instinctive need for solitude; though devoted to the cause of the underprivileged masses through an abstract sense of political justice, his fastidious nature was repelled and disgusted by the crudity of their speech and their animal habits.

As a novelist Gissing was sincere, solid, and animated by strict purposes. During his lifetime and since his death, a substantial minority have rated him as an unfairly neglected author, one to whose powers and principles justice must ultimately be rendered. As time passes and he is viewed in freedom from the irrelevant prejudices and preconceptions of contemporary majority opinion, it may well appear that the four-square honesty of his work is a virtue outweighing the disadvantage that he was inclined to be mastered by his material rather than to be himself truly its master.

I

DURING his writing career of some twenty-three years, Gissing published twenty-four books. It has often been supposed that in less harassing circumstances he would have produced fewer but greater books—an illusory supposition. Gissing was by instinct as well as by early training a classicist, and he would undoubtedly have been drawn to a life of scholarship but for the calamity that shattered his academic career. In the normal course, a brilliant educational record would have culminated in appointment as professor of Greek at one of the newer universities. Looking back, near the end of his life, he speculated upon what he might have become if he could then have begun his intellectual life anew, "keeping before my eyes some definite, some not unattainable good; sternly dismissing the impracticable, the wasteful." He concluded that he might perhaps have developed into nothing better than "an owl-eyed pedant, to whom would be for ever dead the possibility of such enjoyment as I know in these final years."[1]

Gissing's writings, their merits and their imperfections, are the product of Gissing's life *as it was in fact.* No different life could have produced them; nor could they have been produced in a different period. The turmoil of his own affairs coincided in time with the turmoil of accelerated social unrest—the struggle of class against class, of sex against sex. Revolt, or at least a passionate striving for emancipation, was in the air. Imaginative writers, as well as sociologists, were becoming more and more humanitarian in purpose, more and more concerned with the state of the poor, and, consequently, more and more preoccupied with the squalor of destitution. By the time Gissing's first published book, *Workers in the Dawn,* appeared in 1880, the great age of Victorian literature was over and the age of -isms was beginning.

Insofar as Gissing can be said to have had a master among earlier writers, Dickens was that master; and despite the many books written on Dickens since, Gissing's *Charles Dickens: A Critical Study* (1898) remains the classic of its kind. But although the state of the poor certainly disturbed Dickens no less than it disturbed Gissing, their reactions differed immeasurably. The superabundant creative and inventive genius of Dickens enabled him, indeed compelled him, to transcend the nature of his material: the disgusting, without mitigation of its basic disgustingness, could become at Dickens' hands ineffably comic. The prototypes of Squeers, Bumble, Mrs. Gamp, and the many others were not hounded out of existence by moral indignation; they were laughed out of existence. It is a paradox that Dickens, a professionally trained and superb reporter, eschewed

mere reportorial methods in his novels and thus escaped from the crippling limitations of literary realism without neglecting realistic material, whereas the realistic movement that came into prominence after his death stultified itself by raw and frequently inexpert reporting. It is a further paradox that when Gissing was most realistic he was also least convincing. In passages such as the description of Whitecross Street which opens *Workers in the Dawn,* he resembles a foreign visitor who eyes the scene minutely and as minutely itemizes it in his notebook, but who nevertheless fails to sense the "feel" of the place and the mood of its people. Again, the description of the Peckovers' parlor in the fourth chapter of *The Nether World* (1889) is scarcely more illuminating than an auctioneer's catalog.

As a "realist" Gissing attempted a mode alien to his nature. Like many another social theorist he had no fellow feeling or sympathy of the heart for the human unfortunates whose state he lamented and earnestly desired to better. As detailed references will show later, he hated those he would fain have benefited. When demonstrating the state of the poor his prose is at its deadest. His books spring to life and become intellectually exciting when the characters are near to his own class and speak his own language; it is only these whom he represents as being capable of detached thinking.

II

ONE of five children of a pharmaceutical chemist who married a solicitor's daughter, George Robert Gissing was born at Wakefield in Yorkshire on 22 November 1857. His father, Thomas Waller Gissing, first aroused in the boy that passion for reading that was to become a necessity of existence throughout his life and was even to lead him to a somewhat priggish insistence on booklore as a vital qualification in others. From the beginning of his schooling he absorbed knowledge avidly, spurred on partly by a desire to please his father, to whom he was wholly devoted and whose death in 1870 deprived him of a valued guide and companion. He was most unusual in seeming to have no emotional attachment to his mother.

At the age of thirteen, Gissing was taken from the school at Wakefield and sent as a boarder to a Quaker (Society of Friends) school in Worcester-

---

[1]"Winter," pt. 16, in *The Private Papers of Henry Ryecroft* (London, 1903).

shire. He was already showing distinction as a scholar, but also "unsociability and intellectual arrogance" symptomatic of later tendencies.[2] In 1872 he passed first in England in the Oxford local examination and gained a minor scholarship to Owens College, Manchester, where he won almost every available prize and scholarship. Godwin Peak in *Born in Exile* (1892) is in part a self-projection of Gissing, and Whitelaw College reflects Owens. After the prize-giving described in the early pages of the novel,

Godwin Peak stood alone. On the bench where he had sat were heaped the prize volumes (eleven in all, some of them massive) . . . but about this young man was no concourse of admiring kinsfolk. . . . He was not of the young men who easily insinuate themselves into ladies' affections; his exterior was against him, and he seemed too conscious of his disadvantages in that particular.

Earlier in the chapter Peak has been described as

a young man of spare figure and unhealthy complexion. . . . Embarrassment no doubt accounted for much of the awkwardness of his demeanour; but, under any circumstances, he must have appeared ungainly, for his long arms and legs had outgrown their garments, which were no fashionable specimens of tailoring. The nervous gravity of his countenance had a peculiar sternness.

Morley Roberts, Gissing's friend at the college and for the rest of his life, wrote in *The Private Life of Henry Maitland* (1912), a biography-in-disguise, "I know that this chapter [of *Born in Exile*] contains much of what he himself must have felt when I saw him retire to a modest back bench loaded with books bound in calf and tooled in gold" (pp. 27–28, 1958 ed.). The physical description of Peak was less photographic, however, for Roberts describes Gissing as in those days "curiously bright, with a very mobile face. He had abundant masses of brown hair combed backwards over his head, grey-blue eyes, a very sympathetic mouth, an extraordinarily well-shaped chin . . . and a great capacity for talking and laughing" (p. 22).

Gissing, then as ever after, thought continually of the ancient world. The Greek classics fired his imagination, but it was his reading of Gibbon's *Decline*

and Fall of the Roman Empire, won as a school prize, that created his longing for identification with the vanished life of imperial Rome. His lifelong devotion to Gibbon is amusingly and touchingly illustrated by the passage in *The Private Papers of Henry Ryecroft* (1903) in which he recalls buying another copy of the great work:

Sometimes I added the labour of a porter to my fasting endured for the sake of books. At the little shop near Portland Road Station I came upon a first edition of Gibbon, the price an absurdity—I think it was a shilling a volume. To possess those clean-paged quartos I would have sold my coat. As it happened, I had not money enough with me, but sufficient at home. I was living at Islington. Having spoken with the bookseller, I walked home, took the cash, walked back again, and—carried the tomes from the west end of Euston Road to a street in Islington far beyond the Angel. I did it in two journeys—this being the only time in my life when I thought of Gibbon in avoirdupois. Twice—three times, reckoning the walk for the money—did I descend Euston Road and climb Pentonville on that occasion. Of the season and the weather I have no recollection; my joy in the purchase drove out every other thought. Except, indeed, of the weight. I had infinite energy, but not much muscular strength, and the end of the last journey saw me upon a chair, perspiring, flaccid, aching—exultant!

("Spring," pt. 12)

But years later he was compelled by poverty to sell that first edition for less than it had cost him, and it was to the school-prize copy that he clung, to "read and read and read again for more than thirty years."

His unique successes at Owens College were attended by prophecies of a brilliant scholastic future. The prophecies failed, however, and whether the failure is to be considered tragic or only sordid is a problem of moral interpretation. In later years Gissing complained to Morley Roberts: "It was a cruel and most undesirable thing that I, at the age of sixteen, should have been turned loose in a big city, compelled to live alone in lodgings, with nobody interested in me but those at the college"—a complaint that, while not without foundation, has nevertheless some touch of the spiritually corroding self-pity by which Gissing was so long beset.[3] Whether through loneliness, sexual impulse, or sheer quixotry, he became involved with, and aspired to reform, a young prostitute encountered in the streets of Manchester. The money he devoted to Marianne Helen

[2]Article by Thomas Seccombe in the *Dictionary of National Biography, Supplement, 1901–1911* (London, 1912; repr. Oxford, 1920), vol. II, pp. 114–116.

[3]*Henry Maitland* (London, 1958), p. 28.

Harrison in the attempt to establish her in respectability exceeded his small means, and when, in 1876, thefts at the college were traced to him, he received a prison sentence.

On his release, Gissing was assisted to America by friends, and his early impressions of Boston persuaded him that the United States was much less philistine in outlook than England. For a few months he taught languages, but by March 1877 he was destitute in Chicago. In chapter 28 of *New Grub Street* (1891) Whelpdale's account of his journalistic experiences in America reproduces Gissing's own. He persuaded the editor of the *Chicago Tribune* that new fiction would be an attractive feature and, though he had not attempted anything of the kind before, he undertook to write short stories for the paper. Whelpdale begins his reminiscences by declaring: "I have lived for five days on a few cents' worth of pea-nuts in the States," and, after describing the visit to the *Tribune*, continues:

"It was a great thing to be permitted to write a story, but then—*what* story? I went down to the shore of Lake Michigan; walked there for half an hour in an icy wind. Then I looked for a stationer's shop, and laid out a few of my remaining cents in the purchase of pen, ink, and paper—my stock of all these things was at an end when I left New York. Then back to the boarding-house. Impossible to write in my bedroom, the temperature was below zero; there was no choice but to sit down in the common room, a place like the smoke-room of a poor commercial hotel in England. A dozen men were gathered about the fire, smoking, talking, quarreling. Favourable conditions, you see, for literary effort. But the story had to be written, and write it I did, sitting there at the end of a deal table; I finished it in less than a couple of days, a good long story, enough to fill three columns of the huge paper."

It earned him eighteen dollars and for some months he stayed in Chicago, writing for the *Tribune* and other papers.

"But at length the flow of my inspiration was checked; I had written myself out. And I began to grow homesick, wanted to get back to England. The result was that I found myself one day in New York again, but without money enough to pay for a passage home. I tried to write one more story. But it happened, as I was looking over newspapers in a reading-room, that I saw one of my Chicago tales copied into a paper published at Troy. Now Troy was not very far off, and it occurred to me that, if I went there, the editor of this paper might be disposed to employ me, seeing he had a taste for my fiction. And I went, up the Hudson by steam-boat. On landing at Troy I was as badly off as when I reached Chicago; I had less than a dollar. And the worst of it was I had come on a vain errand; the editor treated me with scant courtesy, and no work was to be got. I took a little room, . . . and in the meantime I fed on those loathsome pea-nuts, buying a handful in the street now and then. And I assure you I looked starvation in the face."

Gissing's next venture, like Whelpdale's, was as assistant to an itinerant photographer who traveled about New England reproducing old portraits. By the autumn of 1877 Gissing's original enthusiasm for America had vanished, and he returned home in October, having contracted debts (which he scrupulously repaid later) but having also on a desperate impulse apprenticed himself to the profession he was thenceforth to follow. He was still under twenty.

Before he settled to a new life in England, however, he visited Germany, staying for a while at Jena, where he studied Goethe, Haeckel, Schopenhauer, and the French philosopher, Auguste Comte, who was subsequently to have an important place in Gissing's mental development. A legacy of £300 came to him a year later, but he determined to use only the interest, about £10 a year, and meanwhile lived by private teaching.[4] He renewed his association with Marianne ("Nell") Harrison and lived with her in a succession of dismal lodgings among the back streets off Tottenham Court Road. He craved a woman's companionship, both for the assuaging of his sexual needs and to ward off his ever-pursuing dread of loneliness; and being, as he deemed, responsible for the welfare of Nell, though she had been the instrument of his social downfall, he bound himself to her finally by marriage in 1879. She was already sick with a complication of ailments, both were in dire poverty, and Nell degenerated into a drunken virago whom Gissing at length found intolerable. Yet "clearly there was for him something about this woman, of which no record remains, some charm, some illusion or at any rate some specific attraction, for which he never had words. . . . His home training had made him repressive to the explosive pitch; he felt that to make love to any woman he could regard as a social equal would be too elaborate, restrained and tedious for his urgencies. . . ."[5] Support is given to this diagnosis by H. G. Wells by the fact that

[4]Most of his legacy was eventually used to pay for the publication of his first novel.
[5]H. G. Wells, *Experiment in Autobiography* (London, 1934), p. 569.

almost immediately after Nell's death Gissing again entangled himself.

There are several versions of the beginning of this second access of folly. Wells says that Gissing "created a new situation for himself by picking up a servant girl in Regent's Park one Sunday afternoon and marrying her."[6] Morley Roberts is more explicit:

By now he had come out of the pit of his first marriage, and gradually the horrors he had passed through became dim to his eyes. They were like a badly-toned photograph, and faded. I did foresee that something would happen sooner or later to alter the way in which he lived, but I did not foresee and could not have foreseen or imagined what was actually coming, for no one could have prophesied it. It was absurd, impossible, monstrous, and almost bathos. Yet it fits in with the character of the man as it had been distorted by circumstance. One Sunday when I visited him he told me, with a strange mixture of abruptness and hesitation, that he had made the acquaintance of a girl in the Marylebone Road. Naturally enough I thought at first that his resolution and his habits had broken down and that he had picked up some prostitute of the neighbourhood. But it turned out that the girl was "respectable." He said: "I could stand it no longer, so I rushed out and spoke to the very first woman I came across." It was an unhappy inspiration of the desperate, and the first act in a prolonged drama of pain and misery. It took me some time and many questions to find out what this meant, and what it was to lead to, but presently he replied sullenly that he proposed to marry the girl if she would marry him.

(*Henry Maitland*, pp. 115–116)

In *New Grub Street*, the brothers of Alfred Yule "cried out that he had made an unpardonable fool of himself in marrying so much beneath him; that he might well have waited until his income improved"; but, the narrator observes,

. . . they might just as reasonably have bidden him reject plain food because a few years hence he would be able to purchase luxuries; he could not do without nourishment of some sort, and the time had come when he could not do without a wife. Many a man with brains but no money has been compelled to the same step. Educated girls have a profound distaste for London garrets; not one in fifty thousand would share poverty with the brightest genius ever born. Seeing that marriage is so often indispensable to that very success which would enable a man of parts to mate

[6]Ibid. From a reference in Gissing's manuscript diary M. C. Donnelly infers that they first met in an Oxford Street coffee shop (*George Gissing: Grave Comedian* [Cambridge, Mass., 1954], p. 136).

equally, there is nothing for it but to look below one's own level, and be grateful to the untaught woman who has pity on one's loneliness.

(ch. 7)

Gissing's second marriage took place early in 1891, and he was soon to recognize that Edith Underwood was little better suited to him as a wife than Marianne Harrison had been. They lived at first in Exeter, where poverty continued to stalk Gissing. A son was born at the end of the year, to be followed by a second in December 1892, by which time they had returned to London. In 1894 a further move was made to Epsom, where the already dissatisfied second Mrs. Gissing became increasingly resentful. Like Amy Reardon in *New Grub Street*—though without her mental resources or social pretensions—Edith felt herself cheated by her husband's failure to become a popular and prosperous author. And also like the Reardons, the Gissings parted, but only after a series of distressing quarrels. Years later he wrote in *Henry Ryecroft*:

Every morning when I awake, I thank heaven for silence. This is my orison. I remember the London days when sleep was broken by clash and clang, by roar and shriek, and when my first sense on returning to consciousness was hatred of the life about me. Noises of wood and metal, clattering of wheels, banging of implements, jangling of bells—all such things are bad enough, but worse still is the clamorous human voice. Nothing on earth is more irritating to me than a bellow or scream of idiot mirth, nothing more hateful than a shout or yell of brutal anger.

("Spring," pt. 23)

Through maladroit choice, Gissing found in his wives not the gracious stillness for which his nature craved, but the clamor of human voices, the shouts and yells of anger. A balanced characterization of him can never be written in the absence of vital evidence that Nell and Edith could alone have provided. He sought from them the solace of intimate human companionship and sexual gratification, but nothing is recorded of his wives' compensatory needs nor of his readiness or ability to minister to them. His struggle to reform Nell was a noble endeavor, but nobility of purpose was not enough; and even if the reformation of a whore were not an eternally hopeless enterprise, it is impossible to conceive that a man so fastidious as Gissing could have brought to the task enough of heart-warming sympathy to attract Nell to a life of decency. They had lived apart in her last years, which she spent in drink-sodden, disease-ridden depravity, drawing from her husband a crippling proportion of his meager income until she died in a Lambeth slum in 1888. She was his great failure.

The catastrophe in which Gissing's second marriage ended was relatively commonplace. The social success he enjoyed for a while as his books became better known quickly palled, and he regarded his Epsom home as a refuge from the distractions of London. Edith, on the contrary, craved the gregarious life which he detested, for her days at Epsom were empty of interest and entertainment. She became a complaining and abusive shrew, and Gissing fled from her finally in 1897.

However commonplace marital disturbances may be in general experience, in Gissing's life and work they were both crucial and decisive. In the management of his own affairs, Gissing—it might seem by the malignancy of fate—was the complete fool, and as the direct outcome of this folly the dominant themes in his novels are money, marriage, and the masses, whereas the naturally dominant themes in his mind, when briefly untrammeled by economic necessity, were philosophy and poetry. Greek and Latin were his passion and his way of escape from the pressure of reality, though to him the Athens of Pericles and more particularly the Rome of Augustus were, in truth, less unreal as well as manifestly less ugly than the London of Victoria. He took particular delight in conversing on Greek prosody, and would have liked common education to embrace a wide knowledge of classical meters. It was probably only half in fun that he once said to Morley Roberts, "Why, my dear fellow, do you know that there are actually miserable men who do not know—who have never heard of—the minuter differences between Dochmiacs and Antipasts!"

III

For some time after he came back from America in 1877, Gissing lived near to the starvation line in London. From teaching a few private pupils he earned a pittance, and enforced acquaintance with slum life stirred in him the illusory notion that his place was with the laboring classes. He joined one of the workingmen's clubs that at that time functioned as centers of proletarian enlightenment, and there he became imbued with socialist and rationalist ideas. But it was not in Gissing's nature to become fast dyed in mind or spirit by such dabblings. Though he clung for some years to the theoretical purpose of using his talents in the service of the socially downtrodden, his club-mates soon classed him, he wrote, as an "abominable aristocrat." However steeped in poverty, he remained throughout his life an intellectual aristocrat, subject to acute torment by the speech and conduct of the boorish multitude. "I really don't think, aunt," he makes Miss Haven say in *The Odd Women* (1893), "that there can be any solidarity of ladies with servant girls," Rhoda Nunn having also said, a moment earlier, "I think that as soon as we begin to meddle with uneducated people, all our schemes and views are unsettled. We have to learn a new language, for one thing." Although the opinions of fictional characters are not to be attributed as a matter of course to their creators, such remarks as these occur often enough in Gissing's works to establish a mood. Godwin Peak is vehement on the subject. Having been called an aristocrat by his brother, he replies:

"I hope I am. . . . There's nothing I hate like vulgarity."

"I hate low, uneducated people! I hate them worse than the filthiest vermin! . . . They ought to be swept off the face of the earth! . . . All the grown-up creatures who can't speak proper English and don't know how to behave themselves, I'd transport them to the Falkland Islands, . . . and let them die off as soon as possible. The children should be sent to school and purified, if possible; if not they too should be got rid of."

(*Born in Exile*, pp. 42–43)

From this dilemma of intellectual disgust frustrating theoretically engaged sympathies, Gissing was released first by friendship with a German exile, Eduard Bertz, whose philosopical socialism did not necessitate unhygienic contacts, and later by the influence of Frederic Harrison, one of the foremost English disciples of Comte. This French philosopher held that human thought passes through three progressive stages—the theological, the metaphysical, and what he called the *positive*. Comte's positivism commended itself to a generation that had almost unlimited confidence in the power of the positive (that is, physical) sciences to work for good by developing a community consciousness strong enough to overcome individual self-interest. Capitalists "would be taught to hold their wealth and power as in trust from society to be used for the benefit of all," while workers "would come to regard themselves as . . . serving each in his place." For a while Gissing embraced positivism with ardor, finding in its optimistic materialism an acceptable alternative to the "superstitions" of orthodoxy and sharing its confidence that "science would reconstruct the social fabric." But the positivists' trust in the achievement of perfectibility by mankind through the scientific ordering of human affairs could not for long serve as an antidote to Gissing's pessimism, fed daily by his own desperate economic plight.

Gissing's debt to Harrison was by no means exhausted, however, when the solace of positivism failed. Engagement as tutor to Harrison's sons relieved for the time being the worst of his financial troubles; while as a guest in the Harrisons' home he partook of gracious living such as he was born for but was a stranger to in his own circumstances. Yet in spite of these social contacts Gissing remained hardly more than a friend-by-adoption into a class that was socially other than his own. His dread of loneliness became less insistent, however, as his novels won esteem among a select audience of fellow writers. W. H. Hudson, author of *A Shepherd's Life* and other excellent nature books, was one of the small inner circle, while through Edward Clodd, banker and man of letters, Gissing became acquainted with editors who were ready to take his work and generally extended his acquaintance with other novelists. He met and greatly admired George Meredith; met and disliked Thomas Hardy, of whose forthright Dorset speech and manners he almost prudishly disapproved; and with H. G. Wells had most direct contact in his last years. Wells's article on Gissing's novels in the *Contemporary Review* (August 1897) was the first substantial critical appreciation of his writings, and the pages devoted to him in *Experiment in Autobiography* (1934) sketch his personality vigorously.

His health having been precarious for a considerable period, Gissing was compelled from 1897 to spend much of his time on the Continent. But it was in England in 1898 that he found his ideal woman, Gabrielle Fleury, an intelligent Frenchwoman who called upon him with a proposal to translate *New Grub Street*. Some short time afterward they went to France together, where, to gratify the notions of respectability of Gabrielle's mother, they contracted in 1899 what, in English law, was only a bigamous pseudomarriage, since Gissing's second wife was still living. At last he found, with Gabrielle, a generous measure of the happiness that had hitherto so persistently eluded him. To Edward Clodd, at the beginning of 1902, Gissing said: "You speak of my wife [Gabrielle]. Oh, yes, she is still with me; and, I devoutly hope, will be so until I can no longer benefit by human solace. Our marriage . . . has been justified by the event, and with quietness and indifference to past troubles."

Now his life was ebbing. They moved about from place to place in France, seeking a climate beneficial to his damaged lungs, but the search was ended by an attack of double pneumonia from which he died at St. Jean Pied de Port on 28 December 1903. Wells went out to him as he lay dying, the last of his English friends to see him, and the author of a frank epitaph: "He spent his big fine brain depreciating life, because he would not and perhaps could not look life squarely in the eyes,—neither his circumstances nor the conventions about him . . . nor the limitations of his personal character. But whether it was nature or education that made this tragedy I cannot tell."[7]

IV

A good deal of discussion has centered upon the question of whether Gissing would have written novels at all if some other way of living had been open to him. Since with unexampled audacity he imposed himself as a fiction writer upon the Chicago editor, simply as insurance against imminent starvation, there is ground for the view that he was a novelist perforce rather than by free choice; and the kind of novels he chose to write when his circumstances in England were no more hopeful was determined by the squalid conditions into which he was plunged, by his hope of aiding the abolition of those conditions, and by a desire to shock British prudes who denied to English novelists the moral freedom of presentation he believed to be current among French writers—though, indeed, in the year of Gissing's birth Gustave Flaubert had been hounded in his own country on account of *Madame Bovary*.

If it is a fact that Gissing began with the ambition to become a London Balzac, he was better able to imitate the externals of Balzac's method than to interpret the cockney spirit or to render cockney (that is, uneducated Londoners') speech. He refers in *Born*

[7]Wells, *Experiment in Autobiography*, p. 493.

in Exile to "an ear constantly tormented by the London vernacular," and to the London poor as "of necessity abominable." These Olympian reactions suggest how handicapped Gissing was in his attempts to give an authentic presentation of London life, though not more handicapped than any non-Londoner must be. No one but a native of London is able to distinguish and reproduce the subtle nuances of cockney pronunciation and intonation. The ear needs to be steeped in the dialect from birth, and however strongly a writer may prefer "standard English," he cannot afford to despise cockney if he presumes to use it for any of his fictional characters. Gissing had no ear in this respect; and his reference to the London poor as abominable allowed nothing to their courage, their humor, and their generous capacity for kindliness and neighborly solicitude.

The fact that among the contemporary novelists writing in English he preferred Meredith and that he "manifested an instructive affinity for the lucid and subtle" Turgenev among the Russians, supports much internal evidence in his books that as a realist he was working with subject matter to which he was temperamentally alien. In a drafted prefatory note to an unpublished novel he wrote: "This book is addressed to those to whom Art is dear for its own sake," and he more than once claimed that his books were to be judged as works of literary art. Imperfect though they may be in that respect, those that survive do so because of excellences more numerous than imperfections.

As a literary stylist—in the decades when the niceties of style were uppermost in the minds of Robert Louis Stevenson, Walter Pater, Oscar Wilde, and the whole company of aesthetes—Gissing was unpretentious. His prose attempts no more than to be appropriate to its subject, and is therefore frequently and appropriately drab. When the mood changes, however, the style becomes appropriately changed also, as in chapter 27 of *New Grub Street*. Reardon, during a discussion with Biffen, declares: 'The best moments of life are those when we contemplate beauty in the purely artistic spirit—objectively. I have had such moments in Greece and Italy. . . ."

Reardon's face was illumined with the glow of an exquisite memory.

"Haven't I told you," he said, "of that marvellous sunset at Athens? I was on the Pnyx; had been rambling about there the whole afternoon. For I dare say a couple of hours I had noticed a growing rift of light in the clouds to the west;

it looked as if the dull day might have a rich ending. That rift grew broader and brighter—the only bit of light in the sky. On Parnes there were white strips of ragged mist, hanging very low; the same on Hymettus, and even the peak of Lycabettus was just hidden. Of a sudden, the sun's rays broke out. They showed themselves first in a strangely beautiful way, striking from behind the seaward hills through the pass that leads to Eleusis, and so gleaming on the nearer slopes of Aigaleos, making the clefts black and the rounded parts of the mountain wonderfully brilliant with golden colour. . . . I turned eastward, and there to my astonishment was a magnificent rainbow, . . . stretching from the foot of Parnes to that of Hymettus, framing Athens and its hills, which grew brighter and brighter—the brightness for which there is no name among colours. . . . The Acropolis simply glowed and blazed. As the sun descended all these colours grew richer and warmer; for a moment the landscape was nearly crimson. Then suddenly the sun passed into the lower stratum of cloud, and the splendour died almost at once, except that there remained the northern half of the rainbow, which had become double. In the west, the clouds were still glorious for a time; there were two shaped like great expanded wings, edged with refulgence."

Here, not only is the wonder of the sunset caught into the style, there is also the poetry lover's delight in the exquisite music of the Greek names: Parnes—Hymettus—Lycabettus—Eleusis—Aigaleos.

The semiautobiographical *Private Papers of Henry Ryecroft* is the most consciously stylized of Gissing's books, and nowhere else among his works is a reader so aware of a deliciously cultivated artifice of natural description—lingering echoes of Theocritus and Vergil:

Here, scarce have I assured myself that the last leaf has fallen, scarce have I watched the glistening of hoar-frost upon the evergreens, when a breath from the west thrills me with anticipation of bud and bloom. Even under this grey-billowing sky, which tells that February is still in rule:—

> Mild winds shake the elder brake,
> And the wandering herdsmen know
> That the whitethorn soon will blow.

. . .

I presently found myself on the side of a little valley, in which lay a farm and an orchard. The apple trees were in full bloom, and, as I stood gazing, the sun, which had all that day been niggard of its beams, burst forth gloriously. For what I then saw, I have no words; I can but dream of the still loveliness of that blossomed valley. Near me, a bee was humming; not far away, a cuckoo called; from the pasture of the farm below came a bleating of lambs.

. . .

. . . the surprise of budding branches clothed in a night with green. The first snowy gleam upon the blackthorn did not escape me. By its familiar bank, I watched for the earliest primrose, and in its copse I found the anemone. Meadows shining with buttercups, hollows sunned with the marsh marigold held me long at gaze. I saw the sallow glistening with its cones of silvery fur, and splendid with dust of gold.

("Spring," pt. 8; pt. 15; and pt. 25)

Even if austere contemporary taste should disapprove the occasional mannered touches—"February is still in rule," "niggard of its beams," "held me long at gaze"—or declare that the style is too pervasively mellifluous, *Ryecroft* nevertheless is unstaled and secure: the only one of Gissing's books that has remained in unbroken demand.

While much that is admirable can be found in Gissing's other works, *Ryecroft* is unique among them in arousing affection, or even love. It is one of those rare books that can be read again and again without lessening of enthusiasm: an elderly reader finds that the years have not dimmed the enjoyment given by *Ryecroft* in long-past adolescence. Though it is one of the shortest of Gissing's works, it is the richest and widest-ranging in content. Since there is no theme—other than life in its manifold variety—it is free to conform to the meditations of a liberal and well-stored mind and to the responses of a sensitive heart. Ryecroft is made to say: "one has to distinguish between two forms of intelligence, that of the brain, and that of the heart, and I have come to regard the second as by far the more important."

The preface sets up the fiction that the *Papers* were written by a now-dead Henry Ryecroft and that Gissing is only their editor. A correct title for the book would be "The Meditations of George Gissing," "set down as humour bade him, a thought, a reminiscence, a bit of reverie, a description of his state of mind." Although it began as installments contributed to the *Fortnightly Review,* the sections unite into a coherent whole, the unifying factor being the personality of Gissing himself, freed from the restrictive harness of novel-writing. What he says concerning the imaginary Ryecroft is no less true of Gissing: "in this written gossip he revealed himself more intimately" than at any other time; "when I had read it all through, I knew the man better than before." He succeeded well in preserving the spontaneity at which he aimed and in making "a small volume which, at least for its sincerity's sake, would not be without value for those who read, not with the eye alone, but with the mind."

Nowhere else in Gissing's writings can so much of the whole man be found. Without *The Private Papers of Henry Ryecroft* we could deduce from the novels much of the author's circumstances and external life, but much less of his spirit. From *Ryecroft* alone, however, without other aid, we can reach an understanding of the essential Gissing, a man of infinite variety when released from the imprisoning pressure of "the squalid profession," "the rough and tumble of the literary arena" in which "prices per thousand words" are the prime consideration. Here, in *Ryecroft,* is the lover of England as well as the lover of Italy and Greece. If the names of classical antiquity enchanted him, so also did those of his own country: the valley of the Blythe—Wensleydale—the Cotswolds—the wide vale of Evesham—the hills of Malvern—Ullswater—the South Downs—the Sussex weald. "Unspeakable the charm to my ear of those old names; exquisite the quiet of those little towns, lost amid tilth and pasture, untouched as yet by the fury of modern life, their ancient sanctuaries guarded, as it were, by noble trees and hedges overrun with flowers" ("Summer," pt. 2).

But as well as being in part the idyll of a recluse in country retirement, *Ryecroft* is also in part the retrospective complaint of an impoverished city dweller, remembering his days of squalor, the gloom of London fogs, and a thousand humiliations that accompany the lack of money. Like myriad others from all parts of the world, he found a haven in the British Museum reading room:

At the time when I was literally starving in London, when it seemed impossible that I should ever gain a living by my pen, how many days have I spent at the British Museum, reading as disinterestedly as if I had been without a care! It astounds me to remember that, having breakfasted on dry bread, and carrying in my pocket another piece of bread to serve for dinner, I settled myself at a desk in the great Reading Room with books before me which by no possibility could be a source of immediate profit. At such a time, I worked through German tomes on Ancient Philosophy. At such a time, I read Appuleius and Lucian, Petronius and the Greek Anthology, Diogenes Laertius and—heaven knows what! My hunger was forgotten; the garret to which I must return to pass the night never perturbed my thoughts.

("Spring," pt. 17)

Among the numerous passages of many-sided self-revelation in *Ryecroft*, none is so illuminating of Gissing's fundamental character as the following:

... I never belonged to any cluster; I shrank from casual acquaintance, and, through the grim years, had but one friend with whom I held converse. It was never my instinct to look for help, to seek favour for advancement; whatever step I gained was gained by my own strength. Even as I disregarded favour so did I scorn advice; no counsel would I ever take but that of my own brain and heart. More than once I was driven by necessity to beg from strangers the means of earning bread, and this of all my experiences was the bitterest; yet I think I should have found it worse still to incur a debt to some friend or comrade. The truth is that I have never learnt to regard myself as a "member of society." For me, there have always been two entities—myself and the world, and the normal relation between these two has been hostile. Am I not still a lonely man, as far as ever from forming part of the social order?

("Spring," pt. 8)

It is more than a little unfortunate that the popularity of *Ryecroft* has tended to deprive Gissing of a more substantial reputation by making him appear to many as a one-book writer. While it is true that none of his novels affords constant aesthetic delight, there is much that gives intellectual satisfaction. His admiration of George Meredith's works is understandable in the light of his own mastery of written conversation, though he had no such gifts of wit and lightness of touch as were natural to Meredith. But if Gissing had been free to devote himself to conversation novels—novels of intellectual discussion and ideas—he might have become a distinguished contributor to that popular modern type of fiction. Book after book has extended passages of talk that are not only absorbing in themselves but serve also to create the characters solidly. In descriptive characterization of men and women Gissing is not remarkably successful. The first chapter of *Demos* (1886) introduces the clergyman thus:

... Mr. Wyvern was of vast proportions and leonine in aspect. With the exception of one ungloved hand and the scant proportions of his face which were not hidden by hair, he was wholly black in hue; an enormous beard, the colour of jet, concealed the linen about his throat, and a veritable mane, dark as night, fell upon his shoulders. His features were not ill-matched with this sable garniture. ...

We might take this to be written in the spirit of caricature, and on the evidence of this description, if the immediately following sentences did not qualify it, Mr. Wyvern might be thought destined to play the part of a comic clergyman. More than three hundred pages later we get to know the essential Mr. Wyvern through his discussion with Hubert Eldon, a son of the manor, concerning the socialist demagogue Westlake, a once-esteemed man of letters:

"Now here [says Hubert] is an article signed by Westlake. You know his books? How has he fallen to this? His very style has abandoned him, his English smacks of the street corners, of Radical clubs. The man is ruined; it is next to impossible that he should ever again do good work, such as we used to have from him. . . ."

"It is something of a problem to me," Mr. Wyvern admitted. "Had he been a younger man, or if his writing had been of a different kind. Yet his sincerity is beyond doubt."

"I doubt it," Hubert broke in. "Not his sincerity in the beginning; but he must long since have ached to free himself. It is such a common thing for a man to commit himself to some pronounced position in public life and for very shame shrink from withdrawing. . . ."

"At your age," said Mr. Wyvern, smiling half sadly, "I, too, had a habit of vehement speaking, but it was on the other side. I was a badly paid curate working in a wretched parish. I lived among the vilest and poorest of the people, and my imagination was constantly at boiling-point. . . . At that age and under those conditions it was right and good. I should have been void of feeling and imagination otherwise. Such convictions are among relative truths. To be a social enthusiast is in itself neither right nor wrong, neither praiseworthy nor the opposite, it is a state to be judged in relation to the other facts of a man's life. You will never know that state; if you affected it you would be purely contemptible. And I myself have outgrown it. . . . I used to have a very bleeding of the heart for the half-clothed and quarter-fed hangers-on to civilization; I think far less of them now than of another class in appearance much better off. It is a class created by the mania of education, and it consists of those unhappy men and women whom unspeakable cruelty endows with intellectual needs whilst refusing them the sustenance they are taught to crave. Another generation, and this class will be terribly extended, its existence blighting the whole social state. Every one of these poor creatures has a right to curse the work of those who clamour progress, and pose as benefactors of their race."

"All that strikes me as very good and true," remarked Hubert; "but can it be helped? Or do you refuse to believe in the modern conception of laws ruling social development?"

"I wish I could do so. No; when I spoke of the right to curse, I should have said, from their point of view. In truth, I fear we must accept progress. But I cannot rejoice in it; I will even do what little I can in my own corner to support the old order of things. You may be aware that I was on very friendly terms with the Mutimers, that I even seemed to encourage them in their Socialism. Yes, and because I felt that in that way I could best discharge my duty. What I really encouraged was sympathy and humanity. . . ."

(ch. 29)

To economize space, much has been omitted in this extract from a conversation extending over several pages. Enough has been quoted, however, to show not only Wyvern's self-revelation of mind and character, but also to illustrate Gissing's occasional gift of prophetic foresight. What Wyvern calls "the mania of education" has in fact produced the very consequences adumbrated in his words.

Although, like Bernard Shaw rather later, Gissing crusaded against the degradations of poverty by preaching that money is an indispensable social regenerator—Richard Mutimer in *Demos* "early discerned . . . that to one who lacks money the world is but a great debtor's prison"—he was also acutely conscious of the potential dangers of money and social rank as demoralizing temptations. Richard Mutimer, artisan and fervent socialist, inherits unexpectedly a large fortune from a great-uncle who is thought to have died intestate. Mutimer devotes his wealth to establishing an industrial village on socialist lines, but before long he jilts the plebeian girl to whom he had been engaged and marries a young woman of good family. On this and other counts, rival socialists work up a campaign against him, and at a riotous open-air meeting the chief agitator incites the crowd to mob-hysteria:

"Look at this man!" he cried, pointing at Mutimer, who had drawn as far aside as the cart would let him. "He's been a-tellin' you what he did when somebody died an' left him a fortune. There's just one thing he's forgot, an' shall I tell you what that is? When he was a workin' man like ourselves, mates, he was a-goin' to marry a pore girl, a workin' girl. When he gets his money, what does he do? Why, he pitches her over, if you please, an' marries a fine lady, as took him because he was rich—that's the way *ladies* always chooses their husbands, y'understand."

He was interrupted by a terrific yell, but by dint of vigorous pantomime secured a hearing again.

"But wait a bit, maties; I haven't done yet. He pitches over the pore girl, but he does worse afterwards. He sets a tale a-goin' as she'd disgraced herself, as she wasn't fit to be a honest man's wife. An' it was all a damned lie, as lots of us knows. Now what d'ye think o' that! This is a friend o' the People, this is! This is the man as 'as your interests at 'art,

mates! If he'll do a thing like that, won't he rob you of your savin's?"

(ch. 35)

The mob attacks Mutimer, and he is killed when "a heavy fragment of stone, hurled with deadly force and precision" strikes him on the temple. Mutimer's degeneration of character is displayed with convincing power. He not only covets the social elevation to which his marriage gives access, but also his growing hunger for adulation culminates in what can only be called philanthropic megalomania.

V

GISSING's reputation as a novelist will no doubt continue to depend upon four books: *Demos, New Grub Street, Born in Exile,* and *The Odd Women.* The last-named, concerned with the problem of the numerical surplus of women over men, contains what is perhaps the most substantial group of characters in any single novel by Gissing. Of the six orphaned Madden sisters—"it never occurred to Dr. Madden that his daughters would do well to study with a professional object"—three are dead by the time the story begins. The survivors, in 1888, are Alice (forty-one), Virginia (thirty-nine), and Monica (twenty-one)—precariously employed as nursery governess, companion to a gentlewoman, and draper's assistant. It was Gissing's habit to be ruthless rather than indulgent to his unfortunates, and the reader's sense of probability may stir some suspicion that the author jogged the elbow of fate more than a little in the affairs of the Maddens. Of the three who died young, one was "drowned by the over-turning of a pleasure boat," another was consumptive, while "Isabel was soon worked into illness" while teaching at a public school. "Brain trouble came on, resulting in melancholia. A charitable institution ultimately received her, and there, at two-and-twenty, the poor hard-featured girl drowned herself in a bath." Alice suffered from "headaches . . . backaches, and other disorders." Virginia's "cheeks were loose, puffy, and permanently of the hue which is produced by cold; her forehead had a few pimples; her shapeless chin lost itself in two or three fleshy fissures." Monica, however, had "native elegance," and of the sisters it is she who has the largest part in the book.

Monica is persuaded to leave her drapery estab-

433

lishment and learn office work at an embryonic secretarial school run by Miss Barfoot (assisted by Rhoda Nunn), whose aim is "the education of women in self-respect." Monica quickly becomes bored by the change and marries a man of independent means much older than herself, only to find that she is in worse straits through his possessiveness and demoniac jealousy. But although Monica's affairs are in the forefront of the story, the real center of interest is in the feminist principles of Mary Barfoot and Rhoda and in the latter's facing of the personal contest between independence and love. The argumentative love scenes between her and Everard Barfoot no doubt appeared startlingly new to many early readers of *The Odd Women*, and Rhoda's decision must have come as a cold shower to late Victorian romanticism. In conversation with Mary Barfoot, when discussing another young woman, Rhoda exclaims:

"Love—love—love; a sickening sameness of vulgarity. What is more vulgar than the ideal of novelists? They won't represent the actual world; it would be too dull for their readers. In real life, how many men and women *fall in love?* Not one in every ten thousand, I am convinced. . . ."

That outburst is an echo of the one uttered by Amy Reardon in *New Grub Street*, when she complains to a friend that

"novels are all the same. Nothing but love, love, love; what silly nonsense it is! Why don't people write about the really important things of life? Some of the French novelists do; several of Balzac's, for instance. I have just been reading his *Cousin Pons*, a terrible book, but I enjoyed it ever so much because it was nothing like a love story. What rubbish is printed about love!"

It might be argued that neither Rhoda Nunn the confirmed spinster nor Amy the thwarted wife is a disinterested authority on this subject, but behind both women stands Gissing himself, a slave and a victim to the illusions and the torments of love. Whether *New Grub Street* is or is not the best of his novels (many readers have judged it to be so), it is certainly the centerpiece of his fiction as a whole, for it is largely a transposition of his own literary and emotional plight, but set in a larger imaginative framework.

In Samuel Johnson's great dictionary, published in 1755, appeared the entry: "*Grub-street*, the name of a street in London, much inhabited by writers of small histories, dictionaries, and temporary poems; whence any mean product is called *Grub-street*." Later the street was renamed Milton Street (*not* after the poet) and under that name can still be visited in the City of London, though it is now occupied by business premises instead of hovels and garrets of slaves of the pen. The term "Grub Street" continues to be used in reference to authors and journalists who are compelled to struggle desperately to make a bare livelihood, and also to those who have no scruples about what they write so long as it brings them profit or popularity. Gissing's novel is concerned with the conflict between these two types: Edward Reardon is the unsuccessful conscientious writer who resists attempts to persuade him to lower his standards; Jasper Milvain has only the determination to make money and win social success by writing whatever will bring him to the notice of influential people. An early reviewer of *New Grub Street* suggested that in real life Milvain would have chosen an easier path to prosperity by becoming a stockbroker; but (altogether apart from the fact that money is needed in the first place to become a stockbroker) that suggestion ignores the powerful motive force of vanity in Milvain's character. Stockbrokers, however successful, are not as a class admired or flattered; but, in the eyes of the nonliterary public, a romantic glow encompasses authors, however ludicrously vain or individually unimportant they may be. Milvain's vanity is social, Reardon's is ethical: Milvain desires the easy flattery of fashion, Reardon the more austere and enduring flattery of fame on his own high-principled terms. Amy has married Reardon in the expectation that as an author's wife she will be an envied figure in at least their own circle of acquaintances, but his refusal (or inability) to write frivolous salable stuff disappoints all her hopes and plunges the couple into grinding poverty.

The main thread of the story thereafter leads Amy away from Reardon and, after his death, to Milvain and prosperity. Around this central trio moves a finely drawn group of lesser characters: Alfred Yule the second-rate scholar, whose unfulfilled ambition to become editor of some influential literary journal causes him to degenerate into a pitifully mean character; his daughter and research assistant, Marian, whose hope of marriage to Milvain is shattered when he learns that she will not inherit an expected legacy of £5,000; Biffen, the sympathetically and attractively drawn author of a realistic novel,

Mr. Bailey, Grocer; and a large number of others, among whom Alfred Yule's wife—undereducated and uncultured in speech, and agonizingly aware of her husband's consequent contempt—is a deeply pathetic figure. The account in chapter 31 of the peril of *Mr. Bailey, Grocer* when a drunkard sets the house on fire and Biffen climbs to the roof with his manuscript is the most exciting piece of writing that Gissing achieved. But what may linger more permanently in the reader's memory is the bitter irony of the last few pages of *New Grub Street*, as Amy and Jasper Milvain gloat over their prosperity and happiness in entire forgetfulness of the miserable end of the finer Edward Reardon.

VI

THE mainly sad music of most of Gissing's work was lightened by the happier coda of his last five years. In the book on Dickens, which he was commissioned to write and which appeared in 1898, he wrote: "Dickens had a weapon more efficacious than mere honest zeal. He could make people laugh; and if once the crowd has laughed with you, it will not object to cry a little—nay, it will make good resolves and sometimes carry them out." Gissing's own few attempts at comedy can have provoked very little laughter. The nearest he approached to a Dickensian scene is in the early chapter of *Workers in the Dawn* where he enters into the family life of the curate Orlando Whiffle and his wife and eight children. It is a long way after Dickens, however, though at least one of Whiffle's sayings may be gratefully remembered: "I have never given much attention to natural history. The Church does not encourage it." Nor should it soon be forgotten that the Bloomford Ladies' Sewing Club disapproved astronomy as "a sinful prying into the mysteries of the Almighty." Such flashes of exuberance were not repeated in Gissing's subsequent realistic novels. The posthumously published *Will Warburton* (1905), detailing the experiences of a bankrupted city gentleman who turns retail grocer, is lighthearted enough, but its wan satire is mostly superficial. Though he could not emulate "that overflowing cheeriness which conquered Dickens's first public," Gissing nevertheless understood Dickens well both as man and as writer; and even if by more recent standards of criticism *Charles*

Dickens: A Critical Study is not a scholarly book, it is something more valuable—an illuminating one.

In the year of his death Gissing was enthusiastically engaged on a long-contemplated historical novel, the book he called "my sixth-century story." He expected to finish it before the end of 1903 and in October wrote that he was "past the middle." *Veranilda* remained unfinished, however, breaking off in the twentieth chapter. This need cause little regret. The dialogue is in the now outmoded style once considered imperative in historical fiction, and the story is heavy with learning. It was published in its unfinished state in 1904.

The travel book *By the Ionian Sea: Notes of a Ramble in Southern Italy* (1901) carries its learning far more easily because of its spontaneity. At Cosenza, inland between the instep and the heel of the peninsula, Gissing went to think about Alaric "and with my own eyes to behold the place of his burial":

Ever since the first boyish reading of Gibbon, my imagination has loved to play upon that scene of Alaric's death. Thinking to conquer Sicily, the Visigoth marched as far as to the capital of the Bruttii, those mountain tribes which Rome herself never really subdued; at Consentia he fell sick and died. How often had I longed to see this river Busento, which the "labour of a captive multitude" turned aside, that its flood might cover and conceal for all time the tomb of the Conqueror! I saw it in the light of sunrise, flowing amid low, brown, olive-planted hills; at this time of the year it is a narrow but rapid stream running through a wide, waste bed of yellow sand and stones. The Crati, which here has only just started upon its long seaward way from some glen of Sila, presents much the same appearance, the track which it has worn in flood being many times as broad as the actual current. They flow, these historic waters, with a pleasant sound, over-borne at moments by the clapping noise of Cosenza's washerwomen, who cleanse their linen by beating it, then leave it to dry on the riverbed. Along the banks stood tall poplars, each a spire of burnished gold, blazing against the dark olive foliage on the slopes behind them; plane trees also, very rich of colour, and fig trees shedding their latest leaves.

(ch. 3)

Gissing did not find this ambitious ramble uniformly pleasant, but the variety of his experiences makes the book far more interestingly human than if it had been only a rhapsody of travel. He met men and women of all sorts, was treated sometimes well and sometimes uncouthly; and while his eye for the beauties of nature was richly gratified, he also saw at close quarters much that was ignoble in the living conditions of the people in the days before tourism became a leading international industry. Yet though on his route from Naples to Reggio he was brought into immediate contact with the modern Italians, that was not his purpose in undertaking the journey. "Every man," he wrote, "has his intellectual desire; mine is to escape life as I know it and dream myself into that old world. . . ." On the boat, off Capri, "The stillness of a dead world laid its spell on all that lived. Today seemed an unreality, an idle impertinence; the real was that long-buried past which gave its meaning to all about me. . . ." What he desired was to bring to life again the dry bones of history, a desire realized in mysterious fashion as he lay ill of congestion of the lungs in a miserable inn at one stage of his wanderings. He fell into a visionary state and had his "glimpse of history." When Hannibal, after the Second Punic War at the end of the third century B.C., withdrew from Italy to Carthage:

He then had with him a contingent of Italian mercenaries, and unwilling that these soldiers should go over to the enemy, he bade them accompany him to Africa. The Italians refused. Thereupon Hannibal had them led down to the shore of the sea, where he slaughtered one and all. This event I beheld. I saw the strand by Croton; the promontory with its temple; not as I know the scene today, but as it must have looked to those eyes more than two thousand years ago. . . . And over all lay a glory of sunshine, an indescribable brilliancy which puts light and warmth into my mind whenever I try to recall it. The delight of these phantasms was well worth the ten days' illness which paid for them. . . . I shall always feel that, for an hour, it was granted me to see the vanished life so dear to my imagination.

(ch. 9)

VII

HAD there not been *The Private Papers of Henry Ryecroft*, Gissing would have been remembered mostly as a dour figure, a man defeated by the life of the modern world. *Ryecroft*, however, at least proves that Gissing's imagination was far from wholly dark. It ranges widely in subject and through time and place, but it is peculiarly and cherishably an *English* book. The last of his writings to be published before he died, it may be said to have brought his life "to port after stormy seas": "The dark days are drawing to an end. Soon it will be spring once more;

I shall go out into the fields, and shake away . . . thoughts of discouragement and fear." He died abroad, but *Ryecroft* traverses the English seasons from spring to spring again:

Impatient for the light of spring, I have slept lately with my blind drawn up, so that at waking, I have the sky in view. This morning, I awoke before sunrise. . . . After breakfast, I could not sit down by the fireside; indeed a fire was scarce necessary; the sun drew me forth, and I walked all the morning about the moist lanes, delighting myself with the scent of earth.

On my way home, I saw the first celandine. . . .

I could wish for many another year; yet, if I knew that not one more awaited me, I should not grumble. When I was ill at ease in the world, it would have been hard to die; I had lived to no purpose that I could discover; the end would have seemed abrupt and meaningless. Now, my life is rounded; it began with the natural irreflective happiness of childhood, it will close in the reasoned tranquillity of the mature mind. How many a time, after long labour on some piece of writing, brought at length to its conclusion, have I laid down the pen with a sigh of thankfulness; the work was full of faults, but I had wrought sincerely, had done what time and circumstance and my own nature permitted. Even so may it be with me in my last hour. May I look back on life as a long task duly completed—a piece of biography; faulty enough, but good as I could make it—and, with no thought but one of contentment, welcome the repose to follow when I have breathed the word *Finis*.

("Winter," pt. 26)

Thus, uniquely, Gissing steered his mostly unreposeful life into a final peace of self-comprehension and self-acceptance, looking back neither boastfully nor yet apologetically on "a long task duly completed . . . faulty enough, but good as I could make it."

SELECTED BIBLIOGRAPHY

I. BIBLIOGRAPHIES. *George Gissing 1857–1903* (New York, 1954), catalog of exhibition in the New York Public Library, J. D. Gordan, the compiler, enriches entries with much illuminating information and comment; M. C. Donnelly, *George Gissing* (Cambridge, Mass., 1954), contains an exhaustive list of writings on Gissing, most of them contributed to periodicals; M. Collie, *George Gissing: A Bibliography* (London, 1976). *Note:* Gissing's diary from 1887 to 1903, together with certain collections of letters and other MS material, is in the Berg Collection in the New York Public Library; it has been repr. in P. Coustillas, ed.

(London, 1978). Other letters, notes, and miscellaneous MSS are in the Yale University Library. See F. Niebling, "The Adams Gissing Collection," *Yale University Library Gazette* 16 (1942).

II. SEPARATE WORKS. *Workers in the Dawn*, 3 vols. (London, 1880), novel, "which he subsequently declined to claim" (F. Harrison in the preface to *Veranilda*), repr. in 2 vols. with intro. by R. Shafer (New York, 1935); *The Unclassed*, 3 vols. (London, 1884), novel, also in J. Korg, ed. (London, 1976); *Demos: A Story of English Socialism*, 3 vols. (London, 1886), novel; *Isabel Clarendon*, 2 vols. (London, 1886), novel; *Thyrza*, 3 vols. (London, 1887), novel, also in J. Korg, ed. (London, 1974); *A Life's Morning*, 3 vols. (London, 1888), novel, repr. with intro. by W. Plomer (London, 1947); *The Nether World*, 3 vols. (London, 1889), novel, also in J. Goode, ed. (London, 1974).

The Emancipated, 3 vols. (London, 1890), novel, also in P. Coustillas, ed. (London, 1977); *New Grub Street*, 3 vols. (London, 1891), novel, repr. in Newnes's Sixpenny series (London, 1910) and in the World's Classics, with intro. by G. W. Stonier (London, 1958), also in B. Bergonzi, ed. (Harmondsworth, 1968), the Penguin English Library; *Denzil Quarrier*, 3 vols. (London, 1892; repr. 1979), novel; *Born in Exile*, 3 vols. (London, 1892), novel, repr. in Nelson's Sevenpenny series (London, 1907; repr. 1979); *The Odd Women*, 3 vols. (London, 1893), novel, repr. in Nelson's Sevenpenny series (London, 1907; repr. 1980); *In the Year of the Jubilee*, 3 vols. (London, 1894), novel., repr. in the Watergate Classics with intro. by W. Plomer (London, 1947), also in P. Kropholler, ed. (London, 1976); *Eve's Ransom* (London, 1895), novel; *The Paying Guest* (London, 1895), novel, the Cassell's Pocket Library; *Sleeping Fires* (London, 1895), novel, the Antonym Library, also in P. Coustillas, ed. (London, 1974); *The Whirlpool* (London, 1897), novel, also in P. Parrinder, ed. (London, 1977); *Human Odds and Ends* (London, 1898), short stories, contains "Comrades in Arms," "The Justice and the Vagabond," "The Firebrand," "An Inspiration," "The Poet's Portmanteau," "The Day of Silence," "In Honour Bound," "The Prize Lodger," "Our Mr. Jupp," "The Medicine Man," "Raw Material," "Two Collectors," "An Old Maid's Triumph," "The Invincible Curate," "The Tout of Yarmouth Bridge," "A Well-meaning Man," "A Song of Sixpence," "A Profitable Weakness," "The Beggar's Nurse," "Transplanted," "A Parent's Feelings," "Lord Dunfield," "The Little Woman from Lancashire," "In No-Man's Land," "At High Pressure," "A Conversation," "A Free Woman," "A Son of the Soil," "Out of Fashion"; *The Town Traveller* (London, 1898), novel; *Charles Dickens: A Critical Study* (London, 1898), criticism, repr. in Blackie's Victorian Era series (London, 1903), frequently repr.; *The Crown of Life* (London, 1899; repr. 1979), novel.

By the Ionian Sea: Notes of a Ramble in Southern Italy (London, 1901), travel, repr. in Travellers Library, with intro. by V. Woolf (London, 1933), also repr. with foreword by F. Swinnerton (London, 1956); *Our Friend the Charlatan* (London, 1901), novel, also in P. Coustillas, ed. (London, 1976); *The Private Papers of Henry Ryecroft* (London, 1903), semiautobiography, frequently repr.; *Veranilda: A Romance* (London, 1904), novel, repr. in the World's Classics, preface by F. Harrison (London, 1929); *Will Warburton: A Romance of Real Life* (London, 1905), novel, repr. in the World's Classics (London, 1929); *The House of Cobwebs* (London, 1906), short stories, contains intro. survey by T. Seccombe, a chronological record, "The House of Cobwebs," "A Capitalist," "Christopherson," "Humplebee," "The Scrupulous Father," "A Poor Gentleman," "Miss Rodney's Leisure," "A Charming Family," "A Daughter of the Lodge," "The Riding-Whip," "Fate and the Apothecary," "Topham's Chance," "A Lodger in Maze Pond," "The Salt of the Earth," "The Pig and Whistle."

V. Starrett, ed., *Sins of the Fathers and Other Tales* (Chicago, 1924), short stories, contains "The Sins of the Fathers" (unsigned) from the *Chicago Tribune* (10 March 1877), "R. I. P." (unsigned) from the *Chicago Tribune* (31 March 1877), "Too Dearly Bought" (signed G. R. G.) from the *Chicago Tribune* (4 April 1877), "Gretchen" (signed G. R. G.) from the *Chicago Tribune* (12 May 1877); *Critical Studies of the Works of Charles Dickens* (New York, 1924), criticism, intro. and biblio. by T. Scott, contains intros. to *Sketches by Boz, Pickwick Papers, Oliver Twist, Nicholas Nickleby, Martin Chuzzlewit, Dombey and Son, Barnaby Rudge, The Old Curiosity Shop*, and an article, "Dickens in Memory," from the *Critic* (January 1902), intros. commissioned for the Rochester ed. of Dickens' works; *The Immortal Dickens* (London, 1925), same as the preceding, without the biblio.; *A Victim of Circumstances and Other Stories* (London, 1927), short stories, preface by A. C. Gissing, contains "A Victim of Circumstances," "One Way of Happiness," "The Fate of Humphrey Snell," "A Despot on Tour," "The Elixir," "The Light on the Tower," "The Schoolmaster's Vision," "The Honeymoon," "The Pessimist of Plato Road," "The Foolish Virgin," "Lou and Liz," "The Tyrant's Apology," "Spellbound," "Our Learned Fellow-Townsman," "Fleet-footed Hester."

G. E. Hastings, V. Starrett, and T. O. Mabbott, eds., *Brownie: Now First Reprinted from the Chicago Tribune* (New York, 1931), short stories, contains "Brownie" (signed G. R. G.) from the *Chicago Tribune* (29 July 1877), "The Warden's Daughter" (unsigned) from the *Chicago Evening Journal* (28 April 1877), "Joseph Yates' Temptation" (unsigned) from the *Chicago Post* (2 June 1877), "Twenty Pounds" (unsigned) from the *Chicago Evening Journal* (19 May 1877), "The Death Clock" (signed "Felix Brown") from the *Chicago Tribune* (21 April 1877), "The Serpent-Charm" (signed "Dr. Vargrave") from the *Chicago Tribune* (28 April 1877), "Dead and Alive" (signed "Dr. Vargrave") from the *Chicago Tribune* (14 July 1877).

III. SELECTIONS. *Selections, Autobiographical and Imaginative* (London, 1929), biographical and critical notes by A. C. Gissing and intro. by V. Woolf; *Selected Tales* (London, 1929), short stories, in Harrap's Short Stories of Today and Yesterday series, intro. note by F. H. P., contains "The Prize Lodger," "Miss Rodney's Leisure," "The Firebrand," "A Victim of Circumstances," "An Inspiration," "The Justice and the Vagabond," "One Way of Happiness," "An Old Maid's Triumph," "The Poet's Portmanteau," "A Charming Family," "Our Mr. Jupp," "Comrades in Arms"; *Stories and Sketches* (London, 1938), short stories, preface by A. C. Gissing, contains "Phoebe," "Letty Coe," "Snapshall's Youngest," "His Brother's Keeper," "Under an Umbrella," "A Calamity at Tooting," "A Yorkshire Lass," "The Hapless Boaster," "The Ring Finger," "The Peace Bringer," "The Friend in Need," "A Drug in the Market," "Of Good Address," "Humble Felicity," "A Man of Leisure."

IV. LETTERS. *Letters of Edward Clodd* (London, 1914), privately printed; *Letters to an Editor* [Clement K. Shorter] (London, 1915), privately printed; *Letters to Members of His Family* (London, 1927), collected and arranged by A. Gissing and E. Gissing; E. Gissing, "George Gissing. A Character Sketch," in *Nineteenth Century* 102 (1927); A. C. Gissing, "George Gissing—Some Aspects of His Life and Work," in *National Review* 93 (1929); E. Gissing, "Some Personal Recollections," in *Blackwood's* 225 (1929).

V. BIOGRAPHICAL AND CRITICAL STUDIES. M. Roberts, *The Private Life of Henry Maitland* (London, 1912; rev. ed., 1923), new ed. with intro. by M. Bishop (1958), biography in form of novel, in 1923 ed. Roberts changed fictional names to actual names of persons who had died in the meanwhile, in 1958 ed. Bishop identified all persons, candid yet sympathetic and understanding book; F. Swinnerton, *George Gissing: A Critical Study* (London, 1912; rev. ed., 1923), author deleted some earlier strictures in rev. ed.; R. C. McKay, *George Gissing and His Critic, Frank Swinnerton* (Philadelphia, 1933); H. G. Wells, *Experiment in Autobiography* (London, 1934); Q. D. Leavis, "Gissing and the English Novel," in *Scrutiny* 7 (1938); M. C. Donnelly, *George Gissing: Grave Comedian* (Cambridge, Mass., 1954), indispensable though unstimulating biographical and critical study, draws on MS sources at the New York Public Library and at the Yale University Library as well as on published material; P. Coustillas, ed., *Collected Articles on George Gissing* (London, 1968); P. Coustillas and E. Partridge, eds., *George Gissing: The Critical Heritage* (London, 1972); P. Coustillas, ed., *Recollections of George Gissing* (London, 1973); P. Coustillas, ed., *George Gissing: Letters to Henry Hick* (London, 1973); M. Collie, *George Gissing: A Biography* (London, 1977); J. Goode, *George Gissing: Ideology and Fiction* (London, 1978); J. Korg, *George Gissing, A Critical Biography* (London, 1980).

FRANCIS THOMPSON
(1859-1907)

Peter Butter

INTRODUCTION

WHEN Francis Thompson's first volume, *Poems*, appeared in 1893 Alfred Tennyson and Robert Browning were dead, Alfred Austin was poet laureate, the members of the Rhymers' Club were meeting at the Cheshire Cheese and were producing, in general, rather pale and world-weary verses. It was the era of *The Yellow Book*, when the predominant mood among writers was desire to escape from the ugliness and materialism of the time. Thompson, once a silent guest at the Rhymers' Club, was also a refugee from the nineteenth century, but his verses were neither pale nor world-weary; they were highly colored and sought to express a positive vision of a realm of spiritual realities rather than a rejection of the world of every day. A few thought they found in him true splendor and profound vision; but others thought the splendor merely one of rags and patches, the vision the product of drugs and dreams, of the sentimental reveries of one too weak to deal with the real world. His circle of enthusiastic admirers grew, however, and the collected edition of 1913 had a remarkably good sale; since then he has held the allegiance of a considerable number of ordinary readers of poetry, but the critics have remained predominantly hostile.

Everyone agrees that there are some fine things in Thompson's work, but he is blamed for overornate diction, imprecise and pretentious imagery, lack of form, derivativeness, and pseudoprofundity. If the severer critics are right, we may safely ignore all but a few anthology pieces; but we ought to take a close look at Thompson before deciding that they are so. For it may be that he possesses qualities that are all the more valuable to us for being unfashionable. The most admired work of the younger poets today is precise, controlled, intelligent, but rather lacking in fire and in range and depth of vision. These poets are, admirably, intent on being honest, on not say-

ing more than they have really felt and known to be true—and this often means that they do not say very much. In contrast, Thompson comes to us as the bard, claiming inspiration, claiming to reveal a vision of the kingdom of God to be found "in no strange land," but all around us; for, though humble about himself, he was confident of his vision—"this my seeing is not weak." This confidence gives his work an exhilarating quality rare in modern poetry. The doubt remains, however, to what extent he succeeded in adequately embodying his vision in words.

LIFE

SOMETHING of the same doubt exists about the man as about the poet. To what extent was he a truly religious seer, to what extent merely a neurotic dreamer?

He was born in 1859, the son of a Lancashire doctor. Both his parents were Roman Catholic converts and seem to have been kind and deeply religious people. He was a dreamy, impractical, gentle child, and from early days a great reader. Even in childhood he was rather a solitary, living in a realm of thoughts and imaginings that he could not, or would not, convey to others. He wrote of himself:

There is a sense in which I have always been and even now remain a child. But in another sense I never was a child, never shared children's thoughts, ways, tastes, manner of life, and outlook on life. I played, but my sport was solitary sport, even when I played with my sisters; from the time I began to read (about my sixth year) the game often (I think) meant one thing to me and another (quite another) to them—my side of the game was part of a dream-scheme invisible to them. And from boys, with their hard practical objectivity of play, I was tenfold wider apart than from girls with their partial capacity and habit of make-believe.

A solitary, but at the same time affectionate—that is one of the paradoxes of his life. In a late notebook he wrote of the "desolation and terror of, for the first time, realizing that the mother can lose you, or you her, and your own abysmal loneliness and helplessness without her," and compared this feeling to that of first fearing oneself to be without God.

Thompson did not want to grow up. His time at school—from 1870 to 1877 at St. Cuthbert's College, Ushaw, near Durham—did something, but not much, to take him out of himself. He began to write there, not only serious verse and prose, but also humorous verses that were much admired; and the liturgical life of the seminary must have had an effect upon him; but he seems to have made no close friends. He attracted the affectionate interest of the masters, but was considered too impractical and absent-minded to be acceptable for the priesthood, for which he had been intended. His failure in the course laid out for him brought an inability to explain himself to his parents.

The next ten years were, outwardly at least, a time of uninterrupted failure. For the first six, Thompson was a medical student, but he disliked and neglected his studies, not being able to stand the sight of blood. At about the age of twenty he fell ill and began to take opium (then still freely prescribed by doctors and easily obtainable), perhaps influenced by the gift from his mother, shortly before her death in 1880, of *The Confessions of an English Opium Eater* by Thomas De Quincey, to whose character and situation then and later his own were in some ways remarkably similar. When it became clear that he would never pass his medical examinations, various other openings were tried for him, but in vain. In 1885, after a painful interview with his father, whom he was never able to take into his confidence and who, he later insisted, was in no way to blame, he departed abruptly for London, apparently with no particular object or hope. At first his father sent a small allowance, but after a time he stopped collecting it. He was befriended and given work by a kindly bootmaker, but would settle to no regular employment. He fiercely defended the privacy of the intense inner life that he was to be able to reveal only in his writing. Instinctively he knew what were not the right paths for him, but did not yet know what was. So he became a down-and-out on the streets—sleeping in a shelter on the Embankment or even in the open air, picking up a precarious living by selling matches or unloading trunks from cabs or by other casual expedients, often spending what he earned on

opium to dull the pain of his already disease-racked body, too ragged to dare even to go into a public library to read. He would have drifted to a useless and unnecessary death if help of just the right kind had not come in time.

In 1888 a poem Thompson had sent to the Catholic literary monthly *Merry England* was published, and soon afterward he arrived at the office of the editor, Wilfred Meynell—to all appearance a ragged, dirty, diseased tramp. Meynell displayed extraordinary goodness and patience in giving him not only immediate practical help, but friendship, respect, and admiration, and in continuing to give these things for the next nineteen years. Thompson was persuaded, not without difficulty, to go to a hospital, was in part restored to health, and conquered for a time the opium habit. Release from opium and contact with people who appreciated him set free the vein of poetry that had lain hidden under his diffidence, that flowed strongly for the next seven years, 1889 to 1896, and then almost dried up.

After his rescue he remained the same wayward, incompetent, gentle creature as before, and his life continued to be in some ways sad, solitary, and painful. From 1889 to 1890 he stayed with a community of Franciscan monks in Sussex, and from 1892 to 1896 he was most of the time near another Franciscan community in Wales. At other times he lived a nomadic life in various London lodgings, constant visits to the large Meynell family giving him the nearest to a home that he was to know. He was often ill and in pain and at such times tended, especially toward the end of his life, to relapse into taking opium. In a distant and adoring way he was in love with Alice Meynell, and was briefly attracted by Katherine King, a vivacious and intelligent girl he met in London, and by Maggie Brien, with whose family he lodged in Wales; but none of these affairs went, outwardly, beyond shy affection, and he was to remain always on the fringe of the ordinary human community. Nevertheless, the few who knew Thompson well sensed a serenity, even gaiety, in him, and felt that he was someone to be admired more than pitied. During his last ten years he made his living as a reviewer for literary periodicals, writing a large number of articles of a very high and consistent standard. In 1907 he died of tuberculosis at the age of forty-seven.

Not having faced his difficulties, it is not for us to pass judgment on Thompson the man; but our attitude toward him will make some difference to the way in which we approach his poetry. It is sentimental to deny his weaknesses. His sufferings—physical (illness and privation), mental (loneliness), and spiritual (consciousness of his failings)—were to a large extent self-induced. His withdrawn temperament led him to opium, which increased his isolation and sapped his willpower. He constantly sought to escape from the responsibilities of adult life; hence arose his inconsiderate behavior to his parents and others, his choosing to love women who could not return his love and so make a claim on him, his unpunctuality, his self-pity. This is part of the truth, but not the whole. His notebooks reveal a constant struggle to make his life conform to what he knew his religion demanded. All who knew him well found him a gentle and lovable person, whose sweetness of character had been quite unstained by his three years on the London streets. Those to whom he could reveal himself admired his intelligence and spiritual insight. Coventry Patmore, a fierce, outwardly haughty and intolerant old man, of whom young poets were justifiably in awe, had, Katherine Tynan records, "an enormous opinion of Francis Thompson. He would talk to few people and listen to few people; but he would talk and listen to Francis Thompson by the hour."

On the surface, it may seem that Thompson just drifted through life—first carried downstream to beggary and near death, then was saved by Meynell and allowed his life to be organized for him; but at deeper emotional and spiritual levels, he showed great toughness. One sees this by comparing him to some of the minor poets of the 1890's, such as Ernest Dowson. He wrote in a notebook of Dowson: "A frail and (in an artistic sense) faint minor poet. . . . The major poet moulds, rather than is moulded by, his environment." Out of the sad life of Dowson came only some palely beautiful cries of pain; but Thompson was able, at his best, to rise above his suffering and use it. If he had really been a drifter, what bitter and sordid fruit might have been expected as the product of the environment of much of his life— pain, loneliness, the London streets and the characters he met there? The product in fact was a considerable body of verse, expressing a joyous vision, not of the sordid, but of the kingdom of God seen all around him in people and in nature; a large quantity of very intelligent and well-written prose; and his own unembittered and gentle character. Some purpose after all was served by those apparently wasted years.

Given Thompson's temperament and other difficulties, it may well be that his life should be regarded as a triumph. Nevertheless, the truly religious man in him and the true artist in him never wholly overcame the dreamer and escapist.

POETRY

Survey

The poems can be roughly classified, as to content, into those that deal with people, nature, poetry, and religion. Of course, nearly all of them are in a broad sense religious, but we can distinguish those that deal more directly with man's relationship to God from those that approach him through people, nature, and poetry.

The first category includes poems connected with Alice Meynell (the two series "Love in Dian's Lap" and "Ultima" and a few others), with Katie King (the "Ad Amicam" sonnets and others), and with Maggie Brien ("A Narrow Vessel"); and poems addressed to children. It is typical of Thompson (perhaps of poets in general) that these poems celebrate relationships in which the current of feeling, checked in real life, was able to flow freely only in poetry. Alice Meynell was able to be his muse, the inspirer of poetry, all the better for being safely inaccessible. These poems cover rather a narrow range of emotions. They tell us little about human behavior or the day-to-day changes in human relationships. The people mentioned are present only in a shadowy way. There is little description—of what they did, of what they looked like, or even, in a precise way, of their characters. Thompson is concerned not with them, but with his own emotions, his own insights. (Does not love poetry tend, paradoxically, to be very egocentric?) If we want to know social life or the more superficial levels of feeling, we must turn to a man of wider experience, like Byron. Thompson claims to give us something different: an insight into the nature of love and into the relationship of human to divine love. Together the poems make up a spiritual autobiography.

Thompson's love is checked, restricted; he feels isolated, and succumbs for a time to self-pity; then works through self-pity to acceptance; then is able to see the very checks themselves as a grace, because they have enabled him to see beyond merely natural love to that to which natural love should lead. He sums it up in a notebook: "The function of natural love is to create a craving which it cannot satisfy. And then only has its water been tasted in perfect purity, if it awakens an insatiate thirst for wine." A woman loved can be a Jacob's ladder leading toward God. Human love is an emblem of, and preparation for, the union of the soul with God. The poems contain not only passionate feeling, but also quite clear and precise ideas as to the nature and function of love. Only intermittently does the expression rise to the height of the theme, but several of the poems contain touches at least of greatness, for instance "Before her Portrait in Youth," "Manus Animam Pinxit," "Love Declared," "Grace of the Way," "Arab Love Song," and "A Fallen Yew." Collectively, Thompson's love poetry is, for me, more valuable than the more perfect works of others who deal with the more superficial and obvious levels of experience; it widens horizons.

As a poet of nature also, Thompson has little to tell us of the surface appearance of things. He is capable of the occasional vivid descriptive line ("Green spray showers lightly down the cascade of the larch") and of evoking the atmosphere of a scene (London the night before the Diamond Jubilee: "Night; and the street a corpse beneath the moon,/ Upon the threshold of the jubilant day"), but these are not the things at which he especially excels. He is not concerned to describe the surface of things, but rather to express an imaginative vision of all things as alive, as connected, and as the art of God. The landscape of his poems is a strange and violent one. Suns die weltering in their blood, stars are blown to a flare by great winds or are puffed out by the morning hours; large cosmic forces are handled with a sometimes too easy assurance that tends to trivialize them. But even the less good poems (even the in parts absurd "Corymbus for Autumn") have a Dionysian energy and joy behind them that most modern poems, with all their intelligence and control, lack. They convey a vision of things rather similar to that of Vincent Van Gogh, another neurotic who was also a true visionary and a true, if imperfect, artist.

One of the best nature poems is "Contemplation," which reveals a pattern of energy-within-calm, existing in nature, in the spiritual life, and in the life of the artist. It begins with a description of a beautiful natural scene on a bright morning after a shower; everything seems quiet and at rest:

> The river has not any care
> Its passionless water to the sea to bear;
> The leaves have brown content;
> The wall to me has freshness like a scent,

And takes half-animate the air,
Making one life with its green moss and stain, . . .
(20–25)[1]

Underneath the stillness, great energies are present. This state is compared to that of the soul in contemplation, and especially to that of the poet's mind when, calm and receptive, it is really at its most creative:

> No hill can idler be than I;
> No stone its inter-particled vibration
> Investeth with a stiller lie. . . .
> (30–32)

In poets, as in skies, "lurk un-tumultuous vortices of power." In writing of the "inter-particled vibration" within the apparent stillness of the stone, Thompson shows a capacity, which is rather rare, to assimilate scientific knowledge into poetry. Elsewhere he writes of the "shy universes" unseen by normal eyesight but revealed by the microscope, through which one sees:

> The dusted anther's globe of spiky stars
> . . .
> And every water-drop a-sting with writhing wars . . .
> ("The Nineteenth Century," 95; 98)

and of the vital activity within the insignificant-looking green scale that is the prothallus of the fern and that contains within itself the two sexes.

Thompson is perhaps at his most effective, not when handling in a rather facile way sun, moon, stars, great winds, and so on, but when showing great things in small:

> I do not need the skies'
> Pomp, when I would be wise
> . . .
> One grass-blade in its veins
> Wisdom's whole flood contains . . .

if one is able to see in it

> God focussed to a point
> ("All Flesh," 1–2; 5–6; 36)

For him:

---

[1] All quotations from the poems are from T. L. Connolly, ed., *Poems*, rev. ed. (New York, 1941).

442

Nature is whole in her least things expresst,
Nor know we with what scope God builds the worm.
("The Heart, II," 10–11)

Nature, for Thompson, is the art of God and expresses, even in small things, something of his nature. But he is not, like many nineteenth-century poets, sentimental about her. Many of his contemporaries, turning from their sorrows in the world of men, sought to lay their heads in the lap of mother nature and to find there some response, some tenderness, even to find in her a guide, a teacher. Thompson replies that if one imagines that one hears any response from the great heart of nature to one's longing for sympathy, it is only the echo of one's own heartbeat.

Lo, here stand I and Nature, gaze to gaze,
And I the greater.
("Of Nature: Laud and Plaint," 1–2)

Nature "nor gives nor teaches"; she "has no hands to bless" and has no use for the obeisance of man.

A considerable proportion of Thompson's poetry is concerned with his own experience as a poet. One sometimes gets impatient with his self-consciousness (typical of him and of modern poets in general); but in a few passages (parts of *Sister Songs*, "Contemplation," "From the Night of Forebeing," and "The Cloud's Swan Song") he does succeed in conveying powerfully something of what it feels like to be a poet, and he has interesting things to say about the nature of poetic inspiration:

The poet is not lord
Of the next syllable may come . . .
(*Sister Songs*, part 2, 382–383)

What he plans today may turn out differently tomorrow. Vision cannot be commanded, will not become his mate "by law and vow," but:

Disguised in life's most hodden-grey,
By the most beaten road of everyday
She waits him, unsuspected and unknown.
(394–396)

To a poet a dream may come:

And suddenly his limbs entwine,
And draw him down through rock as sea-nymphs
might through brine.
(401–402)

Into the depths of his own self, perhaps; and possibly the dream is something rising out of the depths of his own mind. But it does not seem like that; the dream, the vision, seems to be something coming to him from the outside and taking hold of him, and so it is spoken of as another being, with whom he can—is forced to—have relations. The moment passes, and the work of art that is born from it can never be a complete embodiment of it.

What is the significance of the vision that meets the poet unexpectedly on life's road? Is it simply a release of energy from the depths of the self? Is the belief in inspiration an illusion? Thompson would deny it. In a state of calm and receptiveness, he says, the poet is able to become a vehicle:

His heart's a drop-well of tranquillity;
His mind more still is than the limbs of fear,
And yet its unperturbed velocity
The spirit of the simoom mocks.
He round the solemn centre of his soul
Wheels like a dervish, while his being is
Streamed with the set of the world's harmonies . . .
("Contemplation," 64–70)

The strong images used here are not mere flourishes; they are seriously intended. Thompson wrote in a review: "The insight of the poet springs from intuition, which is the highest reason, and is acquired through contemplation, which is the highest effort." By his use of the word "contemplation" he deliberately links the activity of the poet to that of the mystic. "The weapon of the poet or saint is intuition, and contemplation is the state, the attitude, which disposes the mind to receive intuitions." By contemplation the poet makes his mind still, and in this state is able to receive intuitions that are not mere whimsies created by his imagination, but perceptions given to it. By linking poet and saint he does not, of course, imply that the poet is necessarily, in his life, a saintly man; but he does seriously mean that a kind of submission, a kind of fidelity (an absolute honesty, a fidelity to his own experience, his own vision), is required of the poet that is parallel to that required of the mystic. He was well aware of the dangers of false mysticism, and of the possibility of its being confused with the true. False mysticism is mere emotionalism, whereas true mysticism is insight reached by contemplation, and is not contrary to reason. There is the same kind of difference between the undisciplined outpourings of the sentimental writer and the work of the true poet, and the same kind of criteria can be used to distinguish false from true in the two realms. In both realms the condition in which true intuitions can be received is reached by discipline, by a self-naughting that clears the sight of the distortions of personal desire. The greatest art may start from a personal dilemma, but reaches beyond it; it can stand up to the scrutiny of reason, though again it goes beyond it.

It would take us too far to argue here whether Thompson's view of the nature of inspiration is true. It can, perhaps, be agreed that there is on the one side a state of slack daydreaming that produces work of a sentimental and derivative kind, and on the other a state of receptiveness reached by discipline and concentrated effort that is quite different and produces work of a quite different kind—work at once intensely personal and something more than that. Some of Thompson's own work is dreamy and derivative—"Dream-Tryst," for example, and "Absence": these poems are less than personal. But usually he writes in a way that is unmistakably and distinctively his own, though many of his poems are no more than personal, being weighed down with his own sorrows. Sometimes, however, he rises to that mixture of passion and calm that is characteristic of major poetry.

In his religious poems Thompson tried, with varying success, to reach beyond absorption with his own sorrows to a state of calm and acceptance. He wrote in a notebook: "The core of mysticism is a *fact*, not an understanding or a feeling. Still less is it an *endeavour* after a something nameless and unattainable. All true mystics know well about what they seek; and that it can be gained or missed according to the fidelity of their own effort. The thing sought is the *Union*." In another notebook: "A mystic poet who is vaporous fancy will not go far. Every such poet should be able to give a clear and logical prose resumé of his teaching as terse as a page of scholastic philosophy." One could give such a résumé of the content of Thompson's religious poems, and show that what he had to say is in accordance with what the great adepts of the spiritual life have taught. That would not, of course, prove the poems to be good as poems; the quality of the emotion and the adequacy of the expression vary greatly. But it would show that such epithets as "vague, cloudy, vaporous" apply much *less* to his than to most nineteenth-century religious poems.

He believed himself to have been given unusual insight into spiritual facts, but was well aware of the inadequacy of the response he had made in life to his vision:

> "Friend, whereto art thou come?" Thus Verity;
> Of each that to the world's sad Olivet
> Comes with no multitude, but alone by night,
> Lit with the one torch of his lifted soul,
> Seeking her that he may lay hands on her;
> Thus: and waits answer from the mouth of deed.
> ("Whereto Art Thou Come," 1–6)

Knowing the insufficiency of his answer from the mouth of deed he was afraid lest he might be among those who, like Judas, had taken the immortal kiss of Truth and then betrayed it—or rather, betrayed himself—and so earned with Judas a guerdon of despair.

"The Dread of Height" well conveys a sense of the mixture of joy and fear with which Thompson visited the high places of the spiritual life. He has drunk "the drink which is divine," has heard:

> . . . secret music, sweetest music,
> From distances of distance drifting its lone flight
> (14–15)

and yet when he has victoriously climbed to the high place:

> My soul with anguish and recoil
> Doth like a city in an earthquake rock,
> As at my feet the abyss is cloven then,
> With deeper menace than for other men,
> Of my potential cousinship with mire.
> (80–84)

He has been shown more than most men: so much the greater his danger of falling, and his guilt if he does so. The sense of awe that these poems convey is a proof of the authenticity of the experience behind them. A mere dreamer would surely imagine a tamer God, a mere escapist, a cozier retreat.

These poems explore mainly the lower—the purgatorial, with some glimpses of the illuminative—stages of the mystic way. In the canceled preface to *New Poems* (1897) Thompson modestly disclaimed any higher intention: "The first section [which includes most of his best mystical poems] exhibits mysticism in a limited and varying degree. I feel my instrument yet too imperfect to profane by it the higher ranges." "Any Saint" is, perhaps, the only one that attempts to enter these higher ranges, to suggest something of the nature of the union.

Some Poems

> The hunchèd camels of the night
> Trouble the bright
> And silver waters of the moon.
> The Maiden of the Morn will soon
> Through Heaven stray and sing,
> Star-gathering.
>
> Now while the dark about our loves is strewn,
> Light of my dark, blood of my heart, O come!
> And night will catch her breath up, and be dumb.
>
> Leave thy father, leave thy mother
> And thy brother;
> Leave the black tents of thy tribe apart!
> Am I not thy father and thy brother,
> And thy mother?
> And thou—what needest with thy tribe's black tents
> Who hast the red pavilion of my heart?
>   ("Arab Love-Song")

This is one of the most deservedly famous of Thompson's poems, and here at least he achieves the maximum effect by the most economical means. The opening lines set the scene in a few words, conjuring up the atmosphere of night, the East, of mystery and beauty and expectancy. The image of the hunched camels (for cloud shapes) links up with the last line of the poem; for the red pavilion referred to is the small tent, lined inside with red, in which women rode on the backs of camels. The girl is to be taken to the heart of her lover, and within that she will be secure; at the same time one sees a picture of her within the red-lined tent on his camel.

The poem is quite satisfying as a simple love song, but, following Father Connolly, I am sure there is a second level of meaning beneath the obvious one. The first six lines of the final section are reminiscent of the passages in the Gospels (Mark 10:28–30; Matthew 12:50) in which Christ calls on his followers to leave parents and brethren for his sake. So the lover here is, as well as the Arab, Christ, who calls the soul (always feminine to God in Thompson and other mystical writers) to leave the black tents of sin and come to the love and protection of the Sacred Heart. Looking back to the earlier parts of the poem we see that the images there are consonant with this interpretation, though they would not by themselves suggest it. The night under whose cover the lovers are to meet before the dawning is also the night of this life, in which the soul must give itself to Christ before the dawning of eternity. In both cases there is a sense of urgency in the call to the beloved. It is significant that the dawn is not here spoken of with any hostility as it is in most night love poems.

Thompson's frequent association of the moon with the Virgin Mary may also be significant here; in the night of this life Mary the mediatrix helps the soul to find Christ, just as in the physical night the moon guides the lovers to their meeting.

In this apparently simple poem there is considerable density of meaning. The images work well together, and they work well on both levels of significance.

The bulk of Thompson's poetry consists of longish poems, mostly odes written in no regular stanza form. The lack of a tight metrical pattern allows him to sprawl, but on the other hand enables him to achieve some of his most characteristic effects. The sections into which they are divided and the poems as wholes are seldom firmly enough constructed; but as one gets to know the poems better, one usually comes to see a more definite progression of thought and feeling and a greater density of meaning than one at first suspected.

"The Hound of Heaven" is the greatest of these odes. Here we have a single great theme and a clear progression of feeling to give unity to the whole; and the sections, though some are too long, are given some shape by the refrain. The theme, of course, is God's pursuit of man—an unusual one in modern religious verse, which more commonly deals with man's fumbling search for God. The poem has a wonderful speed and urgency, expressing in its rhythms the restlessness of the soul's flight and the majestic instancy of God's pursuit. Criticism of details may seem niggling in the face of the power with which it brings to the imagination a sense of the presence of the supernatural as alive and active. Very few, especially modern, religious poems do anything like this; most make us feel in contact only with the author, who tells us what he did, thought, felt, and so on, not with any power outside him. Nevertheless, even here some of Thompson's weaknesses as well as his greatness are displayed.

At first reading there may seem to be some needless repetition and turning back in the first three sections, which deal with the poet's flight from the love of God, which seems to make too great claims upon him. He seeks refuge in the thoughts and emotions of his own mind, in human love, in external nature, in children, and then (in the latter part of the third section) returns to nature. Why this return? On examination, one sees that the two passages on nature are not repetitive, but deal with different experiences, presumably with different periods of the poet's life. In the first (when quite young?) he delighted in the power and beauty of nature and felt in himself something of the same vitality, but did not imagine natural things as sympathizing with his emotions; the winds swept by, unheeding. Later (perhaps when he became a poet?) he began to imagine a response from nature, to cultivate sentimentally the pathetic fallacy:

> I triumphed and I saddened with all weather,
>   Heaven and I wept together,
> And its sweet tears were salt with mortal mine.
>   (88–90)

His failing as a poet is that when he expresses such a weak mood, even if only to transcend it later, he tends to let the standard of the writing drop, as in:

> Let me twine with you caresses,
>   Wantoning
> With our Lady-Mother's vagrant tresses,
>   Banqueting
> With her in her wind-walled palace . . .
>   (64–68)

A greater poet would have been able to inject an undercurrent of irony under the sentimentality, so as to prepare us for the rejection of it in the stronger lines:

> For ah! we know not what each other says,
>   These things and I; in sound *I* speak—
> *Their* sound is but their stir, they speak by silences.
>   (96–98)

And, having reached this point, a greater poet would not have relapsed into the rather infantile:

> Nature, poor stepdame, cannot slake my drouth;
>   Let her, if she would owe me,
> Drop yon blue bosom-veil of sky, and show me
>   The breasts o' her tenderness.
>   (99–102)

At the beginning of the fourth section the turning point is reached:

> Naked I wait Thy Love's uplifted stroke!
>   (111)

After this we may expect the poem to proceed rapidly to its conclusion; and we may be puzzled to find that nothing decisive happens for more than another forty lines, until we reach:

> That Voice is round me like a bursting sea.
>   (157)

The uplifted stroke of love seems to remain suspended for an inordinate length of time; and during this time the protagonist is in a state of even greater depression than before. In the lines:

> And now my heart is as a broken fount,
>   Wherein tear-drippings stagnate . . .
>   (137–138)

he seems to have slipped back into an unpleasing self-pity. One has a sense of anticlimax. All this becomes intelligible, however, once one grasps that there are not just two, but three major stages in the protagonist's progress. In the first he flees from God and vainly seeks satisfaction in other things. In the second he no longer actively flees, but does not yet accept the love of God with any joy; his old life has been destroyed, but he has not yet entered upon a new; he realizes his own nothingness before God, but still apprehends him primarily as the jealous God, who has deprived him of what he had wanted. This part culminates in the impressive vision:

> I dimly guess what Time in mists confounds;
> Yet ever and anon a trumpet sounds
> From the hid battlements of Eternity;
> Those shaken mists a space unsettle, then
> Round the half-glimpsèd turrets slowly wash again.
>   But not ere him who summoneth
>   I first have seen, enwound
> With glooming robes purpureal, cypress-crowned.
>   (143–150)

Is this figure just physical death, or death to self, or Christ in his Passion? Perhaps one does not need to choose. It is a vision of death seen as being necessary for the production of harvest, both in man's heart (where death to self is the kind of death demanded) and in life in general. The figure is primarily death rather than Christ, but its majesty and its presence on the battlements of eternity suggest the idea that God himself in Christ has accepted the principle it embodies. The feeling behind the lines is still fearful rather than joyous, but the petulant complaint of the lines before has been worked through. The vision enables the poet to see his sufferings in perspective, and so to accept them. This leads on to the third stage, in which he inwardly surrenders and sees that he will find in God all that he previously sought elsewhere; fear yields to love. The writing in the last three sections is impressively simple and strong.

One sees, then, that there is a clear line of development in the poem. The weaknesses present, both spiritual and literary, are contained in a context in which they are transcended.

The difficult "The Mistress of Vision" is placed in the prominent first position in Thompson's best volume, *New Poems*. It is intentionally a fantasy, and has a lulling, dreamy rhythm. The meaning, of course, must be felt, and cannot be fully explained, but a discussion of some of the images may help toward feeling them more accurately. The mistress of vision sits at the heart of a secret garden, walled round with emerald; life is its warden, and it is to be reached only by passing over the fosse of death. Father Connolly[2] says that the garden has a threefold significance; it is heaven, the state of sinlessness on earth, and the realm of poetic achievement. Life, then, is eternal life in heaven, the life of grace on earth, and the life of the worthy poet; and death is physical death, death to self, and the particular death to self demanded by the poet's vocation. To the garden come birds (souls), and they hang in air, enchanted by the singing of the lady (primarily the Virgin Mary). In her song she prays:

> That the bowers might stay,
> Birds bate their winging,
> Nor the wall of emerald float in wreathèd haze away.
>
> (18–20)

That is, that the garden may be preserved and that the souls may find permanent rest there. Here Father Connolly's first meaning does not quite apply, since there could be no question of the walls of heaven dissolving away nor of souls who have once reached it ever departing. Here the garden seems to be a sort of paradisal state reached in moments of vision, but one in which there is as yet no secure abode.

The garden is lit by the light of the sun (Christ), which is low in the sky (reference to the Incarnation?), and in particular the lady's body is aureoled and interstrewn with light. Mary is the perfection of sensible nature and as such the reflection (she is referred to as the moon) of the divine. But the lady is,

as well as Mary, the muse, the inspirer of poetry; her words apply to the religious life, and also, more specifically, to the life of the poet and his means of attaining to that state of vision (the garden) out of which great poetry can arise. The garden includes the meanings Father Connolly sees in it, but it evokes also a whole complex of feelings connected with Eden, the lost paradise, the Golden Age. It is the lost Eden to which in some special moments we seem to come home. The lady and the garden are archetypal images, which Thompson interprets in terms of his beliefs, without banishing from them an indefinable richness of suggestion.

The first nine stanzas describe the lady and the garden; in the rest of the poem Thompson tries to reconstruct what he can dimly remember of the lady's song, but he knows that his own song is but a pale reflection of hers. (One is reminded here of that other visionary poem, *Kubla Khan*, which Coleridge breaks off with an implied confession of his inability to revive within him the song of the damsel with the dulcimer; Thompson, more boldly, presses on.) The burden of the lady's song is the necessity, both for man and poet, of accepting suffering, and secondly of being able to see how all things are linked:

> "When to the new eyes of thee
> All things by immortal power,
> Near or far,
> Hiddenly
> To each other linkèd are,
> That thou canst not stir a flower
> Without troubling of a star;
> When thy song is shield and mirror
> To the fair snake-curlèd Pain,
> Where thou dar'st affront her terror
> That on her thou may'st attain
> Perséan conquest; seek no more,
> O seek no more!
> Pass the gates of Luthany, tread the region Elenore."
>
> (149–162)

The poem here turns upon itself and rebukes the mood of escapism that it itself in parts expresses and induces:

> "Where is the land of Luthany,
> And where the region Elenore?
> I do faint therefor."
>
> (146–148)

The facile alliteration, the rather precious sound of "Luthany" and "Elenore," the word "faint" all suggest a daydreamy mood of desire to escape from the troubles of life into some cozy retreat; but the answer from the garden is an astringent reminder that entry to it is to be attained by acceptance of pain and by a new innocence of vision reached by discipline. So this poem, like others of Thompson's, contains both escapist dreaming and real insight.

Other long odes worth careful reading are "From the Night of Forebeing," "Orient Ode," and "An Anthem of Earth." The first of these deals with the times of dryness and unproductiveness in the spiritual life, compared with the similar periods of preparation before the flowering in the natural world (winter preluding spring) and in the whole plan of the creation (death as a prelude to rebirth, the cosmos arising out of chaos, the life of heaven being prepared for in the life of earth). The themes are well combined, so as to illuminate each other. "Orient Ode" is a hymn to the sun—as the physical sun, as an emblem of Christ, and as Apollo, god of poetry. The sun is to the earth as Christ is to the soul, bringing to fruition the seeds of beauty that are contained in her. This emblematic way of looking at the natural world links Thompson with the medieval and metaphysical poets. Like them, he would say that he was not inventing conceits, but showing correspondences between different levels of being, correspondences that really exist. He makes much use of symbolism that is older than Christianity—deliberately, for, he says, "primitive symbolism is really the recognition of a system of analogy inherent in the divine plan of the universe. All creation being an image of God, everything in man is constructed on an identical plan, and one Divine analogy runs through all." "Orient Ode" is shorter, more concentrated, and better constructed than the earlier poem on a similar theme, "Ode to the Setting Sun." A close study of the two would demonstrate Thompson's development.

Some of these odes are too long and some of the sections are lacking in definite shape. But they are not lacking in thought. They do not usually have an argumentative structure, proceeding from point to point in a chain of reasoning; and they do not usually show such a clear progression of feeling as "The Hound of Heaven." They progress by unfolding the various meanings of an idea or symbol or group of symbols.

Diction

Thompson has been blamed for his "passion for polysyllables," his too consistently high-colored language, and his too frequent use of archaic, poetical, and coined words. There is some justification for these criticisms. His language is apt to be as grandiose when writing of a poppy or of some trivial event, as of the largest subjects. Sometimes this is deliberate, when he is showing how great things are contained in small, but sometimes it is due to a sort of automatism. When not inspired by strong feeling or deep thought, his writing seems turgid and verbose. Further, he is sometimes too concerned about the sound of words, to the neglect of immediate intelligibility. Some of his best lines are those in which he uses simple and short words.

Nevertheless, I believe that the objection to Thompson's language is partly due to a prejudice we ought to try to remove from our minds, a modern prejudice against poetic diction as such. Much of the greatest poetry in the world has been written in a language different from the current language of prose. The idea that poetry ought to be as like prose or ordinary speech as possible is not a primitive and natural, but a sophisticated and modern, one. Of course in periods when there was an accepted convention of poetic diction, it was much easier than it has been recently for a poet to write in a high style without seeming odd. The trouble with using a more "poetical" diction than is customary is that it tends at first to draw the reader's attention to itself; the reader is puzzled, perhaps annoyed, perhaps delighted, by the words themselves, which may therefore, to a certain extent, stand between him and the meaning instead of revealing it. But it is not fair to judge by first impressions only. The test is whether, as one gets to know a poet's work better, the words become more luminous, come to seem more and more the fitting expression of the author's personality and of what he intends to convey. A careful reader of Thompson will, I believe, find this happening—at any rate, with many of the poems—as he begins to feel his way into Thompson's world. One of the reasons for the dislike of Thompson's diction is failure to read him with enough care, failure to appreciate the density of meaning that his words often contain.

It is certainly not true to say that Thompson was careless in his choice of words. He wrote:

There are word-tasters and word-swillers. Unfortunately the two are confounded. Because the tasteless many among writers indulge in orgies of "strong" and "picturesque" language unrecking of fitness and delicate adjustment of meaning, a hue and cry goes out against the few whose love of language goes down to the sensitive roots of words, the few who never bang on a strong word like a tin kettle to deafen the ears of the groundlings, but use it because it is the exact vehicle for a strong thing; because it is not *a* strong word, but *the* strong word culled carefully from many strong words.

He suggested using a special diction for a special purpose:

Essays dealing with subtle thoughts, like books dealing with scientific subjects, cannot be precisely expressed without the use of a specialized language, that is to say, from the point of view of the man in the street. His language is too narrow and limited for their purpose—and, in another sense, not limited enough. That is, it is too vague and imprecise.

His aim was to express precisely a special content, to use *the* strong word. The state of his manuscripts confirms that he worked hard at his writing. It was his habit to write alternative versions of words and phrases above or below the words he first wrote down; in many cases there are five or six variants for a single word. In the manuscripts I have seen, less than half the lines were written straight out without variants in the first draft and remained unaltered through the often numerous revisions to the final version.

To say that Thompson chose carefully and with purpose is not, of course, to say that he always chose well. A fair judgment could be reached only by an extensive and detailed examination of his words, for which there is not space here. He was verbally inventive—coining words and making new compounds, reviving archaic words, using noun for verb. The following are a few examples, with the words I would draw attention to italicized:

And so you said
Things sweet *immeditatably* and wise.

Wintered of sunning song

Now with wan ray that other sun of Song
Sets in the *bleakening* waters of my soul.

The passing shower that rainbows *maniple*

Music that is too *grievous* of the height

Ill is *statured* to its opposite

The *abashless* inquisition of each star

She turned, with the *rout* of her dusk South hair

While in a *moted* trouble the vexed gnats
Maze, and vibrate, and tease the noontide hush.

The following are examples of his original hyphenated combinations: *wood-browned* pools, a *greening-sapphire* sea, the *snow-cloistered* penance of the seed, *wind-besomed* chambers of the air.

All the above are attempts, variously successful, to express an exact meaning in a concentrated way. *Maniple*, for instance, is rather obscure, but full of meaning once understood. Normally a noun, it is used as a verb here. It is an ecclesiastical vestment like a small stole that hangs from the priest's left arm and was originally used by the celebrant at mass to wipe away tears or perspiration. "Manipulus" is a sheaf of grain, hence a symbol of joy. The rainbow appearing against the black cloud like a thin stole makes of the passing shower a maniple, a symbol of joy. The word not only expresses the idea of joy being associated with the acceptance of passing, death, tears, and penitence, but also brings together the pageant of nature and ecclesiastical ritual—appropriately in the context (in "Ode to the Setting Sun"). On the other hand, many passages could be quoted (parts of *Sister Songs*, for instance) where the unusual words are, at best, merely decorative. There are examples both of preciosity and of verbal invention to express precise and concentrated meanings in most of Thompson's poems. The task of criticism is to distinguish between the two, not to condemn the unusual or the "poetical" as such.

In considering Thompson's use of words one should not think only of his oddities. He was capable of concentrated plain statement and of making good use of short and ordinary words—as in "Arab Love Song." He quite often effectively puts a single long word in the midst of short ones, as in:

I fled Him, down the nights and down the days;
I fled Him, down the arches of the years;
I fled Him, down the *labyrinthine* ways
Of my own mind.
("Hound of Heaven," 1–4)

A similar good effect is obtained by the single longish words among the monosyllables in the first stanza of "The Kingdom of God":

449

> O world invisible, we view thee,
> O world intangible, we touch thee,
> O world unknowable, we know thee,
> Inapprehensible, we clutch thee!
>
> (1–4)

This skillful and restrained use of long words can be contrasted with the absurdity of, for instance, the description in *Sister Songs* of the evening sun shining on the child Sylvia:

> . . . sinking day, which, pouring its abundance,
> Sublimed the illuminous and volute redundance
> Of locks . . .
>
> (232–234)

Thompson's search for concentration, for density of meaning, is seen in his frequent construction of adjectives by adding *-ed* to nouns. In the first twenty lines of "The Hound of Heaven" we find *vistaed* hopes, *chasmed* fears, and *hearted* casement. This last phrase is rich in meaning in its context:

> I pleaded, outlaw-wise,
> By many a hearted casement, curtained red.
>
> (16–17)

One can understand this as a window shaped like a heart, and see the poet knocking outside the window, pleading to be admitted into the intimacy of the house; or one may think of the window of the heart itself, the heart of another person into which he wants to enter for refuge. It is the advantage of poetical over logical language that one does not need to choose between the two meanings, but can accept both.

PROSE

THERE is space here to deal only very briefly with Thompson's prose writings. They can be divided into three groups.

(1) *Essays in poetic prose, written during his first few years as a writer.* These are written in a mannered, rhythmical, metaphorical style, and include *Shelley* and "Moestitiae Encomium." They are, unfortunately, the best known of his prose works, but make up only a small proportion of his total output.

(2) *Books and other writings on religious subjects.* His short life of John Baptist de la Salle was composed—one supposes, hastily—for a special number of *Merry England* in 1891. It is written for the most part in a plain, undistinguished style, but breaks into eloquence in the final chapter, in which Thompson welcomes the increased concern for social justice to be found in his day, especially in his own church. By the time he wrote his other two religious works—the pamphlet *Health and Holiness* (1905) and a full-scale life of St. Ignatius Loyola, written probably at almost the same time—he had found a mean in style between undistinguished plainness and excessive elaboration. The biography of St. Ignatius is a compilation, based on secondary sources, but shows a poet's imagination at work in bringing events and people to life.

(3) *Journalism.* In a notebook Thompson wrote:

> 1897. End of Poet. Beginning of Journalist.
> The years of transition completed.

Before this he had contributed only a few articles and reviews to periodicals; for the last ten years of his life he was to make his living as a regular reviewer. Father Connolly has brought together about two hundred of his previously uncollected reviews and articles in *Literary Criticisms by Francis Thompson* (1948) and *The Real Robert Louis Stevenson and Other Critical Essays* (1959). These are impressive volumes, displaying the wide range of Thompson's knowledge of literature, his sanity, his intelligence, his humor. The prose is consistently good, always lucid, sometimes eloquent, and seldom too ornate for the purpose in hand. Anyone who wants to get a quick view of the quality of Thompson's mind would do well to turn to the last three of the reviews grouped under the heading "Mysticism: Genuine and Spurious" in the first of the above-mentioned collections. Thompson writes with great authority and precision on a subject that often leads to woolly thinking and inflated writing.

No one who reads much of Thompson's later prose could ever dismiss him as a fool or a mere neurotic dreamer.

CONCLUSION

ONE takes poems apart to look at words and images, but in the end it is the total effect of the poems as wholes, of the poet's works as a whole, that matters.

Every writer has strengths and weaknesses, and one should be aware of both; but one's final opinion is not arrived at by coldly subtracting points against from points for. A major writer's fire seems to burn up the chaff; and I believe Thompson is a major writer, a great flawed writer, much more interesting and valuable than lesser ones of more even quality. If one were to demand artistic perfection, one would have to discard nearly all his poems, and might be left with only one or two short ones. In so doing one would have to cast out much of great value. He himself wrote of the ill effects of the cult of perfection:

Over the whole contemporary mind is the trail of the serpent perfection. . . . It leads in poetry to the love of minute finish, and *that* in turn (because minute finish is most completely attainable in short poems) leads to the tyranny of sonnet, ballade, rondeau, triolet and their kind. The principle leads again to aestheticism, which is simply the aspiration for a hot-house seclusion of beauty in a world which Nature has tempered by bracing gusts of ugliness

("The Way of Imperfection")

Later in the same essay he goes on:

Critics have erected the ideal of a style stripped of everything special or peculiar, a style which should be to thought what light is to the sun. Now this pure white light of style is as impossible as undesirable; it must be splintered into colour by the refracting media of the individual mind, and humanity will always prefer the colour. Theoretically we ought to have no mannerisms; practically we cannot help having them, and without them style would be flavourless. . . . We should avoid as far as possible the mannerisms of our age, because they corrupt originality. But in essence mannerisms—individual mannerisms, are a season of style, and happily unavoidable

Thompson did not altogether avoid the mannerisms of his own and earlier ages; sometimes his mannerisms are derivative, and corrupt originality; more often they are the natural expression of his personality and vision. Few of his poems could possibly have been written by anyone else, and few are without fine things in them.

So I end with a confession rather than an attempt at judicial summing up. For me Thompson's poems —in bulk, not just in a small selection—open new horizons, give a sense of exhilaration, and enhance the feeling of wonder.

SELECTED BIBLIOGRAPHY

I. BIBLIOGRAPHY. C. A. Stonehill and H. W. Stonehill, *Bibliographies of Modern Authors,* 2nd ser. (London, 1925), includes a bibliography of Thompson's books; T. L. Connolly, ed., *Account of Books and Manuscripts of Francis Thompson* (Boston, 1937), catalog of a collection at Boston College; M. P. Pope, "A Critical Bibliography of Works by and about Francis Thompson," in *Bulletin of the New York Public Library,* vol. 62, no. 11 and vol. 63, nos. 1, 3, 4 (1958–1959). *Note:* Comprehensive bibliographies are contained in T. L. Connolly's ed. of Thompson's poems and (more complete and up to date) in P. Danchin, *Francis Thompson* (see below). Bibliographies of Thompson's reviews and literary criticism in periodicals are contained in T. L. Connolly, ed., *Literary Criticisms by Francis Thompson* and *The Real Robert Louis Stevenson* (see below). The Oxford Standard Authors ed. of Thompson's poems has an appendix showing when and where the poems were first published.

II. COLLECTED EDITIONS. *Selected Poems* (London, 1908), with biographical note by W. Meynell; W. Meynell, ed., *Works,* 3 vols. (London, 1913), vols. I and II contain all the poems Meynell considered worth preserving, vol. III contains a selection of his prose, mostly early work; T. L. Connolly, ed., *Poems* (New York, 1932; rev. ed., 1941); *Poems* (Oxford, 1937), the Oxford Standard Authors ed.

III. SEPARATE WORKS. *The Life and Labours of Blessed John Baptist De La Salle* (London, 1891; rev. ed., 1911), originally published in *Merry England; Poems* (London, 1893); *Sister Songs: An Offering to Two Sisters* (London, 1895), also privately printed as *Songs Wing to Wing* (London, 1895); *New Poems* (London, 1897); *Victorian Ode for Jubilee Day, 1897* (London, 1897), privately printed; *Health and Holiness* (London, 1905), prose, with preface by G. Tyrrell, included in vol. III of the *Works; Shelley* (London, 1909), prose, with intro. by G. Wyndham, included in vol. III of the *Works;* J. H. Pollen, ed., *Saint Ignatius Loyola* (London, 1909), prose; *A Renegade Poet and Other Essays* (Boston, 1910), prose, with intro. by J. O'Brien; *Uncollected Verse* (London, 1917), privately printed; T. L. Connolly, ed., *Literary Criticisms by Francis Thompson: Newly Discovered and Collected by Terence L. Connolly* (New York, 1948), prose; T. L. Connolly, ed., *Minor Poets by Francis Thompson* (Los Angeles, 1949), reprs. of criticism by Thompson; T. L. Connolly, ed., *The Man Has Wings* (New York, 1957), includes hitherto unpublished poems and plays; T. L. Connolly, ed., *The Real Robert Louis Stevenson and Other Critical Essays* (New York, 1959), includes some uncollected articles and reviews by Thompson; J. E. Walsh, ed., *The Letters of Francis Thompson* (New York, 1969).

IV. BIOGRAPHICAL AND CRITICAL STUDIES. E. Meynell, *The Life of Francis Thompson* (London, 1913; repr. 1926), sympathetic but not uncritical biography by one who knew Thompson well; R. L. Mégroz, *Francis Thompson, the Poet of Earth in Heaven* (London, 1927), enthusiastic, rather uncritical, but interesting; V. Meynell, *Francis Thompson and Wilfred Meynell, a Memoir* (London, 1952), good account by Meynell's daughter of the friendship of the two men, contains new material; J. C. Reid, *Francis Thompson, Man and Poet* (London, 1959), in-teresting critical study; P. Danchin, *Francis Thompson: La Vie et L'Oeuvre d'un Poète* (Paris, 1959), a thorough and learned account of Thompson's life and work; P. van K. Thomson, *Francis Thompson: A Critical Biography* (New York–Edinburgh, 1961); J. E. Walsh, *Strange Harp, Strange Symphony* (London, 1968), contains new material.